Women's Lives
Multicultural Perspectives

Second Edition

Gwyn Kirk

Margo Okazawa-Rey

Mayfield Publishing Company
Mountain View, California
London • Toronto

Library of Congress Cataloging-in-Publication Data
Kirk, Gwyn.
   Women's lives : multicultural perspectives / Gwyn Kirk, Margo
Okazawa-Rey — 2nd ed.
      p.   cm.
   Includes bibliographical references.
   ISBN 0-7674-1643-0
      1. Women — United States — Social conditions.   2. Women — United
States — Economic conditions.   3. Feminism — United States.   I. Title.

HQ1421.K573   2000
305.42'0973 — dc21   00-056079
                                                                        CIP

Manufactured in the United States of America
10   9   8   7   6   5   4   3   2

Mayfield Publishing Company
1280 Villa Street
Mountain View, CA 94041

Sponsoring editor, Serina Beauparlant; production editor, Julianna Scott Fein; manuscript editor, Margaret Moore; design manager, Susan Breitbard; text designer, Carolyn
Deacy; cover designer, Ellen Pettengell; art editor, Rennie Evans; illustrator, Joan Carol;
manufacturing manager, Randy Hurst. The text was set in 9/11 Palatino by ColorType
and printed on acid-free 45# Highland Plus by Malloy Lithographing, Inc.

Cover art: San Francisco Women's Building. Detail of Lucia, Aztlán. Representing the
mestizo heritage of the Chicano. She is surrounded by Native American, Ecuadorian,
West African, and Korean fabrics. Copyright © 1994 by MaestraPeace. All rights
reserved. Mural by Juana Alicia, Miranda Bergman, Edythe Boone, Susan Kelk
Cervantes, Meera Desai, Yvonne Littleton, and Irene Perez.

Acknowledgments and copyrights continue at the back of the book on pages 611–615
which constitute an extension of the copyright page.

To those who connect us to the past,
our mothers,
who birthed us, raised us,
taught us, inspired us, and took no nonsense from us
Edwina Davies, Kazuko Okazawa, Willa Mae Wells
and to those who connect us to the future
Charlotte Elizabeth Andrews-Briscoe
Gabrielle Raya Clancy-Humphrey
Hansoo Lim
Uma Talpade Mohanty
Camille Celestina Stovall-Ceja

Contents

CHAPTER ONE

Theories and Theorizing: Integrative Frameworks for Understanding 7

CHAPTER TWO

Identities and Social Locations: Who Am I? Who Are My People? 49

CHAPTER THREE

Women's Bodies 100

CHAPTER FOUR

Women's Sexuality 132

CHAPTER FIVE

Relationships, Families, and Households 160

CHAPTER SIX

Violence against Women 217

CHAPTER SEVEN

Living in a Global Economy 264

CHAPTER EIGHT

Work, Wages, and Welfare 314

CHAPTER NINE

Women's Health 360

CHAPTER TEN

Women, Crime, and Criminalization 418

CHAPTER ELEVEN

Women and the Military 465

CHAPTER TWELVE

Women and the Environment 491

CHAPTER THIRTEEN

Creating Change: Theory, Vision, and Action 533

Preface

An introductory course is perhaps the most challenging women's studies course to conceptualize and teach. Depending on their overall goals for the course, instructors must make difficult choices about what to include and what to leave out. Students come into the course for a variety of reasons and with a range of expectations and prior knowledge, and most will not major in women's studies. The course may fulfill a distribution requirement for them, or it may be a way of taking one women's studies course during their undergraduate education out of a personal interest to broaden their knowledge of women's lives. For women's studies majors, the course plays a very different role, offering a foundation for their area of study.

Several factors related to the wider university setting and societal context also shape women's studies. Women's studies programs continue to build their reputations in terms of academic rigor and scholarly standards. Nowadays there is increasing awareness of the difficulties of what it means for mainly White instructors to teach about the broad diversity of women's experiences in the United States. Outside the academy, a range of economic changes and government policies have made many women's lives more difficult in the United States—a loss of factory and office work as jobs continue to be moved overseas or become automated; government failure to introduce a health care system that will benefit everyone or to introduce an adequate system of childcare; cuts in welfare programs; greater restriction of government support to immigrants and their families; and a dramatic increase in the number of women now incarcerated compared with a decade ago.

This text started out as two separate readers that we used in our classes at Antioch College (Gwyn Kirk) and San Francisco State University (Margo Okazawa-Rey) from 1993 to 1995. Serendipitously, as it seemed at the time, we were introduced to each other by a mutual friend. We talked about our teaching and discovered many similarities in approach despite our very different institutional settings. We decided to take what we thought were the best parts of our readers and combine them into a book that would work for an introductory course.

What We Want in an Introductory Women's Studies Book

Several key issues concern us as teachers. We want to present a broad range of women's experiences to our students in terms of class, race, culture, disability, age, and sexual orientation. We assume that hierarchies based on these factors create systems of disadvantage as well as systems of privilege and that women's multiple positions along these dimensions shape our life experiences in important and unique ways. Although the national discourse on race, for example, is presented in Black/White terms, we want teaching materials that do justice to the diversity and complexity of race and ethnicity in this country. We also want materials that address the location of the United States in the global economy. Students need to understand the economic forces that affect the availability of jobs in this country and elsewhere. They also need to understand the significance of U.S. dominance abroad in terms of language and popular culture, the power of the dollar and U.S.-based corporations, and the prevalence of the U.S. military.

In our introductory courses, we both included some discussion of theory because a basic understanding of various theoretical frameworks is a powerful tool not only for women's studies courses but also for other courses students take. Another shared concern we have is women's activism. As women's studies has become more established and professionalized, it has tended to grow away from its roots in the women's liberation movement, a trend that troubles us. As we talked about our own lives, it was clear that we both value our involvements in political movements. This activism has taught us a great deal and provided us with vital communities of like-minded people. Currently, there are myriad women's activist and advocacy projects across the country, but many students do not know about them. In our teaching, we make it a point to include examples of women's activism and urge students to think of themselves as people who can make a difference in their own lives and in the world around them. Much of the information that students learn in women's studies concerning the difficulties and oppression of women's lives can be discouraging. Knowing about women's activism can be empowering, even in the face of daunting realities. This knowledge reinforces the idea that current inequalities and problems are not fixed but have the potential to be changed.

Linking Individual Experiences to National and International Trends and Issues

We are both trained in sociology. We have noticed that students coming into our classes are much more familiar with psychological explanations for behavior and experience than they are with structural explanations. They invariably enjoy first-person accounts of women's experiences, but a series of stories, even wonderfully insightful stories, leaves us unsatisfied. In class, we provide a context for the various issues students study. Taking a story about a woman with cancer, for example, we add details about how many women in the United States have

cancer, possible explanations for this, the effects of age, race, and class on treatment and likelihood of recovery. The overview essay for each chapter provides some broader context for the personal accounts. We have tried to integrate the many aspects of women's lives. We abandoned separate sections on aging and disability in favor of threading these aspects of women's experience through each chapter. We've included readings that reflect the complexity of women's identities, where the authors wrote, for example, about being Chinese American, working class, and lesbian in an integrated way. We added a section on crime and criminalization in response to the great increase in women caught up in the criminal justice system in the past decade, and added a chapter on women and the environment.

Challenges for the Twenty-First Century: Security and Sustainability

We find ourselves thinking about the challenges facing women and men in the twenty-first century: challenges concerning work and livelihood, personal and family relationships, violence on many levels, and the fragile physical environment. These issues pose major questions concerning the distribution of resources, personal and social values, and the definition of security. How is our society going to provide for its people in the years to come? What are the effects of the increasing polarization between rich and poor in the United States and between rich and poor countries of the world? Genuine security—at personal, community-wide, national, and planetary levels—is a key issue for the future, and, similarly, sustainability. These themes of security and sustainability provide a wider framework for the book.

As teachers, we are concerned with students' knowledge and understanding, and beyond that, with their aspirations, hopes, and values. One of our goals for this book is to provide a series of lenses that will help students understand their own lives and the lives of others, especially women. The second goal is that, through this understanding, they will be able to participate in some way in the creation of a secure and sustainable future.

New to the Second Edition

After considering the comments and reactions we received from students and faculty who have used the first edition of this book, we have made a number of changes. We have benefited enormously from opportunities to hear students discuss the book, to read teachers' syllabi, and to learn how students and faculty are using the book in a range of courses. This edition relies on the analyses, principles, and style of the first edition but with some important additions:

- two new chapters, one on sexuality and another on violence against women, which greatly expand the discussion of these key topics
- explicit attention to the role of women in politics — in both feminist movements and electoral politics — and to the development of feminist theories in their historical contexts
- more articles that give historical or theoretical accounts as a complement to the first-person writings in each chapter
- updated statistics and reference to new legislation (e.g., on welfare reform) and new developments (e.g., the growth of the World Trade Organization)
- reference to a broader literature than before so that students and teachers can easily find additional works
- explicit acknowledgment that women's studies students include a growing number of men; inclusion of several readings by male authors; and suggestions for ways that men can contribute to women's opportunities, self-development, and liberation as well as the creation of a secure and sustainable future
- web site addresses for key organizations

A number of considerations — sometimes competing and contradictory — influenced these decisions. We are committed to including established writers and lesser-known writers, and writers from a range of racial and ethnic backgrounds and with differences in ability, age, class, culture, nation of birth, and sexuality. As before, we have looked for writers who, implicitly or explicitly, integrate several levels of analysis (micro, meso, macro, and global) in their work. Teachers want more theory, more history, and more research-based pieces. The students we talked with, including our own, invariably loved the first-person pieces and said that this kind of writing helped to draw them into the more theoretical discussions. We have included more articles that give historical or theoretical accounts as a complement to the first-person writings in each chapter, recognizing that if teachers do not assign the book, students will never see it. As we searched for materials, however, we found much more theoretical work by White women than by women of color. We assume this is because there are far fewer women of color in the academy, because White women scholars and writers have greater access to publishers, and because prevailing ideas about what theory is and what form it should take tend to exclude work by women of color. This can give the unfortunate impression that, aside from a few notable exceptions, women of color are not theorists. This raises the whole issue of what theory is and who can theorize, questions we take up in the first chapter. We have tried hard not to reproduce this bias in our selection, but we note this problem here to make this aspect of our process visible.

This new edition represents our best effort to balance these considerations, as we sought to provide information, analysis, and inspiration concerning the myriad daily experiences, opportunities, limitations, oppressions, hopes, joys, and satisfactions that make up U.S. women's lives.

Acknowledgments

Many people made it possible for us to complete the first edition of this book, some four years in the making, especially our students at Antioch College and San Francisco State University who first inspired us to do it.

In terms of practical support, several people helped us get through the day-to-day tasks of writing, preparing the manuscript, and staying healthy: Alice Feldman, Trina Histon, Erwin Morgenthaler, Alan Ng and Mark Gin at Copy Edge, Diane Sabin, and the School of Social Work at San Francisco State

University. Research assistants Marieka Brown, Anna Lisa Couturier, and Carolyn Reyes were part of this team.

The following people pushed us intellectually, read parts of the manuscript, or provided new ideas and information: Molly Andrews, Grace Lee Boggs, Alice Cook, Annette Dula, Vitka Eisen, Ann Filemyr, Jewelle Gomez, Mark Gross, Anna Gruver, Ynestra King, Martha Matsuoka, Chandra Talpade Mohanty, Cassandra O'Neill, Freddy Paine, Megan Reynolds, Eric Rofes, Anne Simon, and Sondra Stein. Other friends supported and encouraged us: D. Kamili Anderson, Ondwéwe Chymes, Adrienne Cool, Crispin Hollings, Catherine Joseph, Nancy Knipe, Nobu Tomita, Julie Torgeson, and Lisa Vuong.

We acknowledge those who wrote pieces especially for the first edition: Lynore B. Gause, Barbara Bloom, Cynthia Cohen, Monique Corbin, Eric De-Meulenaere, Jean Grossholtz, Teresa Luftus, Shannon Murray, Carolyn Reyes, Melinda Smith-Wells, Rita Takahashi, Elizabeth Wilson-Compton, and Wendy A. Young. We also appreciate all the feminist scholars and activists whose work we have reprinted here and those whose research and writings have informed not only our work but also shaped the field of women's studies.

We are grateful to outside reviewers Teri Ann Bengiveno, San Jose State University; Shamita Das Dasgupta, Rutgers University; Torry Dickinson, Kansas State University; Dana Dunn, University of Texas at Arlington; and Patricia Huckle, San Diego State University, who asked good questions and made useful suggestions.

We also thank our teachers, from whom we've learned information and new ways of thinking, and those key people who provided support and opportunities at various turning points in our lives: Il Soon Ahn, the late James Boggs, Lillian Gonzalez Brown, Steve Brown, Charlotte Bunch, Bryan Burdick, Kathleen Casey, Susan Cavin, Max Culver, Eleanor Duckworth, Kat Duff, Margaret Duncombe, Carolyn Francis, G. William Freeman, Virginia Glennon, Rachel Hare-Mustin, Joseph Jordan, Josephine Lambert, Yoko Lee, Sara Lawrence Lightfoot, Donald Oliver, Grace Paley, Shirley Royster, Josephine Shaddock, David O. Shipp, Judith Sturnick, Suzuyo Takazato, Wendy Grayson Thunderchief, and the late James C. Wells.

Many people have helped us with this revision and we acknowledge them here. We have been par-

ticularly fortunate to have the support of Hamilton College as Jane Watson Irwin Co-Chairs in Women's Studies (1999–2001). Women's studies colleagues have given generously of their friendship, encouragement, and insights: Vivyan Adair, Nesecan Balkan, Susan Sanchez Casal, Margaret Gentry, Shelley Haley, and Chandra Talpade Mohanty. Other colleagues welcomed and supported us: Jennifer Borton, Bobby Fong, Gillian Gane, Barbara Gold, Cheryl Morgan, Doug Raebeck, Carl Rubino, Natsu Sato, and Emiko Yasumoto. Research librarians Julia Dickinson, Lynn Mayo, and Kristin Strohmeyer gave great assistance, as did Interlibrary Loan Coordinator Glynis Asu, department assistant Amy Gowans, and Yvonne Brady at the Print Shop. Meaghan Carey, Jamie Crowley, Jennie Galluccio, David Kolb, and Julie Loder were invaluable proofreaders. Richard Ver Weibe provided research assistance. Erol Balkan, Nancy Bereano, Minnie Bruce Pratt, Eric Rofes, and Michael Scarce gave us information and useful leads. Margaret Duncombe, Margaret Gentry, and Ann Russo made very helpful comments on drafts of the new chapters.

Many thanks to other friends at Hamilton and elsewhere for the cards, calls, e-mails, hospitality, and care packages that nurtured us and got us through the upstate New York winter, especially: Carol Cantwell, Adrienne Cool, John Davies, Arla Ertz, Carolyn Francis, Darrell Gane, Robin Gane, Jewelle Gomez, Crispin Hollings, Rachel Lanzerotti, Debbie Lee, Robin T. K. Lee, Yoto Lee, Martha Matsuoka, Satya Mohanty, Janet Moomaw, Diane Sabin, Anne Simon, and Paul Venet. For helping to keep us healthy: Phil Argus, Zoë Brenno, Alice Feldman, and Mackay Rippey.

We are grateful to everyone at Mayfield who worked on this project: Serina Beauparlant, our editor, who urged us to do this revision and shaped it in significant ways; Julianna Scott Fein, production editor, who was a pleasure to work with again; the production team; and Margaret Moore, a wonderful copy editor. Outside reviewers provided detailed suggestions and advice, challenged us to rethink in places, and gave us the benefit of their experience as scholars and teachers: Jill M. Bystydzienski, Iowa State University; Elizabeth Hackett, University of Michigan; Chun-Hui Sophie Ho, Purdue University; Gail Landberg, Western Michigan University; Dyan Mazurana, University of Wyoming, Laramie; Sally Mitchell, Temple University; Val Moghadam, Illinois

State University; Nancy A. Naples, University of California, Irvine; Jean L. Potuchek, Gettysburg College; Anne Sisson Runyan, Wright State University; Marian Sciachitano, Washington State University; and Julia F. Weber, Washington University.

Thanks to students at Hamilton who taught us more about teaching and learning, and the Class of 2000 at San Francisco State University, School of Social Work.

Lastly, we acknowledge the importance of our friendship, deepening over the years, that provides a firm foundation for our shared understandings and our work together. We continue to be inspired by the cultural work of Sweet Honey in the Rock, whose blend of music and politics touches the head, heart, and hands, and also by the "sociological imagination" — C. Wright Mills' concept — that draws on the need for complex social analysis in order to make change.

To everyone, very many thanks.

We have chosen each other
and the edge of each other's battles
the war is the same
if we lose
someday women's blood will congeal
upon a dead planet
if we win
there is no telling
we seek beyond history
for a new and more possible meeting.

— AUDRE LORDE

The Framework of This Book

The Focus of Women's Studies

To study alongside men, to have access to the same curriculum, and to be admitted to male professions were goals that dominated women's education in the United States for several generations, from the early nineteenth century onward. In the late 1960s and early 1970s, however, the gendered nature of knowledge itself—with its focus on white, male, and middle-class perspectives that are assumed to be universal—was called into question by feminists. The early 1970s saw the start of many women's studies programs across the country, building on the insights and energies of the women's liberation movement. Early courses had titles like "Women's Liberation," "The Power of Patriarchy," or "Sexist Oppression and Women's Empowerment." Texts often included mimeographed articles from feminist newsletters and pamphlets, as there was so little appropriate material in books. By contrast, women's studies is now an established field of study with over six hundred programs nationwide in universities and colleges and a rapidly growing and extensive body of literature (National Women's Studies Association 1994). Women's studies graduates are employed in many fields, including law, business, publishing, health, social and human services, and education and library work (Luebke and Reilly 1995). Students report that women's studies courses

are informative and empowering; they provide a perspective on one's own life and on other college courses in ways that are often life changing (Luebke and Reilly 1995; Musil 1992).

Women's studies seeks new ways of understanding—more comprehensive than those offered by traditional academic disciplines that so often view women in stereotypical ways, if at all. In addition, women's studies goes beyond description and analysis to focus on the consequences and applications of knowledge. In a women's studies class you are encouraged to share your own experiences and to relate the readings and discussions to your own life. Women's studies courses provide data that are often absent in the rest of the curriculum. You may be challenged by this and pushed to rethink some of your assumptions about gender, your own experiences of schooling, family, and relationships, and your positions on a number of complex issues. This kind of study often evokes strong emotional reactions, as your own life may be deeply affected by issues under discussion. These aspects of women's studies have given rise to criticisms that it is too "touchy-feely," more like therapy than serious study, or that it is an extended gripe session against men. We discuss these criticisms later in this introduction. Women's studies also often generates anger in students at the many forms of women's oppression, at other students' ignorance or lack of concern for this,

1

at being female in a male-dominated world, and at the daunting nature of the issues and problems faced by women.

The Framework for This Book: Collective Action for a Sustainable Future

This book is concerned with women in the United States and the rich diversity of their life experiences. We have selected readings that reflect this diversity. Each chapter also includes an overview essay to give some historical and contemporary context for the specific readings. As writers and editors, a big challenge for us has been to choose effective writings and salient facts from the vast wealth of materials available. There has been a groundswell of women's writing and publishing in the past thirty years, as well as a proliferation of popular and scholarly books and journals on issues of interest to women's studies students. When opinion polls, academic studies, government data, public debates, and grassroots research, available in print and through electronic media, are added to this, it is easy to be swamped with information and opposing viewpoints.

In making our selections, we have filtered this wealth of material according to a number of principles—our particular road map.

An Activist Approach

We argue that women and men in the United States face a range of serious problems in the years ahead if we are to sustain our lives and the lives of our children. Although some women have benefited from greater opportunities for education and wage earning, many are now working harder, or working longer hours, than their mothers did, under pressure to keep a job and to juggle their work lives with family responsibilities. In the 1980s and 1990s, a range of economic changes and government policies have made many women's lives more difficult. Examples include a loss of factory and office work as jobs are moved overseas or become automated; government failure to introduce an adequate system of child care or a health-care system that will benefit everyone; cuts in welfare; greater restriction of government support to immigrants and their families; and a dra-

matic increase in the number of women now incarcerated compared with the number from a decade ago. While the U.S. military budget consumes a massive 47 percent of federal income tax (for the fiscal year 2001), according to the War Resisters League (2000), and some states spend more public money on new jails and prisons than on higher education, countless thousands of people are homeless, inner-city schools lack basic resources, and Head Start and other preschool programs are cut back. Individual women and men are personally affected by these changes and policies as they negotiate intimate relationships and family life.

We see collective action for progressive social change as a major goal of scholarly work, and thus, in the face of these economic and political trends, we take a deliberately activist approach in this book. We mention many practical projects and organizations to give students a sense of how much activist work is going on that is often not visible in the mainstream media. Throughout our discussion we emphasize the diversity of women's experiences. These differences have often divided women. We assume no easy "sisterhood" across lines of race, class, age, or sexual orientation, for example, but we do believe that alliances built firmly on the recognition and understanding of such differences make collective action possible.

A Sustainable and Secure Future

We see sustainability and security as central issues for the twenty-first century. These involve questions about the distribution of wealth, both within the United States and between the rich and poor countries of the world, and about the direction of future economic development. Another concern is the rapid deterioration of the physical environment on our overburdened planet. In many chapters security is an underlying theme. This includes the individual security of knowing who we are; having secure family relationships; living in freedom from threats, violence, or coercion; having adequate income or livelihood; and enjoying health and well-being. It also involves security for the community, the nation, and the planet, and includes issues like crime, the role of the military, and the crucial importance of the physical environment. Throughout the book we emphasize severe structural inequalities between people: women and men, White people and people of color, older people and young people, for example. We see these inequalities as a major threat to long-term security because they create literal and metaphorical walls, gates, and fences that separate people and maintain hierarchies among us. We also argue that a more sustainable future means rethinking materialism and consumerism and finding new ways to distribute wealth so that everyone has the basics of life. These issues affect not only women, of course, and are not solely the responsibility of women, but women are actively involved in community organizing and movements for economic and environmental justice in the United States and many other countries, often in greater numbers than men.

The United States in a Global Context

This is not a book about global feminism. Its focus is on the United States, but we also comment on the wider global context within which the United States operates. We recognize the racial and ethnic diversity of this country; many people in the United States were not born here and come with hopes for a better future, but they also have no illusions about inequalities in the United States. We argue that people in the United States need to understand the significance of this country's preeminence in the world, manifested culturally—through the dominance of the English language and in widespread distribution of U.S. movies, pop music, books, and magazines—as well as economically, through the power of the dollar as an international currency and the impact of U.S.-based corporations abroad. We need to understand the significance of the globalization of the economy for people in the United States as well as throughout the world. We must understand the connections between domestic policy issues like health care, child care, and welfare, and foreign policy issues such as military expenditures and foreign aid.

Linking the Personal and the Global

Throughout the book we use the terms **micro level** (personal or individual), **meso level** (community, neighborhood, or school, for example), **macro level** (national), and **global level.** To understand people's experiences or the complexity of a particular issue,

it is necessary to look at all these levels and how they interconnect. For instance, a personal relationship between two people might be thought to operate on a micro level. However, both partners bring all of themselves to the relationship. Thus, in addition to micro-level factors such as appearance, generosity, or their determination not to repeat the mistakes of their parents' relationships, there are also meso-level factors—such as their connections to people of other faiths or races—and macro-level factors—such as the obvious or hidden ways in which men or White people are privileged in this society. As editors we have made these connections in our overview essays and looked for writings that make these links between levels of analysis.

A Matrix of Oppression

Underlying our analysis throughout the book is the concept of oppression, which we see as a group phenomenon, regardless of whether individuals in a group think they are oppressed or want to be in dominant positions. Men, as a group, are advantaged by sexism, for example, while women, as a group, are disadvantaged. Every form of oppression—for instance, **sexism, racism, classism, heterosexism, anti-Semitism, able-bodyism**—is rooted in our **social institutions**—such as the family, education, religion, and the media. Oppression, then, is systemic, and it is systematic. It is used consistently by one group of people—those who are dominant in this society—to rule, control, and exploit (to varying degrees) another group—those who are subordinate—for the benefit of the dominant group.

Oppression works through systems of inequality, as well as the dominance of certain values, beliefs, and assumptions about people and how society should be organized. These are institutional and ideological controls. Members of dominant groups generally have built-in economic, political, and cultural benefits and power, regardless of whether they are aware of, or even want, these benefits. This process of accruing benefits and power from institutional inequalities is often referred to as **privilege.** Those most privileged are often those least likely to be aware of it or to recognize it (McIntosh 1988). Oppression works on personal (micro), community (meso), national (macro), and global levels.

Oppression involves **prejudice**, which we define as unreasonable, unfair, and hostile attitudes toward people, and **discrimination**, differential treatment favoring those who are in positions of dominance. But oppression reaches beyond individual bigotry or good intentions: It is promoted by the **ideologies** and practices of every institution we encounter and are part of and cannot be fully changed without fundamental changes in these institutions (Anderson and Collins 1995). Our definition of oppression assumes that everyone is socialized to participate in oppressive practices, thereby helping to maintain them. People may be involved as direct perpetrators or passive beneficiaries, or they may direct **internalized oppression** at members of their own group. Oppression results in appropriation—the loss—both voluntary and involuntary—of voice, identity, and agency of oppressed peoples.

It is important to think about oppression as an intricate system, at times blatantly obvious and at others subtly nuanced, rather than an either/or dichotomy of privileged/disadvantaged or oppressor/oppressed. We use the term **matrix of oppression** to describe the interconnection and interrelatedness of various forms of oppression. People can be privileged in some respects (race or gender, for example) and disadvantaged in others (class or sexual orientation, for example).

Feminisms: Tangling with the "F" Word

Whether or not you consider yourself a feminist as a matter of personal identity, in women's studies you will study feminist perspectives and theories because these seek to understand and explain gender. *Feminism* is a term with a great deal of baggage. For some it is positive and empowering. For others it conjures up negative images of "ugly" women in overalls and flannel shirts, women who do not wear makeup or shave their legs or underarms and who are said to be lesbians, man-haters, or "ball-busters." Many women do not want to be associated with the label "feminist." They may agree that women deserve higher pay, sexual freedom, or greater opportunity, but they are careful to start their comments with a disclaimer: "I'm not a feminist, but . . ."

In the past several years, virtually every major U.S. publication has published a "feminism has gone too far" or "feminism is dead" piece. Some lament the difficulties of being White and male; others blame women's dissatisfactions on "too much equality"; and still others equate feminism with a "victim" mentality. A number of women are highly visible in this discourse, courted by talk-show hosts and interviewed in the Sunday newspapers. Naomi Wolf (1993), for example, has promoted "power feminism"—the idea that real feminists are go-getting, smart, and equal contenders for power with men. Karen Lehrman (1993) has attempted to discredit women's studies as unacademic, inappropriately personal, providing easy credits, and selling women short in terms of education. Elizabeth Fox-Genovese (1994) has criticized "the new Puritanism" of feminism. Katie Roiphe (1993) has attacked "rape crisis feminism." Camille Paglia (1990) has commented that women who go to frat houses on campus deserve to be raped. An *Esquire* magazine article talked approvingly of "do me feminism" and quoted a woman academic who claimed that there are a lot of "homely girls" in women's studies (Quindlen 1994).

When women talk of violence—battering, incest, rape, sexual abuse, and harassment—or racism, or living in poverty, or aging without health insurance, they are said to be "victim" feminists or, perhaps worse, "feminazis"—antisex, no fun, whining critics who are out to destroy men and the male establishment. This is part of what Faludi (1991) means when she talks of a backlash against feminism and women's rights and an erosion of the gains made for and by women in the past thirty years or so. In our society, women are socialized to care for men and to spare their feelings, but recognizing and discussing institutional inequalities between women as a group and men as a group are very different from "man-bashing." This garbled, trivializing media framework contributes to the many myths and misunderstandings about women's studies on the part of students and scholars in other fields. We consider three of these myths here.

Myth 1: Women's Studies Is Ideological

Some people assume that women's studies is not "real" scholarship but feminist propaganda. Yet feminist inquiry, analysis, and activism have arisen from real problems experienced by real women, from well-documented inequalities and discrimination. For instance, data on women's wages recorded for more than one hundred years in the United States show that women's wages, on average, have never risen above 75 percent of what men earn on average—that is, on average, women earn seventy-five cents for every dollar earned by men. And women of color fare much worse in this respect than White women. As we mentioned earlier, women's studies arose out of feminist organizing, and it values scholarly work that is relevant to activist concerns. Women's studies courses and projects seek to link intellectual, experiential, and emotional forms of connected knowing with the goal of improving women's lives. Women's studies is a rigorous endeavor, but its conception of rigor differs from that of much traditional scholarship, which values abstract, in-depth knowledge, narrowly defined. By contrast, women's studies scholarship places a high value on breadth and connectiveness; this kind of rigor requires broad understandings grounded in a range of experiences and the ability to make connections between knowledge and insights from different fields of study. Knowledge is never neutral, and in women's studies this is made explicit.

To some students and scholars, feminism is something to believe in because it provides a perspective that makes sense of the world and is personally empowering. But students who blithely blame everything on "rich White men" or "the patriarchy" without taking the trouble to read and think critically are anti-intellectual and inadvertently reinforce the notion that women's studies is anti-intellectual.

Myth 2: Women's Studies Is a White, Middle-Class Thing

Some White middle-class feminists have made, and still make, untenable claims about all women based on their own, necessarily partial, experience. Since the writings of Aphra Behn in the early 1600s, however, there have been White women who have thought about race and class as well as gender. Some White feminists worked against slavery in the nineteenth century, organized against the Ku Klux Klan,

and participated in the civil rights movement of the 1950s and 1960s. Indeed, the 1970s revitalization of feminism in the United States came out of civil rights organizing. In the past thirty years or so, White feminists like Charlotte Bunch, Ruth Frankenberg, Peggy McIntosh, Minnie Bruce Pratt, Adrienne Rich, and Mab Segrest have worked to integrate race and gender in their work. Much more can be done in this regard, but there is a foundation to build on. Many notable scholars, writers, and activists of color are also feminists. Among African Americans these include Toni Cade Bambara, Linda Burnham, Patricia Hill Collins, Angela Davis, bell hooks, June Jordan, Audre Lorde, Barbara Omolade, Sonia Sanchez, and Barbara Smith; among Asian Americans, Maxine Hong Kingston, Janice Mirikitani, Miriam Ching Louie, Chandra Talpade Mohanty, Sonia Shah, Nellie Wong, and Merle Woo; among Latinas, Gloria Anzaldua, Aida Hurtado, Elizabeth Martínez, Cherrie Moraga, and Aurora Levins Morales; among Native Americans, Paula Gunn Allen, Beth Brant, Chrystos, and Joy Harjo. Many of these writers are included in this anthology.

Myth 3: Women's Studies Is Narrowly Concerned with Women's Issues

Although women's studies aims to focus on women's experiences—in all their diversity—we do not see this as catering to narrow "special interests." On the contrary, feminist analyses provide a series of lenses to examine many topics and academic disciplines, including psychology, sociology, anthropology, political science, law, international relations, economic development, national income accounting, human biology, philosophies of science, and physics. Feminist scholarship is on the cutting edge of many academic fields, especially literature, history, philosophy, and film and media studies. It also raises crucial questions about teaching and learning, research design and methodologies, and theories of knowledge. Far from narrow, women's studies is concerned with thinking critically about the world in all its complexity.

It is important to acknowledge that women's studies students include a growing number of men. Although most of the readings in this book are by women, we have included several articles by men.

We are mindful that our readership includes male students, and in places we pose questions and give specific suggestions to them. There are many ways that men can contribute to and support wider opportunities for women—as sons, brothers, fathers, partners, friends, coworkers, supervisors, labor organizers, spiritual leaders, teachers, doctors, lawyers, police officers, judges, legislators. The questions at the end of each chapter and suggestions for taking action provide pointers in this direction. There is a long history of men's support for women's equality in the United States (see, for example, Kimmel and Mosmiller 1992 and Movement for a New Society 1983), and a training in women's studies can provide a powerful impetus for this. Clearly, the changes we discuss in this book cannot be achieved by women alone without male allies. But we also assume that there is something for men in this whole project, beyond being allies to women (Johnson 1997). We believe that those in dominant positions (on any social dimension, be it gender, race, class, age, ability, and so forth) are also limited by oppressive structures, that masculinity is socially constructed and highly constrained in our society. Despite the obvious benefits, privilege separates people and makes us ignorant of important truths. To be able to look others in the eye openly and completely, to join together to create a secure and sustainable future for everyone, we have to work to end systems of inequality. This repudiation of privilege, we believe, is not a sacrifice but rather the possibility of entering into genuine community, where we can all be more truly human.

Scope of the Book

The book is concerned with the project of theorizing about the oppressive conditions facing women today and the long-term work of transforming those conditions. Therefore, we begin with a discussion about the process of theory making and the importance of theory for social change. In the next five chapters we analyze women's experiences of self and home in terms of identity, body, sexuality, relationships and families, and violence. We then examine, in Chapter 7, the significance of living in a global economy and what it means, at all the levels of analysis mentioned earlier, to be a part of the United States. This discussion of the global economy is part of the theoretical framework for understanding women's experiences of work, wages, and welfare, health, crime and criminalization, the military, and the environment; these are treated in Chapters 8–12. We end, in Chapter 13, with a discussion of social change and focus on the importance of theories, visions, and action for creating change. Our overall argument is that to improve the lives of women in the United States also means redefining security and directing ourselves, our communities, this society, and the wider world toward a more sustainable future.

CHAPTER ONE

Theories and Theorizing:
Integrative Frameworks for Understanding

W hy are girls in the United States generally better at creative writing than at math? Has this always been so? Is this difference inevitable? Is rape about sexuality? Power? Both? Or neither? What is pornography? Is it the same as erotica? Do lesbians really want to be men? Why do so many marriages end in divorce? Why are so many children in the United States brought up in poverty? Why are more women going to jail than ever before?

People often say that facts speak for themselves. On the contrary, we argue that facts are always open to interpretation. They are "made to speak" according to your particular point of view. This is why we open this book about U.S. women's lives with a chapter on theory and theory making. How you think about women's situations and experiences affects what you see and what you understand by what you see. This chapter may seem abstract in the beginning, and you may want to return to it as you work with the material in the book. It would also be a good idea to review it at the end of your course. In this chapter we look at theory and theory making in general terms and give a brief account of feminist theoretical perspectives in preparation for understanding and interpreting women's experiences and issues presented in the rest of the book. During the course of the discussion we will consider these questions: What is a theory? Who creates theory, and how is it created? What is the purpose of theory?

Definition of a Theory

Consider the following assertion about poverty that many people in our society make: Poor people are poor because they are lazy. Think about the following questions:

1. What is the purpose of this statement?
2. What are the underlying assumptions on which it is based?
3. If the statement were true, what would it imply about action that should be taken?
4. Who came up with this idea, under what circumstances, and when?
5. How did this idea become popular?
6. What would you need to know to decide whether this statement is really true?

The statement above is a theory. It is one explanation of poverty, of why people are poor. It is built on a set of assumptions, or certain factors taken for granted. For example, this theory assumes there are well-paying jobs for all who want to work and that everyone meets the necessary requirements for those jobs, such as education, skills, or a means of providing for child care. These factors are proposed as facts or truths. This explanation of poverty takes a moral perspective. A psychological explanation of poverty may argue that people are poor because they have low self-esteem, lack self-confidence, and take on self-defeating behaviors. A sociological explanation might conclude that structures in our society, such as the educational and economic systems, are organized to exclude certain groups from being able to live above the poverty line. Each theory explicitly or implicitly suggests how to address the problem, which could then lead to appropriate action. If the problem is defined in terms of laziness, a step to ending poverty might be to punish people who are poor; if it is defined in psychological terms, assertiveness training or counseling might be suggested; and if it is defined in terms of structural inequality, ending discrimination would be the answer.

Every human being participates in theorizing, the activity of creating theory. For instance, we analyze the causes of poverty in our communities, the impact of immigration on the state we live in, or the experience of date rape. Theories generated by ordinary people, however, are not regarded as worthy of consideration beyond their own spheres of influence, among friends or coworkers, for example. Historically, Western, university-educated men from the upper classes — most often academics — and their theories, which are supported by societal institutions such as education and government, have had the greatest impact on how human beings and social phenomena are explained and understood. Their considerable influence, indeed, has even compelled many people simply to accept what is presented to them as conventional wisdom. For instance, a proposition that most people apparently agree with is "There will always be poverty," though this is not necessarily true. In the following sections, we discuss how only certain kinds of theories have been legitimized in this society and suggest another way of theorizing and developing knowledge that engages ordinary people.

Theories, Theorizing, and Ways of Knowing

The Dominant Perspective

From the perspective of the **dominant culture** — the values, symbols, means of expression, language, and interests of the people in power in this society — only certain types of theories have authority. Generally,

the authoritativeness of a theory about human beings and society is evaluated primarily along two dimensions. One is its degree of formality, which is determined according to how closely its development followed a particular way of theorizing, the so-called scientific method, the basics of which most of us learned in high school science classes. The second is the scope and generality of the theory (Smelser 1994).

Although in practice there are several variations of the scientific method, key elements must be present for a theory to fit in this category. The scientific method, originally devised by natural scientists, rests on the presumption of **objectivity,** "an attitude, philosophy, or claim . . . independent of the individual mind [through emotional detachment and social distance] . . . verified by a socially agreed-upon procedure such as those developed in science, mathematics, or history" (Kohl 1992, p. 84). Objectivity is seen as both a place to begin the process of theorizing and the outcome of that process. It has been long argued that "if done properly, [science] is the epitome of objectivity" (Tuana 1989, p. xi). Therefore, theories developed correctly using the scientific method are held out as value-free and neutral. The method is also empirical. That is, for something to be a fact, it must be physically observable and countable or measurable. This proposition is extended to include the notion that something is either true or not true, fact or not fact. Last, the experimental method, commonly used in science, "attempts to understand a whole by examining its parts, asking how something works rather than why it works, and derives abstract formulas to predict future results" (Duff 1993, p. 51). In summary, these elements add up to research methods that

> generally require a distancing of the researcher from her or his subjects of study; . . . absence of emotions from the research process; ethics and values are deemed inappropriate in the research process, either as the reason for scientific inquiry or as part of the research process itself; . . . adversarial debates, whether written or oral, become the preferred method of ascertaining truth: the arguments that can withstand the greatest assault and survive intact become the strongest truth.
>
> *(Collins 1990, p. 205)*

The scientific method was adopted by theorists in the social sciences as a way to validate and legitimate social scientific knowledge beginning in the late nineteenth century, as disciplines such as psychology and sociology were being developed. Since that time, academic disciplines like education, nursing, and social work have also adopted it as the primary method with which to develop new knowledge in their fields.

The second dimension for evaluating and judging theory is concerned with its scope and generality. The range is from the most specific explanation with the narrowest scope and most limited generality to the other end of the continuum, the general theory, which is the most abstract and is assumed to have the most general application (Smelser 1994). Many general theories have been promoted and accepted as being universally applicable. One of them, **biological determinism,** holds that a group's biological or genetic makeup shapes its social, political, and economic destiny. In mainstream society, biology is often assumed to be the basis of women's and men's different roles, especially women's ability to bear children. Most social scientists and feminist theorists see behavior as socially constructed and learned through childhood socialization, education, and the media, as argued by Judith Lorber (Reading 2). They explain differences in women's and men's roles in these terms and argue that variations in gender roles from one society to another provide strong evidence for a **social constructionist** view.

Alternative Perspectives

Evaluating and judging theories according to the scientific method has come under heavy criticism from theorists who typically have been viewed as outsiders to traditional academic circles, such as scholars in women's studies, ethnic studies, gay/lesbian studies, and some mainstream academics (e.g., Bleier 1984; Collins 1990; Duran 1998; Shiva 1988). These theorists have seen the fallacies, biases, and harmful outcomes of that way of creating knowledge. The primary criticisms are that knowledge created by the scientific method is not value-free, neutral, or generalizable to the extent it is claimed to be. Science, as with other academic disciplines, is "a cultural institution and as such is structured by the political, social, and economic val-

ues of the culture within which it is practiced" (Tuana 1989, p. xi). As Hubbard (1989) argues:

> To be believed, scientific facts must fit the worldview of the times. Therefore, at times of tension and upheaval, such as during the [1970s and 1980s], some researchers always try to prove that differences in the social, political, and economic status of women and men, blacks and whites, poor people and rich people, are inevitable because they are the results of people's inborn qualities and traits. Such scientists have tried to "prove" that blacks are innately less intelligent than whites, or that women are innately weaker, more nurturing, less good at math than men.
>
> *(p. 121)*

Rather than being neutral, all knowledge is socially constructed, value-laden, and biased and reflects and serves the interests of the culture that produced it, in this case the dominant culture.

The problem is not that theories are value-laden or biased, but that the values and biases of many theories are hidden under the cloak of "scientific objectivity." Moreover, there is the assumption that "if the science is 'good,' in a professional sense [following closely the rules of scientific method], it will also be good for society" (Hubbard 1989, p. 121). Many theories are applied not only to the United States but also to the rest of the world, often without acknowledgment that they primarily serve the interests of the dominant group in the United States. These theories are used to justify the inequalities in our society as well as differences and inequalities between the United States and other societies. Despite claims to the contrary, general theories created by mainstream scholars serve a political purpose in addition to whatever other purpose they are intended to serve. And, as Collins (1990) asserts, "Because elite white men and their representatives control structures of knowledge validation, white male interests pervade thematic content of traditional scholarship" (p. 201).

We further argue that theorizing is a political project, regardless of whether this is acknowledged. Social theories—explaining the behavior of human beings and society—serve to support the existing social order or can be used to challenge it. For women and men of color, White women, poor people, members of oppressed groups, and people with privilege who are interested in progressive social change, the political work of theorizing is to generate knowledge that challenges conventional wisdom and those formal theories that do not explain their real lived experiences, provide satisfactory solutions to their difficulties, or lead to their liberation. Charlotte Bunch divides theory into four interrelated parts: describing what exists, analyzing why that reality exists, determining what should exist, and hypothesizing how to change what is to what should be (Reading 1).

Theoretical Frameworks for Understanding Women's Lives

As an interdisciplinary field of study, women's studies incorporates theoretical insights from several academic disciplines, including anthropology cultural studies, economics, history, literature, philosophy, politics, psychology, and sociology. In turn, feminist scholarship has made significant contributions to these disciplines.

Feminist Theories

Women's studies also draws on feminist theories that primarily seek to understand and explain women's experiences. Many of these theories were developed in the context of women's organizing for change—for the abolition of slavery, for women's suffrage, for labor rights, the civil rights of people of color, women's rights, and gay/lesbian/bisexual/transgender rights. Feminist theories have been concerned with fundamental questions: Why are women in a subordinate position in our society and, indeed, worldwide? What are the origins of this subordination, and how is it perpetuated? Various answers to these questions have provided several approaches for explaining and challenging gender inequality.

Jackie Stacey (1993) notes that the concept of **patriarchy,** meaning "the systematic organization of male supremacy" (p. 53), is one that many theorists have found useful. Allan Johnson discusses this concept, emphasizing its systemic nature (Reading 3). For **radical feminists,** for example, patriarchy is a

core concept. Radical feminist analysis was a major contribution to what is sometimes called **second-wave feminism** in the United States (late 1960s to late 1980s). On this view, male domination manifests itself in women's sexuality, gender roles, and family relationships, and is carried over into the male-dominated world of work, government, religion, and law (Daly 1976; Echols 1989; Harne and Miller 1996; Koedt, Levine, and Rapone 1973). For radical feminists, women's liberation requires the eradication of patriarchy and the creation of alternative ways of living. Lesbians have been particularly influential in developing this strand of feminist thought and alternative women's institutions, including women's health projects, publishing, bookstores, coffeehouses, recording studios, and music festivals (Shugar 1995). Blee (1998) notes that "through women's culture, women-owned cooperative workplaces, and women-only households, radical feminists have fashioned highly participatory and egalitarian institutions separate from and opposed to the hierarchical, male-centered institutions of mainstream society" (p. 501). This approach is still significant in contemporary U.S. women's movements and is especially concerned with reproductive rights, as well as sexual exploitation in marriage, prostitution, pornography, and the trafficking of women and girls for the international sex trade.

Socialist feminist perspectives grew out of Marxist theories of the economy and concern for the emancipation of workers as a class from economic exploitation and drudgery. Feminist activists and writers who draw from this Marxist tradition see the oppression of women in terms of two interconnected systems, patriarchy and capitalism, and they are particularly concerned with the economic-class aspects of women's lives (Eisenstein 1979; Ferguson 1989; Hartmann 1981; Hennessy and Ingraham 1997; Roberts and Mizuta 1993). Eisenstein (1998) notes that "the language of socialism" seems foreign nowadays in the United States, due to the collapse of the former Soviet Union and the discrediting of the political philosophy of socialism along with it. She argues that an anticapitalist, feminist politics is currently of great relevance given the increasing integration of the world economic system, though "whether those politics are named socialist feminism remains to be seen" (p. 219).

Liberal feminist perspectives grew out of the political philosophy of liberalism, a theory about individual rights, freedom, choice, and privacy with roots in seventeenth-century European political thought. Liberalism has been a significant strand in the U.S. political discourse since the inception of the nation, although political and legal rights were originally limited to White men who owned land and property. Liberal feminists explain the oppression of women in terms of unequal access to existing political, economic, and social institutions (Bird and Briller 1969; Friedan 1963; Steinem 1983). They are concerned with women's rights being equal to those of men and that women have equal access to opportunities within existing economic and social structures. Much feminist organizing — for example, for the vote, abortion rights, equal pay, and women's access to professions — is based on this view.

In the late 1960s and the 1970s, many U.S. feminist activists tended to emphasize similarities in women's subordination, which has occurred in many cultures and historical periods. Activists and writers seemed to assume that the case for women's liberation would be stronger if they could show that the oppression of women was widespread, even universal. They spoke in dramatic terms, often making sweeping generalizations, in order to break through the silence about women's issues in this country, especially concerning sexuality, rape, and domestic violence. Nowadays it may be hard to imagine how significant this was at a time when there was virtually no public discourse on such matters.

Many of these activists and writers were White, middle-class, heterosexual women who generalized from their own experiences or those of women like them. They also focused on their subordination as women without paying attention to their privilege on other dimensions, notably race, class, and sexual orientation. These limitations have been roundly criticized by women of color (hooks 1984a; Moraga and Anzaldua 1983; Smith 1983; Trujillo 1998), working-class women (Kadi 1996; Steedman 1986), women from outside the United States (Mohanty, Russo, and Torres 1991), women with disabilities (Fiduccia and Saxton 1997), and lesbians and bisexual women (Harne and Miller 1996; Lorde 1984; Pharr 1988; Rich 1986a). They pointed out that women's experiences are structured by ability, age, class, race/ethnicity, sexuality, and nation as well as by gender. African American writers and activists challenged the idea that abortion is the key issue in reproductive rights — as is the case for many White women — and argued that the right to have children is often more important for Black women (Davis 1983b; Roberts 1997). Working-class women challenged the idea that working for wages is necessarily liberating, in contrast to upper-middle-class women's frustration at being stuck in the suburbs, especially in the 1950s and 60s, as housewives and mothers (Steedman 1986). Lesbian feminists analyzed heterosexuality in a way that few heterosexual women have done (e.g., Rich 1986a). As a result, feminist theorizing has become more nuanced, accurate, and useful.

The now-classic Combahee River Collective statement, written in the late 1970s by a group of Black feminists in the Boston area, integrates gender, race, class, and nation in its analysis (Reading 4). This statement also includes an anti-imperialist strand, reflecting the fact that, in the 1960s, 70s, and 80s, many U.S. feminists of color supported liberation movements in Africa, Asia, and Central America. Chandra Talpade Mohanty also writes about the intersection of gender, race, class, and nation in her experience as a South Asian woman in the United States (Reading 5). An integrative perspective that emphasizes **intersectionality** is not only the prerogative of women of color, though White women have been much slower to develop this kind of analysis (Frankenberg 1993; Segrest 1994; Spelman 1988). It is essential to a multicultural approach and a fundamental assumption throughout this anthology.

Postmodern feminism, developed by academic feminists, also repudiates broad-brush theorizing and emphasizes the particularity of women's experiences in specific cultural and historical contexts (Ferguson and Wicke 1992; Nicholson 1990). Some feminists have asked whether it is meaningful to talk of women as a group, when there are so many differences among women (Weedon 1987). Denise Riley (1988) argues that the category "woman" has not meant the same thing throughout history and that its specific meaning should be investigated in different historical contexts, not assumed. An emphasis on difference also raises the question as to whether women can engage in collective action, something which 1970s feminists usually took for granted. Stacey (1993) argues that postmodern theorists have also emphasized the ways people's **subjectivity**—our thoughts, feelings, and actions—are produced and limited by external constraints. This has been useful in thinking about why women "accept" their subordinate position. Previous explanations of power and subordination, Stacey notes, emphasized coercion, or social conditioning through childhood socialization, schooling, and media representations. Where appropriate, we advance both of these explanations in this book. But in discussing body image and eating disorders, for example, Susan Bordo (1993) writes about power as inherent in institutions and technologies to explain why women might willingly accept norms and practices that limit them.

Theoretical perspectives are developed in response to particular circumstances and with reference to previous theories. They are refined and adapted as understanding grows and as events shed new light on issues or problems. Theory is never finished but is continuously evolving. In the 1990s, the mainstream media consistently depicted facile stereotypes of feminism and feminists that have deterred many younger women from using the term, even though they often support feminist ideas. Young women may think of themselves as **third-wave feminists,** challenging the second-wave feminism of their mothers' generation as no longer relevant and emphasizing personal voice, ambiguity, contradiction, and multiple identities (Findlen 1995; Heywood and Drake 1997; Walker 1995; Zita 1997). The wave metaphor suggests both continuity and discontinuity with the past as women shape theoretical understandings for their generation and historical period. Second-wave feminism was specific to its time and also built on the work of suffragists and women's rights advocates active toward the end of the nineteenth century and into the twentieth century (**first-wave feminism**). Note that these shorthand labels make very powerful transformative movements, with their divergent and overlapping strands, seem much neater, more unitary, and more static than they are in reality.

In seeking to understand U.S. women's lives, we need theoretical lenses that allow us to see their complexity—the generalities as well as differences. We rely on a perspective that integrates gender, race,

class, and nation, and includes four levels of analysis—micro (personal or individual), meso (community or neighborhood), macro, and global—to understand and explain women's experiences and the social system we are a part of. We argue for cultural specificity but also believe that collective action—based on full acknowledgment of differences, as well as some shared goals—is possible and necessary. Kalima Rose exemplifies this approach in an international context in her account of the 1995 Beijing women's conference (Reading 6).

We are also concerned with the deterioration of the physical environment that provides the basis for all human life. This leads us to relatively new **ecofeminist** approaches. Ynestra King (1998) notes that for ecofeminists, "Modern Western science and technology . . . capitalism and Eurocentric masculinist culture together pose a threat to the continuation of life on earth" (p. 207). A core point in ecofeminist analysis involves the concept of dualism, where various attributes are thought of in oppositional terms: culture/nature, mind/body, male/female, civilized/primitive, self/other, and so on. Val Plumwood (1993) argues that these dualisms are mutually reinforcing and should be thought of as an interlocking set. In each pair, one side is valued over the other. Culture, mind, male, civilized, for example, are valued over nature, body, female, primitive, which are thought of as "other" and inferior. This perspective draws on strands found in radical feminism and socialist feminism, and it can link the domination of women and the domination of nature with exploitation based on race and class.

"Socially Lived" Theorizing

As discussed earlier, traditional scholarship primarily validates knowledge that is produced using some form of the scientific method, by White men and others who form an elite group of scholars or subscribe to their views and approaches. We argue that theorizing is not the sole domain of elites. Catharine MacKinnon (1991) talks about "articulating the theory of women's practice—resistance, visions, consciousness, injuries, notions of community, experiences of inequality. By practic[e], I mean socially lived" (p. 20). Much of the work included in this book exemplifies socially lived theorizing. A notable example is provided by Abra Fortune Chernik (Reading 14), who discusses her personal struggle with an eating disorder and the process of understanding and overcoming it. Our framework for theory making is based on the following assumptions:

- All knowledge is socially constructed; there is no value-free or neutral knowledge.

- Everyone has the capacity to be a creator of knowledge.

- What one knows comes out of a specific historical and cultural context, whether one is an insider or outsider to that context.

- It is the responsibility of everyone to reflect on, evaluate, and judge the world around us, and our places in that world, as an essential element of theorizing.

- Knowledge should be used for the purposes of helping to liberate oppressed people and to transform the current social and economic structures of inequality into a sustainable world for all people.

As Catharine MacKinnon (1991) remarks, "It is common to say that something is good in theory but not in practice. I always want to say, then it is not such a good theory, is it?" (p. 1).

In writing about the Holocaust—the mass murder primarily of Jewish people but also of Roma people, people with disabilities, and gay people in Europe during World War II—Alan Rosenberg (1988) makes a profound distinction between knowing and understanding something. According to Rosenberg, knowing is having the facts about a particular event or condition. One knows the Holocaust happened: Eight million people were murdered, and countless others were tortured, raped, and otherwise devastated; the Nazis, under the leadership of Adolph Hitler, were the perpetrators; others, both inside and outside Germany, including the United States initially, were unable or refused to help; the result was the slaughter of six million Jewish people. Traditional educational practices, epitomized by the scientific method, teach us primarily to know. For Rosenberg, knowing is the first step to understanding, a much deeper process that, in the case of the Holocaust, involves not only comprehending its significance and

longer-term effects but also trying to discover how to prevent similar injustices in the future.

> Knowing . . . refers to factual information or the process by which it is gathered. Understanding refers to systematically grasping the significance of an event in such a way that it becomes integrated into one's moral and intellectual life. Facts can be absorbed without their having any impact on the way we understand ourselves or the world we live in; facts in themselves do not make a difference. It is the understanding of them that makes a difference.
>
> *(Rosenberg 1988, p. 382)*

Recognizing theory making as a political project helps us understand, in the way Rosenberg describes it, the conditions facing women in particular, as well as others in subordinate positions. So how do we begin to understand?

Early in the U.S. women's liberation movement of the sixties and seventies, the slogan "The personal is political" was popularized to validate individual women's personal experiences as a starting point for recognizing and understanding discrimination against women as a group. This promoted the practice of "starting from one's own experiences" as a legitimate way to theorize and create new knowledge. This practice was also useful in counteracting the dominant view of theorizing that personal experience, along with emotions and values, contaminates the "purity" of the scientific method. As a first step, starting from what we know the most about—our experiences, our subjectivity—is helpful, but it also contains obvious problems. On the one hand, there is self-centeredness, as reflected in comments such as "I can only know my experience," "I can only speak for myself," and "What does all this have to do with me?" On the other hand, a naive generalization like "As a woman, I assume that all women have experienced the same things I have" also limits the extent to which we can understand diverse women's experiences.

As mentioned earlier in our brief discussion of feminist theories, different social and historical situations give rise to very different experiences and theories about those experiences, hence the importance of **situated knowledge** (Belenky, Clinchy, Goldberger, and Tarnle 1986; Collins 1990) or **standpoint**

theory (Hartsock 1983). What we know is the direct result of our experience, is understood in a specific historical and cultural context, and cannot be generalized. For instance, the experience of being a single mother as a poor teenager in a rural community in the 1990s would be very different from that of being a single mother as an established professional in a big city in the twenty-first century. One could not apply her experience to the other, and neither could speak authoritatively about being a single mother in the 1960s.

Our task of socially lived theorizing involves several important challenges. We are faced with the self-centeredness of pure subjectivity, "in which knowledge and meaning [are] lodged in oneself and one's own experiences" (Maher and Tetreault 1994, p. 94). We must also negotiate the problem of the **cultural relativism** of situated knowledge, in which the authenticity of subjective knowledge is not challenged because it is seen as someone's, or some group's, "real experience," and consequently, others do not have the authority to question it. Thus, the White supremacist views of Ku Klux Klan members might be considered equally as valid as those held by antiracist activists, or a New York judge could sentence a Chinese immigrant man to a mere five years' probation for killing his wife on the argument that the murder was the result of "cultural differences" (Yen 1989).

Given these major challenges arising out of pure subjectivity and cultural relativism, how can we generate knowledge that reflects the perspectives and interests of a broad range of people, communities, and life circumstances, that is visionary, not just reactive, and that could lead to social change? Socially lived theorizing requires a methodology that includes collective dialogue and **praxis**—reflection and action on the world to transform it. Paulo Freire (1989) calls this methodology **conscientization,** or gaining a "critical consciousness," and describes it as "learning to perceive social, political, and economic contradictions, [the effects of the push and pull of opposing forces], and to take action against the oppressive elements of this reality" (p. 19).

"Learning to perceive social, political, and economic contradictions" is a tall order for many of us who have been formally educated by what Freire calls the "banking method," whereby teachers deposit knowledge—dates, historical facts, formulas for problem solving, for example—into the minds of students and expect them to be able to withdraw this information at a given time, such as during exams, quizzes, and class presentations. During our schooling most of us are not often asked such questions as, What are the assumptions in the statement you are making? How do you know what you know? Why do you think so? What are the implications of your position? Many of us may have sat in class listening to a teacher or other students and have kept quiet when we knew what was being said did not match our experience. When we put forward our ideas and observations, they might have been shot down as silly, naive, or too idealistic. We were expected to back up our experience with facts. We were encouraged to accept facts and ideas as they were given to us and to accept social conditions as they are. Indeed, we may often have accepted things as they are without thinking about them, or simply not noticed injustices happening around us. Most likely, too, we have had little opportunity to engage in honest dialogue with others—both people like ourselves and those from different backgrounds—about important issues.

Having honest dialogues and asking critical questions move us beyond excessive subjectivity because we are compelled to see and understand many different sides of the same subject. Creating theory for social change—something that will advance human development and create a better world for all—gives us a basis for making critical judgments of facts and experiences. This in turn provides a framework for deciding where to draw the line on cultural relativism. Through ongoing, detailed discussion and conscientious listening to others, we can generate a carefully thought-out set of principles that lead to greater understanding of issues and of acceptable actions in a given situation.

Many assume that the scientific method involves authoritativeness and rigor. We believe this alternative way of theorizing redefines rigor by demanding the engagement of our intellectual, emotional, and spiritual selves. It compels us to think systematically and critically, requires us to face the challenges of talking about our differences, and obligates us to consider the real implications and consequences of our theories. Knowledge created in this way helps us "to systematically grasp . . . the significance of an event in such a way that it becomes integrated into [our] moral and intellectual life," also a form of rigor (Rosenberg 1988, p. 382).

◆◆◆
Questions for Reflection

In attempting to understand any theoretical perspective, we find the following questions helpful:

1. What does the theory aim to explain?

2. How does it do this? What are the basic arguments and assumptions?

3. What does the theory focus on? What does it ignore?

4. What is the cultural and historical context giving rise to the theory?

5. Do you find this perspective useful? If so, why?

6. Are you convinced by the arguments? Why or why not?

7. What kinds of research questions does this perspective generate?

8. What kinds of actions and projects follow from this perspective?

As you read and discuss the readings in this chapter, think about these questions:

1. How do you explain poverty?

2. How do you explain inequality between women and men in this country? Between White people and people of color in this country?

3. How do you think change happens? How is knowledge related to social change?

◆◆◆
Taking Action

1. Pay attention to the theoretical ideas incorporated into TV news reports. When the presenter says, "Now for the stories behind the headlines," whose stories are these? Who is telling them? What, if anything, is missing from these accounts? What else do you need to know in order to have a full explanation?

2. Analyze what happens when you get into an argument with a friend, classmate, or teacher about an issue that matters to you. Are you both using the same assumptions? Do you have compatible understandings of the issue? If not, how can you explain your position more clearly? Are facts enough to convince someone who is skeptical of your views?

ONE

Not by Degrees
Feminist Theory and Education
Charlotte Bunch

The development of feminist theory and a rigorous analysis of society are more important for us today than ever before. Feminists need to understand the forces working against us, as well as to analyze our experiences as a movement, if we are to survive the antiwoman backlash and keep our visions alive. When feminists despair, burn out, or give up, it is often because the forces against us are strong and because our theoretical framework does not give us a sense of how individual activities contribute to significant victories in the future. A solid feminist theory would help us understand present events in a way that would enable us to develop the visions and plans for change that sustain people engaged in day-to-day political activity.

When I left the university to do full-time work in "the movement" in the 1960s, it didn't occur to me that I would return one day to teach or write feminist theory. Like many others who chose to become movement activists then, I felt that I was leaving behind not only the academic world, but also what I saw as irrelevant theorizing. However, as I experienced the problems of movement organizing when an overall analysis was lacking, felt the frustration of conflicts where issues were not clear, and observed people dropping out of political activity, I became aware of the critical role of theory in the movement. I began to see feminist theory not as academic, but as a process based on understanding and advancing the activist movement.

While my growing sense of the importance of theory applied to all my feminist work, the urgency that I felt about it became clearest during my involvement with lesbian-feminism. When the lesbian issue became a major controversy in the women's movement in the early 1970s, I realized that in order for lesbians to function openly, we would have to understand *why* there was so much resistance to this issue. It was not enough to document discrimination against homosexuals or to appeal to fairness. We had to figure out why lesbianism was taboo, why

it was a threat to feminists, and then devise strategies accordingly. I saw that my life as a lesbian in the movement depended on, among other things, the development of a theory that would explain our immediate conflicts in the context of a long-term view of feminism. This theoretical perspective developed along with our activism, but it required us to consciously ask certain questions, to look at our experiences in and out of the movement, and to consider existing feminist theory in new ways. Through this process, new interpretations of the relationship between lesbianism and feminism, and new strategies for ending lesbian oppression, emerged.

For example, as we examined feminists' fear of being called lesbians, we were able to confront directly the role that such name-calling played in the oppression of all women. Having a theory about lesbian oppression did not tell us what to do tactically, but it did provide a framework for understanding situations, for placing them in a broader context, and for evaluating possible courses of action. This experience showed me that theory was not simply intellectually interesting, but was crucial to the survival of feminism.

The Functions of Feminist Theory

Theory enables us to see immediate needs in terms of long-range goals and an overall perspective on the world. It thus gives us a framework for evaluating various strategies in both the long and the short run, and for seeing the types of changes that they are likely to produce. Theory is not just a body of facts or a set of personal opinions. It involves explanations and hypotheses that are based on available knowledge and experience. It is also dependent on conjecture and insight about how to interpret those facts and experiences and their significance.

No theory is totally "objective," since it reflects the interests, values, and assumptions of those who created it. Feminist theory relies on the underlying assumption that it will aid the liberation of women. Feminist theory, therefore, is not an unengaged study of women. It is an effort to bring insights from the movement and from various female experiences together with research and data-gathering to produce new approaches to understanding and ending female oppression.

While feminist theory begins with the immediate need to end women's oppression, it is also a way of viewing the world. Feminism is an entire world view or *gestalt,* not just a list of "women's issues." Feminist theory provides a basis for understanding every area of our lives, and a feminist perspective can affect the world politically, culturally, economically, and spiritually. The initial tenets of feminism have already been established — the idea that power is based on gender differences and that men's illegitimate power over women taints all aspects of society, for instance. But now we face the arduous task of systematically working through these ideas, fleshing them out and discovering new ones.

When the development of feminist theory seems too slow for the changes that we seek, feminists are tempted to submerge our insights into one of the twentieth century's two dominant progressive theories of reality and change: democratic liberalism or Marxist socialism. However, the limitations of these systems are increasingly obvious. While feminism can learn from both of them, it must not be tied to either because its greatest strength lies in providing an alternative view of the world.

The full implications of feminism will evolve over time, as we organize, experiment, think, analyze, and revise our ideas and strategies in light of our experiences. No theory emerges in full detail overnight; the dominant theories of our day have expanded and changed over many decades. That it will take time should not discourage us. That we might fail to pursue our ideas — given the enormous need for them in society today — is unconscionable.

Because feminist theory is still emerging and does not have agreed-upon answers (or even approaches to many questions), it is difficult to work out strategies based on that theory. This difficulty can lead feminists to rely on the other theories of change or to fall into the "any action/no action" bind. When caught in this bind, one may go ahead with action — any action — for its own sake, or be paralyzed, taking no action for lack of a sense of what is "right." To

escape this bind, we must remember that we do not need, and indeed never will have, all the answers before we act, and that it is often only through taking action that we can discover some of them. The purpose of theory, then, is not to provide a pat set of answers about what to do, but to guide us in sorting out options, and to keep us out of the "any action/no action" bind. Theory also keeps us aware of the questions that need to be asked, so that what we learn in each activity will lead to more effective strategies in the future. Theory thus both grows out of and guides activism in a continuous, spiraling process.

In pursuing feminist theory as an activist, I have become increasingly aware of the need to demystify it. Theory is not something set apart from our lives. Our assumptions about reality and change influence our actions constantly. The question is not whether we have a theory, but how aware we are of the assumptions behind our actions, and how conscious we are of the choices we make daily among different theories. For example, when we decide whether to put our energies into a rape-crisis center or into efforts to change rape laws, we are acting according to certain theories about how service projects and legislation affect change. These theories may be implicit or explicit, but they are always there.

A Model for Theory

Theory doesn't necessarily progress in a linear fashion, but examining its components is useful in understanding existing political theory as well as in developing new insights. In the model I have developed, I divide theory into four interrelated parts: description, analysis, vision, and strategy.

1. Description: *Describing what exists* may sound simple, but the choices that we make about interpreting and naming reality provide the basis for the rest of our theory. Changing people's perceptions of the world through new descriptions of reality is usually a prerequisite for altering that reality. For example, thirty years ago, few people would say that women in the United States were oppressed. Today, the oppression of women is acknowledged by a large number of people, primarily because of feminist work which described that oppression in a number of ways. This work has involved consciousness-raising, as well as gathering

and interpreting facts about women in order to substantiate our assertions. Description is necessary for all theory; unfortunately for feminism, much of our work has not yet gone beyond this point.

2. Analysis: *Analyzing why that reality exists* involves determining its origins and the reasons for its perpetuation. This is perhaps the most complex task of theory and is often seen as its entire function. In seeking to understand the sources of women's oppression and why it is perpetuated, we have to examine biology, economics, psychology, sexuality, and so on. We must also look at what groups and institutions benefit from oppression, and why they will, therefore, strive to maintain it. Analyzing why women are oppressed involves such things as sorting out how the forms of oppression change over time while the basic fact of oppression remains, or probing how the forms of oppression vary in different cultures while there are cross-cultural similarities.

Analysis of why something happens sometimes gets short-circuited by the temptation to ascribe everything to one single factor, such as capitalism or motherhood. In developing an analysis, I find that it is useful to focus initially on a phenomenon in a limited context and consider a wide range of factors that may affect it. Then, as that context is understood, the analysis can be expanded. Above all, we need not feel that we must answer the "why" of everything all at once with a single explanation.

3. Vision: *Determining what should exist* requires establishing principles (or values) and setting goals. In taking action to bring about change, we operate consciously or unconsciously out of certain assumptions about what is right or what we value (principles), and out of our sense of what society ought to be (goals). This aspect of theory involves making a conscious choice about those principles in order to make our visions and goals concrete. We must look at our basic assumptions about such things as "human nature" and how it can be changed, about the relationships of individuals to groups, about whether men and women are essentially different, for example. We may choose not to address some of these issues yet, but since every action carries implicit assumptions, we must be conscious of them so that we do not operate out of old theoretical frameworks by default. The

clearer we are about our principles—for example, whether we think that women should gain as much power as possible in every area, or believe, instead, that power itself should be eliminated—the more easily we can set our long-term goals. Immediate goals can then be based on an assessment of what can be accomplished that may be short of our long-term vision, but moves toward, not away, from it. Visions, principles, and goals will change with experience, but the more explicit we make them, the more our actions can be directed toward creating the society we want, as well as reacting to what we don't like.

4. Strategy: *Hypothesizing how to change what is to what should be* moves directly into questions of changing reality. Some people see strategy not as part of theory, but rather as a planning process based on theory. But I include strategy here in its broadest sense—the overall approach one takes to how to accomplish one's goals. The descriptive and analytic process of theory help develop a more systematic understanding of the way things work, but they usually do not make obvious what one should do. Developing a strategy requires that we draw out the consequences of our theory and suggest general directions for change.

Like the other aspects of theory, this involves a combination of information-gathering and creative speculation. It entails making judgments about what will lead to change—judgments that are based both on description and analysis of reality, and on visions, principles, and goals. Developing a strategy also involves examining various tools for change—legislative, military, spiritual—and determining which are most effective in what situations. There are many questions to consider, such as what sectors of society can best be mobilized to carry out which types of action. In working out which strategies will be most effective, the interaction between developing theory and actively experimenting with it becomes most clear. For in all aspects of theory development, theory and activism continually inform and alter each other.

Using the Model

This four-part model for theory can be used in many ways. In my feminist-theory classes, we have tried to understand different theories by outlining how various authors address each of its developmental parts. For example, we take Shulamith Firestone's *Dialectic of Sex* and discuss her approach to description, analysis, vision, and strategy. Then we compare her ideas in each area with those of other radical feminists, in an effort to see the common tenets of radical feminism, the important areas of disagreement, and the strategy implications of those differences. We then take the same approach to socialist-feminist authors, compare them to each other and to radical feminist works, and so on.

Another way to use this approach to theory is to examine possible ways of addressing a specific issue in terms of these processes. For example, on the issue of reproductive freedom, we can use theoretical work to understand the implications behind various strategies. Considerable work has been done detailing the variety of ways in which women lack control over reproduction, from forced sterilization to negligence in the development of contraceptives. Several analyses of why women do not have control over our bodies have been suggested. These range from the idea that men fear women's powers to create life and therefore compensate by controlling reproduction, to the proposition that capitalism is the primary cause because it must control the number of workers produced, to the view that the Catholic Church is the dominant perpetuator of this situation because its control over reproduction and matters of family life is central to its power. Most analyses also look at which institutions are most influential and which are most vulnerable to change, and the relations between them—e.g., how the Catholic Church affects hospital and government policies.

There are considerable differences of opinion about how reproduction should be treated. Some feminists argue that women should have absolute control over our bodies and reproduction at all times and in all circumstances. Others contend that there can be some legitimate limits on an individual woman's control; in the case of abortion, for example, limiting a woman's right to abortion on demand to the first trimester. Some argue that the state should prescribe standards of control that "protect" women such as the requirement of a thirty-day waiting period for any sterilization; and still others hold that a woman's control must be subordinate to the obligation of government to supervise overall population growth.

The practical consequences of these differences in theory become clear when strategies for gaining women's reproductive rights are discussed. Even among those who agree that women's lack of control over reproduction is central to our oppression, there are differences in strategy based on differences in analysis and vision. Those who think that the Catholic Church is the primary enemy of women's reproductive rights may focus on efforts to remove Church influence on the state, the fight against religious tax exemptions, and so on, while those who see multinational corporations as the primary controller of population issues would focus on them. The controversy among feminists over whether having the government require a thirty-day waiting period for all sterilizations would protect women or further abridge our rights to control our bodies illustrates how disagreement over vision and goals leads to different strategies and often to conflict over what we will demand.

This example, though simplified here, illustrates how the four-part model in particular, and theory in general, can be used to clarify practical political problems. When we understand the basis of our disagreements and the nature of the forces against us, we are better equipped to come to some agreement or to realize when compromise may not be possible. Theory helps clarify how things work and what our choices are, and thus aids in determining where to put our energies and how to challenge the sources of our oppression most effectively.

Theory is also a tool for passing on the knowledge we have gained from our life experiences and movement projects. Feminists need to analyze personal experiences as well as political developments—to sort out our initial assumptions about goals and analysis, to look at the strategies we used and why, and to evaluate the results in terms of what could be learned for the future.

◆◆◆

The Social Construction of Gender

Judith Lorber

Talking about gender for most people is the equivalent of fish talking about water. Gender is so much the routine ground of everyday activities that questioning its taken-for-granted assumptions and presuppositions is like thinking about whether the sun will come up. Gender is so pervasive that in our society we assume it is bred into our genes. Most people find it hard to believe that gender is constantly created and re-created out of human interaction, out of social life, and is the texture and order of that social life. Yet gender, like culture, is a human production that depends on everyone constantly "doing gender" (West and Zimmerman 1987).

And everyone "does gender" without thinking about it. Today, on the subway, I saw a well-dressed man with a year-old child in a stroller. Yesterday, on a bus, I saw a man with a tiny baby in a carrier on his chest. Seeing men taking care of small children in public is increasingly common—at least in New York City. But both men were quite obviously stared at—and smiled at, approvingly. Everyone was doing gender—the men who were changing the role of fathers and the other passengers, who were applauding them silently. But there was more gendering going on that probably fewer people noticed. The baby was wearing a white crocheted cap and white clothes. You couldn't tell if it was a boy or a girl. The child in the stroller was wearing a dark blue T-shirt and dark print pants. As they started to leave the train, the father put a Yankee baseball cap on the child's head. Ah, a boy, I thought. Then I noticed the gleam of tiny earrings in the child's ears, and as they got off, I saw the little flowered sneakers and lace-trimmed socks. Not a boy after all. Gender done.

Gender is such a familiar part of daily life that it usually takes a deliberate disruption of our expectations of how women and men are supposed to act to pay attention to how it is produced. Gender signs and signals are so ubiquitous that we usually fail to note them—unless they are missing or ambiguous. Then we are uncomfortable until we have successfully placed the other person in a gender status; otherwise, we feel socially dislocated. In our society, in addition to man and woman, the status can be *transvestite* (a person who dresses in opposite-gender clothes) and *transsexual* (a person who has had sex-change surgery). Transvestites and transsexuals construct their gender status by dressing, speaking, walking, gesturing in the ways prescribed for women or men—whichever they want to be taken for—and so does any "normal" person.

For the individual, gender construction starts with assignment to a sex category on the basis of what the genitalia look like at birth. Then babies are dressed or adorned in a way that displays the category because parents don't want to be constantly asked whether their baby is a girl or a boy. A sex category becomes a gender status through naming, dress, and the use of other gender markers. Once a child's gender is evident, others treat those in one gender differently from those in the other, and the children respond to the different treatment by feeling different and behaving differently. As soon as they can talk, they start to refer to themselves as members of their gender. Sex doesn't come into play again until puberty, but by that time, sexual feelings and desires and practices have been shaped by gendered norms and expectations. Adolescent boys and girls approach and avoid each other in an elaborately scripted and gendered mating dance. Parenting is gendered, with different expectations for mothers and for fathers, and people of different genders work at different kinds of jobs. The work adults do as mothers and fathers and as low-level workers and high-level bosses, shapes women's and men's life experiences, and these experiences produce different feelings, consciousness, relationships, skills—ways of being that we call feminine or masculine. All of these processes constitute the social construction of gender.

Gendered roles change—today fathers are taking care of little children, girls and boys are wearing unisex clothing and getting the same education, women and men are working at the same jobs.

Although many traditional social groups are quite strict about maintaining gender differences, in other social groups they seem to be blurring. Then why the one-year-old's earrings? Why is it still so important to mark a child as a girl or a boy, to make sure she is not taken for a boy or he for a girl? What would happen if they were? They would, quite literally, have changed places in their social world.

To explain why gendering is done from birth, constantly and by everyone, we have to look not only at the way individuals experience gender but at gender as a social institution. As a social institution, gender is one of the major ways that human beings organize their lives. Human society depends on a predictable division of labor, a designated allocation of scarce goods, assigned responsibility for children and others who cannot care for themselves, common values and their systematic transmission to new members, legitimate leadership, music, art, stories, games, and other symbolic productions. One way of choosing people for the different tasks of society is on the basis of their talents, motivations, and competence — their demonstrated achievements. The other way is on the basis of gender, race, ethnicity — ascribed membership in a category of people. Although societies vary in the extent to which they use one or the other of these ways of allocating people to work and to carry out other responsibilities, every society uses gender and age grades. Every society classifies people as "girl and boy children," "girls and boys ready to be married," and "fully adult women and men," constructs similarities among them and differences between them, and assigns them to different roles and responsibilities. Personality characteristics, feelings, motivations, and ambitions flow from these different life experiences so that the members of these different groups become different kinds of people. The process of gendering and its outcome are legitimated by religion, law, science, and the society's entire set of values.

Gender as Process, Stratification, and Structure

As a social institution, gender is a process of creating distinguishable social statuses for the assignment of rights and responsibilities. As part of a stratification system that ranks these statuses un-

equally, gender is a major building block in the social structures built on these unequal statuses.

As a *process*, gender creates the social differences that define "woman" and "man." In social interaction throughout their lives, individuals learn what is expected, see what is expected, act and react in expected ways, and thus simultaneously construct and maintain the gender order: "The very injunction to be given gender takes place through discursive routes: to be a good mother, to be a heterosexually desirable object, to be a fit worker, in sum, to signify a multiplicity of guarantees in response to a variety of different demands all at once" (J. Butler 1990, 145). Members of a social group neither make up gender as they go along nor exactly replicate in rote fashion what was done before. In almost every encounter, human beings produce gender, behaving in the ways they learned were appropriate for their gender status, or resisting or rebelling against these norms. Resistance and rebellion have altered gender norms, but so far they have rarely eroded the statuses.

Gendered patterns of interaction acquire additional layers of gendered sexuality, parenting, and work behaviors in childhood, adolescence, and adulthood. Gendered norms and expectations are enforced through informal sanctions of gender-inappropriate behavior by peers and by formal punishment or threat of punishment by those in authority should behavior deviate too far from socially imposed standards for women and men.

Everyday gendered interactions build gender into the family, the work process, and other organizations and institutions, which in turn reinforce gender expectations for individuals. Because gender is a process, there is room not only for modification and variation by individuals and small groups but also for institutionalized change (J. W. Scott 1988, 7).

As part of a *stratification* system, gender ranks men above women of the same race and class. Women and men could be different but equal. In practice, the process of creating difference depends to a great extent on differential evaluation. As Nancy Jay (1981) says: "That which is defined, separated out, isolated from all else is A and pure. Not-A is necessarily impure, a random catchall, to which nothing is external except A and the principle of order that separates it from Not-A" (45). From the individual's point of view, whichever gender is A, the other is Not-A; gender boundaries tell the individual who is like him or her, and all the rest are unlike.

From society's point of view, however, one gender is usually the touchstone, the normal, the dominant, and the other is different, deviant, and subordinate. In Western society, "man" is A, "wo-man" is Not-A. (Consider what a society would be like where woman was A and man Not-A.)

The further dichotomization by race and class constructs the gradations of a heterogeneous society's stratification scheme. Thus, in the United States, white is A, African American is Not-A; middle class is A, working class is Not-A, and "African-American women occupy a position whereby the inferior half of a series of these dichotomies converge" (P. H. Collins 1989, 70). The dominant categories are the hegemonic ideals, taken so for granted as the way things should be that white is not ordinarily thought of as a race, middle class as a class, or men as a gender. The characteristics of these categories define the Other as that which lacks the valuable qualities the dominants exhibit.

In a gender-stratified society, what men do is usually valued more highly than what women do because men do it, even when their activities are very similar or the same. In different regions of southern India, for example, harvesting rice is men's work, shared work, or women's work: "Wherever a task is done by women it is considered easy, and where it is done by [men] it is considered difficult" (Mencher 1988, 104). A gathering and hunting society's survival usually depends on the nuts, grubs, and small animals brought in by the women's foraging trips, but when the men's hunt is successful, it is the occasion for a celebration. Conversely, because they are the superior group, white men do not have to do the "dirty work," such as housework; the most inferior group does it, usually poor women of color (Palmer 1989).

Freudian psychoanalytic theory claims that boys must reject their mothers and deny the feminine in themselves in order to become men: "For boys the major goal is the achievement of personal masculine identification with their father and sense of secure masculine self, achieved through superego formation and disparagement of women" (Chodorow 1978, 165). Masculinity may be the outcome of boys' intrapsychic struggles to separate their identity from that of their mothers, but the proofs of masculinity are culturally shaped and usually ritualistic and symbolic (Gilmore 1990).

The Marxist feminist explanation for gender inequality is that by demeaning women's abilities and keeping them from learning valuable technological skills, bosses preserve them as a cheap and exploitable reserve army of labor. Unionized men who could be easily replaced by women collude in this process because it allows them to monopolize the better-paid, more interesting, and more autonomous jobs: "Two factors emerge as helping men maintain their separation from women and their control of technological occupations. One is the active gendering of jobs and people. The second is the continual creation of sub-divisions in the work processes, and levels in work hierarchies, into which men can move in order to keep their distance from women" (Cockburn 1985, 13).

Societies vary in the extent of the inequality in social status of their women and men members, but where there is inequality, the status "woman" (and its attendant behavior and role allocations) is usually held in lesser esteem than the status "man." Since gender is also intertwined with a society's other constructed statuses of differential evaluation—race, religion, occupation, class, country of origin, and so on—men and women members of the favored groups command more power, more prestige, and more property than the members of the disfavored groups. Within many social groups, however, men are advantaged over women. The more economic resources, such as education and job opportunities, are available to a group, the more they tend to be monopolized by men. In poorer groups that have few resources (such as working-class African Americans in the United States), women and men are more nearly equal, and the women may even outstrip the men in education and occupational status (Almquist 1987).

As a *structure*, gender divides work in the home and in economic production, legitimates those in authority, and organizes sexuality and emotional life (Connell 1987, 91–142). As primary parents, women significantly influence children's psychological development and emotional attachments, in the process reproducing gender. Emergent sexuality is shaped by heterosexual, homosexual, bisexual, and sadomasochistic patterns that are gendered—different for girls and boys, and for women and men—so that sexual statuses reflect gender statuses.

When gender is a major component of structured inequality, the devalued genders have less power, prestige, and economic rewards than the valued genders. In countries that discourage gender discrimination, many major roles are still gendered; women still do most of the domestic labor and child rearing, even while doing full-time paid work; women and men are segregated on the job and each does work considered "appropriate"; women's work is usually paid less than men's work. Men dominate the positions of authority and leadership in government, the military, and the law; cultural productions, religions, and sports reflect men's interests.

In societies that create the greatest gender difference, such as Saudi Arabia, women are kept out of sight behind walls or veils, have no civil rights, and often create a cultural and emotional world of their own (Bernard 1981). But even in societies with less rigid gender boundaries, women and men spend much of their time with people of their own gender because of the way work and family are organized. This spatial separation of women and men reinforces gendered differences, identity, and ways of thinking and behaving (Coser 1986).

Gender inequality—the devaluation of "women" and the social domination of "men"—has social functions and social history. It is not the result of sex, procreation, physiology, anatomy, hormones, or genetic predispositions. It is produced and maintained by identifiable social processes and built into the general social structure and individual identities deliberately and purposefully. The social order as we know it in Western societies is organized around racial, ethnic, class, and gender inequality. I contend, therefore, that the continuing purpose of gender as a modern social institution is to construct women as a group to be the subordinates of men as a group.

The Paradox of Human Nature

To say that sex, sexuality, and gender are all socially constructed is not to minimize their social power. These categorical imperatives govern our lives in the most profound and pervasive ways, through the social experiences and social practices of what Dorothy Smith calls the "everday/evernight world" (1990, 31–57). The paradox of human nature is that it is *always* a manifestation of cultural meanings, social relationships, and power politics; "not biology, but

culture, becomes destiny" (J. Butler 1990, 8). Gendered people emerge not from physiology or sexual orientation but from the exigencies of the social order, mostly, from the need for a reliable division of the work of food production and the social (not physical) reproduction of new members. The moral imperatives of religion and cultural representations guard the boundary lines among genders and ensure that what is demanded, what is permitted, and what is tabooed for the people in each gender is well known and followed by most (C. Davies 1982). Political power, control of scarce resources, and, if necessary, violence uphold the gendered social order in the face of resistance and rebellion. Most people, however, voluntarily go along with their society's prescriptions for those of their gender status, because the norms and expectations get built into their sense of worth and identity as [the way we] think, the way we see and hear and speak, the way we fantasy, and the way we feel.

There is no core or bedrock in human nature below these endlessly looping processes of the social production of sex and gender, self and other, identity and psyche, each of which is a "complex cultural construction" (J. Butler 1990, 36). *For humans, the social is the natural.* Therefore, "in its feminist senses, gender cannot mean simply the cultural appropriation of biological sexual difference. Sexual difference is itself a fundamental—and scientifically contested—construction. Both 'sex' and 'gender' are woven of multiple, asymmetrical strands of difference, charged with multifaceted dramatic narratives of domination and struggle" (Haraway 1990, 140).

References

Almquist, Elizabeth M. 1987. "Labor market gendered inequality in minority groups," *Gender & Society* 1:400–14.

Bernard, Jessie. 1981. *The Female World.* New York: Free Press.

Butler, Judith. 1990. *Gender Trouble: Feminism and the Subversion of Identity.* New York and London: Routledge.

Chodorow, Nancy. 1978. *The Reproduction of Mothering.* Berkeley: University of California Press.

Cockburn, Cynthia. 1985. *Machinery of Dominance: Women, Men and Technical Know-how.* London: Pluto Press.

Collins, Patricia Hill. 1989. "The social construction of black feminist thought," *Signs* 14:745–73.

Connell, R. [Robert] W. 1987. *Gender and Power: Society, the Person, and Sexual Politics.* Stanford, Calif.: Stanford University Press.

Coser, Rose Laub. 1986. "Cognitive structure and the use of social space," *Sociological Forum* 1:1–26.

Davies, Christie. 1982. "Sexual taboos and social boundaries," *American Journal of Sociology* 87:1032–63.

Dwyer, Daisy, & Judith Bruce (eds.). 1988. *A Home Divided: Women and Income in the Third World.* Palo Alto, Calif.: Stanford University Press.

Gilmore, David D. 1990. *Manhood in the Making: Cultural Concepts of Masculinity.* New Haven: Yale University Press.

Haraway, Donna. 1990. "Investment strategies for the evolving portfolio of primate females," in *Jacobus, Keller, and Shuttleworth.*

Jacobus, Mary, Evelyn Fox Keller, & Sally Shuttleworth (eds.). 1990. *Body/politics: Women and the Discourse of Science.* New York and London: Routledge.

Jay, Nancy. 1981. "Gender and dichotomy," *Feminist Studies* 7:38–56.

Mencher, Joan. 1988. "Women's work and poverty: Women's contribution to household maintenance in South India," in *Dwyer and Bruce.*

Palmer, Phyllis. 1989. *Domesticity and Dirt: Housewives and Domestic Servants in the United States, 1920–1945.* Philadelphia: Temple University Press.

Scott, Joan Wallach. 1988. *Gender and the Politics of History.* New York: Columbia University Press.

———. 1990. *The Conceptual Practices of Power: A Feminist Sociology of Knowledge.* Toronto: University of Toronto Press.

West, Candace, & Don Zimmerman. 1987. "Doing gender," *Gender & Society* 1:125–51.

THREE

Patriarchy, the System
An It, Not a He, a Them, or an Us

Allan G. Johnson

"When you say patriarchy," a man complained from the rear of the audience, "I know what you *really* mean—me!" A lot of people hear "men" whenever someone says "patriarchy," so that criticism of gender oppression is taken to mean that all men—each and every one of them—are oppressive people. Not surprisingly, many men take it personally if someone merely mentions patriarchy or the oppression of women, bristling at what they often see as a way to make them feel guilty. And some women feel free to blame individual men for patriarchy simply because they're men. Some of the time, men feel defensive because they identify with patriarchy and its values and don't want to face the consequences

these produce or the prospect of giving up male privilege. But defensiveness more often reflects a common confusion about the difference between patriarchy as a kind of society and the people who participate in it. If we're ever going to work toward real change, it's a confusion we'll have to clear up.

To do this, we have to realize that we're stuck in a model of social life that views everything as beginning and ending with individuals. Looking at things in this way, we tend to think that if evil exists in the world, it's only because there are evil people who have entered into an evil conspiracy. Racism exists, for example, simply because white people are racist bigots who hate members of racial and ethnic minorities and want to do them harm. There is gender oppression because men want and like to dominate women and act out hostility toward them. There is poverty and class oppression because people in the upper classes are greedy, heartless, and cruel. The flip side of this individualistic model of guilt and blame is that race, gender, and class oppression are actually not oppression at all, but merely the sum of individual failings on the part of blacks, women, and the poor, who lack the right stuff to compete successfully with whites, men, and others who know how to make something of themselves.

What this kind of thinking ignores is that we are all participating in something larger than ourselves or any collection of us. On some level, most people are familiar with the idea that social life involves us in something larger than ourselves, but few seem to know what to do with that idea. When Sam Keen laments that "THE SYSTEM is running us all,"[1] he strikes a deep chord in many people. But he also touches on a basic misunderstanding of social life, because having blamed "the system" (presumably society) for our problems, he doesn't take the next step to understand what that might mean. What exactly *is* a system, for example, and how could it run us? Do *we* have anything to do with shaping *it*, and if so, how? How, for example, do we participate in patriarchy, and how does that link us to the consequences it produces? How is what we think of as "normal" life related to male dominance, women's oppression, and the hierarchical, control-obsessed world in which they, and our lives, are embedded?

Without asking such questions we can't understand gender fully and we avoid taking responsibility either for ourselves or for patriarchy. Instead, "the system" serves as a vague, unarticulated catchall, a dumping ground for social problems, a scapegoat that can never be held to account and that, for all the power we think it has, can't talk back or actually *do* anything. Both Sam Keen and Robert Bly, for example, blame much of men's misery on industrialization and urbanization. The solutions they offer, however, amount to little more than personal transformation and adaptation, not changing society itself.[2] So, the system is invoked in contradictory ways. On the one hand, it's portrayed as a formidable source of all our woes, a great monster that "runs us all." On the other hand, it's ignored as a nebulous blob that we think we don't have to include in any solutions.

But we can't have it both ways. If society is a powerful force in social life, as it surely is, then we have to understand it and how we are connected to it. To do this, we have to change how we think about it, because how we think affects the kinds of questions we ask. The questions we ask in turn shape the kinds of answers and solutions we'll come up with. If we see patriarchy as nothing more than men's and women's individual personalities, motivations, and behavior, for example, then it probably won't even occur to us to ask about larger contexts — such as institutions like the family, religion, and the economy — and how people's lives are shaped in relation to them. From this kind of individualistic perspective, we might ask why a particular man raped, harassed, or beat a woman. We wouldn't ask, however, what kind of society would promote persistent *patterns* of such behavior in everyday life, from wife-beating jokes to the routine inclusion of sexual coercion and violence in mainstream movies. We are quick to explain rape and battery as the acts of sick or angry men; but we rarely take seriously the question of what kind of society would produce so much male anger and pathology or direct it toward sexual violence rather than something else. We rarely ask how gender violence might serve other more "normalized" ends such as male control and domination. We might ask why a man would like pornography that objectifies, exploits, and promotes violence against women; or debate whether the Constitution protects the individual's right to produce and distribute violent pornography. But it's hard to stir up interest in asking what kind of society would give violent and degrading visions of women's bodies and human sexuality such a prominent and pervasive place in its culture to begin with.

In short, we ignore and take for granted what we can least afford to overlook in trying to understand and change the world. Rather than ask how social systems produce social problems such as male violence against women, we obsess over legal debate and titillating but irrelevant case histories soon to become made-for-television movies. If the goal is to change the world, this won't help us. We need to see and deal with the social roots that generate and nurture the social problems that are reflected in the behavior of individuals. We can't do this without realizing that we all participate in something larger than ourselves, something we didn't create but that we have the power to affect through the choices we make about *how* to participate.

That something larger is patriarchy, which is more than a collection of individuals (such as "men"). It is a system, which means it can't be reduced to the people who participate in it. If you go to work in a corporation, for example, you know the minute you walk in the door that you've entered "something" that shapes your experience and behavior, something that isn't just you and the other people you work with. You can feel yourself stepping into a set of relationships and shared understandings about who's who and what's supposed to happen and why, and all of this limits you in many ways. And when you leave at the end of the day you can feel yourself released from the constraints imposed by your participation in that system; you can feel the expectations drop away and your focus shift to other systems such as family or a neighborhood bar that shape your experience in different ways. To understand a system like a corporation, we have to look at more than people like you, because all of you aren't the corporation, even though you make it run. If the corporation were just a collection of people, then whatever happened to the corporation would by definition also happen to them, and vice versa; but this clearly isn't so. A corporation can go bankrupt, for example, or cease to exist altogether without any of the people who work there going bankrupt or disappearing. Conversely, everyone who works for the corporation could quit, but that wouldn't necessarily mean the end of the corporation, only the arrival of a new set of participants. We can't understand a corporation, then, just by looking at the people who participate in it, for it is something larger and has to be understood as such.

So, too, with patriarchy, a kind of society that is more than a collection of women and men and can't be understood simply by understanding them. *We are not patriarchy,* no more than people who believe in Allah *are* Islam or Canadians *are* Canada. Patriarchy is a kind of society organized around certain kinds of social relationships and ideas. As individuals, we participate in it. Paradoxically, our participation both shapes our lives and gives us the opportunity to be part of changing or perpetuating

it.[3] But *we are not it,* which means that patriarchy can exist without men having "oppressive personalities" or actively conspiring with one another to defend male privilege. To demonstrate that gender oppression exists, we don't have to show that men are villains, that women are good-hearted victims, that women don't participate in their own oppression, or that men never oppose it. If a society is oppressive, then people who grow up and live in it will tend to accept, identify with, and participate in it as "normal" and unremarkable life. That's the path of least resistance in any system. It's hard not to follow it, given how we depend on society and its rewards and punishments that hinge on going along with the status quo. When oppression is woven into the fabric of everyday life, we don't need to go out of our way to be overly oppressive in order for an oppressive system to produce oppressive consequences. As the saying goes, what evil requires is simply that ordinary people do nothing.

"The System"

In general, a system is any collection of interrelated parts or elements that we can think of as a whole. A car engine, for example, is a collection of parts that fit together in certain ways to produce a "whole" that is identifiable in many cultures as serving a particular purpose. A language is also a collection of parts — letters of the alphabet, words, punctuation marks, and rules of grammar and syntax — that fit together in certain ways to form something we can identify as a whole. And societies include a variety of interrelated parts that we can think of as a whole. All of these are systems that differ in the kinds of parts they include and how those parts are related to one another.

The crucial thing to understand about patriarchy or any other kind of social system is that it's something people participate in. It's an arrangement of shared understandings and relationships that connect people to one another and something larger than themselves. In some ways, we're like players who participate in a game. Monopoly, for example, consists of a set of shared understandings about things such as the meaning of property and rent, the value of competition and accumulating wealth, and various rules about rolling dice, moving around a board, buying, selling, and developing property, collecting rents, winning, and losing. It has positions—player, banker, and so on—that people occupy. It has material elements such as the board, houses and hotels, dice, property deeds, money, and "pieces" that represent each player's movements on the board. As such, the game is something we can think of as a social system whose diverse elements cohere with a unity and wholeness that distinguish it from other games and from nongames.[4] Most important, we can describe it as a system without ever talking about the personal characteristics or motivations of the individual people who actually play it at any given moment.

If we watch people play Monopoly, we notice certain routine patterns of feeling and behavior that reflect paths of least resistance that are inherent in the game itself. If someone lands on a property I own, for example, I collect the rent (if I happen to notice), and if they can't pay, I take their assets and force them from the game. The game encourages me to feel good about this, not necessarily because *I'm* greedy and merciless, but because the game is about winning, and this is what winning consists of in Monopoly. Since everyone else is also trying to win by driving me out of the game, each step I take toward winning protects me and alleviates some anxiety about landing on a property whose rent *I* can't pay.

Since these patterns are shaped by the game far more than by the individual players, we can find ourselves behaving in ways that might seem disturbing in other situations. When I'm not playing Monopoly, I behave quite differently, even though I'm still the same person. This is why I don't play Monopoly anymore—I don't like the way it encourages me to feel and behave in the name of "fun," especially toward people I care about. The reason we behave differently outside the game doesn't lie in our personalities but in the *game's* paths of least resistance, which define certain behavior and values as appropriate and expected. When we see ourselves as Monopoly players, we feel limited by the rules and goals the game defines, and experience it as something external to us and beyond our control. It's important to note how rarely it ever occurs to people to simply change the rules. The relationships, terms, and goals that organize the game aren't presented to

us as ours to judge or alter. The more attached we feel to the game and the more closely we identify ourselves as players, the more likely we are to feel helpless in relation to it. If you're about to drive someone into bankruptcy, you can excuse yourself by saying "I've got to take your money, those are the rules," but only if you ignore the fact that you could choose not to play or could suggest a change in the rules. Then again, if you can't imagine life without the game, you won't see many alternatives to doing what's expected of you.

If we try to explain patterns of social behavior only in terms of individual people's personalities and motives—people do greedy things, for example, because they *are* greedy—then we ignore how behavior is shaped by paths of least resistance found in the systems people participate in. The "profit motive" associated with capitalism, for example, is typically seen as a psychological motive of individuals that explains capitalism as a system: capitalism exists because there are individuals who want to make a profit. But this puts the cart before the horse by avoiding the question of where wanting to make a profit comes from in the first place. We need to ask what kind of world makes such wants possible and encourages people to organize their lives around them, for although we may pursue profit as we play Monopoly or participate in real-world capitalism, the psychological profit motive doesn't originate with us. We aren't born with it. It doesn't exist in many cultures and was unknown for most of human history. The profit motive is a historically developed aspect of market systems in general and capitalism in particular that shapes the values, behavior, and personal motives of those who participate in it. To argue that managers lay off workers, for example, simply because managers are heartless or cruel ignores the fact that success under capitalism often depends on this kind of competitive, profit-maximizing "heartless" behavior. Most managers probably know in their hearts that the practice of routinely discarding people in the name of profit and expedience is hurtful and unfair. This is why they feel so bad about having to be the ones to carry it out, and protect their feelings by inventing euphemisms such as "downsizing" and "outplacement." And yet they participate in a system that produces these cruel results anyway, not because of cruel personalities or malice toward workers, but because a capitalist system makes this a path of least resistance and exacts real costs from those who stray from it.

To use the game analogy, it's a mistake to assume that we can understand the players without paying attention to the game they're playing. We create even more trouble by thinking we can understand the *game* without ever looking at it as something more than what goes on inside individuals. One way to see this is to realize that systems often work in ways that don't reflect the experience and motivations of the people who participate in them. If we try to explain warfare, for example, by looking at what soldiers actually do and the consequences that result, we might attribute war to some human tendency to be aggressive and slaughter one another, to some "natural" murderousness and taste for blood. But if we look for such tendencies in the participants themselves, the soldiers, we won't find much, for account after account shows that the typical soldier is motivated by anything but aggressive, bloodthirsty impulses to kill, maim, and destroy. Most soldiers are simply following paths of least resistance. They want nothing more than to do what they think is expected of them—especially to live up to cultural images of what it means to be a man—and to get themselves and their friends home alive and unharmed. Many are there because they couldn't find any other way to make a living or wanted job training or a subsidized college education and never imagined they'd wind up in combat. Or they got caught up in a wave of nationalism that sent them off to fight for things they dimly perceived and barely understood. Once in battle, their aggressive behavior is more often than not a defensive reaction to fear created by confronting them with men who feel compelled to kill them so that *they* can do what's expected of them and get home safely.[5] . . .

In spite of all the good reasons not to use individual models to explain social life, they are a path of least resistance because individual experience and motivation are what we know best. As a result, we tend to see something like sexism as the result of poor socialization through which men learn to act dominant and masculine and women to act subordinate and feminine. While there is certainly some truth to this, it doesn't work as an explanation of patterns like gender oppression. It's no better than trying to explain war as simply the result of training men to be warlike, without looking at economic systems that equip armies at huge profits and political

systems that organize and hurl armies at one another. It's like trying to understand what happens during Monopoly games without ever talking about the game itself and the kind of society in which it would exist. Of course, soldiers and Monopoly players do what they do because they've learned the rules; but this doesn't tell us much about the rules themselves and why they exist to be learned in the first place. Socialization is merely a process, a mechanism for training people to participate in social systems. Although it tells us how people learn to participate in systems, it doesn't illuminate the systems themselves. As such, it can tell us something about the *how* of a system like patriarchy, but very little about the *what* and the *why*.

Since focusing just on individual women and men won't tell us much about patriarchy, simply trying to understand people's attitudes or behavior won't get us very far so long as patriarchy goes unexamined and unchallenged as the only gender game in town. And if we don't look beyond individuals, whatever change we accomplish won't have much more than a superficial, temporary effect. Systemic paths of least resistance provide powerful reasons for people to go along with the status quo. This is why individual change is often restricted to people who either have little to lose or who are secure and protected enough to choose a different path. So change typically gets limited to the most oppressed, who have the least to lose and are in the weakest position to challenge the system as a whole, and the most privileged, who can afford to attend workshops or enter therapy or who can hire someone (typically a woman) to take care of their children. In this latter group in particular, it's easy for men to fool themselves into thinking they can find nicer, less oppressive ways to participate in an oppressive system without challenging it, and therefore without disturbing the basis for male privilege. It's like the myth of a kinder, gentler capitalism in which managers still overwork and lay off employees in order to bolster the bottom line and protect shareholders' interests; but now they do it with greater interpersonal sensitivity. The result is pretty much the same as it was before, but now they can feel better about it. After all, if changing the system isn't a goal, then it makes sense to accommodate to it while maintaining the appearance of regretting its oppressive consequences. And an individualistic approach is perfectly suited to those ends, for the privileged can feel bad about the people who suffer even as they shield from scrutiny the system that makes both suffering and privilege inevitable.

Without some sense of how systems work and how people participate in them, we can't do much about either. Robert Bly and others in the mythopoetic men's movement, for example, want to change cultural definitions of masculinity and femininity. They want men to become "spiritual warriors" in touch with the "deep masculine," who feel good about themselves as men and who don't need to rely on coercion and violence. And they want the "old men"—the fathers—to initiate the young men into this new way of being. Presumably, however, this is going to happen without doing anything about patriarchy as a system, since this concept has no place in their analysis. In other words, masculinity is going to be transformed without confronting the control-driven system of patriarchal power relations and male competition and all the ways it's embedded in social institutions. Where, then, will we find all these old men who are prepared to give up their gender privilege and adopt, promote, and welcome young men into ways of seeing men (and women) that contradict the prevailing order that gives those same old men the most to lose? And where will we find young men willing to follow their lead? Quite simply, we won't, except among a relative few who adopt "new masculinities" as personal styles. These new masculinities, however, are generally reserved for ritual observances among the like-minded and otherwise kept from public view; or, as seems to be the case in the "new men's movement," they turn out to be not so new after all.[6]

Either way, the individualistic model offers little hope of changing patriarchy because patriarchy is more than how people think, feel, and behave. As such, patriarchy isn't simply about the psychic wounding of sons by their fathers, or the dangers and failures of heterosexual intimacy, or boys' feelings about their mothers, or how men treat women and one another. It *includes* all of these by producing them as symptoms that help perpetuate the system; but these aren't what patriarchy *is*. It is a way of organizing social life through which such wounding, failure, and mistreatment can occur. If fathers neglect their sons, it is because fathers move in a world that makes pursuit of goals other than deeply committed fatherhood a path of least resistance.[7] If heterosexual intimacy is prone to fail, it is because

patriarchy is organized in ways that set women and men fundamentally at odds with one another in spite of all the good reasons they otherwise have to get along and thrive together. And if men's use of coercion and violence against women is a pervasive pattern—and it is—it is because force and violence are supported in patriarchal society; it is because women are designated as desirable and legitimate objects of male control, and because in a society organized around control, force and violence *work.*

We can't find a way out of patriarchy or imagine something different without a clear sense of what patriarchy is and what that's got to do with us. Thus far, the alternative has been to reduce our understanding of gender to an intellectual gumbo of personal problems, tendencies, and motivations. Presumably, these will be solved through education, better communication skills, consciousness raising, "heroic journeys," and other forms of individual transformation. Since this isn't how social systems actually change, the result is widespread frustration and cycles of blame and denial, which is precisely where we[8] seem to have been for the better part of thirty years.

We need to see more clearly what patriarchy is about as a system. This includes cultural ideas about men and women, the web of relationships that structure social life, and the unequal distribution of rewards and resources that underlies oppression. We need to see new ways to participate by forging alternative paths of least resistance, for the system doesn't simply "run us" like hapless puppets. It may be larger than us, it may not *be* us, but it doesn't exist except *through* us. Without us, patriarchy doesn't *happen.* And that's where we have power to do something about it and about ourselves *in* it.

Patriarchy

The key to understanding any system is to identify its various parts and how they're arranged to form a whole. To understand a language, for example, we have to learn its alphabet, vocabulary, and rules for combining words into meaningful phrases and sentences. With a social system such as patriarchy, it's more complicated because there are many different kinds of parts, and it is often difficult to see just how they're connected. Patriarchy's defining elements are its male-dominated, male-identified, and male-centered character, but this is just the beginning. At its core, patriarchy is a set of symbols and ideas that make up a culture embodied by everything from the content of everyday conversation to literature and film. Patriarchal culture includes ideas about the nature of things, including men, women, and humanity, with manhood and masculinity most closely associated with being human and womanhood and femininity relegated to the marginal position of "other." It's about how social life is and how it's supposed to be; about what's expected of people and about how they feel. It's about standards of feminine beauty and masculine toughness, images of feminine vulnerability and masculine protectiveness, of older men coupled with young women, of elderly women alone. It's about defining women and men as opposites, about the "naturalness" of male aggression, competition, and dominance and of female caring, cooperation, and subordination. It's about the valuing of masculinity and maleness and the devaluing of femininity and femaleness. It's about the primary importance of a husband's career and the secondary status of a wife's, about child care as a priority in women's lives and its secondary importance in men's. It's about the social acceptability of anger, rage, and toughness in men but not in women, and of caring, tenderness, and vulnerability in women but not in men.

Above all, patriarchal culture is about the core value of control and domination in almost every area of human existence. From the expression of emotion to economics to the natural environment, gaining and exercising control is a continuing goal of great importance. Because of this, the concept of power takes on a narrow definition in terms of "power over"—the ability to control others, events, resources, or oneself in spite of resistance—rather than alternatives such as the ability to cooperate with others, to give freely of oneself, or to feel and act in harmony with nature.[9] To have power over and to be prepared to use it are defined culturally as good and desirable (and characteristically "masculine"), and to lack such power or to be reluctant to use it is seen as weak if not contemptible (and characteristically "feminine").

The main use of any culture is to provide symbols and ideas out of which people construct their sense of what is real. As such, language mirrors social reality in sometimes startling ways. In contemporary usage, for example, the words "crone," "witch," "bitch," and "virgin" describe women as threaten-

ing, evil, or heterosexually inexperienced and thus incomplete. In prepatriarchal times, however, these words evoked far different images.[10] The crone was the old woman whose life experience gave her insight, wisdom, respect, and the power to enrich people's lives. The witch was the wise-woman healer, the knower of herbs, the midwife, the link joining body, spirit, and Earth. The bitch was Artemis-Diana, goddess of the hunt, most often associated with the dogs who accompanied her. And the virgin was merely a woman who was unattached, unclaimed, and unowned by any man and therefore independent and autonomous. Notice how each word has been transformed from a positive cultural image of female power, independence, and dignity to an insult or a shadow of its former self so that few words remain to identify women in ways both positive and powerful.

Going deeper into patriarchal culture, we find a complex web of ideas that define reality and what's considered good and desirable. To see the world through patriarchal eyes is to believe that women and men are profoundly different in their basic natures, that hierarchy is the only alternative to chaos, and that men were made in the image of a masculine God with whom they enjoy a special relationship. It is to take as obvious the idea that there are two and only two distinct genders; the patriarchal heterosexuality is "natural" and same-sex attraction is not; that because men neither bear nor breast-feed children, they cannot feel a compelling bodily connection to them; that on some level every woman, whether heterosexual or lesbian, wants a "real man" who knows how to "take charge of things," including her; that females can't be trusted, especially when they're menstruating or accusing men of sexual misconduct. To embrace patriarchy is to believe that mothers should stay home and that fathers should work out of the home, regardless of men's and women's actual abilities or needs.[11] It is to buy into the notion that women are weak and men are strong, that women and children need men to support and protect them, all in spite of the fact that in many ways men are not the physically stronger sex, that women perform a huge share of hard physical labor in many societies (often larger than men's), that women's physical endurance tends to be greater than men's over the long haul, that women tend to be more capable of enduring pain and emotional stress.[12] And yet such evidence means little in the face of a patriarchal culture that dictates how things *ought* to be and, like all cultural mythology,

> will not be argued down by facts. It may seem to be making straightforward statements, but actually these conceal another mood, the imperative. Myth exists in a state of tension. It is not really describing a situation, but trying by means of this description *to being about* what it declares to exist.[13]

To live in a patriarchal culture is to learn what's expected of us as men and women, the rules that regulate punishment and reward based on how we behave and appear. These rules range from laws that require men to fight in wars not of their own choosing to customary expectations that mothers will provide child care, or that when a woman shows sexual interest in a man or merely smiles or acts friendly, she gives up her right to say no and control her own body. And to live under patriarchy is to take into ourselves shared ways of feeling — the hostile contempt for femaleness that forms the core of misogyny and presumptions of male superiority, the ridicule men direct at other men who show signs of vulnerability or weakness, or the fear and insecurity that every woman must deal with when she exercises the right to move freely in the world, especially at night and by herself. Such ideas make up the symbolic sea we swim in and the air we breathe. They are the primary well from which springs how we think about ourselves, other people, and the world. As such, they provide a taken-for-granted everyday reality, the setting for our intentions with other people that continually fashion and refashion a shared sense of what the world is about and who we are in relation to it. This doesn't mean that the ideas underlying patriarchy determine what we think, feel, and do, but it does mean they define what we'll have to *deal with* as we participate in it.

The prominent place of misogyny in patriarchal culture, for example, doesn't mean that every man and woman consciously hates all things female. But it does mean that to the extent that we don't feel such hatred, it's *in spite of* paths of least resistance contained in our culture. Complete freedom from such feelings and judgments is all but impossible. It is certainly possible for heterosexual men to love women without mentally fragmenting them into breasts, buttocks, genitals, and other variously de-

sirable parts. It is possible for women to feel good about their bodies, to not judge themselves as being too fat, to not abuse themselves to one degree or another in pursuit of impossible male-identified standards of beauty and sexual attractiveness. All of this is possible; but to live in patriarchy is to breathe in misogynist images of women as objectified sexual property valued primarily for their usefulness to men. This finds its way into everyone who grows up breathing and swimming in it, and once inside us it remains, however unaware of it we may be. So, when we hear or express sexist jokes and other forms of misogyny we may not recognize it, and even if we do, say nothing rather than risk other people thinking we're "too sensitive" or, especially in the case of men, "not one of the guys." In either case, we are involved, if only by our silence.

The symbols and ideas that make up patriarchal culture are important to understand because they have such powerful effects on the structure of social life. By "structure," I mean the ways that gender privilege and oppression are organized through social relationships and unequal distributions of rewards, opportunities, and resources. This appears in countless patterns of everyday life in family and work, religion and politics, community and education. It is found in family divisions of labor that exempt fathers from most domestic work even when both parents work outside the home, and in the concentration of women in lower-level pink-collar jobs and male predominance almost everywhere else. It is in the unequal distribution of income and all that goes with it, from access to health care to the availability of leisure time. It is in patterns of male violence and harassment that can turn a simple walk in the park or a typical day at work or a lovers' quarrel into a life-threatening nightmare. More than anything, the structure of patriarchy is found in the unequal distribution of power that makes oppression possible, in patterns of male dominance in every facet of human life, from everyday conversation to global politics. By its nature, patriarchy puts issues of power, dominance, and control at the center of human existence, not only in relationships between men and women, but among men as they compete and struggle to gain status, maintain control, and protect themselves from what other men might do to them.

To understand patriarchy, we have to identify its cultural elements and see how they are related to the structure of social life. We must see, for example, how cultural ideas that identify women primarily as mothers and men primarily as breadwinners support patterns in which women do most domestic work at home and are discriminated against in hiring, pay, and promotions at work. But to do anything with such an understanding, we also must see what patriarchy has to do with us as individuals—how it shapes us and how we, in choosing how to participate, shape *it*.

The System in Us in the System

One of the most difficult things to accept about patriarchy is that we're involved in it, which means we're also involved in its consequences. This is especially hard for men who refuse to believe they benefit from women's oppression, because they can't see how this could happen without their being personally oppressive in their intentions, feelings, and behavior. For many men, being told they're *involved* in oppression can only mean they *are* oppressive.

A common defense against this is to attribute everything to "society" as something external and autonomous, with wants, needs, interests, and the power to control people by making them into one sort of person or another. "It's not men, it's society," and society supposedly does what it does for mysterious reasons known only to itself. Like many others, Sam Keen resorts to this when he writes that men are "assigned" dominant roles in warfare and economics, that women are assigned emotion and men are assigned reason, or that male dominance can be attributed simply to warfare, industrialization, urbanization, or capitalism.[14] But he never asks just who or what does all this assigning or whose interests are served by it. He doesn't ask how things like capitalism came into being, for example, or how this might be connected to core patriarchal values of dominance and control and, hence, to men and male control over major social institutions.[15] Presumably there are no issues of sexism, racism, or class to be reckoned with here—nothing for men, whites, or privileged classes to be concerned about—just the workings of "society."

But societies aren't sentient beings capable of knowing, wanting, or doing anything, including forcing people to perform particular roles. Societies

don't exist without people participating in them, which means that we can't understand patriarchy unless we also ask how people are connected to it and how this connection varies, depending on social characteristics such as race, gender, ethnicity, age, and class. Capitalism, for example, didn't just happen on its own but emerged as an economic system in a patriarchal world dominated by men and their interests, especially white European men of the newly emerging merchant class. The same can be said of industrialization, which was bound up with the development of capitalism in eighteenth- and nineteenth-century Europe. This line of thinking might seem to undermine the argument I've made about including systems in our thinking—"It really comes down to individuals after all"—but it's more complicated than that. The problem isn't society and it isn't us. It's the relationship between the two that we have to understand, the nature of the thing we participate in and how we choose to participate in it and how both are shaped in the process. In this sense, it's a mistake to equate patriarchy with men; but it's also wrong to act as though systems like patriarchy or capitalism have nothing to do with gender and differences in power and interests that distinguish and separate men and women. It's equally wrong to act as though all men or all women are the same, as though dynamics such as racism and class oppression don't affect how patriarchy operates and affects people's lives in different ways.

One way to see how people connect with systems is to think of us as occupying social positions that locate us in relation to people in other positions. We connect to families, for example, through positions such as "mother," "daughter," and "cousin"; to economic systems through positions such as "vice president," "secretary," or "unemployed"; to political systems through positions such as "citizen," "registered voter," and "mayor"; to religious systems through positions such as "believer" and "clergy." How we perceive the people who occupy such positions and what we expect of them depend on cultural ideas—such as the belief that mothers are naturally better than fathers at child care or the expectation that fathers will be the primary breadwinners. Such ideas are powerful because we use them to construct a sense of who we and other people are. When a woman marries, for example, how people (including her) perceive and think about her changes as cultural ideas about what it means to be a wife come into play—ideas about how wives feel about their husbands, for example, what's most important to wives, what's expected of them, and what they may expect of others.

From this perspective, *who* we and other people think we are has a lot to do with *where* we are in relation to social systems and all the positions that people occupy. We wouldn't exist as social beings if it weren't for our participation in one social system or another. It's hard to imagine just who we'd be and what our existence would consist of if we took away all of our connections to the symbols, ideas, and relationships that make up social systems. Take away language and all that it allows us to imagine and think, starting with our names. Take away all the positions that we occupy and the roles that go with them—from daughter and son to occupation and nationality—and with these all the complex ways our lives are connected to other people. Not much would be left over that we'd recognize as ourselves.[16]

We can think of a society as a network of interconnected systems within systems, each made up of social positions and their relations to one another. To say, then, that I'm white, male, college educated, and a writer, sociologist, U.S. citizen, heterosexual, middle-aged, husband, father, brother, and son identifies me in relation to positions which are themselves related to positions in various social systems, from the entire world to the family of my birth. In another sense, the day-to-day reality of a society only exists through what people actually do as they participate in it. Patriarchal culture, for example, places a high value on control and maleness. By themselves, these are just abstractions. But when men and women actually talk and men interrupt women more than women interrupt men, or men ignore topics introduced by women in favor of their own or in other ways control conversation,[17] or when men use their authority to sexually harass women in the workplace, then the reality of patriarchy as a kind of society and people's sense of themselves as female and male within it actually happen in a concrete way.

In this sense, like all social systems, patriarchy exists only through people's lives. Through this, patriarchy's various aspects are there for us to see over and over again. This has two important implications for how we understand patriarchy. First, to some extent people experience patriarchy as external to them; but this doesn't mean that it's a distinct and separate thing, like a house in which we live. Instead, by participating in patriarchy we are *of* patriarchy and it is *of* us. Both exist *through* the other and neither can exist without the other. Second, patriarchy isn't static; it's an ongoing *process* that's continuously shaped and reshaped. Since the thing we're participating in is patriarchal, we tend to behave in ways that create a patriarchal world from one moment to the next. But we have some freedom to break the rules and construct everyday life in different ways, which means that the paths we choose to follow can do as much to change patriarchy as they can to perpetuate it.

We're involved in patriarchy and its consequences because we occupy social positions in it, which is all it takes. Since gender oppression is, by definition, a system of inequality organized around gender categories, we can no more avoid being involved in it than we can avoid being female or male. *All* men and *all* women are therefore involved in this oppressive system, and none of us can control *whether* we participate, only *how*. . . .

Notes

1. Sam Keen, *Fire in the Belly: On Being a Man* (New York: Bantam, 1991), 207.

2. Robert Bly, *Iron John: A Book About Men* (Reading, Mass.: Addison-Wesley, 1990).

3. This is one of the major differences between organisms like the human body and social systems. Cells and nerves cannot "rebel" against the body and try to change it into something else.

4. Although the game analogy is useful, social systems are quite unlike a game in important ways. The rules and other understandings on which social life is based are far more complex, ambiguous, and contradictory than those of a typical game and much more open to negotiation and "making it up" as we go along.

5. For some insightful analysis of why men fight, see Charles Moskos, "Why Men Fight: American Combat Soldiers in Vietnam," *Transaction* 7, no. 1 (1969); and E. A. Shils and Morris Janowitz, "Cohesion and Disintegration in the Wehrmacht in World War II," *Public Opinion Quarterly* 12 (summer 1948). For a powerful personal account of experiences in Vietnam, see Philip Caputo, *A Rumor of War* (New York: Holt, Rinehart and Winston, 1977).

6. . . . For a more thorough treatment than I can offer here, see Michael Kimmel, ed., *The Politics of Manhood: Profeminist Men Respond to the Mythopoetic Men's Movement (And the Mythopoetic Leaders Answer)* (Philadelphia: Temple University Press, 1995).

7. For a history of American fatherhood, see Robert L. Griswold, *Fatherhood in America: A History* (New York: Basic Books, 1993).

8. By "we" I refer to the mainstream of public and private conversation about patriarchy. Feminists — radical feminists in particular — have been quite clear about the futility of individual solutions and the importance of focusing on patriarchy as a system for a long time.

9. For a thorough discussion of this distinction, see Marilyn French, *Beyond Power: On Men, Women, and Morals* (New York: Summit Books, 1985).

10. For discussions of language and gender, see Jane Caputi, *Gossips, Gorgons, and Crones* (Santa Fe: Bear and Company, 1993); Mary Daly, *Gyn/Ecology: The Metaethics of Radical Feminism* (Boston: Beacon Press, 1978); Dale Spender, *Man Made Language* (London: Pandora, 1980); Barbara G. Walker, *The Woman's Encyclopedia of Myths and Secrets* (San Francisco: Harper and Row, 1983); idem, *The Woman's Dictionary of Symbols and Sacred Objects* (San Francisco: Harper and Row, 1988). For a very different slant on gender and language, see Mary Daly (in cahoots with Jane Caputi), *Webster's First New Intergalactic Wickedary of the English Language* (Boston: Beacon Press, 1987).

11. See Arlie Hochschild (with Anne Machung), *The Second Shift* (New York: Avon Books, 1989).

12. See, for example, Rosalyn Baxandall, Linda Gordon, and Susan Reverby, eds., *America's Working Women: A Documentary History — 1600 to the Present* (New York: Vintage Press, 1976); Ashley Montagu, *The Natural Superiority of Women* (New York: Collier, 1974); Robin Morgan, ed., *Sisterhood Is Global* (New York: Anchor, 1990); and Marilyn Waring, *If Women Counted: A New Feminist Economics* (San Francisco: HarperCollins, 1988).

13. Elizabeth Janeway, *Man's World, Woman's Place: A Study in Social Mythology* (New York: Dell, 1971), 37.

14. Sam Keen, *Fire in the Belly*, 47, 65, 241. Keen's statements rest on the highly arguable assumption that such divisions of labor even exist and that things such as reason and emotion are mutually exclusive opposites.

15. Keen bases much of *Fire in the Belly* on the supposedly independent and autonomous influence of warfare as a system. Robert Bly in *Iron John* builds much of his argument around similarly uncritical attributions to industrialization and urbanization.

16. Some would no doubt argue, with good reason, that our social selves mask more essential selves, but that's another argument for another place.

17. There is a substantial research literature documenting such genderized patterns of conversation. See, for example, P. Kollock, P. Blumstein, and P. Schwartz, "Sex and Power in Interaction," *American Sociological Review* 50, no. 1 (1985): 34–46; N. Henley, M. Hamilton, and B. Thorne, "Womanspeak and Manspeak: Sex Differences and Sexism in Communication," in *Beyond Sex Roles*, ed. A. G. Sargent (New York: West, 1985), 168–185; and L. Smith-Lovin and C. Brody, "Interruptions in Group Discussions: The Effect of Gender and Group Composition," *American Sociological Review* 51, no. 3 (1989): 424–435.

FOUR

A Black Feminist Statement

*Combahee River Collective**

We are a collective of Black feminists who have been meeting together since 1974.[1] During that time we have been involved in the process of defining and clarifying our politics, while at the same time doing political work within our own group and in coalition with other progressive organizations and movements. The most general statement of our politics at the present time would be that we are actively committed to struggling against racial, sexual, heterosexual, and class oppression and see as our particular task the development of integrated analysis and practice based upon the fact that the major systems of oppression are interlocking. The synthesis of these oppressions creates the conditions of our lives. As Black women we see Black feminism as the logical political movement to combat the manifold and simultaneous oppressions that all women of color face.

We will discuss four major topics in the paper that follows: (1) the genesis of contemporary Black feminism; (2) what we believe, i.e., the specific province of our politics; (3) the problems in organizing Black feminists, including a brief herstory of our collective; and (4) Black feminist issues and practice.

1. The Genesis of Contemporary Black Feminism

Before looking at the recent development of Black feminism we would like to affirm that we find our origins in the historical reality of Afro-American women's continuous life-and-death struggle for survival and liberation. Black women's extremely negative relationship to the American political system (a system of white male rule) has always been determined by our membership in two oppressed racial and sexual castes. As Angela Davis points out in "Reflections on the Black Woman's Role in the Community of Slaves," Black women have always embodied, if only in their physical manifestation, an adversary stance to white male rule and have actively resisted its inroads upon them and their communities in both dramatic and subtle ways. There have always been Black women activists— some known, like Sojourner Truth, Harriet Tubman, Frances E. W. Harper, Ida B. Wells Barnett, and Mary Church Terrell, and thousands upon thousands unknown—who had a shared awareness of how their sexual identity combined with their racial identity to make their whole life situation and the focus of their political struggles unique. Contemporary Black feminism is the outgrowth of countless generations of personal sacrifice, militancy, and work by our mothers and sisters.

A Black feminist presence has evolved most obviously in connection with the second wave of the American women's movement beginning in the late 1960s. Black, other Third World, and working women have been involved in the feminist movement from its start, but both outside reactionary forces and racism and elitism within the movement itself have served to obscure our participation. In 1973 Black feminists, primarily located in New York, felt the necessity of forming a separate Black feminist group. This became the National Black Feminist Organization (NBFO).

Black feminist politics also have an obvious connection to movements for Black liberation, particularly those of the 1960s and 1970s. Many of us were active in those movements (civil rights, Black nationalism, the Black Panthers), and all of our lives were greatly affected and changed by their ideology, their goals, and the tactics used to achieve their goals. It was our experience and disillusionment

---

*The Combahee River Collective is a Black feminist group in Boston whose name comes from the guerrilla action conceptualized and led by Harriet Tubman on June 2, 1863, in the Port Royal region of South Carolina. This action freed more than 750 slaves and is the only military campaign in American history planned and led by a woman.

within these liberation movements, as well as experience on the periphery of the white male left, that led to the need to develop a politics that was antiracist, unlike those of white women, and antisexist, unlike those of Black and white men.

There is also undeniably a personal genesis for Black feminism, that is, the political realization that comes from the seemingly personal experiences of individual Black women's lives. Black feminists and many more Black women who do not define themselves as feminists have all experienced sexual oppression as a constant factor in our day-to-day existence. As children we realized that we were different from boys and that we were treated differently. For example, we were told in the same breath to be quiet both for the sake of being "ladylike" and to make us less objectionable in the eyes of white people. As we grew older we became aware of the threat of physical and sexual abuse by men. However, we had no way of conceptualizing what was so apparent to us, what we *knew* was really happening.

Black feminists often talk about their feelings of craziness before becoming conscious of the concepts of sexual politics, patriarchal rule, and most importantly, feminism, the political analysis and practice that we women use to struggle against our oppression. The fact that racial politics and indeed racism are pervasive factors in our lives did not allow us, and still does not allow most Black women, to look more deeply into our own experiences and, from that sharing and growing consciousness, to build a politics that will change our lives and inevitably end our oppression. Our development must also be tied to the contemporary economic and political position of Black people. The post–World War II generation of Black youth was the first to be able to minimally partake of certain educational and employment options, previously closed completely to Black people. Although our economic position is still at the very bottom of the American capitalistic economy, a handful of us have been able to gain certain tools as a result of tokenism in education and employment which potentially enable us to more effectively fight our oppression.

A combined antiracist and antisexist position drew us together initially, and as we developed politically we addressed ourselves to heterosexism and economic oppression under capitalism.

2. What We Believe

Above all else, our politics initially sprang from the shared belief that Black women are inherently valuable, that our liberation is a necessity not as an adjunct to somebody else's but because of our need as human persons for autonomy. This may seem so obvious as to sound simplistic, but it is apparent that no other ostensibly progressive movement has ever considered our specific oppression as a priority or worked seriously for the ending of that oppression. Merely naming the pejorative stereotypes attributed to Black women (e.g. mammy, matriarch, Sapphire, whore, bulldagger), let alone cataloguing the cruel, often murderous, treatment we receive, indicates how little value has been placed upon our lives during four centuries of bondage in the Western hemisphere. We realize that the only people who care enough about us to work consistently for our liberation are us. Our politics evolve from a healthy love for ourselves, our sisters and our community which allows us to continue our struggle and work.

This focusing upon our own oppression is embodied in the concept of identity politics. We believe that the most profound and potentially the most radical politics come directly out of our own identity, as opposed to working to end somebody else's oppression. In the case of Black women this is a particularly repugnant, dangerous, threatening, and therefore revolutionary concept because it is obvious from looking at all the political movements that have preceded us that anyone is more worthy of liberation than ourselves. We reject pedestals, queenhood, and walking ten paces behind. To be recognized as human, levelly human, is enough.

We believe that sexual politics under patriarchy is as pervasive in Black women's lives as are the politics of class and race. We also often find it difficult to separate race from class from sex oppression because in our lives they are most often experienced simultaneously. We know that there is such a thing as racial-sexual oppression which is neither solely racial nor solely sexual, e.g., the history of rape of Black women by white men as a weapon of political repression.

Although we are feminists and lesbians, we feel solidarity with progressive Black men and do not advocate the fractionalization that white women who are separatists demand. Our situation as Black people necessitates that we have solidarity around the fact of race, which white women of course do not need to have with white men, unless it is their negative solidarity as racial oppressors. We struggle together with Black men against racism, while we also struggle with Black men about sexism.

We realize that the liberation of all oppressed peoples necessitates the destruction of the political-economic systems of capitalism and imperialism as well as patriarchy. We are socialists because we believe the work must be organized for the collective benefit of those who do the work and create the products, and not for the profit of the bosses. Material resources must be equally distributed among those who create these resources. We are not convinced, however, that a socialist revolution that is not also a feminist and antiracist revolution will guarantee our liberation. We have arrived at the necessity for developing an understanding of class relationships that takes into account the specific class position of Black women who are generally marginal in the labor force, while at this particular time some of us are temporarily viewed as doubly desirable tokens at white-collar and professional levels. We need to articulate the real class situation of persons who are not merely raceless, sexless workers, but for whom racial and sexual oppression are significant determinants in their working/economic lives. Although we are in essential agreement with Marx's theory as it applied to the very specific economic relationships he analyzed, we know that his analysis must be extended further in order for us to understand our specific economic situation as Black women.

A political contribution which we feel we have already made is the expansion of the feminist principle that the personal is political. In our consciousness-raising sessions, for example, we have in many ways gone beyond white women's revelations because we are dealing with the implications of race and class as well as sex. Even our Black women's style of talking/testifying in Black language about what we have experienced has a resonance that is both cultural and political. We have spent a great deal of energy delving into the cultural and experiential nature of our oppression out of necessity because none of these matters has ever been looked at before. No one before has ever examined the multilayered texture of Black women's lives. An example of this kind of revelation/conceptualization occurred at a meeting

as we discussed the ways in which our early intellectual interests had been attacked by our peers, particularly Black males. We discovered that all of us, because we were "smart" had also been considered "ugly," i.e., "smart-ugly." "Smart-ugly" crystallized the way in which most of us had been forced to develop our intellects at great cost to our "social" lives. The sanctions in the Black and white communities against Black women thinkers are comparatively much higher than for white women, particularly ones from the educated middle and upper classes.

As we have already stated, we reject the stance of lesbian separatism because it is not a viable political analysis or strategy for us. It leaves out far too much and far too many people, particularly Black men, women, and children. We have a great deal of criticism and loathing for what men have been socialized to be in this society: what they support, how they act, and how they oppress. But we do not have the misguided notion that it is their maleness, per se—i.e., their biological maleness—that makes them what they are. As Black women we find any type of biological determinism a particularly dangerous and reactionary basis upon which to build a politic. We must also question whether lesbian separatism is an adequate and progressive political analysis and strategy, even for those who practice it, since it so completely denies any but the sexual sources of women's oppression, negating the facts of class and race.

3. Problems in Organizing Black Feminists

During our years together as a Black feminist collective we have experienced success and defeat, joy and pain, victory and failure. We have found that it is very difficult to organize around Black feminist issues, difficult even to announce in certain contexts that we *are* Black feminists. We have tried to think about the reasons for our difficulties, particularly since the white women's movement continues to be strong and to grow in many directions. In this section we will discuss some of the general reasons for the organizing problems we face and also talk specifically about the stages in organizing our own collective.

The major source of difficulty in our political work is that we are not just trying to fight oppression on one front or even two, but instead to address a whole range of oppressions. We do not have racial, sexual, heterosexual, or class privilege to rely upon, nor do we have even the minimal access to resources and power that groups who possess any one of these types of privilege have.

The psychological toll of being a Black woman and the difficulties this presents in reaching political consciousness and doing political work can never be underestimated. There is a very low value placed upon Black women's psyches in this society, which is both racist and sexist. As an early group member once said, "We are all damaged people merely by virtue of being Black women." We are dispossessed psychologically and on every other level, and yet we feel the necessity to struggle to change the condition of all Black women. In "A Black Feminist's Search for Sisterhood," Michele Wallace arrives at this conclusion:

> "We exist as women who are Black who are feminists, each stranded for the moment, working independently because there is not yet an environment in this society remotely congenial to our struggle—because, being on the bottom, we would have to do what no one else has done: we would have to fight the world."[2]

Wallace is pessimistic but realistic in her assessment of Black feminists' position, particularly in her allusion to the nearly classic isolation most of us face. We might use our position at the bottom, however, to make a clear leap into revolutionary action. If Black women were free, it would mean that everyone else would have to be free since our freedom would necessitate the destruction of all the systems of oppression.

Feminism is, nevertheless, very threatening to the majority of Black people because it calls into question some of the most basic assumptions about our existence, i.e., that sex should be a determinant of power relationships. Here is the way male and female voices were defined in a Black nationalist pamphlet from the early 1970s.

> "We understand that it is and has been traditional that the man is the head of the house. He is the leader of the house/nation because his

knowledge of the world is broader, his awareness is greater, his understanding is fuller and his application of this information is wiser . . . After all, it is only reasonable that the man be the head of the house because he is able to defend and protect the development of his home . . . Women cannot do the same things as men—they are made by nature to function differently. Equality of men and women is something that cannot happen even in the abstract world. Men are not equal to other men, i.e. ability, experience or even understanding. The value of men and women can be seen as in the value of gold and silver—they are not equal but both have great value. We must realize that men and women are a complement to each other because there is no house/family without a man and his wife. Both are essential to the development of any life."[3]

The material conditions of most Black women would hardly lead them to upset both economic and sexual arrangements that seem to represent some stability in their lives. Many Black women have a good understanding of both sexism and racism, but because of the everyday constrictions of their lives cannot risk struggling against them both.

The reaction of Black men to feminism has been notoriously negative. They are, of course, even more threatened than Black women by the possibility that Black feminists might organize around our own needs. They realize that they might not only lose valuable and hard-working allies in their struggles but that they might also be forced to change their habitually sexist ways of interacting with and oppressing Black women. Accusations that Black feminism divides the Black struggle are powerful deterrents to the growth of an autonomous Black women's movement.

Still, hundreds of women have been active at different times during the three-year existence of our group. And every Black woman who came, came out of a strongly-felt need for some level of possibility that did not previously exist in her life.

When we first started meeting early in 1974 after the NBFO first eastern regional conference, we did not have a strategy for organizing, or even a focus. We just wanted to see what we had. After a period of months of not meeting, we began to meet again late in the year and started doing an intense variety of consciousness-raising. The overwhelming feeling that we had is that after years and years we had finally found each other. Although we were not doing political work as a group, individuals continued their involvement in Lesbian politics, sterilization abuse and abortion rights work, Third World Women's International Women's Day activities, and support activity for the trials of Dr. Kenneth Edelin, Joan Little, and Inéz García. During our first summer, when membership had dropped off considerably, those of us remaining devoted serious discussion to the possibility of opening a refuge for battered women in a Black community. (There was no refuge in Boston at that time.) We also decided around that time to become an independent collective since we had serious disagreements with NBFO's bourgeois-feminist stance and their lack of a clear political focus.

We also were contacted at that time by socialist feminists, with whom we had worked on abortion rights activities, who wanted to encourage us to attend the National Socialist Feminist Conference in Yellow Springs. One of our members did attend and despite the narrowness of the ideology that was promoted at that particular conference, we became more aware of the need for us to understand our own economic situation and to make our own economic analysis.

In the fall, when some members returned, we experienced several months of comparative inactivity and internal disagreements which were first conceptualized as a Lesbian-straight split but which were also the result of class and political differences. During the summer those of us who were still meeting had determined the need to do political work and to move beyond consciousness-raising and serving exclusively as an emotional support group. At the beginning of 1976, when some of the women who had not wanted to do political work and who also had voiced disagreements stopped attending of their own accord, we again looked for a focus. We decided at that time, with the addition of new members, to become a study group. We had always shared our reading with each other, and some of us had written papers on Black feminism for group discussion a few months before this decision was made. We began functioning as a study group and also began discussing the possibility of starting a Black

feminist publication. We had a retreat in the late spring which provided a time for both political discussion and working out interpersonal issues. Currently we are planning to gather together a collection of Black feminist writing. We feel that it is absolutely essential to demonstrate the reality of our politics to other Black women and believe that we can do this through writing and distributing our work. The fact that individual Black feminists are living in isolation all over the country, that our own numbers are small, and that we have some skills in writing, printing, and publishing makes us want to carry out these kinds of projects as a means of organizing Black feminists as we continue to do political work in coalition with other groups.

4. Black Feminist Issues and Projects

During our time together we have identified and worked on many issues of particular relevance to Black women. The inclusiveness of our politics makes us concerned with any situation that impinges upon the lives of women, Third World and working people. We are of course particularly committed to working on those struggles in which race, sex and class are simultaneously factors in oppression. We might, for example, become involved in workplace organizing at a factory that employs Third World women or picket a hospital that is cutting back on already inadequate health care to a Third World community, or set up a rape crisis center in a Black neighborhood. Organizing around welfare and daycare concerns might also be a focus. The work to be done and the countless issues that this work represents merely reflect the pervasiveness of our oppression.

Issues and projects that collective members have already worked on are sterilization abuse, abortion rights, battered women, rape and health care. We have also done many workshops and educationals on Black feminism on college campuses, at women's conferences, and most recently for high school women.

One issue that is of major concern to us and that we have begun to publicly address is racism in the white women's movement. As Black feminists we are made constantly and painfully aware of how little effort white women have made to understand and combat their racism, which requires among other things that they have a more than superficial comprehension of race, color, and Black history and culture. Eliminating racism in the white women's movement is by definition work for white women to do, but we will continue to speak to and demand accountability on this issue.

In the practice of our politics we do not believe that the end always justifies the means. Many reactionary and destructive acts have been done in the name of achieving "correct" political goals. As feminists we do not want to mess over people in the name of politics. We believe in collective process and a nonhierarchical distribution of power within our own group and in our vision of a revolutionary society. We are committed to a continual examination of our politics as they develop through criticism and self-criticism as an essential aspect of our practice. In her introduction to *Sisterhood Is Powerful* Robin Morgan writes:

I haven't the faintest notion what possible revolutionary role white heterosexual men could fulfill, since they are the very embodiment of reactionary-vested-interest-power.

As Black feminists and Lesbians we know that we have a very definite revolutionary task to perform and we are ready for the lifetime of work and struggle before us.

Notes

1. This statement is dated April 1977.
2. Michele Wallace, "A Black Feminist's Search for Sisterhood," *The Village Voice*, 28 July 1975, pp. 6–7.
3. Mumininas of Committee for Unified Newark, Mwanamke Mwananchi (The Nationalist Woman), Newark, N.J., © 1971, pp. 4–5.

F I V E

◆◆◆

Defining Genealogies
Feminist Reflections on Being South Asian in North America
Chandra Talpade Mohanty

My local newspaper tells me that worldwide migration is at an all-time high in the early 1990s. Folks are moving from rural to urban areas in all parts of the Third World, and from Asia, Africa, the Caribbean and Latin America to Europe, North America and selected countries in the Middle East. Apparently two percent of the world's population no longer lives in the country in which they were born. Of course, the newspaper story primarily identifies the "problems" (for Europe and the USA) associated with these transnational migration trends. One such "problem" is taking jobs away from "citizens." I am reminded of a placard carried by Black and Third World people at an anti-racism rally in London: We Are Here Because You Were There. My location in the USA then, is symptomatic of large numbers of migrants, nomads, immigrants, workers across the globe for whom notions of home, identity, geography and history are infinitely complicated in the late twentieth century. Questions of nation(ality),

and of "belonging" (witness the situation of South Asians in Africa) are constitutive of the Indian diaspora. This essay is a personal, anecdotal meditation on the politics of gender and race in the construction of South Asian identity in North America.

On a TWA flight on my way back to the U.S. from a conference in the Netherlands, the professional white man sitting next to me asks: (a) which school do I go to? and (b) when do I plan to go home?—all in the same breath. I put on my most professional demeanor (somewhat hard in crumpled blue jeans and cotton T-shirt—this uniform only works for white male professors, who of course could command authority even in swimwear!) and inform him that I teach at a small liberal arts college in upstate New York, and that I have lived in the U.S. for fifteen years. At this point, my work is in the U.S., not in India. This is no longer entirely true—my work is also with feminists and grassroots activists in India, but he doesn't need to know this. Being "mistaken" for a graduate student seems endemic to my existence in this country—few Third World women are granted professional (i.e. adult) and/or permanent (one is always a student!) status in the U.S., even if we exhibit clear characteristics of adulthood, like grey hair and facial lines. He ventures a further question: what do you teach? On hearing "women's studies," he becomes quiet and we spend the next eight hours in polite silence. He has decided that I do not fit into any of his categories, but what can you expect from a *Feminist* (an *Asian* one!) anyway? I feel vindicated and a little superior—even though I know he doesn't really feel "put in his place." Why should he? He has a number of advantages in this situation: white skin, maleness and citizenship privileges. From his enthusiasm about expensive "ethnic food" in Amsterdam, and his J. Crew clothes, I figured class difference (economic or cultural) wasn't exactly an issue in our interaction. We both appeared to have similar social access as "professionals."

I have been asked the "home" question (when are you going home) periodically for fifteen years now. Leaving aside the subtly racist implications of the question (go home—you don't belong), I am still not satisfied with my response. What is home? The place I was born? Where I grew up? Where my parents live? Where I live and work as an adult? Where I locate my community—my people? Who are "my people"? Is home a geographical space, an historical space, an emotional, sensory space? Home is always so crucial to immigrants and migrants—I even write about it in scholarly texts, perhaps to avoid addressing it as an issue that is also very personal. Does two percent of the world's population think about these questions pertaining to home? This is not to imply that the other ninety-eight percent does not think about home. What interests me is the meaning of home for immigrants and migrants. I am convinced that this question—how one understands and defines home—is a profoundly political one.

Since settled notions of territory, community, geography, and history don't work for us, what does it really mean to be "South Asian" in the USA? Obviously I was not South Asian in India—I was Indian. What else could one be but "Indian" at a time when a successful national independence struggle had given birth to a socialist democratic nation-state? This was the beginning of the decolonization of the Third World. Regional geographies (South Asia) appeared less relevant as a mark of identifica-

tion than citizenship in a post-colonial independent nation on the cusp of economic and political autonomy. However, in North America, identification as South Asian (in addition to Indian, in my case) takes on its own logic. "South Asian" refers to folks of Indian, Pakistani, Sri Lankan, Bangladeshi, Kashmiri, and Burmese origin. Identifying as South Asian rather than Indian adds numbers and hence power within the U.S. State. Besides, regional differences among those from different South Asian countries are often less relevant than the commonalities based on our experiences and histories of immigration, treatment and location in the U.S.

Let me reflect a bit on the way I identify myself, and the way the U.S. State and its institutions categorize me. Perhaps thinking through the various labels will lead me back to the question of home and identity. In 1977, I arrived in the USA on an F1 visa—a student visa. At that time, my definition of myself—a graduate student in Education at the University of Illinois, and the "official" definition of me (a student allowed into the country on an F1 visa) obviously coincided. Then I was called a "foreign student," and expected to go "home" (to India—even though my parents were in Nigeria at the time) after getting my Ph.D. Let's face it, this is the assumed trajectory for a number of Indians, especially the post-independence (my) generation, who come to the U.S. for graduate study.

However, this was not to be my trajectory. I quickly discovered that being a foreign student, and a woman at that, meant being either dismissed as irrelevant (the quiet Asian woman stereotype), treated in racist ways (my teachers asked if I understood English and if they should speak slower and louder so that I could keep up—this in spite of my inheritance of the Queen's English and British colonialism!), or celebrated and exoticized (you are so smart! your accent is even better than that of Americans—a little Anglophilia at work here, even though all my Indian colleagues insist we speak English the Indian way!).

The most significant transition I made at that time was the one from "foreign student" to "student of color." Once I was able to "read" my experiences in terms of race, and to read race and racism as it is written into the social and political fabric of the U.S., practices of racism and sexism became the analytic and political lenses through which I was able to anchor myself here. Of course, none of this happened in isolation—friends, colleagues, comrades, classes, books, films, arguments, and dialogues were constitutive of my political education as a woman of color in the U.S.

In the late 1970s and early 1980s feminism was gaining momentum on American campuses — it was in the air, in the classrooms, on the streets. However, what attracted me wasn't feminism as the mainstream media and white Women's Studies departments defined it. Instead, it was a very specific kind of feminism, the feminism of U.S. women of color and Third World women, that spoke to me. In thinking through the links between gender, race and class in their U.S. manifestations, I was for the first time enabled to think through my own gendered, classed post-colonial history. In the early 1980s, reading Audre Lorde, Nawal el Sadaawi, Cherríe Moraga, bell hooks, Gloria Joseph, Paula Gunn Allen, Barbara Smith, Merle Woo and Mitsuye Yamada, among others, generated a sort of recognition that was intangible but very inspiring. A number of actions, decisions and organizing efforts at that time led me to a sense of home and community in relation to women of color in the U.S. Home not as a comfortable, stable, inherited and familiar space, but instead as an imaginative, politically charged space where the familiarity and sense of affection and commitment lay in shared collective analysis of social injustice, as well as a vision of radical transformation. Political solidarity and a sense of family could be melded together imaginatively to create a strategic space I could call "home." Politically, intellectually and emotionally I owe an enormous debt to feminists of color — and especially to the sisters who have sustained me over the years. Even though our attempt to start the Women of Color Institute for Radical Research and Action fell through, the spirit of this vision, and the friendships it generated, still continue to nurture me. A number of us, including Barbara Smith, Papusa Molina, Jacqui Alexander, Gloria Joseph, Mitsuye Yamada, Kesho Scott, and myself, among others met in 1984 to discuss the possibility of such an Institute. The Institute never really happened, but I still hope we will pull it off one day.

For me, engagement as a feminist of color in the U.S. made possible an intellectual and political genealogy of being Indian that was radically challenging as well as profoundly activist. Notions of home and community began to be located within a deeply political space where racialization and gender and class relations and histories became the prism through which I understood, however partially, what it could mean to be South Asian in North America. Interestingly, this recognition also forced me to re-examine the meanings attached to home and community in India.

What I chose to claim, and continue to claim, is a history of anti-colonialist, feminist struggle in India. The stories I recall, the ones that I retell and claim as my own, determine the choices and decisions I make in the present and the future. I did not want to accept a history of Hindu chauvinist (bourgeois) upward mobility (even though this characterizes a section of my extended family). We all choose partial, interested stories/histories — perhaps not as deliberately as I am making it sound here. But consciously, or unconsciously, these choices about our past(s) often determine the logic of our present.

Having always kept my distance from conservative, upwardly mobile Indian immigrants for whom the South Asian world was divided into green-card holders and non-green-card holders, the only South Asian links I allowed and cultivated were with Indians with whom I shared a political vision. This considerably limited my community. Racist and sexist experiences in graduate school and after made it imperative that I understand the U.S. in terms of its history of racism, imperialism and patriarchal relations, specifically in relation to Third World immigrants. After all, we were into the Reagan-Bush years, when the neo-conservative backlash made it impossible to ignore the rise of racist, anti-feminist, and homophobic attitudes, practices and institutions. Any purely culturalist or nostalgic/sentimental definition of being "Indian" or "South Asian" was inadequate. Such a definition fueled the "model minority" myth. And this subsequently constituted us as "outsiders/foreigners" or as interest groups who sought or had obtained the American dream.

In the mid-1980s, the labels changed: I went from being a "foreign student" to being a "resident alien." I have always thought that this designation was a stroke of inspiration on the part of the U.S. State, since it accurately names the experience and status of immigrants — especially immigrants of color. The flip side of "resident alien" is "illegal alien," another inspired designation. One can be either a resident or illegal immigrant, but one is always an alien. There is no confusion here — no melting pot ideology or narratives of assimilation—one's status as an "alien" is primary. Being legal requires identity papers. (It is useful to recall that the "passport"—and by extension the concept of nation-states and the sanctity of their borders—came into being after World War I.)

One must be stamped as legitimate (that is, not-gay-or-lesbian and not-communist!) by the Immigration and Naturalization Service (INS). The INS is one of the central disciplinary arms of the U.S. State. It polices the borders and controls all border crossings—especially those into the U.S. In fact, the INS is also one of the primary forces which institutionalizes race differences in the public arena, thus regulating notions of home, legitimacy and economic access to the "American dream" for many of us. For instance, carrying a green card documenting resident alien status in the U.S. is clearly very different from carrying an American passport, which is proof of U.S. citizenship. The former allows one to enter the U.S. with few hassles; the latter often allows one to breeze through the borders and ports of entry of other countries, especially countries which happen to be trading partners (much of Western Europe and Japan, among others) or in an unequal relationship with the U.S. (much of the noncommunist Third World). At a time when notions of a capitalist free-market economy seem (falsely) synonymous with the values attached to democracy, an American passport can open many doors. However, just carrying an American passport is no insurance against racism and unequal and unjust treatment within the U.S. It would be important to compare the racialization of first-generation immigrants from South Asia to the racialization of second-generation South Asian Americans. For example, one significant difference between these two generations would be between experiencing racism as a phenomenon specific to the U.S., versus growing up in the ever-present shadow of racism in the case of South Asians born in the U.S. This suggests that the psychic effects of racism would be different for these two constituencies. In addition, questions of home, identity and history take on very different meanings for South Asians born in North America. But to be fair, this comparison requires a whole other reflection that is beyond the scope of this essay.

Rather obstinately, I have refused to give up my Indian passport and have chosen to remain as a res-

ident alien in the U.S. for the last decade or so. Which leads me to reflect on the complicated meanings attached to holding Indian citizenship while making a life for myself in the USA. In India, what does it mean to have a green card—to be an expatriate? What does it mean to visit Bombay every two to four years, and still call it home? Why does speaking in Marathi (my mother tongue) become a measure and confirmation of home? What are the politics of being a part of the majority and the "absent elite" in India, while being a minority and a racialized "other" in the U.S.? And does feminist politics, or advocating feminism, have the same meanings and urgencies in these different geographical and political contexts?

Some of these questions hit me smack in the face during my last visit to India, in December 1992—post-Ayodhya (the infamous destruction of the Babri Masjid in Ayodhya by Hindu fundamentalists on 6 December 1992). In earlier, rather infrequent visits (once every four or five years was all I could afford), my green card designated me as an object of envy, privilege and status within my extended family. Of course the same green card has always been viewed with suspicion by left and feminist friends who (quite understandably) demand evidence of my ongoing commitment to a socialist and democratic India. During this visit, however, with emotions running high within my family, my green card marked me as an outsider who couldn't possibly understand the "Muslim problem" in India. I was made aware of being an "outsider" in two profoundly troubling shouting matches with my uncles, who voiced the most incredibly hostile sentiments against Muslims. Arguing that India was created as a secular state and that democracy had everything to do with equality for all groups (majority and minority) got me no where. The very fundamentals of democratic citizenship in India were/are being undermined and redefined as "Hindu."

Bombay was one of the cities hardest hit with waves of communal violence following the events in Ayodhya. The mobilization of Hindu fundamentalists, even paramilitary organizations, over the last half century and especially since the mid-1980s had brought Bombay to a juncture where the most violently racist discourse about Muslims seemed to be woven into the fabric of acceptable daily life. Racism was normalized in the popular imagination such that it became almost impossible to publicly raise questions about the ethics or injustice of racial/ethnic/religious discrimination. I could not assume a distanced posture towards religion any more. Too many injustices were being done in my name.

Although born a Hindu, I have always considered myself a non-practicing one—religion had always felt rather repressive when I was growing up. I enjoyed the rituals but resisted the authoritarian hierarchies of organized Hinduism. However, the Hinduism touted by fundamentalist organizations like the RSS (Rashtriya Swayamsevak Sangh, a para-military Hindu fundamentalist organization founded in the 1930s) and the Shiv Sena (a Maharashtrian chauvinist, fundamentalist, fascist political organization that has amassed a significant voice in Bombay politics and government) was one that even I, in my ignorance, recognized as reactionary and distorted. But this discourse was real—hate-filled rhetoric against Muslims appeared to be the mark of a "loyal Hindu." It was unbelievably heart-wrenching to see my hometown become a war zone with whole streets set on fire, and a daily death count to rival any major territorial border war. The smells and textures of Bombay, of home, which had always comforted and nurtured me, were violently disrupted. The scent of fish drying on the lines at the fishing village in Danda was submerged in the smell of burning straw and grass as whole bastis (chawls) were burned to the ground. The very topography, language and relationships that constituted "home" were quietly but surely exploding. What does community mean in this context? December 1992 both clarified as well as complicated for me the meanings attached to being an Indian citizen, a Hindu, an educated woman/feminist, and a permanent resident in the U.S. in ways that I have yet to resolve. After all, it is often moments of crisis that make us pay careful attention to questions of identity. Sharp polarizations force one to make choices (not in order to take sides, but in order to accept responsibility) and to clarify our own analytic, political and emotional topographies.

I learned that combating the rise of Hindu fundamentalism was a necessary ethical imperative for all socialists, feminists and Hindus of conscience. Secularism, if it meant absence of religion, was no longer a viable position. From a feminist perspective, it became clear that the battle for women's minds and hearts was very much center-stage in the Hindu

fundamentalist strategy. Feminists in India have written extensively about the appeal of fundamentalist rhetoric and social position to women. (The journals *The Economic and Political Weekly of India* and *Manushi* are good sources for this work.)

Religious fundamentalist constructions of women embody the nexus of morality, sexuality and Nation—a nexus of great importance for feminists. Similar to Christian, Islamic and Jewish fundamentalist discourses, the construction of femininity and masculinity, especially in relation to the idea of the Nation, are central to Hindu fundamentalist rhetoric and mobilizations. Women are not only mobilized in the "service" of the Nation, but they also become the ground on which discourses of morality and nationalism are written. For instance, the RSS mobilizes primarily middle-class women in the name of a family-oriented, Hindu nation, much like the Christian Right does in the U.S. But discourses of morality and nation are also embodied in the normative policing of women's sexuality (witness the surveillance and policing of women's dress in the name of morality by the contemporary Iranian State). Thus, one of the central challenges Indian feminists face at this time is how to rethink the relationship of nationalism and feminism in the context of religious identities. In addition to the fundamentalist mobilizations tearing the country apart, the recent incursions of the International Monetary Fund and the World Bank with their structural adjustment programs which are supposed to "discipline" the Indian economy, are redefining the meaning of postcoloniality and of democracy in India. Categories like gender, race, caste/class are profoundly and visibly unstable at such times of crisis. These categories must thus be analyzed in relation to contemporary reconstructions of womanhood and manhood in a *global* arena increasingly dominated by religious fundamentalist movements, the IMF and the World Bank, and the relentless economic and ideological colonization of much of the world by multinationals based in the U.S., Japan and Europe. In all these global economic and cultural/ideological processes, women occupy a crucial position.

In India, unlike most countries, the sex ratio has declined since the early 1900s. According to the 1991 census, the ratio is now 929 women to 1000 men, one of the lowest (if not *the* lowest) sex ratios in the world. Women produce seventy to eighty percent of all the food in India, and have always been the hardest hit by environmental degradation and poverty. The contradictions between civil law and Hindu and Muslim personal laws affect women — rarely men. Horrific stories about the deliberate genocide of female infants as a result of sex determination procedures like amniocentesis, and recent incidents of sati (self-immolation by women on the funeral pyres of their husbands) have even hit the mainstream American media. Gender and religious (racial) discrimination are thus urgent, life-threatening issues for women in India. In 1993, politically-conscious Indian citizenship necessitates taking such fundamentally feminist issues seriously. In fact, these are the very same issues South Asian feminists in the U.S. need to address. My responsibility to combat and organize against the regressive and violent repercussions of Hindu fundamentalist mobilizations in India extends to my life in North America. After all, much of the money which sustains the fundamentalist movement is raised and funneled through organizations in the U.S.

Let me now circle back to the place I began: the meanings I have come to give to home, community and identity. By exploring the relationship between being a South Asian immigrant in America and an expatriate Indian citizen in India, I have tried, however partially and anecdotally, to clarify the complexities of home and community for this particular feminist of color/South Asian in North America. The genealogy I have created for myself here is partial, interested and deliberate. It is a genealogy that I find emotionally and politically enabling — it is part of the genealogy that underlies my self-identification as an educator involved in a pedagogy of liberation. Of course, my history and experiences are far messier and not at all as linear as this narrative makes them sound. But then the very process of constructing a narrative for oneself — of telling a story — imposes a certain linearity and coherence that is never entirely there. But that is the lesson, perhaps, especially for us immigrants and migrants: i.e., that home, community and identity all fall somewhere between the histories and experiences we inherit and the political choices we make through alliances, solidarities and friendships.

One very concrete effect of my creating this particular space for myself has been my recent involvement in two grassroots organizations, one in India and the other in the U.S. The former, an organization called *Awareness,* is based in Orissa and works to empower the rural poor. Their focus is political education (similar to Paolo Freire's notion of "conscientization"), and they have recently begun to very consciously organize rural women. *Grassroots Leadership of North Carolina* is the U.S. organization I work with. It is a multiracial group of organizers (largely African American and White) working to build a poor and working peoples movement in the American South. While the geographical, historical and political contexts are different in the case of these two organizations, my involvement in them is very similar, as is my sense that there are clear connections to be made between the work of the two organizations. In addition, I think that the issues, analyses and strategies for organizing for social justice are also quite similar. This particular commitment to work with grassroots organizers in the two places I call home is not accidental. It is very much the result of the genealogy I have traced here. After all, it has taken me over a decade to make these commitments to grassroots work in both spaces. In part, I have defined what it means to be South Asian by educating myself about, and reflecting on, the histories and experiences of African American, Latina, West Indian, African, European American, and other constituencies in North America. Such definitions and understandings do provide a genealogy, but a genealogy that is always relational and fluid as well as urgent and necessary.

This essay is dedicated to the memory of Lanubai and Gauribai Vijaykar, maternal grandaunts, who were single, educated, financially independent, and tall (over six feet) at a time when it was against the grain to be any one of these things; and to Audre Lorde, teacher, sister, friend, whose words and presence continue to challenge, inspire and nurture me.

S I X

◆◆◆

Taking On the Global Economy

Kalima Rose

The rain was with us every day, washing us, a metaphor for the tears of women from across the planet who came to share the pains and victories of their peoples. The earth turned to bog, wheelchairs became stranded and events were canceled. For some, the inconvenience of incessant rain symbolized the expected relegation of women to substandard facilities. For others, we felt the monsoon working on us, softening the definitions of land and boundaries of peoples, preparing the ground for the new seed that women carried here to share.

The distributed seeds held the kernels of analysis that women first brought to trial at the 1985 world women's conference in Nairobi. There, women from countries of the south were raising their analysis of the social disinvestment that was making women poorer in their countries. The disinvestment they experienced in '85 was a result of their countries' overdue foreign debts. The financial institutions that could help them out were dictating structural adjustment policies which compelled them to restructure their economies along free market principles to help exact the debt payments. Things like food, health, and other social infrastructure subsidies were jettisoned to meet these alignments. In 1985, this was news to women from the U.S., where, by the way, the financial institutions enforcing these policies are located.

A Tighter Analysis

At the Beijing conference in 1995, women from around the world, and particularly women of color, carried a further-developed version of this analysis.

Structural adjustment policies were only one component of what women could now more specifically name as the detrimental aspects of the globalization of the economy. They brought criticism of the destructive nature of a world economic system that is driven by consumption and western industrial values. By 1995, women were much more unified in their understanding of the global deregulation that allows market capitalism to run more freely in its pursuit of "maximizing profits." From country after country, women reported disinvestment in social support programs, privatization, increasing domination by western media, and the "westernizing-down" of cultural integrity because of these influences. It was this discussion, about the effects of globalization on communities around the world, that marked a defining change in the world women's movement. World economic issues were now women's issues.

Winona LaDuke, an Anishinabe of the White Earth reservation in northern Minnesota, rejected any notion of gender equity within western, consumer, industrial development, which continually exploits the lands and natural resources of others. She noted the inherent difficulties of seeking gender equity within a system based on exploitation, that denies self-determination of peoples.

Vandana Shiva, a scientist from India associated with the international Women's Environment and Development Organization (WEDO), brought an understanding of how transnational corporations are using intellectual property rights, a particularly western notion of "owning" information, to privatize collective knowledge. For example, if a corporation names the genetics of a seed, or the chemical structure of a medicine, it can then copyright it and claim royalty rights. Farmers saving seed from crops they have grown can now be charged royalty payments, and medicines developed by women in communities as collective knowledge must be purchased.

Margaret Prescod, an African American member of the International Wages for Housework campaign, carried the analysis that economies are supposed to

---

Kalima Rose attended the NGO Forum of the United Nations Fourth World Conference on Women in Beijing, in 1995. She reports on theoretical perspectives discussed by participants, focusing on the globalization of the economy and its implications for women in the U.S.

facilitate the exchange of goods and services necessary in caring for societies. But our contemporary economic system commodifies everything except caretaking work, which largely falls to and is carried out by women. Because it has no value, anyone performing that work is impoverished and anyone out working to earn a living can minister little caretaking. This campaign succeeded in persuading the official conference to adopt their position that governments should start quantifying and keeping account in national accounting systems of all the caretaking work that women do.

Regulating the Corporate Rampage

A common analysis that emerged from these women, is that we need ways of internationally and personally monitoring and regulating an out-of-control, profit-driven system. This has special meaning for women in the U.S., because while we are victims of this growing capitalism, we are also residents of its home territory. So while we can learn from women in other countries who deal with more extreme versions of increasing poverty, social dissolution, forced migration and homelessness, and share strategies to fight these trends, one of the key things we will learn from them is that we also need to rein in our own.

Consider, for example, that while the negative effects of the globalization of the economy was one of the largest issue areas raised at the conference, it got zero press coverage in the U.S. press. Human rights and violence against women got a lot more ink here, but the analysis of human rights is intimately linked to economic rights: women's experiences of violence are interwoven with economic insecurity and militarism. The western media drops its human rights coverage when women leaders challenge how the sacred tenets of capitalism feed human rights abuses.

While women at the NGO forum dealt significantly with this issue, and while the Platform for Action (the official document emerging from the UN forum) was supposed to address problems of poverty, the Clinton administration opposed including language advocating international regulation of transnational corporations, or investigation of the links between the structural adjustment policies of international financial institutions and the increasing poverty of people living under those policies.

Our administration also opposed language that affirmed the importance of including environmental and labor protections in trade agreements. So you can see that the solutions that women presented from around the world to deal with the social disenfranchisement codified by a global economy are in direct opposition to the direction that our congress and our administration propose.

Though the Platform was supposed to address women's increasing poverty, solutions focus on improving women's access to credit and markets. This assumes that the problem is discrimination against women and not in how markets inherently work. Women from the Economic Justice Caucus (an international coalition of women's nongovernmental organizations that work on economic justice issues) tried to raise the issue that there are also inherent problems in the nature of the markets. This is a very important issue for women in the U.S. to continue to raise. Because, while the document specifically mentions providing adequate safety nets; doing macroeconomic analysis that includes a gender analysis; exploring how excess military spending, arms production, and trade contribute to women's poverty; and ensuring the full human rights of all migrants (not just the documented), the current federal government is actually undoing those things.

Strategies on the Homefront

What does this suggest that we should do here in the U.S.? First, we must develop an astute political and economic analysis of the global economy. We must not simply swallow the conservative rhetoric that decries the role of governments and characterizes regulations that protect the interests of citizens as bad. Every economy of every country on earth is undergoing dramatic changes that have to do with commodifying goods and services, specializing the products of each country, and using women as much of the labor force in this specialization, in low-paid and unpaid ways.

Second, we must analyze the kinds of democratic structures that can uphold community visions of what values we want our economy to serve. This means looking at policies that deal with both access and protection. While the U.S. signs international documents that endorse "access," it at the same time is actively undoing "access" regulations that we have in place (affirmative action). And current public rhetoric opposes regulating toxics, protecting workers or ecosystems, or targeting human rights abuses within our own borders.

Third, we should deeply question the idealized industrial model of development whose central tenet is profits dependent on increasing consumption throughout the world. Women from India sang a powerful song, "Coca cola, Pepsi cola, whatever cola, Why can I get any brand of cola, but when I turn on the tap, nothing comes out?" They boycotted the opening of Kentucky Fried Chicken in south India, and they clearly do not think that it is an improvement that western commercials can now be beamed into any hut in India, promoting Nikes, Reeboks, and Levis, along with the panoply of violent U.S. television shows.

Finally, we can strengthen our commitments to democracy, diversity, and human rights by building on the strengths of women. I believe these strengths include tremendous intelligence and the ability to carry cultural relevance and celebration from one generation to the next. Women from South Africa were a tremendous inspiration. They had just participated in drafting the most progressive constitution on earth, where gender rights were codified. The highest ranking member of the ANC [African National Congress] gave a rousing analysis of involving women in democratic participation, then she proceeded to embrace all the other women leaders who were on her panel, and later that night led

the dance of women from South Africa in the cultural celebration. While that was an inspiring display of the rich gifts women leaders bring, our job is more challenging here at home. In the regional tents where cultural celebrations were rampant, the North American/Europe tent was anemic, to be generous. Factory clothes, no food, little art, no music. Our insipid cultural expression is closely linked with our consumerism.

So I close with an offering of the seeds passed to me in the rain of China. Like my sisters from other parts, I urge you to buck these trends. Educate yourself on these issues, educate other women, make friends and do organizing with people of other races, ages, abilities. It will expand your humanity. Bring celebrations to this work across difference, encourage art and music within it. Take a new track by looking deeply inside the negative values American "democracy" is pursuing. Do your best to change them. Forward yourself and encourage other women forward to take on these challenges. Because despite the power and inspiration of gatherings like this Fourth World Conference on Women, despite the important advances made in naming and overcoming the inequities faced by women around the world, we return home to an increasing military budget, decreasing investment in education and jobs, greater poverty and more obscene wealth, more goods and less natural beauty — and these decisions still made mostly by men.

CHAPTER TWO

Identities and Social Locations: Who Am I? Who Are My People?

Our identity is a specific marker of how we define ourselves at any particular moment in life. Discovering and claiming our unique identity is a process of growth, change, and renewal throughout our lifetime. As a specific marker, identity may seem tangible and fixed at any given point. Over the life span, however, identity is more fluid. For example, an able-bodied woman who suddenly finds herself confined to a wheelchair after an automobile accident, an assimilated Jewish woman who begins the journey of recovering her Jewish heritage, an immigrant woman from a traditional Guatemalan family "coming out" as a lesbian in the United States, or a young, middle-class college student, away from her sheltered home environment for the first time and becoming politicized by an environmental justice organization on campus, will probably find herself redefining who she is, what she values, and what "home" and "community" are. Many of the authors in this chapter write about the cultural contexts they grew up in and how their lives were shaped by these contexts as well as by particular events. Looking back, they are able to see how their sense of identity has changed over time.

Identity formation is the result of a complex interplay among individual decisions and choices, particular life events, community recognition and expectations, and societal categorization, classifica-tion, and socialization. It is an ongoing process that involves several key questions:

Who am I? Who do I want to be?

Who do others think I am and want me to be?

Who and what do societal and community institutions, such as schools, religious institutions, the media, and the law, say I am?

Where/what/who are my "home" and "community"?

Which social group(s) do I want to affiliate with?

Who decides the answers to these questions, and on what basis?

Answers to these questions form the core of our existence. In this chapter, we examine the complex issue of identity and its importance in women's lives.

The *American Heritage Dictionary* (1993) defines *identity* as

the collective aspect of the set of characteris-tics by which a thing is definitely known or recognizable;

a set of behavioral or personal characteristics by which an individual is recognizable as a member of a group;

the distinct personality of an individual regarded as a persisting entity;

individuality.

The same dictionary defines *to identify* as "to associate or affiliate (oneself) closely with a person or group; to establish an identification with another or others."

These definitions point to the connections between us as individuals and how we are perceived by other people and classified by societal institutions. They also involve a sense of individual agency and choice regarding affiliations with others. Gender, race, ethnicity, class, nationality, sexual orientation, age, religion, disability, and language are all significant social categories by which people are recognized by others. Indeed, on the basis of these categories alone, others often think they know who we are and how we should behave. Personal decisions about our affiliations and loyalties to specific groups are also shaped by these categories. For example, in many communities of color women struggle over the question of race versus gender. Is race a more important factor than gender in shaping their lives? If a Latina speaks out publicly about sexism within the Latino community, is she betraying her people? This separation of categories, mirrored by our segregated social lives, tends to set up false dichotomies in which people often feel that they have to choose one aspect of their identity over another. It also presents difficulties for mixed-race or bisexual people, who do not fit neatly into such narrow categories.

In order to understand the complexity and richness of women's experiences, we must examine them from the micro, meso, macro, and global levels of social relations. In the selections included in this chapter, several writers make connections between these levels of analysis. Frederica Y. Daly (Reading 7) focuses on the macro level in her over view essay. Each level involves the standards—beliefs, behaviors, customs, and worldview—that people value. But it is important to emphasize that in a society marked by serious social and economic inequality, such as the United States, oppressed peoples rarely see their values reflected in the dominant culture. Indeed, this absence is an important aspect of their oppression. For example, writing about her family whom she describes as "the ungrateful poor," Dorothy Allison (Reading 8) states: "My family's lives were not on television, not in books, not even comic books. There was a myth of the poor in this country; but it did not include us, no matter how hard I tried to squeeze us in."

Critically analyzing the issue of identity at all of these levels of analysis will allow us to see that identity is much more than an individual decision or choice about who we are in the world. Rather, it is a set of complex and often contradictory and conflicting psychological, physical, geographical, political, cultural, historical, and spiritual factors, as shown in the readings that follow.

Being Myself: The Micro Level

At the micro level, individuals usually feel the most comfortable as themselves. Here one can say, for example, "I am a woman, heterosexual, middle class, with a movement disability; but I am also much more than those categories." At this level we define ourselves and structure our daily activities according to our own preferences. At the micro level we can best feel and experience the process of identity formation, which includes naming specific forces and events that shape our identities. At this level we also seem to have more control of the process, although there are always interconnections between events and experiences at this level and the other levels.

Critical life events, such as entering kindergarten, losing a parent through death, separation, or divorce, or the onset of puberty, may all serve as catalysts for a shift in how we think about ourselves. A five-year-old Vietnamese American child from a traditional home and community may experience the first challenge to her sense of identity when her kindergarten teacher admonishes her to speak only in English. A White, middle-class professional woman who thinks of herself as "a person" and a "competent attorney" may begin to see the significance of gender and "the glass ceiling" for women when she witnesses younger, less experienced male colleagues in her law office passing her by for promotions. A woman who has been raped who attends her first meeting of a campus group organizing against date rape feels the power of connection with other rape survivors and their allies. An eighty-year-old woman, whose partner of fifty years has just died, must face the reality of having lost her lifetime companion, friend, and lover. Such experiences shape each person's ongoing formulation of self, whether or not the process is conscious, deliberate, reflective, or even voluntary.

Identity formation is a lifelong endeavor that includes discovery of the new; recovery of the old, forgotten, or appropriated; and synthesis of the new and old, as illustrated by several writers in this chapter who reflect on how their sense of identity has developed over the course of their lives. At especially important junctures during the process, individuals mark an identity change in tangible ways. An African American woman may change her name from the anglicized Susan to Aisha, with roots in African culture. A Chinese Vietnamese immigrant woman, on the other hand, may adopt an anglicized name, exchanging Nu Lu for Yvonne Lu as part of becoming a U.S. citizen. Another way of marking and effecting a shift in identity is by altering your physical appearance: changing your wardrobe or makeup; cutting your hair very short, wearing it natural rather than permed or pressed, dyeing it purple, or letting the gray show after years of using hair coloring. More permanent changes might include having a tattoo, having your body pierced, having a face lift or tummy tuck, or, for Asian American women, having eye surgery to "Europeanize" their eyes. Transsexuals — female to male and male to female — have surgery to make their physical appearance congruent with their internal sense of self. Other markers of a change in identity include redecorating your home, setting up home for the first time, or physically relocating to another neighborhood, another city, or another part of the country in search of a new home.

For many people home is where we grow up until we become independent, by going to college, for example, or getting married; where our parents, siblings, and maybe grandparents are; where our needs for safety, security, and material comfort are met. In reality, what we think of as home is often a complicated and contradictory place where some things we need are present and others are not. Some people's homes are comfortable and secure in a material sense but are also places of emotional or physical violence and cruelty. Some children grow up in homes that provide emotional comfort and a sense of belonging, but as they grow older and their values diverge from those of their parents, home becomes a source of discomfort and alienation.

Regardless of such experiences — perhaps because of them — most people continue to seek places of comfort and solace and others with whom they feel they belong and with whom they share common values and interests. Home may be a geographic, social, emotional, and spiritual space where we hope to find safety, security, familiarity, continuity, acceptance, and understanding, and where we can feel and be our best, whole selves. Home may be in several places at once or in different places at different times of our lives. Some women may have a difficult time finding a home, a place that feels comfortable and familiar, even if they know what it is. Finally, this search may involve not only searching outside ourselves but also piecing together in some coherent way the scattered parts of our identities — an inward as well as an outward journey.

Community Recognition, Expectations, and Interactions: The Meso Level

It is at the meso level — at school, in the workplace, or on the street — that people most frequently ask "Who are you?" or "Where are you from?" in an attempt to categorize us and determine their relationship to us. Moreover, it is here that people experience the complexities, conflicts, and contradictions of multiple identities, which we consider later.

The single most visible signifier of identity is physical appearance. How we look to others affects their perceptions, judgments, and treatment of us. Questions such as "Where do you come from?" and questioning behaviors, such as feeling the texture of your hair or asking if you speak a particular language, are commonly used to interrogate people whose physical appearances especially, but also behaviors, do not match the characteristics designated as belonging to established categories. At root, we are being asked, "Are you one of us or not?" These questioners usually expect singular and simplistic answers, assuming that everyone will fit existing social categories, which are conceived of as undifferentiated and unambiguous. Among people with disabilities, for example, people wanting to identify each other may expect to hear details of another's disability rather than the fact that the person being questioned also identifies equally strongly as, say, a woman who is White, working class, and bisexual.

Community, like home, may be geographic and emotional, or both, and provides a way for people to express group affiliations. "Where are you from?" is a commonplace question in the United States among strangers, a way to break the ice and start a conversation, expecting answers like "I'm from Tallahassee, Florida," or "I'm from the Bronx." Community might also be an organized group like Alcoholics Anonymous, a religious group, or a political organization like the African American civil rights organization, the National Association for the Advancement of Colored People (NAACP). Community may be something much more abstract, as in "the women's community" or "the queer community," where there is presumed to be an identifiable group. In all of these examples there is an assumption of some kind of shared values, goals, interests, culture, or language.

At the community level, individual identities and needs meet group standards, expectations, obligations, responsibilities, and demands. You compare yourself with others and are subtly compared. Others size up your clothing, accent, personal style, and knowledge of the group's history and culture. You may be challenged directly, "You say you're Latina. How come you don't speak Spanish?" "You say you're working class. What are you doing in a professional job?" These experiences may both affirm our identities and create or highlight inconsistencies, incongruities, and contradictions in who we believe we are, how we are viewed by others, our role and status in the community, and our sense of belonging.

Some individuals experience **marginality** if they can move in two or more worlds and, in part, be accepted as insiders (Stonequist 1961). Examples include bisexuals, mixed-race people, and immigrants, who all live in at least two cultures. Margaret, a White, working-class woman, for instance, leaves her friends behind after high school graduation as she goes off to an elite university. Though excited and eager to be in a new setting, she often feels alienated at college because her culture, upbringing, and level of economic security differ from those of the many upper-middle-class and upper-class students. During the winter break she returns to her hometown, where she discovers a gulf between herself and her old friends who remained at home and took full-time jobs. She notices that she is now speaking a slightly different language from them and that her interests and preoccupations are different from theirs. Margaret has a foot in both worlds. She has become sufficiently acculturated at college to begin to know that community as an insider, and she has

retained her old community of friends, but she is not entirely at ease or wholly accepted by either community. Her identity is complex, composed of several parts.

Dorothy Allison (Reading 8) describes her experience of marginality in high school and in college. First-generation immigrants invariably experience marginality, as described by Chandra Talpade Mohanty (Reading 5). In *Letter to Ma*, Merle Woo, who was born in the United States, addresses her frustration with and admiration for her Chinese immigrant parents. She also analyzes the structures of inequality that all three of them are caught in (Reading 10). The positive effect of marginality—also mentioned by several writers—is the ability to see both cultures more clearly than people who are embedded in any one context. This gives bicultural people a broader range of vision and allows them to see the complexity and contradictions of both cultural settings. It also helps them to be cultural interpreters and bridge builders, especially at the micro and meso levels (Kich 1992; Okazawa-Rey 1994; Root 1996).

Social Categories, Classifications, and Structural Inequality: Macro and Global Levels

Classifying and labeling human beings, often according to real or assumed physical, biological, or genetic differences, is a way to distinguish who is included and who is excluded from a group, to ascribe particular characteristics, to prescribe social roles, and to assign status, power, and privilege. People are to know their places. Thus social categories such as gender, race, and class are used to establish and maintain a particular kind of social order. The classifications and their specific features, meanings, and significance are socially constructed through history, politics, and culture. The specific meanings and significance were often imputed to justify the conquest, colonization, domination, and exploitation of entire groups of people, and although the specifics may have changed over time, this system of categorizing and classifying remains intact. For example, Native American people were described as brutal, uncivilized, and ungovernable savages in the writings of early colonizers on this continent. This justified the genocide of Native Americans by White settlers and the U.S. military and public officials, as well as the breaking of treaties between the U.S. government and Native American tribes (Zinn 1995). Today, Native Americans are no longer called savages but are often thought of as a vanishing species, or a nonexistent people, already wiped out, thereby rationalizing their neglect by the dominant culture and erasing their long-standing and continuing resistance. Frederica Y. Daly speaks to the oppression of Native American people, as well as their success in retaining traditional values and the cultural revival they have undertaken in recent years.

These social categories are at the foundation of the structural inequalities present in our society. In each category there is one group of people deemed superior, legitimate, dominant, and privileged while others are relegated—whether explicitly or implicitly—to the position of inferior, illegitimate, subordinate, and disadvantaged.

Category	Dominant	Subordinate
Gender	Men	Women, transgender people
Race	White	Peoples of color
Class	Middle and upper class	Poor, working class
Nation	U.S./First World	Second, third Worlds
Ethnicity	European	All other ethnicities
Sexual orientation	Heterosexual	Lesbian, gay, bisexual, transgender
Religion	Christian	All other religions
Physical ability	Able-bodied	Persons with disabilities
Age	Youth	Elderly persons
Language	English	All other languages

This hierarchy of advantage and disadvantage has meant that the preponderance of analytical writing about identity has been done by those in subordinate positions: women of color, lesbians, bisexual women, and working-class women (e.g., Allen 1986;

Bird 1995; Brant 1988; Kaye/Kantrowitz and Klepfisz 1989; Kim, Villaneuva, and Asian Women United of California 1989, 1997; Kingston 1976; Klepfisz 1990; Moraga and Anzaldua 1983; Rich 1986; Smith 1983; Tyagi 1996). The readings selected for this chapter also follow this overall pattern. For White people descended from European immigrants to this country, the advantages of being White are not always fully recognized or acknowledged. In Reading 12, Mary C. Waters describes how, at the macro level, this country's racial hierarchy benefits European Americans who can choose to claim an ethnic identity as, for example, Irish Americans or Italian Americans. These symbolic identities are individualistic, she argues, and do not have serious social costs for the individual compared with racial and ethnic identities of people of color in the United States. As a result, White people in the United States tend to think of all identities as equal: "I'm Italian American, you're Polish American. I'm Irish American, you're African American." This assumed equivalence ignores the very big differences between an individualist symbolic identity and a socially enforced and imposed racial identity. In Reading 13, Minnie Bruce Pratt writes about becoming more aware of her advantaged position. "As a white woman, raised small-town middle-class, Christian, in the Deep South," she describes her fear of losing her familiar place as she becomes conscious of how her White privilege affects people of color. She sees the positive side of this process—"I gain truth when I expand my constricted eye"—and asks what White women have to gain by changing systems of inequality.

Maintaining Systems of Structural Inequality

Maintaining this system of inequality requires the objectification and dehumanization of subordinated peoples. Appropriating their identities is a particularly effective method of doing this, for it defines who the subordinated group/person is or ought to be. This happens in several ways:

Using the values, characteristics, features of the dominant group as the supposedly neutral standard against which all others should be evaluated. For example, men are generally physically larger and stronger than women. Many of the clinical trials for new pharmaceutical drugs are conducted using men's bodies and activities as the standard. The results, however, are applied equally to both men and women. Women are often prescribed the same dosage of a medication as men are even though their physical makeup is not the same. Thus women, as a distinct group, do not exist in this research.

Using terms that distinguish the subordinate from the dominant group. Terms such as "non-White" and "minority" connote a relationship to another group, White in the former case and majority in the latter. A non-White person is the negative of the White person; a minority person is less than a majority person. Neither has an identity on her or his own terms.

Stereotyping. Stereotyping involves making a simple generalization about a group and claiming that all members of the group conform to this generalization. Stereotypes are behavioral and psychological attributes; they are commonly held beliefs about groups rather than individual beliefs about individuals; and they persist in spite of contradictory evidence. Lesbians hate men. Latinas are dominated by macho Latinos. Women with physical disabilities are asexual. Fat women are good-humored but not healthy. As Andre (1988) asserts, "A 'stereotype' is pejorative; there is always something objectionable in the beliefs and images to which the word refers" (p. 260).

Exoticizing and romanticizing. These two forms of appropriation are particularly insidious because on the surface there is an appearance of appreciation, as described by Joanna Kadi in Reading 11. For example, Asian American women are described as personifying the "mysterious orient," Native American women as "earth mothers" and the epitome of spirituality, and Black women as perpetual towers of strength. In all three cases, seemingly positive traits and cultural practices are identified and exalted. This "positive" stereotyping prevents people from seeing the truth and complexity of who these women are.

Another way to think about the appropriation of identity concerns representation—the images that are circulated and popularized about a group of people. How are various groups of women typically depicted in this society? The fundamental problem with the representation of women, as with all oppressed peoples, is that "they do not have central control over the production of images about themselves" (McCarthy & Crichlow 1993, p. xvii). The

four processes of identity appropriation described earlier are used to project images of women that generally demean, dehumanize, denigrate, and otherwise violate their basic humanity, a point elaborated in Chapter 3.

In the face of structural inequalities, the issue of identity and representation can literally and metaphorically be a matter of life and death for members of subordinated groups for several reasons. They are reduced to the position of the "other"—that is, fundamentally unlike "us"—made invisible, misunderstood, misrepresented, and often feared. Equally significant, designating a group as "other" justifies its exploitation, its exclusion from whatever benefits the society may offer, and the violence and, in extreme cases, genocide committed against it. Therefore, at the macro and global levels, identity is a matter of collective well-being and survival. Individual members of subordinate groups tend to be judged by those in dominant positions according to negative stereotypes. If any young African American women, for example, are poor single mothers, they merely reinforce the stereotype the dominant group holds about them. When young African American women hold advanced degrees and are economically well off, they are regarded as exceptional by those in the dominant group, who rarely let disconfirming evidence push them to rethink their stereotypes.

Given the significance of identity appropriation as an aspect of oppression, it is not surprising that many liberation struggles have included projects and efforts aimed at changing identities and taking control of the process of positive identity formation and representation. Before liberation struggles, oppressed people often use the same terminology to name themselves as the dominant group uses to label them. One crucial aspect of liberation struggles is to get rid of pejorative labels and use names that express, in their own terms, who people are in all their humanity. Thus the name a group uses for itself gradually takes on more of an insider perspective that fits the evolving consciousness growing out of the political movement.

As with individual identity, naming ourselves collectively is an important act of empowerment. One example of this is the evolution of the names African Americans have used to identify themselves, moving from Colored, to Negro, to Black, to

Afro-American, and African American. Similarly, Chinese Americans gradually rejected the derogatory label "Chink," preferring to be called Orientals and now Chinese Americans or Asians. These terms are used unevenly, sometimes according to the age and political orientation of the person or the geographic region, where one usage may be more popular than another. Among the very diverse group of people connected historically, culturally, and linguistically to Spain, Portugal, and their former colonies (parts of the United States, Mexico, the Caribbean, and Central and South America), some use more inclusive terms such as Latino or Hispanic; others prefer more specific names such as Chicano, Puerto Rican, Nicaraguan, Cuban, and so on. Elizabeth Martínez discusses this terminology in Reading 9.

Colonization, Immigration, and the U.S. Landscape of Race and Class

Other macro-level factors affecting people's identities include colonization and immigration. Popular folklore would have us believe that the United States has welcomed "the tired, huddled masses yearning to breathe free" (Young 1997). This ideology that the United States is "a land of immigrants" obscures several important issues excluded from much mainstream debate about immigration: Not all Americans came to this country voluntarily. Native American peoples and Mexicans were already here on this continent, but the former experienced near-genocide and the latter were made foreigners in their own land. African peoples were captured, enslaved, and forcibly imported to this country to be laborers. All were brutally exploited and violated — physically, psychologically, culturally, and spiritually — to serve the interests of those in power. The relationships between these groups and this nation and their experiences in the United States are fundamentally different from the experiences of those who chose to immigrate here, though this is not to negate the hardships the latter may have faced. These differences profoundly shaped the social, cultural, political, and economic realities faced by these groups throughout history and continue to do so today.

Robert Blauner (1972) makes a useful analytical distinction between colonized minorities, whose original presence in this nation was involuntary, and all of whom are people of color, and immigrant mi-

norities, whose presence was voluntary. According to Blauner, colonized minorities faced insurmountable structural inequalities, based primarily on race, that have prevented their full participation in social, economic, political, and cultural arenas of U.S. life. Early in the history of this country, for example, the Naturalization Law of 1790 (which was repealed as recently as 1952) prohibited peoples of color from becoming U.S. citizens, and the Slave Codes restricted every aspect of life for enslaved African peoples. These laws made race into an indelible line that separated "insiders" from "outsiders." White people were designated insiders and granted many privileges while all others were confined to systematic disadvantage. As Mary C. Waters points out, the stories that White Americans learn of how their grandparents and great-grandparents triumphed in the United States "are usually told in terms of their individual efforts." The role of labor unions, community organizations, and political parties, as well as the crucial importance of racism, is usually left out of these accounts, which emphasize individual effort and hard work.

Studies of U.S. immigration "reveal discrimination and unequal positioning of different ethnic groups" (Yans-McLaughlin 1990, p. 6), challenging the myth of equal opportunity for all. According to Fuchs (1990), "Freedom and opportunity for poor immigrant Whites in the seventeenth and eighteenth centuries were connected fundamentally with the spread of slavery" (p. 294). It was then that European immigrants, such as the Irish, Poles, and Italians, began to learn to be White (Roediger 1991). Thus the common belief among descendants of European immigrants that the successful assimilation of their foremothers and forefathers against great odds is evidence that everyone can pull themselves up by the bootstraps if they work hard enough does not take into account the racialization of immigration that favored White people.

On coming to the United States, immigrants are drawn into the racial landscape of this country. In media debates and official statistics, this is still dominated by a Black/White polarization in which everyone is assumed to fit into one of these two groups. Demographically, the situation is much more complex and diverse, but people of color, who comprise the more inclusive group, are still set off against White people, the dominant group. Immigrants

An Outline of U.S. Immigration Law and Policy[*]

Throughout U.S. history tens of millions of newcomers have made their way to the United States, sometimes at the express invitation of the government and sometimes not. The United States has resettled on a permanent basis more refugees fleeing persecution than any other industrialized nation. By contrast with other countries, it is relatively easy to qualify for and obtain U.S. citizenship. These newcomers have transformed and invigorated their adopted country; the United States would not be what it is today without them. At the same time, U.S. immigration law and policy have not always been fairly or evenly applied. Particularly in times of economic stress or when there is a perceived threat to national security, the United States has quickly turned inward and raised legal barriers to the admission of individuals from other countries. Blaming immigrants for the country's economic and social problems is nothing new.

1790   The first immigration law, the Naturalization Law of 1790, which was not repealed until 1952, limited naturalization to "free white persons" who had resided in the United States for at least two years. Slave Codes restricted every aspect of life for enslaved African peoples.

1875   The Immigration Act of 1875 denied admission to individuals considered "undesirable," including revolutionaries, prostitutes, and those carrying "loathsome or dangerous contagious diseases."

1882   The Chinese Exclusion Act, one of the most blatant racially biased immigration laws in U.S. history, was adopted and subsequently upheld by the U.S. Supreme Court; variations were enforced until 1943. The act was a response to fear of the large numbers of Chinese laborers brought to the United States to lay railroads and work in the mines.

1917   Congress designated Asia (with the exception of Japan and the Philippines) as a barred zone from which no immigrants were to be admitted.

1921   The Immigration Act of 1921 set an overall cap on the number of immigrants admitted each year and established a nationalities quota system that strongly favored northern Europeans at the expense of immigrants from southern and eastern Europe and Asia.

1924   The Immigration Act of 1924 (the Johnson-Reed Act) based immigration quotas on the ethnic composition of the U.S. population in 1920; it also prohibited Japanese immigration.

1945   President Harry Truman issued a directive after World War II allowing for the admission of 40,000 refugees.

1946   The War Brides Act permitted 120,000 foreign wives and children to join their husbands in the United States.

1948   The Displaced Persons Act of 1948 permitted entry to an additional 400,000 refugees and displaced persons as a result of World War II.

1952   The Immigration and Nationality Act of 1952 (the McCarren-Walter Act) was a response to U.S. fear of communism and barred the admission of anyone who might engage in acts "prejudicial to the public interest, or that endanger the welfare or safety of the United States." It allowed immigration for all nationalities, however, thus opening the doors to immigrants previously excluded on racial grounds; it also established family connections as a criterion for immigrant eligibility.

[*] Thanks to Wendy A. Young for this material.

An Outline of U.S. Immigration Law and Policy (continued)

1953   The Refugee Relief Act of 1953 admitted another 200,000 individuals, including Hungarians fleeing communism and Chinese emigrating after the Chinese revolution.

1965   The Immigration Act of 1965, which established an annual quota of 120,000 immigrants from the Eastern Hemisphere, increased the number of Asian immigrants, especially middle-class and upper-middle-class people.

1980   The Refugee Act of 1980 codified into U.S. law the 1951 United Nations Convention Relating to the Status of Refugees and its 1967 Protocol; it includes a definition of a refugee as a person who is outside her or his country of nationality and has a well-founded fear of persecution on account of race, religion, nationality, political opinion, or membership in a particular social group.

1986   The Immigration Reform and Control Act of 1986 was introduced to control the growth of illegal immigrants by introducing an "amnesty" program to legalize undocumented people resident in the United States before January 1, 1982, and imposing sanctions against employers who knowingly employ undocumented workers.

1990   The Immigration Act of 1990 affirmed family reunification as the basis for most immigration cases; redefined employment-based immigration; created a new system to diversify the nationalities immigrating to the United States, ostensibly to compensate for the domination of Asian and Latin American immigration that had occurred since 1965; and created new mechanisms to provide refuge to those fleeing civil strife, environmental disasters, or other forms of upheaval in their homelands.

1996   The Illegal Immigration Reform and Immigrant Responsibility Act was adopted, the first legislation in recent years to target both legal and illegal immigration. It provides for increased border controls and penalties for document fraud; changes in employer sanctions; restrictions on immigrant eligibility for public benefits, including benefits for those lawfully in the United States; and drastic streamlining of the asylum system.

The Personal Responsibility and Work Opportunity Reconciliation Act, which mainly dealt with changes in the welfare system, also made legal immigrants ineligible for various kinds of federal welfare assistance. In 1997, Congress restored benefits for some immigrants already in the United States when this law took effect. There is a five-year waiting period before noncitizens can receive Medicaid or Temporary Assistance for Needy Families.

The "pull" factors drawing immigrants to the United States include the possibility of better-paying jobs, better education—especially for children—and greater personal freedom. "Push" factors include poverty, the dire effects of wars, political upheaval, authoritarian regimes, and fewer personal freedoms in the countries they have left. Immigration will continue to be a thorny issue in the United States as the goals of global economic restructuring, filling the country's need for workers, and providing opportunities for family members to live together are set off against the fears of those who see continued immigration as a threat to the country's prosperity and to the dominance of European Americans.

identify themselves according to nationality — for example, as Cambodian or Guatemalan. Once in the United States they learn the significance of racial divisions in this country and may adopt the term *people of color* as an aspect of their identity here. Chandra Mohanty notes her transition from "foreign student" to "student of color" in the United States. "Racist and sexist experiences in graduate school and after made it imperative that I understand the U.S. in terms of its history of racism, imperialism and patriarchal relations, specifically in relation to Third World immigrants."

This emphasis on race tends to mask differences based on class, another important distinction among immigrant groups. For example, the Chinese and Japanese people who came in the nineteenth century and early twentieth century to work on plantations in Hawai'i, as loggers in Oregon, or building roads and railroads in several western states were poor and from rural areas of China and Japan. The 1965 immigration law made way for "the second wave" of Asian immigration (Takaki 1987). It set preferences for professionals, highly skilled workers, and members of the middle and upper-middle classes, making this group "the most highly skilled of any immigrant group our country has ever had" (quoted in Takaki 1987, p. 420). The first wave of Vietnamese refugees who immigrated between the mid-1970s and 1980 were from the middle and upper classes, and many were professionals; by contrast, the second wave of immigrants from Vietnam was composed of poor and rural people. The class backgrounds of immigrants affect not only their sense of themselves and their expectations but also how they can succeed as strangers in a foreign land. For example, a poor woman who arrives with no literacy skills in her own language will have a more difficult time learning to become literate in English than one who has several years of formal schooling in her country of origin that may have included basic English.

Multiple Identities, Social Location, and Contradictions

The social features of one's identity incorporate individual, community, societal, and global factors, as discussed in the accounts that follow. The point

where all the features embodied in a person overlap is called **social location.** Imagine a diagram made up of overlapping circles, with a circle representing one specific feature of identity such as gender, class, ability, age, and so on. A person's social location is the point at which a part of each circle touches all others — where all elements are present simultaneously. Social location is a way of expressing the core of a person's existence in the social and political world. It places us in particular relationships to others, to the dominant culture of the United States, and to the rest of the world. It determines the kinds of power and privilege we have access to and can exercise, as well as situations in which we have less power and privilege.

Because social location is where all the aspects of one's identity meet, our experience of our own complex identities is sometimes contradictory, conflictual, and paradoxical. We live with multiple identities that can be both enriching and contradictory and that push us to confront questions of loyalty to individuals and groups. This is discussed by Dorothy Allison and Chandra Mohanty.

It is also through the complexity of social location that we are forced to differentiate our inclinations, behaviors, self-definition, and politics from how we are classified by larger societal institutions. An inclination toward bisexuality, for example, does not mean that one will necessarily act on that inclination. Defining oneself as working class does not necessarily lead to activity in progressive politics based on a class consciousness.

Social location is also where we meet others socially and politically. Who are we in relation to people who are both like us and different from us? How do we negotiate the inequalities in power and privilege? How do we both accept and appreciate who we and others are, and grow and change to meet the challenges of a multicultural world? In the readings that follow, the writers note significant changes in the way they think about themselves over time. Some mention difficulties in coming to terms with who they are, describing things that have happened to them and the complexities of their contradictory positions. They also write about the empowerment that comes from a deepening understanding of identity, enabling them to claim their place in the world.

◆◆◆
Questions for Reflection

As you read and discuss the readings in this chapter, think about these questions:

1. Where do you come from? Who are you? How has your identity changed? How do you figure out your identity?

2. Which parts of your identity do you emphasize? Which do you underplay? Why?

3. Who are your "people"? Where or what are your "home" and "community"?

4. How many generations have your family members been in the United States? What was their first relationship to it? Under what conditions did they become a part of the United States?

5. What do you know of your family's culture and history before it became a part of the United States?

6. What is your social location?

7. Which of the social dimensions of your identity provide power and privilege? Which provide less power and disadvantage?

◆◆◆
Taking Action

1. Talk to your parents or grandparents about your family history. How have they constructed their cultural and racial/ethnic identities?

2. Look critically at media representations of people in your group and other groups. How are they portrayed? What is left out of these representations? What stereotypes do they reinforce?

3. Find out about women who are very different from you (in terms of culture, class, race/ethnicity, nationality, or religion) and how they think about their identities.

4. Research identity-based organizations. Why did they form? Who are their members? What are their purposes and goals? Did they have a vision of justice and equality?

SEVEN

Perspectives of Native American Women on Race and Gender

Frederica Y. Daly

. . . Native Americans constitute well over five hundred recognized tribes, which speak more than two hundred (mostly living) languages. Their variety and vital cultures notwithstanding, the official U.S. policy unreflectively, and simply, transforms them from Indians to "Americans" (Wilkinson 1987). Some consideration will be given to their unifying traditions, not the least of which are their common history of surviving genocide and their strong, shared commitment to their heritage.

Any discussion of Indian people requires a brief review of the history of the violent decimation of their populations as well as the massive expropriation of their land and water holdings, accomplished with rare exception with the approval of American governments at every level. To ignore these experiences prevents us from understanding the basis for their radical and profound desire for self-determination, a condition they enjoyed fully before the European incursions began. . . .

Historical Overview

Indian history, since the European invasion in the early sixteenth century, is replete with incidents of exploitation, land swindle, enslavement, and murder by the European settlers. The narration includes well-documented, government-initiated, biological warfare, which included giving Indians clothing infected with smallpox, diphtheria, and other diseases to which Indians were vulnerable. Starvation strategies were employed, with forced removal from their lands and the consequent loss of access to basic natural resources, example, the Cherokee and Choctaw experiences in the famous "trail of tears."

Wilkinson as well as Deloria and Lytle (1983) assert that Indian history is best understood when presented within a historical framework established by four major, somewhat overlapping, periods. The

events dominate federal policy about Indians, subsequent Indian law, and many of the formational forces described in Indian sociology, anthropology, and culture.

Period 1: 1532–1828

This period is described by Europeans as one of "discovery" and is characterized by the conquest of Indians and the making of treaties. The early settlers did not have laws or policies governing their relationships with the indigenous tribes until the sixteenth-century theologian Francisco de Vitorio advised the king of Spain in 1532 that the tribes should be recognized "as legitimate entities capable of dealing with the European nations by treaty." As a result, writes Deloria, treaty making became a "feasible method of gaining a foothold on the continent without alarming the natives" (1970, 3). Deloria explains further that inherent in this decision was the fact that it encouraged respect for the tribes as societies of people and, thus, became the workable tool for defining intergroup relationships. By 1778 the U.S. government entered into its first treaty, with the Delaware Indians, at which point the tribe became, and remains, the basic unit in federal Indian law. . . .

Period 2: 1828–87

The second period, beginning little more than a few decades before the Civil War, witnessed massive removal of Indians from their ancestral lands and subsequent relocation, primarily because of their resistance to mainstream assimilation and the "missionary efforts" of the various Christian sects.

Early in his presidency Andrew Jackson proposed voluntary removal of the Indians. When none of the tribes responded, the Indian Removal Act of 1830 was passed. The act resulted in the removal of the tribes from the Ohio and Mississippi valleys to the plains of the West. "Nearly sixteen thousand Cherokees walked from Georgia to Eastern Oklahoma . . . the Choctaws surrendered more than ten million acres and moved west" (Deloria and Lytle 1983, 7). Soldiers, teachers, and missionaries were sent to reservations for policing and proselytizing purposes, activities by no means mutually exclusive and which represented the full benefit of the act as far as the tribes were concerned. Meanwhile, discovery of gold (especially "strikes" on or near Indian land) in the West, coupled with the extension of the railroad, once again raised the "Indian Problem." But at this point, with nowhere else to be moved, Indian tribes were even more in jeopardy, setting the basis for the third significant period.

Period 3: 1887–1928

During the final years of the nineteenth century, offering land allotments seemed to provide a workable technique for assimilating Indian families into the mainstream. The Dawes Act of 1887 proposed the formula for allotment. "A period of twenty-five years was established during which the Indian owner [of a specified, allotted piece of reservation property] was expected to learn proper methods of self-sufficiency, e.g., business or farming. At the end of that period, the land, free of restrictions against sale, was to be delivered to the allottee" (Deloria and Lytle 1983, 9). At the same time, the Indian received title to the land and citizenship in the state.

The Dawes Act and its aftermath constitute one of the most sordid narratives in American history involving tribal peoples. Through assimilation, swindling, and other forms of exploitation, more than ninety million acres of allotted land were transferred to non-Indian owners. Furthermore, much of the original land that remained for the Indians was in the "Great American Desert," unsuitable for farming and unattractive for any other kind of development. During this same period, off-reservation boarding schools began to be instituted, some in former army barracks, to assist in the overall program of assimilation, and the Dawes Act also made parcels of reservation land available to whites for settlement. The plan to assimilate the Indian and thereby eradicate the internal tribal nations caused immense misery and enormous economic loss. But as we know, it

failed. Phyllis Old Dog Cross, a nurse of the North Dakota Mandan Tribe, mordantly puts it, "We are not vanishing" (1987, 29).

Period 4: 1928–Present

The fourth period is identified by Wilkinson especially as beginning just before the Depression in 1928. It is characterized by reestablishment of tribes as separate "sovereignties" involving moves toward formalized self-government and self-determination, and cessation, during World War II, of federal assistance to the tribes.

Prucha (1985) reminds us that, with the increased belief in the sciences in the 1920s and the accompanying beliefs that the sciences could solve human problems, attitudes toward Indians hardened. At this point the professional anthropologist began to be sent and be seen on the reservations to study and live with the people, alongside the missionaries. The changing attitudes continued into the 1930s with the Roosevelt administration. It was during this period that John Collier became commissioner of Indian Affairs, and the reforms of the Indian Reorganization Act of 1934 invalidated the land allotment policies of the Dawes Act, effectively halting the transfer of Indian land to non-Indians. As Deloria indicates, the Reorganization Act provided immense benefits, including the establishment and reorganization of tribal councils and tribal courts.

After about a decade of progress the budgetary demands of World War II resulted in deep reductions in domestic programs, including assistance to the tribes. John Collier resigned in 1945 under attack from critics and amid growing demands in Washington to cancel federal support for Indians. . . .

Deloria writes that Senator Watkins of Utah was "firmly convinced that if the Indians were freed from federal restrictions, they would soon prosper by learning in the school of life those lessons that a cynical federal bureaucracy had not been able to instill in them" (1970, 18). He was able to implement his convictions during the Eisenhower administration into the infamous Termination Act of 1953, in consequence of which several tribes in at least five states were eliminated. In effect, as far as the government was concerned, the tribes no longer existed and could make no claims on the government. Contrary to its original intent as a means of releasing the tribes from their status as federal wards under BIA [Bureau of Indian Affairs] control, the Termination Act did just the opposite, causing more loss of land, further erosion of tribal power, and literally terrorizing most of the tribes with intimidation, uncertainty, and, worst of all, fear of the loss of tribal standing.

Deloria quotes HR Doc. 363 in which, in 1970, President Nixon asserted, "Because termination is morally and legally unacceptable, because it produces bad practical results, and because the mere threat of termination tends to discourage greater self-sufficiency among Indian groups, I am asking the Congress to pass a new concurrent resolution which would expressly renounce, repudiate, and repeal the termination policy" (1970, 20). This firm repudiation by Nixon of the termination policy earned him the esteem of many Indian people, in much the same way that presidents Kennedy and Johnson are esteemed by many African Americans for establishing programs designed to improve their socioeconomic conditions.

From the Nixon administration through the Carter administration, tribal affairs were marked by strong federal support and a variety of programs aimed at encouraging tribal self-determination. The Indian Child Welfare Act of 1978, which gave preference to Indians in adoptions involving Indian children and authorized establishment of social services on and near reservations, was one of the major accomplishments of this period.

Prucha believes that the tribes' continued need for federal programs is an obstacle to their sovereignty. He asserts that dependency persists but that no one knows how to eliminate it (1985, 97). Deloria insists that Indians are citizens and residents of the United States and of the individual states in which they live and, as such, "are entitled to the full benefits and privileges that are offered to all citizens" (246). . . .

Contemporary Native American Women and Sexism

I have just presented a very abbreviated statement of the general, post-European influx historical experiences of Indians in America, drawing from the research and insights of lawyers and social scientists. Without this introduction it would be difficult to understand Native American women and their contemporary experiences of sexism and racism.

Although many tribes were matrilineal, Indian women were seldom mentioned prominently in the personal journals or formal records of the early settlers or in the narratives of the westward movement. They were excluded from treaty-making sessions with federal government agents, and later ethnologists and anthropologists who reported on Indian women frequently presented distorted accounts of their lives, usually based on interviews with Christianized women, who said what they believed would be compatible with the European worldview. Helen Carr, in her essay in Brodzki and Schenck's *Life-Lines: Theorizing Women's Autobiographies*, offers some caveats about the authenticity of contemporary autobiographies of Indian women, when they are written in the Euro-American autobiographical tradition. She cautions that, in reading the autobiographies collected by early anthropologists, we need to be "aware that they have been structured, consciously or unconsciously, to serve particular 'white' purposes and to give credence to particular white views" (1988, 132).

Ruby Leavitt, writing in Gornick and Moran's *Women in Sexist Society*, states: "Certainly the status of women is higher in the matrilineal than the patrilineal societies. Where women own property and pass it on to their daughters or sisters, they are far more influential and secure. Where their economic role is important and well defined . . . they are not nearly so subject to male domination, and they have much more freedom of movement and action" (1972, 397).

We do not learn from social scientists observing Indian communities that women also were the traders in many tribes. With this history of matrilinealism and economic responsibilities it is not surprising that some Indian women deny the existence of an oppressed, nonparticipatory tribal female role. Yet just as other North American women, they are concerned with child care needs, access to abortion, violence against women, and the effects of alcoholism on the family, all symptomatic of sexism experiences. They are also aware of these symptoms as prevalent throughout our society in the United States; they do not view them as specifically Indian related.

Bea Medicine, Lakota activist, anthropologist, and poet *as quoted* in the preface of *American Indian Women — Telling Their Lives*, states "Indian women do not need liberation, they have always been liberated within their tribal structure" (1984, viii). Her view is the more common one I have encountered in my readings and in conversations with Native American women. In the middle 1970s Native American women who were in New York City to protest a U.S. treaty violation, in a meeting to which they had invited non-Indian women, were adamant that they did not need the "luxury of feminism." Their focus, along with that of Indian men, concerned the more primary needs of survival.

The poet Carol Sanchez writes in *A Gathering of Spirit*, "We still have Women's societies, and there are at least thirty active woman-centered Mother rite cultures existing and practicing their everyday life in that manner on this continent" (1984, 164). These groups are characterized by their "keeping of the culture" activities.

Medicine and Sanchez concur about the de-emphasis of the importance of gender roles in some tribes as reflected in the "Gia" concept. *Gia* is the word in the Pueblo Tewa language which signifies the earth. It is also used to connote nurturance and biological motherhood. The tribal core welfare role, which can be assumed by a male or a female, is defined by the tribe in this Gia context. To be a nurturing male is to be the object of much respect and esteem, although one does not act nurturing to gain group approval. Swentzell and Naranjo, educational consultant and sociologist, respectively, and coauthors, write, "The male in the gia role is a person who guides, advises, cares, and universally loves and encompasses all." The authors describe the role, saying, "The core gia was a strong, stable individual who served as the central focus for a large number of the pueblo's members . . . [for example], 'she' coordinated large group activities such as marriages, feast days, gathering and preparing of food products, even house building and plastering" (1986, 37). With increasing tribal governmental concerns the role of core group Gia has lessened, "so that children are no longer raised by the core group members" (39). Interestingly, the Gia concept is being used currently by social ecologists. For them it parallels the notion of Mother Earth and corresponds with the increasingly widespread understanding of the earth as a living organism.

Charles Lange, in *Cochiti — A New Mexico Pueblo, Past and Present*, says: "Among the Cochiti, the woman is boss; the high offices are held by men, but in the households and in the councils of the clans,

woman is supreme. . . . She has been arbiter of destinies of the tribe for centuries" (1959, 367). The important role performed by the "Women's Society," Lange continues, includes "the ceremonial grinding of corn to make prayer meal" (283). Compatible with women's having spiritual role assignments is the fact that in some tribes the gods are women — example, in the matrifocal Cherokee and Pueblo nations Corn Mother is a sacred figure.

A Cheyenne saying reflects the tribe's profound regard for women: "A nation is not conquered until the hearts of its women are on the ground. Then it is done, no matter how brave its warriors, nor how strong its weapons" (Kutz 1988, 143–58). Historically, in some tribes women were warriors and participated in raiding parties. The Apache medicine woman and warrior Lozen lived such a role and was the last of the women warriors (Kutz 1988, 143–58). Paula Gunn Allen, in *The Sacred Hoop* (1986), notes that "traditional tribal lifestyles are more often gynocratic . . . women are not merely doomed victims of Western progress; they are also the carriers of the dream. . . . Since the first attempts at colonization . . . the invaders have exerted every effort to remove Indian women from every position of authority, to obliterate all records pertaining to gynocratic social systems and to ensure that no Americans . . . would remember that gynocracy was the primary social order of Indian America" (2–3). Later she alludes to the regeneration of these earlier roles: "Women migrating to the cities are regaining self-sufficiency and positions of influence they had held in earlier centuries" (31). "Women's traditions," she says, "are about continuity and men's are about change, life maintenance/risk, death and transformation" (82).

When Indian women deny having experienced sexism they seem mainly to be referring to their continuing historical roles within their tribes, in which they are seen as *the keepers of the culture*. There exists a general consensus that the powerful role of tribal women, both traditionally and contemporarily, is not paralleled in the non-Indian society. Additionally, they allude to the women serving in various tribes as council members, and they point to such prominent, well-known leaders as Wilma Mankiller, chief of the Oklahoma Cherokee Nation; Verna Williamson, former governor of Isleta Pueblo; and Virginia Klinekole, former president of the Mescalero Apache Tribal Council.

Contemporary Native American Women and Racism

The relentless system of racism, in both its overt and covert manifestations, impacts the lives of Indian women; most are very clear about their experiences of it, and they recognize it for what it is. Although many are reticent about discussing these experiences, a growing number of Native American women writers are giving voice to their encounters with racism.

Elizabeth Cook-Lynn, a poet and teacher with combined Crow, Creek, and Sioux heritage, writes about an editor who questioned her about why Native American poetry is so incredibly sad. Cook-Lynn describes her reaction in her essay "You May Consider Speaking about Your Art," published in the anthology *I Tell You Now:* "Now I recognize it as a tactless question asked out of astonishing ignorance. It reflects the general attitude that American Indians should have been happy to have been robbed of their land and murdered" (1987, 60–61).

In the same anthology Linda Hogan, from the Chickasaw Tribe in Oklahoma, writes with concern about the absence of information about Native American people throughout the curricula in our educational systems: "The closest I came to learning what I needed was a course in Labor Literature, and the lesson there was in knowing there were writers who lived similar lives to ours. . . . This is one of the ways that higher education perpetuates racism and classism. By ignoring our lives and work, by creating standards for only their own work" (1987, 243). Earlier she had written that "the significance of intermarriage between Indian and white or between Indian and black [has not] been explored . . . but the fact remains that great numbers of apparently white or black Americans carry notable degrees of Indian blood" (216). And in Brant's *A Gathering of Spirit* Carol Sanchez says, "To be Indian is to be considered 'colorful,' spiritual, connected to the earth, simplistic, and disappointing if not dressed in buckskin and feathers" (1984, 163).

These Indian women talk openly about symptoms of these social pathologies, example, experiencing academic elitism or the demeaning attitudes of employees in federal and private, nonprofit Indian agencies. Or they tell of being accepted in U.S. society in proportion to the lightness of skin color. The few who deny having had experiences with racism mention the equality bestowed upon them through the tribal sovereignty of the Indian nations. In reality the tribes are not sovereign. They are controlled nearly completely by the U.S. Department of Interior, the federal agency that, ironically, also oversees animal life on public lands.

Rayna Green, a member of the Cherokee nation, in her book *That's What She Said* (1984), makes a strong, clear statement about racism and sexism: "The desperate lives of Indian women are worn by poverty, the abuse of men, the silence and blindness of whites. . . . The root of their problem appears attributable to the callousness and sexism of the Indian men and white society equally. They are tightly bound indeed in the double bind of race and gender. Wasted lives and battered women are part of the Indian turf" (10). It is not surprising to find some Indian men reflecting the attitudes of the white majority in relating to Indian women. This is the psychological phenomenon found in oppressed people, labeled as identification with the oppressor.

Mary Tallmountain, the Native Alaskan poet, writes in *I Tell You Now* (1987) that she refused to attend school in Oregon because her schoolmates mocked her "Indianness": "But, I know who I am. Marginal person, misfit, mutant; nevertheless, I am of this country, these people" (12). Linda Hogan describes the same experience, saying, "Those who are privileged would like for us to believe that we are in some way defective, that we are not smart enough, not good enough" (237). She recalls an experience with her former employer, an orthodontist, whom she says, "believed I was inferior because I worked for less than his wife's clothing budget or their liquor bill . . . and who, when I received money to attend night school and was proud, accused me of being a welfare leech and said I should be ashamed" (242). In her poem "Those Who Thunder" Linda translated the experience into verse:

> *Those who are timid are sagging in the soul,*
> *And those poor who will inherit the earth*
> *already work it*
> *So take shelter you*
> *because we are thundering and beating on floors*
> *And this is how walls have fallen in other cities.*
> *(242)*

In the United States we do not know one another, except from the stereotypes presented in the media. As a result, there is the tendency to view people of a differing group vicariously, through the eyes of media interpreters.

Louise Erdrich and Michael Dorris, both Indian and both university professors and eminent writers, reported in Bill Moyers's *World of Ideas* (1989): "We had one guy come to dinner, and we cleaned our house and made a nice dinner, and he looks and says, kind of depressed, 'Do you always eat on the table?'" (465). They used the example to demonstrate how people "imagine" (as distinguished from "know") Indians on the basis of movie portrayals, usually as figures partially dressed or dressed in the fashion of the nineteenth century and typically eating while seated on the ground. It is difficult to form accurate perceptions of the people and worldview of another group. Carol Sanchez seems to challenge us to do just that when she asks us not to dismiss Native Americans and then asks, "How many Indians do you know?" (163). . . .

Sanchez charges non-Indians with the wish to have Indians act like whites, so they will be more acceptable to whites, another example of accommodation, assimilation. She is describing the attitude cited by the young child care worker who said to me, "They like our food, our drum music, our jewelry, why don't they like us!?" Activist Winona La Duke, of the Ojibwa Tribe and by profession an economist, asserts in her offering in *A Gathering of Spirit*: "As far as the crises of water contamination, radiation, and death to the natural world and her children are concerned, respectable racism is as alive today as it was a century ago . . . a certain level of racism and ignorance has gained acceptance . . . in fact respectability . . . we either pick your bananas or act as a mascot for your football team . . . in this way, enlightened people are racist. They are arrogant toward all of nature, arrogant toward the children of nature, and ultimately arrogant toward all of life" (65–66). . . .

Continuing Tensions

That since the sixteenth century the history of Native Americans is one of racist oppression has become an integral part of contemporary historical understanding. Indian women are speaking with increasing frequency and force about their experiences of the double jeopardy of racism and sexism. I wish now to consider three factors that continue to contribute to serious tensions within the tribes and between the tribes and the so-called dominant culture. The factors are, first, the tension within the Indian community between accommodation and traditionalism; second, the erosion of tribal life which is resulting in what has become known as cultural marginality; and third, the problems that arise because of conflicts between reservation law and federal and state laws.

Tensions within the Indian Community

Indian People who wish to retain their identity and culture by continuing reservation life have constantly to struggle with choices regarding adaptation to the dominant culture. They realize that extremism in either direction will result in destruction of their ways of life. Those who resist any adaptation will be made to do so involuntarily, and those who accept "white men's ways" completely and without modification by that very fact forgo their heritage. For well over a century governmental policy favored assimilation and the concomitant dissolution of Indian tribal existence. Real estate value and greed for precious natural resources were crucial motivating factors throughout the period. Indians simply were in the way of the invaders' efforts to amass money. . . .

At the Flathead reservation in Montana, attempts are under way to "revive the traditional Salish culture and preserve the rugged land from development" (Shaffer 1990, 54). Attempts to protect the Indian land for future generations are buttressed by the traditional, nearly universal Indian belief that we do not own the land, that we are simply caretakers of it and will pass it on to future generations. Thus, how the land is used can become an issue of deep tension between strict traditionalists and those who want to assimilate contemporary economic development thinking into tribal life and institutions. Likewise, nearly universally held precepts include the prevailing rights of the tribe over individual rights and the discouragement of aggression and competitiveness, which are seen as threats to tribal harmony and survival. Phyllis Old Dog Cross, a Sioux and a nurse, speaking at a health conference in Denver in 1987, stated: "The need not to appear aggressive and competitive within the group is still seen among contemporary Indians . . . even quite

acculturated Indians tend to be very unobtrusive. . . .
[If not,] they receive strong criticism . . . also anything that would seem to precipitate anger, resentment, jealousy was . . . discouraged, for it is believed
that tribal group harmony is threatened" (1987, 20).

Acknowledging their need for self-sufficiency as
reductions in federal funding continue, the tribes are
searching intensively for economic solutions. Some
have introduced organized gambling onto the reservations and the leasing of land to business corporations; others are considering storage on reservation
land of toxic wastes from federal facilities. Many of
these measures are resisted, especially by traditionalists within the tribes, who see them as culturally
destructive.

Erosion of Tribal Life: Cultural Marginality

Cultural marginality is increasingly experienced by
Indian people because of the confusion resulting
from ambiguities about what defines Indian identity,
individually and tribally. The questions "Who is an
Indian?" and "What is a tribe?" no longer permit
neat unequivocal answers.

Different tribes have different attitudes toward
people of mixed heritage. In some a person with
white blood may be accepted, while a person with
some African-American blood may or may not be
identified as Indian. Indian women, if they marry
non-Indians, may or may not be identified within
their tribes as Indians. To be a member of a tribe a
person must meet that tribe's requirements. Many
tribes require proof of a person's being one-sixteenth
or one-quarter or more of Indian descent to receive
tribal affiliation. . . .

A group or an individual may qualify as an Indian for some federal purposes but not for others. A
June 1977 statement by the U.S. Department of Labor on American Indian Women reads: "For their
1970 Census, the Bureau included in their question-
naire the category, 'American Indian,' persons who
indicated their race as Indian. . . . In the Eastern U.S.,
there are certain groups with mixed white, Negro,
and Indian ancestry. In U.S. censuses prior to 1950,
these groups had been variously classified by the
enumerators, sometimes as Negro and sometimes
as Indian, regardless of the respondent's preferred
racial identity." LeAnne Howe, writing in Paula
Gunn Allen's *Spider Woman's Granddaughters*, says

"Half-breeds live on the edge of both races . . .
you're torn between wanting to kill everyone in the
room or buying them all another round of drinks"
(1989, 220).

Paula Gunn Allen, of the Laguna Pueblo tribe
and a professor of literature, in her essay in *I Tell
You Now,* writes: "Of course I always knew I was an
Indian. I was told over and over, 'Never forget that
you're an Indian.' My mother said it. Nor did she
say, 'Remember you're part Indian'" (1987, 144).

Conflicts between Tribal and Other Governmental Laws

The Bureau of Indian Affairs, which has specific
oversight responsibilities for the reservations, has
played, at best, an ambivalent role, according to
its very numerous critics. There have been many
rumors of mishandled funds, especially of failure
of funds to reach the reservations. It is the source of
endless satire by Indian humorists, who, at their
kindest, refer to it as the "Boss the Indian Around"
department. By federal mandate the BIA is charged
with coordinating the federal programs for the reservations. Originally, it was a section of the War Department, but for the last century and a half it has
operated as part of the Department of the Interior.

Continuing skirmishes occur over violations of
reservation land and water rights. Consequently, the
tribes continue to appeal to the Supreme Court and
to the United Nations for assistance in redressing
federal treaty violations. When these cases are made
public they become fodder for those who continue
to push for the assimilation of Indians into the dominant society as well as for the ever-present cadre of
racial bigots.

Federal law and policy have too often been paternalistic, detrimental, and contrary to the best interests of the Indian people. Further, the federal
dollar dominance of the tribes has a controlling interest on Indian life. Levitan and Johnston conclude
that, "for Indians, far more than for any other group,
socio-economic status is a federal responsibility, and
the success or failure of federal programs determines the quality of Indian lives" (1975, 10).

To receive eligibility for government services requires that the person live on or near a reservation,
trust, or restricted land or be a member of a tribe recognized by the federal government. To be an Indian

in America can mean living under tribal laws and traditions, under state law, and under federal laws. The situation can become extremely complex and irksome, for example, when taxes are considered. The maze and snarl of legalese over such questions as whether the Navajo tribe can tax reservation mineral developments without losing its "trust status" and accompanying federal benefits would defeat, and does, the most ardent experts of jurisprudence. And the whole question of income tax for the Indian person living on a reservation and working in a nearby community requires expertise that borders on the ridiculous.

University of New Mexico law professor Fred Ragsdale, describing the relationship of reservation Indians with the federal government, compares it to playing blackjack: "Indians play with their own money. They can't get up and walk away. And the house gets to change the rules any time it wants" (1985, 1).

The outlawing of certain Indian religious practices occurred without challenge until the 1920s, when the laws and policies prohibiting dancing and ceremonies were viewed as cultural attacks. With the passage of the Indian Civil Rights Act in 1964, Indians have been able to present court challenges to discrimination based on their religious practices. Members of the North American Church use peyote, a psychoactive drug, in their ceremonies. Many consider their religion threatened by the recent Supreme Court ruling that removes First Amendment protection of traditional worship practiced by Native Americans.

The negative impact of the 1966 Bennett freeze, a federally attempted solution to the bitter Navajo-Hopi land dispute, continues to cause pain to the Hopi, who use this 1.5 million-acre land mass for grazing, and to the Navajo, many of whom have resided on this land for generations. Sue Ann Presley, a *Washington Post* reporter, describes the area as being among the poorest in the nation and notes that the people living there are prohibited by law from participating in federal antipoverty programs. She reports that 90 percent of the homes have neither electricity nor indoor plumbing, and home repairs are not permitted. She quotes Navajo chair, Peterson Zah: "There are many Navajos who want to live in what we call the traditional way. But that does not mean they want to live with inadequate sewers, un-

paved roads, no running water or electricity and under the watchful eye of the Hopi Tribe" (1993, B1). The forced removal of some of the Navajos from this area to border town housing caused a tremendous increase in the number of people who sought mental health treatment for depression and other disorders, according to the clinical observations of Tuba City, Arizona, psychologist Martin Topper. . . .

Conclusions

This closing decade of the twentieth century, as a promise for continuing scientific discovery and almost geometric progress, offers a special framework as a time for healing. The healing should be aligned with bias-free hope, and it should be as universally inclusive as possible. I think it a modest suggestion to say that it could well start with sharper identification and diagnosis by the scientific community of Native American women's experience of sexism and racism. Studies showing the impact of the privileged culture and dominant race on the development of Native Americans deserve continued exposure and extended development. We need medical research that investigates the health conditions and illnesses of minorities, including Native American women, whose general health status has to be among the worst in America. . . .

The development of new theories must include appropriate, representative definitions of the total population, free of gender bias and not derived disproportionately from the observation of middle-class white men and women. Curriculum offerings with accurate and comprehensive historical data about gender-specific Native American experiences are needed. . . .

As a country, we have failed to acknowledge our despicable treatment of the Indians. . . . It is hoped that the Indian quest for self-determination and proper respect will be realized, and with it will come our healing as a nation as well. There exists a tremendous need to help the U.S. public begin to understand the real significance of Indian history. . . .

References

Allen, P. G. 1986. *The Sacred Hoop.* Boston: Beacon Press.

————. 1987. "The Autobiography of a Confluence." In *I Tell You Now,* ed. B. Swann and A. Krupat. Lincoln: University of Nebraska Press, 141–54.

————. ed. 1989. *Spider Woman's Granddaughters.* Boston: Beacon Press.

Bataille, G., and K. Sands. 1984. *American Indian Women — Telling Their Lives.* Lincoln: University of Nebraska Press.

Bergman, R. 1971. "Navajo Peyote Use: Its Apparent Safety." *American Journal of Psychiatry* 128:6.

Canby, W. C. 1981. *American Indian Law.* St. Paul, Minn.: West Publishing.

Carr, Helen. 1988. "In Other Words: Native American Women's Autobiography." In *Life-Lines: Theorizing Women's Autobiographies,* ed. Bella Brodzki and Celeste Schenck. Ithaca, N.Y.: Cornell University Press, 131–53.

Cook-Lynn, E. 1987. "You May Consider Speaking about Your Art." In *I Tell You Now,* ed. B. Swann and A. Krupat. Lincoln: University of Nebraska Press, 55–63.

Deloria, V. 1970. *We Talk, You Listen.* New York: Dell Publishing.

Deloria, V., and C. Lytle. 1983. *American Indians, American Justice.* Austin: University of Texas Press.

Erdrich, Louise, and M. Dorris. 1989. "Interview." in *Bill Moyers: A World of Ideas,* ed. B. S. Flowers. New York: Doubleday, 460–69.

Gornick, V., and B. Moran, eds. 1972. *Women in Sexist Society.* New York: Signet.

Green, R. 1984. *That's What She Said.* Bloomington: University of Indiana Press.

Hogan, L. 1987. "The Two Lives." In *I Tell You Now,* ed. B. Swann and A. Krupat. Lincoln: University of Nebraska Press, 231–49.

Howe, L. 1989. "An American in New York." In *Spider Woman's Granddaughters,* ed. P. G. Allen. Boston: Beacon Press, 212–20.

Kutz, J. 1988. *Mysteries and Miracles of New Mexico.* Corrales, N.M.: Rhombus Publishing.

La Duke, Winona. 1988. "They Always Come Back." In *A Gathering of Spirit,* ed. B. Brant. Ithaca, N.Y.: Firebrand Books, 62–67.

Lange, C. 1959. *Cochiti — A New Mexico Pueblo, Past and Present.* Austin: University of Texas Press.

Levitan, S., and W. Johnston. 1975. *Indian Giving.* Baltimore: Johns Hopkins University Press.

Old Dog Cross, P. 1987. "What Would You Want a Caregiver to Know about You?" *The Value of Many Voices Conference Proceedings,* 29–32.

Presley, S. 18 July 1993. "Restrictions Force Deprivations on Navajos." *The Washington Post,* G1–G2.

Prucha, F. 1985. *The Indians in American Society.* Berkeley: University of California Press.

Ragsdale, F. 1985. Quoted in Sherry Robinson's "Indian Laws Complicate Development." *Albuquerque Journal,* 1.

Sanchez, Carol. 1984. "Sex, Class and Race Intersections: Visions of Women of Color." In *A Gathering of Spirit,* ed. B. Brant. Ithaca, N.Y.: Firebrand Books.

Shaffer, P. January/February 1990. "A Tree Grows in Montana." *Utne Reader,* 54–63.

Swentzell, R., and T. Naranjo. 1986. "Nurturing the Gia." *El Palacio* (Summer–Fall): 35–39.

Tallmountain, M. 1987. "You Can Go Home Again: A Sequence." In *I Tell You Now,* ed. B. Swann and A. Krupat. Lincoln: University of Nebraska Press, 1–13.

Wilkinson, C. 1987. *American Indians, Time, and the Law.* New Haven, Conn.: Yale University Press.

A Question of Class

Dorothy Allison

. . . My people were not remarkable. We were ordinary, but even so we were mythical. We were the *they* everyone talks about, the ungrateful poor. I grew up trying to run away from the fate that destroyed so many of the people I loved, and having learned the habit of hiding, I found that I also had learned to hide from myself. I did not know who I was, only that I did not want to be *they,* the ones who are destroyed or dismissed to make the real people, the important people, feel safer. By the time I understood that I was queer, that habit of hiding was deeply set in me, so deeply that it was not a choice but an instinct. Hide, hide to survive, I thought, knowing that if I told the truth about my life, my family, my sexual desire, my real history, then I would move over into that unknown territory, the land of *they,* would never have the chance to name my own life, to understand it or claim it.

Why are you so afraid? my lovers and friends have asked me the many times when I have suddenly seemed to become a stranger, someone who would not speak to them, would not do the things they believed I should do, simple things like applying for a job, or a grant, or some award they were sure I could acquire easily. Entitlement, I have told them, is a matter of feeling like *we,* not *they.* But it has been hard for me to explain, to make them understand. You think you have a right to things, a place in the world, I try to say. You have a sense of entitlement I don't have, a sense of your own importance. I have explained what I know over and over again, in every possible way I can, but I have never been able to make clear the degree of my fear, the extent to which I feel myself denied, not only that I am queer in a world that hates queers but that I was born poor into a world that despises the poor. The need to explain is part of why I write fiction. I know that some things must be felt to be understood, that despair can never be adequately analyzed; it must be lived. . . .

I have known I was a lesbian since I was a teenager, and I have spent a good twenty years making peace with the effects of incest and physical abuse. But what may be the central fact of my life is that I was born in 1949 in Greenville, South Carolina, the bastard daughter of a poor white woman from a desperately poor family, a girl who had left the seventh grade the year before, who worked as a waitress and was just a month past fifteen when she had me. That fact, the inescapable impact of being born in a condition of poverty that this society finds shameful, contemptible, and somehow deserved, has dominated me to such an extent that I have spent my life trying to overcome or deny it. I have learned with great difficulty that the vast majority of people pretend that poverty is a voluntary condition, that the poor are different, less than fully human, or at least less sensitive to hopelessness, despair, and suffering.

The first time I read Melanie Kaye Kantrowitz's poems, I experienced a frisson of recognition. It was not that my people had been "burned off the map" or murdered as hers had. No, we had been erased, encouraged to destroy ourselves, made invisible because we did not fit the myths of the middle class. Even now, past forty and stubbornly proud of my family, I feel the draw of that mythology, that romanticized, edited version of the poor. I find myself looking back and wondering what was real, what true. Within my family, so much was lied about, joked about, denied or told with deliberate indirection, an undercurrent of humiliation, or a brief pursed grimace that belies everything that has been said—everything, the very nature of truth and lies, reality and myth. What was real? The poverty depicted in books and movies was romantic, a kind of backdrop for the story of how it was escaped. The reality of self-hatred and violence was either absent or caricatured. The poverty I knew was dreary, deadening, shameful. My family was ashamed of being poor, of feeling hopeless. What was there to work for, to save money for, to fight for or struggle against? We had generations before us to teach us that nothing ever changed, and that those who did try to escape failed.

My mama had eleven brothers and sisters, of whom I can name only six. No one is left alive to tell me the names of the others. It was my grandmother who told me about my real daddy, a shiftless pretty man who was supposed to have married, had six children, and sold cut-rate life insurance to colored people out in the country. My mama married when I was a year old, but her husband died just after my little sister was born a year later. When I was five, Mama married the man she lived with until she died. Within the first year of their marriage Mama miscarried, and while we waited out in the hospital parking lot, my stepfather molested me for the first time, something he continued to do until I was past thirteen. When I was eight or so, Mama took us away to a motel after my stepfather beat me so badly it caused a family scandal, but we returned after two weeks. Mama told me that she really had no choice; she could not support us alone. When I was eleven I told one of my cousins that my stepfather was molesting me. Mama packed up my sisters and me and took us away for a few days, but again, my stepfather swore he would stop, and again we went back after a few weeks. I stopped talking for a while, and I have only vague memories of the next two years.

My stepfather worked as a route salesman, my mama as a waitress, laundry worker, cook, or fruit packer. I could never understand how, since they both worked so hard and such long hours, we never had enough money, but it was a fact that was true also of my mama's brothers and sisters, who worked in the mills or the furnace industry. In fact, my parents did better than anyone else in the family, but eventually my stepfather was fired and we hit bottom—nightmarish months of marshals at the door, repossessed furniture, and rubber checks. My parents worked out a scheme so that it appeared my stepfather had abandoned us, but instead he went down to Florida, got a new job, and rented us a house. In the dead of night, he returned with a U-Haul trailer, packed us up, and moved us south.

The night we left South Carolina for Florida, my mama leaned over the back seat of her old Pontiac and promised us girls, "It'll be better there." I don't know if we believed her, but I remember crossing Georgia in the early morning, watching the red clay hills and swaying gray blankets of moss recede through the back window. I kept looking back at the trailer behind us, ridiculously small to contain everything we owned. Mama had, after all, packed nothing that wasn't fully paid off, which meant she had only two things of worth, her washing and sewing machines, both of them tied securely to the trailer walls. Through the whole trip, I fantasized an accident that would burst that trailer, scattering old clothes and cracked dishes on the tarmac.

I was only thirteen. I wanted us to start over completely, to begin again as new people with nothing of the past left over. I wanted to run away completely from who we had been seen to be, who we had been. That desire is one I have seen in other members of my family, to run away. It is the first thing I think of when trouble comes, the geographic solution. Change your name, leave town, disappear, and make yourself over. What hides behind that solution is the conviction that the life you have lived, the person you are, are valueless, better off abandoned, that running away is easier than trying to change anything, that change itself is not possible, that death is easier than this life. Sometimes I think it is that conviction—more seductive than alcoholism or violence and more subtle than sexual hatred or gender injustice—that has dominated my life, and made real change so painful and difficult.

Moving to central Florida did not fix our lives. It did not stop my stepfather's violence, heal my shame, or make my mother happy. Once there our lives became dominated by my mother's illness and medical bills. She had a hysterectomy when I was about eight and endured a series of hospitalizations for ulcers and a chronic back problem. Through most of my adolescence she superstitiously refused to allow anyone to mention the word cancer. (Years later when she called me to tell me that she was recovering from an emergency mastectomy, there was bitter fatalism in her voice. The second mastectomy followed five years after the first, and five years after that there was a brief bout with cancer of the lymph system which went into remission after prolonged chemotherapy. She died at the age of fifty-six with liver, lung, and brain cancer.) When she was not sick, Mama, and my stepfather, went on working, struggling to pay off what seemed an insurmountable load of debts.

By the time I was fourteen, my sisters and I had found ways to discourage most of our stepfather's sexual advances. We were not close but we united against our stepfather. Our efforts were helped along when he was referred to a psychotherapist after losing his temper at work, and was prescribed psychotropic drugs that made him sullen but less violent. We were growing up quickly, my sisters moving toward dropping out of school, while I got good grades and took every scholarship exam I could find. I was the first person in my family to graduate from high school, and the fact that I went on to college was nothing short of astonishing.

Everyone imagines her life is normal, and I did not know my life was not everyone's. It was not until I was an adolescent in central Florida that I began to realize just how different we were. The people we met there had not been shaped by the rigid class structure that dominated the South Carolina Piedmont. The first time I looked around my junior high classroom and realized that I did not know who those people were — not only as individuals but as categories, who their people were and how they saw themselves — I realized also that they did not know me. In Greenville, everyone knew my family, knew we were trash, and that meant we were supposed to be poor, supposed to have grim low-paid jobs, have babies in our teens, and never finish school. But central Florida in the 1960s was full of runaways and immigrants, and our mostly white working-class suburban school sorted us out, not by income and family background, but by intelligence and aptitude tests. Suddenly I was boosted into the college-bound track, and while there was plenty of contempt for my inept social skills, pitiful wardrobe, and slow drawling accent, there was also something I had never experienced before, a protective anonymity, and a kind of grudging respect and curiosity about who I might become. Because they did not see poverty and hopelessness as a foregone conclusion for my life, I could begin to imagine other futures for myself.

Moving into that new world and meeting those new people meant that I began to see my family from a new vantage point. I also experienced a new level of fear, a fear of losing what before had never been imaginable. My family's lives were not on television, not in books, not even comic books. There was a myth of the poor in this country, but it did not include us, no matter how hard I tried to squeeze us in. There was an idea of the good poor — hardworking, ragged but clean, and intrinsically noble. I understood that we were the bad poor, the ungrateful: men who drank and couldn't keep a job; women, invariably pregnant before marriage, who quickly became worn, fat, and old from working too many hours and bearing too many children; and children with runny noses, watery eyes, and bad attitudes. My cousins quit school, stole cars, used drugs, and took dead-end jobs pumping gas or waiting tables. We were not noble, not grateful, not even hopeful. We knew ourselves despised.

But in that new country, we were unknown. The myth settled over us and glamorized us. I saw it in the eyes of my teachers, the Lions' Club representative who paid for my new glasses, and the lady from the Junior League who told me about the scholarship I had won. Better, far better, to be one of the mythical poor than to be part of the *they* I had known before. *Don't let me lose this chance,* I prayed, and lived in fear that I might suddenly be seen again as what I knew I really was.

As an adolescent, I thought that the way my family escaped South Carolina was like a bad movie. We fled like runaway serfs and the sheriff who would have arrested my stepfather seemed like a border guard. Even now, I am certain that if we had remained in South Carolina, I would have been trapped by my family's heritage of poverty, jail, and illegitimate children — that even being smart, stubborn, and a lesbian would have made no difference. My grandmother died when I was twenty and after Mama went home for the funeral, I had a series of dreams in which we still lived up in Greenville, just down the road from where Granny had died. In the dreams I had two children and only one eye, lived in a trailer, and worked at the textile mill. Most of my time was taken up with deciding when I would finally kill my children and myself. The dreams were so vivid, I became convinced they were about the life I was meant to have had, and I began to work even harder to put as much distance as I could between my family and me. I copied the dress, mannerisms, attitudes, and ambitions of the girls I met in college, changing or hiding my own tastes, interests, and desires. I kept my lesbianism a secret, forming a relationship with an effeminate male friend that served to shelter and disguise us both. I explained to friends that I went home so rarely because my stepfather and I fought too much for me to be comfortable in his house. But that was only part of the reason I avoided home, the easiest reason. The truth was that I feared the person I might become in my mama's house.

It is hard to explain how deliberately and thoroughly I ran away from my own life. I did not forget where I came from, but I gritted my teeth and hid it. When I could not get enough scholarship money to pay for graduate school, I spent a year of blind rage working as a salad girl, substitute teacher, and maid. I finally managed to get a job by agreeing to take any city assignment where the Social Security Administration needed a clerk. Once I had a job and my own place far away from anyone in my family, I became sexually and politically active, joining the Women's Center support staff and falling in love with a series of middle-class women who thought my accent and stories thoroughly charming. The stories I told about my family, about South Carolina, about being poor itself, were all lies, carefully edited to seem droll or funny. I knew damn well that no one would want to hear the truth about poverty, the hopelessness and fear, the feeling that nothing you do will make any difference, and the raging resentment that burns beneath the jokes. Even when my lovers and I formed an alternative lesbian family, sharing all our resources, I kept the truth about my background and who I knew myself to be a carefully obscured mystery. I worked as hard as I could to make myself a new person, an emotionally healthy radical lesbian activist, and I believed completely that by remaking myself I was helping to remake the world.

For a decade, I did not go home for more than a few days at a time.

It is sometimes hard to make clear how much I have loved my family, that every impulse to hold them in contempt has sparked in me a counter-surge of stubborn pride. (What is equally hard to make clear is how much that impulse toward love and pride is complicated by an urge to fit us into the acceptable myths and theories of both mainstream society—

Steven Spielberg movies or Taylor Caldwell novels, the one valorizing and the other caricaturing—and a lesbian feminist reinterpretation—the patriarchy as the villain and the trivialization of the choices the men and women of my family have made.) I have had to fight broad generalizations from every possible theoretical viewpoint. Traditional feminist theory has had a limited understanding of class differences or of how sexuality and self are shaped by both desire and denial. The ideology implies that we are all sisters who should turn our anger and suspicion only on the world outside the lesbian community. It is so simple to say the patriarchy did it, that poverty and social contempt are products of the world of the fathers. How often I felt a need to collapse my sexual history into what I was willing to share of my class background, to pretend that both my life as a lesbian and my life as a working-class escapee were constructed by the patriarchy. The difficulty is that I can't ascribe everything that has been problematic or difficult about my life simply and easily to the patriarchy, or even to the invisible and much-denied class structure of our society. . . .

One of the things I am trying to understand is how we internalize the myths of our society even as we hate and resist them. Perhaps this will be more understandable if I discuss specifically how some of these myths have shaped my life and how I have been able to talk about and change my own understanding of my family. I have felt a powerful temptation to write about my family as a kind of moral tale with us as the heroes and the middle and upper classes as the villains. It would be within the romantic myth, for example, to pretend that we were the kind of noble Southern whites portrayed in the movies, mill workers for generations until driven out of the mills by alcoholism and a family propensity to rebellion and union talk. But that would be a lie. The truth is that no one in my family ever joined a union. Taken as far as it can go, the myth of the poor would make my family over into union organizers or people broken by the failure of the unions. The reality of my family is far more complicated and lacks the cardboard nobility of the myth.

As far as my family was concerned, union organizers, like preachers, were of a different class, suspect and hated as much as they might be admired for what they were supposed to be trying to achieve.

Serious belief in anything—any political ideology, any religious system, or any theory of life's meaning and purpose—was seen as unrealistic. It was an attitude that bothered me a lot when I started reading the socially conscious novels I found in the paperback racks when I was eleven or so. I particularly loved Sinclair Lewis's novels and wanted to imagine my own family as part of the working man's struggle. But it didn't seem to be that simple.

"We were not joiners," my Aunt Dot told me with a grin when I asked her about the union. My cousin Butch laughed at that, told me the union charged dues and said, "Hell, we can't even be persuaded to toss money in the collection plate. An't gonna give it to no fat union man." It shamed me that the only thing my family wholeheartedly believed in was luck, and the waywardness of fate. They held the dogged conviction that the admirable and wise thing to do was to try and keep a sense of humor, not to whine or cower, and to trust that luck might someday turn as good as it had been bad—and with just as much reason. Becoming a political activist with an almost religious fervor was the thing I did that most outraged my family and the Southern working-class community they were part of.

Similarly, it was not my sexuality, my lesbianism, that was seen by my family as most rebellious; for most of my life, no one but my mama took my sexual preference very seriously. It was the way I thought about work, ambition, and self-respect that seemed incomprehensible to my aunts and cousins. They were waitresses, laundry workers, and counter girls. I was the one who went to work as a maid, something I never told any of them. They would have been angry if they had known, though the fact that some work was contemptible was itself a difficult notion. They believed that work was just work, necessary, that you did what you had to do to survive. They did not believe so much in taking pride in doing your job as they did in stubbornly enduring hard work and hard times when you really didn't have much choice about what work you did. But at the same time they did believe that there were some forms of work, including maid's work, that were only for black people, not white, and while I did not share that belief, I knew how intrinsic it was to how my family saw the world. Sometimes I felt as if I straddled cultures and belonged on neither side. I would grind my teeth at what I knew was my family's unquestioning racism but still take pride in their pragmatic endurance, but more and more as I grew older what I truly felt was a deep estrangement from the way they saw the world, and gradually a sense of shame that would have been completely incomprehensible to them.

"Long as there's lunch counters, you can always find work," I was told by both my mother and my aunts, and they'd add, "I can always get me a little extra with a smile." It was obvious that there was supposed to be nothing shameful about it, that needy smile across a lunch counter, that rueful grin when you didn't have rent, or the half-provocative, half-begging way my mama could cajole the man at the store to give her a little credit. But I hated it, hated the need for it and the shame that would follow every time I did it myself. It was begging as far as I was concerned, a quasi-prostitution that I despised even while I continued to use it (after all, I needed the money). But my mother, aunts, and cousins had not been ashamed, and my shame and resentment pushed me even further away from them.

"Just use that smile," my girl cousins used to joke, and I hated what I knew they meant. After college, when I began to support myself and study feminist theory, I did not become more understanding of the women of my family but more contemptuous. I told myself that prostitution is a skilled profession and my cousins were never more than amateurs. There was a certain truth in this, though like all cruel judgments made from the outside, it ignored the conditions that made it true. The women in my family, my mother included, had sugar daddies, not johns, men who slipped them money because they needed it so badly. From their point of view they were nice to those men because the men were nice to them, and it was never so direct or crass an arrangement that they would set a price on their favors. They would never have described what they did as prostitution, and nothing made them angrier than the suggestion that the men who helped them out did it just for their favors. They worked for a living, they swore, but this was different.

I always wondered if my mother had hated her sugar daddy, or if not *him* then her need for what he offered her, but it did not seem to me in memory that she had. Her sugar daddy had been an old man, half-crippled, hesitant and needy, and he treated my mama with enormous consideration and, yes, respect. The relationship between them was painful because it was based on the fact that she and my stepfather could not make enough money to support the family. Mama could not refuse her sugar daddy's money, but at the same time he made no assumptions about that money buying anything she was not already offering. The truth was, I think, that she genuinely liked him, and only partly because he treated her so well.

Even now, I am not sure whether or not there was a sexual exchange between them. Mama was a pretty woman and she was kind to him, a kindness he obviously did not get from anyone else in his life, and he took extreme care not to cause her any problems with my stepfather. As a teenager with an adolescent's contempt for moral failings and sexual complexity of any kind, I had been convinced that Mama's relationship with that old man was contemptible and also that I would never do such a thing. The first time a lover of mine gave me money, and I took it, everything in my head shifted. The amount she gave me was not much to her but it was a lot to me and I needed it. I could not refuse it, but I hated myself for taking it and I hated her for giving it to me. Worse, she had much less grace about my need than my mama's sugar daddy had displayed toward her. All that bitter contempt I had felt for my needy cousins and aunts raged through me and burned out the love I had felt. I ended the relationship quickly, unable to forgive myself for *selling* what I believed should only be offered freely—not sex but love itself.

When the women in my family talked about how hard they worked, the men would spit to the side and shake their heads. Men took real jobs—hard, dangerous, physically daunting work. They went to jail, not just the hard-eyed, careless boys who scared me with their brutal hands and cold eyes, but their gentler, softer brothers. It was another family thing, what people expected of my mama's family, my people. "His daddy's that one was sent off to jail in Georgia, and his uncle's another. Like as not, he's just the same," you'd hear people say of boys so young they still had their milk teeth. We were always driving down to the county farm to see somebody, some uncle, cousin, or nameless male relation. Shaven-headed, sullen and stunned, they wept on Mama's shoulder or begged my aunts to help. "I didn't do nothing, Mama," they'd say and it might have been true, but if even we didn't believe them, who would? No one told the truth, not even about how their lives were destroyed.

When I was eight years old, Butch, one of my favorite cousins, went to jail for breaking into pay phones with another boy. The other boy was returned to the custody of his parents. Butch was sent to the boys' facility at the county farm and after three months, my mama took us down there to visit, carrying a big basket of fried chicken, cold cornbread, and potato salad. Along with a hundred others we sat out on the lawn with Butch and watched him eat like he hadn't had a full meal in the whole three months. I stared at his head, which had been shaved near bald, and his ears, which were newly marked with fine blue scars from the carelessly handled razor. People were laughing, music was playing, and a tall lazy man in uniform walked past us chewing on toothpicks and watching us all closely. Butch kept his head down, his face hard with hatred, only looking back at the guard when he turned away.

"Sons-a-bitches," he whispered, and my mama shushed him. We all sat still when the guard turned back to us. There was a long moment of quiet and then that man let his face relax into a big wide grin.

"Uh-huh," he said. That was all he said. Then he turned and walked away. None of us spoke. None of us ate any more. Butch went back inside soon after and we left. When we got back to the car, my mama sat there for a while crying quietly. The next week Butch was reported for fighting and had his stay extended by six months.

Butch was fifteen. He never went back to school and after jail he couldn't join the army. When he finally did come home we never talked, never had to talk. I knew without asking that the guard had had his little revenge, knew too that my cousin would break into another phone booth as soon as he could, but do it sober and not get caught. I knew without asking the source of his rage, the way he felt about clean, well-dressed, contemptuous people who looked at him like his life wasn't as important as a dog's. I knew because I felt it too. That guard had looked at me and Mama with the same expression he used on my cousin. We were trash. We were the ones they built the county farm to house and break. The boy who had been sent home had been the son of a deacon in the church, the man who managed the hardware store.

As much as I hated that man, and his boy, there was a way in which I also hated my cousin. He should have known better, I told myself, should have known the risk he ran. He should have been more careful. As I became older and started living on my own, it was a litany that I used against myself even more angrily than I used it against my cousin. I knew who I was, knew that the most important thing I had to do was protect myself and hide my despised identity, blend into the myth of both the "good" poor and the reasonable lesbian. Even when I became a feminist activist, that litany went on reverberating in my head, but by then it had become a ground-note, something so deep and omnipresent, I no longer heard it even when everything I did was set to the cadence that it established.

By 1975, I was earning a meager living as a photographer's assistant in Tallahassee, Florida, but the real work of my life was my lesbian feminist activism, the work I did with the local Women's Center and the committee to found a Feminist Studies Department at Florida State University. Part of my role as I saw it was to be a kind of evangelical lesbian feminist, and to help develop a political analysis of this woman-hating society. I did not talk about class, more than by giving lip service to how we all needed to think about it, the same way I thought we all needed to think about racism. I was a serious and determined person, living in a lesbian collective, studying each new book that purported to address feminist issues and completely driven by what I saw as a need to revolutionize the world. . . .

The idea of writing fiction or essays seemed frivolous when there was so much work to be done, but everything changed when I found myself confronting emotions and ideas that could not be explained away or postponed for a feminist holiday. The way it happened was simple and completely unexpected. One week I was asked to speak to two completely divergent groups: an Episcopalian Sunday School class and a juvenile detention center. The Episcopalians were all white, well-dressed, highly articulate, nominally polite, and obsessed with getting me to tell them (without their having to ask directly) just what it was that two women did together in bed. The delinquents were all women, eighty percent black and Hispanic, dressed in green uniform dresses or blue jeans and workshirts, profane, rude, fearless, witty, and just as determined to get me to talk about what it was that two women did together in bed.

I tried to have fun with the Episcopalians, teasing them about their fears and insecurities, and being as bluntly honest as I could about my sexual practices. The Sunday School teacher, a man who had assured me of his liberal inclinations, kept blushing and stammering as the questions about my growing up and coming out became more detailed. When the meeting was over, I stepped out into the sunshine angry at the contemptuous attitude implied by all their questions, and though I did not know why, also so deeply depressed that I couldn't even cry. The delinquents were different. Shameless, they had me blushing within the first few minutes, yelling out questions that were partly curious and partly a way of boasting about what they already knew.

"You butch of femme?" "You ever fuck boys?" "You ever want to?" "You want to have children?" "What's your girlfriend like?" I finally broke up when one very tall confident girl leaned way over and called out, "Hey girlfriend! I'm getting out of here next weekend. What you doing that night?" I laughed so hard I almost choked. I laughed until we were all howling and giggling together. Even getting frisked as I left didn't ruin my mood. I was still grinning when I climbed into the waterbed with my lover that night, grinning right up to the moment when she wrapped her arms around me and I burst into tears.

It is hard to describe the way I felt that night, the shock of recognition and the painful way my thoughts turned. That night I understood suddenly everything that happened to my cousins and me, understood it from a wholly new and agonizing perspective, one that made clear how brutal I had been to both my family and myself. I understood all over again how we had been robbed and dismissed, and why I had worked so hard not to think about it. I had learned as a child that what could not be changed had to go unspoken, and worse, that those who cannot change their own lives have every reason to be ashamed of that fact and to hide it. I had accepted that shame and believed in it, but why? What had I or my cousins really done to deserve the contempt directed at us? Why had I always believed us contemptible by nature? I wanted to talk to someone about all the things I was thinking that night, but I could not. Among the women I knew there was no one who would have understood what I was thinking, no other working-class women in the women's collective where I was living. I began to suspect that we shared no common language to speak those bitter truths.

In the days after that I found myself remembering that afternoon long ago at the county farm, that feeling of being the animal in the zoo, the thing looked at and laughed at and used by the real people who watched us. For all his liberal convictions, that Sunday School teacher had looked at me with eyes that reminded me of Butch's long-ago guard. Suddenly I felt thrown back into my childhood, into all the fears and convictions I had tried to escape. Once again I felt myself at the mercy of the important people who knew how to dress and talk, and would always be given the benefit of the doubt while I and my family would not.

I felt as if I was at the mercy of an outrage so old I could not have traced all the ways it shaped my life. I understood again that some are given no quarter, no chance, that all their courage, humor, and love for each other is just a joke to the ones who make the rules, and I hated the rule makers. Finally I also realized that part of my grief came from the fact that I no longer knew who I was or where I belonged. I had run away from my family, refused to go home to visit, and tried in every way to make myself a new person. How could I be working-class with a college degree? As a lesbian activist? I thought about the guards at the detention center, and the way they had looked at me. They had not stared at me with the same picture-window emptiness they turned on the girls who came to hear me, girls who were closer to the life I had been meant to live than I could bear to examine. The contempt in their eyes was contempt for me as a lesbian, different and the same, but still contempt. . . .

In the late 1970s, the compartmentalized life I had created burst open. It began when I started to write and work out what I really thought about my family. . . . I went home again. I went home to my mother and my sisters, to visit, talk, argue, and begin to understand.

Once home I saw that, as far as my family was concerned, lesbians were lesbians whether they wore suitcoats or leather jackets. Moreover, in all that time when I had not made peace with myself, my family had managed to make a kind of peace with me. My girlfriends were treated like slightly odd versions of my sisters' husbands, while I was simply the daughter who had always been difficult but was still a part of their lives. The result was that I started trying to confront what had made me unable to really talk to my sisters for so many years. I discovered that they no longer knew who I was either, and it took time and lots of listening to each other to rediscover my sense of family, and my love for them.

It is only as the child of my class and my unique family background that I have been able to put together what is for me a meaningful politics, gained a sense of why I believe in activism, why self-revelation is so important for lesbians, reexamining the way we are seen and the way we see ourselves. There is no all-purpose feminist analysis that explains away all the complicated ways our sexuality and core identity are shaped, the way we see ourselves as parts of both our birth families and the extended family of friends and lovers we invariably create within the lesbian community. For me the bottom line has simply become the need to resist that omnipresent fear, that urge to hide and disappear, to disguise my life, my desires, and the truth about how little any of us understand—even as we try to make the world a more just and human place for us all. Most of all I have tried to understand the politics of *they*, why human beings fear and stigmatize the different while secretly dreading that they might be one of the different themselves. Class, race, sexuality, gender, all the categories by which we categorize and dismiss each other need to be examined from the inside.

The horror of class stratification, racism, and prejudice is that some people begin to believe that the security of their families and community depends on the oppression of others, that for some to have good lives others must have lives that are mean and horrible. It is a belief that dominates this culture; it is what made the poor whites of the South so determinedly racist and the middle class so contemptuous of the poor. It is a myth that allows some to imagine that they build their lives on the ruin of others, a secret core of shame for the middle class, a goad and a spur to the marginal working class, and cause enough for the homeless and poor to feel no constraints on hatred or violence. The power of the myth is made even more apparent when we examine how within the lesbian and feminist communities, where so much attention has been paid to the politics of marginalization, there is still so much exclusion and fear, so many of us who do not feel safe even within our chosen communities.

I grew up poor, hated, the victim of physical, emotional, and sexual violence, and I know that suffering does not ennoble. It destroys. To resist destruction, self-hatred, or lifelong hopelessness, we have to throw off the conditioning of being despised, the fear of becoming that *they* that is talked about so dismissively, to refuse lying myths and easy moralities, to see ourselves as human, flawed and extraordinary. All of us — extraordinary.

NINE

A Word about the Great Terminology Question

Elizabeth Martínez

When you have a name like Martínez, sooner or later someone will ask the Great Terminology Question. Say that you prefer to be called a Chicana, not Mexican American, and you'll have to explain it at some length. Say that you prefer to be called Latina rather than Hispanic, and prepare for an even longer discussion. Say you are indigenous, and you'd better make another pot of coffee for a long night's debate. So it goes in this land of many identities, with new ones emerging all the time.

On one hand, there are real grounds for confusion. The term "Chicano" or "Chicana" eludes simple definition because it stands for a mix that is both racial and cultural. It refers to a people who are neither strictly Mexican nor strictly Yankee — as well as both. Go to Mexico and you will quickly realize that most people there do not see Chicanos as Mexican. You may even hear the term "brown gringo." Live in the United States, and you will quickly discover that the dominant population doesn't see Chicanos as real Americans.

Confusion, ignorance and impassioned controversy about terminology make it necessary, then, to begin . . . with such basic questions as: what is a Chicana or Chicano? (And remember, Spanish is a gendered language, hence Chicana/Chicano.)

For starters, we combine at least three roots: indigenous (from pre-Columbian times), European (from the Spanish and Portuguese invasions) and African (from the many slaves brought to the Americas, including some 200,000 to Mexico alone). A smattering of Chinese should be added, which goes back to the sixteenth century; Mexico City had a

Chinatown by the mid-1500s, some historians say. Another *mestizaje,* or mixing took place — this time with Native Americans of various nations, pueblos and tribes living in what is now the Southwest — when Spanish and Mexican colonizers moved north. Later our Chicano ancestors acquired yet another dimension through intermarriage with Anglos.

The question arises: is the term "Chicano" the same as "Mexican American" or "Mexican-American"? Yes, except in the sense of political self-definition. "Chicano/a" once implied lower-class status and was at times derogatory. During the 1960s and 1970s, in an era of strong pressure for progressive change, the term became an outcry of pride in one's peoplehood and rejection of assimilation as one's goal. Today the term "Chicano/a" refuses to go away, especially among youth, and you will still hear jokes like "A Chicano is a Mexican American who doesn't want to have blue eyes" or "who doesn't eat white bread" or whatever. (Some believe the word itself, by the way, comes from "Mexica" — pronounced "Meshica" — which was the early name for the Aztecs.)

People ask: are Chicanos different from Latinos?

At the risk of impassioned debate, let me say: we are one type of Latino. In the United States today, Latinos and Latinas include men and women whose background links them to some 20 countries, including Mexico. Many of us prefer "Latino" to "Hispanic," which obliterates our indigenous and African heritage, and recognizes only the European, the colonizer. (Brazilians, of course, reject "Hispanic" strongly because *their* European heritage is Portuguese, not

Spanish.) "Hispanic" also carries the disadvantage of being a term that did not emerge from the community itself but was imposed by the dominant society through its census bureau and other bureaucracies, during the Nixon administration of the 1970s.

Today most of the people who say "Hispanic" do so without realizing its racist implications, simply because they see and hear it everywhere. Some who insist on using the term point out that "Latino" is no better than "Hispanic" because it also implies Eurocentricity. Many of us ultimately prefer to call ourselves "La Raza" or simply "Raza," meaning "The People," which dates back many years in the community. (Again we find complications in actual usage: some feel that Raza refers to people of Mexican and perhaps also Central American origin, and doesn't include Latinos from other areas.)

We are thus left with no all-embracing term acceptable to everyone. In the end, the most common, popular identification is by specific nationality: Puerto Rican, Mexican, Guatemalian, Colombian and so forth. But those of us who seek to build continental unity stubbornly cling to some broadly inclusive way of defining ourselves. In my own case, that means embracing both "Chicana" and "Latina."

At the heart of the terminology debate is the historical experience of Raza. Invasion, military occupation and racist control mechanisms all influence the evolution of words describing people who have lived through such trauma. The collective memory of every Latino people includes direct or indirect (neo-)colonialism, primarily by Spain or Portugal and later by the United States.

Among Latinos, Mexicans in what we now call the Southwest have experienced U.S. colonialism the longest and most directly, with Puerto Ricans not far behind. Almost one-third of today's United States was the home of Mexicans as early as the 1500s, until Anglos seized it militarily in 1848 and treated its population as conquered subjects. (The Mexicans, of course, themselves occupied lands that had been seized from Native Americans.) Such oppression totally violated the Treaty of Guadalupe Hidalgo, which ended the 1846–48 war and promised respect for the civil and property rights of Mexicans remaining in the Southwest. The imposition of U.S. rule involved taking over millions of acres of Mexican-held land by trickery and violence. Colonization also brought the imposition of Anglo values and institutions at the expense of Mexican culture, including language. Hundreds of Mexicans were lynched as a form of control.

In the early 1900s, while colonization continued, the original Mexican population of the Southwest was greatly increased by an immigration that continues today. This combination of centuries-old roots with relatively recent ones gives the Mexican-American people a rich and varied cultural heritage. It means that Chicanos are not by origin an immigrant people in the United States (except compared with the Native Americans); their roots go back four centuries. Yet they also include immigrants. Too many Americans see only the recent arrivals, remaining blind to those earlier roots and what they signify.

We cannot understand all that history simply in terms of victimization: popular resistance is its other face. Raza resistance, which took the form of organized armed struggle in the Southwest during the last century, continues today in many forms. These include rejecting the colonized mentality, that pernicious, destructive process of internalizing a belief in the master's superiority and our inferiority.

The intensity of the terminology debate comes as no surprise, then, for it echoes people's struggles for non-racist—indeed, anti-racist—ways of defining themselves. Identity continues to be a major concern of youth in particular, with reason. But an obsession with self-definition can become a trap if that is all we think about, all we debate. If liberatory terminology becomes an end in itself and our only end, it ceases to be a tool of liberation. Terms can be useful, even vital tools, but the house of La Raza that is waiting to be built needs many kinds.

Letter to Ma

Merle Woo

January, 1980

Dear Ma,

I was depressed over Christmas, and when New Year's rolled around, do you know what one of my resolves was? Not to come by and see you as much anymore. I had to ask myself why I get so down when I'm with you, my mother, who has focused so much of her life on me, who has endured so much; one who I am proud of and respect so deeply for simply surviving.

I suppose that one of the main reasons is that when I leave your house, your pretty little round white table in the dinette where we sit while you drink tea (with only three specks of Jasmine) and I smoke and drink coffee, I am down because I believe there are chasms between us. When you say, "I support you, honey, in everything you do except... except..." I know you mean except my speaking out and writing of my anger at all those things that have caused those chasms. When you say I shouldn't be so ashamed of Daddy, former gambler, retired clerk of a "gook suey" store, because of the time when I was six and saw him humiliated on Grant Avenue by two white cops, I know you haven't even been listening to me when I have repeatedly said that I am not ashamed of him, not you, not who we are. When you ask, "Are you so angry because you are unhappy?" I know that we are not talking to each other. Not with understanding, although many words have passed between us, many hours, many afternoons at that round table with Daddy out in the front room watching television, and drifting out every once in a while to say "Still talking?" and getting more peanuts that are so bad for his health.

We talk and we talk and I feel frustrated by your censorship. I know it is unintentional and unconscious. But whatever I have told you about the classes I was teaching, or the stories I was working on, you've always forgotten within a month. Maybe you can't listen—because maybe when you look in my eyes, you will, as you've always done, sense more than what we're actually saying, and that makes you fearful. Do you see your repressed anger manifested in me? What doors would groan wide open if you heard my words with complete understanding? Are you afraid that your daughter is breaking out of our shackles, and into total anarchy? That your daughter has turned into a crazy woman who advocates not only equality for Third World people, for women, but for gays as well? Please don't shudder, Ma, when I speak of homosexuality. Until we can all present ourselves to the world in our completeness, as fully and beautifully as we see ourselves naked in our bedrooms, we are not free.

After what seems like hours of talking, I realize it is not talking at all, but the filling up of time with sounds that say, "I am your daughter, you are my mother, and we are keeping each other company, and that is enough." But it is not enough because my life has been formed by your life. Together we have lived one hundred and eleven years in this country as yellow women, and it is not enough to enunciate words and words and words and then to have them only mean that we have been keeping each other company. I desperately want you to understand me and my work, Ma, to know what I am doing! When you distort what I say, like thinking I am against all "caucasians" or that I am ashamed of Dad, then I feel anger and more frustration and want to slash out, not at you, but at those external forces which keep us apart. What deepens the chasms between us are our different reactions to those forces. Yours has been one of silence, self-denial, self-effacement; you believing it is your fault that you never fully experienced self-pride and freedom of choice. But listen, Ma, only with a deliberate consciousness is my reaction different from yours.

When I look at you, there are images: images of you as a little ten-year-old Korean girl, being sent alone from Shanghai to the United States, in steerage with only one skimpy little dress, being sick and lonely on Angel Island for three months; then growing up in a "Home" run by white missionary women. Scrubbing floors on your hands and knees, hauling coal in heavy metal buckets up three flights of stairs, tending to the younger children, putting hot bricks on your cheeks to deaden the pain from the terrible toothaches you always had. Working all your life as a maid, waitress, salesclerk, office worker, mother. But throughout there is an image of you as strong and courageous, and persevering: climbing out of windows to escape from the Home, then later, from an abusive first husband. There is so much more to these images than I can say, but I think you know what I mean. Escaping out of windows offered only temporary respites; surviving is an everyday chore. You gave me, physically, what you never had, but there was a spiritual, emotional legacy you passed down which was reinforced by society: self-contempt because of our race, our sex, our sexuality. For deeply ingrained in me, Ma, there has been that strong, compulsive force to sink into self-contempt, passivity, and despair. I am sure that my fifteen years of alcohol abuse have not been forgotten by either of us, nor my suicidal depressions.

Now, I know you are going to think I hate and despise you for your self-hatred, for your isolation. But I don't. Because in spite of your withdrawal, in spite of your loneliness, you have not only survived, but been beside me in the worst of times when your company meant everything in the world to me. I just need more than that now, Ma. I have taken and taken from you in terms of needing you to mother me, to be by my side, and I need, now, to take from you two more things: understanding and support for who I am now and my work.

We are Asian American women and the reaction to our identity is what causes the chasms instead of connections. But do you realize, Ma, that I could never have reacted the way I have if you had not provided for me the opportunity to be free of the binds that have held you down, and to be in the process of self-affirmation? Because of your life, because of the physical security you have given me: my education, my full stomach, my clothed and starched back, my piano and dancing lessons — all those gifts you never received — I saw myself as having worth; now I begin to love myself more, see our potential, and fight for just that kind of social change that will affirm me, my race, my sex, my heritage. And while I affirm myself, Ma, I affirm you.

Today, I am satisfied to call myself either an Asian American Feminist or Yellow Feminist. The two terms are inseparable because race and sex are an integral part of me. This means that I am working with others to realize pride in culture and women and heritage (the heritage that is the exploited yellow immigrant: Daddy and you). Being a Yellow Feminist means being a community activist and a humanist. It does not mean "separatism," either by cutting myself off from non-Asians or men. It does not mean retaining the same power structure and substituting women in positions of control held by men. It does mean fighting the whites and the men who abuse us, straightjacket us and tape our mouths; it means changing the economic class system and psychological forces (sexism, racism, and homophobia) that really hurt all of us. And I do this, not in isolation, but in the community.

We no longer can afford to stand back and watch while an insatiable elite ravages and devours resources which are enough for all of us. The obstacles are so huge and overwhelming that often I do become cynical and want to give up. And if I were struggling alone, I know I would never even attempt to put into action what I believe in my heart, that (and this is primarily because of you, Ma) Yellow Women are strong and have the potential to be powerful and effective leaders.

I can hear you asking now, "Well, what do you mean by 'social change and leadership'? And how are you going to go about it?" To begin with we must wipe out the circumstances that keep us down in silence and self-effacement. Right now, my techniques are education and writing. Yellow Feminist means being a core for change, and that core means having the belief in our potential as human beings. I will work with anyone, support anyone, who shares my sensibility, my objectives. But there are barriers to unity: white women who are racist, and Asian American men who are sexist. My very being declares that those two groups do not share my complete sensibility. I would be fragmented, mutilated, if I did not fight against racism and sexism together.

And this is when the pain of the struggle hits home. How many white women have taken on the responsibility to educate themselves about Third World people, their history, their culture? How many white women really think about the stereotypes they retain as truth about women of color? But the perpetuation of dehumanizing stereotypes is really very helpful for whites; they use them to justify their giving us the lowest wages and all the work they don't want to perform. Ma, how can we believe things are changing when as a nurse's aide during World War II, you were given only the tasks of changing the bed linen, removing bed pans, taking urine samples, and then only three years ago as a retired volunteer worker in a local hospital, white women gave themselves desk jobs and gave you, at sixty-nine, the same work you did in 1943? Today you speak more fondly of being a nurse's aide during World War II and how proud you are of the fact that the Red Cross showed its appreciation for your service by giving you a diploma. Still in 1980, the injustices continue. I can give you so many examples of groups which are "feminist" in which women of color were given the usual least important tasks, the shitwork, and given no say in how that group is to be run. Needless to say, those Third World women, like you, dropped out, quit.

Working in writing and teaching, I have seen how white women condescend to Third World women because they reason that because of our oppression, which they know nothing about, we are behind them and their "progressive ideas" in the struggle for freedom. They don't even look at history! At the facts! How we as Asian American women have always been fighting for more than mere survival, but were never acknowledged because we were in our communities, invisible, but not inaccessible.

And I get so tired of being the instant resource for information on Asian American women. Being the token representative, going from class to class, group to group, bleeding for white women so they can have an easy answer—and then, and this is what really gets to me—they usually leave to never continue their education about us on their own.

To the racist white female professor who says, "If I have to watch everything I say I wouldn't say anything," I want to say, "Then get out of teaching."

To the white female poet who says, "Well, frankly, I believe that politics and poetry don't necessarily have to go together," I say, "Your little taste of white privilege has deluded you into thinking that you don't have to fight against sexism in this society. You are talking to me from your own isolation and your own racism. If you feel that you don't have to fight for me, that you don't have to speak out against capitalism, the exploitation of human and natural resources, then you in your silence, your inability to make connections, are siding with a system that will eventually get you, after it has gotten me. And if you

think that's not a political stance, you're more than simply deluded, you're crazy!"

This is the same white voice that says, "I am writing about and looking for themes that are 'universal.'" Well, most of the time when "universal" is used, it is just a euphemism for "white": white themes, white significance, white culture. And denying minority groups their rightful place and time in U.S. history is simply racist.

Yes, Ma, I am mad. I carry the anger from my own experience and the anger you couldn't afford to express, and even that is often misinterpreted no matter how hard I try to be clear about my position. A white woman in my class said to me a couple of months ago, "I feel that Third World women hate me and that *they* are being racist; I'm being stereotyped, and I've never been part of the ruling class." I replied, "Please try to understand. Know our history. Know the racism of whites, how deep it goes. Know that we are becoming ever more intolerant of those people who let their ignorance be their excuse for their complacency, their liberalism, when this country (this world!) is going to hell in a handbasket. Try to understand that our distrust is from experience, and that our distrust is power*less*. Racism is an essential part of the status quo, power*ful,* and continues to keep us down. It is a rule taught to all of us from birth. Is it no wonder that we fear there are no exceptions?"

And as if the grief we go through working with white women weren't enough; so close to home, in our community, and so very painful, is the lack of support we get from some of our Asian American brothers. Here is a quote from a rather prominent male writer ranting on about a Yellow "sister":

> . . . I can only believe that such blatant sucking off of the identity is the work of a Chinese American woman, another Jade Snow Wong Pochahontas yellow. Pussywhipped again. Oh, damn, pussywhipped again.

Chinese American woman: "another Jade Snow Wong Pochahontas yellow." According to him, Chinese American women sold out—are contemptuous of their culture, pathetically strain all their lives to be white, hate Asian American men, and so marry white men (the John Smiths)—or just like Pochahontas: we rescue white men while betraying our fathers; then marry white men, get baptized, and go to dear old England to become curiosities of the civilized world. Whew! Now, that's an indictment! (Of all women of color.) Some of the male writers in the Asian American community seem never to support us. They always expect us to support them, and you know what? We almost always do. Anti-Yellow men? Are they kidding? We go to their readings, buy and read and comment on their books, and try to keep up a dialogue. And they accuse us of betrayal, are resentful because we do readings together as Women, and so often do not come to our performances. And all the while we hurt because we are rejected by our brothers. The Pochahontas image used by a Chinese American man points out a tragic truth: the white man and his ideology are still over us and between us. These men of color, with clear vision, fight the racism in white society, but have bought the white male definition of "masculinity": men only should take on the leadership in the community because the qualities of "originality, daring, physical courage, and creativity" are "traditionally masculine."[1]

Some Asian men don't seem to understand that by supporting Third World women and fighting sexism, they are helping themselves as well. I understand all too clearly how dehumanized Dad was in this country. To be a Chinese man in America is to be a victim of both racism and sexism. He was made to feel he was without strength, identity, and purpose. He was made to feel soft and weak, whose only job was to serve whites. Yes, Ma, at one time I was ashamed of him because I thought he was "womanly." When those two white cops said, "Hey, fat boy, where's our meat?" he left me standing there on Grant Avenue while he hurried over to his store to get it; they kept complaining, never satisfied, "That piece isn't good enough. What's the matter with you, fat boy? Don't you have respect? Don't wrap that meat in newspapers either; use the good stuff over there." I didn't know that he spent a year and a half on Angel Island; that we could never have our right names; that he lived in constant fear of being deported; that, like you, he worked two full-time jobs most of his life; that he was mocked and ridiculed because he speaks "broken English." And Ma, I was so ashamed after that experience when I was only six years old that I never held his hand again.

Today, as I write to you of all these memories, I feel even more deeply hurt when I realize how many people, how so many people, because of racism and sexism, fail to see what power we sacrifice by not joining hands.

But not all white women are racist, and not all Asian American men are sexist. And we choose to trust them, love and work with them. And there are visible changes. Real tangible, positive changes. The changes I love to see are those changes within ourselves.

Your grandchildren, my children, Emily and Paul. That makes three generations. Emily loves herself. Always has. There are shades of self-doubt but much less than in you or me. She says exactly what she thinks, most of the time, either in praise or in criticism of herself or others. And at sixteen she goes after whatever she wants, usually center stage. She trusts and loves people, regardless of race or sex (but, of course, she's cautious), loves her community and works in it, speaks up against racism and sexism at school. Did you know that she got Zora Neale Hurston and Alice Walker on her reading list for a Southern Writers class when there were only white authors? That she insisted on changing a script done by an Asian American man when she saw that the depiction of the character she was playing was sexist? That she went to a California State House Conference to speak out for Third World students' needs?

And what about her little brother, Paul? Twelve years old. And remember, Ma? At one of our Saturday Night Family Dinners, how he lectured Ronnie (his uncle, yet!) about how he was a male chauvinist? Paul told me once how he knew he had to fight to be Asian American, and later he added that if it weren't for Emily and me, he wouldn't have to think about feminist stuff too. He says he can hardly enjoy a movie or TV program anymore because of the sexism. Or comic books. And he is very much aware of the different treatment he gets from adults: "You have to do everything right," he said to Emily, "and I can get away with almost anything."

Emily and Paul give us hope, Ma. Because they are proud of who they are, and they care so much about our culture and history. Emily was the first to write your biography because she knows how crucial it is to get our stories in writing.

Ma, I wish I knew the histories of the women in our family before you. I bet that would be quite a story. But that may be just as well, because I can say that *you* started something. Maybe you feel ambivalent or doubtful about it, but you did. Actually, you should be proud of what you've begun. I am. If my reaction to being a Yellow Woman is different than yours was, please know that that is not a judgment on you, a criticism or a denial of you, your worth. I have always supported you, and as the years pass, I think I begin to understand you more and more.

In the last few years, I have realized the value of Homework: I have studied the history of our people in this country. I cannot tell you how proud I am to be a Chinese/Korean American Woman. We have such a proud heritage, such a courageous tradition. I want to tell everyone about that, all the particulars that are left out in the schools. And the full awareness of being a woman makes me want to sing. And I do sing with other Asian Americans and women, Ma, anyone who will sing with me.

I feel now that I can begin to put our lives in a larger framework. Ma, a larger framework! The outlines for us are time and blood, but today there is a breadth possible through making connections with others involved in community struggle. In loving ourselves for who we are — American women of color — we can make a vision for the future where we are free to fulfill our human potential. This new framework will not support repression, hatred, exploitation and isolation, but will be a human and beautiful framework, created in a community, bonded not by color, sex or class, but by love and the common goal for the liberation of mind, heart, and spirit.

Ma, today, you are as beautiful and pure to me as the picture I have of you, as a little girl, under my dresser-glass.

I love you,
Merle

Reference

1. *Aiieeeee! An Anthology of Asian American Writers*, editors Frank Chin, Jeffrey Paul Chan, Lawson Fusao Inada, Shawn Wong (Howard University Press, 1974).

ELEVEN

◆◆◆

Moving from Cultural Appropriation toward Ethical Cultural Connections[1]

Joanna Kadi

My grandmother trudged from the hills of rural Lebanon to the shores of the Mediterranean, carrying clothes and a derbeke.[2] She and the drum survived several weeks in the steerage compartment of a large boat. No small feat. And now she's dead, and the derbeke sits on a shelf far away from me. But I ended up with my sittee's determination, which I've needed to navigate through the stormy waters of drumming.

After experiencing so much anti-Arab hatred growing up, I cut myself off from my culture as soon as I could. I tried hard to assimilate, with the attendant craziness and confusion; but thankfully, my journey into political awareness and action brought me back to my racial/cultural heritage, and in particular to its music. Hearing familiar rhythms, I found myself thinking about — and wanting — a brass derbeke with a chrome finish and intricate engraving. Just like the one my grandmother brought from Lebanon.

So my lover and I embarked on a grand search to ferret out my derbeke. It took a long time, partly because I didn't know where to look, partly because white people's interest in drumming hadn't fully impacted the market. In January 1991, a year after the search began, Jan and I marched in Washington, D.C. to protest the slaughter of Arabs in the vicious outbreak of U.S. imperialism known as the Gulf War. During that weekend, alternating between grief and numbness, we chanced upon a store specializing in musical instruments from around the world. I found my derbeke.

The end of my search? No. Just the beginning. Now I needed a teacher and a community that would offer technical assistance and political respect.

I attended drumming workshops, but each proved as problem-laden as my first, where I found an overwhelmingly white group of women who apparently hadn't given much thought to the issue of playing congas or derbekes. I'm using the word "play" loosely, because even as an unskilled beginner I could tell these women didn't know the traditional Arabic techniques and rhythms I knew simply from listening to Arabic music. Further dismay resulted when I questioned two women and discovered they didn't know the name of their drums; they had just been drawn to the derbeke for some unknown reason and made a purchase. They spent the workshop banging happily on their drums in ways bearing no resemblance to proper derbeke-playing style.

I sat through this drumming workshop, and subsequent ones, with a familiar mix of anger and fear. Anger at the casual (mis)use by white people of important aspects of culture from various communities of color, fear that such groups would prove the only resource available and I would simply have to put up with crap in order to learn. These disheartening experiences led to another year of my derbeke gathering dust as I grew more certain I'd never find what I needed.

But after much searching, I found a wonderful teacher, Mick Labriola, as well as drumming friends/ acquaintances I connect with politically and musically. Because of this, and because of my deep determination to forge ahead in spite of obstacles, drumming has proved an incredible positive experience. I've re-connected with my roots. Experiencing how much beauty and importance Arabs have given the world has helped me feel pride, as opposed to shame, about being Arab.

Then there's anger and grief. My initial experiences at drumming workshops proved common. I continually see derbekes in white people's homes, played by white musicians, banged on at drumming circles. Many players don't even know the name of the instrument, or where it comes from. They don't play properly, and they don't know traditional Arabic rhythms.

But none of this seems to raise any concern, as more and more white people jump on the drumming bandwagon. Why drumming? Why so popular? Because it's a powerful activity? Because it's a wonderfully communal instrument? Because it allows people to learn about other cultures through music? Most days I think these explanations provide a more positive interpretation than the situation warrants, especially when I notice the apolitical spirituality of the New Age movement embracing the concept of "getting in touch with inner rhythms" via the drums of people of color; white people dredding their hair and buying African drums; people "playing" an instrument without knowing its name.

Within these actions, I sense an imperialist attitude in which privileged people want to own segments of other people's cultures. To me, it's cultural appropriation, a subject I'm confused about and infuriated by. I have many questions and ideas, but few answers. The complexity of the subject lends itself more to books (*not* written by white people) than single essays, so be forewarned; I can't tackle everything. I've tried to streamline this by focusing it around drumming, and in particular derbekes, since issues and questions relating to drumming carry over to other types of cultural appropriation.

I've thought long and hard about defining cultural appropriation. Culture includes any and all aspects of a community that provide its life force, including art, music, spirituality, food, philosophy, and history. To "appropriate" means to take possession of. "Cultural" appropriation means taking possession of specific aspects of someone else's culture in unethical, oppressive ways.

While helpful, this basic definition simplifies rather than deepens. It doesn't examine various aspects of cultural appropriation. To do that, I'll analyze what happens when white people play derbekes incorrectly.

It seems to me those white people use derbekes perceiving them as generic, no-name drums unencumbered by hard political/historical/cultural realities, never asking themselves the questions that would uncover these realities, such as: whose music is this? What has imperialism and racism done to the people who created this music? Do I have a right to play this instrument? What kind of beliefs do I hold about Arabs? Ignoring these questions and ignoring Arab musical traditions translates into cultural appropriation—white people taking possession of Arabic culture by commandeering an important instrument and the music it produces. The derbeke and its playing style are important pieces of Arab culture, with thousands of years of history attached. To disregard that and play however one chooses whitewashes the drum, and by implication Arab culture. When stripped of its historical legacy, the drum is placed outside Arab culture, suggesting that Arab culture and history aren't worth taking seriously; even though Arabs have created something valuable and life-enhancing in our music, that doesn't matter. White people can and will choose to perceive the drum as ahistorical and culturally empty—a plaything that can be given whatever meaning the player chooses.

To perceive a derbeke as a plaything is to carry the privileged attitude that has wrought devastation all over our planet: "Everything is here for me to play with and use." Whether peoples, lands, our cultures, it's there for the grabbing. This take-take-take attitude pushed white colonizers through whole peoples and lands on the Asian, African, and American continents. Although brown, black, and yellow people filled those continents, white people perceived them as empty.

That kind of colonization continues, and new forms have evolved. The colonialist attitude has affixed itself to our music, clothing, religions, languages, philosophies and art. I overheard a white shopper in a music store examining a derbeke. "Cool drum. I'll take a couple." He perceived the derbeke as an empty vessel waiting to have meaning infused into it, as opposed to an important cultural symbol/reality embodying centuries of meaning.

I don't believe every white person who buys a derbeke holds that attitude, or that no other issues or desires are mixed in. But I do believe large and small vestiges of colonialist ideas live in many places, and it frightens and angers me. These ideas and their practice have already destroyed so many of our people and may well destroy more. Many white people don't know they possess such a mindset, and unthinking, unexamined ignorance can cause irreparable harm.

These political questions must be raised, along with the psychological effects of cultural appropriation. Many times people of color gloss over these, possibly because we don't want to admit the extent of our pain. I want to try.

Cultural appropriation causes me anger and grief. Anger about flagrant disregard and disrespect for me and my community, about unexamined privilege and power, about cavalier white people who use important cultural symbols/realities and turn them into no-name items. And grief, which stems from a hopeless, powerless feeling that I/my com-

munity will never get the respect and consideration we deserve, that no matter how hard we struggle, no one hears our words or heeds our demands.

Along with those responses is one that so far hasn't been examined in our thinking and writing about cultural appropriation; for me this causes deep pain. Cultural appropriation cuts away at and undermines my basic racial identity.

It's been hard for me to create a clear, strong identity as Arab-American. It's been hard for me to believe I really exist as such a person, when dominant society categorically trivializes, diminishes, and whitewashes Arabs. I've struggled with this for years, and recently my identity has been strengthened, thanks in part to my derbekes. They help me realize I come from somewhere, my community exists, and we've created wonderful cultural expressions over the centuries.

When, as happens frequently, I come across the attitude that clearly says the derbeke is an empty vessel, I begin doubting myself and my community, doubting our very existence. I fight constantly against internalizing the message—if the derbeke means nothing, if it comes from nowhere, I don't exist.

It's impossible to examine increased derbeke sales or the increased numbers of white "shamans" without discussing multiculturalism. Strange things are happening under the guise of "honoring diversity," because multiculturalism, as defined and practiced by white people, is partly responsible for the increase in cultural appropriation. While I'm not opposed to *authentic* multiculturalism, I do believe unauthentic or artificial or perverse multiculturalism simply feeds and reinforces imperialist attitudes. Examples of this abound. Young white schoolchildren aren't taught to connect ethically with other cultures; they're taught to take whatever they want from other cultures and use it. White adult consumers snatch our various arts, wanting the stuff but not caring if its creators are systematically destroyed.

Given the brutal racism endemic to our society, it makes sense that much of what passes for multiculturalism is actually covert and overt cultural appropriation, actually a form of cultural genocide. As dominant white society casually buys and sells our symbols/realities, their cultural meaning is watered down and their integrity diminished. Today items from various communities of color are all the rage, but I'm not happy to see the walls of white people's homes adorned with African masks, Asian paintings, and Native ceremonial objects. Behind the rhetoric and hype about multiculturalism and honoring diversity lurk the same attitudes of entitlement and privilege that form part of structural racism. For the most part, these white people haven't done the work necessary to become allies to people of color. They know little or nothing about current global struggles of people of color, as we define and articulate them. They don't engage in acts of solidarity around specific issues such as Native self-determination or Palestinian liberation. They don't read books by radical authors of color.

Further, these white people haven't analyzed a monster related to racism, that is, classism and the global capitalist system. All of us need to be clear about how and where and why the capitalist system fits into the picture. We need to ask critical questions. Is "multiculturalism" the latest capitalist fad? Who's in control? Who's benefiting? And who's making money, now that it's popular to hang Native dream webs on bedroom walls? Could it be people of color? Hardly. As more and more people of color are forced to live on the streets, white entrepreneurs are getting rich selling our art, music, and spirituality. Watching them profit as they exploit and appropriate our cultures, when for years we experienced hostility and scorn trying to preserve them in a racist society, is truly galling. I grew up with white people belittling and "joking" about my family's choice of music and dancing; now I can watch those same people rush to sign up for "real" belly-dancing lessons. Taught by a white woman, of course.

Economics impact culture, as the belly dance example shows. The particular combination of racism and classism that has popularized belly dancing taught by white people has several implications for Arab-American culture. Arab dancers who can't make a living teaching may be eventually forced to give up their serious studies of traditional dance altogether; this is one factor that eventually leads to cultural genocide. If a certain type of belly dancing becomes popular and another particular strain never catches on with white teachers, the latter could slowly disappear. Again, this factors into cultural genocide. For every cultural form happily adopted by the dominant culture's racist and classist system, another falls by the wayside. Some expressions discarded by dominant society will continue to thrive among marginalized communities, some will be lost forever.

Further, class exploitation crosses over with racism in certain ways, and thus many people of color are working-class or working-poor. Consequently, we can't afford to buy the now-available music, paintings, instruments, and books from our cultures. We can't afford travel to our countries of origin. Observing white, middle-class people engaging in these activities adds yet another layer of anguish and complexity to these issues.

Recently I talked over the phone with a white, middle-class man who has traveled extensively in various Arab countries, attended Arabic language schools, and now speaks Arabic fluently. Upon discovering I was Arab-American, he began speaking Arabic to me.

As is all too usual, I got so choked up with rage I couldn't think clearly. I said curtly, "I don't speak Arabic," and hung up. Next time, I have a response all planned out: "Gee, if only my grandparents hadn't experienced so much racism and been so isolated! Then they wouldn't have tried to assimilate. Then they would have taught us to speak Arabic. Which would be so helpful these days, now that multiculturalism is in. For those who can afford it, which of course precludes most people of color. Oh well, I hope you're having a splendid time with it all."

The discussion of cultural appropriation between white people and people of color is critically important, but I want to push further. If we keep the focus on relationships between colored and white, we come up with an overly simplistic analysis that ignores the fact that many people of color are just as inattentive to these issues and thus act inappropriately toward each other. It implies the only groups worth discussing are *the* white people and *the* people of color, two broad categories which are sometimes helpful but also present problems in terms of understanding the complexities of race. These simplistic categories feed into the myth that people of color constitute a monolithic group unscathed by differences of skin color, immigrant status, gender, ability, sexuality, language, class, and religion. Further, reductionist categories support the lie that we can only be discussed in relation to white people, that our only important relationships exist with white people.

A simplistic analysis of cultural appropriation minimizes and trivializes what we as people of color from different communities do to each other, glossing over the fact that we can and do commit acts of cultural appropriation, and thus hurt each other badly. I've had the painful experience of watching other people of color using derbekes as no-name drums. Our racial identity doesn't rule out unjust acts toward each other. If I were drawn to an African mask in a store and bought it without knowing where it came from, what it represents, and who made it, would that be acceptable? Of course not. I'd be committing an act of cultural appropriation as surely as any white person who did the same thing.

Our existence as people of color doesn't mean we know much—if anything—about other communities of color. It doesn't mean we've done the hard work of freeing ourselves from stereotypes and lies about other racial/ethnic groups. I've heard, time and again, the same kind of anti-Arab racism out of the mouths of people of color that I've heard from white people. Unless people of color do the same anti-racist work we want white people to do, we can't become true allies and friends.

However, I don't equate the actions of people of color with those of white people. There's a difference between a white person and a person of color playing derbekes incorrectly. The white person's actions feed into structural racism; they're part and parcel of the systemic oppression by white people of people of color. The person of color's actions stem, I think, from a mix of structural racism and horizontal violence in which the dominant white power structure keeps us carefully divided from each other, duplicating their mistreatment, and ignorant about the many ways our lives connect.

Even with this understanding, it still hurts when a Latino uses a derbeke as a generic drum. In some ways, because I so badly want and need solidarity from other people of color, these actions hurt more. I don't expect as much from white people, so I'm not as shocked and hurt by their actions. But betrayal from other people of color cuts deeply.

Betrayal appears in varied forms, and I briefly want to mention sexism. Many men of color bring a problematic and divisive note to discussions of drumming and culture by insisting women can't drum because it's not "traditional." I have two responses to this. First, there's historical documenta-

tion from many cultures, including Arabic ones, of women drumming in earlier times. Second, even in relation to preserving our cultures, I find the label "traditional" almost irrelevant. If women didn't drum in the past, why would we want to carry on with that aspect of our culture? Are the men who propose this anxious to continue every traditional cultural practice, from the most inane to the most misogynist?[3] Plenty of manifestations of sexism and misogyny in Arab cultures need to be kissed goodbye.

As a person of color, I want to do more than react to oppression by white people. It's important that, as a subject and moral agent with power in the world, I state what I want and what I consider acceptable. For starters, do I want to share cultural traditions?

There are several reasons I do. First, when healthy cultural connections occur, it's personally and communally affirming. Someone has taken the time and energy to understand and appreciate the derbeke. She's taken me and my community/culture seriously, and shown respect. This affirms me and helps strengthen racial identity.

Second, I'm enriched by participating in an authentic multiculturalism that involves having friends, listening to the music, learning the histories, and being allies in struggle with people from various cultures. This type of multiculturalism has, at its root, respect, thoughtfulness, a political analysis, and openness.

Third, in practical terms, I don't know how to separate. I was born of an interracial marriage. I live in a racially mixed community and belong to organizations and groups that cut across cultures. I've read and listened to and integrated perspectives of people from different racial/ethnic communities. How to undo this mixing? Forget the books, the stories, the poems, the music that have become part of me? Give up friends? Return to my places of origin—which isn't physically possible, and where I may not feel at home for other reasons? It seems foolhardy to consider this.

I support the idea of sharing across cultures, but I also believe some things should never be shared. For starters, sacred instruments, rhythms, and rituals. Yet, unbelievably, this has happened, continues to happen. Several years ago I attended a music festival where two white women planned to perform with a sacred instrument from a community of Australian indigenous people. Although an Australian aboriginal woman was present and voiced objections, it didn't matter to the musicians. At the last minute, outcries from a larger group prevented the show. I don't know if these two musicians used the instrument other times, but given the depth of their resistance to restriction of their "artistic freedom," I wouldn't be surprised if they did.

Of course, I question whether those women should have been performing at all, since their show consisted of playing instruments from various communities of color. I'm tired of seeing white people get the praise, money, and publicity from public performance. However, I can't deal with these questions and issues here. The topic needs an essay of its own and quite possibly its own book.

Back to making and preserving connections across communities. How to make such links? And what to call them? Words carry critical weight in liberation struggles. Naming ourselves and our desires is vital. The term "ethical cultural connection" embodies my ideas. It focuses clearly on culture, on the lifeforce of a community. "Connection" speaks to a freely-chosen bonding experience between two people or two groups. The adjective "ethical" clarifies the type of connection—one based on respect, justice, and integrity.

Ethical cultural connections are comprised of respect for the community involved, a desire to learn and take action, an openness to being challenged and criticized, a willingness to think critically about personal behavior, and a commitment to actively fighting racism. These cornerstones remain the same whether I'm getting to know one Native person or buying a carving from a Native museum. They apply to people of color and white people.

I've come to the conclusion that I'm not opposed to non-Arabs playing derbekes if it's done with respect, knowledge, and seriousness, and if these attitudes manifest themselves in concrete action. I want drummers to learn the derbeke's culture and history, and the proper way to play. And to take this knowledge a step further by actively countering the imperialism, racism, and genocide Arabs experience today. It's not enough to celebrate cultural difference by learning language, music, or history, when people's whole worlds are at risk.

Of course, this raises a critical question. How do I know if someone's doing those things? By watch-

ing? Maybe the person plays the derbeke correctly, maybe he knows Arab rhythms. But that doesn't tell me how much he knows and cares about my people.

I can only know for sure if I talk to the drummer. That's the only way any of us will know. Typing out guidelines or policing cultural events won't do it. We need to talk—across cultures and classes. I've spent days and days and days writing this essay, and months pondering it, and I've been unable to think of any other way to know where a person stands. My analysis doesn't help in isolation. It helps as we communicate across all racial groups—Asian (including Arabs), Latino, Native, African, and white.

And talking to one person won't cut it. I'm sure any white person interested in assuaging her conscience could find enough white-identified Arabs to assure her whatever she does with the derbeke is okay. There are many such people in all communities—people who for whatever reasons have become so alienated from their roots and their communities that they casually approve of the worst kinds of cultural appropriation. At the music festival I mentioned earlier, participants discussed cultural appropriation several times, and it appeared the women of color shared a clear and unified response. That is, until a well-known woman of color, a superb drummer, announced from the stage that anyone who wanted a drum from whatever culture should buy it and play it. So much for solidarity.

I don't want white people seeking out white-identified people of color to give them the stamp of approval. I want white people to talk to many people, including political activists. I want discussion around power and privilege, about who benefits from cultural appropriation and in what ways, about who will decide how cultural connections happen and what makes them ethical. I want discussion about actions and the meanings they carry.

In these discussions, participants need to take emotional reactions into account without letting them dictate the whole discussion. If I'm so sick and tired of watching non-Arabs thoughtlessly pound away on derbekes, I might not notice when someone's doing it right. I might not even care. I'm entitled to my anger, but one person's emotions can't set the tone and agenda for these discussions.

I believe politicized people of color and our white allies must start framing discussions with helpful guidelines that make sense to us. Discussions must be cross-cultural and focussed on tough questions about racism, classism, unauthentic multiculturalism, power, and privilege. And I suggest we include the ways in which personal experience can help frame critical thinking on cultural appropriation.

Looking at the five derbekes that now grace this home, I'm struck by the connection between my drumming and my political thinking. The deeper I go with one, the deeper I go with the other. The political analysis I push myself to do translates into more meaningful drumming. Playing the derbeke helps deal with the pain I experience around vivid examples of cultural appropriation. I offer this personal example not as a "feel-good," quick, on-the-surface remedy for oppression and cultural genocide, but rather as a somber statement of possibility. We can plumb the depths of the worst in our society while participating in meaningful cultural activities that ground us and keep hope alive.

Notes

1. Many thanks to Jan Binder for her help with this article.

2. A *derbeke* (pronounced der-beck-ee) is a traditional Arabic hand drum. I've seen several different spellings, but this is the one I prefer. The drum is also known as a *dumbek* (pronounced doom-beck)—there are varied spellings for that word as well.

3. Another problem with this attitude is that it feeds into the dangerous lie/myth that cultures are static and unchanging entities.

T W E L V E

Optional Ethnicities
For Whites Only?
Mary C. Waters

This paper reviews the current meaning of ethnicity for the descendants of nineteenth- and early twentieth-century European immigrants to the United States and contrasts that experience with the identities of people with non-European origins—the descendants of earlier forced immigrants and conquered peoples and the growing number of voluntary immigrants from non-European countries. The paper proceeds as follows. First the proposition that ethnic identity is optional for most Americans of European background is put forth. Empirical evidence that this is the case is reviewed. The social and historical forces that allow ethnicity to be an option are described.

The experience of non-Whites in the United States is then contrasted. Non-Whites have much more limited options with regard to their ethnicity because of particular historical and social circumstances in the United States. Using the example of current relations on college campuses between Blacks and Whites, I trace the influence that different degrees of options have on everyday encounters between people and the everyday social psychological consequences of failing to recognize this key difference between race and ethnicity.

Ethnic Identity for Whites in the 1990s

What does it mean to talk about ethnicity as an option for an individual? To argue that an individual has some degree of choice in their ethnic identity flies in the face of the common sense notion of ethnicity many of us believe in—that one's ethnic identity is a fixed characteristic, reflective of blood ties and given at birth. However, social scientists who study ethnicity have long concluded that while ethnicity is based in a *belief* in a common ancestry, ethnicity is primarily a *social* phenomenon, not a biological one (Alba 1985, 1990; Barth 1969; Weber

[1921] 1968, p. 389). The belief that members of an ethnic group have that they share a common ancestry may not be a fact. There is a great deal of change in ethnic identities across generations through intermarriage, changing allegiances, and changing social categories. There is also a much larger amount of change in the identities of individuals over their life than is commonly believed. While most people are aware of the phenomenon known as "passing" — people raised as one race who change at some point and claim a different race as their identity — there are similar life course changes in ethnicity that happen all the time and are not given the same degree of attention as "racial passing."

White Americans of European ancestry can be described as having a great deal of choice in terms of their ethnic identities. The two major types of options White Americans can exercise are (1) the option of whether to claim any specific ancestry, or to just be "White" or American (Lieberson [1985] called these people "unhyphenated Whites"), and (2) the choice of which of their European ancestries to choose to include in their description of their own identities. In both cases, the option of choosing how to present yourself on surveys and in everyday social interactions exists for Whites because of social changes and societal conditions that have created a great deal of social mobility, immigrant assimilation, and political and economic power for Whites in the United States. Specifically, the option of being able to not claim any ethnic identity exists for Whites of European background in the United States because they are the majority group — in terms of holding political and social power, as well as being a numerical majority. The option of choosing among different ethnicities in their family backgrounds exists because the degree of discrimination and social distance attached to specific European backgrounds has diminished over time.

The Ethnic Miracle

When European immigration to the United States was sharply curtailed in the late 1920s, a process was set in motion whereby the European ethnic groups already in the United States were for all intents and purposes cut off from any new arrivals. As a result, the composition of the ethnic groups began to age generationally. The proportion of each ethnic group made up of immigrants or the first generation began to gradually decline, and the proportion made up of the children, grandchildren, and eventually great-grandchildren began to increase. Consequently, by 1990 most European-origin ethnic groups in the United States were composed of a very small number of immigrants, and a very large proportion of people whose link to their ethnic origins in Europe was increasingly remote.

This generational change was accompanied by unprecedented social and economic changes. The very success of the assimilation process these groups experienced makes it difficult to imagine how much the question of the immigrants' eventual assimilation was an open one at the turn of the century. At the peak of immigration from southern and central Europe there was widespread discrimination and hostility against the newcomers by established Americans. Italians, Poles, Greeks, and Jews were called derogatory names, attacked by nativist mobs, and derided in the press. Intermarriage across ethnic lines was very uncommon — castelike in the words of some sociologists (Pagnini and Morgan 1990). The immigrants and their children were residentially segregated, occupationally specialized, and generally poor.

After several generations in the United States, the situation has changed a great deal. The success and social mobility of the grandchildren and great-grandchildren of that massive wave of immigrants from Europe has been called "The Ethnic Miracle" (Greeley 1976). These Whites have moved away from the inner-city ethnic ghettos to White middle-class suburban homes. They are doctors, lawyers, entertainers, academics, governors, and Supreme Court justices. But contrary to what some social science theorists and some politicians predicted or hoped for, these middle-class Americans have not completely given up ethnic identity. Instead, they have maintained some connection with their immigrant ancestors' identities — becoming Irish American doctors, Italian American Supreme Court justices, and Greek American presidential candidates. In the tradition of cultural pluralism, successful middle-class Americans in the late twentieth century maintain some degree of identity with their ethnic backgrounds. They have remained "hyphenated Americans." So while social mobility and declining discrimination have created the option of not identifying with any European ancestry, most White Americans continue to report some ethnic background.

With the growth in intermarriage among people of European ethnic origins, increasingly these people are of mixed ethnic ancestry. This gives them the option of which ethnicity to identify with. The U.S. census has asked a question on ethnic ancestry in the 1980 and 1990 censuses. In 1980, 52 percent of the American public responded with a single ethnic ancestry, 31 percent gave multiple ethnic origins (up to three were coded, but some individuals wrote in more than three), and only 6 percent said they were American only, while the remaining 11 percent gave no response. In 1990 about 90 percent of the population gave some response to the ancestry question, with only 5 percent giving American as a response and only 1.4 percent reporting an uncodeable response such as "don't know" (McKenney and Cresce 1992; U.S. Bureau of the Census 1992).

Several researchers have examined the pattern of responses of people to the census ancestry question. These analyses have shown a pattern of flux and inconsistency in ethnic ancestry reporting. For instance, Lieberson and Waters (1986, 1988, p. 93) have found that parents simplify children's ancestries when reporting them to the census. For instance, among the offspring in situations where one parent reports a specific single White ethnic origin and the other parent reports a different single White origin, about 40 percent of the children are not described as the logical combination of the parents' ancestries. For example, only about 60 percent of the children of English-German marriages are labeled as English-German or German-English. About 15 percent of the children of these parents are simplified to just English, and another 15 percent are reported as just German. The remainder of the children are either not given an ancestry or are described as American (Lieberson and Waters 1986, 1993).

In addition to these intergenerational changes, researchers have found changes in reporting ancestry that occur at the time of marriage or upon leaving home. At the ages of eighteen to twenty-two, when many young Americans leave home for the first time, the number of people reporting a single as opposed to a multiple ancestry goes up. Thus while parents simplify children's ancestries when they leave home, children themselves tend to report less complexity in their ancestries when they leave their parents' homes and begin reporting their ancestries themselves (Lieberson and Waters 1986, 1988; Waters 1990).

These individual changes are reflected in variability over time in the aggregate numbers of groups determined by the census and surveys. Farley (1991) compared the consistency of the overall counts of different ancestry groups in the 1979 Current Population Survey, the 1980 census, and the 1986 National Content Test (a pretest for the 1990 census). He found much less consistency in the numbers for northern European ancestry groups whose immigration peaks were early in the nineteenth century — the English, Dutch, Germans, and other northern European groups. In other words, each of these different surveys and the census yielded a different estimate of the number of people having this ancestry. The 1990 census also showed a great deal of flux and inconsistency in some ancestry groups. The number of people reporting English as an ancestry went down considerably from 1980, while the number reporting German ancestry went up. The number of Cajuns grew dramatically. This has led officials at the Census Bureau to assume that the examples used in the instructions strongly influence the responses people give. (Cajun was one of the examples of an ancestry given in 1990 but not in 1980, and German was the first example given. English was an example in the 1980 instructions, but not in 1990.)

All of these studies point to the socially variable nature of ethnic identity — and the lack of equivalence between ethnic ancestry and identity. If merely adding a category to the instructions to the question increases the number of people claiming that ancestry, what does that mean about the level of importance of that identity for people answering the census? Clearly identity and ancestry for Whites in the United States, who increasingly are from mixed backgrounds, involve some change and choice.

Symbolic Ethnicities for White Americans

What do these ethnic identities mean to people and why do they cling to them rather than just abandoning the tie and calling themselves American? My own field research with suburban Whites in California and Pennsylvania found that later-generation descendants of European origin maintain what are called "symbolic ethnicities." Symbolic ethnicity is a term coined by Herbert Gans (1979) to refer to ethnicity that is individualistic in nature and without real social cost for the individual. These symbolic identifications are essentially leisure time activities, rooted in nuclear family traditions and reinforced by the voluntary enjoyable aspects of being ethnic (Waters 1990). Richard Alba (1990) also found later-generation Whites in Albany, New York, who chose to keep a tie with an ethnic identity because of the enjoyable and voluntary aspects to those identities, along with the feelings of specialness they entailed. An example of symbolic ethnicity is individuals who identify as Irish, for example, on occasions such as Saint Patrick's Day, on family holidays, or for vacations. They do not usually belong to Irish American organizations, live in Irish neighborhoods, work in Irish jobs, or marry other Irish people. The symbolic meaning of being Irish American can be constructed by individuals from mass media images, family traditions, or other intermittent social activities. In other words, for later-generation White ethnics, ethnicity is not something that influences their lives unless they want it to. In the world of work and school and neighborhood, individuals do not have to admit to being ethnic unless they choose to. And for an increasing number of European-origin individuals whose parents and grandparents have intermarried, the ethnicity they claim is largely a matter of personal choice as they sort through all of the possible combinations of groups in their genealogies.

Individuals can choose those aspects of being Italian, for instance, that appeal to them, and discard those that do not. Or a person whose father is Italian, and mother part Polish and part French, might choose among the three ethnicities and present herself as a Polish American. For instance, a nineteen-year-old college student, interviewed in California in 1986, told me he would have answered Irish on the 1980 census form that asked about ethnic ancestry. These are his reasons:

Q: Why would you have answered that?
A: Well my Dad's name is Kerrigan and my mom's name is O'Leary, and I do have some German in me, but if you figure it out, I am about 75% Irish, so I usually say I am Irish.
Q: You usually don't say German when people ask?
A: No, no, I never say I am German. My dad just likes being Irish. . . . I don't know I just never think of myself as being German.
Q: So your dad's father is the one who immigrated?
A: Yes. On his side is Irish for generations. And then my grandmother's name is Dubois, which is French, partly German, partly French, and

then the rest of the family is all Irish. So it is only the maternal grandmother who messes up the line. (Waters 1990, p. 10)

Thus in the course of a few questions, this man labeled himself Irish, admitted to being part German but not identifying with it, and then as an afterthought added that he was also part French. This is not an unusual case. With just a little probing, many people will describe a variety of ancestries in their family background, but do not consider these ancestries to be a salient part of their own identities. Thus the 1990 census ancestry question, which estimated that 30 percent of the population is of mixed ancestry, most surely underestimates the degree of mixing among the population. My research, and the research of Richard Alba (1990), shows that many people have already sorted through what they know of their ethnic ancestries and simplified their responses before they ever answer a census or survey question (Waters 1990).

But note that this freedom to include or exclude ancestries in your identification to yourself and others would not be the same for those defined racially in our society. They are constrained to identify with the part of their ancestry that has been socially defined as the "essential" part. African Americans, for example, have been highly socially constrained to identify as Blacks, without other options available to them, even when they know that their forebears included many people of American Indian or European background. Up until the mid-twentieth century, many state governments had specific laws defining one as Black if as little as one-thirty-second of one's ancestors were defined as Black (Davis 1991; Dominguez 1986; Spickard 1989). Even now when the one drop rule has been dropped from our legal codes, there are still strong societal pressures on African Americans to identify in a particular way. Certain ancestries take precedence over others in the societal rules on descent and ancestry reckoning. If one believes one is part English and part German and identifies in a survey as German, one is not in danger of being accused of trying to "pass" as non-English and of being "redefined" English by the interviewer. But if one were part African and part German, one's self identification as German would be highly suspect and probably not accepted if one "looked" Black according to the prevailing social norms.

This is reflected in the ways the census collects race and ethnic identity. While the ethnic ancestry question used in 1980 and 1990 is given to all Americans in the sample regardless of race and allows multiple responses that combine races, the primary source of information on people defined racially in the United States is the census race question or the Hispanic question. Both of these questions require a person to make a choice about an identity. Individuals are not allowed to respond that they are both Black and White, or Japanese and Asian Indian on the race question even if they know that is their background. In fact, people who disobey the instructions to the census race question and check off two races are assigned to the first checked race in the list by the Census Bureau.

In responding to the ancestry question, the comparative latitude that White respondents have does not mean that Whites pick and choose ethnicities out of thin air. For the most part, people choose an identity that corresponds with some element of their family tree. However, there are many anecdotal instances of people adopting ethnicities when they marry or move to a strongly identified neighborhood or community. For instance Micaela di Leonardo (1984) reported instances of non-Italian women who married into Italian American families and "became Italian." Karen Leonard (1992) describes a community of Mexican American women who married Punjabi immigrants in California. Some of the Punjabi immigrants and their descendants were said to have "become Mexican" when they joined their wives' kin group and social worlds. Alternatively she describes the community acknowledging that Mexican women made the best curry, as they adapted to life with Indian-origin men.

But what do these identities mean to individuals? Surely an identity that is optional in a number of ways—not legally defined on a passport or birth certificate, not socially consequential in terms of societal discrimination in terms of housing or job access, and not economically limiting in terms of blocking opportunities for social mobility—cannot be the same as an identity that results from and is nurtured by societal exclusion and rejection. The choice to have a symbolic ethnicity is an attractive and widespread one despite its lack of demonstrable content, because having a symbolic ethnicity combines individuality with feelings of community. People reported to me that they liked having an eth-

nic identity because it gave them a uniqueness and feeling of being special. They often contrasted their own specialness by virtue of their ethnic identities with "bland" Americanness. Being ethnic makes people feel unique and special and not just "vanilla" as one of my respondents put it. For instance, one woman describes the benefits she feels from being Czech American:

> I work in an office and a lot of people in there always talk about their background. It's weird because it is a big office and people are of all different backgrounds. People are this or that. It is interesting I think to find out. Especially when it is something you do not hear a lot about. Something that is not common like Lithuania or something. That's the good part about being Czech. People think it is something different. (Waters 1990, p. 154)

Because "American" is largely understood by Americans to be a political identity and allegiance and not an ethnic one, the idea of being "American" does not give people the same sense of belonging that their hyphenated American identity does. When I asked people about their dual identities—American and Irish or Italian or whatever—they usually responded in a way that showed how they conceived of the relationship between the two identities. Being an American was their primary identity; but it was so primary that they rarely, if ever, thought about it—most commonly only when they left the country. Being Irish American, on the other hand, was a way they had of differentiating themselves from others whom they interacted with from day to day—in many cases from spouses or inlaws. Certain of their traits—being emotional, having a sense of humor, talking with their hands—were understood as stemming from their ethnicity. Yet when asked about their identity as Americans, that identity was both removed from their day-to-day consciousness and understood in terms of loyalty and patriotism. Although they may not think they behave or think in a certain way because they are American, being American is something they are both proud of and committed to.

Symbolic ethnicity is the best of all worlds for these respondents. These White ethnics can claim to be unique and special, while simultaneously finding the community and conformity with others that they also crave. But that "community" is of a type that will not interfere with a person's individuality. It is not as if these people belong to ethnic voluntary organizations or gather as a group in churches or neighborhoods or union halls. They work and reside within the mainstream of American middle-class life, yet they retain the interesting benefits—the "specialness"—of ethnic allegiance, without any of its drawbacks.

It has been suggested by several researchers that this positive value attached to ethnic ancestry, which became popular in the ethnic revival of the 1970s, is the result of assimilation having proceeded to an advanced stage for descendants of White Europeans (Alba 1985; Crispino 1980; Steinberg 1981). Ironically, people celebrate and embrace their ethnic backgrounds precisely because assimilation has proceeded to the point where such identification does not have that much influence on their day-to-day life. Rather than choosing the "least ethnic" and most bland ethnicities, Whites desire the "most ethnic" ones, like the once-stigmatized "Italian," because it is perceived as bringing the most psychic benefits. For instance, when an Italian father is married to an English or a Scottish or a German mother, the likelihood is that the child will be reported to the census with the father's Italian ancestry, rather than the northern European ancestries, which would have been predicted to have a higher social status. Italian is a good ancestry to have, people told me, because they have good food and a warm family life. This change in the social meaning of being Italian American is quite dramatic, given that Italians were subject to discrimination, exclusion, and extreme negative stereotyping in the early part of the twentieth century.

Race Relations and Symbolic Ethnicity

However much symbolic ethnicity is without cost for the individual, there is a cost associated with symbolic ethnicity for the society. That is because symbolic ethnicities of the type described here are confined to White Americans of European origin. Black Americans, Hispanic Americans, Asian Americans, and American Indians do not have the option of a symbolic ethnicity at present in the United States. For all of the ways in which ethnicity does

not matter for White Americans, it does matter for non-Whites. Who your ancestors are does affect your choice of spouse, where you live, what job you have, who your friends are, and what your chances are for success in American society, if those ancestors happen not to be from Europe. The reality is that White ethnics have a lot more choice and room to maneuver than they themselves think they do. The situation is very different for members of racial minorities, whose lives are strongly influenced by their race or national origin regardless of how much they may choose not to identify themselves in terms of their ancestries.

When White Americans learn the stories of how their grandparents and great-grandparents triumphed in the United States over adversity, they are usually told in terms of their individual efforts and triumphs. The important role of labor unions and other organized political and economic actors in their social and economic successes are left out of the story in favor of a generational story of individual Americans rising up against communitarian, Old World intolerance and New World resistance. As a result, the "individualized" voluntary, cultural view of ethnicity for Whites is what is remembered.

One important implication of these identities is that they tend to be very individualistic. There is a tendency to view valuing diversity in a pluralist environment as equating all groups. The symbolic ethnic tends to think that all groups are equal; everyone has a background that is their right to celebrate and pass on to their children. This leads to the conclusion that all identities are equal and all identities in some sense are interchangeable—"I'm Italian American, you're Polish American. I'm Irish American, you're African American." The important thing is to treat people as individuals and all equally. However, this assumption ignores the very big difference between an individualistic symbolic ethnic identity and a socially enforced and imposed racial identity.

My favorite example of how this type of thinking can lead to some severe misunderstandings between people of different backgrounds is from the *Dear Abby* advice column. A few years back a person wrote in who had asked an acquaintance of Asian background where his family was from. His acquaintance answered that this was a rude question and he would not reply. The bewildered White asked Abby why it was rude, since he thought it was a sign of respect to wonder where people were from, and he certainly would not mind anyone asking HIM about where his family was from. Abby asked her readers to write in to say whether it was rude to ask about a person's ethnic background. She reported that she got a large response, that most non-Whites thought it was a sign of disrespect, and Whites thought it was flattering:

Dear Abby,
I am 100 percent American and because I am of Asian ancestry I am often asked "What are you?" It's not the personal nature of this question that bothers me, it's the question itself. This query seems to question my very humanity. "What am I? Why I am a person like everyone else!"

Signed, A REAL AMERICAN

Dear Abby,
Why do people resent being asked what they are? The Irish are so proud of being Irish, they tell you before you even ask. Tip O'Neill has never tried to hide his Irish ancestry.

Signed, JIMMY

In this exchange JIMMY cannot understand why Asians are not as happy to be asked about their ethnicity as he is, because he understands his ethnicity and theirs to be separate but equal. Everyone has to come from somewhere—his family from Ireland, another's family from Asia—each has a history and each should be proud of it. But the reason he cannot understand the perspective of the Asian American is that all ethnicities are not equal; all are not symbolic, costless, and voluntary. When White Americans equate their own symbolic ethnicities with the socially enforced identities of non-White Americans, they obscure the fact that the experiences of Whites and non-Whites have been qualitatively different in the United States and that the current identities of individuals partly reflect that unequal history. . . .

Institutional Responses

Our society asks a lot of young people [on college campuses]. We ask young people to do something that no one else does as successfully on such a wide scale—that is to live together with people from very different backgrounds, to respect one another, to ap-

preciate one another, and to enjoy and learn from one another. The successes that occur every day in this endeavor are many, and they are too often overlooked. However, the problems and tensions are also real, and they will not vanish on their own. We tend to see pluralism working in the United States in much the same way some people expect capitalism to work. If you put together people with various interests and abilities and resources, the "invisible hand" of capitalism is supposed to make all the parts work together in an economy for the common good.

There is much to be said for such a model—the invisible hand of the market can solve complicated problems of production and distribution better than any "visible hand" of a state plan. However, we have learned that unequal power relations among the actors in the capitalist marketplace, as well as "externalities" that the market cannot account for, such as long-term pollution, or collusion between corporations, or the exploitation of child labor, means that state regulation is often needed. Pluralism and the relations between groups are very similar. There is a lot to be said for the idea that bringing people who belong to different ethnic or racial groups together in institutions with no interference will have good consequences. Students from different backgrounds will make friends if they share a dorm room or corridor, and there is no need for the institution to do any more than provide the locale. But like capitalism, the invisible hand of pluralism does not do well when power relations and externalities are ignored. When you bring together individuals from groups that are differently valued in the wider society and provide no guidance, there will be problems. In these cases the "invisible hand" of pluralist relations does not work, and tensions and disagreements can arise without any particular individual or group of individuals being "to blame." On college campuses in the 1990s some of the tensions between students are of this sort. They arise from honest misunderstandings, lack of a common background, and very different experiences of what race and ethnicity mean to the individual.

The implications of symbolic ethnicities for thinking about race relations are subtle but consequential. If your understanding of your own ethnicity and its relationship to society and politics is one of individual choice, it becomes harder to understand the need for programs like affirmative action, which recognize the ongoing need for group struggle and group recognition, in order to bring about social change. It also is hard for a White college student to understand the need that minority students feel to band together against discrimination. It also is easy, on the individual level, to expect everyone else to be able to turn their ethnicity on and off at will, the way you are able to, without understanding that ongoing discrimination and societal attention to minority status makes that impossible for individuals from minority groups to do. The paradox of symbolic ethnicity is that it depends upon the ultimate goal of a pluralist society, and at the same time makes it more difficult to achieve that ultimate goal. It is dependent upon the concept that all ethnicities mean the same thing, that enjoying the traditions of one's heritage is an option available to a group or an individual, but that such a heritage should not have any social costs associated with it.

As the Asian Americans who wrote to *Dear Abby* make clear, there are many societal issues and involuntary ascriptions associated with non-White identities. The developments necessary for this to change are not individual but societal in nature. Social mobility and declining racial and ethnic sensitivity are closely associated. The legacy and the present reality of discrimination on the basis of race or ethnicity must be overcome before the ideal of the pluralist society, where all heritages are treated equally and are equally available for individuals to choose or discard at will, is realized.

References

Alba, Richard D. 1985. *Italian Americans: Into the Twilight of Ethnicity.* Englewood Cliffs, NJ: Prentice-Hall.

———. 1990. *Ethnic Identity: The Transformation of White America.* New Haven, CT: Yale University Press.

Barth, Frederik. 1969. *Ethnic Groups and Boundaries.* Boston: Little, Brown.

Crispino, James. 1980. *The Assimilation of Ethnic Groups: The Italian Case.* Staten Island, NY: Center for Migration Studies.

Davis, Floyd James. *Who Is Black? One Nation's Definition.* University Park, PA: Pennsylvania State University Press, 1991.

di Leonardo, Micaela. 1984. *The Varieties of Ethnic Experience: Kinship, Class and Gender among Italian Americans.* Ithaca, NY: Cornell University Press.

Dominguez, Virginia. 1986. *White by Definition: Social Classification in Creole Louisiana.* New Brunswick, NJ: Rutgers University Press.

Farley, Reynolds. 1991. "The New Census Question about Ancestry: What Did It Tell Us?" *Demography* 28:411–29.

Gans, Herbert. 1979. "Symbolic Ethnicity: The Future of Ethnic Groups and Cultures in America." *Ethnic and Racial Studies* 2:1–20.

Greeley, Andrew M. 1976. "The Ethnic Miracle." *Public Interest* 45 (Fall):20–36.

Leonard, Karen. 1992. *Making Ethnic Choices: California's Punjabi Mexican Americans.* Philadelphia: Temple University Press.

Lieberson, Stanley. 1985. "Unhyphenated Whites in the United States." *Ethnic and Racial Studies* 8:159–80.

Lieberson, Stanley, and Mary Waters. 1986. "Ethnic Groups in Flux: The Changing Ethnic Responses of American Whites." *Annals of the American Academy of Political and Social Science* 487:79–91.

———. 1988. *From Many Strands: Ethnic and Racial Groups in Contemporary America.* New York: Russell Sage.

———. 1993. "The Ethnic Responses of Whites: What Causes Their Instability, Simplification, and Inconsistency?" *Social Forces* 72(2): 421–50.

McKenney, Nampeo R., and Arthur R. Cresce. 1992. "Measurement of Ethnicity in the United States: Experiences of the U.S. Census Bureau." Paper presented at the Joint Canada–United States Conference on the Measurement of Ethnicity, Ottawa, Canada, April 1–3.

Pagnini, Deanna L., and S. Philip Morgan. 1990. "Intermarriage and Social Distance among U.S. Immigrants at the Turn of the Century." *American Journal of Sociology* 96(2): 405–32.

Spickard, Paul R. 1989. *Mixed Blood.* Madison: University of Wisconsin Press.

Steinberg, Stephen. 1981. *The Ethnic Myth: Race, Ethnicity, and Class in America.* Boston: Beacon Press.

U.S. Bureau of the Census. 1992. *Census of Population and Housing, 1990: Detailed Ancestry Groups for States.* Supplementary Reports CP-S-1–2.

Washington, DC: U.S. Government Printing Office.

Waters, Mary C. 1990. *Ethnic Options: Choosing Identities in America.* Berkeley and Los Angeles: University of California Press.

Weber, Max. 1921. *Economy and Society: An Outline of Interpretive Sociology,* edited by Guenther Roth and Claus Wittich, translated by Ephraim Fischoff. New York: Bedminster Press.

THIRTEEN

"Who Am I If I'm Not My Father's Daughter?"

Minnie Bruce Pratt

As a white woman, raised small-town middle-class, Christian, in the Deep South, I was taught to be a *judge,* of moral responsibility and punishment only in relation to *my* ethical system; was taught to be a *preacher,* to point out wrongs and tell others what to do; was taught to be a *martyr,* to take all the responsibility for change and the glory, to expect others to do nothing; was taught to be a *peacemaker,* to mediate, negotiate between opposing sides because *I* knew the right way. When I speak, or speak up, about anti-Semitism and racism, I struggle not to speak with intonations, the gestures, the assumption of these roles, and not to speak out of any role of ought-to; I ask that you try not to place men in that role. I am trying to speak today to women like myself, out of need: as a woman who loves other women passionately and wants us to be able to be together as friends in this unjust world.

But where does the need come from, if by skin color, ethnicity, birth culture, we are women who are in a position of material advantage, where we gain at the expense of others, of other women? A place where *we* can have a degree of safety, comfort, familiarity, just by staying put. Where is our *need* to change what we were born into? What do we have to gain?

When I try to think of this, I think of my father, of how, when I was about eight years old, he took me up the front marble steps of the courthouse in my town. He took me inside, up the worn wooden steps, stooped under the feet of the folks who had gone up and down to be judged, or to gawk at others being judged, up past the courtroom where my grandfather had leaned back in his chair and judged for more than 40 years, up to the attic, to some narrow steps that went to the roof, to the clock tower with a walled ledge.

What I would have seen at the top: on the streets around the courthouse square: the Methodist church, the limestone building with the county health department, board of education, welfare department (my mother worked there), the yellow brick Baptist church, the Gulf station, the pool hall (no women allowed), Cleveland's grocery, Ward's shoe store; then all in a line, connected: the bank, the post office, Dr. Nicholson's office, one door for whites, one for blacks, then separate: the Presbyterian church, the newspaper office, the yellow brick jail, same brick as the Baptist church, and as the courthouse.

What I could not have seen from the top: the sawmill, or Four Points where the white mill folks lived, or the houses of blacks in Veneer Mill quarters.

This is what I would and would not have seen, or so I think, for I never got to the top. When he told me to go up the steps in front of him, I tried to, crawling on hands and knees, but I was terribly afraid. I couldn't—or wouldn't—do it. He let me crawl down: he was disgusted with me, I thought. I think now that he wanted to show me a place he had climbed to as a boy, a view that had been his father's, and his, and would be mine. But I was *not* him. I had not learned to take that height, that being set apart as my own: a white girl, not a boy.

And yet I know I have been shaped by my relation to those buildings, and to the people in the buildings, by ideas of who should be working in the board of education, of who should be in the bank handling money, of who should have the guns and the keys to the jail, of who should be *in* the jail; I have been shaped by what I didn't see, or didn't notice, on those streets.

Each of us carries around with us those growing-up places, the institutions, a sort of backdrop, a stage-set. So often we act out the present against a backdrop of the past, within a frame of perception that is so familiar, so safe that it is terrifying to risk changing it even when we know our perceptions are distorted, limited, constricted by that old view.

So this is one gain for me as I change: I learn a way of looking at the world that is more accurate, complex, multilayered, multidimensioned, more truthful: to see the world of overlapping circles, like movement on the millpond after a fish has jumped, instead of the courthouse square with me in the middle. I feel the *need* to look differently because I've learned that what is presented to me as an accurate view of the world is frequently a lie: so that to look through an anthology of women's studies that has little or no work by women of color is to be up on that ledge above the town and be thinking that I see the town, without realizing how many lives have been pushed out of sight, beside unpaved roads. I'm learning that what I think that I *know* is an accurate view of the world is frequently a lie: as when I was in a discussion about the Women's Pentagon Action with several women, four of us Christian-raised, one Jewish. In describing the march through Arlington Cemetery, one of the four mentioned the rows of crosses. I had marched for a long time through that cemetery; I nodded to myself, visualized rows of crosses. No, said the Jewish woman, they were headstones, with crosses or Stars of David engraved above the names. We four objected; we had all seen crosses. The Jewish woman had some photographs of the march through the cemetery, laid them on the table. We saw rows and rows of rectangular gravestones, and in the foreground, clearly visible, one inscribed with a name and a Star of David.

So I gain truth when I expand my constricted eye, an eye that has only let in what I have been taught to see. But there have been other constrictions: the fear around my heart when I must deal with the *fact* of folk who exist, with their own lives, in other places besides the narrow circle I was raised in. I have learned that my fear of these folks is kin to a terror that has been in my birth culture for years, for centuries, the terror of people who have set themselves apart and *above,* who have wronged others and feel they are about to be found out and punished. It is the terror that in my culture has been expressed in lies about dirty Jews who kill for blood, sly Arab hordes who murder, brutal Indians who massacre, animal blacks who rise in rebellion in the middle of the night and slaughter. It is the terror that has *caused* the slaughter of all these peoples. It is the terror that was my father with his stack of John Birch newspapers, his belief in a Communist-Jewish-Black conspiracy. It is the desperate terror, the knowledge that something is *wrong,* and tries to end fear by attack.

I get afraid when I am trying to understand myself in relation to folks different from me, when there are discussions, conflicts about anti-Semitism and racism among women, criticisms, criticisms of *me;* when, for instance, in a group discussion about race and class, I say I feel we have talked too much about race, not enough about class, and a woman of color asks me in anger and pain if I don't think her skin has something to do with class; when, for instance, I say carelessly to a Jewish friend that there were no Jews where I grew up, she begins to ask me: How do I know? Do I hear what I'm saying? and I get afraid; when I feel my racing heart, breath, the tightening of my skin around me, literally defenses to protect my narrow circle, I try to say to myself: yes, that fear is there, but I will try to be at the edge between my fear and the outside, on the edge at my skin, listening, asking what new thing will I hear, will I see, will I let myself feel, beyond the fear. I try to say to myself: that to acknowledge the complexity of another's existence is not to deny my own. I try to say: when I acknowledge what my people, what those who are like me, have done to people with less power and less safety in the world, I can make a place for things to be different, a place where I can feel grief, sorrow, not to be sorry *for* the others, but to mourn, to expand my circle of self, follow my need to loosen the constrictions of fear, be a break in the cycle of fear and attack.

To be caught within the narrow circle of the self is not just a fearful thing, it is a *lonely* thing. When I could not climb the steps that day with my father, maybe I knew on some level that my place was with women, not with men, that I did not want his view of the world. Certainly, I have felt this more and more strongly since my coming out as a lesbian. Yet so much has separated me from other women, ways in which my culture set me apart by race, by ethnicity, by class. I understood abruptly one day how lonely this made me when a friend, a black woman, spoke to me casually in our shared office: and I heard how she said my name: the lingering accent, so much like how my name is said at home. Yet I knew enough of her history and mine to know how much separated us: the chasm of murders, rapes, lynchings, the years of daily humiliations done by my people to hers. I went and stood in the hallway and cried, thinking of how she said my name like home, and how divided our lives were.

It is a pain I come to over and over again when, for instance, I realize how *habitually* I think of my culture, my ethics, my morality, as the culmination of history, as the logical extension of what has gone before; the kind of thinking represented by my use, in the past, of the word *Judeo-Christian,* as if Jewish history and lives have existed only to culminate in Christian culture, the kind of thinking that the U.S. government is using now to promote Armageddon in the Middle East; the kind of thinking that I did until recently about Indian lives and culture in my region, as if Indian peoples have existed only in museums since white folks came in the 1500s; the kind of thinking that separates me from women in cultures different from mine, makes their experience less central, less important than mine. It is painful to keep understanding this separation, within myself and in the world. Yet I have felt that the need to be

with other women can be the breaking through the shell around me, painful, but a coming through into a new place, where with understanding and change, the loneliness won't be necessary.

If we have these things to gain, and more, by struggling against racism and anti-Semitism in ourselves, what keeps us from doing so, at any one moment, what keeps us from action? In part, I know I hesitate because I have struggled painfully, for years, to make this new place for myself with other women, and I hesitate to disrupt it.

In part I hesitate because the process of uncovering my complicity is so painful: it is the stripping down, layer after layer, of my identity: skin, blood, heart: to find out how much of what I am has been shaped by my skin and family, to find out which of my thoughts and actions I need to change, which I need to keep as my own. Sometimes I fear that stripping away the layers will bring me to nothing, that the only values that I and my culture have are based on negativity, exclusion, fear.

Often I have thought: *what* of who I am is worth saving? worth taking into the future? But I have learned that as the process of shaping identity was long, so the process of change is long. I know that change speeds up the more able I am to put into material shape what I have learned from struggling with anti-Semitism and racism, to begin to act for change can widen perception, loosen fear, ease loneliness. I know that we can choose to act in ways that get us closer to the longed-for but unrealized world, a world where we each are able to live, but not by trying to make someone less than us, not by someone else's blood or pain.

◆◆◆

CHAPTER THREE

Women's Bodies

Body Image and the Beauty Ideal

Our bodies grow and develop from the first moments of life. They provide us with a living, physical basis for our identity where all aspects of our selves are literally embodied. The life cycle—from birth to youth to aging to dying—plays itself out through our bodies, minds, and emotions as we experience these life stages. Through our bodies we feel pain, and we experience sexuality, healing, and the complex physical, hormonal, neurological, and emotional changes that come with menstruation and menopause, pregnancy, and aging. Many of us develop and experience physical strength, agility, concentration, and coordination through exercise, dance, sports, martial arts, and outdoor activities. We show our dexterity in such things as handling tools, from kitchen knives to hammers and saws, or in fixing cars. We experience our bodies' suppleness through yoga. Pregnancy and childbirth provide intense understanding of our elasticity, strength, and stamina and the wonder of being able to sustain another body developing inside us. We have an awareness of our bodily rhythms throughout the day or through the menstrual cycle—the ups and downs of mental and physical energy, tiredness, stiffness, and cramps—and of bodily changes that are part of growing older.

The dominant culture often reduces women to bodies, valuing us only as sex objects or as bearers of children. Postmenopausal women, for example, are sometimes thought of as no longer "real" women, their lifework over. This chapter is concerned with how women think and feel about our bodies, the impact of idealized images of beauty, and the ways gender and sexuality are both grounded in our bodies and socially constructed. Something as intimate and personal as how we feel about our bodies is thus also profoundly cultural and political.

Although there are physiological, financial, and technological limits to how much we can shape them, up to a point our bodies are malleable and we can change how we look, who we are, or who we appear to be. We make choices about clothing, hair, makeup, tattoos or piercing, as well as gestures and mannerisms. We may diet or exercise, use skin-lightening creams or tanning salons, have a nose job or tummy tuck, and consciously adopt particular postures and body language. We may have corrective surgeries for disabilities; our bodies may be altered by mastectomy due to breast cancer; we may need to use reading glasses, wheelchairs, or hearing aids. Transsexual people may choose to have surgery to make their physical appearance congruent with their internal sense of self. Others may deliberately defy cultural boundaries by looking as androgynous as possible or by changing their appearance in **gender-bending** ways. As in the previous chapter, the four levels of analysis—micro, meso, macro, and global—are helpful in understanding the range of factors that shape women's bodies. Thus, individual, micro-level choices about our bodies should also be seen within the context of a system that is White-supremacist, patriarchal, and capitalist.

The Beauty Ideal

Starting in childhood with dolls like Barbie, women and girls in the United States are bombarded with images showing what they should look like and how to achieve this look. Movies, TV programs, posters, billboards, magazine articles, and ads all portray images of the "ideal" woman. She is young and tall, with long legs, small breasts and hips, smooth skin, and well-groomed hair. Her body is trim, toned, and very lean. In some years, cleavage is the desired trait; in others, it may be fuller lips; but the basic formula holds. Thus, Wolf (1991) comments that "450 full time American fashion models who constitute the elite corps [are] deployed in a way that keeps 150 million women in line" (p. 41). In most of these images, the women are White. Where women of color are used, they are often light-skinned and conform to this same body type.

By contrast, in real life, women come in all shapes, sizes, and skin tones. Many of us have rounded—even sagging—breasts and stomachs. We may have varicose veins, scars, stretch marks, warts, wrinkles, or blemishes, and definitely body hair. Many are short and stocky and will never look tall and willowy no matter how many diets and exercise routines they follow. The ideal standard of beauty is one that even the models themselves cannot achieve. Magazine ads and feature photos are airbrushed and enhanced photographically using computer-based image processing to get rid of imperfections and promote the illusion of flawlessness (Dziemianowicz 1992). Not only do these images show no blemishes; they rarely even show pores. Because this ideal of beauty is all around us, it is not surprising that many women and girls—including models and film stars—think there is something wrong with their bodies and work hard, even obsessively, to eliminate, or at least reduce, their "flaws" (Lakoff and Scherr 1984; Naidus 1993).

As girls and teenagers, many of us learn to inspect our bodies critically and to loathe ourselves. Young children pick up the idea that fat is bad; girls aged eight or nine are on self-imposed diets; many teenage girls think they are overweight; and by college age one in eight young women in the United States is bulimic, imagining herself to be much fatter than she actually is (Bordo 1993; Fraser 1997; Russell 1995; Thompson 1994). In a study for *Psychology Today,* psychologist D. M. Garner (1997) found that body dissatisfaction in the United States is increasing at a faster rate than ever before, especially among younger women. He reports that 89 percent of the 3,452 female respondents wanted to lose weight. Liz Dittrich (1997) found no ethnic differences in body-image dissatisfaction levels among her diverse sample of 234 women attending a junior college. Myers et al. (1998) argue that heterosexual-beauty mandates also affect lesbians to the extent that they continue to worry about their weight. These negative attitudes are increasingly common at a global level as U.S. images of women are distributed worldwide. In Korea and Japan, for example, dieting has increased due to changes in beauty standards linked to an influx of foreign (read Western, especially U.S.) TV programs and advertising (Efon, 1997).

In *The Body Project,* social historian Joan Brumberg (1997) argues that U.S. girls' self-scrutiny and anxiety about their bodies has intensified during the course of the last hundred years. Her analysis is based on the diaries of girls aged thirteen to eighteen, from the mid-nineteenth century to the 1990s. She notes a range of "body projects" including hair care and styling, skin care, external constraints on body shape (like corsets), internal constrains (diets and exercise), orthodontia, and shaving. Greater personal freedom, earlier menarche, and earlier sexual activity, as well as the availability of running water, mirrors, bathroom scales, contact lenses, women's razors, and a myriad "beauty products" have all contributed to many U.S. girls thinking of their bodies as their primary project.

The Beauty Business

Ideal standards of beauty are reinforced by, and a necessary part of, the multi-billion-dollar beauty industry that sees women's bodies only in terms of a series of problems in need of correction. These notions of ideal beauty are very effective ways for men—as well as women—to compare and judge women and to keep them on the treadmill of "body management." Allan Johnson (1997) comments: "To live in patriarchy is to breathe in misogynist images of women as objectified sexual property valued primarily for their usefulness to men" (p. 87).

The beauty business creates needs by playing on our insecurities about our bodies and selling us creams, lotions, sprays, and handy roll-ons to improve our complexions, deodorize body scents, curl, color, condition, and straighten hair, or get rid of unwanted body hair altogether. Americans spend more than $10 billion a year on diet drugs, exercise tapes, diet books, diet meals, weight-loss classes, diet doctors, diet surgery, and "fat farms" even though research reveals that most diets don't work (Fraser 1997). We buy exercise equipment and pay for fitness classes or join a gym. We buy magazines that continually urge us to improve ourselves:

> Bored with your looks? Create a new you
>
> Work off those extra pounds! Be a successful eater
>
> Do you have lazy skin? The over-40 look is over
>
> Do you dress to hide your body? Shape up for summer
>
> Learn to dress thin

Women's magazines suggest that anyone who is comfortable with her body must be lazy or undisciplined, "letting herself go" rather than "making the best of herself."

Despite the fact that genes, metabolism, shape, and size set limits on the possibilities for drastic bodily changes, surgery and hormone therapies are pushing back the boundaries of what once was possible, defying natural processes. Liposuction, for example, described in ads as body "sculpting," is designed to remove unwanted body fat from people of normal weight and is one of the fastest-growing operations in the country. It is the most common cosmetic surgery procedure. The average surgeon's fee for liposuction is $1,800, not including anesthesia, operating room facilities, or other related expenses (American Society of Plastic Surgeons 1998). Ads emphasize the benefits of slimmer knees and thighs or smoother hips, but like any surgery, liposuction has risks: the chance of injuries to capillaries, nerves,

and skin or the possibility of infection. Despite "problems ranging from pulmonary embolisms (which killed about a dozen patients during the early 1980s) to uneven skin tone and texture, it has been judged hugely successful by doctors and patients alike" (Haiken 1997, p. 290). Such risks, taken together with greater public awareness and discussion of the dangers of silicon breast implants, for example, have not stopped women—and some men—from wanting surgical procedures to achieve their desired body profiles.

Commodification and Co-option

Striving to achieve and then maintain a perfect body is an ongoing project that takes time, energy, money, and determination. Laura Fraser (1997) describes women's attempts to be thin as a third job, in addition to being a desirable woman, wife, and mother and to working for a living. Our bodies become objects, commodities, somehow separate from ourselves, something to deplore and strive to change. Nancy Mairs (1990) emphasizes the separation of body and mind as a fundamental element of Western thought, where the body is considered inferior to the mind. "I *have* a body, you are likely to say if you talk about embodiment at all; you don't say, I *am* a body" (p. 84). Further, we learn to see ourselves as disconnected parts: ankles, thighs, hips, bottoms, breasts, upper arms, noses, and chins, all in need of improvement; and this **objectification** of women by the advertising media paves the way for women's dismemberment (literal and figurative) in pornography. While women's bodies are used in ads to sell "beauty" products, they are also used to sell virtually everything else—soft drinks, beer, tires, cars, fax machines, chain saws, or gun holsters. The underlying message in a Diet Coke ad is: If someone as beautiful as this drinks Diet Coke, you should, too. You can look like this if you drink Diet Coke. The smiling women draped over cars or caressing fax machines in ads have nothing to do with the product; they are merely tools to draw men's attention and increase sales.

Ads are costly to produce and carefully thought out, with great attention to every detail: the style of the product, its name, color, the shape of the packaging, and the text and layout of the ads (Kilbourne 1994, 1999). Ad designers make it their business to know women's interests and worries, which they use, co-opt, and undermine. The Nike slogan "Just Do It!" appeals to women's sense of independence and self-directedness while co-opting it for the consumption of products. Another slogan, "Running like a Girl," takes the commonplace put-down and turns it into a compliment. Over twenty years ago, Virginia Slims pioneered this kind of co-option with "You've Come a Long Way, Baby," to advertise a new brand of cigarettes designed specifically for women. The use of the word "Slims" is no accident, as many women smoke to control their weight. For the first time in history the smoking rate of girls is now higher than that of boys, with weight control as a key motivation. Wendy Chapkis (1986) notes that 1970s feminists' insistence that a woman is beautiful just as she naturally appears has also been co-opted by the cosmetics industry and "re-written in a commercial translation as the Natural Look. The horrible irony of this is, of course, that only a handful of women have the Natural Look naturally" (p. 8).

Whites Only? Forever Young? Always Able?

These ideal notions of beauty are racist, ageist, and ableist. Even though White women are held to unreasonable beauty standards, they see beauty all around them defined as White. Women of color, by contrast, rarely see themselves reflected in mainstream images of beauty. Veronica Chambers (1995) criticizes White women who do not acknowledge or understand that this may make women of color hate their looks. "To say simply, 'I don't look like Cindy Crawford either,' or 'I think Whitney Houston is really beautiful,' doesn't address the real pain that many black women have experienced. We are still acculturated to hate our dark skin, our kinky hair, our full figures" (p. 26). For example, Naomi Wolf (1991) discusses how expectations of beauty affect women in the paid workforce but does not refer to African American women. Chambers criticizes Wolf for

> failing to give voice to the many ways that black women are instructed to look as "white" as possible, especially with regard to their hair. She doesn't mention the African American flight attendant who brought a famous suit against her employers, who had fired her be-

cause she wore braids. She doesn't mention how often braids, dreads and even Afros are strictly prohibited in many workplaces, forcing black women to straighten their hair and wear styles that are more "mainstream."

> *(p. 27)*

Indeed, White standards of beauty together with internalized racism are responsible for a hierarchy of value based on skin color among some people of color in the United States. Reading 15, "The Coming of Maureen Peal," an excerpt from Toni Morrison's novel, *The Bluest Eye,* shows the affirmation and validation given to a light-skinned African American girl by her teachers, other adults, and her peers. Judith Ortiz Cofer describes how her light skin, which she describes as *leche con café,* was praised in her Puerto Rican community, but that White people in the United States saw her as dark (Reading 16). In Reading 17, Nellie Wong expresses the pain of having wanted to look White.

The ideal standard of beauty emphasizes youth and associates youth with sexuality, especially for women. Gray-haired men are often thought distinguished or wise. Women are urged to look young and are thought old at least a decade before men of the same age. The phrase "old woman" is used negatively in mainstream culture. Many middle-aged women do not like others to know their age or are flattered to be told that they look younger than they are. A combination of beauty products, diet, exercise, surgery, and wealth has made movie stars in their fifties and sixties, like Raquel Welch, Sophia Loren, and Jane Fonda, look much younger than their years. These women reinforce ageist standards of beauty as well as selling thousands of copies of their exercise videos and other products. Oprah Winfrey's accounts of her struggles with diet, exercise, and weight losses and gains have also become best sellers.

Books, tapes, and magazine articles advise women in their sixties and seventies about fitness, nutrition, and sexuality, with an emphasis on new interests, productive lives, and personal growth. Although these images are positive, they assume that older women have the money for dancing lessons, vacations, and retirement financial planning, for example, and give no suggestion that many older women live in poverty and poor health. Eleanor

Palo Stoller and Rose Campbell Gibson (1994) note that contemporary U.S. culture reflects mixed images of older people—as wise, understanding, generous, happy, knowledgeable, and patriotic, but also as forgetful, lonely, dependent, demanding, complaining, senile, selfish, and inflexible. Not all middle-aged or older women mourn the passing of their youth. Many in their fifties, sixties, or older feel that they have really come into themselves, into their own voice, with newfound confidence and purpose (Bird 1995). They find that these years may be a time of self-definition and autonomy when they can resist earlier pressures to conform to dominant beauty standards or to set a good example. At the same time, older women must come to terms with their changing looks, physical limitations, and loss of independence and loved ones, as described by Barbara Macdonald (Reading 18). Elders are highly respected among many cultural groups including Native Americans, African Americans, Asia Americans, and Latinos, by contrast with White U.S. society. In these cultures gray hair, for example, is a mark of honor associated with experience and wisdom, which, if they are lucky, young people may be able to share. Annette Dula's description of "Miss Mildred," an elderly African American woman, included in Chapter 9, is relevant here.

In addition to being racist and ageist, this ideal standard of beauty is profoundly ableist. Even if one is not born with a disability, everyone ages and dies. Aging is a fact of life that cannot be prevented, despite face creams, hair dyes, or hormone treatments. Most people have less physical energy, poorer eyesight and hearing, or weaker immune systems as they age. Susan Wendell (1992) writes that "aging is disabling. Recognizing this helps us to see that disabled people are not 'other,' but that they are really 'us.' Unless we die suddenly, we are all disabled eventually" (p. 66). Ynestra King (1993a) notes:

> The common ground for the person—the human body—is a place of shifting sand that can fail us at any time. It can change shape and properties without warning; this is an essential truth of embodied existence. Of all the ways of becoming "other" in our society, disability is the only one that can happen to anyone, in an instant, transforming that person's life and identity forever.
>
> (p. 75)

In *Aché: A Journal for Lesbians of African Descent,* Aisha (1991) writes:

> I personally feel that we all have challenges, some are visible and some are hidden, mine just happens to be physical but yours is still there! . . . Get in touch with the ways in which you are challenged by being able to share openly my challenge . . . and not become frightened by FEAR (False Evidence Appearing Real) superiority and bigotry.
>
> (p. 28)

Thanks to untiring campaigning on the part of people with disabilities and their nondisabled allies, the U.S. government passed the Americans with Disabilities Act (ADA) in 1990, the only piece of legislation quite like it in the world, though its provisions are not consistently observed or enforced. Under this act, a person with a disability is defined as having "a physical or mental impairment that substantially limits one or more . . . major life activities." According to the Disability Statistics Center (2000), 14.5 percent of the 246 million people residing in the United States in 1990 are covered by the ADA. A more recent estimate suggests that roughly 20 percent of people in this country have some form of disability, including movement and orthopedic problems, poor physical or mental health that is disabling in some way, blindness, deafness, and learning disabilities (*Mainstream* 1997, p. 14). Despite their numbers, people with disabilities are largely absent from the mainstream media, or they are portrayed as pitiful victims—helpless and passive—or as freaks. In the readings that follow, Donna Walton (Reading 19) argues that she is handicapped by the mental limitations of nondisabled people, not by being an amputee.

Resisting Beauty Stereotypes

Many women flout dominant beauty standards: by not using makeup, for example, by wearing sensible shoes and practical clothes, or by showing hairy legs and underarms. Some breast cancer survivors who have had one or both breasts removed have chosen to go without artificial breasts or have had their mastectomy scars tattooed. Some women challenge conventional standards by gender-bending, pushing a boyish look beyond the dictates of current mainstream fashion into a more genuinely androgynous area. Others do not buy into this ideal but may need to make concessions at times, such as wearing appropriate clothes and makeup for work or family gatherings.

Beauty standards are always cultural constructions and vary among different groups, hence the importance of a meso-level analysis. For instance, in African American communities, very thin, boyish-looking women are not necessarily thought beautiful. Queen T'isha notes:

> Racism and sexism as practiced in America includes body hostilities. I didn't grow up with the belief that fat women were to be despised. The women in my family were fat, smart, sexy, employed, wanted, married, and the rulers of their households.
>
> *(Quoted in Edison and Notkin 1994, p. 106)*

Extreme thinness may be associated with poverty, malnutrition, and illnesses such as cancer or AIDS, which eat the body away from the inside. Women who are large, fleshy, and rounded embody strength, sexiness, comfort, and nurturance. American Jewish culture has the word *zaftig,* a positive term for voluptuous women (St. Paige 1999).

Large women challenge many stereotypes and taken-for-granted assumptions: that they are undisciplined, depressed, sexless, unwanted, or unhealthy; and that they have only themselves to blame for letting themselves go. Elise Matthesen argues,

> We have a right to take up space. We have a right to stretch out, to be big, bold, to be "too much to handle." To challenge the rest of the world to grow up, get on with it, and become big enough themselves to "handle" us. . . .
>
> *(Quoted in Edison and Notkin 1994, p. 107)*

And Dora Dewey-McCracken confounds common assumptions about fatness with regard to health:

> I've been diabetic since I was nineteen. . . . All my life I gained and lost at least sixty pounds each year. . . . I tried all diets, eating disorders, and fasts, only to gain the fat back, and more each time. I'm the fattest I've ever been, and yet my diabetic blood work is the best it's ever been. My doctor once told me, "As long as your disease is controlled and your blood chemistry

is good, your fat is just a social issue." I'm extremely lucky to have this doctor; with most doctors, fat-phobia is the rule, not the exception. They see the fat and their brains turn off.

(Quoted in Edison and Notkin 1994, p. 104)

There are many ways to be a woman—a spectrum of looks and behaviors, ranging from the conventionally feminine at one end to being able to pass for a man at the other, with various femme/butch combinations in between. Lesbians in the 1950s and 1960s who identified as butch or femme adopted dress and hairstyles accordingly. Joan Nestle (1992) argues that this was not a replication of heterosexual gender polarization but rather "a lesbian-specific way of deconstructing gender that radically reclaims women's erotic energy" (p. 14). Many 1970s lesbian feminists saw idealized notions of beauty as oppressive to women and also critiqued butch-femme roles as inherently patriarchal. They adopted flannel shirts, overalls, and short hair, as a rejection of conventional womanly looks. Silva Tenenbein (1998) comments that in mainstream culture women have power in their physical beauty. "I want to reverse the beauty-is-power equation. For dykes it's not beauty which makes us powerful but power that makes us beautiful . . . our passion, our strength, and our courage to choose to be 'other' . . . our adamant refusal to be deflected from what we want" (pp. 159, 160). Current fashion includes practical boots and shoes and leather jackets for women, and fashion ads portray androgynous women, suggesting bisexuality or lesbianism. Lesbian and gay characters are turning up in films and TV shows, and *Vanity Fair* has done an issue on "lesbian chic." As women, and men too, push the boundaries of gender and sexual categories, this is represented in the media and also co-opted (Hamer and Budge 1994).

Numerous women's organizations and projects across the country are working on these issues. Self-help books (e.g., Erdman 1995; Newman 1991) and publications like *Radiance: The Magazine for Large Women* are a source of information and positive attitudes. Organizations that challenge sexist media images include the Body Image Task Force (Santa Cruz, Calif.), Challenging Media Images of Women (Framingham, Mass.), and Media Watch and Media Action Alliance (Circle Pines, Minn.). Those challenging fat oppression include the Boston Area Fat Liberation (Cambridge, Mass.), the Council on

Size and Weight Discrimination (Mount Marion, N.Y.), Largess — the Network for Size Esteem (New Haven, Conn.), and the National Association to Advance Fat Acceptance (Sacramento, Calif.). The Grey Panthers (Washington, D.C.) and the Older Women's League (Washington, D.C.) both have many local chapters that advocate for older women around a range of issues, including prejudice and discrimination based on age and looks. Senior Action in a Gay Environment (New York) and the National Pacific/Asian Resource Center on Aging (Seattle, Wash.) support particular groups. Centers for independent living in many cities work with women with disabilities, as do projects like the Disabled Women's Theater Project (New York) and dance groups for women with disabilities.

Brumberg (1997) argues that girls should be encouraged to be physically active and taught from an early age that their power is in other things than their appearance. They need to be informed, to know what they want, and to be able to articulate it. She comments that it is an important political/personal mental-health decision not to let a preoccupation with the perfect body rule one's life.

Feminist Theorizing about Body Image and Beauty Ideals

Explanations of women's dissatisfaction with their bodies are often linked to psychological factors like low self-esteem; depression; childhood teasing, disappointment, and trauma; and family structure and dynamics (Bloom, Chesney-Lind, and Owen 1994; Chernin 1985). Women who diet obsessively, for example, may do it as a way of maintaining control over their bodies, in contrast to the many pressures they experience in other areas of their lives from parents, teachers, and peers. Abra Fortune Chernik (Reading 14) confirms this: "I felt powerful as an anorexic. Controlling my body yielded an illusion of control over my life." Part of her recovery was to face the many ways she had denied herself contact with family and friends, and the social and educational opportunities of college life, so as to avoid eating or to maintain her exercise regime. She comments that she needed to go beyond psychological explanations "to understand why society would reward my starvation and encourage my vanishing," and concludes: "Gaining weight and getting my head out of the toilet bowl

was the most political act I have ever committed." Chernik reflects on her experience of anorexia and also theorizes about it. This is an excellent example of how women develop theory from our lived experience by raising broader questions — analyzing our micro-level experiences and also seeking to understand the meso- and macro-level contexts that affect us.

The constant promotion of an ideal body image is a very effective way of oppressing women and girls, taking up time, money, and attention that could be devoted to other aspects of life, like education or self-development, or to wider issues such as the need for affordable health care, child care, elder care, and jobs with decent pay and benefits. Striving for a better body keeps us in check. Alisa Valdés discusses the contradictions of working as an aerobics instructor in these terms (Reading 20). Although ideals of beauty — and fashions in clothes, makeup, hairstyles, and body shape — are not new, Hesse-Biber (1991, 1996) notes that they have become increasingly stringent and elusive. Over the past twenty-five years or so, women in the United States have made significant gains toward greater equality with men in education and admission to professions and manual trades with higher pay scales. But, as Faludi (1991) notes in her analysis of backlash against women's progress, as women have gained more independence socially and economically, body standards have become harder to achieve.

Susan Bordo (1993) discusses the contradictory ideals and directives girls and women receive about femininity from contemporary culture that may affect their attitudes to food and eating. She argues that the **gendered division of labor**, under which women have the main responsibility for home and nurturing and men are mainly active in the public sphere, has barely changed despite women's entry into jobs and professions once closed to them. Women are supposed to nurture and care for men — their fathers, brothers, boyfriends, husbands, lovers, bosses, colleagues, and sons. Thus women learn to feed others — emotionally and literally — rather than themselves.

Bordo (1993) notes that women who aspire to be successful professionally "must also learn to embody the 'masculine' language and values of that arena — self control, determination, cool, emotional discipline, mastery, and so on" (p. 171). The boyish body ideals of current fashion ads suggest a new freedom from the limitations of reproductive femininity, but when placed next to solid, muscular male models, these ultra-slim women look fragile and powerless. Part of their allure, it seems, is in this relative powerlessness, in their image as little girls who will never grow up to be true equals. Bordo (1993) analyzes the prevalence of hysteria among middle-class, U.S. women in the nineteenth century, agoraphobia in the 1950s and 60s, and anorexia in the 1980s and 90s. She shows how women may attempt to resist assigned gender roles "paradoxically, by pursuing conventional feminine behavior . . . to excess" (p. 179). Following Foucault, she suggests that a conception of power as a "network of practices, institutions, and technologies that sustain positions of dominance and subordination" (p. 167) is helpful in understanding why women would willingly accept norms and practices that limit them.

Becky Thompson (1994) criticizes those who claim that eating disorders are primarily due to an obsession with thinness. Based on her research with a diverse group of women, she argues that struggles with food and appetite for women of color, White lesbians, and working-class women may not be about wanting to be thin. Her respondents' compulsive eating, she argues, is a response to the stress of living with physical and psychic atrocities such as sexism, racism, classism, heterosexism, and physical, emotional, and sexual abuse. Food can be a significant source of comfort and pleasure, numbing bad feelings, anxiety, and anger. Food is available, inexpensive, and socially acceptable, and it is a safer way to buffer pain than drugs or alcohol. Thompson sees the women she interviewed as courageous survivors dealing with trauma. She argues that freedom from eating problems depends on long-term psychological work at a personal level as well as macro-level political change to transform systems of oppression.

Compared with men, most women in the United States have little structural power in terms of money,

professional status, inherited wealth, or political influence. Women who are considered beautiful, though, have this personal power, which may help them "catch" a man but is no guarantee that he will stay. Robin Lakoff and Raquel Scherr (1984) argue that this power is more illusory than real when compared with material wealth and political clout. Moreover, beauty, as conventionally defined, does not last. To the extent that beautiful women have personal power, they will probably lose it as they age.

Body Politics

The body is central to patriarchal oppression of women and is a crucial site of resistance, as mentioned here. We develop this discussion in other chapters: with a focus on sexuality (Chapter 4) and on violence against women (Chapter 6). In Chapter 9, we note that the professionalization of medicine and the development of medical technology have affected women's experience and knowledge of our bodies, and our ability to participate in our own healing and bodily processes. Political as well as technological forces also impact reproductive rights. In Chapter 2, we noted the significance of marking and effecting shifts in identity by changing physical appearance, and the writers in that chapter refer to their bodies as physical markers of gender, race/ethnicity, class, and nation.

The body is where everything is played out: our choices and desires, as well as the societal forces that shape our lives. Institutions such as the mass media, technology, law, government, and religion all have a profound influence on who we are, who we become, and how we imagine ourselves. Retaining control of our bodily lives is an important aspect of women's autonomy and liberation, and it is a theme that recurs in various chapters of this book.

◆◆◆
Questions for Reflection

As you read and discuss the readings that follow, consider these questions:

1. How do you feel about your own body?
2. Do you think that makeup, piercing, tattooing, dieting, and body building make women look beautiful? Sexy? Are looking beautiful and looking sexy the same thing?
3. What makes you feel good about your body? About yourself? Are they different?

4. What images of women do you consider positive? Where do you find them?

5. What are positive images of aging? How can aging be celebrated in women's lives?

6. Why is there currently no significant political movement against the ideal of bodily perfection?

7. How would you organize activities among your peers, on your campus, or in your home community to draw attention to the issue of body image for women and to challenge common stereotypes?

8. How can women with disabilities and nondisabled women work together on the issue of body image?

9. How can young women and older women work together on this issue?

10. How much did you eat while reading this section? How much exercise did you do?

◆◆◆
Taking Action

1. Make it your daily practice to affirm your body. What do/can you do to feel good about your body?

2. Write a letter to a TV station or magazine that shows positive (or negative) images of women and let them know what you think.

3. Find out more about how your body works, for example, by reading *Our Bodies, Ourselves for the New Century.*

4. Learn about the body concerns of women from a different group than your own.

5. Attend a meeting of an organization concerned with body issues.

FOURTEEN

The Body Politic

Abra Fortune Chernik

My body possesses solidness and curve, like the ocean. My weight mingles with Earth's pull, drawing me onto the sand. I have not always sent waves into the world. I flew off once, for five years, and swirled madly like a cracking brown leaf in the salty autumn wind. I wafted, dried out, apathetic.

I had no weight in the world during my years of anorexia. Curled up inside my thinness, a refugee in a cocoon of hunger, I lost the capacity to care about myself or others. I starved my body and twitched in place as those around me danced in the energy of shared existence and progressed in their lives. When

I graduated from college crowned with academic honors, professors praised my potential. I wanted only to vanish.

It took three months of hospitalization and two years of outpatient psychotherapy for me to learn to nourish myself and to live in a body that expresses strength and honesty in its shape. I accepted my right and my obligation to take up room with my figure, voice and spirit. I remembered how to tumble forward and touch the world that holds me. I chose the ocean as my guide.

Who disputes the ocean's fullness?

Growing up in New York City, I did not care about the feminist movement. Although I attended an all-girls high school, we read mostly male authors and studied the history of men. Embracing mainstream culture without question, I learned about womanhood from fashion magazines, Madison Avenue and Hollywood. I dismissed feminist alternatives as foreign and offensive, swathed as they were in stereotypes that threatened my adolescent need for conformity.

Puberty hit late; I did not complain. I enjoyed living in the lanky body of a tall child and insisted on the title of "girl." If anyone referred to me as a "young woman," I would cry out, horrified, "Do not call me the *W* word!" But at sixteen years old, I could no longer deny my fate. My stomach and breasts rounded. Curly black hair sprouted in the most embarrassing places. Hips swelled from a once-flat plane. Interpreting maturation as an unacceptable lapse into fleshiness, I resolved to eradicate the physical symptoms of my impending womanhood.

Magazine articles, television commercials, lunchroom conversation, gymnastics coaches and write-ups on models had saturated me with diet savvy. Once I decided to lose weight, I quickly turned expert. I dropped hot chocolate from my regular breakfast order at the Skyline Diner. I replaced lunches of peanut butter and Marshmallow Fluff sandwiches with small platters of cottage cheese and cantaloupe. I eliminated dinner altogether and blunted my appetite with Tab, Camel Lights, and Carefree bubble gum. When furious craving overwhelmed my resolve and I swallowed an extra something, I would flee to the nearest bathroom to purge my mistake.

Within three months, I had returned my body to its preadolescent proportions and had manipulated my monthly period into drying up. Over the next five years, I devoted my life to losing my weight. I came to resent the body in which I lived, the body that threatened to develop, the body whose hunger I despised but could not extinguish. If I neglected a workout or added a pound or ate a bite too many, I would stare in the mirror and drown myself in a tidal wave of criticism. Hatred of my body generalized to hatred of myself as a person, and self-referential labels such as "pig," "failure" and "glutton" allowed me to believe that I deserved punishment. My self-hatred became fuel for the self-mutilating behaviors of the eating disorder.

As my body shrank, so did my world. I starved away my power and vision, my energy and inclinations. Obsessed with dieting, I allowed relationships, passions and identity to wither. I pulled back from the world, off of the beach, out of the sand. The waves of my existence ceased to roll beyond the inside of my skin.

And society applauded my shrinking. Pound after pound the applause continued, like the pounding ocean outside the door of my beach house.

The word "anorexia" literally means "loss of appetite." But as an anorexic, I felt hunger thrashing inside my body. I denied my appetite, ignored it, but never lost it. Sometimes the pangs twisted so sharply, I feared they would consume the meat of my heart. On desperate nights I rose in a flannel nightgown and allowed myself to eat an unplanned something.

No matter how much I ate, I could not soothe the pangs. Standing in the kitchen at midnight, spotlighted by the blue-white light of the open refrigerator, I would frantically feed my neglected appetite: the Chinese food I had not touched at dinner; ice cream and whipped cream; microwaved bread; cereal and chocolate milk; doughnuts and bananas. Then, solid sadness inside my gut, swelling agitation, a too-big meal I would not digest. In the bathroom I would rip off my shirt, tie up my hair, and prepare to execute the desperate ritual, again. I would ram the back of my throat with a toothbrush handle, crying, impatient, until the food rushed up. I would vomit until the toilet filled and I emptied, until I forgave myself, until I felt ready to try my life again. Standing up from my position over the toilet, wiping my mouth, I would believe that I was safe. Looking in the mirror through puffy eyes in a tumescent face, I would promise to take care of myself. Kept awake by the fast, confused beating of my heart and the ache in my chest, I would swear I did not miss the world outside. Lost within myself, I almost died.

By the time I entered the hospital, a mess of protruding bones defined my body, and the bones of my emaciated life rattled me crazy. I carried a pillow around because it hurt to sit down, and I shivered with cold in sultry July. Clumps of brittle hair clogged the drain when I showered, and blackened eyes appeared to sink into my head. My vision of reality wrinkled and my disposition turned mercurial as

I slipped into starvation psychosis, a condition associated with severe malnutrition. People told me that I resembled a concentration camp prisoner, a chemotherapy patient, a famine victim or a fashion model.

In the hospital, I examined my eating disorder under the lenses of various therapies. I dissected my childhood, my family structure, my intimate relationships, my belief systems. I participated in experiential therapies of movement, art and psychodrama. I learned to use words instead of eating patterns to communicate my feelings. And still I refused to gain more than a minimal amount of weight.

I felt powerful as an anorexic. Controlling my body yielded an illusion of control over my life; I received incessant praise for my figure despite my sickly mien, and my frailty manipulated family and friends into protecting me from conflict. I had reduced my world to a plate of steamed carrots, and over this tiny kingdom I proudly crowned myself queen.

I sat cross-legged on my hospital bed for nearly two months before I earned an afternoon pass to go to the mall with my mother. The privilege came just in time; I felt unbearably large and desperately wanted a new outfit under which to hide gained weight. At the mall, I searched for two hours before finally discovering, in the maternity section at Macy's, a shirt large enough to cover what I perceived as my enormous body.

With an hour left on my pass, I spotted a sign on a shop window: "Body Fat Testing, $3.00." I suggested to my mother that we split up for ten minutes; she headed to Barnes & Noble, and I snuck into the fitness store.

I sat down in front of a machine hooked up to a computer, and a burly young body builder fired questions at me:

"Age?"

"Twenty-one."

"Height?"

"Five nine."

"Weight?"

"Ninety-nine."

The young man punched my statistics into his keyboard and pinched my arm with clippers wired to the testing machine. In a moment, the computer spit out my results. "Only ten percent body fat! Un-believably healthy. The average for a woman your age is twenty-five percent. Fantastic! You're this week's blue ribbon winner."

I stared at him in disbelief. *Winner? Healthy? Fantastic?* I glanced around at the other customers in the store, some of whom had congregated to watch my testing, and I felt embarrassed by his praise. And then I felt furious. Furious at this man and at the society that programmed him for their ignorant approbation of my illness and my suffering.

"I am dying of anorexia," I whispered. "Don't congratulate me."

I spent my remaining month in the hospital supplementing psychotherapy with an independent examination of eating disorders from a social and political point of view. I needed to understand why society would reward my starvation and encourage my vanishing. In the bathroom, a mirror on the open door behind me reflected my backside in a mirror over the sink. Vertebrae poked at my skin, ribs hung like wings over chiseled hip bones, the two sides of my buttocks did not touch. I had not seen this view of myself before.

In writing, I recorded instances in which my eating disorder had tangled the progress of my life and thwarted my relationships. I filled three and a half Mead marble notebooks. Five years' worth of: *I wouldn't sit with Daddy when he was alone in the hospital because I needed to go jogging; I told Derek not to visit me because I couldn't throw up when he was there; I almost failed my comprehensive exams because I was so hungry; I spent my year at Oxford with my head in the toilet bowl; I wouldn't eat the dinner my friends cooked me for my nineteenth birthday because I knew they had used oil in the recipe; I told my family not to come to my college graduation because I didn't want to miss a day at the gym or have to eat a restaurant meal.* And on and on for hundreds of pages.

This honest account of my life dissolved the illusion of anorexic power. I saw myself naked in the truth of my pain, my loneliness, my obsessions, my craziness, my selfishness, my defeat. I also recognized the social and political implications of consuming myself with the trivialities of calories and weight. At college, I had watched as classmates involved themselves in extracurricular clubs, volunteer work, politics and applications for jobs and graduate schools. Obsessed with exercising and exhausted by starvation, I did not even consider joining in such pursuits. Despite my love of writing and painting and literature, despite ranking at the top of my class, I wanted only to teach aerobics. Despite my adolescent days as a loud-mouthed, rambunctious class leader, I had grown into a silent, hungry young woman.

And society preferred me this way: hungry, fragile, crazy. *Winner! Healthy! Fantastic!* I began reading feminist literature to further understand the disempowerment of women in our culture. I digested the connection between a nation of starving, self-obsessed women and the continued success of the patriarchy. I also cultivated an awareness of alternative models of womanhood. In the stillness of the hospital library, new voices in my life rose from printed pages to echo my rage and provide the conception of my feminist consciousness.

I had been willing to accept self-sabotage, but now I refused to sacrifice myself to a society that profited from my pain. I finally understood that my eating disorder symbolized more than "personal psychodynamic trauma." Gazing in the mirror at my emaciated body, I observed a woman held up by her culture as the physical ideal because she was starving, self-obsessed and powerless, a woman called beautiful because she threatened no one except herself. Despite my intelligence, my education, and my supposed Manhattan sophistication, I had believed all of the lies; I had almost given my life in order to achieve the sickly impotence that this culture aggressively links with female happiness, love and success. And everything I had to offer to the world, every tumbling wave, every thought and every passion, nearly died inside me.

As long as society resists female power, fashion will call healthy women physically flawed. As long as society accepts the physical, sexual and economic abuse of women, popular culture will prefer women who resemble little girls. Sitting in the hospital the summer after my college graduation, I grasped the absurdity of a nation of adult women dying to grow small.

Armed with this insight, I loosened the grip of the starvation disease on my body. I determined to recreate myself based on an image of a woman warrior. I remembered my ocean, and I took my first bite.

Gaining weight and getting my head out of the toilet bowl was the most political act I have ever committed.

I left the hospital and returned home to Fire Island. Living at the shore in those wintry days of my new life, I wrapped myself in feminism as I hunted sea shells and role models. I wanted to feel proud of my womanhood. I longed to accept and honor my body's fullness.

During the process of my healing, I had hoped that I would be able to skip the memory of anorexia like a cold pebble into the dark winter sea. I had dreamed that in relinquishing my obsessive chase after a smaller body, I would be able to come home to rejoin those whom I had left in order to starve, rejoin them to live together as healthy, powerful women. But as my body has grown full, I have sensed a hollowness in the lives of women all around me that I had not noticed when I myself stood hollow. I have made it home only to find myself alone.

Out in the world again, I hear the furious thumping dance of body hatred echoing every place I go. Friends who once appeared wonderfully carefree in ordering late-night french fries turn out not to eat breakfast or lunch. Smart, talented, creative women talk about dieting and overeating and hating the beach because they look terrible in bathing suits. Famous women give interviews insulting their bodies and bragging about bicycling twenty-four miles the day they gave birth.

I had looked forward to rejoining society after my years of anorexic exile. Ironically, in order to preserve my health, my recovery has included the development of a consciousness that actively challenges the images and ideas that define this culture. Walking down Madison Avenue and passing emaciated women, I say to myself, *those women are sick*. When smacked with a diet commercial, I remind myself, *I don't do that anymore*. I decline invitations to movies that feature anorexic actors, I will not participate in discussions about dieting, and I refuse to shop in stores that cater to women with eating-disordered figures.

Though I am critical of diet culture, I find it nearly impossible to escape. Eating disorders have woven their way into the fabric of my society. On television, in print, on food packaging, in casual conversation and in windows of clothing stores populated by ridiculously gaunt mannequins, messages to lose my weight and control my appetite challenge my recovered fullness. Finally at home in my body, I recognize myself as an island in a sea of eating disorder, a sea populated predominantly by young women.

A perversion of nature by society has resulted in a phenomenon whereby women feel safer when starving than when eating. Losing our weight boosts self-esteem, while nourishing our bodies evokes feelings of self-doubt and self-loathing.

When our bodies take up more space than a size eight (as most of our bodies do), we say, *too big.* When our appetites demand more than a Lean Cuisine, we say, *too much.* When we want a piece of a friend's birthday cake, we say, *too bad.* Don't eat too much, don't talk too loudly, don't take up too much space, don't take from the world. Be pleasant or crazy, but don't seem hungry. Remember, a new study shows that men prefer women who eat salad for dinner over women who eat burgers and fries.

So we keep on shrinking, starving away our wildness, our power, our truth.

Hiding our curves under long T-shirts at the beach, sitting silently and fidgeting while others eat dessert, sneaking back into the kitchen late at night to binge and hating ourselves the next day, skipping breakfast, existing on diet soda and cigarettes, adding up calories and subtracting everything else. We accept what is horribly wrong in our lives and fight what is beautiful and right.

Over the past three years, feminism has taught me to honor the fullness of my womanhood and the solidness of the body that hosts my life. In feminist circles I have found mentors, strong women who live with power, passion and purpose. And yet, even in groups of feminists, my love and acceptance of my body remains unusual.

Eating disorders affect us all on both a personal and a political level. The majority of my peers—including my feminist peers—still measure their beauty against anorexic ideals. Even among feminists, body hatred and chronic dieting continue to consume lives. Friends of anorexics beg them to please start eating; then these friends go home and continue their own diets. Who can deny that the millions of young women caught in the net of disordered eating will frustrate the potential of the next wave of feminism?

Sometimes my empathy dissolves into frustration and rage at our situation. For the first time in history, young women have the opportunity to create a world in our image. But many of us concentrate instead on recreating the shape of our thighs.

As young feminists, we must place unconditional acceptance of our bodies at the top of our political agenda. We must claim our bodies as our own to love and honor in their infinite shapes and sizes. Fat, thin, soft, hard, puckered, smooth, our bodies are our homes. By nourishing our bodies, we care for and love ourselves on the most basic level. When we deny ourselves physical food, we go hungry emotionally, psychologically, spiritually and politically. We must challenge ourselves to eat and digest, and allow society to call us too big. We will understand their message to mean too powerful.

Time goes by quickly. One day we will blink and open our eyes as old women. If we spend all our energy keeping our bodies small, what will we have to show for our lives when we reach the end? I hope we have more than a group of fashionably skinny figures.

FIFTEEN

The Coming of Maureen Peal

Toni Morrison

My daddy's face is a study. Winter moves into it and presides there. His eyes become a cliff of snow threatening to avalanche; his eyebrows bend like black limbs of leafless trees. His skin takes on the pale, cheerless yellow of winter sun; for a jaw he has the edges of a snowbound field dotted with stubble; his high forehead is the frozen sweep of the Erie, hiding currents of gelid thoughts that eddy in darkness. Wolf killer turned hawk fighter, he worked night and day to keep one from the door and the other from under the windowsills. A Vulcan guarding the flames, he gives us instructions about which doors to keep closed or opened for proper distribution of heat, lays kindling by, discusses qualities of coal, and teaches us how to rake, feed, and bank the fire. And he will not unrazor his lips until spring.

Winter tightened our heads with a band of cold and melted our eyes. We put pepper in the feet of our stockings, Vaseline on our faces, and stared through dark icebox mornings at four stewed prunes, slippery lumps of oatmeal, and cocoa with a roof of skin.

But mostly we waited for spring, when there could be gardens.

By the time this winter had stiffened itself into a hateful knot that nothing could loosen, something did loosen it, or rather someone. A someone who splintered the knot into silver threads that tangled us, netted us, made us long for the dull chafe of the previous boredom.

This disrupter of seasons was a new girl in school named Maureen Peal. A high-yellow dream child with long brown hair braided into two lynch ropes that hung down her back. She was rich, at least by our standards, as rich as the richest of the white girls, swaddled in comfort and care. The quality of her clothes threatened to derange Frieda and me. Patent-leather shoes with buckles, a cheaper version of which we got only at Easter and which had disintegrated by the end of May. Fluffy sweaters the color of lemon drops tucked into skirts with pleats so orderly they astounded us. Brightly colored knee socks with white borders, a brown velvet coat trimmed in white rabbit fur, and a matching muff. There was a hint of spring in her sloe green eyes, something summery in her complexion, and a rich autumn ripeness in her walk.

She enchanted the entire school. When teachers called on her, they smiled encouragingly. Black boys didn't trip her in the halls; white boys didn't stone her, white girls didn't suck their teeth when she was assigned to be their work partners; black girls stepped aside when she wanted to use the sink in the girls' toilet, and their eyes genuflected under sliding lids. She never had to search for anybody to eat with in the cafeteria—they flocked to the table of her choice, where she opened fastidious lunches, shaming our jelly-stained bread with egg-salad sandwiches cut into four dainty squares, pink-frosted cupcakes, sticks of celery and carrots, proud, dark apples. She even bought and liked white milk.

Frieda and I were bemused, irritated, and fascinated by her. We looked hard for flaws to restore our equilibrium, but had to be content at first with uglying up her name, changing Maureen Peal to Meringue Pie. Later a minor epiphany was ours when we discovered that she had a dog tooth—a charming one to be sure—but a dog tooth nonetheless. And when we found out that she had been born with six fingers on each hand and that there was a little bump where each extra one had been removed, we smiled. They were small triumphs, but we took what we could get—snickering behind her back and calling her Six-finger-dog-tooth-meringue-pie. But we had to do it alone, for none of the other girls would cooperate with our hostility. They adored her.

When she was assigned a locker next to mine, I could indulge my jealousy four times a day. My sister and I both suspected that we were secretly prepared to be her friend, if she would let us, but I knew it would be a dangerous friendship, for when my eye traced the white border patterns of those Kelly-green knee socks, and felt the pull and slack of my brown stockings, I wanted to kick her. And when I thought of the unearned haughtiness in her eyes, I plotted accidental slammings of locker doors on her hand.

As locker friends, however, we got to know each other a little, and I was even able to hold a sensible conversation with her without visualizing her fall off a cliff, or giggling my way into what I thought was a clever insult.

One day, while I waited at the locker for Frieda, she joined me.

"Hi."

"Hi."

"Waiting for your sister?"

"Uh-huh."

"Which way do you go home?"

"Down Twenty-first Street to Broadway."

"Why don't you go down Twenty-second Street?"

" 'Cause I live on Twenty-first Street."

"Oh. I can walk that way, I guess. Partly, anyway."

"Free country."

Frieda came toward us, her brown stockings straining at the knees because she had tucked the toe under to hide a hole in the foot.

"Maureen's gonna walk part way with us."

Frieda and I exchanged glances, her eyes begging my restraint, mine promising nothing.

It was a false spring day, which, like Maureen, had pierced the shell of a deadening winter. There were puddles, mud, and an inviting warmth that deluded us. The kind of day on which we draped our coats over our heads, left our galoshes in school, and came down with croup the following day. We always responded to the slightest change in weather, the most minute shifts in time of day. Long before seeds were stirring, Frieda and I were scruffing and poking at the earth, swallowing air, drinking rain. . . .

As we emerged from the school with Maureen, we began to molt immediately. We put our head scarves in our coat pockets, and our coats on our heads. I was wondering how to maneuver Maureen's fur muff into a gutter when a commotion in the playground distracted us. A group of boys was circling and holding at bay a victim, Pecola Breedlove.

Bay Boy, Woodrow Cain, Buddy Wilson, Junie Bug—like a necklace of semiprecious stones they surrounded her. Heady with the smell of their own musk, thrilled by the easy power of a majority, they gaily harassed her.

"Black e mo. Black e mo. Yadaddsleepsnekked. Black e mo black e moya dadd sleeps nekked. Black e mo . . ."

They had extemporized a verse made up of two insults about matters over which the victim had no control; the color of her skin and speculations on the sleeping habits of an adult, wildly fitting in its incoherence. That they themselves were black, or that their own father had similarly relaxed habits was irrelevant. It was their contempt for their own blackness that gave the first insult its teeth. They seemed to have taken all of their smoothly cultivated ignorance, their exquisitely learned self-hatred, their elaborately designed hopelessness and sucked it all up into a fiery cone of scorn that had burned for ages in the hollows of their minds—cooled—and spilled over lips of outrage, consuming whatever was in its path. They danced a macabre ballet around the victim, whom, for their own sake, they were prepared to sacrifice to the flaming pit.

Black e mo Black e mo Ya daddy sleeps nekked.
Stch ta ta stch ta ta
stach ta ta ta ta ta

Pecola edged around the circle crying. She had dropped her notebook, and covered her eyes with her hands.

We watched, afraid they might notice us and turn their energies our way. Then Frieda, with set lips and Mama's eyes, snatched her coat from her head and threw it on the ground. She ran toward them and brought her books down on Woodrow Cain's head. The circle broke. Woodrow Cain grabbed his head.

"Hey, girl!"

"You cut that out, you hear?" I had never heard Frieda's voice so loud and clear.

Maybe because Frieda was taller than he was, maybe because he saw her eyes, maybe because he had lost interest in the game, or maybe because he had a crush on Frieda, in any case Woodrow looked frightened just long enough to give her more courage.

"Leave her 'lone, or I'm gone tell everybody what you did!"

Woodrow did not answer; he just walled his eyes.

Bay Boy piped up, "Go on, gal. Ain't nobody bothering you."

"You shut up, Bullet Head." I had found my tongue.

"Who you calling Bullet Head?"

"I'm calling you Bullet Head, Bullet Head."

Frieda took Pecola's hand. "Come on."

"You want a fat lip?" Bay Boy drew back his fist at me.

"Yeah. Gimme one of yours."

"You gone get one."

Maureen appeared at my elbow, and the boys seemed reluctant to continue under her springtime eyes so wide with interest. They buckled in confusion, not willing to beat up three girls under her watchful gaze: So they listened to a budding male instinct that told them to pretend we were unworthy of their attention.

"Come on, man."

"Yeah. Come on. We ain't got time to fool with them."

Grumbling a few disinterested epithets, they moved away.

I picked up Pecola's notebook and Frieda's coat, and the four of us left the playground.

"Old Bullet Head, he's always picking on girls."

Frieda agreed with me. "Miss Forrester said he was incorrigival."

"Really?" I didn't know what that meant, but it had enough of a doom sound in it to be true of Bay Boy.

While Frieda and I clucked on about the near fight, Maureen, suddenly animated, put her velvet-sleeved arm through Pecola's and began to behave as though they were the closest of friends.

"I just moved here. My name is Maureen Peal. What's yours?"

"Pecola."

"Pecola? Wasn't that the name of the girl in *Imitation of Life*?"

"I don't know. What is that?"

"The picture show, you know. Where this mulatto girl hates her mother 'cause she is black and ugly but then cries at the funeral. It was real sad. Everybody cries in it. Claudette Colbert too."

"Oh." Pecola's voice was no more than a sigh.

"Anyway, her name was Pecola too. She was so pretty. When it comes back, I'm going to see it again. My mother has seen it four times."

Frieda and I walked behind them, surprised at Maureen's friendliness to Pecola, but pleased. Maybe she wasn't so bad, after all. Frieda had put her coat back on her head, and the two of us, so draped, trotted along enjoying the warm breeze and Frieda's heroics.

"You're in my gym class, aren't you?" Maureen asked Pecola.

"Yes."

"Miss Erkmeister's legs sure are bow. I bet she thinks they're cute. How come she gets to wear real shorts, and we have to wear those old bloomers? I want to die every time I put them on."

Pecola smiled but did not look at Maureen.

"Hey." Maureen stopped short. "There's an Isaley's. Want some ice cream? I have money."

She unzipped a hidden pocket in her muff and pulled out a multifolded dollar bill. I forgave her those knee socks.

"My uncle sued Isaley's," Maureen said to the three of us. "He sued the Isaley's in Akron. They said he was disorderly and that that was why they wouldn't serve him, but a friend of his, a policeman, came in and beared the witness, so the suit went through."

"What's a suit?"

"It's when you can beat them up if you want to and won't anybody do nothing. Our family does it all the time. We believe in suits."

At the entrance to Isaley's, Maureen turned to Frieda and me, asking, "You all going to buy some ice cream?"

We looked at each other. "No," Frieda said.

Maureen disappeared into the store with Pecola.

Frieda looked placidly down the street; I opened my mouth, but quickly closed it. It was extremely important that the world not know that I fully expected Maureen to buy us some ice cream, that for the past 120 seconds I had been selecting the flavor, that I had begun to like Maureen, and that neither of us had a penny.

We supposed Maureen was being nice to Pecola because of the boys, and were embarrassed to be caught—even by each other—thinking that she would treat us, or that we deserved it as much as Pecola did.

The girls came out. Pecola with two dips of orange-pineapple, Maureen with black raspberry.

"You should have got some," she said. "They had all kinds. Don't eat down to the tip of the cone," she advised Pecola.

"Why?"

"Because there's a fly in there."

"How you know?"

"Oh, not really. A girl told me she found one in the bottom of hers once, and ever since then she throws that part away."

"Oh."

We passed the Dreamland Theatre, and Betty Grable smiled down at us.

"Don't you just love her?" Maureen asked.

"Uh-huh," said Pecola.

I differed. "Hedy Lamarr is better."

Maureen agreed. "Ooooo yes. My mother told me that a girl named Audrey, she went to the beauty parlor where we lived before, and asked the lady to fix her hair like Hedy Lamarr's, and the lady said, 'Yeah, when you grow some hair like Hedy Lamarr's.'" She laughed long and sweet.

"Sounds crazy," said Frieda.

"She sure is. Do you know she doesn't even menstrate yet, and she's sixteen. Do you, yet?"

"Yes." Pecola glanced at us.

"So do I." Maureen made no attempt to disguise her pride. "Two months ago I started. My girl friend in Toledo, where we lived before, said when she started she was scared to death. Thought she had killed herself."

"Do you know what it's for?" Pecola asked the question as though hoping to provide the answer herself.

"For babies." Maureen raised two pencil-stroke eyebrows at the obviousness of the question. "Babies need blood when they are inside you, and if you are having a baby, then you don't menstrate. But when you're not having a baby, then you don't have to save the blood, so it comes out."

"How do babies get the blood?" asked Pecola.

"Through the like-line. You know. Where your belly button is. That is where the like-line grows from and pumps the blood to the baby."

"Well, if the belly buttons are to grow like-lines to give the baby blood, and only girls have babies, how come boys have belly buttons?"

Maureen hesitated. "I don't know," she admitted. "But boys have all sorts of things they don't need." Her tinkling laughter was somehow stronger than our nervous ones. She curled her tongue around the edge of the cone, scooping up a dollop of purple that made my eyes water. We were waiting for a stop light to change. Maureen kept scooping the ice cream from around the cone's edge with her tongue; she didn't bite the edge as I would have done. Her tongue circled the cone. Pecola had finished hers; Maureen evidently liked her things to last. While I was thinking about her ice cream, she must have been thinking about her last remark, for she said to Pecola, "Did you ever see a naked man?"

Pecola blinked, then looked away. "No. Where would I see a naked man?"

"I don't know. I just asked."

"I wouldn't even look at him, even if I did see him. That's dirty. Who wants to see a naked man?" Pecola was agitated. "Nobody's father would be naked in front of his own daughter. Not unless he was dirty too."

"I didn't say 'father.' I just said 'a naked man.'"

"Well . . ."

"How come you said 'father'?" Maureen wanted to know.

"Who else would she see, dog tooth?" I was glad to have a chance to show anger. Not only because of the ice cream, but because we had seen our own father naked and didn't care to be reminded of it and feel the shame brought on by the absence of shame. He had been walking down the hall from the bathroom into his bedroom and passed the open door of our room. We had lain there wide-eyed. He stopped and looked in, trying to see in the dark room whether we were really asleep — or was it his imagination that opened eyes were looking at him? Apparently he convinced himself that we were sleeping. He moved away, confident that his little girls would not lie open-eyed like that, staring, staring. When he had moved on, the dark took only him away, not his nakedness. That stayed in the room with us. Friendly-like.

"I'm not talking to you," said Maureen. "Besides, I don't care if she sees her father naked. She can look at him all day if she wants to. Who cares?"

"You do," said Frieda. "That's all you talk about."

"It is not."

"It is so. Boys, babies, and somebody's naked daddy. You must be boy-crazy."

"You better be quiet."

"Who's gonna make me?" Frieda put her hand on her hip and jutted her face toward Maureen.

"You all ready made. Mammy made."

"You stop talking about my mama."

"Well, you stop talking about my daddy."

"Who said anything about your old daddy?"

"You did."

"Well, you started it."

"I wasn't even talking to you. I was talking to Pecola."

"Yeah. About seeing her naked daddy."

"So what if she did see him?"

Pecola shouted, "I never saw my daddy naked. Never."

"You did too," Maureen snapped. "Bay Boy said so."

"I did not."

"You did."

"I did not."

"Did. Your own daddy, too!"

Pecola tucked her head in—a funny, sad, helpless movement. A kind of hunching of the shoulders, pulling in of the neck, as though she wanted to cover her ears.

"You stop talking about her daddy," I said.

"What do I care about her old black daddy?" asked Maureen.

"Black? Who you calling black?"

"You!"

"You think you so cute!" I swung at her and missed, hitting Pecola in the face. Furious at my clumsiness, I threw my notebook at her, but it caught her in the small of her velvet back, for she had turned and was flying across the street against traffic.

Safe on the other side, she screamed at us, "I *am* cute! And you ugly! Black and ugly black e mos. I *am* cute!"

She ran down the street, the green knee socks making her legs look like wild dandelion stems that had somehow lost their heads. The weight of he remark stunned us, and it was a second or two before Frieda and I collected ourselves enough to shout, "Six-finger-dog-tooth-meringue-pie!" We chanted this most powerful of our arsenal of insults as long as we could see the green stems and rabbit fur.

Grown people frowned at the three girls on the curbside, two with their coats draped over their heads, the collars framing the eyebrows like nuns' habits, black garters showing where they bit the tops of brown stockings that barely covered the knees, angry faces knotted like dark cauliflowers.

Pecola stood a little apart from us, her eyes hinged in the direction in which Maureen had fled. She seemed to fold into herself, like a pleated wing. Her pain antagonized me. I wanted to open her up, crisp her edges, ram a stick down that hunched and curving spine, force her to stand erect and spit the misery out on the streets. But she held it in where it could lap up into her eyes.

Frieda snatched her coat from her head. "Come on, Claudia. 'Bye, Pecola."

We walked quickly at first, and then slower, pausing every now and then to fasten garters, tie shoe-laces, scratch, or examine old scars. We were sinking under the wisdom, accuracy, and relevance of Maureen's last words. If she was cute—and if anything could be believed, she *was*—then we were not. And what did that mean? We were lesser. Nicer, brighter, but still lesser. Dolls we could destroy, but we could not destroy the honey voices of parents and aunts, the obedience in the eyes of our peers, the slippery light in the eyes of our teachers when they encountered the Maureen Peals of the world. What was the secret? What did we lack? Why was it important? And so what? Guileless and without vanity, we were still in love with ourselves then. We felt comfortable in our skins, enjoyed the news that our senses released to us, admired our dirt, cultivated our scars, and could not comprehend this unworthiness. Jealousy we understood and thought natural—a desire to have what somebody else had; but envy was a strange, new feeling for us. And all the time we knew that Maureen Peal was not the Enemy and not worthy of such intense hatred. The *Thing* to fear was the *Thing* that made *her* beautiful, and not us.

The Story of My Body

Judith Ortiz Cofer

Migration is the story of my body.
—Victor Hernandez Cruz

1. Skin

I was born a white girl in Puerto Rico, but became a brown girl when I came to live in the United States. My Puerto Rican relatives called me tall; at the American school, some of my rougher classmates called me "skinny-bones" and "the shrimp," because I was the smallest member of my classes all through grammar school until high school, when the midget Gladys was given the honorary post of front-row center for class pictures and scorekeeper, bench warmer in P.E. I reached my full stature of five feet even in sixth grade.

I started out life as a pretty baby and learned to be a pretty girl from a pretty mother. Then at ten years of age I suffered one of the worst cases of chicken pox I have ever heard of. My entire body, including the inside of my ears and in between my toes, was covered with pustules that, in a fit of panic at my appearance, I scratched off of my face, leaving permanent scars. A cruel school nurse told me I would always have them—tiny cuts that looked as if a mad cat had plunged its claws deep into my skin. I grew my hair long and hid behind it for the first years of my adolescence. This was when I learned to be invisible.

2. Color

In the animal world it indicates danger: The most colorful creatures are often the most poisonous. Color is also a way to attract and seduce a mate. In the human world color triggers many more complex and often deadly reactions. As a Puerto Rican girl born of "white" parents, I spent the first years of my life hearing people refer to me as *blanca,* white. My mother insisted that I protect myself from the in-

tense island sun because I was more prone to sunburn than some of my darker, *triqeno* playmates. People were always commenting within my hearing about how my black hair contrasted so nicely with my "pale" skin. I did not think of the color of my skin consciously, except when I heard the adults talking about complexion. It seems to me that the subject is much more common in the conversation of mixed-race peoples than in mainstream U.S. society, where it is a touchy and sometimes even embarrassing topic to discuss, except in a political context. In Puerto Rico I heard many conversations about skin color. A pregnant woman could say "I hope my baby doesn't turn out *prieto* (slang for dark or black) like my husband's grandmother, although she was a good-looking *negra* in her time." I am a combination of both, being olive-skinned—lighter than my mother yet darker than my fair-skinned father. In America, I am a person of color, obviously a Latina. On the island I have been called everything from a *paloma blanca,* after the song (by a black suitor), to *la gringa.*

My first experience of color prejudice occurred in a supermarket in Paterson, New Jersey. It was Christmastime and I was eight or nine years old. There was a display of toys in the store where I went two or three times a day to buy things for my mother who never made lists but sent for milk, cigarettes, a can of this or that, as she remembered from hour to hour. I enjoyed being trusted with money and walking half a city block to the new, modern grocery store. It was owned by three good-looking Italian brothers. I liked the younger one with the crew-cut blond hair. The two older ones watched me and the other Puerto Rican kids as if they thought we were going to steal something. The oldest one would sometimes even try to hurry me with my purchases, although part of my pleasure in these expeditions came from looking at everything in the well-stocked aisles. I was also teaching myself to read English by sounding out the labels in packages: L&M cigarettes, Borden's homogenized milk, Red Devil pot-ted ham, Nestlé's chocolate mix, Quaker oats, and Bustelo coffee, Wonder bread, Colgate toothpaste, Ivory soap, and Goya (makers of products used in Puerto Rican dishes) everything — these are some of the brand names that taught me nouns. Several times this man had come up to me wearing his blood-stained butcher's apron and, towering over me, had asked in a harsh voice whether there was something he could help me find. On the way out I would glance at the younger brother who ran one of the registers and he would often smile and wink at me.

It was the mean brother who first referred to me as "colored." It was a few days before Christmas and my parents had already told my brother and me that since we were in *los estados* now, we would get our presents on December twenty-fifth instead of *Los Reyes, Three Kings Day,* when gifts are exchanged in Puerto Rico. We were to give them a wish list that they would take to Santa Claus, who apparently lived in the Macy's store downtown — at least that's where we had caught a glimpse of him when we went shopping. Since my parents were timid about entering the fancy store, we did not approach the huge man in the red suit. I was not interested in sitting on a stranger's lap anyway. But I did covet Susie, the talking schoolteacher doll that was displayed in the center aisle of the Italian brothers' supermarket. She talked when you pulled a string on her back. Susie had a limited repertoire of three sentences: I think she could say: "Hello, I'm Susie Schoolteacher; two plus two is four," and one other thing I cannot remember. The day the older brother chased me away, I was reaching to touch Susie's blond curls. I had been told many times, as most children have, not to touch anything in a store that I was not buying. But I had been looking at Susie for weeks. In my mind, she was my doll. After all, I had put her on my Christmas wish list. The moment is frozen in my mind as if there were a photograph of it on file. It was not a turning point, a disaster, or an earthshaking revelation. It was simply the first time I considered — if naively — the meaning of skin color in human relations.

I reached to touch Susie's hair. It seems to me that I had to get on tiptoe since the toys were stacked on a table and she sat like a princess on top of the fancy box she came in. Then I heard the booming "Hey, kid, what do you think you're doing!" spoken very loudly from the meat counter. I felt caught although I knew I was not doing anything criminal. I

remember not looking at the man, but standing there feeling humiliated because I knew everyone in the store must have heard him yell at me. I felt him approach and when I knew he was behind me, I turned around to face the bloody butcher's apron. His large chest was at my eye level. He blocked my way. I started to run out of the place, but even as I reached the door I heard him shout after me: "Don't come in here unless you gonna buy something. You PR kids put your dirty hands on stuff. You always look dirty. But maybe dirty brown is your natural color." I heard him laugh and someone else too in the back. Outside in the sunlight I looked at my hands. My nails needed a little cleaning as they always did since I liked to paint with watercolors, but I took a bath every night. I thought the man was dirtier than I was in his stained apron. He was also always sweaty — it showed in big yellow circles under his shirt sleeves. I sat on the front steps of the apartment building where we lived and looked closely at my hands, which showed the only skin I could see, since it was bitter cold and I was wearing my quilted play coat, dungarees, and a knitted navy cap of my father's. I was not pink like my friend Charlene and her sister Kathy who had blue eyes and light-brown hair. My skin is the color of the coffee my grandmother made, which was half milk, *leche con café* rather than *café con leche*. My mother is the opposite mix. She has a lot of café in her color. I could not understand how my skin looked like dirt to the supermarket man.

I went in and washed my hands thoroughly with soap and hot water, and, borrowing my mother's nail file, I cleaned the crusted watercolors from underneath my nails. I was pleased with the results. My skin was the same color as before, but I knew I was clean. Clean enough to run my fingers through Susie's fine gold hair when she came home to me.

3. Size

My mother is barely four feet eleven inches in height, which is average for women in her family. When I grew to five feet by age twelve, she was amazed and began to use the word tall to describe me, as in: "Since you are tall, this dress will look good on you." As with the color of my skin, I didn't consciously think about my height or size until other people made an issue of it. It is around the preadolescent years that in America the games children play for fun become fierce competitions where everyone is out to "prove" they are better than others. It was in the playground and sports fields that my size-related problems began. No matter how familiar the story is, every child who is the last chosen for a team knows the torment of waiting to be called up. At the Paterson, New Jersey, public schools that I attended, the volleyball or softball game was the metaphor for the battlefield of life to the inner city kids — the black kids vs. the Puerto Rican kids, the whites vs. the blacks vs. the Puerto Rican kids; and I was 4F, skinny, short, bespectacled, and apparently impervious to the blood thirst that drove many of my classmates to play ball as if their lives depended on it. Perhaps they did. I would rather be reading a book than sweating, grunting, and running the risk of pain and injury. I simply did not see the point in competitive sports. My main form of exercise then was walking to the library, many city blocks away from my barrio.

Still, I wanted to be wanted. I wanted to be chosen for the teams. Physical education was compulsory, a class where you were actually given a grade. On my mainly all-A report card, the C for compassion I always received from the P.E. teachers shamed me the same as a bad grade in a real class. Invariably, my father would say: "How can you make a low grade *for playing games*?" He did not understand. Even if I had managed to make a hit (it never happened), or get the ball over that ridiculously high net, I already had a reputation as a "shrimp," a hopeless nonathlete. It was an area where the girls who didn't like me for one reason or another — mainly because I did better than they on academic subjects — could lord it over me; the playing field was the place where even the smallest girl could make me feel powerless and inferior. I instinctively understood the politics even then; how the *not* choosing me until the teacher forced one of the team captains to call my name was a coup of sorts — there you little show-off, tomorrow you can beat us in spelling and geography, but this afternoon you are the loser. Or perhaps those were only my own bitter thoughts as I sat or stood in the sidelines while the big girls were grabbed like fish and I, the little brown tadpole, was ignored until Teacher looked over in my general direction and shouted, "Call Ortiz," or worse, "Somebody's *got* to take her."

No wonder I read Wonder Woman comics and had Legion of Super Heroes daydreams. Although I wanted to think of myself as "intellectual," my body was demanding that I notice it. I saw the little swelling around my once-flat nipples; the fine hairs growing in secret places; but my knees were still bigger than my thighs and I always wore long or half-sleeve blouses to hide my bony upper arms. I wanted flesh on my bones — a thick layer of it. I saw a new product advertised on TV. Wate-On. They showed skinny men and women before and after taking the stuff, and it was a transformation like the 97-pound weakling turned into Charles Atlas ads that I saw on the back cover of my comic books. The Wate-On was very expensive. I tried to explain my need for it in Spanish to my mother, but it didn't translate very well, even to my ears — and she said with a tone of finality, eat more of my good food and you'll get fat — anybody can get fat. Right. Except me. I was going to have to join a circus someday as "Skinny Bones," the woman without flesh.

Wonder Woman was stacked. She had a cleavage framed by the spread wings of a golden eagle and a muscular body that has become fashionable with women only recently. But since I wanted a body that would serve me in P.E., hers was my ideal. The breasts were an indulgence I allowed myself. Perhaps the daydreams of bigger girls were more glamorous, since our ambitions are filtered through our needs, but I wanted first a powerful body. I daydreamed of leaping up above the gray landscape of the city to where the sky was clear and blue, and in anger and self-pity I fantasized about scooping my enemies up by their hair from the playing fields and dumping them on a barren asteroid. I would put the P.E. teachers each on their own rock in space too where they would be the loneliest people in the universe since I knew they had no "inner resources," no imagination, and in outer space, there would be no air for them to fill their deflated volleyballs with. In my mind all P.E. teachers have blended into one large spiky-haired woman with a whistle on a string around her neck and a volleyball under one arm. My Wonder Woman fantasies of revenge were a source of comfort to me in my early career as a shrimp.

I was saved from more years of P.E. torment by the fact that in my sophomore year of high school I transferred to a school where the midget, Gladys, was the focal point of interest for the people who must rank according to size. Because her height was considered a handicap, there was an unspoken rule about mentioning size around Gladys, but of course there was no need to say anything. Gladys knew her place: front-row center in class photographs. I gladly moved to the left or to the right of her, as far as I could without leaving the picture completely.

4. Looks

Many photographs were taken of me as a baby by my mother to send to my father who was stationed overseas during the first two years of my life. With the army in Panama when I was born, he later joined the navy and traveled often on tours of duty. I was a healthy, pretty baby. Recently I read that people are drawn to big-eyed round-faced creatures, like puppies, kittens, and certain other mammals and marsupials, koalas for example, and, of course, infants. I was all eyes, since my head and body, even as I grew older, remained thin and small-boned. As a young child I got a lot of attention from my relatives and many other people we met in our barrio. My mother's beauty may have had something to do with how much attention we got from strangers in stores and on the street. I can imagine it. In the pictures I have seen of us together, she is a stunning young woman by Latino standards: long, curly black hair and round curves in a compact frame. From her I learned how to move, smile, and talk like an attractive woman. I remember going into a bodega for our groceries and being given candy by the proprietor as a reward for being *bonita*, pretty.

I can see in the photographs and I also remember that I was dressed in the pretty clothes, the stiff, frilly dresses, with layers of crinolines underneath, the glossy patent leather shoes, and, on special occasions, the skull-hugging little hats and the white gloves that were popular in the late fifties and early sixties. My mother was proud of my looks, although I was a bit too thin. She could dress me up like a doll and take me by the hand to visit relatives, or go to the Spanish mass at the Catholic church, and show me off. How was I to know that she and the others who called me pretty were representatives of an aesthetic that would not apply when I went out into the mainstream world of school?

In my Paterson, New Jersey, public schools there were still quite a few white children, although the demographics of the city were changing rapidly. The original waves of Italian and Irish immigrants, silk-mill workers and laborers in the cloth industries, had been "assimilated." Their children were now the middle-class parents of my peers. Many of them moved their children to the Catholic schools that proliferated enough to have leagues of basketball teams. The names I recall hearing still ring in my ears: Don Bosco High vs. St. Mary's High, St. Joseph's vs. St. John's. Later I too would be transferred to the safer environment of a Catholic school. But I started school at Public School Number 11. I came there from Puerto Rico, thinking myself a pretty girl, and found that the hierarchy for popularity was as follows: pretty white girl, pretty Jewish girl, pretty Puerto Rican girl, pretty black girl. Drop the last two categories; teachers were too busy to have more than one favorite per class, and it was simply understood that if there was a big part in the school play, or any competition where the main qualification was "presentability" (such as escorting a school visitor to or from the principal's office), the classroom's public address speaker would be requesting the pretty and/or nice-looking white boy or girl. By the time I was in the sixth grade, I was sometimes called by the principal to represent my class because I dressed neatly (I knew this from a progress report sent to my mother, which I translated for her), and because all the "presentable" white girls had moved to the Catholic schools (I later surmised this part). But I was still not one of the popular girls with the boys. I remember one incident where I stepped out into the playground in my baggy gym shorts and one Puerto Rican boy said to the other: "What do you think?" The other one answered: "Her face is okay, but look at the toothpick legs." The next best thing to a compliment I got was when my favorite male teacher, while handing out the class pictures, commented that with my long neck and delicate features I resembled the movie star Audrey Hepburn. But the Puerto Rican boys had learned to respond to a fuller figure: long necks and a perfect little nose were not what they looked for in a girl. That is when I decided I was a "brain." I did not settle into the role easily. I was nearly devastated by what the chicken-pox episode had done to my self-image. But I looked into the mirror less often after I was told that I would always have scars on my face, and I hid behind my long black hair and my books.

After the problems at the public school got to the point where even nonconfrontational little me got beaten up several times, my parents enrolled me at St. Joseph's High School. I was then a minority of one among the Italian and Irish kids. But I found several good friends there—other girls who took their studies seriously. We did our homework together and talked about the Jackies. The Jackies were two popular girls, one blonde and the other red-haired, who had women's bodies. Their curves showed even in the blue jumper uniforms with straps that we all wore. The blond Jackie would often let one of the straps fall off her shoulder, and although she, like all of us, wore a white blouse underneath, all the boys stared at her arm. My friends and I talked about this and practiced letting our straps fall off our shoulders. But it wasn't the same without breasts or hips.

My final two and a half years of high school were spent in Augusta, Georgia, where my parents moved our family in search of a more peaceful environment. There we became part of a little community of our army-connected relatives and friends. School was yet another matter. I was enrolled in a huge school of nearly two thousand students that had just that year been forced to integrate. There were two black girls and there was me. I did extremely well academically. As to my social life, it was, for the most part, uneventful—yet it is in my memory blighted by one incident. In my junior year, I became wildly infatuated with a pretty white boy. I'll call him Ted. Oh, he was pretty: yellow hair that fell over his forehead, a smile to die for, and he was a great dancer. I watched him at Teen Town, the youth center at the base where all the military brats gathered on Saturday nights. My father had retired from the military and we had all our base privileges—one other reason we had moved to Augusta. Ted looked like an angel to me. I worked on him for a year before he asked me out. This meant maneuvering to be within the periphery of his vision at every possible occasion. I took the long way to my classes in school just to pass by his locker, I went to football games that I detested, and I danced (I too was a good dancer) in front of him at Teen Town—this took some fancy footwork since it involved subtly moving my partner toward the right spot on the dance floor. When

Ted finally approached me, "A Million to One" was playing on the jukebox, and when he took me into his arms, the odds suddenly turned in my favor. He asked me to go to a school dance the following Saturday. I said yes, breathlessly, I said yes but there were obstacles to surmount at home. My father did not allow me to date casually. I was allowed to go to major events like a prom or a concert with a boy who had been properly screened. There was such a boy in my life, a neighbor who wanted to be a Baptist missionary and was practicing his anthropological skills on my family. If I was desperate to go somewhere and needed a date, I'd resort to Gary. This is the type of religious nut that Gary was: When the school bus did not show up one day, he put his hands over his face and prayed to Christ to get us a way to get to school. Within ten minutes a mother in a station wagon on her way to town stopped to ask why we weren't in school. Gary informed her that the Lord had sent her just in time to get us there for roll call. He assumed that I was impressed. Gary was even good-looking in a bland sort of way, but he kissed me with his lips tightly pressed together. I think Gary probably ended up marrying a native woman from wherever he may have gone to preach the Gospel according to Paul. She probably believes that all white men pray to God for transportation and kiss with their mouths closed. But it was Ted's mouth, his whole beautiful self that concerned me in those days. I knew my father would say no to our date, but I planned to run away from home if necessary. I told my mother how important this date was. I cajoled and pleaded with her from Sunday to Wednesday. She listened to my arguments, and must have heard the note of desperation in my voice. She said very gently to me: "You better be ready for disappointment." I did not ask what she meant. I did not want her fears for me to taint my happiness. I asked her to tell my father about my date. Thursday at breakfast my father looked at me across the table with his eyebrows together. My mother looked at him with her mouth set in a straight line. I looked down at my bowl of cereal. Nobody said anything. Friday I tried on every dress in my closet. Ted would be picking me up at six on Saturday: dinner and then the sock hop at school. Friday night I was in my room doing my nails or something else in preparation for Saturday (I know I groomed myself nonstop all week) when the telephone rang. I ran to get it. It was Ted. His voiced sounded funny when he said my name, so funny that I felt compelled to ask: "Is something wrong?" Ted blurted it all out without a preamble. His father had asked who he was going out with. Ted had told him my name. "Ortiz? That's Spanish, isn't it?" the father had asked. Ted had told him yes, then shown him my picture in the yearbook. Ted's father had shaken his head. No. Ted would not be taking me out. Ted's father had known Puerto Ricans in the army. He had lived in New York City while studying architecture and had seen how the *spics* lived. Like rats. Ted repeated his father's words to me as if I should understand *his predicament* when I heard why he was breaking our date. I don't remember what I said before hanging up. I do recall the darkness of my room that sleepless night, and the heaviness of my blanket in which I wrapped myself like a shroud. And I remember my parents' respect for my pain and their gentleness toward me that weekend. My mother did not say "I warned you," and I was grateful for her understanding silence.

In college, I suddenly became an "exotic" woman to the men who had survived the popularity wars in high school, who were now practicing to be worldly: They had to act liberal in their politics, in their lifestyles, and in the women they went out with. I dated heavily for a while, then married young. I had discovered that I needed stability more than social life. I had brains for sure, and some talent in writing. These facts were a constant in my life. My skin color, my size, and my appearance were variables—things that were judged according to my current self-image, the aesthetic values of the times, the places I was in, and the people I met. My studies, later my writing, the respect of people who saw me as an individual person they cared about, these were the criteria for my sense of self-worth that I would concentrate on in my adult life.

SEVENTEEN

When I Was Growing Up

Nellie Wong

I know now that once I longed to be white.
How? you ask.
Let me tell you the ways.

    when I was growing up, people told me
    I was dark and I believed my own darkness
    in the mirror, in my soul, my own narrow vision

        when I was growing up, my sisters
        with fair skin got praised
        for their beauty, and in the dark
        I fell further, crushed between high walls

    when I was growing up, I read magazines
    and saw movies, blonde movie stars, white skin,
    sensuous lips and to be elevated, to become
    a woman, a desirable woman, I began to wear
    imaginary pale skin

        when I was growing up, I was proud
        of my English, my grammar, my spelling
        fitting into the group of smart children

    smart Chinese children, fitting in,
    belonging, getting in line

    when I was growing up and went to high
        school,
    I discovered the rich white girls, a few yellow
        girls,
    their imported cotton dresses, their cashmere
        sweaters,
    their curly hair and I thought that I too
        should have
    what these lucky girls had

        when I was growing up, I hungered
        for American food, American styles,
        coded: white and even to me, a child
        born of Chinese parents, being Chinese
        was feeling foreign, was limiting,
        was unAmerican

    when I was growing up and a white man
        wanted

to take me out, I thought I was special,
an exotic gardenia, anxious to fit
the stereotype of an oriental chick

> when I was growing up, I felt ashamed
> of some yellow men, their small bones,
> their frail bodies, their spitting
> on the streets, their coughing,
> their lying in sunless rooms,
> shooting themselves in the arms

when I was growing up, people would ask
if I were Filipino, Polynesian, Portuguese.
They named all colors except white, the shell
of my soul, but not my dark, rough skin

> when I was growing up, I felt
> dirty. I thought that god

made white people clean
and no matter how much I bathed,
I could not change, I could not shed
my skin in the gray water

when I was growing up, I swore
I would run away to purple mountains,
houses by the sea with nothing over
my head, with space to breathe,
uncongested with yellow people in an area
called Chinatown, in an area I later learned
was a ghetto, one of many hearts
of Asian America

I know now that once I longed to be white
How many more ways? you ask.
Haven't I told you enough?

EIGHTEEN

◆◆◆

Do You Remember Me?

Barbara Macdonald

I am less than five feet high and, except that I may have shrunk a quarter of an inch or so in the past few years, I have viewed the world from this height for sixty-five years. I have taken up some space in the world; I weigh about a hundred and forty pounds and my body is what my mother used to call dumpy. My mother didn't like her body and so, of course, didn't like mine. "Dumpy" was her word and just as I have had to keep the body, somehow I have had to keep the word—thirty-eight inch bust, no neck, no waistline, fat hips—that's dumpy.

My hair is grey, white at the temples, with only a little of the red cast of earlier years showing through. My face is wrinkled and deeply lined. Straight lines have formed on the upper lip as though I had spent many years with my mouth pursed. This has always puzzled me and I wonder what years those were and why I can't remember them. My face has deep lines that extend from each side of the nose down the face past the corners of my mouth. My forehead is wide, and the lines across my forehead and between my eyes are there to tes-

tify that I was often puzzled and bewildered for long periods of time about what was taking place in my life. My cheekbones are high and become more noticeably so as my face is drawn further and further down. My chin is small for such a large head and below the chin the skin hangs in a loose vertical fold from my chin all the way down my neck, where it meets a horizontal scar. The surgeon who made the scar said that the joints of my neck were worn out from looking up so many years. For all kinds of reasons, I seldom look up to anyone or anything anymore.

My eyes are blue and my gaze is usually steady and direct. But I look away when I am struggling with some nameless shame, trying to disclaim parts of myself. My voice is low and my speech sometimes clipped and rapid if I am uncomfortable; otherwise, I have a pleasant voice. I like the sound of it from in here where I am. When I was younger, some people, lovers mostly, enjoyed my singing, but I no longer have the same control of my voice and sing only occasionally now when I am alone.

My hands are large and the backs of my hands begin to show the brown spots of aging. Sometimes lately, holding my arms up reading in bed or lying with my arms clasped around my lover's neck, I see my arm with the skin hanging loosely from my forearm and cannot believe that it is really my own. It seems disconnected from me; it is someone else's, it is the arm of an old woman. It is the arm of such old women as I myself have seen, sitting on benches in the sun with their hands folded in their laps; old women I have turned away from. I wonder now, how and when these arms I see came to be my own— arms I cannot turn away from. . . .

I have grown to like living in Cambridge. I like the sharp lines of the reality of my life here. The truth is I like growing old. Oh, it isn't that I don't feel at moments the sharp irrevocable knowledge that I have finally grown old. That is evident every time I stand in front of the bathroom mirror and brush my teeth. I may begin as I often do, wondering if those teeth that are so much a part of myself, teeth I've clenched in anger all my life, felt with my own tongue with a feeling of possession, as a cat licks her paw lovingly just because it is hers—wondering, will these teeth always be mine? Will they stay with me loyally and die with me, or will they desert me before the Time comes? But I grow dreamy brushing my teeth and find myself, unaware, planning—as I always have when I brush my teeth—that single-handed crossing I plan to make. From East to West, a last stop in the Canaries and then the trade winds. What will be the best time of year? What boat? How much sail? I go over again the list of supplies, uninterrupted until some morning twinge in my left shoulder reminds me with uncompromising regret that I will never make that single-handed crossing— probably. That I have waited too long. That there is no turning back.

But I always say probably. Probably I'll never make that single-handed crossing. Probably, I've waited too long. Probably, I can't turn back now. But I leave room now, at sixty-five, for the unexpected. That was not always true of me. I used to feel I was in a kind of linear race with life and time. There were no probably's, it was a now or never time of my life. There were landmarks placed by other generations, and I had to arrive on time or fail in the whole race. If I didn't pass—if the sixth grade went on to the seventh without me, I would be one year behind for the rest of my life. If I graduated from high school in 1928, I had to graduate from college in 1932. When I didn't graduate from college until 1951, it took me another twenty years to realize the preceding twenty years weren't lost. But now I begin to see that I may get to have the whole thing, and that no experience longed for is really going to be missed.

"I like growing old." I say it to myself with surprise. I had not thought that it could be like this. There are days of excitement when I feel almost a kind of high with the changes taking place in my body, even though I know the inevitable course my body is taking will lead to debilitation and death. I say to myself frequently in wonder, "This is my body doing this thing." I cannot stop it, I don't even know what it is doing, I wouldn't know how to direct it. My own body is going through a process that only my body knows about. I never grew old before; never died before. I don't really know how it's done. . . .

So often we think we know how an experience is going to end so we don't risk the pain of seeing it through to the end. We think we know the outcome so we think there is no need to experience it, as though to anticipate an ending were the same as living the ending out. . . .

Of course, this time, for me, I am not going to live beyond this ending. The strangeness of that idea comes to me at the most unexpected moments and always with surprise and shock; sometimes, I am immobilized by it. Standing before the mirror in the morning, I feel that my scalp is tight. I see that the skin hangs beneath my jaw, beneath my arm; my breasts are pulled low against my body; loose skin hangs from my hips, and below my stomach a new horizontal crease is forming over which the skin will hang like the hem of a skirt turned under. A hem not to be "let down," as once my skirts were, because I was "shooting up," but a widening hem to "take up" on an old garment that has been stretched. Then I see that my body is being drawn into the earth— muscle, tendon, tissue and skin is being drawn down by the earth's pull back to the loam. She is pulling me back to herself; she is taking back what is hers. . . .

I think a lot about being drawn into the earth. I have the knowledge that one day I will fall and the earth will take back what is hers. I have no choice, yet I choose it. Maybe I won't buy that boat and that list of supplies; maybe I will. Maybe I will be able to write about my life; maybe I won't. But uncertainty will not always be there, for this is like no other experience I have ever had—I can count on it. I've never had anything before that I could really count on. My life has been filled with uncertainties, some were not of my making and many were: promises I made myself I did not keep; promises I made others I did not keep; hopes I could not fulfill; shame carried like a weight heavier each year, at my failure, at my lack of clear purpose. But this time I can rely on myself, for life will keep her promise to me. I can trust her. She isn't going to confuse me with a multitude of other choices and beckon me down other roads with vague promises. She will give me finally only one choice, one road, one sense of possibility. And in exchange for the multitude of choices she no longer offers, she gives me, at last, certainty. Nor do I have to worry this time that I will fail myself, fail to pull it off. This time, for sure I am going to make that single-handed crossing.

NINETEEN

What's a Leg Got to Do with It?

Donna Walton

What's a leg got to do with it? Exactly what I thought when, during a heated conversation, a female rival told me I was less than a woman because I have one leg.

Excuse me. Perhaps I missed something. How could she make such an insensitive comment about something she had no experience with? Was she some expert on disabilities or something? Was she, too, disabled? Had she—like me—fought a battle with cancer that cost her a limb? For a split second, my thoughts were paralyzed by her insensitivity. But, like a defeated fighter who returns to the ring to regain victory, I bounced back for a verbal round with Ms. Thang.

I am woman first, an amputee second and physically challenged last. And it is in that order that I set out to educate and testify to people like Ms. Thang who are unable to discern who I am—a feisty, unequivocally attractive African-American woman with a gimpy gait who can strut proudly into any room and engage in intelligent conversation with folks anxious to feed off my sincere aura.

It is rather comical and equally disturbing how folks—both men and women—view me as a disabled woman, particularly when it comes to sexuality. They have so many misconceptions. Straight women, for example, want to know how I catch a man, while most men are entertained with the idea that because I have one leg sex with me must be a blast.

I have even been confronted by folks who give me the impression that they think having sex is a painful experience for me. Again, I say, What's a leg got to do with it?

For all of those who want to inquire about my sexual prowess but dare not to, or for those who are curious about how I maintain such positive self-esteem when life dealt me the proverbial "bad hand," this story is for you. But those who have a tough time dealing with reality probably should skip the next paragraph because what I am about to confess is the gospel truth.

I like sex! I am very sexual!! I even consider myself sexy, residual limb and all. You see, I was a sexual being before my leg was amputated 19 years ago. My attitude didn't change about sex. I just had to adjust to the attitudes of others.

For example, I remember a brother who I dated in high school—before my leg was amputated—then dated again five years later. The dating ended abruptly because I realized that the brother could not fathom the one-leg thing. When he and I were home alone, he was cool as long as we got hot and bothered with my prosthesis on. However, whenever I tried to take off my artificial leg for comfort purposes, he immediately panicked. He could not fathom seeing me with one leg.

I tried to put him at ease by telling him Eva's story from Toni Morrison's novel *Sula*—that "my leg just got tired and walked off one day." But this brother just could not deal. He booked.

On the other hand, my experiences with lesbians have varied; they don't all book right away, but some have booked. Not all are upfront with their feelings 'cuz women are socialized to be courteous, emotional, and indirect, sparing one's feelings. Instead, some tend to communicate their discomfort with my missing limb in more subtle ways. For example, one lesbian I dated did not want to take me out to bars, clubs and other social settings. My lop-sided gait was an embarrassment, and the fact that I use a cane garnered unwanted attention for her. Behind closed doors, she did not have any problems with it. How we would be perceived by trendy lesbians was her main concern.

Conversely, I have had positive experiences with lesbians as well. For instance, I have dated and been in love with women who have been affirming and supportive while respecting my difference. My wholeness has been shaped by all of these experiences. Without hesitation, I can now take off my prosthesis, be comfortable hopping around on one-leg and the sex . . . . is still a blast.

How does a woman with one leg maintain such a positive self-esteem in a society where people with disabilities are not valued? Simply by believing in myself. I know you're saying, "That sounds much too hokey." But as I said earlier, this is the gospel truth.

I was 19 years old when my leg was amputated. I was diagnosed with osteogenic sarcoma, bone can-

cer. During the first five years after my surgery, concentrating on other folks' perceptions of me was the least of my concerns. I was too focused on beating the odds against dying. You see, I was given only a 15% chance of survival—with spiritual guidance and support from my family—I had made the very difficult decision to stop taking my chemotherapy treatments. Doctors predicted that, by halting the dreadful chemotherapy, I was writing my own death certificate. However, through what I believe was divine healing, my cancer was eradicated.

Before this cancerous ordeal, I was not strong spiritually, and my faith was rocked when my leg was amputated because I thought I was to keep my leg. At the time, I could not see past the physical. After my amputation, I was preoccupied with the kinds of crippling thoughts that all the Ms. Thangs of the world are socialized to believe: that I was not going to be able to wear shorts, bathing suits or lingerie; that my womanness was somehow compromised by the loss of a limb.

If you have a disability and are in need of some fuel for your spirit, check out any novel by Toni Morrison ("Sula" is my favorite because of the one-legged grandmother, Eva) or Khalil Gibran's "The Prophet." These resources helped me build self-esteem and deal with my reality.

Ultimately, building positive esteem is an ongoing process. To that end, I am currently producing a motivational video that will outline coping strategies for female amputees.

No matter what your disability or circumstance, you cannot give in to a defeatist attitude. When you do, your battle is lost. There is a way of fighting back. It is called self-esteem.

Believe in yourself, and you will survive—and thrive.

◆◆◆

TWENTY

Ruminations of a Feminist Aerobics Instructor

Alisa L. Valdés

Just saying my title is enough to make most people laugh: feminist aerobics instructor. Huh? It's like being a fascist poet. People think you just can't. One day several years ago as I impelled my step class to eat whatever they wanted whenever they wanted, to love their thighs no matter what size, I was overwhelmed by all the uniquely American, female contradictions confronting me. The women in the class just stared at me with these blank, nearly hostile eyes. Hello? What part of "low-fat" didn't I understand? Couldn't I see how fat they were? What kind of aerobics instructor was I, anyway?

The answer was easy: a twenty-something, lower-middle-class musician/writer/social critic cum feminist aerobics instructor with big college loan payments and, therefore, a big, two-sided problem.

Part of the problem is this: In a lecture she gave at the Boston Public Library in 1991, the year of my emerging feminism, Gloria Steinem pointed out that women are a permanent underclass in the United States of America; because of our economic inequity, we comprise a third-world nation within the borders of our own developed country. There is no argument. In 1991, women still earned only seventy-one cents to every dollar earned by a man, and a college-educated woman could (and still can) expect to earn the same as or less than her male colleague with only a high school diploma. If we are ever going to progress, we are going to have to achieve economic equality. Period.

In New York City, aerobics instructors, feminist and otherwise, earn between thirty-five and forty-five dollars an hour.

The second part of my problem is roughly this: In 1986, nutritionist Laurel Mellin did a study through the University of California at San Francisco called "Why Girls as Young as Nine Fear Fat and Go on Diets to Lose Weight." Probably we don't need to know much more than the title to feel depressed, but in this study fifty percent of the nine-year-olds, and nearly eighty percent of the ten- and eleven-year-olds, had "put themselves on a diet because they thought they were too fat." According to some experts, eating disorders were "the disease" of the seventies and have only been getting worse since then, despite being eclipsed by AIDS since the mid-eighties. And this: Studies show that seventy-five percent of adult women in this country think we are too fat, though only twenty-five percent of us actually weigh more than the standards set forth by Metropolitan Life's weight tables. And of course, there's always America's favorite doll, Barbie, by Mattell. If a woman of Barbie's proportions existed, she wouldn't be able to walk, breathe or digest food.

When I first started teaching aerobics I was fifteen years old. I did it for extra money and for a free membership to a health club. I'm not going to lie: I also did it to counter the geek factor of my adolescent existence. I was teased endlessly as a child for being overweight (*fatty fatty two-by-four, can't fit through the kitchen door* was my name), and once I actually lost weight, my parents wouldn't let me be a high school cheerleader like my best friends, Staci and Nana. Instead, they insisted that I go into band. Being a teenage aerobics instructor was a way for me to fight back on both fronts.

Even then I made about eight dollars an hour, which was great compared to the three and change I had earned wearing a greasy orange-and-brown uniform as a cashier at a local restaurant.

In early 1988, at the age of seventeen, I moved to Boston to study saxophone at the Berklee College of Music. One of the first things I did after arriving was secure a job for myself as an aerobics instructor at New England Aerobics and Nautilus, a women's gym a few blocks from school. My peers at Berklee were eighty-five percent male, so it was a good balance for me to enter that sweaty female domain where I could stand in front of the class and command and connect. The gym was one of the few places on earth where I actually felt I possessed an irrefutable degree of power. It hadn't occurred to me yet to analyze why so many brilliant, professional women were wasting so many hours every week hopping around in leotards. All I knew then was that it was a great job with good money, lots of other women, loud music and a kind of ritualized dancing that I got to choreograph. As fun and American as lite beer, buffalo wings and fried cheese.

Gradually, and somewhat to my astonishment, I became a *professional* instructor. By my senior year of college I had actually carved out a secondary career for myself in the aerobics industry in Boston, which was good since not too many jazz saxophonists or poets were making enough bread to pay back a loan such as the twenty-three thousand dollars I suddenly owed after graduation (no thanks to Uncle Reagan). I was teaching at the city's top clubs — places populated by women who carried attaché cases and men in ties, places with names like the Sky Club, Healthworks, the Squash Club and Boston Health and Swim Club — and getting about twenty-five dollars an hour for my perspirational efforts. Other friends from school were working as cashiers at Tower Records or as security guards at the Hines Convention Center, barely breaking minimum wage. I felt lucky.

I even invested in a license to train other instructors for the Aerobics and Fitness Association of America, one of the two major certification organizations in the country, and was soon able to make about three hundred dollars an hour for private clinics. I taught step, funk, Latin, high- and low-impact, body sculpting and stretch. I even entered an aerobics competition in 1992 with a male partner, and we grinned and bounced our way to second place in the New England regionals.

Soon I was heading the aerobics program at a club near Tufts University; at twenty-three I had my own office, a good salary and power over a whole staff of instructors, and I was presenting a master class at the Boston MetroSports Fitness Expo. People in the industry knew my name. Disc jockeys made free tapes for my classes. Reebok invited me to sit on its instructor board to help design its 1993 line of shoes. Reebok, Nike and Rykä shoe companies gave me freebies, just for being a good instructor. And I could pay back my loans. Though I kept telling myself I was really still a feminist, a musician and a writer, I was becoming a career instructor — sweating more, practicing less, writing less — and it was almost comfortable.

Almost, except for the gnawing ache of betrayal. I had read Alice Walker. I knew better than to en-

courage women's obsession with their appearance, including my own. I knew better than to freak out at my own cellulite, staying late after work to pump iron to make it go away. I knew better than to stand skinny in front of a room full of self-doubting women and actually say to them, "Okay, let's tone up." I had betrayed myself, betrayed my dreams; most of all I had betrayed my gender. But it was almost as if I, who spent the first years of my life in a housing project and have been living hand-to-mouth ever since, had no choice. The world had rewarded "Hispanic female" me not for being a writer or musician, but for being an aerobics instructor. I was a cheerleader after all, and I hadn't even noticed. Like many other women who bought the fitness lie, I had been duped into believing there was strength in, well, fat loss. Eventually, my conscience got the better of me. I quit everything fitness-oriented in Boston, packed my bags and moved to New York City to try to be a feminist writer and musician for real. At first it was groovy, but it was only a matter of time before my credit was canceled and the phone company lawyers were threatening me.

I landed a prestigious unpaid internship at the *Village Voice,* but ended up having to leave early and quite sloppily because I was also teaching fifteen to twenty aerobics classes a week to pay my bills. Commuting two hours a day, practicing my saxophone, writing consistently and holding down two jobs was too much; I just couldn't handle the pressure. The physical and emotional stress overwhelmed me: I was physically sick all the time, I slept on the bus home, I craved several boxes of doughnuts at once. So I quit the *Voice* when I really wanted to quit teaching. But there was no money at the *Voice,* and women, remember, are a permanent, albeit fit, underclass in our society.

Before long, I was a full-time aerobics instructor again, this time in Manhattan, at places with names like the Jeff Martin Studio, Molly Fox Fitness and Crunch Fitness, places that had articles written about them in those "women's" magazines, right next to articles about sticking to your diet or ten ways to make Him find you sexy again. I watched as my lifelong dream of being a professional feminist writer slipped through my fingers and back into my spandex and sneakers, all because I needed to pay for a roof over my head and the food in my stomach. I realized that only the children of the rich are able to afford to be entry-level journalists for the progressive publications of our nation. The poor become, well, cheerleaders for the status quo. Give me a "Y"! (Why!)

And that is my problem.

I say I was a cheerleader after all, and a part of me grimaces. I've tried hard to hold on to a shred of fem˙ ˙st dignity in all this jumping around. I made it a ౢoal to battle the common misconception about aerobics instructors—that we are nothing but airheads in thongs.

I rationalized this femifitness philosophy in many ways. I grew convinced that there is actually a great deal of raw, primal energy and force in a room full of women moving together in time; a few of the editors from the *Voice,* feminists all of them (well, Pagliaesque, cutesy, Voicey, Madonna feminists at any rate), took classes at one of the studios I worked for. In real life, I reminded myself, women take aerobics classes in shorts and T-shirts; it is only on television that they all wear tights and thongs. And only on the ESPN programs that air in sports bars at eleven in the morning do aerobics instructors grin wildly and stick their asses in the air.

That dignified instructor part of me thought men, including Woody Allen, had sexified and bubblefied the image of aerobics instructor in order to claim ownership of one of our society's few appealing areas where men simply are not welcome. I thought, What could honestly be more frightening to men than a room full of capable, professional women moving together, in sync, unaware of anything but themselves and each other? Only Hillary Rodham Clinton and a truly lesbian orgy, perhaps.

And I found intellectual polemics to support my misdirected theory. In 1989 Roberta Pollack Seid wrote that "ten years ago vigorous exercise was seen as the province primarily of young men. Today women have smashed the sex barrier that once excluded them from this 'male' domain."* Right on, part of me gurgled over the water fountain. Not only had we smashed the barriers, but through our organized dance exercise, we had also created a girls' club where women work for women and make money off of and for women (albeit with a sociopolitically skewed agenda).

Iris Marion Young, a professor from the University of Pittsburgh who has written extensively on gender differences in motility in our society, wrote that there are "certain observable and rather ordinary ways in which women in our society typically comport themselves and move differently from the ways that men do."[†] She documents that we take proportionally shorter steps than men do, keep our arms in close to us when we walk (whereas men swing freely) and stand with our legs closer together. She argues that the cliché way boys and girls throw a ball differently is an outward manifestation of an across-the-board social conditioning to female inferiority; and she adds that until a human can trust her body to actually comport itself in the direction of its possibilities, the possibilities will remain overlooked. The aerobics studio, then, I told myself, is one of the few places women let go of these inhibitions and trust their bodies to move *big.* By hopping and squatting hundreds of women throughout the week, I was moving women toward self-realization.

Young also writes that in everyday life women "fail to summon the full possibilities of our muscular coordination, position, poise, and bearing."[††] I knew the high of that endorphin-assisted moment in the middle of each class when women summon the very core of their strength, and I had seen it shine. Maybe that's why I taught, because seeing and directing a room full of women who were summoning their full possibilities was a charge, even if the motive was ultimately less than feminist.

Finally, both Young and my hero Robin Morgan have argued that consciousness as a human being is related not to the intellect alone, but also to the body; the body is the vehicle through which everything comes to and goes from us. I think that maybe this is why I taught, as well: to dance, to connect with my body in a tangible way so that I could better connect with my intellect and assist others in doing the same. The process of strengthening the body could also strengthen women's ability to achieve our goals. Never mind that often those goals—to achieve a flat tummy, to fit into that tiny wedding

---

*Roberta Pollack Seid, *Never Too Thin: Why Women Are at War with Their Bodies* (New York: Prentice Hall, 1989), p. 8.

[†]Iris Marion Young, *Throwing Like a Girl and Other Essays in Feminist Philosophy and Social Theory* (Bloomington: Indiana University Press, 1990), p. 143.
[††]Young, p. 145.

dress, to lose ten pounds before going to Club Med to find Mr. Right—do not exactly subvert patriarchy. Creating a psychological space where women could move, really move, was the thrill. Teaching was my way of doing battle with the one idea expressed by Simone de Beauvoir that I vehemently disagreed with: that the female body is ultimately a burden. I tried to bring joy and movement into that body. In a word, I backwardly justified what I did as empowerment.

Interestingly, Young points out that her research does not include "movement that does not have a particular aim—for example, dancing." Ah. But dancing, aerobic dancing in particular, does have an aim, and this is where all of my aerobi-feminist convictions have turned on me. The aim, usually, is to be thin and beautiful, or as one of my fifty-year-old clients wrote on her release form, "to be 21 years old, 115 pounds, and Beautiful [sic]."

Women's fitness as we now know it truly is our newest patriarchal religion, based in principle as much on ritualized pain and suffering as any of the Judeo-Christian ones that came before it. No wonder nobody trusts Jane Fonda anymore. Fitness is a rigid religion of style, as debilitating and oppressive for many as a corset. Anorexics fill my classes like worshipers in a church, and no one stares. Other instructors starve themselves and do cocaine for energy with a regularity that would surprise many of their admirers. *She's so thin,* the members whisper admiringly in the locker room, *she looks great.* "In earlier centuries," writes Seid, "people who exhibited such mastery over hunger were categorized either as saints or as possessed by the devil, or, like the sixteenth-century Fasting Girl of Couflens, they were regarded as marvels whom travelers flocked to see. Today, that awe has become a horrified fascination, not because of the rarity of the phenomenon, but because of its increasing commonplaceness."*

---

*Seid, p. 21.

So by the time I reached twenty-three, I really began to think about my priorities. Might it be worth going into debt to attend graduate school, just so that one day I could pull myself away from the contradictions? I thought about myself, about my assisting other women to betray their potential. And it was a great relief to finally recognize the female obsession with thinness and fitness as an extension of the hurt we suffer at the hands of a patriarchal society, a society that even convinces us to hurt ourselves, so that we are kept from the real business of our lives.

I had to battle the hurt. I'd go into debt. I did. I am. Two years later I owe nearly forty thousand dollars in loans, but I have a gig as a staff writer for the *Boston Globe,* because my graduate degree from Columbia, while it might not have helped my writing, convinced some editors I was made of the right stuff.

This debt, the one I will have to feed from my bank account for the next couple of decades, is what happened to me because of my second-class citizenship and economic disadvantage. I was distracted for a time from the more serious pursuit of actually hustling to make a living as a writer and musician.

The *Globe* has given me a biweekly fitness column, something I find ironic but challenging. I try to avoid fueling fitness obsession. I've written columns on kid-friendly gyms, community centers that have programs for seniors, how to use objects in the home to strengthen muscles—anything that doesn't evoke spandex. I understand now that the gym has really become just another painful way we are all distracted from the serious business of our lives.

It seems that no matter how close I have gotten to empowerment through the modern fitness industry—women bosses and coworkers, good salary, the opportunity to connect with and help other women— there is still the knowledge that none of us, instructors or members, will ever reach our real goals playing by the rules of that industry, no matter how many inches we shed, no matter how much money we make.

◆◆◆

CHAPTER FOUR

Women's Sexuality

The body is the place where biological sex, socially constructed gender, and sexuality come together. Sexual attitudes and behaviors vary considerably from society to society and across historical time periods (Caplan 1987; Lancaster and di Leonardo 1997). Sexuality is not instinctive but learned from our families, our peers, sex education in school, popular culture, negotiations with partners, and listening to our own bodies. Much is learned from what is not said as well as what is made explicit. In this society, sexuality is a source of intimacy and pleasure, vulnerability and danger. Over the course of our lives, women's sexuality may take different forms and take on different degrees of significance. There is a heavy emphasis on sexuality in advertising, news reporting, and popular culture. At the same time, there is a dearth of accurate information about women's sexuality, and there are many constraints on it. To explore your sexuality, ideally you need a comfortable, safe place and freedom from worries about being attractive, getting pregnant, or getting sexually transmitted diseases. You also need time, self-awareness, and a cooperative partner to discover what you want sex to be for you.

This chapter focuses on women's experiences of sexuality, the meso- and macro-level forces that shape these experiences, and the ways that women are defining sexuality for themselves. As you read this chapter, think also about the social construction of

male sexuality discussed by Michael Kimmel in a later chapter (Reading 38).

Stereotypes, Contradictions, and Double Standards

In advertising images and popular culture, sexuality is the prerogative of the young, slender, and able-bodied. Many of these images portray White women. Melba Wilson (1993) notes that racism and sexism converge in mainstream stereotypes of women of color as "exotic creatures of passion" and "oversexed" (p. 66). Contemporary "pornographic images of black women show us as picturesque, removed from self and deserving of—even asking for—enslavement." She argues that this imagery is based in the historical abuse of Black women by White slave masters (p. 76). Asian and Asian American women are stereotyped as "Suzie Wong" or as "exotic flowers," passive, accommodating, and focused on serving men. The film *Slaying the Dragon* (1988; distributed by Women Make Movies) provides an excellent critique of this stereotype. In reality, older women, large women, and women with disabilities are also sexually active, as noted in the previous chapter (Doress and Siegal 1987). Barbara Waxman Fiduccia and Marsha Saxton (1997) comment that women with disabilities have been kept socially isolated and discouraged from expressing their sexuality. In their "Disability Feminism: A Manifesto" (1997), they write: "We want our sexuality accepted and supported with accurate information" (p. 60). Lillian Gonzales Brown, of the Institute on Disability Culture (Las Cruces, New Mexico), notes the influence of the disability rights movement on changing attitudes for people with disabilities. There has been a shift from feeling shame, wanting to assimilate, to disability pride. In workshops on sexuality for women with disabilities, she urges participants to explore their sexuality and to see themselves as sexual beings (L. G. Brown, personal communication, October, 1996).

Ads that use women's bodies to sell products also sell an idea of women's sexuality as passive and accommodating. As sex objects, women are commonly portrayed as child-like or doll-like playthings. These images flow from and reinforce macro-level patriarchal constructions of sexuality and gender based on the following assumptions: Heterosexuality is prescribed or natural for women and men, men are the initiators in heterosexual encounters, and men's sexuality is assumed to be assertive and in need of regular release. Women are expected to be modest and virtuous, to look beautiful, and, simultaneously, to lure men and to fend them off. Traditionally, a woman has been expected to remain a virgin until marriage, untouched except by her husband, and this attitude is still strong in many communities in the United States and around the world. Men's sexual activity is assumed and accepted; after all, "Boys will be boys." Sexually active women and girls are likely to be condemned as "sluts."

This fundamental contradiction between encouraging men's sexuality and expecting women to be chaste results in the construction of two categories of women: "good" women and "bad" women, virgins and whores—the women men marry and the women they fool around with. This double standard controls women's sexuality and autonomy, and serves to divide women from each other. This is significant at the micro, meso, and macro levels. Growing up in a Mexican American community, Sandra Cisneros (Reading 21) writes that *la Virgen de Guadalupe* was the model held up to girls. The boys "were fornicating like rabbits while the Church ignored them and pointed us women towards our destiny—

marriage and motherhood. The other alternative was *puta*hood," being defined a whore. Gloria Wade-Gayles (1993) learned the same double standard, but women in her Memphis neighborhood also divided men into two categories: good men who care for their wives and families, and "dogs" who "only want one thing." This latter category included White men who cruised through the neighborhood "in search of black women who, they assumed, were naturally sensuous, sexually superior, and easy" (p. 84).

It is important to note that many girls and women experience sexual coercion and abuse—in childhood, as adults, or both. Some struggle for many years with the devastating effects of sexual abuse on their confidence, trust, sexuality, and sense of themselves in the world. We take up this issue in detail in Chapter 6.

What Is Women's Autonomous Sexuality?

Given the cultural construction of women as objects of masculine sexual desire, whether women can create an autonomous sexuality is a key question that we return to later. In the 1960s there was much talk of a sexual revolution in the United States, partly made possible by the availability of contraceptive pills for the first time. Women "on the pill" could be sexually active with men without the same fear of pregnancy as in the past. In practice, many feminists argued that this "revolution" was very much on men's terms (Segal 1994), although, since that time, there has been increasing discussion of women's own sexual needs and preferences (Boston Women's Health Book Collective 1998; Cox 1999; Drill, McDonald, and Odes 1999; Ehrenreich, Hess, and Jacobs 1986; Ensler 1998; hooks 1993). Rebecca Chalker (1995) describes this process as a "real woman-friendly sexual revolution in progress" (p. 52). Women's magazines have provided one forum for this discourse, as well as women's erotica (Bright 1994; Reynolds 1992) and images of pop stars like Madonna, who revels in her sexuality in public. Eve Ensler, a playwright and screenwriter, has performed her Obie-winning show, *The Vagina Monologues,* in many parts of the country (Reading 22 is a short excerpt). She notes that, for many women, the word *vagina* is associated with shame, embarrassment, and silencing, even violation.

> And as more women say the word, saying it becomes less of a big deal; it becomes part of our language, part of our lives. Our vaginas become integrated and respected and sacred. They become part of our bodies, connected to our minds, fueling our spirits. And the shame leaves and the violation stops.
>
> *(Ensler 1998, p. xxiv)*

On Valentine's Day 2000, students from over 300 U.S. colleges and universities performed Ensler's script as part of the V-Day College Initiative, a nationwide project to celebrate women and to oppose sexual violence.

Shere Hite is one of the few popular researchers to conduct extensive surveys of men's and women's sexual experiences and preferences. The following questions, from one of her surveys, were written for women, but they are also relevant for men:

> Is sex important to you? What part does it play in your life?
>
> Who sets the pace and style of sex — you or your partner or both? Who decides when it's over?
>
> Do you think your genital area and vagina are ugly or beautiful?
>
> If you are sexually active, do you ever fake orgasms? Why?
>
> What are your best sex experiences? What would you like to try that you never have?
>
> What is it about sex that gives you the greatest pleasure? Displeasure?
>
> Have you chosen to be celibate at any point? What was/is that like for you?
>
> In the best of all possible worlds, what would sexuality be like?
>
> Do you know as much as you'd like to know, about your own body? Orgasm? Conception and pregnancy? Safe sex?
>
> Do your partners know about your sexual desires and your body? If not, do you ask for it or act yourself to get it?
>
> *(Hite 1994, pp. 17–22)*

In the 1980s and 90s, feminists engaged in heated argument about women's sexuality and the possibility of genuine sexual agency (Jaggar 1994; Snitow, Stansell, and Thompson 1983; Vance 1984). Marilyn Frye (1992) notes that "the word 'virgin' did not originally mean a woman whose vagina was untouched by any penis, but a free woman, one not betrothed, not married, not bound to, not possessed by any man. It meant a female who is sexually and hence socially her own person" (p. 133) — virtually an impossibility under patriarchy. Frye argues that radical feminist lesbians are inventing ways of living out this kind of virginity. Is this also possible for heterosexual women? As Frye puts it: "Can you fuck without losing your virginity?" (p. 136). She concludes that this is unlikely, but concedes it may be possible if women are willing to be wild and undomesticated — sexually, socially, and politically. This relates to Naomi Wolf's question about "sleeping with the enemy" (Reading 23).

In Reading 23, Naomi Wolf notes that "all over the country, millions of feminists have a secret indulgence. By day they fight gender injustice; by night they sleep with men. . . . Is sleeping with a man, 'sleeping with the enemy'?" She resolves this question by advocating what she calls "radical heterosexuality." To achieve this, women would need financial independence, marriage would have to be very different, and both women and men would have to give up their "gender benefits." Segal (1994) and Schwartz (1994) describe how some heterosexual couples are negotiating sex to make it more egalitarian. Schwartz notes that in U.S. culture there is a commonly held feeling that "male leadership and control is inherently erotic," that role differences between women and men and "the mystery of not knowing each other" make for a more exciting sex life (p. 70). Against this, she argues:

> Reducing difference can be sexy. Equitable treatment and role innovation can be exciting. . . . Hierarchy and domination are not essential for arousal. The natural ebb and flow of power in a relationship and the gulf between any two human beings that continually needs bridging gives enough natural tension and interest for peer sexuality to include passion.
>
> *(pp. 77–78)*

But only some men, Schwartz writes, "perhaps those with strong mothers, or with a great respect for competence and intelligence, find equality compelling and sexy" (p. 78). And not all women "refuse to be an instrument in male orchestration" (p. 78). She comments that passion is a Western ideal for marriage, although research shows that passion decreases over the length of a relationship. A long-term **peer marriage,** which is intentionally egalitarian, she notes, may be better at providing romance and respect than providing passion—unless, presumably, the notion of passion is reconstructed. Michael Kimmel takes up this issue in his discussion of male sexuality (Reading 38, Chapter 6).

Challenging Binaries

Our society constructs sex in strictly binary terms: female or male. Fausto-Sterling (1993) shows how intersexual people challenge these categories in a fundamental way. Their social, surgical, and hormonal treatment—which makes them a specific gender and pressures them to stick with it—shows how important this dichotomy is. Sexuality, too, has been defined in binary terms. According to Katz (1995), the concept of heterosexuality developed in parallel with the concept of homosexuality, and both date from the end of the nineteenth century. The word *heterosexuality* was first used in the 1890s, an obscure medical term applied to nonprocreative sex—that is, sex for pleasure. At the time this was considered a deviant idea, showing "abnormal or perverted appetite toward the opposite sex" (p. 86). Webster's dictionary did not include the word *heterosexuality* until 1934, and it gradually came into common usage in the United States as a "stable sign of normal sex" (p. 40).

Lesbians and gay men have long challenged the legitimacy and "normalcy" of heterosexuality (Allen 1986; Boswell 1994; Cavin 1985; Duberman, Vicinus, and Chauncey 1989; Faderman 1981; Grahn 1984; History Project 1998). Bisexual people have argued for greater fluidity in sexual desire and behaviors, what Bennett (1992) calls "a both/and option for an either/or world" (see also Hutchins and Kaahumanu 1991; Storr 1999; Weise 1992). Lisa Orlando (Reading 24) notes that stereotypes about bisexuality have grown out of the fact that bisexuals are poised between what "appear as two mutually exclusive sexual cultures" and from a common assumption "that homosexual and heterosexual desires exclude each other." Eridani (1992) argues that many women are probably bisexual and do not fit into a gay/straight categorization. She suggests that sexual orientation, meaning a "deeply rooted sense . . . that serious relationships are possible only with persons of the opposite sex or the same sex" (p. 174), is itself a masculinist perspective. Wilchins (1997) notes the limited notion of the erotic entailed in hetero-homo dualism: "an entire Geography of the Absent—body parts that aren't named, acts one mustn't do, genders one can't perform—because they are outside the binary box" (p. 167).

Those who refuse to tailor their looks and actions to conventional categories—for example, butch lesbians, cross-dressers, drag queens, and queers, described by Feinberg (1996) as "transgender warriors"—are involved in something profoundly challenging and transgressive. Drag, for example, has a long history in Euro-American culture (Bullough and Bullough 1993; Ekins 1997; Garber 1992; Lorber 1994). It plays with the idea of appearance as an illusion; mimics and parodies conventions; and raises questions as to who the person really is in terms of both outside appearance and inner identity. During the 1980s, younger people reclaimed the word *queer,* which for many older lesbians and gay men was a hateful and oppressive term (Bernstein and Silberman 1996). This is a broader definition of queerness, with an emphasis on experimentation and playfulness, and includes all who challenge heteronormativity.

Writing about transgender politics, Leslie Feinberg describes herself:

> I am a human being who unnerves some
> people. As they look at me, they see a kaleido-
> scope of characteristics they associate with
> both males and females. I appear to be a tan-
> gled knot of gender contradictions. . . . I'm
> a female who is more masculine than those
> prominently portrayed in mass culture . . . .
> My life only comes into focus when the word
> *transgender* is added to the equation.
>
> *(Reading 26)*

Feinberg (1998) and Bornstein (1995, 1998) point out that transgender people are creating a broader space for everyone to express their gender and their sexuality. Judith Butler (1990) considers "the binary framework for both sex and gender" to be "regulatory fictions" that consolidate and naturalize the power of masculine and heterosexist oppression (p. 33). Her conception of gender as performative allows and requires us to think of gender and sexuality more fluidly than rigid categories permit. It also opens the possibility that, under less repressive circumstances, people would have a much wider repertoire of behaviors than most currently do. At the same time, Butler notes that people "who fail to do their gender right" by standards held to be appropriate in specific contexts and at particular times, may be punished for it, through name calling, discrimination, hate, and outright violence (p. 140).

Phyllis Burke (1996) argues that transsexuals who choose sexual reassignment surgery both challenge binary gender categories and reinforce them. Judith Lorber (1994) notes that "it is Western culture's preoccupation with genitalia as the markers of both sexuality and gender and the concept of these social statuses as fixed for life that produces the problem and the surgical solution for those who cannot tolerate the personal ambiguities Western cultures deny" (p. 86). Transsexuals do not change their sex completely. Their chromosomes remain the same, and they rely on hormone treatments to alter their body shape, hair distribution, and the development of secondary sex characteristics like breasts or beards. Women-to-men transsexuals, for example, do not produce sperm. Lorber argues that they change *gender,* and have to construct a new gender identity, but that they do not disrupt "the deep genderedness of the modern Western world" (p. 96). Whether transgenderism as a movement can deal with structural inequalities of power between men and women raises the question of how personal freedoms, played out through the construction of sexuality and the body, are connected to other political issues and other progressive groups in society. Two spokespeople for this movement, Leslie Feinberg (1998) and Riki Anne Wilchins (1997), are making those connections.

Theorizing Sexuality

In *The Second Sex,* Simone de Beauvoir (1973) argued that gender is neither biological nor natural but learned. She concluded that one is not born a woman, but, rather, becomes one. In dominant ideology, woman is the Other to the male Self. De Beauvoir's work has been highly influential in shaping later feminist formulations of gender and sexuality. In addition, "Four linked political and intellectual movements—the sexual revolution, feminism, gay liberation, and the civil rights/race-minority power—have altered common perceptions of proper women's and men's lives, of sexual behavior" (Lancaster and di Leonardo 1997, p. 1). Feminists were very critical of the so-called 1960s sexual revolution, mentioned earlier, and began to "discuss sexual and bodily matters with a new, unladylike frankness" (p. 2). Carole Vance (1984) sums up the contradictions of sexuality for women:

> Sexuality is simultaneously a domain of restriction, repression, and danger as well as a domain of exploration, pleasure, and agency. To focus only on pleasure and gratification ignores the patriarchal structure in which women act, yet to speak only of sexual violence and oppression ignores women's experience with sexual agency and choice and unwittingly increases the sexual terror and despair in which women live.
>
> *(p. 1)*

In her now classic essay, Adrienne Rich (1986a) discusses how social institutions like law, religion, philosophy, official kinship, and popular culture support what she terms compulsory heterosexuality. She argues that patriarchy *demands* heterosexuality to keep women serving masculinist interests. For Rich, what needs to be explained is not why women identify as lesbians, but how and why so many women are heterosexual, since, typically, we first experience the intimacy of emotional caring and physical nurture with women—our mothers. In many cultural settings women and girls spend time together, care for and depend on one another, and enjoy each other's friendship—often passionately. Why would women ever redirect that search? Rich asks. As you read this chapter, consider Rich's question: What are "the societal forces which wrench women's emotional and erotic energies away from themselves and other women and from human-identified values" (p. 35), which teach us systematically to see men as appropriate partners?

Many feminists have focused on sexual violence—both theoretically and through active participation in rape crisis centers and shelters for battered women—and understand that sexuality can be a source of profound vulnerability for women. Andrea Dworkin (1987), for example, argues that intercourse is inherently repressive for women, partly for anatomical reasons, but more because of unequal power relations between women and men. As a way of repudiating the eroticization of inequality, some feminists have argued that women's sexuality should be based on sexual acts that are safe, loving, and intimate, in the context of a caring, monogamous relationship. Others have seen this as a new — feminist — restriction on women's freedom of expression (Duggan and Hunter 1995; Jaggar 1994; Leidholdt and Raymond 1990).

Seidman (1992) characterizes this polarization in terms of sexual romanticism on the one hand and sexual **libertarianism** on the other. Carole Vance (1984) compiled papers presented at the Scholar and the Feminist IX Conference, "Towards a Politics of Sexuality," which was held in New York City, April 1982, and intended to advance feminist understandings of sexuality. Gayle Rubin (1984) noted two strains of feminist thought concerning sexuality: one criticizing "restrictions on women's sexual behavior," denouncing "the high costs imposed on women for being sexually active," and calling for "a sexual liberation that would work for women as well as for men"; the other considering "sexual liberation to be inherently a mere extension of male privilege" and full of "conservative, anti-sexual discourse" (p. 301). Critics of the conference argued that some of the presenters are antifeminist and should not have been invited to participate, and that prostitution and other forms of sex work, pornography, and **S/M** are inherently violent to women, never to be accepted by feminists.

After the Stonewall Riots (New York) in 1969, a gay rights movement flourished, drawing on feminist ideas as well as "strands of sex research that did not treat homosexuality as pathological, and on an urban gay subculture that had been expanding since the end of World War II" (Lancaster and di Leonardo 1997, p. 3).

> With varying degrees of success and through struggles that continue today, gay and lesbian activists have publicly championed all that is positive, pleasurable and creative in same-sex desire while opposing the obvious sources of antigay oppression: police harassment, social stigma, religious bigotry, psychiatric persecution, and sodomy laws. In the process, these concrete struggles have revealed the less obvi-
> ous heteronormative premises deeply embedded in law, science, philosophy, official kinship, and vernacular culture.
>
> *(Lancaster and di Leonardo 1997, p. 3).*

This gay and lesbian activism, together with gay men's theorizing and feminist theorizing about sexuality as exemplified in Rubin's approach, mentioned earlier, led to the development of queer theory and queer studies (Alcoff 1988; Fuss 1991; Stein 1997), which take sexuality as the main category of analysis. Sedgwick's (1990) Axiom #2 states: "The study of sexuality is not coextensive with the study of gender; correspondingly, antihomophobic inquiry is not coextensive with feminist inquiry" (p. 27). Though not identical, feminism and antihomophobic work often overlap, as exemplified in Suzanne Pharr's (1988) analysis of homophobia as a weapon of sexism and her comment that "as long as the word lesbian can strike fear in any woman's heart, then work on behalf of women can be stopped; the only successful work against sexism must include work against homophobia" (p. 26). Note the unfortunate use of the term *homophobia,* meaning fear of homosexuals, rather than *heterosexism.* This latter term refers to the system of heterosexuality as a place of institutional privilege, parallel to systems of inequality based on race (racism) or gender (sexism).

Lisa Orlando (Reading 24) comments: "I don't think anyone knows what desire is, where it comes from, or why it takes the general and specific form it does." She hypothesizes that it involves "some kind of interaction between a more or less shapeless biological 'drive' and a combination of individual experiences and larger social forces." She notes that the very notion of sexual identity is specific to our culture and time in history.

Economic changes such as industrialization, the development of the factory system, and the spread of wage labor had a profound impact on family life. Gradually, families stopped producing the goods they needed and supported themselves through wage labor. Children, who had been an economic advantage to their families by contributing to household production, became a liability and an expense. The U.S. birthrate dropped dramatically during the twentieth century as a result. Further, developments like the contraceptive pill, alternative insemination, in vitro fertilization, and other reproductive technologies have made possible the separation of intercourse and procreation. Heterosexual women can be sexually active without becoming pregnant, and lesbians as well as heterosexual women can become pregnant without having intercourse. Historian John D'Emilio (1984) argues that these trends create conditions "that allow some men and women to organize a personal life around their erotic/emotional attraction to their own sex" (p. 104). They have "made possible the formation of urban communities of lesbians and gay men, and more recently, of a politics based on a sexual identity" (p. 104). On this analysis, sexual identity has a basis in macro-level circumstances rather than personal factors (D'Emilio and Freedman 1997), although cultural acceptance of lesbians and gay men does not always follow economic possibilities, in White communities or communities of color (Anzaldua 1987; Eng and Hom 1998; Smith 1998; Trujillo 1991). D'Emilio (1984) accepts that there have been same-sex partnerships for generations, as claimed by Adrienne Rich (1986a) and many other authors and researchers cited above. He complicates this claim, however, by differentiating homosexual *behavior* from homosexual *identity,* and argues that only under certain economic conditions are homosexual identity and community possible.

This links to the experience of Surina A. Khan (Reading 25), a Pakistani American woman who struggled to reconcile the various parts of her identity. Despite the fact that images of same-sex couples have been part of the history of South Asia for hundreds of years, she notes that most people from South Asia do not have words for homosexuality and regard it as a Western phenomenon. This apparent paradox is exactly what D'Emilio's distinction between behavior and identity helps to explain. Further, it may be useful to think of four distinctive categories: inclination, behavior, identity, and politics. One may have sexual inclinations but may decide not to act on them. One may engage in certain sexual behaviors but not adopt a bisexual or gay identity, for example. One may identify as a lesbian or transgender woman but not act on that identity in a political way.

The Erotic as Power

The issue of sexuality is part of our wider concern with security in the sense that sexuality can be a source of restriction and vulnerability—hence insecurity—for women. This is true for women whose sexual activities and identities fit patriarchal norms and expectations, and also for those who challenge or repudiate them. Like beauty—however it is defined, sexuality can be a source of power, affirmation, and self-definition for women. Many women are exploring their sexuality, claiming the right to sexual pleasure on their own terms, and challenging the limitations of conventional expressions of sexuality. Sexuality is a key element in personal relationships, of course, and we explore this in the next chapter, focused on relationships and families.

Black lesbian poet and activist Audre Lorde discusses the power of the erotic in the broadest way (Reading 27). She sees the erotic as "our most profoundly creative source." She notes that women have been "taught to separate the erotic . . . from most vital areas of our lives other than sex." By contrast, she writes: "When I speak of the erotic . . . I speak of it as an assertion of the life-force of women: of that creative energy empowered, the knowledge and use of which we are now reclaiming in our language, our history, our dancing, our loving, our work, our lives." Lorde sees the distortion and suppression of the erotic as one of the ways that women are oppressed, and concludes: "Recognizing the power of the erotic in our lives can give us the energy to pursue genuine change within our world."

Activism and Sexuality

Many informal networks, local groups, and national organizations support and advocate for lesbians, bisexual and transgender women, and gay men, especially in urban areas. Some are primarily social groupings; others are support groups that provide information, encouragement, and social connections. Still others focus on particular issues like women's health, HIV/AIDS, lesbian and gay parenting, community or police violence, religious bigotry, or the situation of gays in the military. Others run gay and lesbian journals, magazines, newsletters, bookstores, presses, churches, bars, coffeehouses, bands, sports teams, and theater companies; support political candidates for local, state, or national office; oppose city and state ordinances designed to limit lesbian and gay rights; or raise funds for lesbian and gay organizations. These various networks and organizations span a broad political spectrum. Some are overtly feminist; others are more closely aligned with queer politics. Examples include Queer Nation, and Lesbian Avengers—national networks with local participating groups, the Boston Bisexual Women's Network, the Detroit Women's Coffeehouse, Older Lesbians Organizing for Change (Houston, Texas), the National Gay and Lesbian Taskforce (Washington, D.C.), and the International Gay and Lesbian Human Rights Commission (San Francisco). In addition, lesbians and bisexual women are active in antiracist organizing, rape crisis centers, shelters for battered women, labor unions, antimilitarist organizations, and women's studies programs where they link their knowledge and experiences of oppression based on sexuality with other oppressions.

♦♦♦
Questions for Reflection

As you read and discuss the readings that follow, consider the questions raised by Shere Hite, listed on page 134.

♦♦♦
Taking Action

1. Write in your journal or have a candid conversation with a friend about your ideas about sexuality. How do you recognize the power of the erotic as Andre Lorde describes it?

2. Analyze the way women's magazines and men's magazines discuss women's sexuality.

3. Look critically at the way women's sexuality is portrayed in movies, on TV, and in ads.

4. However you define your sexuality, participate in campus or community events to commemorate National Coming-Out Day (usually in October) or Gay Pride (usually in June).

TWENTY-ONE

♦♦♦

Guadalupe the Sex Goddess

Sandra Cisneros

In high school I marveled at how white women strutted around the locker room, nude as pearls, as unashamed of their brilliant bodies as the Nike of Samothrace. Maybe they were hiding terrible secrets like bulimia or anorexia, but, to my naive eye then, I thought of them as women comfortable in their skin.

You could always tell us Latinas. We hid when we undressed, modestly facing a wall, or, in my case, dressing in a bathroom stall. We were the ones who still used bulky sanitary pads instead of tampons, thinking ourselves morally superior to our white classmates. *My mama said you can't use tampons till after you're married.* All Latina mamas said this, yet how come none of us thought to ask our mothers why they didn't use tampons *after* getting married?

Womanhood was full of mysteries. I was as ignorant about my own body as any female ancestor who hid behind a sheet with a hole in the center when husband or doctor called. Religion and our culture, our culture and religion, helped to create that blur, a vagueness about what went on "down there."

So ashamed was I about my own "down there" that until I was an adult I had no idea I had another orifice called the vagina; I thought my period would arrive via the urethra or perhaps through the walls of my skin.

No wonder, then, it was too terrible to think about a doctor — a man! — looking at you down there when you could never bring yourself to look yourself. ¡*Ay, nunca!* How could I acknowledge my sexuality, let alone enjoy sex, with so much guilt? In the guise of modesty my culture locked me in a double chastity belt of ignorance and *vergüenza,* shame.

I had never seen my mother nude. I had never taken a good look at myself either. Privacy for self-exploration belonged to the wealthy. In my home a private space was practically impossible; aside from the doors that opened to the street, the only room with a lock was the bathroom, and how could anyone who shared a bathroom with eight other people stay in there for more than a few minutes? Before college, no one in my family had a room of their own except me, a narrow closet just big enough for my twin bed and an oversized blond dresser we'd bought in the bargain basement of *el Sears*. The dresser was as long as a coffin and blocked the door from shutting completely. I had my own room, but I never had the luxury of shutting the door.

I didn't even see my own sex until a nurse at the Emma Goldman Clinic showed it to me — *Would you like to see your cervix? Your os is dilating. You must be ovulating. Here's a mirror; take a look.* When had anyone ever suggested I take a look or allowed me a speculum to take home and investigate myself at leisure!

I'd only been to one other birth control facility prior to the Emma Goldman Clinic, the university medical center in grad school. I was 21 in a strange town far from home for the first time. I was afraid and I was ashamed to seek out a gynecologist, but I was more afraid of becoming pregnant. Still, I agonized about going for weeks. Perhaps the anonymity and distance from my family allowed me finally to take control of my life. I remember wanting to be fearless like the white women around me, to be able to have sex when I wanted, but I was too afraid to explain to a would-be lover how I'd only had one other man in my life and we'd practiced withdrawal. Would he laugh at me? How could I look anyone in the face and explain why I couldn't go see a gynecologist?

One night, a classmate I liked too much took me home with him. I meant all along to say something about how I wasn't on anything, but I never quite found my voice, never the right moment to cry out — *Stop, this is dangerous to my brilliant career!* Too afraid to sound stupid, afraid to ask him to take responsibility too, I said nothing, and I let him take me like that with nothing protecting me from motherhood but luck. The days that followed were torture, but fortunately on Mother's Day my period arrived, and I celebrated my nonmaternity by making an appointment with the family planning center.

When I see pregnant teens, I can't help but think that could've been me. In high school I would've thrown myself into love the way some warriors throw themselves into fighting. I was ready to sacrifice everything in the name of love, to do anything, even risk my own life, but thankfully there were no takers. I was enrolled at an all-girls' school. I think if I had met a boy who would have me, I would've had sex in a minute, convinced this was love. I have always had enough imagination to fall in love all by myself, then and now.

I tell you this story because I am overwhelmed by the silence regarding Latinas and our bodies. If I, as a graduate student, was shy about talking to anyone about my body and sex, imagine how difficult it must be for a young girl in middle school or high school living in a home with no lock on the bedroom door, perhaps with no door, or maybe with no bedroom, no information other than misinformation from the girlfriends and the boyfriend. So much guilt, so much silence, and such a yearning to be loved; no wonder young women find themselves having sex while they are still children, having sex without sexual protection, too ashamed to confide their feelings and fears to anyone.

What a culture of denial. Don't get pregnant! But no one tells you how not to. This is why I was angry for so many years every time I saw a *la Virgen de Guadalupe,* my culture's role model for brown women like me. She was damn dangerous, an ideal so lofty and unrealistic it was laughable. Did boys have to aspire to be Jesus? I never saw any evidence of it. They were fornicating like rabbits while the Church ignored them and pointed us women toward our destiny — marriage and motherhood. The other alternative was *puta*hood.

In my neighborhood I knew only real women, neither saints nor whores, naive and vulnerable *huerquitas* like me who wanted desperately to fall in love, with the heart and soul. And yes, with the *panocha* too.

As far as I could see, *la Lupe* was nothing but a Goody Two-shoes meant to doom me to a life of unhappiness. Thanks, but no thanks. Motherhood and/or marriage were anathema to my career. But being a bad girl, that was something I could use as a writer, a Molotov cocktail to toss at my papa and *el Papa,* who had their own plans for me.

Discovering sex was like discovering writing. It was powerful in a way I couldn't explain. Like writing, you had to go beyond the guilt and shame to get to anything good. Like writing, it could take you to deep and mysterious subterranean levels. With each new depth I found out things about myself I didn't know I knew. And, like writing, for a slip of a moment it could be spiritual, the cosmos pivoting on a pin, could empty and fill you all at once like a Ganges, a Piazzolla tango, a tulip bending in the wind. I was no one, I was nothing, and I was everything in the universe little and large—twig, cloud, sky. How had this incredible energy been denied me!

When I look at *la Virgen de Guadalupe* now, she is not the Lupe of my childhood, no longer the one in my grandparents' house in Tepeyac, nor is she the one of the Roman Catholic Church, the one I bolted the door against in my teens and twenties. Like every woman who matters to me, I have had to search for her in the rubble of history. And I have found her. She is Guadalupe the sex goddess, a goddess who makes me feel good about my sexual power, my sexual energy, who reminds me that I must, as Clarissa Pinkola Estés so aptly put it, "[speak] from the vulva . . . speak the most basic, honest truth," and write from my *panocha.*

In my research of Guadalupe's pre-Columbian antecedents, the she before the Church desexed her, I found Tonantzin, and inside Tonantzin a pantheon of other mother goddesses. I discovered Tlazolteotl, the goddess of fertility and sex, also referred to as Totzin. Our Beginnings, or Tzinteotl, goddess of the rump. *Putas,* nymphos, and other loose women were known as "women of the sex goddess." Tlazolteotl was the patron of sexual passion, and though she had the power to stir you to sin, she could also for-

give you and cleanse you of your sexual transgressions via her priests who heard confession. In this aspect of confessor Tlazolteotl was known as Tlael-cuani, the filth eater. Maybe you've seen her; she's the one whose image is sold in the tourist markets even now, a statue of a woman squatting in childbirth, her face grimacing in pain. Tlazolteotl, then, is a duality of maternity *and* sexuality. In other words, she is a sexy mama.

To me, *la Virgen de Guadalupe* is also Coatlicue, the creative/destructive goddess. When I think of the Coatlicue statue in the National Museum of Anthropology in Mexico City, so terrible it was unearthed and then reburied because it was too frightening to look at, I think of a woman enraged, a woman as tempest, a woman *bien berrinchuda,* and I like that. *La Lupe* as *cabrona.* Not silent and passive, but silently gathering force.

Most days, I too feel like the creative/destructive goddess Coatlicue, especially the days I'm writing, capable of fabricating pretty tales with pretty words, as well as doing demolition work with a volley of *palabrotas* if I want to. I am the Coatlicue-Lupe whose square column of a body I see in so many Indian women, in my mother, and in myself each time I check out my thick-waisted, flat-assed torso in the mirror.

Coatlicue, Tlazolteotl, Tonantzin, *la Virgen de Guadalupe.* They are each telescoped one into the other, into who I am. And this is where *la Lupe* intrigues me—not the Lupe of 1531 who appeared to Juan Diego, but the one of the 1990s who has shaped who we are as Chicanas/*mexicanas* today, the one inside each Chicana and *mexicana.* Perhaps it's the Tlazolteotl-Lupe in me whose *malcriada* spirit inspires me to leap into the swimming pool naked or dance on a table with a skirt on my head. Maybe it's my Coatlicue-Lupe attitude that makes it possible for my mother to tell me, "No wonder men can't stand you." Who knows? What I do know is this: I am obsessed with becoming a woman comfortable in her skin.

I can't attribute my religious conversion to a flash of lightning on the road to Laredo or anything like that. Instead, there have been several lessons learned subtly over a period of time. A grave depression and near suicide in my thirty-third year and its subsequent retrospection. Vietnamese Buddhist monk

Thich Nhat Hanh's writing that has brought out the Buddha-Lupe in me. My weekly peace vigil for my friend Jasna in Sarajevo. The writings of Gloria Anzaldúa. A crucial trip back to Tepeyac in 1985 with Cherríe Moraga and Norma Alarcón. Drives across Texas, talking with other Chicanas. And research for stories that would force me back inside the Church from where I'd fled.

My *Virgin de Guadalupe* is not the mother of God. She is God. She is a face for a god without a face, an *indigena* for a god without ethnicity, a female deity for a god who is genderless, but I also understand that for her to approach me, for me to finally open the door and accept her, she had to be a woman like me.

Once watching a porn film, I saw a sight that terrified me. It was the film star's *panocha*—a tidy, elliptical opening, pink and shiny like a rabbit's ear.

To make matters worse, it was shaved and looked especially childlike and unsexual. I think what startled me most was the realization that my own sex has no resemblance to this woman's. My sex, dark as an orchid, rubbery and blue-purple as *pulpo,* an octopus, does not look nice and tidy, but otherworldly. I do not have little rosette nipples. My nipples are big and brown like the Mexican coins of my childhood.

When I see *la Virgen de Guadalupe* I want to lift her dress as I did my dolls, and look to see if she comes with *chones* and does her *panocha* look like mine, and does she have dark nipples too? Yes, I am certain she does. She is not neuter like Barbie. She gave birth. She has a womb. *Blessed art thou and blessed is the fruit of thy womb. . . .* Blessed art thou, Lupe, and, therefore, blessed am I.

TWENTY-TWO

Smell

Eve Ensler

The script for The Vagina Monologues *is based on dozens of interviews in which Eve Ensler asked women what they thought about their vaginas. This short extract includes some of the responses to the question:*

"What does a vagina smell like?"
Earth.
Wet garbage.
God.
Water.
A brand-new morning.
Depth.
Sweet ginger.
Sweat.
Depends.
Musk.
Me.
No smell, I've been told.
Pineapple.
Chalice essence.
Paloma Picasso.

Earthy meat and musk.
Cinnamon and cloves.
Roses.
Spicy musky jasmine forest, deep, deep forest.
Damp moss.
Yummy candy.
The South Pacific.
Somewhere between fish and lilacs.
Peaches.
The woods.
Ripe fruit.
Strawberry-kiwi tea.
Fish.
Heaven.
Vinegar and water.
Light, sweet liquor.
Cheese.
Ocean.
Sexy.
A sponge.
The beginning.

TWENTY-THREE

Radical Heterosexuality

Naomi Wolf

All over the country, millions of feminists have a secret indulgence. By day they fight gender injustice; by night they sleep with men. Is this a dual life? A core contradiction? Is sleeping with a man "sleeping with the enemy"? And is razor burn from kissing inherently oppressive?

It's time to say you *can* hate sexism and love men. As the feminist movement grows more mature and our understanding of our enemies more nuanced, three terms assumed to be in contradiction— radical feminist heterosexuality—can and must be brought together.

Rules of the Relationship

But how? Andrea Dworkin and Catharine MacKinnon have pointed out that sexism limits women to such a degree that it's questionable whether the decision to live with a man can ever truly be free. If you want to use their sound, if depressing, reasoning to a brighter end, turn the thesis around: radical heterosexuality demands substituting choice for dependency.

Radical heterosexuality requires that the woman be able to support herself. This is not to belittle women who must depend financially on men; it is to recognize that when our daughters are raised with the skills that would let them leave abusers, they need not call financial dependence love.

Radical heterosexuality needs alternative institutions. As the child of a good lifetime union, I believe in them. But when I think of pledging my heart and body to a man—even the best and kindest man—within the existing institution of marriage, I feel faint. The more you learn about its legal structure, the less likely you are to call the caterers.

In the nineteenth century, when a judge ruled that a husband could not imprison and rape his wife, the London *Times* bemoaned, "One fine morning last month, marriage in England was suddenly abolished." The phrase "rule of thumb" descends

from English common law that said a man could legally beat his wife with a switch "no thicker than his thumb."

If these nightmarish echoes were confined to history, I might feel more nuptial; but look at our own time. Do I want the blessing of an institution that doesn't provide adequate protection from marital rape? That gives a woman less protection from assault by her husband than by a stranger? That assigns men 70 percent of contested child custodies?

Of course I do not fear any such brutality from the man I want to marry (no bride does). But marriage means that his respectful treatment of me and our children becomes, despite our intentions, a kindness rather than a legally grounded right.

We need a heterosexual version of the marriages that gay and lesbian activists are seeking: a commitment untainted by centuries of inequality; a ritual that invites the community to rejoice in the making of a new freely chosen family.

The radical heterosexual man must yield the automatic benefits conferred by gender. I had a lover once who did not want to give up playing sports in a club that had a separate door for women. It must be tempting to imagine you can have both—great squash courts *and* the bed of a liberated woman— but in the mess hall of gender relations, there is *no such thing as a free lunch.*

Radical heterosexual women too must give up gender benefits (such as they are). I know scores of women—independent, autonomous—who avoid assuming any of the risk for a romantic or sexual approach.

I have watched myself stand complacently by while my partner wrestles with a stuck window, an intractable computer printer, maps, or locks. Sisters, I am not proud of this, and I'm working on it. But people are lazy—or at least I am—and it's easy to rationalize that the person with the penis is the one who should get out of a warm bed to fix the snow on the TV screen. After all, it's the very least owed to me *personally* in compensation for centuries of virtual enslavement.

Radical heterosexuals must try to stay conscious — at all times, I'm afraid — of their gender imprinting, and how it plays out in their erotic melodramas. My own psyche is a flagrant *son et lumière* of political incorrectness. Three of my boyfriends had motorcycles; I am easy pickings for the silent and dysfunctional. My roving eye is so taken by the oil-stained persona of the labor organizer that myopic intellectuals have gained access to my favors merely by sporting a Trotsky button.

We feminists are hard on each other for admitting to weakness. Gloria Steinem caught flak from her left-wing sisters for acknowledging in *Revolution from Within* that she was drawn to a man because he could do the things with money and power that we are taught men must do. And some were appalled when Simone de Beauvoir's letters revealed how she coddled Sartre.

But the antifeminist erotic template is *in* us. We would not be citizens of this culture if swooning damsels and abandoned vixens had not been beamed at us from our first solid food to our first vote. We can't fight it until we admit to it. And we can't identify it until we drag it, its taffeta billowing and its bosom heaving, into the light of day.

I have done embarrassing, reactionary, abject deeds out of love and sexual passion. So, no doubt, has Norman Schwarzkopf. Only when we reveal our conditioning can we tell how much of our self-abasement is neurotic femininity, and how much is the flawed but impressive human apparatus of love.

In the Bedroom

Those are the conditions for the radical heterosexual couple. What might this new creation look like in bed? It will look like something we have no words or images for — the eroticization of consent, the equal primacy of female and male desire.

We will need to tell some secrets — to map our desire for the male body and admit to our fascination with the rhythms and forces of male arousal, its uncanny counterintuitive spell.

We will also need to face our creature qualities. Animality has for so long been used against us —

bitch, fox, *Penthouse* pet — that we struggle for the merit badges of higher rationality, ambivalent about our animal nature.

The truth is that heterosexual women believe that men, on some level, are animals; as they believe that we are animals. But what does "animal" mean?

Racism and sexism have long used animal metaphors to distance and degrade the Other. Let us redefine "animal" to make room for that otherness between the genders, an otherness fierce and worthy of respect. Let us define animal as an inchoate kinship, a comradeship, that finds a language beyond our species.

I want the love of two unlikes: the look of astonishment a woman has at the sight of a male back bending. These manifestations of difference confirm in heterosexuals the beauty that similarity confirms in the lesbian or gay imagination. Difference and animality do not have to mean hierarchy.

Men We Love

What must the men be like? Obviously, they're not going to be just anyone. *Esquire* runs infantile disquisitions on "Women We Love" (suggesting, Lucky Girls!). Well, I think that the men who are loved by feminists are lucky. Here's how they qualify to join this fortunate club.

Men We Love understand that, no matter how similar our backgrounds, we are engaged in a cross-cultural (if not practically biracial) relationship. They know that we know much about their world and they but little of ours. They accept what white people must accept in relationships with people of other ethnicities: to know that they do not know.

Men We Love don't hold a baby as if it is a still-squirming, unidentifiable catch from the sea.

Men We Love don't tell women what to feel about sexism. (There's a postcard that shows a dashing young fellow, drawn Love-comix-style, saying to a woman, "Let me explicate to you the nature of your oppression.") They do not presume that there is a line in the sand called "enlightened male," and that all they need is a paperback copy of Djuna Barnes and good digital technique. They understand that unlearning gender oppressiveness means untying the very core of how we become female and malc. They know this pursuit takes a lifetime at the minimum.

Sadly, men in our lives sometimes come through on personal feminism but balk at it intellectually. A year ago, I had a bruising debate with my father and brother about the patriarchal nature of traditional religious and literary canons. I almost seized them by their collars, howling "Read Mary Daly! Read Toni Morrison! Take Feminism 101. *No, I can't* explain it to you between the entrée and dessert!"

By spring, my dad, bless his heart, had asked for a bibliography, and last week my brother sent me *Standing Again at Sinai,* a Jewish-feminist classic. Men We Love are willing, sooner or later, to read the Books We Love.

Men We Love accept that successful training in manhood makes them blind to phenomena that are fact to women. Recently, I walked down a New York City avenue with a woman friend, X, and a man friend, Y. I pointed out to Y the leers, hisses, and invitations to sit on faces. Each woman saw clearly what the other woman saw, but Y was baffled. Sexual harassers have superb timing. A passerby makes kissy-noises with his tongue while Y is scrutinizing the menu of the nearest bistro. "There, there! Look! Listen!" we cried. "What? Where? Who?" wailed poor Y, valiantly, uselessly spinning.

What if, hard as they try to see, they cannot hear? Once I was at lunch with a renowned male crusader for the First Amendment. Another Alpha male was present, and the venue was the Supreme Court lunchroom — two power factors that automatically press the "mute" button on the male ability to detect a female voice on the audioscope. The two men began to rev their motors; soon they were off and racing in a policy-wonk grand prix. I tried, once or twice, to ask questions. But the free-speech champions couldn't hear me over the testosterone roar.

Men We Love undertake half the care and cost of contraception. They realize that it's not fair to wallow in the fun without sharing the responsibility. When stocking up for long weekends, they brave the amused glances when they ask, "Do you have this in unscented?"

Men We Love know that just because we can be irrational doesn't mean we're insane. When we burst into premenstrual tears — having just realized the cosmic fragility of creation — they comfort us. Not until we feel better do they dare remind us gently that we had this same revelation exactly 28 days ago.

Men We Love must make a leap of imagination to believe in the female experience. They do not call women nags or paranoid when we embark on the arduous, often boring, nonnegotiable daily chore of drawing attention to sexism. They treat it like adults taking driving lessons: if irked in the short term at being treated like babies, they're grateful in the long term that someone is willing to teach them patiently how to move through the world without harming the pedestrians. Men We Love don't drive without their gender glasses on.

A Place for Them

It's not simple gender that pits Us against Them. In the fight against sexism, it's those who are for us versus those who are against us — of either gender.

When I was 16, my boyfriend came with me to hear Andrea Dworkin speak. While hearing great feminist oratory in a sea of furious women changed my life, it nearly ended my boyfriend's: he barely escaped being drawn and quartered.

It is time to direct our anger more acutely at the Men We Hate — like George Bush — and give the Men We Love something useful to do. Not to take over meetings, or to set agendas; not to whine, "Why can't feminists teach us how to be free?" but to add their bodies, their hearts, and their numbers, to support us.

I meet many young men who are brought to feminism by love for a woman who has been raped, or by watching their single mothers struggle against great odds, or by simple common sense. Their most frequent question is "What can I do to help?"

Imagine a rear battalion of committed "Men Against Violence Against Women" (or Men for Choice, or what have you) — of all races, ages, and classes. Wouldn't that be a fine sight to fix in the eyes of a five-year-old boy?

Finally, the place to make room for radical feminist heterosexuality is within our heads. If the movement that I dearly love has a flaw, it is a tendency toward orthodoxies about other women's pleasures and needs. This impulse is historically understandable: in the past, we needed to define ourselves against men if we were to define ourselves at all. But today, the most revolutionary choice we can make is to affirm other women's choices, whether lesbian or straight, bisexual or celibate.

NOW President Patricia Ireland speaks for me even though our sexual lives are not identical. Simone de Beauvoir speaks for me even though our sexual lives are not identical. Audre Lorde speaks for me even though our sexual lives are not identical. Is it the chromosomes of your lovers that establish you as a feminist? Or is it the life you make out of the love you make?

◆◆◆

Loving Whom We Choose

Lisa Orlando

The struggles of "sexual minorities" within the lesbian and gay and feminist movements have revived interest in issues of sexual freedom. Within our movements such interests seemed, over the years since Stonewall, to have become increasingly confined to our radical margins. Now, however, S/M, man–boy love, butch and femme role-playing, sex workers, cross-dressing, and other sexual behavior are widely discussed in our publications and community meetings, with the result that a renaissance of our early "sex radicalism" seems to be occurring. However, in the midst of all this talk of sex, one sexual practice—bisexuality—is rarely discussed. If we really want a sexually liberating renaissance, we must discuss and rethink bisexuality in the same way that we have other forms of gay "deviance."

In the early days of our movement, many gay liberationists agreed that both homosexual and heterosexual potentials existed in all human beings. They believed that heterosexual culture so vigorously oppresses those who insist on expressing homosexual desire because, as Martha Shelley, one of the first post-Stonewall theorists, wrote, we are heterosexuals' "own worst fears made flesh."* Even later separatist lesbian-feminists like the Furies collective affirmed the inherent bisexuality of human nature. If the feminist and gay liberation movements succeeded, they thought, the gay and straight dichotomy would disappear. Although, as Dennis Altman pointed out, many people would still not *practice* bisexuality, we would nevertheless achieve the "end of the homosexual" as a meaningful category.

Belief in bisexuality as a utopian potential has not always coincided, as it has for Altman, with support for and acceptance of bisexuals. Nevertheless, bisexuals who were active in the earliest days of the gay liberation movement seem to have had little trouble being accepted as gay. But times change. Few gay activists now claim to be striving for a bisexual paradise or to regard bisexuality as a repressed human potential. And while many nonbisexual gays have, as individuals, supported us and encouraged our attempts to organize, the lesbian and gay community abounds with negative images of bisexuals as fence-sitters, traitors, cop-outs, closet cases, people whose primary goal in life is to retain "heterosexual privilege," power-hungry seducers who use and discard their same-sex lovers like so many Kleenex.

These stereotypes result from the ambiguous position of bisexuals, poised as we are between what currently appear as two mutually exclusive sexual cultures, one with the power to exercise violent repression against the other. Others grow out of the popular assumption, contrary to that of early gay liberation, that homosexual and heterosexual *desires* exclude each other. Still others result from lesbian-feminism, which argues that lesbianism is a political choice having little to do with sexual desire *per se.*

---

*Quoted in Dennis Altman, *Homosexual: Oppression and Liberation,* Avon Books, 1971, p. 69.

From this point of view, a bisexual woman "still de-fine[s] herself in terms of male needs"* rather than, as she herself might argue, in terms of her own de-sires. Since lesbian-feminism equates meeting male needs with supporting male supremacy, it considers bisexual women traitors by definition.

Other factors may have played a role in shift-ing attitudes toward bisexuals in the lesbian and gay community: the growth of lesbian and gay "lifestyles" and ghettos, the boundaries produced by constructing gay people as a "minority," the de-velopment of sexual identity as a political concept; and even, as Cindy Patton has argued, the brief hey-day of media-created "bisexual chic" was a factor that trivialized bisexuality as just another fashion.[†]

But these stereotypes also resonate with some people's personal experience and with the gay sub-culture lore developed out of collective experience. Most stereotypes reflect some small aspects of real-ity which they then serve to reinforce. Some bisex-uals do act in stereotypical ways, often because we have internalized our social image. And because nonbisexuals view this behavior through the lens of the stereotype, they perceive it as evidence of the truth of the stereotype rather than as an individual action. As more bisexuals refuse to hide our sexu-ality, as we organize within the gay community, we can better challenge these negative images and demonstrate that they are, like other stereotypes, essentially false. Other gay people will be forced to recognize that as a group bisexuals are no more "promiscuous" or incapable of commitment than anyone else (like many stereotypes of bisexuals, this also runs rampant in the straight world). "Hetero-sexual privilege" doesn't prevent us from being queerbashed on our way home from the bars or hav-ing our children taken away when we come out. We look just like other queers; i.e., we range from bla-tant to indistinguishable from straights. And many of us not only involve ourselves in lesbian and gay

struggles but also identify ourselves primarily with the gay community.

As we challenge people on their more easily disproved beliefs, they may also begin to question whether they perceive their personal experiences with bisexuals in a distorted way. For example, I think we might better explain at least some of the stories about bisexuals who leave their same-sex lovers for heterosexual relationships in the same ways we explain being left, period, rather than as some special form of desertion and betrayal. And if gay people examine the problems we have had with bisexual lovers whose primary relationships are het-erosexual, they resemble quite closely the problems we have had in similar "secondary" relationships with homosexuals.

Since most bisexuals are acutely aware of the dif-ferences between heterosexual and homosexual rela-tionships, some probably do "settle" for heterosexual relationships, at whatever emotional cost, and for all the reasons one might imagine. I find it as difficult to condemn them as to condemn homosexuals who seek therapy to "become" heterosexual — oppres-sion is ugly and we all want out, whether we seek individual or collective solutions. Other gay people rarely notice, however, that most bisexuals continue to have homosexual relationships *despite* the weight of heterosexist oppression. This can only testify to the fact that heterosexual relationships generate their own problems — and that the power of desire often overcomes that of oppression. Many homo-sexuals resent the fact that the thoughtless pleasures of a heterosexual relationship always exist as an op-tion for bisexuals and fear that, as homophobia in-tensifies, more bisexuals will take that option. But "option" seems a strange expression to describe re-pressing an entire aspect of one's sexuality, and the closet exists as an "option" for *all* queers.

We all suffer oppression when we choose to ex-press homosexual desire. We may suffer even more when we force ourselves to repress it. And although the experiences differ, we suffer whether, as with bisexuals, our desire might take other paths or whether, as with homosexuals, the only path is total repression. In each of these cases, our suffering re-sults from the power of a homophobic society. We *all* share an interest in assuring that bisexuals make their choices, conscious or not, on the basis of desire

---

*Loretta Ulmschneider for the Furies, "Bisexuality," in *Lesbianism in the Women's Movement*, ed. Nancy Myron and Charlotte Bunch, Diana Press, 1975, p. 86.

[†]Quoted in Arthur Kroeber, "Bisexuality: Towards a New Understanding of Men, Women, and Their Feelings," *Boston Globe*, October 10, 1983, p. 53.

rather than oppression. And gay liberation offers the only guarantee that this will happen.

Those who view bisexuals as untrustworthy because of our "options" at least acknowledge that we exist. Others insist that we are the closet cases temporarily stuck in a transitional stage in the coming-out process. I hope that as bisexuals begin to speak for ourselves, we will weaken this notion since many of us have identified as such for years—and lifetimes. I wonder, however, if the power of this belief might not resist such evidence. While I would argue that gay identity is essentially political—something we construct to promote solidarity and oppose our oppression—for many people, gay identity seems to imply that we all naturally possess a *sexual* identity and that this identity just as naturally fits into one of two categories.

Why do so many people who oppose the other forms of madness created and perpetuated by the psychiatric and medical establishment so wholeheartedly embrace the notion of a strict division between heterosexuality and homosexuality, a notion which originated alongside that of homosexuality as disease? As much gay historical research has shown, "homosexuality" as we understand it in the West didn't exist until, with the advent of capitalism, religious ideology began to lose ground and medical ideology took its place. What Christianity saw as a sinful potential in everyone, psychiatry reconceptualized as a sickness which permeated one's being, displacing heterosexual desire. But if we reject the psychiatric definition of homosexuality, why do we cling to the notion of homosexual desire as exclusive? That we do testifies, I think, to the incredible power of our need to fit things into neat dichotomies.

Human beings tend to use dual classification when we think about our world—pairs such as up and down and hot and cold as well as pairs such as human and animal and man and woman, where more value is placed on one term—possibly because such oppositions structure the human mind itself. Many anthropologists believe that when some aspect of a culture gains particular prominence or importance people feel an even stronger need to fit it into such a scheme and will become uneasy in the face of ambiguities. The "disorder" resulting from central features of our lives which we cannot fit into dichotomies with sharp boundaries disturbs us deeply. I suspect that the homosexual and hetero-

sexual dichotomy gained acceptance as both sexuality and "personal identity" became central to our culture. Whether or not this is true, most of us feel threatened when the categories we believe in are challenged, especially if they shape our sense of who we are. Not only do bisexuals contradict a primary set of cultural categories—our culture calls us "decadent" because we refuse to play by the rules, thereby undermining the social "order"—but we challenge many people's personal sense of what constitutes sexual identity. Whether we threaten by introducing a third category or by undermining the notion of categories altogether, we cause enough discomfort that many people deny our existence.

If we wish to develop liberating politics, we must ask, as early gay liberation did, whether our need to classify simultaneously violates the truths of at least some people's desires and plays into heterosexism. Obviously we will never stop classifying; we couldn't speak or even think if we did. But we must be wary of both our obsession with order, with getting rid of "dirt," and our tendency to see the categories we use as natural or simply given rather than as the social and political constructions they are. This is particularly true with those categories which bear the most political weight. But the historically specific categories we adopt in order to think about our world, including our selves, do more than merely describe, or violate the truths of, our desires. They also shape and even create them. We must question as well the whole notion of an essential sexual truth which somehow resides in each of us.

I don't think anyone knows what desire is, where it comes from, or why it takes the general and specific forms it does. I'm inclined to believe that some kind of interaction between a more or less shapeless biological "drive" and a combination of individual experiences and larger social forces creates each of our unique sexualities. But the way we as "modern" people experience them, the mere fact that we experience something we call "sexual identity," is peculiar to our particular culture and historical period. Much current historical research argues that all our talk about "identity crisis" and "finding ourselves," even our very notion of sexuality, would mean nothing to people from another time and place. If both the way we view our selves and the categories into which we fit them are modern social constructions, not timeless truths, I can't view my own sense, however subjectively powerful, that I am "really" *anything* with less than suspicion. The human mind too easily interprets — and reinterprets — anything and everything to fit its current beliefs.

But we still have no better way of describing our experience than by saying that we have discovered what we "really" are. In using the term "really," we acknowledge the experience many people have either of having "always known" or of coming to a place where they finally feel at home. I, too, believe, seventeen years after "discovering" my bisexuality and ten years after relinquishing my lesbian identity, that I am "really" bisexual.

Bisexuality: A Stage

Many exclusive homosexuals *do* experience bisexuality as a stage (as indeed do some heterosexuals). This obviously bolsters the belief that "real" bisexuality doesn't exist. People who have had this experience tend to look back at their old selves with condescension and embarrassment. I suspect that the word "bisexual" triggers unpleasant feelings in many of them which they project on anyone claiming a bisexual identity.

While most self-defined homosexuals and heterosexuals may be correct in seeing their own bisexuality as just a stage, inevitably some people who see themselves as exclusively homosexual or heterosexual will have repressed rather than "grown out of" bisexuality. As some lesbians in the fifties who were neither butch nor femme felt forced to choose, so do some bisexuals. Both sides often exert so much pressure to "make up your mind" and direct so much contempt at people who are unwilling to do so — and most of us are so unaware of bisexuality as a legitimate possibility — that a simple need for acceptance and community often forces people (particularly, and often most painfully, young people) to repress one aspect of their desire. Just as closet queers (also perhaps bisexual) often lead the pack in homophobic attacks, so may closet bisexuals be the most intensely biphobic. I think this is particularly true among women who came out via lesbian-feminism.

Many women, in fact, who now identify as bisexual, experienced *lesbianism* as a stage. I identified as bisexual before the women's movement, but as happened with many women, consciousness-raising

and traumatic experiences fueled an acute anger and disgust with men that led me to lesbianism. Some women became lesbians because "feminism is the theory and lesbianism is the practice."* Or they may simply have succumbed to peer pressure (even some heterosexual women "became" lesbians for these reasons). Over the years, many of us, often because of working in political coalitions, have reconnected with the world outside the "women's community" and have discovered our heterosexual desires. We are now attacked for having "gone back into the closet," as traitors, and as self-deceiving fools.

The theoretical and emotional need to keep alive both the notion that all true feminists are lesbians and the belief that no rapprochement with men is possible fuels lesbian-feminist hatred of bisexuals. Many lesbians who oppose other forms of separatism, who work with men politically and have male friends, still see *sexual* separatism as an eternal given. But as political separatism falls into disrepute, sexual separatism also loses its rationale. As many lesbians recognize that class, race, age, etc. may be as powerful sources of oppression as gender and sexual orientation, they also recognize the futility of separatism as more than a stage. Few people — and fewer sexual radicals — really want a movement which forbids us to relate sexually to people whose race, sex, class, physical abilities, age, looks, etc. aren't exactly the same as ours. And many of us also refuse to have our desires and sexual practices dictated by anyone else's idea of "political correctness."

Many bisexuals, like many homosexuals, have never identified with gay politics. But some of us, including many women who have rejected lesbian-feminism, *have* committed ourselves to gay liberation. We see gay identity and solidarity as crucial, since heterosexism oppresses all gay people, whether homosexual or bisexual, and we can only struggle against it as a self-conscious group. The ambiguous nature of our sexuality needn't imply any ambiguity in our politics. By choosing gay identity we acknowledge that sexuality dominates our identity in

---

*The slogan originated with a heterosexual feminist, Ti-Grace Atkinson, who first used it in a speech before the New York chapter of the Daughters of Bilitis, an early homophile organization, in late June 1970. Toby Marotta, *The Politics of Homosexuality,* Houghton Mifflin, 1981, p. 258.

a heterosexist world while recognizing that in a nonoppressive society no one would care who we wanted or who our sexual partners were, and sexuality would no longer be so central to our sense of who we are.

Unfortunately, political movements and embattled subcultures have particular difficulty acknowledging ambiguities of any kind. Add to this the current plethora of "ex-lesbians" and we can see what haunts the political unconscious of the lesbian and gay movement. Clearly, the rest of the gay community ignores or ostracizes us at its peril; embattled as we all are, we need all the forces we can muster. Bisexuals often encounter unusual opportunities to confront and contradict homophobia and, if we have been encouraged to develop a gay consciousness, we will act powerfully and efficiently in such situations.

But if it rejects us, the gay movement loses more than numbers and strategic force. It also loses another opportunity, similar to that offered by other "sexual minorities," to re-examine its commitment to sexual freedom rather than to mere interest-group politics. What would it mean for the gay movement to acknowledge that some people experience their sexuality as a lifelong constant, others as a series of stages, some as a choice, and many as a constant flux? It would certainly mean a drastic reworking of the standard categories which have grounded gay politics over the last decade. And it might mean a renewed commitment to the revolutionary impulse of gay liberation, which, believing that homosexual desire is a potential in everyone, insisted that "gay" is a potentially universal class, since sexual freedom for all people is the ultimate goal of our struggle.

T W E N T Y - F I V E

◆◆◆

The All-American Queer Pakistani Girl

Surina A. Khan

I don't know if my grandmother is dead or alive. I can't remember the last time I saw her — it must have been at least ten years ago, when I was in Pakistan for a visit. She was my only living grandparent, and her health was beginning to fail. Every once in a while, I think she's probably dead and no one bothered to tell me.

I'm completely out of touch with my Pakistani life. I can hardly speak Urdu, my first language; I certainly can't read or write it. I have no idea how many cousins I have. I know my father comes from a large family — eleven brothers and sisters — but I don't know all their names. I've never read the Koran, and I don't have faith in Islam.

As a kid, I remember being constantly reminded that I was different — by my accent, my brown skin color, my mother's traditional clothing, and the smell of the food we ate. And so I consciously Americanized myself. I spent my early childhood perfecting my American accent, my adolescence affirming my

American identity to others, and my late teens rejecting my Pakistani heritage. Now, at the age of twenty-seven, I'm feeling the void I created for myself.

Sometimes I think of what my life would be like if my parents hadn't moved to Connecticut in 1973, when I was five. Most of my family has since moved back to Pakistan, and up until seven years ago, when I came out, I went back somewhat regularly. But I never liked going back. It made me feel stifled, constrained. People were always talking about getting married. First it was, "You're almost old enough to start thinking about finding a nice husband," then, "When are you getting married?" Now I imagine they'd say, with disappointment, "You'll be an old maid."

My family is more liberal than most of Pakistani society. By American standards that translates into conservative (my mother raised money for George Bush). But I was brought up in a family that valued education, independence, integrity, and love. I never had to worry about getting pressured into an arranged marriage, even though several of my first cousins were—sometimes to each other. Once I went to a wedding in which the bride and groom saw each other for the first time when someone passed them a mirror after their wedding ceremony and they both looked into it at once. That's when I started thinking my family was "modern."

Unfortunately they live in a fundamentalist culture that won't tolerate me. I can't even bring myself to visit Pakistan. The last time I went back was seven years ago, for my father's funeral, and sometimes I wonder if the next time will be for my mother's funeral. She asks me to come visit every time I talk to her. I used to tell her I was too busy, that I couldn't get away. But three years ago I finally answered her truthfully. I told her that I didn't like the idea of traveling to a country that lashed lesbians one hundred times in public. More important, I didn't feel comfortable visiting when she and I had not talked about anything important in my life since I had come out to her.

Pakistan has always been my parents' answer to everything. When they found out my sisters were smoking pot in the late 1970s, they shipped all of us back. "You need to get in touch with the Pakistani culture," my mother would say. When my oldest sister got hooked on transcendental meditation and started walking around the house in a trance, my father packed her up and put her on a plane back to the homeland. She's been there ever since. Being the youngest of six, I wised up quickly. I waited to drop my bomb until after I had moved out of the house and was financially independent. If I had come out while I was still living in my parents' home, you can bet I'd have been on the next flight to Islamabad.

When I came out to my mother, she suggested I go back to Pakistan for a few months. "Just get away from it all," she begged. "You need some time. Clear your head." But I knew better. And when I insisted that I was queer and was going to move to Washington, D.C., to live with my girlfriend, Robin (now my ex-girlfriend, much to my mother's delight), she tried another scare tactic: "You and your lover better watch out. There's a large Pakistani community in D.C., and they'll find out about you. They'll break your legs, mutilate your face." That pretty much did it for me. My mother had just validated all my fears associated with Pakistan. I cut all ties with the community, including my family. *Pakistan* became synonymous with *homophobia*.

My mother disowned me when I didn't heed her advice. But a year later, when Robin and I broke up, my mother came back into my life. It was partly motivated by wishful thinking on her part. I do give her credit, though, not only for nurturing the strength in me to live by my convictions with integrity and honesty but also for eventually trying to understand me. I'll never forget the day I took her to see a lawyer friend of mine. She was on the verge of settling a lawsuit started by my father before he died and was unhappy with her lawyer. I took her to see Maggie Cassella, a lawyer/comedian based in Hartford, Connecticut, where I was again living. "I presume this woman's a lesbian," my mother said in the car on the way to Maggie's office. "Yes, she is," I replied, thinking, *Oh, no, here it comes again.* But my mother took me by surprise. "Well, the men aren't helping me; I might as well go to the dykes." I didn't think she even knew the word *dyke.* Now, *that* was a moment.

Her changing attitude about my lesbian identity was instilling in me a desire to reclaim my Pakistani identity. The best way to do this, I decided, would be to seek out other Pakistani lesbians. I barely knew any Pakistanis aside from my family, and I sure as hell didn't know, or even know of, any Pakistani lesbians. I was just naive enough to think I was the only one.

It wasn't easy for me even to arrive at the concept of a Pakistani lesbian. Having rejected my culture from a young age, I identified only as a lesbian when I came out, and in my zeal to be all-American, I threw myself into the American queer liberation movement. I did not realize that there is an active South Asian gay and lesbian community in the United States—and that many of us are here precisely because we're able to be queer and out in the Western world.

South Asian culture is rampant with homophobia—so much so that most people in South Asia literally don't have words for homosexuality, which is viewed as a Western phenomenon despite the fact that images of gays and lesbians have been a part of the subcontinent's history for thousands of years. In the temples of Khajuraho and Konarak in India, there are images of same-gender couples—male and female—in intimate positions. One temple carving depicts two women caressing each other, while another shows four women engaged in sexual play. There are also references to homosexuality in the *Kāma-sūtra,* the ancient Indian text on the diversities of sex. Babar, the founder of the Mughal dynasty in India, is said to have been gay, as was Abu Nawas, a famous Islamic poet. The fact is that homosexuality is as native to South Asia as is heterosexuality. But since the culture pressures South Asian women to reject our sexual identity, many South Asian queers living in the United States reject South Asian culture in turn. As a result, we are often isolated from one another.

Despite the odds, I started my search for queer people from South Asia—and I found them, all across America, Canada, and England. Connecting with this network and talking with other queer South Asians has begun to fill the void I've been feeling. But just as it took me years to reject my Pakistani heritage, it will likely take me as long, if not longer, to reintegrate my culture into my life as it is now.

I'm not ready to go back to Pakistan. But I am ready to start examining the hostility I feel toward a part of myself I thought I had discarded long ago.

T W E N T Y - S I X

◆◆◆

We Are All Works in Progress

Leslie Feinberg

The sight of pink-blue gender-coded infant outfits may grate on your nerves. Or you may be a woman or a man who feels at home in those categories. Trans liberation defends you both.

Each person should have the right to *choose* between pink or blue tinted gender categories, as well as all the other hues of the palette. At this moment in time, that right is denied to us. But together, we could make it a reality. . . .

I am a human being who would rather not be addressed as Ms. or Mr., ma'am or sir. I prefer to use gender-neutral pronouns like *sie* (pronounced like *"see"*) and *hir* (pronounced like *"here"*) to describe myself. I am a person who faces almost insurmountable difficulty when instructed to check off an "F" or an "M" box on identification papers.

I'm not at odds with the fact that I was born female-bodied. Nor do I identify as an intermediate sex. I simply do not fit the prevalent Western concepts of what a woman or man "should" look like. And that reality has dramatically directed the course of my life.

I'll give you a graphic example. From December 1995 to December 1996, I was dying of endocarditis—a bacterial infection that lodges and proliferates in the valves of the heart. A simple blood culture would have immediately exposed the root cause of my raging fevers. Eight weeks of 'round-the-clock intravenous antibiotic drips would have eradicated

every last seedling of bacterium in the canals of my heart. Yet I experienced such hatred from some health practitioners that I very nearly died.

I remember late one night in December my lover and I arrived at a hospital emergency room during a snowstorm. My fever was 104 degrees and rising. My blood pressure was pounding dangerously high. The staff immediately hooked me up to monitors and worked to bring down my fever. The doctor in charge began physically examining me. When he determined that my anatomy was female, he flashed me a mean-spirited smirk. While keeping his eyes fixed on me, he approached one of the nurses, seated at a desk, and began rubbing her neck and shoulders. He talked to her about sex for a few minutes. After his pointed demonstration of "normal sexuality," he told me to get dressed and then he stormed out of the room. Still delirious, I struggled to put on my clothes and make sense of what was happening.

The doctor returned after I was dressed. He ordered me to leave the hospital and never return. I refused. I told him I wouldn't leave until he could tell me why my fever was so high. He said, "You have a fever because you are a very troubled person."

This doctor's prejudices, directed at me during a moment of catastrophic illness, could have killed me. The death certificate would have read: Endocarditis. By all rights it should have read: Bigotry.

As my partner and I sat bundled up in a cold car outside the emergency room, still reverberating from the doctor's hatred, I thought about how many people have been turned away from medical care when they were desperately ill—some because an apartheid "whites only" sign hung over the emergency room entrance, or some because their visible Kaposi's sarcoma lesions kept personnel far from their beds. I remembered how a blemish that wouldn't heal drove my mother to visit her doctor repeatedly during the 1950s. I recalled the doctor finally wrote a prescription for Valium because he decided she was a hysterical woman. When my mother finally got to specialists, they told her the cancer had already reached her brain.

Bigotry exacts its toll in flesh and blood. And left unchecked and unchallenged, prejudices create a poisonous climate for us all. Each of us has a stake in the demand that every human being has a right to a job, to shelter, to health care, to dignity, to respect.

I am very grateful to have this chance to open up a conversation with you about why it is so vital to also defend the right of individuals to express and define their sex and gender, and to control their own bodies. For me, it's a life-and-death question. But I also believe that this discussion will have great meaning for you. All your life you've heard such dogma about what it means to be a "real" woman or a "real" man. And chances are you've choked on some of it. You've balked at the idea that being a woman means having to be thin as a rail, emotionally nurturing, and an airhead when it comes to balancing her checkbook. You know in your guts that being a man has nothing to do with rippling muscles, innate courage, or knowing how to handle a chain saw. These are really caricatures. Yet these images have been drilled into us through popular culture and education over the years. And subtler, equally insidious messages lurk in the interstices of these grosser concepts. These ideas of what a "real" woman or man should be straightjacket the freedom of individual self-expression. These gender messages play on and on in a continuous loop in our brains, like commercials that can't be muted.

But in my lifetime I've also seen social upheavals challenge this sex and gender doctrine. As a child who grew up during the McCarthyite, Father-Knows-Best 1950s, and who came of age during the second wave of women's liberation in the United States, I've seen transformations in the ways people think and talk about what it means to be a woman or a man.

Today the gains of the 1970s women's liberation movement are under siege by right-wing propagandists. But many today who are too young to remember what life was like before the women's movement need to know that this was a tremendously progressive development that won significant economic and social reforms. And this struggle by women and their allies swung human consciousness forward like a pendulum.

The movement replaced the common usage of vulgar and diminutive words to describe females with the word *woman* and infused that word with strength and pride. Women, many of them formerly isolated, were drawn together into consciousness-raising groups. Their discussions—about the root of women's oppression and how to eradicate it—resonated far beyond the rooms in which they took place. The women's liberation movement sparked a mass conversation about the systematic degradation, violence, and discrimination that women faced in this society. And this consciousness raising changed many of the ways women and men thought about themselves and their relation to each other. In retrospect, however, we must not forget that these widespread discussions were not just organized to *talk* about oppression. They were a giant dialogue about how to take action to fight institutionalized anti-woman attitudes, rape and battering, the illegality of abortion, employment and education discrimination, and other ways women were socially and economically devalued.

This was a big step forward for humanity. And even the period of political reaction that followed has not been able to overturn all the gains made by that important social movement.

Now another movement is sweeping onto the stage of history: Trans liberation. We are again raising questions about the societal treatment of people based on their sex and gender expression. This discussion will make new contributions to human consciousness. And trans communities, like the women's movement, are carrying out these mass conversations with the goal of creating a movement capable of fighting for justice—of righting the wrongs.

We are a movement of masculine females and feminine males, cross-dressers, transsexual men and women, intersexuals born on the anatomical sweep between female and male, gender-blenders, many other sex and gender-variant people, and our significant others. All told, we expand understanding of how many ways there are to be a human being.

Our lives are proof that sex and gender are much more complex than a delivery room doctor's glance at genitals can determine, more variegated than pink or blue birth caps. We are oppressed for not fitting those narrow social norms. We are fighting back.

Our struggle will also help expose some of the harmful myths about what it means to be a woman or a man that have compartmentalized and distorted your life, as well as mine. Trans liberation has meaning for you — no matter how you define or express your sex or your gender.

If you are a trans person, you face horrendous social punishments — from institutionalization to gang rape, from beatings to denial of child visitation. This oppression is faced, in varying degrees, by all who march under the banner of trans liberation. This brutalization and degradation strips us of what we could achieve with our individual lifetimes.

And if you do not identify as transgender or transsexual or intersexual, your life is diminished by our oppression as well. Your own choices as a man or a woman are sharply curtailed. Your individual journey to express yourself is shunted into one of two deeply carved ruts, and the social baggage you are handed is already packed.

So the defense of each individual's right to control their own body, and to explore the path of self-expression, enhances your own freedom to discover more about yourself and your potentialities. This movement will give you more room to breathe — to be yourself. To discover on a deeper level what it means to be your self.

Together, I believe we can forge a coalition that can fight on behalf of your oppression as well as mine. Together, we can raise each other's grievances and win the kind of significant change we all long for. But the foundation of unity is understanding. So let me begin by telling you a little bit about myself.

I am a human being who unnerves some people. As they look at me, they see a kaleidoscope of characteristics they associate with both males and females. I appear to be a tangled knot of gender contradictions. So they feverishly press the question on me: woman or man? Those are the only two words most people have as tools to shape their question.

"Which sex are you?" I understand their question. It sounds so simple. And I'd like to offer them a simple resolution. But merely answering woman or man will not bring relief to the questioner. As long as people try to bring me into focus using only those two lenses, I will always appear to be an enigma.

The truth is I'm no mystery. I'm a female who is more masculine than those prominently portrayed in mass culture. Millions of females and millions of males in this country do not fit the cramped compartments of gender that we have been taught are "natural" and "normal." For many of us, the words *woman* or *man, ma'am* or *sir, she* or *he* — in and of themselves — do not total up the sum of our identities or of our oppressions. Speaking for myself, my life only comes into focus when the word *transgender* is added to the equation.

Simply answering whether I was born female or male will not solve the conundrum. Before I can even begin to respond to the question of my own birth sex, I feel it's important to challenge the assumptions that the answer is always as simple as either-or. I believe we need to take a critical look at the assumption that is built into the seemingly innocent question: "What a beautiful baby — is it a boy or a girl?"

The human anatomical spectrum can't be understood, let alone appreciated, as long as female or male are considered to be all that exists. "Is it a boy or a girl?" Those are the only two categories allowed on birth certificates.

But this either-or leaves no room for intersexual people, born between the poles of female and male. Human anatomy continues to burst the confines of the contemporary concept that nature delivers all babies on two unrelated conveyor belts. So are the birth certificates changed to reflect human anatomy? No, the U.S. medical establishment hormonally molds and shapes and surgically hacks away at the exquisite complexities of intersexual infants until they neatly fit one category or the other.

A surgeon decides whether a clitoris is "too large" or a penis is "too small." That's a highly subjective decision for anyone to make about another person's body. Especially when the person making the arbitrary decision is scrubbed up for surgery! And what is the criterion for a penis being "too small"? Too small for successful heterosexual intercourse. Intersexual infants are already being tailored for their sexuality, as well as their sex. The infants have no say over what happens to their bodies. Clearly the struggle against genital mutilation must begin here, within the borders of the United States.

But the question asked of all new parents: "Is it a boy or a girl?" is not such a simple question when transsexuality is taken into account, either. Legions of out-and-proud transsexual men and women demonstrate that individuals have a deep, developed, and valid sense of their own sex that does not always correspond to the cursory decision made by a delivery-room obstetrician. Nor is transsexuality a recent phenomenon. People have undergone social sex reassignment and surgical and hormonal sex changes throughout the breadth of oral and recorded human history.

Having offered this view of the complexities and limitations of birth classification, I have no hesitancy in saying I was born female. But that answer doesn't clear up the confusion that drives some people to ask me "Are you a man or a woman?" The problem is that they are trying to understand my gender expression by determining my sex—and therein lies the rub! Just as most of us grew up with only the concepts of *woman* and *man,* the terms *feminine* and *masculine* are the only two tools most people have to talk about the complexities of gender expression.

That pink-blue dogma assumes that biology steers our social destiny. We have been taught that being born female or male will determine how we will dress and walk, whether we will prefer our hair shortly cropped or long and flowing, whether we will be emotionally nurturing or repressed. According to this way of thinking, masculine females are trying to look "like men," and feminine males are trying to act "like women."

But those of us who transgress those gender assumptions also shatter their inflexibility.

So why do I sometimes describe myself as a masculine female? Isn't each of those concepts very limiting? Yes. But placing the two words together is incendiary, exploding the belief that gender expression is linked to birth sex like horse and carriage. It is the social contradiction missing from Dick-and-Jane textbook education.

I actually chafe at describing myself as masculine. For one thing, masculinity is such an expansive territory, encompassing boundaries of nationality, race, and class. Most importantly, individuals blaze their own trails across this landscape.

And it's hard for me to label the intricate matrix of my gender as simply masculine. To me, branding individual self-expression as simply feminine or masculine is like asking poets: Do you write in English or Spanish? The question leaves out the possibilities that the poetry is woven in Cantonese or Ladino, Swahili or Arabic. The question deals only with the system of language that the poet has been taught. It ignores the words each writer hauls up, hand over hand, from a common well. The music words make when finding themselves next to each other for the first time. The silences echoing in the space between ideas. The powerful winds of passion and belief that move the poet to write.

That is why I do not hold the view that gender is simply a social construct—one of two languages that we learn by rote from early age. To me, gender is the poetry each of us makes out of the language we are taught. When I walk through the anthology of the world, I see individuals express their gender in exquisitely complex and ever-changing ways, despite the laws of pentameter.

So how can gender expression be mandated by edict and enforced by law? Isn't that like trying to handcuff a pool of mercury? It's true that human self-expression is diverse and is often expressed in ambiguous or contradictory ways. And what degree of gender expression is considered "acceptable" can depend on your social situation, your race and nationality, your class, and whether you live in an urban or rural environment.

But no one can deny that rigid gender education begins early on in life—from pink and blue color-coding of infant outfits to gender-labeling toys and games. And those who overstep these arbitrary borders are punished. Severely. When the steel handcuffs tighten, it is human bones that crack. No one knows how many trans lives have been lost to police brutality and street-corner bashing. The lives of trans people are so depreciated in this society that many murders go unreported. And those of us who have survived are deeply scarred by daily run-ins with hate, discrimination, and violence.

Trans people are still literally social outlaws. And that's why I am willing at times, publicly, to reduce the totality of my self-expression to descriptions like masculine female, butch, bulldagger, drag king, cross-dresser. These terms describe outlaw status. And I hold my head up proudly in that police lineup. The word *outlaw* is not hyperbolic. I have been locked up in jail by cops because I was wearing a suit and tie. Was my clothing really a crime? Is it a "man's" suit if I am wearing it? At what point—from field to rack—is fiber assigned a sex?

The reality of why I was arrested was as cold as the cell's cement floor: I am considered a masculine female. That's a *gender* violation. My feminine drag queen sisters were in nearby cells, busted for wearing "women's" clothing. The cells that we were thrown into had the same design of bars and concrete. But when we—gay drag kings and drag queens—were thrown into them, the cops referred to the cells as bull's tanks and queen's tanks. The cells were named after our crimes: gender transgression. Actual statutes against cross-dressing and cross-gendered behavior still exist in written laws today. But even where the laws are not written down, police, judges, and prison guards are empowered to carry out merciless punishment for sex and gender "difference."

I believe we need to sharpen our view of how repression by the police, courts, and prisons, as well as all forms of racism and bigotry, operates as gears in the machinery of the economic and social system that governs our lives. As all those who have the least to lose from changing this system get together and examine these social questions, we can separate the wheat of truths from the chaff of old lies. Historic tasks are revealed that beckon us to take a stand and to take action.

That moment is now. And so this conversation with you takes place with the momentum of struggle behind it.

What will it take to put a halt to "legal" and extralegal violence against trans people? How can we strike the unjust and absurd laws mandating dress and behavior for females and males from the books? How can we weed out all the forms of trans-phobic and gender-phobic discrimination?

Where does the struggle for sex and gender liberation fit in relation to other movements for economic and social equality? How can we reach a point where we appreciate each other's differences, not just tolerate them? How can we tear down the electrified barbed wire that has been placed between us to keep us separated, fearful and pitted against each other? How can we forge a movement that can bring about profound and lasting change—a movement capable of transforming society?

These questions can only be answered when we begin to organize together, ready to struggle on each other's behalf. Understanding each other will compel us as honest, caring people to fight each other's oppression as though it was our own.

TWENTY-SEVEN

Uses of the Erotic
The Erotic as Power
Audre Lorde

There are many kinds of power, used and unused, acknowledged or otherwise. The erotic is a resource within each of us that lies in a deeply female and spiritual plane, firmly rooted in the power of our unexpressed or unrecognized feeling. In order to perpetuate itself, every oppression must corrupt or distort those various sources of power within the culture of the oppressed that can provide energy for change. For women, this has meant a suppression of the erotic as a considered source of power and information within our lives.

We have been taught to suspect this resource, vilified, abused, and devalued within western society. On the one hand, the superficially erotic has been encouraged as a sign of female inferiority; on the other hand, women have been made to suffer and to feel both contemptible and suspect by virtue of its existence.

It is a short step from there to the false belief that only by the suppression of the erotic within our lives and consciousness can women be truly strong. But that strength is illusory, for it is fashioned within the context of male models of power.

As women, we have come to distrust that power which rises from our deepest and nonrational knowledge. We have been warned against it all our lives by the male world, which values this depth of feeling enough to keep women around in order to exercise it in the service of men, but which fears this same depth too much to examine the possibilities of it within themselves. So women are maintained at a distant/inferior position to be psychically milked, much the same way ants maintain colonies of aphids to provide a life-giving substance for their masters.

But the erotic offers a well of replenishing and provocative force to the woman who does not fear its revelation, nor succumb to the belief that sensation is enough.

The erotic has often been misnamed by men and used against women. It has been made into the confused, the trivial, the psychotic, the plasticized sensation. For this reason, we have often turned away from the exploration and consideration of the erotic as a source of power and information, confusing it with its opposite, the pornographic. But pornography is a direct denial of the power of the erotic, for it represents the suppression of true feeling. Pornography emphasizes sensation without feeling.

The erotic is a measure between the beginnings of our sense of self and the chaos of our strongest feelings. It is an internal sense of satisfaction to which, once we have experienced it, we know we can aspire. For having experienced the fullness of this depth of feeling and recognizing its power, in honor and self-respect we can require no less of ourselves.

It is never easy to demand the most from ourselves, from our lives, from our work. To encourage excellence is to go beyond the encouraged mediocrity of our society. To go beyond the encouraged mediocrity of our society is to encourage excellence. But giving in to the fear of feeling and working to capacity is a luxury only the unintentional can afford, and the unintentional are those who do not wish to guide their own destinies.

This internal requirement toward excellence which we learn from the erotic must not be misconstrued as demanding the impossible from ourselves nor from others. Such a demand incapacitates everyone in the process. For the erotic is not a question only of what we do; it is a question of how acutely and fully we can feel in the doing. Once we know the extent to which we are capable of feeling that sense of satisfaction and completion, we can then observe which of our various life endeavors bring us closest to that fullness.

The aim of each thing which we do is to make our lives and the lives of our children richer and more possible. Within the celebration of the erotic in all our endeavors, my work becomes a conscious decision — a longed-for bed which I enter gratefully and from which I rise up empowered.

Of course, women so empowered are dangerous. So we are taught to separate the erotic demand from most vital areas of our lives other than sex. And the lack of concern for the erotic root and satisfactions of our work is felt in our disaffection from so much of what we do. For instance, how often do we truly love our work even at its most difficult?

The principal horror of any system which defines the good in terms of profit rather than in terms of human need, or which defines human need to the exclusion of the psychic and emotional components of that need — the principal horror of such a system is that it robs our work of its erotic value, its erotic power and life appeal and fulfillment. Such a system reduces work to a travesty of necessities, a duty by which we earn bread or oblivion for ourselves and those we love. But this is tantamount to blinding a painter and then telling her to improve her work, and to enjoy the act of painting. It is not only next to impossible, it is also profoundly cruel.

As women, we need to examine the ways in which our world can be truly different. I am speaking here of the necessity for reassessing the quality of all the aspects of our lives and of our work, and of how we move toward and through them.

The very word *erotic* comes from the Greek word *eros*, the personification of love in all its aspects — born of Chaos, and personifying creative power and harmony. When I speak of the erotic, then, I speak of it as an assertion of the lifeforce of women; of that creative energy empowered, the knowledge and use of which we are now reclaiming in our language, our history, our dancing, our loving, our work, our lives.

There are frequent attempts to equate pornography and eroticism, two diametrically opposed uses of the sexual. Because of these attempts, it has become fashionable to separate the spiritual (psychic and emotional) from the political, to see them as contradictory or antithetical. "What do you mean, a poetic revolutionary, a meditating gunrunner?" In the same way, we have attempted to separate the spiritual and the erotic, thereby reducing the spiritual to a world of flattened affect, a world of the ascetic who aspires to feel nothing. But nothing is farther from the truth. For the ascetic position is one of the highest fear, the gravest immobility. The severe abstinence of the ascetic becomes the ruling obsession. And it is one not of self-discipline but of self-abnegation.

The dichotomy between the spiritual and the political is also false, resulting from an incomplete attention to our erotic knowledge. For the bridge which connects them is formed by the erotic — the sensual — those physical, emotional, and psychic expressions of what is deepest and strongest and richest within each of us, being shared: the passions of love, in its deepest meanings.

Beyond the superficial, the considered phrase, "It feels right to me," acknowledges the strength of the erotic into a true knowledge, for what that means is the first and most powerful guiding light toward any understanding. And understanding is a handmaiden which can only wait upon, or clarify, that knowledge, deeply born. The erotic is the nurturer or nursemaid of all our deepest knowledge.

The erotic functions for me in several ways, and the first is in providing the power which comes from sharing deeply any pursuit with another person. The sharing of joy, whether physical, emotional, psychic, or intellectual, forms a bridge between the sharers which can be the basis for understanding much of what is not shared between them, and lessens the threat of their difference.

Another important way in which the erotic connection functions is the open and fearless underlining of my capacity for joy. In the way my body stretches to music and opens into response, hearkening to its deepest rhythms, so every level upon which I sense also opens to the erotically satisfying experience, whether it is dancing, building a bookcase, writing a poem, examining an idea.

That self-connection shared is a measure of the joy which I know myself to be capable of feeling, a reminder of my capacity for feeling. And that deep and irreplaceable knowledge of my capacity for joy comes to demand from all of my life that it be lived within the knowledge that such satisfaction is possible, and does not have to be called *marriage,* nor *god,* nor *an afterlife.*

This is one reason why the erotic is so feared, and so often relegated to the bedroom alone, when it is recognized at all. For once we begin to feel deeply all the aspects of our lives, we begin to demand from ourselves and from our life-pursuits that they feel in accordance with that joy which we know ourselves to be capable of. Our erotic knowledge empowers us, becomes a lens through which we scrutinize all aspects of our existence, forcing us to evaluate those aspects honestly in terms of their relative meaning within our lives. And this is a grave responsibility, projected from within each of us, not to settle for the convenient, the shoddy, the conventionally expected, nor the merely safe.

During World War II, we bought sealed plastic packets of white, uncolored margarine, with a tiny, intense pellet of yellow coloring perched like a topaz just inside the clear skin of the bag. We would leave the margarine out for a while to soften, and then we would pinch the little pellet to break it inside the bag, releasing the rich yellowness into the soft pale mass of margarine. Then taking it carefully between our fingers, we would knead it gently back and forth, over and over, until the color had spread throughout the whole pound bag of margarine, thoroughly coloring it.

I find the erotic such a kernel within myself. When released from its intense and constrained pellet, it flows through and colors my life with a kind of energy that heightens and sensitizes and strengthens all my experience.

We have been raised to fear the *yes* within ourselves, our deepest cravings. But, once recognized, those which do not enhance our future lose their power and can be altered. The fear of our desires keeps them suspect and indiscriminately powerful, for to suppress any truth is to give it strength beyond endurance. The fear that we cannot grow beyond whatever distortions we may find within ourselves keeps us docile and loyal and obedient, externally defined, and leads us to accept many facets of our oppression as women.

When we live outside ourselves, and by that I mean on external directives only rather than from our internal knowledge and needs, when we live away from those erotic guides from within ourselves, then our lives are limited by external and alien forms, and we conform to the needs of a structure that is not based on human need, let alone an individual's. But when we begin to live from within outward, in touch with the power of the erotic within ourselves, and allowing that power to inform and illuminate our actions upon the world around us, then we begin to be responsible to ourselves in the deepest sense. For as we begin to recognize our deepest feelings, we begin to give up, of necessity, being satisfied with suffering and self-negation, and with the numbness which so often seems like their only alternative in our society. Our acts against oppression become integral with self, motivated and empowered from within.

In touch with the erotic, I become less willing to accept powerlessness, or those other supplied states of being which are not native to me, such as resignation, despair, self-effacement, depression, self-denial.

And yes, there is a hierarchy. There is a difference between painting a back fence and writing a poem, but only one of quantity. And there is, for me, no difference between writing a good poem and moving into sunlight against the body of a woman I love.

This brings me to the last consideration of the erotic. To share the power of each other's feelings is different from using another's feelings as we would use a kleenex. When we look the other way from our experience, erotic or otherwise, we use rather than share the feelings of those others who participate in the experience with us. And use without consent of the used is abuse.

In order to be utilized, our erotic feelings must be recognized. The need for sharing deep feeling is a human need. But within the european-american tradition, this need is satisfied by certain proscribed erotic comings-together. These occasions are almost always characterized by a simultaneous looking away, a pretense of calling them something else, whether a religion, a fit, mob violence, or even playing doctor. And this misnaming of the need and the deed give rise to that distortion which results in pornography and obscenity—the abuse of feeling.

When we look away from the importance of the erotic in the development and sustenance of our power, or when we look away from ourselves as we satisfy our erotic needs in concert with others, we use each other as objects of satisfaction rather than share our joy in the satisfying, rather than make connection with our similarities and our differences. To refuse to be conscious of what we are feeling at any time, however comfortable that might seem, is to deny a large part of the experience, and to allow ourselves to be reduced to the pornographic, the abused, and the absurd.

The erotic cannot be felt secondhand. As a Black lesbian feminist, I have a particular feeling, knowledge, and understanding for those sisters with whom I have danced hard, played, or even fought. This deep participation has often been the forerunner for joint concerted actions not possible before.

But this erotic charge is not easily shared by women who continue to operate under an exclusively european-american male tradition. I know it was not available to me when I was trying to adapt my consciousness to this mode of living and sensation.

Only now, I find more and more women-identified women brave enough to risk sharing the erotic's electrical charge without having to look away, and without distorting the enormously powerful and creative nature of that exchange. Recognizing the power of the erotic within our lives can give us the energy to pursue genuine change within our world, rather than merely settling for a shift of characters in the same weary drama.

For not only do we touch our most profoundly creative source, but we do that which is female and self-affirming in the face of a racist, patriarchal, and anti-erotic society.

CHAPTER FIVE

Relationships, Families, and Households

L osing a close friend, asking for support from family and friends at difficult times, falling in love, moving in with a roommate or partner, holding your newborn baby for the first time, breaking up with a partner of many years, struggling to understand a teenage son or daughter, and helping your mother to die with dignity and in peace are commonplace life events. These ties between us, as human beings, define the very texture of our personal lives. They are a source of much happiness, affirmation, and personal growth as well as frustration, misunderstanding, anxiety, and, sometimes, misery. This chapter looks at personal relationships—between women and men, women and women, parents and children—and the ways in which an idealized notion of family masks the reality of family life for many people in the United States. We argue that families—however they are defined—need to be able to care for their members and that specific forms are much less important than the quality of the relationships between people.

Defining Ourselves through Connections with Others

As suggested in Chapter 2, personal and family relationships are central to individual development, the definition of self, and ongoing identity develop-

ment. This happens across cultures, though it may not take the same form or have the same meaning in all cultural settings. It involves relying on others when we are very young and later negotiating with them for material care, nurturance, and security; defining our own voice, space, independence, and sense of closeness to others; and learning about ourselves, our family and cultural heritage, ideas of right and wrong, practical aspects of life, and how to negotiate the world outside the home. In the family we learn about socially defined **gender roles:** what it means to be a daughter, sister, wife, and mother, and what is expected of us. Family resources, including material possessions, emotional bonds, cultural connections and language, and status in the wider community, are also important for the experiences and opportunities they offer children. In Reading 28, Miriam Ching Yoon Louie describes her close relationship with her husband, their shared parenting, and their commitment to teaching their values to their children. Her daughter, Nguyen Louie, describes her parents' support, the lessons she learned from them, and the space she had, within the family, to develop her own independence. They both situate their personal experiences within the wider framework of meso- and macro-level factors. Rachel Aber Schlesinger (Reading 29) writes about the geographical and cultural contexts that shaped the lives of Jewish grandmothers who migrated to North

America and about their role in the transmission of culture to their grandchildren, who live in a very different time and place.

How we are treated by parents and siblings and our observations of adult relationships during childhood provide the foundation for our own adult relationships. Friends and family members may offer rules for dating etiquette. Magazine features and advice columns coach us in how to catch a man (or woman, in the case of lesbian magazines) and how to keep him or her happy once we have. Regardless of sexual orientation, we are all socialized in a heterosexual and heterosexist world, as argued by Adrienne Rich (1986a). The ups and downs of personal relationships are the material of countless magazines, TV talk shows, movies, sit-coms, novels, and pop music. Many women value themselves in terms of whether they can attract and hold a partner. Whole sections of bookstores are given over to books and manuals that analyze relationship problems and teach "relationship skills"; counselors and therapists make a living helping us sort out our personal lives. Fairy tales and romantic stories may end with the characters living happily ever after, but the reality of personal relationships is often very different.

Theories about Personal Relationships: Living in Different Worlds?

Popular writers and academics draw on a range of psychological and sociological explanations of relationship dynamics in terms of differences in **gender socialization,** communication styles, and personal power. In real-life situations all these explanations may be useful; for ease of analysis here we look at these theoretical strands separately. Virtually all this theorizing assumes a heterosexual relationship, though some points we raise below may be applicable to lesbians and bisexual women.

Men and Women: Sex versus Love

Girls and boys generally absorb different messages about relationships from families, peers, and popular culture. Though empirical research is mostly concerned with people of European descent, and there-

fore limited, anecdotal evidence from conversations and observation suggests that differences in socialization also obtain in other cultural groups. Leaflets addressing date rape on college campuses, for example, warn women students that their dates may well expect sex and that many guys have been taught to see sex as "scoring," whereas young women are more likely to see dating as a way of developing a caring relationship. The reporting of date rape has increased significantly on college campuses, and the issue has been taken up by the mass media. The incidence of date rape is difficult to assess, due to underreporting and to different interpretations of the term. Based on the FBI's Uniform Crime Report, the Boston Women's Health Book Collective (1992) noted that one in four American college women is said to be a victim of rape or attempted rape. Given the difficulty of getting complete data and the authority of the source, this estimate is still cited. We take this up further in the next chapter.

Skeptics counter that such figures are highly inflated and that many women who claim to have been raped blame their dates for their own poor judgment in having sex (Paglia 1990; Roiphe 1993). One of the myths about rape is that it is perpetrated by strangers in dark alleyways, though most women are raped by men they know. Other myths are that women want to be raped; that if they stay out late, wear sexy clothes, or get drunk or stoned they are asking for it; that "No" does not mean "No." It is important to note that, over the past twenty-five years or so, many women, including rape-crisis center activists, have challenged the idea that rape is fundamentally about sex and have redefined it as an issue of violation and the abuse of power (Brownmiller 1975; Griffin 1986). We focus on this issue in the next chapter.

Consensual sex is one of the very few ways for people to make intimate connections in this society, especially men, many of whom do not express emotion easily. Shere Hite (1994), for example, found that for men, dating and marriage are primarily about sex, and that they often shop around for varied sexual experiences. For Hite's women respondents, expressing emotion through sexual intimacy and setting up a home were usually much more important than they were for men. Hite attributes much of the frustration in personal relationships to these fundamentally different approaches. She argues that many women give up on their hope for an emotionally satisfying relationship and settle for companionability with a male partner, while devoting much of their emotional energy elsewhere: to their children, work, or other interests. Some women, described by Robin Norwood (1986) as "women who love too much," try hard to make an unsatisfactory relationship work. Their efforts are explained psychologically in terms of their low self-esteem and willingness to make excuses for their partners' insensitivity and lack of consideration for them. As intimate heterosexual relationships are currently structured, Hite claims, they will be a source of struggle for women, who need to resign themselves to some kind of compromise. At the same time, she sees women as "revolutionary agents of change" in relationships, working with men to renegotiate this intimate part of their lives. Naomi Wolf's discussion of "radical heterosexuality" in the previous chapter is also relevant here (Reading 23).

Cross-Cultural Communication: Speaking a Second Language

Basing her work on the premise that boys and girls grow up in essentially different cultures, sociolinguist Deborah Tannen (1990) analyzes everyday conversations between men and women to make sense of the "seemingly senseless misunderstandings that haunt our relationships" (p. 13). She does not claim that differences in conversational style explain all the problems that may arise in relationships between women and men, and she acknowledges that "psychological problems, the failures of love and caring, genuine selfishness—and real effects of political and economic inequity" may also be important (p. 18). But men and women often accuse each other of these things when they are simply "expressing their thoughts and feelings, and their assumptions about how to communicate, in different ways" (p. 17). By taking a sociolinguistic approach, she argues, one can explain the dissatisfactions many women and men feel in their relationships, "without accusing anyone of being crazy or wrong" (p. 17). Boys' socialization with peers involves jockeying for status in a group; from this experience men learn to see themselves as individuals in a hierarchical social order in which they are either one up or

one down. Thus, for men, conversations are negotiations about independence. Girls, by contrast, learn to make connections with a few close friends and later, as adult women, see themselves as individuals in a network of connections, where conversations are negotiations about closeness. Tannen comments that all individuals need closeness and independence, but women tend to focus on the former and men the latter. These differences give women and men different views of the same situation, the root of many misunderstandings in relationships. Partners in heterosexual relationships, she notes, are "living with asymmetry," and each can benefit from learning the other's conversational styles and needs (p. 287).

Tannen and Hite both comment on the significance of heterosexual women's friendships, as described by Andrea Canaan in Reading 30. From time to time U.S. women's magazines observe that often a woman's closest emotional ties are with a woman friend, even if they are both married, and that such friendships provide the intimate connection that many women do not have with their partners (O'Connor 1992; Oliker 1989; Raymond 1986). John Gray, the author of several best-sellers, including *Men Are from Mars, Women Are from Venus* (1992), also makes the argument that men and women have been socialized differently and have different styles of communication (1994). He assumes that women as a group are naturally giving and caring and that men as a group are naturally "wired up" to be providers, an assumption we reject, favoring a social-constructionist view of gender as something learned rather than innate (see Chapter 1).

Inequalities of Power

Personal relationships always include an element of power, though in more egalitarian relationships this shifts back and forth. Our experience of personal relationships as adults often has a lot to do with our experiences as children and the ways in which our parents, siblings, teachers, and other adults used power, rules, and punishments in their relations with us. Hilary Lips (1991) describes this power imbalance in terms of "the principle of least interest" (p. 57), a concept taken from social exchange theory. The person who has the least interest in a relationship—in a heterosexual relationship, often the man—

has the most power in it. His moods and needs will tend to be dominant. Women, instead of thinking about themselves, will focus more on what men need. Men negotiate emotional distance by, for example, calling when it suits them, breaking dates, withdrawing affection, threatening violence, or opposing the woman's desire for a monogamous relationship—if that is what she wants.

Although personal relationships are, by definition, intimate, each person brings to them all of her or his identity—the micro, meso, and macro aspects—what Tannen calls the "real effects of political and economic inequity." In several traditions these inequalities are assumed in marriage. For example, within the U.S. Baptist church there is ongoing discussion of the relationships between husbands and wives. A 1998 amendment to the Baptist Faith and Message Statement of 1963 reads: "A wife is to submit graciously to the servant leadership of her husband, even as the church willingly submits to the headship of Christ," with opinion divided as to whether this is appropriate ("Baptists in Texas" 1999). The relative power positions of women as a group and men as a group in the wider society are crucial factors in personal relationships. These include differences in socialization and in one's sense of agency, efficacy, entitlement, and personal status as a man or a woman.

Pepper Schwartz (1994), for example, looks at power inequalities in her analysis of peer marriage—a marriage of equal companions who collaborate to produce "profound intimacy and mutual respect" (p. 2). She argues that traditional marriage with defined gender roles does not provide the same degree of intimacy, deep friendship, and mutual respect as peer marriage. The "provider role" is "the linchpin of marital inequality" and needs to be eliminated in a peer marriage (p. 111). Although the provider role is not an easy one, the breadwinner has much more power and economic control in the relationship. Schwartz argues that the provider role polarizes men and women and "inevitably . . . causes a loss of respect for women in their husband's eyes" (p. 120). These power relations, which operate at the institutional, or macro, level, are often played out in the relationship, even when the partners are not aware of it. People who are in a subordinate position in some way—through disability, race, or gender, for example—always know more about the dominant group than the other way around. A White person in a relationship with a person of color may objectify his or her partner as "exotic," may unconsciously make racist comments or inappropriate assumptions and criticisms about the partner, may have little respect for aspects of the partner's culture, or may simply fail to see how his or her own white-skin privilege creates a sense of entitlement and confidence that pervades all daily interactions. Similarly, some men consider themselves superior to women, and this may be reflected in the relationship as protectiveness, condescension, lack of respect and emotional support, bad manners, or power plays. From time to time, men's magazines, newsmagazines, and TV talk shows make this issue of power explicit by promoting the idea that men need to reclaim the power they have lost to women in recent years, both personally and in the wider society (Segell 1996).

The Ideal Nuclear Family

For psychologists and sociologists, the family is a key social institution in which children are nurtured and socialized. In much public debate and political rhetoric, the family is touted as the centerpiece of American life. This idealized family, immortalized in the 1950s TV show *Leave It to Beaver,* consists of a heterosexual couple, married for life, with two or three children. The father is the provider while the wife/mother spends her days running the home. This is the family that is regularly portrayed in ads for such things as food, cars, cleaning products, or life insurance, which rely on our recognizing—if not identifying with—this symbol of togetherness and care. It is also invoked by conservative politicians who hearken back to so-called traditional family values. The copious academic and popular literature on the family emphasizes change—some say breakdown—in family life (Coontz 1992, 1997; Mintz and Kellogg 1988; Risman 1998; Skolnick 1991). Conservative politicians and religious leaders attribute many social problems to "broken homes," so-called dysfunctional families, and moral decline, citing divorce rates, teen pregnancy rates, numbers of single-parent families, large numbers of mothers in the paid workforce, a lack of Christian values, and violence. In a *New York Times* article on single mothers, the steady increase in the rate of births to unmarried women since 1952 was called "a predictable metaphor for the fraying of America's collective moral fiber" (Usdansky 1996).

Although this mythic family makes up only a small proportion of U.S. families, much of the literature on U.S. families assumes homogeneity. The prevalence of this ideal family image has a strong ideological impact and serves to both mask and delegitimize the real diversity of family forms. It gives no hint of the range of family forms, the incidence of family violence, or conflicts between work and caring for children. Sociologist Stephanie Coontz (1997) argues that the nostalgia for the so-called traditional family is based on myths. Specifically, the 1950s White, middle-class family was the product of a particular set of circumstances that were short-lived:

> Women who had worked during the depression or World War II quit their jobs as soon as they became pregnant. . . . Fewer women remained childless during the 1950s than in any decade since the late nineteenth century. The timing and spacing of children became far more compressed, so that young mothers were likely to have two more children in diapers at once. . . . At the same time, again for the first time in 100 years, the educational gap between middle-class women and men increased, while job segregation for working men and women seems to have peaked. . . . The result was that family life and gender roles became much more predictable, orderly, and settled in the 1950s than they were either twenty years earlier or would be twenty years later.
>
> *(p. 36)*

Coontz (1997) argues that holding onto these nostalgic ideas creates problems for contemporary families. "The *lag* in adjusting values, behaviors, and institutions to new realities" can make for marital dissatisfaction and divorce, as well as inappropriate policy decisions (p. 109).

Cultural and Historical Variations

The ideal family, with its rigid gender-based division of labor, has always applied more to White families than to families of color. As bell hooks (1984a) argues, many women of color and working-class White women have always had to work outside the home. Children are raised in multigenerational families, by divorced parents who have remarried, by adoptive parents, single parents (usually mothers), or grandparents. Eleanor Palo Stoller and Rose Campbell Gibson (1994) note that "when children are orphaned, when parents are ill or at work, or biological mothers are too young to care for their children alone other women take on childcare, sometimes temporarily, sometimes permanently" (p. 162). Barbara Omolade (1986) describes strong female-centered networks linking African American families and households, in which single mothers support one another in creating stable homes for their children. She challenges official characterization of this kind of family as "dysfunctional." Maxine Baca Zinn (1989) notes that for people of color, the two-parent family is no guarantee against poverty. Anthropologist Leith Mullings discusses the macro-level and global factors that profoundly affect African American households headed by women in New York City (Reading 31). She notes that women-headed households are an international phenomenon, shaped by global as well as local processes like the movement of jobs from industrialized to developing nations. In the United States, they are also affected by historical patterns of discrimination and racism, popular images of low-income women as ineffective mothers, and social policies that limit their already limited options. Mullings describes the transformative work of the women she interviewed in raising children and in sustaining their households and communities under such challenging circumstances. One or both parents may have a disability, as described by Carol Gill and Larry Voss (Reading 32). Some families are split between countries through work, immigration, and war.

Single women (not all of whom are lesbians) have children through alternative insemination. Lesbians and gay men have established networks of friends who function like family. Some have children from earlier, heterosexual relationships; other gay and lesbian couples are fostering or adopting children. According to the Family Pride Coalition, an umbrella organization for gay and lesbian family support groups, at least 2 million gay and lesbian parents in the United States are raising between 3 million and 5 million children, most of them children of heterosexual marriages. The National Adoption Information Clearinghouse, a federal agency, puts the figures much higher—between 2.5 million and 8 million gay and lesbian parents, and 6 million to 14 million children (Lowy 1999). In Reading 33, Ann Filemyr describes "loving across the boundary," as a White woman in partnership with Essie, a woman of color, and comments that "by sharing our lives, our daily survival, our dreams and aspirations, I have been widened and deepened." Their family includes Essie's son and her grandmother. Filemyr makes insightful connections between their personal experiences, other people's reactions to their multiracial household, and the impact of racism and heterosexism on their lives.

Besides providing for the care and socialization of children, families in the United States historically were also productive units. Before the onset of industrialization, work and home were not separated, as happened under the factory system, and women were not housewives but workers. Angela Davis (1983a) cites the following description of domestic work in the colonial era:

> A woman's work began at sunup and continued by firelight as long as she could hold her eyes open. For two centuries, almost everything that the family used or ate was produced at home under her direction. She spun and dyed the yarn that she wove into cloth and cut and hand-stitched into garments. She grew much of the food her family ate, and preserved enough to last the winter months. She made butter, cheese, bread, candles, and soap and knitted her family's stockings.
>
> *(p. 225)*

Thus, housework was directly productive in a home-based economy. In addition, women produced goods for sale—dyed cloth, finished garments, lace, netting, rope, furniture, and homemade remedies. Enslaved African women were involved in such production for their owners and sometimes also for their own families. Native American women were similarly involved in productive work for their family and community. Under such a family system both parents could integrate child care with their daily tasks, tasks in which children also participated. Indeed, childhood was a different phenomenon, with an emphasis on learning skills and responsi-

bilities as part of a community, rather than on play or schooling.

Many shopkeeping and restaurant-owning families today—some of them recent immigrants, others the children or grandchildren of immigrants—continue to blend work and home.

Chinese immigrant life in the United States was very different from these earlier family experiences. At first only Chinese men were allowed to enter the United States—to build roads and railroads, for example—creating a community of bachelors. Later Chinese women were also permitted entry, and the Chinatowns of several major cities began to echo with children's voices for the first time.

Marriage, Domestic Partnership, and Motherhood

Young people in the United States currently face fundamental contradictions concerning marriage and family life. Marriage is highly romanticized: The partners marry for love and are expected to live happily ever after. Love marriages are a relatively recent phenomenon. Although most families in the United States no longer arrange a daughter's marriage, they usually have clear expectations of the kind of man they want her to fall in love with. The ideal of marriage as a committed partnership seems to hold across sexual orientation, with women looking for Mr. or Ms. Right. Marriage and motherhood are often thought to be an essential part of a woman's life, the status to strive for, even if she chooses to keep her own name or rarely uses the coveted title Mrs. People may not refer to unmarried women as "old maids" or "on the shelf" as much as in the past, but there is often still a stigma attached to being single in many cultural groups. Women marry for many reasons, following cultural and religious precepts. They may believe that marriage will make their relationship more secure or provide a stronger foundation for their children. There are material benefits in terms of taxes, health insurance, pension rights, ease of inheritance, and immigration status. It is the conventional and respected way of publicly affirming one's commitment to a partner and being supported in this commitment by family and friends, as well as societal institutions. However, under the excitement and romance of the wedding and despite the fact that many partnerships are thriving, marriage as an institution is taking a buffeting, mainly because of changes in the economy and changing ideas of women's role in society (Coontz 1997; Risman 1998; Skolnick 1991).

Compared with their mothers or grandmothers, fewer U.S. women are marrying, or those who do are marrying later, though they may be involved in committed relationships that last longer than many marriages. Though some research suggests that the vast majority of young people want to marry, a growing number of them see marriage as financially unattainable for a couple who might have to depend on the income of a man without a college degree. Others oppose marriage as the institutionalization of social and economic inequalities between men and women. As Naomi Wolf notes in Reading 23, under English and subsequently U.S. law, a husband and wife were one person in law; married women and children were literally the property of their husbands and fathers. Not for nothing was it called wed*lock*. Marriage is still, at root, a legal contract, though intertwined with social, economic, theological, and emotional aspects. Only a representative of the state can legally marry heterosexual couples, for example. In 1993 rape in marriage became a crime in all fifty states, under at least one section of the sexual offense codes. In seventeen states and the District of Columbia, there are no exemptions for husbands from rape prosecution, while thirty-three states recognize marital rape only under certain circumstances (National Clearinghouse on Marital and Date Rape 1998).

Through concerted lobbying and major national demonstrations, lesbians and gay men have emphasized the validity of their families. Demands for gay marriage in the interests of equal treatment for lesbians, gay men, and heterosexual couples provide an interesting counterweight to feminist critiques of marriage as inherently patriarchal, which we explore below. Efforts to recognize same-sex marriages in Alaska and Hawaii were defeated in state ballot measures. To date, twenty-eight states have passed laws banning same-sex marriage (American Civil Liberties Union [ACLU] 1999). Lesbians and gay men, together with heterosexual couples who have chosen not to marry, have campaigned for the benefits of "domestic partnership"—to be covered by a partner's health insurance, for example, or to be able to draw the partner's pension if he or she dies.

As of December 6, 1999, eighty-one of the Fortune 500 companies offered domestic-partnership health benefits for same-sex partners, including AT&T, Chase Manhattan Bank, Chevron, Costco Wholesale, Mobil, Microsoft, Viacom, and Wells Fargo ("State of the Workplace Report" 1999). The list of state and local governments and academic institutions offering domestic-partnership benefits continues to grow ("State of the Workplace Report" 1999). In a landmark decision on December 20, 1999, the Vermont Supreme Court ruled in *Baker v. Vermont* that lesbian and gay couples are entitled to all of the same "common benefits and protections" that the law gives to married couples (ACLU 1999).

College-educated women in their twenties, thirties, and forties have grown up with much more public discussion of women's rights than did their mothers and with expanded opportunities for education and professional work. Those who work in corporate or professional positions have more financial security in their own right than did middle-class housewives of the 1950s, for example, and are less interested in what Stacey (1996) calls "the patriarchal bargain." Older women, born in the 1920s and brought up during the Great Depression of the 1930s, often valued material security with a man who would be a good provider above emotional closeness or sexual satisfaction. Nowadays, many middle-class women expect much more intimacy in personal relationships than did their mothers.

The idealized family is assumed to provide a secure home for its members, what Lasch (1977) has called "a haven in a heartless world." For some this is generally true. Yet many marriages end in divorce, and a significant number are characterized by violence and abuse. For many women and children—in heterosexual and lesbian families—home is not a safe place but one where they experience emotional or physical violence through beatings, threats, or sexual abuse. Public information and discussion of this "private" issue have gradually grown over the past twenty-five years or so, pushed along by the steady work of shelters for battered women and dramatic public events like the trial of football star O. J. Simpson, accused of killing his wife, Nicole Brown Simpson. We take up this issue in Chapter 6.

Like marriage, motherhood is also currently undergoing change. In 1998, 46 percent of women between the ages of fifteen and thirty-nine had never married (U.S. Bureau of the Census 1998).* In 1997, 32 percent of the live births in the United States were to unmarried women. The percentages varied significantly by race: among Chinese and Japanese American mothers, 6.5 percent and 10 percent; among Native American and Puerto Rican mothers, 58 and 61 percent (Ventura et al. 1999a, pp. 38–39). Generally, more affluent families have fewer children across all racial groups. The fertility rate, the number of children born to women between fifteen and fifty-four, for Mexican American women (116 per 1,000) is about twice that of other groups (Ventura et al. 1999a, p. 39). Children of color are less likely than White children to survive infancy and childhood. Native American infants have the highest rate of death from sudden infant death syndrome and birth defects (Singh and Yu 1995). Although the national infant mortality rate declined at a rate of 3 percent between 1950 and 1991, the rate for Black infants who died before their first birthday (14 per 1,000) was over twice as high as the rate for White and Hispanic infants (6 per 1,000) in 1998 (Martin et al. 1999, p. 31).

At the same time, 43 percent of women between twenty-five and twenty-nine years old had not had children in 1996, compared with 20 percent in 1960; and it was 26 percent of women between thirty and thirty-four years compared with 14 percent for the same years (U.S. Bureau of the Census 1998). Most are childless on purpose, despite the idea, popularized in the media, that women are controlled by a "biological clock," ticking away the years when conception is possible. Many of these women describe themselves as child-free rather than childless, an important shift in emphasis highlighting that this

---

*Official statistics are a key source of information but are limited for discussion of diversity, as they are usually analyzed according to three main categories only: White, Black, and Hispanic. "Hispanic" includes Puerto Ricans, Cubans, Mexican Americans, and people from Central and South America. Some reports give a separate category for Native Americans and Native Alaskans, or for Asians and Pacific Islanders, another very heterogeneous group for whom there are few data at a national level. Data on many social issues are not usually analyzed by class, another serious limitation. We have tried to be as inclusive as possible; sometimes this is limited by the availability of adequate data.

Family Violence

- Up to 50 percent of all homeless women and children in this country are fleeing domestic violence. Approximately 1 out of every 25 elder persons is victimized annually. Of those who experience domestic elder abuse, 37 percent are neglected and 26 percent are physically abused. Of those who perpetrate the abuse, 30 percent are adult children of the abused person.

- As violence against women becomes more severe and more frequent in the home, children experience a 300 percent increase in physical violence by the male batterer.

- Sixty-two percent of sons over the age of 14 were injured when they attempted to protect their mothers from attacks by abusive male partners. Women are 10 times more likely than men to be victims of violent crime in intimate relationships.

Source: National Coalition Against Domestic Violence.

---

is a positive choice for them (Bartlett 1994; Ireland 1993; Morrell 1994; Reti 1992; Safe 1996). Such women challenge the idea that women must have children to be fulfilled. They find great satisfaction and great joy in intimate relationships, friendships, work, travel, community activities, spirituality, and connections with children.

Teen pregnancy rates declined considerably during the 1990s (Ventura et al. 1999). Luker (1996) argues that, contrary to popular stereotypes, teen pregnancy rates were higher in the 1950s than in the mid-1990s. She noted that teenagers—aged fifteen to nineteen—made up less than a third of all unmarried mothers and that two-thirds of teenage mothers were eighteen or nineteen. Fewer young women than in the fifties and sixties have "shotgun" weddings triggered by pregnancy. Fewer babies born to teenage mothers were given up for adoption in the 1980s—4 percent between 1982 and 1988—compared with the late 1960s—21 percent between 1965 and 1972. (Usdansky 1996).

Because women are daughters, we all have some perspective on motherhood through the experience of our own mothers. Many people regard motherhood as the ultimate female experience and disapprove of women who do not want to be mothers, especially if they are married. Magazines and advertising images show happy, smiling mothers who dote on their children and buy them their favorite foods, cute clothes, toys, and equipment. Rearing children is hard work, often tedious and repetitious, requiring humor and patience. Many women experience contradictory emotions, including fear, resentment, inadequacy, and anger about motherhood despite societal idealization of it and their own hopes or expectations that they will find it unreservedly fulfilling.

Adrienne Rich (1986b) has argued that it is not motherhood itself that is oppressive to women, but the way our society constructs motherhood. The contemporary image of a young mother—usually White and middle-class—with immaculate hair and makeup, wearing a chic business suit, briefcase in one hand and toddler in the other, may define an ideal for many young women. But it also sets a standard that is virtually unattainable without causing the mother to come apart at the seams—that is, in the absence of a generous budget for convenience foods, restaurant meals, work clothes, dry cleaning, hairdressing, and good-quality child care. Despite contradictions and challenges, many women are finding joy and affirmation in redefining what it means to be a wife or mother (Abbey and O'Reilly 1998; Blakley 1994; Hochman 1994; Van Every 1995).

Motherhood has been defined differently at different times. During World War II, for example, when women were needed to work in munitions factories and shipyards in place of men drafted overseas, companies often provided housing, canteens, and child care to support these working women (Hayden 1981). After the war women were no longer needed in these jobs, and such facilities were largely discontinued. Psychologists began to talk about the central importance of a mother's care for the healthy physical and emotional development of children (Bowlby 1963). Invoking the notion of maternal instinct, some asserted that a mother's care is qualitatively different from that of others and that only a mother's love will do. Mothers who are not

sufficiently "present" can be blamed for their children's problems. Ironically, mothers who are too present, said to be overidentified with their children and a source of negative pressure, are also blamed. In 1999, 10 million preschoolers had mothers in the paid workforce. But, according to syndicated columnist Ellen Goodman (1999), "the cultural consensus still says that professional mothers should be home with the kids while welfare mothers should be out working." Elizabeth Harvey's (1999) research on children aged three to twelve showed that those whose mothers were in the paid workforce during the first three years were not significantly different in terms of behavior, cognitive development, self-esteem, and academic achievement compared with those whose mothers were at home. Any slight differences disappeared by the time the children were of school age.

Despite the fact that there are more mothers of young children in the paid workforce today than ever before, working mothers, especially women of color, risk being called unfit and perhaps losing their children to foster homes or state agencies if they cannot maintain some conventionally approved standard of family life. Throughout the 1990s, a series of news reports describing low-quality child-care facilities, including some cases in which children were said to have been sexually abused, contributed to the anxiety of working mothers. Cultural ideas about who makes a bad mother are most germane to custody cases. In 1994, for example, a full-time Michigan university student lost custody of her child because the judge decided that she would not be sufficiently available to care for the child properly. The father was awarded custody, even though his mother would be the one to take care of the child because he worked full time. This decision was overturned on appeal. But in a 1996 case involving a lesbian mother, a Florida appeals court judge ruled that the father—who had served eight years in prison for murdering his first wife—would make a better parent than the mother (Navarro 1996).

Motherhood has been a persistent rationale for the unequal treatment of women in terms of access to education and well-paid, professional work, though it has not impeded the employment of African American women, for example, as domestics and nannies in White people's homes or of White working-class women in factories. Not all today's older women were able to choose whether or not to stay out of the paid workforce when their children were young, despite the popular and scholarly rhetoric advocating full-time motherhood.

Juggling Home and Work

In general, U.S. workplaces are still structured on the assumption that men are the breadwinners and women are the homemakers, despite the fact that more U.S. women are in the paid workforce than ever before, including 70 percent of mothers. Many women work part-time jobs with low pay and no benefits. This is particularly stressful for single parents, most of whom are women, especially if they do not have a strong support network. Even with two adults working, many families find it hard to make ends meet. Although middle- and upper-class families have the money to hire help in the home — nannies, maids, or caregivers for the elderly — and may send their children to boarding schools and summer camps, most families, whether there are two wage earners or one, continually juggle the demands of their jobs with running a home and family responsibilities (Barnett and Rivers 1996; Hochschild 1997; Lawe and Lawe 1980; Nadelson and Nadelson 1980). As we noted earlier, this is one of the greatest strains on contemporary family life and a defining life experience for most working women, many of whom do a **second shift** — coming home to household chores after working outside the home (Hochschild 1989). Women who live with husbands or male partners generally do more of the routine housekeeping than the men.

Women's roles have changed much more than men's roles. In a *New York Times* and *CBS News* survey of teenagers, only 58 percent of the boys interviewed expected that their wives would work outside the home, compared with 86 percent of the girls. The boys did not see themselves doing what they considered "women's work," particularly cooking, cleaning, and child care. Some of the girls interviewed saw this difference in terms of boys wanting to be "manly" and powerful at home and anticipated "a lot of fights" negotiating the relationships they want. Most women spend seventeen years of their lives, on average, taking care of children and eighteen years looking after their elderly parents or their husband's parents. In reality these periods overlap, usually when the children are in their teens. An additional factor complicating daily life is the high divorce rate, which means that parents and stepparents are involved in ongoing negotiations over shared child-care arrangements — often a source of hostility and stress.

Breaking Up, Living Alone

As we grow as individuals, our personal relationships may also develop in ways that continue to sustain us. Sometimes they cannot support our changing needs and concerns, and we may have to make the difficult decision to leave. The idealized family image does not include divorce or widowhood. Making a marriage or committed relationship "work" is complex and involves some combination of loving care, responsibility, communication, patience, humor, and luck. Material circumstances may have a significant impact, especially over the longer term. Having money, food, personal security, a home, reliable and affordable child care, and additional care for elderly relatives; being willing and able to move for a job or a chance to study; and having good health are examples of favorable circumstances. Negative factors that especially affect young African American women and Latinas are the high unemployment rates for men of color and the fact that roughly 30 percent of young African American and Latino men between eighteen and twenty-five are caught up in the criminal justice system.

As discussed in several of the readings that follow, the couple may look to each other as friends, partners, and lovers and expect that together they can provide for each other's material and emotional needs and fulfill their dreams. In addition to experiencing the joy and satisfaction of sharing life on a daily basis, the partnership may also bear the brunt of work pressures, money worries, changing gender roles, or stress from a violent community, as well as difficulties due to personal misunderstandings, different priorities, or differing views of what it means to be a husband or a wife.

These stresses and difficulties are compounded when there are children. Half of U.S. marriages end in divorce, usually initiated by women, for reasons of incompatibility, infidelity, mistreatment, economic problems, or sexual problems (Kurz 1995). Many women experience the breakup with a mixture of fear, excitement, relief, and a sense of failure. They almost always suffer a serious drop in their standard of living immediately after divorce — hence the saying, "Poverty is only a divorce away" — whereas men's standard of living goes up (Peterson 1996). Usually mothers retain custody of the children even though fathers may see them on weekends or during school vacations. Relatively few fathers pay regular child support, and in any case child support rates are set too low to be realistic. Boumil and Friedman (1996) estimate that "complete and regular child support payments are received in less than 50% of the cases where there is court-ordered child support" (p. 108). Children are usually affected emotionally and educationally by the ups and downs of parents' marital difficulties. Though a divorce may bring some resolution, children may have to adjust to a new home, school, neighborhood, a lowered standard of living, or a whole new family set-up complete with stepparent, and stepbrothers or sisters. Most children suffer emotionally as a result of divorce but recover their equilibrium within eighteen months (Stewart et al. 1997), and the large majority of children of divorced parents grow up socially and psychologically well-adjusted (Hetherington and Clingempeel 1992).

Most divorced or widowed men marry within a year of the end of their previous relationship, often marrying women younger than themselves. Women wait longer to remarry, and fewer do. The majority of older men are married, while the majority of older women are widows. Women in all racial and ethnic groups outlive men in those same groups, though most people of color have a shorter life expectancy than White people. On average, African American women, for example, are widowed at a younger age than White women. Women alone over sixty-five years of age make up one of the poorest groups in the country—together with single mothers. We take up the issue of poverty in more detail in Chapter 8. Being old and alone is something that women often fear, though some older women feel good about their relative autonomy, especially if they are comfortable financially and have support from family members or friends.

Immigration and the Family

The image of the ideal nuclear family says nothing about how this family happens to be in the United States in the first place. Since 1952, U.S. immigration law and policy have allowed family members to join relatives in this country. This can be a lengthy process, and many families are split between the United States and their native countries. Men and women who immigrate to this country often leave their children back home until they have gained a foothold here. Others send their children, especially teenagers, to the "old country" to keep them from the problems of life in the United States. Some recent Chinese immigrant women, who work long hours for low pay in New York garment factories, are sending their infants back to China to be cared for by family members (Sengupta 1999). They lack affordable child care and the support of an extended family. The children are U.S. citizens by birth and are expected to return to this country when they are school age.

Women who are recent immigrants may be more affected by the customs of their home country, though younger immigrant women see coming to the United States partly in terms of greater personal freedom, as do many young women born here to immigrant parents. Differing aspirations and expectations for careers, marriage, and family life between mothers and daughters may lead to tensions between the generations, as exemplified in Amy Tan's novel *The Joy Luck Club* (1989). According to Stoller and Gibson (1994), many older Asian American women suffer both economic hardship and cultural isolation in this country. Recent elderly immigrants are also affected by cultural isolation, especially if they do not know English and their children and grandchildren are keen to become acculturated. First-generation immigrants who hold traditional views of family obligations, for example, may be disappointed by the treatment they receive from their Americanized children and grandchildren.

Feminist Perspectives on Marriage, Motherhood, and the Family

There is a sense in which marriage and family life are so "normal," so much a part of our everyday lives, that many of us rarely stop to think much about them. Feminists often challenge commonplace beliefs about these bedrock social institutions that people may not even know they hold. Marriage and the family are crucially important in feminist theory, and as we argue earlier, constitute a contested terrain in public discourse.

Challenging the Private/Public Dichotomy

A core idea in much U.S. political thought is that there is a dichotomy between the private and personal (dating, marriage, sexual habits, who does the housework, relationships between parents and children) and the public (religion, law, business). According to this view, these two spheres affect each other but are governed by different rules, attitudes, and behavior. The family, for example, is the only place where love, caring, and sensitivity are assumed to come first. How a man treats his wife or children, then, is a private matter. A woman's right to an abortion in the United States—despite many restrictions in practice—also rests on this principle of the right to privacy. A key aspect of much feminist theorizing and activism has been to challenge this public vs. private dichotomy and to explain the family as a site of patriarchal power summed up in the saying "The working man's home is his castle." Every man may not be the most powerful person in the family, yet this is a culturally accepted idea. Such power may operate in relatively trivial ways—as, for example, when Mom and the kids cater to Dad's preferences in food or TV shows as a way of avoiding a confrontation. Usually, as the main wage earner and "head" of the family, men command loyalty, respect, and obedience. Some resort to violence or sexual abuse, as mentioned earlier. White, middle-class feminists like Betty Friedan (1963), who wrote about her dissatisfactions with suburban life and the boredom of being a full-time homemaker, which she described as "the problem which has no name," identify motherhood as a major obstacle to women's fulfillment. By contrast, working-class women—White women and women of color—name a lack of well-paying jobs, a lack of skills or education, and racism, not motherhood, as obstacles to their liberation.

Given the lower status of women in society, feminists point to marriage as a legal contract between unequal parties (Pateman 1988). As Okin (1989) notes, the much-repeated slogan "the personal is the political" is "the central message of feminist critiques of the public/private dichotomy" (p. 124). She lists four ways in which the family is a political entity:

1. Power is always an element of family relationships.
2. This domestic sphere is governed by external rules—for example, those concerning marriage and divorce, marital rape, or child custody.
3. It is in the family that much of our early socialization takes place and that we learn gender roles.
4. The division of labor within the family raises practical and psychological barriers against women in all other spheres of life.
   (pp. 128–33)

The Family and the Economic System

Other feminist theorists see the family as part of the economic system and emphasize its role in the **reproduction of labor** (Benston 1969; Dalla Costa and James 1972; Mitchell 1971; Zaretsky 1976). In this highly unsentimental view, marriage is compared to prostitution, where women trade sex for economic and social support. The family is deemed important for society because it is responsible for producing, nurturing, and socializing the next generation of workers and citizens, the place where children first learn to be "social animals." This includes basic skills like language and potty training and social skills like cooperation and negotiation with others or abiding by rules. Women's unpaid domestic work and child care, though not considered productive work, directly benefit the state and employers by turning out functioning members of society. The family also cares for its adult members by providing meals and clean clothes, as well as rest, relaxation, love, and sexual intimacy, so that they are ready to face another working day—another aspect of the reproduction of labor. Similarly, it cares for people who are not in the workforce, those with disabilities, the elderly, or the chronically ill. Still other theorists explain the family in terms of patriarchal power linked to a capitalist system of economic relations, with much discussion of exactly how these two systems are connected, and how the gendered division of labor within the family first came about (Hartmann 1981; Jaggar 1983; Young 1980).

Mothering and Maternal Thinking

According to Lauri Umansky (1996), in the late 1970s and early 1980s feminist writing about motherhood increased enormously with an emphasis on the daily experience of mothering (Lazarre 1976; Rich

1976) and the symbolic meaning of motherhood (Chodorow 1978; Dinnerstein 1976). Many writers were deeply ambivalent about mothering and recognized the severe limitations of the gendered division of labor. Chodorow and Dinnerstein both advocated shared parenting as essential to undermining rigid gender roles, under which many men are cut off, practically and emotionally, from the organic and emotional concerns of children and dissociated from life processes. Two decades later, Pepper Schwartz (1994) and Barbara Risman (1998) make similar arguments.

Umansky (1996) notes that maternalist rhetoric and imagery were central to much 1980s ecofeminism and women's peace activism. Examples are Martha Boesing's statement during her trial for criminal trespass at the Honeywell Corporation, a manufacturer of cluster bombs used in the Middle East and South East Asia (Boesing 1994) and the Unity Statement of the Women's Pentagon Action (Reading 72, Chapter 11). Sara Ruddick (1989) argued, further, that the experience and the work of mothering has the potential to generate principles of "maternal thinking" based on the desire to preserve life and foster growth. Such principles could serve as a blueprint for human interaction that would involve genuine peace and security. Responsible mothering has also led women to organize for better working conditions, improvements in welfare programs, and environmental justice (Jetter, Orelck, and Taylor 1997). Leith Mullings takes up this point in her discussion of women's transformative work in Reading 31.

Policy Implications and Implementation

Many feminist scholars, policy makers, and activists have followed through on their analyses of women's roles in the family by taking steps to implement the policies they advocate. They have set up crisis lines and shelters for battered women and children across the country and made family violence and childhood sexual abuse public issues. They have campaigned for higher wages for women, job training, and advancement, which we discuss further in Chapter 8. They have argued for shared parental responsibility for child care, including flexible work schedules, paid parental leave for both parents, payment of child support, after-school programs, and redrawing the terms of divorce such that, in the

event of divorce, both postdivorce households would have the same standard of living. Above all, feminists have campaigned for good-quality child care subsidized by government and employers, on site at big workplaces, and they have organized community child-care facilities and informal networks of mothers who share child care. Although some of these efforts have been successful, there is still a great deal to be accomplished if women are not to be penalized for having children, an issue we discuss in Chapter 8.

Although policy makers and politicians often declare that children are the nation's future and greatest resource, parents are given little practical help in caring for them. The editors of *Mothering* magazine pulled no punches when they asked:

> Why is the United States the only industrial democracy in the world that provides no universal pre- or postnatal care, no universal health coverage; . . . has no national standards for child care; makes no provision to encourage at-home care in the early years of life; . . . has no explicit family policies such as child allowances and housing subsidies for all families; and has not signed the United Nations Convention on the Rights of the Child—a dubious distinction shared with Iraq, Libya, and Cambodia?
>
> *(Brennan, Winklepleck, and MacNee 1994, p. 424)*

At the same time, former first lady Hillary Clinton (1996), adopting an African proverb, argues that "it takes a village to raise a child." Susan Moller Okin (1989) notes that so few U.S. politicians have raised children that it seems almost a qualification for political office not to have done so. Skolnick (1991) notes that other industrialized countries have also experienced "changes in gender roles, divorce rates, and family structure—but their public policy responses have been very different" (p. 218). Most European countries have instituted family policies with provisions for health care, child allowances, child care, prenatal care, parental leave, and services for the elderly. In the United States, family policy is an unfamiliar term and the few policies that support families, like welfare, unemployment assistance, and tax relief, are inadequate and uncoordinated. Randy Albelda and Chris Tilly argue that a comprehensive family policy is needed in this country to resolve the contradictions and inconsistencies that parents and children currently face (Reading 34).

As Stacey (1996) argues, how "family" is defined is also a political matter. Many policy makers, politicians, and commentators still seek to enforce the idealized nuclear family model. Feminist researchers and activists need to argue for the validity of *all* family forms. The form is not the issue. What matters is that parents and other adults are supported in raising children with love and security. Many local community organizations, religious groups, and health projects across the country are involved in this. Parents, Families, and Friends of Lesbians and Gays (PFLAG) is one example, with chapters in many areas.

Toward a Redefinition of Family Values

Elevating the ideal of the nuclear, two-parent family is a major contradiction in contemporary U.S. society, as we argue earlier. Regardless of its form, the family should

> care for family members, emotionally and materially;
>
> promote egalitarian relationships among the adults, who should not abuse their power over children;
>
> share parenting between men and women so that it is not the province of either gender;
>
> do away with a gendered division of labor;
>
> teach children nonsexist, antiracist, anticlassist attitudes and behavior and the values of caring and connectedness to others;
>
> pass on cultural heritage; and
>
> influence the wider community.

Relationships between Equals

As a result of the major U.S. political movements of the past four decades—for civil rights, women's rights, and gay/lesbian rights—many people, particularly women, have understood the connection between inequality in interpersonal relationships and that among social groups. For personal relationships to be more egalitarian, as far as possible the partners should have shared values or compati-

---

Pro-Family Measures

- Restructure work hours and benefits to suit working parents.
- Redistribute work to reduce under- and overemployment.
- Enact comparable worth standards of pay equity so that women as well as men can earn a family wage.
- Provide universal health, prenatal and child care, sex education, and reproductive rights to make it possible to choose to parent responsibly.
- Legalize gay marriage.
- Revitalize public education.
- Pass and enforce strict gun control laws.
- End the economic inequities of property and income dispositions in divorce.
- House the homeless.
- Fund libraries, parks, public broadcasting, and the arts.

Source: Stacey 1999, pp. 489–90.

---

ble nonnegotiables, have some compatible sense of why they are together, and share power in the relationship. They also need to be committed to a clear communication process and be willing to work through difficulties with honesty and openness. If the relationship is to last, it must be flexible and able to change over time so that both partners can grow individually as well as together. Few of us have much experience to guide us. Indeed, most people have experienced and observed unequal relationships—at home, in school, and in the wider community—which give us little basis for change. Pepper Schwartz (1994) notes the costs of peer marriage. The partners may have less intense sex lives and fewer external sources of validation and support. Their closeness may exclude others, and they may not be able to pursue their careers to the fullest extent possible. In spite of these costs, the couples she interviewed had created extremely rewarding marriages. Miriam Ching Yoou Louie and Nguyen Louie (Reading 28) and Carol Gill and Larry Voss (Reading 32) discuss their experiences of egalitarian relationships and shared parenting and the importance of teaching their children nonsexist, antiracist, anticlassist attitudes.

Shared Parenting

Although children, it is hoped, are a great source of pleasure and satisfaction, women generally bear much more responsibility for children than do men. We argue that caring for family members should not be an individual problem or only a woman's problem but an issue for the wider society. Adrienne Rich (1986b), for example, advocated thinking of pregnancy and childbirth, a short-term condition, quite separately from child rearing, a much longer-term responsibility. We noted above various changes that would bring shared parenting closer to being a reality.

Teaching Children Nonsexist, Antiracist, Anticlassist Attitudes

Currently the family is a key institution for teaching gender roles, though this may not be done in the same way across different cultural groups. Many African American mothers, for example, emphasize self-confidence, skills, cultural heritage, and a sense of capability and strength in raising children so that they will have practical abilities and inner resources to cope with the institutionalized racism of the wider society. As members of the dominant group, White children often have very little consciousness of "whiteness." Poor children may not know they are poor until they go to school or mix with those from higher income brackets. Middle-class children often learn classist attitudes about poorer children, ex-

pressed, for example, in criticism of their unfashionable clothes, pushy manners, or nonstandard language. Children learn about gender very early, from everyday observation, toys, games, TV shows, and cartoons, and the way adults interact with them. Current gender roles are required by the gendered division of labor. We see this as inherently limiting to both women and men, a caricature of human potential. Though nonconforming behavior is acceptable in small children, girls can be tomboys for only so long before they are pressured to be more ladylike. Similarly, boys are usually discouraged from playing with dolls or dressing up, often out of fear that this behavior will cause them to grow up to be gay. Transgressive gender behavior in heterosexual adults is equally, or maybe even more, challenging to conventional attitudes. Even if a family encourages assertive girls or gentle boys, the children have to deal with gendered reality in school. A family committed to redefining family values will need to negotiate them with the community it is a part of and seek out appropriate schooling, if possible.

Susan Moller Okin (1989) argues that for society to be just, all social institutions must be just, including the family. We argue that the family must be a source of security for its members, an element in constructing a secure and sustainable future. A sustainable future means that we, in the present generation, must consider how our actions will affect people of future generations. A useful reference here is the Native American "seventh generation" principle: The community is responsible for those not yet born, and because of this, whatever actions are taken in the present must not jeopardize the possibility of well-being seven generations to come. How would we have to restructure our relationships as well as other social institutions in order to honor that principle?

◆◆◆

Questions for Reflection

In reading and discussing this chapter, consider these questions:

1. What do you expect/hope for in a personal relationship?

2. Are you in love now? How can you tell?

3. How does power manifest itself in your relationships with family members, friends, dates, or lovers?

4. Should intimate relationships be monogamous? Why/Why not?

5. Do you have friends or dates with people from a racial/ethnic/cultural group different from your own? If so, how did you meet? How have your differences been a factor in your friendship or relationship?

6. How do you define family? Whom do you consider family in your own life?

7. How do macro-level institutions—in particular the government, media, and organized religion—shape people's relationships and family lives?

8. Should there be gay marriage? Where do you stand on this issue?

9. If women are to have more equal treatment within the family, what kinds of changes in male attitudes and behavior will be needed also? How might this happen?

10. What changes are necessary to involve men in parenting? Look at the micro, meso, macro, and global levels of analysis.

◆◆◆
Taking Action

1. Talk with your peers—women and men—about your nonnegotiables in a personal relationship. What are you willing to compromise on?

2. Talk with your mother or grandmother (or women their age) about their experiences of marriage, motherhood, and family. What choices have they made in their lives in this regard? What options did they have?

3. Look critically at the way women are portrayed in relationships and the family in magazines, movies, and ads, and on TV.

TWENTY-EIGHT
◆◆◆

The Conversation Begins
Miriam Ching Yoon Louie and Nguyen Louie

A Mother's Story

My daughter, Nguyen, was born March 6, 1975, two days before International Women's Day. The Third World Women's Alliance was in charge of organizing a big celebration, and I had to drop off programs and files to another organizer en route to the hospital. My husband, Belvin, was there coaching and taking pictures during the birth, and I was so happy when Nguyen arrived. We named her after Nguyen Thi Dinh, the head of the women's union in Vietnam, who started the armed struggle against French colonialism. Twelve years later, during a women's peace conference in Moscow in 1987, I had the thrill of meeting Madame Nguyen Thi Dinh, by then a salt-and-pepper-haired grandmother. When I showed her a picture of Nguyen, she squeezed my hand and said, "I feel like she is my daughter, too."

I am a third-generation Chinese- and Korean-American, born in Vallejo, California, in 1950, the year the Korean War broke out. My maternal grandfather was a Methodist minister, educated by missionaries in Seoul. He was active in the Korean independence movement while Grandma raised their eleven children. My paternal grandparents came from Guangdong, a province in southern China, and did odd jobs in San Francisco Chinatown. My father upset his family when he married my mother, because she was Korean instead of Chinese.

Vallejo is a naval-shipyard town, and my father worked in the shipyard for over forty years. World War II broke the color line, opening up jobs for minorities in defense industries, but wages were low. To make ends meet, Dad also worked at a Chinese-owned gas station on weekends and moonlighted in a Chinese-owned grocery store at night. Mom took care of us five kids. While I was growing up, my parents fought constantly. As adults we gradually realized that Mom has manic-depression. One of my brothers drank himself to death at twenty-nine; another has had substance abuse problems and a hard time getting a stable job. Half my family can more or less function and get to where they are supposed to be in the morning, and the other half has a real hard time. I suppose we are your typical American working-class dysfunctional family.

After moving out of the projects, we were one of the first minority families to move into another neighborhood in Vallejo. After more black families moved in, some whites began to get hostile. I remember picking up the telephone party line one day and hearing, "Too many niggers are moving into the neighborhood." I thought, "Gee, are they talking about us?" That was my first encounter with racial discrimination. Our Irish-American playmates up the hill called us "Chinks" and "Japs." Mom told us different names we could call whites. One day when they called us "Japs" we called them "Limeys," and they got really mad and broke one of our windows.

When I was a high-school student, a Black Muslim tried to sell me a newspaper on the street, saying, "Hey, they're trying to kill your people in Vietnam." He was way ahead of me. Completely ignorant about Vietnam, I thought, "I'm not Vietnamese." Later my liberal civics teacher raised alternative points of view about the war, which started me thinking. When people at church said, "You know this is a righteous war because those people are Buddhists and we need to Christianize them," I thought, "This is wrong." That was it for me with the Christian religion. I quit going to church, which made Mom furious.

In 1968 I entered the University of California – Berkeley with scholarships and a Higher Educational Opportunity Program grant — the first person in my family to go to college. It was the height of campus activity at Berkeley. Students rioted in solidarity with the French student movement that summer. In the fall they boycotted classes when the school refused to allow Eldridge Cleaver, then a Black Panther, to teach. In the winter students of color organized the Third World Liberation Front to establish a Third World College, and in the spring others launched the People's Park action. When the police stormed the campus, gassing and beating students, I stopped going to classes, too.

I first met my husband in a freshman chemistry class at Berkeley. We were both trying to avoid getting F's for missing class during the Third World strike. Belvin is second-generation Chinese, and I asked if he had heard about the Asian-American Political Alliance, which later launched the larger Third World Liberation Front, which also included the Black Student Union, MEChA (Movimiento Estudiantil Chicano de Aztlan), and the Native American group. He said, "Nope," and that ended the discussion. That summer we met again at the Third World Board office, where I volunteered as a secretary. My typing was pretty bad, but Belvin stuck up for me. In some organizations women complained about doing only clerical work. In the Asian movement women have always been outspoken leaders who did both the typing and the talking.

Eventually I became so involved in organizing activities that I lost interest in quantitative chemistry tests and premed studies and dropped out of college. When Belvin and I started living together, my mother and I got in a big fight about sex before marriage. We cried and screamed on the phone. Over the years Mom mellowed out so that by the time my sister Beth was in a relationship, Mom advised her, "Don't rush into marriage. Maybe you two should live together first to see if it's going to work." Coming from a family that was active in the Korean independence movement, Mom was open to our activism, whereas Dad, with his conservative Chinese working-class background, advised us, "Don't rock the boat; roll with the punches; don't fight city hall."

Belvin and I went to Cuba together in 1969 as part of the first Venceremos Brigade. (*Venceremos* means "we will win" in Spanish.) We cut sugarcane for two months during the big harvest and met with Fidel Castro. The Cuban Revolution, Vietnam War, China's split with the Soviet Union, student movements in Mexico, Japan, and South Korea — all were events that influenced and radicalized youth-of-color movements in the United States. Our racial identification with these movements opened our eyes to what the United States was doing in the third world and shed light on aspects of our own history as third-world people living "within the belly of the beast."

After Belvin and I had been living together for five years, I got pregnant. My mother said, "Miriam, you always do things ass backward. You're supposed to get married first, then have a baby." We had another big fight about that. In late 1974 I was four months pregnant when our friends and relatives helped us celebrate our marriage with a big lunch buffet at a Chinese restaurant. Nguyen likes to say she was there at the buffet, too, eating chow mein, roast pork, and wedding cake — from the inside. At the time, we were under FBI surveillance because of our trip to Cuba. Once on our way to Lamaze classes with pillows under our arms, the FBI showed up on the stairs of our apartment, asking, "Do you want to talk about your trip to Cuba?" "No," we answered, and hurried to class.

When Nguyen was three months old, I took her to a baby-sitter and went to work as an administrative assistant at Asian Manpower Services, a job-training program for new immigrants. When Nguyen was two and a half, I took her to a child-care center in Chinatown that was pretty good. She cried when I left her, which made me feel terrible. Even in the third grade, when she started a new school, Nguyen still burst out crying, "Mom, don't leave me!"

I came into the women's movement by way of the Third World Women's Alliance, shortly before Nguyen was born. Our group did some of the earliest work in this country on the intersection of gender, race, and class, and took up issues ignored by the mainstream women's movement, such as infant mortality, sterilization abuse, abortion access for poor women, affirmative action, and special admissions programs for women of color. The alliance supported women with children because a lot of us had kids. At one point there was a Child Development Committee, and we always organized child care for meetings and events. When Nguyen was little, she got carted to everything. We took a spread for her to crawl around on at big conferences and demonstrations. When she was six, her brother, Lung San, was born.

My husband and I are pretty close, partly because our work in the movement has given us common experiences and reference points. But we also have had our share of ups and downs. We had a fight about my going back to work after Nguyen was born. He said, "We have to figure out if it's worth your going to work, because of the cost of child care. Maybe it's not worth it." We went back and forth until I said, "How come the price of a baby-sitter is deducted from my salary? How come the cost of the baby-sitter is not deducted from *both* our salaries?" After that I went back to work.

Belvin has always shared the housework and taken care of the kids. He is very responsible, partly because he grew up working in a family-owned Chinese restaurant. He chops vegetables super fast, helps when the kids are stumped on homework, attends parent-teacher conferences, and makes a mean dish of soy sauce pork. I have always worked for nonprofit organizations for low pay; he is the stable earner. He helps my various organizations with computer and campaign work, and lends a hand for special events and demonstrations. He got a Best Corporate Sponsor award for all the garment workers' campaign picket lines he walked. Now, like his father, Lung San helps me leaflet, put out bulk mailings, and inputs supporters on our data base. We brainstorm together on issues, and I badger Belvin to edit my writing. Some men are threatened by women who are active, but not Belvin. Rather, he sees me as a window into different experiences. Many of our friends are single or divorced, lesbian and straight, so as a straight married couple we are an aberration — a dying breed. Friends prophesying the end of the nuclear family call us the dinosaurs.

In 1983 I began working for Asian Immigrant Women's Advocates (AIWA), an organization seeking to empower low-income immigrant women who find themselves working for third-world wages. In 1989 I also started working with the Women of Color Resource Center (WCRC), which includes some good friends from Third World Women's Alliance days. Through AIWA I get to support Asian women workers' struggles for justice, while the WCRC allows me to work with and learn from feisty women-of-color organizers across racial lines. In 1990 I went back to Berkeley to get my BA and in 1991 I studied in Korea for a year while Belvin took care of the kids.

With all the running around we did, Nguyen grew up like a wild weed. If there were meetings at night, Belvin and I took turns taking care of her. Sometimes she would say, "Mommy, I don't want you to go," and I would say, "I have to go." Or she would yell at me as I went out the door. For a period after she turned twelve, we had big fights because she wouldn't do things as I saw fit. It took a while before it dawned on me that she wanted to be more independent. I had to realize that bearing down would only make her rebel against me.

I would have liked to spend more time with my kids while they were growing up. At the time I would not have considered giving up my organizing activities, but now I have some regrets. Nguyen still says, "Hey, Mom, where are you going? Who are you going with? When are you getting back?" Our relationship is something of a role reversal. I jump into things and end up being consumed by different activities, rushing from cause to cause and event to event. I probably get that from the Korean, manic-depressive side of my personality. Nguyen used to try to create some order to pressure me to stick around.

Nguyen has good instincts and is very independent. You can count on her to do the right thing and be at the right place at the right time. Despite having grown up like a weed, she turned out pretty well. I wish she didn't have to agonize so much over her decisions, but she is a critical thinker; she works out things in her own methodical way. Her dad is pretty logical, whereas I am impulsive and often get myself out on a limb. Perhaps because her parents have such strong opinions, she works hard to come up with her own independent perspective on everything. In college she works so hard that she barely sleeps or eats. Sometimes her pop and I tell her not to study so hard, to try to get to more student conferences and demonstrations because that's also what a college education is about. Then we catch ourselves and laugh about the kind of parents we are. Nguyen went up to Boston for a training session for our Garment Workers Justice Campaign and demonstrations against manufacturer Jessica McClintock for corporate responsibility. That made her old mom happy.

I need to slow down because I am getting older. I can't get as much done now as I used to, and I can already tell that menopause is not going to be nice to me. Fortunately, a younger generation of women is coming up that is bringing in new points of view and different issues that we had not considered. I hope they can build on and take advantage of our mistakes and experiences.

I am hopeful for the future. Women in grassroots organizations need more resources and visibility. While the mainstream women's movement is considered to represent us in pursuing important electoral, legislative, and judicial battles, they don't deal with a lot of issues minority women face. The consciousness that the women's movement fought so hard for has filtered into different communities. Now women of color are creating distinct kinds of feminism and organizing relevant to their own communities and experiences. No longer do you have to decide whether your allegiance is to the minority community or to the women's liberation movement. That false dichotomy is absent from the organizations and activists of the new generation.

My definition of feminism has changed over the years. When I worked with the Third World Women's Alliance, I was emphatically not a feminist. I saw feminist ideology as placing gender above class and race, thus rendering working-class women, especially women of color, invisible. Now women of color have crafted feminisms that take into account the many oppressions and challenges they face. I've been in women's groups for over twenty years, and today if people call me a feminist I no longer get uptight about it.

Like anyone else, Nguyen has to deal with her identity and what she wants to be. But in terms of knowing who her people are, where she comes from, and what her culture is, she has a solid foundation. My husband and I handed down our values, either through osmosis at the dinner table or just by our kids' seeing how their parents function — what kind of work we do, whom we respect. Nguyen already has the kind of confidence in the way she looks at the world that took me years to achieve. What I had to fight for, she can assume. She takes for granted the principles of feminism and is secure in her ethnic identity. We've seen her stand up against arbitrary practices by authority figures in school and job settings even when fellow students and coworkers were afraid to speak out. The girl can hold her own.

It was rewarding to see how things had changed and developed when I went back to school and majored in ethnic studies. For all its ups and downs, that period of ferment in the 1960s was a turning point. Many of us who started out in those movements ended up forming ethnic and women's studies programs and new community-based organizations and campaigns so that this new generation can start from higher ground. I hope Nguyen can do something she really enjoys that will serve the communities and people who are struggling to get by. Whatever she chooses to do, I know she will put all her energy and heart into it.

A Daughter's Story

I am a Chinese-Korean-American young woman. It may be a mouthful, but that is who I am in my entirety. Each identity is an integral part of me that cannot be separated from the others. Because of this, prejudice is something that I have had to deal with all my life. Whenever I am made fun of or discriminated against, I say something and move on, so that I don't have a whole line of resentments following me. In high school this guy in my class would slant his eyes and ask me if he looked Chinese. One day I pushed my eyes together and asked him if I looked black. It became very apparent that he was being stupid. From that day forward, he treated me with respect.

I was born two days before International Women's Day (IWD), on March 6, 1975. This was always a hectic time of year because my mother was busy going to meetings and organizing programs for the IWD event. I resented the fact that it seemed to take precedence over my birthday. I always wanted a full-fledged birthday party with a dozen or so friends, junk food, and presents. Instead, I stayed in daycare with other children whose mothers were members of the Third World Women's Alliance. On my eleventh birthday I was allowed to be part of the IWD event; I gave a speech in front of three hundred people to raise money for a childcare center in Angola. My mother coached me and bought me a purple jumpsuit for the occasion. For the first time, I was actually doing something that might make a difference on the other side of the world. I think I grew more during that five-minute speech than I had during the previous year. That's when I realized why my mother did what she did and why it was important.

My parents were at Berkeley during the sixties. They agitated for the development of ethnic studies, dropped out of school, and protested against the Vietnam War. They were very liberal. They also gave me a lot of freedom to grow on my own. With that flexibility, I didn't feel the need to rebel. I don't really understand the kinds of relationships my girlfriends have with their mothers. Usually their mothers are overprotective, making my friends want to defy them even more. Although my mom and I are not equals, we are best friends. I can talk to her, confide in her, laugh with her, and cry with her.

We weren't always so close. As a young child, I remember telling her I hated her. I was resentful that she didn't have much time to spend with me. I felt closer to my father; he *did* things with me. We watched videos, ate potato chips, played board games, and went for walks together. When my dad brought his paperwork home, I would poke around and ask him what he was doing. My parents were probably gone from home the same amount of time, but I blamed my mother more. I guess it was because I thought my mother was supposed to be around.

When I was six, my mother became pregnant with my brother, Lung San. I was lonely and looked forward to having a sibling to play with, but I didn't expect my parents to spend so much time with him and not with me. Again, I blamed my mother. I tried to run away but made it only to the corner because I wasn't supposed to cross the street. Consequently I was forced to compromise with my parents and accept my new role as a responsible big sister, one who was too mature to have tantrums and run away. By age twelve I preferred to stay home from the conventions my parents went to and take care of my brother. We ate quick and easy meals, like Kraft macaroni and cheese and ramen noodles. After school and on the weekends when my parents were away, I rarely felt burdened with taking care of my brother or doing housework. I enjoyed being the "little mom."

Looking back, I realize that my mother always made sure we had quality time together. My father and I were content to bum around the house, but my mother insisted that we go out and do things. We went on excursions to the Berkeley marina, Golden Gate Park, and Chinatown, and we took family vacations in Santa Cruz and Hawaii. Although it may sound cheesy, my family is very trusting, loving, and closely knit.

At home we ate a mixture of ethnic and American food. Sometimes my father would fry pork in soy sauce and sugar, sometimes my mother would prepare soft tacos, and other times I would make spaghetti. Most meals were accompanied by rice and kim chee, which is Korean pickled cabbage.

I used to feel pressure to be active in my mother's causes. I felt that I was letting her down if I didn't go to meetings. Being active was the morally right thing to do, but it wasn't always what I wanted to do. I wanted to be a "normal" teenager, to go to the movies or bowling with my friends. Often it seemed like my parents did not have any fun; they were always gone, and they came home exhausted. I wasn't able to see that their work was interesting or worthwhile. To me, it seemed oppressive. Also, I don't like to be pressured into doing things, even if they are "for the best." In a lot of ways I am more conservative than my mom. I often fight change. My mom wants me to get out there and be more active, and sometimes I just don't think I have the time or energy for it. I just want to be myself.

I like the fact that my mom gets an idea into her head and carries through with it. For instance, two years ago she decided to learn how to speak Korean, so she studied abroad at Yonsei University. Sometimes I wish I could do that, but I have a lot of reservations. When I was thirteen my parents sent me to Cuba for a month with an international youth organization. My mother said, "It will open your eyes, and you'll learn so much." But I adamantly did not want to go. My body was changing and I had started to menstruate, and I was insecure and anxious about having to deal with guys or compete with girls on this trip. The mere thought of it terrified me. But my parents were firm; they put me on the plane, and I went.

My parents were right. It was an eye-opening experience. Delegations of young people had come to Cuba from all over the world: Angola, the Soviet Union, Nicaragua. I learned how impoverished some other kids were and the struggles they were going through. When I went home I felt I had a responsibility to do something, to use the information I had gained and become more active. I started out with good intentions, but my resolve dwindled when I went to junior high school. There were many cliques that required being popular and looking cute, and I wanted to be myself. I didn't want to change myself to fit into any clique. Instead, I stayed in the library, and everybody thought I was the nice little Asian girl. I was often lonely and miserable. I hated junior high.

In high school I discovered it was okay to be myself. In fact, it was cool to be an individual. I became secure and comfortable with myself and made a lot of good friends who accepted me for who I was. When I was a sophomore I was a founding member of the Asian Awareness Club. When complaints arose about Asian students getting beaten up and kicked in the hallways, we organized workshops on interracial relationships and Asian stereotypes. Part of what I liked about the club was organizing with my friends and deciding to do it on my own. My parents weren't telling me, "You are going to this meeting and will learn something from it." *I* planned the meetings and the different issues we discussed.

My parents both went back to college when I was in high school. It was hellish for them—having to work, take care of their kids, and maintain honor grades. But their experience made me see that going to college is an opportunity to learn, not just a means to a job. I decided to go to Brown because of its academic diversity and the fact that it offered the flexibility of creating your own major. Also, being at home with my parents was too comfortable; I needed to get out on my own and be more independent. Breaking away from my parents was the hardest thing for me to do. I knew that even though we would see each other in the future, the dynamics of our relationship would change. I would change. But my parents made the transition easier by flying out with me to the East Coast and giving me lots of support.

When I got to Brown, I went through a difficult time. Until I went to college I had never been so aware of my socioeconomic background, but at Brown it seems that the majority of the students have been through private East Coast preparatory schools, and I felt they had the upper hand. I also found it strange to meet so many students whose primary goal is to make money. It seems that many students aspire to be doctors not because they want to help people but in order to have extravagant lifestyles. I was disheartened by this attitude.

The first semester was a struggle for me. My parents stressed that although grades are important, they are not matters of life and death. They never made me feel as though I failed them by getting B's rather than A's. They just said, "Do the best you can." I have learned a lot from my experiences. I know my limitations and can balance my time and priorities better. I still feel the need to work, but the pressure is coming from within myself. And with my parents behind me, I am bound to be a success.

During my first semester, I tacitly went along with the "Asian gravitational pull." It was comfortable and familiar. However, many of the Asians I met grew up in predominantly Caucasian suburbs, and because I grew up in Oakland I found it increasingly difficult to relate. Over the course of the second semester, socioeconomic differences crystallized. I still have a lot of close Asian friends who are Thai, Chinese, Korean, Filipino, and Vietnamese. At the same time, though, I have a lot of close non-Asian friends who are Irish, Jewish, Mexican, and Dominican. I think part of this has to do with the fact that I am Chinese, Korean, and American, and because my parents' friends are of various racial and ethnic backgrounds. At Brown there is a lot of pressure to "stick to your own." But for me, commonalities and true understanding go far beyond race and have to do with cultural, social, and economic complexities.

I am a feminist by my own interpretation: I believe that men and women are equal physically and intellectually; therefore, they are entitled to equal rights, treatment, and respect. I take this for granted, and I immediately assume people are wrong for thinking otherwise. It's almost instinctive. Yet I would never introduce myself as a feminist; I am a Chinese-Korean-American young woman. As such, I must deal with more than uniquely feminist issues. Issues of race, class, and culture are equally important to me. Being a feminist is an integral part of who I am, but it is not all that I am.

At this point in my life, I can't see myself as being as much of an activist as my mother, but activism is definitely a part of me. It's in my blood. I'm not sure whether that's a blessing or a curse. I plan to tap into the activism on campus, but I don't want to devote my life to it. I prefer to deal with things on a personal level. What I want from life is to achieve my maximum potential, to be happy, and to be comfortable. I want to find balance.

Eventually I would like to have the kind of relationship my parents have. They love each other, respect each other, and give each other support, but they are not joined at the hip. They have learned, changed, and grown both individually and "together as one" for the past twenty-five years, and they have encouraged me to do the same. When I went away to college I saw many parts of my mother and my father in myself: the discipline, the curiosity, and the ambition.

You can always hear and know what my mom has to say, whether it is through a bullhorn, a newsletter, or a poem. Her voice is strong, loud, and clear. She's wild; she's out there on her motor scooter. She's in the know. She has traveled around the world and back, working with different organizations and individuals and touching many lives. I am proud to be the daughter of Miriam Ching Louie.

T W E N T Y - N I N E

◆◆◆

Personal Reflections on Being a Grandmother: L'Chol Dor Va Dor

Rachel Aber Schlesinger[1]

My Grandmother

My maternal grandmother lived with us. I learned from her that grandmothers have great power. They

[1] I was able to carry out this research with the help of a grant from Canada Multicultural Department and the Centre of Jewish Studies at York University. I want to thank Sarah Taieb Carlen for conducting some of the interviews with Sephardi women in French, and for her help with this project.

represent a relationship that, like a parent's, demands respect and provides love but is different. *Omamma* was a "queen," she kept religious standards high, passed on a sense of family history, and told wonderful stories. She helped give us a sense of who we were and what we stood for. Our family had religious and family traditions. We were a matriarchal family. The men were important and respected, but the names and the stories were those of the mothers.

The family stories began with my great-grandparents, the rabbi and *rebbitzin* of Luebeck. They had twelve children. My great-grandmother greeted the birth of each child, and indeed every family occasion with a poem, a *Tischlied*. In quiet moments she wrote a book of poetry for the young Jewish bride, stressing the family and religious roles of Jewish women. This book of poems was still given to my older cousin upon marriage. Before the Second World War, the lives of these women and the poems held commonly understood meanings.

My grandmother was the oldest of eight daughters. In her later years she wrote her memoirs. Even in this religious family the important items that she remembered were elegant balls, clothes, and meeting her husband. She lived in the age of romance, and saw her early years in these terms. She was also deeply religious and supervised the early religious teachings of her grandchildren.

Tragically, she was widowed as a young woman. Her life in Germany was devoted to social service activities; her home was filled with interesting people. Upon her death I found correspondence from Bertha Pappenheim dealing with rescue activities for Jewish women and children. Omamma spoke English well and came to America by way of Portugal in the 1940s. Once here, she divided her time between living with her two surviving children, my mother and my uncle. She did small jobs, was a companion to others, and baby-sat, yet this work never diminished her queenly status in her eyes or in the eyes of others.

My Mother as Grandmother

I was able to understand my mother in her role as a grandparent because of the influence of my grandmother. Both women were unique; daughters and wives of distinguished rabbis, they had a strong sense of self, of Jewish values, and of family *Yehus*.

Mutti's world changed with the Nazi era. My mother's stories were told not to her children who experienced the events she recounted, but to her grandchildren. Since I was the youngest of her children I didn't remember these experiences, but my children told me Mutti's stories. Here is one of the stories.

On *Krystallnacht* in November 1938, the synagogue in Bremen was destroyed and my father, the rabbi, was taken to a concentration camp. My mother, known by Jew and non-Jew in this middle-sized port city, worked for his release and that of the other men

taken that night. Each day, as the story goes, she went with her three daughters to the Gestapo headquarters to ask when the men would be released. One day she was told that they would be sent home on a midnight train, but she did not know which night. Every night, at midnight, she walked to the railway station to see if my father would be coming on that train. Every night, she heard footsteps behind her as a Gestapo officer followed her through dingy parts of town. That did not deter her.

Weeks later, after this routine was followed each night, my father did indeed arrive on a train. Mutti turned around at the station. The footsteps behind her had stopped. She looked up to see the Gestapo officer salute her and my father. He had been following her each night for her protection. That is the kind of devotion my beautiful mother inspired.

Mutti believed in the power of the individual, and the vital role of the woman in the family and in the community. She was a deeply committed Jew. Her religion, her vocation, and her belief system were holistic. I know that her grandchildren loved her, respected her, and understood her. My son told me, "Mutti was unusual. She really believed in what she believed in!"

My Own Experience

Now I am a grandmother. I am a living ancestor! My stories will be different, I live in another land, in another time. I wonder if any of us can transmit to our children's children the tastes, the smells, the environment, the understanding of the values that shaped us.

What do I want to pass on to my grandchildren? I find it easier to ask "how," than to pinpoint "what" it is I want to transmit. Like my grandmother I tell stories, sing songs, and recount family history. If my sisters and I have pictures, we put them on the walls. We use the ability to name to perpetuate memories and names. Those of us who were born in other countries speak in our mother tongue. We use language to recall roots. We model our religious practices and holiday observances. We convey our oral traditions in the kitchens of our homes. As our grandchildren get older, we share secrets often not told to our own children.

The bond between grandchild and grandparents may be the strongest, and of the longest duration, next to the parent bond. Can grandparents transmit values, or is this too difficult due to the age gap between the first and third generation, differences in life experiences, and competition from outside agents of socialization?

Immigrant Grandmothers

For the past few years I have been talking with Jewish grandmothers, asking them about their perceptions of being a grandparent and transmitting their own values to their grandchildren. Let me introduce some of the women who shared their thoughts on this question.

Sephardi Grandmothers

Sara comes from Morocco. There is a big difference between her world and that of her grandmother. Her grandmother was married at twelve years of age, and was only fifteen when Sara's mother was born. The role of women in her community was important. Sara recounts that it was often the woman who urged the family to leave, either for Israel, France, or Canada. In Morocco, women lived in separate spheres, yet had valued roles. With the shift to a new country, their roles changed. The family changed from being a large, extended family living with each other to having members dispersed. Sara's family life is strongly linked to religious observance. "If you can't cook, you can't fulfill your religious obligations."

Leaving Morocco meant leaving cultural roles behind. "My grandmother's religious views and her ways will be acknowledged in her home, but maybe not in ours. This means that while we have memory, we may not have continuity of culture." In order for a culture to survive, it must be practiced. It is not good enough to talk of the "old days," if they are not followed today.

Lena, born in Morocco, adds: "Family traditions . . . are very important. They are mostly French traditions, like table manners, classical music, French literature. Yes, in my country, it was our way." She talks about a way of life that combines Jewish and secular culture, a civilized worldview, formed by Continental culture in an Arabic environment, far removed from her present North Toronto setting.

Pina says, "I want to give them an idea of the way we lived. My father taught me wisdom; my

mother's family had been in Iraq for millennia, maybe since Abraham."

Nadia, who comes from Turkey adds: "I have to tell them about our life. . . . Here, there is no Turkish atmosphere, no Turkish synagogue, no Turkish bath, no Turkish schools . . . so I have to talk about our way of life, and it is not always possible to imagine. It's like a dream."

Values grow out of a culture. These Sephardi grandmothers want to pass on respect and obedience to elders, for "they know more than us, they have a whole life behind them. Respect, it's like breathing. It comes naturally; we are born with it" (Mrs. C).

Ashkenazi Grandmothers

While Jews from Eastern Europe also had close associations with their home countries, when they talk of bringing grandchildren "home" it is to teach them what can happen to Jewish communities. It is to put the Holocaust into personal terms. Or it is to put the Russian experience into perspective.

Ada is under five feet tall, and she is a survivor—of the Holocaust, of displaced-person camps, of migrations to several countries, before settling in Canada twenty years ago. She spoke in optimistic terms about her life.

For her, her grandchildren are a miracle, the remnants of a family that is once again extended. She feels the need to transmit memories, and has taken her five grandchildren to Poland, to see the *Camps*, to show them what she has survived. She tells them how she picked up her life after the war. She returned to Poland after the war, met her husband, lived in Israel, then came to Canada.

She wants to perpetuate language, not Polish but Hebrew, and speaks it with her grandchildren. Ada models her values, she still volunteers time as a nurse's aide, and together with her husband, remains active in the community. She lives within walking distance of her children.

She finds it difficult to convey her Jewish values. "One son-in-law does not speak Hebrew; he is a Canadian, and cannot even understand the feelings of being a survivor. He tells me I spoil the children."

Mrs. Z came to Canada seven years ago; she focuses on her Lithuanian experiences. Her grandchildren do not understand why she chose to remain in a Communist country. Indeed, she had a high position in the government. She was eventually able to connect with her grandchildren by telling them about her experiences in the underground during the Second World War. She still has difficulties, since her children in Canada became "very Jewish, and I don't understand this. It was not my way."

These women are survivors — of their generation, of the Holocaust, of war. They can no longer return for a visit with their grandchildren; their world died. Many return to visit the death camps, but some women do not want their grandchildren to associate the Jewish life of their own youth only with death and destruction.

Domestic Religion, Food, and Practice

In our families we model our beliefs, talk about them, emphasize what's important. Religious observance is an area we articulate, often in loud, judgmental terms. The grandmothers speak of learning, religious rituals, and observance.

Religion is often viewed from the perspective of the kitchen. Cooking for holidays, talking in the kitchen, passing on *kashrut* by doing, not by reading; these are all examples of transmitting values. Recipes are handed over from generation to generation; they are part of the oral tradition. This too is religious commentary.

In terms of religious observances and even foods, the Sephardi feel a degree of cognitive dissonance. The foods they ate at home are not common in Canada. Ashkenaza families can find familiar kosher or kosher-style foods in supermarkets; the Sephardi cannot.

Mrs. W. had been unable to follow her religion in her home country. "In Latvia I couldn't be religious. Here I want to be, but my husband is still afraid. My granddaughter helps me."

Grandmothers feel that they have contributions to make to the family in terms of ideas, responsibilities, child care, and even financial assistance. Many of them hope that they are role models, as indeed their grandparents had been to them. It is important to them to be seen as representing the old culture, providing continuity of family traditions, while still being close to their grandchildren. They articulate the values of a Jewish education, family closeness

and the concept of *Shalom Bayit*. They feel a sense of responsibility to ensure this for the next generation.

These grandmothers reflected a wistfulness for times past. Singing together reminds them of their own childhood. The first contacts with a new grandchild are often through singing songs in grandmother's mother tongue. They hope their grandchildren will respect them as older persons, by means of their behavior, such as good manners. They report that their grandchildren do respect their views and opinions, often coming to them before going to parents to ask for advice.

Roadblocks

Some fear they do not have a place in their grandchildren's lives now, but hope this will develop with time. Factors that impede communication and closeness include physical location, distance, family mobility, and family fragmentation.

Grandparents often have less formal education than their children or grandchildren, and some feel that this educational gap creates barriers. Others report feeling "inferior," "not modern enough." They feel inadequate because they can only transmit what is most common to their own life and experience, for example the customs, traditions, and history of their country of origin. Yet their children and grandchildren may not have a frame of reference for the information grandmothers wish to impart. So much is lost, replaced by strange new ways. Grandparents try to fit their culture into a new setting, and that is often a difficult task.

Even the words we use have changed. In Jewish tradition an older person was a *zakena*, a person of wisdom. In modern Hebrew, the terms *Saba* and *Safta* are used to denote grandparents, the father of my father; what has happened to the concept of wisdom?

Some Reflections

Some of the grandmothers felt frustrated, partly because the changes that have taken place during their lifetimes make it difficult to transmit a sense of what was. Their own world has been transformed through transitions.

Family roles have changed and older women see their status as lower in Canada than it might have been in the old society. The pattern of immigration itself has weakened family links. The new buzzword of "individualization" undermines the sense of family and of community as well as woman's and grandmother's role in the family. Grandmothers no longer occupy the same physical space as their children and grandchildren and they fear that their domestic religion is out of their hands. Today's grandmother may really have little influence in conveying her concept of Jewish culture. A way of life has altered in a short span of time.

The grandmothers I interviewed examined the concepts of societal changes and ideological shifts. The Sephardi women spoke of open community life; some of the Eastern Europeans had belonged to the *Bund* and grown up on socialism. One needs to question if it is possible to have cultural transmission when the culture and politics have changed so drastically.

Are Jewish grandmothers different? Perhaps. This generation of women gives great importance to perpetuating the Jewish people. Older grandparents today are a generation who experienced migrations, displacements, and the Holocaust. We cherish the ability to have given birth, to survive as a people. We worry about the Jewishness of our children and grandchildren. We do have values to pass on—from generation to generation.

Can I transmit a sense of family to my grandchildren? Hopefully, yes. I can provide the smells of *hallah* baking; I can surround them with pictures of family members, of places and events. I can record voices for them to listen to; I can even use videos to pinpoint places and people. Modern technology helps, but being there, talking, being willing to listen, trying to explain our perspective, and respecting our own children and grandchildren may be the keys to future communications and continuity. Our grandchildren are not mind readers; contact, open communication, and understanding are also necessary ingredients in a relationship.

It is harder to impart religious values for eventually we each must find our own path and follow it for a time. We too change and may change our perspectives. That is what we can try to pass on—the ability to see and judge for oneself.

What do I want to communicate? I want healthy, thoughtful, creative, and caring family members—the rest is commentary.

L'chol Dor Va Dor, from generation to generation. My grandmother once told me, "listen carefully to what I will tell you . . . then you will tell this story to your children, and they will tell it to their grandchildren.

But will the story lose its meaning? My grandmother's and mother's stories were unique, coming from urgent times and far away places. I am part of the quiet generation. While I was born in Germany and raised by European parents, I grew up in North America. I need to add my own stories to those of the women in my family.

We are links in a long chain—which of the stories will our great-grandchildren repeat?

THIRTY

Girlfriends

Andrea R. Canaan

You know, the kind of woman friend you
can be a girl with.
You know what I mean a woman you giggle
with one minute and can be dead serious
the next.
The kind of friend that you can be a bitch

with and she thinks that you were being
a bitch just then, and tells you so.
The kind of friend that you usually
tell all to and when you forget to tell
her some secret that you have been holding
and casually mention it to her, you are

surprised that you hadn't told her.
You know, the kind of friend that you can
go out with and it's not always dutch.
The kind of woman friend that you
play with and sleep with and go to
the movies with and gossip half the day
or night with and argue politics with and
never agree yet always agree with . . . you know?
The kind of friend that you keep secrets
for and with and can be P.I. with, in fact
you both insist upon it.
I mean the kind of friend that you laugh
and cry with over some woman breaking your
heart even though this is the fourth time
this year it's happened, and she will hold
you and let you wail
just like it was the very first time your
heart was ever broken.
The kind of woman that will leave
no stone unturned to find out why she hurt
your feelings even if she didn't mean to and
especially if she did.
The kind of friend that you will accept
an apology from graciously even when you feel
now that you might have been being hyper-
sensitive that day and revel in the knowing
that someone cares so much how you feel and
you don't have to worry about monogamy or
polygamy or which side of the bed is yours
or nothing.
The kind of woman friend that you can tell
how your lover done you so wrong and she
doesn't get mad when you don't do all those

things you swore you would.
The kind of friend that you can get
mad with or strongly disagree with or lose
it with and she will not give up on you
or stop loving you.
The kind of friend that will give
you space to fall in love even though your
new affair is taking the spontaneity out
of her being able to pop over or to
call you late about some small bit of
info to hear your voice and be assured
about some fear that you can not
yet name.
The kind of friend that doesn't get mad
until she has not seen or heard from you
for two solid weeks and then she comes
over or calls and cusses your ass out for days
and then you go out for an ice cream cone.
I mean the kind of friend that stays mad
with the people that fuck over you long
after you have forgiven them.
The kind of friend that
allows you to wallow in self pity for
just so long and then gives you a swift
kick.
The kind of friend that close or far apart
she will be there for you, the distance wiped
away instantly to meet some outside enemy or
trouble.
I mean the kind of woman who always honors
what is private and vulnerable for you.

You know, I mean girlfriends.

◆◆◆

Households Headed by Women
The Politics of Race, Class, and Gender

Leith Mullings

In 1990, over 20 percent of all families in the United States with children under eighteen were headed by women (U.S. Bureau of the Census 1990a). The precipitous increase in frequency in this household form—from 10.7 percent in 1970 to 21 percent in 1990 (U.S. Bureau of the Census 1973, 1990a)—has generated a great deal of academic debate. But perhaps more pertinent are those discussions that take place in the popular and political arenas: from former Vice President Dan Quayle's attack on *Murphy Brown,* a television portrayal of a professional Euro-American woman who chooses to have a child out of wedlock, to the more insidious and less contested demonization of "welfare mothers."

As people struggle over definitions of the normative family and control of reproduction, divisions of race and class are never far from the surface. For African Americans, the conflict over fertility has always been linked to the political economy, as their efforts to control the conditions of their reproduction clashed with the interests of the dominant class. During slavery, slaveowners encouraged fertility among enslaved women to increase the labor force. In the contemporary economy, as African Americans resist confinement to the low-wage jobs of their parents and grandparents (Collins 1991), they are increasingly considered a "redundant population," an underclass that must be contained. Reproduction is now regulated less directly and less personally than it was during slavery: The structure of the households of women seeking welfare benefits or admission to homeless shelters has come under increasing bureaucratic manipulation and regulation, and women who head households are increasingly stigmatized.

Today, with labor and capital moving around the globe, race, class, and gender, as well as nationality, define boundaries to be held, reclaimed, or challenged. In the global context of population policies, disease, and disasters of all kinds, local populations seek to envision continuity through children and act to ensure that continuity. Using low-income women in Harlem, New York City, as an example, this [essay] describes the global and local socioeconomic relations that form the context for stratified reproduction, the power relations by which "some categories of people are empowered to nurture and reproduce, while others are disempowered" (Ginsburg and Rapp 1995, 3); explores the ways in which ideologies and social policies reinforce stratified reproduction; and discusses "transformative work," through which people seek to sustain themselves, their families, and their communities.

Global, National, and Local Intersections

That women increasingly raise children themselves is an international phenomenon, characteristic of both industrialized and developing nations. Various factors bear on the rise of these households in different parts of the world. A precipitous increase in the proportion of such households may be associated with war, as in Iraq; genocidal policies, as in Guatemala; neocolonial apartheid and separation, as in South Africa; labor migration, as landless peasants search for work in much of the world; or with increasing unemployment, as in parts of the industrialized world. The international labor diaspora places huge burdens on women, and in most areas households headed by women are associated with high rates of poverty as children become a cost particular to them.

Household structure in both developing and industrialized countries is shaped by global as well as local processes, as policies implemented at national or international levels increasingly mold reproductive experiences. The flight of industry from U.S. cities to areas with cheaper and less organized labor and the rapid movement of "hot money" around the world in search of speculative opportunities have local consequences: unemployment, destruction of social services, and infrastructural deterioration plague postindustrial cities in the United States.

In the United States, global processes interact with historical patterns of racism and discrimination, sharpening racial and gender disparities. Minority populations in inner cities are most severely affected by the increasing social and economic polarization. Since the 1980s the African American middle class has expanded. But at the same time a growing number of workers have been expelled from the labor force, and unemployment and underemployment among African American and Latino men has reached staggering proportions.

Because the growth of households headed by women is linked to unemployment and low earnings (see Ross and Sawhill 1975; Wilson 1987), it is not surprising that 50 percent of all African American households and 24.2 percent of all Latino households with children under 18, compared with 15.8 percent of all Euro-American households with children under 18, are headed by women (U.S. Bureau of the Census 1990a). While the rise of feminism, growing labor force, participation (which increases women's economic independence), and changing attitudes toward marriage may be factors in the rising incidence of female headship among Euro-American women (England and Farkas 1986), for African Americans, male unemployment seems to be a major reason for the increase in the number of female-headed households (Wilson 1987). The disappearance of "marriageable" African American men — through disproportionate unemployment, consequent participation in an informal underground economy of which crime is only one aspect, and ensuing high levels of incarceration and "excess" death — means that African American women of all classes are less likely to marry or to remarry. But the consequences are greatest for low-income women, who must deal with poverty. In 1990 almost half (42 percent) of all households with children under 18 headed by women — including 34 percent of Euro-American, 53 percent of African American, and 55 percent of Latino households — fell below the poverty threshold (U.S. Bureau of the Census 1990b). Increasingly concentrated in the inner cities, these households become the subject of considerable critical scrutiny in the context of global discourses linking economic development with population control.

Local Communities: Women, Work, and Family in Central Harlem

Central Harlem, a predominantly African American community in northern Manhattan, presents an example of the havoc wreaked in local communities already disadvantaged by centuries of discrimination. But it is also a complex and variegated community, in which people struggle against increasingly difficult conditions. At the turn of the century, people of African descent began to migrate to Harlem from other parts of New York City, the South, and the Caribbean. Though shaped by segregation and discrimination, Harlem has been a vibrant social, political, and cultural center for African Americans of all classes. In the 1920s it was the hub of a cultural renaissance. Social movements ranging from Marcus Garvey's Universal Negro Improvement Association to the election of Ben Davis as the first Communist city councilman have found fertile ground in Harlem.

Many of Central Harlem's residents are currently experiencing severe difficulties as the effects of global restructuring and the economic policies and cutbacks of the 1970s and 1980s interact with long-standing patterns of racism to produce rapidly deteriorating conditions. Though there is a strong middle class in Harlem, poorer Harlemites' limited access to

well-paying jobs is reflected in the low median income, which was $13,252 in 1989, compared with $29,823 for New York City as a whole, and in levels of unemployment more than double those of New York City (New York City Department of City Planning 1992a, 1992b). Almost half (42.2 percent) of Harlem youth between sixteen and nineteen were unemployed in 1989 (New York City Department of City Planning 1992c), and almost 40 percent of the residents of Central Harlem had incomes below the poverty line (New York City Department of City Planning 1992d).

As the conditions for poor people in the inner cities of the industrial world increasingly resemble those of people without resources in the developing world, it is not surprising that a study found that for men in Central Harlem "the rate of survival beyond the age of 40 is lower . . . than in Bangladesh" (McCord and Freeman 1990, 174). Less well publicized is the situation for women. "For women, overall survival to the age of 65 is somewhat better in Harlem [than in Bangladesh], but only because the death rate among girls under five is very high in Bangladesh" (McCord and Freeman 1990, 1974).

Women find themselves in an increasingly difficult position. In Central Harlem, 69 percent of all families with children under eighteen are headed by women (New York City Department of City Planning 1992b). While some women have been immobilized by the crisis conditions, others succeed in raising their children without a stable income from men and are able to maintain their households despite adverse circumstances.

Historically, most African American women have been compelled — by slaveholders or by necessity — to work outside the home. With the devastating levels of unemployment of African American men, the labor force participation rate of African American women has become roughly equal to that of men. In 1990 women constituted 52.4 percent of the African American work force, though women made up only 45.3 percent of the Euro-American work force (U.S. Bureau of the Census 1992).

Though differences in work force participation rates between African American and Euro-American women are no longer dramatic, their history is. Euro-American women are no longer dramatic, their history is. Euro-American women's aggregate participation in the work force has only recently approached that of African American women, who, as mothers, have always worked outside their homes in large numbers. The obstacles that confront all working mothers are intensified for African American women, who find themselves in the ambiguous position of being primary wage earners in a society where the official ideology designates men as the principal breadwinners. In Central Harlem, 65 percent of women in the labor force have children under eighteen, and 43 percent of them have children under six (New York City Department of City Planning 1993). These difficulties are compounded for those with low-income jobs.

By the 1980s, as a result of the struggle for civil rights and an expanding service economy, African American women had moved into a variety of professions and occupations. But a large proportion of African American women continue to be concentrated in low-wage jobs, with little job security, few benefits, and difficult working conditions. The poorest women are excluded from the job market altogether. In Central Harlem in 1990, more than half (54.7 percent) of women eligible to work were not in the labor force (New York City Department of City Planning 1990b), with 28.9 percent of Harlem residents receiving Aid to Families with Dependent Children (New York City Department of City Planning 1991). Women may work entirely in the informal sector or may augment their income from welfare or low-wage work with such informal-sector jobs as child care and other domestic work, renting out living spaces, or selling various products. Some develop strategies that combine attending school to improve their job chances with one or more low-wage jobs. Nevertheless, 54.3 percent of all Harlem households headed by women that include children under eighteen have incomes below the poverty line (New York City Department of City Planning 1993). In short, many women work a triple shift — work outside the home, additional informal-sector work, and housework — which must be extended to fill the gap left by declining social services.

In addition to responsibility for supporting the household — often on marginal incomes — women must maintain the family in conditions exacerbated by the economic policies of the 1980s. As the federal government decreased its contribution to New York City's budget from 19.8 percent in 1978 to 10.9 percent in 1990 (New York City Office of the Budget 1991), women have had to cope with the problems caused by cutbacks not only in social services but also in education, housing, child care services, and health care.

For example, many African American mothers feel that they can no longer rely on the schools. Education has historically been of great importance to the African American struggle for equality. African Americans have fought for equal access to education, and since emancipation mothers' wages have often been applied to allowing children to continue in school (see Pleck 1979). This strategy has had some successes. Since the 1970s, African Americans have significantly narrowed the gap between themselves and Euro-Americans in the number of school years completed, although this improvement has not resulted in narrowing the income gap.

But the gains in education won during the civil rights era of the 1960s and 1970s have eroded since then, and racial inequality in access to education has increased (Kozol 1991). Children in New York City schools, for example, receive less funding per capita than children in suburban schools (Kozol 1991), and in Central Harlem children and schools receive less funding in almost every category than in other districts in New York City (Breslin and Stier 1987). The "survival rate" in these large, underfunded, understaffed schools is low: The two high schools to which the majority of students from junior high schools in Central Harlem are directed have a four-year graduation rate of approximately 27 percent (Mullings and Susser 1992), which does not include those who drop out between the eighth and ninth grades. There is, nonetheless, a belief in the efficacy of education. Parent and community organizations have been successful in instituting after-school programs and in persuading the Board of Education to establish several special schools and programs, including a high school to serve Central Harlem.

In addition to their concerns about education, women must raise their children in neighborhoods where poverty, neglect, drugs, and crime are threatening the social fabric. Since the 1970s, nearly ten thousand units of housing have been abandoned in Central Harlem (Harlem Urban Development Corporation 1990; Mullings and Susser 1992), and at the same time there has been a major reduction in federal funds for new housing units. Consequently, between 1970 and 1990 the number of available housing units in the community dropped by 27.1 percent (New York City Department of City Planning 1990a). The resulting overcrowding, homelessness, and destruction of neighborhoods have had a ripple effect: As families move away, networks that have historically sustained the community and that might control deviant behavior are destroyed, and deterioration and crime increase (see Wallace, Fullilove, and Wallace 1992).

Drugs are a case in point. With the inability (or unwillingness) of the federal government to halt the importation of drugs into the United States and with police effectiveness significantly curtailed by corruption, strategically located low-income neighborhoods become marketplaces for the sale of drugs to surrounding suburbs. Youth are drawn into the sale and distribution of drugs as meaningful economic or educational opportunities decline. The director of a substance-abuse program in Central Harlem pointed out: "The young people today don't have an anti-work ethic. . . . Those kids are out doing the crack thing, that's work. . . . They have a sophisticated understanding of management, organization, distribution, marketing, and competition. But it's all geared to the wrong thing" (cf. Williams 1989).

The depth of worry about children growing up in these conditions is difficult to convey. The epidemic of violence (the cost of which is borne by these neighborhoods), fueled by the ready availability of firearms, threatens everyone, but people worry most about the youth. Older relatives sometimes give teenage boys guns for protection, and violence spirals. In 1989 Central Harlem had a total of 3,175 violent crimes, ranking seventeenth among seventy-five community districts in New York City in number of violent crimes per person (New York City Office of Management Analysis and Planning 1989).

People are adamant about trying to keep children safe. Women spend an extraordinary amount of time escorting children, limiting their movement, and trying by any means to keep them away from the violence of the streets. There are building-by-building and block-by-block struggles (often unsuccessful) to expel drug dealers. At the same time, proceeds from the sale of illegal drugs may be the only source of income for some families. As I interviewed residents of Central Harlem, people repeatedly expressed acute concern about losing the children — to the drug culture, to early death as a result of substance abuse, to the often random violence associated with illegal drugs in poor neighborhoods. Today, the leap of faith to envision continuity

through children must be as great as it was during the days of slavery.

In these circumstances, it might be argued that women are making adaptive reproductive decisions in a situation where the population is endangered by excessive morbidity and mortality. As with unemployment rates, infant mortality rates among African Americans are over twice the national average. In Central Harlem, the infant mortality rate in 1988 was approximately three times the national rate; between 1985 and 1988, children up to the age of four were dying at three times the expected rate for the United States as a whole (Health and Hospitals Corporation 1991). Indeed, in all age groups except for those between the ages of five and fourteen and those over sixty-five, residents of Central Harlem die at higher rates than the general U.S. population (Mullings and Susser 1992; Health and Hospitals Corporation 1991).

It is not surprising that among pregnant young women I interviewed in Central Harlem, the death of family members was not an unusual occurrence. For example, one unmarried nineteen-year-old stated that her mother had urged her to carry this pregnancy to term, though she had terminated a previous pregnancy by abortion. In the course of the discussion, it became clear that in the last two years several family members had died unexpectedly: her brother had been killed by a stray bullet, a cousin had died of AIDS, and another cousin had died of respiratory distress in a hospital.

Though women through their childbearing behavior may, in a sense, replace people lost to early death (cf. Sharff 1987), it is important not to underestimate the cost of all these burdens to women themselves. Between 1985 and 1988, the annual excess death rate (see Mullings and Susser 1992 for an explanation of this index) of women in Central Harlem was ten times that of New York City as a whole, with heart disease being the leading cause (Mullings and Susser 1992), no doubt reflecting the stresses to which these women are subject. One might conclude that while excess death among men reflects direct confrontation with the social system, women die of indirect effects.

As conditions in these communities decline, the potential for violence directed at the larger society escalates. While AIDS and illegal drugs function as forms of population control, the public discussion of fertility escalates. As women attempt to raise children in crisis conditions, they find themselves the focus of representations that in effect obscure and even blame them for those conditions.

Ideology and Public Policy

Elements of strongly held ideologies concerning race, class, and gender are reflected in the public discussion of women who head households. Ideologies of race portray them as promiscuous women and inadequate mothers; ideologies of class blame them for their poverty; and ideologies of patriarchy label nontraditional family forms as "pathological." The convergence of these beliefs and their reproduction at so many locations render the representation of women who head households particularly deleterious.

Race, Motherhood, and Sexuality

Stratified reproduction is reinforced and reproduced by gender constructions that have emphasized motherhood for Euro-American women (Davin 1978; Laslett and Brenner 1989) but sexuality for African American women. Both sides of this fractured imagery have implications for reproduction, as motherhood, womanhood, and race are symbolically intertwined and contested.

For elite Euro-American women, motherhood has been a major defining element of gender identity. Women as mothers — who are involved in both biological and cultural reproduction — become master symbols of family, race, and civility, and are central to the authorized definition of the national community (cf. Stoler 1989). When boundaries are threatened, rhetoric about fertility and population control escalates, and native Euro-American women, preferably those of the dominant class, are exhorted to have children. Deviation from traditional roles is presumed to promote race suicide, and women who do not or cannot conform are censured as contributing to the decline of civilization. For example, abolitionists were labeled "shameless amazons" and "unsexed females" (Scott 1970, 20); suffragists were accused of contributing to race suicide by concerning themselves with matters outside the home (Rosen 1982, 45).

In the face of rising discontent with the widening division of wealth and challenges to cultural hegemony, and as international migrations again modify the face of the United States, the oratory of the 1992 Republican National Convention bore a striking resemblance to Nazi rhetoric, which demanded motherhood for the "mothers of the master race" versus compulsory sterilization for others and "race hygienic sterilization . . . [as] a prelude to mass murder" (Bock 1983, 408). "Family values" became a ringing slogan, but not just any family would do. The model was the (Euro-American) nuclear family with the father working and the mother at home, characteristic of less than one sixth of U.S. families. Not surprisingly, traditional gender roles, antiabortion laws, attacks on households headed by women, and defense of the traditional educational curriculum were linked to the preservation of the nation.

The dominant class's construction of gender has throughout history portrayed African American women as inadequate mothers and promiscuous women. Not only were enslaved women vulnerable to sexual exploitation, but slavery required fertility without motherhood: children could be and were sold away from them.

When slavery ended, segregation and discrimination dictated that African American women work outside the home, but their opportunities were initially limited to domestic work. Representations of African American women as sexually provocative, which had rationalized the vulnerability of slaves to the sexual advances of Euro-American men, continued to excuse advances toward African American domestic workers.

Images of African Americans as bad mothers, ineffective mothers, and matriarchs (see Collins 1991 and Morton 1991 for a discussion of these notions in popular culture and scholarly literature) also conceal and justify the difficult conditions in which they work and raise children. But, oddly enough, these same women, who are said to run amok in their own communities, are thought to be entirely competent at parenting the children of the elite — as mammies during slavery, as domestic workers during segregation, or as child care workers today. Thus the popular images of low-income African American women who head households emphasize not mothering but sexuality. They are not portrayed as mothers with limited resources struggling to care for children. Their public image as nurturers depends entirely on the care they "offer" to the children of Euro-American families. At the same time, the problem of endangered African American manhood is laid at the door of these "weak" mothers, who cannot adequately "discipline" their children.

Class and Patriarchy

Ideologies of class come into play in depicting these women and their children as the crystallization of the urban underclass. Several works (see, for example, Lemman 1986; Murray 1984; Jenks 1991) attribute contemporary poverty in minority communities to the growth of households headed by women. This literature has been reviewed and critiqued elsewhere (for example Williams 1992; Reed 1992), but these views persist despite the work demonstrating the relationship between unemployment and the rising numbers of female-headed families. By blaming these women for their own poverty and, indeed, for the economic ills of the entire nation, attention is diverted from the injustice of the racial and gendered labor market and from the "savage inequalities" (Kozol 1991) increasingly characterizing U.S. society.

Notions of normative gender roles continue to pervade those works that attempt to analyze the structural conditions that give rise to these households (for example, Wilson 1987). Despite the lack of significant evidence that single-parent households are in themselves harmful, these households are invariably described as inherently pathological (for discussion of these concepts in the social-policy literature, see Schorr and Moen 1979, Schlesinger 1986). One might conclude that the intensity of affect and scrutiny to which these households are subject at some level reflects "a fear of women without men" (cf. Tiffany and Adams 1985 on the "matriarch fixation"); households headed by women are seen as the "other" of the patriarchal family (Sands and Nuccio 1989), just as the underclass is the "other" to the middle class.

Limiting Options through Policies and Representation

Powerful ideas of class, race, and gender are central to social policies, which, by imposing constraints on reproduction according to race and class, replicate and reinforce structural inequality. Public policies regarding child care, women's work, and compensation, rationalized by notions about appropriate gender roles, promote the male-headed nuclear family by reinforcing the dependence on women. For the working class, and increasingly for middle-stratum women who must work, these policies make their lives difficult.

For poor women, however, state policies that structure access to social benefits often reinforce and encourage matrifocality. As the lack of employment and educational opportunities constrains women's access to men's income and they are forced to rely on the state, social policies then function to further encourage matrilocality. Benefits such as income support (Stack 1974) or Medicaid (Davis and Rowland 1983) are virtually unavailable to men or to households that include men (Stack 1974). Susser's (1989) ethnographic study of shelters for the homeless in New York graphically documents the role of the state in structuring the composition of households through its regulation of who may sleep where and with whom and whether parents may stay with children. As low-income housing becomes increasingly unavailable and the homeless population grows, the shelter system routinely separates men from their children and the mothers of the their children. In some facilities, boys over the age of nine are not permitted to stay in the shelters with their mothers. Families are defined as women and young children, and men are considered irrelevant and even dangerous.

These public policies combine with popular perceptions to further limit already limited options. Images of the promiscuous welfare mother deflect attention from the role of the society in producing African American mothers and children who are dependent on the state. Harrington suggested that the image of "a welfare mother with a large family, pregnant once again (the poor as promiscuous and lazy) . . . [has] done more to set back the struggle against poverty than have all efforts of reactionary politicians" (Harrington 1984, 179). These representations are then deployed to rationalize policies ranging from forcing Norplant birth control implants on welfare recipients to cutting welfare benefits of parents whose number of children exceed a designated limit (Reed 1992, 36). The limitations on educational and occupational opportunities, which create the conditions in which young women are likely to have children, are then reinforced.

Some feminists (for example, Hartmann 1987) suggest that households headed by women may be a positive development, contributing to women's autonomy and control. We do need to "denaturalize" (Rapp 1987) the family: to understand the nuclear family as a historically particular form characteristic of a minority of humankind for a relatively small proportion of time. We do need to point out that male or female "headship" in and of itself does not determine the consequences widely attributed to it, but that the social context of the family (whatever its form), especially access to material and social resources, seems to be crucial.

Nevertheless, feminist analyses emphasizing increased independence tend to underplay its costs to women, children, and the community and to verge on adopting the conservative view that these women are making an unrestricted lifestyle choice. While this is a complex issue, I think it reasonable to assume that for a majority of African American women who head households, their situation is both imposed and chosen (cf. Lebsock 1984). To the extent that they choose, they do so within a range of options severely limited by hierarchies of race, class, and gender. The task, then, is to transform the structure that limits options for both men and women.

Women, Reproduction, and Resistance: Transformative Work

As described above, women work outside the home and in the home, rearing children in difficult circumstances. But they also engage in what we might call *transformative work*. I use transformative work in two senses: efforts to sustain continuity under transformed circumstances, and efforts to transform circumstances in order to maintain continuity. These efforts have spanned the domains of work, household, and community.

A History of Struggle

In their efforts to sustain continuity under transformed circumstances, women in Harlem have a long tradition to draw on. In slavery, some women resisted increasing the property of slavers through their fertility by using various contraceptive and abortion techniques that southern medical journals referred to as "medicine," "violent exercise," and "ex-

ternal and internal manipulation" (Gutman 1976, 81). Others imagined their continuity through children even within the "peculiar" institution of slavery. To bear children who became the property of the slave owner must have given an especially poignant meaning to the concept of alienation; nevertheless, women bore and raised children, creating families in which woman-centered networks figured prominently (Gutman 1976; Mintz and Price 1976).

Within the constraints of segregation, African American men and women attempted to maintain some control over the conditions under which they bore children. Though planters (Gutman 1976) and poverty forced many married women to work, they often chose to work as laundresses rather than as live-in domestics, increasing the time they could spend with their families and limiting as best they could their vulnerability to sexual exploitation.

In their effort to maintain continuity and support survival through the conditions of slavery, segregation, and deindustrialization, African American women have often utilized woman-centered networks. These "blood mothers and other mothers" (Collins 1991) embedded in larger networks have a long history in the African American community as an alternative family form (see Omolade 1987). They have sustained and supported survival, caring for children and adults when immediate relatives were unable to do so. In Harlem these networks continue, often supported by community-based organizations.

Efforts to sustain the family have always been inseparable from efforts to assist the community. African American women have a long history of community work (see Gilkes 1988). Inevitably, the attempt to sustain the community requires measures to transform the larger society. Most African American women and men have been actively involved in individual and collective efforts that foster resistance and empowerment.

Conditions and Constraints

African American women, and particularly poor women in communities such as Harlem, now face one of the greatest challenges since slavery. In the face of deteriorating conditions, many women in Harlem continue to engage in efforts directed at both sustaining continuity and transforming conditions. Kin and nonkin networks continue to be important in raising children, but the extent to which these networks are threatened by the crisis conditions (De-Havenon 1988) is indicated by the record number of children in foster care. These networks and other institutions are particularly weakened by the spread of illegal drug use among African American women.

Though the decline of working-class movements has undercut a major area of potential advance, women in Central Harlem, many of whom head households, are the backbone of militant unions, such as Local 1199 of the Hospital Workers Union, and they continue to try to change the workplace. They are active in community efforts to build associations and tenant organizations, to improve housing and schools, and to eliminate drugs from buildings and neighborhoods. Community-based activities such as the church-led movement to protest extensive billboard advertisement of cigarettes and alcohol and two environmental movements focusing attention on pollution in low-income neighborhoods have been highly publicized. These local struggles have sometimes been the building blocks of larger, citywide political actions, such as the election of the first African American mayor of New York City in 1989 and the formation of the New Majority Coalition, a multiracial organization that was active in voter registration, supporting progressive candidates for election to the city council, and organizing for a civilian review board.

However, with the failures of liberal integration (Marable 1992) and the destruction of the left movement (Horne 1993), the political context for collective movements for empowerment and basic social reform has become severely restricted. The current repressive environment, which has a negative impact on efforts for collective empowerment, lends itself to the resurgence of ethnically based political and cultural movements. This development is immediately evident to the casual observer in the rise of various Afrocentrisms; the adoption of neo-African hair styles, jewelry, and clothing; the growing influence of the Nation of Islam; and expressions of concern about loss of history, culture, and community. Explanations such as "We need to return to our values" and "We need to build our own cultural and moral base for our children" were typically given by people I interviewed in Central Harlem. On one hand, this concern with culture may represent an attempt to contest hegemonic constructs of race and culture, to repossess history and to create new definitions of community. On the other hand, fundamentalist nationalist movements are frequently patriarchal and authoritarian. In these cases, the status of women, who are often seen as culture-bearers, becomes highly problematic.

In doing transformative work, then, women seek to construct a space in which they can ensure continuity for themselves, their children, and their communities. We need to increase our understanding of the conditions in which these efforts are successful and the circumstances in which they develop into larger social movements. But what is perhaps unique about the experience of African American women is the dramatic way in which their experience has linked the domains of household, community, and the larger society. For women of color, working-class women, and increasingly for middle-stratum women, protection of their children, which mobilizes their activism, requires the protection and transformation of their households, their communities, and the larger society. For this reason, efforts to sustain and maintain continuity inevitably involve significant social transformations.

References

Baca Zinn, Maxine. 1989. "Family, Race, and Poverty in the Eighties." *Signs* 14: 856–74.

Bock, Gisela. 1983. "Racism and Sexism in Nazi Germany: Motherhood, Compulsory Sterilization and the State." *Signs* 8: 400–21.

Breslin, Susan, and Eleanor Stier. 1987. *Promoting Poverty: The Shift of Resources Away from Low Income New York City School Districts.* New York: Community Service Society of New York.

Collins, Patricia Hill. 1991. *Black Feminist Thought: Knowledge, Consciousness, and the Politics of Empowerment.* New York: Routledge.

Davin, Anna. 1978. "Imperialism and Motherhood." *History Workshop* 5: 9–65.

Davis, Karen, and Diane Rowland. 1983. "Uninsured and Underserved: Inequities in Health Care in the United States." In Peter Conrad and Rochelle Kern, eds., *The Sociology of Health and Illness: Critical Perspectives.* New York: St. Martin's Press.

DeHavenon, Anna Lou. 1988. "Where Did All the Men Go?": An Etic Model for the Cross-Cultural Study of the Causes of Matrifocality." Paper presented at the symposium Female-Headed/Female-Supported Households, Twelfth International Congress of Anthropological and Ethnological Sciences, July 21–31, Zagreb, Yugoslavia.

England, Paula, and George Farkas. 1986. *Households, Employment, and Gender: A Social, Economic, and Demographic View.* New York: Holt, Rinehart, and Winston.

Fox-Genovese, Elizabeth. 1988. *Within the Plantation Household: Black and White Women of the Old South.* Chapel Hill: University of North Carolina Press.

Gilkes, Cheryl. 1988. "Building in Many Places: Multiple Commitments and Ideologies in Black Women's Community Work." In Ann Bookman and Sandra Morgan, eds., *Women and the Politics of Empowerment.* Cambridge: Harvard University Press.

Ginsburg, Faye, and Rayna Rapp. 1995. "Introduction." In Faye Ginsburg and Rayna Rapp, eds., *Conceiving the New World Order: The Global Politics of Reproduction.* Los Angeles: University of California Press.

Gutman, Herbert G. 1976. *The Black Family in Slavery and Freedom, 1750–1925.* New York: Pantheon.

Harlem Urban Development Corporation. 1990. *Bradhurst Revitalization Planning Document.* New York: Harlem Urban Development Corporation.

Harrington, Michael. 1984. *The New American Poverty.* New York: Holt, Rinehart, and Winston.

Hartmann, Heidi I. 1987. "Changes in Women's Economic and Family Roles in Post–World War II United States." In Lourdes Beneria and Catherine R. Stimpson, eds., *Women, Households, and the Economy.* New Brunswick, NJ: Rutgers University Press.

Health and Hospitals Corporation. 1991. *A Summary Examination of Excess Mortality in Central Harlem and New York City.* New York: Office of Strategic Planning, Health and Hospitals Corporation.

Hernandez, Donald J. 1992. *When Households Continue, Discontinue, and Form: Studies on Household and Family Formation.* Current Population Reports, series P23179. Washington, DC: U.S. Bureau of the Census.

Horne, Gerald. 1993. "Myth and the Making of Malcolm X." *American Historical Review* 98: 440–50.

Jenks, Christopher. 1991. "Is the American Underclass Growing?" In Christopher Jenks and D. Peterson, eds., *The Urban Underclass.* Washington, DC: Brookings Institute.

Jones, Jacqueline. 1985. *Labor of Love, Labor of Sorrow: Black Women, Work, and the Family from Slavery to the Present.* New York: Basic Books.

Kozol, Jonathan. 1991. *Savage Inequalities: Children in America's Schools.* New York: Crown.

Laslett, Barbara, and Johanna Brenner. 1989. "Gender and Social Reproduction: Historical Perspectives." *Annual Review of Sociology* 15: 381–404.

Lebsock, Suzanne. 1984. *The Free Women of Petersburg: Status and Culture in a Southern Town, 1784–1860.* New York: W. W. Norton.

Lemman, Nicolas. 1986. "The Origins of the Underclass," Parts 1 and 2. *Atlantic Monthly* (June): 31–35, (July): 54–68.

McCord, Colin, and Harold P. Freeman. 1990. "Excess Mortality in Harlem." *New England Journal of Medicine* 322(3): 173–77.

Marable, Manning. 1992. "Race, Identity and Political Culture." In Gina Dent, ed., *Black Popular Culture.* Seattle: Bay Press.

Mintz, Sidney W., and Richard Price. 1976. *An Anthropological Approach to the Afro-American Past: A Caribbean Perspective.* Philadelphia: Institute for the Study of Human Issues.

Morton, Patricia. 1991. *Disfigured Images: The Historical Assault on Afro-American Women.* New York: Praeger.

Mullings, Leith, and Ida Susser. 1992. *Harlem Research and Development: An Analysis of Unequal Opportunity in Central Harlem and Recommendations for an Opportunity Zone.* New York: Office of the Borough President of Manhattan.

Murray, Charles. 1984. *Losing Ground.* New York: Basic Books.

New York City Department of City Planning. 1990a. *Community District 10.* New York: Department of City Planning.

———. 1990b. *Persons 16 Years and Over by Labor Force Status and Sex, New York City, Boroughs and Community Districts.* DCP 1990, no. 317. New York: Department of City Planning.

———. 1991. *Community District Needs, FY 1993.* DCP no. 91-14. New York: Department of City Planning.

————. 1992a. *Civilian Labor Force 16 Years and Over by Employment Status and Sex, New York City, Boroughs and Community Districts.* DCP 1990, no. 315. New York: Department of City Planning.

————. 1992b. *Demographic Profiles: A Portrait of New York City's Community Districts from the 1980 and 1990 Censuses of Population and Housing.* New York: Department of City Planning.

————. 1992c. *Persons 16–19 Years, Enrollment, Education, and Labor Force/Employment, New York City, Boroughs and Community Districts.* DCP 1990, no. 321. New York: Department of City Planning.

————. 1992d. *Selected Poverty Tabulations in 1989, New York City, Boroughs and Community Districts.* DCP 1990, no. 310. New York: Department of City Planning.

————. 1993. *Socioeconomic Profiles: A Portrait of New York City's Community Districts from the 1980 and 1990 Censuses of Population and Housing.* New York: Department of City Planning.

New York City Office of Management Analysis and Planning. 1989. *Statistical Report: Complaints and Arrests.* New York: Crime Analysis Unit, Office of Management Analysis and Planning.

New York City Office of the Budget. 1991. *1990 Annual Average Labor Force Data Disaggregated by Community District.* New York: New York State Department of Labor.

Omolade, Barbara. 1987. "The Unbroken Circle: A Historical and Contemporary Study of Black Single Mothers and Their Families." *Wisconsin Women's Law Journal* 3: 239–74.

Pleck, Elizabeth. 1979. "A Mother's Wages." In N. Cott and Elizabeth Pleck, eds., *A Heritage of Her Own.* New York: Simon and Schuster.

Rapp, Rayna. 1987. "Toward a Nuclear Freeze? The Gender Politics of Euro-American Kinship Analysis." In Jane Collier and Sylvia Yanagisako, eds., *Gender and Kinship: Essays Toward a Unified Analysis.* Stanford, CA: Stanford University Press.

Reed, Adolph. 1992. "The Underclass as Myth and Symbol: The Poverty of Discourse About Poverty." *Radical America* 24(1): 21–40.

Rosen, Ruth. 1982. *The Lost Sisterhood: Prostitution in America, 1900–1918.* Baltimore: Johns Hopkins University Press.

Ross, Heather L., and Isabel V. Sawhill. 1975. *Time of Transition: The Growth of Families Headed by Women.* Washington, DC: Urban Institute.

Sands, Roberta, and Kathleen Nuccio. 1989. "Mother-Headed Single Parent Families: A Feminist Perspective." *Affilia* 4(3): 25–41.

Schlesinger, Benjamin. 1986. "Single-Parent Families: A Bookshelf, 1978–1985." *Family Relations* 35(1): 199–204.

Schorr, Alvin L., and Phyllis Moen. 1979. "The Single Parent and Public Policy." *Social Policy* 9(5): 15–21.

Scott, Ann Firor. 1970. *The Southern Lady.* Chicago: University of Chicago Press.

Sharff, Jagna. 1987. "The Underground Economy of a Poor Neighborhood." In Leith Mullings, ed., *Cities of the United States: Studies in Urban Anthropology.* New York: Columbia University Press.

Stack, Carol. 1974. *All Our Kin: Strategies for Survival in a Black Community.* New York: Harper and Row.

Stoler, Ann. 1989. "Making Empire Respectable: The Politics of Race and Sexual Morality in Twentieth-Century Colonial Cultures." *American Ethnologist* 16(4): 634–60.

Susser, Ida. 1989. "The Structuring of Homeless Families: New York City, 1980–1990." Paper presented at the annual meeting of the American Anthropological Association, November, Washington, DC.

Tiffany, Sharon, and Kathleen Adams. 1985. *The Wild Woman: An Inquiry into the Anthropology of an Idea.* Cambridge, MA: Schenkman.

U.S. Bureau of the Census. 1973. *1970 Census of Population and Housing, Characteristics of Population, U.S. Summary.* Washington, DC: Government Printing Office.

————. 1990a. *1990 Census of Population and Housing, Summary Tape File 1C.* Washington, DC: Government Printing Office.

————. 1990b. *1990 Census of Population and Housing, Summary Tape File 3C. Poverty Status in 1989 by Family Type and Presence and Age of Children.* Washington, DC: Government Printing Office.

————. 1992. *Detailed Occupation and Other Characteristics from the EEO File for the United States. 1990 Census of Population and Housing, Supplementary Report.* Washington, DC: Government Printing Office.

Wallace, Rodrick, M. Fullilove, and D. Wallace. 1992. "Family Systems and Deurbanization: Implications for Substance Abuse." In Joyce Lowinson, ed., *Substance Abuse: A Comprehensive Textbook*. Baltimore: Williams and Wilkins.

Williams, Brett. 1992. "Poverty Among African Americans in the Urban United States." *Human Organization* 51(2): 164–74.

Williams, Terry. 1989. *The Cocaine Kids*. New York: Columbia University Press.

Wilson, William J. 1987. *The Truly Disadvantaged: The Inner City, the Underclass and Public Policy*. Chicago: University of Chicago Press.

THIRTY-TWO

Shattering Two Molds
Feminist Parents with Disabilities
Carol J. Gill and Larry A. Voss

We are two persons with extensive physical disabilities who have raised a nondisabled son. Countering the stereotype of people with disabilities as childlike, fragile, and suffering, we have nurtured and, we believe, nurtured powerfully. With wonder and relief, we have watched our child's development into a generous, emotionally open, strong, and socially responsible adult. It was not a snap. All three of us waged a long struggle against society's devaluation of human difference to get to this place.

Our war against ableist beliefs began in childhood when we acquired our disabilities in the 1950 polio epidemic. We used braces and wheelchairs and would have had little problem attending our neighborhood school if not for architecture and its real foundation: attitudes. In those days before the disability rights movement, we were barred from mainstream life. No ramps or elevators were installed to ensure our access. Instead, we were bussed miles each day to a "special" school with similarly displaced children.

Undoubtedly, these experiences laid the groundwork for our acceptance of a feminist perspective. We acquired a deep suspicion of unequal treatment and stereotyping in any form. In high school, we identified with the civil rights struggle. In college, our rejection of sexism took definite shape. For Carol, the conscious decision to participate in the women's movement grew from classroom discussion of the work of Greer, Friedan, and Steinem. For Larry, it grew out of heated ideological debates between men and women in radical student collectives during the antiwar movement.

When Larry married a woman from this movement (his first marriage), he found daily life to be a mixture of new and traditional gender roles. During most of the marriage, his partner, who was not disabled, worked as an intensive care nurse while Larry completed his education. Although they shared household duties according to preferences as well as Larry's disability limitations, it was expected that his partner would cook and perform "housewife" chores after coming home from her job.

The decision to have a baby, on the other hand, was planned to be as joint a venture as possible. Larry remained by his wife's side during her prenatal exams and, long before it was accepted practice, he participated in the birth of his son in the hospital delivery room. He remembers this experience as ecstasy and agony—the incomparable joy of watching his child's birth and his sense of helpless horror as the emerging head made an audible tear in his wife's tissues. That painful moment registered clearly in Larry's consciousness—a factor, perhaps, in his later diligence in shouldering childcare duties.

Larry, in fact, became the primary parent. As is true of most children of disabled parents, Brian had little trouble adapting to his father's wheelchair and unconventional strategies for accomplishing daily tasks. When Larry's marriage foundered, he had no intention of parting with his son, then a toddler. Although it was rare for men to get custody of children in divorces, and even rarer for disabled persons, Larry fought to keep Brian with him and won.

Single parenthood was a rich and difficult time for them. Although Larry's sister and mother helped baby-sit, he experienced the loneliness and weight of responsibility that many single parents face. Additionally, there were unique physical and social difficulties. Unemployed and without child support, Larry could afford neither personal assistance nor adequate accessible housing. Consequently, errands such as grocery shopping became all-day feats of endurance. After driving home from the store, he would be forced to leave his wheelchair at the top of the stairs, crawl down the steps several times to his basement apartment and up again, hauling each bag of groceries followed by the baby, and then drag his wheelchair down the steps so he could get back into it and put groceries away!

Even more exhausting were the social hurdles. Strangers as well as family members challenged Larry's decision to keep his child, citing both gender- and disability-based concerns. Brian's first teachers suggested he was being shortchanged by not having a mother or nondisabled parent. (Brian's biological mother moved out of state and maintained very limited contact with him.) Neighborhood children teased or grilled him about his "wheelchair father" and asked why he had no mother. People who knew nothing about Larry's parenting skills would cluck over Brian's misfortune and tell him that having a "crippled daddy" was his cross to bear.

Although we — Carol and Larry — knew each other superficially while attending the same "special" high school, our paths did not cross again until a mutual friend brought us together at the time of Larry's divorce. After several years of intense and romantic friendship, we married.

At first, Brian was thrilled about Carol joining the family. Even before the wedding, which took place when he was seven, he insisted on calling her "Mom." But once it was official, he was ambivalent. Due both to her disability and her feminism, Brian's "new mother" was anything but the traditional nurturing figure people had told him he needed. She was physically incapable of performing many of the cooking and household chores mothers were supposed to do. She was not conventionally pretty. She

was unexpectedly strong in communicating her ideas and affecting household decisions. She was even unwilling to change her name when she got married.

Not that Brian had been raised to be sexist. He had a father who baked cookies, cared for a home, brushed his lover's hair, and became an elementary school teacher. He also knew Larry's fondness for baseball, tools, and macho action movies. Father and son openly shared hugs and kisses between bouts of arm wrestling. Larry's philosophy of child-rearing, like his philosophy of education, stressed openness. He had always been pleased that Brian's early years were fairly non-sex-typed. He had let the toddler's strawberry blond hair grow to shoulder length undaunted by family predictions of gender confusion. He admired Brian's eclectic taste in toy trucks and stuffed animals as well as his drawings of kittens, nudes, Army tanks, Spiderman and posies.

But despite Larry's efforts to raise a child liberated from all the "isms," Brian was exposed to and affected by the sexism and ableism (not to mention racism, ethnocentrism, and heterosexism) of the surrounding culture. Dealing with this in addition to the typical tensions of stepparenting introduced a great deal of struggle into our family life.

It is hard for us to separate where our parenting was guided by feminism or by our experience and values as disabled persons. We believe in both notions of a women's culture and a disabled people's culture. Further, we believe the overlap of cultural values in the two communities is significant. Both feminist analysis and the disability independent living philosophy embrace values of interdependence, cooperative problem-solving, flexibility/adaptability, and the importance of relationships in contrast to traditional male values of autonomy, performance, competition, dominance, and acquisition.

By necessity, a guiding principle of our partnership has always been unfettered cooperation. There has been no "women's work" or "men's work." From the start, we negotiated most tasks of life by deciding who could do it, who was good at it, who wanted to do it, who had time, who needed help, etc. Larry's arm strength meant he had kitchen duty. Carol's greater physical limitations meant she organized the lists and schedules. In our professional jobs, we alternated being the major breadwinner. Everything from lovemaking to getting out of the car was an exercise in cooperation and respect — an orchestration of timing, assistance, and down-to-earth tolerance.

Our parenting was similarly orchestrated. As the only one who could drive, Larry did the car-pooling. Carol's math acuity made her the homework authority. Larry did more of the "hands-on" parenting jobs: cuddling, restraining, washing, roughhousing. Carol nurtured by story-telling, instructing, reprimanding, discussing, and watching endlessly ("Mom, watch this!").

We both did an enormous amount of talking. Larry explained and lectured. Carol questioned motivations and articulated feelings. We even entered family counseling during several difficult times to talk some more. Reflecting back on it, we realize one of the central themes of all this talking was nurturance: caring for and being responsible for people, animals, plants, and the environment. Larry encouraged empathy in Brian through questions like, "How do you think you would feel if that happened to you?" Carol nudged Brian to write notes and make gifts for family members. We gave him regular chores to do for the family and engaged him in many rescues of abandoned and injured stray animals.

Another major theme was prejudice and unfairness. Disability rights and women's rights were frequent topics in our household. Carol often directed Brian's attention to surrounding events, attitudes, and images that contributed to women's oppression, e.g., *Playboy*, sadistic images in rock videos, crude jokes. Most of the time, Brian would roll his eyes and protest that Carol could find sexism in anything. Larry usually backed her up but sometimes he lightened the tension by joining Brian in teasing Carol about her unwillingness to take her menfolk's last name. This was a family joke that ironically conveyed both affection and respect for Carol and got everyone to smile.

We also did a lot of the standard things most people do to raise a nonsexist son, from respecting his need to cry, to encouraging his interests and talents regardless of their traditional "gender appropriateness." Again, this lent a certain eclecticism to Brian's activities, which included sports, cooking, ceramics, drawing, music, reading, swimming and surfing, collecting, etc. On both feminist and pacifist grounds, we tried to avoid the most destructive "macho" stuff. For example, at his request, we enrolled Brian in a karate class. But when we discovered the instructor tested each boy's mettle by getting the class to take turns punching him in the stomach, Larry pronounced it barbaric and encouraged Brian to drop out, which he did. We also kept Brian out of formal team sports run by zealous competitive coaches and pressured him not to join the military when the gung-ho recruiters tried to nab him in high school.

Although we often held little hope that our battle against the "isms" was making an impact, like other parents, we now see that children do pay attention. Brian is now 22 and spontaneously uses words like "sexism" when critiquing the world. He is also our only relative who consistently uses Carol's proper name in introductions and addressing mail. He is comfortable in the friendship of both men and women. He loves sports and still hugs his childhood stuffed dog when he's sick. He has argued for the rights of women, people with disabilities, and other minorities.

Brian has shared his life for four years with a woman who also has strong goals and opinions. They have found a way to support each other, argue, and give space as needed. Like us, they are lover, companion, and family — equals. Seeing them interact is the great payoff to all our years of struggle. We enjoy watching our son laundering his partner's delicate sweaters or lovingly constructing her sandwiches. We listen to him express the depth of his feelings and respect for her. (Yes, he is a talker like his parents!) They have negotiated their course with cooperation, nurturance, and concern about unfairness. They want to have a family, they want to protect the earth.

When we told Brian about writing this piece, we asked his permission to tell the story of our family. He was enthusiastic and helped us reminisce about the past. One of his recollections confirmed how much he had been affected by the equity in his parents' relationship. He told us that sometimes as a child when he would answer the family telephone, callers would ask to speak to the "head of the house." Brian remembers his natural response to this request was to ask "Which one?" Then he and the caller would have a confusing discussion about which parent was needed on the phone. He said it was always simpler when only one of us was home because then the choice was clear: he would just summon whichever "head of the house" happened to be present!

THIRTY-THREE

Loving across the Boundary

Ann Filemyr

Nubian, our puppy, scratches and whines at the bedroom door. Essie sits bolt upright in bed crying out: "What time is it?" Groggy, I squint at the clock, "Almost seven—"

"Granny was supposed to wake us up at six!"

"Maybe she forgot—" I hustle into my bathrobe at the insistent scratching on the door, "I've got to let Nubi out—"

"Granny never forgets to wake us," Essie mutters under her breath as she scrambles out of the tangled sheets.

I race down the stairs, "Granny! GRANNY!"

I find her body on the cold kitchen floor, but she is gone. I can feel her spirit lifting up and out into the golden morning light filtering through the grand old maples that surround the farmhouse. Despite the utter peace in the room, I panic.

"Essie! Essie Carol!" I scream up the stairs to my partner.

Granny's breath is gone, but her body remains. A line from the book *Daughters of Copper Woman* circles through my mind, "*And she left her bag of bones on the beach. . . .*" Sun crowds the kitchen and the golden maple leaves gleam in October light. Essie flies barefoot across cold linoleum, cradling Granny in her arms, the first sob rising in our throats.

Granny was wearing the tee shirt I had given her from my trip to Brazil. Beneath a little refrain in Portuguese about protecting the rainforest for all the forest creatures was a brown-skinned elf with a green leaf hat. It reminded me of Granny's love for the forest, for the "red-birds" (cardinals) and "loud-mouth crows," for the gentle deer. She would wait all day just to catch a glimpse of them, moving from one window to the next or taking the short trail up to Sunset Hill to sit on her bench, waiting, watching for the deer.

Granny had on the green stretch pants Essie had given her, and pinned to the inside of her pants were her house keys. She always carried her keys when she went out on the paths surrounding the wooded farmhouse where we lived. She loved to take her cane and her cat and go out for a morning walk before we left for work. When she didn't have pockets, she would pin her keys to the inside of her pants just in case in our morning rush to get to work we would leave and lock her out; of course, we never did.

Granny had made her bed that morning. She was dressed and ready for her Monday morning walk. But instead of the familiar stroll, Granny had traveled where we could not follow. We shared a long, sad look. Essie's face crumpled in pain. . . .

In the hospital emergency room we wept, our heads bent over Granny's body. Stroking back her wavy black hair (even at 79 her hair had not turned white) we sighed and pleaded. Two years earlier in ICU the doctors had told us she was gone. Her heart would not hold a steady beat. They pointed to the monitor above her unconscious body to show us the erratic yellow line, the uneven blip across the screen. Only the machines kept her breathing. We said no. It was her second heart failure in three months that winter of 1991, but we had plans for our shared lives—Granny, Essie and me. We were anticipating spring. . . .

Granny regained her strength that time. But that was March 1991 and this was October 1993. The doctor nodded to us and spoke with her strong Pakistani accent, "She looks happy. She had a long life. She would die one day." Then she left us alone, but the nurse on duty asked us a million questions about "the body"—about funeral arrangements—about donating organs—about contacting "the family"—we could not respond.

We *are* the family—an elder with her two granddaughters. This is our story of love, though now we are the body of women weeping. Granny was ours to care for, we had taken her into our daily lives because we loved her, and now she is sleeping, and we cannot wake her.

Skin color marked Essie as the one who belonged to Granny. The nurse nodded and smiled at me, "It's so nice of you to stand by your friend at a time like this."

Where else would I be? Granny was my grandmother, too. She loved me like no one else in my life: she loved me fiercely. She knew I had stepped across the line in North America which is drawn across the center of our faces to keep us separate — to keep the great grandchildren of slavekeepers from the great grandchildren of slaves. When she met me as Essie's "friend" twelve years earlier, she had watched me closely, but then she accepted me into her household and into her family. As the elder, her acceptance meant acceptance. She recognized my love for her granddaughter and would say to me, "People talk, but you hold your head up. You walk tall. The Lord sees what you're doing for my granddaughter, how you help her with her son. He sees how you stick together and help each other out." As far as Granny was concerned it was the *quality of our caring* not our sexuality that mattered. In this she was far wiser than most.

For the past three years we had lived together in Yellow Springs, sharing meals and dishes. She would sometimes pull out her old photo albums and tell her stories, laughing at memories of wild times out dancing with her friends in the juke joint or riding horses with her cousin on her father's ranch or traveling cross country in the rig with her husband and his magical black cat when he worked as a truckdriver. Rich, warm memories, and I would sip my coffee and imagine her days and nights. What sustained her? Love — no doubt. Love and greens and cornbread — good food. That's what she craved. And the kitchen was her favorite room next to her bedroom.

She had been raised in the fields and farms of the south. When I was deciding whether or not to take the job in Ohio, Granny was part of the decision-making process. Moving back to the country after four decades in the city felt like coming full circle to her. She said she wanted to come with us. And it was here in Ohio that Granny and I had the luxury of time together to make our own relationship to each other. She would talk to me about "the things white folks do — " how they tend to "put themselves first like they better than other folks — " how foolish they looked on the TV talk shows "tellin' all their business — " or how much she had enjoyed some of the white friends she and her husband once had.

She spoke her mind without embarrassment or apology. I listened. She had survived the jim crow laws of the south. She had survived segregation and desegregation. She kept a gun under her pillow she called "Ole Betsy" in case someone would try to break in or "mess with her." Granny paid attention to details as a matter of survival. She prided herself on the subtle things she observed in watching how people acted and how they treated one another. She would interpret everything: tone of voice, a simple gesture, the hunch of someone's shoulders. She always knew when someone felt sad or tired. You didn't have to say anything. She comforted. She sympathized. She was extremely skilled at making others feel loved, feel noticed, feel good about themselves. But if Essie had not been in my life it is doubtful that I would have ever known this remarkable woman, her namesake, Essie (Granny) Hall.

When I moved in with Essie in 1982, my nomadic tendencies were pulling at me, urging me to convince Essie that it was a perfect time for us to relocate to another city. I had lived in Milwaukee for two and a half years, for me that was long enough. I'd found a new love, an important someone in my life. It seemed like the perfect time to move on with my new partner. But Essie's life was described and defined by different currents. She had roots. She had family. She told me, "I will be here as long as Granny needs me." I was shocked. My feet carried me freely; I fought against family attachments. Was this difference cultural? Personal? Both? But now I have grown to respect and appreciate this way of being, this way of belonging. Is it a middle-class white cultural tendency to break free, to move on, to move up, to move out? Certainly the bonds of family and of commitment were far stronger for Essie than for me. One of the greatest gifts in my life has been that she shared her son and grandmother with me.

I wanted to tell the emergency room nurse all of this. I held Essie Carol in my arms as she cried. I wanted to scream, "Here we are, can't you see us? Lovers and partners holding each other in a time of crisis — What do you need for proof?" . . .

Sunday mornings Granny listened to gospel preachers on her old radio, rocking and clapping to the music. When we weren't home, she'd get up and dance through the rooms of the house, tears flowing freely as she sang outloud. We'd catch her and tease her. Once Granny hung a plastic Jesus in the bathroom; he had his hands folded in prayer and flowing blonde locks thrown back over his shoulders. Essie groaned, "A white man on the bathroom wall!" She took it down and tried to explain to

Granny everybody did not worship the same way she did.

We were not only a multiracial household, but one that held different spiritual beliefs. Essie followed a path she had first been introduced to by Granny's mother, her great-grandmother, Caroline Kelly Wright, affectionately known as Ma. Ma wore her hair in long braids and had been called "the little Indian" most of her life. She had married a freed African slave, but she herself was Blackfoot. Ma smoked a pipe and prayed to the sun. Essie remembered as a child the whole family would gather in Ma's bedroom facing East. The dawn's pale light would begin to appear through the open window only a few city blocks from the enormous freshwater ocean called Lake Michigan. Everyone listened as Ma prayed aloud over the family, telling all secrets, opening up all stories, praying to Creator to provide answers, to help guide them to find their purpose in life and hold to it, to be strong. Everything was said on these Sunday mornings and tears fell as Ma blew her smoke toward the light of the rising sun.

Ma had delivered Essie during a wild January blizzard. Ma was a midwife, herbalist, neighborhood dream interpreter, the community sage and soothsayer. If the term had been as popular then as it is now, Ma would have been honored as a shaman. Essie remembers the Baptist preacher visiting their house and saying to Ma, "I'll pray for you, Miz Caroline," and Ma responding, "You can't pray for me, but I can pray for you."

At the age of eight after a preacher had singled her out to stand up and read the Bible as a punishment for something she hadn't even done, Essie told her great-grandmother that she did not want to attend church anymore. Ma agreed. So Essie had little patience for Granny's Christianity. She was especially offended by refrains such as the "Good Master" and would try to point out to Granny how Black Christian faith was a result of slavery, the product of an enforced cultural genocide. Essie would try to "educate" Granny about the ways slaves were punished for trying to hold on to older beliefs, such as the care and worship of the ancestors or relating to land and nature as an expression of the Sacred. Of course this didn't work, and I would try to negotiate peace settlements between the two generations, between the two Essies, between the centuries, be-

tween the ancestors and the youth. Neither one of them really listened to me. I would take the younger Essie aside and tell her, "Leave Granny alone. You're not going to change her." And the younger Essie would retort, "But she's trying to change me!" . . .

[A]t the funeral the man in the black suit did his best. He tried to save us. He opened the doors of the church and urged us to enter. He forgot about the corpse in the casket behind him, and he called the stray flock home. White men and Black men held each other in the back row. White women held Black women in the front row. And in between were all shades of brown and pink, young and old, from four week old Jade, the last baby Granny had blessed, to Mrs. Cooper, Granny's phone buddy. They had spoken every day on the phone for a year. Granny adored "Cooper" as she called her, though they had never met in person. Here we sat in rows before an open casket: all colors, ages, sexualities, brought together by a mutual love for an exceptional person. As some of Essie's family members called out urgently, encouraging the preacher with *Amen* and *Yes, Lord* others ignored the eulogy, attending to their own prayers.

At the funeral we sat side by side in the front row in dark blue dresses. Essie's sister and son sat on the other side of her. We wept and held each other's hands. If Granny loved us for who we were, then we weren't going to hide our feelings here. Certainly there were disapproving glances from some family members, but not all. During the decade we lived in Milwaukee, we had shared childcare and holidays, made it through illnesses and the deaths of other beloved family members—what else qualifies someone as family? Yet despite this, I knew there were those who despised my presence for what I represented was the alien. I was the lesbian, and I was white. For some my presence was an inexcusable reminder of Essie's betrayal. She had chosen to be different, and I was the visible reminder of her difference. For some this was a mockery of all they valued, but she did not belong to them so they could control her identity. Granny knew this, and Granny loved her because she had the strength to be herself.

My family is liberal Democrat, yet my mother once said to me that my choice to love other women would make my life more difficult. She wanted to discourage me from considering it. She said, *I would tell you the same thing if you told me you loved a Black man.* I was then nineteen. It struck me as curious that to love someone of the same sex was to violate the same taboo as to love someone across the color line. In the end I chose to do both. Does this make me a rebel? Certainly if my attraction was based initially on the outlaw quality of it, that thrill would not have been enough to sustain the trauma of crossing the color line in order to share love. The rebellious young woman that I may have been could not make sense of the other story, the story of her darker-skinned sister, without a willingness to question everything I had been raised to accept as "normal," without an active analysis of the politics of racial subjugation and institutionalized white male supremacy. And without personal determination, courage, a refusal to be shamed, a sheer stubbornness based on our assumption that our lives held unquestionable worth as women, as women together, as women of different colors together, despite the position of the dominant culture—and even at times the position of the women's community—to diminish and deny us, we would not have been able to make a life together.

I have participated in and been witness to a side of American life that I would never have glimpsed if Essie had not been my partner. The peculiar and systematic practice of racial division in this country has been brought into sharp focus through many painful but revealing experiences. By sharing our lives, our daily survival, our dreams and aspirations, I have been widened and deepened. It has made me much more conscious of the privileges of being white in a society rigidly structured by the artificiality of "race."

One of the first awakenings came near the beginning of our relationship when her son came home with a note from the school librarian that said, "Your overdue books will cost 45 cents in fines. Irresponsible handling of school property can lead to problems later including prison." I was shocked—threatening a nine-year-old boy with prison because of overdue books? I couldn't imagine what that librarian was thinking. Did she send these letters home with little white boys and girls? I wanted to call the school and confront her. Essie stopped me by telling me a number of equally horrifying stories about this school so we agreed to take Michael out.

We decided that Michael, who had been staying with Granny and Daddy Son and attending the school near their home during the week, should move in full-time with us. Essie worked first shift at the hospital, and I was a graduate student at the university. She left for work at 6 A.M., and I caught the North Avenue bus at 9:30. I would be able to help Michael get to school before I left for the day. We decided to enroll Michael in our neighborhood school.

The neighborhood we lived in was one of the few mixed neighborhoods in the city. It formed a border between the rundown urban center and the suburbs on the west side. The neighborhood school was across an invisible boundary, a line I did not see but would grow to understand. Somewhere between our house and this building, a distance of approximately six blocks, was a color line. A whites-only-no-Blacks-need-apply distinctly drawn and doggedly patrolled. We scheduled a visit with the principal, and when both of us appeared the next morning, we observed a curious reaction. Though polite, she was absolutely flustered. She could not determine who to direct her comments to. She looked from Essie's closely cropped black hair to my long loose wavy hair, from cream skin to chocolate skin, and stammered, "Who—who is the mother?"

"I am," said Essie.

"I'm sorry," was the reply. "We have already reached our quota of Black students in this school."

"Quota? We live in this neighborhood," I replied. "This is not a question of bussing a child in. He lives here."

She peered at the form we had filled out with our address on it. Then responded coldly, "We are full."

"That's ridiculous," I objected.

"Are you telling me that my child is not welcome to attend the fourth grade in your school?" Essie asked icily.

"We simply don't have room."

Essie stood up and walked out of the room without another word. I wanted to scream. I wanted to force the principal to change her mind, her politics, her preoccupation with the boundaries defined by color. I sat there staring at her. She refused to meet my eyes. I said slowly, "This will be reported to the Superintendent and to the school board," and walked out following Essie to the car.

We scheduled a meeting at the school administration to register a formal complaint and find Michael another school. I was furious. We were tax payers. These are public schools. How can he be refused entrance? How can a child be denied because of some quota determined by an administrator somewhere? I was naive in matters of race.

I would have to say all white people are naive about the persistence of the color line. We prefer naiveté—in fact we insist on it. If we, as white people, actually faced the entrenched injustice of our socioeconomic system and our cultural arrogance, we might suffer tears, we might suffer the enormous weight of history, we might face the iceberg of guilt which is the underside of privilege. We might begin to glimpse our losses, our estrangement from others, our intense fear as the result of a social system that places us in the precarious position of the top. We might be moved to call out and protest the cruelty that passes for normal behavior in our daily lives, in our cities, and on our streets. . . .

Nothing in my life, my education, my reading, my upbringing, prepared me to straddle the color-line with Essie under the Reagan years in Milwaukee, a post-industrial city suffering economic decline and social collapse. The rigidly entrenched division of social power by race and the enormously draining limitations we faced on a daily basis began to tear at the fabric of our daily survival. I began to experience a kind of rage that left me feeling as sharp as broken glass. I was in this inner state when we finally arrived in the long quiet corridors of the central administration of Milwaukee Public Schools.

We were ushered into an office with a man in a suit sitting behind a desk. He could have been an insurance salesman, a loan officer, or any other briefcase-carrying decision-making tall white man in a position of power and control. We were two women of small build and modest dress, but we were carrying the larger presence—righteous anger. We sat down. I leaned across his desk and challenged him to explain to us why Michael had been refused admittance into the school of our choice. He backpedaled. He avoided. He dodged. Essie suddenly said, "I am finished. I am taking my child out of school," and stood up.

I snapped my notebook closed, signaling the end of the conversation. The man had never asked me who I was. Did he assume I was a social worker? a family member? a friend? a lawyer? a journalist? Had it even crossed his mind that he was looking at a pair of lovers, at a family, at the two acting parents of this child? For the first time he looked worried, "I am

sure we can find an appropriate school for your son. Tell me his interests. We'll place him in one of our specialty schools."

We hesitated.

"I'll personally handle his registration," he seemed to be pleading with us. He looked from Essie to me wondering who his appeal would reach first.

We settled on a school with a square of wild prairie, the environmental science specialty school. It was a half hour bus ride from our home. Michael liked the school, but we did not feel completely victorious. How could we? Though we had challenged the system, these policies and practices which place undue emphasis on the color of a child's skin had not been changed. The school system simply accommodated us, perhaps fearing our potential to cause widespread dissent by giving voice to the intense dissatisfaction of the African American community with the public school system. We compromised—perhaps exhausted by the constant fight against feeling invisible and powerless. It was not just that Michael was Black. It was also that his family consisted of a white woman and a Black woman, and regardless of our commitment to him, we were not perceived as a valid family unit though we functioned as a family. . . .

It is heartbreaking to raise an African American boy in the U.S. From an early age he is taught that others fear him. He is taught that he is less than. He is taught that his future is defined by certain streets in certain neighborhoods, or that the only way out is through musical or athletic achievement. Michael played basketball and football. He wrote raps and performed them to the punctuated beat of electronic keyboards and drum machines. When it was fashionable, he would breakdance on the living room floor. He had a few good years in school, but by and large school did not satisfy his quest for knowledge, nor did it provide him with creative avenues for self-expression. . . .

There were so many things I could not do for Michael. I could not clothe him in transparent skin to prevent him from being pre-judged by color-conscious teachers who would label him inferior. I could not surround him with safety on the street corner where he waited for his school bus. One grisly morning in November he came home shaking. He and a small boy had been shot at while waiting on a familiar corner two blocks from the house. It was

7:30 A.M. While he was preparing to attend school, boys his age were shooting guns out of car windows hoping to kill somebody in order to get into a gang so they could make money.

On that gray morning, the capitalist notion of success as the acquisition of material wealth appeared for what it is: an absolute perversion of human dignity. Yet white American culture persists in holding material affluence as the highest symbol of achievement. The way this plays out in the lives of people of color and those who love them can be summed up in one word: cruelty. We suffer for a lack of basic resources because of the hoarding, the feverish consumerism, and the complete lack of concern by people who have more than they will ever possibly need. Fashion crimes, ganking [gang violence targeting rival gang members or other young people], children beating and killing other children to acquire the stingy symbols of status in a society devoid of real meaning—this is what happens on the city streets of the richest nation in the world.

I could not keep Michael from the bullets. I could not move him out into the suburbs where another kind of violence would confront him daily, those who would question his presence and limit his right to move freely from one house to the next. I could not close his eyes to the terror he would see in his friends when death visited among them. I could not hold him against the rage he held inside. A rage that thundered through the house pulverizing everything in its path, terrifying me, tearing at his mother.

What could we say to him about how to live on the mean streets of a bully nation? We did not live on those same streets even though we lived in the same neighborhood. His experience, my experience, his mother's experience—we walked out of the front door into three separate worlds. Worlds we did not define or control except in how we would respond to them. Michael watched the hours I spent typing, writing, scratching out, rewriting. He watched the transformations his mother carried out with color on canvas, making lumps of cold clay into warm red altar bowls with her naked hands. He saw that we took our pain and rage, our grinding frustration and radiant hope, and made something out of it that gave us strength. Michael is still writing, making music, performing in his own music videos. He sees himself as an artist as we see ourselves; this is the thing that has carried us through.

The Westside where we bought a home had always been a working class neighborhood where people invested in their sturdy brick and wood frame houses planting roses in their green squares of grass. The neighborhood had been built in the teens and twenties by German immigrants who took a certain pride in quality. These homes had fireplaces and stained-glass windows, beautifully crafted built-in bookshelves and beveled mirrors. Only a few generations earlier, there was safety and prosperity here. Waves of immigrants—Greek, Polish, Hasidic Jews, African Americans coming North to work in the factories, shared these streets. I can remember walking into the corner bakery and the Greek woman behind the counter asked Essie and I if we were sisters. It was possible there at that time. Blood was shared. Love between the races happened. We laughed and nodded, "Yes—yes, we're sisters." In these moments we utterly and joyfully belonged together.

My friends who lived on the Eastside of the city rarely came to visit after I moved in with Essie. It was as if I had moved to the other side of the moon. . . . I trusted white women less and less as friends because they could not be counted on when things got tough. They tended to retreat. Race issues are ugly and hard, but if white women who want to fight male supremacy can't stand up to their own fears around the issue of color and simultaneously fight white supremacy, how can they really undertake the work of women's liberation? Certainly without an analysis and willingness to deal with race, there is no depth to the commitment. It is simply a get-ahead strategy for a particular middle class white female minority. Today I feel there is a greater commitment to address issues of racism within the feminist movement, but most of the voices I hear are still women of color. . . .

White women are conditioned to stay put, even rebellious daughters who love other women rarely cross the road that divides the races. Any woman who engages in a serious relationship—as friend or family, as lover, or mother to daughter—with a woman of a different shade of skin will find this relationship demanding a deeper vulnerability than any other as long as race relationships continue to be fraught with tension. But if we settle for a divided nation, we settle for social rigidity and police brutality, we settle for ignorance and stereotypes, we settle for emptiness and fear.

I am still learning how to confront racism when I see it, how to educate my friends without alienating them, how to ask for what I need in terms of support. It has been a rare occurrence, but a joyful one, for us to find other mixed-race lesbian couples. When we begin to talk about how difficult it is, we discover certain patterns and find solace that we are not alone. But why should we suffer for being ourselves and finding ourselves in the borderless culture between races, in the undefined space where wakefulness is necessary for survival, where honest communication and self-reflection must replace the simple recipes of romance. . . .

Few of us born in the Americas can trace our bloodline with impunity. So many of our ancestors have been erased or invented as need be. I know very few family names that have not gone without at least one attempt at revision—to anglicize it—simplify it—discard the ethnic or cultural baggage of a *ski* or *stein* or other markers of race/ethnic identity. One who is raised as part of an unwanted people will shift the identity to become acceptable. Note the number of Chippewa and Menominee people in Wisconsin with French last names. One Chippewa man explained to me how in every neighborhood his family adopted another identity: Mexican when living on the Southside, French on the Eastside. Only back up on the reservation could they say aloud their true names. . . .

How many of us are of African descent? Slavery was challenged in part because of the enormous outcry against the "white slave children." Children of enslaved African women who were the result of forced sex with slavemasters ended up on the auction block. Some of these children looked just like the "free" children of "free" European-American mothers. Obviously there was a tremendous outcry resulting from the confusion that the rationale for chattel slavery was based on a strict hierarchy of skin color as the basis of privilege. How could they justify selling these children that by all appearances looked white even if the mother was a light-skinned African American slave? White men in the South parented children on both sides of the yard: women they took as wives, and women who worked the fields. The brown and pale children were half-brothers and half-sisters related by blood through the father. This simple truth was denied, and these children were taught to never consider themselves as one family. There is no doubt that many of us have relatives we never considered before. Part of my work has been beginning to claim these unnamed Ancestors as family.

The day after I wrote that paragraph, I visited my parents. It was a week before Christmas, and I was planning to spend the day with my two grandmothers and my parents for Mimi's birthday. While in my parent's home, I asked about an old photo album that I remembered from childhood. My mother commented that it had recently surfaced from the jumble of daily life and brought it into the kitchen. Tintypes and daguerreotypes, family photographs spanning 1850–1900. Fifty years of Walkers, my mother's father's family.

That night, back in the city, stretched across the guest bed at a friend's house, I slowly turned the pages. There are my Ancestors, among the first generation here from the British Isles. Aunt Mary and Uncle Tom Walker. By pulling the photographs out and inspecting the little leather and brass book, I discovered they settled in Clinton and Seaforth, Ontario. I knew these relatives had lived in Canada, but hadn't known they lived between Lakes Huron, Erie and Ontario! All of the faces were unfamiliar, stiff, caught in frozen poses over a century ago. A few of the photographs I remembered from my childhood, especially the sad-faced child in the unusual robe with straight cropped black hair and Asian eyes. For the first time it occurred to me that this could be the face of a native child—not European at all! Who is this child? Then a particularly striking face caught my attention. A young woman gazed confidently, intently, at what? Her hair hung around her wide face and high cheekbones in thick black ringlets, her full lips barely open, her strong chin—this is a woman of African descent. Who is she to me? She wore a gold hoop earring and a checkered bow over a satin dress. With one arm resting against an upholstered pillow, she posed proudly. Why had I never heard of her before?

I live near Wilberforce College, one of the oldest historically Black colleges in the U.S., which was founded by slaveowners who wanted to train their half-white children in the trades. A friend who used to work there told me a story about a white male teacher at the college who became an important ally to his students. He assisted the African American sons and daughters of slaveowners to escape slavery by helping them relocate to Ontario, Canada after graduation rather than returning them to the South to work for their fathers. Is this woman the daughter of those students of Wilberforce? Is she my great-aunt or a distant cousin or great-great grandmother?

No one in my family seems to know much about these faces, these people, these lives, and how they relate to us. . . . If I am supposed to be a proud daughter of the colonizing English and the migrating Irish, why can't I also be a proud daughter of the Anishinabeg or Haudenausaunee, two of the indigenous peoples of this Great Lakes region, as well as a proud daughter of the African Diaspora? In America the idea of Europe was created, as if my English Ancestors weren't trying to dominate my Irish Ancestors. Why can't we talk about our truly diverse heritages? Nothing has been passed down in my family of these darker-skinned faces in my family's picture album. Is the refusal to see ourselves as something other than Northern European based in a fearful grasping after shreds of white-skinned privilege? What do we lose if we acknowledge our connection? What do we gain?

Granny kept a photo album. The pictures were important. Some were tattered and worn out, but they mattered. They held the faces of relatives — cousins, aunts, sisters — men in fine hats and women in silk dresses looking into the camera, into the future. In the album is a small square black and white snapshot of two plump white babies seated outdoors on a stuffed armchair. The Kelly boys. Irish. Part of the family. Essie remembers her great-grandmother telling her children, grandchildren and great-grandchildren, "These are your cousins." I bet those white boys don't show the dark faces of their cousins to their kin. . . .

The tight little boxes of identity defined by our society keep the building blocks of political and economic power in place. How can we gender-bend,

race-cross, nature-bond, and love ourselves in our plurality enough to rebel against the deadening crush of conformity? Is it a crisis of the imagination which prevents us from extending compassion beyond the boundaries of limited personal experience to listen *and be moved to action* by stories of injustice others suffer. How can we extend the boundaries of our own identities so that they include "the other"? If we have any hope for the future of life, how can we expand our sense of self to include other people as well as beings in nature? The structure of our society is articulated by separation and difference. How do we challenge this by living according to a sense of connection not alienation?

For us, for Essie and I, the greatest challenge has been inventing ourselves as we went along for we could not find a path to follow. Where are our foremothers? Light and Dark women who held each other's hands through childbirth and child-raising? Who stood side by side and loved each other refusing to budge despite everybody's objections? Who pooled their measly resources together to make sure there was food and heat and light enough for everyone's needs? I want to know them. I want to hear their stories. I'll tell them mine. This is the first time anyone has asked me to write anything about the twelve years we have shared.

Despite the absence of role models, we share specific Ancestors, disembodied presences gliding through our lives like a sudden breeze teasing the candle flame on the altar; secret-keepers who come under guard of moonlight, carrying apple baskets full of fresh fruit which they drop into our sleeping; we wake up before dawn with the sweet taste on our lips of good dreams and lucky numbers. We have our shared Ancestors to thank, and we are fortunate to count Granny among them.

◆◆◆

THIRTY-FOUR

Policies As If Families Really Mattered

Randy Albelda and Chris Tilly

... "Family policy" is an unfamiliar term in the United States because our family-friendly public policies are so few and far between, but it forms an integral and accepted part of European society. Most Western European nations offer universally available childcare, extensive paid parental leaves, child and housing allowances to supplement the income of families with children, universal health coverage, and government-guaranteed child support for single parents. To see where we as a nation might go, it is useful to start with a brief examination of the policies of these other countries.

Tell Me I'm Not Dreaming: Family Policy in Western Europe

In the decades since World War II, the countries of Western Europe, explicitly recognizing that raising children takes time and money, have created government policies to support families. Different countries have pursued different approaches. The Scandinavian countries and France have promoted women's paid work, providing services such as childcare to encourage paid labor, while tying many social welfare benefits to current or recent employment. Germany and some other countries in continental Europe have instead stayed closer to the "male breadwinner" model, but offer generous benefits to families who lack an employed breadwinner. Despite these variations, most of the countries of Western Europe offer a package that includes the following:[1]

- *Child or family allowances.* These are cash payments to families with children, typically available to all families at a fixed amount per child. Some countries (for example, France and Denmark) offer higher allowances to poorer families, and the amounts can be substantial: in France, a family with two small children and wages of $13,000 would receive $6,000 a year in allowances.[2]

- *Government-guaranteed child support.* Many Western European countries provide government guarantees of child support to deal with situations where absent parents fail — or are unable — to pay. In most cases, the government guarantee is small (about $1,500 per year), designed to supplement paid work rather than to replace it.[3]

- *Paid parental leave.* European countries have adopted two complementary types of parental leave policies. First, upon childbirth, mothers have the right to leave work for three months (in Luxembourg) to three years (in France and Germany) without losing job rights or seniority. Second, governments and employers together generally pay the mother full or nearly full wages for part of this period (typically, at least three to six months). Most countries offer some parental leave to fathers as well, and Norway and Sweden offer longer total leave times if fathers use part of the benefit.[4]

- *Subsidized childcare services.* Most Western European countries provide free, high-quality preschools for three- to five-year-olds, and many also subsidize childcare for infants and toddlers. An astounding 95 percent of three- to five-year-olds in France and Belgium are in childcare.[5]

- *Housing allowances.* Housing is a major cost for families. Housing allowances provide government cash assistance with housing costs, available to families with children whose income falls below a certain level. Despite the income test, housing allowances often reach far into the middle class — aiding one-third of families with children in Sweden and one-quarter in France. Further, they form part of a comprehensive housing policy, which includes public housing construction as well as subsidies for private construction.[6]

- *Universal, subsidized health care.* The United States is the only wealthy country that lacks a universal health care plan. In addition to guaranteed health care, some European countries, such as France, run special systems of preventive care for pregnant women and preschool children.[7]

This family policy package does not mean that life in Western Europe is paradise for families. There are still economic hardships, gender inequalities, and gaps in the safety net. But it does keep these societies far less stratified than the increasingly polarized United States, and provides families with a basic level of security and flexibility. Government assistance lifts many more poor families out of poverty in Western Europe than in the United States. It allows European families to balance work and family in ways that are relatively sane and sensible. Is it merely a dream to wish for the same in the United States?

Family Policies for the United States

The costs of real welfare reform are high—but so are the costs of poverty, child neglect, and overwork. Under the current system, low-income families, women, and children disproportionately bear these costs, yet that does not mean that the rest of society escapes them. Perhaps the most striking element of Europe's family policies is not any particular policy, but rather the deeply held philosophy of "social solidarity," meaning that "children and young people belong to the entire community, not just to their individual families," in the words of researcher Katherine McFate.[8] Here are eight broad policy approaches the United States should take that embody the notion of social solidarity.

1. Financially Support Full-Time Childcare

This means financially supporting women engaged in full-time childcare or providing alternate sources of childcare for those who work outside the home.

If we acknowledge the reality of children's needs and sincerely value families, then the important work of taking care of young children or relatives who cannot take care of themselves is, at times, best kept within the family. Even with childcare supports, families must be afforded the right to choose who does the work of childrearing. In short, jobs simply cannot be perceived as the answer for all single mothers at all times. For families with only one adult, this means that paid employment will not always be desirable or even possible, and will require some form of cash assistance.

What about parents who do choose paid employment? States currently provide childcare vouchers to women on welfare who are involved in employment and training programs, most often for up to one year after they get a job. One of the main reasons women return to welfare is that they can't make a job work for them, and the inability to find and pay for safe, quality daycare is a key barrier. But women who receive welfare are not the only people who need help securing childcare. *All* parents with children want to see their children cared for properly. Yet, for many families, working for pay and taking care of children is a costly proposition. The only comprehensive childcare program in the United States today is a federal tax deduction, and it is inadequate. Covering only a small portion of childcare costs, it only benefits families who make enough to owe income taxes. Perhaps its largest drawback is that it does not increase the *supply* of childcare. This deduction is supplemented in a limited way by small block grant and subsidy programs, a tax exemption for children, and the Earned Income Credit (a refundable credit for families with at least one child). But all of this does not even come close to creating a childcare *system.* And it falls far short of what most European countries provide: universal, free childcare (at least for ages three to five), plus cash family allowances based on the number of children.

Families that include someone at home doing unpaid work all day long are vanishing quickly. Women realize that their economic independence rests on their ability to earn wages, and increasingly, two incomes are necessary to ensure a reasonable standard of living. Indeed, it is just this fact that has made jobs the cornerstone of welfare reform. If we as a country expect many more women to work, however, we had better be prepared to pay for raising children.

2. Create More Jobs — and Stop Assuming Jobholders Have a Wife at Home

In early 1997, in the midst of economic boom times by all standard business indicators, over seven million Americans were unemployed. Over two million had been unemployed for fifteen weeks or more. And these official unemployment numbers don't include those who have given up looking for work, or those who want full-time work but have only been able to find shorter hours. If we include these people, the number of unemployed swells to thirteen million. Though the Federal Reserve Board and economists in their ivory towers may define this situation as full employment, it most certainly is not. The federal government could do far more to create jobs, from targeting monetary policy toward higher employment goals and increasing economic development investments in depressed areas, to directly funding public service employment. Full employment is an old idea that still makes sense.

While many people who want to work can't find a job, others are overworked. Jobs that can support a family often require a full-time commitment (or more), leaving many people exhausted. It's not just the welfare system that has to come to terms with family needs; it's employers as well. With women making up 46 percent of the workforce — and men also taking on more childcare responsibilities — a change in work styles is overdue.

All workers, men and women, need more time and flexibility on a day-to-day, week-to-week basis. One way to provide everyone with more time is to move to a thirty-hour work week. Short of this, federal and state governments could do more to reward businesses that adopt family-friendly policies. Businesses clearly get benefits from such policies: a [1996] study by Massachusetts Institute of Technology Management Professor Lotte Bailyn and others found that departments at Xerox who took work/family needs into account saw unprecedented reductions in absences, decreases in customer-response times, and on-schedule completions of new product development.[9] Unfortunately many employers place more value on controlling their employees and squeezing out as many hours of labor as possible — and as long as this is true, public policy is needed to tip the balance the other way.

3. Boost Wages to a "Living Wage" Level, and Make Them Fairer

With earnings the main source of income for most families and the key alternative to government support, we can't afford to leave so many adults stuck in low-wage employment. Between 1973 and 1996, the average hourly wage for nonsupervisory workers in the private sector slumped from $13.60 to $11.82 (in 1996 dollars).[10] For the lowest wage earners, even year-round, full-time work is no guarantee of avoiding poverty. Currently, 11 percent of poor families have a head who works full-time, year-round; 14 percent of year-round, full-time workers earn less than their family's poverty line.[11] And job discrimination against people of color, non-English speakers, and women persists, often lowering the wages of these groups.

There is no magic bullet that will solve the problems of low and unfair wage levels, but three measures could make a big difference. First, *mandate equal pay for comparable work.* "Equal pay for equal work" is an important principle, but with women and men segregated into different types of jobs (with very different pay levels!), it does not do enough to overcome gender inequality within specific jobs. Comparable worth — that is, requiring equal pay for work requiring comparable, though not identical, skills, education, and responsibility — could do a lot more to close the gender pay gap. Economists Deborah Figart and June Lapidus estimated the effect of comparable worth, also called pay equity, on women's wages. They concluded that a comprehensive pay equity program would raise women's average hourly wage by 8.5 percent. The biggest effect would be seen at the bottom of the scale: before comparable worth, 25 percent of women would not earn enough to bring a family of three up to the poverty line; after comparable worth, only 15 percent would fall short of this threshold.[12] Poor women need pay equity most, but all women need it.

Second, *raise the minimum wage, and expand requirements for a living wage.* Almost 60 percent of minimum-wage workers are women. Further, women are more likely than men to stay in minimum-wage jobs over the course of their working lives. Between 1979 and 1995, the inflation-adjusted value of the minimum wage tumbled by 30 percent. In 1996, Congress increased the minimum wage from $4.25 an hour to $5.15, still leaving it far below its 1979 level of $6.18 (in 1996 dollars). Some point out that, even at that higher level, a minimum wage still would not be a living wage. A modest definition of a living wage is one that allows a full-time, year-round worker to bring a family of four up to its poverty threshold— $7.71 per hour in 1996. Community-labor coalitions have pressed city governments to require any business receiving city business or tax breaks to pay a living wage, and have recently won such laws in Baltimore, Los Angeles, Milwaukee, and Minneapolis. Figart and Lapidus estimated that bumping the minimum wage up from $4.25 to $4.75 would boost women's average wages by 2 to 4 percent.[13] An important complement to increasing the minimum wage is expanding the Earned Income Credit, a refundable federal income tax credit aimed at low-income families.

Third, *level the playing field for labor unions.* While the track record of unions on diversity remains mixed, the most dynamic unions today are ones aggressively recruiting and supporting women and people of color. Unions raise wages most for the lowest paid—good news for women and minority workers. Union representation increases a woman's wage by an average of 20 percent (over that of an otherwise identical woman without union coverage). Taking this into account, doubling the percentage of unionized women should push women's average wage 3 percent higher.[14] Every bit helps! But union coverage has shrunk from one-third of the workforce in the 1950s to less than one-sixth today. Businesses have discovered that they can run hardball union-busting campaigns—misleading, threatening, and even firing workers—and pay only minimal penalties, usually years after the damage is done. To level this playing field, we need stronger laws protecting workers' rights to unionize without fear of employer retaliation and to strike without fear of being immediately—and permanently—replaced.

4. Tame the Family Budget Busters

Housing is the biggest expense for most families, and paying for health care is a serious problem for those who don't get coverage from an employer or the government. And the growth in both housing and health care costs is outrunning income, leaving increasing numbers of families without adequate shelter or coverage.

Housing costs have grown faster than income since the early 1980s, leading to declining home ownership and rising rent-to-income ratios. The housing squeeze pinches low-income households the hardest. Nearly one-fifth of all renters, but *one-half of low-income renters,* spend more than half of their income on housing costs.[15] Whereas in 1970 there were more low-rent units than low-income renters, by 1993 the situation had dramatically reversed, and there were 4.7 million fewer affordable units than low-income renters.[16] One predictable result has been growing homelessness: a careful 1992 estimate put the ranks of the homeless at 600,000 on any given night, and 1.2 million over the course of a year.[17] And families with children are the fastest-growing group among the homeless.

While a variety of approaches can help make housing more affordable, the best strategy is to combine approaches. Rent vouchers and opportunities for affordable home ownership can assist many families, but we also need public housing as a last resort. Low-income women—like any other group—have particular housing needs, and some nonprofit organizations have specifically targeted those needs. For example, the Women's Development Corporation (WDC) in Providence, Rhode Island, has developed 550 units of housing for low-income women. WDC places a priority on integrating women into a variety of networks in the broader community, "so that they see themselves as the same as others in the community, with the same rights," says Susan Aitcheson, codirector of the WDC. The Boston-based Women's Institute for Housing and Economic Development (WIHED), rather than developing housing itself, gives technical assistance to organizations providing housing for women and children. A partial list of WIHED projects highlights the diversity of women's housing situations, including grandmothers raising their grandchildren, Haitian-American single mothers and their children, teen mothers trying to make it on their own, recovering substance abusers (many of whom are trying to regain custody of their children), elderly women who have been homeless, and younger formerly homeless women and their children. Creative groups like WDC and WIHED deserve support.

Health care is the other major family budget buster. While the average family spent 18 percent of its income on health care in 1992, the burden weighs most heavily on the poorest one-fifth of the population, which shelled out 23 percent of its income for medical care. Thirty-nine million people lacked health insurance in 1992, but even among those who were insured, many reported that they had trouble paying for health care expenses: even among people with private health insurance, one in six reported difficulty paying medical bills.[18]

After all the sound and fury over health care reform in the last few years, the only federal reform in place so far is to guarantee people the right to continue health insurance coverage at their own expense after leaving a job. It is past time to get in step with the rest of the industrialized world and make health care a basic right. The other industrialized countries, which provide universal coverage through "single-payer" plans (meaning that there is a single, government-controlled insurer for all), deliver health care more cheaply than the United States *and* have healthier populations.[19]

5. Expand the Safety Net

Neither welfare recipients nor the general public is enthusiastic about welfare—to put it mildly. But cash assistance . . . remains necessary as the ultimate safety net for families with children. Yet expanding other parts of the social safety net could help to reduce reliance on welfare. Two candidates for expansion are unemployment insurance and temporary disability insurance.

Unemployment insurance (UI), established as part of the 1935 Social Security Act, offers compensation to unemployed workers based on their earnings while employed. Research by the Washington-based Institute for Women's Policy Research indicates, however, that UI is currently a fairly exclusive program.[20] This is true even for men and full-time workers, the traditional beneficiaries of the program: 74 percent of unemployed men, and 62 percent of unemployed full-time workers, do not meet eligibility requirements—including the reasons for leaving a job, number of weeks worked, minimum pay levels, and industry restrictions. But women and part-time workers are most often shut out: 80 percent of un-

employed women, and 90 percent of unemployed part-time workers, fail to meet eligibility criteria for UI. The percentage of the unemployed who receive UI has declined significantly for several reasons: Women and part-time workers now make up a larger share of the workforce; unemployment durations have lengthened, so more unemployed people reach UI's time limits; and states have simply tightened eligibility rules. And although many welfare recipients cycle between welfare and work, only 11 percent of working welfare mothers draw on UI—relying instead on welfare as a "poor woman's unemployment insurance."

What can be done? The Center for Law and Social Policy has suggested a variety of reforms that would enable UI to help more people: widen eligibility, extend time limits, add a component covering temporary disability (including pregnancy and childbirth), and possibly even consolidate the UI program with cash assistance for families with children that include an employable adult.[21]

Another option would be to strengthen and expand temporary disability insurance (TDI) systems. About one-quarter of women who leave their jobs do so because of family reasons, such as pregnancy. The 1993 Family and Medical Leave Act (FMLA) guarantees twelve weeks of unpaid leave for childbirth and family illnesses or other emergencies. This helps, but the FMLA only covers about half of the workforce (those in businesses employing fifty people or more), and a mere 2 to 4 percent of workers eligible for time off actually take leaves.[22] After all, few people can afford to take unpaid time off. Creating universal, paid family leave, as in all Western European countries, would do far more to ease work-family tensions. This could be done by establishing a nationwide temporary disability insurance program—or simply by strengthening the FMLA. Five states (California, Hawaii, New Jersey, New York, and Rhode Island) currently operate temporary disability insurance systems—in effect, replacing the current unpaid Family and Medical Leave Act with paid leave.[23] The programs offer partial wage replacement—starting at about 50 percent of pay and capping at a specified maximum—for personal medical disability (including pregnancy).[24] State TDI systems could be extended to provide paid leave for women and men who need to suspend work in order to take care of sick family members. The Institute for Women's Policy Research estimated the monthly total cost per worker in ten states for current (or proposed) TDI benefits plus paid family leave for care of a sick spouse, elderly parents, sick children, or newborns. The costs ranged from $17.70 per month in New Jersey to $12.60 in Rhode Island — hardly a budget buster.[25] Costs could be shared by employers, employees, and/or the government — since all have much to gain from such a program.

6. Provide Affordable and Available Education and Training for All

The United States boasts one of the best higher-education systems in the world. But the U.S. education and training system stacks up far worse for the 75 percent of the workforce with less than a four-year college degree, and worst of all for those who do not finish high school. Since the large majority of welfare recipients have no more than a high school diploma, they suffer from these shortcomings in the country's school-and-skill system — but so do many other groups: displaced workers, older women re-entering the workforce, and young people who don't follow the college track. And as the tuition costs of postsecondary education mount, the simple afford-ability of college has also become an issue.

The education and training system must be re-built from the bottom up. High school students in noncollege tracks need a curriculum that is richer and more closely linked to actual jobs — possibly adapt-ing Western European apprenticeship programs. The "second-chance" system for those who drop out of high school or who require retraining must be ex-panded and retooled. Currently, publicly subsidized second-chance training is largely limited to people who are persistently poor and unemployed; in many employers' eyes, it is a stigma rather than a creden-tial. An improved second-chance training system would take in a much wider spectrum of people, rec-ognizing that most, if not all, of the workforce needs retraining at some point. It would offer special sup-ports, rather than segregation, for those with greater training needs. Over the last ten years, for every $100 of production taking place in the United States, the government spent 10¢ on training; the rate in Sweden was six times as great.[26]

Both secondary education as well as second-chance education and training must strike a balance: they must provide work-relevant knowledge, often imparted in a work setting, but they must also help people develop broad understanding and critical thinking that go beyond narrow job-specific skills. Without the second component, workers can remain trapped in low-level jobs or be stranded when jobs disappear. A useful model in this regard is the new vocational education goal of studying "all aspects of an industry," including financial and social as well as technical ones.

Public sector education and training can only fill part of the gap. By international standards, U.S. firms themselves do not provide enough training for workers. When Bill Clinton ran for president in 1992, he proposed a payroll tax of 1 to 1.5 percent to fund a pool that employers could draw on to provide training to their workforces. And while nothing ever came of that campaign promise, such an incentive to train makes good sense.

Finally, we need to broaden access to and af-fordability of higher education. The combination of skyrocketing tuition plus a college requirement for a growing number of jobs adds up to a crisis. Presi-dent Clinton's $1,500 tax break for college tuition does little to help. It is small, and aids poor families least, since they often do not pay enough taxes to benefit from the break. One step toward a more com-plete solution is expanded student aid, including aid tied to national service and loans whose repay-ment schedules would depend on actual postcollege earnings. Another part of the solution is bolstering public higher education, which — although in crisis across much of the country — continues to offer the best bargain in postsecondary schooling.

7. Promote Community-Based Economic Development

Private sector–driven development has left increasing numbers of people — and in some cases, entire neigh-borhoods or regions — stranded. And mistrust of gov-ernment is at an all-time high. While government action is needed to set standards and redistribute resources, there is a third option: community-based economic development, in which locally controlled nonprofits take the lead in providing employment opportunities, housing, training, and services.

Community economic development can take a wide variety of forms, such as supporting the cre-ation of small businesses and producer coopera-tives, investing in the revitalization of neighborhood commercial areas, or training community members for better jobs. Some community economic development organizations, such as Chicago's Women's Self-Employment Project or Los Angeles's Coalition of Women's Economic Development, focus specifically on women. The strengths of community control are the flexibility, creativity, and accountability that it brings, plus the fact that community action on economic development helps to build broader social and political cohesion. On the downside, even when a poor community pools its resources, those resources are still quite limited—and communities acting separately can do little to change the large structural forces and the market economy's "rules of the game" that powerfully shape their destinies. Despite these limitations, community-based strategies have made an important difference in many areas and deserve government support.

8. Secure Funding with a Fairer Tax Structure

Let's face up to the fact that wage earnings and child support from absent fathers are not going to be enough to pull single-mother families out of poverty. Some supplemental assistance in the form of child allowances, childcare subsidies, and transfers will be necessary to help bear the costs of childrearing. The best way to share those costs is through government financing. Since the government gets its income from taxes and fees, financing new government programs means raising taxes or cutting spending on other areas.

It may not seem politically and economically feasible to finance new programs when states are strapped for cash and the federal government is concerned with reducing its already large deficit. But the costs of our current system are already unacceptably high. Women, children, and people of color disproportionately bear the costs of child poverty and all its attendant problems. Refusing to fund the programs recommended here may be far more costly.

To finance new programs, the United States needs a fairer tax system at the federal and state levels. This means overhauling the current tax structure so that those who can most afford to pay taxes do so. In the 1980s, the federal government cut taxes for the wealthiest, placing a larger share of the burden on middle- and low-income families. These changes, plus large increases in employee Social Security contributions, have reduced federal tax receipts *and*

made lower-income families pay a higher percentage of their income to fund programs they typically do not get to take part in. Recent tax reforms have helped to correct some of the plunder of the 1980s, but there is still a long way to go at the federal level. In the states and localities, taxes are even less fair: states, for instance, rely heavily on property and sales taxes, which take a bigger chunk, percentage-wise, out of low incomes than high ones. After federal tax deductions, total state and local taxes in 1995 claimed a nationwide average of 12 percent from the incomes of the poorest fifth of families of four, but only 6 percent from the incomes of the richest 1 percent.[27] Graduated state income taxes—tax rates based on the ability to pay, as at the federal level—would be a real step forward.

Surveys show that U.S. citizens would be willing to pay more taxes if the money went to fund policies they believe in. The programs proposed here have important economic and social benefits for everyone. To start with, providing an enhanced sense of economic security in the form of a social floor, for every U.S. citizen—including the rights to health care, childcare, a child allowance, and housing—is likely to improve the productivity of American workers immensely. During and after World War II, American workers' productivity on the job increased because the private and public sectors both offered stronger guarantees of economic well-being. The programs recommended here are also sure to reduce workplace absenteeism, as family-friendly policies at Xerox and other companies have already done. Finally, and most important, these programs will bolster a sense of shared values and commitment in society about the work of raising *all* our children, sending the message: the work of raising and caring for children is important enough to be a social responsibility, not just an individual one.

Replacing Contradictions with Consistencies

[Four contradictions affect] the agenda for women's economic equality. First, we are a country that says we should value families, and above all else children, yet we devalue the *work* of taking care of children. Second, we are a country that expects all able-bodied adults to be in the labor force, yet we leave job creation to a private sector unable to provide a job to everyone who wants one. Third, as a country, we firmly believe that a job is the best way out of poverty, but we have allowed increasing numbers of jobs to slip below a living wage level — even as businesses cut back on essential fringe benefits, such as health insurance. Finally, financial dependency within the family is considered natural, as when a woman stays home to cook, clean, and care for her children. But when she does not have a husband and wants to do exactly the same kind of necessary work in her home, dependency on the government is deplored.

These four contradictions put all women — but especially single mothers — in a no-win situation. If a woman does paid work, she is not taking care of her family. If she is taking care of her family, she is not living up to her obligations to do paid work. And while Murphy Brown may have beaten Dan Quayle in the battle over family values, Quayle and other conservatives are winning the war by blaming women for the problems of insufficient time and money to take care of our families and communities. The right wing has effectively blamed women's rights for problems that are actually caused by a deadly combination of a market system that fails to provide jobs with living wages and a political and economic system that refuses to socialize the cost of raising children. Welfare recipients are cannon fodder in this battle.

Women's economic equality can only be won by completing a broad reform agenda that demands that this country divide up economic resources in a very different, more just way than currently allocated. Only by resolving the contradictions of our current situation — and creating new *consistencies* in values and action — will we overcome the glass ceilings and the bottomless pits that face women today.

Notes

1. The framework for this summary draws on Sheila B. Kamerman and Alfred J. Kahn, "Family Policy: Has the United States Learned from Europe?" *Policy Studies Review,* vol. 8, no. 3 (1989): 581–98. Other useful overviews include: Gosta Esping-Anderson, "The Equality-Employment Trade-Off: Europe's Welfare States at the End of the Century," mimeo, University of Trento and Instituto Juan March, 1995; Karen Gibson and Peter Hall, "American Poverty and Social Policy: What Can Be Learned from the European Experience,"

Social Science Research Council, New York (distributed by the National Center for Children in Poverty, Columbia University, New York), 1993; Jane Lewis, ed., *Women and Social Policies in Europe: Work, Family, and the State* (Aldershot, England: Edward Elgar, 1993); Katherine McFate, Roger Lawson, and William Julius Wilson, eds., *Poverty, Inequality and the Future of Social Policy: Western States in the New World Order* (New York: Russell Sage, 1995).

2. Barbara Bergmann, "The French Child Welfare System: An Excellent System We Could Adapt and Afford," in *Sociology and the Public Agenda,* ed. William Julius Wilson (Newbury Park, CA: Sage Publications, 1993).

3. Lee Rainwater and Timothy Smeeding, "U.S. Doing Poorly — Compared to Others," *National Center for Children in Poverty — News and Issues* (fall/winter 1995).

4. Kamerman and Kahn, op. cit.; Søren Carlsen and Jørgen Larsen, eds., *The Equality Dilemma: Reconciling Working Life and Family Life, Viewed in an Equality Perspective — The Danish Example* (Copenhagen: The Danish Equal Status Council, 1994), figure 14a; Linda Haas, *Equal Parenthood and Social Policy: A Study of Parental Leave in Sweden* (Albany: State University of New York Press, 1992); Raju Narisetti and Rochelle Sharpe, "Take It or Leave It, Norway Tells New Fathers," *Wall Street Journal,* 29 August 1995, p. A1.

5. Kamerman and Kahn, op. cit.; Carlsen and Larsen, op. cit., table 14.b; Sheila Kamerman, "Child Care Policies and Programs: An International Overview," *Journal of Social Issues,* vol. 47, no. 2 (1991).

6. Kamerman and Kahn, op. cit.; Gibson and Hall, op. cit.

7. Bergmann, op. cit.

8. Katherine McFate, *Poverty, Inequality, and the Crisis of Social Policy: Summary of Findings* (Washington, DC: Joint Center for Political and Economic Studies, 1991), p. 23.

9. Sue Shellenbarger, "Family-Friendly Jobs Are the First Step to Efficient Workplace," *Wall Street Journal,* 15 May 1996, p. B1.

10. U.S. Council of Economic Advisors, *Economic Report of the President* (Washington, DC: Government Printing Office, 1997), table B-45.

11. Computed by authors from U.S. Bureau of the Census, Current Population Survey, March 1994, computer tape.

12. Deborah M. Figart and June Lapidus, "A Gender Analysis of U.S. Labor Market Policies for the Working Poor," *Feminist Economics,* vol. 1, no. 3 (1995).

13. Ibid.

14. Calculated by the authors based on the union wage premium of 20 percent (Lawrence Mishel and Jared Bernstein, eds., *The State of Working America 1994–95* [Armonk, NY: M. E. Sharpe, 1994]), and women's 1995 union representation rate of 14 percent (U.S. Bureau of Labor Statistics, *Employment and Earnings,* January 1996, table 40).

15. Peter Dreier and John Atlas, "U.S. Housing Policy at the Crossroads: A Progressive Agenda to Rebuild the Housing Constituency," Working Paper, Occidental College, International and Public Affairs Center, Los Angeles, 1996.

16. Edward B. Lazere, *In Short Supply: The Growing Affordable Housing Gap* (Washington, DC: Center on Budget and Policy Priorities, 1995).

17. Martha Burt, *Over the Edge: The Growth of Homelessness in the 1980s* (New York: Russell Sage Foundation, 1992).

18. Information in this paragraph is from Edith Rassell, "Health Care: Expenditures Exceed Results," in *The State of Working America 1994–95,* eds. Lawrence Mishel and Jared Bernstein (Armonk, NY: M. E. Sharpe, 1994).

19. Ibid. For example, despite lower average income levels, many industrialized countries have lower infant mortality and longer life expectancy than the United States.

20. Institute for Women's Policy Research, "Unemployment Insurance: Barriers to Access for Women and Part-time Workers," Research-in-brief, Washington, DC, 1995; Roberta Spalter-Roth, Heidi Hartmann, and Beverly Burr, "Income Insecurity: The Failure of Unemployment Insurance to Reach Out to Working AFDC Mothers," Institute for Women's Policy Research, presented at the Second Annual Employment Task Force Conference, March 20–22, 1994.

21. Steve Savner and Mark Greenberg, "Reforming the Unemployment Insurance System to Better Meet the Needs of Low-income Families," revised draft, Center for Law and Social Policy, Washington, DC, March 1996.

22. Glenn Burkins, "Family Leave: A Government Survey Shows Few Are Making Use of It," *Wall Street Journal,* 26 March 1996, p. A1.

23. Institute for Women's Policy Research, "Using Temporary Disability Insurance to Provide Paid Family Leave: A Comparison with the Family and Medical Leave Act," Research-in-brief, Washington, DC, 1995.

24. Kirsten Wever, *The Family and Medical Leave Act: Assessing Temporary Wage Replacement for Family and Medical Leave* (Cambridge, MA: Radcliffe Public Policy Institute, 1996).

25. Institute for Women's Policy Research, "Using Temporary Disability Insurance to Provide Paid Family Leave: A Comparison with the Family and Medical Leave Act," Research-in-brief, Washington, DC, 1995.

26. Karen Gibson and Peter Hall, "American Poverty and Social Policy: What Can Be Learned from the European Experience," Social Science Research Council, New York (distributed by the National Center for Children in Poverty, Columbia University, New York), 1993.

27. Citizens for Tax Justice, *Who Pays: A Distributional Analysis of the Tax System in All 50 States* (Washington, DC: Citizens for Tax Justice, 1996).

◆◆◆

CHAPTER SIX

Violence against Women

anadian novelist Margaret Atwood once asked a male friend why men feel threatened by women. He replied: "They are afraid women will laugh at them." She then asked a group of women why they feel threatened by men. They answered: "We're afraid of being killed" (Caputi and Russell 1990).

Gender violence affects women in all societies, all socioeconomic classes, all racial/ethnic groups, and it can occur throughout the life cycle (Heise, Pitanguy, and Germain 1994). Heise (1989) comments: "This is not random violence; the risk factor is being female" (p. 13). In the United States, this includes the interpersonal violence of battering, rape, child sexual abuse, stalking, hassles on the street, obscene phone calls, sexual harassment at school or workplace. Underlying these incidents and experiences are systemic inequalities, also a kind of violence, that maintain women's second-class status — culturally, economically, and politically. In the United States, the fact that Native Americans were dispossessed of their land and enslaved African people forced to work for slave masters was a profound violation, in addition to sexualized violence against women of these groups (Trask 1999). This chapter focuses on violence against women in the United States and the many efforts to stop it. We refer to this issue in other places also: with regard to sexuality (Chapter 4) and to relationships and family (Chapter 5), as a work-

place issue (Chapter 8), regarding women in prison (Chapter 10), and in connection with the military (Chapter 11).

What Counts as Violence against Women?

Most women tolerate a certain amount of what could be defined as sexual violence as part of daily life. We experience hassles on the street, in parks, or in cafés and bars. We put up with sexist comments from bosses or coworkers. We sometimes make compromises as part of maintaining intimate relationships, including going along with sex when we do not really want it, or tolerating put-downs, threats, and inconsiderate behavior. We may define some of these experiences as violence, and others not.

Researchers and writers do not use terms like *sexual assault, sexual abuse, battering,* or *domestic violence* in a standardized way. Differences of definition and terminology have led to marked discrepancies in reporting and have contributed to considerable confusion about these issues, which should be borne in mind throughout this chapter.

The United Nations Declaration on Violence Against Women defines such violence as "any act of gender-based violence that results in, or is likely to result in, physical, sexual or psychological harm or suffering to women, including threats of such acts, coercion or arbitrary deprivation of liberty whether occurring in public or private life" (Heise, Pitanguy, and Germaine 1994, p. 46). This includes physical acts like battering, rape, child sexual abuse, stalking, and inappropriate touching in the case of sexual harassment in the workplace. It includes verbal and psychological violence against intimate partners like yelling, intimidation, and humiliation; inappropriate personal remarks made to coworkers or students; and offensive sexist "jokes." It also includes forced isolation, denial of support, and threats of violence or injury to women in the family. This broad definition implicitly recognizes that men as a group have power over women—the women they are close to and those they encounter in public places. Women may be physically smaller or weaker, they may be economically dependent on their partner, or they may need their boss's support to keep their jobs or to get promotion or a pay raise. Thus, macro-level inequalities are present in violence at the micro level. An important element of this male power is that it is sexualized. This is a given in interactions between intimate partners. It is also often true of interactions that are violent or that border on violence between men and women who are not intimate but who are friends, coworkers, teachers and students, or complete strangers (see Figure 6.1).

Many researchers and commentators do not use such a broad definition of violence against women. They focus on specific physical acts that can be measured. Emotional violence and the fear of threats are impossible to quantify precisely. It is much easier to bring charges of violence if one can show clear evidence of physical coercion or harm. Indeed, the legal system demands demonstrable damage or there is nothing to claim. The problem with this kind of quantification is that one cannot see the wider social and political context within which violence occurs.

The definition of violence against women can also be expanded beyond the United Nations definition quoted earlier. Bulhan (1985), for example, proposes the following:

> Violence is any relation, process, or condition by which an individual or a group violates the physical, social, and/or psychological integrity of another person or group. From this perspective, violence inhibits human growth, negates inherent potential, limits productive living, and causes death.
>
> *(p. 135)*

This would include colonization, poverty, racism, lack of access to education, health care and medical insurance, negative media representations, as well as environmental catastrophes. These factors can affect men as well as women. But women as a group are poorer than men; fewer women have health insurance; women's rights may be limited with regard to reproductive freedom; and women are systematically objectified and commodified in the media. We argue that these macro-level factors jeopardize women's security and should be part of this discussion of violence even though they may not have an explicitly sexual dimension. Some activists and writers use the word *rape*—for example, rape by the economic or legal system—to refer to macro-level violence. We caution against this as it reduces the power of the term to refer to sexual violation.

At micro and meso levels, women as well as men can be violent. Women may abuse children, other family members, their peers, and people who work for them. bell hooks (1984b) notes that women "may employ abusive measures to maintain authority in interactions with groups over whom they exercise power" (p. 119). Research shows that, in general, women hit children more than men do, but they also spend much more time with children. Women may hit their partners first. They may contribute to the dynamic of a violent relationship. Occasionally women kill abusive partners in self-defense, seemingly the only way out of situations in which they believe they would be killed if they did not defend themselves (Jones 1980; Richie 1996). In 1996, 3 percent of all male murder victims were killed by their wives or girlfriends compared to 30 percent of all female murder victims who were killed by their husbands or boyfriends (Federal Bureau of Investigation 1997). Indeed, the vast majority of gender violence is violence against women. According to the Department of Justice (2000), the chance of being victimized by an intimate is significantly greater for a woman than a man; 95 to 98 percent of people beaten by their spouse or intimate partner are women (National Coalition Against Domestic

Figure 6.1 The Dynamics of Domestic Violence: Power and Control Wheel

Source: Asian Women's Shelter, adapted from Domestic Abuse Intervention Project, Duluth, MN. Used with permission.

Gender Violence Worldwide, throughout the Life Cycle

Phase	Type of violence
Prebirth	Sex-selective abortion (e.g. in China, India, Republic of Korea); battering during pregnancy (emotional and physical effects on the woman; effects on birth outcome); coerced pregnancy (for example, mass rape in war).
Infancy	Female infanticide; emotional and physical abuse; differential access to food and medical care for girl infants.
Girlhood	Child marriage; genital mutilation; sexual abuse by family members and strangers; differential access to food and medical care; child prostitution.
Adolescence	Dating and courtship violence (for example, acid throwing in Bangladesh, date rape in the United States); economically coerced sex (African secondary school girls having to take up with "sugar daddies" to afford school fees); sexual abuse in the workplace; rape; sexual harassment; forced prostitution; trafficking in women.
Reproductive age	Abuse of women by intimate male partners; marital rape; dowry abuse and murders; partner homicide; psychological abuse; sexual abuse in the workplace; sexual harassment; rape; abuse of women with disabilities.
Elderly	Abuse of widows; elder abuse (in the United States, the only country where data are now available, elder abuse affects mostly women).

Source: Heise, Pitanguy, and Germain (1994), p. 5.

Violence 1996). We prefer the term "violence against women" over "gender violence" because it makes this inequality explicit.

The Incidence of Violence against Women

Domestic violence, rape, sexual abuse, and child sexual abuse are all illegal in the United States. The incidence of such violence is difficult to estimate accurately because of discrepancies in definition and terminology, limited research, and underreporting. According to the Family Violence Prevention Fund (1998), "Every year, as many as 4 million American women are physically abused by men who promised to love them" (p. 1). The U.S. Department of

Justice (1994) reported that women are more often victims of domestic violence—meaning violence by intimate partners—than victims of burglary, muggings, or other physical crimes combined. The U.S. Department of Justice (1997) reported that 37 percent of all women who sought care in hospital emergency rooms for violence-related injuries in 1997 were injured by a current or former spouse, boyfriend, or girlfriend. Abuse-related injuries include bruises, cuts, burns and scalds, concussion, broken bones, penetrating injuries from knives, miscarriages, permanent injuries such as damage to joints, partial loss of hearing or vision, and physical disfigurement. There are also serious mental health effects of isolation, humiliation, and ongoing threats of violence. As mentioned earlier, many writers and researchers do not take account of psychological and emotional dimensions of domestic violence because they are difficult to measure. They define it as physical assault only, which gives the impression that quantifiable acts of violence—kicking, punching, or using a weapon—tell the whole story.

One in five high school girls surveyed reported that she had been physically or sexually abused; the majority of these incidents occurred at home and happened more than once (Commonwealth Fund 1997). Girls aged sixteen to nineteen experience one of the highest rates of violence by an intimate partner (Greenfeld et al. 1998). Larkin and Popaleni's (1997) interviews with young women reveal how young men use criticism, intimidation, surveillance, threats, and force to establish and maintain control over their girlfriends. O'Toole and Schiffman (1997) note that young women are vulnerable to abuse because they may feel that involvement in a personal relationship is necessary to fit in; they may be flattered by a dating partner who demands time and attention; and they lack experience negotiating affection and sexual behavior.

The legal definition of rape turns on force and nonconsent. Consent to sexual intercourse is not meaningful if given under the influence of alcohol, drugs, or prescription medication. Like domestic violence, rape is not always reported, and the true scope of the problem is difficult to estimate. The 1998 National Crime Victimization Survey estimated that only "31.6% of all rapes/sexual assaults were reported to law enforcement." Rape here is defined as forced sexual intercourse—vaginal, anal, or oral penetration. Sexual assault includes attacks involving unwanted sexual contact; it may involve force and include grabbing or fondling, also verbal threats (Rape Abuse Incest National Network 1999). The groups most at risk for sexual assault are sixteen- to nineteen-year-olds, then twenty- to twenty-four-year-olds. In contrast to popular ideas about rape committed by a stranger in a dark alley, 76 percent of women who reported that they had been raped or physically assaulted since the age of eighteen said that their partner or date committed the assault (National Institute of Justice and Centers for Disease Control and Prevention 1998). An early-1990s survey found that 13 percent of adult women are victims of forcible rape: one woman in seven (National Victim Center 1992). A 1998 survey reported that 18 percent of women had experienced a completed rape or attempted rape at some time in their lives (National Institute of Justice and Centers for Disease Control and Prevention 1998).

A study of date rape on campuses in the mid-1980s found that one in nine college women had been raped and that eight out of ten victims knew their attacker, although as few as 5 percent reported the crime (Koss 1988). One in twelve college men responding to the same survey admitted that they had committed acts that met legal definitions of rape (Koss, Dinero, and Seibel 1988). As mentioned in Chapter 4, the FBI's Uniform Crime Report (compiled from over 16,000 law enforcement agencies covering 96 percent of the nation's population) estimated that one in four U.S. college women is a victim of rape or attempted rape, and this estimate is still widely used by academics, activists, and journalists. Female students are most at risk of date rape in the first few weeks of college. They often do not report a rape because of confusion, guilt, or fear, or because they feel betrayed; they may be ashamed to tell parents or college counselors; and they may not identify the experience as rape. However, the reporting of date rape increased significantly on U.S. college campuses during the 1990s. The psychological effects of rape can be devastating, traumatic, and long-lasting. They include feelings of humiliation, helplessness, anger, self-doubt, self-hate, and fear; and a student may become depressed and withdrawn and do poorly in school.

Effects of Race, Class, Nation, Sexuality, and Disability

Although these forms of violence occur across the board, women's experiences are complicated by race, class, sexual orientation, and disability.

Research The Bureau of Justice Statistics (1995) notes that domestic violence is consistent across racial and ethnic lines. Raphael and Tolman (1997) found that past and current victims of domestic violence were overrepresented among women on welfare and families with extremely low incomes. Estimates that are based on official reports of violence are limited by the fact that many cases are not reported. Those that rely on research are limited by the scope of studies undertaken. Children and adolescents, prostituted women, homeless women,

women with mental disabilities, institutionalized women, very poor women, and women in neighborhoods with high crime rates are rarely included in surveys. Women and girls with physical and mental disabilities may be particularly vulnerable to physical, emotional, and sexual abuse (Young et al. 1997). But there are insufficient data to generalize about this.

Reporting   Violence between intimate partners is illegal in this country, but it is seriously under reported because of confusion, shame, self-blame, loyalty to the abuser, lack of information, or fear of repercussions, including loss of his income. Women may not believe that reporting violence to the police will do any good. Women of color, poor women, and prostituted women often have very negative experiences with the police. Women of color may decide not to report domestic violence or rape to avoid bringing more trouble on husbands, partners, friends, and acquaintances who already suffer discrimination based on race, as mentioned by Fernando Mederos (Reading 35). In many communities of color the police are perceived not as helpful but, rather, as abusive, harassing, and violent. Women as well as men "bear the brunt of police indifference and abuse" and "men are frequently targeted for false arrest," (Smith 1997). Their community may expect women of color to maintain silence about sexual assault, to protect "family honor and community integrity" (Crenshaw 1993, p. 5). Melba Wilson (1993) discusses the conflicting pressures operating here and urges Black women to hold men accountable for sexual abuse of children. Older women may not report acts of violence committed by spouses, adult children, caregivers, relatives, and neighbors, because they fear being rejected, losing their caregiver, being placed in a nursing home, or losing their property — particularly their home or independent access to money. Immigrant women who are dependent on an abusive partner for their legal status may fear repercussions from the INS if they report violence, as discussed by Deanna Jang in Reading 36. Some women have been reluctant to speak about abuse in lesbian relationships, perhaps assuming that domestic violence happens only between women and men or not wanting to feed negative stereotypes of lesbians in the wider society.

Responses of the Police, Support Services, Medical and Legal Systems   The response to reports of violence against women and the provision of services have greatly expanded over the last thirty years as this issue has become recognized publicly. Police officers, judges, doctors, nurses, and emergency-room staff may undergo professional training, although much more still needs to be done in this regard. During slavery times, the rape of Black women in the United States was legal and commonplace. They were chattel, the property of their masters, and available for anything and everything. Currently, negative stereotypes about women of color, poor White women, and lesbians all perpetuate the idea, in the wider society, that these women are not worthy of respect. They are less likely to be taken seriously when they report acts of violence. Crenshaw (1993) notes an early-1990s study of sentences given to convicted rapists in Dallas: "The average sentence given to the rapist of a Black woman was 2 years . . . to the rapist of a Latina . . . five years, and . . . to the rapist of a white woman . . . ten years. Interviews with jurors reveal that the low conviction rate of men accused of raping Black women is based on on-going sexual stereotypes about Black women" (p. 4).

Explanations of Violence against Women

Most explanations of violence against women are social theories. Before discussing some of these, we note the resurfacing of a biological explanation of rape. Thornhill and Palmer (2000) argue that rape evolved historically as a form of male reproductive behavior. These authors base their claims on studies of animal species from the scorpion fly to primates. As with other sociobiological theories, they make huge leaps between animal behavior and human life, they are not grounded in an analysis of social systems, and their claims are not borne out by the experience of women who have suffered acts of violence.

As in other chapters, we focus on social theories and separate micro- and macro-level explanations.

Micro-level Explanations

Whatever form it takes, violence against women is always experienced at the personal or micro level.

Family violence, rape, and child sexual abuse are often explained in terms of an individual mental health problem, innate sexual craving, or personal dysfunction on the part of perpetrators. By contrast, Grossholtz (1983) argues that research on rapists and batterers shows them to be "ordinary men, indistinguishable from nonrapists and nonbatterers" (p. 59). Another explanation for domestic violence is that the partners have an unhealthy relationship.

Three psychological syndromes have been advanced to explain violence against women: battered woman syndrome, rape trauma syndrome, and false memory syndrome.

Battered Woman Syndrome   Feminist analyses of domestic violence emphasize inequalities of power and control and systematic patterns of violence. Violence can "be triggered by a burned meal, a sharp word, a crying child, an expressed desire to get a job or go to school, or simply being in a room" (Grossholtz 1983, p. 65). Shelter workers have noted that calls increase significantly at times of high family stress and alcohol consumption like Thanksgiving and Christmas. Barbara Harman (1996) describes how a woman in an abusive relationship is always in a position of second-guessing and responding to an abusive partner in her attempts to avoid further violence:

> Don't raise your voice. Don't talk back. Don't say no to sex. Like whatever he does. Don't ask him to do anything he has not already done. Get up when he gets up. Go to bed when he goes to bed. Wait. Do what he wants to do. Never contradict him. Laugh at what he thinks is funny. Never ask for his time, attention, his money. Have your own money, but give it to him if he wants it. Never go out alone but do not expect him to go with you. If he is angry in the car, walk home. Be his friend except when he needs an enemy. Defend his family except when he hates them. Understand everything.
>
> *(p. 287)*

Psychologist Lenore Walker (1979, 1984) put forward the notion of a "battered woman syndrome." She noted a pattern of behavior that she termed "learned helplessness," whereby women who are repeatedly battered "learn" it is impossible to escape. After an episode of violence, they are seduced back

by the batterer with declarations of love and promises that he will change. These calm, loving episodes alternate with periods of accelerating violence, isolating the woman further and tying her closer to him. Attorneys have used a "battered woman syndrome" defense for women who kill violent partners by arguing that their clients' judgment was affected "in such a way as to make them honestly believe that they were in imminent danger and that the use of force was their only means of escape" (Gordon 1997, p. 25).

Rape Trauma Syndrome   This term is used by mental health and legal professionals to refer to women's coping strategies following rape. The focus is on women's reactions and responses rather than on the actions of the perpetrators or the prevalence of sexual violence in our society. Rape trauma syndrome has been used to explain women's apparently "counterintuitive" reactions—such as not reporting a rape for days or even months, not remembering parts of the assault, appearing too calm, or expressing anger at their treatment by police, hospital staff, or the legal system—in terms of pathology (Stefan 1994, p. 1274). Women diagnosed with rape trauma syndrome—who are generally White and middle class—are given psychiatric treatment with the goal of recovery and resolution. Expert testimony concerning rape trauma syndrome in rape trials improves the chances that a perpetrator will be convicted but at the cost of representing the woman as a pathetic victim. Stefan (1994) argues that the creation of this syndrome has depoliticized the issue of rape.

False Memory Syndrome   Childhood sexual abuse by parents, older siblings, stepparents, and other family members, exemplified in Dorothy Allison's novel *Bastard Out of Carolina* (1992), is another aspect of family life that has gradually become a public issue through the efforts of survivors, counselors, and feminist advocates (Reading 37, by Grace Caroline Bridges). Many abused children block out memories of what happened to them, and these may not surface again until their adult years, perhaps through flashbacks, nightmares, panic attacks, or pain (Petersen 1991; White 1988). They then gradually piece together fragments of their experience that have been suppressed. Those who have been abused as children often experience confusion, shame, fear, or fear of being crazy. They may spend years thinking they were to blame. They may have feelings of not being worth much, or conversely, they may feel special. The child is invariably told that this special secret must never be spoken about. Healing from the effects of childhood sexual abuse takes time, courage, and support (Bass and Davis 1988; Herman 1992; Petersen 1991; E. C. White 1985; L. White 1988; Wilson 1993), and many families do not want to open up this can of worms. False memory syndrome (FMS) has been invoked by parents who believe they "have been falsely accused [of incest] as a result of their adult children discovering 'memories' in the course of therapy" (Wasserman 1992, p. 18) and by lawyers acting on their behalf. According to FMS, the incest survivor is someone with impaired cognitive functioning. Memory is complex cognitively, and there are well-regarded psychologists on both sides of this issue.

As explanations of violence against women, these syndromes are all inadequate. They pathologize women who suffer acts of violence as helpless victims. These syndromes raise the question of how to get adequate recognition for violence against women without turning them into victims. As legal defenses in cases involving acts of violence, they are also highly problematic. Like the other syndromes mentioned here, a battered-woman-syndrome defense for women who have killed abusive partners represents battered women as impaired, rather than as "rational actors responding to perceived danger" (Gordon 1997, p. 25). Attorneys have tried to get courts to accept that the law of self-defense applies to battered women, but without much success. These syndromes all blame the victim for her situation. The advice that police departments often give to women for their safety also assumes that they bring assaults on themselves: Do not go out alone late at night; do not wear "provocative" clothing; always walk purposefully; do not make eye contact with men on the street; park your car in a lighted area; have your keys ready in your hand before you leave the building; look into the back seat before getting in your car, and so on. This advice assumes that women are responsible for acts of violence against them, either directly "asking for it" by their dress or behavior or indirectly encouraging it by not being sufficiently cautious.

Macro-level Explanations

Micro-level explanations of violence against women can be compelling if one focuses on specific personal interactions, but by themselves they cannot explain such a universal and systemic phenomenon. It is essential to analyze this issue at the meso and macro levels to understand it fully and to generate effective strategies to stop it.

Macro-level explanations focus on the cultural legitimation of male violence and the economic, political, and legal systems that marginalize, discriminate against, and disempower women. Franz Fanon's (1967, 1968) analysis of colonialism and the processes of colonization are very helpful, especially his insights into violence and systems of oppression. In *The Wretched of the Earth* (1968), Fanon notes that "colonialism . . . is violence in its natural state" (quoted in Bulhan 1985, p. 131). Extending Fanon's work, Bulhan (1985) comments:

> A situation of oppression is essentially a cauldron of violence. It is brought into existence and is maintained by dint of violence. This violence gradually permeates the social order to affect everyday living. In time the violence takes on different guises and becomes less blatant and more integral to institutional as well as to interpersonal reality.
>
> *(p. 131)*

Bulhan argues that most people view violence too narrowly, focusing on shocking cases such as incidents of child sexual abuse, a cold-blooded murder, or seemingly senseless wartime atrocities. This limited view is reinforced by the way the news media sensationalize violence. Behavioral scientists and criminologists have tended to study violent acts that have an identifiable perpetrator and an identifiable victim, as mentioned earlier. To get around the limits of this approach, Bulhan uses a very broad definition of violence that rests on several assumptions:

> Violence is not an isolated physical act or a discrete random event. It is a relation, process, and condition undermining, exploiting, and curtailing the well-being of the victim. These violations are not just moral or ethical, but also physical, social, and/or psychological. They involve demonstrable assault on or injury of and damage to the victim. Violence in any of the three domains—physical, social, or psycho-

logical—has significant repercussions in the other two domains. Violence occurs not only between individuals, but also between groups and societies. Intention is less important than consequence in most forms of violence. Any relation, process, or condition imposed by someone that injures the health and well-being of others is by definition violent.

(p. 135)

Applying these ideas to violence against women may make it easier to see violence at the structural level and as it is played out by individuals who have learned their socially accepted roles, as argued by Allan Johnson in his discussion of patriarchy as a system (Reading 3, Chapter 1). Macro-level factors such as sexism, heterosexism, racism, economic opportunities, working conditions, unemployment, poverty, or loss of status and cultural roots that may accompany immigration also affect personal and family relationships from the outside. This is not to excuse men and women who abuse their partners or children but, rather, to provide a wider context for understanding violence. As we noted in Chapter 5, family violence is embedded in institutional roles and relationships, supported by cultural standards and expectations—meso- and macro-level factors.

The Cultural Legitimation of Male Violence   This includes cultural beliefs in male superiority and male control of women's behavior and of the family, which are supported by social institutions such as education, law, religion, and popular culture. The old idea that a wife is the property of her husband still lingers in custom and in law (see Naomi Wolf, Reading 23, Chapter 4); wives are supposed to agree to sex, for example, as part of their wifely duty. Rape in marriage was made a crime in the United States as recently as 1993, but in thirty-three states there are varying exemptions from prosecuting husbands for rape, which indicates that rape in marriage is still treated as a lesser crime than other forms of rape (National Clearinghouse on Marital and Date Rape 1998). Examples of exemptions are when a wife is mentally or physically impaired, unconscious, or asleep (Bergen 1996, 1999). Another example of male control is street harassment, where women may be "touched, harassed, commented upon in a stream of constant small-scale assaults" (Benard and Schlaffer 1997, p. 395). The public street is defined as male

space where women without male escorts are considered "fair game." Benard and Schlaffer note that women need to "plan our routes and our timing as if we are passing through a mine field" (p. 395).

The cultural legitimation of male superiority involves patterns of male and female socialization in the family and in schools, and the social construction of male sexuality, described by Michael Kimmel in Reading 38. In a White-supremacist society, men of color may be attracted to a construction of masculinity that derives from White patriarchal attitudes and behavior. Discussing violence against women in African American communities, bell hooks (1994b) writes:

> Black males, utterly disenfranchised in almost every arena of life in the United States, often find that the assertion of sexist domination is their only expressive access to the patriarchal power they are told all men should possess as their gendered birthright.
>
> *(p. 110)*

Haki Madhubuti takes up this issue in Reading 39.

In addition, we live in a society where war toys, competitive games, violent and aggressive sports, video games, and violence on TV and in movies are integral to children's socialization, especially that of boys. Popular culture, news media, and advertising all reinforce these cultural attitudes and contribute to the objectification and commodification of women. Rape, beating, and verbal abuse of women are commonplace in feature films and TV shows. At the meso level too, in various communities, cultural attitudes and religious beliefs support domestic violence as a husband's prerogative to "discipline" his wife. Some psychological explanations invoke a culture of violence that violent families perpetuate.

Economic Systems That Disempower Women   Because women as a group earn less than men as a group, it may be difficult for a woman to leave a violent marriage or relationship if she is financially dependent on her partner. This is an example of violence "inherent in the established mode of social relations, distribution of goods and services, and legal practices of dispensing justice" (Bulhan 1985, p. 136). It not only is unfair and unjust, but also involves "hidden but lethal inequities" (p. 136). Macro-level violence, writes Bulhan, "imposes a pattern of relations and practices that are deeply ingrained in and dominate everyday living." In the context of the workplace, women may find it difficult to speak up about sexual harassment. As Michael Kimmel notes, sexual harassment "fuses two levels of power: the power of employers over employees and the power of men over women. Thus what may be said or intended as a man to a woman is also experienced in the context of superior and subordinate." We return to this issue in Chapter 8.

Legal Systems That Discriminate against Women
This macro-level factor includes inadequate laws and practices concerning violence against women, and insensitive treatment of women by police and the courts. Mahoney (1994) emphasizes the narrowness of legal categories and procedures in dealing with violence against women. For instance, the "statute of limitations," a limit on the time period allowed for bringing a lawsuit for damages or criminal charges against a perpetrator, stops some women from using the law for redress in cases of rape or childhood sexual abuse. In the latter case, they may be in their twenties, and years past the time limit, before they recognize that they were abused as children and gain the personal strength to confront the perpetrator publicly. Grossholtz (1983) argues that violence against women has not "simply been overlooked by the criminal justice system" (p. 67), but that this is part of the way patriarchal power compels women "through fear and endangerment, to submit to self-depreciation, heterosexuality, and male dominance in all spheres of life" (pp. 67–68).

Political Systems That Marginalize Women's Concerns   Women are still a small minority in elected office in the United States, especially at the congressional level. Violence against women is often not taken seriously by policy makers or legislators. There is a notable gender gap among U.S. voters. Compared to male voters, more women are concerned about violence against women. More women favor universal health care, government support for child care, meaningful gun control, an end to the international trade in arms, reductions in military spending, and disarmament. Women believe such changes would greatly increase their security and the well-being of their communities (Abzug 1984; Gallagher 1993; Smeal 1984). We take up the issue of women in electoral politics in Chapter 13.

The aspects and levels of violence mentioned earlier are interconnected and reinforce each other. Borkovitz (1995) argues that it is necessary to transform prevailing ideas of domination, whether of racism, imperialism, male violence against women, or same-sex battering. Similarly, bell hooks (1984b) argues that violence against women should be seen as part of a general pattern of violence between the powerful and the powerless stemming from the "philosophical notion of hierarchical rule and coercive authority that is the root cause of violence against women, of adult violence against children, of all violence between those who dominate and those who are dominated" (p. 118). She argues that feminists should oppose all forms of coercive domination rather than concentrating solely on male violence against women. Crenshaw (1993) points out that the anti-violence movement must be an anti-oppression movement. This theme was emphasized by speakers at The Color of Violence Conference (University of California/Santa Cruz, April 2000).

Ending Violence against Women

Violence against women has engaged the attention, anger, and activist efforts of scholars, policy makers, and organizers around the world. Linda Gordon (1988, 1997) notes that U.S. feminists challenged wife-beating as part of antidrinking campaigns in the late nineteenth century, then again in the 1930s in campaigns for child custody and welfare for single mothers so that they could leave abusive men. Extremely important feminist work in the 1960s and 70s broke through the prevailing silence on this subject, as mentioned in Chapter 1 (Brownmiller 1975; Griffin 1971; Russell 1975). Feminists reframed the issue of rape, for example, exposing the myth that rape is about sex—a crime of "frustrated attraction, victim provocation, or uncontrollable biological urges, perpetrated only by an aberrant fringe" (Caputi and Russell 1990, p. 34). Rather, rape is about power and control—a "direct expression of sexual politics and an assertion of masculinist norms that reinforce and preserve the gender status quo" (Caputi and Russell 1990, p. 34). Feminist writers and organizers insisted that no woman deserves to be abused, or brings it on herself, or "asks for it."

The Importance of a Political Movement

Judith Herman (1992) argues that changing public consciousness about a traumatic issue like violence against women takes a concerted political movement. In her study of trauma and recovery connected to violence, she writes that perpetrators of violence "ask bystanders to do nothing, simply to ignore the atrocity;" whereas "victims demand action, engagement, and remembering" (pp. 7–8). Feminist writers and workers in shelters and rape crisis projects often use the term *survivor* to refer to women who are coping with acts of violence, rather than calling them victims. Herman's use of the term *victim* in the following discussion is unfortunate, but her comments on the processes of denial and silencing that often surround violence against women are very insightful. Note that similar processes operate with macro-level violations like colonization.

> In order to escape accountability for his crimes, the perpetrator does everything in his power to promote forgetting. Secrecy and silence are the perpetrator's first line of defense. If secrecy fails, the perpetrator attacks the credibility of his victim. If he cannot silence her absolutely, he tries to make sure that no one listens. To this end, he marshals an impressive array of arguments, from the most blatant denial to the most sophisticated . . . rationalization. After every atrocity one can expect to hear the same predictable apologies: it never happened; the victim lies; the victim exaggerates; the victim brought it upon herself; and in any case it is time to forget the past and move on. The more powerful the perpetrator, the greater is his prerogative to name and define reality, and the more completely his arguments prevail.
>
> *(p. 8)*

Herman argues that isolated bystanders are often overwhelmed by the perpetrators' claims. To "hold traumatic reality in consciousness" (p. 9) and to cut through the power of the perpetrators' arguments "requires a social context that affirms and protects the victim and that joins victim and witness in a common alliance" (p. 9). For the individual victim of violence, relationships with family, friends, and lovers create this context. For the wider society, "the social context is created by political movements that give voice to the disempowered," (p. 9), a key example being the feminist movement of the 1960s and 70s.

Nadya Burton (1998) notes that second-wave feminists often used sweeping statements and over-simplistic rhetoric in their attempts to get the issue on the public agenda. They also emphasized fear, passivity, and victimhood in discussing violence against women. While acknowledging the damage suffered as a result of violence, it is also important to see women as resistors and survivors, people who cope with violation, who are not defined by it, and who thrive despite it. As Mahoney (1994) comments, it is easy to see this issue in terms of victimization and, hence, to obliterate women's agency. This tendency led to well-publicized critiques of "feminist whining" and so-called "victim feminism" (Paglia 1992, 1994; Roiphe 1993; Wolf 1993), taken up in media accounts that trivialized feminist perspectives.

Feminist theorizing about the prevalence of violence against women led to concerted efforts to provide supports for women who experienced such violence, to educate the wider society on the issue, and to change public policy. These efforts have expanded significantly over the past thirty years, though women continue to report acts of violence in large numbers.

Providing Support for Victims/Survivors

The first shelter for battered women in the United States opened in 1974. Now there are over 2,500 shelters and service programs nationwide, stretched to capacity. More shelters are needed, and those that exist need to be more accessible—physically and culturally—to women with disabilities, women of color, immigrant women, and lesbians. Shelters that emphasize culturally relevant perspectives and services include the Asian Women's Shelter (San Francisco); Black, Indian, Hispanic and Asian Women in Action—BIHA (Minneapolis); Casa Myrna Vasquez (Boston); the Farmworker Women's Leadership Project (Pomona, Calif.); Hermanas Unidas (Washington, D.C.); the Korean American Family Service Center (New York); Sakhi, a South Asian project (New York); and Uzuri (Minneapolis). They include an analysis and understanding of cultural factors, religious beliefs, economic issues, and language barriers facing their clients, in a way that many shelters organized by White women have not done (Bhat-tacharjee 1997; Tan 1997) as discussed in Reading 35. Domestic violence is not restricted to heterosexual relationships; it occurs between lesbians, bisexual, and transgender women (Lobel 1984; Renzetti 1992; Wingspan Domestic Violence Project 1998).

Similarly, rape crisis centers operate in many cities throughout the country. Volunteers and paid staff answer emergency calls to crisis hotlines, give information, and refer women who have been raped to counseling, medical, and legal services. They may accompany a woman to the police or a doctor or advocate for her in court proceedings. Rape crisis centers often conduct public education and self-defense training for women, and many have peer counselors who are rape survivors. Over the years, some rape crisis projects that mainly served White women have become multicultural by broadening their perspectives to include antiracist work. Other organizations focus their efforts on the needs of women of color, lesbians, bisexual women, and transgender women.

College women reporting rapes have often been blamed for putting themselves in compromising situations, especially if they have been drinking. Generally, the men involved have been protected and punished lightly if at all, especially if they are university athletes. Some administrators have been concerned about the effects of alcohol and drug use and the role of fraternity parties in campus rapes (Sanday 1990). Others seem more concerned to protect their college's reputation. Campus materials and workshops on date rape for incoming students emphasize girls' and boys' different socialization and attitudes toward dating, as mentioned in Chapter 5. Notable among the efforts to deal with this issue is Antioch College's sexual offense policy, which expects students to talk through a sexual encounter step by step, giving verbal consent at each step (Gold and Villari 2000).

Men's projects that work on violence against women are making a crucial contribution to creating change on this issue. Examples include the National Organization for Men Against Sexism (Owego, N.Y.), AMEND (Denver, Colo.), Emerge (Cambridge, Mass.), Men's Rape Prevention Project (Washington, D.C.), and MOVE (Men Overcoming Violence; San Francisco). Michael Kimmel and Haki Madhubuti discuss this issue from male perspectives (Readings 38 and 39), both arguing that men must acknowledge and deal with their sexist socialization and work with other men to stop violence against women.

Public and Professional Education

In response to rape in public places, women's groups in several U.S. cities have organized a "curfew for men." They put up posters announcing that men should be off the streets at night in order to stop incidents of violence against women. Women have also written on sidewalks and buildings in their neighborhood or on campus: "A woman was raped here."

Compared with a generation ago, there is now considerable public information and awareness about violence against women, including public service announcements, bumper stickers, and ads on billboards, buses, and TV. Increasingly, employers and labor unions recognize that domestic violence can interfere with a woman's ability to get, perform, or keep a job. In a 1994 survey of Fortune 1000 companies, nearly half (49 percent) said that domestic violence had a harmful effect on their company's productivity, 44 percent said it had a harmful effect on health-care costs, and 66 percent agreed that a company's financial performance would benefit from addressing the issue among employees (U.S. Department of Labor, Women's Bureau, 1996, p. 3). Some corporations and labor unions have developed education and training programs on domestic violence for managers and workers. Others contribute financially to shelters.

There is a growing body of research as well as theoretical, therapeutic, and political writing on this subject, developing the work of the 1970s and early 80s (Bart and O'Brien 1993; Bass and Davis 1988; Bohmer and Parrot 1993; Buchwald, Fletcher, and Roth 1993; Fineman and Mykitiuk 1994; Herman 1992; Jones 1994b; Koppelman 1996; Koss et al. 1994; NiCarthy 1986, 1987; Russell 1990; White 1985; Zambrano 1985). Public exhibitions like The Clothesline Display Project, described by Elizabeth Wilson-Compton in Reading 87, Chapter 13, also make powerful statements. Another development has been the growth of professional education on violence against women for doctors, nurses, emergency-room staff, and other health-care providers, as well as social workers and teachers. Greater knowledge and understanding are also imperative for police officers, judges, and legislators. National-level organizations like the Family Violence Prevention Fund (Washington, D.C.; San Francisco), the National Clearinghouse on Marital Rape and Date Rape (Berkeley, Calif.), the National Coalition Against Domestic Violence (Denver, Colo.), the National Resource Center on Domestic Violence (Harrisburg, Pa.), and the Network for Battered Lesbians (Boston) provide research and expertise to local organizations, the news media, and policy makers at state and federal levels. The work of the National Latino Alliance for the Elimination of Domestic Violence (Arlington, Va.) is included in the readings that follow.

Policy and Legislative Initiatives

Twenty-five years ago there were no laws concerning domestic violence. Now there is a growing, if uneven, body of law, mainly at the state level, including protection orders that prohibit the abuser from coming near or contacting the woman and her children. The rape laws have also been reformed because of pressure from feminists and rape survivors. This has been a piecemeal process and also varies from state to state. Nowadays, rape laws no longer require the corroboration of a victim's testimony; women are no longer required to have resisted their attackers; and the sexual histories of rape victims are no longer subject for cross-examination, unless shown to be relevant.

On the federal level, the Violence Against Women Act (VAWA) was signed into law as part of the Violent Crime and Law Enforcement Act of 1994. It authorized $1.6 billion to be spent over six years to address and prevent violence against women. VAWA 99 (House Bill H.R. 357) seeks to reauthorize and increase funds for this purpose, including the National Domestic Violence Hotline; $1 billion for battered women's shelters over the next five years; and funding for community initiatives, training for judges and court personnel, improvements in arrest policies, and legal advocacy programs for victims. Also, the bill includes provisions to limit the effects of violence on children, to prevent sexual assault and domestic violence, and to deal with violence against women in the military system (NOW Legal Defense and Education Fund 1999). In Sep-

tember 2000 it was approved by the House for four more years.

Limitations of Current Strategies

An increase in funding and increasing professionalization of work involving violence against women may be seen as major successes. A negative aspect of this development is the fact that shelters and rape crisis centers have come under closer official scrutiny, especially regarding workers' qualifications. Although there is still a vital role for volunteers, many leadership positions require a master's degree in social work (MSW) or a counseling qualification. This is linked to the current emphasis on individual services and therapeutic remedies. Participants in The Color of Violence Conference were clear about the need to repoliticize the issue of violence against women. As hard as women work to help particular individuals, there are always many more—seemingly an endless stream of women needing help. This can lead to burnout among workers who well understand the continuing strength of meso- and macro-level factors that support violence against women. As Grossholtz (1983) points out, "Shelters are radical forces in the midst of social service agencies and radical threats to the ongoing political economy of violence. . . . A battered women's shelter cannot take the maintenance of the nuclear family or sex-role stereotypes as its goal" (p. 67).

There is an inherent contradiction in looking to the government—the State—to solve this problem. The State is a key institution involved in the oppression of women. It supports and requires the maintenance of the nuclear family and the gendered division of labor. It condones and legitimizes violence against women through laws, judges' decisions, and police treatment that discriminate against victims of violence. It gives priority to custom and tradition over women's fundamental human rights. In their capacity as government employees, U.S. prison guards rape and abuse women, as mentioned by Nancy Kurshan (Reading 63, Chapter 10). Border patrols along the U.S.-Mexico border have assaulted undocumented women entering the United States (Light 1996; Martinez 1998). U.S. military personnel based in the United States and overseas commit violent acts against women and girls. As individuals these men may have little power, but by virtue of their role as representatives of the U.S. government they have significant power over others, as well as a sense of entitlement that comes with their position. Suzuyo Takazato, the co-coordinator of Okinawa Women Act Against Military Violence, discusses this in the context of Okinawa (Japan); see Reading 40. This grassroots organization was formed in the fall of 1995 after the rape of a twelve-year-old Okinawan girl by three U.S. military personnel. The group has been active in denouncing military violence against women and girls, and calling for a redefinition of security not based on militarism. It demands the full investigation of all past U.S. military crimes and human rights violations committed against women and girls, and the withdrawal of all U.S. military bases and military forces from Okinawa.

Although many military personnel do not commit acts of violence against women, a significant number do (Guenter-Schlesinger 1999; Morris 1999). Military personnel are socialized into a highly masculinist military culture and are trained to dehumanize "the enemy" to be able to kill in time of war (Reardon 1985). Rape has long been a purposeful act of war-making and an instrument of policy. It is a violation against women of the enemy group or country and, through them, an act of aggression, hostility, and humiliation against their husbands, sons, fathers, and brothers. Tétreault (1997) notes that rape in war,

> like other forms of torture, is frequently performed in front of family members to maximize its effectiveness in achieving social, emotional, and cognitive disorientation, terrorizing the community, and making it easier to control.
>
> *(p. 428)*

Examples include the rape of Vietnamese women by U.S. troops during the Vietnam War (Enloe 1988) and the mass rape and forced impregnation of Muslim and Croatian women by Serbian soldiers in Bosnia-Herzegovina in the early 1990s (MacKinnon 1993, 1998; Pitter and Stilmayer 1993; Tax 1993). In 1992 the United Nations Security Council created a war crimes commission to investigate atrocities in former Yugoslavia, including rape charges, and later established a war crimes tribunal to hear charges of war crimes. Tétreault (1997) argues that this process was limited because there was no international consensus on who was responsible for the conflict and the tribunal did not have access to "those at the top of the pyramid of responsibility for policies that utilized rape as an instrument of terror and genocide" (p. 436). Another well-documented example of war crimes against women is the sexual slavery of "comfort women" recruited by the Japanese Imperial Army in World War II, mentioned by Suzuyo Takazato in Reading 40. The remaining survivors, who are now very elderly, are still waiting for compensation and a full apology from the Japanese government, despite a strong international campaign on this matter (Barry 1995; Hicks 1994; Sajor 1998).

Women's Rights as Human Rights

Much of our discussion focuses on the United States, but we also note the significance of this issue worldwide though cultural differences mean that violence against women may take different forms (see the box on page 220). In December 1979, the United Nations adopted the Convention on the Elimination of All Forms of Discrimination Against Women (CEDAW), which includes violence against women. One hundred sixty-five countries have ratified CEDAW and adopted it as national policy, though often with many reservations so that implementation has been much more limited. Over twenty years later, U.S. women's organizations are still lobbying for the United States to ratify CEDAW.

Lori Heise (1989) notes that "sex-specific violence has not been treated with the same seriousness as other human rights abuses" (p. 13). Defining violence against women as a human rights issue has been a successful strategy to get this issue onto the international agenda (Beasley and Thomas 1994; Bunch and Carillo 1991; Kerr 1993). In June 1993, women from many countries organized the Global Tribunal on Violations of Women's Human Rights to coincide with the Non-Governmental Organization (NGO) Forum of the U.N. World Conference on Human Rights, held in Vienna (Bunch and Reilly 1994). They collected more than 400,000 signatures (representing 124 countries) on a petition demanding that the U.N. Conference recognize violence against women as an abuse of women's human rights. Thirty-three women from twenty-five countries shared personal testimony before an international panel of eminent judges. In 1994 the U.N. Commission on Human Rights created a new position—the Special Rapporteur on Violence Against Women, Its Causes and Consequences—based in Geneva, Switzerland.

Violence against women was a key topic at the U.N. Fourth World Conference on Women in Beijing, as well as at the parallel NGO forum in Hairou, thirty miles away. In Hairou, women from virtually every country discussed this issue and the many ways it manifests itself in their communities. These included the Single Women's Group from Delhi (India), which confronts men who abuse their wives and challenges marriage as women's only option; the Jinglun Family Center (China), which runs the country's first domestic violence hotline and provides education for abusers and violence-prevention training for community mediators and family members; the Fiji Women's Crisis Center, which promotes domestic violence awareness and prevention through radio talk shows and community drama; and the Musasa Project (Zimbabwe), which runs a public education project on domestic violence (Family Violence Prevention Fund 1995).

In 2000, five years after the Beijing Conference, the United Nations is to review progress on the Beijing *Platform for Action*. An international women's educational and lobbying project, initiated by 140 women from 65 countries, is planning national marches and a major gathering outside the United Nations (New York City). This effort is focused on poverty and violence against women worldwide, and its goal is "to generate world political pressure that cannot be ignored" (World March of Women in the Year 2000).

As this chapter makes clear, there is an urgent need for many changes for women to be secure from violence including:

- the socialization and education of all children to respect and value each other;

- changes in the social construction of femininity and masculinity, and the abolition of cultural attitudes that support male superiority;

- an end to the objectification and commodification of women;

- changes in women's work and wages, and support for community-based economic development to give women economic security and independence;

- changes in the law, court decisions, police practices, and the political system so that women's human rights are central; and

- continued collaboration among all who are working to end violence, and challenges to those who are not.

◆◆◆
Questions for Reflection

In reading and discussing this chapter, consider these questions:

1. What beliefs about rape are really myths? How would your life be different if rape and the threat of rape did not exist?

2. How does the intersectionality of gender, race, class, nation, sexuality, and so forth, affect violence against women?

3. How do boys in your community learn to respect women? to disrespect women?

4. How has abuse or violence affected your life? your family? your community?

5. What kinds of masculinity would help to create personal security for women?

6. What is men's responsibility for ending violence against women?

♦♦♦
Taking Action

1. Visit the web sites listed below to find out more about this issue.

2. Talk about this issue with your peers, and initiate public discussion on your campus or in your community. Find out about your college's policy on sexual assault and how it is enforced (or not). Find out about rape crisis centers, shelters, and support groups in your area so that you can support someone who is coping with sexual assault.

3. Volunteer with a rape crisis project on campus or at a shelter for victims of domestic violence. Men students: Work with other men on this issue.

Web Sites

National Organization for Men Against Sexism www.nomas.org

For reports of the U.N. Special Rapporteur on Violence Against Women, Its Causes and Consequences www.aco.org/united-nations/womtitle.html

For details of international campaigns concerning violence against women www.cwgl.rutgers.edu

THIRTY-FIVE
♦♦♦

National Symposium on La Violéncia Doméstica:
An Emerging Dialogue among Latinos (excerpt)
Fernando Mederos

Forty Latinos and Latinas—domestic violence activists, clinicians, researchers, lawyers and survivors of violence from the United States and Puerto Rico—met on November 6 and 7, 1997, in Washington, D.C., for the National Symposium on La Violencia Doméstica: An Emerging Dialogue Among Latinos. Our purpose was to begin a national dialogue about domestic violence, to acknowledge its impact on our children and on our communities, to make recommendations for action, and to increase the allocation of federal resources to eliminate domestic violence in our neighborhoods. The Steering Committee that organized and led this meeting was composed of six women and two men who have provided leadership in domestic violence work in Latino communities. The Symposium was sponsored by the U.S. Department of Health and Human Services (DHHS), which is the lead federal agency in the implementation of the Family Violence Prevention and Services

Act. DHHS recognizes the need to bring in the voices of Latino researchers, practitioners, and activists into policy discussions.

This Symposium operated on two levels. First, it was a policy forum with plenary presentations and in-depth discussions with participants. This was not a hierarchical, experts dictating to the people event, but rather a gathering of people with extensive experience in the field who were selected for their expertise. They came to listen and learn from each other and to contribute to a thoughtful dialogue. . . .

At another level, the Symposium was a force for unity, strength and connection for a very diverse group. Participants came from many parts of the United States. While many were long-term immigrants from Mexico, Central and South America, and the Caribbean, most were born in the United States or Puerto Rico, not unlike the U.S. Latino population.

Steering Committee members were guided by an emerging consensus on the following:

- We Latinos have lived and struggled with domestic violence in unique and unconventional ways and in diverse settings. We have in common a history of silence about this aspect of our lives. In order to make recommendations for action and allocation of federal resources that fit Latino culture, all of us will need an opportunity to affirm our experiences and successes in working with domestic violence.

- We need to connect with those parts of our culture that help our people heal and resist domestic violence. We need to experience our culture as a source of healing and strength. This wisdom will guide the group in the process of developing policy recommendations.

- We will work together in the struggle against domestic violence. We are committed to combine our gifts as Latinas and Latinos, women and men, in this task.

Accordingly, the Symposium began with a Ceremony of Connection with our past and with our spirituality. This celebrated the solemnity and sacredness of the Symposium's purpose, helping the group to recognize the bonds of tradition and belief that link the participants. This was followed by a *Conocimiento,* which is a gathering of acknowledgement and interconnectedness during which participants are encouraged to share their stories. Many persons told their stories, often speaking on behalf of the communities they represented. This broke down many barriers and allowed the participants to recognize the experiences they have in common.

This account will begin with a summary of these exchanges, though it is impossible to convey the passion and intensity of the occasion. At best, it is like using words to describe music.

Building a Vision: Ceremony

In setting the stage for the Ceremony, Steering Committee member Jerry Tello reminded us that as a people, spirituality has always been a part of the Latino people's ethos. He explained the role of the altar in the center of the room. It was to be a place where every person, regardless of faith, could put something that represented themselves and their family. The altar was a centering place that became the focus of our interconnectedness.[1]

Concha Saucedo began the Ceremony with a prayer for healing and balance. She explained that the altar is a *mesa,* a table of spiritual nourishment. She asked us to stand and join hands around the table. In joining together, she reminded us that we all have energy, which is embodied in our words, and that our words can heal. A prayer was said in the four directions (north, south, east and west), representing also the man, the woman, the child, and the elder. She invoked the energy of the east, embodying the sun, the direction of *guerreros* and *guerreras,* male and female warriors and defenders, and the energy of the north, the place of our ancestors, the old ones, the teachers, to strengthen us in our purpose.

Representing the voice of the elders, Isaac Cardenas of San Antonio, Texas, offered this prayer:

> Great-grandfather, holy spirit, great spirit, watch over all of these Latinos and Latinas. Give them strength, give them your love, take care of them, help them to reach their destination, both in their personal life, and in the goals we seek here.

Griselda Tapia, representing the voice of the child, expressed her hope that through education we can overcome the secret of domestic violence that has stayed within families. She offered her prayer on behalf "of all the children who have to live in families where domestic violence is present."

Another participant, representing the voice of men, said:

> Creator, we first want to thank you, and ask for permission, for those first keepers of this land here, that we are on today. . . . And we also give thanks, and ask your blessing for all these people, for all the nations gathered here . . . and open all the barriers that we need, that this organization needs [opened] to complete its goal.

The last prayer, representing the voice of women, was that of Concha Saucedo (translated):

> The seed is one, it comes from the Creator. Our hearts beat together. Yours, mine, with the

same seed, seeds from the Creator, the seed of a universe. And thus you and I are one, we are of the universe. You are my other self, *tu eres mi otro yo,* woman, man, children, elders, ancestors, teachers, grandparents. Thanks, Mother Earth. For those who are part of this movement, thank you. You are my other self.

The Conocimiento: A Gathering of Acknowledgement and Interconnectedness

Continuing the link with the altar, Jerry Tello passed around a basket of polished stones and asked that each person take two, one for themselves and one for those they represent. All were then asked to introduce themselves and those they represent to the group. After receiving our energy, these stones would go on the altar, stay there during our meeting and, at the end of the Symposium, be taken by each person as a continuing connection with the gathering.

Everyone spoke during the next two hours. These shared thoughts, feelings and histories slowly converged throughout the Symposium into a common vision. It is impossible to reproduce each person's account, as valuable as they all were. Instead, here is an edited cross-section of our words, with names omitted to protect participants' privacy:

Man from New Orleans: If I had to say who I represent, gosh, too many people, I feel. I am a person who was born in Cuba.... I feel that any kind of violence is connected one with another, and that the violence that we may find inside of a home or a house, has to do too much with the violence that is outside of the house.... The thing that impresses me the most, are the children. And I'm so impressed to see how much, not only are they suffering from the violence they see between their parents, but the violence they feel from their parents to them. Not only physical violence, but emotional violence.

Woman from New York: I bring my New Yorkrican self, and that transplants to California.... And I think more than anything else I bring truth in the sense that I think we have the ability, within ourselves, to end domestic violence, but we have to do it our way. We can't do it the way that other people want us to do it; we have to do it our way.... And

the other thing I bring, I think, is a challenge to us to work together on this issue as men and women. So stepping out of the box, the traditional box of defining domestic violence as a woman's issue, and really embracing that this is a community issue that when one family, or one child, or one individual is devastated by domestic violence, we are all devastated by it. So, you know, let's be together in every sense of the way, and that is my challenge, and that is my hope.

Woman from California: I'm also a survivor of domestic violence. I survived 23 years ago, and for the past 10 years I've been working with the men, running a Latino batterers' program. And the reason I'm doing that is because when I was living with violence, I had always hoped that there was some help, and particularly some help for my spouse. So I'm here to represent the batterers, who are also in a lot of pain. These are men who have been victims themselves, who are living in a lot of pain.

Man from California: But let me tell you, *yo soy un Chicano de East L.A.* .... (I'm a Chicano from East L.A. . . . .) I'm born, raised, continue to live, work, and I'm probably going to die there.... I don't take drugs anymore.... I come from a background of violence; I know it well. *Yo era lo que se dice bato loco. Era pandillero.* .... (I used to be what they call a wise guy. I was a gangster....) But my blessing has been [a woman I met as] a 15-year-old *chicanita con el nombre de Angelina* (called Angelina).... We have been married 45 years, we have five children, eight grandchildren, three great-grandchildren, and another one that we hope to see when we get back. And, in fact, my children have quit having babies, and my grandchildren are having babies, if you get the picture. So that is who I am, in terms of me as a person. In my professional life, I'm a licensed psychotherapist.... I work with batterers, with men who like to kick women's ass, okay? And in that area I think I'm very good because of my violent background. *A mi no me van a madrear. Que me provocó?* (They can't fool me. She provoked me?) Give me a break, man. Do you know what *provocar* means? She provoked me? It is a classic excuse.

Man from New York: ... I am a black Puerto Rican. I think that is very important to stress.... I represent the races in the Latino community.... As we talk about the reality of what confronts us as people, we need to understand that the brutality and racism in this world, in this country, have affected us in this community, as well. . . . I want us to appreciate the culture, but we need to recognize both its strengths and also its limitations. Because part of the limitations is what is contributing to the violence, and to the harm to the children. . . . I represent East Harlem. . . . I am, indeed, honored to be here with all of you.

Woman from California (all translated): I arrived three years ago from Puerto Rico. . . . I bring the strength of women who, with fewer resources, I think, than all of us here survive in this country . . . and not only domestic violence, which is perhaps what brings them to our programs, but also all of the other oppressions that we suffer as Latinos. . . . I want to leave with the hope that as Latinos and Latinas we can do the work in a different way, even though we are oppressed by institutions that make us do things in certain ways in order to get the money we need to do this work. But I think that having this altar in the center is a symbol that our culture has many ways of doing things, and that we have to rescue those ways if we want to reach our communities.

Woman from Chicago: . . . I am originally from Mexico, I live in Chicago. . . . My kids were the ones that told me, mom, you have to come and work in *el barrio* (the neighborhood). . . . And I went to *Mujeres Latinas en Acción* (Latina Women in Action), and I have to thank that organization, because they gave me — that organization gave me my womanhood. I became a real woman working at Mujeres Latinas. . . . So I embarked in my pioneering mission, and I found myself *completamente sola*, completely isolated . . . after seeing so many battered women who were victims, so much pain on their faces, and in their hearts, so little hope. . . . And in trying to be the rescuer, their protector, I burned out. And under doctor's orders, I had to stop working for over six months. I had to stop doing what I liked the best. . . . I went back to work knowing exactly how to do it. And when I supervised my *compañeras*, my main concern is how are you doing? How are you doing? Are you exhausted, go home, take time off. That is my main concern, because burnout is an awful experience.

Another woman from Chicago: In order to stop domestic violence, I feel we have to face the problem. I mean, I heard over, and over again, my mom and my grandmother say: *pero que va a decir la gente, yo no quiero que se den cuenta de lo que pasa* (but what will people say, I don't want them to know what's going on). You know, I'm sick and tired of hearing

that. I mean, to tell you the truth, I feel that everyone knew about it, but they didn't do anything. . . . Well, I think we have to stop thinking about other people and think about ourselves, especially our families, and our children. We need to unite as a community, and help those families who are in need. Finally, I would like to leave you with a quote that reads: "We did then what we knew then, now that we know better, we do better." And I truly hope we do better for our children.

Conclusion of the Conocimiento

Todas las Relaciones Son Sagradas: All Relationships Are Sacred

At the end of the Conocimiento, Jerry Tello, a Steering Committee member, articulated the collective vision of the eight women and men who had met to plan the Symposium: that in the Latino community men, women, elders, and children will work together against domestic violence, recognizing that doing this will require tremendous trust and a leap of faith and healing among participants. Faith, trust, and healing are not "policy issues"; they are a form of knowledge and conviction that each person has gained from life and from the heart. Jerry was chosen to convey this vision by telling participants the story about the lessons his father and his culture have offered him. In a sense, this is the Steering Committee's collective Conocimiento. It is also a story of marginalization and of struggling for honorable manhood. The following is a summary of his remarks:

> I remember as a little boy, going with my dad to the store to buy milk for my little sister. And he would want to pay and the men who were running the store were sitting in the back playing cards and they wouldn't come to collect the money. My dad would say, "Hey, *quiero pagar,* I want to pay" and they would say, "It's a stupid wetback, make him wait." I would look at my dad and he would begin getting mad. They made him wait a long time and called him ugly names and I would wonder why doesn't he do something — hit them, knock something over, or rip off the milk, but he couldn't because then he would go to jail. Then he wouldn't be able to

work and we wouldn't eat. He just got more angry and when I asked him why he didn't do anything, he slapped me on the head and said "Shut up, you don't understand." He then put on his hat and put the rest of the anger under it. Sometimes that anger would slip out from under the hat and I didn't know why.

When my brother got busted for being on the wrong side of the tracks, my dad would get angry and tell us that my brother was not a good example to follow—so my dad would be angry and my brother would get angry too. At the same time, society was telling us that Mexican men were wetbacks, gang bangers, drunks and womanizers and as a little boy this is what I thought *Macho* was—I thought this was what a Latino man was supposed to be and how he was supposed to act. What I didn't understand was that this was society's way of breaking us down, reinforcing false teachings, and hiding our true knowledge. But the old writings of the *HueHues* (Elders) told us what it meant to be a true *hombre* and *mujer* (man and woman). That in order to be an *Hombre Noble* (Noble Man) you must respect women—that the first lesson in crossing the bridge to manhood is respect for *"El Otro Yo"* (your other self), woman. If you didn't learn that lesson, then you didn't go on. It is our responsibility to reteach these old lessons and to bring harmony and balance to our relationships.

So, struggling with working in this field, I'm a father, I'm a son, I also represent your fathers and your sons, and your partners. I also represent the men that have abused, that have been the perpetrators. And so, for them, and especially to you [women in the audience], I apologize for those of us that have been irresponsible, for those of us that couldn't keep it under our hat, for those of us that made excuses, and for those of us that were violent to any of you, for any of the women you represent, I take responsibility and apologize.

Because the first aspect of anything is *mujer,* creation, you; without you, we would not be. And so in looking back, I begin to understand that *de veras un macho es un hombre* (really a male is a man who is) honorable, dignified, respectful, sensitive, supportive, accountable, all of those things. . . . And I just want to thank

the women here, all of you, that have taught us, that have accepted us, and maybe somehow can forgive us, and to allow us an opportunity to learn and grow, so that maybe your sons, when they grow up, people will not be afraid of them. . . . So I think the task is interconnected, it is about grandparents, it is about children, it is about *mujeres* and about *hombres* (about women and men), and I just feel blessed to be in this room, to be able to be present where there are so many strong mujeres with a lot of experience; elders and people with stories, *jóvenes* (young people), and all of that.

And I think we represent each other, and whether we think we are ready or not, whether we think we are experienced, got degrees or not, *ni modo* (it doesn't matter), we have to do it, because we are the voice for many, many people that are hurting, and many more that we can actually make a better way for.

The interconnectedness between Latinos and Latinas and our desire to work together was voiced again and again by participants throughout the gathering, and the Steering Committee provided leadership in this respect through their example, as women and men working together on the Steering Committee.

Plenary I

Hablando del Sistema: Talking about the System

The first plenary, Hablando del Sistema, addressed current policy crises at the national and local levels and explored strategies that we can use to promote helpful policies. It was chosen as the first theme because recent policy initiatives, such as limits on welfare benefits, and restrictions on health care coverage and disability benefits for residents, have further exacerbated long-term problems such as colonialism, racism, poverty, and police brutality. Other legislation that is troubling includes deportation provisions for legal residents, English-only laws, and Proposition 187 (which denies public education in California to children whose parents are undocumented). Finally, there is the challenge of our own internalized oppression that divides us. . . .

Plenary II

Entre Familia: Among Family

The next plenary, *Entre Familia,* shifted the emphasis to the most intimate arena: our families, how our history has affected us, and how we can use our own resources and our culture to heal our wounds.

Steering Committee member Sonia Davila Williams of the School of Social Work at the University of Minnesota moderated this session. She noted that the extended family is the norm in Latino culture. Family includes uncles, aunts, grandparents, first, second and third cousins, relatives by marriage and their relatives, even compadres and comadres, who may be godparents or long-term intimate friends not related by blood. In a sense, even the community is part of *la familia* since it is made up of families.

She introduced Dr. Concepción Saucedo Martinez, otherwise known in this text as Concha Saucedo. Dr. Saucedo is a clinical psychologist and a Yaquì elder and healer. Currently, she is Executive Director of the Family Institute of La Raza in San Francisco.

Dr. Saucedo was asked to speak about (a) the legacy and impact of colonization, immigration, and acculturation on family values, (b) the ensuing dynamics between child and parent and between child and child, both intergenerational and intergender, that are part of domestic violence in our community, and (c) the strengths (the healing resources within our community), the negatives, and what we can do to promote healing. An attempt has been made to remain faithful to her voice by rendering the essence of her remarks in the first person. . . .

To understand ourselves, we have to go back 500 years to the Spanish invasion. Since then, we have survived and there are things that we carry from that survival, both gifts and burdens. In the struggle to survive, we lost awareness of this legacy of gifts and burdens. And having lost that awareness, we carry and transmit the burdens onto our families, our marriages, and our children. Violence is part of that burden, but we do not recognize it as violence. We see it as endemic and inherent in the culture, and it survives. We also forget our gifts.

In order to change this we must empower ourselves to rename things and to recapture our gifts for healing and growth. For example, we should not accept the limitations and the labels that the federal government places on us. Currently, there is an international movement for everybody to be "documented." This has created certain divisions in our own communities, between the documented and the undocumented. "You are not a person unless you have a *tarjeta* [green card], right?"

So what will we name ourselves? . . . Do we name ourselves Hispanics, do we name ourselves *raza* (the race, the people), do we name ourselves Chicano, do we name ourselves *Indios* (Indians), do we name ourselves *Centroamericanos* (Central Americans), do we name ourselves *immigrantes* (immigrants), do we name ourselves *migrantes* (migrants)? . . . And I say . . . papers for no one, no one needs a paper to be who they are. And I begin looking at myself, and everyone else in this room, as a migrant on this continent, and on these islands, right? And a migrant can move anyplace, that is our right. We did that before the invader came. People in Puerto Rico did business with people on the coast of Mexico. They were entrepreneurs; they traded. People crossed what is now *La Frontera* (the U.S.-Mexico frontier), freely, for years. We've done that for a millennium. . . .

We are not interlopers or outsiders. Our interventions and our work with our communities should acknowledge this.

We must also rename family. The federal definition of family is limited to mother and father and children. For us, family includes not only blood and marriage relations, but also relations based on *compadrazgo* (relationships created through godparenting or long-term intimate friendships). We often use ceremonies to create relationships and sometimes these relationships take the place of blood relations, when they are not able to function in a healthy way. This capacity to create relationships and to be bound by them is one of the gifts of survival and this is a resource that must be used and encouraged in interventions within our community. It is a source of strength, help, and healing.

Renaming family also means accepting gay and lesbian relationships as families. These men and women are part of our circle; they are part of us. They are not a separate circle. Accepting our oneness is a source of strength and healing.

Las pandillas, the gangs, are also families that have gone a little crazy. They are trying to provide sustenance to each other that they did not get in their families. We failed in some way. We did not provide certain directions, and now we have to rectify that. So when working with young people, it is important to include other young people, because that is who they listen to. They can move out of violence if one treats them with respect and responds to them as *familia.*

As we continue renaming, we must remember *respeto* (respect). In our culture, people may have different roles and functions, but they are recognized for their innate value, their essence. In a sense, we are all sacred. This is the core of our understanding of respect. We still have a lot of this in our culture. It is something positive that we can use and teach. If a man says that he wants to be respected, that he was not being respected and that is why he beat his wife up, then he is not talking about *respeto.* We can redefine *respeto* for individuals. Is *respeto* hitting someone or being a provider? Redefining *respeto* is the cornerstone of change.

Respeto also implies acceptance of diversity within our culture. Some of us, like me, have more indigenous background. Others appear more European, but we are all Latinos even though our values may differ somewhat. We share a feeling that family is what is most important—this is a unifying force for us.

We need to redefine and rename our diversity even further. My mother was a full-blood Yaqui and her people were massacred again and again by the Mexican government. I have certain feelings about the Mexicanness that is in me, so I identify more on the native side, and with northern natives here as well, and have learned much from them. Do those issues also appear in Cuban Americans, in Puerto Ricans? You have Africa and Spain and what is left of the native Tainos. What does all that variation and color mean in a family? How does it get played out in violence issues? How does that get played out in our own communities? Exploring these legacies should be a part of our healing practice.

Another element that we need to rename and recover is traditional medicine, which may use herbs, ceremonies, or words. This may provide a better treatment in many situations, and these traditions need to be recognized and fostered.

We have to make changes with or without the money. Sometimes government assistance has hampered us, because we end up forgetting "that we can do it ourselves, and we can do it well, and we can do it as a group." For example, in San Francisco, people try to do things together. Seven years ago 55 deaths of young people were counted over a short period of time. There was no response to this crisis. Finally, the community declared a violence prevention initiative and brought people together without money. They partnered with different sectors: public health, recreation, economic and community development, and arts and culture. This initiative now has a name: the *Comunidad Unida Para La Salud* (the Community United for Health): A Blueprint for a Healthy Mission Community.

Through education, information and the use of community campaigns, cultural norms regarding family, domestic violence, use of alcohol and other drugs can be shifted. If young men get drunk on weekends because it is a way of feeling closeness and brotherhood, then we have to find something that gives them that sense of closeness—a way that they can bond with other men.

The prevention and promotion strategies promote alternatives to violence, drug abuse, and other ills. They present affirming alternatives that center on balance and harmony. Whenever a problem is addressed and described, it is accompanied by other possibilities, or positive ways of living, to help people visualize alternatives to change. Thus, a continuum of strategies that support and promote behaviors that are positive and strengthening is always available. Next, the initiative needs to have a commitment to spiritual healing as a core value to connect with and affirm non-material internal values.

A promotional strategy or campaign is an initiative to create a healthy community. It must respect cultural values of diverse populations of the community, understand differing levels of biculturation, and use a culturally-based filter in program design that is adaptable and flexible. It needs to bring together separate professions, agencies, categories, disciplines, and create a marriage between traditional and conventional approaches. Public and private sectors need to work together, under the leadership of the community. And such a campaign needs to adapt segmented funding, such as substance abuse treatment monies, to family-centered approaches.

Finally, these campaigns must be based on the belief that change is slow and incremental, that it happens in small pieces, and that outcome research has to be done with the indices that the community says are the indices of health. If we save one woman, we save one child. If one child goes on and does whatever they want, whatever dream they had, whether it was to be a television star, or to sing a song, that is a success.

Success with abusive men is a difficult issue with respect to criteria or indices of success. Abusers need accountability and consequences. They have to develop a sense of responsibility. But, if our response is to simply put them in jail, they go into another battering system, and we have lost other souls. In the old, old days, in the village, if certain people did certain things, they were vanished from the village, a *palizas, verdad?* (with a beating, right?) We need community mechanisms for men who batter that are more effective and that react more rapidly than the judicial system.

Dr. Saucedo made specific suggestions for a promotional strategy in the Latino community. Specifically, she emphasized that such a campaign should:

- Integrate the expansive Latino concept of family, addressing not only nuclear and extended families, but also *compadrazgo* (non-blood kin) systems.

- Include lesbian and gay families, expanding and modifying the Latino concept of family.

- Integrate existing community resources, such as having young people become teachers of other young people, as a way of helping youth involved in gangs; involvement of the arts and music both to publicize positive messages and to involve the community in the production of art and culture.

- Incorporate traditional values and healing practices. These can range from the use of native healers to the use of traditional values in the healing process.

- Highlight positive models of relationships and of family life in all aspects of the campaign.

- Create separate spaces for men and women to support and talk to each other and solve problems in ways that make sense to them. This is in accordance with traditional practice and it could be a vehicle for introducing or revisiting ideas of balance and respect.

As the floor was opened for participant comments and questions, Ricardo Carrillo announced that in 1997 no gang-related deaths had occurred in La Misión [Mission District, San Francisco]. This announcement was met with applause. Dr. Carrillo was careful to explain that the police had also had a part in what happened, but he felt much was owed to the initiative that Concha had led with others in the last two years.

In the ensuing commentaries, four main themes were discussed at length. These are presented below, along with a condensed version of the comments:

1. How do consequences for offenders, such as involving the police and incarceration, fit into community responses to domestic violence?

- A participant stated that, on the one hand, there is a profound reluctance to send men to jail, since this amounts to sending them into institutions that brutalize them. On the other hand, some people are so damaged that if they are not restrained (sent to jail), they will hurt someone badly.

- A participant revealed that he had had his son arrested because he was extremely dangerous and out of control. There was no other option in that acute situation. Some participants acknowledged that this is a painful reality. This led to a suggestion that laws should not be categorical, that interventions should fit the offenders' level of dangerousness and that there ought to be provisions for community intervention in the process of holding offenders accountable. There was no consensus about these issues, but a realization that a deeper dialogue needs to take place about offenders and that the Latino community must be a full partner in that discussion.

- In another series of commentaries, three practitioners with extensive experience working with abusive Latinos shared their perspective on their work.

One said that physically abusive men should be considered lost spirits—people who need rebalancing, which involves intense work in the physical, emotional, psychological, and spiritual spheres. This is where the community should have a significant role.

Another stated that these men have a very narrow, insecure, and distorted image of what manhood is: "They bought the lie. . . . They live in the lie (associating manhood with dominance and violence), but they are insecure inside. . . . And if you begin stripping the defenses, they run from any kind of treatment. So we know that what works is building a greater value system that is greater than that very narrow, distorted image of manhood and violence, and you do find that in our *cultura* (culture)."

In the same vein, a third counselor disclosed that instead of calling the men batterers, abusers, perpetrators, he calls them *desenfrenados*—men who are out of control. "They can say I lack control, no *tengo frenos* (literally, I don't have brakes). Their job is to get those brakes, to control themselves." He urged participants to really take into consideration history and colonization, and use that as a backdrop to everything that we do: "Because without that context, we then rename, re-discriminate, re-marginalize the very same people that we want to work with. So that is part of our *historia* (history), part of our tradition that we have to take into account. And maybe seeing it in that way allows us to have some empathy, and maybe some success with the men."

Another participant contested this point, saying that it is important to name the men's behaviors—perpetrator or offender may be accurate, though she also suggested that "oppressor" may be a good choice. How about calling them oppressors?

- There was no consensus about how to name and work with Latinos who are physically abusive, but some cultural perspectives about working with Latino abusers were outlined. It was clear that more dialogue needs to happen.

2. How can one incorporate our spiritual beliefs and our family orientation into domestic violence work?

- One participant reminded the group that the *Ceremonia* (Ceremony) started with acknowledging the four directions, representing men, women, elders, and children. He urged the group to always keep in mind this framework in developing responses to domestic violence: "They all have to be considered, and if we consider them together always, we will not come up with solutions that just see men as perpetrators, but as men who need help being with women, elders and children."

- Another participant shared her experience of developing domestic violence services for Latinos in an isolated community. There was an "organic" growth process as new services were developed to respond to the requests of community members. The first step was to offer women's support groups in Spanish. Participants requested baby-sitting and, once the children were present, an educational and support group was developed for them. The children became very strong and committed participants. Eventually the women said, "Why are you not talking to the men?" This led to a decision to start a men's group and, after a long process, a male facilitator was trained. Now, the agency has groups for Latino men. Currently many men are court-referred, but many are coming voluntarily and many stay after the 24-week standard men's program. Participation in women's groups is voluntary, but there is an enthusiastic response. "We did not know that we were not supposed to do that (have groups for men and women). We were oriented to working with families, so that is what we did." Feedback from women indicates that there have been good results with respect to stopping violent behavior, but less impact on verbal and emotional abuse. Very high levels of sexual abuse have also been reported, both by women and by men (as perpetrators). The staff is thinking about responding to this information as they continue program development.

3. Are we giving enough attention to rape and sexual violence in our work on domestic violence?

- Participants repeatedly mentioned that many Latinas have experienced rape and other forms of sexual violence in relationships and in other settings.

- There was a strong feeling that this issue needs more attention in men's programming, in public education campaigns about violence, and in research with Latinas about violence.

4. Participants strongly acclaimed Dr. Saucedo's affirmation of diversity within diversity—the fact that Latinos are not one group, but many nationalities and histories who share many basic values, but are not all the same. In other words, we are many identities with a common tradition and spiritual base.

- Participants endorsed a diversity-within-diversity approach that acknowledges and embraces the fact that we have various gender preferences and racial identities within our population, and an approach that repudiates growing divisions such as citizen/non-citizen.

- Participants also stated that a diversity-within-diversity approach should not freeze traditional roles. For example, it is important to recognize men as providers, but it is equally important to recognize that women have been providers and that this role will become ever more important. "Provider" should not be a male domain.

- Another participant mentioned the absence of services for people with disabilities who are victims or perpetrators of domestic violence. Isolation is profoundly redoubled for such families. This should not happen.

Entre Familia ended with two spontaneous and somewhat parallel accounts, by a man and a woman, regarding the importance of working together and of learning from each other as men and women.

The man is a Mexican American, a grandfather and a psychotherapist who works with violent Latinos. He stated that he had begun to wonder where the spirituality he uses in his work with men comes from:

Yo soy terapista (I am a therapist), as you all know. And I think I'm a good therapist, I think I have a direct connection to the male ego, in all its beauty and in all its ugliness. I think a great part of my treatment is based on spirituality. And in assessing my life, my career, and my development. . . . I try to look for where my spiritual talent came from in treating these

men. *Lo busqué en mi jefe, en mis carnales, en mis home boys, en mis tíos* (I looked for it in my boss, in my male relatives, in my home boys, in my uncles), in all the males that I have been exposed to, and I couldn't find one that gave me any real spiritual food, you could say. They taught me about a lot of other things, and I learned how to be a male in the male world, but nothing in terms of the spiritual aspects.

He went on to state that as he thought about his life, he remembered various women: first, his blind grandmother, who had taken care of him when he was between the ages of three and five, and spent much time telling him entrancing stories. Then he thought of his mother, who established herself as a supportive and compassionate presence when he was nine years old. She became his adviser and his confidante. After that, his wife took that place in his life. She touched, and still touches, his heart; he has a powerful connection with her. Later on, he had a daughter who had cerebral palsy and died at the age of eight, but she was yet another powerful source of connection and a motivator for change. He recounted the following:

I had already made changes, but I think she was the icing on the cake, which is the source of my life, and she was the one that brought it all together. This has been 15, 20 years now. I guess what I'm trying to say is that I want to publicly thank all you women that are here, because without you, I wouldn't know the way, I wouldn't know that the Creator is very important to me. I'm not a very spiritual person in terms of standing up and saying prayers, but He is in my heart, and I feel Him all the time. So, *otra vez* (again), I love you all, and thank you and thanks to all the women. They are the spiritual seed and the spiritual force in the world. And I believe all that is true and that we have somehow or other kept them down, to keep them from touching us.

The woman who gave a parallel account spoke about the special men in her life. Her grandfather, with whom she lived for a few years in Puerto Rico, was special and unique, someone who made her feel understood and loved. As she came back to the United States to work in the battered women's movement, she confronted again and again the reality of what men do to women. In addition, she resented and distrusted men's lack of involvement in the movement: "I said, but we have to do something, men have to get involved; they have to do something. And I always would criticize that constantly, about how we had men who had survived, who are not living violent lives, but yet weren't coming back to the community and doing anything about it."

The participant explained that she had had two sons, but was reluctant to have a daughter, fearing what kind of world she would bring her into. When she met her partner, her sense of trust grew: "But then I met a man in my life, my *compañero* (my partner) today. He is *casi un santo* (almost a saint) my *compañeras* (my friends) tell me, because of how supportive he is with my work. I would like for him to be a little more involved, but *él no es de las personas que tiene coraje como muchos de nosotros aquí* (but he is not one of those people who carries the same level of passion for this issue as many of us here). But he understands the issues, and believes in them. And then I had my daughter. I decided I wanted a daughter; I couldn't be complete without a daughter. So I had my daughter Margarita, who is four now."

> I'm sharing all of this because for a long, long time, until very recently, I thought and was made to believe by others that this was a woman's issue, and that we have the responsibility . . . to re-educate our sons, our brothers, our compañeros, so that this would stop, this cycle would end. And there is truth in that, lots of it.

However, she went on to explain that in the last few years she also had met and worked with two Latinos from New York, deeply committed men who counsel physically abusive Latinos, and felt understanding, support and partnership. She stated that these men were both at the Symposium and that there presence was important to her. She also felt the presence and commitment of other men in the room, and a sense of trust was in her words and expression:

> And today to sit here, and I really would like for us to look around, one, two, three, four . . . fourteen, fifteen, sixteen [men]. This is the first time, in the fifteen years that I have been doing this work, that I have been among so many men. So I want to thank you, men, for being here.

Perhaps it is not a coincidence that *Entre Familia* — Among Family — ended with these accounts. They acknowledge how we can help each other to grow and to complete our work in this difficult field. . . .

Notes

1. In pre-Columbian times, Mesoamerican teachings about relationships were couched in ceremony. These were taught at home, in schools, and in various aspects of society. These ceremonies were documented in the codices and, more importantly, were also shared through oral traditions.

T H I R T Y - S I X

◆◆◆

Asian Immigrant Women Fight Domestic Violence

Deanna L. Jang

Domestic violence occurs in all communities, and the Asian community is no exception. The lack of statistics regarding the incidence of domestic violence in the Asian community is reflective of this fact as well as other factors, such as the inaccessibility of services for non-English or limited English speaking women, the underutilization of the social or governmental services by Asians, and the need for community education in the Asian community regarding domestic violence.

The profiles of Asian and Pacific battered women are similar to battered women in general. Often they have traditional views of the woman's role as wife and mother, the feeling of isolation, low self-esteem, a belief that the abuse may be justified, are financially and emotionally dependent on the batterer, and have a greater fear of the problems of survival outside the family than the violence inside the family. However, because of the immigrant nature of the Asian and Pacific community, these women also face barriers of language, culture and immigration status.

Asian Immigration

U.S. immigration laws for Asia were not liberalized until 1965, when Congress passed amendments to the Immigration and Nationality Act that ended racist national origin quotas and affirmed family reunification as the cornerstone of U.S. immigration policy. For the Asian community this was the first opportunity in decades for reunification. Of the 270,000 visas currently issued annually, Mexico and five Asian countries, including China, Hong Kong and the Philippines, receive the highest number of visas.

The history of U.S. immigration policy is a reflection of the U.S. need for cheap labor. Early Asian immigrants were men who came to build railroads, dig mines or work in the fields. Today, women and children make up approximately two-thirds of legal immigrants and immigrant women are more able to find jobs in the "hidden" service sectors. Employees in the service, garment, or light manufacturing industries are disproportionately Asian women. Isolated in this country without a command of the language, culture, social and legal systems, these women are often subject to discrimination based on sex, race and immigration status. All too often, they are forced to endure substandard working conditions and are vulnerable to exploitation. Many Asian women immigrate via marriage to a U.S. citizen who they have met in their home country or in the United States. Because of the U.S. military bases in Asia, many Asian women have married U.S. servicemen. Since World War II, nearly 250,000 Asian and Pacific women have married servicemen. Studies indicate that there is a higher incidence of domestic violence within military families. Reasons may include isolation, the culture of military training which emphasizes physical force and obedience to authority, and the high rate of alcoholism.

Cheap labor and marriage, however, do not fully encompass the reasons why Asian women immigrate to the U.S. Some are fleeing economic or political repression. Others immigrate with their entire family or join a family already here, sometimes after long periods of separation due to war or legal restrictions. Finally, there are also an alarming number of "mail-order" bride companies that play on the stereotypes of Asian women as passive, noncomplaining servants and/or exotic sex objects. These sexist and racist stereotypes, reinforced by the media, prevail in Western society and encourage the use of violence against Asian women.

Constant Fear

The common stereotype of an undocumented immigrant or "illegal alien" is that of a Mexican male farmworker who illegally crosses the border. Few studies on the magnitude of undocumented Asians exist. In addition, there are a number of undocumented Asian women who may have entered legally as visitors, students, fiancees, or workers and became undocumented after their temporary visas expired or after their conditional residency terminated, even though they may be married to U.S. citizens or permanent residents. Therefore, an undocumented immigrant woman who is also the victim of battering suffers even greater hardships than other immigrant women. In constant fear of deportation and, in most cases, the resulting fear that she may lose her children, she will heed her partner's threat to call the INS if she leaves him or reports him to the police.

"When my husband married me, he continually talked about my becoming a citizen. He told me he had hired a lawyer, that my application for citizenship was taken care of. . . . Today my immigration status is expired and a mess" (*A Community Secret: The Story of Two Filipinas,* by Jacqueline R. Agtuca).

With the passage of the Immigration Reform and Control Act (IRCA) in 1986, many immigrant women found fewer legal and social resources to draw upon in their continuous struggle to provide for themselves and their families. Although IRCA offered legalization to thousands of undocumented persons, its main provision was employer sanctions. The employer sanctions provision, opposed by civil rights and immigrant rights organizations, imposes monetary and criminal penalties on employers who hire undocumented workers. Under IRCA, employees must provide proof of work authorization (that they are lawfully residing in the United States and have permission from INS to work) to any employer who hires them after the date of IRCA's passage. Employees hired prior to this date were "grandfathered" in and did not have to provide any documentation of work.

Employer sanctions have served to further disenfranchise an already disempowered community. IRCA legalized their nonemployment, their nonentitlement to public benefits, and their systematic exploitation in the workplace. The General Accounting Office, in its final report on the impact of employer sanctions, found widespread discrimination against Latinos and Asians. "Grandfathered" employees became "trapped" in exploitative working conditions because they cannot work anywhere else. Women, particularly those working in the least regulated industries such as the garment industry, became even more vulnerable to wage discrimination and sexual and racial harassment.

Without work authorization, a battered undocumented woman who has left her batterer will have even greater difficulty obtaining employment and gaining financial independence. She is likely to find only the jobs which are offered by unscrupulous employers who subject their workers to low wages and poor working conditions and threaten deportation if the workers resist. In addition, IRCA's provisions further discourage immigrants from seeking public benefits, even when they are entitled to receive them for themselves or their children who are U.S. citizens.

Economically Trapped

In addition to the fear of deportation, undocumented women may find themselves economically trapped in battering relationships because they are precluded from most public benefits and must find employment without work authorization. While some battered Asian immigrant and refugee women seek help from social services in the Asian community and from domestic violence programs, few turn to the criminal justice system or use the civil legal system for help. They fear that the police or government agency will report them or their spouses to INS. On a local level, advocates for the rights of immigrants and refugees have addressed this problem by lobbying local government to pass resolutions or ordinances which bar city officials and local law enforcement from turning over persons to the INS, from providing names and addresses to the INS, or from generally assisting in the arrest, deportation or detention of individuals.

No clear spokesperson or organization advocating for this disenfranchised community of immigrant women exists. Thus, the goal of advocates for immigrant women is to raise these issues to the civil rights, immigrants' rights, women's and other organizations and to form a broader coalition for the rights of immigrant women. Already, local groups for the rights of immigrant women have formed in San Francisco, New York, Los Angeles and Honolulu.

Battered Asian immigrant women, particularly those who are undocumented and/or are dependent upon a battering husband to obtain legal status, have few legal remedies available to them. Therefore, it is crucial for immigrant rights, women's rights and battered women's advocates to coordinate efforts and create a responsive advocacy and service network that addresses the overwhelming challenges faced by immigrant women in a post-IRCA environment. Networking and coalition building efforts should focus on creating multifaceted strategies that range from public policy advocacy to community outreach and public education on domestic violence, the need for accessible, culturally appropriate services and the rights of immigrant women.

THIRTY-SEVEN

Lisa's Ritual, Age 10

Grace Caroline Bridges

Afterwards when he has finished
lots of mouthwash helps
to get rid of her father's cigarette taste.
She runs a hot bath
   to soak away the pain
     like red dye leaking from her
      school dress in the washtub.

She doesn't cry.
When the bathwater cools she adds more hot.
She brushes her teeth for a long time.

Then she finds the corner of her room,
curls against it. There the wall is
hard and smooth
as teacher's new chalk, white
as a clean bedsheet. Smells
fresh. Isn't sweaty, hairy, doesn't stick
to skin. Doesn't hurt much
when she presses her small backbone
into it. The wall is steady
while she falls   away:
   first the hands   lost

arms dissolving   feet gone
   the legs   dis-   jointed
    body cracking down
      the center like a fault
       she falls inside
         slides down like
   dust   like kitchen dirt
          slips off
   the dustpan into
           noplace

  a place where
nothing happens,
nothing ever happened.

When she feels the cool
wall against her cheek
she doesn't want to
come back. Doesn't want to
think about it.
The wall is quiet, waiting.
It is tall like a promise
only better.

THIRTY-EIGHT

Clarence, William, Iron Mike, Tailhook, Senator Packwood, Spur Posse, Magic . . . and Us

Michael S. Kimmel

The 1990s may be remembered as the decade in which America took a crash course on male sexuality. From the national teach-in on sexual harassment that emerged from Clarence Thomas's confirmation hearings, to accusations about sexual harassment against Senator Robert Packwood, to the U.S. Navy Tailhook scandal, to Magic Johnson's revelation that he is infected with the HIV virus, to William Kennedy Smith's and Mike Tyson's date rape trials, to the trials of lacrosse players at St. John's University and high school athletes at Glen Ridge, New Jersey, we've had a steady discussion about male sexuality, about a sexuality that is more about predatory conquest than pleasure and connection.

And there's no end in sight—which explains the title of this essay. In the immediate aftermath of the Clarence Thomas confirmation hearings, the media claimed, as if with one voice, that the hearings would have a "chilling effect" on American women—that women would be far less likely to come forward and report incidents of sexual harassment for fear that they would be treated in the same shameful way as Anita Hill was by the Senate Judiciary Committee. Have the media ever been more wrong?

Since then, we've had less of a "chilling effect," and more of a national thaw, as women have come forward in record numbers to report cases of sexual harassment, date rape, and acquaintance rape. "Every woman has her Clarence Thomas," commented one woman, sadly surveying the workplace over the past two decades. In an op-ed essay in the *New York Times,* novelist Mary Lee Settle commented that Anita Hill had, "by her heroic stance, given not only me but thousands of women who have been silenced by shame the courage and the need to speak out about what we have tried for so long to bury and forget."

Currently, corporations, state and local governments, universities, and law firms are scrambling to implement procedures to handle sexual harassment. Most seem motivated more out of fear of lawsuits than out of general concern for women's experiences; thus, they are more interested in adjudicating harassment *after the fact* than in developing mechanisms to prevent it. In the same way, colleges and universities are developing strategies to handle the remarkable rise in date and acquaintance rape, although only a few are developing programs on prevention.

With more women coming forward now than ever before, many men have reacted defensively; "Men on Trial" has been the common headline linking Smith and Thomas in the media. But it's not *men* on trial here, it's *masculinity,* or, rather, a definition of masculinity that leads to certain behaviors that we now see as problematic and often physically threatening. Under prevailing definitions, men have been and are the "politically incorrect" sex.

But why have these issues emerged now? And why are issues such as sexual harassment and date rape the particular issues we're facing? Since it is certain that we will continue to face these issues for the rest of the decade, how can we understand these changes? And, most important, what can we do about it? How can we change the meanings of masculinity so that sexual harassment and date rape will disappear from our workplaces and our relationships?

The Social Construction of Male Sexuality

To speak of transforming masculinity is to begin with the way men are sexual in our culture. As social scientists now understand, sexuality is less a product of biological urges and more about the meanings that we attach to those urges, meanings that vary dramatically across cultures, over time, and among a variety of social groups within any particular culture. Sexual beings are made, not born. John Gagnon, a well-known theoretician of this approach, argues in his book *Human Sexualities* that

> people learn when they are quite young a few of the things that they are expected to be, and continue slowly to accumulate a belief in who they are and ought to be through the rest of childhood, adolescence, and adulthood. Sexual conduct is learned in the same ways and through the same processes; it is acquired and assembled in human interaction, judged and performed in specific cultural and historical worlds.

And the major item in that assemblage, the chief building block in the social construction of sexuality, is gender. We experience our sexual selves through a gendered prism. The meanings of sex to women and to men are very, very different. There really are a "his" and "hers" when it comes to sex. Just one example: think about the difference in the way we view a man or a woman who has a lot of different partners—the difference, say, between a stud and a slut.

The rules of masculinity and femininity are strictly enforced. And difference equals power. The difference between male and female sexuality reproduces men's power over women, and, simultaneously, the power of some men over other men, especially of the dominant, hegemonic form of manhood—white, straight, middle-class—over marginalized masculinities. Those who dare to cross over—women who are sexually adventurous and men who are sexually passive—risk being seen as *gender,* not sexual, nonconformists. And we all know how homophobia links gender nonconformity to homosexuality. The stakes are high if you don't play along.

Sexual behavior confirms manhood. It makes men feel manly. Robert Brannon has identified the four traditional rules of American manhood: (1) No Sissy Stuff: Men can never do anything that even remotely suggests femininity. Manhood is a relentless repudiation and devaluation of the feminine. (2) Be a Big Wheel: Manhood is measured by power, wealth, and success. Whoever has the most toys when he dies, wins. (3) Be a Sturdy Oak: Manhood depends on emotional reserve. Dependability in a crisis requires that men not reveal their feelings. (4) Give 'em Hell: Exude an aura of manly daring and aggression. Go for it. Take risks.

These four rules lead to a sexuality built around accumulating partners (scoring), emotional distance, and risk taking. In locker rooms and on playgrounds across the country, men are taught that the goal of every encounter with women is to score. Men are supposed to be ever ready for sex, constantly seeking sex, and constantly seeking to escalate every encounter so that intercourse will result, since, as one of my students once noted, "It doesn't count unless you put it in."

The emotional distancing of the sturdy oak is considered necessary for adequate male sexual functioning, but it leads to some strange behaviors. For example, to keep from ejaculating "too soon," men may devise a fascinating array of distractions, such as counting, doing multiplication tables in their heads, or thinking about sports.

Risk taking is a centerpiece of male sexuality. Sex is about adventure, excitement, danger. Taking chances. Responsibility is a word that seldom turns up in male sexual discourse. And this of course has serious medical side effects; the possibilities include STDs, impregnation, and AIDS — currently the most gendered disease in American history.

To rein in this constructed male "appetite," women have been assigned the role of asexual gatekeeper; women decide, metaphorically and literally, who enters the desired garden of earthly delights, and who doesn't. Women's sexual agency, women's sense of entitlement to desire, is drowned out by the incessant humming of male desire, propelling him ever forward. A man's job is to wear down her resistance. One fraternity at a college I was lecturing at last year offered seminars to pledges on dating etiquette that appropriated the book of business advice called *Getting to Yes.*

Sometimes that hum can be so loud that it drowns out the actual voice of the real live woman that he's with. Men suffer from socialized deafness, a hearing impairment that strikes only when women say "no."

Who Are the Real Sexual Revolutionaries?

Of course, a lot has changed along the frontiers of the sexual landscape in the past two decades. We've had a sexual revolution, after all. But as the dust is settling from the sexual revolution, what emerges in unmistakably fine detail is that it's been women, not men, who are our era's real sexual pioneers. Of course, we men like to think that the sexual revolution, with its promises of more access to more partners with less emotional commitment, was tailor-made for male sexuality's fullest flowering. But in fact it's been women's sexuality that's changed in the past two decades, not men's. Women now feel capable, even *entitled,* to sexual pleasure. They have learned to say "yes" to their own desires, claiming their own sexual agency.

And men? We're still dancing the same tired dance of the sexual conquistadors. Look, for a minute, at that new late-night game show "Studs." Here are the results of the sexual revolution in media miniature. The men and women all date one another, and from implicit innuendo to explicit guffaws, one assumes that every couple has gone to bed. What's not news is that the men are joking about it; what *is* news is that the women are equally capable of it.

Now some might argue that this simply confirms that women can have "male sex," that male sexuality was victorious because we've convinced women to be more like us. But then why are so many men wilting in the face of desiring women? Why are the offices of sex therapists crammed with men who complain not of premature ejaculation (the most common sexual problem twenty years ago — a sexual problem that involves being a bit overeager) but of what therapists euphemistically call "inhibited desire." That is, these men don't want to have sex now that all these women are able to claim their sexual rights.

Date Rape and Sexual Predation, Aggression, and Entitlement

As women have claimed the right to say "yes," they've also begun to assert their rights to say "no." Women are now demanding that men be more sexually responsible and are holding men accountable for their sexual behaviors. It is women who have changed the rules of sexual conduct. What used to be (and in many places still is) called male sexual etiquette—forcing a woman to have sex when she says no, conniving, coercing, pushing, ignoring efforts to get you to stop, getting her so drunk that she loses the ability (or consciousness) that one needs to give consent—is now defined as date rape.

In one recent study, by psychologist Mary Koss at the University of Arizona, forty-five percent of all college women said that they had had some form of sexual contact against their will. A full twenty-five percent had been pressed or forced to have sexual intercourse against their will. And Patricia Bowman, who went home with William Kennedy Smith from Au Bar in Palm Beach, Florida, knows all about those statistics. She testified that when she told Smith that she'd called her friends, and she was going to call the police, he responded, "You shouldn't have done that. Nobody's going to believe you." And, indeed, the jury didn't. I did.

I also believed that the testimony of three other women who claimed they were sexually assaulted by Smith should have been allowed in the trial. Such testimony would have established a pattern not of criminal assault, but of Smith's obvious belief in sexual *entitlement,* that he was entitled to press his sexual needs on women despite their resistance, because he didn't particularly care what they felt about it.

And Desiree Washington knows all about men who don't listen when a woman says no. Mike Tyson's aggressive masculinity in the boxing ring was sadly translated into a vicious misogyny with his ex-wife Robin Givens and a predatory sexuality, as evidenced by his behavior with Desiree Washington. Tyson's "grandiose sense of entitlement, fueled by the insecurities and emotions of adolescence," as writer Joyce Carol Oates put it, led to a behavior with women that was as out of control as his homosocial behavior inside the ring.

Tyson's case underscores our particular fascination with athletes, and the causal equation we make between athletes and sexual aggression. From the St. John's University lacrosse team, to Glen Ridge, New Jersey, high school athletes, to dozens of athletic teams and individual players at campuses across the nation, we're getting the message that our young male athletes, trained for fearless aggression on the field, are translating that into a predatory sexual aggression in relationships with women. Columnist Robert Lipsyte calls it the "varsity syndrome—winner take all, winning at any cost, violence as a tool, aggression as a mark of masculinity." The very qualities we seek in our athletes are exactly the qualities we do not want in young men today. Rather, we want to encourage respect for others, compassion, the ability to listen, and attention to process rather than the end goal. Our task is to make it clear that what we want from our athletes when they are on the playing field is *not* the same as what we want from them when they are playing the field.

I think, though, that athletes only illustrate a deeper problem: the problem of men in groups. Most athletes play on teams, so much of their social life and much of a player's public persona is constructed through association with his teammates. Another homosocial preserve, fraternities, are the site of most gang rapes that occur on college campuses, according to psychologist Chris O'Sullivan, who has been studying gang rape for several years. At scores of campus and corporate workshops over the past five years, women have shared the complaint that, while individual men may appear sympathetic when they are alone with women, they suddenly turn out to be macho louts capable of the vilest misogynistic statements when they are in groups of men. The members of the U.S. Navy Tailhook Association are quite possibly decent, law-abiding family men when they are alone or with their families. But put them together at a convention, and they become a marauding gang of hypermasculine thugs who should be prosecuted for felonious assault, not merely slapped on their collective wrists.

I suppose it's true that the members of Spur Posse, a group of relatively affluent Southern California adolescent boys, are also "regular guys." Which makes their sexual predation and homosocial competition as chilling as it is revealing of something at the heart of American masculinity. Before a large group of young women and girls — one as young as ten! — came forward to claim that members of Spur Posse had sexually assaulted and raped them, these guys would have been seen as typical high school fellas. Members of the group competed with one another to have sex with the most girls and kept elaborately coded scores of their exploits by referring to various athletes' names as a way of signifying the number of conquests. Thus a reference to "Reggie Jackson" would refer to 44, the number on his jersey, while "David Robinson" would signify 50 different conquests. In this way, the boys could publicly compete with one another without the young women understanding that they were simply the grounds for homosocial competition.

When some of these young women accused the boys of assault and rape, many residents of their affluent suburb were shocked. The boys' mothers, particularly, winced when they heard that their fifteen-year-old sons had had sex with 44 or 50 girls. A few expressed outrage. But the boys' fathers glowed with pride. "That's my boy," they declared in chorus. They accused the girls of being sluts. And we wonder where the kids get it from?

Spur Posse is only the most recent example of the way masculine sexual entitlement is offered to boys as part of their birthright. Transforming a rape culture is going to mean transforming a view of women as the vessels through which men can compete with one another, trying to better their positions on the homosocial ladders of success and status.

What is it about groups that seems to bring out the worst in men? I think it is because the animating condition for most American men is a deeply rooted fear of other men — a fear that other men will view us as less than manly. The fear of humiliation, of losing in a competitive ranking among men, of being dominated by other men — these are the fears that keep men in tow and that reinforce traditional definitions of masculinity as a false definition of safety. Homophobia (which I understand as more than the fear of homosexual men; it's also the fear of other men) keeps men acting like men, keeps men exaggerating their adherence to traditional norms, so that no other men will get the idea that we might really be that most dreaded person: the sissy.

Men's fear of being judged a failure as a man in the eyes of other men leads to a certain homosocial element within the heterosexual encounter: men often will use their sexual conquest as a form of currency to gain status among other men. Such homosocial competition contributes to the strange hearing impairment that men experience in any sexual encounter, a socialized deafness that leads us to hear "no " as "yes," to escalate the encounter, to always go for it, to score. And this is occurring just at the moment when women are, themselves, learning to say "yes" to their own sexuality, to say "yes" to their own desire for sexual pleasure. Instead of our socialized deafness, we need to become what Langston Hughes called "articulate listeners": we need to trust women when they tell us what they want, and when they want it, and what they don't want as well. If we listen when women say "no," then they will feel more trusting and open to saying "yes" when they feel that. And we need to listen to our own inner voices, our own desires and needs. Not the voices that are about compulsively proving something that cannot be proved, but the voices that are about connection with another and the desires and passions that may happen between two equals.

Escalating a sexual encounter beyond what a woman may want is date rape, not sex; it is one of the most important issues we will face in the 1990s. It is transforming the sexual landscape as earlier sexual behaviors are being reevaluated in light of new ideas about sexual politics. We have to explore the meaning of the word *consent,* explore our own understandings, and make sure that these definitions are in accord with women's definitions.

From the Bedroom to the Boardroom

Just as women have been claiming the right to say "yes" and demanding the right to say "no" and have it listened to and respected in the sexual arena, they've also transformed the public arena, the workplace. As with sexuality, the real revolution in the past thirty years has been women's dramatic entry into the labor force in unprecedented numbers. Almost half of the labor force is female. I often demonstrate this point to my classes by asking the women who intend to have careers to raise their hands. All do. Then I ask them to keep their hands raised if their mothers have had a career outside the home for more than ten years. Half put their hands down. Then I ask them to keep their hands raised if their grandmothers had a career for ten years. Virtually no hands remain raised. In three generations, they can visibly see the difference in women's working lives. Women are in the work force to stay, and men had better get used to having them around.

That means that the cozy boy's club — another homosocial arena — has been penetrated by women. And this, just when that arena is more suffused with doubt and anxieties than ever before. We are, after all, a downwardly mobile culture. Most Americans are less successful now than their parents were at the same age. It now takes two incomes to provide the same standard of living that one income provided about a generation ago. And most of us in the middle class cannot afford to buy the houses in which we were brought up. Since men derive their identity in the public sphere, and the primary public arena where masculinity is demonstrated is the workplace, this is an important issue. There are fewer and fewer big wheels and more and more men who will feel as though they haven't made the grade, who will feel damaged, injured, powerless — men who will need to demonstrate their masculinity all over again. Suddenly, men's fears of humiliation and domination are out in the open, and there's a convenient target at which to vent those anxieties.

And now, here come women into the workplace in unprecedented numbers. It now seems virtually impossible that a man will go through his entire working life without having a woman colleague, co-worker, or boss. Just when men's economic bread-winner status is threatened, women appear on the scene as easy targets for men's anger. Thus sexual harassment in the workplace is a distorted effort to put women back in their place, to remind women that they are not equal to men in the workplace, that they are still just women, even if they are in the workplace.

It seems to me that this is the context in which to explore the meaning of sexual harassment in our society. The Clarence Thomas confirmation hearings afford men a rare opportunity to do some serious soul searching. What is sexual harassment about? And why should men help put an end to it?

One thing that sexual harassment is usually *not* about, although you couldn't convince the Senate Judiciary Committee of this, is a matter of one person telling the truth and the other person lying. Sexual harassment cases are difficult and confusing precisely because there are often a multiplicity of truths. "His" truth might be what appears to him as an innocent indication of sexual interest by harmless joking with the "boys in the office" (even if those "boys" happen to include women workers). "Her" truth is that those seemingly innocent remarks cause stress and anxiety about promotion, firing, and sexual pressure.

Judge Thomas asserted during the course of his testimony that "at no time did I become aware, either directly or indirectly, that she felt I had said or done anything to change the cordial nature of our relationship." And there is no reason to assume that he would have been aware of it. But that doesn't mean his words or actions did not have the effect that Professor Hill states, only that she was successful in concealing the resulting trauma from him — a concealment that women have carefully developed over the years in the workplace.

Why should this surprise us? Women and men often experience the same event differently. Men experience their behavior from the perspective of those who have power, women from the perspective of those upon whom that power is exercised.

If an employer asks an employee for a date, and she declines, perhaps he has forgotten about it by the time he gets to the parking lot. No big deal, he says to himself. You ask someone out, and she says "no." You forget about it. In fact, repairing a wounded male ego often *requires* that you forget about it. But the female employee? She's now frozen, partly with fear. What if I said yes? Would I have gotten promoted? Would he have expected more than a date? Will I now get fired? Will someone else get promoted over me? What should I do? And so, she will do what millions of women do in that situation: she calls her friends, who counsel her to let the matter rest and get on with her work. And she remembers for a long, long time. Who, therefore, is likely to have a better memory: those in power or those against whom that power is deployed?

This is precisely the divergence in experience that characterizes the controversies spinning around Senator Bob Packwood. Long a public supporter of women's causes, Senator Packwood also apparently chased numerous women around office desks, clumsily trying to have affairs with them. He claims, now, that alcoholism caused this behavior and that he doesn't remember. It's a good thing that the women remember. They often do.

Sexual harassment is particularly volatile because it often fuses two levels of power: the power of employers over employees and the power of men over women. Thus what may be said or intended as a man to a woman is also experienced in the context of superior and subordinate, or vice versa. Sexual harassment in the workplace results from men using their public position to demand or exact social relationships. It is the confusion of public and private, bringing together two arenas of men's power over women. Not only are men in positions of power in the workplace, but we are socialized to be the sexual initiators and to see sexual prowess as a confirmation of masculinity.

Sexual harassment is also a way to remind women that they are not yet equals in the workplace, that they really don't belong there. Harassment is most frequent in those occupations and workplaces where women are new and in the minority, like surgeons, firefighters, and investment bankers. "Men see women as invading a masculine environment," says Louise Fitzgerald, a University of Illinois psychologist. "These are guys whose sexual harassment has nothing whatever to do with sex. They're trying to scare women off a male preserve."

When the power of men is augmented by the power of employer over employee, it is easy to understand how humiliating and debilitating sexual harassment can be, and how individual women would be frightened about seeking redress. The workplace is not a level playing field. Subordinates rarely have the resources to complain against managers, whatever the problem.

Some men were confused by Professor Hill's charges, others furious about sexual harassment because it feels as though women are changing the rules. What used to be routine behavior for men in the workplace is now being called sexual harassment. "Clarence Thomas didn't do anything wrong that any American male hasn't done," commented Dale Whitcomb, a thirty-two-year-old machinist. How right he was. The fact that two-thirds of men surveyed said they would be complimented if they were propositioned by a woman at work gives some idea of the vast gulf between women's and men's perceptions of workplace sexual conduct.

Although men surely do benefit from sexual harassment, I believe that we also have a stake in ending it. First, our ability to form positive and productive relationships with women colleagues in the workplace is undermined by it. So long as sexual harassment is a daily occurrence and women are afraid

of their superiors in the workplace, innocent men's behaviors may be misinterpreted. Second, men's ability to develop social and sexual relationships that are both ethical and exciting is also compromised. If a male boss dates a subordinate, can he really trust that the reason she is with him is because she *wants* to be? Or will there always be a lingering doubt that she is there because she is afraid not to be or because she seeks to please him because of his position?

Currently, law firms and corporations all over the country are scrambling to implement sexual harassment policies, to make sure that sexual harassment will be recognized and punished. But our challenge is greater than admonition and post hoc counseling. Our challenge will be to prevent sexual harassment *before* it happens. And that means working with men. Men must come to see that these are not women who happen to be in the workplace (where, by this logic, they actually don't belong), but workers who happen to be women. And we'll need to change the meaning of success so that men don't look back at their careers when they retire and wonder what it was all for, whether any of it was worth it. Again, we'll need to change the definition of masculinity, dislodging it from these misshapen public enactments, including the capacity to embrace others as equals within it, because of an inner security and confidence that can last a lifetime. It is more important than ever to begin to listen to women, to listen with a compassion that understands that women's and men's experiences are different, and an understanding that men, too, can benefit from the elimination of sexual harassment.

AIDS as a Men's Disease

Surely, men will benefit from the eradication of AIDS. Although we are used to discussing AIDS as a disease of gay men and IV drug users, I think we need to see AIDS as a men's disease. Over ninety percent of all AIDS patients are men; AIDS is now the leading cause of death for men aged thirty-three to forty-five nationwide. AIDS is American men's number one health problem, and yet we rarely treat it as a men's issue. But AIDS is also the most gender-linked disease in American history. No other disease has attacked one gender so disproportionately, except those to which only one sex is susceptible, such as hemophilia or uterine or prostrate cancer. AIDS *could* affect both men and women equally (and in Africa that seems to be closer to the case). But in the United States, AIDS patients are overwhelmingly men.

(Let me be clear that in no way am I saying that one should not be compassionate for women AIDS patients. Of course one must recognize that women are as likely to get AIDS from engaging in the same high risk behaviors as men. But that's precisely my point. Women don't engage in those behaviors at rates anything like men.)

One is put at risk for AIDS by engaging in specific high-risk behaviors, activities that ignore potential health risks for more immediate pleasures. For example, sharing needles is both a defiant flaunting of health risks and an expression of community among IV drug users. And the capacity for high-risk sexual behaviors—unprotected anal intercourse with a large number of partners, the ability to take it, despite any potential pain—are also confirmations of masculinity.

And so is accumulation—of money, property, or sexual conquests. It's curious that one of America's most lionized heroes, Magic Johnson, doesn't seem to have been particularly compassionate about the possibility of infection of the twenty-five hundred women he reported that he slept with. Johnson told *Sports Illustrated* that as a single man, he tried to "accommodate as many women as I could, most of them through unprotected sex." Accommodate? When he protested that his words were misunderstood, he told the *New York Times*, "I was a bachelor, and I lived a bachelor's life. And I'm paying the price for it. But you know I respect women to the utmost." (I suppose that Wilt Chamberlain, who boasted in his autobiography that he slept with over twenty thousand women, respected them almost ten times as much.)

As sociologists have long understood, stigmatized gender identity often leads to exaggerated forms of gender-specific behavior. Thus, those whose masculinity is least secure are precisely those most likely to enact behavioral codes and hold fast to traditional definitions of masculinity. In social science research, hypermasculinity as compensation for insecure gender identity has been used to explain the propensity for homophobia, authoritarianism, racism, anti-Semitism, juvenile delinquency, and urban gangs.

Gay men and IV drug users—the two largest risk groups—can be seen in this light, although for different reasons. The traditional view of gay men is that they are not "real men." Most of the stereotypes revolve around effeminacy, weakness, passivity. But following the Stonewall riots of 1969, in which gay men fought back against a police raid on a gay bar in Greenwich Village, New York, and the subsequent birth of the Gay Liberation Movement, a new gay masculinity emerged in major cities. The "clone," as the new gay man was called, dressed in hypermasculine garb (flannel shirts, blue jeans, leather); and short hair (not at all androgynous) and a mustache; and was athletic, highly muscular. In short, the clone looked more like a "real man" than most straight men.

And the clones—who comprised roughly one-third of all gay men living in the major urban enclaves of the 1970s—enacted a hypermasculine sexuality in steamy back rooms, bars, and bathhouses, where sex was plentiful, anonymous, and very hot. No unnecessary foreplay, romance, or post-coital awkwardness. Sex without attachment. One might even say that, given the norms of masculinity (that men are always seeking sex, ready for sex, wanting sex), gay men were the only men in America who were getting as much sex as they wanted. Predictably, high levels of sexual activity led to high levels of sexually transmitted diseases, such as gonorrhea, among the clones. But no one could have predicted AIDS.

Among IV drug users, we see a different pattern, but with some similar outcomes when seen from a gender perspective. The majority of IV drug users are African-American and Latino, two groups for whom the traditional avenues of successful manhood are blocked by poverty and racism. More than half of the black men between eighteen and twenty-five in our cities are unemployed, and one in four are in some way involved with the penal system (in jail, on probation, under arrest). We thus have an entire generation structurally prevented from demonstrating its manhood in that most traditional of ways—as breadwinners.

The drug culture offers an alternative. Dealing drugs can provide an income to support a family as well as the opportunity for manly risks and adventure. The community of drug users can confirm gender identity; the sharing of needles is a demonstration of that solidarity. And the ever-present risk of death by overdose takes hypermasculine bravado to its limits.

Who Asked for It?

The victims of men's adherence to these crazy norms of masculinity—AIDS patients, rape victims, victims of sexual harassment—did not become victims intentionally. They did not "ask for it," and they certainly do not deserve blame. That some women today are also sexual predators, going to swank bars or waiting outside athletes' locker rooms or trying to score with male subordinates at work, doesn't make William Kennedy Smith, Mike Tyson, Magic Johnson, or Clarence Thomas any less predatory. When predatory animals threaten civil populations, we warn the population to stay indoors, until the wild animals can be caught and recaged. When it's men on the prowl, women engage in a voluntary curfew, unless they want to risk being attacked.

And the men—the date rapists, the sexual harassers, the AIDS patients—are not "perverts" or "deviants" who have strayed from the norms of masculinity. They are, if anything, overconformists to destructive norms of male sexual behavior. Until we change the meaning of manhood, sexual risk-taking and conquest will remain part of the rhetoric of masculinity. And we will scatter the victims, both women and men, along the wayside as we rush headlong towards a testosterone-infected oblivion.

The Sexual Politics of Safety

What links the struggle against sexual harassment, date and acquaintance rape, and AIDS is that preventing all of them require that *safety* become the central term, an organizing principle of men's relationships with women, as well as with other men. The politics of safety may be the missing link in the transformation of men's lives, in their capacity for change. Safety is more than the absence of danger, although that wouldn't be such a bad thing itself. Safety is pro-active, the creation of a space in which all people, women and men, gay and straight, and of all colors, can experience and express the fullness of their beings.

Think for a moment about how the politics of safety affects the three areas I have discussed in this essay. What is the best way to prevent AIDS? To use sterile needles for intravenous drug injections and to practice "safer sex." Sterile needles and safer sex share one basic characteristic: they both require that

men act responsibly. This is not one of the cardinal rules of manhood. Safer sex programs encourage men to have fewer partners, to avoid certain particularly dangerous practices, and to use condoms when having any sex that involves the exchange of bodily fluids. In short, safer sex programs encourage men to stop having sex like men. To men, you see, "safer sex" is an oxymoron, one of those juxtapositions of terms that produce a nonsensical outcome. That which is sexy is not safe, that which is safe is not sexy. Sex is about danger, risk, excitement; safety is about comfort, softness, and security.

Seen this way, it is not surprising to find, as some researchers have found, that one-fourth of urban gay men report that they have not changed their unsafe sexual behaviors. What is, in fact, astonishing is that slightly more than three-fourths *have* changed and are now practicing safer sex.

What heterosexual men could learn from the gay community's response to AIDS is how to eroticize that responsibility—something that women have been trying to teach men for decades. Making safer sex into sexy sex has been one of the great transformations of male sexuality accomplished by the gay community. And straight men could also learn a thing or two about caring for one another through illness, supporting one another in grief, and maintaining a resilience in the face of a devastating disease and the callous indifference of the larger society.

Safety is also the animating condition for women's expression of sexuality. While safety may be a turn-off for men (comfort, softness, and security are the terms of postorgasmic detumescence, not sexual arousal), safety is a precondition for sexual agency for women. Only when women feel safe can they give their sexuality full expression. For men, hot sex leaves a warm afterglow; for women, warmth builds to heat, but warmth is not created by heat.

This perspective helps explain that curious finding in the sex research literature about the divergence of women's and men's sexualities as they age. We believe that men reach their sexual peak at around eighteen, and then go into steady, and later more precipitous, decline for the rest of their lives; while women hit their sexual stride closer to thirty, with the years between twenty-seven and thirty-eight as their peak years. Typically, we understand these changes as having to do with differences in biology—that hormonal changes find men feeling soft and cuddly just as women are getting all steamed up. But aging does not produce such changes in every culture; that is, biology doesn't seem to work the same way everywhere.

What biological explanations leave out is the way that men's and women's sexualities are related to each other, and the way that both are shaped by the institution of marriage. Marriage makes one's sexuality more predictable — the partner, the timing, the experience — and it places sex *always* in the context of the marital relationship. Marriage makes sex safer. No wonder women find their sexuality heightening — they finally feel safe enough to allow their sexual desires to be expressed. And no wonder men's sexuality deflates — there's no danger, risk or excitement left.

Safety is a precondition for women's sexual expression. Only when a woman is certain, beyond the shadow of a doubt, that her "no" means "no," can she ever say "yes" to her own sexual desires. So if we men are going to have the sexual relationships with exciting, desiring women that we say we want, then we have to make the environment safe enough for women to express their desires. We have to make it absolutely certain to a woman that her "no" means "no" — no matter how urgently we feel the burning of our own desires.

To do this we will need to transform the definition of what it means to be a real man. But we have to work fast. AIDS is spreading rapidly, and date rape and sexual harassment are epidemic in the nation's colleges and workplaces. As AIDS spreads, and as women speak up about these issues, there are more and more people who need our compassion and support. Yet compassion is in relatively short supply among American men, since it involves the capacity of taking the role of the other, of seeing ourselves in someone else's shoes, a quality that contradicts the manly independence we have so carefully cultivated.

Sexual democracy, just like political democracy, relies on a balance between rights and responsibilities, between the claims of the individual and the claims of the community. When one discusses one's sexual rights — that each person, every woman and man, has an equal right to pleasure — men understand immediately what you mean. Women often look delighted and a little bit surprised. Add to the Bill of Sexual Rights a notion of responsibility, in which each of us treats sexual partners as if they had an integrity equal to our own, and it's the men who look puzzled. "Responsibility? What's that got to do with sex? I thought sex was about having fun."

Sure it is, but it's also political in the most intimate sense. Sexual democracy doesn't have to mean no sex. It means treating your partner as someone whose lust is equal to yours and also as someone whose life is equally valuable. It's about enacting in daily life one's principles, claiming our rights to pleasure, and making sure that our partners also feel safe enough to be able to fully claim theirs. This is what we demand for those who have come to America seeking refuge — safety — from political tyranny. Could we ask any less for those who are now asking for protection and refuge from millennia of sexual tyranny?

T H I R T Y - N I N E

◆◆◆

On Becoming Anti-Rapist

Haki R. Madhubuti

There are mobs & strangers in us who scream of the women we wanted and will get as if the women are ours for the taking.

. . . Male acculturation (or a better description would be males' "seasoning") is antifemale, antiwomanist/ feminist, and antireason when it comes to women's equal measure and place in society. This flawed socialization of men is not confined to the West but permeates most, if not all, cultures in the modern world. Most men have been taught to treat, respond, listen, and react to women from a male's point of view. Black men are not an exception here; we, too, are imprisoned with an intellectual/spiritual/sexual understanding of women based upon antiquated male culture and sexist orientation—or should I say miseducation. For example, sex or sexuality is hardly ever discussed, debated, or taught to black men in a nonthreatening or nonembarrassing family or community setting.

Men's view of women, specifically black women outside of the immediate family, is often one of "bitch," "my woman," "ho," or any number of designations that demean and characterize black women as less than whole and productive persons. Our missteps toward an understanding of women are compounded by the cultural environments where much of the talk of women takes place: street corners, locker rooms, male clubs, sporting events, bars, military service, business trips, playgrounds, workplaces, basketball courts, etc. Generally, women are not discussed on street corners or in bars as intellectual or culturally compatible partners. Rather the discussion focuses on what is the best way to "screw" or control them.

These are, indeed, learning environments that traditionally are not kind to women. The point of view that is affirmed all too often is the ownership of women. We are taught to see women as commodities and/or objects for men's sexual releases and sexual fantasies; also, most women are considered "inferiors" to men and thus are not to be respected or trusted. Such thinking is encouraged and legitimized by our culture and transmitted via institutional structures (churches, workplaces), mass media (*Playboy* and *Penthouse*), misogynist music (rap and mainstream), and R-rated and horror films that use exploitative images of women. And of course there are the ever-present, tall, trim, "Barbie-doll" women featured in advertising for everything from condoms to the latest diet "cures." Few men have been taught, really taught, from birth—to the heart, to the gut—to respect, value, or even, on occasion, to honor women. Only until very recently has it been confirmed in Western culture that rape (unwelcomed/uninvited sex) is criminal, evil, and antihuman.

> *our mothers, sisters, wives and*
> *daughters ceased to be the*
> *women men want we think of them as*
> *loving family music & soul bright wonderments.*

> *they are not locker room talk*
> *not the hunted lust or dirty*
> *cunt burnin hos.*
> *bright wonderments are excluded by association as*
> *blood & heart bone & memory*
> *& we will destroy a rapist's knee caps,*
> *& write early grave on his thoughts*
> *to protect them.*

Human proximity defines relationships. Exceptions should be noted, but in most cultures and most certainly within the black/African worldview, family and extended family ties are honored and respected. One's sexual personhood in a healthy culture is nurtured, respected, and protected. In trying to get a personal fix here, that is, an understanding of the natural prohibitions against rape, think of one's own personhood being violated. Think of one's own family subjected to this act. Think of the enslavement of African people; it was common to have breeding houses on most plantations where one's great-great-grandmothers were forced to open their insides for the sick satisfaction of white slave owners, overseers, and enslaved black men. This forced sexual penetration of African women led to the creation of mixed-race people here and around the world. There is a saying in South Africa that the colored race did not exist until nine months after white men arrived. This demeaning of black women and other women is amplified in today's culture, where it is not uncommon for young men to proclaim that "pussy is a penny a pound." However, we are told that such a statement is not meant for one's own mother, grandmother, sister, daughter, aunt, niece, close relative, or extended family. Yet the point must be made rather emphatically that incest (family rape) is on the rise in this country. Incest between adults and children is often not revealed until the children are adults. At that point their lives are so confused and damaged that many continue incestuous acts.

> *it will do us large to recall*
> *when the animal in us rises*
> *that all women are someone's*
> *mother, sister, wife, or daughter*
> *and are not fruit to be stolen when hungry.*

Part of the answer is found in the question: Is it possible or realistic to view all women as precious persons? Selective memory plays an important role here. Most men who rape are seriously ill and improperly educated. They do not view women outside of their "protected zone" as precious blood, do not see them as extended family, and do not see them as individuals or independent persons to be respected as most men respect other men. Mental illness or brain mismanagement blocks out reality, shattering and negating respect for self and others, especially the others of which one wishes to take advantage. Power always lurks behind rape. Rape is an act of aggression that asserts power by defaming and defiling. Most men have been taught—either directly or indirectly—to solve problems with force. Such force may be verbal or physical. Violence is the answer that is promoted in media everywhere, from Saturday morning cartoons to everyday television to R-rated films. Popular culture has a way of trivializing reality and confusing human expectations, especially with regard to relationships between men and women. For too many black people, the popular has been internalized. In many instances, the media define us, including our relationships to each other.

Women have been in the forefront of the anti-rape struggle. Much of this work has taken place in nontraditional employment, such as serving in police and fire departments, as top professors and administrators in higher education, as elected and appointed public servants in politics, and in the fields of medicine and law. However, the most pronounced presence and "advancement" of women has been seen in the military. We are told that the military, in terms of social development, remains at the cutting edge of changes, especially in the progress of blacks and female soldiers. However, according to Gary A. Warner in the *San Francisco Examiner* (December 30, 1992), the occurrence of rape against women in the military is far greater than in civilian life:

> A woman serving in the Army is 50 percent more likely to be raped than a civilian, newly released military records obtained by the Orange County Register show.
>
> From 1981 to 1987, 484 female soldiers were raped while on active duty, according to Department of the Army records released after a Freedom of Information Act request.

The Army rate of 129 rape cases per 100,000 population in 1990 exceeds nationwide statistics for the same year compiled by the FBI of 80 confirmed rape cases per 100,000 women. The 1990 statistics are the latest comparable ones available.

The brutality of everyday life continues to confirm the necessity for caring men and women to confront inhuman acts that cloud and prevent wholesome development. Much of what is defined as sexual "pleasure" today comes at the terrible expense of girls and often boys. To walk Times Square or any number of big city playgrounds after dark is to view how loudly the popular, throwaway culture has trapped, corrupted, and sexually abused too many of our children. In the United States the sexual abuse of runaway children, and children sentenced to foster care and poorly supervised orphanages, is nothing less than scandalous. The proliferation of battered women's shelters and the most recent revelation of the sexual abuse of women incarcerated in the nation's prisons only underscores the prevailing view of women by a substantial number of men, as sex objects for whatever sick acts that enter their minds.

Such abuse of children is not confined to the United States. Ron O'Grady, coordinator of the International Campaign to End Child Prostitution in Asiatic Tourism, fights an uphill battle to highlight the physical and economic maltreatment of children. Murray Kempton reminds us in his essay "A New Colonialism" (*New York Review of Books*, November 19, 1992) of Thailand's "supermarkets for the purchases of small and disposable bodies." He goes on to state that

> tourism is central to Thailand's developmental efforts; and the attractions of its ancient culture compare but meagerly to the compelling pull its brothels exercise upon foreign visitors. The government does its duty to the economy by encouraging houses of prostitution and pays its debt to propriety with its insistence that no more than 10,000 children work there. Private observers concerned with larger matters than the good name of public officials estimate the real total of child prostitutes in Thailand at 200,000.

The hunters . . . of children find no border closed. They have ranged into South China carrying television sets to swap one per child. The peasants who cursed the day a useless girl was born know better now: they can sell her for consumers overseas and be consumers themselves. Traffickers less adventurous stay at home and contrive travel agencies that offer cheap trips to Kuala Lumpur that end up with sexual enslavement in Japan or Malaysia.

That this state of affairs is not better known speaks loudly and clearly to the devaluation of female children. The war in Sarajevo, Bosnia, and Herzegovina again highlights the status of women internationally. In the rush toward ethnic cleansing and narrow and exclusive nationalism, Serbian soldiers have been indicted for murder and other war crimes. The story of one such soldier, Borislav Herak, is instructive. According to an article by John F. Burnes in the *New York Times* (November 27, 1992) entitled "A Serbian Fighter's Trial of Brutality," Mr. Herak and other soldiers were given the go-ahead to rape and kill Muslim women:

> The indictment lists 29 individual murders between June and October, including eight rape-murders of Muslim women held prisoner in an abandoned motel and cafe outside Vogosca, seven miles north of Sarajevo, where, Mr. Herak said, he and other Serbian fighters were encouraged to rape women and then take them away to kill them in hilltops and other deserted places.
>
> The indictment also covers the killings of at least 220 other Muslim civilians in which Mr. Herak has confessed to being a witness or taking part, many of them women and children. (Also see the January 4, 1993 issue of *Newsweek*.)

Much in the lives of women is not music or melody but is their dancing to the beat of the unhealthy and often killing drums of men and male teenagers. Rape is not the fault of women; however, in a male-dominated world, the victims are often put on the defensive and forced to rationalize their gender and their personhood.

Rape is not a reward for warriors
it is war itself

a deep, deep tearing, a dislocating of
the core of the womanself.
rape rips heartlessly
soul from spirit,
obliterating colors from beauty and body
replacing melody and music with
rat venom noise and uninterrupted intrusion and
*   beatings.*

The brutality of rape is universal. Most modern cultures — European, American, African, Asian, religious, and secular — grapple with this crime. Rarely is there discussion, and, more often than not, women are discouraged from being a part of the debates and edicts. Rape is cross-cultural. I have not visited, heard of, or read about any rape-free societies. The war against women is international. Daily, around the world, women fight for a little dignity and their earned place in the world. And men in power respond accordingly. For example, Barbara Crossette reported in the *New York Times* (April 7, 1991) about an incident in Batamaloo, Kashmir:

> In this conservative Muslim Society, women have moved to the forefront of demonstrations and also into guerrilla conclaves. No single event has contributed more to this rapidly rising militancy among women than reports of a gang rape a month ago by Indian troops in Kunan, a remote village in northwestern Kashmir.
>
> According to a report filed by S. M. Yasin, district magistrate in Kupwara, the regional center, the armed forces "behaved like violent beasts." He identified them as members of the Fourth Rajputana Rifles and said that they rampaged through the village from 11 P.M. on Feb. 23 until 9 the next morning.
>
> "A large number of armed personnel entered into the houses of villagers and at gunpoint they gang-raped 23 ladies, without any consideration of their age, married, unmarried, pregnancy etc.," he wrote. "There was a hue and cry in the whole village." Local people say that as many as 100 women were molested in some way.

As a man of Afrikan descent, I would like to think that Afrikans have some special insight, enlightened hearts, or love in us that calms us in such times of madness. But my romanticism is shattered every day as I observe black communities across this land. The number of rapes reported and unreported in our communities is only the latest and most painful example of how far we have drifted from beauty. However, it is seldom that I have hurt more than when I learned about the "night of terror" that occurred in Meru, Kenya, on July 13, 1991, at the St. Kizito boarding school. A high school protest initiated by the boys, in which the girls refused to join, resulted in a night of death, rapes, and beatings unparalleled in modern Kenya, in Africa or in the world. As Timothy Dwyer reported in the *Chicago Tribune* (April 18, 1991):

> The night of terror a month ago at the boarding school near Mount Kenya has torn the soul of the Kenyan people. What had the girls done to invoke the wrath of their male schoolmates? They dared say no to the boys, who wanted them to join a protest against the school's headmaster, according to police and to those girls who lived through the night.
>
> In Kenya, one-party rule has resulted in a tyranny of the majority. Dissent, even in politics, is not welcome. "Here, the minority must always go along with the majority's wishes," said a businessman who has done a lot of work with the government in the last 15 years and asked not to be named. "And it is said that a woman cannot say no to a man."
>
> Woman's groups have said the rapes and deaths were an extreme metaphor for what goes on in the Kenyan society. The girls of St. Kizito dared to say no to the boys, and 19 paid with their lives while 71 others were beaten and raped. . . .
>
> There have been many school protests in Kenya this year. This summer alone, some 20 protests have turned into riots resulting in the destruction of school property. There have been rapes at other schools when girls have refused to join boys in their protests.

A growing part of the answer is that we men, as difficult as it may seem, must view all women (no matter who they are — race, culture, religion, or nationality aside) as extended family. The question is, and I know that I am stretching: Would we rape our mothers, grandmothers, sisters, or other female relatives, or even give such acts a thought? Can we extend this attitude to all women? Therefore we must:

1. Teach our sons that it is their responsibility to be anti-rapist; that is, they must be counter-rapist in thought, conversations, raps, organizations, and actions.

2. Teach our daughters how to defend themselves and maintain an uncompromising stance toward men and boys.

3. Understand that being a counter-rapist is honorable, manly, and necessary for a just society.

4. Understand that anti-rapist actions are part of the black tradition; being an anti-rapist is in keeping with the best Afrikan culture and with Afrikan family and extended family configurations. Even in times of war we were known to honor and respect the personhood of children and women.

5. Be glowing examples of men who are fighting to treat women as equals and to be fair and just in associations with women. This means at the core that families as now defined and constructed must continually be reassessed. In today's economy most women, married and unmarried, must work. We men must encourage them in their work and must be intimately involved in rearing children and doing housework.

6. Understand that just as men are different from one another, women also differ; therefore we must try not to stereotype women into the limiting and often debilitating expectations of men. We must encourage and support them in their searching and development.

7. Be unafraid of independent, intelligent, and self-reliant women. And by extension, understand that intelligent women think for themselves and may not want to have sex with a particular man. This is a woman's prerogative and is not a comment on anything else other than the fact that she does not want to have sex.

8. Be bold and strong enough to stop other men (friends or strangers) from raping and to intervene in a rape in process with the fury and destruction of a hurricane against the rapist.

9. Listen to women. Listen to women, especially to womanist/feminist/Pan-Africanist philosophies of life. Also, study the writings of women, especially black women.

10. Act responsibly in response to the listening and studying. Be a part of and support anti-rape groups for boys and men. Introduce anti-rape discussion into men's groups and organizations.

11. Never stop growing, and understand that growth is limited and limiting without the input of intelligent women.

12. Learn to love. Study love. Even if one is at war, love and respect, respect and love must conquer, if there is to be a sane and livable world. Rape is anti-love, anti-respect. Love is not easy. One does not fall in love but *grows* into love.

We can put to rest the rape problem in one generation if its eradication is as important to us as our cars, jobs, careers, sport-games, beer, and quest for power. However, the women who put rape on the front burners must continue to challenge us and their own cultural training, and position themselves so that they and their messages are not compromised or ignored.

A significant few of their
fathers, brothers, husbands, sons
and growing strangers
are willing to unleash harm onto the earth
and spill blood in the eyes
of
maggots in running shoes
who do not know the sounds of birth
or respect the privacy of the human form

If we are to be just in our internal rebuilding, we must challenge tradition and cultural ways of life that relegate women to inferior status in the home, church/mosque/temple, workplace, political life, and education. Men are not born rapists; we are taught

very subtly, often in unspoken ways, that women are ours for the taking. Generally, such teachings begin with the family. Enlightenment demands fairness, impartiality, and vision; it demands confrontation of outdated definitions and acceptance of fair and just resolutions. One's sex, race, social class, or wealth should not determine entitlements or justice. If we are honest, men must be in the forefront of eradicating sex stereotypes in all facets of private and public life. I think that being honest, as difficult and as self-incriminating as it may be, is the only way that we can truly liberate ourselves. If men can liberate themselves (with the help of women) from the negative aspects of the culture that produced them, maybe a just, fair, good, and liberated society is possible in our lifetime.

The liberation of the male psyche from preoccupation with domination, power hunger, control, and absolute rightness requires an honest and fair assessment of patriarchal culture. This requires commitment to deep study, combined with a willingness for painful, uncomfortable, and often shocking change. We are not where we should be. That is why rape exists; why families are so easily formed and just as easily dissolved; why children are confused and abused; why our elderly are discarded, abused, and exploited; and why teenage boys create substitute families (gangs) that terrorize their own communities.

I remain an optimistic realist, primarily because I love life and most of what it has to offer. I often look at my children and tears come to my eyes because I realize how blessed I am to be their father. My wife and the other women in my life are special because they know that they are special and have taken it upon themselves, at great cost, to actualize their dreams, making what was considered for many of them unthinkable a few years ago a reality today. If we men, of all races, cultures, and continents would just examine the inequalities of power in our own families, businesses, and political and spiritual institutions, and decide today to reassess and reconfigure them in consultation with the women in our lives, we would all be doing the most fundamental corrective act of a counter-rapist.

It is indeed significant, and not an arbitrary aside, that males and females are created biologically different. These profound differences are partially why we are attracted to each other and are also what is beautiful about life. But too often due to hierarchical and patriarchal definitions one's sex also relegates one to a position in life that is not necessarily respected. Sex should not determine moral or economic worth, as it now does in too many cultures. In a just society, one's knowledge and capabilities, that is, what one is actually able to contribute to the world, are more valuable than if the person is male or female.

Respect for the women closest to us can give us the strength and knowledge to confront the animal in us with regard to the women we consider "others." Also, keep in mind that the "others" often are the women closest to us. If we honestly confront the traditions and histories that have shaped us, we may come to realize that women should be encouraged to go as far as their intellect and talents will take them—burdened only by the obstacles that affect all of us. Most certainly the sexual energies of men must be checked before our misguided

maleness manifests itself in the most horrible of crimes—rape.

> *No!*
> *Means No!*
> *even when men think*
> *that they are "god's gift to women"*
> *even after dropping a week's check & more*
> *on dinner by the ocean,*
> *the four tops, temptations and intruders memory*
>   *tour,*
> *imported wine & rose that captured her smile,*
> *suggested to you private music & low lights*
> *drowning out her inarticulated doubts.*
>
> *Question the thousand years teachings*
> *crawling through your lower depths and*
> *don't let your little head*
> *out think your big head.*
> *No! means No!*
> *even when her signals suggest yes.*

FORTY

Sisters in Okinawa[*]

Suzuyo Takazato

Women in Okinawa have a different identity from "Hondo women"—who live on the main islands of Japan—and this difference is deeply rooted in the history of Okinawa. Okinawa, which was formerly the Ryukyu Kingdom, has only recently been part of Japan. It was just 390 years ago that it was invaded by a clan from Satsuma, and some 120 years ago, in 1872, that it was formally annexed by Japan's Meiji government. Okinawa has managed to maintain a

unique tradition and culture which include performances and handicrafts that have been inherited over its history of cultural and commercial exchanges with China and other Asian countries.

The distance between women in Okinawa and those of the Hondo is rooted in their experiences and how they survived World War II and the postwar era. Okinawa experienced an appalling three-month ground battle at the closing of the war, and following defeat was ruled for 27 years by the suppressive control of the U.S. military forces. On the Japanese mainland, after a shorter U.S. military occupation, a Peace Constitution and the Japan-U.S. Security Treaty were concluded. Okinawa was completely ignored in this decision-making process. Japan's rapid reconstruction from war devastation and economic growth was achieved over the victimization of Okinawa. In other words, Japan gained its pros-

---

[*]In Okinawa, which are known as "islands for U.S. military bases," women have been victimized by both U.S. and Japanese soldiers. They continue to struggle to restore their dignity. Okinawan women, in particular, are trying to revive and review their own traditions. Suzuyo Takazato, an assemblymember from Naha City, has long been active on the issue of women and the U.S. bases.

perity by treating Okinawa as a scapegoat and turning it into "islands of the U.S. military bases."

Now, 23 years after the 1972 restoration to Japan, I would like to recapture the historical experiences of Okinawa from a woman's perspective and look at how Okinawan women are constructing our own identities. This should be accomplished by creating a rich global society through encountering and sharing with other women in Asia and other regions; by examining and exposing the nature of the military; and by organizing women's strengths and capabilities to create a world of non-violence which will never require dependence on military forces.

Structural Violence and Sexploitation by Military Forces

There are plans for a massive visit of 1,000 U.S. military veterans to Okinawa in June [1995]. The veterans, who were in their 20s at the time of the war, will hold a commemoration ceremony at a U.S. base in Okinawa, and will hoist the U.S. flag which they used when they landed on Okinawa. When this news was released, it caused tremendous consternation and anger among many Okinawan people. Above all, this forces women who were victims of a direct violence that went beyond our imagination to relive their pain. The U.S., along with prime ministers from its former allies, such as France and the United Kingdom, held a large scale memorial ceremony for the Normandy Landing Operation (D-Day) last June, and following this were veterans' ceremonies and parades commemorating their victories in Guam, Saipan and the Philippines. What lies behind this series of activities is an ostentatious display of the armed forces of victors or liberators, and the reconfirmation of the political, economic and military leadership of the U.S. in the international community.

Okinawa underwent three dreadful months of ground battle when the U.S. military landed, resulting in the deaths of 200,000 people, including infants and old people. Nonetheless, modern buildings have been constructed today, and the affluent daily life of the people has been restored. However, even now, daily activities on Okinawa are often disturbed by the excavation of large unexploded shells, about three hundred of which are found annually. Furthermore, it is estimated that the removal of remaining shells will take another fifty years. While Okinawa makes up only 0.6% of Japan's total land mass, 75% of active U.S. military facilities are concentrated in the area. People in Okinawa live under very tense circumstances, including the possibility of crashes by U.S. fighters, the constant roar of aircraft, the chance of forest fires or accidents caused by stray shots or shrapnel during drills with live bullets, as well as crimes by U.S. soldiers.

Among all the problems deriving from the U.S. military bases, the one which has been most continuously committed over the past 50 years in Okinawa are those involving sexual transgressions against women. Women survived bombardment during the war only to find themselves facing another kind of aggression against women. Soldiers trampled on women's bodies as they did on the island itself. There were numerous cases of rape. Some were raped in the fields or on the sides of roads, or after being taken away from their families at gunpoint. Some were raped on the military bases where they were working as domestic workers or typists. Whenever the place and time, the sexual violence against women has resulted in pregnancies, murders, and mental disorders. How many of the veterans who plan to visit Okinawa will bear in mind the past crimes they committed against women? Even though they are now retired, 50 years ago were they not members of the military establishment that assaulted with guns and raped women? The structural violence of the military forces is inseparable from their new actions, and we, the women of Okinawa, are making our refusal to allow their planned event very clear.

The suffering of Okinawan women, like that of the Koreans, Taiwanese, and Filipinas whom the Japanese Government owes war compensation — the systematized sexual exploitation by military forces to encourage or reward soldiers' fighting spirit and as an outlet for their sexual desires — was covertly arranged and approved. Patriarchal or military power-oriented societies place women in a subordinate position and legitimate their objectification as sexual machinery in order to achieve the goals of the nation. The sexual victimization of women continues at military bases and in regions of conflict around the world today. The very nature of military forces, with their structural mechanisms of violence, should be fully uncovered so that the silencing of women can be ended and their pain healed.

What this means, first of all, is that it is necessary to dig up past crimes. The peace movement demanded the removal of the bases, but in spite of the progress it made it neglected to recognize the gravity of the crimes and human rights violations against women. Hence the overwhelming majority of the victims were unable to file cases so that the statistical figures on these crimes fail to reflect the real situation, and in many cases offenders have been acquitted without contest. Taking into consideration that, especially regarding the way U.S. bases in Okinawa have functioned to provide sorties, communication, drilling, logistics, and recreation for 50 years, during the Korean War, Vietnam War, Gulf War and other regional conflicts in which the U.S. became involved, the significance of crimes by the military's 50,000 stationed soldiers and personnel has not been sufficiently understood, and has contributed to customs in Okinawa itself which undervalue women's human rights.

This year marks the 50th anniversary of the end of the war. Many newspapers have published special memorial issues with themes such as the experiences of survivors. However, even though crimes against women are social crimes, they have not become a theme and hence these publications have hushed up the past even until today. This explains why the offenders, the military side, can march onto Okinawa with their banner a half century later. Currently women are determined to fill in this gap. Regardless of whether the crimes were committed during a state of War or during the postwar period on the military bases, the crimes must be investigated by the victims themselves.

Prostitution Sanctioned at the Bases

Women who had lost their husbands, elder brothers, or sons in the war, or who had been raped and lost their dignity, were driven into selling sex to American soldiers around the bases in Okinawa after the war. According to 1969 statistics, there were 7,400 such women. Considering the female population aged between 10 and 60, one in every 40 to 50 women were engaged in prostitution. Those women had

no other choice other than to sell their bodies to the last drop of their blood, sweat and tears in order to feed their children and families, and to survive themselves. Eventually, their hard work at the bottom supported the base-dependent economy of Okinawa, with no social consideration given to their contribution.

This society with military priorities allows people to be ruled by violence, weapons, and money. This includes the "Yumiko-chan Case" of 1955 in which a six-year-old girl was raped and murdered, as well as the numerous screams of other rape victims and humiliated women. A woman who was raped by three American soldiers when she was 21 received plastic surgery several times in order to cover up "the stigma," and was repeatedly admitted to mental hospitals. She cried out: "I lost my humanity at the age of 21. But still I am a human. Please remember that." Another woman who engaged in prostitution for U.S. soldiers returning from Vietnam suffers from paranoia and was almost choked to death several times. She suffers from severe mental illness, and stands in the rain and rubs her head on the ground saying "I am an evil woman. I am too ashamed of myself. I am an obscene woman. Please, I am too ashamed of myself to face to others. I'm dirty. Please forgive me." She wandered around the streets days and nights. We hear cries demanding restoration of dignity deprived. We would like to reveal the experience of Okinawan women following the bravery of Korean women who broke their 50 years of silence and began to tell their experiences of sex-enslavement which was long concealed by the Japanese Imperial Army.

War Crime Perspectives

In May 1993, a 19-year-old woman was taken into a base by car and raped. The case was reported only after the offender who was arrested had fled to the U.S. The bar association and the prefectural assembly took up the case. The criminal was sent back from the U.S., but the victim did not pursue the case. A military court in the U.S. in March 1994 gave the soldier a dishonorable discharge. According to police statistics, three to five rape cases are reported annually. These figures reveal only the tip of the iceberg, since for rape cases to be classified as a crime the victim must file a complaint for prosecution. To-day, due to the economic reversal resulting from the yen's evaluation and the dollar's decline, young and poor American soldiers approach women sexually either with sham soft words or they resort to direct violence. They would find it hard to imagine how during the Vietnam War American soldiers were spending greenbacks like tissue papers and buying several women a night.

The soldiers stationed in Okinawa are not re-quired to register as aliens so their period of stay in Japan is unknown. In the recent trend of "interna-tionalization," many Japanese regard U.S. soldiers as friendly foreigners, and this is reinforced by im-ages of movie heroes. Many local residents partici-pate in carnivals and bazaars held on the bases. The number of applicants for colleges on the bases has increased, and young girls dream of the opportun-ity to court U.S. soldiers. Each soldier has a private room thanks to a special "consideration budget," which comes from the Japanese government's de-fence budget. Gate controls stopping young girls from entering bases have become easier. This pol-icy of easing entrance to the bases seems just the opposite from the medical care measures taken to prevent American soldiers from getting venereal dis-eases when, taking advantage of the dollar's evalu-ation, they left bases to play around. However, it is in fact exactly the same in essence. The existence of the U.S. soldiers continues today and the past vio-lence of the soldiers has not been cured. It is a con-tinuing nightmare.

As a result of the changing economic relation be-tween the U.S. military bases and Okinawa society resulting in a fall in demand in areas surrounding the bases, the working conditions of working women, such as Filipino women with entertainment visas, have become harder and human rights violations have increased. Around 180 to 200 Filipino women with entertainment visas are working near Camp Hansen in Kin town, where two Filipinos died in a fire in 1983. Even though Okinawan women are (eco-nomically) equal to or superior in position to U.S. sol-diers, they are still assaulted by groups of male soldiers directly or indirectly. Thus though the ap-pearance has changed, the essential structure has not.

The World Human Rights Conference in Vienna, in June, 1993 gave recognition to the issues of "com-fort women" and to the group rape of Muslim women by Serbian soldiers in Bosnia-Herzegovina, as viola-tions of women's human rights, and labelled the women as victims of war crimes. I also made de-mands for effective measures. At the NGO Forum which was held simultaneously to the conference, various forms of violence against women were raised, demanding an expansion of the concept of human rights to include violence against women. This event encouraged a reinvestigation into the issue of vio-lence against Okinawan women under the long period of control of stationed U.S. military.

In regard to the rape of a 19-year-old girl, the Association for Solidarity with Asia called for an investigation based on the Vienna Declaration. In response, six women's organizations in Okinawa launched a joint petition campaign titled "The State-ment to Investigate the Rape by a U.S. soldier and a Demand for the Prevention of Crimes Against Women," and submitted this to the governor of Okinawa Prefecture in April 1994. In the statement Okinawan women demanded (1) an investigation into the series of human rights violations against women by the military going back to the beginning, and efforts for a revival of women's life which has been torn apart, and (2) the initiation of counseling services for empowerment in order to revive the hu-man dignity and plundered bodies of women by both the Japanese and U.S. military.

CHAPTER SEVEN

Living in a Global Economy

In September 1995 more than thirty thousand women from virtually every country in the world gathered in Huairou, China, to discuss the many issues and problems faced by women and girls around the world and to work together for change (see Reading 6, Chapter 1). This was the forum for nongovernmental organizations (NGOs) and was the largest meeting of women in history. A two-hour bus ride away, at the official United Nations Fourth World Conference on Women in Beijing, some five thousand delegates discussed what their governments are doing to improve women's lives and negotiated an official U.N. document, the *Platform for Action* (Wong 1995).

There were nearly five thousand workshops listed in the NGO Forum schedule. Among the discussions about literacy and the education of women and girls, nutrition and health care for infants and adults, the need for clean water in many rural areas of the world, the need for jobs or guaranteed livelihood, the plight of millions of refugees, disability rights, violence against women, sexual freedom, solar stoves, and prostitution, to take just a few examples, one theme was repeated again and again: the effects on women and girls of the globalization of the economy, and the inequality between the rich countries of the world, often located in the Northern Hemisphere, and the poorer countries of the Southern. This seemingly abstract issue affects everyone and underlies many other problems.

To understand the situations and experiences of women in the United States, it is important to know something of women's lives and working conditions worldwide and the ways we all participate in, and are affected by, the global economy. It is against this global economic background that women's activism for economic and social justice takes place. This chapter takes this wider angle of view, with nation as an additional analytical category together with gender, race, and class. The film *The Global Assembly Line* (distributed by New Day Films, www.newday.com) is an excellent introduction to the topic, and readers are urged to see it, if possible, in conjunction with reading this chapter.

The Global Factory

In the past thirty years or so, electronic communications and air transport have made it increasingly possible for corporations to operate across national boundaries, a practice that is likely to become even more prevalent in the future. Now a company based in the United States, such as Nike, Playtex, IBM, or General Motors, can have much of its manufacturing work done overseas—in, for example, Indonesia, Taiwan, Mexico, the Philippines, Guatemala, or Europe—by workers who are paid much lower wages than U.S. workers (Enloe 1989; Fuentes and Ehrenreich 1983; Greider 1997; Kamel 1990; Kamel

Average Hourly Wages for Garment Workers

Country	U.S. Dollars	Country	U.S. Dollars
Bangladesh	$0.10–0.16* **	India	$0.26*
Burma	$0.10–0.18* **	Indonesia	$0.34*
Canada	$9.88	Italy	$14.00
China	$0.20–0.68* **	Jamaica	$1.80
Colombia	$1.05	Macau	$2.41*
Costa Rica	$2.38	Mexico	$1.08
Dominican Republic	$1.62	Nicaragua	$0.76
Eastern Europe	$1.11	Pakistan	$0.21*
El Salvador	$1.38	Philippines	$0.94*
France	$7.81	Sri Lanka	$0.31*
Germany	$23.19	Thailand	$1.02*
Guatemala	$1.25	United Kingdom	$7.38
Haiti	$0.49	United States	$9.56
Honduras	$1.31	Vietnam	$0.26*
Hong Kong	$4.55*		

*Not including bonuses.
**Low end for state factories, high end for township or foreign-invested joint-venture factories.
Source: *Women's Wear Daily,* December 31, 1996.

and Hoffman 1999; Ross 1997). This organization of work results in inexpensive consumer goods for the U.S. market, particularly clothing, toys, household appliances, and electronic equipment. Thus, our lives are dependent on the labor of a myriad of people in a vast global network.

Roughly 90 percent of the workers in this **off-shore production** are young women in their late teens and early twenties. Some countries, like the Philippines and China, have established Export Processing Zones (EPZs), where transnational corporations (TNCs) set up factories making products for export to Europe, U.S., Canada, and Japan. In Mexico this is done through *maquiladoras* — factories that make goods on contract to a "parent" company, as described by María Patricia Fernández-Kelly in

Reading 41. In 1996 Mexican women in Tijuana started working for Samsung (a South Korean firm) at about $50 for a forty-five-hour week (DePalma 1996). Women in Haiti worked for eleven cents an hour making "Pocohontas" pajamas for J.C. Penney. Aside from paying far lower wages than they would pay to U.S. workers, such companies experience fewer restrictions on their operations.

Even in countries like Mexico, with protective labor and environmental legislation, these regulations are often not enforced in relation to the operations of transnational corporations. Thus, workers experience oppressive working conditions and suffer health problems such as stress from trying to make the assigned quotas; illnesses from exposure to glues, solvents, and other toxic chemicals; and lint and dust in textile factories; or poor eyesight from hours spent at microscopes. In addition, women are often subject to sexual harassment by male supervisors. Mexican women workers in *maquiladoras* have been required to undergo a pregnancy test as a condition of employment and have been denied work if they are pregnant (Human Rights Watch 1999b). Company doctors "routinely administer pregnancy tests and distribute birth control pills" (Tooher 1999, p. 39). Levimex, for example, a Tijuana *maquiladora* owned by the Leviton Manufacturing Co., gave contracts to workers for a month, three months, or one year. Each time the contract was renewed, women had to take a pregnancy test. When workers complain and organize to protest such dire conditions, they are often threatened that the plants will close and move elsewhere; indeed, this has sometimes happened. For example, Nike has moved some of its production from South Korea, where women have campaigned for better wages and working conditions, to Indonesia and the southern part of China, thereby pitting workers in one country against those in another. Cynthia Enloe describes this process in Reading 42.

Many thousands of U.S. workers have been laid off through automation or the movement of jobs overseas. Fewer and fewer products are made in the United States. With a lack of manufacturing jobs, the job market in the United States is becoming increasingly polarized between professional jobs and low-paying service work—flipping burgers at McDonald's, for example—that offers no benefits or job security. Rising unemployment, or underemployment—where people are overqualified for the jobs available—has had devastating social and economic effects in older manufacturing cities like Detroit, Cleveland, and Pittsburgh.

Sweatshops are a feature of the global economic system and are defined by the U.S. General Accounting Office as employers that violate more than one federal or state labor law. Pharis Harvey, executive director of the International Labor Rights Fund, defines a sweatshop as "any workplace where the wages are inadequate, the hours too long, and the working conditions endanger safety or health—whether or not any laws are violated" (Facts on the Global Sweatshop 1997, p. 16). Sweatshops are common in the garment industry and toy manufacturing (Ross 1997). They exist in many countries, including the United States. The U.S. Department of Labor es-

timates that more than half the country's 22,000 sewing shops violate minimum wage and overtime laws. Many of these workers are employed in cramped factories, often with blocked fire exits, unsanitary bathrooms, and poor ventilation. According to Sarah Wood (1997), "The terms 'sweatshop' and 'sweating' were first used in the 19th century to describe a subcontracting system where the middlemen earned their profit from the margin between the amount they received from a contract and the amount they paid their workers. This margin was 'sweated' from the workers," who received minimal wages for excessive hours worked under poor conditions. Nowadays, too, the garment industry is organized in such a way that big-name retailers like Gap, for example, and brand-name manufacturers like Jessica McClintock contract with sewing shops that hire workers to make the finished product, although they do not directly control workers' wages and working conditions. The retailers and manufacturers, in effect, determine wages for garment workers by controlling the price to the contractor.

Despite serious risks to their jobs, workers are organizing for better pay and working conditions. The National Mobilization Against Sweatshops, for example, was formed by the Chinese Staff and Workers' Association and works with women garment workers in New York's Chinatown. Increased consumer awareness in the United States and other industrialized countries has also brought about some changes in wages and working conditions for overseas workers, as consumers have attempted to hold corporations accountable for exploitative conditions. A major campaign against Nike in 1997–98, for example, protested inhumane working conditions in plants making Nike shoes in Vietnam and China (Bourbeau 1998; Greenhouse 1997; Sanders and Kaptur 1997; Saporito 1998; Stewart 1997). In February 1997, North Olmstead, Ohio, a working-class suburb of Cleveland, became the first U.S. city to ban municipal purchases of sweatshop-made products (Facts on the Global Sweatshop 1997, p. 16). In 1999 Duke University students staged a sit-in in the university president's office to ensure that clothing bearing Duke's name is not made in sweatshops. Students from over 100 colleges called on their institutions to honor a strict code of conduct for overseas factories that make goods bearing college names. In response to this public outcry, the U.S. Department of Labor mounted a media campaign focusing on industry "trendsetters," and President Clinton created a task force of industry, labor, and human rights organizations with the goal of eliminating sweatshops (Press 1997).

The existence of sweatshops and the polarization of the U.S. job market are not random or isolated, however, but an integral part of the global economic system. The driving force is the accumulation of wealth by corporations and individuals. Their **capital**—money and property—is invested in manufacturing, communications, or agriculture, for example. By producing goods, services, and crops, workers earn wages and also increase the wealth of their employers. **Capitalism** is an economic and political system in which the major means of production and distribution are privately held and operated for profit. Labor and nature are seen as resources. In practice there is no "pure" capitalism; rather, the system is a mixture of corporate and government decisions that provide the foundation for business operations. Governments levy taxes that may be used to alleviate poor social conditions. Government and corporate elites share assumptions about what makes the economy successful. In extreme circumstances, governments may sanction the use of police or military force against workers who strike for better pay and working conditions. Governments of some small countries may have operating budgets smaller than those of transnational corporations, a situation that makes control of the corporations difficult. For instance, according to Charles Gray (1999) the top three companies in the world—Exxon-Mobil, General Motors, and Ford—each have higher revenues than the national budgets of all but seven countries (United States, Germany, Japan, China, Italy, United Kingdom, and France). Some companies have more revenue than the budgets of their home governments (e.g., Shell/Netherlands and Daewoo/South Korea). It is important to understand the underlying principles of this economic system outlined below.

The Profit Motive

Companies compete with one another to sell their services and products, and they stay in business only as long as it is profitable or while governments are willing to subsidize them, as happens, for example, with agriculture and defense industries in

the United States. If enough people can afford to buy gold faucets or to change their cars every six months, these things will be produced regardless of whether ordinary people have an adequate diet or somewhere to live. Women in Taiwan or Malaysia, for example, spend their working lives producing more and more goods for the U.S. market even if their own daily survival needs are barely met.

Consumerism, Expansionism, and Waste

To expand, companies have to produce more products, develop new products, and find new markets and new needs to supply. The concept of "need" is a tricky one. Many of the things we think we need are not absolute necessities but contrived needs generated by advertising or social pressure. Some needs are also context specific. It is doubtful whether every household in an urban area in the United States with extensive public transportation needs a car, but a car is probably required in a rural area for basic necessities like getting to work, as there is unlikely to be adequate, if any, public transportation. This economic system is intrinsically wasteful. Companies have little or no responsibility to workers left stranded, or for polluted land and water they leave behind when, for example, car assembly plants close down in Detroit, or Mattel moves its Barbie doll factory to Malaysia.

The Myth of Progress

There is an assumption that economic growth is the same as "progress"—a much more complex concept with economic, intellectual, social, moral, and spiritual dimensions. This equation often leads people in a highly material society like the United States to value themselves primarily in terms of the money they make and the things they own. At a national level, too, it leads to an emphasis on material success and material security, with support for government policies that facilitate profit making regardless of social costs.

Emphasis on Immediate Costs

The business definition of costs—the immediate costs of raw materials, plant, payroll, and other operating expenses—is a narrow one. It does not take into account longer-term considerations like the

The Village

If we could shrink the earth's population to a village of precisely 100 people, with all the existing human ratios remaining the same, it would look like the following. There would be

57 Asians
21 Europeans
14 from the Western Hemisphere, both north and south
8 Africans

52 would be female
48 would be male

70 would be non-white
30 would be white

70 would be non-Christian
30 would be Christian

89 would be heterosexual
11 would be homosexual

6 people would possess 59% of the entire world's wealth and all 6 would be from the United States

80 would live in substandard housing

70 would be unable to read

50 would suffer from malnutrition

1 would be near death; 1 would be near birth

1 (yes, only 1) would have a college education

1 would own a computer

Source: E-mail widely circulated in 2000.

them out of business. In the nineteenth century, European and U. S. factory owners said the same thing about proposals to abolish child labor and reduce working hours to an eight-hour day, both of which were implemented through legislation.

The Global Economy

Complex Inequalities

Our economic system generates profound inequalities within countries—of wealth, material comfort, safety, opportunities, education, social standing, and so on. Members of wealthy elites in Brazil, Saudi Arabia, Indonesia, Turkey, Germany, South Africa, and the United States, to take a few random examples, often have more in common with one another than they do with many of their fellow citizens. Poor people living in Oakland, Detroit, or the south Bronx have rates of illiteracy and infant mortality as high as poor people in parts of Africa, Latin America, and the Caribbean. This has led some commentators to talk of "the Third World within the First World" as a way of emphasizing inequalities within countries and drawing connections among poor people worldwide, overwhelmingly people of color.

These inequalities are enhanced in a global economy, which produces inequalities between rich and poor nations. The richest 20 percent of the world's population receives 83 percent of the world's income, while the poorest 60 percent receives 5.6 percent. The richest 20 percent of the world's population in northern industrial countries uses 70 percent of the world's energy, 75 percent of the world's metals, 85 percent of the world's wood, and 60 percent of the world's food (Danaher n.d.). Workers in one country are pitted against those in another in the corporations' scramble for profits, as mentioned in the articles that follow, and this generally erodes their bargaining power. The internationalization and mobility of capital calls for an international labor movement to standardize wages and working conditions. The fact that standards of living and wage rates differ from country to country means that this process of moving work and factories around the world is likely to continue and to become increasingly complex. In addition to U.S.-based corporations, Japanese, Western European, and South Korean firms also operate in other countries, seeking lower wages, better tax breaks, and other financial incentives.

effects of production on the environment or workers' well-being. Government regulation of pollution, for example, is frequently resisted by corporations on the grounds that it will increase costs and drive

What's in a Name?

The various overlapping terms used in the discourse on the global economy offer a convenient shorthand but often obscure as much as they explain.

First World, Second World, Third World

These terms refer to countries that can be roughly grouped together according to their political alliances and economic status. The "First World" refers to North America, Western Europe, Australia, New Zealand, and Japan. The "Second World" includes Russia and countries of Eastern Europe. The "Third World" includes most of Asia, Latin America, Africa, and the Caribbean. There is an assumption of a hierarchy built into this terminology, with First World countries superior to the rest. Some Native Americans and indigenous peoples in Canada, Latin America, Australia, and New Zealand use the term "First Nations" to emphasize the fact that their ancestral lands were colonized and settled by Europeans. Some environmentalists use the term "Fourth World" to refer to a scattered collection of small-scale, environmentally sound projects, suggesting an alternative economic and political model. Some commentators use the term "Two-Thirds World" to draw attention to the fact that the majority of the world's population (approximately 68 percent) lives in Asia, Latin America, Africa, and the Caribbean.

Developed, Undeveloped, Underdeveloped, Developing, Maldevelopment

These terms refer to economic development, assuming that all countries will become industrialized like North America and Western Europe. Ranging these terms on a continuum from "undeveloped" to "developed" suggests that this process is linear and the best way for a nation to progress. Indeed, economic growth is often unquestioningly assumed to be synonymous with progress. This continuum masks the fact that much of the wealth of developed countries comes from undeveloped countries and is a key reason for their lack of economic development. Vandana Shiva (1988) emphasizes this connection by using the term "devastated" instead of "underdeveloped" economies. Other commentators speak of "maldevelopment" to refer to exploitation of undeveloped countries by developed ones.

East/West; North/South

The division between East and West refers to a political and military division between North America and Western Europe—the West—countries which, despite differences, have stood together against the East—the former Soviet Union and Eastern Europe. Clearly this notion of East and West excludes many countries in the Western and Eastern Hemispheres. This distinction also obscures the similarities between these blocs, which are both highly industrialized with massive military programs. Some writers use the terms North/South to distinguish between rich and poor countries; "rich" in this context usually means rich with cash rather than with land, resources, or people's skills, creativity, and hard work.

Legacies of Colonialism

Current inequalities between countries are often based on older inequalities resulting from colonization. British colonies included India, Ghana, Kenya, Nigeria, Pakistan, and Hong Kong. France had colonial possessions in Algeria, Senegal, Togo, and Vietnam. Although the details varied from place to place and from one colonial power to another, several factors were central to this process:

the imposition of legal and political institutions;

cultural devastation and replacement of language;

International Economic Institutions and Trade Agreements

Several groups of countries have joined together, forming trading blocs such as the Economic Community of West African States (ECOWAS) and the European Union (EU), and agreements such as the North American Free Trade Agreement (NAFTA). The goal of these regional institutions is to strengthen the economies of the member countries, although the various countries may not all have the same economic power or influence in the group.

The World Bank

Headquartered in Washington, D.C., the World Bank was set up in 1944 to provide loans for reconstruction after the devastation of World War II and to promote development in countries of the South, where the bank's emphasis has been on major, capital-intensive projects such as roads, dams, hydroelectric schemes, irrigation systems, and the development of large-scale, chemical-dependent, cash-crop production. The bank's investors are the governments of rich countries who make money on the interest on these loans. Because the World Bank assigns voting power in proportion to the capital provided by its shareholders, its decisions are dominated by the governments of the North, and its policies are in line with their concerns.

International Monetary Fund (IMF)

Also based in Washington, the IMF is an international body with 140 member countries. It was founded at the same time as the World Bank to promote international trade and monetary cooperation. It makes loans to governments for development projects and in times of severe budget deficits. France, Germany, Japan, Britain, and the United States have over 50 percent of the votes, which are allocated according to financial contribution to the fund. If member countries borrow from the fund, they must accept a range of conditions, such as structural adjustment programs, and must put export earnings above any other goal for the country's economy.

General Agreement on Tariffs and Trade (GATT)

This trade agreement was started after World War II to regulate international trade. Since its inception, over a hundred nations, responsible for four-fifths of world trade, have participated in the agreement. The latest round of GATT negotiations, which began in 1986, significantly changed the agreement in response to transnational corporations' demand for a reduction of import tariffs, in

---

psychological dimensions such as internalized racism; and

distortions of the economy with dependence on a few agricultural products or raw materials for export.

Colonial powers extracted raw materials—timber, minerals, and cash crops—which were processed into manufactured goods in the colonial centers for consumption there and for export. During the second half of the twentieth century, virtually all former colonies gained political independence, but they remain linked to their colonizers—politically through organizations like the British Common-

wealth and economically through the activities of established firms in operation since colonial times, from the more recent activities of transnational corporations, and by loans from governments and banks of countries of the North (that is, the rich countries of the developed world). Many members of the new political and business elites were educated at prestigious universities in colonial capitals. Whether the handover of political power was relatively smooth or accompanied by turmoil and bloodshed, newly independent governments have been under pressure to improve living conditions for their populations and have borrowed capital to finance economic development. This combination of what Nader (1993) described as "an unprecedented corporate power grab" (p. 1). (The changed agreement was adopted by the United States in 1994.) Transnational corporations will pay fewer tariffs on the goods they move around the world —data, components, partly finished products, and goods ready for sale. Proponents argued that a global market and free trade mean global prosperity. Labor organizers, environmentalists, and consumer advocates who opposed these changes in GATT argued that governments would lose tax income from imports; that countries like the United States, where wage rates and benefits are high in international terms, would be likely to lose jobs; and that legislation protecting workers and the environment might be set aside or ruled to be an unlawful limitation on the operations of corporations.

North American Free Trade Agreement (NAFTA)

This agreement among the United States, Canada, and Mexico, established in 1994, allows for greater freedom of movement of jobs and products among the three countries. Its proponents argued that these countries needed to collaborate to remain as competitive internationally as the economically powerful European Union and Pacific Rim trading groups. Like GATT, NAFTA was discussed in terms of a liberalization of trade but is in effect a liberalization of capital expansion, again serving the interests of transnational corporations against opposition in all three countries from labor, environmentalists, and consumers.

Proponents argued that NAFTA would create more jobs in the United States, though this has not been the case. The Clinton administration has admitted that 75,000 U.S. jobs were lost because of NAFTA. Workers in the Mexico-U.S. border region have suffered a sharp drop in their standard of living, "speed-ups" in the labor process, and opposition to labor rights and union organizing (Comité Fronterizo de Obreras-American Friends Service Committee 1999). In all three NAFTA countries, increases in real wages have lagged behind increases in productivity (Anderson, Cavanagh, and Ranney 1999).

World Trade Organization (WTO)

The World Trade Organization (WTO) is the GATT ruling body, established in 1995 in the "Uruguay Round" of GATT negotiations (Working Group on the WTO 1999). This is an unelected international body over which member nations and their peoples have no democratic control. The WTO allows national governments to challenge each others' laws and regulations as violations of WTO rules against restraints to trade. Cases are decided by a panel of three trade experts. WTO tribunals are secret, binding on member states, and provide no outside appeal or review. Once a WTO ruling is issued, losing countries have a set time to change their law to conform to WTO requirements, pay compensation to the winning country, or face non-negotiated trade sanctions. All environmental or public health laws that have been challenged so far at the WTO have been ruled illegal (Working Group on the WTO 1999, p. 5).

circumstances has led many commentators to characterize the continuing economic inequalities between rich and poor countries as **neocolonialism.** The United States is part of this picture because of its colonial relationships with the Philippines, Hawaii (now a state), and Puerto Rico (a commonwealth); the strength of U.S. corporations worldwide; the dominance of U.S. news media and popular culture; the strength of the dollar as an international currency; and the fact that key international institutions like the World Bank and the International Monetary Fund have their headquarters in the United States and are heavily influenced by U.S. investments and policies.

External Debt

All countries are involved in international trade, buying and selling goods and services. Currently many countries pay more for imports than they earn in exports, leading to external debt, or a balance of payments deficit. In 1991 over $1.3 trillion was jointly owed by governments of Latin America, Asia, Africa, and the Caribbean to Northern governments and commercial banks. The sixteen major borrowers in Latin America owed a total of $420 billion, a situation that has not changed significantly since then (O'Reilly 1991). Researchers at the Caribbean Association for Feminist Research and Action note that more money has gone out from Third World countries than has come in, in loans and investments (Reading 43). The United States, too, has had an enormous budget deficit, dropping from $290 billion in 1992 to $164 billion in 1995 because of major budget cuts (Sivard 1996).

Repayment of Loans Partly because countries of western Europe and North America have serious balance-of-payments problems themselves, they have pressured other debtor countries to repay loans. Like a person who acquires a second credit card to cover the debt on the first, a country may take out additional loans to cover interest repayments on earlier ones, thus compounding its debt. This situation is complicated by the fact that loans usually have to be repaid in hard currency that can be exchanged on world currency markets: U.S. dollars, Japanese yen, British pounds, French francs, Swiss francs, and German marks. To repay the loans, debtor nations have to sell goods and services that richer countries want to buy or that can earn hard currency from poorer countries. These include raw materials (hardwoods, oil, copper, gold, diamonds), cash crops (sugar, tobacco, coffee, tea, tropical fruits and flowers), illegal drugs and drug-producing crops (coca, marijuana, opium poppies), and weapons. Debtor countries may also earn foreign exchange by encouraging their people to work abroad as construction workers or maids or to become mail-order brides. They may lease land for foreign military bases or trash dumps that take toxic waste from industrialized countries, or they may develop their tourist assets — sunny beaches, beautiful landscapes, and "exotic" young women and children who are recruited into sex tourism.

Structural Adjustment Programs In addition to selling goods and services to offset their external debt, debtor nations have also been under pressure from the World Bank and the IMF to make stringent changes in their economies to qualify for new loans. The aim of such structural adjustment programs is to increase the profitability of the economy. Required measures include

- cutting back government spending on health, education, child care, and social welfare provisions;

- cutting government subsidies and abolishing price controls, particularly on food, fuel, and public transportation;

- adding new taxes, especially on consumer goods, and increasing existing taxes and interest rates;

- selling nationalized industries, or at least a majority of the shares, to private corporations, often from outside the country;

- reducing the number of civil servants on the government payroll;

- improving profitability for corporations through wage controls, tax breaks, loans, and credit, or providing infrastructure by building ports, better roads, or rail transportation;

- devaluing local currency to discourage imports and encourage exports; and

- increasing the output of cash crops, by increasing yields and/or increasing the amount of land in cash crop production.

Though not required to do so by the World Bank, the Reagan, Bush, and Clinton administrations all adopted similar policies for use in the United States, and they were enshrined in the "Contract with America" introduced by the Republican Congress in 1994. Such policies are in line with global economic restructuring with the goal of increasing corporate profitability. Examples include the deregulation of air transport and the privatization of public utilities and aspects of the prison industry. In addition, these administrations restructured government spending by making reductions in the government workforce and cuts in, for example, Medicaid, Medicare, and welfare programs.

Implications of the Debt Crisis for Women   Despite women's increased opportunities for paid work in urban areas and export-processing zones in Asia, Latin America, and the Caribbean, the external debt crisis and structural adjustment programs have had a severe impact on women's lives and livelihoods. Addressing the U.N. Commission on the Status of Women in March 1998, Rini Soerojo of Indonesia spoke on behalf of 132 developing countries. She emphasized that "the full and effective enjoyment of human rights by women could never be achieved in the absence of sustainable economic growth and a supportive social and international order" (Deen 1998, p. 2). Cuts in social services and health care, often already woefully inadequate, have increased women's responsibilities for child care, health, and family welfare. Cuts in government subsidies for food and other basic items and devaluation of local currencies have reduced women's wages and raised prices, thus doubly reducing their buying power. Women's wages fell by as much as 50 percent in many countries during the 1980s (Steinberg 1989), and they continued to fall in the 1990s. The emphasis on cash crops at the expense of subsistence crops has devastating environmental consequences and makes subsistence agriculture—very often the responsibility of women—much more difficult. Growing cash crops on the flatter land, for instance, pushes subsistence farmers to use steep hillsides for food crops, which is harder work and often less productive and which increases soil erosion. Clearing forests to plant cash crops or raise cattle, as McDonald's did in parts of Central and Latin America, for example, increased soil erosion and reduced the supply of fuel wood, which has further added to women's daily burden of work (Dankelman and Davidson 1988; Sen and Grown 1987; Shiva 1988). Other consequences of the debt crisis include an increase in the number of people seeking work overseas as temporary migrant workers or permanent immigrants; increasing unemployment and underemployment, with growth in the exploitative and unregulated informal sector of the economy (such as sweatshops and low-paid work in homes); an increase in the number of students who have to drop out of school and college because of financial pressures; and a general increase in poverty and hardship. Grace Chang shows how structural adjustment in the Philippines economy has affected Filipina workers, thousands of whom go abroad each year for work—particularly to Canada, western Europe, the Middle East, and the United States (Reading 44).

Debt Cancellation   Between 1982 and 1990, $160 billion was transferred from Latin America to the developed world in debt repayments (O'Reilly 1991), but this was only the interest on 50 percent of their loans (George 1988). In 1982 Mexico announced that it could not repay its debt, and other countries suspended their repayments throughout the 1980s. This led to much political and financial debate concerning the legitimacy of debts owed by countries of the South to the North. According to Oxfam International (1998):

> In Ethiopia over 100,000 children die annually from easily preventable diseases, but debt payments are four times more than public spending on health care.

> In Tanzania, where 40 percent of people die before the age of thirty-five, debt payments are six times as much as spending on health care.

> In Africa as a whole, where one out of every two children doesn't go to school, governments transfer four times more to northern creditors in debt payments than they spend on the health and education of their citizens.

Many activist organizations worldwide support debt cancellation. They argue that much of the money borrowed has benefited only upper-class and professional elites or has gone into armaments, nuclear power plants, or luxuries such as prestige buildings, especially in urban areas. As summed up in the lyrics to *Ode to the International Debt:* "Guns you can't eat /And buildings you can't live/And trinkets you can't wear / It is a debt not owed by the people" (Reagon 1987). In some countries, large sums of money borrowed by governments were kept by corrupt politicians and businesspeople and then reinvested in the lender countries. As the authors of the Caribbean Association for Feminist Research and Action Newsletter argue in Reading 43, poor people have rarely benefited from such investments and should not be held responsible for this debt. Susan George (1988) claims that "cancellation would turn recipient countries into financial pariahs" who would not be able to borrow further loans. She argues that the goals of a debt campaign "should be to get money and the political power that goes with it directly into the hands of the poor majorities, by-passing the elites, and insofar as possible, the State; and to ensure much greater popular control over the development process" (p. 20).

It is an inescapable fact that the world's poorest countries are getting poorer and will never be able to pay their international debts. Although this debt is not the only cause of their poverty, the debt burden makes their situation significantly worse. With the agreement of the leading industrialized nations, the governing boards of the IMF and World Bank adopted a debt-relief proposal in 1996. A few countries benefited under this scheme, but progress was extremely slow. During the 1990s, people in rich and poor countries took part in major protests against world economic priorities. In June 1999, a worldwide alliance of NGOs and religious groups known as the Jubilee 2000 Coalition presented the leaders of the G-8 (Group of Eight) nations (United States, Japan, Britain, France, Germany, Italy, Canada, and Russia) with a petition signed by 17 million people from rich nations urging debt cancellation (Francis 1999). The G-8 proposed an expansion of the World Bank/IMF debt-relief initiative, though by December 1999 not one country had seen its debt payments reduced. In December 1999, Britain announced that it would write off all debts owed by the world's most impoverished countries as a way of starting "the international drive . . . to get much needed financial help flowing to more than two dozen countries" by the end of 2000 (Elliott 1999, p. 1).

Free Trade

Governments have attempted to protect their own economies by restricting imports from overseas competitors, or they have augmented national revenues by imposing taxes on imported goods, including components, partly finished products, and goods ready for sale. As corporations move their operations around the world in search of higher profit margins, they want to be rid of such restrictions, and international trade agreements like NAFTA and GATT have made this increasingly possible, as mentioned earlier. The language of free trade suggests that such agreements are concerned with the promotion of commerce. Kamel and Hoffman (1999) argue

they might better be described as attempts to rewrite the framework for international economic relations . . . placing severe restrictions on the right of governments to regulate the activities of transnational corporations in order to protect the environment, safeguard labor rights, protect the standard of living or food security of their populations, or promote the development of their own economies.

(p. 102)

Implications of Global Economic Inequalities

Addressing a vast crowd in Havana at the end of a visit to Cuba in January 1996, Pope John Paul II criticized unsustainable economic programs imposed by rich countries on the poor and "the resurgence of a certain capitalist neoliberalism that subordinates the human person to blind market forces"; he also deplored the fact that "a small number of countries [are] growing exceedingly rich at the cost of the increasing impoverishment of a great number of other countries" (News Services 1998, p. A1).

In principle, inequality is unjust. Some people's freedom and comfort cannot be bought at the expense of other people's oppression, degradation, and poverty. More pragmatically, inequality is a continual source of violence and conflict. On an international level it is one of the main causes of war; on a community level it can lead to alienation, anger, violence, theft, and vandalism.

Connections to U.S. Policy Issues

Two issues of national importance in the United States that are greatly affected by global inequalities are immigration and drugs. Vast differences in living standards between the United States and many other countries are a source of continuing pressure for immigration into this country (Ong, Bonacich, and Cheng 1994), as argued by Saskia Sassen in Reading 45. These same inequalities also drive the international drug trade, a lucrative earner of hard currency for producer countries as well as for those who procure and sell illegal drugs or launder drug money (Lusane 1991). It is important to understand the global economic forces driving the drug trade and pressures for immigration and to recognize the inadequacy of control measures that do not address underlying causes.

Discussion of the drug trade is beyond the scope of this book, but we consider the issue of immigration here, building on the brief history of immigration law and policy included in Chapter 2. The 1990s saw controversial and acrimonious debate in the United States over immigration, along with a range of new legislation, like the 1996 Illegal Immigration Reform and Immigrant Responsibility Act, which aims to control it. Anti-immigration politicians and countless media reports have invoked the specter of "alien hordes" poised on the borders, ready to overrun the country, take jobs away from the native born, and drain the welfare system. Wendy Young (1997) counters this perception, arguing that undocumented people "typically fill service-sector jobs and are ineligible for most benefits, even though they pay $7 billion annually in taxes and social security contributions. Moreover, 85% of immigrants come to the United States through legal channels" (p. 9). In 1995, 54 percent of documented immigrants to the United States were women (U.S. Immigration and Naturalization Service 1996).

At the heart of much of this debate are racism and xenophobia. White people particularly see the country changing demographically with the arrival of more people from Asia, Mexico, and Central and South America. This poses a threat to the dominance of "the Anglo-Saxon part of America's culture" (Holmes 1995b). Such fears have provided leverage for a greatly increased Immigration and Naturalization Service budget and tighter border control, especially along the long land border with Mexico, which has been strongly fortified (Ayres 1994), as described by Leslie Marmon Silko in Reading 46. Congress cut government funding for virtually all agencies except the military in the mid-1990s, but the INS received an increase of $1 billion, which brought its 1996 budget to $2.6 billion (Freedberg 1996).

The distinction between legal and illegal immigrants has been drawn more sharply. Young (1997) noted that undocumented migration is currently estimated at some 300,000 people each year. Undocumented women entering the United States are often subject to sexual harassment and rape in the process, including assaults by INS border patrols (Light 1996). The 1986 Immigration Act introduced sanctions against employers, making it illegal to knowingly hire undocumented workers, with fines for those who violate the law. This controversial program was intended to eliminate the "pull" factor of jobs attracting undocumented migrants into the country. Illegal immigrants are hired at low wages by agricultural growers, construction firms, landscaping and cleaning businesses, and the garment industry, for example, as well as by private individuals as maids and baby-sitters. Evidence indicates that employer sanctions have been ineffective; employers are not always prosecuted, and if they are, they tend to consider the relatively small fines as a hazard of doing business. However, as Young (1997) observes, "Numerous studies have shown that employer sanctions have caused employment discrimination against U.S. citizens and permanent residents who look or sound 'foreign.' Some employers will avoid hiring such individuals rather than risk being subjected to sanctions and fines" (p. 8).

Increasing numbers of undocumented workers were deported during the early 1990s (Holmes 1995a), and legal immigrants applied for citizenship in record numbers in response to growing controversy over immigration and moves to deny legal immigrants access to government supports. Migration policy will continue to be a contentious issue in the United States, particularly in states like California, Florida, New York, and Texas, which have large proportions of immigrants.

International Alliances among Women

Women's organizations worldwide are concerned with economic issues, including economic development, loans to start small businesses, and other job opportunities for women, as well as the lack of government spending on health care, child care, or care for the elderly. At international feminist meetings and conferences, such as the NGO Forum in September 1995, these global inequalities are central to many discussions. Women from countries of the South invariably challenge those from the North to take up the issue of external debt and structural adjustment with our governments and banks.

Some U.S. feminist organizations focus their work on women's rights in this country, which is understandable, as earlier gains are being eroded. But the separation of domestic and foreign policy masks crucial connections and continuities and can lead to an insularity and parochialism on the part of women in the United States, an important aspect of the ignorance that comes with national privilege. In the context of trade agreements like GATT and NAFTA, Mary McGinn, the North American coordinator for Transnationals Information Exchange, comments, "Unfortunately, most U.S. women's advocacy groups took no position on GATT. But clearly, all women have a lot to lose: expanded freedom for multinational corporations jeopardizes social justice everywhere" (McGinn 1995, p. 15).

In order to build more effective international campaigns and alliances, women in the North need to learn much more about the effects of corporate and government policies on women in Asia, Africa, Latin America, and the Caribbean, and to understand the connections between these women's situations and our own.

Many women in the United States who attended the NGO Forum spoke to public meetings, religious organizations, women's groups, and school and college classes about their impressions and brought back a heightened understanding of global linkages to their ongoing efforts. The Women of Color Resource Center (Berkeley, Calif.), for instance, decided to give priority to the globalization of the economy in its organizing and educational work: "Global economics was at the top of the Beijing agenda; it is now at the top of ours as well" (1996, p. 2). A campaign titled Women's Eyes on the World Bank-U.S., based at Oxfam America (Washington, D.C.), began "to monitor Bank progress toward bringing its lending operations in line with the Beijing Platform" (Williams 1997, p. 1). This is the importance of international gatherings like the NGO Forum at Huairou or the U.N. *Platform for Action,* which

> criticizes structural adjustment programs; advises cuts in military spending in favor of social spending; urges women's participation at all peace talks and in all decision-making affecting development and environment; confronts violence against women; calls for measuring women's unpaid work; and refers to "the family" in all its various forms.
>
> *(Morgan 1996, p. 20)*

United Nations documents have to be ratified by the governments of individual countries to be accepted as national policy. Even if governments do not ratify them—and the U.S. on several occasions has not—they are still useful for activists in their attempts to hold governments accountable and to show what others have pledged to do for women and girls. Wangari Maathai, coordinator of the Kenyan Women's Green Belt, comments:

> It's very hard to push governments on issues that affect all aspects of society, let alone those that affect women. But the U.N. document has given us a tool with which to work. Now it's up to the women to push their issues into the boardrooms where political and economic decisions are made by those who did not even bother to come to Beijing.
>
> *(Quoted in Morgan 1996, p. 18)*

The Women's Environment and Development Organization evaluated governments' progress since the 1995 U.N. Conference in Beijing (WEDO 1998) and reported that "over 70% of the world's 187 countries have drawn up national action plans or drafts as required by the Beijing Platform" (WEDO press release, March 1, 1998). Sixty-six governments have set up national offices for women's affairs, thirty-four of them with the power to initiate legislation. Fifty-eight countries have adopted new legislation or policies to address women's rights, particularly concerning violence against women (Latin American and Caribbean countries, China, and New Zealand), female genital mutilation (Egypt), and the trafficking of women and children (Thailand). However, organizations from a majority of countries reported that economic restructuring has severely affected the realization of the Beijing commitments and reduced women's access to jobs, health care, and equal opportunity.

The global economic situation has generated new alliances and organizations working across national borders. Examples include STITCH (Support Team International for Textileras), a network of women organizers in the United States and Guatemala, and Comité Fronterizo de Obreras (CFO), or Border Committee of Women Workers, a Mexican worker-controlled organization that works closely with the American Friends Service Committee, a social justice organization. They have won several significant victories, such as winning wages that have been withheld illegally; pressuring companies to implement laws requiring safety equipment and protective clothing; challenging illegal layoffs and dismissals and winning legally mandated severance pay; curbing pollution in communities and factories; teaching workers practical exercises to alleviate repetitive strain injuries; testifying at shareholder meetings to give details of how companies treat their workers; and building the confidence of women workers so that they can stand up for their rights (http://www.afsc.org/border/maquila.htm). Diverse Women for Diversity are an international network with a secretariat in India. They oppose the corporate assault on biological and cultural diversity as argued in the statement they prepared for the WTO's Third Ministerial Conference, in Seattle, November 1999 (Reading 47). Thousands of people, including environmentalists, union members, indigenous people, feminists, and people of many faiths, came from all continents to participate in alternative workshops on economic and environmental issues, as well as to protest the WTO. This coordinated opposition was successful in stalling the "Seattle round" of talks aimed at further opening up global trade.

The Seeds of a New Global Economy

In Latin America, the Caribbean, Africa, and Asia, thousands of workers' organizations, environmentalists, feminists, and religious groups are campaigning for better pay and working conditions and for economic development that is environmentally sound (Braidotti et al. 1994; De Oliveira et al. n.d.; Leonard 1989), and they are protesting the poverty caused by external debt. Similarly, social and economic justice organizations and networks in countries of the North advocate that we in the United States learn more about the global economy and the impact of global inequalities on people's lives and livelihoods (Benjamin and Freedman 1989). They also urge us to live more simply: to recycle materials, wear secondhand clothing, barter for things we need, establish collectives and cooperatives, engage in socially responsible shopping and investing, and buy directly from farmers and craftspeople. A number of nonprofit organizations are involved in supporting fair trade between producers and craftspeople in the South and consumers in the North, including Equal Exchange (Cambridge, Mass.), Global Exchange (San Francisco Bay Area), Pueblo to People (Houston, Tex.), SELF-

HELP Crafts (Akron, Pa.), and Thread of Hope (Eugene, Ore.) Other projects include dialogue projects linking workers of the North and South, such as North-South Dialogue of the American Friends Service Committee's Latin American/Caribbean Program; campaigns urging a debt amnesty for countries of the South, like Jubilee 2000; campaigns to get institutions to stop buying World Bank bonds; Third World study tours; and direct support through work brigades such as those in Cuba and Nicaragua.

In the 1960s and 1970s, those active in U.S. movements for liberation and civil rights made theoretical and practical connections with anticolonial struggles in such countries as South Africa, Vietnam, Cuba, Angola, and Mozambique. In the twenty-first century, these international linkages are crucial, not merely, as Angela Davis (1997) remarked, "as a matter of inspiration or identification, but as a matter of necessity," because of the impact of the globalization of the economy.

Mary Zepernick (1998a, 1998b) and Virginia Rasmussen (1998) both argue that corporate dominance is not inevitable. In the eighteenth and nineteenth centuries, U.S. city and state governments watched corporations closely and revoked or amended their charters if they harmed the general welfare or exceeded the powers granted them by government. In 1843, for example, the Pennsylvania Legislature declared: "A corporation in law is just what the incorporation act makes it. It is the creature of the law and may be moulded to any shape or for any purpose the Legislature may deem most conducive for the common good" (quoted in Grossman 1998a, p. 1). In 1890 the highest court in New York revoked the charter of the North River Sugar Refining Corporation in a unanimous decision (*People v. North River Sugar Refining Corp.,* 24 N.E. 834.1890). In its judgment, the court noted:

> The judgment sought against the defendant is one of corporate death. The state which created, asks us to destroy, [sic] and the penalty invoked represents the extreme rigor of the law. The life of a corporation, is, indeed, less than that of the humblest citizen. . . . Corporations may, and often do, exceed their authority only where private rights are affected. When these are adjusted all mischief ends and all harm is averted. But where the transgression has a wider scope, and threatens the welfare of

the people, they may summon the offender to answer for the abuse of its franchise and the violation of corporate duty. . . . The abstract idea of a corporation, the legal entity . . . is itself a fiction. . . . The state permits in many ways an aggression of capital, but, mindful of the possible dangers to the people, overbalancing the benefits, keeps upon it a restraining hand, and maintains over it prudent supervision.

(Quoted in Grossman 1998a, p. 2)

Corporate owners worked hard to change the law and were successful over time. In an 1886 decision, the U.S. Supreme Court declared corporations legal persons. Gradually they were given a long list of civil and political rights, such as free speech, property rights, and the right to define and control investment, production, and the organization of work (Gross-

man 1998b). They became entitled to the Fourteenth Amendment protection that was added to the Constitution in 1870 to provide due process to freed African Americans (Zepernick 1998b). This resulted in a gradual reversal of the sovereignty of the people over corporations—originally mere legal entities—and an undermining of democracy, for people who are subordinate to corporations are not citizens. Zepernick and Rasmussen note that corporations are *things;* they cannot care or be responsible. The Program on Corporations, Law and Democracy (POCLAD) promotes public discussion of this fundamental contradiction between democracy and corporate control. It advocates that city governments, for example, create policies and programs to ensure control over corporations conducting business with the city, as a step toward reclaiming people's power over corporate entities.

◆◆◆

Questions for Reflection

In thinking about the issues raised in this chapter, consider these questions:

1. Why does the impact of the globalization of the economy matter to people living in the United States? What does it tell us about structural privilege (which we may not know we have and may not want)? If some of this material is new to you, why do you think you have not learned it before?

2. How does global inequality reinforce sexism, racial prejudice, and institutionalized racism in the United States?

3. How do you define wealth, aside from material possessions? List all the ways you are enriched.

4. Does wealth equal political power? Are rich people always in the **power elite**—the group that influences political and economic decisions in the country? Who makes up the power elite in the United States?

5. How do people in elite positions justify the perpetuation of inequalities to others? To themselves? How are the ideologies of nationalism, racial superiority, male superiority, and class superiority useful here?

◆◆◆

Taking Action

1. Look at the labels in your clothes and on all products you buy. Where were they made? Look up these countries on a map if you don't know where they are.

2. Do you need all you currently own? List everything you need to sustain life. Which items do you need to buy? Which might you make yourself, share, or barter with others?

3. Find out who manufactures the clothing that bears your college's name, and whether there are sweatshops in your region.

4. Get involved with a campaign that is tackling the issue of sweatshop production or debt relief.

Web Sites

Community Aid Abroad www.caa.org.au/campaigns/nike/sweating.html

Corporate Watch www.corpwatch.org

Global Exchange www.globalexchange.org

Human Rights Watch—Women's Division www.hrw.org/about/projects/women.html

Jubilee 2000 www.j2000usa.org/debt/edpac/debt.html

Student Alliance to Reform Corporations www.corpreform.org

Sweatshop Watch www.sweatshopwatch.org/swatch/industry

Women's Environment and Development Organization www.wedo.org

FORTY-ONE

Maquiladoras
The View from Inside
María Patricia Fernández-Kelly

What is it like to be female, single and eager to find employment at a maquiladora? Shortly after arriving in Ciudad Juárez and after finding stable lodging, I began looking through the pages of newspapers hoping to find a "wanted" ad. My intent was to merge with the clearly visible mass of women who roam the streets of industrial parks of Ciudad Juárez searching for jobs. They are, beyond doubt, a distinctive feature of the city, an effervescent expression of the conditions that prevail in the local job market.

My objectives were straightforward: I was to spend from four to six weeks applying for jobs and obtaining direct experience about the employment policies, recruitment strategies and screening mechanisms used by companies in the process of hiring

---

As part of the fieldwork for her study of the *maquiladora* industry in Mexico, anthropologist María Patricia Fernández-Kelly worked in a textile factory in Ciudad Juárez.

assembly workers. Special emphasis would be given to the average investment of time and money expended by individual workers in trying to gain access to jobs. In addition, I was to spend an equal amount of time working at a plant, preferably at one involved in the manufacture of apparel.

With this I expected to learn more about working conditions, production quotas and wages at a particular plant. In general both research stages were planned as exploratory devices that would elicit questions relevant to the research project from the perspective of workers themselves.

In retrospect, it seems odd that the doubt as to whether these goals were feasible or not never entered my design. However, finding a job at a maquiladora is not a self-evident proposition. For many women, actual workers, the task is not an easy one. This is due primarily to the large number of women they must compete with. Especially for those who are older than twenty-five years of age the probability of getting work in a maquiladora is low. At every step of their constant peregrination women are confronted by a familiar sign at the plants, "No applications available," or by the negative response of a guard or a secretary at the entrance of the factories. But such is the arrogance of the uninformed researcher. I went about the business of looking for a job as if the social milieu had to comply with the intents of my research rather than the reverse. Moreover, I was pressed for time. It was indispensable that I get a job as quickly as possible.

By using newspapers as a source of information for jobs available, I was departing from the common strategy of potential workers in that environment. As my own research would show, the majority of these workers avail themselves of information by word of mouth. They are part of informal networks which include relatives, friends and an occasional acquaintance in the personnel management sector. Most potential workers believe that a personal recommendation from someone already employed at a maquiladora can ease their difficult path.

This belief is well founded. At many plants, managers prefer to hire applicants by direct recommendation of employees who have proven to be dependable and hard-working. For example, at Electro Componentes de Mexico, the subsidiary of General Electric and one of the most stable maquiladoras in Juárez, it is established policy not to hire "outsiders." Only those who are introduced personally to the manager are considered to fill up vacancies.

Such a policy is not whimsical. It is the result of evaluations performed on a daily basis during the interactions between company personnel and workers. By resorting to the personal linkage, managers attenuate the dangers of having their factories infiltrated by unreliable workers, independent organizers and "troublemakers." . . .

On the other hand, the resemblance of a personal interest in the individual worker at the moment of hiring enables management to establish a bond often heavily colored by paternalism. From the point of view of workers this is a two-faceted proposition. Some complain of the not unusual practice of superintendents and managers who are prone to demand special services, for example, overtime, in exchange for personal favors: a loan, an exemption from work on a busy day when the presence of the worker at home is required by her children, and so on. As in other similar cases, personal linkages at the

workplace can and will be used as subtle mechanisms to exert control.

Workers, in turn, acknowledge a personal debt to the individual who has hired them. In the majority of cases, commitment to the firm is not distinct from the commitment to a particular individual through whom access to employment presumably has been achieved. A job becomes a personal favor granted through the kindness of the personnel manager or the superintendent of a factory. . . .

Only those who are not part of tightly woven informal networks must rely on impersonal ways to find a job. In this situation are recently arrived migrants and older women with children, for whom the attempt to find maquiladora employment may be a new experience after many years spent caring for children and the home. In objective terms my own situation as a newcomer in Ciudad Juárez was not markedly different from that of the former. Both types of women are likely to be found in larger numbers in the apparel manufacturing sector.

This is not a random occurrence. One of the basic propositions in the present work is that differences in manufacturing activity are related to variations in the volume of capital investments. In turn this combined variable determines recruitment strategies. Therefore different types of persons are predominately employed in different manufacturing sectors. Ciudad Juárez electronics maquiladoras, for example, tend to employ very young, single women. This is, in effect, a preferred category of potential workers from the point of view of industry.

Workers, on their part, also prefer the electronics sector, which is characterized by the existence of large stable plants, regular wages and certain additional benefits. In contrast, the apparel manufacturing sector is frequently characterized by smaller, less stable shops where working conditions are particularly strenuous. Because of their low levels of capital investment, many of these shops tend to hire personnel on a more or less temporary basis. The lack of even the smallest of commitments to their employees and the need to maintain an elastic work force to survive as capitalist enterprises in a fluctuating international market forces management to observe crude and often ruthless personnel recruitment policies.

One of such firms was Maquiladoras Internacionales. . . .

Attached to the tent-like factory where women work from 7:30 A.M. to 5:00 P.M. from Monday to Friday there is a tiny office. I entered that office wondering whether my appearance or accent would elicit the suspicion of my potential employers. The personnel manager looked me over sternly and told me to fill out a form. I was to return the following morning at seven to take a dexterity test.

I tried to respond to the thirty-five questions contained in the application in an acceptable manner. Most of the items were straightforward: name, age, marital status, place of birth, length of residence in Ciudad Juárez, property assets, previous jobs and income, number of pregnancies, general state of health, and so on. One, however, was unexpected: What is your major aspiration in life? I pondered briefly upon the superfluous character of that inquiry given the general features of the job sought. . . .

The following morning I was scheduled to take an on-the-job test. I assumed that this would consist of a short evaluation of my skills as a seamstress. I was to be proven wrong. At 7 A.M. I knocked at the door of the personnel office where I had filled out the application the day before. But no one was there yet. I peeked into the entrance of the factory in a state of moderate confusion. A dark-haired woman wearing false eyelashes ordered me to go in and promptly led me to my place. Her name was Margarita and she was the supervisor.

I had never been behind an industrial sewing machine of the kind I confronted at this time. That it was old was plain to see; how it worked was difficult to judge. An assortment of diversely cut denim parts was placed on my left side while I listened intently to Margarita's instructions. I was expected to sew patch-pockets on what were to become blue jeans. Obediently, I started to sew. The particulars of "unskilled" labor unfolded before my eyes.

The procedure involved in this operation required perfect coordination of hands, eyes and legs. The left hand was used to select the larger part of material from the batch next to the worker. Upon it, the pocket (swiftly grabbed by the right hand) had to be attached. There were no markers to guide the placement of the pocket on its proper place. This was achieved by experienced workers on a purely visual basis. Once the patch-pocket had been put on its correct position, the two parts had to be directed under a double needle while applying pressure on the machine's pedal with the right foot.

Because the pockets were sewed on with thread of a contrasting color, it was of peak importance to maintain the edge of the pocket perfectly aligned with the needles so as to produce a regular seam and an attractive design. Due to the diamond-like shape of the pocket, it was also indispensable to slightly rotate the materials three times while adjusting pressure on the pedal. Too much pressure inevitably broke the thread or resulted in seams longer than the edge of the pocket. Even the slightest deviation from the needles produced lopsided designs which had to be unsewed and gone over as many times as necessary to achieve an acceptable product. According to the instructions of the supervisor, once trained, I would be expected to sew a pocket every nine to ten seconds. That is, between 360 and 396 pockets every hour, between 2,880 and 3,168 every shift.

For this, velocity was a central consideration. The vast majority of apparel manufacturing maquiladoras operate through a combination of the minimum wage and piecework. At the moment of being hired, workers receive the minimum wage. During 1978 this amounted to 125 pesos a day (approximately $5.00). However, they are responsible for a production quota arrived at by time-clock calculations. Workers receive slight bonus payments when they are able to fulfill their production quotas on a sustained basis throughout the week. In any case they are not allowed to produce less than 80% of their assigned quota without being admonished. And a worker seriously endangers her job when unable to improve her level of productivity.

At Maquiladoras Internacionales a small blackboard indicated the type of weekly bonus received by those able to produce certain percentages of the quota. These fluctuated between 50.00 pesos (approximately $2.20) for those who completed 80% to 100.00 pesos (about $4.40) for those who accomplished 100%. Managers call this combination of steep production quotas, minimum wages and modest bonuses, "incentive programs."

I started my test at 7:30 A.M. with a sense of embarrassment about my limited skills and disbelief at the speed with which the women in the factory worked. As I continued sewing, the bundle of material on my left was renewed and grew in size, although slowly. I had to repeat the operation many times before the product was considered acceptable. But that is precisely what was troubling about the "test." I was being treated as a new worker while presumably being tested. I had not been issued a contract and, therefore, was not yet incorporated into the Instituto Mexicano del Seguro Social (the National Security System). Nor had I been instructed as to working hours, benefits and system of payment.

I explained to the supervisor that I had recently arrived in the city, alone, and with very little money. Would I be hired? What was the current wage? When would I be given a contract? Margarita listened patiently while helping me unsew one of many defective pockets, and then said, "You are too curious. Don't worry about it. Do your job and things will be all right." I continued to sew aware of the fact that every pocket attached during the "test" was becoming part of the plant's total production.

At 12:30 during the thirty-minute lunch break, I had a chance to better see the factory. Its improvised aura was underscored by the metal folding chairs behind the sewing machines. I had been sitting in one of them during the whole morning, but not until then did I notice that most of them had the well-known emblem of Coca-Cola painted on their backs. I had seen this kind of chair many times in casual parties both in Mexico and in the United States. Had they been bought or were they being rented from the local concessionary? In any event they were not designed in accordance to the strenuous requirements of a factory job, especially one needing the complex bodily movements of sewing. It was therefore necessary for women to bring their own colorful pillows to ameliorate the stress on their buttocks and spines. Later on I was to discover that chronic lumbago was, and is, a frequent condition among factory seamstresses.

My curiosity did not decrease during the next hours, nor were any of my questions answered. At 5 P.M. a bell rang signaling the end of the shift and workers quickly prepared to leave. I marched to the personnel office with the intent of getting more information about a confusing day. But this time my inquiry was less than welcome. Despite my over-shy approach to the personnel manager, his reaction was hostile. Even before he was able to turn the disapproving expression on his face into words, Margarita intervened with energy. She was angry. To the manager she said, "This woman has too many questions: Will she be hired? Is she going to be insured?" And

then to me, "I told you already we do piecework here; if you do your job you get a wage, otherwise you don't. That's clear, isn't it? What else do you want? You should be grateful! This plant is giving you a chance to work! What else do you want? Come back tomorrow and be punctual."

This was only the first in a number of application procedures that I underwent. Walking about the industrial parks while following other job-seekers was especially informative. Most women do not engage in this task alone. Rather, they do it in the company of friends or relatives. Small groups of two or three women looking for work may be commonly seen in the circumvicinity of the factories. Also frequent is the experience of very young women, ages between sixteen and seventeen, seen in the company of their mothers. . . .

At the times when shifts begin or end, the industrial parks of Juárez form a powerful visual image as thousands of women arrive in buses, taxi-cabs and *ruteras* while many others exit the factories. During working hours only those seeking jobs may be seen wandering about. Many, but not the majority, are "older women." They confront special difficulties due both to their age and to the fact that they often support their own children. These are women who, in most cases, enter the labor force after many years dedicated to domestic chores and child-care. The precipitant factor that determines their entry into the labor force is often the desertion by their male companions. The bind they are placed in at that time is well illustrated by the experience of a thirty-one-year-old woman, the mother of six children: "I have been looking for work since my husband left me two months ago. But I haven't had any luck. It must be my age and the fact that I have so many children. Maybe I should lie and say I've only one. But then the rest wouldn't be entitled to medical care once I got the job." Women often look for jobs in order to support their children. But being a mother is frequently the determining factor that prevents them from getting jobs.

In early June, 1978, Camisas de Juárez, a recently formed maquiladora, was starting a second (evening) shift. Until then it had hired approximately 110 workers operating in the morning hours. As it expanded production, a new contingent of workers had to be recruited. Advertisements to that effect appeared in the daily newspapers. I responded to them. So did dozens of other women.

Camisas de Juárez is located in the modern Parque Industrial Bermúdez. On the morning that I arrived with the intent of applying for a job, thirty-seven women had preceded me. Some had arrived as early as 6 A.M. At 10 the door which separated the front lawn from the entrance to the factory had not yet been opened. A guard appeared once in a while to peek at the growing contingent of applicants, but these were given no encouragement to stay on, nor was the door unlocked.

At 10:30 the guard finally opened the door and informed us that only those having personal recommendation letters would be permitted to walk inside. This was the first in a series of formal and informal screening procedures used to reduce the number of potential workers. It was an effective screening device: Thirteen women left immediately, as they did not have the letter of recommendation alluded to by the guard. Others tried to convince him that although they had no personal recommendation, they "knew" someone already employed at the factory. It was through the recommendation of these acquaintances that they had come to apply for a job.

One of them, Xochitl, lacked both a written or verbal recommendation but she insisted. She had with her a diploma issued by a sewing academy. She was hopeful that this would work in her favor. "It is better to have proof that you are qualified to do the job than to have a letter for recommendation, right?" I wondered whether the personnel manager would agree.

Indeed her diploma gave Xochitl claim to a particular skill. But academies such as the one she had attended abound in Ciudad Juárez. For a relatively small sum of money they offer technical and vocational courses which presumably qualify young men and women for skilled work. However, in an environment lacking in employment opportunities, their value is in question. In many cases maquiladora managers prefer to hire women who have had direct experience on a job or those who are young and inexperienced but who can be trained to suit the needs of a particular firm. As one manager put it to me, "We prefer to hire women who are unspoiled, that is, those who come to us without preconceptions about what industrial work is. Women such as these are easier to shape to our own requirements." . . .

We waited upon the benevolence of the guard who seemed unperturbed by the fluctuating number of women standing by the door. To many of us he was the main obstacle lying between unemployment and getting a job from someone inside the factory in a decision-making position. If only we could get our foot in, maybe there was a chance. . . . The young man dressed in uniform appeared to the expectant women as an arrogant and insensitive figure. I asked him how long he had worked there. With the air of one who feels he has gained mastery over his own fate he answered, "Uy! I've been working here for a very long time, I assure you: almost two years."

To me his words sounded a bit pathetic. But Beatríz and Teresa, two sisters of twenty-three and nineteen years of age, respectively, were not pleased by his attitude. Their patience had been exhausted and their alternating comments were belligerent: "Why must these miserable guards always act this way? It would seem that they've never had to look for a job. Maybe this one thinks he's more important than the owner of the factory. What a bastard!" But their dialogue failed to elicit any response. Guards are accustomed to similar outbursts.

Teresa wanted to know whether I had any sewing experience. "Not much," I told her, "but I used to sew for a lady in my hometown." "Well, then you're very lucky," she said, "because they aren't hiring anyone without experience." The conversation having begun, I proceeded to ask a similar question, "How about you, have you worked before?"

> Yes, both my sister and I used to work in a small shop on Altamirano Street in downtown Juárez. There were about seventy women like us sewing in a very tiny space, about twenty square meters. We sewed pants for the minimum wage, but we had no insurance.
>
> The boss used to bring precut fabric from the United States for us to sew and then he sold the finished products in El Paso. When he was unable to get fabric we were laid-off; sent to rest without pay! Later on he wanted to hire us again but he still didn't want to insure us even though we had worked at the shop for three years.
>
> When I was sixteen I used to cut thread at the shop. Afterwards one of the seamstresses taught me how to operate a small machine and I started doing serious work. Beatríz, my sister, used to sew the pockets on the pants. It's been

three months since we left the shop. Right now we are living from the little that my father earns. We are two of nine brothers and sisters (there were twelve of us in total but three died when they were young). My father does what he can but he doesn't have a steady job. Sometimes he does construction work; sometimes he's hired to help paint a house or sells toys at the stadium. You know, odd jobs. He doesn't earn enough to support us.

I am single, thanks be to God, and I do not want to get married. There are enough problems in my life as it is! But my sister married an engineer when she was only fifteen. Now she is unmarried and she has three children to support. They live with us too. Beatríz and I are the oldest in the family, you see, that's why we really have to find a job. . . .

At that point Beatríz intervened. I asked whether her husband helped support the children. Her answer was unwavering: "No, and I don't want him to give me anything, not a cent, because I don't want him to have any claim or rights over my babies. As long as I can support them, he won't have to interfere." I replied, "But aren't there better jobs outside of maquiladoras? I understand you can make more money working at a *cantina*. Is that true?"

Both of them looked at me suspiciously. Cantinas are an ever present reminder of overt or concealed prostitution. Teresa said,

That is probably true, but what would our parents think? You can't stop people from gossiping, and many of those cantinas are whorehouses. Of course, when you have great need you can't be choosy, right? For some time I worked as a waitress but that didn't last. The supervisor was always chasing me. First he wanted to see me after work. I told him I had a boyfriend, but he insisted. He said I was too young to have a steady boy-friend. Then, when he learned I had some typing skills, he wanted me to be his secretary. I'm not stupid! I knew what he really wanted; he was always staring at my legs. So I had to leave that job too. I told him I had been rehired at the shop although it wasn't true. He wasn't bad looking, but he was married and had children. . . . Why must men fool around?

At last the guard announced that only those with previous experience would be allowed to fill out applications. Twenty women went into the narrow lobby of Camisas de Juárez, while the rest left in small quiet groups. For those of us who stayed a second waiting period began. One by one we were shown into the office of the personnel manager where we were to take a manual dexterity test. The point was to fit fifty variously colored pegs into fifty similarly colored perforations on a wooden board. This had to be accomplished in the shortest possible time. Clock in hand, the personnel manager told each woman when to begin and when to stop. Some were asked to adjust the pegs by hand, others were given small pliers to do so. Most were unable to complete the test in the allotted time. One by one they came out of the office looking weary and expressing their conviction that they wouldn't be hired.

Later on we were given the familiar application form. Again, I had to ponder what my greatest aspiration in life was. But this time I was curious to know what Xochitl had answered. "Well," she said, "I don't know if my answer is right. Maybe it is wrong. But I tried to be truthful. My greatest aspiration in life is to improve myself and to progress." . . .

After completing the application at Camisas de Juárez there was still another test to take. This one consisted of demonstrating sewing skills on an industrial machine. Again many women expressed doubts and concern after returning to the lobby where other expectant women awaited their turn. In the hours that had been spent together a lively dialogue had ensued. Evidently there was a sense that all of us were united by the common experience of job seeking and by the gnawing anxiety that potential failure entails. Women compared notes and exchanged opinions about the nature and difficulty of their respective tests. They did not offer each other overt reassurance or support, but they made sympathetic comments and hoped that there would be work for all.

At 3:30 P.M., that is, seven hours after the majority of us had arrived at the plant, we were dismissed. We were given no indication that any of us would be hired. Rather, we were told that a telegram would be sent to each address as soon as a decision was made. Most women left disappointed and certain that they would probably not be hired.

Two weeks later, when I had almost given up all hope, the telegram arrived. I was to come to the plant as soon as possible to receive further instructions. Upon my arrival I was given the address of a small clinic in downtown Ciudad Juárez. I was to bring two pictures to the clinic and take a medical examination. Its explicit purpose was to evaluate the physical fitness of potential workers. In reality it was a simple pregnancy test. Maquiladoras do not hire pregnant women, although very often these are among the ones with greater need for employment. . . .

Having been examined at the clinic, I returned to the factory with a sealed envelope containing certification of my physical capacity to work. I was then told to return the following Monday at 3:30 P.M. in order to start work. After what seemed an unduly long and complicated procedure, I was finally being hired as an assembly worker. For the next six weeks I shared the experience of approximately eighty women who had also been recruited to work the evening shift at Camisas de Juárez. Xochitl, Beatríz and Teresa had been hired too.

On weekdays work started at 3:45 P.M. and it ended at 11:30 P.M. At 7:30 P.M. a bell signaled the beginning of a half-hour break during which workers could eat their dinner. Some brought homemade sandwiches, but many bought their food at the factory. Meals generally consisted of a dish of *flautas* or *tostadas* and carbonated drinks. The persistence of inadequate diets causes assembly workers numerous gastric problems. On Saturdays the shift started at 11:30 A.M. and it ended at 9:30 P.M. with a half-hour break. We worked in total forty-eight hours every week and earned the minimum wage, that is, 875 pesos per week; 125 pesos per day; an hourly rate of approximately $0.60. . . .

From the perspective of workers, medical insurance is as important as a decorous wage. This is particularly true in the case of women who have children in their care. Thus, it was not surprising to find out that some new workers at Camisas de Juárez were there mainly because of the *seguro*. María Luisa, a twenty-nine-year-old woman, told me, "I don't have a lot of money, but neither do I have great need to work. My husband owns a small restaurant and we have a fairly good income. But I have four children and one of them is chronically sick. Without insurance medical fees will render us poor. That's the main reason why I am working."

As do the majority of garment maquiladoras, Camisas de Juárez operates by a combination of piecework and the minimum wage. Upon being hired by the plant every worker earns a fixed wage. However, all workers are expected to fulfill production quotas. On the first day at the job I was trained to perform a particular operation. My task was to sew narrow biases around the cuff-openings of men's shirts. As with other operations I had performed before, this one entailed coordination and speed. . . .

As for the production quota, I was expected to complete 162 pairs of sleeves every hour, that is, one every 2.7 seconds, more than 1,200 pairs per shift. It seemed to me that to achieve such a goal would require unworldly skill and velocity. In six weeks as a direct production operator I was to fall short of this goal by almost 50%. But I was a very inexperienced worker. Sandra, who sat next to me during this period, assured me that it could be done. It wasn't easy, but certainly it could be done. . . .

The factory environment was all-embracing, its demands overwhelmed me. Young supervisors walked about the aisles asking for higher productivity and encouraging us to work at greater speed. Periodically their voices could be heard throughout the workplace: "Faster! faster! Come on, girls, let us hear the sound of those machines!" They were personally responsible before management for the efficiency of the workers under their command.

Esther, who oversaw my labor, had been a nurse prior to her employment in the factory. I was intrigued by her polite manner and her change of jobs. She dressed prettily, seeming a bit out of place amidst the heated humdrum of the sewing machines, the lint and the dispersed fabric that cluttered the plant. She told me it was more profitable to work at a maquiladora than at a clinic or a hospital.

Esther saw her true vocation as that of a nurse, but she had to support an ill and aging father. Her mother had died three years earlier, and although her home was nice and fully owned, she was solely responsible for the family debts. Working at a factory entailed less prestige than working as a nurse, but it offered a better wage. She was now earning almost one thousand pesos a week. As a nurse she had earned only a bit more than half that amount. From her I also learned, for the first time, about the dubious advantages of being a maquiladora supervisor.

As with the others in similar positions, Esther had to stay at the plant long after the shift ended and the workers left. Very often the hours ran until one in the morning. During that time she verified quotas, sorted out production, tried to detect errors and, not seldom, personally unseamed defective garments. With the others she was also responsible for the preparation of shipments and the selection of material for the following day's production. In other words, her supervisory capacities included quality control and some administrative functions.

When productivity levels are not met, when workers fail to arrive punctually or are absent, or when there is trouble in the line, it is the supervisor who is first admonished by management. Thus, supervisors occupy an intermediary position between the firm and the workers, which is to say that they often find themselves between the devil and the deep blue sea.

As with the factory guard, supervisors and group leaders are frequently seen by workers as solely responsible for their plight at the workplace. Perceived abuses, unfair treatment and excessive demands are thought to be the result of supervisors' whims rather than the creature of a particular system of production. That explains, in part, why workers' grievances are often couched in complaints about the performance of supervisors.

But while supervisors may be seen by workers as close allies of the firms, they stand at the bottom of the administrative hierarchy. They are also the receivers of middle and upper management's dissatisfaction, but they have considerably less power and their sphere of action is very limited. Many line supervisors agree that the complications they face in their jobs are hardly worth the differences in pay. . . .

The Organization of Labor in the Factory

The pressures exerted by supervisors at Camisas de Juárez were hard to ignore. Esther was considerate and encouraging: "You're doing much better now. Soon enough you'll be sewing as fast as the others." But I had doubts, as she was constantly asking me to repair my own defective work, a task which entailed an infinite sense of frustration. I began to skip dinner breaks in order to continue sewing in a feeble attempt to improve my productivity level. I was not alone. Some workers fearful of permanent dismissal also stayed at their sewing machines during the break while the rest went outside to eat and rest. I could understand their behavior; their jobs were at

stake. But presumably my situation was different. I had nothing to lose by inefficiency, and yet I felt compelled to do my best. I started pondering upon the subtle mechanisms that dominate will at the workplace and about the shame that overwhelms those who fall short of the goals assigned to them.

The fact is that as the days passed it became increasingly difficult to think of factory work as a stage in a research project. My identity became that of the worker; my immediate objectives those determined by the organization of labor at the plant. Academic research became an ethereal fiction. Reality was work, as much for me as for the others who labored under the same roof.

These feelings were reinforced by my personal interactions during working hours. I was one link in a rigidly structured chain. My failure to produce speedily had numerous consequences for others operating in the same line and in the factory as a whole. For example, Lucha, my nineteen-year-old companion, was in charge of cutting remnant thread and separating the sleeves five other seamstresses and I sewed. She also made it her business to return to me all those parts which she felt would not meet Esther's approval. According to her she did this in order to spare me further embarrassment. But it was in her interest that I sewed quickly and well; the catch in this matter was that she was unable to meet her quota unless the six seamstresses she assisted met theirs.

Therefore, a careless and slow worker could stand between Lucha and her possibility to get a weekly bonus. The more a seamstress sewed, the more a thread cutter became indispensable. As a consequence, Lucha was extremely interested in seeing improvements in my level of productivity and in the quality of my work. Sometimes her attitude and exhortations verged on the hostile. As far as I was concerned, the accusatory expression on her face was the best work incentive yet devised by the factory. It was not difficult to discern impinging tension. I was not surprised to find out during the weeks spent at Camisas de Juárez that the germ of enmity had bloomed between some seamstresses and their respective thread cutters over matters of work.

Although the relationships between seamstresses and thread cutters were especially delicate, all workers were affected by each other's level of efficiency. Cuffless sleeves could not be attached to shirts.

Sleeves could not be sewed to shirts without collars or pockets. Holes and buttons had to be fixed at the end. Unfinished garments could not be cleaned of lint or labeled. In sum, each minute step required a series of preceding operations effectively completed. Delay of one stage inevitably slowed up the whole process.

From the perspective of the workers, labor appeared as the interconnection of efficiently performed individual activities rather than as a structured imposition from above. Managers are nearly invisible, but the flaws of fellow workers are always apparent. Bonuses exist as seemingly impersonal rewards whose access can be made difficult by a neighbor's laziness or incompetence. As a result, complaints are frequently directed against other workers and supervisors. The organization of labor at any particular plant does not immediately lead to feelings of solidarity.

On the other hand, common experiences at the workplace provide the basis for dialogue and elicit a particular kind of humor. In this there is frequently expressed a longing for relief from the tediousness of industrial work. One of Sandra's favorite topics of conversation was to reflect upon the possibility of marriage. She did so with a witty and self-deprecatory attitude.

She thought that if she could only find a nice man who would be willing to support her, everything in her life would be all right. She didn't mind if he was not young or good-looking, as long as he had plenty of money. Were there men like that left in the world? Of course, with the children it was difficult, not to say impossible, to find such a godsend. Then again, no one kept you from trying. But not at the maquiladora. All of us were female. Not even a lonely engineer was to be found at Camisas de Juárez. One could die of boredom there.

However, the fact that there weren't men around at the plant had its advantages according to Sandra. At many factories men generally occupied supervisory and middle- and upper-management positions. Sandra knew many women who had been seduced and then deserted by engineers and technicians. In other cases women felt they had to comply with the sexual demands of fellow workers because they believed otherwise they would lose their jobs. Some were just plain stupid. Things were especially difficult for very young women at large plants like RCA. They needed guidance and information to stay out of trouble, but there was no one to advise them. Their families had too many problems to care. . . .

Fortunately, there were the bars and the discotheques. Did I like to go out dancing? She didn't think so; I didn't look like the kind who would. But it was great fun; we should go out together sometime (eventually we did). The Malibú, a popular dancing hall, had good shows. But it was tacky and full of kids. It was better to go to the Max Fim, and especially the Cosmos. The latter was always crowded because everyone liked it so much. Even people from the other side (the United States) came to Juárez just to visit Cosmos. Its décor was inspired by outerspace movies like *Star Wars*. It was full of color and movement and shifting lights. They played the best American disco music. If you were lucky you could meet a U.S. citizen. Maybe he would even want to get married and you could go and live in El Paso. Things like that happen at discotheques. Once a Jordanian soldier in service at Fort Bliss had asked her to marry him the first time they met at Cosmos. But he wanted to return to his country, and she had said no. Cosmos was definitely the best discotheque in Juárez, and Sandra could be found dancing there amidst the deafening sound of music every Saturday evening.

The inexhaustible level of energy of women working at the maquiladoras never ceased to impress me. How could anyone be in the mood for all-night dancing on Saturdays after forty-eight weekly hours of industrial work? I had seen many of these women stretching their muscles late at night, trying to soothe the pain they felt at the waist. After the incessant noise of the sewing machines, how could anyone long for even higher levels of sound? But as Sandra explained to me, life is too short. If you don't go out and have fun, you will come to the end of your days having done nothing but sleep, eat and work. And she didn't call that living. . . .

FORTY-TWO

The Globetrotting Sneaker

Cynthia Enloe

Four years after the fall of the Berlin Wall marked the end of the Cold War, Reebok, one of the fastest growing companies in United States history, decided that the time had come to make its mark in Russia. Thus it was with considerable fanfare that Reebok's executives opened their first store in downtown Moscow in July 1993. A week after the grand opening, store managers described sales as well above expectations.

Reebok's opening in Moscow was the perfect post–Cold War scenario: commercial rivalry replacing military posturing; consumerist tastes homogenizing heretofore hostile peoples; capital and managerial expertise flowing freely across newly porous state borders. Russians suddenly had the "freedom" to spend money on U.S. cultural icons like athletic footwear, items priced above and beyond daily subsistence: at the end of 1993, the average Russian earned the equivalent of $40 a month. Shoes on display were in the $100 range. Almost 60 percent of single parents, most of whom were women, were living in poverty. Yet in Moscow and Kiev, shoe promoters had begun targeting children, persuading them to pressure their mothers to spend money on stylish, Western sneakers. And as far as strategy goes, athletic shoe giants have, you might say, a good track record. In the U.S. many inner-city boys who see basketball as a "ticket out of the ghetto" have become convinced that certain brand-name shoes will give them an edge.

But no matter where sneakers are bought or sold, the potency of their advertising imagery has made it easy to ignore this mundane fact: Shaquille O'Neal's Reeboks are stitched by someone; Michael Jordan's Nikes are stitched by someone; so are your roommate's, so are your grandmother's. Those someones are women, mostly Asian women who are supposed to believe that their "opportunity" to make sneakers

for U.S. companies is a sign of their country's progress—just as a Russian woman's chance to spend two month's salary on a pair of shoes for her child allegedly symbolizes the new Russia.

As the global economy expands, sneaker executives are looking to pay women workers less and less, even though the shoes that they produce are capturing an ever-growing share of the footwear market. By the end of 1993, sales in the U.S. alone had reached $11.6 billion. Nike, the largest supplier of athletic footwear in the world, posted a record $298 million profit for 1993—earnings that had nearly tripled in five years. And sneaker companies continue to refine their strategies for "global competitiveness"—hiring supposedly docile women to make their shoes, changing designs as quickly as we fickle customers change our tastes, and shifting factories from country to country as trade barriers rise and fall.

The logic of it all is really quite simple; yet trade agreements such as the North American Free Trade Agreement (NAFTA) and the General Agreement of Tariffs and Trade (GATT) are, of course, talked about in a jargon that alienates us, as if they were technical matters fit only for economists and diplomats. The bottom line is that all companies operating overseas depend on trade agreements made between their own governments and the regimes ruling the countries in which they want to make or sell their products. Korean, Indonesian, and other women workers around the world know this better than anyone. They are tackling trade politics because they have learned from hard experience that the trade deals their governments sign do little to improve the lives of workers. Guarantees of fair, healthy labor practices, of the rights to speak freely and to organize independently, will usually be left out of trade pacts—and women will suffer. The [1994] passage of both NAFTA and GATT ensures that a growing number of private companies will now be competing across borders without restriction. The result? Big business will step up efforts to pit working women in industrialized countries against much

---

This article draws from the work of South Korean scholars Hyun Sook Kim, Seung-kyung Kim, Katharine Moon, Seungsook Moon, and Jeong-Lim Nam.

lower-paid working women in "developing" countries, perpetuating the misleading notion that they are inevitable rivals in the global job market.

All the "New World Order" really means to corporate giants like athletic shoemakers is that they now have the green light to accelerate long-standing industry practices. In the early 1980s, the field marshals commanding Reebok and Nike, which are both U.S.-based, decided to manufacture most of their sneakers in South Korea and Taiwan, hiring local women. L.A. Gear, Adidas, Fila, and Asics quickly followed their lead. In short time, the coastal city of Pusan, South Korea, became the "sneaker capital of the world." Between 1982 and 1989 the U.S. lost 58,500 footwear jobs to cities like Pusan, which attracted sneaker executives because its location facilitated international transport. More to the point, South Korea's military government had an interest in suppressing labor organizing, and it had a comfortable military alliance with the U.S. Korean women also seemed accepting of Confucian philosophy, which measured a woman's morality by her willingness to work hard for her family's well-being and to acquiesce to her father's and husband's dictates. With their sense of patriotic duty, Korean women seemed the ideal labor force for export-oriented factories.

U.S. and European sneaker company executives were also attracted by the ready supply of eager Korean male entrepreneurs with whom they could make profitable arrangements. This fact was central to Nike's strategy in particular. When they moved their production sites to Asia to lower labor costs, the executives of the Oregon-based company decided to reduce their corporate responsibilities further. Instead of owning factories outright, a more efficient strategy would be to subcontract the manufacturing to wholly foreign-owned—in this case, South Korean—companies. Let them be responsible for workers' health and safety. Let them negotiate with newly emergent unions. Nike would retain control over those parts of sneaker production that gave its officials the greatest professional satisfaction and the ultimate word on the product: design and marketing. Although Nike was following in the footsteps of garment and textile manufacturers, it set the trend for the rest of the athletic footwear industry.

But at the same time, women workers were developing their own strategies. As the South Korean pro-democracy movement grew throughout the 1980s, increasing numbers of women rejected tradi-

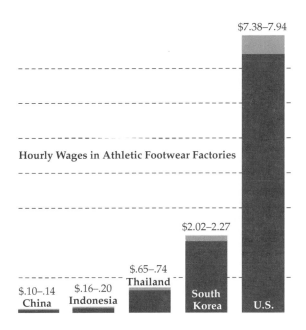

Hourly Wages in Athletic Footwear Factories

$7.38–7.94

$2.02–2.27

$.65–.74
Thailand

$.10–.14
China

$.16–.20
Indonesia

South Korea

U.S.

tional notions of feminine duty. Women began organizing in response to the dangerous working conditions, daily humiliations, and low pay built into their work. Such resistance was profoundly threatening to the government, given the fact that South Korea's emergence as an industrialized "tiger" had depended on women accepting their "role" in growing industries like sneaker manufacture. If women reimagined their lives as daughters, as wives, as workers, as citizens, it wouldn't just rattle their employers; it would shake the very foundations of the whole political system.

At the first sign of trouble, factory managers called in government riot police to break up employees' meetings. Troops sexually assaulted women workers, stripping, fondling, and raping them "as a control mechanism for suppressing women's engagement in the labor movement," reported Jeong-Lim Nam of Hyosung Women's University in Taegu. It didn't work. It didn't work because the feminist activists in groups like the Korean Women Workers Association (KWWA) helped women understand and deal with the assaults. The KWWA held consciousness-raising sessions in which notions of feminine duty and respectability were tackled along with wages and benefits. They organized independently of the male-led labor unions to ensure

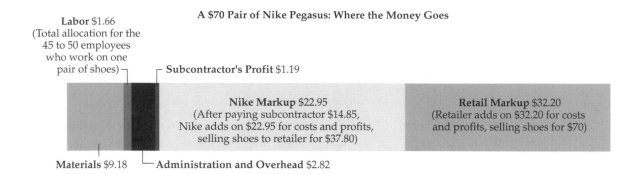

A $70 Pair of Nike Pegasus: Where the Money Goes

Labor $1.66
(Total allocation for the
45 to 50 employees
who work on one
pair of shoes)

Subcontractor's Profit $1.19

Nike Markup $22.95
(After paying subcontractor $14.85,
Nike adds on $22.95 for costs and profits,
selling shoes to retailer for $37.80)

Retail Markup $32.20
(Retailer adds on $32.20 for costs
and profits, selling shoes for $70)

Materials $9.18   **Administration and Overhead** $2.82

that their issues would be taken seriously, in labor negotiations and in the pro-democracy movement as a whole.

The result was that women were at meetings with management, making sure that in addition to issues like long hours and low pay, sexual assault at the hands of managers and health care were on the table. Their activism paid off: in addition to winning the right to organize women's unions, their earnings grew. In 1980, South Korean women in manufacturing jobs earned 45 percent of the wages of their male counterparts; by 1990, they were earning more than 50 percent. Modest though it was, the pay increase was concrete progress, given that the gap between women's and men's manufacturing wages in Japan, Singapore, and Sri Lanka actually *widened* during the 1980s. Last but certainly not least, women's organizing was credited with playing a major role in toppling the country's military regime and forcing open elections in 1987.

Without that special kind of workplace control that only an authoritarian government could offer, sneaker executives knew that it was time to move. In Nike's case, its famous advertising slogan—"Just Do It"—proved truer to its corporate philosophy than its women's "empowerment" ad campaign, designed to rally women's athletic (and consumer) spirit. In response to South Korean women workers' newfound activist self-confidence, the sneaker company and its subcontractors began shutting down a number of their South Korean factories in the late 1980s and early 1990s. After bargaining with government officials in nearby China and Indonesia, many Nike subcontractors set up shop in those countries, while some went to Thailand. China's government remains nominally Communist; Indonesia's ruling generals are staunchly anti-Communist. But

both are governed by authoritarian regimes who share the belief that if women can be kept hard at work, low paid, and unorganized, they can serve as a magnet for foreign investors.

Where does all this leave South Korean women —or any woman who is threatened with a factory closure if she demands decent working conditions and a fair wage? They face the dilemma confronted by thousands of women from dozens of countries. The risk of job loss is especially acute in relatively mobile industries; it's easier for a sneaker, garment, or electronics manufacturer to pick up and move than it is for an automaker or a steel producer. In the case of South Korea, poor women had moved from rural villages into the cities searching for jobs to support not only themselves, but parents and siblings. The exodus of manufacturing jobs has forced more women into the growing "entertainment" industry. The kinds of bars and massage parlors offering sexual services that had mushroomed around U.S. military bases during the Cold War have been opening up across the country.

But the reality is that women throughout Asia are organizing, knowing full well the risks involved. Theirs is a long-term view; they are taking direct aim at companies' nomadic advantage, by building links among workers in countries targeted for "development" by multinational corporations. Through sustained grassroots efforts, women are developing the skills and confidence that will make it increasingly difficult to keep their labor cheap. Many are looking to the United Nations conference on women in Beijing, China, this September [1996], as a rare opportunity to expand their cross-border strategizing.

The Beijing conference will also provide an important opportunity to call world attention to the hypocrisy of the governments and corporations doing business in China. Numerous athletic shoe companies followed Nike in setting up manufacturing sites throughout the country. This included Reebok—a company claiming its share of responsibility for ridding the world of "injustice, poverty, and other ills that gnaw away at the social fabric," according to a statement of corporate principles.

Since 1988, Reebok has been giving out annual human rights awards to dissidents from around the world. But it wasn't until 1992 that the company adopted its own "human rights production standards"—after labor advocates made it known that the quality of life in factories run by its subcontractors was just as dismal as that at most other athletic shoe suppliers in Asia. Reebok's code of conduct, for example, includes a pledge to "seek" those subcontractors who respect workers' rights to organize. The only problem is that independent trade unions are banned in China. Reebok has chosen to ignore that fact, even though Chinese dissidents have been the recipients of the company's own human rights award. As for working conditions, Reebok now says it sends its own inspectors to production sites a couple of times a year. But they have easily "missed" what subcontractors are trying to hide—like 400 young women workers locked at night into an overcrowded dormitory near a Reebok-contracted factory in the town of Zhuhai, as reported last August in the *Asian Wall Street Journal Weekly.*

Nike's cofounder and CEO Philip Knight has said that he would like the world to think of Nike as "a company with a soul that recognizes the value of human beings." Nike, like Reebok, says it sends in inspectors from time to time to check up on work conditions at its factories; in Indonesia, those factories are run largely by South Korean subcontractors. But according to Donald Katz in a recent book on the company, Nike spokesman Dave Taylor told an in-house newsletter that the factories are "[the subcontractors'] business to run." For the most part, the company relies on regular reports from subcontractors regarding its "Memorandum of Understanding," which managers must sign, promising to impose "local government standards" for wages, working conditions, treatment of workers, and benefits.

In April, the minimum wage in the Indonesian capital of Jakarta will be $1.89 *a day*—among the highest in a country where the minimum wage varies by region. And managers are required to pay only 75 percent of the wage directly; the remainder can be withheld for "benefits." By now, Nike has a well-honed response to growing criticisms of its low-cost labor strategy. Such wages should not be seen as exploitative, says Nike, but rather as the first rung on the ladder of economic opportunity that Nike has extended to workers with few options. Otherwise, they'd be out "harvesting coconut meat in the tropical sun," wrote Nike spokesman Dusty Kidd, in a letter to the *Utne Reader.* The all-is-relative response craftily shifts attention away from reality: Nike didn't move to Indonesia to help Indonesians; it moved to ensure that its profit margin continues to grow. And that is pretty much guaranteed in a country where "local standards" for wages rarely take a worker over the poverty line. A 1991 survey by the International Labor Organization (ILO) found that 88 percent of women working at the Jakarta minimum wage at the time—slightly less than a dollar a day—were malnourished.

A woman named Riyanti might have been among the workers surveyed by the ILO. Interviewed by the *Boston Globe* in 1991, she told the reporter who had asked about her long hours and low pay: "I'm happy working here. . . . I can make money and I can make friends." But in fact, the reporter discovered that Riyanti had already joined her coworkers in two strikes, the first to force one of Nike's Korean subcontractors to accept a new women's union and the second to compel managers to pay at least the minimum wage. That Riyanti appeared less than forthcoming about her activities isn't surprising. Many Indonesian factories have military men posted in their front offices who find no fault with managers who tape women's mouths shut to keep them from talking among themselves. They and their superiors have a political reach that extends far beyond the barracks. Indonesia has all the makings for a political explosion, especially since the gap between rich and poor is widening into a chasm. It is in this setting that the government has tried to crack down on any independent labor organizing—a policy that Nike has helped to implement. Referring to a recent strike in a Nike-contracted factory, Tony Nava, Nike representative in Indonesia, told the *Chicago Tribune* in November 1994 that the "troublemakers" had been fired. When asked about Nike policy on the issue, spokesman Keith Peters struck a conciliatory note: "If the government were to allow and encourage independent labor organizing, we would be happy to support it."

Indonesian workers' efforts to create unions independent of governmental control were a surprise to shoe companies. Although their moves from South Korea have been immensely profitable [see chart on p. 290], they do not have the sort of immunity from activism that they had expected. In May 1993, the murder of a female labor activist outside Surabaya set off a storm of local and international protest. Even the U.S. State Department was forced to take note in its 1993 worldwide human rights report, describing a system similar to that which generated South Korea's boom 20 years earlier: severely restricted union organizing, security forces used to break up strikes, low wages for men, lower wages for women—complete with government rhetoric celebrating women's contribution to national development.

Yet when President Clinton visited Indonesia last November, he made only a token effort to address the country's human rights problem. Instead, he touted the benefits of free trade, sounding indeed more enlightened, more in tune with the spirit of the post–Cold War era than do those defenders of protectionist trading policies who coat their rhetoric with "America first" chauvinism. But "free trade" as actually being practiced today is hardly *free* for any workers—in the U.S. or abroad—who have to accept the Indonesian, Chinese, or Korean workplace model as the price of keeping their jobs.

The not-so-new plot of the international trade story has been "divide and rule." If women workers and their government in one country can see that a sneaker company will pick up and leave if their labor demands prove more costly than those in a neighbor country, then women workers will tend to see their neighbors not as regional sisters, but as competitors who can steal their precarious livelihoods. Playing women off against each other is, of course, old hat. Yet it is as essential to international trade politics as is the fine print in GATT.

But women workers allied through networks like the Hong Kong–based Committee for Asian Women are developing their own post–Cold War foreign policy, which means addressing women's needs: how to convince fathers and husbands that a woman going out to organizing meetings at night is not sexually promiscuous; how to develop workplace agendas that respond to family needs; how to work with male unionists who push women's demands to the bottom of their lists; how to build a global movement.

These women refuse to stand in awe of the corporate power of the Nike or Reebok or Adidas executive. Growing numbers of Asian women today have concluded that trade politics have to be understood by women on their own terms. They will be coming to Beijing this September [1995] ready to engage with women from other regions to link the politics of consumerism with the politics of manufacturing. If women in Russia and Eastern Europe can challenge Americanized consumerism, if Asian activists can solidify their alliances, and if U.S. women can join with them by taking on trade politics—the post–Cold War sneaker may be a less comfortable fit in the 1990s.

FORTY-THREE

The Debt Crisis
Who Really Owes Whom?
Caribbean Association for Feminist Research and Action

Africa, Asia, Latin America and the Caribbean are all suffering in similar manner from the policies applied by the IMF and World Bank for the "development" of these regions. The same "structural adjustment" policies are being applied everywhere: devaluations that put up the prices of food, housing, transportation, clothing, books, etc.; wage freezes which make it impossible to cope with the rapidly increasing cost of living; massive breakdown of social services such as health and education; no consultation with the ordinary people whose living conditions are the most affected by these policies; repression of people's protest; and the confinement of decision-making to elites within the local populations. In this model, development is about big projects that serve big business. For example, on the three continents, hundreds of thousands of indigenous peoples are being moved from their lands to make way for huge dams to service the enterprises of multinational corporations while ordinary people have no access to clean drinking water.

Women across all the regions are the main burden-bearers of this "development." In the Caribbean, they are the ones employed in the Export Processing Zone (EPZ) factories which are the main "solution" offered. The idea that a woman's wage is supplementary to that of some man is being used to justify paying the women extra low wages. In actual fact, in the Caribbean, as in Africa, Asia and Latin America, women's income and labour are critical to family survival. Faced with the deepening economic crisis, women must work longer and longer hours of overtime to make ends meet, and also do more work at home so as not to spend cash, or to make up for declining social services. With less leisure time for themselves, their children, their families, and their social relationships, the quality of life declines. Despite the women's efforts, thousands of children have had their life chances damaged by these policies, and the effect will be felt for generations to come. In 1989, for example, Jamaica recorded the lowest ever percentage of passes in the Caribbean Examinations Council (CXC) Exams. This is a direct result of the high cost of books and school materials; the low morale of teachers as a result of grossly inadequate pay; and the fact that parents have less and less time to see to their children as they fight the desperate battle for survival. This increased desperation is a direct result of IMF conditionalities placed on loans made to the governments.

Who Is NOT Suffering?

While the quality of life is getting worse for ordinary people, the banks and corporations are flowing with funds. While we have been suffering, U.S. and other corporations have had record profits during the 1980s, particularly since 1987.

Where Does All This Money Come From?

With all this talk about Third World debt, it may come as a surprise to learn that we are subsidising the U.S. and other western banks and big companies, and not the other way round. In 1988–89, US$50 billion more went out from the Third World in profits than what we got in loans, investments, etc. Over the last three years, the net "capital outflow," as it is called, was US$120 billion.

This money does not stay in our countries to contribute to our own development. We need money for this. How do the banks respond? They rush to give us "loans." So then our governments have to put out more (capital plus interest) to pay them back. Furthermore, they can increase the interest rates whenever they wish; then we have to pay back even more.

In reality, the root of the problem lies in the historical colonial relationship between the South ("Third World") and the North ("developed countries"), where the South was colonised mainly to provide cheap raw materials and labour for the profit-oriented machineries of the North. The North sets the prices, and the priority is to get what they need at the cheapest possible rate.

In the late 1970s, this exploitation took on a new phase because there was extra money in the big banks from increased petroleum profits from which the multinational corporations were the main ones to benefit. Of course, small countries which had no oil suffered from this. Then came the banks with their petrodollars to "bail us out," but only if our governments would allow the companies to have a free hand to exploit us through cheap labour, no taxes, no price controls, no unions, etc. The economic situation of the poor countries has therefore gone from bad to worse. But WHO REALLY OWES WHOM?

The Debt Squeeze

Our governments feel powerless to fight the banks and the corporations, so they squeeze us instead, by cutting back social services and by levying more and more taxes on the majority of us. All over the Caribbean, we are seeing more taxes being placed on the backs of the poor rather than on the rich: taxes on traders (also called hucksters, higglers, etc.), VAT (Value Added Tax), consumption taxes, etc.

When taxes are not enough, the IMF and the World Bank and the big foreign corporations that they serve say, "We will accept your land, your successful enterprises, your hotels, in exchange for the debt." This is what they call "debt-equity swaps." In this way, they get our governments to sell out our countries to them.

Debt of Selected Caribbean Countries (US$)

Jamaica	4,048m
Trinidad & Tobago	1,860m
Guyana	1,039m
Haiti	957m
Barbados	650m
St. Vincent and the Grenadines	59m

(Source: World Bank Debt Tables 1989)

Much of what we owe is due to the changes in interest rates; in other words, we are paying for money we never actually got.

What Are People Doing about This?

There has been resistance all over the Third World.

In the Caribbean, there have been riots and demonstrations in Jamaica, the Dominican Republic, Venezuela, Trinidad and Tobago, Haiti and Guyana. Women in particular have had to confront harassment and brutality from customs officers and police all over the region in their efforts to expand and increase their informal trading activity to maintain themselves and their families. In many of our territories, state forces have driven them from the streets, destroying their stalls, and relocated them away from the areas where it is easiest to get sales. Prostitutes have also come under fire. None of the authorities have concerned themselves very much with the conditions that drive women more and more to these activities.

The women traders have responded with a variety of strategies. In Caracas, Venezuela, traders lay out goods on oil-cloths. When the police sirens are heard, goods are scooped into a bundle in the twinkling of an eye, and disappear into all kinds of hiding places. Minutes after the police leave, the goods are out again. In Africa, traders in Accra, the capital of Ghana, were forcibly removed from the streets. In response, they took to sitting at the roadside with brooms — sweeping at least is a legitimate activity! On the brooms, they tied strips of cloth or other indicators of the goods they had to sell. Interested buyers would come by and sit as if in conversation. They would absent-mindedly fondle the item they wanted to purchase. Purchaser and trader would then walk to where the goods were hidden.

Women have also been organising themselves into vendors' associations, housing groups, co-operatives, etc. The non-governmental organisations (NGOs) of the South and the North, including women's groups, are building links to share experiences, to develop strategies, and to inform people about the reasons for the sharpened economic crisis. NGOs are also beginning to discuss alternatives to the IMF/World Bank prescription which has turned out to be medicine which kills us while they grow fat selling it to us. There is a growing view that the debt should not be paid, and that the money should be used instead to promote regional and inter-regional development which locates people as the main focus of development.

FORTY-FOUR

The Global Trade in Filipina Workers

Grace Chang

Since the 1980s, the World Bank, the International Monetary Fund, and other international lending institutions based in the North have routinely prescribed structural adjustment policies (SAPs) to the governments of indebted countries of the South as pre-conditions for loans. These prescriptions have included cutting government expenditures on social programs, slashing wages, liberalizing imports, opening markets to foreign investment, expanding exports, devaluing local currency, and privatizing state enterprises. While SAPs are ostensibly intended to promote efficiency and sustained economic growth in the "adjusting" country, in reality they function to open up developing nations' economies and peoples to imperialist exploitation.

SAPs strike women in these nations the hardest and render them most vulnerable to exploitation both at home and in the global labor market. When wages and food subsidies are cut, wives and mothers must adjust household budgets, often at the expense of their own and their children's nutrition. As public healthcare and education vanishes, women suffer from a lack of prenatal care and become nurses to ill family members at home, while girls are the first to be kept from school to help at home or go to work. When export-oriented agriculture is encouraged, indeed coerced, peasant families are evicted from their lands to make room for corporate farms, and women become seasonal workers in the fields or in processing areas. Many women are forced to find work in the service industry, in manufacturing, or in home work, producing garments for export.[1]

When women take on these extra burdens and are still unable to sustain their families, many have no other viable option but to leave their families and migrate in search of work. Asian women migrate by the millions each year to work as servants, service workers, and sex workers in the United States, Canada, Europe, the Middle East, and Japan. Not coincidentally, the demand for service workers, and especially for private household caregivers and domestic workers, is exploding in wealthy nations of the First World undergoing their own versions of adjustment.

For example, in the United States, domestic forms of structural adjustment, including cutbacks in healthcare and the continued lack of subsidized childcare, contribute to an expanded demand among dual-career, middle-class households for workers in childcare, eldercare, and housekeeping. The slashing of benefits and social services under "welfare reform" helps to guarantee that this demand is met by eager migrant women workers. The dismantling of public supports in the United States in general, and the denial of benefits and services to immigrants in particular, act in tandem with structural adjustment abroad to force migrant women into low-wage labor in the United States. Migrant women workers from indebted nations are kept pliable not only by the dependence of their home countries and families on remittances, but also by stringent restrictions on immigrant access to almost all forms of assistance in the United States. Their vulnerability is further reinforced by U.S. immigration policies, designed to recruit migrant women as contract laborers or temporary workers who are ineligible for the protections and rights afforded to citizens.[2]

Both in their indebted home countries and abroad, women suffer the most from the dismantling of social programs under structural adjustment. In the Third World, women absorb the costs of cuts in food subsidies and healthcare by going hungry and foregoing proper medical care. Ironically, these same women continue to take up the slack for vanishing social supports in the First World, by nursing the elderly parents and young children of their employers for extremely low wages. Thus, there is a transfer of costs from the governments of both sending and receiving countries to migrant women workers from indebted nations. In both their home and "host" countries, and for both their own and their employers' families, these women pay most dearly for "adjustment."

Testimonies of Women Living under SAPs

At the 1995 Women's NGO Forum in China, women from the Third World gave first-hand testimony on the impact of SAPs on their daily lives and struggles for survival. The phenomenon consistently reported is that overall standards of living, and conditions for women and girls in particular, have deteriorated dramatically since the onset of SAPs. Often this has occurred after periods of marked improvement in women's employment, health, education, and nutrition following national independence movements prior to the institution of SAPs.

In a workshop on the impact of SAPs on women, an organizer from rural India spoke of the particular hardships women face, as those most affected by cuts in social programs and those first displaced from their farm lands. She reported that lands in India formerly used to produce rice have been rapidly converted to shrimp farms and orange orchards. While rice has always been a staple for local consumption, shrimp are purely cash crops for export to Japan, and the oranges are for export to the United States for orange juice. In her community, peasant women ran in front of bulldozers to try to prevent these lands from being taken over, but to no avail.[3]

Women from many other Third World countries reported similar conditions. An organizer from Malaysia observed, "We are adjusting with no limits to capital mobilizing everywhere. Malaysia has used all of the SAP principles, including privatization of services and deregulation of land acquisition." This woman reported that in Malaysia, land once held by small farmers has also been shifted to shrimp cultivation, while in Sri Lanka, peasants see their lands being taken up to cultivate strawberries for export to other countries.[4] Similarly, peasant women from the Philippines testified that, under SAPs, they have had to relinquish all the profits of their labor to landlords, and that lands once used to grow rice, corn, and coffee have been converted to growing orchids and "other exotic flowers that you can't eat" for export.[5]

In each of these countries, women bear the brunt of SAP-induced poverty daily through lack of healthcare, housing, and food.[6] Filipina rural women have reported going without power for four to eight hours each day and coping with little or no water.[7] Urban women from the Philippines reported working an average of 18 hours a day doing domestic work, laundry work outside their homes, and begging, while men face increasing unemployment. Their children are most often on the street rather than in school, and many families are becoming homeless with the high price of housing and the demolition of houses under development. Families may eat only once or twice a day because they can't afford more, and most go without any healthcare as the public hospitals demand payment up front and prescription medicines become prohibitively expensive.[8] Similarly, one rural organizer from India reported that prices for essential medicines have gone up 600 percent since the onset of SAPs, severely reducing Indian women's access to proper healthcare.[9]

Consistently, women from around the Third World testified that, as women have been displaced from their lands and homes under structural adjustment, women who were once small farmers have been forced to do home work, to migrate to the cities to work in manufacturing and the electronic industry, or to migrate overseas to do nursing, domestic work, sex work, and "entertainment."[10] The women's testimony demonstrates their clear recognition that they bear the brunt of hardships under structural adjustment, while their nations' governments and elites reap fat rewards in the form of women's cheap or unpaid labor and remittances from migrant women workers abroad. Commentary of women organizing in countries affected by SAPs reflects an acute awareness of the ways in which the governments and economic elites of their countries and First World countries profit at the expense of women's labor conditions, education, nutrition, health, and safety. As one labor organizer from India remarked:

> Our governments are surrendering to these multinational corporations and Western agencies. These magnate[s] and mafias, in the name of globalization, want to exploit our workers and resources. Our real concerns are food, water, clean sanitary conditions, health, shelter, and no exploitation. These are the human rights we want. All these governments are telling us to talk about human rights. What are they doing?[11]

Exporting Women:
The "New Heroes"

Each day, thousands of Filipinas leave their homes and families in search of work abroad. The Philippine government estimates that more than 4 percent of the country's total population are contract workers overseas. About 700,000 Filipinas/os were deployed through a government agency, the Philippine Overseas Employment Administration (POEA), in each of the past two years.[12] In 1991, women constituted a larger proportion of the country's overseas workforce (41 percent) than its domestic workforce (36 percent). Of those overseas, approximately 70 percent are women working as domestic servants in middle- and upper-class homes in the United States, Britain, Europe, Japan, and the Middle East. Many of the others work as nurses, sex workers, and entertainers.[13] Such massive migrations of women have led to public charges that the Philippines government is selling or trafficking in women.

Indeed, this massive migration is no mere coincidence of individual women's choices to leave the Philippines. The Philippine government receives huge sums of remittances from its overseas workers each year. "Host" country governments and private employers welcome the migrant women workers for the cheap labor they provide. These governments and employers save money not only by paying abominably low wages, but by failing to provide public benefits or social services to these temporary workers. Finally, recruiting agencies and other entrepreneurs on each end of the trade route reap tremendous profits for providing employers in "host" countries with ready and willing service workers and caregivers of all kinds.

In 1994, the Central Bank of the Philippines recorded the receipt of USD $2.9 billion in remittances by overseas workers. Remittances through informal channels have been estimated at six to seven billion U.S. dollars each year. These remittances are the country's largest source of foreign exchange—surpassing income from either sugar or minerals—and provide currency for payments towards the country's USD $46 billion debt. In 1993, overseas contract workers' remittances were estimated at 3.4 percent of the gross domestic product, which is the equivalent of 30 percent of the trade deficit or of the entire sum of interest payments on the country's foreign debt. These estimates are based on official figures alone and do not include moneys that enter through informal channels. As the Freedom from Debt Coalition (FDC), an organization working to counter SAPs, has put it: "What the country cannot achieve through export of goods, it compensates for through the export of human resources."[14]

Of less importance to the Philippine government but certainly significant in explaining the continued massive migration of women workers are estimates that approximately 30 to 50 percent of the entire Filipino population are dependent on migrant worker remittances.[15] Furthermore, it has been found that women migrant workers send home a larger proportion of their wages than their male counterparts do, even though they tend to earn less than men.[16] Such contributions led one ambassador from the Philippines to Canada to proclaim: "The migrant workers are our heroes because they sustain our economy."[17]

"Host" countries are eager to receive these female mercenaries, as they bolster their economies, too. As many countries of the North undergo downsizing and the dismantling of public supports, migrant women workers offer the perfect solution. The steady flow of migrant women provides an ideal source of cheap, highly exploitable labor. These women are channeled directly into the service sector, where they do every form of care work for a pittance and no benefits. Ironically, immigrant domestic workers, nannies, in-home caregivers, and nurses pick up the slack for cuts in government services and supports that pervade the North as well as the South. Overseas, they provide care for the ill, elderly, and children, while their own families forego this care because of the economic restructuring that drives them overseas.

Filipina Nurses
and Homecare Workers

Currently, there are 100,000 registered nurses in the Philippines, but almost none actually reside in the country. Similarly, 90 percent of all Filipino/a medical school graduates do not live in the Philippines. Since the 1970s, the United States has imported women from the Philippines to work as nurses, ostensibly in response to domestic shortages in trained nurses. This importation system became institutionalized with the H-1 nursing visa, which enables a hospital or nursing home to sponsor or bring a nurse with a professional license from abroad to work in the United States for two years.

Under the [earlier] H-1 program, a migrant woman must take the U.S. nurses' licensing exam. If she passes, she can gain permanent residency after two years. During those two years, she is almost captive to her original sponsoring employer. If she fails the exams she loses her sponsorship, and technically she must leave the country. More often, such women go underground until they can take the exam again. Sometimes, they work in nursing homes where they are underpaid at five dollars an hour. Others buy green-card marriages.

In 1988, the Filipina Nurses Organization fought for the Nursing Relief Act, which has provided some rights and stability to H-1 nurses in the last decade. The law grants nurses permanent residency after five years of living in the United States and working in the nursing profession. Prior to this act's passage, H-1 nurses had to go home after five years and could return after one year's residence in their home countries. Only after this period of absence could they apply to have their H-1 visas renewed. This system kept nurses in low-wage, temporary positions, forcing them to begin again and again at entry level with no seniority or benefits. The Immigration and Naturalization Service routinely conducted raids at hospitals to ensure that this turnover of temporary workers occurred.

Mayee Crispin, a Filipina nurse, organizes foreign nurse graduates (FNGs) at St. Bernard's Hospital on the south side of Chicago. At St. Bernard's, 80 percent of the nurses are single Filipina women on H-1. The starting wage at St. Bernard's is $14 an hour, in contrast to $16 an hour at other hospitals, and the ratio of patients to nurses is high. But many of the FNGs are reluctant to organize, fearful of losing their jobs or their employers' immigration sponsorship if they are identified as being pro-union. Many are sending remittances to their families at home and struggling to pay off their debts from migration.

Crispin proposes that importing nurses from the Philippines is a money-making venture for hospitals and the nursing recruiters they contract. According to Crispin, a hospital typically gets workers from overseas by making an official certification that they cannot find U.S. workers to fill its nursing positions. (This is usually because the hospital offers wages that no U.S. worker is willing to accept.) The hospital is then free to contract a recruiter to go to the Philippines in search of nurses. An FNG must pay, on average, between USD $7,000 and $9,000 to the recruiter. Ostensibly, a portion of this fee goes to the recruiter's salary, and a portion goes to a lawyer to arrange the woman's visa. Often both are employed by the hospital, which also gets a cut of the fee. Since most women cannot afford this fee, they agree to have it deducted from their wages. After paying off such fees and sending roughly 25 to 30 percent of their wages to their families at home, their monthly wages quickly disappear. In essence, most of these women live in a situation much like indentured servitude or debt bondage for at least two years. Crispin says that hospitals, by hiring FNGs, not only get cheap labor, they also get a workforce that is extremely vulnerable, fearful, uninformed of their rights, and thus likely to resist unionization.

Ninotchka Rosca of Gabriela Network USA observes the ironic history of Filipina nurses in the United States. In the 1980s, the nursing profession was extremely low-paying, with salaries at about $20,000 a year in the United States, so the country experienced a drastic shortage of nurses. With few U.S. citizens going into the field or willing to do nursing at such low wages, many Jamaican and Filipina women migrated here to do this work. With the downsizing in healthcare, many of the migrant nurses who have been here for over a decade are now finding themselves just as vulnerable as new migrants. Hospitals are attempting to reduce costs by firing their most experienced, and thus highest-paid, nurses. Rosca suggests that U.S. hospitals and the healthcare industry would collapse without Filipina nurses. "We take care of everybody else's weaker members of society, while we let our own society go to hell."[18]

Homecare Workers

Home healthcare is another industry in which immigrant women are highly concentrated and fall prey to both profit-seeking agencies and the cost-cutting U.S. government. Many homecare workers are employees of the state, under a state-funded program called "in-home support services" (IHSS). Some of these women are registered nurses, while others are not trained as nurses at all. The program provides no training, no regulations, and no monitoring of the work, which includes everything from performing medical procedures, preparing meals, and cleaning to helping elderly, frail, or ill clients go to the toilet, bathe, and move about. To keep costs down, the state pays workers a minimum wage of $4.50 an hour and provides no benefits, including no sick leave, family leave, overtime pay, compensation for injuries on the job, or reimbursement for bus fares or gasoline used to run errands for patients or to take them to the doctor.[19] In California, there are 170,000 of these workers statewide, of which approximately 80 percent are women, 60 to 70 percent are people of color, and 40 percent are immigrants.

Josie Camacho is an organizer with Service Employees International Union. Camacho points out that, particularly with the restructuring of hospitals under the ongoing privatization of healthcare, patients are being sent home too early and thus homecare workers are having to provide what should be trained nursing care, often without any formal training. For example, routine duties can include giving enemas and insulin shots, changing bandages, and hooking up dialysis machines.[20] In addition to the grueling work and low pay, immigrant workers in particular frequently report sexual harassment and other forms of abuse from their clients, including threats of deportation and general treatment as slaves. One worker was ordered to clean the bathroom with a toothbrush.[21]

The union is demanding the workers' rights to dignity and respect, to proper training in health and safety procedures, and to better wages. Camacho explains that these demands are aimed not only at improving the standard of living and rights for the workers, but at improving the quality of care provided to clients. Patients are typically Supplementary Security Income (SSI) recipients and must have assets under $2,000 to qualify for care under the state program. Thus, the government is relying on the weak positions of both impoverished patients, who have no control over the quality of care offered them, and low-wage workers, who have little recourse to fight these low wages and highly exploitative conditions.

Employing an IHSS worker saves taxpayers approximately $30,000 a year, the difference between the cost of keeping a patient in a nursing home and

the typical salary of $7,000 a year earned by an IHSS worker who works 30 hours a week. This savings is reaped by the state, county, and (through Medicaid) federal governments, which all share the program's annual cost. Robert Barton, manager of the adult services branch of the California Department of Social Services overseeing the program, commented: "It's a good deal for the government." The union's director of organizing in Washington, D.C., David Snapp, retorts: "It's a scam."[22] The IHSS program provides perhaps the best illustration available of the tremendous savings to local, state, and federal governments through the low-wage labor of migrant care workers. Other savings to the state and employers have not been measured, such as those reaped from not providing public benefits, services, and protections to these workers.

In the private sector, the situation is no better. Agencies and companies turn a profit from placing these workers, just as the state saves money by underpaying workers. Homecare agencies, just like hospitals, make huge profits from recruiting and placing homecare workers. For example, an agency will typically contract out a live-in caregiver to a client for $120 to $200 a day, while the worker herself receives only $80 of that daily rate.

Domestic Workers and Nannies

The majority of migrant Filipina workers are domestic workers and nannies. Many of them work in Canada, which has had a "live-in caregiver program" since 1992 to facilitate the importation of these migrants. Through this program, a Canadian employer (either an individual or employment agency) may apply through the Canadian Employment Office for a prospective employee. The employer must show that it has first tried to find a Canadian to do the job. The prospective employee must have six months of formal training or 12 months' experience in caregiving work and be in good health. If approved, the employee can gain temporary employment authorization for one year, and this can be extended for an additional year. A nanny must undergo a personal interview with Canadian consular officials and obtain security clearance. Once matched with an employer, she must notify the Ministry of Citizenship and Immigration if she wishes to change employers. After two years of live-in work, a nanny can apply for landed-immigrant status. She can then sponsor immediate family members to join her if they can prove they have a source of steady income. Three years after applying for landed-immigrant status, she can become a Canadian citizen.[23]

The film *Brown Women, Blonde Babies,* produced by Marie Boti, documents the conditions for Filipina migrant women working as domestics and nannies in Canada. Typically, women work around the clock, from 7 A.M. to 10 P.M. and beyond, and are always considered on call. They earn an average of $130 a month after taxes. Women who wish to leave their employers must persuade an immigration officer to let them. In response to one woman's pleas for release from an employer, one immigration officer coldly responded, "You didn't come here to be happy."

In stark contrast to the conditions revealed in this documentary, employers of domestic workers and nannies in Canada romanticize the work and the "opportunities" they offer to immigrant women. For example, *The Globe and Mail,* a Toronto newspaper, boasted that Canada is the first-choice destination for Filipina migrant workers, claiming:

> For the women themselves, improving their economic status helps them challenge the Philippines' traditional stereotype of women as submissive homemakers who need to rely on their husbands, fathers, or brothers to survive. The huge exodus of female contract workers from the country in the past decade has created a generation of women who are more confident and independent about their role in a society that has now been forced to ask some hard questions about many of its traditional paternalistic attitudes.[24]

Clearly, if Filipina women's roles in their society are subservient, as this statement implies, then those roles are not overturned but reinforced when migrant women are forced to serve as low-wage workers overseas instead of homemakers. The only difference is that they provide domestic services to employers in the North instead of their own families, while servicing their government's foreign debt at the same time.

According to the Kanlungan Foundation Centre, an advocacy group for Filipina migrant workers,

> We do not migrate as totally free and independent individuals. At times, we have no choice but to migrate, to brave the odds. . . . Even

from the very start, we are already victims of illegal recruitment, victims of our government's active marketing of our cheap labor, . . . and suffering the backlash of states that fail to provide adequate support for childcare services, we enter first world countries that seek to preserve patriarchal ideology.[25]

This statement reflects migrant women workers' clear understanding that they are being used to maintain patriarchy in the First World, as governments in these wealthy nations cut social supports.

Just as employers try to justify exploiting servants by romanticizing the "opportunities" they provide these women, the Philippine government attempts to rationalize the trade in women by glorifying its migrant women exports: In 1988, on a state visit to Hong Kong, President Aquino declared migrant women the new heroes of the Philippine economy.[26] Since then, many officials have taken this up as the party line in justifying the trade in women. In response, the FDC states: "Because of their economic contributions, migrant workers are hailed by the administration as the new heroes, and labor export is elevated into a national policy, the appalling social costs and the prevalence of abuses notwithstanding."[27]

Women's Resistance

In July of 1994, Sarah Balagaban, a 15-year-old Filipina working as a maid in the United Arab Emirates (UAE), was raped at knifepoint by her employer. In self-defense, Balagaban stabbed and killed her rapist/employer and was sentenced to seven years in prison. In response to protests, Balagaban was retried, but was then sentenced to death. In outrage, many overseas Filipinas joined protests staged by Gabriela Network USA in front of the UAE mission and the Philippine government consulate in the United States. Again, Balagaban's sentence was revised. This time, she was sentenced to one year in prison and 100 lashes, and ordered to pay her deceased employer's family 150,000 dirhams, the equivalent of USD $41,995. Gabriela's Ninotchka Rosca speculates that the main reason the UAE government rescinded the death sentence was for fear of a walkout by the approximately 75,000 Filipina/os working in the UAE—a walkout that would paralyze the country.

Protests continued after this last sentence, with objections that 100 lashes could actually kill Balagaban. The Philippine government agreed to the final sentence over these protests, reinforcing outrage that the Philippine government refuses to protect its overseas workers and is clearly willing to sacrifice women's lives to maintain good relations with its chief trade partners. Many Filipinas working in the UAE have collected a scholarship fund for Balagaban to complete her education once she finishes her prison sentence. She had quit school in order to work in the UAE to support her parents and to help pay for her brother's education. Balagaban has since become a symbol for overseas Filipinas fighting for their rights.[28]

Teresita Tristan is a widow who left two children behind in the Philippines for a job in Britain as a domestic worker. Before leaving, she had been promised a salary of $400 a month, but when she arrived, her employers took her passport and informed her she would be paid $108 a month. On her first day in the country, she was taken for a medical exam, given medicine to clean her stomach, and was instructed to take a bath and not to touch the dishes with her bare hands until five days had passed. Her daily work consisted of cleaning the entire house, taking the children to school, and preparing the family's meals, while she ate leftovers. She was not allowed to eat from plates or glasses or to use the toilet inside the house. When her employer kept making sexual advances and asking her to go to the guest house with him, she asked to be released so she could return home. Instead, she was transferred to her employers' daughter's home, where she was likewise treated badly.[29]

One day Tristan went to the park and met an Englishwoman who took her phone number and called the police for her. The Commission for Filipina Migrant Workers helped her to leave her employer's home and find shelter. For many weeks, she feared that her employer would come to find her. Now, Tristan belongs to an organization of unauthorized workers fighting for migrant worker rights.

Tristan's story is typical of that of migrant workers, according to Kalayaan, an organization working for justice for overseas domestic workers in Britain. Between January 1992 and December 1994, Kalayaan interviewed 755 migrant domestic workers who had left their employers. The results of these interviews revealed widespread abuses of migrant domestic

workers from the Philippines, Sri Lanka, India, Ghana, Nigeria, Colombia, and Brazil. Eighty-eight percent had experienced psychological abuse, including name-calling, threats, and insults, and 38 percent had endured physical abuse of some form. Eleven percent had experienced attempted, threatened, or actual sexual assault or rape. A full 60 percent had received no regular meals, 42 percent had no bed, and 51 percent had no bedroom and were forced to sleep in a hallway, kitchen, bathroom, or storeroom. Thirty-one percent reported being imprisoned or not being allowed to leave the house. Ninety-one percent reported working for an average of 17 hours a day with no time off. Fifty-five percent were not paid regularly, and 81 percent were paid less than was agreed upon in their contracts, with an average monthly wage of USD $105.

A spokeswoman from Kalayaan says that these widespread abuses are made possible by British immigration law. In 1979, the British government abolished work permits for overseas domestic workers but continued to allow overseas employers and returning British residents to bring domestic workers into the country. This concession was granted to wealthy people returning from traveling abroad with employees. As Maria Gonzalez of the Commission on Filipina Overseas Domestic Workers puts it: "In the United Kingdom, migrant women are brought into the country like the baggage of their employers."[30] Migrant women enter with their employers' names stamped on their passports, and they cannot change employers after entering. Even in the rare case that a woman negotiates a contract with her employer, she has no bargaining power or legal recourse if the employer violates it.

Migrant workers have mobilized worldwide to expose these abuses and to fight for protection of their rights. Women in many "host" countries, including Canada, Japan, Britain, and the United States, have organized grassroots organizations to offer support and legal advocacy, and to lobby for the protection of Filipina and other migrant workers abroad. Kalayaan lobbies to change British law to allow migrant workers to receive permits directly, to change employers freely, and to stay and work in the country while pursuing legal action against former employers.

INTERCEDE is a similar organization, based in Toronto, that conducts research and advocacy for Filipina and Caribbean migrant domestic worker rights. It provides direct services, such as individual counseling on labor and immigration rights and educational meetings and social activities to aid settlement, and lobbies the Canadian government. In 1981, INTERCEDE succeeded in convincing the Canadian Parliament to grant the rights of Canadian citizens under labor laws to foreign domestic workers on temporary visas.[31] Currently, INTERCEDE is pressuring the government to recognize domestic work as an occupation, to do away with the live-in requirement, and to allow immigrants to gain "landed-immigrant" status immediately upon entering Canada, instead of having to wait two years.

In the United States, healthcare workers (many of whom are migrant women) are the fastest-growing service workers. As some of the most exploited and, until recently, least organized workers, they are a prime target for labor organizers.[32] A recent victory by SEIU against the California government represents the fruits of a five-year struggle by the union on behalf of over 50,000 homecare workers in the state. In the summer of 1990, the California legislature and Governor Pete Wilson failed to reach an agreement on a budget, and the state stopped issuing paychecks. IHSS homecare workers were the first to feel the impact of the budget crisis — some workers' paychecks were delayed up to two months. During the budget impasse of 1992, workers suffered the same series of events.

SEIU brought a class-action suit against the State of California on behalf of more than 10,000 IHSS workers. SEIU argued that the workers suffered extreme hardship because of the delayed payments, including having electricity turned off in their homes and not having enough money for food, among other necessities. A U.S. District Court judge ruled on March 17, 1994, that the delayed payments violated the Fair Labor Standards Act. A settlement reached in May 1995 awarded damages of four million dollars, to be divided among the approximately 50,000 workers who joined the action.[33] This SEIU struggle represents a dramatic victory.

Josie Camacho points to the ongoing challenges of organizing homecare workers: First, there is no central workplace, with workers scattered among as many as 6,000 different worksites in a county. Second, some immigrant workers feel indebted to their employers and are reluctant to join the union. They are afraid and don't know their rights. This has challenged the union to recruit organizers who are multilingual and able to inform workers of their rights. Third, no party is willing to admit responsibility for, or can be held accountable for, the rights and protection of these workers. All parties, including both the sending and receiving countries' governments, employers, and employment agencies, evade or completely deny responsibility. Yet all benefit immensely from these workers' labor, extracting foreign currency, profits, savings, and care services.

Groups such as Kalayaan, INTERCEDE, and SEIU focus on organizing migrant workers and providing direct services to them in "host" countries while lobbying these "host" governments to change oppressive immigration and labor policies. Other organizations have a different emphasis, putting pressure on the Philippine government to recognize the impact of SAPs on poor women of the Third World at home and abroad. They aim to expose how the Philippine government facilitates the exportation of women migrant workers, sacrificing women in the futile effort to keep up with debt payments. Finally, they pressure the Philippine government to redirect expenditures away from debt servicing, to institute protections for migrant workers abroad, and to stop the export of women from the Philippines and other impoverished countries.

While many organizations focus on fighting for protections for migrant workers overseas, others propose that ultimately the global trafficking in women must stop. Gabriela Network has led the fight against the trade in Filipina and other migrant women. Gabriela accused the Philippine government of feeding young Filipinas into the sex industry in Japan after the Philippine government's policy prohibiting women under 23 years old from migrating to Japan to work as entertainers was found to have been violated 35 times within a four-month period. Gabriela found that the government made exceptions to the policy for four "favored" recruitment agencies.[34] Gabriela has called for the government to stop labor exportation as its chief economic strategy. The Philippine government denies that it participates in such a trade.[35]

Mainstream U.S. feminist responses to the trade in women have been lukewarm at best. When Gabriela called on women's organizations around the world to put the issue of global trafficking of women on their agendas, the National Organization for Women (NOW) declined to do so, stating that it does not deal with international issues.[36] The real issue may be that privileged women of the First World, even self-avowed feminists, are some of the primary consumers and beneficiaries in this trade. Middle- and upper-class professional women generally have not joined efforts to improve wages or conditions for care workers in the United States, since they have historically relied on the "affordability" of women of color and migrant women working in their homes, daycare centers, and nursing homes. As Cynthia Enloe observes:

> Politically active maids have not always found feminists in the host countries to be reliable allies. Too often local feminist groups in countries importing maids either from overseas or from the poor regions of their own countries were led by women of precisely the social class that hired domestic workers.[37]

Major U.S. women's groups were conspicuously silent during the Zoe Baird controversy, when Baird, the nominee for attorney general, was found to have employed two undocumented migrant workers as a babysitter and gardener. Shortly after the Baird scandal, proposals for a "homecare worker" or "nanny" visa, modelled after the Canadian Live-in Caregiver program, were discussed at the Immigration Reform Commission hearings. Only a few individuals from NOW attended the hearings, but they were not representing NOW.

Even among grassroots organizations fighting for justice for migrant women workers, it may prove difficult to develop a unified position or strategy. The effectiveness and viability of one strategy, imposing a ban on recruitment of Filipinas for migrant work, has been debated since such a ban was imposed by the Aquino administration in 1988. A coalition of 22 migrant worker groups in Hong Kong formed to press the Aquino government to repeal the ban, arguing that it hindered Filipinas' ability to secure employment, actually debilitating rather than protecting them.[38]

Almost ten years later, debate over the efficacy of the ban continues. Felicita Villasin, executive director of INTERCEDE and executive board member of the National Action Committee on the Status of Women (NAC) in Canada, says that a ban on migrant workers will only drive women to face greater danger and abuses as illegal migrants. Instead, she calls for structural changes in the Philippine economy that will

make migration a choice and not a necessity. At least on this last point, Villasin asserts, there seems to be consensus among the women's groups involved in Filipina migrant worker struggles.

Asian/Pacific Islander and other women of color feminists in the First World would do well to take the lead from groups like INTERCEDE and many of our Third World sisters who have been mobilizing around the issues of SAPs and the traffic in women for years now. At the NGO Forum, many First World women remarked that they were the least well-informed or organized on global economic issues. Many First World feminists of color came home from the Forum resolved to undertake or redouble efforts to understand and expose the links between economic restructuring in the First World, SAPs in the Third World, and the global trade in women.

In Canada, NAC and the Canadian Labour Congress co-sponsored a month-long, nationwide Women's March Against Poverty in May and June of 1996. The march culminated in a rally at the nation's capital to bring to Parliament demands for measures to redress women's poverty in Canada and globally. Its call to action included the need to strengthen employment conditions and opportunities for women, to reinforce social services, and to adopt "as a foreign policy objective" the elimination of women's poverty.[39]

In the United States, Miriam Ching Louie and Linda Burnham of the Women of Color Resource Center, returned from the NGO Forum committed to designing a popular education project, Women's Education in the Global Economy (WEdGE). The project includes a curriculum and set of trainings focused on a broad range of global economic issues and trends affecting women: the global assembly-line; SAPs; women's unpaid, contingent, and informal work; welfare; environmental justice; women's human rights, sex trafficking, and migration; and organizing around these issues.[40]

SAPs and other economic restructuring policies affect Third World women in similar ways the world over, making survival more precarious, making women's unpaid labor burdens heavier, and exacerbating women's exploitation as low-wage workers both at home and abroad. First World variations of structural adjustment bring consequences that are less well-known but no less insidious. Walden Bello describes the effects of "welfare reform" as the domestic version of SAPs in the United

States: In 1992, by the end of the Republicans' assault on social welfare programs, the living standards of many Americans had deteriorated to Third World levels. Approximately 20 million U.S. residents lived in hunger, and infant mortality rates among African Americans reached rates higher than those of countries such as Jamaica, Trinidad, and Cuba.[41]

Bello says that the original intentions of SAPs were: first, to resubordinate the Third World—particularly those nations threatening to become developed—by crippling the authority of their governments and, second, to repress labor globally in order to free corporate capital from any hindrances to maximum profits. Clearly SAPs in the Philippines have been an uncontested success by these measures. The Philippine government has been unable to protect its own female citizens abroad and apparently has given up any intention of doing so. The trade in women from the Philippines has proven immensely profitable to the Philippine government and entrepreneurs, and highly "economical" to the governments that recruit them and the elites who employ them. Yet the struggles and triumphs of women like Balagaban and Tristan, and groups such as Kalayaan, INTERCEDE, Gabriela, and SEIU stand as testament to the ability of women to resist this global assault on Third World women workers.

Notes

This article is extracted from a chapter in my forthcoming book, *Gatekeeping and Housekeeping.* I would like to thank Luisa Blue, Josie Camacho, Mayee Crispin, Ninotchka Rosca, Carole Salmon, and Felicita Villasin for sharing their great insights, expertise, and time in interviews. I am also indebted to Miriam Ching Louie and Linda Burnham for bravely leading the Women of Color Resource Center delegation to Huairou, and for their pioneering work on Women's Education in the Global Economy. I am grateful to Nathaniel Silva for his insights and comments in developing this piece.

1. Sparr, Pamela. *Mortgaging Women's Lives: Feminist Critiques of Structural Adjustment.* London: Zed Books, 1994.

2. Chang, Grace. "Disposable Nannies: Women's Work and the Politics of Latina Immigration." *Radical America* 26. 2 (October 1996): 5–20.

3. Testimony of Fatima. Workshop on the impact of SAPs, NGO Forum, September 2, 1995.

4. Testimony of Eileen Fernandez. Workshop on the impact of SAPs, NGO Forum, September 2, 1995.

5. Gabriela Workshop, NGO forum, September 3, 1995.

6. The "official" figures corroborate these first-hand testimonies of women in countries under structural adjustment: Between 1969 and 1985, per capita food production declined in 51 out of 94 developing countries. Simultaneously, access to food has been severely limited by increased food prices with the devaluation of local currencies under SAPs. Expenditures on education in all poor developing countries except India and China declined from 21 percent of national budgets in 1972 to 9 percent in 1988. Healthcare expenditures were also reduced from 5.5 percent to 2.8 percent of national budgets during this period. See UNICEF report cited by Peter Lurie, Percy Hintzen, and Robert A. Lowe, "Socioeconomic Obstacles to HIV Prevention and Treatment in Developing Countries: The Roles of the International Monetary Fund and the World Bank." *AIDS* 9(6): 542–543.

7. Testimony of Merceditas Cruz. Workshop on Migration and the Globalizing Economy, NGO Forum, September 6, 1995.

8. Testimony of Carmen. Organization of Free & United Women under Gabriela, NGO Forum.

9. Workshop on the Impacts of SAPs, NGO Forum, September 2, 1995.

10. Testimony of representative from International Organization of Prostitutes. Gabriela Workshop, NGO Forum, September 3, 1995.

11. Plenary on Globalization, NGO Form, September 3, 1995.

12. This number does not include women who are trafficked or illegally recruited, those who migrate for marriage, students, or tourists who eventually become undocumented workers. Compiled by Kanlungan Center Foundation from Philippine Overseas Employment Administration (POEA) and Department of Labor and Employment (DOLE) statistics.

13. Vincent, Isabel. "Canada Beckons Cream of Nannies: Much-sought Filipinas Prefer Work Conditions." *The Globe and Mail.* 20 January 1996: A1, A6. Other authors address more extensively trafficking in women for the sex work, entertain-

ment, and mail-order bride industries. See Rosca, Ninotchka. "The Philippines' Shameful Export." *The Nation.* 17 April 1995: 523–525; Kim, Elaine. "Sex Tourism in Asia: A Reflection of Political and Economic Equality." *Critical Perspectives of Third World America* 2.1 (Fall 1984): 215–231; *Sisters and Daughters Betrayed: The Trafficking of Women and Girls and the Fight to End It.* Video. Prod. Chela Blitt. Global Fund for Women.

14. "Flor Contemplacion: Victim of Mismanaged Economy." Editorial. *PAID! (People Against Immoral Debt).* Newsletter of Freedom from Debt Coalition, April 1995: 7.

15. Kanlungan Center Foundation, Inc. fact sheet prepared for the 1995 UN Conference on Women.

16. Freedom from Debt Coalition, based on DOLE figures.

17. *Brown Women, Blonde Babies.* Film. Prod. Marie Boti. Multimonde Productions.

18. Rosca, Ninotchka. Personal interview. 29 April 1996.

19. Kilborn, Peter T. "Union Gets the Lowly to Sign Up: Home Care Aides Are Fresh Target." *New York Times.* 21 November 1995.

20. Ibid.

21. Camacho, Josie. Personal interview. 18 April 1996.

22. Kilborn, op cit.

23. Ms. Greenhill of the Canadian Consulate in Los Angeles, CA. Personal interview. December 1993; Vincent A1.

24. Vincent A6.

25. *A Framework on Women and Migration.* Kanlungan Center Foundation; prepared for the NGO Forum of 1995.

26. Rosca, Ninotchka. Personal interview. 29 April 1996.

27. Freedom from Debt Coalition, statement prepared for NGO Forum, 1995.

28. *Kapihan Sa Kanlungan: A Quarterly Digest of Migration News,* newsletter produced by Kanlungan Center Foundation. April-June 1995; Rosca, Ninotchka. Personal interview. 29 April 1996; Vincent A6.

29. Testimony, Workshop on Violence and Migration, NGO Forum, 1995.

30. Ibid.

31. Enloe, Cynthia. *Bananas, Beaches and Bases: Making Feminist Sense of International Politics.* Berkeley: University of California Press, 1989. 190.

32. Kilborn, op cit.

33. "Delayed Payment Case for Home Care Workers Settled with State for $4 Million." SEIU press release. May 30, 1995.

34. Press conference. National Press Club in Manila, Philippines, March 1994; "Gabriela Accuses Philippine Government of Pimping." *Gabriela International Update.* August 1995.

35. Rosca, Ninotchka. Personal interview. 29 April 1996.

36. Ibid.

37. Enloe 194.

38. Enloe 188. Slowly, the Aquino government exempted one government after another from its requirements, and by 1989, 22 countries enjoyed exemption from the ban.

39. NAC bulletins on the March.

40. For information, contact: Women of Color Resource Center, 2288 Fulton Street, Suite 103, Berkeley, CA 94704.

41. Bello, Walden, Shea Cunningham, and Bill Rau, *Dark Victory: The United States, Structural Adjustment and Global Poverty.* London: Pluto Press and Food First and Transnational Institute, 1994.

Immigrants in a Global Economy

Saskia Sassen

Current immigration policy in developed countries is increasingly at odds with other major policy frameworks in the international system and with the growth of global economic integration. All highly developed countries have received rapidly growing numbers of legal and undocumented immigrants over the last decade; none has found its immigration policy effective. These countries are opening up their economies to foreign investment and trade while deregulating their financial markets. In developed countries, the emergence of a new economic regime sharply reduces the role of national governments and borders in controlling international transactions. Yet the framework of immigration policy in these countries remains centered on older conceptions of the nation-state and of national borders.

How can immigration policy account for the facts of rapid economic internationalization and the corresponding transformation of national governments? This is the subject I briefly discuss here.

Shift in Global Economy

The 1980s saw a major shift in the global economy. In that decade, the developed countries opened their economies to foreign investment, international financial markets, and imports of goods and services; deregulation and internationalization of a growing range of economic activities became hallmarks of economic policy. As economic doors have opened to others, many developing countries have implemented export-oriented growth strategies. Export-manufacturing zones and the sale of once-public sector firms on world markets became key venues for this internationalization.

Global economic trends engendered a new framework for national economic policy-making. This new framework is evident in the formation of regional trading blocks: the U.S.-Canada Free Trade Agreement, the European Community (EC), the new trading blocks being formed in Southeast Asia as well as the proposed NAFTA agreement. At the heart of this framework is a new conception of the role of national borders. Borders no longer are sites for imposing levies. Rather, they are transmitting membranes guaranteeing the free flow of goods, capital and information. Eighteenth-century concepts of free trade assumed freedom of movement between distinct national economies: 21st-century concepts of free trade are about an economy which is itself global, and about governments that coordinate rather than control economic activities.

To be sure, neither the old border-wall nor the nation-state has disappeared. The difficulties and complexities involved in this transformation are evident in the many obstacles to the ratification of the Uruguay Round of the GATT talks, which aims at further opening economies to the circulation of services. But the relentless effort to overcome these difficulties also signals the pressure to depart from an old conception of national economic policy and the emergence of a new conception of how economic activity is to be maximized and governed.

The framework for immigration policy in the highly developed countries, on the other hand, is still rooted in the past. Immigration policy has yet to address global economic integration in the 21st century and its implications. Border-control remains the basic mechanism for regulating immigration—an increasingly troubled effort given new policies aimed at opening up national economies, such as the lifting of restrictions on foreign investment, the deregulation of financial markets, and the formation of financial free zones in major cities. Those policies amount to a partial denationalizing of national territory for the flow of capital, and they in turn globalize certain sectors of the workforce, notably the high-level transnational professional and managerial class.

Moreover, the policy framework for immigration treats the flow of labor as the result of individual actions, particularly the decision to migrate in search of better opportunities. Such a policy puts responsibility for immigration on the shoulders of immigrants. Policy commentary which speaks of an immigrant "influx" or "invasion" treats the receiving country as a passive agent. The causes for immigration appear to be outside the control or domain of receiving countries; immigration policy becomes a decision to be more or less benevolent in admitting immigrants. Absent from this understanding is the notion that the international activities of the governments or firms of receiving countries may have contributed to the formation of economic linkages with emigration countries, linkages that may function as bridges not only for capital but also for migration flows. That older view emphasizes individual "push" factors and neglects systemic linkages.

The worldwide evidence shows rather clearly that there is considerable patterning in the geography of migrations, and that the major receiving countries tend to get immigrants from their zones of influence. This holds for countries as diverse as the U.S., France or Japan. A transnational analysis of immigration contributes to its redefinition and allows us to see migrations as happening within global systems. The periods known as Pax Britannica and Pax Americana are but two representations of such transnational systems. The formation of systems for the internationalization of manufacturing production, or the formation of regional trading blocks, are other instances. These systems can be characterized in a multiplicity of ways: economic (the Atlantic economy of the 1800s, the EC, NAFTA); politico-military (the colonial systems of several European countries, U.S. involvement in Central America); transnational war zones (formation of massive refugee flows as a result of major European wars); cultural-ideological zones (impact in socialist countries of the image of Western democracies as offering the "good life").

Recent developments in Japan capture the intersection of economic internationalization and immigration. They also illuminate the intersection of immigration policy and reality. Japan's closed door policy has not prevented a growing influx of immigrants. Nor has its 1990 immigration law, which opens up the country to high-level foreign workers but closes it to all low-wage workers, kept out the latter. Furthermore, despite a strong anti-immigration culture, immigrants have become incorporated into various labor markets and have begun to form immigrant communities in major cities in Japan. A detailed exploration of the dynamic at work provides useful insights into immigration processes.

What makes the disparity between the framework for immigration policy and the facts of the world economy particularly urgent is that all highly developed countries have experienced sharp increases in migration of both legal and undocumented immigrants. In some countries there is a resurgence of immigration after inflows had fallen sharply in the 1970s: this is the case for Germany and Austria. In other countries, notably the U.S., immigration policy opened up the country in 1965, yet in the 1980s, the number of entries doubled compared with the 1965–1980 period. Still other countries are becoming immigration countries for the first time in their contemporary histories: this is the case with Italy and Spain, long-time emigration countries, and with Japan, a nation of deep anti-immigration beliefs and policies.

Discard Old Notions

A detailed analysis of cross-country immigration patterns suggests that some key notions about immigration may be inadequate, particularly the notion that the developed countries may be facing a massive invasion of people from less developed countries. These cross-country regularities suggest that there is more room for effective and equitable policies than the imagery of "invasion" allows:

1. **Emigration is a minority event in demographic terms.** Except for terror-driven refugees, we now know that most people are reluctant to leave their home villages or towns: For example, most people in Mexico have not gone to the U.S. A minority is determined to come no matter what, while a gray area of potential emigrants may or may not leave, depending on pull factors; but the vast mass of people in a poor country are not likely to emigrate.

2. **There is considerable return migration** except when the military/political situation in countries of origin makes it unsafe. For example, we now know that about 60 percent of Italians who left for the U.S. around the turn of the century returned to Italy.

3. Rather than an uncontrolled "invasion," what we see over time is a **tendency towards the formation of permanent settlements** for a variable share of immigrants, but never all. This tendency is likely even when there are high return rates and even when a country's policies seek to prevent permanent settlement. We see this happening in

all countries receiving immigrants, including such extremely closed countries as Japan and Saudi Arabia, as well as in the more liberal Western nations.

4. No matter what the political culture and the particular migration policies of a country, **"illegal" immigration has emerged as a generalized fact in all Western economies in the post–World War II era,** including Japan. This has raised a whole set of questions about the need to rethink regulatory enforcement and the sites for such enforcement.

5. **Immigration is a highly differentiated process:** it includes people seeking permanent settlement and those seeking temporary employment who want to circulate back and forth. One important question is whether recognizing these differences might facilitate the formulation of policy today. There is a growing presence of immigrants who are not searching for a new home in a new country; they think of themselves as moving in a cross-country and even global labor market. We know that when illegal immigrants are regularized, they often establish permanent residence in their country of origin and work a few months in the immigration country, an option that becomes available when they can circulate freely.

Towards New Policies

How should the new reality shape our thinking about immigration? A more comprehensive approach can provide more analytic and empirical footholds towards a better understanding of migration and towards more effective policy. The various transnational economic, cultural, political systems now evident in the world all tend to have very specific geographies. They are not planet-wide events, but occur in the relation of cities to cities, or in production chains linking factories in rather remote areas of developing countries to manufacturing and distribution centers in developed countries. Considerable migration flows within these new geographies for economic transactions. By understanding the nature of these geographies we can understand where to intervene for regulatory purposes. Further, international migrations themselves are patterned in geographic, economic and temporal terms. These two types of patterning provide maps within which to search for new policies to regulate immigration.

If immigration is partly an outcome of the actions of the governments and major private economic actors in receiving countries, the latter could conceivably recognize the migration impact of such actions and make decisions accordingly. For instance, economic policies that facilitate overseas operations of firms, particularly in developing countries, should recognize the migration impact of such operations. Economic internationalization suggests that the responsibility for immigration may not be exclusively the immigrant's. Refugee policy in some countries does lift the burden of immigration from the immigrant's shoulders. U.S. refugee policy, particularly for Indochinese refugees, does acknowledge partial responsibility on the part of the government. Clearly, in the case of economic migrations, such responsibility is far more difficult to establish, and by its nature far more indirect. As governments increasingly coordinate rather than contain economic activity, their role in immigration policy, as in other aspects of political economy, becomes elusive. Despite this complexity, the responsibilities for the consequences of globalization do not disappear. If economic internationalization contributes to migration flows, recognition of this fact can only help in designing more effective immigration policy.

FORTY-SIX

The Border Patrol State

Leslie Marmon Silko

I used to travel the highways of New Mexico and Arizona with a wonderful sensation of absolute freedom as I cruised down the open road and across the vast desert plateaus. On the Laguna Pueblo reservation, where I was raised, the people were patriotic despite the way the U.S. government had treated Native Americans. As proud citizens, we grew up believing the freedom to travel was our inalienable right, a right that some Native Americans had been denied in the early twentieth century. Our cousin, old Bill Pratt, used to ride his horse 300 miles overland from Laguna, New Mexico, to Prescott, Arizona, every summer to work as a fire lookout.

In school in the 1950s, we were taught that our right to travel from state to state without special papers or threat of detainment was a right that citizens under communist and totalitarian governments did not possess. That wide open highway told us we were U.S. citizens; we were free. . . .

Not so long ago, my companion Gus and I were driving south from Albuquerque, returning to Tucson after a book promotion for the paperback edition of my novel *Almanac of the Dead*. I had settled back and gone to sleep while Gus drove, but I was awakened when I felt the car slowing to a stop. It was nearly midnight on New Mexico State Road 26, a dark, lonely stretch of two-lane highway between Hatch and Deming. When I sat up, I saw the headlights and emergency flashers of six vehicles — Border Patrol cars and a van were blocking both lanes of the highway. Gus stopped the car and rolled down the window to ask what was wrong. But the closest Border Patrolman and his companion did not reply; instead, the first agent ordered us to "step out of the car." Gus asked why, but his question seemed to set them off. Two more Border Patrol agents immediately approached our car, and one of them snapped, "Are you looking for trouble?" as if he would relish it.

I will never forget that night beside the highway. There was an awful feeling of menace and violence straining to break loose. It was clear that the uniformed men would be only too happy to drag us out

of the car if we did not speedily comply with their request (asking a question is tantamount to resistance, it seems). So we stepped out of the car and they motioned for us to stand on the shoulder of the road. The night was very dark, and no other traffic had come down the road since we had been stopped. All I could think about was a book I had read — *Nunca Más* — the official report of a human rights commission that investigated and certified more than 12,000 "disappearances" during Argentina's "dirty war" in the late 1970s.

The weird anger of these Border Patrolmen made me think about descriptions in the report of Argentine police and military officers who became addicted to interrogation, torture and the murder that followed. When the military and police ran out of political suspects to torture and kill, they resorted to the random abduction of citizens off the streets. I thought how easy it would be for the Border Patrol to shoot us and leave our bodies and car beside the highway, like so many bodies found in these parts and ascribed to "drug runners."

Two other Border Patrolmen stood by the white van. The one who had asked if we were looking for trouble ordered his partner to "get the dog," and from the back of the van another patrolman brought a small female German shepherd on a leash. The dog apparently did not heel well enough to suit him, and the handler jerked the leash. They opened the doors of our car and pulled the dog's head into it, but I saw immediately from the expression in her eyes that the dog hated them, and that she would not serve them. When she showed no interest in the inside of our car, they brought her around back to the trunk, near where we were standing. They half-dragged her up into the trunk, but still she did not indicate any stowed-away human beings or illegal drugs.

Their mood got uglier; the officers seemed outraged that the dog could not find any contraband, and they dragged her over to us and commanded her to sniff our legs and feet. To my relief, the strange violence the Border Patrol agents had focused on us now seemed shifted to the dog. I no longer felt so strongly that we would be murdered. We exchanged looks—the dog and I. She was afraid of what they might do, just as I was. The dog's handler jerked the leash sharply as she sniffed us, as if to make her perform better, but the dog refused to accuse us: She had an innate dignity that did not permit her to serve the murderous impulses of those men. I can't forget the expression in the dog's eyes; it was as if she were embarrassed to be associated with them. I had a small amount of medicinal marijuana in my purse that night, but she refused to expose me. I am not partial to dogs, but I will always remember the small German shepherd that night.

Unfortunately, what happened to me is an everyday occurrence here now. Since the 1980s, on top of greatly expanding border checkpoints, the Immigration and Naturalization Service and the Border Patrol have implemented policies that interfere with the rights of U.S. citizens to travel freely within our borders. I.N.S. agents now patrol all interstate highways and roads that lead to or from the U.S.-Mexico border in Texas, New Mexico, Arizona and California. Now, when you drive east from Tucson on Interstate 10 toward El Paso, you encounter an I.N.S. check station outside Las Cruces, New Mexico. When you drive north from Las Cruces up Interstate 25, two miles north of the town of Truth or Consequences, the highway is blocked with orange emergency barriers, and all traffic is diverted into a two-lane Border Patrol checkpoint—ninety-five miles north of the U.S.-Mexico border.

I was detained once at Truth or Consequences, despite my and my companion's Arizona driver's licenses. Two men, both Chicanos, were detained at the same time, despite the fact that they too presented ID and spoke English without the thick Texas accents of the Border Patrol agents. While we were stopped, we watched as other vehicles—whose occupants were white—were waved through the checkpoint. White people traveling with brown people, however, can expect to be stopped on suspicion they work with the sanctuary movement, which shelters refugees. White people who appear to be clergy, those who wear ethnic clothing or jewelry and women with very long hair or very short hair (they could be nuns) are also frequently detained; white men with beards or men with long hair are more likely to be detained, too, because Border Patrol agents have "profiles" of "those sorts" of

white people who may help political refugees. (Most of the political refugees from Guatemala and El Salvador are Native American or mestizo because the indigenous people of the Americas have continued to resist efforts by invaders to displace them from their ancestral lands.) Alleged increases in illegal immigration by people of Asian ancestry means that the Border Patrol now routinely detains anyone who appears to be Asian or part Asian, as well.

Once your car is diverted from the Interstate Highway into the checkpoint area, you are under the control of the Border Patrol, which in practical terms exercises a power that no highway patrol or city patrolman possesses: They are willing to detain anyone, for no apparent reason. Other law-enforcement officers need a shred of probable cause in order to detain someone. On the books, so does the Border Patrol; but on the road, it's another matter. They'll order you to stop your car and step out; then they'll ask you to open the trunk. If you ask why or request a search warrant, you'll be told that they'll have to have a dog sniff the car before they can request a search warrant, and the dog might not get there for two or three hours. The search warrant might require an hour or two past that. They make it clear that if you force them to obtain a search warrant for the car, they will make you submit to a strip search as well.

Traveling in the open, though, the sense of violation can be even worse. Never mind high-profile cases like that of former Border Patrol agent Michael Elmer, acquitted of murder by claiming self-defense, despite admitting that as an officer he shot an "illegal" immigrant in the back and then hid the body, which remained undiscovered until another Border Patrolman reported the event. (Last month, Elmer was convicted of reckless endangerment in a separate incident, for shooting at least ten rounds from his M-16 too close to a group of immigrants as they were crossing illegally into Nogales in March 1992.) Or that in El Paso, a high school football coach driving a vanload of his players in full uniform was pulled over on the freeway and a Border Patrol agent put a cocked revolver to his head. (The football coach was Mexican-American, as were most of the players in his van; the incident eventually caused a federal judge to issue a restraining order against the Border Patrol.) We've a mountain of personal experiences like that which never make the newspapers. A history professor at U.C.L.A. told me she had been traveling by train from Los Angeles to Albuquerque twice a month doing research. On each of her trips, she had noticed that the Border Patrol agents were at the station in Albuquerque scrutinizing the passengers. Since she is six feet tall and of Irish and German ancestry, she was not particularly concerned. Then one day when she stepped off the train in Albuquerque, two Border Patrolmen accosted her, wanting to know what she was doing, and why she was traveling between Los Angeles and Albuquerque twice a month. She presented identification and an explanation deemed "suitable" by the agents, and was allowed to go about her business.

Just the other day, I mentioned to a friend that I was writing this article and he told me about his 73-year-old father, who is half Chinese and had set out alone by car from Tucson to Albuquerque the week before. His father had become confused by road construction and missed a turnoff from Interstate 10 to Interstate 25; when he turned around and circled back, he missed the turnoff a second time. But when he looped back for yet another try, Border Patrol agents stopped him and forced him to open his trunk. After they satisfied themselves that he was not smuggling Chinese immigrants, they sent him on his way. He was so rattled by the event that he had to be driven home by his daughter.

This is the police state that has developed in the southwestern United States since the 1980s. No person, no citizen, is free to travel without the scrutiny of the Border Patrol. In the city of South Tucson, where 80 percent of the respondents were Chicano or Mexicano, a joint research project by the University of Wisconsin and the University of Arizona recently concluded that one out of every five people there had been detained, mistreated verbally or nonverbally, or questioned by I.N.S. agents in the past two years.

Manifest Destiny may lack its old grandeur of theft and blood — "lock the door" is what it means now, with racism a trump card to be played again and again, shamelessly, by both major political parties. "Immigration," like "street crime" and "welfare fraud," is a political euphemism that refers to people of color. Politicians and media people talk about "illegal aliens" to dehumanize and demonize undocumented immigrants, who are for the most part people

of color. Even in the days of Spanish and Mexican rule, no attempts were made to interfere with the flow of people and goods from south to north and north to south. It is the U.S. government that has continually attempted to sever contact between the tribal people north of the border and those to the south.*

Now that the "Iron Curtain" is gone, it is ironic that the U.S. government and its Border Patrol are constructing a steel wall ten feet high to span sections of the border with Mexico. While politicians and multinational corporations extol the virtues of NAFTA and "free trade" (in goods, not flesh), the ominous curtain is already up in a six-mile section at the border crossing at Mexicali; two miles are being erected but are not yet finished at Naco; and at Nogales, sixty miles south of Tucson, the steel wall has been all rubber-stamped and awaits construction likely to begin in March. Like the pathetic multimillion-dollar "antidrug" border surveillance balloons that were continually deflated by high winds and made only a couple of meager interceptions before they blew away, the fence along the border is a theatrical prop, a bit of pork for contractors. Border entrepreneurs have already used blowtorches to cut passageways through the fence to collect "tolls," and are doing a brisk business. Back in Washington, the I.N.S. announces a $300 million computer contract to modernize its record-keeping and Congress passes a crime bill that shunts $255 million to the I.N.S. for 1995, $181 million earmarked for border control, which is to include 700 new partners for the men who stopped Gus and me in our travels, and the history professor, and my friend's father, and as many as they could from South Tucson.

It is no use; borders haven't worked, and they won't work, not now, as the indigenous people of the Americas reassert their kinship and solidarity with one another. A mass migration is already under way; its roots are not simply economic. The Uto-Aztecan languages are spoken as far north as Taos Pueblo near the Colorado border, all the way south

---

*The Treaty of Guadalupe Hidalgo, signed in 1848, recognizes the right of the Tohano O'Odom (Papago) people to move freely across the U.S.-Mexico border without documents. A treaty with Canada guarantees similar rights to those of the Iroquois nation in traversing the U.S.-Canada border.

to Mexico City. Before the arrival of the Europeans, the indigenous communities throughout this region not only conducted commerce, the people shared cosmologies, and oral narratives about the Maize Mother, the Twin Brothers and their Grandmother, Spider Woman, as well as Quetzalcoatl the benevolent snake. The great human migration within the Americas cannot be stopped; human beings are natural forces of the Earth, just as rivers and winds are natural forces.

Deep down the issue is simple: The so-called "Indian Wars" from the days of Sitting Bull and Red Cloud have never really ended in the Americas. The Indian people of southern Mexico, of Guatemala and those left in El Salvador, too, are still fighting for their lives and for their land against the "cavalry" patrols sent out by the governments of those lands. The Americas are Indian country, and the "Indian problem" is not about to go away.

One evening at sundown, we were stopped in traffic at a railroad crossing in downtown Tucson while a freight train passed us, slowly gaining speed as it headed north to Phoenix. In the twilight I saw the most amazing sight: Dozens of human beings, mostly young men, were riding the train; everywhere, on flat cars, inside open boxcars, perched on top of boxcars, hanging off ladders on tank cars and between boxcars. I couldn't count fast enough, but I saw fifty or sixty people headed north. They were dark young men, Indian and mestizo; they were smiling and a few of them waved at us in our cars. I was reminded of the ancient story of Aztlán, told by the Aztecs but known in other Uto-Aztecan communities as well. Aztlán is the beautiful land to the north, the origin place of the Aztec people. I don't remember how or why the people left Aztlán to journey farther south, but the old story says that one day, they will return.

◆◆◆

Seattle Declaration

Diverse Women for Diversity

We, Diverse Women for Diversity, diverse in culture, race, religion, socio-economic conditions, have one common goal: biological and cultural diversity as the foundation of life on earth. Therefore we stand for self-sufficiency, self-reliance and solidarity, locally and globally.

For this reason we have gathered in Seattle in November 1999 to struggle against the WTO.

The WTO was created to further and stabilize the freedom of trade and profit on behalf of a few multinationals. Going far beyond this goal, however, it acts as a new World Government.

The WTO is a non-elected institution, based on secrecy and non-representation. It erodes the substance of democracy in our countries. Through its rules it imposes economic policies in favor of gigantic global corporate interests.

The WTO promises to create growth and wealth for all, equality, jobs, ecological sustainability through a "free globalized market."

The reality, however, is that the free market mechanism has led to increased poverty, to more unemployment, to more ecological destruction, and more violence against women, children and [subordinated peoples].

Our food and agricultural system has been brought under corporate control of global grain merchants like Cargill and ADM through WTO Agreements on Agriculture. This has robbed women and peasant producers of their livelihood and has denied consumers worldwide access to sufficient, safe and healthy food.

The WTO rejects precautionary principle and thus allows corporations like Monsanto (USA), Novartis

(Switzerland), DuPont (USA), Astrazeneca (UK/Netherlands) and Aventis (Germany) to spread genetically modified seeds and foods without people's knowledge and consent, thus creating unprecedented ecological and health hazards. These corporations are a danger to life on earth.

For thousands of years, indigenous people, women and men have protected, nurtured and sustained the Biodiversity of food, crops and medicinal plants. This rich Biodiversity is now being stolen by monopolistic "life science" corporations, under the legal protection of the Agreement on Trade Related Intellectual Property Rights (TRIPs). TRIPs forces countries to introduce patents on life and promotes the piracy of millennia of innovation and creativity by millions of women and peasants through the privatization of traditional knowledge.

After the Multilateral Agreement on Investment was defeated by worldwide citizens' resistance in De-cember 1998, the same proponents of unlimited free markets are now pushing for a new round of negotiation on the same issue in WTO. They also include new areas for liberalization, namely, TRIMs Services [Trade Related Investment Measures], Investment, Public Procurement and Competition. All these areas, if further liberalized, will have further negative effect, particularly on women.

In summary, this so called "free market" system is indeed a global war system, based on violence against nature, humanity, especially women and children.

Together with the thousands of children, women and men gathered here in Seattle, we, Diverse Women for Diversity, reject this global war system and the WTO. We pledge to build an economy and a society where nature and human beings can live and prosper in peace and happiness.

Seattle, 1st December 1999

CHAPTER EIGHT

◆◆◆

Work, Wages, and Welfare

Virtually all women in the world work. They are farmers, artists, craft workers, factory workers, businesswomen, maids, baby-sitters, engineers, secretaries, soldiers, teachers, nurses, sex workers, journalists, bus drivers, lawyers, therapists, waitpersons, prison guards, doctors, cashiers, airline pilots, executives, sales staff, professors, carpenters, dishwashers, filmmakers, mail carriers, dancers, homemakers, mothers, and wives. Many find satisfaction and challenge, even enjoyment, in their work; for others it is a necessary drudgery. This chapter looks at women's experiences of work in the United States, how work is defined in this country, the effects of changes in the economy over the last thirty-five years, women's wages, and income supports for women without paid work. We argue that economic security is fundamental to women's well-being and the security of our families and communities.

Defining Women's Work

According to dictionary definitions, the English word *economy* comes from two Greek words: *oikos,* meaning "house," and *nemo,* meaning "to manage." Thus, economy can be understood as managing the affairs of the household, and beyond the household, of the wider society. Modern-day professional economists make a distinction between "productive" and "un-

productive" work, however, which is not implied in this original definition. So-called productive work is done for money; work not done for money is defined as unproductive. By this analysis, a woman who spends her day making meals for her family, doing laundry, finding the schoolbooks and football shoes, packing school lunches, making beds, washing the kitchen floor, remembering her mother-in-law's birthday, changing diapers, waiting in for the TV repair person, taking the toddler to the park, walking the dog, meeting the older children after school, making calls about an upcoming PTA meeting, changing the cat litter, paying bills, and balancing her checkbook is not involved in productive work (Waring 1988). A United Nations study released in Nairobi, Kenya, in 1985 at the end of the International Decade on Women (1975–85) stated that women do 75 percent of the world's work; they earn 10 percent of the world's wages and own 1 percent of the world's property (Pharr 1988, p. 9). Worldwide, then, most of women's work is unpaid and hence unproductive.

Leith Mullings (1997) distinguishes four kinds of women's work: paid work in the formal sector; reproductive work, including housework and raising children as well as paid work taking care of children, the elderly, and the sick; work in the informal sector, which may be paid under the table or in favors returned; and transformational work, volunteering in community organizations, professional groups, and

314

clubs of all kinds (see Reading 31, Chapter 5). As we discussed in Chapter 5, one effect of the gendered division of labor in the home has been a similar distinction between women's work and men's work in the paid workforce.

Although in recent years some women have broken into professions and jobs that were once the preserve of men, most paid jobs in the United States are divided along gender lines, and women are greatly overrepresented in low-paying jobs. Most women in the workforce do "women's work" in service and administrative support jobs, as secretaries, waitresses, and health aides. They work in day-care centers, elder-care facilities, garment factories, food processing, retail stores, restaurants, laundries, and other women's homes. In addition to earning low wages, such workers are often treated as expendable by employers, as Hattie Gossett points out in Reading 48. Women in professional jobs tend to be elementary school teachers, social workers, nurses, and health-care workers. There is an emphasis on caring for and serving others in many of these jobs; some may also require being on display and meeting dominant beauty standards. As Tucker (1996) remarked, "You do not have to look to Venus or Mars to find the difference in men and women. Just look at their paychecks" (p. 3).

In the idealized nuclear family described in Chapter 5, middle-class White women were not expected to be wage earners. Despite the fact that they were responsible for all the tasks involved in maintaining a home and taking care of a family, many said of themselves, "I don't work; I'm just a housewife." By contrast, women on welfare are thought lazy or work-shy if they concentrate on looking after their children and do not participate in the paid workforce.

Women in the U.S. Workforce

Before wage labor developed, several economic systems coexisted in this country. Amott (1993) identifies

> family farming, the *hacienda* system of large ranches in the Southwest, plantation slavery in the South, the economies of the different Native American nations, and the early capitalist industrial enterprises.
>
> (p. 15)

Economic Inequalities

- In the 1,500 biggest companies in the United States, men are 95 percent of the senior managers (*Women . . . A World Survey*, Ruth Sivard, 1995).

- The wealth of the world's 358 billionaires exceeds the combined annual incomes of countries that are home to 45 percent of the world's population (*London Guardian*, 16 July 1996, p. 11).

- The average CEO in the United States makes about 149 times the average factory worker's pay.

- The poverty rate in 1997, 13.7 percent, was higher than in 1989, despite seven years of economic growth. Approximately 50 million Americans—19 percent of the population—live below the national poverty line (defined as $8,122, or half of the 1991 median U.S. income). This includes one in four children under eighteen, one in five senior citizens, and three out of five single-parent households (*The Nation*, Jan. 12–19, 1998, p. 3).

- Between 1973 and 1994, the number of U.S. children living in poverty grew by 50 percent; now 22 percent grow up poor, and the number is rising (Richard Barnett, *The Nation*, 19 December 1994, p. 754).

- An estimated 250 million children between the ages of five and fourteen work full and part time in countries of the South (U.N. International Labor Report).

- Nike CEO Philip Knight's personal fortune is estimated at $5.2 billion; Michael Jordan has a $20 million endorsement deal; a pair of Air Jordans retails generally around $135 per pair. Women workers in Indonesia who make Nikes earn $2.20 per day (Global Exchange 1997).

She notes that race and ethnicity were central in determining who was assigned to each of these labor systems; gender and class determined what work people performed. The U.S. labor market is still structured hierarchically, as discussed by Amott and Matthaei (Reading 49). Significant inequalities in women's work opportunities may mask economic interconnections among women:

> In a very real sense, the lives of any one group of women have been dependent upon the lives of others. . . . Unfortunately the ties which have joined us have rarely been mutual, equal, or cooperative; instead, our interdependence has been characterized by domination and exploitation. American Indian women's lost lands were the basis for European immigrant wealth. The domestic work of African American and poor European immigrant women, along with the labors of their husbands, sons, and daughters in factories, underwrote the lavish lifestyles of upper-class European American women. The riches enjoyed by the wives and children of Mexican American *hacienda* owners were created by the poverty of displaced and landless Indians and Chicanas. And U.S. political and economic domination of the Philippines and Puerto Rico allowed U.S. women to maintain higher standards of living, and encouraged the migration of impoverished Filipina and Puerto Rican women to U.S. shores.
>
> *(Amott and Matthaei 1996, p. 3)*

As pointed out in Chapter 7, the economy of the United States is undergoing fundamental changes because of automation in manufacturing and office work and the movement of jobs overseas. Many U.S. companies have laid off workers, sometimes by the thousands, as they scramble to downsize their operations as a way to cut costs and maintain, or even increase, profits. Innovations such as ATMs, voice mail, salad bars, and self-service gas stations, to name a few everyday examples, all mean fewer jobs. One result has been a growing inequality in earnings between people in professional and technical positions and those without college educations who are working low-income jobs. Despite the influx of relatively inexpensive consumer goods into the United States, especially clothing and electronic items from

"global factories" around the world, it has become much harder for many families to make ends meet. Several factors have made it imperative that more and more women are income earners. Rents and housing payments, health insurance, and the cost of college tuition, for example, have increased. Much manufacturing, such as car assembly and related engineering work, which was relatively well paid and largely done by men, has been automated or moved out of the United States. Divorce rates are high, and many fathers pay little or no child support.

According to the U.S. Department of Labor, Women's Bureau (1999), 59.8 percent of U.S. women were in the paid labor force in 1998, the highest rate ever, and women accounted for 46 percent of all workers. Labor force participation was highest for women in the thirty-five–forty-four age group (77 percent), who were closely followed by those aged twenty-five–thirty-four and forty-five–fifty-four (each 76 percent). Of older women, 51 percent between fifty-five and sixty-four years of age are employed; the rate for younger women (sixteen–nineteen years) is similar: 52 percent. Most women work full time, but 26 percent held part-time jobs. Two-thirds of all part-time workers (66 percent) and temporary workers are women. Withorn (1999) notes that this is often a "devil's bargain," because wages are low and there are no benefits, but women take these jobs because they need flexibility in their lives to look after children or aging parents. The labor market is structured so that the best positions are reserved

> for those adults who have someone on call to handle the life needs of an always-available worker. Economist Randy Albelda calls these positions "jobs with wives."
>
> *(Withorn 1999, p. 9)*

Data examining the relationship between employment and marital status show that 74 percent of divorced women are in the paid labor force, as are 66 percent of single, never-married women and 62 percent of married women with spouses present. Seventy-one percent of U.S. women with children under eighteen are in paid employment. Sixty-four percent of mothers with preschoolers were income earners in 1997. Black mothers are more likely to be in the paid workforce than White or Latina mothers. Although 18 percent of all families were maintained solely by women in 1992, the detailed figures show a wide disparity based on race. Forty-seven percent of Black families, 24 percent of Latino families, and 14 percent of White families were maintained by women.

Women's Wages: The Effects of Gender, Race, Class, Disability, and Education

Julianne Malveaux, an economist and syndicated columnist, points out that popular culture gives a very misleading view of women's work by featuring women in well-paying jobs in TV shows and movies (Reading 51). The best-paid jobs for women are as lawyers, physicians, pharmacists, engineers, computer analysts, and scientists, but many more women earn the minimum wage. Ida Castro, acting director of the Women's Bureau of the U.S. Department of Labor, commented that "society needs to really look critically at the value given to work performed predominantly by women," and cites child-care workers, home-care attendants, and nursing home workers as persons who earn the minimum wage but do the vitally important work of looking after children and older people (Angwin 1996). Women on average earn roughly seventy-five cents for every dollar that men earn on average. This gap has slowly narrowed in the past two decades, partly because women's wages are improving but also because men's wages are falling. The average salary of a Black woman college graduate in full-time work is less than that of a White male high school drop-out. Women with disabilities earn much less than nondisabled women, partly because so few women with disabilities have college degrees. Women of color with disabilities earn less than White women with disabilities.

According to the U.S. Bureau of the Census (1999b), average annual earnings for full-time workers in 1998 were as follows:

All women	$25,862
White women	26,243
Black women	22,648
Latinas	19,221
All men	35,345
White men	36,172
Black men	27,050
Latinos	22,285

Working wives contribute significantly to household income. According to the U.S. Department of Labor, Women's Bureau (1999), in 1997 the average income of married couples with both partners in the paid workforce was $60,669. In families where the wife was not earning, the average income was $36,027. On divorce, the income of a mother and her children usually drops drastically from its predivorce level. More than 75 percent of divorced mothers with custody of their children are employed. Many fathers (more than 50 percent by some estimates) pay little or no child support. The average annual income of families maintained by women was $21,023 in 1997, compared with $32,960 for families maintained by men and $60,669 for two-earner families. White single mothers earn more than Black and Latina single mothers, on average. Bear in mind that averages always conceal extremes. Many women and men earn less than the average figures cited above and less than the official **poverty level**, which in 1998 was $12,800 for a family of three.

The more education a woman has the more likely she is to be employed. Among women aged twenty-five and over in 1998, 31 percent of those without a high school diploma were income earners; for high school graduates this rose to 56 percent; and for college graduates, to 75 percent (U.S. Department of Labor, Bureau of Labor Statistics, 1999). The close relationship between a woman's level of educational attainment and higher wage levels is expected to continue in many jobs, often linked to developments in computer technology. Workers need to keep skills up-to-date, which requires access to opportunities to keep learning and a willingness to do so. A lack of educational qualifications is a key obstacle for women on welfare who need greater educational opportunity if they are to acquire meaningful work.

Even with a college education, however, and equivalent work experience and skills, women are far less likely than men to get to the top of their professions or corporations. They are halted by unseen barriers, such as men's negative attitudes to senior women and low perceptions of their abilities, training, and skills. This barrier has been called a **glass ceiling.** Women can see what the senior positions in their company or their field look like, but few women reach them (Franklin and Sweeney 1988; Morrison et al. 1992). The Federal Glass Ceiling Commission, appointed by President George Bush, reported in 1995 that in the top Fortune 1000 industrial and 500 service companies 95 percent of senior-level managers were men and, of this number, 97 percent were White (Redwood 1996, p. 2).

Discrimination against Working Women: Sexual Harassment, Age, and Disability

The segmented labor market is reproduced through micro-, meso-, and macro-level factors. These include unequitable educational opportunities for women, especially women of color; social attitudes and assumptions regarding women's skills, abilities, ambitions, and family responsibilities; and discriminatory practices — many of them subtle — in decisions about hiring, firing, and promotion, as well as the day-to-day organization of work. Reading 50 refers to different assumptions about women workers compared with men workers.

Sexual Harassment   According to the American Federation of State, County and Municipal Employees (AFSCME), sexual harassment is "a serious problem for over two-thirds of working women and some working men" (AFSCME 1988). It is defined by the federal Equal Opportunity Commission guidelines as

> unwelcome sexual advances, requests for sexual favors and other verbal or physical conduct of a sexual nature when
>
> 1. submission to such conduct is made either explicitly or implicitly a term or condition of employment;
>
> 2. submission to or rejection of such conduct by an individual is used as the basis for employment decisions affecting such individual; or
>
> 3. such conduct has the purpose or effect of unreasonably interfering with an individual's work performance or creating an intimidating, hostile or offensive working environment.

Sexual harassment at work can include verbal abuse, visual abuse, physical abuse, and rape and is against the law. In 1986 the first case concerning sexual harassment (*Meritor Savings Bank v. Vinson*) reached the Supreme Court and established that sexual harassment includes the creation of a hostile or abusive work environment. The Court also held that the appropriate question is not whether the victim tolerated the harassment "voluntarily" but whether it was "unwelcome." The testimony of Anita Hill in November 1991 before a Senate Judiciary Committee considering the confirmation of Clarence Thomas to the Supreme Court made this issue a lead story for virtually every TV talk show, magazine, and newspaper in the country (Morrison 1992). As women talked about their experiences of sexual harassment, its very widespread nature was publicly acknowledged. Employers hastily set up workshops and seminars for their staffs, mindful of the costs of losing sexual harassment lawsuits. Public figures who were sued for sexual harassment in 1996 included President Bill Clinton and Senator Bob Packwood, who was forced by his Republican colleagues to resign his Senate seat, as mentioned by Michael Kimmell (Reading 38, Chapter 6). It is important to note that the federal law against sexual harassment applies only to behavior in the workplace or in schools, not to sexual intimidation and abuse in other situations. Daphne Patai (1998) goes so far as to claim that "the mere allegation of 'sexual harassment' now provides women with an extraordinarily effective weapon to wield against men." However, the Supreme Court strengthened protections against sexual harassment in 1998 (Mason 1998), and many women acknowledge the serious difficulties involved in making such allegations.

Age Discrimination   The wage gap between women and men increases with age. One effect of corporate downsizing and layoffs is that a growing number of older, experienced workers are unemployed. They are too young to retire but often considered too old or too expensive to hire. For women over forty, particularly, age complicates the job search. It takes longer for such women to find new work than it does men, and their new jobs usually pay less than they were earning before or are part time. There are several myths about older women in the workforce: it is not cost-effective to hire an older woman; she will be hard to train and is likely to have difficulty with new technology; her insurance costs will be higher than for a younger person; and she will not have a strong commitment to work. According to the American Association of Retired Persons (n.d.), none of these myths are borne out by research findings.

Discrimination against Women with Disabilities
Nancy Russo and Mary Jansen (1988) noted that women with disabilities have not participated in the "women's employment revolution" (p. 229). They argued that people with disabilities are generally stereotyped as dependent, passive, and incompetent, qualities that are also often attributed to women in general. More African American women and Latinas report a work disability, a disabling condition that makes them unable to work outside the home, than do White women. Work disabilities are more prevalent among older women. At the same time, many women with disabilities that keep them out of the paid workforce do their own cooking, laundry, and housekeeping. Increasing numbers of students with disabilities are going to college. They tend to be older (36 percent are thirty-five or older) and married, financially independent, and/or veterans. In 1993, 6 percent of all undergraduates reported having some kind of disability, with the most common related to orthopedic conditions (37 percent), health conditions (20 percent), hearing (18 percent), sight (11 percent), and speech (7 percent) (*Mainstream* 1997).

Women with disabilities generally have much lower educational attainment than nondisabled women, which bars them from entering higher-paying professional work. They may have missed a lot of school as children or may not have been provided with relevant special education programs. Vocational schools and rehabilitation programs for women who suffer a disability after completing their education also tend to channel them into dependent roles within the family or to low-paid "women's work" in the labor force. Added to these limitations are the prejudices and ignorance of employers and coworkers and the ableist attitudes of this culture. Women with disabilities may also have to make what Mudrick (1988) describes as "significant and sometimes costly special arrangements" (p. 246) to maintain their employment, such as transportation or extra help at home.

The Americans with Disabilities Act (ADA) of 1990 is a landmark piece of legislation, as mentioned in Chapter 3. A 1999 Supreme Court decision narrowed the law's reach in the area of employment discrimination. The Court declared that individuals with physical impairments that can be easily corrected (for example, by medication or eyeglasses) are not disabled and not allowed protection under the ADA—even though the disabilities have cost them their jobs (Greenhouse 1999).

Balancing Home and Work

Until the 1950s many companies would not hire married women, and there is still a fear that married women will be less committed to their work than men. In Chapter 6 we discussed the difficulties many women face, juggling paid work and family responsibilities (Gould 1997; Hochschild 1989; Peters 1997). Despite some men's involvement in housekeeping and child care, women are still largely responsible for raising children and running the home. Inadequate or unaffordable child care and difficulties in taking time off work to care for a sick child, for example, make many working women's lives extremely stressful and difficult. Also, more people are working longer hours. By some estimates, parents spend 40 percent less time with their children than they did thirty years ago, because of other pressures (Brennan, Winklepleck, and MacNee 1994, p. 373).

Flextime, Part-Time Work, Home Working, and the Mommy Track   In Reading 52 Jeannine Ouellette Howitz describes her experiences of juggling work and caring for children. Mothers in the paid workforce may try to find a job with hours that are compatible with children's school schedules. This might mean working jobs that allow some flexible scheduling, seeking part-time work, or working at home—whether sewing, minding children, or "telecommuting." Thanks to innovations like fax-modems, electronic mail, and pagers, home working is currently touted for professional and corporate workers as a way to work flexible hours with greater personal freedom and no stressful commute. This may alleviate the problem of child care for some professional families and greatly help the commuter marriage, but for garment workers and child-care providers, who account for the majority of home workers, the pay is poor and there are no benefits. Garment workers on piecework rates put in long hours, often working into the night. They are also isolated from one another, which makes it much more difficult to improve their pay through collective bargaining.

Another solution to the problem for professional women, put forward in the late 1980s, was that firms adopt a "mommy track." Professional women who

Home and Work: Caring for Children and Elders

- Sixty-three percent of women with children under the age of six, and 78 percent of women with children aged six to seventeen, are in the paid workforce. Sixty-two percent of working parents say their main problem with child care is finding affordable high-quality care (AFL-CIO, *Bargaining for Child Care Fact Sheet* n.d.).

- The average annual cost of child care for a four-year-old in an urban center ($4,000–$6,000) is more than the average annual cost of public college tuition in almost every state. Costs for infants are higher than those for a four-year-old (Children's Defense Fund 1998).

- Middle-aged people—especially women—are increasingly a "sandwich" generation who care for their children and their aging parents at the same time. Seventy percent of informal, unpaid caregivers—for children and elders—are women. The typical caregiver is a 46-year-old working woman (National Alliance for Care Giving, American Association of Retired Persons n.d.).

- Of the 7.1 million elderly with some kind of disability, almost three-fourths live at home and receive unpaid care from relatives and friends (Urban Institute 1996).

- Paid caregivers (of children and elders) earn around $6.12 an hour, or about $10,000 a year. This is almost $3,000 lower than the 1998 poverty threshold ($12,800) for a family of three. Nationwide, child-care workers earn 63 percent of the average wage. This ranges between 55 percent of the state's average wage (Pennsylvania) and 70 percent (Maine) (Center for Policy Alternatives, *Balancing Family and Work: Facts about Working Families*, 1999).

- Nearly 5 million school-aged children in the United States spend time as latchkey kids without adult supervision (Child Care Bureau 1997). Studies show that latchkey children are at greater risk for truancy, stress, poor grades, and substance abuse (Children's Defense Fund 1998).

- Nationally, only one in ten eligible families gets federal child-care assistance (U.S. Department of Health and Human Services 1999).

wanted career advancement comparable to that of men either would not have children or would somehow manage their lives so as to combine having children with working long hours, attending out-of-town meetings, taking little vacation time, and doing whatever the job demanded. Otherwise, they could "opt" for the mommy track and be recompensed accordingly.

Child Care   Child care is a family's fourth highest expense, after housing, food, and taxes. For some women who want to work, the cost of child care is prohibitive, even if they can find suitable child-care providers. Federal and state governments, employers, and labor unions offer some assistance to child-care providers and parents in the form of tax credits, grants to child-care programs, on-site care in the case

of some large employers, provisions for child care as part of a benefits package, flextime, and leave for family emergencies, such as sickness. Taken overall, these provisions are woefully inadequate. It is particularly difficult to obtain child care for the hours before and after school and during school vacations. Head Start programs, for example, which offer preschool education to low-income children, are usually available only for a half day and serve approximately 17 percent of eligible children. The Family and Medical Leave Act of 1993 provides for leave in family emergencies like the birth of a child or illness of a family member, but it covers only firms with fifty or more workers, and the leave is unpaid. Most workers cannot take advantage of full unpaid leave without severe financial hardship. By 1999 an estimated 20 million workers had used the law to take time off for family needs, but there was no information concerning how many low- to moderate-income families had been forced to forgo such leave because they could not afford to lose a paycheck. The Family Leave Commission reported that nearly 10 percent of workers who take family or medical leave are forced onto public assistance during that time (Gardner 1999).

Another aspect of this issue is the working conditions for child-care workers, the vast majority of whom are women who work in their own homes or at child-care centers and preschool programs. Although parents often struggle to afford child care, child-care workers are poorly paid. Many are not paid overtime; they do not receive health insurance or paid vacations. Even fewer have retirement plans. Child-care workers, on average, earn less than animal caretakers, parking lot attendants, and garbage collectors. Low pay and difficult working conditions mean that turnover among these workers is high.

The Second Shift Women employed outside the home still carry the main responsibility for housework and raising children and are left with very little time for themselves. Although this is particularly acute for single parents, many women living with men also do more housework and child care than their partners (Mainardi 1992). Undoubtedly, this pattern varies among couples and perhaps also at different stages in their lives. Arlie Hochschild (1989) has estimated that women in the labor force work a second shift of at least fifteen hours a week more than men, or an extra month of twenty-four-hour days over a year, and argues that men need to do more in the home. A 1990 Virginia Slims Opinion Poll uncovered great resentment among women over housework. "Fully 52 percent of wives said they feel resentful about how little their husband does at home" (Brennan, Winklepleck, and MacNee 1994, p. 395). In households where men are present, housework is often divided along gendered lines. Husbands and fathers take care of the car, do yard work and household repairs, and take out the trash. Women usually have major responsibility for food shopping, meals, laundry, and child care. These tasks have to be done every day and take more time and emotional energy than "men's" tasks. Negotiating household responsibilities and the stress of juggling home and paid work is a key source of friction in many families. Upper-middle-class households pay

cleaners, maids, and baby-sitters, which helps to free such women from the time crunch and stress of balancing home and work. These domestic workers are usually paid low wages without benefits. In seeking greater freedom for themselves, upper-middle-class women thus find themselves perpetuating poor working conditions for poorer women.

Organized Labor

Historically, the male-dominated labor movement has been weak in pressing for changes that would benefit women workers, and women have not been taken seriously as labor leaders. Some male workers were hostile to women in the workforce, fearing for their own jobs and their authority as breadwinners. In support of women in unions, the Coalition of Labor Union Women (CLUW) has four main goals: to organize the unorganized, to promote affirmative action in the workplace, to stimulate political action and legislation on women's issues, and to increase the participation of women in their unions. The coalition emphasizes such issues as equal pay, child care, universal access to health care, and reproductive freedom. It aims to educate working women about their rights, to provide training in dealing with management, and to prepare women for union leadership positions.

Workers usually make significant gains in wage levels and working conditions when they are members of a labor union. In 1997 women union members earned 40 percent more than nonunion women, and the differential is slightly higher for women of color (U.S. Department of Labor, Bureau of Labor Statistics 1999). In 1996 women accounted for 39 percent of all union members and the majority of new ones (Waldman 1997, p. 12). Erika Jones discusses recent changes in the U.S. labor movement due to globalization of the economy and women's growing union participation in an interview with Jeanette Huezo and Susan Winning from the Women's Institute for Leadership Development (Reading 53).

The majority of women in the U.S. workforce are not union members. This is partly due to the decline of unions nationally in recent decades. Also many women work in jobs that are hard to unionize, such as retailing or the fast-food business, where they are scattered at many separate locations. The United Farm Workers of America (UFW), founded by Cesar Chavez and Dolores Huerta, has pressured growers to sign union contracts to improve the pay and working conditions of its members—women and men—many of whom are migrant workers and immigrants to the United States whose health is continually compromised by chemical pesticides. The UFW has called for boycotts of non-organic table grapes, and now strawberries, which are heavily sprayed with pesticides, as a means of leverage in its struggle with growers (Ferriss and Sandoval 1997).

The Working Poor   Organized labor also calls attention to low wages, a contributory factor in the raise in the minimum wage in 1996. More than 9 million working people were living in poverty in 1997, and one-quarter of them worked full time, year round. Nearly 60 percent of the working poor are women, and women of color are more than twice as likely to be poor compared with White women. Almost 3 million poor workers were in families with children under the age of six. Ten percent of people with significant disabilities working full time fell below the poverty line. In public debate poor people are usually assumed to be on welfare, masking the reality of life for the many working poor. This includes legal immigrants, who often start off at the bottom of the employment hierarchy. Some people with very low incomes are working minimum-wage jobs, and others work part time or seasonally. They may be involved in the informal economy as maids, baby-sitters, or gardeners, for example, doing home work for the garment trade, fixing cars, carrying and selling small amounts of drugs, getting money for sex, selling roses at off-ramps.

Others work in sweatshops, as mentioned in Chapter 7, which are also unregulated in terms of wages, hours, and conditions of work. These are on the rise in many major U.S. cities and often employ undocumented workers. In the mid-1990s there were several media exposés of clothing companies whose subcontractors operate sweatshops, including The Gap, Macy's, and Mervyn's. The Union of Needletrades, Industrial and Textile Employees (UNITE) has organized demonstrations outside department stores to encourage shoppers to boycott brands that use sweatshop labor. In 1996 Asian Immigrant Women Advocates, after a three-year campaign, won a significant agreement from Jessica McClintock to improve labor practices. Workers filed a class-action lawsuit against Guess and sixteen of its contracting shops for "systematic violations of basic labor laws" (Sharf 1997).

Affirmative Action   Labor unions, as well as many women's organizations and civil rights organizations, also support affirmative action in employment, introduced as part of the Civil Rights Act of 1964 to improve job possibilities for women, people of color, and military veterans, whose opportunities in education, job training, and hiring are not equal to those of White men. Affirmative action is not a quota system, as is often claimed; it is not reverse discrimination; and it is not a system for hiring unqualified people. The need for and desirability of affirmative action policies—which have benefited White women more than any other group—were called into question increasingly in the 1990s and were the subject of public campaigns. The affirmative action policy for state agencies in California was overturned in a ballot initiative in 1996, and in 1998 the University of California banned affirmative action in student admissions. Also in 1998, Washington State voters supported a ban on all state affirmative action programs for all women and men of color in education, contracting, and employment.

Challenges of the Global Economy   A great challenge for organized labor in the future is the continued impact of the globalization of the economy on the availability of work, wage rates, working conditions in the United States, and continued pressure for immigration into this country, as discussed in Chapter 7. As capital becomes increasingly international in its movements, labor will need to become increasingly international in its strategies. This country has a vital tradition of labor organizing, including actions in support of workers in other countries. Although circumstances have changed, there is much to be learned from this history that can be applied today (Cobble 1993; Milkman 1985).

Pensions, Disability Payments, and Welfare

For women who cannot work because of illness, age, or disability, for those who are made redundant or who cannot leave their children, there is a complex patchwork of income-support measures and means-tested allowances provided by federal and state governments and private pension plans. Community organizations, particularly religious organizations, also provide much-needed informal support to poor

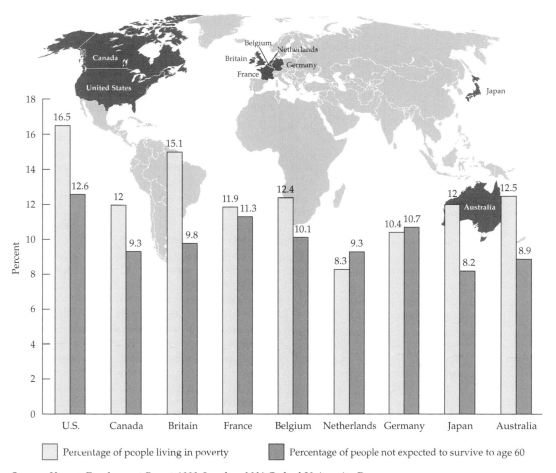

Poverty and Life Expectancy in Industrialized Countries

Percentage of people living in poverty

Percentage of people not expected to survive to age 60

Source: *Human Development Report 1999*, London, N.Y. Oxford University Press.

people. Before the Great Depression of the 1930s, when the economy collapsed and many thousands were suddenly destitute, there was a commonly held belief that poverty was due to laziness and that there was plenty of work available for those willing to roll up their sleeves and get on with it. But the severity of the collapse, which put so many people on bread lines, desperate to feed their families, called for government intervention in the labor market to protect people from the worst effects of the booms and slumps inherent in the economy. This provided the impetus and the political justification for the establishment of Social Security and Medicare programs under the Social Security Act of 1935.

These programs are based on people's relationship to work and are rooted in the principle of the work ethic. Older people can claim pensions because they have already done their share and paid into the Social Security fund during their working lives; people with disabilities may be excused if they are not able to work as long or as vigorously as non-disabled people; those who are laid off because of plant closures or other company changes can usually claim unemployment benefits for a few months while they look for other jobs. Such people are considered "deserving" in contrast to the "undeserving," meaning those who are young and able-bodied but who "simply don't want to work," as is often said nowadays, no less than in the 1930s. This distinction underlies two kinds of benefits: one is based on the concept of social insurance, which allows individuals to draw from an insurance fund to which they have contributed during their working lives; the other is based on the concept of public assistance, under which the needy are given "means-tested" allowances.

Significantly for women today, this Social Security legislation was designed to assist the ideal nuclear family, where the male head of the household was in regular, full-time, paid employment until his death or retirement, and the woman was a full-time homemaker. More than sixty-five years later most U.S. families are not of this type, and women's benefits are adversely affected because their employment histories, upon which payments are calculated, are usually not the same as men's.

Pensions and Retirement

Retirement pensions are a crucial source of income for older people, but women generally receive significantly lower pension payments than men. Pensions are based on wage levels while the person was working and on the number of years in employment. This assumes that only paid work is productive work, so no amount of housekeeping or caring for children and elderly relatives will count. As mentioned earlier, women generally earn lower wages than men and are more likely to work part time and to move in and out of the workforce as they balance paid work with raising children and family responsibilities. Currently, few part-time jobs provide health insurance or a pension plan. When women retire, many have to rely on a Social Security pension that will be lower than that for most men, because women were not able to contribute as much to it during their working lives. Only 31 percent of retired women aged sixty-five or over have a private-sector pension; the average benefit for women who do have pensions is only 38 percent of the average amount received by men (U.S. Department of Labor, Women's Bureau, 1997, p. 11). For divorced women this is particularly serious. Many have not planned independently for retirement. Financial concerns

for older women are further aggravated by the fact that women tend to live longer than men, so their retirement assets must be spread over a longer period of time.

Because work and retirement are defined according to the labor market experiences of White middle-class men, this penalizes not only many women but also men of color and people with disabilities. Poor or working-class men have lower wages, fewer benefits, and less job security and are more likely to have suffered occupational injury than middle-class men and women. Poor women and men of color often have to piece together an income, depending on seasonal or part-time work, sometimes working informally for cash or favors returned. These factors make them less able to retire from paid work completely when they are older.

A new stereotype of affluent older people in ads for cruises, cars, vitamins, health insurance, and hearing aids suggests that all older people are physically fit and enjoying their retirement. As noted by Stoller and Gibson (1994), this is a welcome change from negative images of elderly people, but it deflects attention from those who are poor. These authors found that 11.4 percent of people over sixty-five in the United States have incomes below the poverty line, but this figure rises to 20 percent for Latinos and 31 percent for African Americans. For elderly African Americans living alone the poverty rate increases to 60 percent (p. 55). Because of broken treaties and oppressive policies, elderly Native Americans as a group have the lowest incomes and the worst housing in the country. At the same time, many older people provide valuable services for themselves and others: participating in community organizations, helping family and friends, looking after children, maintaining and repairing their homes, and doing daily cooking, cleaning, and other housework. Stoller and Gibson point out that the advantages of a job with good pay and benefits, a comfortable home, and stimulating opportunities tend to accumulate across the life course. Similarly, disadvantages may also accumulate, producing large differences in economic resources, and often also in health, in old age (p. 107).

The country's elderly population will rise dramatically in the next two decades as baby boomers now in their middle years reach retirement age. The elderly will also be a much larger proportion of the population than previously, giving rise to the notion of the affluent older person collecting unearned benefits at the expense of less affluent younger workers. There is concern over the future of the Social Security system, as a larger number of people will be drawing pensions than will be paying into it. Some, claiming that Social Security will become bankrupt, with nothing left for those who are now young, have gone so far as to call for its privatization. Others argue that Social Security can be fixed with relatively modest increases in contributions in the short term, rather than by wholesale privatization (Lieberman 1997). Sixty percent of Social Security beneficiaries are women, and Social Security is the major source of retirement income for the majority of them. Social Security benefits are guaranteed for life, which is important because of women's longer life span (Institute for Women's Policy Research 1998).

Disability Payments

For reasons similar to those we outlined above in connection with pensions, women with disabilities also receive less from public income support than do men with disabilities. As a result, fewer women with disabilities are able to claim Social Security Disability Insurance (DI), which was designed with the needs of working men in mind, and must rely on the Supplemental Security Income program (SSI), which is subject to a means test for eligibility and greater bureaucratic scrutiny, often demeaning. Some disabled elderly people may choose disability benefits over Social Security pensions, depending on their work histories. The future of income support for people with disabilities is likely to be influenced by two opposing trends: the growing political clout of the disability rights movement and the desire of many politicians to cut government spending.

Welfare

The issue of government support for poor families became especially controversial in the mid-1990s. In 1996, Aid to Families with Dependent Children (AFDC) was replaced by block grants for Temporary Assistance for Needy Families (TANF), as Title I of the Personal Responsibility and Work Opportunity Reconciliation Act (Blau 1999; Goldberg and Collins 1999). This was signed into law by President Clinton

against opposition from many welfare rights organizations and advocates for poor women and children, such as the National Welfare Rights Union, the Children's Defense Fund, and local campaigns like Survivors Inc. (Roxbury, Mass.) and the Coalition for Basic Human Needs (Cambridge, Mass.). Gwendolyn Mink (Reading 54) roundly criticizes feminist organizations and feminist policy makers for not opposing welfare reform more forcefully. The new law ended federal entitlement to assistance dating back to the Social Security Act of 1935.

The Department of Health and Human Services described TANF as "work-based antipoverty programs." States are required by the federal government to set the following conditions for TANF payments: time limits of two years or less, a five-year lifetime limit on benefits, and a work requirement whereby welfare recipients have to spend at least thirty hours a week in "work experience." This does not include basic education, college classes, or training not related to a specific job. States have flexibility to provide other benefits, such as health care, transportation, or child-care subsidies to cushion the transition from welfare to work. The challenge is to find jobs for former welfare recipients, and this is one of the great contradictions of this issue. They are pitted against other low-paid workers, some of whom have been displaced by "workfare 'trainees' working off their welfare grant at less than minimum-wage equivalents" (Cooper 1997, p. 12). They also need affordable child care, a major obstacle for most working mothers. The advantage of workfare trainees to employers is that TANF —in place of wages— is paid out of state funds.

Welfare rolls dropped by roughly 50 percent from 1994 to 1999, and government officials claimed welfare reform a great success. In Wisconsin, early efforts to establish what had happened to former welfare recipients found that 38 percent were unemployed (*Los Angeles Times* 1999, p. A21). Studies from 21 states found that those who got jobs did not leave poverty in most cases (Associated Press May 12, 1999); all jobs obtained by former welfare recipients were low-paying, and many were short-term (Havemann 1999). There was considerable confusion about the new programs and uneven implementation. A majority of states had unspent TANF funds by 1999, estimated to be at least $4 billion overall. Critics of welfare reform argued that the changes had reduced the numbers on welfare but had done nothing to end poverty.

Myths about welfare recipients were central to the public discourse on this issue, stigmatizing those who need to rely on assistance and serving to erode the possibility of empathy by those who are better-off for those who are poor. The mass media gave prominence to stories about welfare "cheats." The prevailing image of a welfare mother is a Black woman with a large family. In 1994, of all AFDC recipients 38 percent were White, 37 percent Black, 17 percent Latina, 2.8 percent Asian, and 1.4 percent Native American (Martinez 1996, p. 62). Forty-two percent of AFDC families had only one child; 30 percent had two (Abramovitz and Newton, 1996). Proponents justified cuts in welfare programs on the grounds that this would help to reduce the federal budget deficit. Welfare payments accounted for approximately 1 percent of the federal budget and 2 to 3 percent of states' budgets. Compare this with other public expenditures, especially the military budget, and note the alternative ways of allocating federal funding proposed by the Women's International League for Peace and Freedom (Reading 71, Chapter 11).

It is important to note here that many people in this society receive some kind of government support, be it through income-tax deductions for homeowners, medical benefits for those in the military, tax breaks for corporations, agricultural subsidies to farmers, government bailouts to savings and loans companies, or government funding for high-tech military-related research conducted by universities and private firms. This is often not mentioned in discussions of welfare, but it should be.

Feminist Approaches to Women's Work and Income

Comparable Worth

Feminist researchers and policy analysts have been concerned with women's overall working conditions and women's labor history (Amott 1993; Amott and Matthaei 1996; Bergmann 1986; Jones 1985; Kessler-Harris 1990; Zavella 1987). They have questioned why the job market is segregated along gender lines and have challenged traditional inequities in pay between women and men. These may be partly explained by differences in education, quali-

fications, and work experience, but part of this wage gap is simply attributable to gender. This has led to detailed discussion of the **comparable worth** of women's jobs when considered next to men's jobs requiring comparable levels of skill and knowledge. Why is it, for example, that secretaries or child-care workers, who are virtually all women, earn so much less than truck drivers or mail carriers, who are mainly men? What do wage rates say about the importance of a job to the wider society? What is being rewarded? Advocates for comparable worth have urged employers to evaluate employees without regard to gender, race, or class, but in terms of knowledge and skills needed to perform the job, mental demands or decision making involved in the job, accountability or the degree of supervision involved, and working conditions, such as how physically safe the job is (Tong 1989). Such calculations reveal many discrepancies in current rates of pay between women's work and men's work. Indeed, if pursued, this line of argument opens up the thorny question of how to justify wage differentials at all.

Feminization of Poverty

Feminist researchers have also pointed to the **feminization of poverty** (Abramovitz 1996; Dujon and Withorn 1996; Sidel 1996). The two poorest groups in the United States are women raising children alone and women over sixty-five living alone. According to the Children's Defense Fund, roughly one-quarter of U.S. children are currently living in poverty, and more children are abused, neglected, committing suicide, running away, and living without health insurance than was the case twenty-five years ago. *Poverty* is a complex term with economic, emotional, and cultural dimensions. One may be materially well-off but emotionally impoverished, for example, and vice versa. Poverty also needs to be thought about in the context of costs — for housing, food, transportation, health care, child care, and clothes needed to go to work — and the social expectations of this materialist culture. Many poor children in the United States today clamor for Nikes, for example, in response to high-pressure advertising campaigns.

There is no consistent national policy in the United States designed to lift people out of poverty. Katha Pollitt (1994) argues forcefully that welfare is a feminist issue because it weakens women's dependence on men. It means that pregnant women can choose to give birth and keep their babies even if abandoned by their boyfriends and families; it means that battered women can leave abusive men, and miserable working-class wives, like their middle-class sisters, can get a fresh start without reducing their children to starvation. It protects women at a time when the patriarchal family is disintegrating, and that is why family-values conservatives hate it, even though opposition to welfare forces them to laud employed mothers, whom—in another part of the policy forest—they usually attack.

(p. 45)

Marxist theorists of the economy used to see women as a reserve army of labor to be brought into the workforce when necessary, as, for instance, during World War II. More recently such theorists note that currently it is women workers who are specifically hired for export production in the Third World, as mentioned in Chapter 7. They are paid low wages and also valued by employers as "docile" and "dexterous." Maria Mies (1986) argues that this international division of labor divides the world into producers and consumers. Third World women producers are linked to First World women consumers through commodities bought by the latter. This division renders many women and men in the First World expendable as far as paid work is concerned; hence the high unemployment rates for young people of color in the United States. In this connection, note the high numbers of African American women and Latinas who enlist in the military, mainly as a way to get a steady paycheck and health insurance. In 1997, 60 percent of women in the Army's enlisted ranks were African Americans and Latinas.

Impact of Class

A key concept in any discussion of work, income, and wealth is class. In the United States today, most people describe themselves as "middle class," a term that includes a very wide range of incomes, occupations, levels of security, and life situations. Indicators of class include income, occupation, education, culture and language, neighborhood, clothes, cars, and, particularly important, unearned wealth. As noted in Chapter 2, some people raised in a working-class community may have a middle-class education and occupation later in life and a somewhat mixed class identity as a result. A woman's class position is usually linked to that of her father and husband. For Marxists, a person's class is defined in relation to the process of economic production—whether she or he works for a living. There is currently no politically accepted way for most people to make a livelihood except by working for it, and in this society work, in addition to being an economic necessity, carries strong moral overtones. Note that this same principle is not applied to those among the very rich who live on trust funds or corporate profits. In much public debate in the United States, class is more of a psychological concept—what we think and feel about our class position—than an economic one. Poverty is often explained as resulting from individual low self-esteem, laziness, or dysfunctional families, as we pointed out in Chapter 1. In public discourse on inequality, race is invariably emphasized at the expense of class. Government census data, for example, are analyzed for racial differences much more than for class differences, which gives the impression that race is the most salient disparity among people. In practice race and class overlap, but greater attention to class differences would show different patterns of inequality. It would also show more similarities and more of a basis for alliances between people of color and White people who are economically disadvantaged.

Policy Implications and Activist Projects

Feminists have tackled the issue of women and work from many angles. In addition to working for comparable worth in wage rates, they have encouraged women to return to school to improve their educational qualifications, opposed sexual harassment on the job, campaigned for decent, affordable childcare arrangements, exposed the dangers of occupational injury and the health hazards of toxic work environments, and advocated for women in senior positions in all fields, and that math, science, and computer education be more available and effective for girls. The "Take Our Daughters to Work Day" initiated by the Ms. Foundation, for example, exposes girls to jobs they may know little about and provides role models for them, which can have a powerful impact. Several organizations have worked to open up opportunities for women to enter well-paying trades such as carpentry and construction, including Women in the Building Trades (Jamaica Plain, Mass.), Minnesota Women in the Trades, and Northern New England Tradeswomen (Barre, Vt.). Many local groups help women to start small businesses, utilizing existing skills. The Women's Bean Project (Denver) and the Navaho Weaving Project (Kykotsmovi, Ariz.) are group projects that promote self-sufficiency.

Promoting Greater Economic Security for Women

A lack of jobs, low wages, low educational attainment, having children, and divorce all work against women's economic security and keep many women in poverty, dependent on men, or both. As we concluded in Chapter 5, an aspect of security and sustainability for family relationships involves equal opportunities and responsibilities for parenting, which in turn means a redefinition of work. Yet if current workplace trends continue, many young people in the United States — especially young people of color — will never be in regular, full-time employment in their lives. Politicians and businesses promote almost any venture — building convention centers, ballparks, jails, and prisons and maintaining obsolete military bases — on the argument that it will create jobs. Changes in the economy force us to confront some fundamental contradictions that affect women's work and the way work is thought about generally:

What should count as work?

Does the distinction between "productive" and "unproductive" work make sense?

How should work be rewarded?

How should those without paid work, many of them women, be supported?

How can the current inequalities between haves and have-nots be justified?

Is the work ethic useful? Should it be redefined?

Is materialism the mark of success?

Years ago, pushed by the impact of the Great Depression of the 1930s, social commentators saw great potential for human development promised by (then) new technologies like telephones, Dictaphones, and washing machines, by means of which people could provide for their needs in a relatively short time each week. The British philosopher Bertrand Russell (1935), for example, favored such "idleness" as an opportunity to become more fully human, to develop oneself in many dimensions of life. Recognizing that this could not happen if material living standards had to keep rising, he put forth a modest notion of what people "need." He also understood that these kinds of changes would require political imagination and will.

Nowadays, people in many inner-city areas of the United States are faced with a related challenge: how to make a living if there are no jobs. Grace Lee Boggs (1994) and others in Detroit, for example, are exploring how communities can support one another now that the auto industry has all but abandoned the city. Neighborhood businesses, community bartering schemes, and community currencies like Ithaca HOURS all suggest possibilities. Participants in Ithaca HOURS (in Ithaca, New York) trade their time and skills for Ithaca money, where one hour is the equivalent of $10. In effect they buy goods and services with their own labor. This system helps people to connect with one another rather than making them competitors. Since its start in 1991, some $50,000 worth of Ithaca HOURS have recirculated in the local community buying goods and services worth an estimated $2,000,000 (Glover 1997). Berkeley Bread (Berkeley, Calif.) and Great Lakes Dollars (Detroit) are other examples.

◆◆◆
Questions for Reflection

As you read and discuss this chapter, think about these questions:

1. What are your experiences of work?

2. What have you learned through working? About yourself? About other people's lives? About the wider society? How did you learn it? Who were your teachers?

3. What have you wanted to change in your work situations? What would it take to make these changes? What recourse do you have as a worker to improve your conditions of work?

4. How might pension policies be changed to reflect the range of productivity of women across the life course?

Taking Action

1. Draw up a detailed budget of your needs, expenses, income, and savings.

2. Discuss work experiences with your mother or grandmother (or women of their ages). What opportunities did they have? What choices did they make? What similarities and differences do you notice between your own life and theirs at the same age?

3. Analyze representations of women workers in ads, news reports, TV shows, and movies.

4. Consult the web sites listed below for additional information on the wage gap, poverty levels, and welfare reform.

Web Sites

AFL-CIO Working Women www.aflcio.org/women

Center for Law and Social Policy www.clasp.org

Children's Defense Fund www.childrensdefense.org

Institute for Women's Policy Research www.iwpr.org

National Jobs for All Coalition www.njfac.org/jobnews.html

Welfare Information Network www.welfareinfo.org

FORTY-EIGHT

the cleaning woman/labor relations #4

Hattie Gossett

the doctors knew.

the lab people knew.

the secretaries knew.

the volunteers knew.

the patients knew.

the clinic was moving to a new spot and would be closed for a while and everybody knew ahead of time.

everybody except the cleaning woman.

she only found out on closing day.

i dont know why no one thought to tell you before this the woman doctor said to the cleaning woman over the phone annoyance all up in her voice at being asked by the cleaning woman why they hadnt given her an earlier notice.

i dont know why no one thought to tell you. anyway i have patients now and have no time for you.

it was the cleaning womans dime so she went for broke. but i am dependent on the salary you pay me and now suddenly it wont be there she protested. wouldnt it be fair to give me some kind of severance pay?

severance pay! shrieked the woman doctor. look she snapped you havent been with us that long. only a few weeks. besides i have help at home you know and i . . .

its like this the cleaning woman interrupted not wanting to hear about the doctors help at home (at least not what the doctor was going to say) when you work for a salary you need some kind of reasonable notice when its going to be discontinued so you can prepare yourself. how would you like it if you were in my place?

the woman doctor then tried to offer the cleaning woman a job in the new clinic plus a job in her own new private office but neither of these jobs would start for some weeks. she never did say how she would feel being in the cleaning womans place. the cleaning woman realized she was dealing with people who really didnt care about her. as far as they were concerned she could starve for those few weeks. she wondered how long you would have to work for these people before it was long enough for them to tell you at least 2weeks ahead of time that they were closing. how long is long enough?

forget it the cleaning woman told the woman doctor. she was pissed. she didnt like knowing that she was being shafted and that there wasnt anything she could do. when do you want me to bring back your keys? because she cleaned at night or very early in the morning she had keys to the clinic.

as soon as the woman doctor said anytime in a somewhat startled voice the cleaning woman hung up. she didnt slam down the phone. she put it down gently. but she didnt say goodbye or have a nice day.

damn the cleaning woman said to herself after she had hung up. here these people are supposed to be progressive and look at how they act. here they are running an alternative clinic for lesbians and gays and straights and yet they treat their help just as bad as the american medical association fools treat theirs. are they really an alternative she asked herself.

sure they treat their help bad herself answered laughingly.

the cleaning woman looked up a little surprised because she hadnt heard herself come in. now herself sat down and started eating some of the cleaning womans freshly sliced pineapple.

what do you mean girlfriend the cleaning woman asked herself.

have you forgotten that every sister aint a sister and every brother aint a brother herself began. where did you get this pineapple? its really sweet and fresh.

come on now. dont play games. tell me what you mean the cleaning woman said.

look herself said. some of these sisters and brothers aint nothing but secondhand reprints out of the bidness as usual catalogue in spite of all their tongue flapping to the contrary. and these secondhand reprints can be worse than the originals. like they have to prove that they know how to abuse people even more cold-heartedly than the originals do. its getting harder and harder to tell the real alternatives from the rank rapscallions. of course everybody else on the staff knew that the gig was moving but you. in their book you aint nothing no way.

what could the cleaning woman say?

herself was right once again and the cleaning woman tried to tell herself this but that girl didnt hear anything cuz she had already tipped on out taking the last piece of pineapple with her.

so the cleaning woman laughed for a minute. then she stopped brooding over those fools at the clinic.

she got on the phone and started lining up some more work.

later she sat down and wrote this story which she put in the envelope with the clinic keys. she wrote the woman doctors name on the front of the envelope cuz she wanted to be sure the woman doctor would be able to share the story. at the bottom of the story the cleaning woman put not to be copied or reproduced by any means without written permission from the author.

cuz one monkey sho nuff dont stop no show.

◆◆◆

FORTY-NINE

The Transformation of Women's Wage Work

Teresa Amott and Julie Matthaei

Over the last two centuries, the paid work performed by women has changed dramatically. This [essay] focuses on the transformation of women's occupations over the course of the twentieth century and on the changes in the racial-ethnic, gender, and class hierarchies within paid work. . . .

The Growth and Decline of Women's Paid Domestic Work

Along with agricultural work, domestic service was one of the first major occupations for women in all racial-ethnic groups. Although early domestic work was unpaid, performed by indentured servants, slaves, or apprentices, the job gradually came to be compensated in wages (although live-in servants still receive a substantial proportion of their pay in the form of room and board). Over the course of the twentieth century, employment in domestic service declined dramatically, moving much of women's paid employment out of the home sphere. At the same time, much of the work once assigned to women domestic servants is now performed by women employed by profit-motivated firms.

Homemaking was an arduous task from early colonial times through much of the nineteenth century, involving not simply child care and housework, but also the production of many household goods. Families of means employed others to do most of this work, and very wealthy families had large staffs of servants of both sexes, from maids and butlers to coachmen and cooks. In 1870, over half of all wage-earning women were found in domestic service, either as servants, laundresses, or boarding and lodging housekeepers—and 89 percent of all domestic servants were women.[1]

Regional differences in the racial-ethnic nature of the employer-servant relationship produced distinct differences in women's work experiences. In the South, Southwest, and West, domestic service usually involved a woman of color laboring for a white woman or family, and thus the work both reflected and reinforced racial domination. As slavery took hold in the South, domestic service there became a Black occupation. African American intellectual W. E. B. Du Bois noted, "Blacks . . . became associated with servitude generally . . . wherever Blacks served, domestic service was labeled 'nigger's work.'"[2] After the Civil War, domestic service continued to be seen in the East as an occupation dominated by Black women. In the Southwest and West, domestic service was also racially typed and devalued, and Mexicans, American Indians, and Asians predominated. On the West Coast, Asian men were often employed in domestic service since there was a shortage of women of all racial-ethnic groups.

Live-in servants in the North and Midwest generally enjoyed better treatment than those in the South and the West, particularly from the Revolution to about 1850, since servants and employers usually belonged to the same racial-ethnic group. During that period, most northern and midwestern servants were U.S.-born whites who worked under relatively egalitarian conditions—indeed, they were often referred to as "help," not servants. The North's egalitarian view of domestic help began to change in the nineteenth century as U.S.-born servants were replaced by immigrants, especially Irish women. The combination of ethnic, religious, and class difference opened up a vast social distance between white, U.S.-born employers and their immigrant servants. However, this process took decades; as late as 1900, there were still twice as many U.S.-born white women employed as private household workers as there were foreign-born white women.[3]

During the nineteenth century, domestic service coincided with and promoted the cult of domesticity. Domestic servants were essential to wealthy women's aspirations toward ideal womanhood. Servants freed the homemaker from the drudgery of housework so that she could attend to the "higher" functions of homemaking: mothering, socializing, and for some, the volunteer work that was a form of social homemaking. At the same time, a large pool of women willing to work as domestic servants for low wages was guaranteed by the lack of other jobs for poor, racially subordinated, and immigrant women. Roughly half of African American and European immigrant women were in domestic service, compared to only 28 percent of U.S.-born white women. A substantial share of African and Asian men were also so employed. On the other hand, less than 1 percent of European American men performed domestic work.

Through the early twentieth century, most domestic servants lived in their employers' homes. Single women were far more likely to live in than married women, since living in provided a roof over their heads. Most worked for married, middle- and upper-class white homemakers in what was seen as helpful training for their servants' futures as homemakers. Hence, domestic service often involved a generational relationship (as well as one between classes and racial-ethnic groups) in which an older, married woman used her husband's income to pay a younger, single woman—and where the servant's pay was then often transferred to her parents.

However, taking on another woman's domestic work did not always involve living in the employer's home. Married women servants, who were disproportionately Black, preferred day work to live-in service whenever they could obtain it. Large numbers of married Black women took in laundry in their own homes in order to escape the direct supervision of a white mistress. On the West Coast, the Chinese, especially men, did laundry work. Caring for other women's children—the precursors of today's daycare centers—was another form of domestic service which could be performed in one's own home.

In urban areas, taking in boarders and lodgers provided yet another path to escape from domestic service in another woman's home, allowing married women and their daughters to contribute cash income to their families through cooking, cleaning, and laundering for their clients; this was especially common in immigrant communities. Boarding services were also in high demand by adult men in communities where women were scarce, such as among Asian plantation workers in Hawaii. Unlike domestic service, boarding and lodging appears rarely to have involved racial inequality. Boarding and lodging was, instead, an exchange between persons of the same class and racial-ethnic group who were of different ages and phases in their working lives.

Although domestic service was the single most important occupation for women in 1900, its significance declined dramatically in the course of the twentieth century. Between 1900 and 1990, although the population tripled and per capita output more than quadrupled, the total number of private household workers fell from about two million to under one-half million. The share of women employed in private household service fell from 35 percent to less than 1 percent.[4]

Both supply and demand factors contributed to the decline in women's paid domestic work. Many family needs formerly filled by women's domestic work—such as health care, child care and education, and meal preparation—are now serviced by hospitals, convalescent homes, medical and health professionals, schools, daycare centers, and hotels and restaurants, lowering the economy's overall demand for domestic workers. In addition, new commodities that reduce the amount of physical work necessary to fill family needs have become available and affordable: hot and cold running water, electricity and telephones; durable goods such as refrigerators, washing machines, and vacuum cleaners; and processed foods. All these changes have reduced the need for domestic servants, laundresses, and women who take in boarders and lodgers. At the same time, the growing availability of other jobs for women—many of them in the service sector, as well as in manufacturing and clerical work—has decreased the supply of women available for domestic work, and consequently increased the wages of domestic servants.

The movement out of domestic service has, however, been uneven across racial-ethnic groups, as shown in Table 1. African American women have remained the most likely to work as domestic servants. Since the overwhelming majority of the families employing domestics have been white, through the first third of the twentieth century, the majority of African American women's working experiences entailed housework, child care, and laundry for white women and their families. This direct, personal, and continuing experience of racial subordination has been central to the lives of contemporary Black women's mothers and grandmothers.[5] On the other extreme, white and Asian American women

Table 1   Share of Employed Women Working in Private Household Service,
by Racial-Ethnic Group, 1900–1990

	1900	1930	1960	1980	1990
American Indian	13.4	22.5	16.8	1.4	1.0
Chicana	n.a.	33.1	11.5	2.4	2.6
European American	29.8	12.0	4.4	0.8	0.6
African American	43.5	53.5	39.3	5.0	2.2
Chinese American	35.6	12.1	1.7	0.8	0.6
Japanese American	28.6	29.9	8.2	1.4	0.6
Filipina American	n.a.	34.4	3.7	0.9	0.6
Island Puerto Rican	78.4	27.5	13.7	1.4	1.4
U.S. Puerto Rican	n.a.	n.a.	1.2	0.7	0.7

NOTES: Asian American data include Hawaii for all years; 1980 and 1990 data for American Indians include Eskimo and Aleut peoples; for 1900–1960, African American and European American include Latinas.

were able to leave domestic service most rapidly. By 1990, no more than three in a hundred women worked in domestic service in any racial-ethnic group; the share for Blacks and Chicanas, however, remained much greater than that for other groups.

Thus, women left employment in the homes of other women for jobs in new settings, such as factories, offices, schools, nursing homes, and restaurants. In this process, they exchanged the direct supervision of a mistress or master for a more complicated and bureaucratic hierarchy of supervision. In some cases, this meant that supervision became less personal, and it often meant that the supervisor was no longer another woman.

The New Service Work

As we have seen, domestic service declined partially because women's traditional work of caring for the personal needs of others was taken over by firms. Whereas in the past, domestic servants were hired by individual employers and worked in their households, today this work is increasingly organized by capitalist entrepreneurs in search of profits. Domestic work is now performed by daycare center workers, cooks and waitresses in restaurants, nurses and aides in hospitals, and commercial laundry workers. While the form and usually the location of service work changed in this process, today's personal service workers—like the domestic servants before

them—are still confined to the bottom of the labor market hierarchy.

Employment in service occupations grew rapidly between 1900 and 1990, from about 2 to 15 million workers, nearly 9 million of them women. Today, service occupations outside the private household include food preparation and service (waiters and waitresses, cooks, counter workers, and kitchen workers), health service (dental assistants, nurse's aides, orderlies, and attendants), cleaning and building service (maids, janitors, and elevator operators), personal service (barbers, hairdressers, guides, and childcare workers), and protective service (police officers, firefighters, and guards).

The expansion of service occupations in the twentieth century drew in large numbers of women workers. Service occupations employed 17 percent of women workers in 1990, compared to less than 3 percent of women workers in 1900. As shown in Table 1, the representation of women in these new service jobs varied across racial-ethnic groups. American Indian, Chicana, and African American women were more likely than other women to hold new service jobs in 1990, just as they were more likely to be domestic servants.

Women are overconcentrated in service jobs other than protective service: although they make up less than half of the workforce, women are two-thirds of these service workers. Many service jobs involve traditionally female tasks, such as cooking, cleaning, and caring for the sick, the aged, and the

Table 2   **Share of Employed Women Working in Service Occupations (Other than Private Household Service), by Racial-Ethnic Group, 1900–1990**

	1900	1930	1960	1980	1990
American Indian	12.1	2.9	25.8	23.9	22.4
Chicana	n.a.	3.8	16.5	20.4	21.1
European American	3.8	8.1	13.2	15.3	14.5
African American	7.9	7.5	23.0	24.2	22.9
Chinese American	8.7	8.8	9.2	13.0	13.0
Japanese American	3.8	10.1	12.9	15.8	13.1
Filipina American	n.a.	4.1	16.6	15.8	13.1
Island Puerto Rican	n.a.	1.3	12.2	14.8	12.9
U.S. Puerto Rican	n.a.	n.a.	7.3	14.4	16.7

NOTES: Asian American data include Hawaii for all years; 1980 and 1990 data for American Indians include Eskimo and Aleut peoples; for 1900–1960, African American and European American include Latinas.

very young. However, service work is not simply or only a women's job. First, there are racial-ethnic hierarchies within female-dominated service jobs. For instance, according to the 1980 Census, white and Asian women were about 50 percent more likely than other women to be supervisors. Black women were three times as likely as white and Asian American women to be janitors and cleaners, while American Indian and Latina women were about twice as likely.[6] (Unfortunately, detailed occupational data for these racial breakdowns are not available in the published reports of the 1990 Census, but there is no reason to believe that the relative positions have changed dramatically between 1980 and 1990.) Racial-ethnic typing is even more severe when we look within a region or within a place of work. In many northeastern and midwestern cities, all of the nurse's aides and cleaning-service workers are women of color; in most restaurants, waitresses are all of the same racial-ethnic group.

Second, just as men of color were significantly represented in domestic service jobs during the nineteenth and early twentieth centuries, so also a significant share are employed in non-protective service work today. Indeed, certain service jobs are dominated by poor or immigrant white men and men of color, such as janitors, bellhops, and elevator operators.

Another exception to women's dominance in service work occurs in the elite service jobs known as protective service, consisting predominantly of police officers and firefighters. Protective service was monopolized by white men for decades. In 1900, white men accounted for only 72 percent of the labor force, but made up 97 percent of all policemen, firemen, and watchmen. Men of color, in contrast, were seriously underrepresented, and women's shares were insignificant. Over the course of the century, struggles by white women and people of color, especially in the 1960s and 1970s, have brought them a greater share of these jobs. By 1990, men of color's share had grown from 3 percent to almost 20 percent, while their share of all jobs increased from 10 to 12 percent. Women of all racial-ethnic groups other than Chinese Americans have also increased their relative concentrations in protective service, with American Indian, Black, and Puerto Rican women making the greatest gains. Despite these inroads, white men are still overrepresented.[7]

Were women's working conditions improved by moving out of domestic service into new service jobs? Certainly, most women have seen these jobs as an improvement over live-in domestic service, involving as they do more limited hours and the ability to live in one's own home and with one's children. Furthermore, earnings are higher, on the average: with median weekly earnings of $256 for full-time, full-year women workers in 1994, service occupations offered better pay than private household and agriculture ($177 and $234, respectively). However, women working in service occupations continued to earn considerably less than those in manufacturing, sales, or clerical jobs. In addition, 50 percent of women's new service jobs are part-time (compared to about 35 percent of all women's jobs), and 45 percent of service jobs involve work on weekends.[8]

New unionizing efforts promise to bring new service workers some measure of justice and dignity on the job. By using a variety of creative organizing tactics (modeled on the approaches of the National Welfare Rights Organization, the United Farm Workers, and community-based groups), unions have increased organizing among workers, such as home healthcare aides. By 1995, over 70,000 home healthcare aides had organized, reaching out to form client-worker coalitions that made the case for higher pay for aides as a way of increasing the quality of services delivered to clients. The Service Employees International Union has built a major campaign to raise wages for office building cleaners, most of whom are recent immigrants and people of color, by organizing 200,000 workers, one-fifth of the janitorial workforce.[9]

Out of the Fields

Through 1870, the majority of workers in the United States worked in agriculture. However, agriculture meant very different things to different people: for some, self-employment and a chance at earning wealth; for others, slavery, extreme exploitation as a migrant or plantation worker, or the perpetual debt of sharecropping or tenant farming.

The types and conditions of agricultural work depended in great measure on race-ethnicity, which to a large extent determined access to land. European immigrants, especially before the late 1800s, were able to homestead on lands stolen from Native Americans; thus, they were most likely to be self-employed farmers or ranchers. However, an elite of white farmers and ranchers held large parcels of land, squeezing smaller farmers; in the South, many poor whites were forced into tenant farming and sharecropping. During slavery, most African Americans worked in agriculture. Once freed, most were kept by Jim Crow racist practices from acquiring land of their own, and continued to labor for whites as sharecroppers or tenant farmers. The colonization of the Mexican Southwest stripped land from the indigenous peoples and concentrated ownership among a wealthy few. The remaining American Indians and Mexicans were reduced to the status of landless peasants or subsistence farmers. After the U.S. takeover, Anglos acquired most of the Mexican lands, leaving Chicanas/os to work as tenant farmers, sharecroppers, or migrant workers. American Indians, forced onto smaller, less fertile land areas, tried to continue the self-sufficient farming and ranching in which most had been occupied before the European invasion. Island Puerto Ricans also suffered from the concentration of lands in the hands of a few, with many small family farmers driven gradually into agricultural wage labor for wealthy farmers. Chinese, Japanese, and Filipinas/os were brought to the United States and Hawaii as plantation laborers and migrant workers, and prohibited by law from acquiring land in the United States. Nonetheless, some were able to escape this landless status into family farming and gardening.

The degree to which women participated in agricultural work varied greatly among these groups, depending both upon the overall importance of agricultural work for the racial-ethnic group as a whole and on the share of the work allocated to women. Census data on women's agricultural employment are unreliable, since they probably undercount women's participation; nevertheless, they may be useful for comparative purposes.

In 1900 over half of all American Indian, African American, Chicana/o, Puerto Rican, and Japanese workers were employed in agriculture, compared to only one-third of all whites and less than one-fourth of Chinese. This is due to a number of different reasons, including the rural nature of American Indian life, the importation of African and Asian workers to the United States specifically to perform agricultural work, the Great Driving Out of Chinese in the late 1800s, and the exclusion of people of color, especially Blacks, from non-agricultural employment. In general, however, a higher share of people of color remained in agriculture in 1900 than that of whites.

The share of agricultural work done by women within each racial-ethnic group was also higher among women of color in 1900 (except among Asians, whose population was still mostly male). Among American Indians, this stemmed from a cultural tradition involving women in farming. African American women's participation can be traced both to African traditions and to slaveowners' practice of employing women in the fields. Among Puerto Ricans, farming was traditionally men's work. On the other hand, these data may understate the share of agricultural work performed by European American and

**Table 3   Share of Employed Women Working in Agriculture,
by Racial-Ethnic Group, 1900–1990**

	1900	1930	1960	1980	1990
American Indian	47.2	26.1	10.5	1.2	1.1
Chicana	n.a.	21.2	4.3	2.9	2.5
European American	9.8	4.1	1.5	1.0	0.9
African American	44.2	24.7	3.7	0.5	0.3
Chinese American	7.3	2.5	0.7	0.3	0.2
Japanese American	58.1	22.9	6.7	1.3	0.8
Filipina American	n.a.	27.5	4.3	1.2	0.8
Island Puerto Rican	3.9	9.5	1.6	0.3	0.3
U.S. Puerto Rican	n.a.	n.a.	0.3	0.4	0.4

NOTES: Asian American data include Hawaii for all years; 1980 and 1990 data for American Indians include Eskimo and Aleut peoples; for 1900–1960, African American and European American include Latinas.

Puerto Rican women, especially on family farms, where women usually contributed to cash crop production through harvesting, dairying, gardening, and cooking and cleaning for hired hands.

In the course of the twentieth century, agricultural productivity increased greatly as a result of labor-saving technological changes, especially mechanization. Consequently, agricultural employment fell from over 10 million to less than 3 million, and vast numbers of people left rural areas for the cities. In 1900, agriculture employed more than one in three workers; in 1990, the share had fallen to fewer than one in forty. Table 3 shows the changing shares of women workers employed in agriculture from 1900 through 1990. Through the first third of the twentieth century, substantial shares of American Indian, African, Chicana, and Japanese women continued to work in agriculture; however, by 1990, no more than 3 percent of women in any racial-ethnic group were so employed.

For those women, disproportionately Chicanas, who remain in agricultural wage labor, conditions have barely improved since the early twentieth century. Wages continue to be extremely low, as the presence of substantial numbers of undocumented workers allows super-exploitation by growers and foremen. The recent employers' offensive against unions has also taken its toll on farm worker organizing, although the 1995 victory at the Sainte Michelle winery has given new hope to the United Farm Workers.

Women family farmers have also suffered reversals in the past two decades. As farm indebtedness and bankruptcy soared in the 1980s, huge corporate firms increasingly came to dominate the agricultural landscape, absorbing family farms and turning farm owners into farm managers and tenants. Black farm ownership has fallen disproportionately, and farm women of all racial-ethnic groups have taken on a triple day: work on the farm, a second job in town, and continued responsibility for child care and other family work.[10] Despite this punishing schedule, women throughout the Midwest and South have organized to fight foreclosures, lobbied for aid to farmers, and developed farmer cooperatives. Many of these groups draw on old Populist traditions, exhorting farmers to raise "less corn and more hell."[11]

Manufacturing Inequality

As capitalism developed in the United States, labor shifted out of agriculture and domestic service into manufacturing. Manufacturing itself gradually changed from predominantly skilled craft and artisan work to unskilled and semi-skilled factory work.

By 1900, manufacturing made up approximately one-fourth of total employment. There was great variation in the proportions of women and men workers of the different racial-ethnic groups who were employed in manufacturing occupations. Among

Table 4   Share of Employed Women Working in Manufacturing,
by Racial-Ethnic Group, 1900–1990

	1900	1930	1960	1980	1990
American Indian	24.9	37.6	18.1	17.0	14.2
Chicana	n.a.	24.7	29.1	26.0	20.0
European American	32.6	21.2	18.5	12.6	9.4
African American	2.6	8.4	15.5	18.4	14.5
Chinese American	41.1	20.8	24.0	20.8	16.2
Japanese American	7.7	12.2	19.0	12.5	8.4
Filipina American	n.a.	15.3	17.4	13.8	8.4
Island Puerto Rican	14.6	52.4	31.3	22.0	17.5
U.S. Puerto Rican	n.a.	n.a.	69.3	29.1	16.1

NOTES: Asian American data include Hawaii for all years; 1980 and 1990 data for American Indians include Eskimo and Aleut peoples; for 1900–1960, African American and European American include Latinas.

women, more than one-fourth of European American, American Indian, and Chinese American women held manufacturing jobs, while for Japanese American, island Puerto Rican, and African American women the share in manufacturing was much lower, as shown in Table 4. Among men, only European Americans held more than their labor market share of manufacturing jobs; men of color remained relatively concentrated in agriculture. Thus, in 1900, manufacturing jobs still represented a white preserve from which most men and women of color were excluded.

Particular manufacturing occupations were typed by gender and/or by race-ethnicity. For example, skilled garment making — performed by dressmakers, seamstresses, shirt, collar, and cuff makers, tailors and tailoresses — was a job undertaken by women of all racial-ethnic groups, often in their own homes. Women made up 78 percent of these workers in 1900, and only African American women had less than their labor market share. European American women had five times their share (with immigrant women more likely to be so employed than U.S.-born), American Indian women four times, and Japanese and Chinese at least twice.[12] Needlework jobs were also important for Puerto Rican and Chicana women.

In contrast, in 1900, textile mill operatives were almost exclusively white, and about half men and half women. White men held less than their labor market share of these jobs (since they could find more lucrative jobs), while white women held more

than three times their labor market share. Within the mills, jobs were typed according to sex and ethnicity. European immigrants, especially Irish, Italian, English, and Welsh, had higher relative concentrations in mill jobs than did U.S.-born whites. On the other hand, no group of men or women of color had achieved more than one-twentieth of their labor market share of textile mill jobs, which paid considerably more than the agricultural and domestic service jobs into which they were crowded.

A third set of jobs was monopolized by white males: traditional, masculine crafts, such as carpentry, masonry, plumbing, blacksmithing, cabinetmaking, and machine-making (machinists). In all of these jobs, European American men maintained a near monopoly. Many slave men, trained in these crafts, were prevented by white men from practicing their trades after Emancipation. However, this exclusion worked unevenly: in 1900, African American men held about their labor market share of masonry and plastering jobs, a little less than half their share of carpentry and blacksmithing, and only about one-tenth their share of plumbing and machinist jobs. No other group of men held even half its labor market share, although Chinese, Japanese, and American Indian men had a significant part of their shares in carpentry and blacksmithing. Women of all racial-ethnic groups were the most excluded from the crafts, with none receiving more than 6 percent of their labor market share.[13] Exclusion was costly since the crafts were generally much higher-paid than other manufacturing jobs.

Between 1900 and 1980, as the economy grew and changed, the number of manufacturing jobs quadrupled and manufacturing's share of total employment increased. Women's manufacturing employment also quadrupled, but women's total employment grew even faster, so the share of women in manufacturing fell. However, the decline in women's manufacturing employment was very uneven across racial-ethnic groups. Only among white women was there a smooth decline, as white women found better-paid jobs as sales, clerical, and professional and managerial workers. Not until the mid-twentieth century did Black women gain entry to manufacturing as a result of organizing, war-time labor shortages, and white women's exodus. Very high percentages of Puerto Rican women have been employed in manufacturing, both in Puerto Rico and in the United States, at rates which have fluctuated widely with the movement of firms in and out of Puerto Rico or New York.

If we look at the overall pattern, an interesting change is clear. In 1900, when manufacturing represented a relatively good job, white women's share was greater than that of most women of color. In contrast, in 1980, most women of color, other than Japanese, had higher participation in manufacturing than white women. This signifies not a reversal of the racial-ethnic hierarchy, but the movement of white women into higher-paid, higher-status jobs such as clerical and professional work.

Since 1980, overall U.S. employment in manufacturing (excluding construction) has fallen in absolute terms as a result of a combination of factors, including productivity increases, the transfer of plants abroad, and competition from foreign producers. Ironically, the share of women workers in manufacturing actually rose between 1970 and 1990. In research on heavy manufacturing jobs such as steelworking, European American sociologist Joan Smith found that white men were likely to be replaced by workers of color and/or white women in sectors where profits were slipping and firms were not investing in new equipment. In those sectors, the strategy to boost profits was to employ lower-wage workers.[14]

Thus, even though factory jobs were in decline, employers have increasingly relied on two forms of manufacturing work common in the nineteenth and early twentieth century, sweatshops and industrial homework. Now, as then, these jobs employ a disproportionate number of immigrant women. Many Southeast Asian refugee women, undocumented Mexican immigrant women, and recent Chinese immigrant women are finding employment in the newly resurgent sweatshops. Industrial homework—manufacturing work contracted out to workers in their own homes—has also been on the rise. For employers, homework offers freedom from unionization, government regulations, and overhead costs. Women, on the other hand, turn to homework in the hopes of combining work and family, or because no other work is available. Under the Reagan administration, regulations prohibiting homework were dismantled. As a result, capitalists are opting to locate more work in workers' homes and have expanded the range of manufacturing jobs contracted out to homeworkers to include electronic component assembly as well as the traditional garment work.[15]

Today, as in the past, women of different racial-ethnic groups are unevenly represented within different manufacturing jobs. Garment work—both by dressmakers and by sewing-machine operators—continues to be female-dominated. However, Black women are no longer excluded, and in 1980 they held more than twice their labor market share of these jobs; Asian American and Latina women each occupied five to six times their labor market share, while white women held twice theirs. (1990 data are not available at this level of racial and occupational detail.)

Although women continue to be overrepresented in garment work, there has been progress in more lucrative areas of manufacturing as a result of the anti-discrimination struggles of the past 20 years. The most significant improvement has been for men of color, who were overrepresented in the crafts in 1990. In contrast, women of all racial-ethnic groups held less than one-third of their labor market share; these crafts, then, shifted from white-male-dominated to male-dominated. Women of color were doing better than white women at gaining representation in the crafts: in 1990, Chicana, American Indian, Asian, and U.S. Puerto Rican women had the highest relative concentrations in craft work, ranging from 33 to 26 percent respectively, with white women at 19 percent. Since craft work offers relatively high-paying and secure employment to people who cannot afford higher education, it is not

Table 5   Share of Employed Women Working in Clerical Occupations, by Racial-Ethnic Group, 1900–1990

	1900	1930	1960	1980	1990
American Indian	0.1	3.3	14.2	27.4	24.9
Chicana	n.a.	2.8	21.8	26.2	24.7
European American	6.9	25.3	34.5	32.3	28.2
African American	0.1	0.6	8.0	25.8	25.8
Chinese American	0.5	11.7	32.1	24.7	20.7
Japanese American	0.1	3.7	30.5	31.6	28.0
Filipina American	n.a.	1.6	24.3	28.2	28.0
Island Puerto Rican	1.2	2.3	16.9	26.9	26.6
U.S. Puerto Rican	n.a.	n.a.	13.9	31.9	31.0

NOTES: Asian American data include Hawaii for all years; 1980 and 1990 data for American Indians include Eskimo and Aleut peoples; for 1900–1960, African American and European American include Latinas.

surprising that women of color, who continue to have less access to higher education than white women, choose this route to economic security.

The Rise of Office Work

One of the most important occupational changes for women in the twentieth century has been the growth of clerical work. Women's clerical employment grew from 320,000 in 1900 to over 2 million in 1930 and nearly 15 million in 1990. Clerical work provides an interesting example of the transformation and reproduction of gender and racial-ethnic hierarchies. In the nineteenth century, a clerk was typically an educated white man who worked in an office as training for managerial work. When the typewriter was introduced, young European American middle-class women were hired to operate the machine, and the job was feminized: the clerical worker's career path to management was eliminated, and clerical workers found themselves acting as low-level assistants to male managers and treated as office wives.

The feminization of the office, as this process is called by European American sociologist Margery Davies, was at first a European American phenomenon. White immigrant women other than the English were kept out of offices, and women of color's access to clerical occupations was severely restricted through World War II. In 1900, as shown in Table 5, only among white women were a significant share employed in clerical work; a smaller share of Japanese and Chinese women were able to find clerical jobs in firms serving their communities. Black women and American Indian women were almost totally excluded from this new, relatively high-status job. Indeed, the relative concentration of white men among stenographers and typists (about one-third of their labor market share) was eight times higher than that of Black women.[16]

Clerical employment grew by over one and a half million jobs between 1900 and 1930. Most of these new jobs were taken by European women, although women of color made small gains. Black women continued to face the greatest obstacles. However, as clerical jobs continued to multiply in the post–World War II era, racial barriers eventually broke down as a result of both the persistence of women of color and the economy's burgeoning demand for workers. Education and urbanization have also provided opportunities for women of color to gain access to clerical work. At the same time, the two groups most highly represented in clerical work in 1960 — European and Chinese American women — reduced their share in the subsequent 20 years, as educated women in these groups took advantage of new opportunities in professional and managerial fields. As a result of all these changes, the differences between women of various racial-ethnic groups were greatly reduced: in 1990, from one-fourth to almost one-third of each group's employed women worked as clericals. Since women's clerical jobs pay substantially more than their jobs in services, manufacturing, and sales (with 1994 weekly earnings of $374, compared to $257, $293, and $324, respectively), and since many women prefer office working conditions to those in the factory or in service work, this movement has represented a genuine step forward for women of color.[17]

While clerical work is no longer reserved for white women, racial-ethnic and gender segregation persists. For instance, in 1980, 31 percent of white women were secretaries, compared to 18 percent of African American women. In contrast, women of color were more likely to be typists, data entry keyers, and file clerks — all occupations that were lower in pay and status than those dominated by white women. (As mentioned above, 1990 data are not available at this level of detail.) Furthermore, automation threatens to displace many lower-skilled clerical jobs, and it is likely that women of color, whose hold on clerical work is more tenuous, will be more affected by a retrenchment in this sector than white women. While women of color were concentrated in lower-level clerical jobs, the men in clerical work were concentrated in supervisory work in 1980, where they made up 41 percent of all workers, compared to only 2 percent of secretaries, stenographers, typists, and receptionists.[18]

Union organizing among clerical workers is succeeding in raising wages, much of it through the strategy of comparable worth (which demands equal pay for jobs of comparable skill, responsibility, and working conditions, regardless of the gender of the worker or the sex-typing of the job). Pressure from women of color has extended the concept of comparable worth to ensure equity between whites and people of color along with equity between men and women. Some of today's women office workers have also successfully fought to remove from their job descriptions such "wifely" tasks as preparing the office coffee and shopping for their bosses' anniversary gifts. However, many clerical workers continue to perform these tasks, receiving little recognition and low wages in return. Worse, office workers, like other women workers, continue to experience sexual harassment by male supervisors and co-workers.

Career Women: Women in Professional Jobs

Managerial and professional jobs offer women the highest wages and status. Like other jobs, they have been typed by gender and race-ethnicity, with white men at the top, although white women and people of color have made progress recently into some jobs which once were dominated by white men.

In 1900, over one-tenth of European American women were employed in managerial or professional jobs, compared to less than one in fifty workers among women of color. European American women were largely confined to a small set of managerial and professional jobs, including teaching, library science, and social work, all jobs which extended and professionalized woman's nurturing and caring roles. Indeed, educated white women played a major role in the fight to develop and feminize these professions, which they saw as outgrowths of social homemaking.

Before the Civil War, most teachers were white men; during the war, white women were hired to replace them, and after the war, they remained, arguing that teaching was, after all, a form of mothering. For Black women, teaching played a special role as a means to elevate and emancipate their people.[19] In 1900, white women had five times their labor market share of elementary and secondary school teaching jobs. The only other group of men or women to have at least their labor market share was Native American women. Next came Black women with 78 percent of their labor market share, Chinese women with 64 percent, and white men with 33 percent. Just as schools were racially segregated, so teachers of color were assigned to teach children of their own racial-ethnic group; however, given the underrepresentation of men and women of color in teaching, white women also commonly taught students of color.

By 1900, women, mostly but not entirely white, had begun to professionalize nursing, elevating it from a form of domestic service to a skilled job which required professional education. As a broad occupational category, it was women's work; women of color had three times their labor market share of these jobs, and white women over five times, while men of color and white men each had less than one-tenth their labor market share. Within nursing, however, as within teaching, jobs were racially typed according to clientele, and access to nursing schools was limited for women of color.[20]

Other professions — physicians and surgeons, lawyers, and engineers, among others — became the province of white men. These jobs typically offered higher pay than white women's professions, called

Table 6   Share of Employed Women Working in Professional and Technical Occupations, by Racial-Ethnic Group, 1900–1990

	1900	1930	1960	1980	1990
American Indian	1.9	4.6	9.1	14.5	15.7
Chicana	n.a.	2.7	5.9	8.4	10.8
European American	10.2	16.2	14.6	18.0	21.4
African American	1.2	3.4	7.8	15.2	17.0
Chinese American	1.4	22.0	17.9	20.4	17.0
Japanese American	0.3	6.6	12.3	17.8	23.5
Filipina American	n.a.	6.0	26.4	27.1	19.3
Island Puerto Rican	0.7	4.5	15.5	21.1	21.9
U.S. Puerto Rican	n.a.	n.a.	4.0	10.9	12.2

NOTES: Asian American data include Hawaii for all years; 1980 and 1990 data for American Indians include Eskimo and Aleut peoples; for 1900–1960, African American and European American include Latinas.

for more formal training, and involved control over, rather than service of, others. Indeed, they often required assistance by women, as nurses, receptionists, or legal secretaries. In 1900, no group other than white men held even half its labor market share of these elite professions, although a few individuals had gained admittance. Chinese men, American Indian men, and white women had made the most progress in medicine; American Indian men, Black men, and white women in law.[21] Women of color were almost totally excluded. The greatest relative concentration for women of color in white men's professions was that of Black women in law, at one-twentieth their labor market share; in most of the white men's professions, no Chinese, Japanese, or American Indian women were even recorded in 1900.[22]

Over the course of the twentieth century, professional and managerial employment has increased by a factor of nine, and the share of these jobs in total employment has risen from one-tenth to over one-quarter. Although men continue to make up the majority of workers, women's share of managerial and professional jobs has more than doubled, from 20 to 48 percent.

Central to women's entrance into professional and managerial jobs have been their successful struggles for access to higher education, which constitute an important part of African American, Chinese American, and Japanese American economic history, as well as of that of whites. Not surprisingly, the share of women in professional and managerial occupations by racial-ethnic group is highly corre-

lated with the share of college graduates.[23] Because educational opportunity has such an important effect on labor market opportunities for women, lower educational attainment is also related to lower labor force participation rates, and may be both a cause and a result of Chicanas' and U.S. Puerto Rican women's relatively low labor force participation rates.[24]

While women's representation in professional work increased for all racial-ethnic groups between 1900 and 1990, levels and rates of growth differ (see Table 6). The share in the professions increased most dramatically for women of color, who had been almost entirely excluded from such jobs in 1900. By 1990, Japanese American and island Puerto Rican women were more likely to hold professional and technical jobs than European American women. However, in 1990, African American, Chicana, and U.S. Puerto Rican women were still less likely to hold professional and technical jobs than European American women had been in 1930.

Much of the growth in women's professional employment occurred in jobs that have historically been dominated by women: pre-kindergarten, kindergarten, and elementary school teacher; nurse; librarian; dietitian; and social worker. In 1994, these professions (each of which was at least 69 percent female) employed 48 percent of women professionals. Women made up 94 percent of all registered nurses and 86 percent of all elementary school teachers.[25]

The racial-ethnic composition of women's professions has also changed as the near-monopoly of white women has been challenged. Between 1900 and 1990, white women's relative concentration in teaching fell from 525 to 178, while that of women of color rose. In 1990, all racial-ethnic groups of women, except Chinese women and Filipinas, were over-represented in elementary and secondary teaching, and even those two underrepresented groups had a higher relative concentration than any racial-ethnic group of men. Nursing has continued to be dominated by women, and women in all racial-ethnic groups except Chicanas and American Indians hold more than their employment share of nursing jobs.[26]

In 1990, despite increased representation of other groups, white men continued to make up the majority of such professions as engineering and medicine. In fact, between 1900 and 1990, white men's share of all jobs fell much more rapidly than their share of these professions, increasing their relative concentrations. However, all previously excluded groups (especially Asian American women and men) have made significant progress, increasing both their share of these jobs and their relative concentrations between 1900 and 1990 in almost all cases.[27] Among engineers, Filipinas and all three groups of Asian American men had equal or higher relative concentrations than white men—approximately two and three times their labor market shares, respectively. However, most groups of color continued to be underrepresented relative to their share of all jobs. For instance, African American men held less than half their employment share of physicians' jobs, and African American women held only one-fifth their share. Chicanas/os and American Indians were even more seriously underrepresented.

Although the increasing presence of people of color and white women in previously restricted occupations is a victory, racial-ethnic and gender hierarchies persist *within* the professions (and indeed, within all occupations) in the form of different job assignments, different treatment, and unequal pay for equal work. For example, women lawyers in corporations tend to work for smaller firms, where they earn lower pay and have fewer opportunities for advancement. Data on law school faculties show that women are more likely to be working in non-tenure-track jobs or to have achieved tenure at lower-status law schools. According to one study, women of color constituted less than 10 percent of women law faculty in 1986, and only 2 percent of all faculty.[28]

The Persistence of Racial-Ethnic, Gender, and Class Hierarchies in the Labor Market

This survey of occupations reveals a mixed picture: racial-ethnic and gender hierarchies have been reproduced and maintained in some ways at the same time as they have broken down in others. Asian Americans have surpassed European Americans according to many average indicators, and small shares of previously marginalized groups have broken into the elite jobs from which they were once excluded. Yet men still earn much more than women, on average, as do whites compared to non-Asian people of color.

Notes

1. Julie Matthaei, *An Economic History of Women in America: Women's Work, the Sexual Division of Labor, and the Development of Capitalism* (New York: Schocken Books, 1982), 284; *1870 Census of the United States*, Population and Social Statistics, Table XXIX.

2. Quoted in Judith Rollins, *Between Women: Domestics and Their Employers* (Philadelphia: Temple University Press, 1985), 51.

3. Ibid., 50–53; 1900 Census.

4. Constant dollar per GNP increased from $1,011 in 1900 to $3,555 in 1970, and has risen 45 percent since then. U.S. Bureau of the Census, *Historical Statistics of the United States, Colonial Time to 1970*, vol. 1 (Washington, DC: 1970); U.S. Bureau of the Census, *Statistical Abstract of the United States 1994*, 451; U.S. Census, 1900 and 1990.

5. bell hooks, presentation at New Words Bookstore, 5 March 1989, Cambridge, MA, on the occasion of the publication of *Talking Back: Talking Feminist, Talking Black* (Boston: South End Press, 1989).

6. Calculated from 1980 Census, provisional volume, U.S. Summary, Table 278.

7. Relative concentration can rise for all groups. White men's share of protective service jobs only dropped by 13 percentage points, while white men's share of all jobs dropped by 24 percentage points (as a result of women's movement into the labor force); thus, the relative concentration of

white men in protective service rose. The 1980 data include police officers and firefighters.

8. *Employment and Earnings* (January 1995), 195 and 209–13; *Employment and Earnings* (March 1980), 35.

9. Michael Ybarra, "Janitors' Union Uses Pressure and Theatrics to Expand Its Ranks," *Wall Street Journal,* 21 March 1994, A1–6.

10. Blacks fell from 14.5 percent of all farm operators in 1910 to only 3.8 percent of the total in 1969, and only 2.1 percent in 1980. *Black Population,* 81, and 1980 Census.

11. One such group is the Rural Women's Leadership Development Project of Prairiefire Rural Action, which organizes an annual conference, "Harvesting Our Potential," and publishes a journal entitled "Women of the Land." Their address is 550 11th St., Des Moines, Iowa 50309.

12. The 1900 Census data presented here include only workers within the continental United States, and hence excludes island Puerto Ricans. The numbers for Chinese women are very low, and data for Chicanas are not available.

13. Calculated from 1900 Census.

14. Joan Smith, "Impact of the Reagan Years: Race, Gender, and the Economic Restructuring," First Annual Women's Policy Research Conference Proceedings (Washington, DC: Institute for Women's Policy Research, 1989), 20.

15. An excellent set of essays on homework can be found in Eileen Boris and Cynthia R. Daniels, eds., *Homework: Historical and Contemporary Perspectives on Paid Labor at Home* (Urbana: University of Illinois Press, 1989).

16. Calculated from 1900 Census.

17. *Employment and Earnings* (January 1995), 210–13.

18. U.S. Department of Labor, Women's Bureau, *Women and Office Automation: Issues for the Decade Ahead* (Washington, DC: GPO, 1985), 20–22; *Statistical Abstract of the United States, 1988,* 376–77.

19. See Matthaei, 178–82.

20. Susan Reverby, *Ordered to Care: The Dilemma of American Nursing, 1850–1945* (New York: Cambridge University Press, 1987).

21. In medicine, Chinese men, American Indian men, and white women held 61, 44, and 40 percent of their labor market shares, respectively, with Black men and women at 13 and 3 percent. In law, American Indian men held 33 percent, Black men 7 percent, and white women 6 percent of their labor market shares. Calculated from 1900 Census.

22. Calculated from the 1900 Census. For a study of white and Black women's struggles to enter medicine, and white men's organizing to keep them out, see Gloria Moldow, *Women Doctors in Gilded-Age Washington: Race, Gender, and Professionalization* (Chicago: University of Illinois Press, 1987).

23. The shares of women with a college education are as follows: Filipina (41.2 percent), Chinese American (29.5 percent), Japanese American (19.7 percent), island Puerto Rican (18.3 percent), European American (13.5 percent), African American (8.3 percent), American Indian (6.4 percent), U.S. Puerto Rican (4.8 percent), and Chicana (3.7 percent). See U.S. Census, 1980, Tables 160 and 166, and Junta de Planificación de Puerto Rico, *Indicadores Socio-Económicos de la Mujer en Puerto Rico* (San Juan, Puerto Rico; La Junta, March 1987), A-3.

24. Elizabeth Almquist, *Minorities, Gender and Work* (Lexington, MA: D.C. Heath, 1972), 149–52.

25. *Employment and Earnings* (January 1995), 175–76.

26. Calculated from the 1900 and 1990 Censuses. In 1990, the job category for nursing is "health assessment and treating." Filipinas are especially overrepresented in nursing, with a relative concentration over 600.

27. 1900 data for Latinas/os were not available. The two exceptions to rising relative concentrations are Chinese men, who experienced a decrease in their relative concentration in physicians' and surgeons' jobs, and white women, whose relative concentration held steady. Calculated from 1900 and 1990 Censuses.

28. Susan Erlich Martin and Nancy C. Jurik, *Doing Justice, Doing Gender: Women in Law and Criminal Justice Occupations* (Thousand Oaks, CA: Sage Publications, 1996), 115–27.

◆◆◆

FIFTY

He Works, She Works,
but What Different Impressions They Make

Have you ever found yourself up against the old double standard at work? Then you know how annoying it can be and how alone you can feel. Supervisors and coworkers still judge us by old stereotypes that say women are emotional, disorganized, and inefficient. Here are some of the most glaring examples of the typical office double standard.

The family picture is on HIS desk:
Ah, a solid, responsible family man.

The family picture is on HER desk:
Hmm, her family will come before her career.

HIS desk is cluttered:
He's obviously a hard worker and busy man.

HER desk is cluttered:
She's obviously a disorganized scatterbrain.

HE'S talking with coworkers:
He must be discussing the latest deal.

SHE'S talking with coworkers:
She must be gossiping.

HE'S not at his desk:
He must be at a meeting.

SHE'S not at her desk:
She must be in the ladies' room.

HE'S having lunch with the boss:
He's on his way up.

SHE'S having lunch with the boss:
They must be having an affair.

HE'S getting married.
He'll get more settled.

SHE'S getting married:
She'll get pregnant and leave.

HE'S having a baby:
He'll need a raise.

SHE'S having a baby:
She'll cost the company money in maternity benefits.

HE'S leaving for a better job:
He recognizes a good opportunity.

SHE'S leaving for a better job:
Women are undependable.

HE'S aggressive.

SHE'S pushy.

HE'S careful.

SHE'S picky.

HE loses his temper.

SHE'S bitchy.

HE'S depressed.

SHE'S moody.

HE follows through.

SHE doesn't know when to quit.

HE'S firm.

SHE'S stubborn.

HE makes wise judgments.

SHE reveals her prejudices.

HE is a man of the world.

SHE'S been around.

HE isn't afraid to say what he thinks.

SHE'S opinionated.

HE exercises authority.

SHE'S tyrannical.

HE'S discreet.

SHE'S secretive.

HE'S a stern taskmaster.

SHE'S difficult to work for.

FIFTY-ONE

Work, Worth, and Popular Culture

Julianne Malveaux

Although work is the central factor in the lives of most Americans, popular culture tends to depict work in ways so unrealistic that the naive cannot be blamed for getting the wrong impression. A television romp through workplace-centered programs would lead one to believe that we all work in hospitals, as lawyers or police officers, or in the media, as professionals with a fair amount of discretion over our time and our surroundings. While this is true for some workers, many dance to the beat of their bosses' drummer. This is why I had to smirk when I read about Arlie Hochschild's new book, *The Time Bind* (Metropolitan Press, [1997]) which asserts that many parents are so pressed for time that they find the office a refuge, a place to "goof off."

No doubt, Ms. Hochschild is writing the reality for well-paid professional and managerial workers who, seeped in the culture of "quality circles" and "bonding," spend more face time with their subordinates than with their children (and, perhaps, enjoy it more). The reality for clerical, service, and other workers is likely to be quite the opposite. Who will voluntarily work unpaid overtime to more closely "bond" with a typewriter or word processor, to serve just a few more burgers, or to empty just a few more bedpans (although at the rate some hospitals are going, patients are going to be charged with emptying those themselves)?

The gulf between professionals/managers and clerical/service workers is not so much a gulf in workplace orientation as it is a gulf in pay. There are 27 million full-time managers and professional specialty workers in the workplace, earning a median weekly wage of $718. That sum ranges from a median high of around $1100 for lawyers, engineers, and physicians, to a median low of around $500 for food service managers, social workers, and clergy. In contrast, there are 26 million full-time technical, sales and administrative support workers, at a median weekly wage of $474. Clerical workers have a median wage of $405 per week, while some technical workers have wages that are much higher.

Guess whose world you are more likely to be introduced to in a television sitcom? Guess whose world more closely fits with the one Arlie Hochschild depicts in *The Time Bind*? To be sure, the challenges that professionals face are no less pressing than those that clerical workers face. Still, with so many women, especially, juggling household, family, and low wages (about 80 percent of all women earn less than $25,000 per year), our notion of workplace reality is somewhat skewed if we suggest these women are piddling around at the office because their lives are too busy at home.

Further, the issue of juggling is a challenge, at best, for families where both parents are present. What about single-parent families, those more likely to be headed by someone with a modest income? How does *The Time Bind* reflect their world?

I am concerned about work and popular culture because so many policy makers have had so little exposure to the world of real work. They seem to think that public assistance recipients, for example, can be effortlessly integrated into productive workplaces without any consequences. They seem to think that workers so crave flexibility that they will shrug off hard-earned overtime for it. Arlie Hochschild's book presents a vision of the office as such a delightful place that some prefer it to the home. Some workers have the luxury of such preferences, and the support system to back them up. Others have neither luxury nor support. The sewing machine operator who makes $254 per week (there are more than half a million such workers), the assembler that makes $378 (1.1 million workers in this category), the janitors that earn $301 per week (nearly 1.5 million of these workers), or the typists that earn $395 per week (half a million of these) aren't often depicted in popular culture, aren't often considered in the policy context. These are the workers, though, that often make it possible for professional and managerial workers to find their offices such safe havens from the rest of their responsibilities.

◆◆◆

FIFTY-TWO

Reflections of a Feminist Mom

Jeannine Ouellette Howitz

I am seven months pregnant, slithering along my kitchen floor. The ruler I clutch is for retrieving small objects lost in the dust jungle beneath my refrigerator. After several swipes I come up with a pile of dirt and a petrified saltine, so I get serious and press my cheek against the floor, positioning my left eye just inches from the target zone. I spot it — the letter "G," a red plastic refrigerator magnet. "Here it is!" I cry, hoisting myself up to offer this hard-won prize to Sophie, my momentarily maniacal toddler. Her face collapses into a sob as she shrieks, "NOT THAT ONE!"

Sophie is 22 months old, and in the final stages of potty training, which I remember as I feel a gush of warm and wet on my outstretched leg. Wet clothes bring more tears (hers, not mine), and I quickly strip off her clothes, then pull off my own with one hand while I slice and peel an apple with the other. I might have barely enough time while she eats to run upstairs, grab dry clothes, and toss the dirty ones into the basket before I'm urgently missed.

That was how I came to be standing in the middle of my kitchen with the magnificence of my naked abdomen hanging low and wide on a clammy June afternoon. The sweat of my exertion had just begun trickling between my breasts when the phone rang. It was an old friend with whom I'd been out of touch for a while. I panted hello, eyeing Sophie as she climbed up and out of her booster chair to totter precariously on the table top. "What are you doing home?" my friend wanted to know. "Don't you work at all anymore?"

Don't you work at all anymore? Again and again since entering the life phase which positioned my work in the home, I have encountered the judgments, however unconscious, of those whose definition of work excludes most of what I do. The same system that discounts my labor scoffs at its rewards, which, like my productivity, are impossible to measure by conventional standards. By limiting our view to one which allows only for paid employment, usually only that located outside the home, to be included in the understood meaning of the word "work," we support the process through which all that we do and all that we are as women is ultimately devalued and despised.

Like most labels applied to women's roles, "working mother" is extremely inaccurate and defeating, because it foolishly implies that there is another type of mother: the non-working variety. Being a mother is work. On the other hand, it is equally absurd to call mothers who are not employed outside the home "full-time mothers," as this unfairly suggests that employed mothers are only mothers part-time. Ridiculous as they are, these labels go largely unchallenged, even by many feminists. They are a sinister trap, imprisoning women in feelings of inadequacy about whatever roles we have chosen or been required to perform.

The same process that forces a woman to say "I don't work" when she performs 12 to 16 hours of unpaid labor every single day at home ultimately transforms most female-dominated professions into mere chores that women and men alike come to consider less desirable and important than other types of work. Once stamped with the kiss of death "women's work," we can forget entitlement to the same respect and fair wages a man would get for equivalent labor.

Before motherhood, I sold advertising at a newspaper, with hopes of working my way into editorial. However, my sales performance exceeded standards, and I was quickly promoted to a well-paying position in management which required me to build a classified department from the ground up. I forged ahead until my daughter was born, when, after reexamining our options, my husband and I decided one of us should stay home with her. Although he was happily working in his chosen field, John's income as a schoolteacher was half that of mine, which rendered him the financially logical choice for at-home parenthood. But it was I who jumped at the chance, albeit scary, to shift the gears of my career and of my life.

When my maternity leave was up, I told the publishers that I wouldn't be returning to the office. Surprisingly, they offered me the chance to bring my daughter to work with me. I was thrilled; those long days at home with an infant weren't exactly what I had imagined. I discovered that although I didn't always enjoy my job, I did enjoy the recognition it provided me — something I found was not a part of the package for home-working moms. While my sister spoke with unveiled envy about all the reading and writing I would now be accomplishing, in reality I was lucky if I brushed my teeth. So I took the deal.

Seven weeks old on her first day at work, Sophie fascinated the staff as only a newborn can. A two-minute trip to the copier often turned into a half-hour social ordeal as one person after the next stopped to exclaim over her. She was a great diversion for a young and predominantly single staff. I had no idea, as a new mother, how fortunate I was to have an extroverted baby. It was my own introverted nature that suffered from the constant sensory bombardment. I was uncomfortably aware of my special status, and fighting a losing battle to hide how much time it actually took to care for Sophie on the job.

In a culture where women feel guilty to call in sick to work when a child is sick, it was tremendously difficult to be in an office setting, drawing a full salary, and to say, "Sophie's crying now — this phone call, this meeting, this project, whatever it is, will have to wait." In a society that expects workers to give 150 percent dedication to the job, and considers motherhood a terrible detriment to productivity, it was incredibly stressful and even painful at times to experience such a personal conflict in a very public setting when the two worlds collided.

For six months, I toted a baby, a briefcase, and a diaper bag back and forth from home to my office, which at first housed the crib and swing, after which came the walker, the play gym, and the toy box — not to mention the breast pump equipment and mini-diaper pail. I could hardly see my desk, let alone get to it. Not that it mattered, because by that time I wasn't doing any work that required a desk. It had gotten crazy, and I knew it. The circles under my eyes and my continued weight loss told me it was time for a change.

I explored every alternative I could think of, from researching and visiting daycares to negotiating with my employers for a part-time or home-based position, or a combination of the two. However, my key position on the management team required a full-time presence in the office.

Offering my resignation was an extremely difficult decision, particularly in light of my gratitude for the progressive opportunity to have my daughter on-site. My employers and I finally agreed to view my departure as the beginning of an indefinite unpaid leave that left the door open for my possible return at some unpredictable future date.

A two-month notice allowed me to finish up the last big sales project of the quarter, while my daughter was cared for by a neighbor. I got an unforgettable taste of the superwoman syndrome, rising at 5 A.M. and dashing out the door by 6 to drop Sophie off and commute an hour to the office for a grueling nine-hour day. This was followed by a long drive in Minnesota winter rush-hour traffic to pick my daughter up and go home, and was topped off with a couple of frantic hours that my husband and I spent getting everyone fed and Sophie bathed and to bed so that we could start all over again after what felt like a quick catnap. Relief overcame me as my last day at the office arrived, and I packed my diaper bags for good.

Our plans had always included my return to full-time paid employment upon our children's entry to school, which meant that, for the benefit of our financial solvency, we should have another baby quickly if at all. We chose "quickly," and shortly after our daughter's first birthday I was pregnant again.

I started stringing for our local newspaper, rushing out to city council and school board meetings as soon as my husband dragged himself through the door at seven o'clock. I got paid a measly 25 dollars a story, but since the meetings were at night and I could write the stories at home, I didn't have to pay for childcare. Moreover, it was the first time I saw my writing published; it signaled a turning point for me as I finally made the leap from advertising to editorial.

Since then, I've stuck to what I'm passionate about as I navigate the uncertain waters of these transitional years. I've redefined my priorities, and am using this time to lay the groundwork for a career that is going to work for me long after my children are grown. Like the many women who grow home businesses while growing young ones, I've discovered meaning in my personal work that was previously absent.

These days, since I do perform paid work from home, I could have an easy answer to "Don't you work at all anymore?" I could say that I am a freelance writer working at home. It's true, and since I know, based upon my own research, that it gains me a great deal more respect in the eyes of the asker than saying that I'm home with the kids, I'm tempted to offer it up. But I won't because every time I do, I'm perpetuating a system that defines work only in terms of what men have traditionally been paid to do, and discounts most of what women have traditionally done for centuries.

I have to make perfectly clear when I say that I work at home, I'm talking about the childcare and the home maintenance activities which utilize my talents as a manager, nurturer, healer, wise woman, acrobat . . . and retriever of small objects lost in the dust jungle beneath my refrigerator. Otherwise, people automatically dismiss these activities and conjure up a false image of an orderly day spent at the computer doing paid work. This strain toward clarity requires a lot more effort than calling myself a full-time mom, or proclaiming that I'm taking time off to be with my kids (motherhood is not a vacation), or worst of all, concurring that no, "I really don't work at all anymore." It demands concentration and patience, but it can be done.

We must find new words, or new combinations of and meanings for old words that more accurately reflect our reality. When we don't—when we resign ourselves to the old words that apportion us less worth than we deserve because it's less awkward and just plain easier—we are validating a description of ourselves that we know to be false. This danger is like that of looking into a fun house mirror, without challenging the falsehood of the contorted stranger staring back at you. Eventually, you're going to believe what you see is you, and that twisted version of yourself becomes the only truth you know.

FIFTY-THREE

◆◆◆

Toward a More Perfect Union

Erika Jones

In the past decade, workers have come under attack within the new global economy. The profit demand of ever-larger corporations has made instant "downsizing"—the elimination of jobs with higher pay and benefits—commonplace. Operations have moved out of the country. Real wages are falling, and the fastest growing sector of the work force is temporary work without benefits. Welfare-to-work policies have also added to labor's woes, driving wages downward as women are forced into low paying—"any job is a good job"—situations with little worker leverage. Meanwhile, union membership has dwindled over the years, cut by a decline in industrial production—the bedrock of many established unions—and a tarnished public image of unions characterized by leadership scandals and membership exclusivity.

Given the depth and breadth of these challenges, union leaders are becoming more aware that they can no longer afford to ignore or ostracize large segments of the working population. Simultaneously, over the last five years, women's committees within unions have gained renewed strength by addressing issues important to women and making unions more accessible to women, people of color and immigrants. And, the scope of unionized work has also expanded because women, people of color, and immigrants have organized within previously nonunionized sectors such as heath care and the service industry.

As more and more women and people of color join unions and organize, labor has begun to reconnect with broader social issues beyond "bread and butter." In their organizing work, women's committees often make connections between the importance of immigrant rights, welfare reform, and a living wage, and push for a more diverse and open national union culture.

WILD, the Women's Institute for Leadership Development, has supported women's organizing in the labor movement since 1986. WILD's educational and networking programs promote women's leadership and address issues of oppression within the labor movement. *Sojourner* talked with two women from WILD, Jeanette Huezo and Susan Winning, about the status of women and people of color in the labor movement today, and the slow shift toward a more inclusive, representative labor movement of the future.

For more information about WILD's work, contact them at 33 Harrison Avenue, 4th Floor, Boston, MA 02111; (617) 426-0520.

Jeanette Huezo, a Community Organizer for WILD, works with immigrant women in the Latino community who organize around labor issues.

Erika Jones: Do you see a changing role for women in the labor movement, particularly for women of color?

Jeanette Huezo: I don't want to say that it is changing dramatically, but we have started the process. We are educating women about unions, and women are realizing that unions are a way they can have better jobs and opportunities. Not all unions are working for the workers, however, and that is another reason why it is important that women be involved in union work. Women working together can make changes in how the union operates and create unions that truly represent workers. At WILD, we are working to have women of color in power positions within unions. Unions usually are only white men, and white men have had the powerful positions in the past. There are white women in a few powerful positions, but they still represent women. There are a few women who are presidents of unions, and that is a big improvement. However, we are still waiting to have someone represent women of color at the Massachusetts AFL-CIO.

In the past, unions were typically created by white men in industrial sector jobs. What kinds of jobs are union women coming from today?

They are coming from different perspectives. There are women in the building trades. There are women in hospitals, in libraries, women in cleaning jobs, and women working in nursing homes. Everywhere there are women in the workplace, we have women becoming organized. Women are also becoming involved at all levels of the unions.

What difficulties do immigrant women face when trying to organize today?

Being an immigrant, especially a woman immigrant, in the labor movement is not an easy thing. I think one of the barriers to immigrant women organizing is the lack of introduction to what a union is

in the United States. There are a lot of stereotypes, and the perception of what a union is differs among communities. For example, if you're talking about unions to many Latin Americans, if they are coming from a country where there was an armed conflict, they will probably feel threatened because they have a different perception [of unions]. For example, I am from El Salvador. In El Salvador ten or fifteen years ago, if you were part of a union that was not part of the government, you were in big trouble. You could lose your life; you could be murdered. So immigrants make connections with their experiences in their home countries and their experiences here. That is one obstacle. Women do not know that they have the right to be a union member and the right to organize for their rights.

Unauthorized residents are threatened with deportation if they protest illegal or unfair treatment at their workplace. What is being done in the labor movement about the rights of these workers?

Immigration is a very hot issue not only in the labor movement. It is a very large social problem. Women who are here illegally are not able to defend their rights. For example, I know a woman who is suffering from sexual harassment, but if she files a grievance, then she can be deported. The woman is scared and doesn't want to lose her job. What is she supposed to do?

How are women working to organize within the labor movement?

I think the key thing is education about our rights. WILD is a great example of a tool for women in the labor movement. Our last Summer Institute was amazing. I was with 150 women for a weekend. It's a lot of fun, a lot of support. We learn from each other, and you feel as though you can change the world.

When women are able to organize and form a union in their workplace, what changes do you see in women's lives and their communities?

Women who work in places without a union get paid less than women that work in a place with a union, and that's a big thing. That can change your life and your community. Even if a woman is paid two, three, or four dollars less for a day's labor, if you multiply that by a week, a month, or a year, that is a lot of money she is losing. Community people are seeing that to make changes, we have to make them together. Labor and community working together is the only way we can make changes. If we isolate our problems we will never get anywhere.

Susan Winning has been the Director of WILD since 1993. She is actively involved with WomenLead, a project of WILD that seeks to support women's organizing within the labor movement.

Do you see a general trend in what women labor activists are pushing for, and how they are organizing?

Susan Winning: Women are actively organizing around having access to unions, and having the labor movement include a culture that is welcoming to people other than white, straight men. Women are also organizing again into women's committees. Committees are being formed by women at many different levels: in individual unions, by region or around an interest, and also on a community basis. The women's committees are addressing what makes it difficult for women to participate in unions, and also are organizing around issues that are important to women in general, like the Massachusetts campaign for paid family medical leave.

What has been the reaction of members from the older union structure to the inclusion of women leaders and women's issues in labor organizing?

There is a recognition that there needs to be a change to really involve current members and increasingly to be more attractive to the new work force that is more and more women and immigrants and people of color, not just white men, who, primarily, have been the labor movement in the past.

There is some support for these changes from the organized labor movement. For example, the Massachusetts AFL-CIO has created a Diversity Task Force, which is going to be making some recommendations to the AFL-CIO convention next month, and that's a big change.

Can you give examples of recent victories women have had in gaining a louder voice in unions, and participating in labor organizing at the national level?

In Massachusetts and nationally, women are now in top union leadership positions. Four or five years ago Linda Chavez Thompson was elected Executive Vice President of the national AFL-CIO, the highest union leadership position a woman has held ever in the United States. In the Massachusetts AFL-CIO, Kathy Cassavant is the first woman to hold the

position of Secretary Treasurer. (We are also very proud to have her on the WILD board.) So there has been some success with women gaining top leadership positions, but there is still a long way to go.

Women are also organizing together nationally. The national AFL-CIO has created a Working Women's Department, and they are having their second large conference in 2000. They bring together union and non-union women who are in the work place together to explore issues and to talk about women's needs in the workplace.

Another emphasis in the labor movement today is recruiting new union members. As industrial manufacturing—the traditional sector of labor organizing—has declined in this country, the number of people organizing with unions has steadily declined. So there is a very big push for new organizing. The organizing effort has been successful to a large extent in the service industry, which is primarily women and people of color; those are the folks who are joining unions now and those are the women who are participating in campaigns on several levels. That is how the union organizing demographics are really changing—new union members are tending to be women and people of color.

What remains the biggest challenge to all workers who wish to organize for their rights?

The biggest obstacle to organizing is labor law, which is totally on the side of the employer. It's almost as big an obstacle as employers breaking the law and firing people despite their right to organize.

Workers have to be extremely motivated to unionize because the obstacles are fairly great, although legally they have every right to organize without intimidation.

On both the state and the national level the labor movement is really trying to promote a much more positive support for people organizing. There have been resolutions introduced in city councils to support workers' rights' to organize and to help create a more supportive culture and to sort of shame employers into adhering to the law.

How have unions addressed the "booming" U.S. economy in which workers' real wages have been declining as corporate profits have skyrocketed?

The decline of unions over the years has had a negative effect on people's general wages and benefits. Money has been going upward to the CEOs and upper management rather than to workers. In contrast, a high percentage of unionization in an industry or in an area has a real upward push on wages and benefits. For instance, since there are very few nursing homes that are organized, nursing home owners can keep wages and benefits as low as they want. But once nursing homes begin to organize, workers have the option to move near an organized nursing home and work as part of a union, instead of accepting the lower wages of a non-unionized nursing home. This puts pressure on other nursing homes to be more competitive [with salaries and benefits] to attract workers.

At the same time, welfare reform is a source of downward pressure on wages and benefits, particularly for low-income people. Welfare recipients are being forced into the workplace and often, due to a lack of skills, are working lower level jobs. As more people are available to do those jobs, there is a tendency for the wage floor to be pushed down for everybody. That is one of the reasons why a number of people in unions are organizing around welfare recipients and around welfare law. Welfare reform hurts everybody — besides the fact that people believe there needs to be a safety net. A large percentage of women who are on welfare are victims of domestic violence and that's another topic, but it's all connected.

How have women in unions organized around welfare reform, and broadened the focus of organized labor campaigns?

WILD tries to bring union women in to support issues that traditionally have not been considered labor issues. In the past, the labor movement really didn't touch on the issue of welfare reform, and there was a struggle with union members who believe that everybody's problems are caused by welfare recipients. For example, many low income women [in the unions] thought welfare recipients were getting all the breaks while they were out there struggling and not getting any support or help. But I think there has really been a change. There has been a lot of organizing to educate union members, both women and men, about how people are really in the same boat. In many ways, they are just in a slightly different position — and kicking people off welfare will not help other people's economic position.

Also, within the leadership of the labor movement there are some similar stands to take on issues which actually don't even affect organized union members, but do affect workers. For example, the AFL-CIO has been very active in the campaign to increase the minimum wage. Although most union members already make at least a minimum wage, this is something which tends to be a floor for workers and is a standard by which other wages are set.

F I F T Y - F O U R

Feminists, Welfare Reform, and Welfare Justice[1]

Gwendolyn Mink

Over 95% of adult welfare recipients are women. This is not surprising since women are usually the caregivers in their families. What is surprising is that during two years of formal legislative debate about ending welfare, the adverse consequences of such a decision for poor women were scarcely mentioned. Even in liberal circles, where tears flowed prodigiously for poor children, few rued the effects of punitive welfare provisions on poor women.

To be sure, the leaders of many women's and feminist organizations (ranging from the American

Association for University Women to the National Organization for Women) did oppose punitive welfare reform — calling press conferences, holding vigils, and even engaging in dramatic acts of civil disobedience. Yet the millions of women who have made feminism a movement did not rally around their leaders' cause. The Personal Responsibility Act is the most aggressive invasion of women's rights in this century, and most feminists did little to resist it. Many feminists actually endorsed the new law's core principles — namely, that poor single mothers should move from welfare to work and into financial relationships with their children's fathers.

Such feminists collaborated with welfare reformers—either by their silence or in their deeds. Mainly middle class and white, many with ties to the organized women's movement, and some with high electoral positions, these feminists often speak for all of feminism. When mobilized, they can wield impressive political clout—enough to inspire an otherwise wishy-washy President Clinton to hang tough on such knotty issues as late-term abortion, for example. Resilient and resourceful, these feminists have campaigned vigorously over the years—for women candidates, against the Hyde Amendment, and for the Violence Against Women Act. They have worked aggressively for women's rights and gender justice, even when the odds for success have been poor. When it came to welfare, however, they sat on their hands. Ignoring appeals from sister feminists and welfare rights activists to defend "welfare as a women's issue" and to oppose "the war against poor women" as if it were "a war against *all* women," many even entered the war on the anti-welfare side.[2]

Some examples are: on Capitol Hill, all white women in the U.S. Senate—including four Democratic women who call themselves feminists—voted *for* the new welfare law when it first came to the Senate floor in the summer of 1995. In the House of Representatives in 1996, 26 of 31 Democratic women, all of whom call themselves feminists, voted *for* a Democratic welfare bill that would have stripped recipients of their entitlement to welfare.[3] Meanwhile, across the country, a NOW-Legal Defense and Education Fund appeal for contributions to support an economic justice litigator aroused so much hate mail that NOW-LDEF stopped doing direct mail on the welfare issue (Kornbluh, 1996: 25).

Feminist members of Congress did not write the Personal Responsibility Act, of course. Neither did members of the National Organization for Women or contributors to Emily's List comprise the driving force behind the most brutal provisions of the new welfare law. My claim is not that feminists were uniquely responsible for how welfare has been reformed. My point is that they were uniquely positioned to make a difference. They have made a difference in many arenas across the years, even during inauspicious Republican presidencies—overturning judicial evisceration of Title IX (in the Civil Rights Restoration Act of 1988), for example, and

winning damage rights for women in discrimination claims under Title VII (in the Civil Rights Act of 1991). They certainly could have made a difference when a friendly Democratic president began casting about for ways to reform welfare in 1993; although they could not have changed Republican intentions in the 104th Congress, they surely could have pressured the Democrat they helped elect to the White House to veto the Republican bill.

Welfare reform did not directly bear on the lives of most feminists, though, and did not directly implicate their rights. The new welfare law did not threaten middle-class feminists' reproductive choices, their sexual privacy, their right to raise their own children, or their occupational freedom. So they did not raise their voices as they would have if, say, abortion rights had been at stake. Solipsism induced silence among many feminists, giving permission to policymakers to treat punitive welfare reform as a no-lose situation.

Silence among feminists was not the only problem, however. Even while feminists remained silent about the effects of new welfare provisions on poor women's rights, they were quite vocal about the need to reform welfare so as to improve the personal and family choices poor single mothers make. Many feminists did, indeed, see that welfare is a women's issue—because almost all adult recipients are mothers. Yet they also viewed welfare as an issue for feminism: as a social policy that has promoted the dependency of single mothers on government rather than independence in the labor market; that has discouraged poor women from practicing fertility control, which in turn has compensated for the sexual and paternal irresponsibility of individual men.

Without a doubt, welfare never has been a feminist policy. Its goal never has been to enhance women's independence or to honor women's choices. Benefits always have been conditional and stigmatized, forcing poor mothers to conform to government rules and to suffer suspicion that they cheat on those rules. Though critiques of state patriarchy are common among academic feminists, I don't think they are what lay behind most feminists' reservations about defending poor women's entitlement to welfare.

During the welfare debate, most feminists focused on the deficiencies of welfare mothers, rather than on the deficiencies of the welfare system. They trafficked in the tropes of "illegitimacy" "pathology," "dependency," and "irresponsibility," much as did conservative male politicians in both parties. Kinder and gentler than the men who repealed welfare, however, they viewed mothers who need welfare as mothers who need feminism, not punishment. They saw welfare mothers as victims—of patriarchy, maybe of racism, or possibly of false consciousness. However, they didn't see welfare mothers as agents of their own lives—as women who are entitled to and capable of making independent and honorable choices about what kind of work they will do and how many children they will have and whether they will marry. If anything, many feminists agreed with conservatives that welfare mothers do not make good choices.

Feminist reservations about welfare mothers' choices strengthened the bipartisan consensus that there is something wrong with mothers who need welfare and that cash assistance should require their reform. The two pillars of the new welfare law—work and marriage—were born from this consensus. The harshness of the law's work requirements and the brutality of its sanctions against nonmarital childrearing may be Republican and patriarchal in execution. But the law's emphasis on women's labor market participation and on men's participation in families were Democratic and feminist in inspiration.

With feminist complicity, the new welfare law—the Personal Responsibility Act of 1996—hardens legal differences among women based on their marital, maternal, class, and racial statuses. It segregates poor single mothers into a separate caste, subject to a separate system of law. While middle-class women may choose to participate in the labor market, poor single mothers are forced by law to do so (work requirements and time limits). While middle-class women may choose to bear children, poor single mothers may be punished by government for making that choice (the family cap and illegitimacy ratios). While middle-class women enjoy still-strong rights to sexual and reproductive privacy, poor single mothers are compelled by government to reveal the details of intimate relationships in exchange for survival (mandatory maternal cooperation in establishing paternity). And while middle-class mothers may choose their children's fathers by marrying them or permitting them to develop relationships with children—*or not*—poor single mothers are required by law to make room for biological fathers in

their families (mandatory maternal cooperation in establishing and enforcing child support orders).

Feminist Themes in the Personal Responsibility Act

Feminists contributed to this new welfare regime in two major ways: first, in their emphasis on work outside the home, and second, in their insistence on "making fathers pay." Although there is plenty of evidence that women in general and feminists in particular don't like the draconian aspects of the new welfare law, they do not necessarily eschew the law's basic assumptions. One assumption is that poor single mothers should move from welfare to work.

Feminists did not invent the "work" solution to welfare.[4] Yet their emphasis on women's right to work outside the home—in tandem with women's increased presence in the labor force—gave cover to conservatives eager to require wage work of single mothers even as they championed the traditional family. Moreover, it legitimated a view popular among many feminists—that wage earning is "good for" mothers who need welfare.

Most of the policy claims made by second-wave feminists have emphasized women's right to be equal to men in a men's world—to be leaders and breadwinners, too. The white and middle-class women who rekindled feminism in the 1960s responded to their particular historical experiences, experiences drawn by an ethos of domesticity that had confined middle-class white women to the home and that had used such women's domesticity to justify their inequality. Middle-class feminists understandably spurned the domesticity they had been assigned and keyed on work outside the home as a defining element of women's full and equal citizenship.

As they entered the labor market, these women did not spurn family work; rather, they found their energy doubly taxed by the dual responsibility of earning and caring. Accordingly, many feminists called for labor market policies to address the family needs that fall disproportionately on women—parental leave and childcare policies, for example. Their concern has been to ease the contradictions between wage work and family life. They have focused on how family needs impede opportunities and achievements in the labor market, and their goals have been labor policies that relieve women's family responsibilities (e.g., childcare) and strengthen women's rights in the workplace (e.g., wage equity). They have not been so interested in winning social policies to support women where we meet our family responsibilities: in the home.

The popular feminist claim that women earn independence, autonomy, and equality through wages historically has divided feminists along class and race lines, as women of color and poor white women have not usually earned equality from sweated labor. To the contrary. Especially for women of color, wage work has been a mark of inequality: expected by the white society for whom they work, necessary because their male kin cannot find jobs or cannot earn family-supporting wages, and exploitative because their earnings keep them poor. Thus, the right to care for their own children—to work inside the home—has been a touchstone goal of their struggles for equality. The fact that women are positioned divergently in the nexus among caregiving, wage-earning, and inequality separated feminists one from another on the welfare issue. It separated many white feminists from many feminists of color and separated employed middle-class feminists from mothers who need welfare.

Out of second-wave feminism's emphasis on winning rights in the workplace emerged, *sotto voce,* a feminist expectation that women *ought* to work outside the home and an assumption that *any* job outside the home—including caring for other people's children—is more socially productive than caring for one's own. Although feminism is fundamentally about winning women choices, our labor market bias has put much of feminism not on the side of vocational choice—the choice to work inside or outside the home—but on the side of wage-earning for all women. Thus, most congressional feminists, along with many feminists across the country, have conflated their *right* to work outside the home with poor single mothers' *obligation* to do so. Thus, many feminists agreed with Bill Clinton and the Republicans that poor single mothers should "move from welfare to work."

The labor market focus of second-wave feminism has accomplished much for women—most importantly establishing equality claims for women as wage-earners. Contemporary feminist calls for further labor market reforms—for an increased minimum wage, gender-sensitive unemployment insurance, comparable worth, and childcare—rightly point out the persisting impediments to women's equality as labor market citizens. The problem is not with the specific content of feminist agendas, but with their one-sidedness and prescriptivity.

Many feminists have worked ardently to attenuate the new welfare law's harshest provisions. For example, NOW-LDEF, working especially with Lucille Roybal-Allard in the U.S. House and Patti Murray in the U.S. Senate, has fought hard to exempt battered women from some of the new welfare rules. This initiative, along with Patsy Mink's efforts in the U.S. House to secure vocational education funds for single mothers and grass-roots struggles to enforce fair labor standards in welfare mothers' jobs, could improve some women's fate in the new welfare system. However, feminists' attempts to mitigate disaster do not disturb the principles behind the new welfare law: they do not refute the idea that poor single mothers *should* seek work outside the home. Except among welfare rights activists and a handful of feminists, no one has defended the right of poor mothers to raise their children, and no one has questioned the proposition that poor single mothers should *have to*—should be compelled by law to—work outside the home.

The enlistment of feminists in work-ethical welfare reform reflected their gender goals and biases. In the welfare context, these goals and biases have racial effects. Although work requirements aim indiscriminately at all poor single mothers, it is mothers of color who bear their heaviest weight. African American and Latina mothers are disproportionately poor, and, accordingly, are disproportionately enrolled on welfare: in 1994, adult recipients in AFDC families were 37.4% white, 36.4% Black, 19.9% Latina, 2.9% Asian, and 1.3% Native American.[5] So when welfare rules indenture poor mothers as unpaid servants of local governments (in workfare programs), it is mothers of color who are disproportionately harmed. Moreover, when time limits require poor mothers to forsake their children for the labor market, it is mothers of color who are disproportionately deprived of their right to manage their family's lives and it is children of color who are disproportionately deprived of their mothers' care.

The view of feminists that labor market participation is good for women skewed discussions of single mothers' poverty and raised the costs of caregiving, especially for mothers who are poor and of color. At the same time, the feminists' view that tough child support enforcement is good for mothers and children raised the costs of childbearing and child-raising for mothers who are poor and never married.

Feminists in Congress have been particularly emphatic about "making fathers pay" for children through increased federal involvement in the establishment and enforcement of child support orders.[6] In fact, without white, middle-class feminist interventions, especially in the House of Representatives, paternity-based child support would not be the major pillar of the new welfare policy that it has become. The only reason the Personal Responsibility Act contains child support provisions is because feminists in Congress embarrassed Republicans into adopting them.

The child support provisions impose stringent national conditions on nonmarital childrearing by poor women. The first condition is the mandatory establishment of paternity. Welfare law stipulates that a mother's eligibility for welfare depends upon her willingness to reveal the identity of her child's father. Since the purpose of paternity establishment is to assign child support obligations to biological fathers, the second condition is that mothers who need welfare must cooperate in establishing, modifying, and enforcing the support orders for their children. The law requires states to reduce a family's welfare grant by at least 25% when a mother fails to comply with these rules and permits states to deny the family's grant altogether.[7]

The view that the dereliction of fathers creates or feeds mothers' need for welfare is quite popular among middle-class feminists. Finding the costs of childbearing that fall disproportionately on women a wellspring of gender inequality, many feminists want men to provide for their biological children, even if they have no relationship with them. Incautious pursuit of this objective aligned middle-class feminists behind a policy that endangers the rights of poor single mothers.

Paternity establishment rules compel nonmarital mothers to disclose private matters in exchange for cash and medical assistance—to answer questions like: Whom did you sleep with? How often? When? Where? How? Meanwhile, child support rules require nonmarital mothers to associate with biological fathers, and in so doing to stoke such fathers' claims to parental rights. In these and other

ways, paternity establishment and child support provisions set poor single mothers apart from other mothers, subjecting them to stringent legal requirements because of their class and marital status. While they beef up services that deserted middle-class mothers may *choose* to enlist, they *impose* such services on—and compel intimate revelations from—poor mothers who have chosen to parent alone.

Middle-class feminist energy behind vigorous paternity establishment and child support enforcement is no doubt animated in part by exasperation with some men's cost-free exploitation of the sexual revolution. From this perspective, men ought to be held responsible for the procreative consequences of their heightened access to women's bodies. The quest for fairness in procreative relations drives the increasingly punitive proposals designed to force fathers to meet their obligations to children. Yet it doesn't explain why middle-class feminists believe maternal coercion is an acceptable means to paternal responsibility.

A reading of congressional debates suggests that the main impetus behind middle-class feminists' advocacy of punitive paternity establishment and child support enforcement rules is their own class and marital experiences. When middle-class women think of the circumstances that might lead them to welfare, they think of divorce—from middle-class men who then refuse to chip in for the care and maintenance of children. California Congresswoman Lynn Woolsey is a case in point. Something of a Beltway icon during the welfare debate, she described herself and was described by others as "a typical welfare mother." Thirty years earlier, she had had to turn to welfare following her divorce from a man she describes as "very successful."[8] Though she had a support order, she "never received a penny in child support."[9] Woolsey's story provided a useful strategic intervention into the welfare debate, countering the stereotypic image of welfare mothers as Black and unmarried. Yet marking one mother's story, however uplifting, as representative of a whole population invites the kind of solipsism that produces one-size-fits-all policy prescriptions. Such prescriptions are not only unworkable, they also neglect the needs of people who must and do live their lives differently.

The compulsory features of paternity establishment and child support enforcement may be unremarkable to a divorced mother with a support order: she escapes compulsion by choosing to pursue child support, and what matters to her is that the support order be enforced. However, some mothers do not have support orders because they do not want them. A mother may not want to identify her child's father because she may fear abuse for herself or her child. She may not want to seek child support because she has chosen to parent alone — or with someone else. She may know her child's father is poor and may fear exposing him to harsh penalties when he cannot pay what a court tells him he owes.[10] She may consider his emotional support for his child to be worth more than the $100 the state might collect and that she will never see.[11]

"Making fathers pay" may promote the economic and justice interests of many custodial mothers. Yet *making mothers* make fathers pay means making mothers pay for subsistence with their own rights — and safety. The issue is not whether government should assist mothers in collecting payments from fathers. Of course it should. Neither is the issue whether child support enforcement provisions in welfare policy help mothers who have or desire child support awards. Of course they do. Nor is the issue whether it is a good thing for children to have active fathers — of course it can be. The issue is coercion, coercion directed toward the mother who has eschewed patriarchal conventions — whether by choice or from necessity. It is also coercion directed toward the mother whose deviation from patriarchal norms has been linked to her racial and cultural standing.

Paternity establishment and child support became strategies for welfare reform not because of the unjust effects of divorce on mothers, but because of the allegedly unsavory behavior of mothers of nonmarital children. It is nonmarital childbearing, not divorce, that has been blamed for social pathologies like crime and dependency. The preamble to the new welfare law legislates precisely this point of view. Such patriarchal reasoning leaches into racial argument, as welfare discourse specifically correlates nonmarital childbearing rates among African Americans with social and moral decay.[12]

Like work requirements, the coercive aspects of paternity establishment and child support policy are aimed against single mothers in general. However, like work requirements, they have decidedly racial effects. The mandatory maternal cooperation rule targets mothers who are not and have not been married, as well as mothers who do not have and do not want child support. Nonmarital mothers are the

bull's-eye, and among nonmarital mothers receiving welfare, only 28.4% are white.[13] This means that the new welfare law's invasions of associational and privacy rights will disproportionately harm mothers of color. Inspired by white feminist outrage against middle-class "deadbeat dads," the paternity establishment and child support provisions both reflect and entrench inequalities among women.

Should Feminists Defend Welfare?

How might feminists have intervened differently in the welfare debate? We could have begun with the feminist method — with listening to welfare mothers' stories rather than inferring from our own. We could have begun by defending poor mothers' rights as we would defend our own — by resisting reforms that coerce poor mothers to surrender rights in exchange for cash assistance and that make poor mothers' choices for them.

We did, indeed, need to end welfare — but as poor single mothers knew it, not as middle-class moralizers imagined it. *Why* we end welfare dictates *how* we end it — whether we end it by subordinating poor single mothers or by improving their prospects for equality.

What kind of social policy *would* enable poor single mothers' equality? During the welfare debate, feminists who did mobilize against punitive reforms found common ground in opposition to the initiatives proposed by the Republicans, as well as to some proposed by President Clinton. Yet we were far from united behind a common vision of welfare justice. Although we could all agree on the urgency of childcare and health care and jobs, we were less certain about what social policy should say to single mothers who want to or need to care for their own children in their own homes. That we were collectively ambivalent about social policy toward caregiving didn't matter during the welfare debate, for the terms of debate were so narrow. No one was asking: "What should welfare be for?" or "How might welfare work *for* women?" Although it doesn't look like these questions will soon be ripe, feminists must push and prepare for the day when they will be.

Toward that end, I offer my own assessment, one based on 10 years of welfare research and welfare activism. In my view, welfare is not only a survival issue for poor families, it is also an equality issue for poor mothers. It is an equality issue because the assumptions and prescriptions embedded in welfare law and rife in the welfare debate disable poor mothers' independent citizenship. Equality requires us to repudiate the existing basis of welfare, which we can do most effectively by establishing a new one — namely, that poor single women who give care to their children are mothers whose caregiving *is work.*

We all know that family work — household management and parenting — takes skill, energy, time, and responsibility. We know this because people who can afford it *pay* other people to do this work. Many wage-earning mothers pay for childcare; upper-class mothers who work outside the home pay for nannies; very wealthy mothers who don't even work outside the home pay household workers to assist them with their various tasks. Moreover, even when we are not paying surrogates to do our family caregiving, we pay people to perform activities in the labor market that caregivers also do in the home. We pay drivers to take us places; we pay nurses to make us feel better and help us get well; we pay psychologists to help us with our troubles; we pay teachers to explain our lessons; we pay cooks and waitresses to prepare and serve our food.

If economists can measure the value of this work when it is performed for other people's families, why can't we impute value to it when it is performed for one's own? In 1972, economists at the Chase Manhattan Bank did just that, translating family caregiving work into its labor market components — nursemaid, dietitian, cook, laundress, maintenance man, chauffeur, food buyer, cook, dishwasher, seamstress, practical nurse, and gardener. The economists concluded that the weekly value of family caregivers' work was at least $257.53, or $13,391.56 a year (in 1972 dollars) (Scott, 1972: 56–59). Had poor single mothers received welfare benefits in 1996 at even 1972 values for caregiving work, they would have had incomes above the poverty line! Moreover, had their benefits explicitly compensated them for the work that they do, poor single mothers would not have had to live under the stigma of "welfare dependency."

Once we establish that *all* caregiving is work — whatever the racial, marital, or class status of the caregiver and whether or not it is performed in the labor market — we can build a case for economic arrangements that enable poor single mothers to do their jobs. In place of stingy benefits doled out begrudgingly to needy mothers, welfare would become an income owed to nonmarket, caregiving workers — owed to anyone who bears sole responsibility for children (or for other dependent family members).

We could model this income on survivors' insurance, which since 1939 has supported widowed mothers who work inside the home raising their children. More generous than welfare, survivors' insurance is free from stigma and social controls. It is nationally uniform and paid automatically to widows (or caregiving widowers) and minor children of deceased workers covered by the Social Security Act. Mothers who are eligible for survivors' insurance do not have to submit to governmental scrutiny to receive benefits and do not have to live by the government's moral and cultural rules. Survivors' insurance gives widowed mothers the means to make *their own* choices about caregiving and wage-earning. It designates caregiving as a socially necessary and valuable activity, deserving of social assistance.

All family caregivers are owed an income in theory, for all caregiving is work. However, a caregiver's income should redistribute resources to mothers without means, for their capacity to sustain families and to make independent choices hangs on their ability to provide. The cardinal purpose of such an income should be to redress the unique inequality of solo caregivers — usually mothers — who shoulder the dual responsibilities of providing care for children and financing it. Although some single mothers may be able to afford both responsibilities, most cannot, because they are time-poor, cash-poor, or both. A caregiver's income would relieve the disproportionate burdens that fall on single mothers and in so doing would lessen inequalities among women based on class and marital status, and between male and female parents based on default social roles. Though paid to single caregivers only, this income support should be universally guaranteed, assuring a safety net to all caregivers if ever they need or choose to parent — or to care for other family members — alone. The extension of the safety net to caregivers as independent citizens would promote equality, as it would enable adults to exit untenable — and often violent — relationships of economic dependency and to retain reproductive and vocational choices when they do.

We need to end welfare in this way to enable equality — in the safety net, between the genders, among women, and under the Constitution. Income support for all caregivers who are going it alone would permit solo parents to decide how best to manage their responsibilities to children. It might even undermine the sexual division of labor, for some men will be enticed to do family caregiving work once they understand it to have economic value. Offering an income to all solo caregivers in a unitary system—to nonmarital mothers as well as to widowed ones—would erase invidious moral distinctions among mothers and eliminate their racial effects. Further, universal income support for single parents would restore mothers' constitutional rights—to not marry, to bear children, and to parent them, even if they are poor. It would promote occupational freedom, by rewarding work even when work cannot be exchanged for wages. So redefined, welfare would become a sign not of dependency, but of independence, a means not to moral regulation, but to social and political equality.

Ending welfare this way will remedy inequality where it is most gendered—in the caregiving relations of social reproduction. Yet, it will not be enough to end welfare by replacing it with a caregiver's income. The end of welfare—the goal of feminist social policy—must be to enhance women's choices across their full spectrum. We need to improve women's opportunities as *both* nonmarket and market workers, so that the choice of caregivers to work inside the home is backed up by the possibility of choosing not to. Middle-class feminists were correct to reject *ascribed* domesticity, and they have taught us well that fully independent and equal citizenship for women entails having the right *not* to care. So we must also win labor market reforms to make outside work feasible even for mothers who are parenting alone. Unless we make outside work affordable for solo caregivers, a caregiver's income would constrain choice by favoring caregiving over wage-earning.

The end of welfare, then, includes "making work pay," not only by remunerating caregiving work, but also by making participation in the labor market equitable and rewarding for women, especially mothers. To make work pay, we must improve women's position in the labor market through the following measures: a minimum wage that provides an income at least at the poverty threshold, comparable worth policies that correct the low economic value assigned to women's jobs, unemployment insurance reforms covering women's gendered rea-

sons for losing or leaving jobs, paid family leave, guaranteed childcare, universal health care, a full employment policy, massive investment in education and vocational training, and aggressive enforcement of anti-discrimination laws.

This end to welfare will take us down many paths, in recognition of women's diverse experiences of gender and diverse hopes for equality.

Notes

1. This essay was originally delivered to the Dean's Symposium, University of Chicago, November 7, 1997. Portions are drawn from Gwendolyn Mink, *Welfare's End,* copyright © 1998 by Cornell University. Used by permission of the publisher. Some portions are also reprinted in Gwendolyn Mink, "The Lady and the Tramp (II): Feminist Welfare Politics, Poor Single Mothers, and the Challenge of Welfare Justice," *Feminist Studies,* spring 1998).

2. This was the rallying cry of the Women's Committee of One Hundred, a feminist mobilization against punitive welfare reform co-chaired by the author. See the full-page ad by Women's Committee of One Hundred, "Why Every Woman in America Should Beware of Welfare Cuts" (*New York Times,* August 8, 1995).

3. Castle-Tanner substitute amendment to H.R. 3734, "The Personal Responsibility and Work Opportunity Act of 1996," *Congressional Record* (July 18, 1996: H7907–7974).

4. One example of the labor market focus of feminist thinking about women's poverty can be found in Bergmann and Hartmann (1995: 85–91).

5. U.S. House of Representatives, Committee on Ways and Means, *1996 Green Book,* Table 8-32.

6. Congresswoman Barbara Kennelly (D-Connecticut) played a crucial role in winning strengthened child support enforcement provisions in welfare law in the mid-1980s. She and other feminist congressmembers also have sponsored standalone child support enforcement bills, especially to improve collections across state lines and to toughen penalties on delinquent fathers.

7. P.L. 104–193, *The Personal Responsibility and Work Opportunity Act of 1996,* Title I, Section 408 (a) (2).

8. Congresswoman Lynn Woolsey (D-California), "Remarks," in Mink (1993).

9. "Remarks of Mrs. Woolsey," *Congressional Record* (February 1, 1995: H1031).

10. In 1989, the average annual child support award for poor mothers was only $1,889 (Bassuk, Browne, and Buckner, 1996: 62).

11. The Personal Responsibility Act ended the $50 "pass-through," the amount of collected child support state governments were required to share with mothers enrolled in the Aid to Families with Dependent Children program.

12. On the "implicit stories of race and gender" in welfare politics, see Dowd (1995: 19, 26, 45–46), Austin (1993: 575–594), Fineman (1995: Chapter 5), and the works of Dorothy Roberts.

13. U.S. House of Representatives, Committee on Ways and Means, *1996 Green Book,* Table 8-2.

References

Kornbluh, Felicia. 1996. "Feminists and the Welfare Debate: Too Little? Too Late?" *Dollars and Sense* (November–December): 25.

Scott, Ann Crittenden. 1972. "The Value of Housework: For Love or Money'?" *Ms.* (July): 56–59.

CHAPTER NINE

Women's Health

Health, healing, and learning how our bodies work are all issues of major concern to women, helping us to take care of ourselves and others more effectively. Although women make up a majority of health care providers in clinics, doctors' offices, nursing homes, and hospitals, professionalization and the medicalization of health care have given doctors—mostly White men—authority in medical matters. In times gone by, women made teas, tinctures, oils, and salves and gave baths and massages to heal sickness and alleviate pain. Some women still study the medicinal properties of plants and treat many complaints with herbal remedies (Perrone, Stockel, and Krueger 1989). Currently, the medical care available to women in the United States is dominated by drug treatments and surgery. Women's health conditions vary greatly depending on individual factors like diet, exercise, smoking, stress, or violence, as well as macro-level factors such as race and class. This chapter reviews data about women's health, discusses the economic basis of the U.S. medical industry, and considers ways to move the emphasis in medical care away from an overreliance on drugs and surgery to a more balanced conception of health. Health is related to many aspects of our lives, and the chapters on women's bodies, relationships and family, work, and the environment are also relevant here.

Causes of Death for Women: Effects of Race and Class

Like many of the issues covered in this book, health is both a personal concern and a political issue. It is also somewhat intangible—a complex mix of physical, mental, emotional, and spiritual states of well-being. The transition from health to illness is often gradual and rather subjective. By contrast, death is a more clearly defined event and is used as an indicator—though admittedly rather crude—of the health of the population.

Like men, women in the United States are most likely to die from heart disease or cancer, followed by strokes, pneumonia, pulmonary diseases, accidents, and diabetes. Overall, men have higher cancer rates than women. In all racial groups, however, women aged thirty to fifty-four have higher rates than men of the same age because of the high incidence of breast and gynecological cancers (Stocker 1991, 1993). Among women, cancer is the most common among White women, though the death rate from cancer is highest in Alaska Native women (National Cancer Institute 1996). Women who earn less than $15,000 a year and who do not have private medical insurance are more likely to have a late diagnosis of cancer. In general, late diagnoses are directly related to higher mortality rates. Women of color are more likely to live and work in areas with high levels of toxic waste, which increases their risk of developing cancer. They are also more likely to receive late diagnosis and poorer medical treatment because of the racism of the wider society and within the medical system. Heart disease is 44 percent lower for Asian American women than for White women. Schulman et al. (1999) found that the race and gender of patients with chest pain influenced whether they were sent for the most definitive tests for heart disease. All other things being equal, African American men and all women are 40 percent less likely than White men to be referred by their physicians for cardiac catheterization; Black women are 60 percent less likely to be referred for this procedure than White men. Among the top ten causes of death for African American women and Latinas are conditions connected to pregnancy and childbirth, not found in the top ten causes of death for White women. Significantly more (25 percent more) African American women die in their twenties than do White women of that age as a result of HIV/AIDS, maternal mortality, drug use, and homicide (see White 1990 for discussions of Black women's health issues). Native American women aged fifteen to twenty-four show a 50 percent higher death rate than White women of the same age for similar reasons. In Reading 7 (Chapter 2), Frederica Daly provides a detailed historical, legal, and economic context for her brief discussion of Native American women's health, which, she notes, is among the worst in the country. Native American women have lower life-expectancy rates compared with the overall population, and they have high mortality rates due to violence, alcoholism, treatable diseases like diabetes and tuberculosis, as well as suicide (LaFramboise, Berman, and Sohi 1994). Taken as a whole, the health of African American women, Native American women, and Latinas is significantly worse than that of White women and Asian American women.

Breast Cancer. This affects one woman in nine nationwide, though there are much higher incidences in certain geographic areas, as noted by Rita Arditti and Tatiana Schreiber in Reading 55. Breast cancer is the most frequently diagnosed cancer among all women, though Vietnamese women living in the United States have higher rates of cervical cancer (National Cancer Institute 1996). The incidence of breast cancer increases with age, though African American women are more likely than White women to get it at younger ages. Fewer Black women get cancer than White women, but their mortality rate is 28 percent higher, presumably because they wait longer than White women to seek medical treatment. Although there is some controversy about the effectiveness of mammograms, they are generally recommended for women in their forties for early detection of breast cancer. Women with more education are more likely to know about this screening procedure, and are more likely to have insurance to cover it and to be registered with a doctor who encourages it. Research suggests that even when Black women have insurance, doctors are less likely to suggest mammograms. White women with cancer also get what the literature refers to as "more aggressive" treatment than Black women, meaning that Black women are not told about all relevant treatment options, given the full range of tests, or always prescribed the most effective medications.

Hypertension. This is a major risk factor for heart disease and stroke, the first and third leading causes of death for women. During 1988–91, the prevalence of hypertension for African American women was 31 percent, for Mexican American women 22 percent, and for White women 21 percent (National Center for Health Statistics 1996a). According to Krieger and Sidney (1996), more African Americans than White people have high blood pressure, a fact attributable to stress related to racism.

Diabetes. Three times as many African American women as White women have diabetes, and more die from it than do White women. Similarly, Latinas have a significantly higher incidence of diabetes, especially Puerto Ricans and Mexican Americans (Torre 1993). Native American rates for diabetes are twice as high as the rate for the United States as a whole and have risen significantly in the past forty-five years (F. Daly 1994).

Tuberculosis. Compared with people in the United States as a whole, Native Americans are four times as likely to have tuberculosis, an infectious disease prevalent in the late nineteenth and early twentieth centuries and usually associated with poverty and poor living conditions (F. Daly 1994).

HIV/AIDS. For younger people (twenty-five to forty-four), complications from HIV/AIDS were the leading cause of death in 1993; in that year women's deaths increased more than men's, and African American women's and Latinas' more than White women's (Hammonds 1995). Forty percent of all AIDS patients under thirteen in New York were Latino (Torre 1993). Women have not been diagnosed as early as men because their symptoms are not so clear-cut and doctors were less likely to look for symptoms of HIV/AIDS in women. Moreover, because there were fewer women involved in clinical trials, they did not receive the better treatment that men received. Ogur (1996) points out that negative stereotypes of HIV-positive women (as drug users and women with multiple sex partners) have affected their visibility and their care. Overall, the number of AIDS cases reported each year is falling, but African Americans and Latinos account for a larger share of the caseload. They were 47 percent and 20 percent, respectively, of people diagnosed with AIDS in 1998 (Morrow 1999b). Women were 23.5 percent of those diagnosed with AIDS in 1998, up from 19.7 percent in 1995 (Morrow 1999b). In 1998–99, young people (aged thirteen–twenty-four) accounted for 15 percent of all reported HIV cases, and women were 49 percent of this group. Seventy-seven percent of women with HIV and 80 percent of women with AIDS were African Americans and Latinas (Centers for Disease Control and Prevention 1999).

Stress. Common stressors include such things as new demands, sadness, or fear due to the death of somebody we love or need, ending or beginning a new relationship, starting a new job, having a baby, and moving. In addition, financial insecurity, job loss, illness, injury, legal problems, and being discriminated against because of race or culture cause stress, especially for poor people and people of color.

Domestic Violence and Sexual Abuse. Women of all race and class groups who are beaten by their partners or suffer emotional violence or sexual abuse are subject to a significant health hazard. (For more on this issue, see Chapter 6.)

Reproductive Health

The ability to become pregnant and have a baby is one of the most fundamental aspects of women's lives. A woman becomes pregnant for many reasons: she wants to have a child; she wants to experience pregnancy and childbirth; she believes it will make her a "real" woman; she hopes it will keep her relationship together or make her partner happy. Some women plan to be pregnant; others get pregnant by accident, still others as a result of being raped. Having a child is a profoundly personal experience, usually with far-reaching consequences for the mother's life, and it is also a public issue. The government has an interest in the numbers of children born, who their parents are, whether they are married, whether they are teens, poor, or recent immigrants. This interest is reinforced by, and also influences, dominant notions of what kinds of women should be mothers. For some women—especially teenagers, lesbians, and mothers receiving welfare—there may be a serious tension between the personal event of pregnancy and societal attitudes to it. African American women have consistently tried to be self-determining in their reproductive lives despite having been used as breeders by slaveholders and despite subsequent systematic state interventions to control their fertility (Dula 1996; Roberts 1997). Dula also argues that the state is interested in the literal reproduction of labor power—producing more workers and citizens—and in keeping down the birthrates of women of color so as to reduce the number of people of color. According to Ventura et al. (2000), Black women have almost twice as many pregnancies as White women. Latinas have substantially more births than either of these groups.

Infant Mortality

The number of infants who die in their first year is an important indicator of infant and maternal health. Infant mortality is commonly a result of low birth weight, poor nutrition, inadequate prenatal care, the mother's level of education, and her overall health, whether due to poor diet, stress, smoking, drinking and drug use, or HIV/AIDS. Infant mortality in babies born between 1983 and 1991 showed Chinese Americans with the lowest rate (5.1 deaths per 1,000 live births), White infants (7.4), Hawaiian and Puerto Rican infants (10.4), Native Americans (12.6), and African American babies with the highest rate (17.1) (National Center for Health Statistics 1996a). More African American babies than babies from other groups were HIV-positive, and more Native American babies suffered from fetal alcohol syndrome.

Infant mortality for babies born in 1997 showed Asian and Pacific Islanders with the lowest rate

(5 deaths per 1,000 live births), White infants (6.0), Puerto Rican (7.9), and African American (13.7) (Ventura et al. 2000). During the 1990s, infant mortality rates decreased as a whole, but Black infants continue to die at twice the rate of White infants and are four times as likely to die from causes related to low birthweight, resembling infant mortality rates of developing countries. In 1997 the rate of sudden infant death syndrome was 2.5 times higher for Native American infants than for White infants. Infant mortality rates are linked to both race and class. They were higher for infants whose mothers did not have prenatal care in the first trimester, did not complete high school, were unmarried, were teenagers or older than forty, or smoked during pregnancy. Rates of first-trimester care are low for Native American, Mexican American, and African American women, compared with White women and Asian American women.

Controlling Fertility

Women's fertility is both a blessing and a liability, and many women in the United States want to control their fertility—perhaps to limit the number of children they have, to avoid pregnancy with a particular partner, to postpone pregnancy until they are older, or to avoid it altogether—or to have the freedom to bear children. To do this they need some combination of sex education that is accurate and culturally appropriate; affordable and reliable birth control; safe, legal, affordable abortion; prenatal care and care through childbirth; health care for children to decrease infant mortality; and alternative insemination. In addition they need good general health care and widespread cultural acceptance that they have a right to control their lives in this way. Once a woman learns that she is pregnant, the decision to have a child or to have an abortion depends on a broad range of factors, including her age, personal circumstances, economic situation, whether or not she already has children, her level of overall health, cultural attitude to abortion, and the circumstances that led her to become pregnant (Arcana 1994; Lunneborg 1992; Townsend and Perkins 1992). As argued by Marsha Saxton in Reading 56, women with disabilities must also fight for the right to have children in the face of a dominant view that they are nonsexual beings who could not cope with being mothers (see also Finger 1990).

The World's Deadliest Disease Is Poverty

- Ten million children born in 1997, worldwide, will die before their fifth birthday, mainly from malnutrition, malaria, acute respiratory infections, measles, and diarrhea.

- Because of the strong preference for male children in many parts of the world, many girls receive inferior nutrition and health care from birth onward.

- Ill health, poor nutrition, and the need to work for wages affect children's attendance and performance at school.

- Complications associated with pregnancy and childbirth (obstructed labor, sepsis, and unsafe abortion) are among the ten leading causes of death and disability for women aged fifteen to forty-four years in developing countries. Maternal conditions, HIV/AIDS, and tuberculosis are the three main causes of the burden of disease in developing regions.

- Most of these conditions can be prevented or cured with improvements in sanitation, clean water supply, better housing, an adequate food supply, general hygiene, and inexpensive vaccines.

Source: World Health Organization.

Birth Control   Barrier methods like condoms and diaphragms have been used for many years. In the 1960s the intrauterine device (IUD), often called the coil, was introduced despite severe unwanted side effects for some women, such as heavy bleeding, pain, and cramps. The pill, introduced around the same time, was the first chemical contraceptive to be taken every day. It affects the whole body continuously, as do Depo-Provera (an injectable contraceptive) and Norplant (implanted under the skin). Poor African American and Native American women and Latinas are much more likely than White women to be encouraged to use these long-acting contraceptives. Official policy seeks to limit their pregnancies and assumes that these women would be unreliable using other methods, thereby continuing the long connection between birth control and eugenics. Depo-Provera is currently used in the United States though previously banned because of its many side effects. The Black Women's Health Network, the National Latina Health Organization, and other women's health advocates have called for its withdrawal as unsafe and have also called attention to the fact that many women using Norplant have had difficulty finding anyone to remove it. In addition, these methods compound many of the health problems suffered by poor women of color, including hypertension, diabetes, and stress. In 1999 American Home Products Corporation, which sells Norplant, agreed to offer cash settlements to 36,000 women who filed suit claiming that they had not been adequately warned about possible negative effects of using Norplant (Morrow 1999a). These included excessive menstrual bleeding, headaches, nausea, dizziness, and depression.

A new barrier method is the female condom, a loosely fitting, polyurethane (not latex) pouch with a semiflexible plastic ring at each end that lines the vagina. Ideally it allows women more control over their reproduction. The pregnancy rate with normal use of the female condom is expected to be similar to the rate with use of the male condom, though early findings show that it has a failure rate of between 21 percent and 26 percent, compared with 13 percent for the male condom (Boston Women's Health Book Collective 1998). Pharmaceutical companies have all but abandoned the field of contraceptive research in this country. Of the nine major companies that were involved in the 1960s and 70s, only two remain. This is due to a decline in funding from the government, international sources, and private foundations, as well as political opposition (Fund for a Feminist Majority 1997).

Abortion   Attitudes toward abortion have varied greatly from one society to another. Historically, the Catholic Church, for example, held the view that the soul did not enter the fetus for at least forty days after conception and allowed abortion up to that point. In 1869, however, Pope Pius IX declared that life begins at conception, and thus all abortion became murder in the eyes of the Church. In the United States up until the mid-nineteenth century, women were allowed to seek an abortion in the early part of pregnancy before they felt the fetus moving, a subjectively determined time, referred to as the quickening. After the Civil War more restrictive abortion laws were passed, partly to increase population and partly to shift authority over women's reproductive lives to the medical profession. By 1900 the only legal ground for an abortion was to save the life of the mother. Many women were forced to bring unwanted pregnancies to term in poverty, illness, or appalling personal circumstances. Thousands died trying to abort themselves or at the hands of "backstreet" abortionists. Some upper- and middle-class women found doctors to perform safe abortions for a high price, though they and the doctors risked prosecution if they were found out, as described by Grace Paley (1998) in her short article, "The Illegal Days." Women with knowledge of herbs or medicine tried to help other women. The Jane Collective organized a clandestine feminist abortion service in the Chicago area in the early 1970s.

In 1973 the landmark case *Roe v. Wade* made abortion legal, though despite that decision, the right to have an abortion has continued to be contested. In 1977 the Hyde Amendment withdrew state funding for abortion for poor women as the first of many restrictions, which include rules requiring waiting periods and parental consent. The 1970s' feminist call for "Free Abortion on Demand" was modified in the 1980s to "A Woman's Right to Choose," in the face of increasingly violent protests in support of fetal rights at abortion clinics, the bombing of clinics, and fatal attacks on doctors known to perform abortions as part of their practice (Jaggar 1994; Petchesky 1990). The Freedom of Access to Clinic Entrances Act (1994) has reduced harassment outside clinics, but there has been a 14 percent reduction in the number of abortion providers, and in 1999, 86 percent of counties had no abortion provider (Family Planning and Choice Protection Bill, H.R. 2624/S1400, 1999). Fewer doctors are being trained to carry out the procedure. Thirty-nine states have adopted laws requiring a young woman to get the consent of, or notify, one or both parents prior to an abortion, and thirty states are enforcing these measures. Congressional opponents continued to challenge abortion rights in the 1990s, and this was a fiercely contested election issue at state and federal level, with well-funded right-wing groups financing antichoice candidates. The Family Planning and Choice Protection Bill (H.R. 2624/S1400, 1999) was introduced in 1999 to safeguard women's rights to abortion and to information about reproductive health, and to address the fact that many women have medical insurance that does not cover contraception.

In 1997, 20 of every 1,000 women of reproductive age (fifteen–forty-four) had abortions, the same rate as the previous two years and the lowest since 1975 (Ventura et al. 2000). Factors assumed to be responsible for this decline include reduced access to abortion, an increased willingness to use contraception, and negative attitudes toward abortion. Fifty-two percent of women who had an abortion in 1997 were twenty-four or younger; most were White and unmarried; and 55 percent of the procedures were done in the first two months of pregnancy. Sixteen states reported drug-induced abortions, using methotrexate. Mifepristone (known as RU-486), designed specifically to end pregnancy was mired in antiabortion politics for many years. The National Organization for Women, the Fund for a Feminist Majority, the National Abortion Rights Action League, and others campaigned for RU-486 to be made available in this country. It has been prescribed in France since 1989. In September 2000 the U.S. Food and Drug Administration approved this drug for use under very specific conditions. It can only be dispensed by physicians who are able to provide a surgical abortion or to refer a woman to such a provider in the small number of cases (estimated at 5 percent) where it does not work. It is expected to be generally available early 2001 and to cost roughly the same as a surgical abortion.

White feminists made abortion the centerpiece of reproductive rights activism in the 1980s and 90s. According to the Black Women's Health Project (1995), when faced with an unintended pregnancy, the percentage of Black women who choose abortion is about equal to that of White women. Because Black women experience unintended pregnancies twice as often as White women, they are twice as likely to have abortions. Women of color have generally seen abortion as one piece in a wider reproductive-health agenda that includes health care for women and children and the freedom to have children.

Sterilization Abuse   Sterilization abuse, rather than the right to abortion, has been a concern of poor women, especially women of color, for many years (Davis 1983a; Roberts 1997). Sterilization, without women's full knowledge or under duress, has been a common practice in the United States for poor Latina, African American, and Native American women. Roberts (1997) notes that sterilization was a key tool in repressing the fertility of women of color in the 1930s, 40s, and 50s. Discussing sterilization of women of color in the 1960s, she comments:

> It is amazing how effective governments— especially our own—are at making sterilization and contraceptives available to women of color, despite their inability to reach these women with prenatal care, drug treatment, and other health services.
>
> *(p. 95)*

By 1982, 24 percent of African American women, 35 percent of Puerto Rican women, and 42 percent of Native American women had been sterilized, compared with 15 percent of White women (Black Women's Health Project 1995). Currently, sterilization is federally funded under the Medicaid program and is free on demand to poor women.

Teen Pregnancy   U.S. teenagers are having sex at younger ages, despite the risk of contracting sexually transmitted diseases and HIV. Unintended teenage pregnancies have declined 15 percent since 1991, apparently because of increased condom use, the adoption of injectable and implant contraceptives (Depo-Provera and Norplant), and the leveling off of teenage sexual activity (Ventura et al. 2000). Analyzed by race and ethnicity, teen birthrates were highest for Mexican American, African American, Native American, and Puerto Rican teenagers. In many cases the fathers of these babies are considerably older than the young women. According to syndicated columnist Ellen Goodman (1996), "two out of every three teenage mothers are impregnated by a man over 20" (p. A17). Twenty percent of the fathers are at least six years older than the mothers. Babies born to teens present a tremendous responsibility for young women and their families. Many community programs seek to prevent teen pregnancy, although sex education in schools and programs to distribute condoms, to prevent the spread of HIV/AIDS as much as pregnancy, have run into opposition from some parents, school boards, and conservative religious groups.

Sexually Transmitted Diseases (STDs)   Sexually transmitted diseases affect some 10 million people each year (Boston Women's Health Book Collective

1992), but women and infants disproportionately bear their long-term effects (Centers for Disease Control and Prevention 1996). The term STD refers to more than twenty diseases, including herpes, genital warts, pubic lice ("crabs"), chlamydia, gonorrhea, syphilis, and HIV. With the exception of gonorrhea, all STDs are increasing at an alarming rate. One reason for this is that women often do not have any symptoms or, if they do, the symptoms are mistaken for something else. Sexually transmitted diseases can affect how a woman feels about her body and her partner and can make her infertile or more susceptible to other diseases. Knowing about safer sexual practices is important in reducing the risk of sexually transmitted diseases, including HIV/AIDS.

Toxic Hazards   Working in toxic workplaces is a serious health hazard for many poor women and disproportionately for women of color. Some companies have kept women out of the most hazardous work—often the highest paid among blue-collar jobs—or required that they be sterilized first, to avoid being sued if these workers later give birth to babies with disabilities (Chavkin 1984).

Medicalization of Reproductive Life

Childbirth   Before there were male gynecologists, midwives helped women through pregnancy and childbirth (Ehrenreich and English 1978). As medicine became professionalized in the nineteenth century, gynecology and obstetrics developed as an area of medical specialization. Doctors eroded the position of midwives and ignored or scorned their knowledge as "old wives' tales." Largely for the convenience of the doctor, women began to give birth lying on their backs, perhaps the hardest position in which to deliver a child. Forceps and various painkilling medications were widely used. From the 1950s onward cesarean sections (C-sections) became more common, often for the doctors' convenience or from fear of malpractice suits. In 1998, 21.2 percent of births in the United States were C-sections, the highest rate in the world (Martin et al. 1999). The past twenty-five years have seen a further extension of this medicalization process as doctors monitor pregnancy from the earliest stages with a battery of new techniques such as amniocentesis, sonograms, and ultrasound. Although this technology allows

medical practitioners, and through them, pregnant women, to know details about the health and condition of the fetus, as well as its sex, it also changes women's experiences of pregnancy and childbirth and can erode their knowledge of and confidence in their bodily processes. In Reading 57, Joy Harjo describes changes in Native American women's experiences of childbirth.

Menopause   Another aspect of this medicalization process concerns menopause. This natural life process is increasingly treated as a disease rather than as a series of complex bodily and emotional changes. Many middle-aged women are advised to take hormone-replacement therapy (HRT) for the rest of their lives to control the symptoms of menopause (Klein and Dumble 1994; Komesaroff, Rothfield, and Daly 1997).

Reproductive Technologies   Technologies like in vitro fertilization (IVF), in which a woman's eggs are fertilized by sperm outside her body and the fertilized embryo is then implanted into her womb, are an important development. They push the medicalization of pregnancy and childbirth one step further and hold out the hope that infertile couples or postmenopausal women will be able to have children. Bearing a child as a surrogate mother under contract to an infertile couple is one way a relatively poor young woman, usually White, can earn $10,000 or so, plus medical expenses, for nine months' work. Fertility clinics also need ovum donors and seek to harvest the eggs of young, college-educated women from a range of specified racial and ethnic groups. Infertility treatments so far have had a spectacularly low success rate, and they are very expensive. They are aimed at middle- and upper-middle-class women as a way of widening individual choice. Infertility may stem from a range of causes such as sexually transmitted diseases, the effects of IUDs, delayed childbearing, and occupational and environmental factors. Infertility rates were lower in the 1990s than in previous decades, but this issue has a higher profile nowadays because of technological developments.

These reproductive technologies open up an array of economic, legal, and moral questions (Donchin and Purdy 1999; Hubbard 1990). Are they liberating for women? for which women? and at what costs? Some feminists have argued that women's biology and the ability to reproduce have been used to justify their social and economic subordination. Shulamith Firestone (1970), for example, was convinced that women's liberation requires freedom from biological reproduction and looked forward to developments in reproductive technology that would make it possible for a fetus to develop outside the womb. This is in stark contrast to Katz-Rothman (1986) and the myriad women who believe that if women lose their ability to reproduce they lose a "quintessential female experience" (p. 111). Other feminist critics of reproductive technologies focus on their invasiveness and consumers' lack of power over and knowledge about these methods, as compared with that of medical experts or "medocrats" (Arditti, Klein, and Minden 1984; Corea 1985, 1987; Lublin 1998; Petchesky 1997; Stanworth 1987).

Health and Aging

The health of women in middle age and later life is partly linked to how healthy they were when they were younger. The effects of stress, poor nutrition, smoking, or not getting enough exercise build up over time. Exposure to toxic chemicals, the physical and emotional toll of pregnancies, accidents, injuries, and caring for others all affect our health as we grow older. A lifetime of poverty often translates into poor health later in life.

On average, women in the United States live longer than men, with a life expectancy of 79 years for women and 72.3 years for men. The majority of old people in the United States are women, who accounted for 60 percent of those aged 65 and over and 72 percent of the population over 85 in the early 1990s (Brennan, Winklepleck, and MacNee 1994). African American women have a life expectancy of 74.7 years, significantly lower than that of White women (79.9 years) but much higher than that of African American men (67.2 years), while Asian Americans of both sexes live several years longer than Whites (National Center for Health Statistics 1999b). If African Americans live to be 85, they often live longer than Whites.

Of course, the mere fact of living longer says nothing about the quality of a person's life, and older women suffer higher rates of disabling diseases such as arthritis, Alzheimer's, diabetes, deafness, cataracts, broken bones, digestive conditions, and osteoporosis than do men (Doyal 1995). Women over 45 use hospitals less often than men do, reflecting a basic health difference between the sexes: men are more likely to have fatal diseases, whereas women have chronic conditions that worsen with age. These lingering diseases seriously affect the quality of women's lives. Older women often have to accept the fact that they need support and care. They have to face their changed looks, physical limitations, and the loss of independence and loved ones, which calls on their emotional and spiritual resources, including patience, forbearance, optimism, and religious faith. Older women's health is also adversely affected by caring for their sick partners when they themselves are old and sick. Healey (1997) argues that confronting ageism in society, as well as individual women's negative feelings about aging, is a must for women's mental health, a point made by Barbara Macdonald (Reading 18, Chapter 3).

Mental and Emotional Health

Mental Illness in Women: Difficulties of Diagnosis

Women are overrepresented among people with some sort of mental illness and are most likely to be diagnosed with depression. Men are most likely to be diagnosed with alcohol- and drug-related conditions. There are many problems with diagnostic categories, however, and a great deal of room for interpretation based on individual and cultural factors. The American Psychological Association did not drop homosexuality from its list of mental disorders until 1973. Lesbianism was thought to be caused by dominant mothers and weak fathers or, conversely, by girls' having exclusively male role models. Those who "came out" in the 1950s and 1960s risked being sent to psychotherapists or mental institutions for a "cure." Since the 1980s, young women who do not conform to traditional gender roles may be diagnosed with "gender identity disorder."

Hopelessness and anger at one's life circumstances—which may include childhood sexual abuse, rape, domestic violence, poverty, homelessness, or simply dull routines—are not irrational reactions. Women's symptoms can seem vague to doctors, who may not really try to find out what is troubling them. In Reading 58, Eileen Nechas and Denise Foley discuss this issue in connection with alcohol abuse. Even when understood by doctors, women's traumas and difficulties are not easy to cure. According to the U.S. Department of Health and Human Services (1996), in 1990–92, almost 50 percent of all women between fifteen and fifty-four had experienced symptoms suggestive of a psychiatric disorder at some time in their lives; however, only 55 percent of them had ever received mental health treatment. More women than men attempt suicide, but men are more likely to use guns and to be successful, whereas women tend to use drug overdoses and are often found before their attempts are fatal. Patients in mental hospitals represent a relatively small proportion of those who are suffering mentally and emotionally. In general, women are admitted to mental hospitals as inpatients in roughly the same numbers as men. Women aged twenty-five–forty-four are more likely than women in other age groups to be admitted to a psychiatric hospital.

One reason why more women are classified as having mental illness may be that the proportion of women seeking help for personal or emotional problems is twice as high as it is for men. It increases with educational attainment for both men and women. For both men and women, more persons who were formerly married seek help than do those currently married or never married. Employment is also a factor here, with a higher percentage of men and a slightly higher percentage of women who are unemployed seeking help (Dargan 1995). However, one cannot infer from these data that everyone who "seeks help" is doing so voluntarily; sometimes seeing a counselor or therapist is required by a social service agency or is a condition of probation. Voluntarily seeking help for emotional problems is linked to one's ability to pay, finding a suitable therapist, and cultural attitudes toward this kind of treatment.

Many people of all classes and racial groups attempt to deal with the pain and difficulty of their lives through drugs and alcohol. Frederica Daly (1994) notes that rates of alcoholism, homicide, and suicide among Native Americans are significantly higher than the national rates. In the United States, drug addiction is generally thought of as a crime rather than as a health issue. We discuss it further under the topic of crime and criminalization in Chapter 10, but we also see it as a symptom of stress brought on by

the pressures of life, often caused by social and economic inequality. There are far fewer drug-treatment programs than required, and fewer for women than for men.

Feminist Perspectives on Mental Illness

A number of feminist writers have argued that contemporary approaches to mental distress, as illness, can be harmful to women (Chesler 1972; Ehrenreich and English 1978; Russell 1995; Showalter 1987; Ussher 1991). Russell (1995) briefly traces the history of definitions of madness from medieval Europe, where it was thought of as a combination of error and sin. During the seventeenth century, economic crises and rising unemployment in Europe prompted local officials to build houses of confinement for beggars, drunks, vagabonds, and other poor people and petty criminals, as well as for those who were thought mad. Through the eighteenth and nineteenth centuries, psychiatry gradually developed as a new medical specialty and asylums in Europe and the United States were headed by doctors, who theorized that much mental distress experienced by women was due to their reproductive capacities and sexuality. Hysteria, thought to be due to a disturbance of the womb, became a catchall category to describe women's mental illness. (The English word *hysterical* comes from the Greek word *husterikos,* meaning "of the womb.") Showalter (1987) and Chesler (1972) show how definitions of madness have been used to suppress women's creativity, education, and political involvement. Nineteenth-century White upper- and middle-class women who wanted to write, paint, travel, or speak out in public on issues of the day were assumed by their husbands — and by psychiatrists — to be insane. Charlotte Perkins Gilman's powerful fictional work *The Yellow Wallpaper,* for example, describes this experience and was written as a result of having lived through it. In the twentieth century, depression and premenstrual syndrome (PMS) replaced "hysteria" as stock phrases used in describing mental illness in women.

Feminist writers offer scathing critiques of the alleged objectivity of much contemporary mental health theorizing and of the value judgments and blatant sexism involved in many diagnostic categories like depression, behavioral disorders, and personality disorders that affect women more than men. Symptoms for these disorders are often very general, vague, and overlapping, and, according to Russell (1995), there is little agreement among practitioners as to what conditions are indicated by the symptoms. She questions the assumption that there is a biological or neurological basis for mental distress and argues that drug therapies based on this assumption have very mixed results in practice. Rather, she points to many external factors affecting women's mental equilibrium, including childhood sexual abuse, domestic violence, restricted educational or economic opportunities, and pressure to look beautiful, to be thin, to be compliant wives and long-suffering mothers, any of which could reasonably make women depressed or "crazy." Fallon (1994) notes that young White women from middle- and upper-middle-class families currently suffer from eating disorders such as anorexia and bulimia in what are described as epidemic proportions, especially on college campuses (also see Chapter 3). This condition is less common for women of color and is relatively unknown outside industrialized countries, all factors that point to its cultural basis.

Medical Care: Business as Usual?

Since the seventeenth century, Western thought has consistently viewed organic, bodily processes as separate from those of the mind. The Western medical model separates physical, mental, emotional, and spiritual states of well-being and focuses on illness and disease rather than on the wholeness of people's lives, often treating symptoms rather than causes (Candib 1995). For example, though stressors generated by racism are a strong influence in the hypertension that disproportionately affects African Americans, the medical response is to treat the symptoms with medication, rather than to involve doctors, patients, and the wider society in combating racism. Similarly, many women are prescribed antidepressants rather than being empowered and supported in changing their life circumstances. Kat Duff (1993) comments: "Our concepts of physical and psychological health have become one-sidedly identified with the heroic qualities most valued in our culture: youth, activity, productivity, independence, strength, confidence, and optimism" (p. 37). This Western medical model also contributes to fantasies of immortality to be achieved by life-prolonging

surgeries and drug treatments, as well as expensive cosmetic surgeries.

Because medical care is provided on a fee-paying basis in the United States, the medical industry has many of the characteristics of any business venture (see the discussion of the global economy in Chapter 7). Hospitals are bought and sold like factories. Hospitals, nursing homes, and clinics that cannot balance their books are forced to lower their standards of treatment or are taken over by more profitable companies. The emphasis is on high-tech treatments, particularly drug therapies and surgery, as these are the most profitable for drug companies and manufacturers of medical equipment. Most people have benefited from vaccines and antibiotics, and the use of drugs and surgery may improve the lives of cancer patients, give relief from constant arthritic pain, or restore good vision to elderly people with cataracts. However, this overall emphasis has severely skewed the range of treatments available. It has led to an overproduction of intensive-care equipment, for example, while many people, especially the poor, have little access to the most rudimentary medical services. Vincente Navarro (1993) noted that 65 percent of medical expenditures in the United States went to *curing* disease even though more people — especially women — suffer from chronic conditions for which *caring* is the more appropriate mode of treatment. This emphasis on drugs, surgery, and high-tech procedures has also shaped public policy through the testing and use of new drugs, the routine use of mammograms in breast cancer screening, sonograms and amniocentesis in pregnancy, and the prevalence of hysterectomies and births by cesarean section.

Paying for Medical Care

How we pay for medical care as a nation and who can afford it are questions much discussed in recent years, especially in connection with proposals for a national health plan put forward by President Clinton in his first term of office. This plan was successfully opposed by medical insurers, some doctors, and the American Medical Association, who convinced enough voters, editorial writers, and members of Congress that standards of care would inevitably decline under a nationalized health system. The United States is the only industrialized country in the world, except South Africa, that does not have such a system.

Although 70 percent of people in the United States do have some kind of private medical insurance (Campbell 1999), this often covers only emergencies and hospitalization. Only 7 to 8 percent of participants in group plans are fully covered for hospital maternity charges. In the early 1990s, over 5 million women of reproductive age had private insurance that did not cover maternity care at all, and some 550,000 babies a year were born to uninsured mothers, many of them teens (Brennan, Winklepleck, and MacNee 1994). Adela de la Torre (1993) notes that only 60 percent of Latinas initiate prenatal care in the first trimester of pregnancy, at least in part because they lack insurance coverage; by contrast, 80 percent of White women seek early prenatal care. Women's Wellness programs are currently a profitable screening service provided by hospitals, though many insurance policies do not cover them, and they are not always culturally sensitive for all women's needs, especially women of color, women with disabilities, and lesbians. Forty-nine percent of large-group insurance plans do not routinely cover any kind of contraception, including some health plans offered to federal, state, and city workers (Center for Reproductive Law and Policy n.d.).

For most people who have private medical insurance (62 percent), this is employment-related. The figures for men and women with private coverage are very similar. Twenty-five percent of the population receive government coverage — Medicaid or Medicare. More women (11.7 percent) have government coverage than men (8.3 percent), reflecting Medicaid eligibility criteria that focus on mothers and children, and the greater numbers of women among the elderly who rely on Medicare. Cuts in Medicaid and Medicare during the 1990s mean that some of these people lost medical coverage altogether or in part. In 1998, 16 percent of the U.S. population was uninsured (U.S. Bureau of the Census 1999a). This rose to 30 percent for those in the $14,000 to $25,000 income group and to 35 percent among people with the lowest family income (less than $14,000). In the highest income group ($50,000 or more), only 6 percent had no health-care coverage. Young adults between the ages of eighteen and twenty-four constituted the highest proportion (30 percent) of uninsured among age groups (Campbell 1999). These statistics may be misleading, since they do not distinguish those with coverage for only part of the year from those insured the entire year,

and since some people are insured by more than one plan.

Analyzed by race, the data for medical coverage show approximately 12 percent Whites, 21.5 percent Blacks, and 35 percent Latinos with no insurance (Campbell 1999). These people are concentrated in small businesses with low rates of unionization or are working part time or on a temporary basis. Immigration status is another factor affecting the rate of medical coverage. In 1995, a higher proportion of immigrants (33 percent) than those born in the United States (13.6 percent) was without health-care insurance. Among the immigrants, naturalized citizens had a coverage rate more than double that of noncitizens — 40 percent versus 16 percent. Poor immigrants were even worse off, with 52 percent of them uninsured (National Center for Health Statistics 1996a). Recent immigrants are often employed in low-paying jobs without benefits. It is not surprising, then, to note that states with large immigrant populations have the highest proportion of uninsured people: Arizona, California, Louisiana, New Mexico, and Texas (National Center for Health Statistics 1996a). Since the mid-1990s, changes in government policy have sought to bar undocumented people and some legal immigrants from public health-care services, including emergency care. Undocumented women may risk jeopardizing their work and residence in the United States if they seek medical care for themselves or their children (Calvo 1996).

Managed Care

Hospitals, health maintenance organizations (HMOs), and nursing homes increasingly use a managed-care approach. In 1994 almost half the people in the United States with medical insurance were enrolled in a managed-care plan. Ellen Freudenheim (1995) defines this as "a comprehensive approach to health care delivery that encompasses planning and coordination of care, patient and provider education, monitoring of care quality, and cost control" (p. 155). It works on a prepayment system: If the care provided costs more than the prepayment, the HMO loses money. Although the managed-care approach started out with an emphasis on prevention and coordination among providers, there is always pressure to lower costs in order to increase profits. Treatment tends to be parceled out according to preset formulas that may not meet individual needs. As childbirth became medicalized, for example, women used to be hospitalized for a week or more. This was gradually cut back by insurers to the point where many women had to go home after only one night (increased to two in 1996). Medicaid is moving to a managed-care approach, though working out the cost of care for the elderly or chronically sick is difficult. In Reading 59, Annette Dula creates the character of Miss Mildred, an elderly African American woman, to make the point that people are not standardized machines and that they need medical care that is appropriate physically, emotionally, culturally, and financially.

Other Barriers to the Use of Medical Services

Other barriers to people's use of medical services, beyond those imposed by managed care and lack of insurance, include fear of treatment, transportation difficulties, long waiting times, not being able to take time off work or losing pay for doing so, child-care responsibilities, language and cultural differences, and residential segregation, which may mean that there are few medical facilities in some communities of color or rural communities. Most inner cities have large teaching hospitals that treat local people, predominantly people of color, in their emergency rooms, but this treatment may be slanted toward the educational needs of the hospital's medical students rather than to the health needs of the patients. Taken overall, women visit doctors and other health practitioners more often than men do. In 1992, on average, for people between the ages of fifteen and sixty-four, women made 66 percent more visits than men. African Americans tend to be diagnosed or seek treatment later than Whites for many chronic diseases, which may reduce the effectiveness of treatment and their ability to survive. Once under medical treatment, they receive what official reports describe as "less aggressive" treatment than Whites.

Gender and Race Bias in Medical Research

Despite the relative frequency of women's visits to the doctor, there is a clear male bias in medical knowledge (Candib 1995). Most doctors in the United States are White, upper-middle-class men, and a meager 13 percent of government research funds was spent on women's health in the early 1990s (Doyal 1995). Federal law now requires that women and men of color be included in research, but it will be a long time before this makes a big difference to the state of medical knowledge. Heart disease, which affects both men and women, was thought of as a man's disease for many years. As a result, it was studied much more than breast cancer (Dickersin and Schnaper 1996). Research samples have mainly consisted of White men even when women's illnesses were being studied. Preliminary testing of antidepressant medications—prescribed mainly to women—was done only on men, despite evidence suggesting a difference in the drugs' effects between men and women. Research into health problems that men and women share was done on men and made to seem universal, not accounting for specific factors that might affect women differently. For example, the NIH-sponsored five-year Physicians Health Study concerning the effects of aspirin on heart disease used a sample of 22,071 men and no women, even though heart disease is also the number one killer of women (Nechas and Foley 1994). Recommended drug treatments are also tested on men and then prescribed for women on the assumption that they will be equally effective, though whether this is so is not known (Nechas and Foley 1994). Although women make up one of the fastest-growing groups to contract HIV/AIDS, there has been very little research concerning women and AIDS. Similarly, there is little research on the long-term effects of birth control pills, estrogen-replacement therapy prescribed for menopausal women, or safe, reliable forms of contraception. Too little is known about the health needs of women of color, older women, and women with disabilities (Gill 1996; Krieger and Fee 1996). Ann Pollinger Haas gives a historical view of lesbian health issues (noting limitations that persist today. Reading 60).

Caring for People with Disabilities and Chronic Illness: A Labor of Love?

An aspect of health that generally affects women much more than men is caring for relatives and friends. Many people with disabilities and chronic illness rely on others to provide meals, shop, do laundry, clean, help with personal care such as bathing and dressing, and give emotional support, love, and encouragement. Over 3 million women in the United States provide personal assistance to family members who are sick or disabled, and over

10 million women provide care to people outside their own households, usually their elderly parents and their husbands' elderly parents. This caretaking of elders may go on for as much as fifteen years and often overlaps with the women's other responsibilities—holding jobs, taking care of growing children, and managing homes. This regimen can be very trying; it involves physical and emotional stress and added expense and can seriously affect the quality of life and health for women in their middle years, who may have to give up opportunities for education, social life, or leisure-time activities. These women may be reluctant and resentful at times but accept their situation as part of what it means to be a good wife or daughter. It is important to recognize that women who care for others need support and respite themselves.

Health as Wellness

Requirements for Good Health

Health is not just the absence of illness, as implied by the medical model described earlier. Feeling well involves a complex mix of physical, mental, and emotional factors. Many aspects of life are not under our control. For example, living in damp housing or near a busy freeway or polluted industrial area, working in hazardous factories and mines, being exposed to toxic pesticides in agricultural work, doing repetitive tasks all day, and sitting in the same position for long periods of time are all aspects of daily life that can compromise one's health. The many newspaper and magazine articles that focus on individual lifestyle factors—diet, cigarette smoking, weight, exercise, and a positive attitude to coping with stress—urge us to take more personal responsibility for our health. Although this is valuable advice, lifestyle is only part of the story. Rita Arditti and Tatiana Schreiber present data on links between breast cancer and environmental contamination in Reading 55. Cancer research efforts that focus on individual neurological or genetic factors miss this crucial environmental connection.

Health requires clean water, air, and food, adequate housing, safety and security, healthy working conditions, and emotional and material supports. Thus, seemingly unconnected issues like poverty, racism, and sexism are also health issues. Illness is not just a series of symptoms to be eliminated but an indicator that our bodies are telling us something important. Many critics of the current medical system differentiate health care from medical treatment and argue that the medical model, with its emphasis on high-tech equipment and procedures, drug treatments and surgeries, does not adequately protect or promote health.

Feminist Approaches to Wellness

Women's health has been a central issue for activists for the past thirty years or more (Norsigian 1996). Sia Nowrojee and Jael Silliman discuss contemporary Asian women's health organizing in Reading 61. Because many women's health needs are not currently met under the current system, feminist health practitioners and advocates urge a fundamental shift in emphasis toward a more holistic system of health care that recognizes that physical, emotional, and mental health are intimately connected and which emphasizes self-education, prevention, self-help, alternative therapies, a restructuring of medical financing, and a wider provision of basic facilities. As a means to this end, and depending on their view of the cause of the problem, some groups concentrate on changing current health policies while others choose to work with self-help projects on the grounds that this is a more effective use of their time and resources. Still other groups have been active in opposing Operation Rescue and other so-called pro-life organizations that have tried to close down clinics where abortions are performed.

Self-Education and Preventive Care   Preventing illness through self-education has low priority in the United States, and beyond basic immunization for infants and some minimal sex education for teens, it has generally been left to interested practitioners, organizations like the American Cancer Society, or self-help health-care projects. It involves learning to listen to our bodies and becoming more conscious of what they can tell us; learning to eat well and to heal common ailments with home remedies; taking regular exercise; quitting smoking; doing breast self-exams; and practicing safer sex. Self-education and preventive care also include various types of self-help, such as programs dealing with substance abuse or codependence. Many of these, like Alcoholics Anonymous, Al-Anon, Narcotics Anonymous, and other twelve-step programs, have been successful in helping people change negative habits and attitudes, though they usually do not address macro-level factors like institutionalized racism, sexism, and heterosexism. A self-help approach also means taking a greater degree of personal responsibility for one's health and being able to make informed decisions about possible remedies and treatments, rather than simply consuming services. Finally, preventive care encompasses all the creative activities and projects, like dancing, music, poetry, sports, and homemaking, that give us joy and make us feel alive.

Alternative Therapies   Therapies such as acupuncture, homeopathy, deep tissue massage, and chiropractic care that do not rely on drug treatments and surgery may be highly beneficial for a range of complaints. Although they have been scorned as quackery by many mainstream medical practitioners, they are being used more often, sometimes in conjunction with Western medicine. At present most alternative therapies are not financially accessible even for people with medical insurance, as they are not routinely covered, and they are usually available only in larger cities.

Reform of Health Care Financing   As mentioned earlier, a proposal for a national health plan put forward by President Clinton in his first term of office was abandoned because of lack of political, financial, and professional support. Many advocates for women's health argue for a fundamental change in the way health care is paid for. In May 1993, for example, the Women's Convergence for National Health Care, attended by over five hundred women from twenty states, called for a universal health-care plan to provide equal access, comprehensive benefits, freedom to choose doctors and other caregivers, health education and prevention, reproductive health, public account-

ability, and progressive, fair financing (Baker 1993). Participants argued that universal health care is a major component of a social justice agenda.

Feminist Health Projects   Such projects have been active since the early 1970s. Examples include courses in women's health; informal self-health groups like the Bloomington Women's Health Collective (Bloomington, Ind.); women's health centers (e.g., in Concord, N.H., and Burlington, Vt.); campaigns for reproductive rights (e.g., National Abortion Rights Action League and regional affiliates) or public funding for breast cancer research and treatment (e.g., Women's Community Cancer Project, Cambridge, Mass.); community health campaigns (e.g., Boston Health Access Project); and national organizations like the Black Women's Health Project (Atlanta), the National Asian Women's Health Organization (San Francisco), the National Latina Health Organization (Oakland, Calif.), the National Women's Health Network (Washington, D.C.), and the Native American Women's Health and Education Resource Center (Lake Andes, S.Dak.). The Boston Women's Health Book Collective's groundbreaking book *Our Bodies, Ourselves* first started as mimeographed notes for a course in women's health and was later developed for publication. It has become an essential resource on women's health and sexuality for women of all ages. A key emphasis of this women's health movement is a recognition of the politics of health and illness and that individual health is inescapably linked to macro-level factors.

Feminist perspectives, research, lobbying, and policy making have significantly changed how women's health is perceived and how women are treated as patients. There is still a great deal to be done before quality health care is available to all women in this country.

◆◆◆
Questions for Reflection

As you read and discuss this chapter, consider these questions:

1. How do you know when you're healthy? Sick?

2. How can you learn more about your own body and your health?

3. What is a health crisis? For an individual person? At the national level?

4. Who should pay for health care? How? Why do you think this?

5. How does an individual, a family, or a society construct definitions of illness?

6. How do you define reproductive health? Reproductive rights?

◆◆◆
Taking Action

1. List all the steps you take to care for yourself and any additional ones you could take.

2. Find out more about what your family and community consider effective self-care practices.

3. Find out where women can go to keep healthy or get quality health care in your community.

FIFTY-FIVE
◆◆◆

Breast Cancer: The Environmental Connection—a 1998 Update
Rita Arditti and Tatiana Schreiber

Today in the United States we live in the midst of a cancer epidemic. Cancer is currently the second leading cause of death; one out of every three people will get some kind of cancer, and one out of four will die from it. [Twenty-nine] years have gone by since the National Cancer Act was signed, yet the treatments offered to cancer patients are the same ones as those offered fifty years ago: surgery, radiation, and chemotherapy (or slash, burn, and poison, as they are called bitterly by both patients and increasingly disappointed professionals). And in spite of sporadic pronouncements from the cancer establishment, survival rates for the three main cancer killers — lung, breast, and colorectal cancer — have remained virtually unchanged and depressingly low.

In the 1960s and 1970s environmental activists and a few scientists emphasized that cancer was linked to environmental contamination, and their concerns began to make an impact on the public awareness of the disease.[1] In the 1980s and early 1990s, however, with an increasingly conservative political climate and concerted efforts on the part of industry to play down the importance of chemicals in causing cancer, we were presented with a new image of the disease. It was portrayed as an individual problem that could be overcome only with the help of experts and then only if one had the money and

the know-how to recruit them for one's personal survival efforts. The emphasis on personal responsibility, lifestyle, and genetic factors has reached absurd proportions. People with cancer are asked "why they brought this disease on themselves" and why they don't work harder at "getting well." Testing for "cancer genes" is presented as one of the most important new developments in cancer research, with little or no evidence of the usefulness of this testing for the vast majority of the population.

While people with cancer should be encouraged not to fall into victim roles and to do everything they can to strengthen their immune systems (our primary line of defense against cancer), the sociopolitical and economic dimensions of cancer have been pushed almost completely out of the picture by the conservative backlash of our times. "Blaming the victim" is a convenient a way to avoid looking at the larger environmental and social issues that frame individual experiences. This retrenchment has happened in spite of the fact that many lines of evidence indicate that cancer *is* an environmental disease. Even the most conservative scientists[2] agree that approximately 80% of all cancers are avoidable and in some way related to environmental factors (this includes smoking). Support for this view relies on four lines of evidence: (1) the dramatic differences in the incidence of cancer between communities (the incidence of cancer among people of a given age in different parts of the world can vary by a factor of 10 to 100); (2) changes in the incidence of cancer (either lower or higher rates) in groups that migrate to a new country; (3) changes in the incidence of particular types of cancer over time; and (4) the actual identification of specific causes of certain cancers (such as beta-naphthylamine, responsible for an epidemic of bladder cancer among dye workers employed at DuPont factories in the 1930s).[3] Other well-known environmentally linked cancers are lung cancer (linked to asbestos, arsenic, chromium, several other chemicals, and, of course, smoking); endometrial cancer, linked to estrogen use; thyroid cancer, often the result of childhood exposure to irradiation; and liver cancer, linked to exposure to vinyl chloride.

The inescapable conclusion is that if cancer is largely environmental in origin, it is largely preventable. "Environment" as we use it here includes not only air, water, and soil, but also our diets, medical procedures, and living and working conditions. This means that the food we eat, the water we drink, the air we breathe, the radiation to which we are exposed, where we live, what kind of work we do, and the stress that we suffer are responsible for up to 80 percent of all cancers. In this article we discuss some of the recent research on possible environmental links to breast cancer, the controversies that surround it, and the need for prevention-oriented research and political organization around cancer and the environment.

Breast Cancer and Chemicals

In the United States breast cancer has reached epidemic proportions: in 1998, estimates are that 178,700 women will develop breast cancer and 43,900 will die from it.[4] In other words, in 1998 nearly as many women will die from breast cancer as the number of American lives lost in the entire Vietnam War. Cancer is the leading cause of death among women of ages thirty-five to fifty-four, and approximately one-third of these deaths are due to breast cancer. African American women occupy a special place in this picture: in spite of the fact that their breast cancer incidence rate is lower than white women's, African American women have a higher breast cancer mor-

tality rate and are more likely to get breast cancer at an earlier age.[5] Evidence indicates that breast cancer fulfills three of the four lines of reasoning regarding its nature as an environmental disease: (1) the rates of incidence of breast cancer between communities can vary by a factor of 7, (2) the rate for breast cancer among populations that have migrated conforms to that of their new residence within one generation, and (3) the lifetime incidence of breast cancer in the United States has increased from one in twenty in 1950 to one in eight in the 1990s.

A number of factors have been linked to breast cancer: age (the risk of breast cancer increases with age), a first blood relative (parent, sibling, or child) with the disease, early onset of menstruation, late menopause, no childbearing or late age at first full-term pregnancy, and higher education and socioeconomic status. However, for the overwhelming majority of breast cancer patients (70 to 80 percent), their illness is not clearly linked to any of these factors. Furthermore, only 5 to 7 percent of breast cancer is hereditary, making the discovery of the so-called breast cancer genes, BRCA1 and BRCA2, irrelevant to the vast majority of breast cancer patients. As for those women who may carry one of these genes, Kay Dickerson, an epidemiologist who has had breast cancer and is herself a likely carrier of the gene, has put it clearly: "We have nothing to offer women who test positive."[6]

In the early 1990s work began to appear focusing on the chemical–breast cancer connection. Elihu Richter and Jerry Westin reported that Israel had seen a real drop in breast cancer mortality in the decade of 1976–1986, despite a worsening of all known risk factors.[7] Westin and Richter could not account for the drop solely in terms of demographic changes or improved medical intervention. Instead, they suspected that the change may have been related to the 1978 ban on three carcinogenic pesticides (benzene hexachloride, lindane, and DDT) that heavily contaminated milk and milk products in Israel. These pesticides are known as inducers of a superfamily of enzymes called the cytochrome P450 system. These enzymes can promote cancer growth, can weaken the immune system, and are capable of destroying anticancer drugs. The researchers suspected that these induced enzymes could have increased the virulence of breast cancer in women and thereby increased the mortality rates. They speculated that the removal of the pesticides from the diet resulted in much less virulent cancer and reduced mortality from breast cancer. Other researchers then began to directly measure chemical residues in women who had breast cancer and compare them with those who didn't. Mary Wolff and Frank Falk did a case-controlled study of fifty women in which a number of chemical residues, including DDE (a DDT metabolite) and PCBs, were measured, and they found that these were significantly elevated in cases of malignant disease as compared with non-malignant cases.[8] A follow-up study by Wolff, Paolo Toniolo, and colleagues examined DDE and PCB residues in stored blood samples of women enrolled in the New York University Women's Health Study between 1985 and 1991. The study matched 58 women who developed breast cancer with 171 similar women who did not. After controlling for confounding factors (such as first-degree family history of breast cancer, lifetime lactation, and age at first full-term pregnancy), the data showed a four-fold increase in the risk of developing breast cancer for women who had a higher level of DDE in their blood sera.[9] Another study compared data among women in different racial groups[10] and looked at the level of DDE and PCBs in the stored blood of white, Asian American, and African American women who developed breast cancer, as compared with matched controls. At first glance, this study did not reveal statistically significant differences. However, reanalysis of the data showed that the white and African American subjects with the highest level of exposure to the chemicals were two to three times more likely to acquire breast cancer than those with lower levels.[11]

A critical point to bear in mind in assessing these studies is that DDE and PCBs in our bodies may be associated with other chemicals that have not yet been identified. Also, in the real world we are exposed to dozens of chemicals, many of which have effects on our metabolism and may potentiate each other. So although these studies are important, they hardly reflect the conditions in which we live.

Additional research has implicated plastics in breast cancer development because of their ability to leach substances that have estrogenic effects. Ana Soto and Carlos Sonneschein discovered this effect unexpectedly while studying the role of estrogen on the development of breast cancer cells in the lab. Using methods they had long successfully employed to remove all estrogen from their blood samples, they were surprised to find one day that their samples continued to show estrogenic activity. The reason turned out to be that a new type of centrifuge tube they were using was leaching *p*-nonyl-phenol into the cultures, causing the estrogenic effect. Nonylphenols are part of a group of compounds, alkylphenols, that are widely used in plastics, as lubricants in condoms, and in spermicides and vaginal foams. While many of these chemicals are individually present in the environment at levels too low to produce an effect of their own, Soto reports that "when you take the 10 estrogenic chemicals and combine each of them at one-tenth of their effective dose, you now have an effective dose."[12]

Out of these (and other) studies a hypothesis started to emerge. It is a generally accepted fact that estrogen, a hormone produced by the ovaries, is a risk factor for breast cancer. The hormone influences cell growth by binding to an intracellular protein known as the estrogen receptor. Complexes of the hormone and receptor can bind to DNA in the nucleus and activate the genes that direct cell division, increasing the likelihood that a carcinogenic mutation will take place. The new hypothesis suggested that certain substances that are introduced into the body from the environment mimic the action of estrogen produced in cells or alter the hormone's activity. These substances were named xenoestrogens (foreign estrogens), and some of them, found in pesticides, drugs, fuel, and plastics, could amplify the effects of estrogen and promote breast cancer. However, other xenoestrogens (phytoestrogens), found in plant foods such as soy, cauliflower, and broccoli, could alter the hormone's activity and protect against breast cancer. This helps to explain the lower breast cancer incidence of Asian women whose diets are rich in phytoestrogens.[13] Timing of exposure may also be an important factor in breast cancer development. According to Devra Lee Davis and Leon Bradlow, "Various investigations suggest that unusually high exposure to estrogen during prenatal development, adolescence, or the decade or so before menopause primes breast cells to become malignant. At those times, the estrogen presumably programs the cells to respond strongly to stimulation later in life."[14]

The work on xenoestrogens and other endocrine-disrupting materials suggests that they may also be contributing to abnormal development in animals and to a range of reproductive disorders in men worldwide, such as testicular cancer, undescended testis, urinary tract defects, and lowered sperm counts. For some researchers, the disruption of the hormonal balance of many species and the transgenerational effects are, in the long run, even more frightening than their carcinogenic effects. Carlos Sonneschein believes that "the effect of these pollutants can wipe out the whole species. . . . It's not that one species disappears and that's it; the disappearance of one species affects others, for example, when we don't have bees, fruits and vegetables are affected. . . . One has to have a strategy that concerns both the short-term and the long-term effects of these compounds."[15]

Breast Cancer and Radiation

Another area that demands urgent investigation is the role of radiation in breast cancer development. It is widely accepted that high doses of ionizing radiation cause breast cancer, whereas low doses are generally regarded as safe. Questions remain, however, regarding the shape of the dose-response curve, the length of the latency period, and the significance of age at time of exposure. These questions are of great importance to women because of the emphasis on mammography for early detection. Few voices dare challenge mammography screening. One of them is Rosalie Bertell, who criticized the breast cancer screening program of the Ontario Health Minister in Canada in 1989. Bertell argued that the program would "increase breast cancer death by increasing breast cancer incidence" and presented a risk-benefit assessment of the program to support her criticism.[16]

According to Bertell, the present breast cancer epidemic is a direct result of "above ground weapons testing" carried out in Nevada between 1951 and 1963, when two hundred nuclear bombs were set off and the fallout dispersed across the country. Because the latency period for breast cancer peaks at about 40 years, this is an entirely reasonable hypothesis. Chris Busby in the United Kingdom has recently come up with results that support Bertell's hypotheses. In the UK the increases in cancer incidence began in areas of high rainfall, such as Wales, Scotland, and the west country; cancer incidence did not increase in the dry areas. A good explanation for this is that the cancers were the result of atmospheric nuclear bomb testing in the period 1955 to 1963 by the

nuclear superpowers in Kazakhstan, Nevada, and the South Pacific. The explosions drove "large quantities of radioactive material into the stratosphere, and this was circulated globally, falling to Earth everywhere, but particularly in high rainfall areas." At the peak of the testing (1961–1963) infant mortality began to rise and there was concern that strontium-90, accumulating in the milk, might be affecting babies. At the World Conference on Breast Cancer in 1997, in Ontario, Canada, Busby reported that this cohort of women, the nursing mothers exposed at the peak of testing, have shown the largest increase in breast cancer.[17]

Questions have also been raised about the possible effect of electromagnetic fields (EMFs). Studies on telephone company and electrical workers have raised the possibility of a connection between EMF exposure and breast cancer in *males*. Genevieve Matanoski of Johns Hopkins University studied breast cancer rates on male New York Telephone employees from 1976 to 1980 and observed a dose-response relationship to cancer and two cases of male breast cancer.[18] Another study, by Paul Demers of the Hutchinson Cancer Research Institute in Seattle, Washington, also found a strong correlation between breast cancer risk for men and jobs that involved exposure to EMFs.[19] Finally in 1994, a study appeared on *female* electrical workers in the United States. It showed excessive breast cancer mortality relative to other women workers.[20] While this study has limitations because it is based on mortality statistics, which do not include information on other known risk factors, its results are consistent with the work of David Blask and others concerning melatonin. This work has shown that exposure to low-frequency electromagnetic fields, as well as exposure to light at night, reduces the pineal gland's production of its main hormone, melatonin. Melatonin, when given in normal physiological doses, is able to inhibit the growth of breast cancer cells in culture and in animals; it does so by decreasing the production of the cell's estrogen receptors.[21] Clearly, further investigation is strongly warranted in this area.

The Precautionary Principle

The importance of environmental factors to the current breast cancer epidemic is often dismissed; their contribution is considered too small to worry about.

But as Rachel Carson succinctly explained in her groundbreaking work in 1962, repeated small doses of a carcinogen can be more dangerous than a single large dose. She wrote, "The latter may kill cells outright, whereas the small doses allow some to survive, though in a damaged condition. These survivors may then develop into cancer cells. This is why there is no 'safe' dose of a carcinogen."[22]

In November 1996 the Harvard Center for Cancer Prevention released a report claiming to summarize the current knowledge about the causes of human cancer. Shockingly, the report claimed that only 2 percent of U.S. cancer deaths can be attributed to environmental pollution. However, the definition of "environmental pollution" used in the report was extremely limited ("air pollution and hormonally active aromatic organochlorines") and has been sharply criticized by other scientists and environmental activists. All other environmental hazards were covered under separate categories. For example, adding the percentage of risk that the report attributed to factors we would consider "environmental," such as occupational factors, radiation, and food additives and contaminants, brings the figure to 10 percent, and since a half million deaths are caused by cancer in the United States each year, that means that 50,000 deaths are due to environmental factors. The report suggests that an additional 30 percent of cancer mortality is due to diet and obesity, but it does not discuss the issue of environmental carcinogens in food, particularly those stored in fat. Water contamination (a significant source of pesticide residues in the diet) was not included in the environmental pollution section. The report also discusses socioeconomic status as a risk factor without clarifying that money or education does not *cause* cancer and that socioeconomics is always a surrogate for something else. Minimizing environmental factors through this kind of manipulation of statistics, while emphasizing "lifestyle" factors instead, obstructs real progress in the struggle against cancer.

"It's a blame-the-victim perspective," said Peter Montague, the editor of *Rachel's Environment and Health Weekly.* "You can make a choice about eating spinach or not. It's more difficult to choose not to eat pesticides, or to control what's in your water or what's in your food. The choice just isn't available to most people to pick clean or contaminated food."[23] Cancer activists saw the report as a backlash against the small inroads being made on the topic of cancer

and the environment, and pointed out that the Harvard School of Public Health, which sponsored the report, lists in its 1996 annual report dozens of major chemical manufacturers among its large donors. These include ARCO Chemical Company; Asarco, Inc.; Chevron; CIBA-GEIGY, Ltd.; Dow Chemical; DuPont; Eastman Chemical Company; General Electric; Monsanto; Shell Oil; Texaco; Union Carbide; and Procter & Gamble. DuPont and Asarco were among the companies reporting the highest release of toxic substances in 1994, according to an Environmental Protection Agency report. CIBA-GEIGY is the brains behind Atrazine and Simazine (widely used herbicides that have been classified as possible human carcinogens), and Monsanto is the maker of bovine somatropin (also called BGH), the growth hormone given to cows to increase milk production.[24] Clearly, it is not in the interest of chemical manufacturers to support a major report that would accurately name environmental pollution as a significant causal factor in cancer risk.

The question that screams to be addressed is, what should be considered sufficient proof to take action to eliminate potentially harmful substances from the environment? Or, as the Ontario Task Force on the Primary Prevention of Cancer put it in their March 1995 report,

> The central issue facing those involved in the primary prevention of cancer attributable to environmental sources is how much evidence is required and how strong the evidence must be before remedial action is taken to reduce or eliminate exposures.[25]

The Precautionary Principle is a public health guideline requiring that we act to prevent illness and death. Framing an issue from a public health perspective means that we recognize the existence of other factors apart from personal habits—such as economic, political, and cultural factors—that determine the parameters of the problem. We do not need to wait for absolute proof of harm. The Precautionary Principle emphasizes prevention and puts the burden of proof on those who risk the public health by introducing potentially harmful chemicals into the environment. As a public health principle, it has an honorable history and has been incorporated into several international agreements. The case of the Great Lakes is a good example of its application in

North America. For more than forty years the Great Lakes have been a dumping ground for toxic chemicals produced by industry. More than eight hundred chemicals have been identified in the Great Lakes, many of them implicated in cancer, birth defects, and damage to the nervous and immune systems. An outpouring of concern forced the United States and Canada to sign a sweeping document requiring an end to the discharge of toxic substances. A binational commission responsible for monitoring and assessing the progress made after the agreement took a responsible view and came down clearly on the side of the Precautionary Principle. They wrote, "It is first necessary to shift the burden of responsibility for demonstrating whether substances should be allowed in commerce. The concept of reverse onus, or requiring proof that a substance is not toxic or persistent before use, should be the guiding philosophy of environmental management agencies, in both countries."[26] The Precautionary Principle takes a "weight of evidence" approach to assessing environmental health risks. It synthesizes the evidence gathered from epidemiological and biochemical research, wildlife observation, and other approaches, taking into account the cumulative weight of the studies that focus on the question of injury (or the likelihood of injury) to life, instead of narrowly focusing on one type of study alone. It brings an interdisciplinary and much needed holistic perspective to the sciences, and it introduces an important value: prudence. If there is not enough evidence, let's err on the side of caution!

The Precautionary Principle is necessary in order to protect public health and the environment, since the regulation of toxic chemicals in the United States is ineffective and out of date. The Toxic Substances Control Act (TSCA) was established in 1976 to determine which chemicals are dangerous and how the public can be protected from them. There are some 70,000 chemicals now in use, and every year about 1000 new chemicals enter the commercial market. During a typical year, the National Toxicology Program—a consortium of eight federal agencies—studies the cancer effects of one or two dozen chemicals. It is impossible, given the resources allocated to the program, to evaluate the dangers of all the chemicals now in circulation. A corporate self-regulation provision of the law proved completely ineffective, with chemical corporations failing to report scientific data on adverse health effects from chemicals. The overall outcome of twenty-one years of work under the TSCA has been to remove nine chemicals from the market.[27]

In her recent book *Living Downstream*, ecologist Sandra Steingraber writes that we all live downstream from toxic wastes dumped into the environment, and that to end cancer we need to go upstream and stop the pollution that is poisoning our lives.[28] In practice, however, national cancer policies emphasize early diagnosis and treatment, with minimal attention directed toward prevention. The recent highly publicized Breast Cancer Prevention Trial using tamoxifen (an antiestrogen synthetic hormone) on healthy volunteers considered to be at high risk for breast cancer raises troubling questions about what prevention really means for the medical establishment. In this study, although breast cancer incidence decreased among those taking tamoxifen, the number of deaths was the same between the treated and untreated groups because of other life-threatening conditions that developed among the group taking tamoxifen.[29] It is estimated that 29 million healthy women would be "potentially eligible" for preventive treatment with tamoxifen. At a cost of $80 to $100 for a month's supply, this is truly a "big deal" for Zeneca, the company that manufactures the drug under the name Nolvadex.

Biochemist Ross Hume Hall's analysis of the reasons we are making so little progress on cancer is compelling.[30] In discussing who directs cancer policy, he takes a look at a coalition of shared interests, which he calls the "medical industrial complex," that conducts research, develops drugs and medical equipment, and provides treatment. The medical part of the complex controls a vast number of cancer institutes, all focusing on diagnosis, treatment, and the search for a cure; the industrial part of the complex, on the other hand, has no interest in prevention because healthy people do not need their products or services. The hugely powerful chemical industry fights every initiative that would reduce the number of pollutants in the environment and funds much of cancer research. A striking example of this conflict of interest is offered by the case of Zeneca, the company mentioned previously. Zeneca owns and manages eleven cancer treatment centers in the United States; it is also the primary sponsor of October as Breast Cancer Awareness Month and has veto power over any materials produced in connection with this month of activities. Not surprisingly, the literature of Breast Cancer Awareness Month never mentions the word carcinogen, and it relentlessly emphasizes mammography as the "best protection" for women. Given the results of the Breast Cancer Prevention Trial, it is likely that tamoxifen will be included in their list of recommendations for breast cancer prevention. Zeneca is also the producer of a carcinogenic herbicide, acetochlor, and has been involved in litigation stemming from environmental damage to California harbors. Thus, Breast Cancer Awareness Month reveals the close connection between the chemical industry and the cancer research establishment.

Women's cancer groups at both the local and international levels have been at the forefront of criticism of the medical-industrial complex and have asked for the development of a true prevention approach, summarized by the phrase "Stop cancer before it starts." At the 1997 World Conference on Breast Cancer, delegates from fifty-four countries emphasized that breast cancer not only is a medical issue, but is also a social problem that needs to be addressed by international activism. Environmental factors were discussed in depth. Nancy Evans, a delegate from California, was clear about the need for environmental activism: "We are losing the war on cancer because we are fighting the wrong enemies," she said. "The cancer establishment has taught us to look for the enemy within—within our genes, our unwise reproductive choices or our stressful lifestyle. Although these factors may contribute to breast cancer and other cancers, our real enemies are faceless transnational corporations that spread their poisons around the globe in the name of free trade. . . . Prevention activism means understanding who these enemies are."[31]

Indeed, if we want to stop not just breast cancer but all cancers, we need to think in global terms and link across nations and disciplines, building a perspective that incorporates the knowledge gained from public health science, grassroots environmental groups, and people living with cancer. Only then will we be able to reverse the trend that has resulted in the present epidemic, and set the basis for a healthy future for ourselves and the following generations.

Notes

1. See, for instance, Epstein, Samuel. *The Politics of Cancer.* Garden City, NY: Anchor Press/ Doubleday, 1979; and Agran, Larry. *The Cancer Connection.* New York: St. Martin's Press, 1977.

2. Doll, Richard, and Richard Peto. *The Causes of Cancer: Quantitative Estimates of Avoidable Risks of Cancer in the United States Today.* New York: Oxford University Press, 1981.

3. Proctor, Robert N. *Cancer Wars: How Politics Shapes What We Know and Don't Know about Cancer.* New York: Basic Books, 1995, p. 38. See also Clayson, D. B., "Occupational Bladder Cancer," *Preventive Medicine,* Vol. 5, 1976, pp. 228–244.

4. American Cancer Society. *Cancer Facts & Figures—1998.* Atlanta, GA: American Cancer Society, 1998.

5. Moormeier, Jill. "Breast Cancer in Black Women," *Annals of Internal Medicine,* Vol. 124, No. 10, May 15, 1996, pp. 897–905.

6. Quoted in Batt, Sharon. *Patient No More.* Charlottetown, PEI, Canada: Gynergy Books, 1994, p. 169.

7. Westin, Jerome B., and Elihu Richter. "The Israeli Breast-Cancer Anomaly," *Annals of the New York Academy of Science,* "Trends in Cancer Mortality in Industrial Countries," edited by Devra Davis and David Hoel. 1990, pp. 269–279.

8. Falk, Frank, Andrew Ricci, Mary S. Wolff, James Gobold, and Peter Deckers. "Pesticides and Polychlorinated Biphenyl Residues in Human Breast Lipids and Their Relation to Breast Cancer," *Archives of Environmental Health,* Vol. 47, No. 2, March/April 1992, pp. 143–146.

9. Wolff, Mary S., Paolo G. Toniolo, Eric W. Lee, Marilyn Rivera, and Neil Dubin. "Blood Levels of Organochlorine Residues and Risk of Breast Cancer," *Journal of the National Cancer Institute,* Vol. 85, No. 8, April 21, 1993, pp. 648–652.

10. Krieger, Nancy, Mary S. Wolff, Robert A. Hiatt, Marilyn Rivera, Joseph Vogelman, and Norman Orentreich. "Breast Cancer and Serum Organochlorines: A Prospective Study Among White, Black, and Asian Women," *Journal of the National Cancer Institute,* Vol. 86, No. 8, April 20, 1994, pp. 589–599.

11. Davis, Devra Lee, and H. Leon Bradlow. "Can Environmental Estrogens Cause Breast Cancer?" *Scientific American,* October 1995, pp. 166–172.

12. Soto, Ana M., Honorato Justiia, Jonathan W. Wray, and Carlos Sonneschein, "p-Nonyl-Phenol: An Estrogenic Xenobiotic Released from 'Modified' Polysterene," *Environmental Health Perspectives,*

Vol. 92, 1991, pp. 167–173; and personal communication with Ana Soto and Carlos Sonneschein, October 1994.

13. See note 11, p. 170.

14. See note 11, p. 168. See also vom Saal, Frederick. "Getting to the Truth: What We Know and Don't Know about the Hazards of Endocrine Disrupting Chemicals," *Pesticides and You*, Vol. 17, No. 3, 1997, pp. 9–16.

15. Arditti, Rita, and Tatiana Schreiber. "Breast Cancer: Organizing for Prevention," *Resist*, Vol. 3, No. 9, November 1994, p. 4. See also Colborn, Theo, Dianne Dumanoski, and John Peterson Myers. *Our Stolen Future*. New York: Dutton, 1996.

16. The paper can be obtained by writing to Dr. Rosalie Bertell, President, International Institute of Concern for Public Health, 830 Bathurst Street, Toronto, Ontario, Canada, M5R 3G1. See also Bertell, Rosalie. "Breast Cancer and Mammography," *Mothering*, Summer 1992, pp. 949–957.

17. Busby, Chris. "Cancer and the 'Risk-Free' Radiation," *The Ecologist*, March/April 1998, Vol. 28, No. 2, pp. 54–56.

18. Matanoski, G. M., P. N. Breysse, and E. A. Elliott. "Electromagnetic Field Exposure and Male Breast Cancer," *Lancet*, No. 337, 1991, p. 737.

19. Demers, P. A., D. B. Thomas, K. A. Rosenblatt, et al. "Occupational Exposure to Electromagnetic Fields and Breast Cancer in Men." *American Journal of Epidemiology*, Vol. 134, 1991, pp. 340–347.

20. Loomis, Dana P., David A. Savitz, and Cande V. Ananth. "Breast Cancer Mortality among Female Electrical Workers in the United States," *Journal of the National Cancer Institute*, Vol. 86, No. 12, June 15, 1994, pp. 921–925.

21. Personal communication with Dr. David E. Blask, September 1994. See also Hill, Steven M., and David E. Blask. "Effects on the Pineal Hormone Melatonin on the Proliferation and Morphological Characteristics of Human Breast Cancer Cells (MCF-7) in Culture," *Cancer Research*, No. 48, November 1, 1988, pp. 6121–6126.

22. Carson, Rachel. *Silent Spring*. Boston: Houghton Mifflin, 1962, p. 232.

23. Schreiber, Tatiana. "Misleading and Irresponsible: Cancer Activists Decry Harvard Report," *Resist*, Vol. 6, No. 3, April 1997, p. 5.

24. See note 23.

25. *Recommendations for the Primary Prevention of Cancer*. Report of the Ontario Task Force on the Primary Prevention of Cancer, Ministry of Health, March 1995, p. 33. See also Arditti, Rita. "The Precautionary Principle: What It Is and Why We Should Embrace It," *Women's Community Cancer Project Newsletter*, Summer 1997, pp. 1–2.

26. *Seventh Biennial Annual Report on Great Lakes Water Quality*. International Joint Commission, Windsor, Ontario, 1994, pp. 1–2.

27. Montague, Peter. "Is Regulation Possible?" *Ecologist*, Vol. 28, No. 2, March/April 1998, pp. 59–61.

28. Steingraber, Sandra. *Living Downstream: An Ecologist Looks at Cancer and the Environment*. Reading, MA: Addison-Wesley, 1997.

29. Arditti, Rita. "Tamoxifen: Breast Cancer Prevention That Is Hard to Swallow," *Sojourner*, July 1998, p. 32.

30. Hume Hall, Ross. "The Medical-Industrial Complex," *Ecologist*, Vol. 28, No. 2, March/April 1998, pp. 62–68.

31. John, Lauren. "World Conference Calls for Global Action Plan," *Breast Cancer Action Newsletter*, No. 44, October/November 1997, p. 9.

◆◆◆

Reproductive Rights
A Disability Rights Issue
Marsha Saxton

In recent years, the women's movement has broadened its definition of "reproductive rights" to include not only abortion, but all aspects of sexuality, procreation, and parenthood. The priorities of the National Abortion Reproductive Rights Action League also reveal this broader agenda: protecting adolescent reproductive health, preventing unintended pregnancy and sexually transmitted disease, eliminating restrictive or coercive reproductive health policies, and promoting healthy pregnancy and early childhood health.

Some women may take for granted birth control, reproductive health care, and sex education, forgetting that people with different life experiences based on class, race, or physical or mental ability may not have access to these fundamental aspects of reproductive freedom. But for people with disabilities, *all* the reproductive rights are still at stake.

For centuries, the oppression of people with disabilities has denied us "choice": choice about who should be regarded as "a sexual being," who should have babies, which babies should be born, which babies should be allowed to live after they're born, who should raise these babies into adulthood. These choices were made, for the most part, by others. People with disabilities are beginning to demand a say in these decisions now that the Americans with Disabilities Act (ADA) has forced the public to perceive our issues as civil rights issues. In the decades to come, we hope to see a transformation in the public's perception of disability and of people with disabilities. The issue of reproductive rights can serve as a catalyst for this transformation.

The stereotype of asexuality is slowly lifting. There are now a few disabled characters in the popular literature and media who are portrayed as sexual beings participating in intimate activities. (Some of these movie personalities, such as actress Marlee Maitlin, themselves are deaf or have physical disabilities. However, most disabled characters on TV or in the movies are still played by non-disabled actors.)

New and complex issues are emerging in regard to disability and procreation. Many relate to new developments in reproductive technologies. Others reflect changing social values. What follows is a discussion of how these new issues affect people with disabilities.

Reproductive Health Care

Because of patronizing attitudes about disabled people, many medical practitioners and health care facilities do not consider offering reproductive health care services to their patients who have disabilities. Many people with disabilities or with chronic illness, because of the "preexisting condition" exclusion in most health insurance, have been denied access to *any* health care, not only reproductive health care. There are few medical or nursing schools that offer any training on the reproductive health of people with disabilities. Only in the last five years has there been any research on the effects of various birth control methods for people with different kinds of disabilities or chronic illness, and these studies are limited, often focusing only on spinal cord injury. Even people with the more common disabling conditions like diabetes, arthritis, or multiple sclerosis have little or no information about whether they should or shouldn't use particular methods of birth control.

In Chicago, a group of disabled women have created a "disability accessible" gynecological clinic through the Chicago Rehabilitation Institute and the Prentice Women's Hospital, staffed with practitioners who have been trained to serve disabled women. The Health Resource Center for Women with Disabilities is unique. One day a week, it offers accessible core gyn services for women with disabilities and now serves more than 200 women. The staff includes nurse practitioners and midwives; and a nurse who has a disability has been hired. The clinic program plans to expand its resources to include a project director to monitor clinic services and to oversee a library with health-related videos and publications. It will also add an 800 telephone number staffed by a woman with a disability to respond to questions about accessible health care services. The center has initiated research directed at documenting the medical experiences of women with disabilities and improving services for traditionally underserved populations, including developmentally disabled, learning disabled, and mentally retarded women.

Sex Education

Disabled children and adults need information about dating, sex, menstruation, pregnancy, birth control, AIDS, and other sexually transmitted diseases. Attitudes have changed, and increasingly, parents and educators are recognizing that disabled children need sex education. But this is not the norm. Disabled children are still often overprotected by adults who don't know how to teach them about "the facts of life." Questions such as the following tend to provoke confusion: how can blind children be given information about gender anatomy? How should retarded children be told about AIDS? How can deaf children, children who use wheelchairs, or any child who may have felt the stigma of disability be encouraged to interact positively with non-disabled and disabled peers and to learn positive sexual self-esteem? Many disabled adults never received important information about sex. They are vulnerable to confusing or dangerous misinformation and serious difficulties with their own sexuality, difficulties that result not from actual physical limitations but simply from exclusion from information and experience.

Marriage Disincentives

In the United States, people with disabilities who receive certain kinds of Social Security or Medicaid benefits are discouraged from getting married by threat of reduced or eliminated benefits. These "marriage disincentives" (like "employment disincentives," which discourage disabled people from employment by threat of reduced medical coverage) reveal the serious disability discrimination fundamentally built into our disability policies. If an SSI (Supplemental Security Income) recipient marries, his or her spouse's earnings are considered income, thus reducing the recipient's benefits, jeopardizing essential medical and personal care attendant services, and often placing enormous financial burden on the couple to finance prohibitively expensive services or equipment. The current law has the effect of forcing people with disabilities to accept "living together" as temporary sweethearts rather than an adult, community-sanctioned marriage. A recent attempt by disability rights advocates to urge Donna Shalala of the federal Department of Health and Human Services to legislate a more equitable system failed. While the outward rationale for the law is to save taxpayer money on people who could be supported by a spouse (based on the assumption that two can live as cheaply as one), social scientists and disability rights activists suspect that drafters of these marriage disincentive laws were also intending to thwart marriage and potential procreation for disabled people.

"Reproducing Ourselves"

The very idea of disabled persons as parents scares some people and exposes discriminatory attitudes that might otherwise remain hidden. Acceptance of disabled people as parents simply requires the larger community's acceptance of us as human beings. By denying our rights to be mothers and fathers, it is not only our competence to care for our young, but our very existence, our desire to "reproduce ourselves," that is forbidden.

In late 1991, TV news anchor Bree Walker, who has a genetic disability and who was pregnant, became the brunt of a call-in radio talk show when the host Jane Norris asked listeners, "Should disabled people have children?" Callers aired their opinions about whether Walker should have her baby or, as Norris posed the question, "Is it 'fair' to bring a child with a disability into the world?" The incident became the focal point of the disabled women's community's challenge to the idea that people with disabilities should not be born.

Qualifications for Parenthood

The Earls are a married Michigan couple, both severely disabled with cerebral palsy. They had a baby, Natalie, and sought assistance from the Michigan

Home Help Program in providing physical care for the infant. Their desire to raise their own child and to demonstrate their competence as loving parents was thwarted by state regulations that bar the personal care assistant (PCA) of a disabled client from touching the client's child during paid work hours. One result of this regulation seems to be that disabled people who rely on the PCA program for help in daily living cannot have children.

Of course, people with disabilities must take seriously the responsibilities of adult sexuality and the potential for pregnancy and parenthood. We must also educate ourselves, the disability community, and our families and friends about what it means to be a parent and be disabled. And we must be prepared to take on the discriminatory policies of a variety of institutions: medical, social services, legal, and media. But we must also do battle within ourselves. We must overcome the voices we've internalized that say, "You can't possibly do this, you can't be good parents, and you don't deserve the benefits or the assistance required to raise your own children."

In Berkeley, California, an agency called Through the Looking Glass offers the first program specifically designed to assist parents with disabilities in skills development, community resources, and peer support. Looking Glass also publishes a newsletter, which can be ordered at [2198 Sixth St., Suite 100, Berkeley, CA 94710].

Custody Struggles

Tiffany Callo is a young woman who wanted to raise her newborn son. Because of her cerebral palsy, the California Department of Social Services challenged her ability to care for the child. Armed with lawyers and court orders, the department refused to allow her to demonstrate her parenting skills in an appropriate environment that would enable her to show the creative approaches she had developed to handle the baby. *Newsweek* reporter Jay Mathews picked up her story, and Callo became a spokesperson for the cause of mothers with disabilities who fight for the right to raise their own children. Social service and child protection agency professionals need training and awareness to allow them to perceive the *abilities* of disabled parents, not only the stereotyped limitations.

Adoption

A large number of children adopted or waiting for adoption are disabled. Many disabled adults were adopted or placed in foster homes. It is still largely the case that adoption agencies do not consider disabled people as prospective parents for either disabled or non-disabled children. We need to challenge this stereotype that people with disabilities cannot be good adoptive parents. A few adoption agencies are changing policies, allowing disabled people to adopt, and in some cases even encouraging disabled adults to adopt children with disabilities. For example, Adoption Resource Associates in Watertown, Massachusetts, has taken a special interest in prospective disabled parents and makes specific mention in their brochure that they do not discriminate on the basis of disability in their placement services.

Sterilization Abuse

Consider this story of a woman with a psychiatric disability: "When I was twenty, I got pregnant by my boyfriend at the state mental school. Of course, there was no birth control for patients. We weren't allowed to have sex, but it went on all the time, even between patients and attendants. A doctor forced my mother to sign a paper giving me an abortion, even though I wanted to give up the baby for adoption. When I woke up, I found out I had had a hysterectomy. Maybe I couldn't take care of the baby then, but nobody even asked me what I wanted to do, or what I hoped for when I got older."

When a guardian or medical professional decides that people labeled retarded, mentally ill, or with other disabilities should not be parents, sterilization without consent may occur. Often, guardians or other decision makers who intervene on behalf of these disabled people have little exposure to the Independent Living Movement, or other community disability resources. As disabled people, we need to be empowered to make our own decisions regarding sexuality and procreation.

Abortion

Women with disabilities have reported significant difficulties with regard to abortion. These include being pressured to undergo an abortion because it is assumed that a disabled woman could not be a good parent, or, conversely, being denied access to abortion because a guardian decides the woman was incapable of making her own reproductive choices. Sometimes, after birth, a disabled woman's child is taken away from her. Women with disabilities experience the same kinds of abortion access difficulties as non-disabled women, but these difficulties are often magnified by disability discrimination.

Prenatal Screening

Scientific advances in the field of genetics have created technologies that can detect an increasing number of genetic conditions in the womb. While the general public seems to regard this medical technology as a wonderful advance and a way to reduce the incidence of disability and improve the quality of life, people with disabilities often have a very different view. As revealed in the Bree Walker case mentioned above, the unchallenged assumption often accompanying the use of these screening tests is that the lives of people with genetically related disabilities (such as muscular dystrophy, Down syndrome, cystic fibrosis, sickle cell anemia, and spina bifida) are simply not worth living and are a burden that families and society would rather not endure. The options to abort a fetus who might die early in life, or to abort in order to preclude the birth of a child with severe disabilities, are framed as "reproductive options." But in this era of health care cost containment, the notion of controlling costs by eliminating births of disabled babies may become a requirement, rather than an option. Then it ceases to be reproductive freedom and becomes quality control of babies — eugenics. The availability of these tests reinforces these notions, and the tests are actually marketed to women and to health care providers on this basis. Women are increasingly pressured to abort a fetus identified as disabled. Real choice must include the right to bear children with disabilities.

We in the disabled community must voice our ideas about selective abortion and attest to the true value of our lives. Only when a valid picture of the quality of our lives is available can prospective parents make choices about the use of tests for genetic disabilities in fetuses.

The Reproductive Rights Movement

The women's movement has begun to reach out to women with disabilities as a group. Women's organizations have begun to understand and challenge their own discriminatory attitudes and behaviors. More and more events in the women's movement are beginning to be wheelchair accessible and interpreted for the hearing impaired. But we have a long way to go to make the women's community fully welcoming of disabled people. This is a good time to get involved and share our thinking and energies. To be fully integrated into society, we must get involved and take leadership in all movements, and the movement for reproductive health care and real choice is an especially important one for people with disabilities to take on.

As disabled people, we have unique perspectives to share. Our views can enlighten everyone about the fundamental issues of sexuality and reproduction. We have gained much knowledge and experience with medical intervention, asking for and effectively managing help, dealing with bureaucracy, and fighting for access and power. Other controversial issues to which we can contribute our thinking include surrogate motherhood, population concerns, birthing technologies, artificial insemination, and *in vitro* fertilization.

The movement for reproductive rights needs to include people with disabilities as much as disabled people need to be included in the movement.

◆◆◆

FIFTY-SEVEN

Three Generations of Native American Women's Birth Experience

Joy Harjo

It was still dark when I awakened in the stuffed back room of my mother-in-law's small rented house with what felt like hard cramps. At 17 years of age I had read everything I could from the Tahlequah Public Library about pregnancy and giving birth. But nothing prepared me for what was coming. I awakened my child's father and then ironed him a shirt before we walked the four blocks to the Indian hospital because we had no car and no money for a taxi. He had been working with another Cherokee artist silk-screening signs for specials at the supermarket and making $5 a day, and had to leave me alone at the hospital because he had to go to work. We didn't awaken his mother. She had to get up soon enough to fix breakfast for her daughter and granddaughter before leaving for her job at the nursing home. I knew my life was balanced at the edge of great, precarious change and I felt alone and cheated. Where was the circle of women to acknowledge and honor this birth?

It was still dark as we walked through the cold morning, under oaks that symbolized the stubbornness and endurance of the Cherokee people who had made Tahlequah their capital in the new lands. I looked for handholds in the misty gray sky, for a voice announcing this impending miracle. I wanted to change everything; I wanted to go back to a place before childhood, before our tribe's removal to Oklahoma. What kind of life was I bringing this child into? I was a poor, mixed-blood woman heavy with a child who would suffer the struggle of poverty, the legacy of loss. For the second time in my life I felt the sharp tug of my own birth cord, still connected to my mother. I believe it never pulls away, until death, and even then it becomes a streak in the sky symbolizing that most important warrior road. In my teens I had fought my mother's weaknesses with all my might, and here I was at 17, becoming as my mother, who was in Tulsa, cooking breakfasts and preparing for the lunch shift at a factory cafeteria as I walked to the hospital to give birth. I should be with her; instead, I was far from her house, in the house of a mother-in-law who later would try to use witchcraft to destroy me.

After my son's father left me I was prepped for birth. This meant my pubic area was shaved completely and then I endured the humiliation of an enema, all at the hands of strangers. I was left alone in a room painted government green. An overwhelming antiseptic smell emphasized the sterility of the hospital, a hospital built because of the U.S. government's treaty and responsibility to provide health care to Indian people.

I intellectually understood the stages of labor, the place of transition, of birth—but it was difficult to bear the actuality of it, and to bear it alone. Yet in some ways I wasn't alone, for history surrounded me. It is with the birth of children that history is given form and voice. Birth is one of the most sacred acts we take part in and witness in our lives. But sacredness seemed to be far from my lonely labor room in the Indian hospital. I heard a woman screaming in the next room with her pain, and I wanted to comfort her. The nurse used her as a bad example to the rest of us who were struggling to keep our suffering silent.

The doctor was a military man who had signed on this watch not for the love of healing or out of awe at the miracle of birth, but to fulfill a contract for medical school payments. I was another statistic to him; he touched me as if he were moving equipment from one place to another. During my last visit I was given the option of being sterilized. He explained to me that the moment of birth was the best time to do it. I was handed the form but chose not to sign it, and am amazed now that I didn't think too much of it at the time. Later I would learn that many Indian women who weren't fluent in English signed, thinking it was a form giving consent for the doctor to deliver their babies. Others were sterilized without even the formality of signing. My light skin had probably saved me from such a fate. It wouldn't be the first time in my life.

When my son was finally born I had been deadened with a needle in my spine. He was shown to me—the incredible miracle nothing prepared me for—then taken from me in the name of medical progress. I fell asleep with the weight of chemicals and awoke yearning for the child I had suffered for, had anticipated in the months proceeding from his unexpected genesis when I was still 16 and a student at Indian school. I was not allowed to sit up or walk because of the possibility of paralysis (one of the drug's side effects), and when I finally got to hold him, the nurse stood guard as if I would hurt him. I felt enmeshed in a system in which the wisdom that had carried my people from generation to generation was ignored. In that place I felt ashamed I was an Indian woman. But I was also proud of what my body had accomplished despite the rape by the bureaucracy's machinery, and I got us out of there as soon as possible. My son would flourish on beans and fry bread, and on the dreams and stories we fed him.

My daughter was born four years later, while I was an art student at the University of New Mexico. Since my son's birth I had waitressed, cleaned hospital rooms, filled cars with gas (while wearing a miniskirt), worked as a nursing assistant, and led dance classes at a health spa. I knew I didn't want to cook and waitress all my life, as my mother had done. I had watched the varicose veins grow branches on her legs, and as they grew, her zest for dancing and sports dissolved into utter tiredness. She had been born with a caul over her face, the sign of a gifted visionary.

My earliest memories are of my mother writing songs on an ancient Underwood typewriter after she had washed and waxed the kitchen floor on her hands and knees. She too had wanted something different for her life. She had left an impoverished existence at age 17, bound for the big city of Tulsa. She was shamed in a time in which to be even part Indian was to be an outcast in the great U.S. system. Half her relatives were Cherokee full-bloods from near Jay, Oklahoma, who for the most part had nothing to do with white people. The other half were musically inclined "white trash" addicted to country-western music and Holy Roller fervor. She thought she could disappear in the city; no one would know her family, where she came from. She had dreams of singing and had once been offered a job singing on the radio but turned it down because she was shy. Later one of her songs would be stolen before she could copyright it and would make someone else rich. She would quit writing songs. She and my father would divorce and she would be forced to work for money to feed and clothe four children, all born within two years of each other.

As a child growing up in Oklahoma, I liked to be told the story of my birth. I would beg for it while my mother cleaned and ironed. "You almost killed me," she would say. "We almost died." That I could kill my mother filled me with remorse and shame. And I imagined the push-pull of my life, which is a legacy I deal with even now when I am twice as old as my mother was at my birth. I loved to hear the story of my warrior fight for my breath. The way it was told, it had been my decision to live. When I got older, I realized we were both nearly casualties of the system, the same system flourishing in the Indian hospital where later my son Phil would be born.

My parents felt lucky to have insurance, to be able to have their children in the hospital. My father came from a fairly prominent Muscogee Creek family. *His* mother was a full-blood who in the early 1920s got her degree in art. She was a painter. She gave birth to him in a private hospital in Oklahoma City; at least that's what I think he told me before he died at age 53. It was something of which they were proud.

This experience was much different from my mother's own birth. She and five of her six brothers were born at home, with no medical assistance. The only time a doctor was called was when someone was dying. When she was born her mother named her Wynema, a Cherokee name my mother says means beautiful woman, and Jewell, for a can of shortening stored in the room where she was born.

I wanted something different for my life, for my son, and for my daughter, who later was born in a university hospital in Albuquerque. It was a bright summer morning when she was ready to begin her journey. I still had no car, but I had enough money saved for a taxi for a ride to the hospital. She was born "naturally," without drugs. I could look out of the hospital window while I was in labor at the bluest sky in the world. I had support. Her father was present in the delivery room—though after her birth he disappeared on a drinking binge. I understood his despair, but did not agree with the painful means to describe it. A few days later Rainy Dawn was presented to the sun at her father's pueblo and given a name so that she will always be recognized as a part of the people, as a child of the sun.

That's not to say that my experience in the hospital reached perfection. The clang of metal against metal in the delivery room had the effect of a tuning fork reverberating fear in my pelvis. After giving birth I held my daughter, but they took her from me for "processing." I refused to lie down to be wheeled to my room after giving birth; I wanted to walk out of there to find my daughter. We reached a compromise and I rode in a wheelchair. When we reached the room I stood up and walked to the nursery and demanded my daughter. I knew she needed me. That began my war with the nursery staff, who deemed me unknowledgeable because I was Indian and poor. Once again I felt the brushfire of shame, but I'd learned to put it out much more quickly, and I demanded early release so I could take care of my baby without the judgment of strangers.

I wanted something different for Rainy, and as she grew up I worked hard to prove that I could make "something" of my life. I obtained two degrees as a single mother. I wrote poetry, screenplays, became a professor, and tried to live a life that would be a positive influence for both of my children. My work in this life has to do with reclaiming the memory stolen from our peoples when we were dispossessed from our lands east of the Mississippi; it has to do with restoring us. I am proud of our history, a history so powerful that it both destroyed my father and guarded him. It's a history that claims my mother as she lives not far from the place her mother was born, names her as she cooks in the cafeteria of a small college in Oklahoma.

When my daughter told me she was pregnant, I wasn't surprised. I had known it before she did, or at least before she would admit it to me. I felt despair, as if nothing had changed or ever would. She had run away from Indian school with her boyfriend and they had been living in the streets of Gallup, a border town notorious for the suicides and deaths of Indian peoples. I brought her and her boyfriend with me because it was the only way I could bring her home. At age 16, she was fighting me just as I

had so fiercely fought my mother. She was making the same mistakes. I felt as if everything I had accomplished had been in vain. Yet I felt strangely empowered, too, at this repetition of history, this continuance, by a new possibility of life and love, and I steadfastly stood by my daughter.

I had a university job, so I had insurance that covered my daughter. She saw an obstetrician in town who was reputed to be one of the best. She had the choice of a birthing room. She had the finest care. Despite this, I once again battled with a system in which physicians are taught the art of healing by dissecting cadavers. My daughter went into labor a month early. We both knew intuitively the baby was ready, but how to explain that to a system in which numbers and statistics provide the base of understanding? My daughter would have her labor interrupted; her blood pressure would rise because of the drug given to her to stop the labor. She would be given an unneeded amniocentesis and would have her labor induced—after having it artificially stopped! I was warned that if I took her out of the hospital so her labor could occur naturally my insurance would cover nothing.

My daughter's induced labor was unnatural and difficult, monitored by machines, not by touch. I was shocked. I felt as if I'd come full circle, as if I were watching my mother's labor and the struggle of my own birth. But I was there in the hospital room with her, as neither my mother had been for me, nor her mother for her. My daughter and I went through the labor and birth together.

And when Krista Rae was born she was born to her family. Her father was there for her, as were both her grandmothers and my friend who had flown in to be with us. Her paternal great-grandparents and aunts and uncles had also arrived from the Navajo Reservation to honor her. Something *had* changed.

Four days later, I took my granddaughter to the Saguaro forest before dawn and gave her the name I had dreamed for her just before her birth. Her name looks like clouds of mist settling around a sacred mountain as it begins to speak. A female ancestor approaches on a horse. We are all together.

FIFTY-EIGHT

Fallen Women
Alcoholics and Drug Abusers
Eileen Nechas and Denise Foley

These days, the biggest challenge facing Julianne Harris (not her real name) is getting her four-month-old twins to settle down for a nap. She relishes that hour or so of peace and tranquility, a rare treat in a day jam-packed with diapers, feedings, and bathings. But for Julianne, a twenty-nine-year-old former bookkeeper and Joan Lunden look-alike, it's a challenge she embraces with joy and optimism. Indeed, she sails through her days with confidence and energy, the picture of young motherhood, a baby perched on each jean-clad hip.

But up until a few years ago, Julianne faced a different kind of daily existence, one she endured alone and in an alcoholic haze. Her days were spent sprawled on the sofa with a glass in one hand and the TV remote control in the other. She didn't even bother to eat. "At my worst, the only thing I managed to do was walk to the liquor store to replenish my supply," she says, "and I would think I had accomplished a lot." Over a period of seven years she saw her life spiral out of control, fueled by the 2 gallons of vodka that she downed each week.

Although her family suspected that she probably drank too much, they didn't know the extent of it. Like so many women alcoholics, Julianne remained hidden to them, her friends, her co-workers, even her doctor. She became one of the millions of closet drinkers, overwhelmed by guilt and shame, shunned by society and ignored by medicine and research.

Although 40 percent of those who abuse alcohol or drugs are women, it's easy for them to remain virtually unnoticed, like so much dirt swept under a carpet. In fact, they feel like dirt much of the time. Like Julianne Harris, most chemically dependent women must contend with the disgust and repulsion of family and friends. In fact, those reactions often reinforce an addicted woman's reluctance to admit to a problem or to seek help for it. "I would make excuses so I didn't have to be around other people," says Julianne. "I didn't want to see their looks of disap-

proval. I knew I had a problem, but I didn't want anyone else to know. It was too humiliating."

The scientific community has hardly been more open-minded. Traditionally, substance abuse has been regarded almost entirely as a male affliction, an unfortunate assumption that has compounded the invisibility problem for addicted women. Researchers, who have had little interest in studying those who didn't fit the "norm," simply excluded women from their studies or just averaged their data in with the men's. Indeed, of the more than 110,000 substance abusers studied by various researchers over a period of thirty years, only about 7 percent (8,000) were women. Even when looking for possible hereditary predisposition, researchers have more often chosen to study the biological connections between sons and their alcoholic parents, disregarding whether the findings would be applicable to daughters of alcoholics. And because recovery programs have been studied using only addicted men, they have remained insensitive to the special needs of addicted women.

What little is known about substance abuse in women has only served to underscore the desperate need for more research. Women alcoholics, for example, develop severe liver disease after a shorter period of time than men drinkers do and after consuming far less alcohol, although no one has bothered to find out why. The disease progresses faster, too. More women than men die from cirrhosis of the liver, the most common health complication of alcoholism. According to the National Institute of Alcohol Abuse and Alcoholism, women alcoholics have death rates 50 to 100 percent higher than those of male alcoholics. A greater percentage of female alcoholics die from suicides, alcohol-related accidents, and circulatory disorders.

Women are also at an increased risk of developing multiple addictions, far more so than men. Women are prescribed two-thirds of all psychoactive drugs, such as Valium and Librium, and are more likely to be prescribed excessive dosages. Indeed, 25 percent of women in treatment for alcoholism have serious prescription drug problems as well.

Apparently the interest of the scientific community has yet to be stirred to any significant degree. In 1990, for example, the National Institute of Alcohol Abuse and Alcoholism spent under $7 million on research related to women out of a total budget of $132 million, while pleas from those who study and treat women with chemical dependencies are largely ignored. When research money is spent, most goes to studies of the role of drugs and alcohol on women's reproductive functions or on the influence of substance abuse on women's positions as wives and mothers. The research community, as it does in other arenas, fails to recognize that "women are more than just baby carriers and care givers," says substance abuse researcher Tonda Hughes, Ph.D., R.N., of the University of Illinois. The effect of alcohol and drugs on women themselves, on their psychological and physical health, remains unmapped ground as do the social and economic pressures that influence their addictive behaviors. As long as both interest and money remain in short supply, chemical dependencies in women will continue to be ignored, underreported, underdiagnosed, and most definitely undertreated. Consequently, it will be decades or longer before knowledge of the causes, risk factors, long-term effects, and treatment of addictions in women approaches that of men's.

The Stigma of the Female Addict

In society's eyes, women are still held to a higher code of conduct than men. They are seen as the gatekeepers of social standards and morality. Excessive drinking is simply incompatible with that narrow view. No one likes a drunk, but when the drunk is a woman, she is despised. In ancient Roman times, women who were caught drinking were put to death by stoning or starvation. Although the penalty for drinking isn't death anymore, it's still torture for most women. Indeed, drunken women are labeled as fallen women, dangerously promiscuous, and generally out of control. Snubbed by society and riddled with guilt, they are driven into hiding, becoming

closet drinkers, like Julianne Harris, or secret pill poppers or both.

Not so for men, however. In typical double-standard fashion, a drunken man is not only tolerated, but is either viewed as "macho" by his buddies or excused with a wink and a boys-will-be-boys attitude. Julianne, who used to play in a coed softball league, says that she eagerly guzzled beer with the guys until she noticed the dirty looks shot her way. "They made it clear that drinking the way *they* did wasn't ladylike."

But by far the most damaging stigma that women who drink or use drugs must contend with is that of sexual promiscuity. The prevailing attitude is that women who drink excessively become far more sexually aggressive. Yet the research simply does not support that notion, no matter how popular it remains. One study showed, for example, that only 8 percent of 1,000 women surveyed said they became less particular about their choice of sexual partner when they had been drinking. And the proportion hardly varied whether the women were light or heavy drinkers. Instead, the majority of the women reported that they were the targets of sexual aggression by men who had been drinking.

This stereotype of promiscuity among women who drink is not only inaccurate, says psychiatry professor Sheila B. Blume, M.D., of the State University of New York at Stony Brook, it results in promoting the sexual victimization of drinking women. In other words, if she drinks, "well, she's just asking for it." Studies have shown that she gets it, too. In one survey that compared alcohol-dependent women with nondrinking women, 16 percent of the alcoholic women reported being raped, whereas none of the nonalcoholic women had been.

Women who drink in bars are particularly vulnerable to victimization even if they are not themselves heavy or problem drinkers. Julianne Harris says that men often became more brazen when she was out drinking. "They became less afraid to make the first move. Once when I was drunk, a man took advantage of me. It wasn't rape, but I still felt so dirty afterward. It made me want to drink more just to hide the pain," she says, her voice growing soft with embarrassment.

Sadly, women who abuse alcohol or drugs are likely to believe the low opinion that many have of them. "Since the chemically dependent woman grows up in the same society as the rest of us, she applies these stereotypes to herself," says Blume, who also treats alcoholics at South Oaks Hospital in Amityville, New York. When she fails to meet society's standards, she is acutely aware of her own failures, reacting with extreme guilt and shame. Harris says that people called her a slut when she was drunk even though there was no reason for that. Or they'd say "I was just a drunk. It was bad enough to be called a drunk, but '*just* a drunk' made me feel even more diminished and worthless."

The effect of these social stigmas is to drive addicted women into hiding, into invisibility. Indeed, alcoholic women are much more likely to drink alone, at home, early in the mornings or on weekends, and to go to great lengths to hide their problems from themselves and others. Julianne Harris used to make some excuse to go to her room or to the basement or wherever she had stashed a bottle of vodka, and there, alone and hidden away from disapproving stares, she would drink. "Sometimes I'd pour vodka into a glass and put it behind the microwave oven," she recalls. "Since I was always alone in the kitchen when I cooked, I could sip from my secret source without fear of discovery. But when the house was empty, I would drink all day."

Slipping through the Cracks

The fact is that it's far too easy for women addicted to alcohol or drugs to remain in hiding. It's as if no one cares enough to even look for them, and in a sense that's true. The existing systems that expose men with addictions and get them into treatment programs don't necessarily work for women. That's because they were all designed with the male substance abuser in mind. It's *his* behavior when he drinks or uses drugs that has been used as the model for detection. Women simply don't follow the same behavior patterns that men do when they're addicted.

When men have chemical dependency problems, they are more likely to have trouble on the job or trouble with the law. Women, because they are more likely to drink alone and at home are, consequently, far less likely to be caught driving under the influence, drunk at work, or making a public scene. Not

surprisingly, employee assistance programs, drunk driver rehabilitation programs, and public intoxication programs are all heavily male dominated. Indeed, the male-to-female ratio among the latter two programs is nine to one. Adds Blume, "Employee assistance programs, which use impaired job performance as a problem indicator and job jeopardy as a motivator, have also been more successful with men."

Families, too, whether intentional or not, often undermine any efforts the addicted member makes to seek treatment. Julianne Harris's family tried to get her committed to a mental hospital, a choice *they* felt was more respectable for their upper-class daughter than the drug rehab program she preferred, which they equated with street junkies. Sadly, studies have shown that about 25 percent of women's families are actually opposed to their seeking treatment of any kind, contributing to these women's invisibility and prolonging their addictions. Aware of and sensitive to the social stigmas associated with female substance abuse, these families fear exposure of their shameful secret. Or more selfishly, they may not want to lose the services of the person who also happens to be the primary family caretaker.

Drug-dependent women are also far more likely to be divorced or separated, so the only people who might be aware of their problem are their own children, and the kids are not about to turn in the people who care for them. Besides, women fear losing custody of their children if they acknowledge that they need help for an addiction — with good reason. In some states, a woman who is addicted to drugs or alcohol is legally labeled as a child abuser or child neglecter. Paradoxically, a woman who continues her dependency without seeking help does not have to face this charge. By remaining invisible, she gets to keep her children, although it comes at the expense of her own recovery efforts. Only the state of New York has recognized what a disincentive this rule is for women who want to kick their habits. There, a woman who is participating in a treatment program is not automatically assumed to be an abusive or neglectful parent, at least not without additional evidence.

When women do decide to seek help, it's usually because of trouble with their health or trouble with their families. But unlike the drunk driver and public intoxication programs that favor the needs of men addicts, there are no public assistance programs for the marriage or health problems that are more consistent with women's addictions. The best these women can hope for is that the people they most often turn to—their doctors, health clinics, or even family and social service agencies—will somehow detect their drug or alcohol problems. In fact, divorce lawyers could be good at detecting chemical dependencies in their women clients if they would allow themselves to do so, claims Blume.

What *about* doctors? Who could be better equipped to uncover the hidden alcoholic than a doctor talking face to face with his or her patient? Although this sounds perfectly logical, it simply doesn't happen—not nearly as often as it should, considering that diagnosing ills is what doctors are trained to do. Yet physicians are often reluctant to diagnose *this* particular problem, especially in their women patients, because they're as aware of the negative stereotypes as everyone else is. In surveys, doctors admit that they often shy away from alcoholic patients because evaluating them, confronting them with their suspicions, and then managing their cases all take large blocks of time, the same excuse many use for not diagnosing patients who are victims of domestic violence.

Doctors are at a disadvantage. Like battered women, women with chemical dependencies are more likely to visit their doctors with vague symptoms such as headaches, anxiety, or insomnia. And, like victims of domestic violence, they leave with a prescription for Valium or some other sedative rather than what they really need—a referral to a drug treatment program. It's the vigilant and concerned doctor who can see through the facade. Julianne Harris's doctor was fooled every time. No matter what illness drove her to the doctor, she'd always mention something about being under a great deal of stress, which, she says, was a complete lie. "I would say that for the past two weeks I've really been drinking a lot. I'd never tell him that I'd been drinking heavily for the past five years. The doctor always took my word for it and never probed further." Instead, Julianne would occasionally receive a prescription for Valium for her so-called stress problem.

Granted, doctors don't have a great deal to go on in their quest to identify a substance abuser. Alcohol screening tests, for example, sound like a good idea. But even if these screening devices were used all the

time (which they're not), they're still bound to miss a proportion of women with addictions, because the tests were developed for and tested on men. The Michigan Alcoholism Screening Test, for example, was tested on men at first, and then repeated with another group of people, only 5.5 percent of whom were women, says chemical dependency researcher Tonda Hughes, Ph.D. A shorter version of the same scale (called the Short Michigan Alcoholism Screening Test) was also originally tested on only male subjects. Although some questions have been changed to incorporate women's life experiences, they are still more geared to uncovering men with addictions than women. Questions about getting into fights or arguments, for example, or drinking-related arrests, trouble at work, or being hospitalized due to alcohol problems are not nearly as relevant for women as they are for men, she says.

Neither are the questions that ask the patient if they ever drink first thing in the morning or before noon. Though women whose addiction is limited to alcohol might be detected with that line of questioning, those are still the patterns more typical of men alcoholics. The fact is, alcoholic women are twice as likely to combine their alcoholism with a dependence on sedative drugs, so they may be more inclined to start their days with Valium or other tranquilizers. Indeed, women who have multiple addictions may not touch a drop of alcohol until the evening hours.

A clinician who asks his women patients how much alcohol they drink each day may also be missing the ones with problems. Studies show that women who drink excessively consume only about *half* what their male counterparts do, although both have the same level of impairment. Until recently, doctors blamed body water content for the difference. According to that theory, because women have less body water than men do, alcohol becomes more concentrated in their systems. But there's more to it than that. When researchers finally got around to studying alcohol metabolism in both men *and* women, they uncovered the most important difference. They found that women have far less of the stomach enzyme that breaks down alcohol, gastric alcohol dehydrogenase, than men do. This enzyme decreases the availability of alcohol to the whole body, so that the less of this enzyme there is, the more intoxicated the person becomes. Because women have less of the enzyme, more alcohol enters their systems. Alcoholic women, the researchers found, have virtually none of this alcohol-metabolizing enzyme.

In spite of this new knowledge, the charts and tables that are used to calculate blood alcohol levels have yet to be revised. Those tables are designed to determine when it's safe to drive by taking into account the number of drinks a person has had, body weight, and time elapsed since the last alcoholic beverage. But those tables still apply to men only, so regardless of what they say, women would be well advised to consume half the amount of alcohol recommended as safe on the charts before attempting to get behind the wheel.

Treatment Insensitivity

When women manage to emerge from the shadows of alcohol or drug addictions and attempt treatment programs, they are likely to find the road to recovery a particularly difficult and lonely one. Detection systems have failed women so completely that there are from four to ten times as many men as women being treated for their addictions, even though addicted men outnumber addicted women only two to one. Vast numbers of women with dependencies still go untreated, whereas those who do get help are forced to participate in programs that have been designed with the male addict in mind.

As in other areas of medical research, women have been systematically neglected, particularly by those who study treatments for alcoholism and other drug dependencies. Researchers have relied almost entirely on male volunteers, and the results are simply generalized to both men and women, a process that does nothing to advance the knowledge of women's addictions or how best to treat them. "It's like operating in a vacuum," says addictions therapist Marsha Vannicelli, Ph.D., of Harvard University Medical School. "Maybe the study results based on men do apply, and then again, maybe they don't."

Because men have been the ones most often studied, they have also become the standard or norm against which women are measured whether women fit that particular picture of "normal" or not. Most often, of course, they don't. Instead, women are relegated to what's called a special population group, a designation that allows those who design treatment programs to exclude their needs in favor of the

needs of those all-purpose standard setters — white males. In that way researchers, policy makers, and doctors can leave existing programs as they are whether they work for all their patients or not.

For women, they are often quite problematic. Male-based treatment programs commonly fail to recognize the importance of the excessive guilt and shame that women suffer, to understand the impact of women's life experiences on their addictions, and to treat them as grown-up individuals who want and need to take responsibility for their lives. Julianne Harris, for example, went through three different rehab programs over a period of one and a half years and fell off the wagon each time before finding a therapist who was sensitive to her style of coping.

As with many women alcoholics, Harris found the therapy strategies used by her counselors to be confrontational rather than supportive, a method that has proven to suit men's behavior patterns much more than women's, says Hughes. Women are already so shamed and demoralized by their addictions that a confrontational approach is counterproductive for them, diminishing their already low self-esteem even further. Typically, says Julianne, the therapist would "scream at the group and tell us that we were idiots. They wanted us to get angry and yell right back to get it out of our systems," she says. In all the groups she participated in, nearly every man did just that. In fact, they got so worked up that she expected to see fist fights break out. "But the men really seemed to get something out of it; you could see that they felt better afterward, relieved," she says. "The women, though, would completely shut down. They'd start to cry and simply freeze and not be able to speak at all. I always felt worse about myself after those sessions and would dread each and every one."

Male-based treatments also tend to discount or trivialize the impact of women's social and economic experiences on the development of their chemical dependencies. Women are not just rationalizing when they relate the onset of their addiction problems to life events such as divorce, sexual abuse, joblessness, or childbirth, says Blume, and those events need to be addressed for treatment to be successful. Julianne's drinking, for example, began as an antidote to the humiliation of discovering her first husband in bed with their next-door neighbor. But it progressed rapidly to needing alcohol to boost her confidence for everyday situations, too, even something as routine as picking up the phone to call about a potential job. Yet, the programs she participated in didn't seem interested in her personal story. "The impression I got was that they had heard it all before many, many times, and so they didn't have to listen to what I thought or felt. Instead, they just wanted to tell me what the problem was and then give me the standard treatment."

Just as detrimental to successful treatment outcomes are the stereotypes and false beliefs that many therapists themselves have of chemically dependent women. The fact is, therapists hold the same negative attitudes as society in general. Women, particularly addicted women, are considered weak and therefore needing extra protection. Julianne found, for example, that the rehab programs tended to treat her as if she were a helpless child who needed constant tending. "It was as if, because I was a woman, I couldn't be trusted on my own to follow the program and do what was expected," she says.

Though therapists may believe that they are being supportive and helpful, the effect is anything but that. Says Vannicelli, "In my experience I have found that many women patients, and alcoholic women in particular, need to learn a different message about themselves, namely, that they are or have the potential to be competent, mature women and that they are not doomed to be helpless little girls forever." Indeed, Julianne says that it felt good to take responsibility for herself. "To say, wait a minute, I can do this. If I really want to stop drinking, then it's up to me. Being successful was the best confidence builder."

Chemically dependent women have also been falsely stereotyped as being sicker and harder to treat than their male counterparts. The fact is, however, that women *appear* sicker or less motivated to recover only if they are compared against the male standard. In actuality, of fifty-one studies that compared the treatment outcomes of both sexes, forty-three showed no difference between men and women, seven showed that women had done better than men, and five showed that men had done better than

women.* The notion that women have a poorer response to treatment is simply not supported by the existing research, says Vannicelli, who reviewed thirty years' worth of medical literature. "If anything, the weight of the evidence seems to lean slightly in the opposite direction."

And that's with treatment programs designed specifically for the chemically dependent male. What if there were programs sensitive to women's needs? What if there were programs that provided child care for those who needed it; that took women's social and economic status into consideration; that addressed the greater guilt and shame that women experience; that offered supportive rather than the male-oriented confrontational strategies; that included vocational training to improve women's employment opportunities; that worked on assertiveness training and building up long beaten-down self-esteem; that compared results with what's typical for women, not men? Would the outcomes be even better? The truth is, practically no research has been done to find out. Nobody even knows for sure if women do better in all-female groups rather than the more traditional mixed-sex groups, whether a female therapist is better for women than a male therapist, or whether individual counseling is better than group therapy.

"If treatment is done the right way, women respond well, too," says Julianne Harris, who says a day doesn't go by that she doesn't feel blessed. She had her turnaround, which has given her a new life, filled with hope "and diapers," she laughs. But she lost valuable time—most of her twenties—in her search for the right treatment. "I was lucky that I found someone who listened to me," she says. "But I shouldn't have had to find that someone in the Yellow Pages."

---

*The number of studies adds up to more than fifty-one because some studies reported data on more than one sample.

FIFTY-NINE

The Life and Death of Miss Mildred
An Elderly Black Woman
Annette Dula

Who is the elderly black woman? What do health care workers need to know about her life when they treat her for her numerous chronic ailments? What social factors are important when those chronic illnesses ultimately require decisions about withholding or withdrawing treatment? What must health care providers consider when they approach African American elderly to find out whether they have designated a power of attorney or documented their preferences in case they become incompetent? What are the implications of the Patient Self-Determination Act (PSDA) for elderly African Americans and members of other ethnic populations who also have disproportionately poor health outcomes?

This paper presents the life story of an elderly black woman in the rural south. It is a story about Miss Mildred's history, family, community, work, religion, health, and death. I focus on the elderly black woman simply because she is more likely to live beyond the age of 65 than her male counterpart. Miss Mildred is a composite of elderly black women in the rural southern community where I grew up: They are my mothers, grandmothers, aunts, great aunts, and cousins. They are blood and nonblood relatives. This narrative attempts to link the life, the chronic illnesses, and the death of a black elderly woman.

I have chosen to present a life story because many health care workers do not know the elderly black woman outside the private office, the emergency room, or the clinic. Because what they know about elderly blacks comes from the experts, this paper attempts to let Miss Mildred speak for herself. After all, she is the expert on her life. If one listens carefully, it is clear what she thinks* about her illnesses, her folk health beliefs, her health care providers, life-sustaining therapies, and her approaching death.

Certainly, it is the responsibility of health practitioners — as specified by the PSDA — to educate elderly blacks about advance directives. It is equally, perhaps even more, important to educate elderly blacks so that they themselves can participate in managing and controlling their illnesses, thereby improving the current quality of their lives. Before health care providers can effectively educate, however, they must have a firm grasp of the life challenges that elderly African Americans have faced at every stage of their lives: They must learn about and then understand and accept the culture. To do this, they need to enter the world of the elderly black patient and . . . enter that world cautiously. So let us now enter the world of Miss Mildred.

In the black community, traditionally, the elderly black woman sits on a throne of grace, emanating an aura of dignity that permeates her being. She is respected for her wisdom, admired for her strength, and honored for her contributions to the health and well-being of both the black family and its community. She is tapped as a valuable resource and a knowledgeable advisor because of her life experiences. Her presence provides a "certain steadiness, a calming effect on younger adults and young middle-aged adults as they are moving through the critical periods of adult development." She is an upright, upstanding member of the community; her very presence has served as a buttress against racism and discrimination. She plays a critical role in imparting values on work, education, religion, and family and community responsibility.

She is never referred to by her first name; she is Miss Mildred† to non-family members, Sister

---

*In Miss Mildred's story, references are included to substantiate Miss Mildred's reflections.

†Regardless of marital status, adult or elderly black women in the south are called "Miss." Hence, throughout this narrative, "Miss Mildred" rather than "Mrs. Mildred" is used. Also, "Aint" is a synonym for "Aunt" used extensively in some southern communities.

Mildred to her age peers and church ladies, and Aint Mildred to her dozens of younger relatives. She is called Big Mama by her grandchildren, her great grandchildren, and all the other blood and nonblood relatives that she has raised and cared for over the years. Almost never is she called just "Mildred."

Her beautiful flower garden with the snapdragons, zinnias, and azaleas is the talk of the neighborhood. She still cans, or "puts up," apples, blackberries, peaches, and tomatoes— all harvested from her own garden with her own hands. At church fetes, members line up to make sure they get some of Sister Mildred's famous fried chicken and deep-dish peach cobbler.

She is somewhat overweight, but *no one* in the community would have the nerve to call her fat. One of her church Sisters might dare to say, "You looking right healthy, Sister Mildred. Life must be treating you pretty good."

Sister Mildred might piously, yet playfully, reply, "Yes Sister, the Lord's been right good to me. I can't complain. If he calls me tomorra, I'm ready to go. And Sister, I hope you can say the same thing, too." And under her breath, she might be heard to mumble indignantly, "Don't you be getting all se-ditty and uppity on me, Tillie Mae. I knowed you before you became a Christian—when you wasn't nothing but a old fast gal, giving your life to the devil."

Elderly black women have a very strong faith; they believe in the Lord with all their hearts. They may show it inside or outside the church. As active church participants, they sing in the choir, teach Sunday School, or head a missionary group. Indeed, they are more active than elderly black males. Elderly black women occupy a most respected role as elders of the church and loudly extol the glory and the grace of God through shouting. They have given to the church all their lives, and when they become sick, the church gives back to them. The church provides some material sustenance, particularly in hard economic times or in sickness. Most of all, however, it provides spiritual sustenance.

Indeed, the older they get, the more religious elderly black women often become. A friend of mine recently said to me, "Chile, every time I go home, Mama done got more religious than she was the last

time I was home. One of these days, she's going to fly right off to heaven."

There is another group of elderly black women who do not spend so much time in the church, perhaps because of poor health, employment requirements, or lack of transportation. But their faith is just as strong. They pray and read the bible frequently, listen to religious radio, and watch religious TV. They have been faithful supporters of evangelical ministers like Oral Roberts, Jimmy Swaggart, Jim Bakker, and Billy Graham for a good number of years. Even if they cannot attend church services regularly, they do manage to attend the bigger and more famous of the traveling church revivals and camp meetings. Elderly black women contribute financially to the church, even though their income is meager.

> Although Sister Mildred may have little, she will share her food and visit with the infirm and others doing less well than she. As she puts it "I ain't got much, but the Good Lord done said that we got to help them that needs help. We got to give food to the hungry, visit the old folks and the lonely folks, and minister to the sick. Don't matter what color they is neither. We're all God's children."

Outside the black community, there is a different portrait of the elderly black woman. There, she is often seen just as a poor old black auntie or as an uneducated, domineering matriarch. Her main interactions in the white community are as a patient in the health care system and as a domestic in private or public service.

A number of surveys reveal that she thinks that her health is poor. If she is not doing too poorly, she may still be working in a private white household; some studies show that 72% of employed blacks over the age of 55 work as service workers in private homes and businesses. Although her health care provider and employers may recognize her strength, they do not often see her dignity, her nobility, her beauty, or her importance to her family and the black community.

She may not speak standard English very well, and most likely she has not received formal education beyond the eighth grade. Public school education in the pre-war south revolved around the picking of cotton, the cutting of sugar cane, the harvesting of tobacco, and the explicit and purposeful exclusion of blacks from equal education.

Miss Mildred cooks for the white folks and does a bit of light cleaning. She does not work nearly as hard as she did when she first started working for the Braehills. (She's been working for them off and on for the past four decades.) Over the years, she has worked as hard as any man or woman: She has picked cotton and tobacco; she has nursed white children; she has worked as a domestic worker for several white families; she has washed and ironed white folks' laundry in her own home. (Of all her jobs, she preferred taking in laundry, because working at home meant that she could be her own boss.)

"I even worked in a textile mill and in a furniture factory back in the 60s, when they first began letting us women work the shifts. That was the time I said I wasn't going to be no maid for white folks no more. But I had to quit both them jobs. Those chemicals and dust made me dizzy and sick to the stomach. So I had to go back to work for Miss Braehill."

Things have changed a lot since she first started working for Miss Braehill. In fact, Miss Mildred's white folks treat her pretty decently now, except at holidays. On Thanksgiving and Christmas, they expect her to bake ten cakes and ten pies and cook enough food for all Miss Braehill's relatives who come in for the holidays.

"It ain't so easy for me to do all that cooking nowadays. My bunions hurt me sometimes. I sure get mighty tired when I have to stand up for a long time. But Miss Braehill is pretty good to me. Since I got old she hired somebody else to do most of the cleaning. Now she even lets me leave early on holidays with hardly no fuss a'tall. After all these years, it finally come to her mind that I've got to spend some time with my own family and my own children on holidays. I remember in the old days, I used to hate it real bad when Christmas would fall on a Sunday. That meant I couldn't go to church. And that pained me a heap."

Sister Mildred started her own Thanksgiving dinner this year about a week before the holiday, so all the food was prepared by Thanksgiving day. She cooked candied yams, a 20-pound turkey, two sweet potato pies, 20 pounds of chitlins cooked with hot peppers, potato salad, a pork roast, some buttermilk biscuits, and collard greens seasoned with ham hocks and fat back.

"I know I ain't supposed to be eating these foods. And I done cut back on them some. These is the foods that make your blood hot, and rich, and thick. That's when you get 'high blood.' High blood is a disease that done killed lots o' us black folks. Now, you can cool down and thin the blood if you take a little bit of garlic water, or lemon juice, or vinegar. That's what my herb doctor told me to do. And I believe it works. But you've got to stop eating pork and grease. That's the hard part, 'cause that's what us old folks was raised on. The chitlins, and the ears, and the tails was the parts o' the pig that the white folks didn't want."

Miss Mildred invited all of her family to Thanksgiving dinner. They include her two remaining blood sisters and five middle-aged children. Only ten of the grandchildren came to dinner, but 20 great grandchildren showed up at Big Mama's. Uncle Boy was there too. He has no blood family, but the ladies in the community look out for him and make sure he has at least one good hot meal every day.

All the grandchildren and great grandchildren call Sister Mildred "Big Mama." Big Mama and Daddy Joe raised their nine children, two grandchildren, and the two Jones kids. The Jones kids lost their parents in the big fire of 1945. They didn't have anyplace to go, so Big Mama took them in. Aint Hominy still lives with Big Mama. Nobody knows where she came from—she just showed up one day and started living with the family. Now she is family. Thirty years later, Miss Hominy and Sister Mildred have the big house to themselves, except when somebody needs a place to stay.

Although the black family structure is showing signs of stress, it has traditionally been the strongest African American institution. One function of the black family has been to act as a buffer against the stress of living in a racist society. The African American family includes nuclear, extended, and augmented family forms. Strong kinship bonds in which relatives and friends support and reinforce one another are based on African heritage and the slavery experience. Often, a multigenerational family lives under the same roof. It is likely that our composite elderly woman lives in a multigenerational family. Some of those members are relatives, and some are not, but it doesn't matter. They are all considered family.

Sister Mildred has been feeling poorly lately. In fact, she hasn't felt too good ever since she had that operation 2 years ago. They took out her gallbladder. If she had had her druthers, she would not go back to Miss Braehill's. Lord knows she hasn't felt like it. She likes Miss Braehill; she is a nice white lady. The other day, Sister Mildred told Miss Hominy, "I'm so tired. I been cleaning up after white folks nigh on 60 years now. But I needs to take care of my burial. So I needs to keep working."

Miss Mildred had thought about retiring but decided, "Us poor colored women can't retire; that's what white folks do. We just keep on working and getting sicker and sicker. And then we die.

"Sister Hominy, at my funeral, I want you to make sure they put some gladiolas on top o' the hearse that carries m' body. I get a little bit o' money from the government, but honey, you know it ain't much. But one thing's for sure. I ain't got to ask nobody for nothing. I been paying two dollars a week for my burial ever since I turned 50. Soon's I die, Ebony Funeral Home's going to put up two thousand dollars for my burial. I done picked out and paid for my tombstone and a little plot o' land over in Freedman cemetery. Don't want none of the kin folks to have to put me away.

"I been planning for my death a long time. I know the Lord is coming after me soon. And I'm gonna be ready to go. I want to be buried in that pretty white dress my baby granddaughter give me two years ago. I ain't never wore it but twice. I want little Donna—how old is she now? 'Bout 30, I reckon—I want her to sing 'I am Climbing Jacob's Ladder.' That sure is a pretty song."

No matter how poor they may be, many elderly black folks have a little burial insurance on the side.

"I still has to pay for some of my medicine and I have to pay for it out o' that little bit o' money that I get from the government and from Miss Braehill. I also set a little money aside each month for the herb doctor. But if I don't have the money, she doctors me just the same."

Although Miss Mildred has been working since she was 11 years old, for the most part, none of her employers have contributed to her Social Security fund. She does receive Supplemental Security Income (SSI), which is pretty meager but keeps the wolf from the door. She doesn't quite understand that Medicare and Medicaid business. Medicaid is supposed to be for poor folks and Medicare for old folks. But even with Medicaid and Medicare help, it is still hard for Miss Mildred to pay for all of her health care needs. Still, she thinks, "Things is much better for us elderly since Mama died. Didn't have no Medicare and Medicaid to help the elderly then. But even if things is better for us than they used to be, I don't believe colored folks get the same care that white folks get."

Yes, Sister Mildred *has* been feeling poorly lately. It is all she can do to drag herself out of bed every day and do her housework and put in a few hours at Miss Braehill's. But she isn't quite ready to tell the family how lowly she's been feeling lately. Black elderly describe illness according to their ability to perform the activities of daily living: cooking their meals, cleaning their homes, doing their laundry, shopping, and going to the bathroom without aid. Although they may consider themselves in poor health, they do not regard themselves as really ill until they are no longer able to function on their own.

Sister Mildred will go see Dr. McBee. She doesn't think that Doc McBee is helping her much but since Dr. McBee likes her, Sister Mildred humors the doctor a little bit. "Dr. McBee treats me real good. But she ain't so good at explaining things. She uses these big words, and I don't know a bit more what she's talking about. She told me I had a tumor in my lung that was going to kill me. I didn't know she was talking about cancer until one of my grandchildren asked me if it was malignant. (I didn't know what that word meant either.) I don't know why them doctors can't just come on out and use plain language. Sometimes *she* don't understand things too good neither. One time my hip was hurting me real bad, and she wanted me to tell her what the pain was like. Now the only thing I could think of was that time I fell off the old mule and got kicked in the side. I told the doctor it had hurt so much that I liked to uh' died.

"And that fool doctor, much as I like her, thought I was saying I wanted to kill myself. That's when she asked me if I knew what euthanasia is. First I thought it had something to do with young people—youthanasia. When she told me what euthanasia is, I looked at her like she was crazy. I was kind of surprised that she even brought it up, since sometimes black folks can be mighty touchy about white folks trying to get rid of us. Maybe she went to one of them conferences that she's always going to and they told her to talk to her patients about these things. They sure didn't teach her how to talk to me about it though.

"But you know what? Ever since we talked about it, looks like every time I turn on the TV, somebody's talking about euthanasia, and doctors helping kill off old and sick folks. Well, I ain't seen them ask nary a elderly black on none of them TV shows and news programs what they thought about euthanasia. I believe the Lord will take me away when it's time to go. Ain't nobody going to hurry me along. You got to be careful what you tell these doctors. Even the good ones.

"Now, McBee's been talking about a living will. I'm kinda confused. I thought about signing that thing. But I didn't know whether they was going to try to kill me by not giving me good doctoring, or keep me alive on them machines, or keep me doped up on them medicines. I just ain't sure about this living will thing. I don't want to be kept alive on no machines. To tell you the truth, I wouldn't put it past them doctors to kill me off anyhow. Well, I don't really think McBee would kill me off, but she ain't the only doctor that tends me. So I ain't about to make it easy for them. I done

told Sister Hominy what I want done if I get to the place that I can't talk for myself. That way the doctors can't play God and decide that I done lived long enough. Them doctors think a pore old colored lady ain't got no sense a'tall. Well, I'm here to tell 'em different.

"Chile, they had Sister Johnny doped up so bad that she did not know nothing. Lordy, it was pitiful to see her. She couldn't do nothing for herself. If the family hadn't come in and combed her hair and greased her skin, why, she'da looked like nobody cared nothing about her. The nurses tried to do right, but they don't know how to take care of colored people's skin and hair. Sister Johnny woulda just died of pure dee shame if she coulda knowed that she was messing all over herself. And them nurses, honey. If they was busy, they'd just let her lay in her own mess. I do declare, I don't want to be no burden to nobody. But I don't want them to kill me off, neither. I'm afraid if I sign that living will thing, them doctors will use that piece of paper to kill me off.

"My blood has been real high, and the medicine that Dr. McBee give me just ain't working. So I been goin' to the herb doctor over in WestEnd and she's been treating my high blood. She told me to take some garlic for my high blood. And I been rubbing my side in alcohol and camphor for that pain that I been having for so long. My sugar's been high, too. My eyesight is bad because of the diabetes; I don't read nothing but the Bible and the newspaper these days. McBee is worried that I am going to get glaucoma and go blind. Well, I'm a bit worried about that, too. Even if I ain't got long for this world, I want to see it while I'm here.

"She didn't help me none, neither, when she told me twice as many black people die each year from sugar diabetes than white people. I don't know why she's telling me all this stuff, 'cause I ain't going nowhere till the Lord calls me. She just caused me to have an attack of 'high-pertension.' I don't care what them doctors say, there ain't nothing you can do for high-pertension except to stop worrying and try to get your nerves under control."

Miss Mildred has also been "bleeding from down below." She told her granddaughter that it was like having a period again. It sure is a nuisance, particularly since she had thought that her bleeding was all done with. Now Sister Mildred thinks that if she can just get through Christmas dinner, she will go see Dr. McBee the next day. She has decided that as a last resort, once it became clear that the herb doctor's medications weren't working either. She knows that Dr. McBee will find time to see her. She always does.

Miss Mildred has made it through Christmas dinner, but just barely. It was obvious to other members of the family that Sister Mildred was not herself. She seemed to be in a lot of pain. And she had to take to the bed a couple of times to rest a bit.

"I'm just tired," she told the family when they all tried to make her go to the emergency room of the hospital. "I ain't going to no doctor tonight. I just needs me some rest. Besides, the doctor can't do me no good. But I'll go tomorrow if ya'll will quit pestering me. All this aggregation is sure to kill me off. There won't be no need to worry about the doctors doing it."

After a family discussion, they have decided that 16-year-old BettyeLou will stay with her great grandmother and Miss Hominy that night, in case Big Mama has to go to the hospital.

In her heart of hearts, Miss Mildred does not want to go to the doctor this time. She is afraid that she will be hospitalized, and for Miss Mildred, the hospital is a place for old people to go and die. She'd rather die at home. She is getting along in age; she'll be 85 years old come Valentine's Day. That is already longer than most black folks live. She knows her time is coming soon, and she has no regrets. All in all, she has had a good life. And she is ready. Most of her friends have already "gone home." She is tired, too, and about ready to go and see her husband Daddy Joe and her own Mama and Papa.

She thinks to herself, "Daddy Joe sure was a good man. He worked real hard for me and the young'uns. But they beat him to death back in 1959. I always told Daddy Joe that his big mouth was going to get him kilt. Them policemen said he had a heart attack in the jail house. Humph! I knows they beat him to

death. And there weren't nothing I could do about it. Yes, I'm tired and I'm ready to move on where there ain't no more sickness, and meanness, and racial hatred."

Miss Mildred goes back and forth to and from the hospital several times over the next few months. Although her condition has noticeably deteriorated, collapses in cognition have not occurred. She has been approached on several occasions by her physician, who has requested that she "legalize" her treatment preferences through an advance directive. Dr. McBee understands that Miss Hominy is an informal proxy and that informal directives may be just "as ethically compelling as any formal document." But since Miss Mildred had so many relatives, her provider is afraid there will be some difficulties and lack of family consensus in carrying out Miss Mildred's wishes. Miss Mildred — after careful consultation with Miss Hominy, her siblings, her youngest daughter, and her pastor — finally agrees to document her preferences. She formally designates Miss Hominy as her proxy. She particularly lets it be known that food and water — whether artificially administered or ingested through the mouth — are to be provided under all conditions.

"Food and water ain't medication. I don't care how they give it to you. If you take away food and water from a person, you might as well kill 'em. I ain't saying that they have to do every blessed thing. I just want them to respect me and give me good care. Why, you'd give even a thirsty dog some water, wouldn't you? I just want the doctors and the nurses and all these young people learning how to be doctors to treat me just as good as they do the white patients. Like the Good Book say, 'Give comfort to all the sick, not just to some o' them.'"

It has been a couple of weeks since Miss Mildred signed the advance directive. She is certainly getting weaker and weaker each day, but her mind is still clear. She has spent some time in the intensive care unit, but now she is back on the floor. She wonders whether she has been returned to the floor because they have given up on her. She's heard that they do that sometimes — to make room for white patients. But to be fair, she doesn't really think

Doc McBee would let them abandon her, just like that. After all, wasn't it Doc McBee who got the hospice people to come over every day when she was home?

Miss Mildred doesn't feel too good within herself about how she is being treated. Since she has come back from intensive care, she feels that the nurses and doctors are just waiting for her to die. They are kind enough; it just seems that they have already disengaged themselves from her, they don't seem to care anymore whether she is comfortable or not. When she signed that living will, they'd been oh so careful to promise her that she would get good care and comfort.

Miss Mildred has her good days and her bad days. Yesterday, she choked on her phlegm. BettyeLou cleared the phlegm from Big Mama's mouth and kept her lips and tongue moistened with a wet cloth. The worst part, though, was when she had to go to the toilet. Usually someone in the family is around to help her. But every now and then she has to depend on the staff. She does not mind using the bedpan if she only has to make water, but it is a matter of self-respect and pride to get up and go to the toilet for a bowel movement. Thank God she can still get to the bathroom, even though she needs a little help. That morning, though, she'd rung and rung, but no one had come to see about her. That was the straw that broke the camel's back. That was when she decided that she would just tear up that darn advance directive.

One of the nurses finally showed up, cheerily inquiring, "Hi there, Hon. How are we doing this morning?"

Big Mama, with all the dignity and iciness that she could muster, answered, "I don't know how *we* are doing, Nurse, but I want you to go and get me that living will that I signed and bring it here to me so that I can tear it up. Maybe then I can get some attention. Ain't nobody paid no attention to me since I signed that thing."

Miss Mildred decides that she wants to spend as much of her remaining time as possible in her own home among friends and family, who are honored and happy to take care of her. Dr. McBee makes arrangements for her

to be as comfortable as possible. Different hospice workers spend a couple of hours with her every day. Dr. McBee also manages to find time to drop in each day or so, just to check up on her state and to chat with her. (After all, Mildred has been her patient for 25 years.)

The community will prepare itself and the family for her death; they will talk about all the good Miss Mildred has done, the people she has helped, the wise counsel she has given. They will joke about how she loved to go fishing almost as much as she loved to go to church. The few old friends who are still living will bring her food (which she will pretend to eat) and sit with her for a spell. Neighbors, friends, or family will clean her house; others will make sure she has clean sheets every day. And the younger ones will comb, brush, and braid her hair daily. Friends and family will come in and sit up with Miss Mildred—all night if it seems necessary. She will never be left alone. When she dies, someone in the community will most likely be with her to help her cross over into the other land.

Conclusion

Miss Mildred should not be regarded as a stereotype of the elderly black woman. Although a great many elderly black women are religious, live in southern states, and are surrounded by family and friends, a sizable portion do not fit that mold. Many do bask in the warmth and love of family, friends, church, and community, but some live alone in dangerous and poor urban neighborhoods—without either kin or social, psychological, and spiritual support.

Nor should the elderly black woman be romanticized. There is nothing romantic about having a nutritionally deficient diet or living in unhealthy and substandard housing with the constant threat of utility shutoffs or even evictions and homelessness, as is the case for many elderly black women and men. Whatever lens one uses to try to understand their life situations, it is clear that elderly blacks, as a group, are sicker and poorer than any other adult group in this country.

I have presented the life story of an elderly black woman because her biography is insufficiently appreciated, and because she is more likely than the black man to live long enough to be considered elderly. Although there may be other portraits, I have tried to present one picture of an elderly black woman's life—one that is embedded in a matrix of family, religion, and community. It is a profile in which health disparities in access, inequalities in health status, and end-of-life discussions cannot be considered apart from historical, social, and economic aspects of life. We have seen that Miss Mildred is an example of an important and respected member of a multigenerational extended family that includes both blood relatives and members who are not related. When decisions about life and death are being made, various family members will be involved. For the health care practitioner who is unfamiliar with black culture, it may be difficult to sort out who is who. She may not know that "Mamma Sis," "Aunt Tubby," "Aint Sister," and "Elizabeth" are all the same person.

After the family, religion is the most important institution in the biographies of many elderly black women and is intricately tied to family life. Religious involvement provides not only spiritual succor, but also social life, practical information, and political consciousness.*

If an elderly black woman is 75 years old, she has probably been working for at least 60 of those years, yet has not accumulated wealth or assets. Furthermore, she is unlikely to be enrolled in supplementary medical insurance or to receive Social Security benefits, and she may have only a vague understanding of the intricacies of Medicare and Medicaid. Small SSI payments do little to ameliorate her poverty. Therefore, she may still be employed part-time as a service worker, not because she wants to work but because she needs to supplement her income. If she is among the few elderly blacks enrolled in supplementary medical insurance, some of her small earned income will go to pay for that coverage.

The elderly black woman understands white middle-class people because she has been the recipient of intimacies that the white mistress would not even tell her best friend. Because of race, class, and

ethnicity barriers, however, health care practitioners do not know the elderly poor black outside the clinical setting. To morally intervene in the lives of their patients, providers need to understand those patients' culture, including family and community norms. They need to be familiar with the life stories of their patients, for it is through stories that we get to walk in other people's shoes. Stories open our eyes to other people's ethical dilemmas and dramas surrounding life and death. In a health care system in which the providers are mostly white and the sickest people are elderly African Americans, a larger sense of each patient's story will improve the quality of the everyday practice of medicine as well as the quality of communication with the person who is ill or approaching death.

As we see with Miss Mildred, differences in use of language contribute to misunderstanding and distrust. Health care workers may use unfamiliar terms and medical jargon that Miss Mildred is unlikely to understand. Conversely, the physician is likely to misconstrue or simply fail to understand what Miss Mildred considers the plainest description of her experience. Understanding and appreciating life histories can go a long way to eliminating the distrust that many elderly blacks may have for the health care system.

Miss Mildred teaches us that the elderly black woman is a proud and independent being. She is used to taking care of others—not being taken care of. She is used to doing things for herself. One of her greatest fears in life is that she will be a burden to her family, friends, and community. She would rather die than do that. Preparation for and control of one's own death have always been a part of black culture. There are accounts in black history and literature in which death is preferable to life. The idea of controlling the circumstances of one's death does not necessarily contradict the image of a self-sufficient elderly black woman. Rather, the difficulty will be in persuading her that health care providers and the larger society are just as committed to improving access to care and reducing health disparities based on race as they are to getting her to execute a living will. Only then will she be convinced that the living will is neither an excuse to kill her off by stopping treatment prematurely or to prolong her life beyond God's will, but rather simply a tool to protect her rights and preferences.

---

*Langston Hughes, highly acclaimed African American author, pointed out that many of the old Negro spirituals were really calls for political action. For example, "Swing Low, Sweet Chariot," is a song about a "chariot of freedom from slavery," not about a "chariot of death."

SIXTY

Lesbian Health Issues: An Overview

Ann Pollinger Haas

The biggest issue in lesbian health is that health care practitioners know so little about it. As in the general society, lesbians are a virtually invisible segment of health services consumers and are not identified as a subgroup in clinical reporting or in mainstream health research. Perhaps more disturbing, lesbians have remained quite solidly locked behind the closet door within the women's health movement (Stern, 1992).

For most health care providers, as for most women (including many lesbians), "lesbian health" prompts the question of whether and how the health issues of lesbians differ from those of other women. The aim of this [essay] is to address this question first through examining what is currently known about the health status, problems, needs, and concerns of lesbians. Following this, strategies are identified and suggestions made about ways in which women's health care providers can better serve this unrecognized minority among their clientele.

Background

Prior to the late 1970s, lesbians were rarely mentioned within medical literature, with the notable exception of psychiatric treatises and case reports, which invariably depicted sexual relationships among women as pathological and self-destructive (Berg, 1958; Caprio, 1954; Saghir, Robins, Walbran, & Gentry, 1970; Wilbur, 1965; Wolff, 1971). Around 1980 papers began appearing in the literature of medical disciplines other than psychiatry (Owen, 1980; Whyte & Capaldini, 1980) that urged practitioners toward greater sensitivity in dealing with homosexual patients. These made few distinctions, however, between the health status or needs of lesbians and gay men.

In 1976 a survey of gynecologists was conducted that provided the first empirical evidence of lesbians' invisibility within medical practice (Good, 1976). Among the 110 respondents to the survey, fully half said they had never treated a woman they knew or thought to be a lesbian; not a single physician could identify more than six lesbians in their practice.

This study was followed shortly by the first articulation of specific lesbian health concerns (O'Donnell, 1978; O'Donnell, Leoffler, Pollock, & Saunders, 1979; Santa Cruz Women's Health Collective, 1977) and the first systematic attempts to study lesbian health and health care experiences. [In the 1980s] a considerable amount of research has been done in this area, much of it emanating from the discipline of nursing. The bulk of the studies conducted to date have been surveys (Bradford & Ryan, 1988; Buenting, 1992; Cochran & Mays, 1988; Dardick & Grady, 1980; Deevy, 1990; Harvey, Carr, & Bernheine, 1989; Hitchcock & Wilson, 1992; Johnson, Guenther, Laube, & Keettel, 1981; Johnson, Smith, & Guenther, 1987; Lucas, 1992; Olesker & Walsh, 1984; Parowski, 1987; Reagan, 1981; Robertson, 1992; Saunders, Tupac, & MacCulloch, 1988; Smith, Johnson, & Guenther, 1985; Stevens & Hall, 1988; Trippet & Bain, 1992; Zeidenstein, 1990), focused primarily on lesbians' experiences with health care professionals.

Only a small number of these surveys have attempted to assess the actual status of lesbian health. These include a survey of 117 lesbians recruited through lesbian organizations in the Iowa City area by Johnson and her colleagues (1981), a survey by some of the same authors (Johnson et al., 1987; Smith et al., 1985) of 1,921 geographically diverse lesbians attending women's music festivals in the Midwest and New England in 1980, and a national survey of 1,917 lesbians conducted in the mid-1980s by Bradford and Ryan (1988) and sponsored by the National Lesbian and Gay Health Foundation. An even smaller number of lesbian health studies have involved physical examinations (Robertson & Schecter, 1981) or reviews of medical records (Degan & Waitkavicz, 1982).

While reporting extensive descriptive data, virtually all studies of lesbian health have suffered from significant methodological weaknesses that have limited the generalizability of their findings and resulted in sometimes considerable variations in their conclusions. Of primary importance is the fact that they have relied almost exclusively on samples of self-identified lesbians, typically volunteers recruited from among individuals engaged in lesbian social organizations or activities. Respondents have been overwhelmingly white, middle-class, under the age of 40, well educated, and, on the whole, relatively open regarding disclosure of their lesbianism. Survey findings thus provide extremely limited information about lesbians who are poor, old, from minority backgrounds, and not at all open about their sexual orientation.

A second weakness is that studies of lesbian health have generally not obtained data from comparable heterosexual women, making it difficult to draw conclusions about differences between the two groups. In some cases, notably the Bradford and Ryan survey (1988), attempts have been made to draw comparisons from general women's health surveys, but these have been limited by variations in the wording of questions and by the presumed inclusion of unspecified numbers of lesbians within the figures reported for women in general.

Third, studies have not used a consistent definition of what constitutes a lesbian for the purposes of health research. In determining their samples, most researchers have used measures based on Kinsey's original scale (Kinsey, Pomeroy, Martin, & Gebbard, 1953), with extremes ranging from "exclusively lesbian" to "exclusively heterosexual." There has been considerable variation, however, in whether the scale has been used to measure specific sexual activity as opposed to general sexual orientation and whether the samples have been limited to those who describe themselves as "exclusively lesbian." Moreover, the use of the word *lesbian* in these measures may have excluded some appropriate subjects who do not identify with this label.

Of final concern is the fact that most findings about lesbians' actual health status that have been reported have been based solely on self-report data and have not been validated through either physical examination or medical records. In spite of these methodological weaknesses and inconsistencies, a number of conclusions are suggested from the accumulated research on lesbian health. These are summarized below under the key categories that have been investigated.

Lesbians' Interactions with Health Care Professionals

In virtually all surveys reported to date, substantial numbers of lesbians have described hostile, intimidating, and humiliating experiences with health care providers. In some cases, these appear to reflect the blatantly homophobic ideas and attitudes that have been documented among significant numbers of nurses and physicians (Douglas, Kalman, & Kalman, 1985; Gerbert, Maguire, Bleeker, Coates, & McPhee, 1991; Mathews, Booth, Turner, & Kessler, 1986; Randall, 1989; Young, 1988), in particular physicians in the specialties of obstetrics/gynecology, family practice, and surgery.

The most common manifestation of bias among health professionals is the routine presumption of heterosexuality, which lesbians in all studies have identified as the biggest barrier to obtaining quality health care. In an excellent review of the literature on lesbians' health care experiences, Stevens (1992) notes that lesbians have overwhelmingly described their providers as presuming they had male sexual partners and as providing little opportunity to learn otherwise. In addition to making lesbians feel invisible, this presumption has been reported to lead providers to misdiagnose conditions, ask insensitive questions, offer irrelevant information, and provide inadequate treatment to lesbians. Although lesbians clearly feel more comfortable and less vulnerable with female health care providers, most studies have found that female providers are not significantly more likely to specifically inquire about sexual orientation and activity.

Although a large majority of lesbians in all surveys say they would like to be able to disclose their lesbian status to their health care provider, at least half express clear reluctance to do so out of fear of being humiliated or rejected or having their care compromised. Some lesbians say they would refuse to disclose their lesbianism even if asked directly or if they believed their condition to be related to their sexual activity (Dardick & Grady, 1980). Among those who have been open, reported responses include voyeuristic curiosity, shock, withdrawal, physical roughness, insults, and breaches of confidentiality (Stevens, 1992).

Not a surprise, such negative experiences lead many lesbians away from mainstream health services and discourage them from obtaining routine, preventive care. Almost 60%, for example, have been found to seek gynecological care only when a specific problem occurred (Smith et al., 1985), and almost a third describe their usual health care provider as "myself" (Bradford & Ryan, 1988). Studies have also reported a tendency among lesbians to delay seeking medical help and to turn to lesbian friends for advice and help rather than to health professionals (Deevy, 1990; Reagan, 1981; Stevens & Hall, 1988; Zeidenstein, 1990).

Researchers reporting these findings have noted their disturbing implications for the timely detection and treatment of health problems among lesbians. In addition, the lack of trust and comfort so many lesbians experience in their relationships with health care professionals may have negative implications in terms of lesbians' compliance with medical advice as well as their physiological and psychological responses to the treatments they receive.

An additional factor that has been found through several surveys to limit lesbians' interactions with health care providers is financial. For a complex of reasons, lesbians generally have been found to earn incomes considerably below what would be expected given their education, and to report widespread financial concerns (Bradford & Ryan, 1988). In addition, up to 50% in some surveys report having no, or very limited, health insurance coverage. . . .

In spite of the fact that considerable numbers of lesbians report infrequent and unsatisfying health care experiences, studies have reported a generally positive picture of their overall health status (Bradford & Ryan, 1988; Johnson et al., 1981). Further, research to date has not identified any health problems specifically linked to female homosexual activity (Johnson et al., 1981).

Legal and Partnership Issues Related to Lesbian Health

Of considerable importance and interest to lesbians are issues concerning their own and their partners' rights in the event of illness or disability. Half of all respondents to the Bradford and Ryan survey (1988) expressed a need to know more about their legal rights related to health, and the apprehension that rights might be violated within the mainstream

health care system appears to be widespread among lesbians (Simkin, 1991). Very few, however, have reported taking specific measures to protect their interests in the event of illness or incapacity, through such measures as executing a durable power of attorney, naming a conservator or health proxy, or signing a living will.

Although these procedures offer important sources of control to all persons, for lesbians and gay men they are essential. In cases where no power of attorney or nomination of conservator has been made by the individual while competent, courts have proven to be largely unsympathetic to the claims of lesbian or gay lovers or friends and have most often appointed a parent or sibling to take control of the incapacitated person's affairs (Hunter, Michaelson, & Stoddard, 1992).

Another very difficult problem faced by lesbians who are seriously ill or hospitalized is the exclusion of their partners from participating in decision making regarding medical treatment, receiving information about the ill person's medical status from care providers, or visiting in the intensive care unit (Simkin, 1991). At the time that a serious illness or condition is diagnosed, lesbians are likely to be particularly reluctant to risk any compromising of care that might follow from disclosing their lesbianism. Thus, unless the care provider specifically asks whether the patient wishes to involve any other person in her treatment, the existence of the partner is likely to remain unknown. This not only alienates the patient from the provider but deprives her of the opportunity to integrate the partner's emotional and practical support into the treatment.

Strategies for Improving Lesbian Health and Health Care

The picture of lesbian health that emerges from the accumulated research literature suggests room for significant improvement in the delivery of care to this minority population. Although they share many of the same screening, prevention, and treatment needs as heterosexual women, lesbians appear to be less likely to have these needs met. And, in the face of lesbians' unique problems and concerns, the mainstream medical system remains largely uninformed and disinterested and far too often provides care that is discriminatory and offensive (Denenberg, 1992).

On an organizational level, there is much that advocates for women's health can do to bring lesbian issues into the mainstream of the women's health agenda as well as into the consciousness of women's health practitioners: speaking out on behalf of the needs and concerns of lesbians, along with those of other minorities; taking a proactive approach to encourage the inclusion of lesbian health issues in the publications, conferences, and workshops of professional groups and organizations; publicly identifying and working to change the systems of health care education and delivery that perpetuate homophobic attitudes and practices; lobbying for identification of sexual orientation in all government-sponsored research on women's health and for support of much-needed research on the key health problems of lesbians, particularly cancer and stress; and disseminating the results of lesbian health research among women's health care providers.

Regarding the critical area of research, pilot efforts are needed to explore solutions to the unique methodological problems involved in studying the diverse lesbian population whose parameters are largely unknown and in which key segments are not readily identifiable. This includes the development of strategies to identify and recruit appropriate comparison groups of heterosexual women. Women's health care advocates can play an effective role by encouraging and facilitating broad-based awareness and discussion of these methodological issues among both researchers and funding agencies.

There is also much that can be done on the level of the individual practitioner to improve the status of lesbian health care. First and most basic, women's health care practitioners must themselves become knowledgeable about lesbians' needs and concerns through availing themselves of the considerable literature in this area and networking with the several different groups and organizations that are actively working for lesbian health on both the national and the local levels. Much can be learned by inviting and listening to the stories and experiences of individual lesbian patients.

Given that all women's health care providers will inevitably be working with lesbians, specific efforts should be made to ensure that one's practice is welcoming and respectful of women of all sexual orientations. It is difficult to escape the conclusion that adequate care cannot be provided to any women whose sexual orientation and activity remains hidden, and special efforts must be made to create an atmosphere of safety and respect that encourages lesbian patients to accurately disclose this information. Much can be conveyed to patients by the presence in the waiting room of educational materials that specifically mention sexual orientation or that directly address issues related to lesbian health. Routine office forms should be reviewed for heterosexist presumptions in questions about marital status or use of birth control. The inclusion of phrases such as *living with a spouse/sexual partner* in place of simply *married* signals the practitioner's openness toward the patient's sexual orientation and relationship status and provides much more useful information than what is obtained when lesbians in committed relationships are forced into the categories of "single" or "divorced."

The health history should include specific, neutrally worded questions on sexual activity (i.e., "Are you sexually active with men, with women, or both?"). Patients indicating current relationships only with women should be asked about past heterosexual activity.

Women who relate sexually with women vary widely in their identification with such sexual orientation labels as *lesbian, gay, homosexual,* or *bisexual,* and it is generally best to avoid using these terms in initial inquiries. Other terms to avoid are sexual *preference* or *lifestyle choice,* which many lesbians feel misrepresent their sexual identity and trivialize their relationships. The key to building rapport with lesbian patients is to express interest in their *lives* rather than simply their "lifestyles."

When patients disclose lesbian sexual activity, it is important to discuss the issue of whether or not they wish such information to be documented in the chart. This may be of particular concern in a clinic setting where the patient may be seen by a number of different practitioners or where review of the record by third parties may be of consequence. Although some practitioners use a code to remind them of the patient's sexual orientation, this too should be done only with the patient's knowledge and consent.

Once an initial relationship of respect and concern has been established with the lesbian patient, an effective partnership can be developed around the mutual goal of discovering and learning about the complex ways in which lesbianism affects health status and the health care experience. Most lesbians do not demand that their care providers be "experts" on lesbian health. Like all patients, they do expect that those from whom they seek help be attentive to and willing to learn about their particular problems, needs, and concerns.

Much needs to be done to persuade lesbians that they can be "out," safe, and well cared for within the U.S. health care system. Clearly, it is time for practitioners, educators, researchers, and policymakers to recognize and address the factors that have limited lesbians' access to medical care, fostered and maintained their invisibility as patients, and denied them appropriate treatment.

References

Berg, C. (Ed.). (1958). *The problem of homosexuality.* New York: Citadel.

Bradford, J., & Ryan, C. (1988). *The national health care survey: Final report.* Washington, DC: National Lesbian and Gay Health Foundation.

Buenting, J. A. (1992). Health life-styles of lesbian and heterosexual women. *Health Care of Women International, 13,* 165–171.

Caprio, F. S. (1954). *Female homosexuality: A psychodynamic study of lesbianism.* New York: Citadel.

Cochran, S. D. & Mays, V. M. (1988). Disclosure of sexual preference to physicians by black lesbian and bisexual women. *Western Journal of Medicine, 149,* 616–619.

Dardick, L., & Grady, K. E. (1980). Openness between gay persons and health professionals. *Annals of Internal Medicine, 93,* 115–119.

Deevy, S. (1990). Older lesbian women: An invisible minority. *Journal of Gerontological Nursing, 16,* 35–39.

Degan, K., & Waitkavicz, H. J. (1982, May). Lesbian health issues. *British Journal of Sexual Medicine,* pp. 40–47.

Denenberg, R. (1992, Spring). Invisible women: Lesbians and health care. *Health/PAC Bulletin,* pp. 14–21.

Douglas, C. J., Kalman, C. M., & Kalman, T. P. (1985). Homophobia among physicians and nurses: An empirical study. *Hospital and Community Psychiatry, 36,* 1309–1311.

Gerbert, B., Maguire, B. T., Bleeker, T., Coates, T. H., & McPhee, S. J. (1991). Primary care physicians and AIDS: Attitudinal and structural barriers to care. *Journal of the American Medical Association, 266,* 2837–2842.

Good, R. S. (1976). The gynecologist and the lesbian. *Clinical Obstetrics and Gynecology, 19,* 473–483.

Harvey, S. M., Carr, C., & Bernheine, S. (1989). Lesbian mothers: Health care experiences. *Journal of Nurse-Midwifery, 34,* 115–119.

Hitchcock, J. M., & Wilson, H. S. (1992). Personal risking: Lesbian self-disclosure of sexual orientation to professional health care providers. *Nursing Research, 41,* 178–183.

Hunter, N. D., Michaelson, S. E., & Stoddard, T. B. (1992). *The rights of lesbians and gay men: The basic ACLU guide to a gay person's rights* (3rd ed.). Carbondale: Southern Illinois University Press.

Johnson, S. R., Guenther, S. M., Laube, D. W., & Keettel, W. C. (1981). Factors influencing lesbian gynecological care: A preliminary study. *American Journal of Obstetrics & Gynecology, 140,* 20–28.

Johnson, S. R., Smith, E. M., & Guenther, S. M. (1987). Comparison of gynecologic health care problems between lesbians and bisexual women. *Journal of Reproductive Medicine, 32,* 805–811.

Kinsey, A. C., Pomeroy, W., Martin C. E., & Gebbard, P. E., (1953). *Sexual behavior in the human female.* New York: W. B. Saunders.

Lucas, V. A. (1992). An investigation of health care preferences of the lesbian population. *Health Care of Women International, 13,* 221–228.

Mathews, W. C., Booth, M. W., Turner, J. D., & Kessler, L. (1986). Physicians' attitudes toward homosexuality: Survey of a California county medical society. *Western Journal of Medicine, 144,* 106–110.

O'Donnell, M. (1978). Lesbian health care: Issues and literature. *Science of People, 10,* 8–19.

O'Donnell, M., Leoffler, V., Pollock, K., & Saunders, Z. (1979). *Lesbian health matters!* Santa Cruz, CA: Santa Cruz Women's Health Center.

Olesker, E., & Walsh, L. V. (1984). Childbearing among lesbians: Are we meeting their needs? *Nurse-Midwife, 29,* 322–329.

Owen, W. E., Jr. (1980). The clinical approach to the homosexual patient. *Annals of Internal Medicine, 93,* 90–92.

Parowski, P. A. (1987). Health care delivery and the concerns of gay and lesbian adolescents. *Journals of Adolescent Health Care, 8,* 188–192.

Randall, C. E. (1989). Lesbian phobia among BSN educators: A survey. *Journal of Nursing Education, 28,* 302–306.

Reagan, P. (1981). The interaction of health professionals and their lesbian clients. *Patient Counselling and Health Education, 3,* 21–25.

Robertson, M. M. (1992). Lesbians as an invisible minority in the health services arena. *Health Care of Women International, 13,* 155–163.

Robertson, P., & Schecter, J. (1981). Failure to identify venereal disease in lesbian population. *Sexually Transmitted Diseases, 8,* 75–76.

Saghir, M. J., Robins, E., Walbran, E., & Gentry, K. (1970). Homosexuality: IV. Psychiatric disorders and disability in the female homosexual. *American Journal of Psychiatry, 127,* 147–154.

Santa Cruz Women's Health Collective. (1977). *Lesbian health care: Issues and bibliography.* Santa Cruz, CA: Santa Cruz Women's Health Center.

Saunders, J. M., Tupac, J. D., & MacCulloch, D. (1988). *A lesbian profile: A survey of 1000 lesbians.* West Hollywood: Southern California Women for Understanding.

Simkin, R. J. (1991). Lesbians face unique health care problems. *Canadian Medical Association Journal, 145,* 1620–1623.

Smith, E. M., Johnson, S. R., & Guenther, S. M. (1985). Health care attitudes and experiences during gynecological care among lesbians and bisexuals. *American Journal of Public Health, 75,* 1085–1087.

Stern, P. N. (1992). Helping sisters. *Health Care of Women International, 13,* v–vi.

Stevens, P. E. (1992). Lesbian health care research: A review of literature from 1970 to 1990. *Health Care of Women International, 13,* 91–120.

Stevens, P. E., & Hall, J. M. (1988). Stigma, health beliefs, and experiences with health care in lesbian women. *Image: Journal of Nursing Scholarship, 20,* 69–73.

Trippet, S. E., & Bain, J. (1992). Reasons American lesbians fail to seek traditional health care. *Health Care of Women International, 13,* 145–153.

Whyte, J., & Capaldini, L. (1980). Treating the lesbian or gay patient. *Delaware Medical Journal, 52,* 271–280.

Wilbur, C. B. (1965). Clinical aspects of female homosexuality. In J. Marmor (Ed.), *Sexual inversion: The multiple roots of homosexuality* (pp. 268–281). New York: Basic Books.

Wolff, C. (1971). *Love between women.* New York: Harper & Row.

Young, E. W. (1988). Nurses' attitudes toward homosexuality: Analysis of change in AIDS workshops. *Journal of Continuing Education in Nursing, 19,* 9–12.

Zeidenstein, L. (1990). Gynecological and childbearing needs of lesbians. *Journal of Nurse-Midwifery, 35,* 10–18.

SIXTY-ONE

Asian Women's Health
Organizing a Movement
Sia Nowrojee and Jael Silliman

Over the last decade, several pan-Asian organizations have been established. Many address the particular needs of women and girls. These include the National Asian Women's Health Organization (NAWHO), Asian Immigrant Women Advocates (AIWA), the Committee Against Anti-Asian Violence (CAAAV), Asian American Pacific Islanders in Philanthropy (AAPIP), Asian AIDS Project, National Asian Pacific American Legal Consortium (NAPALC), Congressional Asian Pacific American Caucus Institute, Asian American Health Forum, and Asian American AIDS Foundation, as well as the Asian Women's Shelter in San Francisco. Pan-Asian organizations have challenged the "model minority" myth which has been perpetuated, albeit with different intentions, by both "successful Asians" and the mainstream culture. The myth masks the economic disparities and ethnic differences among Asian Americans.[1] Moreover, it exacerbates tensions between Asian communities and other communities of color, who are often compared pejoratively with this model minority. Asian Americans are often scapegoated by low-income whites and other minority groups who claim they take away educational and job opportunities.

The model minority myth perpetuates the false notion that Asian American communities are generally wealthy, with broad access to health and other social services. This false assumption translates into little funding for services earmarked for Asian communities. Asian women's health needs, in particular, have not been identified as research priorities in any advocacy or policy arena.[2] Improving Asian women's health requires organizing for change both within and outside of our communities, with an understanding of the global forces that impact our health.

Despite our growing numbers, most national research projects still identify Asian populations as "statistically insignificant." This makes it difficult to access even basic epidemiological information on Asian communities. A lack of knowledge of the immense diversity that exists within Asian America, in terms of cultural and ethnic background, language, immigration and/or refugee status, degree of assimilation, and socioeconomic and health status, has resulted in a lack of understanding about the kinds of interventions that would be most effective in reaching different Asian populations. As a result, health programs to assess and respond to the health risks and needs of Asian women and girls have been limited.

What we do know about the health of Asian women and girls is not promising. Though they are the most likely among women of color to have health insurance, selected subpopulations of Asians lack coverage. Asian American women are the least likely to have had a gynecological exam or pap smear in the last year, often because they lack knowledge about risk factors and believe that cancer is inevitably fatal.[3] A 1996 NAWHO survey examined the use of reproductive health technologies by Asian American women in six California counties with significant populations of Asian Americans. It found that half of the women had not visited a healthcare provider within the last year for reproductive or sexual health services. Moreover, one fourth had never received any reproductive or sexual health information in their lives.[4] Another study involving Chinese American women found that only 18 percent had annual pelvic examinations.[5] At least one third of Vietnamese, Laotian, and Cambodian women in the United States receive no first-trimester prenatal care; nearly half of Cambodian and Laotian American women consequently have higher-risk births.[6]

Rates of cervical cancer are higher among Chinese and Southeast Asian women than among their European American counterparts.[7] The national breast cancer rates of Asian American women are still the lowest of all women in the United States; however, as women move to the United States from Asian countries, their chances of getting breast cancer increase; the risk of breast cancer in successive generations increases, as well. This increased risk is presumably related to the loss of protective factors from low-incidence Asian countries and greater risk for breast cancer associated with residence in the United States.[8] Over half of the 600 Asian Americans responding to a 1995 national Asian American sex survey reported that they did not regularly use contraception or protection against sexually transmitted diseases (STDs).[9] Respondents also reported that sexual violence, sexual stereotypes, and shame impeded their sexual health. In another national reproductive health poll, one third of Asian American women respondents did not know where to obtain an abortion.[10] The poll also found that Asian American women are the least likely of all women of color to receive information about HIV/AIDS and the most likely to believe that they are not at risk for HIV/AIDS.[11]

Rates of STDs in Asian communities may currently be severely underestimated. In 1992, the state of California reported just 32 cases of syphilis among Asians, compared to 420 Hispanic and 781 African American cases. There were 482 cases of gonorrhea among Asians, compared to almost 6,000 Hispanic and over 16,000 African American cases. These disproportionate statistics strongly suggest the likelihood of underreporting of STDs within Asian communities.[12]

The First National Asian Women's Conference, organized by NAWHO in November 1995, brought over 500 Asian American women together to discuss the health risks confronting them and to outline priorities for action and research. A broad cross-section of the Asian American community attended this historic event, including government officials, health professionals and advocates, and community leaders. Over 12 states were represented, girls and women ranging from ages 13 to 65 participated, and translation was provided in two Asian languages.

The topics addressed in the conference shattered the silence of the Asian American community on a broad spectrum of issues.[13] They challenge the notion of a "model minority" community that does not need resources, research, services, or advocacy on health and socioeconomic issues. Participants unequivocally identified sexism, racism, homophobia, and violence—from within their communities, mainstream society, and the state—among the key threats to Asian women's health. This analysis demands a community and a feminist response to challenge the multiple oppressive structures that affect Asian American

women's health, in contrast to an individual or self-help approach.

Conference participants noted that Asian women perceive health broadly to encompass mental, physical, emotional, social, and sexual well-being. Spirituality, which includes the performance of rituals, ceremonies, meditations, and the use of traditional medicines and consultations with traditional leaders, is often considered an important aspect of maintaining one's health. Many Asian American women report using traditional health practices and medicines. There is a high rate of non-compliance with Western prescriptions among them, perhaps in deference to traditional treatments. In addition, research on Korean American women found that many avoid going to U.S. physicians because of "communication difficulties" and because they are "treated disrespectfully" by "impatient doctors and nurses."[14]

While many progressive Asian American organizations do not make health their central concern, they include health issues in their advocacy, organizing, and analysis. Thus there is a great diversity in the ways in which Asian organizations are approaching health concerns.

Asian Women's Roles and Health

Asian American women's notions of health are shaped by the ways in which our roles are constructed in our families and communities, as well as by mainstream socioeconomic, political, and cultural structures. As in most cultures, Asian families often place women in the taxing role of primary caregiver. Selfless devotion to the needs of other family members is held up as an ideal. This concept of selfless devotion can prevent Asian women from viewing their own health needs as legitimate and worthy of attention. Both community-specific cultural norms and the mainstream economy and culture reinforce these gender-based expectations. For example, economic pressures often require women to work outside the home. However, there is little public support for working mothers, and Asian communities often do not recognize or acknowledge the central role women play in family maintenance and survival. Thus, both the household and caregiving work of Asian American women is invisible within Asian American communities and in mainstream U.S. society.

Notions of sexuality and body image imposed by both Asian culture and the dominant culture also affect the ways in which Asian women think about themselves and their health. The silences within Asian communities regarding women's sexuality are based on several assumptions: that sex only occurs within the confines of heterosexual marital relationships, primarily for the goal of reproduction, that sex is another duty that women should perform for their husbands, and that there are different standards of sexual conduct for men and women. These assumptions often deny the spectrum of sexual relationships among Asian American women, which include consensual and pleasurable sex between partners, both heterosexual and homosexual, as well as the prevalence of violent, coerced sex; infection; unwanted pregnancy; incest; and unsafe abortions.

Issues relating to sexuality are extremely difficult for Asian American women and girls to discuss openly among family members, partners, or within the community. The recent NAWHO survey of Asians in California confirmed that one third of the 734-person sample never discussed pregnancy, STDs, birth control, or sexuality in their households. More than half were uncomfortable discussing reproductive health with their mothers and were even more uncomfortable discussing these concerns with their fathers and brothers.[15] Lesbian and bisexual women face particular challenges in finding supportive and safe environments to discuss their relationships and health concerns. As one South Asian lesbian activist states, "Because most teenagers are assumed to be heterosexual, it is common to feel that your sexuality just 'happened' without any sense of active participation in sexual choice and behavior."[16] The Asian Lesbian and Bisexual Women's health project reports that "sexuality is often not discussed in Asian households. . . . This lack of knowledge silences Asian lesbian and bisexual women, not only in terms of discussing their sexuality, but by preventing them from recognizing symptoms of disease or dysfunction and seeking appropriate healthcare services."[17]

There are direct health consequences stemming from the ways in which Asian women's roles and relationships have been defined by others, be they from within or outside of our communities. A NAWHO assessment of Asian women's use of reproductive and sexual health services found that there is a tendency among Asian American women to view gynecological ailments as important and legitimate only when they concern reproductive functions. This narrow view of reproductive and sexual health often prevents Asian women from seeking proper medical help when they experience symptoms unrelated to pregnancy. This has particular consequences for women who are either not likely to become pregnant, or do not perceive that they are, such as young or menopausal women, users of contraceptives, and lesbians. The assumption that women's sexual health is only linked to reproduction translates into Asian women's failure to seek out broader health information and services for STDs, including HIV/AIDS, basic gynecological care, and sexuality education.

The Commodification of Asian Women's Sexuality and Bodies

The history of immigration in the United States has played a role in the construction of Asian women's sexuality. In the 1800s, Chinese immigrants to the United States found their sexual interactions both within and beyond their community tightly controlled through immigration and segregation laws. Chinese women were not allowed to migrate to the United States, and Chinese men in the United States were prohibited from having sexual relations with white women.[18] The stereotype of Asian male asexuality that developed then persists today. In direct contrast, the stereotype of Asian women as being cheap, submissive, accessible sexual objects also pervades U.S. culture. The exponential growth in the global trafficking of women, particularly Asian women and girls, for industrial, domestic, and sexual work contributes to the view of Asian women as commodities rather than individuals with rights. The Western pornography industry, with its interpretations of the *Kama Sutra,* its specialized marketing of Asian women as passive yet artful and willing to please, and tourism in Asian countries, all contribute to the objectification of Asian women.

Asian women's sexuality—both in this country and abroad—cannot be disengaged from its global context. Economic forces and militarism have defined and exploited Asian women's sexuality for profit and as the spoils of war. U.S. servicemen abroad have worn T-shirts that describe Asian women as "Little Brown Fucking Machines." The potential consequences of these views were brought to the fore by the rape of a 12-year-old girl by U.S. soldiers in Okinawa in September 1995.

For Asian American and other immigrant women in the United States, these images and stereotypes have an immediate impact on health and self-esteem. One national sexuality survey found that 17 percent of Asian women have been forced to perform sexual acts against their will. In another survey, one respondent whose mother had been raped by a white American GI said, "A lot of Vietnamese American women and/or our mothers have experienced rape, so that's how we learn about sex."[19]

Many Asian American women work in the sex industry, where they are advertised as "exotic." Their workplaces may be massage parlors, strip joints, bars, informal brothels, or, for mail-order brides, their homes. These women face poverty, imprisonment, deportation, racist and sexist violence, rape, isolation, degradation, and lack of access to information, as well as other health hazards. The Asian AIDS Project, which provides health education and support services to women in the massage parlors of San Francisco, finds that sex workers often do not have even the most basic information on how to protect themselves against work-related health risks.

CAAAV, through its Community Courts Project, conducts outreach to women workers in massage parlors in New York City. It provides health education in different Asian languages and works with women to organize for better working conditions. For example, CAAAV has discussed how women can resist customer and police violence on the job, and has begun a self-education program on the issues that affect Asian women sex workers. CAAAV also links sex workers with organizations that provide health services for STDs, tuberculosis testing, drug use, and gynecological care, as well as immigration services. Still, much more work needs to be done to improve not only the health and working conditions of Asian American sex workers, but the larger economic and social conditions that enable their exploitation.

Immigration and Health

Many recent immigrants, particularly women, find themselves isolated in their new homes. For instance, in 1992, 42 percent of the Vietnamese American pop-

ulation five years of age and older lived in linguistically isolated households—that is, a household in which no person aged 14 years or older speaks only English, and no person aged 14 years or older who speaks another language speaks English "very well."[20] Linguistic isolation severely limits access to healthcare. Many immigrants have left extensive support networks in their home countries, and there is little in U.S. culture that replicates these connections. These factors exacerbate their sense of isolation and heighten stress. The NAWHO South Asian women's health project found that while many young women follow traditional behavioral norms in their homes and with their families, they try to assimilate into mainstream U.S. culture outside. This creates a cultural schizophrenia that causes unique stress conditions. Additionally, many immigrant and refugee women bring with them health histories rooted in their countries of origin. For example, for many Southeast Asian refugee women, the trauma of dislocation and resettlement results in medical conditions such as the psychosomatic or non-organic blindness reported among Cambodian women 40 years of age and older. Even when they seek care, language barriers make these conditions difficult to diagnose and treat. Their stress and trauma are compounded as they resettle in violent, inner-city environments.[21]

Increasing rates of HIV infection in many Asian countries make STD and HIV screening and treatment, as well as support services for immigrant Asian women, particularly important. Yet, these services are few and far between. Fear of communicating, coupled with shame and guilt regarding stigmatized conditions such as HIV/AIDS, deters Asian Americans from seeking healthcare. In fact, many refugee and immigrant women are at increased risk of both interpersonal and institutional abuse by virtue of their vulnerable immigration status. Current federal health proposals seek to further reduce even basic healthcare services for immigrants.

Asian women's residency in the United States is particularly vulnerable due to existing and pending immigration legislation that reflects both labor needs and heterosexist assumptions.[22] Most Asian women come to the United States as spouses of male immigrants. Men have the right to confer or withhold legal status for their wives, just as a U.S. citizen does for a mail-order bride. Mail-order brides who are allowed into the United States on 90-day fiancée visas can be sent back to their home countries if they do not meet with "customers'" approval. The undocumented status of many Asian women immigrants makes their health needs invisible.

Asian women are beginning to question the gender- and class-biased assumptions of U.S. citizenship laws. Immigration policies currently favor professional males as the "desired" or "right" kind of immigrants. This devalues the labor of women in the domestic and service sectors. While there is a high demand in the United States for domestic workers, they are not considered a priority for receiving immigration status. Thus many domestic workers are undocumented, making them even more vulnerable to exploitation and abuse from their employers. Similarly, sex workers are criminalized, even as the sex industry makes huge profits. The large number of undocumented male and female Asian workers in the hotel, restaurant, garment, and sex industries are subject to unfair labor practices as well as severe occupational health risks with little access to healthcare.

Domestic Violence

Asian American households are often intergenerational; older Asian women live with their sons, daughters, and other relatives, documented or undocumented, but remain invisible outside the family and community. Linguistic and educational barriers often prevent their integration into U.S. society. Moreover, many elderly Asians are extremely poor and financially dependent on their children, who are often their only connection with the outside world. The mainstream U.S. concept of the household as a nuclear unit ignores the needs of these extended family members. It masks their poverty and lack of access to resources, even within what appear to be privileged or comfortable households. Women in extended family households often experience abuse from other household members. Wives and domestic workers are particularly subject to abuse, more so when they are undocumented. Their "illegal" status translates into fear of public institutions. They are denied or deny themselves support services and forego legal challenges even in deeply abusive relationships or situations.

It is noteworthy, therefore, that for many Asian American women, organizing around social change has begun with organizing in response to violence against women in the forms of elder and spouse abuse. This is particularly evident in South Asian communities, where domestic violence organizations such as Sakhi, Apna Ghar, and Manavi reflect the extent of violence in these communities and the capacity of women to form effective organizations to counter violence. There have also been attempts by activists within Sakhi and Workers' Awaaz to address employer violence towards domestic workers in their homes.

In addition to community-specific organizations, pan-Asian organizations such as the Asian Women's Shelter [San Francisco] work across Asian communities to counter violence. The establishment and growth of these organizations explodes the myths that "Asians take care of their own" or that "Asian women do not experience violence." These organizations have sought to advocate on behalf of Asian women in the court system, where they are greatly disadvantaged. Many states, for example, do not require interpreters for victims of domestic violence. Consequently, many Asian women have lost custody of their children. Many organizations have also worked against the use of the cultural defense, which purports to "explain" abusive behavior as acceptable practice in Asian cultures and therefore beyond the pale of U.S. law. However, the mental, emotional, and physical health of many Asian women is seriously undermined by violence in their homes.

The sensitivity and familiarity required to work across Asian communities at the level of service provision is demonstrated by the Asian Women's Shelter. A group of Asian women formed the shelter in 1988 to create a "safe" space for Asian women. As Beckie Masaki, Executive Director and cofounder of the shelter, puts it, "A sense of safety does not only mean having locks on the doors and a secret location." It means a place where women feel safe, surrounded by what is familiar to them. To create a nurturing and safe environment, the Asian Women's Shelter provides its clients with language-appropriate services, as well as five kinds of rice, because each Asian community has its own way of preparing rice and knows its rice is the best! Also, familiarity with the culture makes the shelter staff aware of the fact that for many Asians, rice is a source of survival and nurturance that will help women heal.

Complexity of the Healthcare System

A range of structural barriers, such as anti-immigrant sentiment, linguistic differences, and budget cuts, affect Asian women's access to and use of existing healthcare services. The increasing complexity of the healthcare system, driven by market forces and increased privatization, has only exacerbated these barriers. Abuse and violence within the healthcare industry towards poor women, especially those who cannot speak English, further fuels Asian women's distrust of the healthcare system. A 1986 national survey found that 81 percent of women who are forced by court orders to undergo Cesarean sections are African American, Latina, or Asian. Twenty-four percent of those Asian and Latina women did not speak English as their first language. Even those Asian women who can speak and read English avoid services that are culturally alien at best and inappropriate at worst. Lack of outreach by existing community services to women who are often unaware of their existence further contributes to underuse of services, feeding the stereotype that Asian communities do not need public, easily accessible health and social services.

Organizing an Asian Women's Health Movement

Asian American women organizing together—both within and across our communities—is important now, perhaps more than ever. Anti-poor legislation is having an increasingly detrimental effect on the poorer sectors of Asian American communities. Asian Americans are the fastest growing group of welfare recipients, and they are not all single mothers. This negates the much-bandied notion that it is women's licentiousness that is the cause of poverty in the United States. In 1975, only 0.5 percent of parents receiving Aid to Families with Dependent Children (AFDC) were Asians, but by 1990 the percentage had grown to 2.8 percent. In 1979, 14,020 Asians received AFDC in California, comprising 2.6 percent of the total AFDC population; by 1992 the number of Asians on AFDC jumped over 480 percent to 82,177—approximately 9.5 percent of the state's total AFDC population. Southeast Asians, whose welfare dependency rates reach over 50 percent, have the highest dependency rates of any ethnic or racial group nationwide. In California, they comprise 87 percent of the total Asian welfare population and constitute the largest group of Asians on AFDC.[23] Many refugees from Laos, Cambodia, and Vietnam with no formal education or English proficiency have been channeled into welfare programs as part of a national strategy to facilitate their economic assimilation.[24]

Welfare cuts hit these immigrants particularly hard. Welfare cuts also seriously impact those Asians who work in low-security, high-risk jobs, such as those in sweatshops, canneries, and the sex industry, as well as in taxicab and kiosk management. Welfare reform is having a devastating impact on poor women, and even legal immigrants are denied social security, food stamps, cash assistance, and other social services. Immigration restrictions—and the fear of them—have serious implications for both the availability and use of health and other social services. In the days after Proposition 187, an anti-immigrant bill, was passed in California, crisis calls to the Asian Women's Shelter in San Francisco dropped by 38 percent. School attendance by Asian and Latino children also dropped in several counties of California, and use of health clinics serving Asians in Los Angeles declined. For primarily immigrant communities, fear of Proposition 187 diminished their access to potentially life-saving services.

In this hostile external environment, Asian American organizations must be committed to real power-sharing and equal representation within their ranks. Asian American organizations need to share information about existing resources, in spite of competition for funds. Established leaders must be prepared to serve as mentors to less-established activists, providing guidance as well as the willingness and opportunities to act on new ideas using new methodologies. In particular, Asian organizations must be especially careful not to claim to be pan-Asian if in fact they are not, either in services or representation. Pan-Asian organizations must allow time for their memberships to learn about the historical differences and stereotypes regarding country of origin, ethnicity, age, educational level, socioeconomic class, and political affiliation among Asian communities. The need to be open and honest about differences is critical. The need to organize within different communities is still essential, while advocacy efforts can be more broad-based or pan-Asian in scope.

NAWHO: A Case Study

NAWHO provides an interesting model from which to examine health advocacy for and by Asian Americans. It is a nonprofit, community-based health advocacy organization committed to improving the overall health of Asian women and girls. Formed in 1993, it is representative of the new wave of pan-Asian organizing that has developed over the last decade. From its inception, NAWHO has organized across a broad cross-section of Asian women with the understanding that the needs and concerns of women of Asian descent are at the same time specific and diverse. NAWHO is aware of the incredible diversity embedded in the term "Asian." However, it has made a conscious decision to work under this banner with a clear understanding of the strengths and pitfalls of doing so. The category "Asian" carries a political weight and strength that individual ethnic or national groups cannot garner. Moreover, working under this rubric may counteract the isolation of Asian women and has the potential for forging creative political partnerships across ethnicities and nationalities (NAWHO does not claim to represent Pacific Islanders, while it is committed to supporting their work).

Through an informal affirmative action policy, NAWHO has hired staff and recruited volunteers and board members who represent a range of Asian communities, immigration status, ages, and education levels. The staff currently includes a Korean immigrant, a Japanese American *sansei* [a person whose grandparents were immigrants], a first-generation Indian American, and a Laotian immigrant. NAWHO develops projects that focus on specific communities while addressing cross-cutting concerns. In so doing, it has emphasized the need for conducting outreach and advocacy in specific communities because language, cultural differences, and immigration status and histories make meaningful grassroots work across Asian communities close to impossible.

NAWHO's South Asian women's health project and the Southeast Asian reproductive health education project are both geared toward eliciting and sharing much-needed information on health issues within these different communities while involving them in their own advocacy. In contrast, NAWHO's assessment of the factors influencing Asian American women's use of reproductive and sexual health services and its Asian lesbian and bisexual women's

health report were not community-specific. Women from a range of communities were included, based on an understanding that Asian women face similar issues, albeit in different ways, and that developing common advocacy strategies can be very effective.

While underlining the need to be inclusive and to work across Asian communities, NAWHO has committed itself from the outset to working with other women of color. Women of color activists serve on the board of directors and advisors, and NAWHO works with established women of color health organizations, such as the National Black Women's Health Project and the National Latina Health Organization.

Racism both within and beyond the Asian community has led many Asians to distance themselves from or deny that they are in fact people of color; this, in spite of the racism these communities face daily. So while Black and Latino communities, in spite of their differences, have established both internal and external recognition of the value of collective organizing of people of color, Asian organizations have little history of organizing in this manner. It is therefore significant that NAWHO is a founding member and current Secretariat of the Women of Color Coalition for Reproductive Health Rights. The process of coalition-building across communities of color is not without its challenges, particularly for Asian women. As newcomers to this arena, Asian women have the difficult task of representing the diverse Asian community, often to communities who, if they are not in fact more homogeneous, at least have a longer tradition of identifying as one community with one common language.

NAWHO worked with the Women of Color Coalition to participate in the 1994 International Conference on Population and Development in Cairo and the 1995 Fourth World Conference on Women in Beijing. At both conferences, NAWHO played a critical role in ensuring that U.S. women of color were heard in both domestic and global negotiations, and that Asian American women and organizations, such as AIWA and Asian Health Project, were represented. For the first time, Asian American perspectives on immigration, reproductive and sexual health and rights, violence against women, community organizing, and sustainable development were represented in national and international policy dialogues.

In its second biennial health conference in May 1997, NAWHO focused on creating a political presence and voice for Asian American women to advocate for improving the quality of their lives. Local, state, and national leaders heard directly from Asian women about their key health concerns and aspirations. Since then, NAWHO has provided an educational forum for Congressional members and their staff, government agencies, and women's health organizations, focusing on gaps in breast cancer prevention efforts for Asian American women.

The emerging Asian American women's health movement has begun the process of deconstructing the stereotypes and structural barriers that have prevented Asian women from realizing good health. With careful strategizing that includes a vision of respect both for diversity and pan-Asian strength, Asian women are laying the foundation for empowering themselves and improving their health while building stronger and safer communities.

Notes

NAWHO's efforts to organize stem from its feminist orientation; it is part of the transnational women's health movement. We would like to acknowledge the critical suggestions, comments, and information provided by Mary Chung, Priya Jaganathan, and Anannya Bhattacharjee.

1. Although only 15 percent of all Asian and Pacific Islanders and only 29 percent of all households headed by Asian and Pacific Islander females reported incomes below the poverty level in 1995, there is great variation among subpopulations. For instance, 6 percent of Japanese Americans, compared to 60 percent of Laotians, were below the poverty level in 1990. The proportion of Vietnamese families reporting incomes below the poverty level was more than three times greater than that of Asian Indian families in 1990. Leigh, Wilhelmina A., and Melinda Lindquist. *Women of Color Data Book*. Draft. 1997. National Institute of Health, Office of Research on Women's Health, 55.

2. Chen, M. S., and B. L. Hawks. "A Debunking of the Myth of Healthy Asian Americans and Pacific Islanders." *American Journal of Health Promotion* 9. 4 (March/April 1994): 261–268.

3. Communications Consortium Media Center (CCMC) and the National Council of Negro Women (NCNW). *The 1991–1992 Women of Color Reproductive Health Poll*. Washington, DC: CCMC and NCNW, n.d.; Leigh and Lindquist, 55.

4. National Asian Women's Health Organization (NAWHO). *Expanding Options: A Reproductive and Sexual Health Survey of Asian American Women*. San Francisco: NAWHO, 1997.8.

5. Mo, B. "Modesty, Sexuality, and Breast Health in Chinese-American Women." *Western Journal of Medicine* 157. 3 (1992).

6. Leigh and Lindquist 55. Zane, N., D. Takeuchi, and K. Young, eds. *Confronting Critical Health Issues of Asian Pacific Islander Americans*. Thousand Oaks, CA: Sage Publications, 1994.

7. Jenkins, C., and M. Kagawa-Singer. *Confronting Critical Health Issues of Asian Pacific Islander Americans*. Eds. N. Zane, D. Takeuchi, and K. Young. Thousand Oaks, CA: Sage Publications, 1994. 105–147.

8. National Asian Women's Health Organization (NAWHO). *National Plan of Action on Asian American Women and Breast Cancer*. San Francisco: NAWHO, May 1997. 4.

9. "1995 Asian American Sex Survey." *A. Magazine: Inside Asian America* August–September 1995.

10. CCMC and NCNW, op cit.

11. op cit, Nowrojee, Sia. *Perceptions of Risk: An Assessment of the Factors Influencing Use of Reproductive and Sexual Health Services by Asian American Women*. San Francisco: NAWHO, 1995.

12. Nowrojee, Sia. "Asian Women's Sexual Health: A Framework for Advocacy." Keynote address. Coming Together, Moving Strong: Mobilizing an Asian Women's Health Movement Conference. San Francisco. November 1995.

13. Conference sessions addressed the overall status of Asian women's health; environmental and occupational health; reproductive and sexual health, including the needs of Asian lesbians and bisexual women; violence against women; cancer prevention and treatment; breast health; substance abuse; HIV/AIDS; holistic approaches to wellness; alternative medicine and nutrition; mental health issues; the implications of managed care for the Asian American community; and the need for aggressive political advocacy in defending a progressive policy agenda.

14. Duluquisen, E. M., K. M. Groessl, and N. H. Puttkammer. *The Health and Well-Being of Asian and Pacific Islander Women*. Oakland, CA: Asian and Pacific Islanders for Reproductive Health, 1995.

15. NAWHO, *Expanding Options* 10–11.

16. Bannerji, K. "No Apologies." *A Lotus of Another Color: An Unfolding of the South Asian Gay and Lesbian Experience.* Ed. R. Ratti. Boston: Alyson Publications, 1993.

17. National Asian Women's Health Organization (NAWHO). Asian Lesbian and Bisexual Women's Health Project. San Francisco: NAWHO, Spring 1996.

18. Takaki, R. *Strangers from a Different Shore.* Boston: Little Brown & Company, 1989.

19. Nowrojee, Sia, Crystal Jang, Dawn Pessaffo, Cianna Steward, and Jennifer Lee. "A Frank Conversation about Sex." Nowrojee, Sia, "Asian Women's Sexual Health: A Framework for Advocacy." Keynote Address. Coming Together, Moving Strong: Mobilizing an Asian Women's Health Movement Conference. National Asian Women's Health Organization. San Francisco. November 1995.

20. Martin, J. A. "Birth Characteristics for Asian or Pacific Islander Subgroups, 1992." *Monthly Vital Statistics Report* 43. 10 (1995). Supplement.

21. Rozee, P. D., and G. Van Boemel. "The Psychological Effects of War Trauma and Abuse on Older Cambodian Refugee Women." *Women and Therapy* 8. 4 (1989): 23–50; Frye, B. A., and C. D. Avanzo. "Cultural Themes in Family Stress and Violence Among Cambodian Refugee Women in the Inner City." *Adv. Nurs. Sci.* 16. 3. (1994): 64–77.

22. Masaki, Beckie, Anannya Bhattacharjee, and Karen Narasaki. "Violence Against Women: A Public Health Issue." Coming Together, Moving Strong: Mobilizing an Asian Women's Health Movement Conference. National Asian Women's Health Organization. San Francisco. November 1995.

23. Ong, Paul, and Evelyn Blumenberg, eds. "Welfare and Work Among Southeast Asians." *The State of Asian Pacific America: Economic Diversity, Issues, and Policies.* Los Angeles: LEAP, 1994.

24. NAWHO. *Welfare Reform Information Packet: Why This Packet Is Important to Asian Americans.* San Francisco: NAWHO, 1995.

◆◆◆

CHAPTER TEN

Women, Crime, and Criminalization

I n the mid-1990s, movie audiences were entertained by a new Hollywood depiction of women as violent criminals. *Thelma and Louise* (two White women run from the police after one kills the man who tried to rape the other), *Set It Off* (four young Black women in dire straits go on a spree of bank robberies), and *Bound* (two White lesbians try to steal $2 million from the Mob), among others, introduced images of women — Black and White, heterosexual and lesbian, working class and middle class — seeking revenge, money, fun, a sense of being in charge, adventure, and even "liberation" through criminal activity. Many moviegoers reacted with approval and excitement to these images of women breaking out of stereotypical roles, no longer the moll, sister, mother, or wife of the main character, a criminal man. In reality, the life stories of women in the United States who commit crimes and who are caught up in the criminal justice system are very different. Some steal from stores, bounce checks, use stolen credit cards, and use illegal drugs;

some are pickpockets and small-scale drug dealers; some are simply in the wrong place at the wrong time. They are disproportionately Latina and African American, and most are poor.

The National Context: "Get Tough on Crime"

From the end of 1990 to the end of 1998, the number of people incarcerated in the United States grew by 700,000 inmates, and by December 1998 the number of incarcerated people was 461 per 100,000 U.S. residents, the highest rate in the world. The criminalization of women must be understood in the context of a pro-punishment mind-set fueled by the "get tough on crime" rhetoric that has proliferated in the United States for the past twenty-five years, especially in the 1990s. In the 1988 presidential election, the Republican candidate George Bush used the case of Willie Horton, a Black inmate from a Massachusetts prison who committed murder while out of prison on the state's furlough program, to establish street crime — burglary, auto theft, mugging, murder, and rape committed by strangers — as one of the most important national issues. This tactic implied that Black people, especially men, were the ones to fear most. Since then, politicians and the media have reinforced that view by promoting and reporting on

This chapter was written by Barbara Bloom, MSW, Ph.D., a criminal justice consultant and researcher specializing in the development and evaluation of programs serving girls and women under criminal justice supervision; it has been edited and updated by Gwyn Kirk and Margo Okazawa-Rey.

legislation such as the "three-strikes-you're out" law, which requires a life sentence without parole for three-time felons, and by continually publicizing crime stories, particularly high-profile cases such as those involving murder and abduction of children. This trend continues although national and many local crime statistics show a decline in crime rates. According to the U.S. Department of Justice (1998), both violent crimes and property crimes are at their lowest since 1973.

This "get tough on crime" rhetoric taps into people's sense of futility and fear—especially White people's fear of people of color. People are led to believe that no one is safe from street crime anywhere, but especially around African American and Latino men, and that everyone labeled "criminal" is an incorrigible street tough or "gangsta." Contrary to this rhetoric, the facts show that women are least safe in their own homes or with male friends (as we argued in Chapter 6) and that the greatest economic losses from crime do not happen on the street. According to Lichtenstein and Kroll (1996), "Society's losses from 'white collar crime' far exceed the economic impact of all burglaries, robberies, larcenies, and auto thefts combined" (p. 20). Nonetheless, high-income criminals who commit such crimes as fraud and embezzlement are not only less likely to be incarcerated but also less likely even to be considered hardened criminals; rather, they may be regarded as people who used bad judgment or went "off track" (Sherrill 1997). According to Human Rights Watch (1999a), "get tough" anticrime policies, which have enjoyed significant public support, have become the vehicle for abusive policies and constitutional rights violations, documented by international human rights monitors. Although the United States regards itself highly in the area of human rights, "Both federal and state governments have nonetheless resisted applying to the U.S. the standards that, rightly, the U.S. applies elsewhere" (Human Rights Watch 1999a, p. 1).

Women in the Criminal Justice System

I stood with my forehead pressed as close as possible to the dark, tinted window of my jail cell. The window was long and narrow, the foot-deep wall that framed it made it impossible to stand close. The thick glass blurred everything outside. I squinted and focused, and I concentrated all my attention on the area where my mother said the family would stand and wave. . . . It would be good to see my grandparents and my mother, but it was my daughter I really wanted to see. My daughter who would be two years old in two months.

A couple of minutes passed, and in that small space of time, I rethought my entire life and how it had come to this absurd moment, when I became a twenty-one-year-old girl in jail on a drug charge, a mother who had to wait for someone to bring my own daughter to glimpse me. I could not rub my hands across her fat, brown cheeks, or plait her curly hair the way I like it.

(Gaines 1994, p. 1)

On any given day, over 120,000 women are incarcerated in jails—where people are held before trial and when convicted of a misdemeanor with a sentence of less than one year—and prisons—where people convicted of felony charges and serving more than a one-year sentence are held. Historically, women offenders were ignored by researchers and media reports because their numbers were small in comparison with those of men. During the last decade, however, the rate of growth in women's imprisonment has far outstripped that of men's. Between 1990 and 1997, there was a 49 percent increase among men and a 71 percent increase among women. In 1980 there were roughly 12,000 women in state and federal prisons compared with approximately 84,000 in 1998 (Bureau of Justice Statistics, 1999a), an increase of 88 percent between 1990 and 1998. There are ten times more incarcerated women in the United States than in Western Europe. Indeed, the United States leads the world in women's incarceration, but, according to Chesney-Lind (2000), it is

not alone in the mania to imprison. . . . Women's cell space in Canada has tripled since 1992; in Great Britain, the number of women in prison jumped nineteen percent between 1996 and 1997; and in New Zealand, the same two-year period showed a twenty percent increase. Essentially, it appears that around the world there is an increased willingness to incarcerate women.

(p. 7)

In 1998 almost 1 million women were involved with the criminal justice system, or 1 woman for every 109 women in the U.S. population (Bureau of Justice Statistics, 1998, p. 1). See Richie (1996), Rierden (1997), Ross (1993), Serna (1992), Stein (1991), and Watterson (1996) for firsthand accounts of women's experiences of incarceration. Shannon Murray (Reading 62) and Nancy Kurshan (Reading 63) describe prison life.

This dramatic increase in the imprisonment of women has been driven primarily by "the war on drugs" and mandatory sentencing for drug offenses. The majority of female arrests are for drug offenses, such as possession and dealing, and crimes committed to support a drug habit, particularly theft and prostitution, sometimes referred to as drug-related crimes. According to Drug Use Forecasting (DUF) data, more than half of the women arrested test positive for drugs (Bureau of Justice Statistics 1991). Between 1990 and 1997, the number of women serving time in state prisons doubled. This increase is also related to declining release rates and increasing time served. Almost 34 percent of women in state prisons and 72 percent in federal prisons have been convicted of drug-related offenses. Bush-Baksette (1999, p. 223) argues that the war on drugs targeted women intentionally. The sentencing guidelines, mandatory nature of the imprisonment laws, focus on first-time offenders, and mandatory minimums (prison sentences) for persons with prior felony convictions all brought more women into the criminal justice system and led to a tremendous increase in the number of incarcerated women.

Under current punishment philosophies and practices, women are also increasingly subject to criminalization of noncriminal actions and behaviors. For example, poor and homeless women — many of them mothers — are subject to criminalization as many cities pass ordinances prohibiting begging and sleeping in public places. Another disturbing trend has been the criminalization of HIV-positive women and pregnant drug-addicted women. For example,

in 1992, a woman in North Carolina, allegedly HIV-positive, became entangled in the criminal justice system when she went to a public health facility for a pregnancy test. The test was positive, and she was arrested and prosecuted for "failure to follow public health warning." Her crimes were not advising her sexual partners of her HIV status and not using ing condoms whenever she had sexual intercourse (Cooper 1992; Seigel 1997). Although this may seem an extreme example, it is part of a growing trend, as discussed by Dorothy Roberts in Reading 64. Pregnant women using illegal drugs are characterized as "evil women" and "bad mothers" who are willing to endanger the health of their unborn children in pursuit of drug-induced highs. There also has been a trend to arrest and prosecute these women for "the 'delivery' of controlled substances to their newborns; their alleged mode of 'delivery' to the newborn is through the umbilical cord between birth and the time the cord is cut" (Cooper 1992, p. 11).

Characteristics of Incarcerated Women

Women prisoners have a host of medical, psychological, and financial problems and needs. Substance abuse, compounded by poverty, unemployment, physical and mental illness, and homelessness, often propels women into a revolving cycle of life inside and outside jails and prisons. They are predominantly single heads of households, with at least two children. They are undereducated and unskilled, with sporadic employment histories. The majority of jailed and imprisoned women are unemployed prior to arrest (53 percent), and only some (23 percent) have completed high school. They frequently have histories of physical and sexual abuse as children, adults, or both. Nearly 60 percent of women in state prisons report having been physically or sexually abused at least once at some time in their lives prior to incarceration (Bureau of Justice Statistics 1999a). Imprisoned women are at least three times more likely than men to have been physically abused and at least six times more likely to have been sexually abused since age eighteen (Bureau of Justice Statistics 1999a).

The median age of women in prison is approximately thirty-five years; jailed women are a little younger, with an average age of thirty-one years.

Daily Life of Incarcerated Women

- Women prisoners spend on average 17 hours a day in their cells with 1 hour outside for exercise. By contrast, men prisoners spend on average 15 hours a day in their cells with 1.5 hours outside.

- Eighty percent of imprisoned women have children, and of those women, 70 percent are single mothers. Prior to imprisonment, 84.7 percent of female prisoners (compared with 46.6 percent of male prisoners) had custody of their children.

- Mothers in prison are less likely to be visited by their children than are fathers because women are sent away to other counties or remote areas of a state more often than men.

- A survey conducted in 38 states revealed that 58 percent of the prisons or jails serve exactly the same diet to pregnant prisoners as to others, and in most cases these meals do not meet the minimum recommended allowances for pregnancy.

- Many women come to prison pregnant; some become pregnant in prison. They receive virtually no prenatal care and suffer a high rate of miscarriage as a result. Congress has banned the use of federal funds for abortion in prison; women who can pay for an abortion themselves may be able to get one at a clinic, but will need to convince prison authorities to get them there. Women who carry their pregnancies to term are often treated inhumanely, denied prompt medical attention, and may be forced to undergo labor and childbirth in shackles (Siegal 1998).

- Health care for prisoners is practically nonexistent. It is common practice for prisoners to be denied medical examinations and treatments outright. Incarcerated HIV-infected women have no access to experimental drug trials or to use of new drug protocols.

- Sexual abuse of women inmates by male staff is common. This includes rape, harassment, voyeurism in showers and during physical exams, and touching women's breasts and genitals during pat-downs and strip searches (Amnesty International USA 1999).

- It costs more to send a person to prison for a year than to an Ivy League university for a year.

Source: Prison Activist Resource Center 1997, unless otherwise noted.

Most are unmarried (43 percent never married), and approximately 65 percent have children, two-thirds of whom are under age eighteen. It is estimated that 200,000 children under eighteen are affected by the incarceration of their mothers. The majority of those children live with relatives, primarily grandparents, and approximately 10 percent of them are in foster care, a group home, or other social service agency. About 8 to 10 percent of women are pregnant when they are incarcerated. For most women under correctional supervision, their problems began as girls. One national study of incarcerated women indicates that nearly half (46.7 percent) had run away from home as girls, and two-thirds of these women ran away more than once (American Correctional Association 1990).

Incarcerated women use more serious drugs and use them somewhat more frequently than do incarcerated men (Bureau of Justice Statistics 1992). In addition, women are more likely than men to report having used a needle to inject drugs prior to incarceration. The rate of HIV infection is higher for women prisoners than for men prisoners according to the Bureau of Justice Statistics (1999c). An estimated 3.5 percent of the women report being HIV-positive, compared with 2.2 percent of the men.

Offenses Committed by Women and Patterns of Arrest

Studies have consistently shown that women generally commit fewer crimes than men and that their offenses tend to be less serious, primarily nonviolent property offenses such as fraud, forgery, and theft, as well as drug offenses (Bloom, Chesney-Lind, and Owen 1994; Gilfus 1992; Pollack 1994). Notwithstanding movie images of violent female criminals, violent offenses committed by women continue to decline. When women do commit acts of violence, these are usually in self-defense against abusive spouses or partners. Forty-four percent of women who have committed murder have killed their abusive partners (Bureau of Justice Statistics 1999a).

Although it is commonly assumed that women addicts engage in prostitution to support their drug habits, their involvement in property crimes is even more common. In a sample of 197 female crack cocaine users in Miami, Inciardi, Lockwood, and Pottieger (1993) found that in the women's last ninety days on the street, 76 percent had engaged in drug-related offenses, 77 percent had committed minor property crimes, and 51 percent had engaged in prostitution (p. 120). Anglin and Hser (1987) found that the women in their sample supported their habits with a variety of crimes. Felony conviction data illustrate that the highest percentage of women were convicted of fraud and larceny, which includes forgery, embezzlement, and auto theft (39 percent), followed by drug possession (16 percent) and trafficking (21 percent) (Bureau of Justice Statistics 1999a).

Sentence Length and Time Served

Bureau of Justice Statistics (1991, 1994a) provided some information on the length of women's sentences and the time they actually served, which was much shorter. The average time served for those released in 1986 was 16 months. Violent offenders served an average of 27 months, property offenders about 13 months, and drug offenders around 14 months. In a 1991 sample, women received somewhat shorter maximum sentences than men but served much less time than men. Half of the female prisoners served a sentence of 60 months or less, whereas half of the men served a sentence of 120 months or less. Twenty-four percent of the female prison population received

sentences of less than 36 months. Women drug offenders received an average sentence of 79 months, property offenders 74 months, and violent offenders 178 months. For all female prisoners, the average sentence received was 105 months (Bureau of Justice Statistics 1994a).

Because female prisoners tend to receive shorter sentences than men overall, it has been assumed by some researchers that women benefit from chivalrous treatment (a so-called chivalry factor) by sentencing judges. Although the chivalry factor does have some statistical support, there is more evidence that women may receive harsher sentences for some crimes or that women who do not fit traditional female stereotypes—such as butch lesbians—may receive more punitive sentences than men (Chesney-Lind 1987; Erez 1992). When women receive shorter sentences, this is due to gender differences in the offenses for which they are incarcerated, their criminal histories, and the roles they played in the crime, such as whether they were accessories to men or were the "masterminds," and whether they acted alone. On average, women incarcerated in state prisons in 1991 had fewer previous convictions than men, and the crimes of which they had been convicted in the past were less violent (Mauer and Huling 1995).

Race and Class Disparities

Most women in the U.S. criminal justice system are marginalized by race and class. Poor women are pushed into the "underground economies" of drugs, prostitution, and theft as a way of supporting themselves and their children. African American women constitute 44 percent of women in jails, 48 percent in state prisons, and 35 percent in federal prisons; Latinas 15 percent of women in jails, 15 percent in state prisons, and 32 percent in federal prisons; White women 36 percent in jails, 33 percent in state prisons, and 29 percent in federal prisons (Bureau of Justice Statistics 1999a). According to Bureau of Justice Statistics (1998), young African American women and Latinas experienced the greatest rates of incarceration of all demographic groups studied. Nationally, between 1990 and 1997, the number of Black women imprisoned grew by 72 percent, Latinas by 71 percent, and White women by 67 percent. Women of color are also disproportionately represented on the death rows of this country (O'Shea 1998).

Many crimes committed on Native American reservations are classified as federal offenses, and lawbreakers are held in federal prisons, usually in remote places long distances away from home and hard to get to by public transportation, two factors that increase the isolation of such prisoners.

Racial bias is a factor in arrests, pretrial treatment, and differential sentencing of women offenders. Mann (1995) documents disparity in prison sentences by comparing arrest rates with sentencing rates of women offenders in California, Florida, and New York. She found that, in all three states, women of color, particularly African Americans, were disproportionately arrested. The few studies that report race-specific differences indicate more punitive treatment of women of color. In their study of one Missouri institution over a sixteen-year period, Foley and Rasche (1979) found that, in general, African American women received longer sentences (55.1 months) than White women (52.5 months). They also discovered differences based on race in sentencing for the same offense. For example, White women imprisoned for murder served one-third less time than African American women for the same offense. In a study of gender differences in felony court processing in California in 1988, Farnsworth and Teske (1995) found that White women defendants were more likely to have charges of assault changed to nonassault than were women of color. In 1996 the issue of differential sentencing for cocaine use surfaced as a public issue. Currently the sentences for possession and use of crack cocaine, mainly used by poor people of color, are much higher than sentences for the possession of powdered cocaine, mainly used by middle- and upper-middle-class White people.

The current "war on drugs," initiated by the Reagan administration and continued under Bush and Clinton, has been aggressively pursued in poor urban neighborhoods, especially poor African American and Latino communities, and in Third World countries, despite the fact that White people make up the majority of drug users and traffickers. A presidentially appointed "drug czar" is responsible for overseeing this policy. Proponents justify massive government intervention as necessary to quell the drug epidemic, gang violence, and "narco-terrorism." However, critics charge that "Blacks, Latinos, and third world people are suffering the worst excesses of a program that violates . . . civil

rights, human rights, and national sovereignty" (Lusane 1991, p. 4).

The declared intention to get rid of drugs and drug-related crime has resulted in the allocation of federal and state funding for more police officers on the streets, more federal law enforcement officers, and more jails and prisons, rather than for prevention, rehabilitation, and education. Poor women of color have become the main victims of these efforts in two ways: They are trying to hold their families and communities together while so many men of color are incarcerated, and they are increasingly incarcerated themselves. As Lusane (1991) observes, "The get-tough, mandatory-sentencing laws are forcing judges to send to prison first-time offenders who a short time ago would have gotten only probation or a fine. . . . It is inevitable that women caught selling the smallest amount of drugs will do time" (p. 56). As argued in Chapter 7, the international drug trade must be understood at the global level, as one way producer countries earn hard currency to repay foreign debt. Mandatory minimum prison sentences have had negligible effects on the drug trade in this country (Siegal 1998).

Girls in the Criminal Justice System

When people think of juvenile crime they often think of boys, but roughly two-thirds of incarcerated women were first arrested as juveniles, and about half of them spent time in detention when they were minors (Siegal 1995). Girls are likely to be held in detention for lesser offenses than boys, and a higher percentage of girls are in detention for offenses such as shoplifting, violations of probation and parole, minor public order disturbances, and driving without a license. African American girls are much more likely to be held in detention than White girls or Latinas. There are fewer options for girls as compared with boys in terms of rehabilitation and housing, so girls spend more time in detention awaiting placement. The great majority of girls in the criminal justice system have been physically or sexually abused; many have learning disorders; many use drugs and alcohol (Chesney-Lind 1997). According to Siegal (1995), "Probation officers, counselors, and placement staffers prefer to work with boys because they say girls' problems are more complex and more difficult to address" (p. 16). Girls express more emotional needs than boys. "Middle class girls with the same problems might end up in therapy, treatment programs, boarding schools, or private hospitals. But girls in Juvenile Hall have fallen through the system's proverbial safety net" (p. 17).

Dating from the 1890s, the early juvenile justice system held to the principle of rehabilitation, but the "get tough on crime" attitude has meant that many states have changed their approach. California, for example, has reduced the age at which minors can be tried as adults from sixteen to fourteen for twenty-four different crimes. The state has also changed the law on confidentiality so that the names of juvenile offenders can become public knowledge.

Women Political Prisoners

The International Tribunal on Human Rights Violations of Political Prisoners and Prisoners of War in the United States, held in New York City, December 1990, defined a political prisoner as "a person incarcerated for actions carried out in support of legitimate struggles for self-determination or for opposing illegal policies of the United States government" (Bin Wahad 1996, p. 277). A small but significant group of women in federal prisons is there as a result of such political activities. In Reading 65, Silvia Baraldini, Marilyn Buck, Susan Rosenberg, and Laura Whitehorn describe conditions at the Women's Control Unit in Marianna, Florida, which housed ninety women, including members of the Puerto Rican Socialist Party, supporters of Native American sovereignty movements, and participants in Black revolutionary movements in the United States and abroad. Silvia Baraldini, who was given a forty-year sentence, is an Italian citizen, arrested on conspiracy charges arising out of militant political activities in solidarity with national liberation movements, including assisting in the escape of Black activist Assata Shakur. She was active in the women's movement and the anti–Vietnam War movement, and was a supporter of the national liberation movement in Zimbabwe. Laura Whitehorn and Marilyn Buck define themselves as anti-imperialist activists. They were charged with a number of bombings claimed by the Armed Resistance Unit and the Red Guerrilla Resistance (Browne 1996). Susan Rosenberg was involved in the student

movement, the anti–Vietnam War movement, and the women's movement. According to Rosenblatt (1996), "She was targeted by the FBI for her support of the liberation of Assata Shakur from prison, and her support of the Black Liberation Army. After going underground in the 1980s she was arrested . . . in 1984, convicted of weapons possession, and sentenced to 58 years" (p. 355). From 1986 to 1988, Silvia Baraldini and Susan Rosenberg were held in the "High Security Unit" (HSU), a specially built underground prison for political prisoners in Lexington, Kentucky. Although this sixteen-bed prison housed no more than six women at a time, it became the center of intense scrutiny by national and international human rights organizations, including Amnesty International, and "became direct proof that political prisoners not only exist in the United States but are the targets of a well-organized counter-insurgency campaign" (O'Melveny 1996, p. 322). As a result of ongoing political pressure from activists and the Italian government, Silvia Baraldini was released to Italian authorities in 1999 so that she could return to Italy due to serious complications associated with cancer. Laura Whitehorn was released to a halfway house in 1999 having served a fourteen-year sentence.

Since about the mid-1950s, the federal government has operated "counter-insurgency programs," complete with special police forces and lockup facilities, to track, undermine, and destroy left-wing political organizations it deemed radical and militant and to imprison or kill activists. The Federal Bureau of Investigation (FBI) in its Counter Intelligence Programs (COINTELPRO) launched campaigns against the Communist Party in 1954 and, subsequently, against the Socialist Workers Party, the Puerto Rican independence movement, the Black Power Movement, particularly the Black Panther Party, and the American Indian Movement (AIM) in the 1960s and 1970s (Churchill 1992). Mumia Abu-Jamal, Leonard Peltier, and Geronimo Pratt were all convicted of murder, although they all claim to have been framed by the FBI. Geronimo Pratt was freed in 1997 after over twenty-five years in prison. A judge ruled that the evidence used to convict him had indeed been tampered with, as both Pratt and prison rights activists had been arguing all along (Booth 1997). Angela Davis, an internationally known scholar and activist, was imprisoned for two years for murder, conspiracy, and kidnapping charges but later aquitted.

Women jailed in the early 1900s for opposition to government policy were suffragists, whose crime was peacefully picketing the White House in their campaign for votes for women. In 1917, for example, hundreds of suffragists, mainly White, middle-class women, organized pickets around the clock. At first they were ignored by the police. By June they began to be arrested, and in August they received thirty-day and sixty-day sentences for obstructing traffic. A number of those who were jailed went on hunger strikes; they were forcibly fed and threatened with transfer to an insane asylum. They were released the following year by order of President Wilson, and the Washington, D.C., Court of Appeals ruled that their arrests, convictions, and imprisonment were illegal (Gluck 1976). This kind of political action was very different from that of revolutionary organizations committed to self-defense and armed struggle if necessary. But, like the sentences of political women prisoners active in the 1970s and 80s, suffragists also received disproportionately long sentences and harsh treatment, clearly intended to discourage this kind of sustained opposition to government policy. Browne (1996) notes: "A Ku Klux Klansman, charged with violations of the Neutrality Act and with possessing a boatload of explosives and weapons to be used in an invasion of the Caribbean island of Dominica, received eight years. Yet Linda Evans [charged with bombings claimed by militant left-wing groups], convicted of purchasing four weapons with false ID, was sentenced to 40 years — the longest sentence ever imposed for this offense" (p. 285).

Another example of politically motivated incarceration was the internment of thousands of Japanese Americans in remote camps following the bombing of Pearl Harbor by Japanese troops during World War II, as described by Rita Takahashi in Reading 66. Most of these people were U.S. citizens, living in West Coast states. They were forced to leave their homes and property, and were kept in the camps for the duration of the war. In Reading 67, Wendy Young describes the experiences of three Chinese women who came to the United States in 1993 to escape China's coercive "one child" family-planning policy and who, in 1997, were still being held in detention by the Immigration and Naturalization Service (INS) under extremely harsh conditions, waiting for decisions on their applications for political asylum.

Theories of Women and Crime

There is a lack of research specifically on women in conflict with the law in the United States. This is partly because until the 1980s far fewer women than men were caught up in the criminal justice system and also because it is difficult for researchers to obtain access to women in prison. Official data collected by the Bureau of Justice are limited and often date back several years by the time they are published, a limitation of the data cited in this chapter.

Theories of female criminality have been developed primarily from two strands of thought. The first approach is taken by those who attempt to explain female criminality in individual terms. These theories often apply assumptions and stereotypes about the "female psyche" that are blatantly sexist and without much evidence to support their claims. They include biological arguments — for example, that women commit crimes as a result of premenstrual syndrome (PMS) — and psychological notions — that "hysterical" women behave criminally, or that women are conniving and manipulative, and so resort to using poison rather than a gun to kill a person.

The second approach applies traditional theories of crime, developed to explain male criminality, to women. These include theories of *social learning* (crime is learned), *social process* (individuals are affected by institutions such as the family, school, and peers), and *social structure* (individuals are shaped by structural inequalities), and *conflict theory,* a specific social structure theory, which generally claims that the law is a weapon of social control used by the powerful against the less powerful (Turk 1995).

An apparent increase in female crime in the 1960s and 1970s prompted new theories attributing female criminality to the women's liberation movement. The female offender was identified as its "dark side" (Chesney-Lind 1986). More recently, the phenomenon of girls in gangs has been blamed on the women's movement (Chesney-Lind and Shelden 1992). Sociologist Freda Adler (1975), for example, proposed that women were committing an increasing number of violent crimes because the women's movement had created a liberated, tougher class of women, a view that became known as the "masculinity thesis." Similarly, Simon (1975) argued that a rise in women's involvement in property crimes, such as theft, embezzlement, and fraud, was due to women entering previously male occupations, such as banking and business, and to their consequent exposure to opportunities for crime that were previously the preserve of men. This theory is called the "opportunity thesis." Neither of these theses is supported by much empirical evidence.

A third theory of female criminality, the "economic marginalization thesis," posits that it is the absence, rather than the availability, of employment opportunity for women that appears to lead to increases in female crime (Giordano, Kerbel, and Dudley 1981; Naffine 1987). According to this view, most crime committed by women is petty property crime, such as theft, a rational response to poverty and economic insecurity. The increasing numbers of single women supporting dependent children mean that more women may risk the benefits of criminal activity as supplements or alternatives to employment (Rafter 1990). Noting that the majority of female offenders are low-income women who committed nonemployment-related crimes, rather than middle- and upper-middle-class professional women who committed employment-related crimes, proponents of economic marginalization theory argue that the feminization of poverty, not women's liberation, is the social trend most relevant to female criminality.

Contemporary feminist research on women and crime, though still in its early stages, has contributed to our understanding of women's experiences on their own terms, not simply by contrasting women's experiences to men's. Feminist scholars have attempted to explain crime, gender differences in crime rates, and the exploitation of female victims from different perspectives. Some view the cause of female crime as originating in male supremacy, which subordinates women through male domination and aggression, and in men's efforts to control women sexually. Such scholars attempt to show how physical and sexual victimization of girls and women can be underlying causes of criminal behavior (Chesney-Lind 1995; Owen and Bloom 1995). They argue that the exploitation of women and girls causes some to run away or to begin abusing drugs at an early age,

which often leads to criminal activity. This links to our discussion of violence against women in Chapter 6. Note that the research and activism concerning violence against women, and that concerning incarcerated women, generally remain separate, though there are important connections between them. Many women in the prison system are victims of gender violence, as mentioned earlier, and some of them are there precisely because of this.

Other feminists view gender inequality as stemming from the unequal power of women and men in a capitalist society (Connell 1990; Messerschmidt 1986). They trace the origins of gender differences to the development of private property and male domination over the laws of inheritance, asserting that within the current economic system, men control women economically as well as socially. Such theorists argue that women commit fewer crimes than men because women are isolated in the family and have fewer opportunities to engage in white-collar crimes or street crimes. Since capitalism renders women relatively powerless both in the home and in the economic arena, any crimes they commit are less serious, nonviolent, self-destructive crimes such as drug possession and prostitution. Moreover, women's powerlessness also increases the likelihood that they will be the target of violent acts, usually by men.

Although these feminist theories break some new ground in explaining women's criminal behavior, they do not explain why some women commit crimes and others from the same backgrounds and similar life circumstances do not. Compelling theoretical explanations for women's crime do not yet exist, and further research is needed.

"Equality with a Vengeance": Is Equal Treatment Fair Treatment?

Feminist legal scholars have been very concerned about women's treatment in the criminal justice system. Pollack (1994) asks, are women receiving more equal treatment today? If equal treatment relates to equal incarceration, then the answer appears to be a resounding yes. More women offenders are likely to be incarcerated than at any other time in U.S. history. There is a continuing debate among feminist legal scholars about whether equality under the law is necessarily good for women (Chesney-Lind 1995; K. Daly 1994). On the one hand, some argue that the only way to eliminate the discriminatory treatment and oppression that women have experienced in the past is to push for continued equalization under the law. Though equal treatment may hurt women in the short run, in the long run it is the only way to guarantee that women will be treated as equal partners economically and socially. For example, MacKinnon (1987) states, "For women to affirm difference, when difference means dominance, as it does with gender, means to affirm the qualities and characteristics of powerlessness" (pp. 38–39). Even legal scholars who do not view women as an oppressed group conclude that women will be victimized by laws created out of "concern and affection" and designed to protect them.

Another view maintains that any approach focusing on equality and inequality always presumes that the norm is men. Hence studies of criminal justice always compare the treatment of women with that of men, and men remain the standard against which all are judged (Smart 1995). Some feminist scholars call for a recognition of the differential, or "special" needs of women. Critics of both of these positions note that the equal-treatment and special-needs approaches accept the domination of male definitions: Equality is defined as having rights equal to those of males, and differential needs are defined as needs different from those of males. Women are the "other" under the law; the bottom line is a male one (Smart 1989).

Although these scholars have identified the limitations of an equal-treatment model in law or in research into legal practices, that model, and the evidence on which it is based, is the centerpiece for sentencing reforms throughout the United States. These gender-neutral sentencing reforms aim to reduce disparities in sentencing by punishing like crimes in the same way. Through this emphasis on parity and the utilization of a male standard, more women are being imprisoned (K. Daly 1994). New prison beds for women take the place of alternatives to prison, and gender-blind mandatory sentencing statutes, particularly for drug-law violations, contribute to the rising numbers of women in prison. A Phoenix, Arizona, sheriff proudly boasted, "I don't believe in discrimination" after he established the first female chain gang in the United States, where women, whose work boots are chained together, pick up trash in downtown Phoenix (In Phoenix chain gangs for women 1996). This is what Lahey (1985) has called "equality with a vengeance."

Another effect of the equalization approach has been in the types of facilities women are sentenced to. For example, boot camps have become popular with prison authorities as an alternative to prison for juvenile and adult offenders. New York, for instance, operates a boot camp for women that is modeled on those for men. This includes uniforms, shorn hair, humiliation for behaviors considered to be disrespectful of staff, and other militaristic approaches.

Carlen (1989) argues that equality with men in the criminal justice system means more punitive measures applied to women. Instead, she advocates the supervision of women in noncustodial settings in their communities, where they can remain connected with their children and families, and calls for reducing the number of prison beds for women and using nonprison alternatives for all but the most dangerous offenders. She bases her argument on the fact that most women commit nonviolent crimes and are themselves victims of physical, sexual, and emotional abuse. Therefore, she claims, programs that acknowledge women's victimization and support their emotional needs are more appropriate than punitive measures.

The "Prison Industrial Complex"

Public policy, however, is going in the other direction, with an emphasis on incarceration. Currently there are more than 2 million people — women and men — in U.S. jails and prisons. Government funding for the building and operation of new jails and prisons has increased while funding for social services, education, welfare, and housing has been cut.

Some critics of the criminal justice system argue that this current trend has created what they term the "prison industrial complex" (Browne 1996; Davis 1997; Walker 1996). Borrowing from the term "military industrial complex," coined by President Dwight Eisenhower in the 1950s, the phrase "prison industrial complex" refers to the increasingly interconnected relationship between private corporations, the public prison system, and public interests. The Corrections Corporation of America manages many

The U.S. Criminal Justice System and Violations of Human Rights

- In 1998 approximately 3.9 million U.S. citizens (most of them African American men) were denied the right to vote because of felony convictions. No other democratic country in the world denies as many people in absolute or proportional terms (Human Rights Watch 1999a).

- Drug control policies emphasize surveillance in poor urban communities, especially communities of color, resulting in a higher number of arrests, convictions, and imprisonment. The use and sale of crack cocaine result in much harsher sentences than those for powder cocaine (mainly used by Whites), which means that African Americans and Latinos are punished more severely than Whites for cocaine use (Human Rights Watch 1999a).

- Two-thirds of women on probation are White; two-thirds of women in jails and prisons are women of color.

- Fifty percent of incarcerated women were living below the poverty line when arrested (Amnesty International USA 1999).

- Male correctional officers subject female inmates to rape, other sexual assault, sexual extortion, and groping during body searches, as well as retaliating—often brutally—against female inmates who complain about sexual harassment. According to the U.S. Justice Department, in 1997 only ten prison employees in the entire federal system were disciplined for this; seven were prosecuted. Such human rights violations are routine (Amnesty International USA 1999).

prisons in this country. The construction and servicing of prisons and jails have become big business—indeed, the big growth industry of the 1990s (Walker 1996). Profits are being generated not only by archi-

tecture firms designing prisons, security companies supplying equipment, and food distribution companies providing food service but also, in part, by the direct and indirect exploitation of prisoners. For example, TWA and Best Western (the international motel chain) use prisoners to take calls from customers during times when there is an overflow, such as before holidays and certain vacation periods. Microsoft, Victoria's Secret, and Boeing are also using low-cost prison labor. Blue jeans and Spice Girls paraphernalia are made in U.S. prisons (Parenti 1999). The prison industry employs some 500,000 people, more than any Fortune 500 corporation except General Motors transportation (Light 1999). This is being done for a number of reasons: It is difficult to attract regular workers for seasonal employment, prisoners do not have to be paid minimum wage or be covered by workers' compensation (a tax employers must pay for regular employees), and they cannot unionize (Lichtenstein and Kroll 1996). Telephone companies also profit because people outside jails and prisons are not allowed to call prisoners directly; prisoners are allowed only to call collect, which is one of the most expensive ways of making telephone calls. Telecommunications industry officials estimate that the corrections communications market generates about $1 billion annually, and it is expected to grow in the future (Walker 1996).

Inside/Outside Connections

The issue of crime and criminality is an important one for women because of the massive increase in the number of women who are serving time in U.S. jails and prisons and because the criminalization of women is one of the most dramatic ways in which gender, race, and class position shape women's lives. Many in this society are shielded from this reality because incarcerated women are literally locked away, behind bars, and out of sight. In many cases, society has given up on them.

The societal assumptions that justify and reinforce this separation between "inside" and "outside" are that these are bad women, perhaps foolishly involved with criminal men, a little crazy from drink, drugs, or the pain of their lives, but that they must have done something *terrible* to end up in jail. Criminal and noncriminal women often share the same life situations. Many have experienced physical, sexual, and emotional abuse, racism, sexism, classism, and other forms of exploitation. Most women who commit crimes are economically marginalized, involved in drug and alcohol abuse, and single heads of households. The crimes they commit reflect their marginalization in our society and generally are a result of being poor, women of color, or both.

Women who have never been incarcerated can be allies to incarcerated and formerly incarcerated women by getting involved in advocacy organizations or by attending activities involving former prisoners and activists. Examples include Aid to Incarcerated Mothers (Atlanta), Let's Start (St. Louis, Mo.), the National Women's Law Center Women's Prison Project (Washington, D.C.), National Network for Women in Prison (San Francisco), and Social Justice for Women (Boston). Women on the outside are working with women prisoners in literacy classes and creative writing projects, such as the Medea Project: Theater for Incarcerated Women (San Francisco) and the Women in Prison Project, sponsored by *Woman's Way* (Utah and Boulder, Colo.), or supporting self-help groups run by prisoners, such as Convicted Women against Violence at the California Institution for Women. AIDS awareness programs for people in prison are sponsored by the ACLU National Prison Project (Washington, D.C.) and the AIDS in Prison Project (New York). Women in a maximum-security prison have organized HIV peer education (Members of the AIDS Counseling and Education Program of the Bedford

Hills Correctional Facility 1998). Films by and about women who killed abusive partners include *Defending Our Lives* (Cambridge Documentary Films), which tells the story of Battered Women Fighting Back! a group of inmates at a prison in Framingham, Massachusetts. *From One Prison . . .* (Michigan Battered Women's Clemency Project) was produced in collaboration with women at a Michigan prison who are serving life or long-term sentences for killing their batterers.

Advocates for incarcerated women critique the funding priorities of successive administrations that give a higher priority to building more jails and prisons than to education, social services, and welfare; they urge a fundamental redirection of these resources. They also critique the inadequate provision of health care, drug treatment, and educational, therapeutic, and life-skills programs for incarcerated women.

After the cancellation of New York state funding, a consortium of private organizations, including several colleges, established a fund to continue the college program at Bedford Hills, recognizing the importance of education for women to rebuild their lives. The Bedford Hills Correctional Facility Education Center enrolled over 200 women in its first 2½ years. The Rocky Mountain Peace and Justice Center's Prison Moratorium Project (Boulder, Colo.) challenges the idea that prisons can solve social problems. It seeks to halt prison expansion and redirect resources toward the development of alternative sentencing, prevention, and treatment programs.

◆◆◆
Questions for Reflection

As you read and discuss this chapter, consider these questions:

1. Why is there such attention by politicians and the media to street crimes?

2. Why are women so afraid of street crimes when they are least safe in the company of men they know?

3. Where is the prison nearest to where you live? Are men, women, or both incarcerated there? Who are they in terms of class, race, and age?

4. What do you know about prison conditions for women?

5. What conditions "outside" would compel a woman to think that a jail or prison is the best place for her to be?

◆◆◆
Taking Action

1. Analyze the way the news media reports crime, or analyze the portrayal of criminals in movies and TV shows. How are women who have committed crimes portrayed? Pay particular attention to issues of race and class.

2. Find out about the daily conditions for women in the jail or prison nearest to you.

3. Find out about activist groups in your area that support incarcerated women. What can you do on behalf of women in prison?

Shannon's Story

Shannon Murray

I was born in Detroit Lakes, Minnesota, on September 21, 1969. I grew up in the Old Colony projects in South Boston. The neighborhoods in them days were quiet. The parents kept to themselves and the children were well behaved. We would play games like kick ball or Red Rover. There was a huge park across the street from the complex with a playground so there was always something to do.

My family consisted of my mother, my stepfather, my older sister Janine, and my younger brother Robbie. We were a close family that showed a lot of affection for each other. My parents were alcoholics so it was a struggle. We made the best of what we had. We weren't any worse off than other families; in some ways we had more. Somehow my parents managed to send me and my younger brother to Catholic school. In this way I felt more fortunate than others.

My sister and I are American Indians. My mother, stepfather, and brother are Irish. It was hard because my sister and I were often singled out. I've always felt different from everyone else at home and at school.

I first started smoking pot and drinking at the age of twelve. By this time, I was more aware of the drug abuse in my neighborhood. The older teens would hang in the hallways smoking pot and drinking. I started to "use" to fit in. It also helped me to escape the feelings I had surrounding my parents' alcoholism.

My first arrest was at the age of 16 for drinking in public. Over the next four years I was able to avoid the arms of the law. I was put into Protective Custody a few times for disorderly conduct. By this time I was drinking and drugging daily. My disease had taken over. I supported my habits by babysitting and selling pot. I dropped out of school in the tenth grade because it was getting in the way of me partying the way I wanted to. I had a few jobs here and there but was unable to hold one because they also got in the way of my using.

After I had my daughter Jaquelin at the age of 18, I started smoking coke more and more often. I had used before that but I stopped during my pregnancy, only smoking pot because I was more afraid of the effects coke could have on my baby than the effect of pot.

The cocaine caused me to lose custody of my daughter to my parents and eventually my apartment. I couldn't deal with the pain of losing my daughter so I turned to heroin. This led to many arrests for shoplifting and possession. My first incarceration was at the age of 25. I was to do three months with probation upon my release.

I was scared because of the stories I had heard about jail. I just felt alone and cut off from reality. I kept to myself and didn't get involved with any of the programs except going to the AA meetings for my good time. I was released with the intention of never coming back.

About nine months later I was incarcerated again, this time for a year. I kind of welcomed the incarceration. This time I am taking advantage of the time I have here to learn more about myself. Being here has given me the chance to take a good look at my lifestyle and what I need to change. I am in the Recovery Program here and I have taken classes like Peace at Home, HIV Prevention, Voices Within, Graphic Arts, and I tutor for pre-GED.

It is hard being locked up in a man's prison. I feel there are prejudices against women here at the Suffolk County House of Corrections. We don't have yard privileges except for a caged-in area that we are only allowed access to during the summer months. We aren't allowed to work in the kitchen or anywhere else in the prison except for the two floors which hold female inmates. We are only allowed to go to the other parts of the prison during the night for things like the library or computers.

I think poverty has a lot to do with people being incarcerated. Where there is poverty there is a lot of drug abuse and less access to structured programs. I think prejudice has a lot to do with being incarcerated because there aren't many jobs for minorities and people have to resort to crime to get things they need that you aren't able to at low-paying jobs.

I have learned that I want a better way of life and that I really don't want to come back here. I know I need to lead an honest life if I truly want to stay out of prison. I hope to become a productive person in society by taking on my responsibilities. I am afraid of failing but I know if I pick up by first dealing with my addictions then I won't have to resort to criminal behavior.

Behind the Walls
The History and Current Reality of Women's Imprisonment
Nancy Kurshan

Prisons serve the same purpose for women as they do for men; they are instruments of social control. However, the imprisonment of women, as well as all the other aspects of our lives, takes place against a backdrop of patriarchal relationships. We refer here to Gerda Lerner's definition of patriarchy: "The manifestation and institutionalization of male dominance over women and children in the family and the extension of male dominance over women in society in general. It implies that men hold power in all the important institutions of society and that women are deprived of access to such power." Therefore, the imprisonment of women in the United States has always been a different phenomenon than that for men; the proportion of women in prison has always differed from that of men; women have traditionally been sent to prison for different reasons; and once in prison, they endure different conditions of incarceration. Women's "crimes" have often had a sexual definition and been rooted in the patriarchal double standard. Furthermore, the nature of women's imprisonment reflects the position of women in society.

In an effort to examine these issues further, this essay explores how prisons have historically served to enforce and reinforce women's traditional roles, to foster dependency and passivity, bearing in mind that it is not just incarcerated women who are affected. Rather, the social stigma and conditions of incarceration serve as a warning to women to stay within the "proper female sphere." Needless to say this warning is not issued equally to women of all nationalities and classes. For this reason, our analysis will also take into account the centrality of race in determining female prison populations, both in the North and the South and pre– and post–Civil War. We believe that white supremacy alters the way that gender impacts on white women and women of color. The final avenue of exploration of this [essay] will thus concern the relationship between race and women's imprisonment. We will attempt to show that the history of the imprisonment of women is consistent with Audre Lorde's comment that in "a patriarchal power system where white skin privilege is a major prop, the entrapments used to neutralize Black women and white women are not the same."

As long as there has been crime and punishment, patriarchal and gender-based realities and assumptions have been central determinants of the response of society to female "offenders." In the late Middle Ages, reports reveal differential treatment of men and women. A woman might commonly be able to receive lenient punishment if she were to "plead her belly," that is, a pregnant woman could plead leniency on the basis of her pregnancy. On the other hand, women were burned at the stake for adultery or murdering a spouse, while men would most often not be punished for such actions. Such differential treatment reflected ideological assumptions as well as women's subordinate positions within the family, church, and other aspects of society. Although systematic imprisonment arose with industrialization, for centuries prior to that time unwanted daughters and wives were forced into convents, nunneries, and monasteries. In those cloisters were found political prisoners, illegitimate daughters, the disinherited, the physically deformed, and the mentally "defective."

A more general campaign of violence against women was unleashed in the witch-hunts of 16th- and 17th-century Europe, as society tried to exert control over women by labeling them as witches. This resulted in the death by execution of at least tens of thousands and possibly millions of people. Conservative estimates indicate that over 80 percent of all the people killed were women. Here in the United States, the witchcraft trials were a dramatic chapter in the social control of women long before systematic imprisonment. Although the colonies were settled relatively late in the history of European witch-hunts, they proved fertile ground for this misogynist campaign. The context was a new colonial society, changing and wrought with conflicts. There were arguments within the ruling alliance, a costly war with the indigenous people led by King Philip, and land disputes. In the face of social uncertainty, unrest and "uncivilized Indians," the Puritans were determined to recreate the Christian family way of life in the wilderness and reestablish the social patterns of the homeland. The success of their project was an open question at the time, and the molding of the role of women was an essential element in the defense of that project.

Hundreds were accused of witchcraft during the New England witchcraft trials of the late 1600s, and at least 36 were executed. The primary determinant of who was designated a witch was gender; overwhelmingly, it was women who were the objects of witch fear. More women were charged with witchcraft, and women were more likely than men to be convicted and executed. In fact, men who confessed were likely to be scoffed at as liars. But age, too, was an important factor. Women over 40 were most likely to be accused of witchcraft and fared much worse than younger women when they were charged. Women over 60 were especially at high risk. Women who were alone, not attached to men as mothers, sisters, or wives were also represented disproportionately among the witches. Puritan society was very hierarchal, and the family was an essential aspect of that hierarchy. According to Carol Karlsen, the Puritan definition of woman as procreator and "helpmate" of man could not be ensured except through force. Most of the witches had expressed dissatisfaction with their lot, if only indirectly. Some were not sufficiently submissive in that they filed petitions and court suits, and sometimes sought divorces. Others were midwives and had influence over the well-being of others, often to the chagrin of their male competitors, medical doctors. Still others exhibited a female pride and assertiveness, refusing to defer to their male neighbors.

Karlsen goes on to offer one of the most powerful explanations of the New England witchcraft trials. She argues that at the heart of the hysteria was an underlying anxiety about inheritance. The inheritance system was designed to keep property in the hands of men. When there were no legitimate male heirs, women inheritors became aberrations who threatened the orderly transmission of property from one male generation to the next. Many of the witches were potential inheritors. Some of them were already widowed and without sons. Others were married but older, beyond their childbearing years, and therefore no longer likely to produce male heirs. They were also "disposable" since they were no longer performing the "essential" functions of a woman, as reproducer and, in some cases, helpmate. Many of the witches were charged just shortly after the death of the male family member, and their witchcraft convictions meant that their lands could easily be seized. Seen in this light, persecution of "witches" was an attempt to maintain the patriarchal social structure and prevent women from becoming economically independent. These early examples of the use of criminal charges in the social control of women may be seen as precursors to the punitive institutions of the 1800s. Up until this time, there were few carceral institutions in society. However, with the rise of capitalism and urbanization come the burgeoning of prisons in the United States. It is to those initial days of systematic imprisonment that we now turn.

The Emergence of Prisons for Women

The relatively few women who were imprisoned at the beginning of the 19th century were confined in separate quarters or wings of men's prisons. Like the men, women suffered from filthy conditions, overcrowding, and harsh treatment. In 1838 in the New York City Jail (the "Tombs"), for instance, there were 42 one-person cells for 70 women. In the 1920s at Auburn Penitentiary in New York, there were no separate cells for the 25 or so women serving sentences up to 14 years. They were all lodged together in a one-room attic, the windows sealed to prevent communication with men. But women had to endure even more. Primary among these additional negative aspects was sexual abuse, which was reportedly a common occurrence. In 1826, Rachel Welch became pregnant while serving in solitary confinement as a punishment and shortly after childbirth she died as a result of flogging by a prison official. Such sexual abuse was apparently so acceptable that the Indiana state prison actually ran a prostitution service for male guards, using female prisoners.

Women received the short end of even the prison stick. Rather than spend the money to hire a matron, women were often left completely on their own, vulnerable to attack by guards. Women had less access to the physician and chaplain and did not go to workshops, mess halls, or exercise yards as men did. Food and needlework were brought to their quarters, and they remained in that area for the full term of their sentence.

Criminal conviction and imprisonment of women soared during and after the Civil War. In the North,

this is commonly attributed to a multitude of factors, including men's absence during wartime and the rise of industrialization, as well as the impact of the dominant sexual ideology of 19th-century Victorianism. The double standard of Victorian morality supported the criminalization of certain behaviors for women but not for men. In New York in the 1850s and 1860s, female "crimes against persons" tripled while "crimes against property" rose 10 times faster than the male rate.

Black people, both women and men, have always been disproportionately incarcerated at all times and all places. This was true in the Northeast and Midwest prisons before the Civil War. It was also the case in the budding prison system in the western states, where Blacks outstripped their very small percentage of the population at large. The only exception was in the South, where slavery, not imprisonment, was the preferred form of control of African-American people. Yet while the South had the lowest Black imprisonment rate before the Civil War, this changed dramatically after the slaves were freed. This change took place for African-American women as well as men. After the Civil War, as part of the re-entrenchment of Euro-American control and the continuing subjugation of Black people, the post-war southern states passed infamous Jim Crow laws that made newly freed Blacks vulnerable to incarceration for the most minor crimes. For example, stealing a couple of chickens brought three to ten years in North Carolina. It is fair to say that many Blacks stepped from slavery into imprisonment. As a result, southern prison populations became predominately Black overnight. Between 1874 and 1877, the Black imprisonment rate went up 300 percent in Mississippi and Georgia. In some states, previously all-white prisons could not contain the influx of African-Americans sentenced to hard labor for petty offenses.

These spiraling rates in both the North and South meant that by mid-century there were enough women prisoners, both in the North and South, to necessitate the emergence of separate women's quarters. This practical necessity opened the door to changes in the nature of the imprisonment of women. In 1869, Sarah Smith and Rhoda Coffin, two Indiana Quakers, led a campaign to end the sexual abuse of women in that state's prison, and in 1874 the first completely separate women's prison was constructed. By 1940, 23 states had separate women's prisons. The literature refers to these separate prisons for women as "independent" women's prisons. This is ironic usage of the word since they were independent only in their physical construction. In every other way they fostered all forms of dependency in the incarcerated women and were an integral part of the prison system. Although these prisons were not initiated as separate institutions until almost a century after men's prisons, it is not so much this time lag that differentiates the development of prisons for women from those for men. The difference comes from the establishment of a bifurcated (two-part) system, the roots of which can be found in the patriarchal and white supremacist aspects of life in the United States at the time. Understanding this bifurcation is a step towards understanding the incarceration of women in the United States.

On the one hand, there were custodial institutions that corresponded by and large to men's prisons. The purpose of custodial prisons, as the name implies, was to warehouse prisoners. There was no pretense of rehabilitation. On the other hand, there were reformatories that, as the name implies, were intended to be more benevolent institutions that "uplifted" or "improved" the character of the women held there. These reformatories had no male counterparts. Almost every state had a custodial women's prison, but in the Northeast and Midwest the majority of incarcerated women were in reformatories. In the South, the few reformatories that existed were exclusively white. However, these differences are not, in essence, geographical; they are racial. The women in the custodial institutions were black whether in the North or the South, and had to undergo the most degrading conditions, while it was mainly white women who were sent to the reformatories, institutions that had the ostensible philosophy of benevolence and sisterly and therapeutic ideals.

The Evolution of Separate Custodial Prisons for Women

In the South after 1870, prison camps emerged as penal servitude and were essentially substituted for slavery. The overwhelming majority of women in the prison camps were Black; the few white women who were there had been imprisoned for much more serious offenses, yet experienced better conditions of confinement. For instance, at Bowden Farm in Texas, the majority of women were Black, were there for property offenses, and worked in the field. The few white women who were there had been convicted of homicide and served as domestics. As the techniques of slavery were applied to the penal system, some states forced women to work on the state-owned penal plantations but also leased women to local farms, mines, and railroads. Treatment on the infamous chain gangs was brutal and degrading. For example, women were whipped on the buttocks in the presence of men. They were also forced to defecate right where they worked, in front of men.

An 1880 census indicated that in Alabama, Louisiana, Mississippi, North Carolina, Tennessee, and Texas, 37 percent of the 220 Black women were leased out whereas only 1 of the 40 white women was leased. Testimony in an 1870 Georgia investigation revealed that in one instance "There were no white women there. One started there, and I heard Mr. Alexander (the lessee) say he turned her loose. He was talking to the guard; I was working in the cut. He said his wife was a white woman, and he could not stand it to see a white woman worked in such places." Eventually, as central penitentiaries were built or rebuilt, many women were shipped there from prison farms because they were considered "dead hands" as compared with the men. At first, the most common form of custodial confinement was attachment to male prisons; eventually, independent women's prisons evolved out of these male institutions. These separate women's prisons were established largely for administrative convenience, not reform. Female matrons worked there, but they took their orders from men.

Like the prison camps, custodial women's prisons were overwhelmingly Black, regardless of their location. Although they have always been imprisoned in smaller numbers than African-American or Euro-American men, Black women often constituted larger percentages within female prisons than Black men did within men's prisons. For instance, between 1797 and 1801, 44 percent of the women sent to New York state prisons were African-Americans as compared to 20 percent of the men. In the Tennessee state prison in 1868, 100 percent of the women were Black, whereas 60 percent of the men were of African descent. The women incarcerated in the custodial prisons tended to be 21 years of age or older. Forty percent were unmarried, and many of them had worked in the past.

Women in custodial prisons were frequently convicted of felony charges; most commonly for "crimes" against property, often petty theft. Only about a third of female felons were serving time for violent crimes. The rates for both property crimes and violent crimes were much higher than for the women at the reformatories. On the other hand, there were relatively fewer women incarcerated in custodial prisons for public order offenses (fornication, adultery, drunkenness, etc.), which were the most common in the reformatories. This was especially true in the South, where these so-called morality offenses by Blacks were generally ignored, and where authorities were reluctant to imprison white women at all. Data from the Auburn, New York prison on homicide statistics between 1909 and 1933 reveal the special nature of the women's "violent" crimes. Most of the victims of murder by women were adult men. Of 149 victims, two-thirds were male; 29 percent were husbands, 2 percent were lovers, and the rest were listed as "man" or "boy" (a similar distribution exists today). Another form of violent crime resulting in the imprisonment of women was performing "illegal" abortions.

Tennessee Supreme Court records offer additional anecdotal information about the nature of women's violent crimes. Eighteen-year-old Sally Griffin killed her fifty-year-old husband after a fight in which, according to Sally, he knocked her through a window, hit her with a hammer, and threatened to "knock her brains out." A doctor testified that in previous months her husband had seriously injured her ovaries when he knocked her out of bed because she refused to have sex during her period. Sally's conviction stood because an eye-witness said she hadn't been threatened with a hammer. A second similar case was also turned down for retrial.

Southern states were especially reluctant to send white women to prison, so they were deliberately screened out by the judicial process. When white women were sent to prison, it was for homicide or sometimes arson; almost never did larceny result in incarceration. In the Tennessee prison, many of the African-American property offenders had committed less serious offenses than the whites, although they were incarcerated in far greater numbers. Frances Kellor, a renowned prison reformer, remarked of this screening process that the Black female offender "is

first a Negro and then a woman—in the whites' estimation." A 1922 North Carolina report describes one institution as being "so horrible that the judge refuses to send white women to this jail, but Negro women are sometimes sent." Hundreds of such instances combined to create institutions overwhelmingly made up of African-American women.

The conditions of these custodial prisons were horrendous, as they were in prisons for men. The southern prisons were by far the worst. They were generally unsanitary, lacking adequate toilet and bathing facilities. Medical attention was rarely available. Women were either left totally idle or forced into hard labor. Women with mental problems were locked in solitary confinement and ignored. But women suffered an additional oppression as well.

> The condition of the women prisoners is most deplorable. They are usually placed in the oldest part of the prison structure. They are almost always in the direct charge of men guards. They are treated and disciplined as men are. In some of the prisons children are born . . . either from the male prisoners or just "others." . . . One county warden told me in confidence, "That I near kill that woman yesterday. . . ." One of the most reliable women officials in the South told me that in her state at the State Farm for women the dining room contains a sweat box for women who are punished by being locked up in a narrow place with insufficient room to sit down, and near enough to the table so as to be able to smell the food. Over the table there is an iron bar to which women are handcuffed when they are strapped.

Generally speaking, the higher the proportion of women of color in the prison population, the worse the conditions. Therefore, it is not surprising that the physical conditions of incarceration for women in the custodial prisons were abysmal compared to the reformatories (as the following section indicates). Even in mainly Black penal institutions, Euro-American women were treated better than African-American women.*

---

*Estelle B. Freedman, *Their Sisters' Keepers: Women's Prison Reform in America, 1830–1930* (Ann Arbor: University of Michigan Press, 1981). Ch. 4, note 44.

Early Twentieth Century: Female Reformatories

Reformatories for women developed alongside custodial prisons. These were parallel, but distinct, developments. By the turn of the century, industrialization was in full swing, bringing fundamental changes in social relations: shifts from a rural society to an urban one, from a family to market economy; increased geographic mobility; increased disruption of lives; more life outside the church, family, and community. More production, even for women, was outside the home. By 1910, a record high of at least 27 percent of all women in New York state were "gainfully" employed. Thousands of women worked in the New York sweatshops under abominable conditions.

There was a huge influx of immigration from Southern and Eastern Europe; many of these were Jewish women who had come straight from Czarist Russia and brought with them a tradition of resistance and struggle. The division between social classes was clearly widening and erupted in dynamic labor struggles. For example, in 1909, 20,000 shirt-waist makers, four-fifths of whom were women, went on strike in New York. Racism and national chauvinism were rampant in the United States at the turn of the century in response to the waves of immigrants from Europe and Black people from the South. The Women's Prison Association of New York, which was active in the social purity movement, declared in 1906 that

> if promiscuous immigration is to continue, it devolves upon the enlightened, industrious, and moral citizens, from selfish as well as from philanthropic motives, to instruct the morally defective to conform to our ways and exact from them our own high standard of morality and legitimate industry. . . . Do you want immoral women to walk our streets, pollute society, endanger your households, menace the morals of your sons and daughters . . . ? Do you think the women here described fit to become mothers of American citizens? Shall foreign powers generate criminals and dump them on our shores?*

*Nicole Hahn Rafter, *Partial Justice: Women in State Prisons 1800–1935* (Boston: New England University Press, 1985), pp. 93–94.

Also at the turn of the century various currents of social concern converged to create a new reform effort, the Progressive movement, that swept the country, particularly the Northeast and Midwest, for several decades. It was in this context that reformatories for women proliferated. Reformatories were actually begun by an earlier generation of female reformers who appeared between 1840 and 1900, but their proliferation took place during this Progressive Era as an alternative to the penitentiary's harsh conditions of enforced silence and hard labor. The reformatories came into being as a result of the work of prison reformers who were ostensibly motivated to improve penal treatment for women. They believed that the mixed prisons afforded women no privacy and left them vulnerable to debilitating humiliations.

Indeed, the reformatories were more humane and conditions were better than at the women's penitentiaries (custodial institutions). They did eliminate much male abuse and the fear of attack. They also resulted in more freedom of movement and opened up a variety of opportunities for "men's" work in the operation of the prison. Children of prisoners up to two years old could stay in most institutions. At least some of the reformatories were staffed and administered by women. They usually had cottages, flower gardens, and no fences. They offered discussions on the law, academics, and training, and women were often paroled more readily than in custodial institutions. However, a closer look at who the women prisoners were, the nature of their offenses, and the program to which they were subjected reveals the seamier side of these ostensibly noble institutions.

It is important to emphasize that reformatories existed for women only. No such parallel development took place within men's prisons. There were no institutions devoted to "correcting" men for so-called moral offenses. In fact, such activities were not considered crimes when men engaged in them and therefore men were not as a result imprisoned. A glance at these "crimes" for women only suggests the extent to which society was bent on repressing women's sexuality. Despite the hue and cry about prostitution, only 8.5 percent of the women at the reformatories were actually convicted of prostitution. More than half, however, were imprisoned because of "sexual misconduct." Women were incarcerated in reformatories primarily for various public order offenses or so-called "moral" offenses: lewd and lascivious carriage, stubbornness, idle and disorderly conduct, drunkenness, fornication, serial premarital pregnancies, keeping bad company, adultery, venereal disease, and vagrancy. A woman might face charges simply because a relative disapproved of her behavior and reported her, or because she had been sexually abused and was being punished for it. Most were rebels of some sort.

Jennie B., for instance, was sent to Albion reformatory for five years for having "had unlawful sexual intercourse with young men and remain[ing] at hotels with young men all night, particularly on July 4, 1893." Lilian R. quit school and ran off for one week with a soldier, contracting a venereal disease. She was hospitalized, then sentenced to the reformatory. Other women were convicted of offenses related to exploitation and/or abuse by men. Ann B. became pregnant twice from older men, one of whom was her father, who was sentenced to prison for rape. She was convicted of "running around" when she was seven months pregnant. One woman who claimed to have miscarried and disposed of the fetus had been convicted of murdering her illegitimate child. There was also the increasing practice of abortion that accounted for at least some of the rise in "crime against persons."

As with all prisons, the women in the reformatories were of the working class. Many of them worked outside the home. At New York State's Albion Reformatory, for instance, 80 percent had, in the past, worked for wages. Reformatories were also overwhelmingly institutions for white women. Government statistics indicate that in 1921, for instance, 12 percent of the women in reformatories were Black while 88 percent were white.

Record keeping at the Albion Reformatory in New York demonstrates how unusual it was for Black women to be incarcerated there. The registries left spaces for entries of a large number of variables, such as family history of insanity and epilepsy. Nowhere was there a space for recording race. When African Americans were admitted, the clerk penciled "colored" at the top of the page. African-American women were much less likely to be arrested for such public order offenses. Rafter suggests that Black women were not expected to act like "ladies" in the first place and therefore were reportedly not deemed worthy of such rehabilitation.

The program of these institutions, as well as the offenses, was based on patriarchal assumptions. Reformatory training centered on fostering ladylike behavior and perfecting housewifely skills. In this way it encouraged dependency and women's subjugation. Additionally, one aspect of the retraining of these women was to isolate them, to strip them of environmental influences in order to instill them with new values. To this end family ties were obstructed, which is somewhat ironic since the family is at the center of the traditional role of women. Letters might come every two months and were censored. Visits were allowed four times a year for those who were on the approved list. The reformatories were geographically remote, making it very difficult for loved ones to visit. Another thorn in the rosy picture of the reformatory was the fact that sentencing was often open-ended. This was an outgrowth of the rehabilitative ideology. The incarceration was not of fixed length because the notion was that a woman would stay for as long as it took to accomplish the task of reforming her.

Parole was also used as a patriarchal weapon. Ever since the Civil War, there was a scarcity of white working-class women for domestic service. At the same time, the "need for good help" was increasing because more people could afford to hire help. It was not an accident that women were frequently paroled into domestic jobs, the only ones for which they had been trained. In this way, vocational regulation went hand-in-hand with social control, leading always backwards to home and hearth, and away from self-sufficiency and independence. Additionally, independent behavior was punished by revoking parole for "sauciness," obscenity, or failure to work hard enough. One woman was cited for a parole violation for running away from a domestic position to join a theater troupe; another for going on car rides with men; still others for becoming pregnant, going around with a disreputable married man, or associating with the father of her child. And finally, some very unrepentant women were ultimately transferred indefinitely to asylums for the "feeble-minded."

Prison reform movements have been common; a reform movement also existed for men. However, all these institutions were inexorably returned to the role of institutions of social control. Understanding this early history can prepare us to understand recent developments in women's imprisonment and indeed imprisonment in general. Although the reformatories rejected the more traditional authoritarian penal regimes, they were nonetheless concerned with social control. Feminist criminologists claim that in their very inception, reformatories were institutions of patriarchy. They were part of a broad attack on young working-class women who were attempting to lead somewhat more autonomous lives. Women's sexual independence was being curbed in the context of "social purity" campaigns. As more and more white working-class women left home for the labor force, they took up smoking, frequenting dance halls, and having sexual relationships. Prostitution had long been a source of income for poor women, but despite the fact that prostitution had actually begun to wane about 1900, there was a major morality crusade at the turn of the century that attacked prostitution as well as all kinds of small deviations from the standard of "proper" female propriety.

Even when the prisons were run by women, they were, of course, still doing the work of a male supremacist prison system and society. We have seen how white working-class women were punished for "immoral behavior" when men were not. We have seen how they were indoctrinated with a program of "ladylike" behavior. According to feminist criminologists such as Nicole Hahn Rafter and Estelle Freedman, reformatories essentially punished those who did not conform to bourgeois definitions of femininity and prescribed gender roles. The prisoners were to embrace the social values, although, of course, never to occupy the social station of a "lady." It is relevant to note that the social stigma of imprisonment was even greater for women than men because women were supposedly denying their own "pure nature." This stigma plus the nature of the conditions of incarceration served as a warning to all such women to stay within the proper female sphere.

These observations shed some light on the role of "treatment" within penal practice. Reformatories were an early attempt at "treatment," that is, the uplifting and improvement of the women, as opposed to mere punishment or retribution. However, these reforms were also an example of the subservience of "treatment" to social control. They demonstrate that the underlying function of control continually reasserts itself when attempts to "improve" people take place within a coercive framework. The reformatories are an illustration of how sincere efforts at reform may only serve to broaden the net and extend the state's power of social control. In fact, hundreds and hundreds of women were incarcerated for

public order offenses who previously would not have been vulnerable to the punishment of confinement in a state institution were it not for the existence of reformatories.

By 1935, the custodial prisons for women and the reformatories had basically merged. In the 1930s, the United States experienced the repression of radicalism, the decline of the progressive and feminist movements, and the Great Depression. Along with these changes came the demise of the reformatories. The prison reform movement had achieved one of its earliest central aims, separate prisons for women. The reformatory buildings still stood and were filled with prisoners. However, these institutions were reformatories in name only. Some were administered by women, but they were women who did not even have the progressive pretenses of their predecessors. The conditions of incarceration had deteriorated miserably, suffering from cutbacks and lack of funding.

Meanwhile, there had been a slow but steady transformation of the inmate population. Increasingly, the white women convicted of misdemeanors were given probation, paroled, or sent back to local jails. As Euro-American women left the reformatories, the buildings themselves were transformed into custodial prisons, institutions that repeated the terrible conditions of the past. As custodial prison buildings were physically closed down for various reasons, felons were transferred to the buildings that had housed the reformatories. Most of the women were not only poor but also were Black. African-American women were increasingly incarcerated there with the growth of the Black migration north after World War I. These custodial institutions now included some added negative dimensions as the legacy of the reformatories, such as the strict reinforcement of gender roles and the infantilization of women. In the end, the reformatories were certainly not a triumph for the women's liberation. Rather, they can be viewed as one of many instances in which U.S. institutions are able to absorb an apparent reform and use it for continuing efforts at social control.

Women and Prison Today

. . . What are the conditions women face when they are imprisoned? Women are confined in a system designed, built and run by men for men, according to a fall 1990 issue of *Time Magazine*. Prison authorities rationalize that because the numbers of women have been so relatively low, there are no "economies of scale" in meeting women's needs, particularly their special needs. Therefore, women suffer accordingly, they say. There are a wide range of institutions that incarcerate women and conditions vary. Some women's prisons look like "small college campuses," remnants of the historical legacy of the reformatory movement. Bedford Hills state prison in New York is one such institution; Alderson Federal Prison in West Virginia is another. Appearances, however, are deceptive. For instance, Russell Dobash describes the "underlying atmosphere [of such a prison] as one of intense hostility, frustration, and anger."

Many institutions have no pretenses and are notoriously overcrowded and inadequate. The California Institution for Women at Frontera houses 2,500 women in a facility built for 1,011. Overcrowding sometimes means that women who are being held for trivial offenses are incarcerated in maximum-security institutions for lack of other facilities. Women's prisons are often particularly ill-equipped and poorly financed. They have fewer medical, educational, and vocational facilities than men's prisons. Medical treatment is often unavailable, inappropriate, and inconsistent. Job training is also largely unavailable; when opportunities exist, they are usually traditional female occupations. Courses concentrate on homemaking and low-paid skills like beautician and launderer. Other barriers exist as well. In an Alabama women's prison, there is a cosmetology program, but those convicted of felonies are prohibited by state law from obtaining such licenses.

In most prisons, guards have total authority, and the women can never take care of their basic intimate needs in a secure atmosphere free from intrusion. In the ostensible name of security, male guards can take down or look over a curtain, walk into a bathroom, or observe a woman showering or changing her clothes. In Michigan, for instance, male guards are employed at all women's prisons. At Huron Valley, about half the guards are men. At Crane prison, approximately 80 percent of the staff is male and there are open dormitories divided into cubicles. In one section the cubicle walls are only four feet high and there are no doors or curtains on any cubicles anywhere at Crane. The officers' desks are right next to the bathroom and the bathroom doors must be left open at all times. Male guards are also allowed to do body shakedowns where they run their hands all over the women's bodies.

Incarceration has severe and particular ramifications for women. Eighty percent of women entering state prisons are mothers. By contrast 60 percent of men in state prisons are fathers and less than half of them have custodial responsibility. These mothers have to undergo the intense pain of forced separation from their children. They are often the sole caretakers of their children and were the primary source of financial and emotional support. Their children are twice as likely to end up in foster care than the children of male prisoners. Whereas when a man goes to prison, his wife or lover most often assumes or continues to assume responsibilities for the children, the reverse is not true. Women often have no one else to turn to and are in danger of permanently losing custody of their children. For all imprisoned mothers the separation from their children is one of the greatest punishments of incarceration, and engenders despondency and feelings of guilt and anxiety about their children's welfare.

Visiting with children often is extremely difficult or impossible. At county jails where women are awaiting trial, prisoners are often denied contact visits and are required to visit behind glass partitions or through telephones. Prisons are usually built far away from the urban centers where most of the prisoners and their families and friends live. Where children are able to visit, they have to undergo frightening experiences like pat-downs under awkward and generally anti-human conditions. When women get out of prison, many states are supposed to provide reunification services, but in fact most do not. Although even departments of corrections admit that family contact is the one factor that most greatly enhances parole success, the prison system actively works to obstruct such contact.

Reproductive rights are nonexistent for the 10 percent of the women in prison who are pregnant. Massachusetts is one of the few states to provide Medicaid funds for poor women to get abortions, but these funds are unavailable for imprisoned women. All the essentials for a healthy pregnancy are missing in prison: nutritious food, fresh air, exercise, sanitary conditions, extra vitamins, and prenatal care. Women in prison are denied nutritional supplements such as those afforded by the Women Infants and Children (WIC) program. Women frequently undergo bumpy bus rides, and are shackled and watched throughout their delivery. It is no wonder then that a 1985 California Department of Health study indicated that a third of all prison pregnancies end in late-term miscarriage, twice the outside rate. In fact, only 20 percent have live births. For those women who are lucky enough to have healthy deliveries, forced separation from the infant usually comes within 24 to 72 hours after birth.

Many commentators argue that, at their best, women's prisons are shot through with a viciously destructive paternalistic mentality. According to Rafter, "Women in prison are perpetually infantilized by routines and paternalistic attitudes." Assata Shakur describes it as a "pseudo-motherly attitude . . . a deception which all too often successfully reverts women to children." Guards call prisoners by their first names and admonish them to "grow up," "be good girls," and "behave." They threaten the women with a "good spanking." Kathryn Burkhart refers to this as a "mass infancy treatment." Powerlessness, helplessness, and dependency are systematically heightened in prison while what would be most therapeutic for women is the opposite—for women to feel their own power and to take control of their lives. Friendship among women is discouraged, and the homophobia of the prison system is exemplified by rules in many prisons that prohibit any type of physical contact between women prisoners. A woman can be punished for hugging a friend who has just learned that her mother died. There is a general prohibition against physical affection, but it is most seriously enforced against known Lesbians. One Lesbian received a disciplinary ticket for lending a sweater and was told she didn't know the difference between compassion and passion. Lesbians may be confronted with extra surveillance or may be "treated like a man." Some Lesbians receive incident reports simply because they are gay.

Many prison administrators generally agree that community-based alternatives would be better and cheaper than imprisonment. However, there is very little public pressure in that direction. While imprisonment rates for women continue to rise, the public outcry is deafening in its silence. Ruth Ann Jones of the Division of Massachusetts Parole Board says her agency receives no outside pressure to develop programs for women. However, around the country small groups of dedicated people are working to introduce progressive reforms into the prisons. In Michigan, there is a program that buses family and friends to visit at prisons. In New York, at Bedford Hills, there is a program geared towards enhancing and encouraging visits with children. Chicago Legal Aid for Imprisoned Mothers (CLAIM), Atlanta's Aid to Imprisoned Mothers, and Madison, Wisconsin's Women's Jail Project are just some of the groups that have tirelessly and persistently fought for reforms as well as provided critical services for women and children.

The best programs are the ones that can concretely improve the situation of the women inside. However, many programs that begin with reform-minded intentions become institutionalized in such a way that they are disadvantageous to the population they are supposedly helping. Psychological counselors may have good intentions, but they work for the departments of corrections and often offer no confidentiality. And of course, even the best of them tend to focus on individual pathology rather than exposing systematic oppression. Less restrictive alternatives like halfway houses often get turned around so that they become halfway in, not halfway out. That is, what we are experiencing is the widening of the net of state control. The results are that women who would not be incarcerated at all wind up under the supervision of the state rather than decreasing the numbers of women who are imprisoned.

Prison Resistance

One topic that has not been adequately researched is the rebellion and resistance of women in prison. It is only with great difficulty that any information was found. We do not believe that is because resistance does not occur, but rather because those in charge of documenting history have a stake in burying this herstory. Such a herstory would challenge the patriarchal ideology that insists that women are, by nature, passive and docile. What we do know is that as far back as 1943 there was a riot in Sing Sing Prison in New York, which was the first woman's prison. It took place in response to overcrowding and inadequate facilities.

During the Civil War, Georgia's prison was burned down, allegedly torched by women trying to escape. It was again burned down in 1900. In 1888, similar activity took place at Framingham, Massachusetts, although reports refer to it as merely "fun." Women rebelled at New York's Hudson House of Refuge in response to excessive punishment. They forced the closing of "the dungeon," basement cells and a diet of bread and water. Within a year, similar cells were reinstituted. The story of Bedford Hills is a particularly interesting one. From 1915 to 1920 there were a series of rebellions against cruelty to inmates. The administration had refused to segregate Black and white women up until 1916, and reports of the time attribute these occurrences to the "unfortunate attachments formed by white women for the Negroes." A 1931 study indicated that "colored girls" revolted against discrimination at the New Jersey State Reformatory.

Around the time of the historic prison rebellion at Attica Prison in New York State, rebellions also took place at women's prisons. In 1971, there was a work stoppage at Alderson simultaneous with the rebellion at Attica. In June of 1975, the women at the North Carolina Correctional Center for Women staged a five-day demonstration "against oppressive working atmospheres, inaccessible and inadequate medical facilities and treatment, and racial discrimination, and many other conditions at the prison." Unprotected, unarmed women were attacked by male guards armed with riot gear. The women sustained physical injuries and miscarriages as well as punitive punishment in lockup and in segregation, and illegal transfers to the Mattawan State Hospital for the Criminally Insane. In February of 1977, male guards were for the first time officially assigned to duty in the housing units where they freely watched women showering, changing their clothes, and performing all other private functions. On August 2, 1977, a riot squad of predominantly male guards armed with tear gas, high pressure water hoses, and billy clubs attacked one housing unit for five hours. Many of the women defended themselves and were brutally beaten; 28 women were illegally transferred to Mattawan where they faced a behavior modification program.

This short exposition of the rebellions in women's prisons is clearly inadequate. Feminist criminologists and others should look towards the need for a detailed herstory of this thread of the women's experience in America.

Conclusion

We began this research in an attempt to understand the ways that patriarchy and white supremacy interact in the imprisonment of women. We looked at the history of the imprisonment of women in the United States and found that it has always been different for white women and African-American women. This was most dramatically true in the social control of white women, geared toward turning them into "ladies." This was a more physically benign prison track than the custodial prisons that contained Black women or men. But it was insidiously patriarchal, both in this character and in the fact that similar institutions did not exist to control men's behavior in those areas. We also saw that historically the more "Black" the penal institution, the worse the conditions. It is difficult to understand how this plays out within the walls of prisons today since there are more sophisticated forms of tracking. That is, within a given prison there are levels of privileges that offer a better or worse quality of life. Research is necessary to determine how this operates in terms of white and African-American female prisoners. However, we can hypothesize that as women's prisons become increasingly Black institutions, conditions will, as in the past, come more and more to resemble the punitive conditions of men's prisons. This is an especially timely consideration now that Black women are incarcerated eight times more frequently than white women.

Although the percentage of women in prison is still very low compared to men, the rates are rapidly rising. And when we examine the conditions of incarceration, it does appear as if the imprisonment of women is coming more and more to resemble that of men in the sense that there is no separate, more benign, track for women. Now more than ever, women are being subjected to more maximum-security, control units, shock incarceration; in short, everything negative that men receive. We thus may be looking at the beginning of a new era in the imprisonment of women. One observation that is consistent with these findings is that the purpose of prisons for women may not be to function primarily as institutions of patriarchal control. That is, their mission as instruments of social control of people of color generally may be the overriding purpose. Turning women into "ladies" or "feminizing" women is not the essence of the mission of prisons. Warehousing and punishment are now enough, for women as well as men.

This is not to suggest that the imprisonment of women is not replete with sexist ideology and practices. It is a thoroughly patriarchal society that sends women to prison; that is, the rules and regulations, the definition of crimes are defined by the patriarchy. This would include situations in which it is "okay" for a husband to beat up his wife, but that very same wife cannot defend herself against his violence; in which women are forced to act as accessories to crimes committed by men; in which abortion is becoming more and more criminalized. Once in prison, patriarchal assumptions and male dominance continue to play an essential role in the treatment of women. As discussed previously, women have to deal with a whole set of factors that men do not, from intrusion by male guards to the denial of reproductive rights. Modern day women's imprisonment has taken on the worst aspects of the imprisonment of

men. But it is also left with the sexist legacy of the reformatories and the contemporary structures of the patriarchy. Infantilization and the reinforcement of passivity and dependency are woven into the very fabric of the incarceration of women.

The imprisonment of women of color can be characterized by the enforcement of patriarchy in the service of the social control of people of color as a whole. This raises larger questions about the enormous attacks aimed at family life in communities of color, in which imprisonment of men, women, and children plays a significant role. However, since this area of inquiry concerns the most disenfranchised elements of our society, it is no wonder that so little attention is paid to dealing with this desperate situation. More research in this area is needed as there are certainly unanswered questions. But we must not wait for this research before we begin to unleash our energies to dismantle a prison system that grinds up our sisters.

SIXTY-FOUR

Punishing Drug Addicts Who Have Babies
Women of Color, Equality, and the Right of Privacy

Dorothy E. Roberts

In July 1989, Jennifer Clarise Johnson, a twenty-three-year-old crack addict, became the first woman in the United States to be criminally convicted for exposing her baby to drugs while pregnant.[1] Florida law enforcement officials charged Johnson with two counts of delivering a controlled substance to a minor after her two children tested positive for cocaine at birth. Because the relevant Florida drug law did not apply to fetuses, the prosecution invented a novel interpretation of the statute. The prosecution obtained Johnson's conviction for passing a cocaine metabolite from her body to her newborn infants during the sixty-second period after birth and before the umbilical cord was cut.

A growing number of women across the country have been charged with criminal offenses after giving birth to babies who test positive for drugs. The

majority of these women, like Jennifer Johnson, are poor and Black.[2] Most are addicted to crack cocaine. The prosecution of drug-addicted mothers is part of an alarming trend toward greater state intervention into the lives of pregnant women under the rationale of protecting the fetus from harm. Such government intrusion is particularly harsh for poor women of color. They are the least likely to obtain adequate prenatal care, the most vulnerable to government monitoring, and the least able to conform to the white middle-class standard of motherhood. They are therefore the primary targets of government control.

The prosecution of drug-addicted mothers implicates two fundamental tensions. First, punishing a woman for using drugs during pregnancy pits the state's interest in protecting the future health of a child against the mother's interest in autonomy over her reproductive life—interests that until recently had not been thought to be in conflict. Second, such prosecutions represent one of two possible responses to the problem of drug-exposed babies. The government may choose either to help women have healthy pregnancies or to punish women for their prenatal conduct. Although it might seem that the state could pursue both of these avenues at once, the two responses are ultimately irreconcilable. Far from deterring injurious drug use, prosecution of drug-addicted mothers in fact deters pregnant women from using available health and counseling services because it causes women to fear that, if they seek help, they could be reported to government authorities and charged with a crime. Moreover, prosecution blinds the public to the possibility of nonpunitive solutions and to the inadequacy of the nonpunitive solutions that are currently available.

The debate between those who favor protecting the rights of the fetus and those who favor protecting the rights of the mother has been extensively waged in the literature.[3] This [essay] seeks to illuminate the current debate by examining the experiences of the class of women who are primarily affected—poor Black women.

Providing the perspective of poor Black women offers two advantages. First, examining legal issues from the viewpoint of those they affect most helps to uncover the real reasons for state action and to explain the real harms it causes. It exposes the way the prosecutions deny poor Black women a facet of their humanity by punishing their reproductive choices. The government's choice of a punitive response perpetuates the historical devaluation of Black women as mothers. Viewing the legal issues from the experiential standpoint of the defendants enhances our understanding of the constitutional dimensions of the state's conduct.

Second, examining the constraints on poor Black women's reproductive choices expands our understanding of reproductive freedom in particular and the right of privacy in general. Much of the literature discussing reproductive freedom has adopted a white middle-class perspective, which focuses narrowly on abortion rights. The feminist critique of privacy doctrine has also neglected many of the concerns of poor women of color.

My analysis presumes that Black women experience various forms of oppression simultaneously, as a complex interaction of race, gender, and class

that is more than the sum of its parts. It is impossible to isolate any one of the components of this oppression or to separate the experiences that are attributable to one component from experiences attributable to the others. The prosecution of drug-addicted mothers cannot be explained as simply an issue of gender inequality. Poor Black women have been selected for punishment as a result of an inseparable combination of their gender, race, and economic status. Their devaluation as mothers, which underlies the prosecutions, has its roots in the unique experience of slavery and has been perpetuated by complex social forces.

This [essay] advances an account of the constitutionality of prosecutions of drug-addicted mothers that explicitly considers the experiences of poor Black women. The constitutional arguments are based on theories of both racial equality and the right of privacy. I argue that punishing drug addicts who choose to carry their pregnancies to term unconstitutionally burdens the right to autonomy over reproductive decisions. Violation of poor Black women's reproductive rights helps perpetuate a racist hierarchy in our society. The prosecutions thus impose a standard of motherhood that is offensive to principles of both equality and privacy.

Although women accused of prenatal crimes can present their defenses only in court, judges are not the only government officials charged with a duty to uphold the Constitution. Given the Supreme Court's current hostility to claims of substantive equality and reproductive rights, my arguments might be directed more fruitfully to legislatures than to the courts.

Background: The State's Punitive Response to Drug-Addicted Mothers

The Crack Epidemic and the State's Response

Crack cocaine appeared in America in the early 1980s, and its abuse has grown to epidemic proportions. Crack is especially popular among inner-city women.[4] Most crack-addicted women are of childbearing age, and many are pregnant.[5] This phenomenon has contributed to an explosion in the number of newborns affected by maternal drug use. Some experts estimate that as many as 375,000 drug-exposed infants are born every year.[6]

Babies born to drug-addicted mothers may suffer a variety of medical, developmental, and behavioral problems, depending on the nature of their mother's substance abuse. Data on the extent and potential severity of the adverse effects of maternal cocaine use are controversial.[7] The interpretation of studies of cocaine-exposed infants is often clouded by the presence of other fetal risk factors, such as the mother's use of additional drugs, cigarettes, and alcohol and her socioeconomic status.

The response of state prosecutors, legislators, and judges to the problem of drug-exposed babies has been punitive. They have punished women who use drugs during pregnancy by depriving these mothers of custody of their children, by jailing them during their pregnancy, and by prosecuting them after their babies are born.

The Disproportionate Impact on Poor Black Women

Poor Black women bear the brunt of prosecutors' punitive approach. These women are the primary targets of prosecutors, not because they are more likely to be guilty of fetal abuse, but because they are Black and poor. Poor women, who are disproportionately Black,[8] are in closer contact with government agencies, and their drug use is therefore more likely to be detected. Black women are also more likely to be reported to government authorities, in part because of the racist attitudes of health care professionals. Finally, their failure to meet society's image of the ideal mother makes their prosecution more acceptable.

It is also significant that, out of the universe of maternal conduct that can injure a fetus, prosecutors have focused on crack use. The selection of crack addiction for punishment can be justified by neither the number of addicts nor the extent of the harm to the fetus. Excessive alcohol consumption during pregnancy, for example, can cause severe fetal injury, and marijuana use may also adversely affect the unborn.[9] The incidence of both these types of substance abuse is high as well. In addition, prosecutors do not always base their claims on actual harm to the child, but on the mere delivery of crack by the mother.

Focusing on Black crack addicts rather than on other perpetrators of fetal harms serves two broader social purposes. First, prosecution of these pregnant women serves to degrade women whom society views as undeserving to be mothers and to discourage them from having children. If prosecutors had instead chosen to prosecute affluent women addicted to alcohol or prescription medication, the policy of criminalizing prenatal conduct very likely would have suffered a hasty demise. Society is much more willing to condone the punishment of poor women of color who fail to meet the middle-class ideal of motherhood.

In addition to legitimizing fetal rights enforcement, the prosecution of crack-addicted mothers diverts public attention from social ills such as poverty, racism, and a misguided national health policy and implies instead that shamefully high Black infant death rates[10] are caused by the bad acts of individual mothers. Poor Black mothers thus become the scapegoats for the causes of the Black community's ill health.

Punishing Black Mothers and the Perpetuation of Racial Hierarchy

The legal analysis of the prosecutions implicates two constitutional protections: the equal protection clause of the Fourteenth Amendment and the right of privacy. These two constitutional challenges appeal to different but related values. A basic premise of equality doctrine is that certain fundamental aspects of the human personality, including decisional autonomy, must be respected in all persons. Theories of racial equality and privacy can be used as related means to achieve a common end of eliminating the legacy of racial discrimination that has devalued Black motherhood. Both aim to create a society in which Black women's reproductive choices, including the decision to bear children, are given full respect and protection.

The equal protection clause[11] embodies the Constitution's ideal of racial equality. State action that violates this ideal by creating classifications based on race must be subjected to strict judicial scrutiny. The equal protection clause, however, does not explicitly define the meaning of equality or delineate the nature of prohibited government conduct. As a result, equal protection analyses generally have divided into two visions of equality: one that is informed by an antidiscrimination principle, the other by an antisubordination principle.[12]

The antidiscrimination approach identifies the primary threat to equality as the government's "failure to treat Black people as individuals without regard to race."[13] The goal of the antidiscrimination principle is to ensure that all members of society are treated in a color-blind or race-neutral fashion. The Supreme Court's current understanding of the equal protection clause is based on a narrow interpretation of the antidiscrimination principle.[14] The Court has confined discrimination prohibited by the Constitution to state conduct performed with a discriminatory intent. State conduct that disproportionately affects Blacks violates the Constitution only if it is accompanied by a purposeful desire to produce this outcome.

Black women prosecuted for drug use during pregnancy may be able to make out a prima facie case of discriminatory purpose.[15] The Court has recognized that a selection process characterized by broad government discretion that produces unexplained racial disparities may support the presumption of discriminatory purpose.[16]

A Black mother arrested in Pinellas County, Florida, could make out a prima facie case of unconstitutional racial discrimination by showing that a disproportionate number of those chosen for prosecution for exposing newborns to drugs are Black. In particular, she could point out the disparity between the percentage of defendants who are Black and the percentage of pregnant substance abusers who are Black. A *New England Journal of Medicine* study of pregnant women in Pinellas County found that only about 26 percent of those who used drugs were Black.[17] Yet over 90 percent of Florida prosecutions for drug abuse during pregnancy have been brought against Black women. The defendant could buttress her case with the study's finding that, despite similar rates of substance abuse, Black women were ten times more likely than white women to be reported to public health authorities for substance abuse during pregnancy. In addition, the defendant could show that both health care professionals and prosecutors wield a great deal of discretion in selecting women to be subjected to the criminal justice system. The burden would then shift to the state "to dispel the inference of intentional discrimination" by justifying the racial discrepancy in its prosecutions.

The antisubordination approach to equality would not require Black defendants to prove that the prosecutions are motivated by racial bias. Rather than requiring victims to prove distinct instances of discriminating behavior in the administrative process, the antisubordination approach considers the concrete effects of government policy on the substantive condition of the disadvantaged. Under this conception of equality, the function of the equal protection clause is to dismantle racial hierarchy by eliminating state action or inaction that effectively preserves Black subordination.

The prosecution of drug-addicted mothers demonstrates the inadequacy of antidiscrimination analysis and the superiority of the antisubordination approach. First, the antidiscrimination approach may not adequately protect Black women from prosecutions' infringement of equality, because it is difficult to identify individual guilty actors. Who are the government officials motivated by racial bias to punish Black women? The hospital staff who test and report mothers to child welfare agencies? The prosecutors who develop and implement policies to charge women who use drugs during pregnancy? Legislators who enact laws protecting the unborn?

It is unlikely that any of these individual actors intentionally singled out Black women for punishment based on a conscious devaluation of their motherhood. The disproportionate impact of the prosecutions on poor Black women does not result from such isolated, individualized decisions. Rather, it is a result of two centuries of systematic exclusion of Black women from tangible and intangible benefits enjoyed by white society. Their exclusion is reflected in Black women's reliance on public hospitals and public drug treatment centers, in their failure to obtain adequate prenatal care, in the more frequent reporting of Black drug users by health care professionals, and in society's acquiescence in the government's punitive response to the problem of crack-addicted babies.

In contrast to the antidiscrimination approach, antisubordination theory mandates that equal protection law concern itself with the concrete ways government policy perpetuates the inferior status of Black women. From this perspective, the prosecutions of crack-addicted mothers are unconstitutional because they reinforce the myth of the undeserving Black mother by singling out—whether intentionally or not—Black women for punishment. The government's punitive policy reflects a long history of denigration of Black mothers dating back to slavery, and it serves to perpetuate that legacy of unequal respect. The prosecutions should therefore be upheld only if the state can demonstrate that they serve a compelling interest that could not be achieved through less discriminatory means. A public commitment to providing adequate prenatal care for poor women and drug treatment programs that meet the needs of pregnant addicts would be a more effective means for the state to address the problem of drug-exposed babies.

Claiming the Right of Privacy for Women of Color

Identifying the Constitutional Issue

In deciding which of the competing interests involved in the prosecution of drug-addicted mothers prevails — the state's interest in protecting the health of the fetus or the woman's interest in preventing state intervention — we must identify the precise nature of the woman's constitutional right at stake. In the *Johnson* case, the prosecutor framed the constitutional issue as follows: "What constitutionally protected freedom did Jennifer engage in when she smoked cocaine?" That was the wrong question. Johnson was not convicted of using drugs. Her "constitutional right" to smoke cocaine was never at issue. Johnson was prosecuted because she chose to carry her pregnancy to term while she was addicted to crack. Had she smoked cocaine during her pregnancy and then had an abortion, she would not have been charged with such a serious crime. The proper question, then, is "What constitutionally protected freedom did Jennifer engage in when she decided to have a baby, even though she was a drug addict?"

Understanding the prosecution of drug-addicted mothers as punishment for having babies clarifies the constitutional right at stake. The woman's right at issue is not the right to abuse drugs or to cause the fetus to be born with defects. It is the right to choose to be a mother that is burdened by the criminalization of conduct during pregnancy. This view of the constitutional issue reveals the relevance of race to the resolution of the competing interests. Race has historically determined the value society places on an individual's right to choose motherhood. Because of the devaluation of Black motherhood, protecting the right of Black women to choose to bear a child has unique significance.

Overview of Privacy Arguments

Prosecutions of drug-addicted mothers infringe on two aspects of the right to individual choice in reproductive decision making. First, they infringe on the freedom to continue a pregnancy that is essential to an individual's personhood and autonomy. This freedom implies that state control of the decision to carry a pregnancy to term can be as pernicious as state control of the decision to terminate a pregnancy. Second, the prosecutions infringe on choice by imposing an invidious government standard for the entitlement to procreate. Such imposition of a government standard for childbearing is one way society denies the humanity of those who are different. The first approach emphasizes a woman's right to autonomy over her reproductive life; the second highlights a woman's right to be valued equally as a human being.

Toward a New Privacy Jurisprudence

In this section, I will suggest two approaches that I believe are necessary in order for privacy theory to contribute to the eradication of racial hierarchy. First, we need to develop a positive view of the right of privacy. Second, the law must recognize the connection between the right of privacy and racial equality.

The definition of privacy as a purely negative right serves to exempt the state from any obligation to ensure the social conditions and resources necessary for self-determination and autonomous decision making. Based on this narrow view of liberty, the Supreme Court has denied a variety of claims to government aid.[18] Laurence Tribe has suggested an alternative view of the relationship between the government's negative and affirmative responsibilities in guaranteeing the rights of personhood: "Ultimately, the affirmative duties of government cannot be severed from its obligations to refrain from certain forms of control; both must respond to a substantive vision of the needs of human personality."[19]

Thus, the reason legislatures should reject laws that punish Black women's reproductive choices is not an absolute and isolated notion of individual autonomy. Rather, legislatures should reject these laws as a critical step toward eradicating a racial hierarchy that has historically demeaned Black motherhood. Respecting Black women's decision to bear children is a necessary ingredient of a community that affirms the personhood of all its members.

Our understanding of the prosecutions of drug-addicted mothers must include the perspective of the women who are most directly affected. The prosecutions arise in a particular historical and political context that has constrained reproductive choice for poor women of color. The state's decision to punish drug-addicted mothers rather than help them stems from the poverty and race of the defendants and society's denial of their full dignity as human beings.

A policy that attempts to protect fetuses by denying the humanity of their mothers will inevitably fail. The tragedy of crack babies is initially a tragedy of crack-addicted mothers. Both are part of a larger tragedy of a community that is suffering a host of indignities, including, significantly, the denial of equal respect for its women's reproductive decisions.

It is only by affirming the personhood and equality of poor women of color that we will ensure the survival of their future generation. The first principle of the government's response to the crisis of drug-exposed babies should be the recognition of their mothers' worth and entitlement to autonomy over their reproductive lives. A commitment to guaranteeing these fundamental rights of poor women of color, rather than punishing them, is the true solution to the problem of unhealthy babies.

Notes

1. *See* State v. Johnson, No. E89–890-CFA, slip op. at 1 (Fla. Cir. Ct. July 13, 1989), *aff'd,* 578 So. 2d 419 (Fla. Dist. Ct. App. 1991), *rev'd,* 602 So. 2d 1288 (Fla. 1992).

2. According to a memorandum prepared by the ACLU Reproductive Freedom Project, of the fifty-two defendants, thirty-five are African American, fourteen are white, two are Latina, and one is Native American. *See* Lynn Paltrow and Suzanne Shende, State by State Case Summary of Criminal Prosecutions against Pregnant Women (Oct. 29, 1990). In Florida, where two women have been convicted for distributing drugs to a minor, ten out of eleven criminal cases were brought against Black women. *Id.* at 3–5.

3. For arguments supporting the mother's right to autonomy, see, e.g., Goldberg, *Medical Choices during Pregnancy: Whose Decision Is It Anyway?,* 41 Rutgers L. Rev. 591 (1989). For arguments advocating protection of the fetus, see, e.g., Walker and Puzder, *State Protection of the Unborn after Roe v.*

Wade: A Legislative Proposal, 13 Stetson L. Rev. 237, 253–63 (1984).

4. Approximately half of the nation's crack addicts are women. *See* Alters, *Women and Crack: Equal Addiction, Unequal Care,* Boston Globe, Nov. 1, 1989, at 1. The highest concentrations of crack addicts are found in inner-city neighborhoods. *See* Malcolm, *Crack, Bane of Inner City, Is Now Gripping Suburbs,* N.Y. Times, Oct. 1, 1989, at 1.

5. Many crack-addicted women become pregnant as a result of trading sex for crack or turning to prostitution to support their habit. *See* Alters, *supra* note 4, at 1.

6. *See* Besharov, *Crack Babies: The Worst Threat Is Mom Herself.* Wash. Post, Aug. 6, 1989, at B1.

7. *See* Koren et al., *Bias against the Null Hypothesis: The Reproductive Hazards of Cocaine,* Lancet, Dec. 16, 1989, at 1440.

8. Black women are five times more likely to live in poverty, five times more likely to be on welfare, and three times more likely to be unemployed than are white women. *See* United States Comm'n on Civil Rights, The Economic Status of Black Women 1 (1990).

9. *See, e.g.,* Fried et al., *Marijuana Use during Pregnancy and Decreased Length of Gestation,* 150 Am. J. Obstetrics & Gyn. 23 (1984).

10. In 1987, the mortality rate for Black infants was 17.9 deaths per 1,000, compared to a rate of 8.6 deaths per 1,000 for white infants. *See* U.S. Dep't of Commerce, Bureau of Census, Statistical Abstract of the United States 77 (table 110) (1990).

11. The Fourteenth Amendment provides, in relevant part, that "[n]o State shall make or enforce any law which shall . . . deny to any person within its jurisdiction the equal protection of the laws." U.S. Const. amend. XIV, § 1.

12. These competing views of equal protection law have been variously characterized by commentators. *See, e.g.,* L. Tribe, American Constitutional Law §§ 16–21, at 1514–21 (2d ed. 1988).

13. Dimond, *The Anti-Caste Principle: Toward a Constitutional Standard for Review of Race Cases,* 30 Wayne L. Rev. 1, 1 (1983).

14. *See* Strauss, *Discriminatory Intent and the Taming of Brown,* 56 U. Chi. L. Rev. 935, 953–54 (1989).

15. For a discussion of equal protection challenges to racially selective prosecutions, see

Developments in the Law: Race and the Criminal Process, 101 Harv. L. Rev. 1472, 1532–49 (1988).

16. *See* Kennedy, McCleskey v. Kemp: *Race, Capital Punishment and the Supreme Court,* 101 Harv. L. Rev. 1388, 1425–27 (1988).

17. *See* Chasnoff et al., *The Prevalence of Illicit Drug or Alcohol Use during Pregnancy and Discrepancies in Mandatory Reporting in Pinellas County, Florida,* 322 New Eng. J. Med. 1202, 1204 (table 2) (1990).

18. *See, e.g.,* DeShaney v. Winnebago County Dep't of Social Servs., 489 U.S. 189, 196 (1989) ("[O]ur cases have recognized that the Due Process Clauses generally confer no affirmative right to governmental aid, even where such aid may be necessary to secure life, liberty, or property interests of which the government itself may not deprive the individual").

19. Tribe, *supra* note 12, § 15–2, at 1305.

Women's Control Unit
Marianna, FL

Silvia Baraldini,* Marilyn Buck, Susan Rosenberg, and Laura Whitehorn

Shawnee Unit, at the Federal Correctional Institution in Marianna, Florida, was opened by the Federal Bureau of Prisons (BOP) in August 1988, after the small group-isolation experiment at Lexington High Security Unit (HSU) was shut down in response to a lawsuit by prisoners housed there and a national and international campaign. The political and security mission of Shawnee is the same as that of the HSU: to control, isolate, and neutralize women who, for varying reasons, pose either a political, escape, or disruption threat. Neutralization ensures that the women imprisoned here will never leave prison with the full capacity to function. Central to the mission is the understanding that Washington can decide at any point to transfer any female political prisoner or prisoner of war here. The recent transfer of Laura Whitehorn is a case in point.

The unit serves as a public admonishment to those who would challenge the supremacy of the United States—deterrence and isolation are central to its mission. It also serves to maintain control over all women in BOP prisons: 12 women who were targeted as leadership of the recent demonstration against police violence by women at Lexington were transferred here in less than 24 hours.

Once a control unit is set up, it fulfills many needs. The BOP operates Shawnee with some flexibility. Protected witnesses, disciplinary cases, high profile individuals, members of various Colombian cartels, and women with successful escape histories are imprisoned here. What distinguishes them from the political prisoners is their ability to transfer out of Shawnee. Over the past year, there has been a massive movement out of the unit. But political prisoners, despite repeated requests to be transferred, have been excluded from this.

Psychological Control

To wash away the brutal image of the HSU, the BOP has created the deception that life at Shawnee is normal, not designed or manipulated. The physical plant is designed to deflect any concern from the outside about human rights abuses—it looks comfortable and attractive. This appearance is a lie.

The women of Shawnee live in a psychologically assaultive environment that aims at destabilizing women's personal and social identities. This is true of the prison system as a whole; here it has been elevated to a primary weapon, implemented through a physical layout and day-to-day regimen that pro-

---

*In 1999, Silvia Baraldini, an Italian citizen, was released to Italian authorities after a concerted international lobbying effort that included the Italian government. She was seriously ill with cancer.

duce inwardness and self-containment. The unit is a small triangle with a small yard. Within this severely limited space, women are under constant scrutiny and observation. In the unit, cameras and listening devices (the latter are installed in every cell) ensure constant surveillance and control of even the most intimate conversation. Lockdown is not necessary because there is nowhere to go, and individuals can be observed and controlled better while having the illusion of some mobility.

The fences around the yard—the only place where one could have any sense that an outside world existed—were recently covered with green cloth, further hammering into the women the sense of being completely apart and separate. It is one thing to be imprisoned in this tiny isolation unit for a year or two, another to be told one will be here for three more decades—that this small unit will be one's world for the rest of one's life.

Compared to the other federal prisons for women, Shawnee is like being in a suffocating cocoon. What replaces visual stimulation and communication is TV. As in the Marion control unit, there is a TV in every cell—the perfect answer to any complaints about isolation or boredom. TV provides the major link to the world—a link that conveniently produces passivity and inculcates "family values."

The intense physical limitations are compounded by a total lack of educational, training, or recreational programs. At a time when such programs are being expanded at other women's prisons, here, at the end of the line, women are not worthy of even the pretense of rehabilitation. The geographical location of Shawnee makes contact with family and community an almost impossible task. Gradually, women here begin to lose their ability to relate to the outside world. As time moves on, frustration sets in, accompanied by alienation and despair. The result is the creation of dysfunctional individuals who are completely self-involved, unable to participate in organized social activities, and unprepared for eventual reintegration into life on the outside: women who resist less, demand less, and see each other as fierce competitors for the few privileges allowed.

Competition and individualism become the defining characteristics of personality distortion here. The staff seeks out the most needy personalities and molds them into informants. Unit life has been rocked by a number of internal investigations begun

when individual prisoners "confided" in ambitious staff members. Snitching and cooperation are the pillars of the "justice system." Those who refuse to go along are isolated and targeted by those who do. In the tiny world of the unit, this can have a massive effect on one's daily life.

A system of hierarchical privileges governs the unit and destroys any potential unity. Small comforts, such as pieces of clothing, have become the mechanism through which cooperation and collaboration are obtained. The latest wrinkle is the institution of "privileged housing"—the arbitrary designation of a limited number of cells on the upper tier as a reward for acceptable behavior. This is classic behavior modification. The unit is in a constant state of uproar over the daily moves that enforce the fall from privileged status.

White Supremacy and Racism

There are close to 90 women imprisoned at Shawnee: one-third Black women from various parts of the world, one-third Latin women, one-third white women, and a very small number of Native-American women. The numerical balance belies the hegemony of white supremacist ideology. As outside the walls, a permanent conflict exists between Black people and those in power. Prisoners experience and are affected by the sharpening of conflict on the outside and the increasing national oppression experienced by Black people in particular. Events in California have given focus to the discontent and heightened the contradictions. Since May 1992, an unprecedented number of Black women have been put in the hole—more than the total for the past two years. Currently, five women from the unit are in the hole; all are Black. And while the administration says that they do not deal with gangs, "Boyz 'N the Hood" and "Jungle Fever" were banned from the prison after the Aryan Brotherhood protested.

A strict segregationist policy determines who gets the jobs. After four years, no Black women have ever worked for education or recreation, except for janitorial jobs. It has taken as long to place a Black woman in commissary and to promote one woman to be a trainer in the UNICOR* factory. All Black staff

*[Ed. note: The federal prison industry.]

have left the unit, eliminating the small cushion they provided. This is significant, as staff in the federal system determine everything from access to family to release conditions.

Racism governs how religion can be practiced. Islam, Judaism, and Native-American religions are either totally ignored or marginalized. One cannot help but notice this, since there is a daily diet of fundamentalist Protestant and Catholic services, seminars and retreats.

Superexploitation of Women's Labor

Like B block at Marion, there is no productive labor at Shawnee besides UNICOR. Unit life is organized to facilitate the functioning of the Automated Data Processing (ADP) factory. Nearly 40 women work here, 12 hours a day and 5 more hours on Saturday. The forced rhythm of this work has made the ADP factory the most profitable UNICOR operation in the BOP for its size. The complete lack of any other jobs, the need for funds, the lack of family support, the enormous expense of living in Shawnee, all push women into UNICOR, into intense competition and into an acceptance of their exploitation. Unlike general population prisons, Shawnee prisoners are not even permitted to work in jobs maintaining the physical plant. Removing productive labor is an element in destroying human identity and self-worth.

Increasing Violence, Misogyny and Homophobia

The recent physical attacks by male guards at Lexington, and a similar incident here at Shawnee, illustrate the marked tendency towards using greater force to control women prisoners. While lower security women are being sent to minimum-security facilities, those left in high-security prisons will be more and more vulnerable to physical attack—justified by being characterized by the BOP as "dangerous."

Women in prison are at the very bottom. The misogyny and contempt for women in the society as a whole are compounded by the way the prison system is organized to exploit and utilize women's oppression. The BOP characterizes some women as "dangerous" and "terrorist" (having gone beyond the bounds of acceptable female behavior in the United States), making them the target of particularized repression, scorn, and hatred. To be classified maximum-security is to be seen as less than human, by definition not eligible for "rehabilitation."

All women's prisons operate based on the all-pervasive threat of sexual assault, and the dehumanizing invasion of privacy. Throughout the state and federal prison system in the United States, invasive "pat searches" of women by male guards ensure that a woman prisoner is daily reminded of her powerlessness: she cannot even defend her own body.

In the control unit, there is absolutely no privacy: windows in cell doors (which cannot be covered), patrolling of the unit by male guards, and the presence of the bathrooms in the cells guarantee this. The voyeuristic nature of the constant surveillance is a matter of record: in the past year alone, there have been three major internal investigations of sexual harassment and misconduct by male officers—including rape.

Programs that exist in other women's prisons, addressing the particular needs of women, are deemed frivolous at Shawnee. Most women here are mothers, but no support at all is given to efforts to maintain the vital relationship between mother and child. Similarly, if Shawnee were not a control unit, then education, recreation, religious, and cultural programs should be on a par with those at Lewisburg, Leavenworth, and Lompoc (three men's high-security prisons). But not a single program available in those prisons is available here.

The median age of the women here is 37—a situation distinct from any other women's prison. Nearly everyone is doing more than 15 years; more than 10 women are serving life sentences without parole. Menopause is the main medical problem in the unit. Menopause is an emotional as well as a physiological process. Ignoring this is a pillar of misogynist Western medicine. In the repressive reality of Shawnee, refusal to recognize and treat the symptoms of menopause becomes a cruel means of punishment and an attack on the integrity of one's personality.

Security determines all medical care. Two women who have suffered strokes here were both denied access to necessary treatment in a hospital, a life-threatening decision, made solely for "security reasons."

Intense isolation and lack of activities mean that the loving relationships that provide intimacy and comfort to women in all prisons are of heightened importance here. Until recently, a seemingly tolerant attitude towards Lesbian relationships was actually a form of control. For Lesbian relationships to function without disciplinary intervention by the police, the women had to negotiate with, and in some instances work for, the staff. This tolerance was viewed as necessary because the relationships served as a safety valve for the tensions and anger in the population. As a result of the system of police-sanctioned tolerance, people tended to elevate the individual relationships above any collective alliances that might endanger the administration's rule over the unit.

This situation served to increase the already intense homophobia in the population. A new administration has now ended the tolerance, and Lesbian women are now suffering greater harassment and discrimination. A witch hunt is underway to identify Lesbians and couples engaging in homosexual behavior.

Misogyny and homophobia, together with racism, define conditions here. When coupled with the repressive practices of a control unit, psychological disablement can result—fulfilling the Shawnee mission.

Conclusion

Partly as a result of the astronomic rise in the number of women in prison and the resulting public in-

terest in women's prisons, and partly as a result of the struggle against the Lexington HSU, the BOP has to be very careful not to appear to be brutal in its treatment of women prisoners. The investigations of the HSU by Amnesty International, the Methodist Church, the American Civil Liberties Union and others struck a nerve in Washington. The experiment carried out within the walls of the HSU failed because of the personal and political resistance of those inside and outside the walls. But this defeat did not deter the BOP-stated goals. It just drove them to hide those goals cosmetically behind a veneer of new paint and the momentary elimination of the most notorious abuses. The BOP always denies the truth of its workings. It denies the existence of control units and this unit in particular, not even listing it in the BOP Register of Prisons. Nevertheless, Shawnee is the present women's version of the Marionization of the prison system. The next one is supposed to be opened in North Carolina in 1994. [At the time of publication, this prison has not opened.] The movement should not fall into the trap and ignore the particular control strategy aimed at women. Uncovering and exposing the reality that Shawnee Unit is a control unit will contribute to the movement against all control units.

Anti-imperialist Political Prisoners
Marianna, Florida
Fall 1992

U.S. Concentration Camps and Exclusion Policies
Impact on Japanese American Women
Rita Takahashi

During World War II, most women of Japanese ancestry residing in the United States received the same sentence from their government. Under Executive Order 9066, signed by President Franklin Delano Roosevelt on 19 February 1942, people of Japanese ancestry living on the West Coast were excluded from their communities and incarcerated in concentration camps. The government justified its

actions on grounds of "military necessity," although more than two-thirds of the incarcerated people were U.S.-born citizens. The camps were initially established and temporarily operated by the U.S. Army, under the name of the Wartime Civil Control Administration (WCCA). Later, jurisdiction was transferred to a newly-created civilian federal agency, the War Relocation Authority (WRA).

U.S. Incarceration Policy for People of Japanese Ancestry

A documented 120,313 persons of Japanese ancestry fell under the jurisdiction of the WRA. Of this number, 112,603 people were forced to leave their homes and enter U.S. concentration camps in seven states — Arizona, Arkansas, California, Colorado, Idaho, Utah, and Wyoming. A third of those incarcerated were classified as resident "aliens," despite the fact that they lived in the United States for many years prior to World War II. Less than one-third of one percent of all evacuated persons of Japanese ancestry (native and foreign-born) had been living in the U.S. for less than ten years.

"Aliens" of Japanese ancestry were "non-citizens" because of discriminatory laws that made them ineligible for naturalized citizenship. At the time of incarceration, 30,619 (80.2%) of the first generation "aliens" (known as *Isseis*) had resided in the United States for 23 or more years. Almost all *Isseis* had been residents for more than fifteen years, since the 1924 Immigration Act excluded Japan from further immigration to the United States. Only 345 alien Japanese had resided in the U.S. for less than ten years.

Banished individuals had the choice of moving "voluntarily" to inland states (they had about a three-week period to do so), and approximately 9,000 people did this, to avoid being sent to concentration camps. Approximately 4,000 of these "voluntary resettlers" moved to the eastern half of California. This group was subsequently forced to move again when the Government announced that the entire state of California, not just the western half, was off limits to people of Japanese ancestry. Some 4,889 persons "voluntarily" moved to states outside of California (1,963 to Colorado; 1,519 to Utah, 305 to Idaho; 208 to eastern Washington; 115 to eastern Oregon; and the remainder scattered throughout the United States).

This incarceration policy was consistent with previous discriminatory local, state, and federal policies affecting Asian Americans in the United States. Japanese Americans were targeted, in part because of the economic competition they posed in various states, particularly on the West Coast (California, Oregon, and Washington). Many government officials saw World War II as the perfect opportunity to get rid of Japanese Americans from their states, once and for all. For the U.S. government, under President Roosevelt, the war was a good opportunity to institute its assimilation policy and "Americanization" plan: to disperse persons of Japanese ancestry throughout the U.S., in a deliberate plan to break up the "Little Tokyos" and "Japantowns."

The U.S. Constitution calls for equal protection under the law and prohibits deprivation of life, liberty, or property without "due process of law." These "protective" guarantees were suspended in this case, and the Government was able to implement this massive program with few questions asked. Congress sanctioned the plan and the U.S. Supreme Court failed to challenge its constitutionality. Few dared to oppose such a plan, presented as an urgent necessity to secure a nation under what was rhetorically stated as a dire military threat.

Intelligence Reports Dispute "Military Necessity"

Although military necessity and national security were the stated reason and goal for mass incarceration, decision-making elites knew that there was no threat to U.S. security from Japanese Americans. Top officials had access to years of intelligence reports from a variety of sources, including the Department of State, Department of Justice (through the Federal Bureau of Investigation), Navy Intelligence, and Army Intelligence. In October 1941, Jim Marshall reported:

> For five years or more there has been a constant check on both Issei [first generation immigrants from Japan] and Nisei [second generation, U.S.-born persons of Japanese ancestry] — the consensus among intelligent people is that an overwhelming majority is loyal. The few who are suspect are carefully watched. In event of war, they would be behind bars at once. In case of war, there would be some demand in California for concentration camps into which Japanese and Japanese-Americans would be herded for the duration. Army, Navy or FBI never have suggested officially that such a step would be necessary. . . . Their opinion, based on intensive and continuous investigation, is that the situation is not dangerous and that, whatever happens, there is not likely to be any trouble — with

this opinion west coast newspapermen, in touch with the problem for years, agree most unanimously.[1]

In an intelligence report submitted in November 1941 (only three months before President Roosevelt signed Executive Order 9066), Curtis Munson, a Special Representative to the State Department, said that:

> As interview after interview piles up, those bringing in results began to call it the same old tune. . . . There is no Japanese "problem" on the Coast. There will be no armed uprising of Japanese. . . .[2]

Just two days before President Roosevelt signed Executive Order 9066, the Head of the Justice Department, Francis Biddle, encouraged Roosevelt to say something in defense of persons of Japanese ancestry, and wrote, "My last advice from the War Department is that there is no evidence of planned sabotage."[3]

Despite the evidence presented to President Roosevelt—all confirming that there was no threat that warranted *en masse* incarceration—he proceeded with the incarceration policy. He also maintained a consistent pattern of not "setting the record straight" based on intelligence facts.

Experiences of Japanese American Women

All Japanese American women felt the impact of World War II, and the exclusion policy caused major disruptions and upheavals in their lives. It affected their professional careers, impinged on the ways in which they viewed the world, and changed the course and direction of their lives.

Although the exclusion orders affected all women of Japanese ancestry, their specific experiences varied broadly due to many factors, including residence at the time of the exclusion order, age at the time of incarceration (adult or child), the camp that one went into, the job that one was able to get (inside and outside of camp), the college one was admitted to, the degree of co-operation one exhibited toward the concentration camp administrators, and one's status and socio-economic class.

From 1991 to 1997 this author conducted over 300 interviews with Japanese Americans, all of whom were affected by the U.S. Government's policy to banish, exclude, and incarcerate this population, *en masse,* because of their Japanese heritage. This author discovered that, although the same policies were directed at the entire group, the personal experiences were as diverse as the individuals themselves.

The following discussion represents a sampling of five Japanese American women's experiences during World War II derived from interviews conducted by this writer.[4]

Meriko Hoshiyama Mori

A Teenager Left to Fend for Herself after FBI Picked Up Both Parents

Meriko Hoshiyama Mori, born in Hollywood, California, is the only child of Suematsu Hoshiyama (of Niigata-ken, Japan) and Fuki Noguchi Hoshiyama (of Tochig-ken, Japan). Her parents owned a nursery / gardening business in West Los Angeles until World War II. Her mother, who taught at a Japanese language school before the war, was picked up and detained by the Federal Bureau of Investigation (FBI) on 22 February 1942. Fuki Noguchi Hoshiyama was among the few women who were picked up by the FBI (she was later released and sent to Santa Anita Assembly Center, a converted race track). She had the presence of mind to collect the personal thoughts of detainees — other Japanese women who were also picked up by the FBI. These quotations, collected at the time of internment, are hand-written in Japanese.

A few weeks later, in March 1942, Meriko Mori's father, who was the Japanese Language School treasurer, was also picked up by the FBI. Consequently, Meriko Mori was left, by herself, to take care of all the family and business matters. She was only nineteen years of age when both parents were picked up.

As a teenager desperate for help, Meriko Mori went to the social welfare office to get aid. According to Mori, they told her that they could do nothing for her because there were no rules or regulations for cases like hers. Therefore, Mori got no assistance from them. Reflecting back on this experience in a letter dated 10 February 1997, Mori wrote:

When I was left alone, it was a shock, but perhaps not as great as it might have been because by the time my father was picked up, the FBI had come several times, and did not find him at home, because he was at work. I recall the FBI sitting in the car waiting for him to come home. . . . Although I had said I would be all alone, I recall following them [FBI] to Mr. Hayashida's home a block away where he was picked up. Even now as I write this, tears come to my eyes. It is very difficult to recall unpleasant memories.

My Caucasian neighbors expressed concern and wrote to me in camp. My Japanese neighbors were so concerned [about] their own families and situation of packing, moving, etc. they expressed concern but did not have the time to be involved in my predicament. If my Aunt Maki and Uncle Iwamatsu Hoshiyama did not offer to include me in their family (they had 3 girls and 2 boys), I don't know what I could have done when the welfare department didn't know what to do. To say the least, I was very fortunate and am forever grateful to Maki and Iwamatsu Hoshiyama.

When the U.S. entered World War II, Meriko Mori was a sophomore at the University of California at Los Angeles. She was surprised that she was treated like an enemy alien, and angered by her exclusion. In the words of her letter (1997):

> I was angry at the U.S. Government for its treatment of a U.S. citizen, and felt forsaken by my country and lost faith in the U.S. . . . We had lost our freedoms on which the country was founded.

Her studies were disrupted when she had to leave for Manzanar Camp, where she was watched and controlled by the U.S. Army's armed guards. In 1997, she thought about her camp experience, and said, "My memories of Manzanar are [that it was a] very hot or cold desert. I recall many sand storms and walking against the wind backwards." This camp, originally established under the U.S. Army's WCCA, later became a WRA camp. While at Manzanar, Mori earned the top salary of $19 a month for her work as a school teacher. Fifty-five years later, in her 1997 letter, Mori addressed the impact of her experiences:

These experiences have taught me to be self-reliant, independent, resourceful, and aware of how injustices can be perpetrated on innocent victims who are weak and have no voice. We need to be constantly vigilant.

Kiyo Sato-Viacrucis

A Student Who Left Camp for a Midwest School and Who Returned to Stolen Property

Kiyo Sato-Viacrucis was born in Sacramento, California, the eldest of nine children born to Shinji "John" Sato (from Chiba-ken, Japan) and Tomomi "Mary" Watanabe Sato (from Aizuwakamatsu, Fukushima-ken). When World War II broke out, the Sato family was farming in the Sacramento area. Having graduated from Sacramento High School in Spring 1941, Kiyo Sato-Viacrucis was attending Sacramento Junior City College at the time of the incarceration orders.

In May 1942, the Sato family was ordered to go to Pinedale Assembly Center, a WCCA facility set up and run by the U.S. Army. Ironically, while her family was sent to a concentration camp, under armed Army guard, her brother was serving in the U.S. Army. He had volunteered after Pearl Harbor was bombed by Japan, and ended up serving for the duration of the war. When Kiyo Sato-Viacrucis volunteered her services to the military, and when she attempted to gain admission into institutions of higher education, she was rejected. Later she wrote to the institutions, saying: "My brother and others are fighting to uphold democratic principles. I cannot understand that an institution of your standing would have such a policy." She was eventually accepted by Western Reserve University in 1945.

After four and one half months at Pinedale, she and her family were shipped, via train and open army truck, to Poston (Arizona) Camp, which was operated by the newly-established civil federal agency, the WRA. Upon her family's arrival in July 1942, the temperature was 127 degrees Fahrenheit. Viewing all the sage brush and experiencing the heat, Kiyo Sato-Viacrucis literally passed out.

Sato-Viacrucis did what she could to leave Poston quickly. After three and one half months, she managed to depart for Hillsdale College in Michigan. Since the college was located in an inland state, she was released only if she would agree to attend this private Baptist college.

After the West Coast was opened to Japanese Americans, Kiyo Sato-Viacrucis was one of the early returnees to Sacramento in 1945. She found that her family's home had been occupied by unknown and unauthorized persons, and that all their stored goods had been stolen. Further, she saw that the Mayhew Japanese Baptist Church (in Sacramento), which had stored the incarcerated Japanese Americans' belongings, had been burned to the ground the night before her return.

The incarceration experience had continuous and long-term impact on excludees. Reflecting on the implications for her and other women, Sato-Viacrucis said, "Partly because of our background, we *nisei* women retreated from a hostile world into our shells like turtles. Even after fifty years, we are afraid to come out and tell what happened." Reminiscing in 1997, fifty-five years after the exclusionary policies and programs, she said:

> *Nisei* [U.S.-born and second generation Japanese American] men were able to go to war and be recognized for their heroic efforts, but we *nisei* women were "war casualties" on two fronts. Not only were we not of the right color for the Navy or Air Force, but we were not acceptable by many institutions of higher learning "due to policy." It was certainly devastating to be rejected by the Navy because of my color, and then by Yale, Johns Hopkins, Western Reserve University schools of nursing, again because of their "policy." It is hard to believe that even our country's most prestigious institutions of higher learning succumbed to social pressure. That is scary. It happened so easily; will it happen again?

Yoshiye Togasaki

A Medical Doctor Who Took Her Practice to the Concentration Camps

Yoshiye Togasaki was born in an upstairs room of the Geary Theater, located in San Francisco. She was the fifth of six children born to Kikumatsu Togasaki (from Ibaraki-ken, Japan) and Shige Kushida Togasaki

(from Tokyo). In 1892, her mother had been sent to the United States as an activist in the Women's Christian Temperance Union. This Japanese immigrant woman was a most unique person who did not shy away from publicly expressing her opinions and speaking her mind. She had stood out on the streets of San Francisco, preaching Christian doctrine.

When World War II broke out, Yoshiye Togasaki was already established in her profession as a medical doctor. In those days, women doctors — especially women of color — were a small minority. After her December 1921 graduation from Lowell High School in San Francisco, Togasaki attended the University of California, Berkeley, where she received a bachelor's degree in public health in 1929. With her medical doctor's degree from Johns Hopkins University in June 1935, she took an internship at the Los Angeles General Hospital.

In 1938, Togasaki became chief resident for communicable diseases at the L.A. General Hospital. She remained in this position until just six months before the U.S. entered World War II. At the time of the Pearl Harbor bombing, Togasaki was an assistant to the City of Los Angeles's epidemiologist. Because she knew she would be terminated when the war broke out, she resigned.

Togasaki spent time trying to correct public perceptions about Japanese Americans. Because the President of the Council on Churches harangued persons of Japanese ancestry, Togasaki went directly to him to try to change his belief that Japanese Americans were "untrustworthy." According to Togasaki, his mind was rigidly set.

After the incarceration orders were announced, and when it became clear that Manzanar, California, would be one of the WCCA Assembly Centers, Togasaki volunteered to help set it up. She arrived at the camp on 21 March 1942, and remained there until October 1942. Open trenches and hygienic problems were prevalent throughout the camp. According to Togasaki, she worked sixteen hours a day, dealing with public health and medical matters. For her services, she earned a salary of $16 per month. She managed to get scarce medical supplies, such as vaccines, from friends or associates outside the camp.

Due to overwork, Togasaki became ill, so she went to Tule Lake Camp (also in California) to join her two sisters. Because there were few resources to diagnose and care for her illness, she went to San

Francisco's Children's Hospital for diagnosis. This was a rare event, since Japanese Americans were supposed to be excluded from the area. After five or six days at Children's Hospital, Togasaki stayed at the home of a doctor friend in San Francisco. In Togasaki's words, "No one complained that a Japanese American was there."

Togasaki worked as a pediatric doctor at Tule Lake, where she worked with Dr. Pedicord, a retired doctor from the Kentucky mountains who had failed to keep abreast of the latest developments in medicine. He stirred up a lot of antagonism around Tule Lake because of his attitude toward Japanese Americans, whom he viewed as inferior, foreign, and un-American. Considered whistle blowers and antagonists, Togasaki and her two sisters, Kazue (an obstetrician) and Chiye, were transferred to Manzanar in April 1943. Yoshiye Togasaki remained at Manzanar a few months before she left, in July 1943, for a pediatric position at New York's Bellevue Hospital.

Masako Takahashi Hamada

An Excludee Who "Voluntarily" Moved Inland to Idaho

Masako Takahashi Hamada was born in Seattle, Washington, the sixth of seven children born to Kumato Takahashi and Toshi Kato Takahashi, both of Niigata-ken, Japan. After graduating from Garfield High School, she was studying in Seattle when World War II broke out.

During a three-week period in March 1942, Japanese Americans were given the option to "voluntarily" leave their homes in the military exclusion zones (the entire West Coast of the U.S. mainland) and to resettle in an inland state outside the military zones, or be sent to a concentration camp. Masako Takahashi, her mother, and five siblings decided to move and join their oldest brother and his wife in Idaho, where his wife's family [Tamura] resided. Leaving most of their valuable possessions behind, they moved to avoid going into concentration camps. They were among the 305 "voluntary movers" who entered Idaho from the restricted military zones. Another older brother, who was living in Washington at the time of the exclusion, did not move because he was originally unaware of the or-

ders. Consequently, he was incarcerated in a concentration camp.

In the Southern Idaho area where she settled, travel was restricted in certain areas, and "NO JAPS ALLOWED" signs were posted in various businesses, alerting the public that "Japs" would not be served. Of course, it did not matter whether one was a citizen or not; service was denied, regardless. This discriminatory behavior was matched by the Idaho Governor's attitude toward Japanese Americans. Governor Chase Clark openly expressed his aversion to any Japanese American migration into the State of Idaho.

Masako Takahashi and her family faced very tough times in the new area. They struggled to make enough money to live, as they encountered new work environments and life situations. They worked for the E. H. Dewey family, who are related to Colonel W. H. Dewey of Silver City, Idaho. Although her goal, at that time, was to be a dress designer, she spent her days working in the fields, hoeing, weeding, and toiling in the hot sun for minimal rewards.

She and her sister (Yuki) went to Chicago to further their education. After the war, she married an Idaho-born Japanese American veteran of World War II, who served with the 442nd Regimental Combat Team, whose motto was "Go For Broke." She remained in Idaho, where she served as a nurse for twenty-five years and where she volunteers her services in Mountain Home, Idaho.

Reflecting upon her experiences in a 3 February 1997 letter, Hamada said, "I hope that such a sad [and] shocking experience will never be repeated again in history. . . . Let us hope that each and every one of us [will] live in peace and harmony."

Tsuru Fukui Takenaka

A Businesswoman Outside the Military Zone Who Faced Government Restrictions

Tsuru Fukui Takenaka was born on 26 August 1900, in Wakayama-ken, Japan. In 1920, after marrying Sennosuke Takenaka in Japan, she came to the United States with her husband who had been working in the U.S. prior to marriage. Upon her arrival in San Francisco, she was detained and quarantined a week by the U.S. immigration authorities at Angel

Island. In her words, her immigration detention was "just like jail."

In 1930, she and her husband went to Lovelock, Nevada, and took over the Up-to-Date Laundry from the Nakamuras. They owned and worked in this hand laundry throughout World War II, and they maintained the business for years thereafter. In fact, Tsuru Takenaka continued to work in the laundry until 1990, when she was 90 years of age. During the years at the laundry, she strenuously worked long hours.

The Takenakas did not have to leave their home and go into concentration camps because they were situated in a non-military exclusion zone. Therefore, the family continued to run the laundry business throughout the war. Although some established customers did not return after the start of World War II, the Takenakas remained busy enough to keep their business going. But the military restrictions, imposed during World War II, affected the Takenakas' free movement. They were restricted to a fifty-mile radius and could not go to the closest large town, Reno. Further, according to Tsuru Takenaka, the Reno Mayor was known to harbor anti-Japanese sentiments.

Until after World War II, the Takenaka family was the only Japanese American family in Lovelock, and they did experience some discriminatory treatment. Takenaka's daughter, for example, was not allowed to board a train, and her husband, Sennosuke, was subjected to harassment and "bad" talk when he went to the Persian Hotel and Restaurant in downtown Lovelock.

Final Comments

The World War II experiences of Japanese American women are as varied as the number of people involved. In this paper, only five examples are presented, to illustrate the variety in experience. While some women were already established in their profession (e.g., Togasaki), others were just beginning their careers (e.g., Sato-Viacrucis). Some women owned their own businesses in the non-exclusion areas (e.g., Takenaka), while others were employees. All were affected by their residential location. Some living in the military exclusion zones were subjected to FBI raids (e.g., Mori), and most were forced, *en masse,* to go into concentration camps (Mori, Sato-

Viacrucis, and Togasaki). With mandatory removal imminent, some chose to move from military exclusion zones prior to being incarcerated in concentration camps (Takahashi Hamada).

Nearly 40 years after this incarceration policy was instituted, the U.S. Commission on Wartime Relocation and Internment of Civilians (CWRIC) was established, in 1980, to "review the facts and circumstances surrounding Executive Order Number 9066 . . . and the impact of such Executive Order on American citizens and permanent resident aliens." The Commission concluded that these policy decisions were shaped by "race prejudice, war hysteria and a failure of political leadership." In summary, "a grave personal injustice was done." Furthermore,

> The excluded people suffered enormous damages and losses, both material and intangible. To the disastrous loss of farms, businesses and homes must be added the disruption for many years of careers and professional lives, as well as the long-term loss of income and opportunity. . . .

Following these findings, there were years of debate in the U.S. House of Representatives and in the U.S. Senate concerning compensation to those who had suffered this injustice. After many Congressional sessions, compromises, and legislative drafts, the U.S. House of Representatives passed the Civil Liberties Act on 17 September 1987, by a vote of 243 to 141. The U.S. Senate passed a similar bill on 20 April 1988, also after lengthy discussion, by a vote of 69 to 27. To bring the two congressional versions together, a conference bill was worked out between the U.S. House and U.S. Senate leaders. This conference bill passed in the Senate on 17 July 1988 and in the House on 4 August 1988. President Ronald Reagan signed the Civil Liberties Act of 1988 into law on 10 August 1988.

Because the new law was an authorization bill, there was no provision for actual appropriations of $20,000 payments to each eligible individual. In November 1989, President George Bush signed an authorization bill into law, entitling the U.S. Government to pay up to $500 million each fiscal year, up to a total of $1.25 billion. With this entitlement in place, the Government was able to begin payments in October 1990.

The redress policy included provisions for a U.S. Government apology for discriminatory wrongs it committed and for individual monetary compensation. The following letter, signed by President George Bush, accompanied each individual redress check:

A monetary sum and words alone cannot restore lost years or erase painful memories; neither can they fully convey our Nation's resolve to rectify injustice and to uphold the rights of individuals. We can never fully right the wrongs of the past. But we can take a clear stand for justice and recognize that serious injustices were done to Japanese Americans during World War II.

In enacting a law calling for restitution and offering a sincere apology, your fellow Americans have, in a very real sense, renewed their traditional commitment to the ideals of free-

dom, equality, and justice. You and your family have our best wishes for the future.

Notes

1. Carey McWilliams. *Prejudice: Japanese-Americans: Symbol of Racial Intolerance.* Hamden, CT: Shoe String Press (Reprint), 1971, p. 114.

2. Curtis B. Munson. "Japanese on the West Coast," reprinted in *Hearings before the Joint Committee on the Investigation of the Pearl Harbor Attack* (79th Congress, 1st Session, Part 6). Washington, D.C.: Government Printing Office, January, 1946, p. 2686.

3. Bill Hosokawa, *Nisei: The Quiet American.* New York: William Morrow and Company, Inc., 1969, p. 277.

4. Quotes from the five women were taken from interviews conducted by Rita Takahashi or from their letters to her.

SIXTY-SEVEN

◆◆◆

Three Chinese Women in Search of Asylum Held in U.S. Prisons

Wendy A. Young

Founded in 1989, the Women's Commission for Refugee Women and Children is a nonprofit membership organization that seeks to improve the lives of refugee women and children through a vigorous and comprehensive program of public education and advocacy. Its goal is to secure for refugee women and children around the world the protection, assistance, education, and health care they deserve. Moreover, the Women's Commission promotes the empowerment of refugee women by ensuring that women themselves are the leaders and decision makers in their quest for personal safety and a secure family life.

In December 1996, the Women's Commission for Refugee Women and Children sponsored a delegation to assess conditions of detention for female asylum seekers in the Kern County Lerdo Detention Center in Bakersfield, California. At that time, the Immigration and Naturalization Service (INS) was

holding seven Chinese women in detention there. Members of the delegation included experts in immigration, refugees, and social work.

The delegation interviewed three Chinese women,* who had been incarcerated in a variety of county prisons for three and a half years. Two of the women, Chi and Zheng, entered the United States on board the *Golden Venture,* a ship that received extensive media coverage when it ran aground off Rockaway Beach, New York, carrying more than 300 Chinese asylum seekers, 23 of whom were women. As far as the delegation could ascertain, the five other Chinese women held in Kern County had been in detention for a similar length of time.

---

*Throughout this report, the women will be referred to as Chi, Zheng, and Su to protect their privacy.

Most of the women have based their political asylum claims on China's coercive family planning policy. Whether their fear of sterilization or punishment for having, or planning to have, more than one child is grounds for asylum has been the subject of much controversy. Both the Bush and Clinton Administrations, as well as the Justice Department's Board of Immigration Appeals and various federal courts, have issued conflicting directives on the issue. Most recently, Congress included a section in the "Illegal Immigration Reform and Immigration Responsibility Act of 1996" (Immigration Act of 1996), signed into law by President Clinton on September 28, 1996, stating that a person fleeing her homeland to escape involuntary family planning shall be deemed to have been persecuted on account of her political opinion.

Because of the confusion on this issue and the Clinton Administration's fear that releasing the Chinese would invite increased "alien smuggling," the Chinese have been subjected to prolonged detention. Many of the women have been transferred from county prison to county prison, caught up in a system they do not understand and losing hope that the United States will answer their dream of freedom.

The Women's Commission for Refugee Women and Children first addressed the situation of the Chinese women in March 1995 when it sponsored a delegation to New Orleans and Bay St. Louis, Mississippi, where the *Golden Venture* women were first detained. The delegation raised serious concerns about the effect prolonged detention was having on the women's mental health. These concerns were even more evident in 1996; the confusion, fear, depression, and anger the women were experiencing had clearly been exacerbated to a point of crisis as a result of their continued incarceration. It was extremely difficult for the 1996 delegation to solicit much information from the women, because they were so distraught when speaking about their experience.

Delegation Findings

Physical Setting

The Bakersfield Lerdo Detention Center is approximately a five-and-a-half hour drive from San Francisco and two hours from Los Angeles. Bakersfield is an isolated community that lacks a strong immigrant or immigrant advocate presence. The prison is located several miles outside of town, and is surrounded by fences and concertina wire.

Although owned and administered by Kern County, the detention center is only used to house federal detainees held by the INS, Marshals Service, or Bureau of Prisons. Kern County is paid approximately $57 per day for each detainee. The overall capacity of the prison is approximately 300 inmates. In contrast to other county prisons visited by the Women's Commission, the Kern County facility does not clearly delineate between space in which women are housed as opposed to men. Instead, detainees are moved around to meet the facility's space needs on any particular day. This means that women may be housed in close proximity to male detainees, although locked doors separate them.

Of the three federal agencies contracting with the facility, the INS uses it most frequently. According to the prison staff, the INS contract allows the county "to keep the lights on." The detention center is used by both the INS San Francisco District Office and the Los Angeles District Office to detain individuals in immigration proceedings. The Chinese women are being held under the jurisdiction of the San Francisco office.

The facility was constructed in the mid-1970s. It contains a variety of cell units of different sizes and levels of security. The Chinese women have been moved from unit to unit depending on the size of the prison population and the needs of the facility. At the time of the Women's Commission's visit, they were housed together in a 12-person cell, which contains six bunk beds. As far as the delegation could tell, the women are not commingled with criminal detainees, and the prison staff stated that it is their practice to house criminal and civil detainees separately. However, one woman had recently been transferred to another building within the complex, which the delegation did not tour. It remained unclear who else was housed in that facility with her.

The prison design and atmosphere are extremely oppressive. The walls are painted a dull yellow and gray, and the floors are cement. Little or no natural light reaches the cells. The large cells have some windows too high for an inmate to look out, while the smaller cells, including the one in which the women had been held for several months, have no natural light. The ventilation seemed poor, as the air was stagnant and smelled bad. The temperature is erratic, a problem acknowledged by the prison staff. The women also complained that their cell is infested with insects that bite them. All detainees wear prison uniforms and are shackled when they leave the facility.

In December 1995, when the women participated in a 50-day hunger strike to protest their prolonged detention, they were held in isolation in a row of "disciplinary isolation" cells, each of which is approximately 6' by 15' without natural light and with only televisions locked outside each cell for entertainment.

Most disturbing was an isolation cell used to house inmates experiencing behavioral problems, including suicidal tendencies. Approximately 10' by 10', the padded cell is painted brown and dimly lit by an overhead light. The cell is completely bare, lacking a bed, a chair, and even a toilet. Detainees are forced to urinate and defecate in a grate in the middle of the floor. Prison staff reported that detainees held in the cell are checked every 15 minutes, including by psychiatric staff, but that there is no overall limit on how long they can be held there.

The prison also contains holding and processing cells, several attorney visiting rooms, a visiting area where detainees can speak to family members and friends through a glass partition via a telephone, a clinic, and a classroom.

Translation Assistance

Neither the prison staff nor the INS staff posted on-site include full-time trained interpreters. One INS officer speaks Mandarin; however, it did not appear that he attempts to speak with the Chinese detainees in any regular or systematic way, unless the women request his assistance in writing.

Interpretation is also occasionally provided by telephone through AT&T in situations such as medical emergencies or routine examinations. The prison staff also indicated that they sometimes rely on inmates to translate for each other, although they admitted they do not like to do so.

Education

The only education provided in the prison is English as a Second Language (ESL) classes, which are offered through an adult education program in Bakersfield.

However, the women detainees are not even provided this service, because there are so few of them. The prison staff said it is open to providing access to volunteer teachers for the women.

Diet

The women complained that the food they are served is geared toward a Latino diet, which is unfamiliar and unappealing to them. They therefore rely on dried ramen noodles that they purchase through the prison commissary to satisfy their hunger. They crave such staples of the Chinese diet as rice.

Meals are served at odd times. Breakfast is scheduled before dawn at approximately 4:00 A.M. Lunch is at 10 A.M., and dinner is at 3:00 or 4:00 P.M. As a result, one woman reported that they are often very hungry in the evening. The prison staff stated that the odd meal times are necessary because of "security concerns."

Both the women and advocates who have had contact with them reported that the water in the facility is undrinkable and "foul smelling." For a time, the women were able to purchase bottled water through the commissary but that service has been discontinued, leaving them with no alternative but to drink the tap water.

The prison has publicly stated that it has fixed the water problem, which is attributable to a high level of hydrogen sulfate, and advocates reported that there has been some improvement. The women indicated that they notice little difference. When the delegation tested the water, it was flat and sulfuric.

Recreation and Exercise

The prison staff reported that the women are allowed outside for three hours a week, for one-and-a-half hours at a time, weather permitting. Su said that they actually had been allowed out 3–4 times per week, after her attorney complained to the facility about the limited outdoor access. This access, however, was often provided during non-daylight hours, such as 6 A.M. or 11 P.M.

The outdoor recreation area is approximately the size of one-fourth a football field and is completely paved, with no grass or trees. It is also fully enclosed with cement walls, over which it is impossible to see, topped by fencing and a roof. It contains a volley-ball net and some balls.

The prison contains a small library and a book cart that makes the rounds every Sunday. However, all the literature is in English.

The women reported that they spend their time reading Chinese newspapers that have been donated to them; talking among themselves; writing letters; watching English language television, which is kept on all day long; and sleeping. They reported that they are very bored.

Visitor Access and Isolation

After frequent attempts over the course of several months to obtain permission to visit the Bakersfield facility, the Women's Commission was finally able to interview the Chinese women and tour the facility. The day before its scheduled visit, however, the INS San Francisco District staff indicated that they had revoked this agreement due to ongoing national litigation dealing with INS detention policy. The District cited an INS General Counsel "e-mail" to support its decision. After intervention by the INS Central Office in Washington, DC, however, the visit was rescheduled.

Once in Bakersfield, the delegation was given a thorough tour of the facility and allowed to interview three women. The prison staff answered all questions addressed to them. The delegation, however, was not allowed to interview the INS staff in the San Francisco District Office.

Access to the facility is generally limited by its remote location. Attorneys representing the women have found it difficult to visit their clients because of the amount of time it takes them to travel from San Francisco to Bakersfield. One attorney has managed to make the trip once a month, but at great cost in terms of time.

According to advocates, two of the women have boyfriends who wish to marry them. However, the prison has refused to allow this to happen. One of the men regularly visits his fiancée. The other has been forbidden to visit, as he was expelled for "disturbing the peace." Some of the women have family in the United States, but they live in New York.

Members of a local organization, Voice for Life, have taken a strong interest in the women's situation, and visit the women almost every week. The group has also organized occasional visits from members of the community concerned about the women. The prison staff indicated that the detainees otherwise receive few visitors.

The women have had only limited access to Chinese language religious services. Initially, advocates reported, the prison chaplain refused to allow Chinese-speaking ministers into the facility. Now, a Chinese Baptist minister is allowed to provide a weekly service, but only with the prison chaplain present. He is not allowed to provide individual counseling. When the Women's Commission requested an interview with the Baptist minister, he responded that the chaplain had forbidden him to speak with the delegation.

Health Care

The Bakersfield facility has a nurse on duty 24 hours a day and a doctor on call. The facility maintains a clinic to handle routine medical problems, and transports detainees to the local county hospital in emergency situations.

Chi was very concerned about her health. Since her detention, she has developed high blood pressure, which she attributed to the stress caused by her incarceration. She is currently on medication for the condition. She also said that she has "something growing in her throat." She is confused about the exact nature of this but has been receiving medication for it for over a year. She also reported that her eyes and feet are swelling. In addition, she appeared jaundiced. She expressed anxiety about her condition, and stated that she feared that she would die in prison without seeing her children again.

Su, who is 24 years old, is taking pain killers for stomach problems. She also reported that she had been three months pregnant when she was first picked up by the U.S. Border Patrol. She had been experiencing abdominal and stomach pains for approximately a month prior to this, and said that she was immediately taken to a hospital in San Diego, where she lost the fetus. It was unclear to the delegation whether she had experienced a spontaneous abortion or if she had been given an abortion without her consent. It appeared to the delegation that she was experiencing medical complications with her pregnancy that needed immediate attention. However, Su herself was obviously very confused about why she required an "abortion." She stated that the translation services she received in the hospital were very poor. She reported that she frequently dreams about her child.

Zheng did not report any medical problems. However, she appeared very gaunt and had a rash on her face.

All the women were exhibiting signs of stress and anxiety. They were feeling tremendous pressure as a result of their fleeing from China, their arduous trip to the United States, and their subsequent incarceration. They were anxious to see their loved ones. They exhibited symptoms of Post-Traumatic Stress Disorder, including intense fear, helplessness, anxiety, social withdrawal, somatic complaints, feelings of ineffectiveness, shame, feeling permanently damaged, and feeling constantly threatened.

All of the women feared the future. Adding to this was the fact that they had seen several of their compatriots removed from the facility without explanation. The delegation confirmed that one woman was moved to a separate building within the Bakersfield complex. At least one was deported, and another was transferred back to New Orleans where she was released. These transfers, however, were never explained to the women left behind.

Chi sobbed as she told the delegation about her nightmare the night before. She reported that she is having problems sleeping and frequently has bad dreams. She was haunted by the notion that she may never see her two children again, including a teenage son who has gone blind during her time in detention. However, she is also ashamed of her detention and fears what her children might think of her. She said, "I feel as if there is something wrong with me when I wear these prison clothes."

Zheng was visibly outraged by her experience in detention. She had been moved from the cell in which the other Chinese women are held into a solitary cell, because she had an argument with a fellow detainee. She was distraught that the prison had failed to move her personal belongings with her, such as letters from home and her commissary purchases. She reported that she was not even able to bring her attorney's telephone number with her.

Su said that "she thinks too much" and constantly worries about her future. Despite their obvious distress, none of the women reported having received mental health care while in detention.

Treatment by the Prison Guards

Other than with each other, the most regular human contact the women have is with the prison staff. The women reported that some of the guards are "nice," while others are "bad" and "rude." Chi stated, "The guards treat me as less than a person." It was obvious to the delegation that the overall atmosphere in the facility was institutional and punitive in nature.

For example, the women are patted down or strip searched (but not cavity searched) every time they return from the outside exercise area. The staff reported that women guards perform these searches on women detainees, but advocates said that men have occasionally filled this function. Advocates indicated that one woman refuses to go outside, because she is so intimidated by these searches. Reportedly, she was subjected to spousal abuse in China.

In addition, the women have been placed in solitary confinement for infraction of minor "rules" of prison. Chi was in solitary for five days, because she failed to use a pencil sharpener properly. Exacerbating this treatment is the fact that no one has explained the facility rules to the women in Chinese, forcing them to learn by trial and error.

Monitoring of the women's residential area is performed by male guards as well as female guards. The staff noted that they are required to have a female guard on duty, but she is not necessarily stationed in the women's cell area. The staff admitted that male guards occasionally see the women showering or dressing, but blamed that on the women "not caring." Screens are provided to block the view of the showers and toilets.

Su complained that a guard used to deny her sanitary napkins. She was forced to use toilet paper. The guard got upset with her for using too much toilet paper, shoved her, and then placed her in disciplinary isolation for 15 days.

The prison staff indicated that the women must request sanitary napkins on an as-need basis. One male guard said that male guards are uncomfortable with the whole issue, and that they give the women as many napkins as they request, stating, "We are typical guys. We don't like to talk about it. We don't care as long as they don't turn the napkins into art work or use them to plug up the toilets."

Access to Counsel and Asylum Proceedings

Attorneys can visit their clients in Bakersfield at any time. However, as previously mentioned, their access is effectively limited by the remote location of the detention center. This is particularly troublesome due to the complexity of the law forming the basis of the women's asylum claims.

The INS occasionally will transport a detainee to San Francisco to meet with an attorney if the attorney so requests and a van is transporting detainees there for other reasons. Attorneys representing the women, however, reported that this service was discontinued for the women for some time because the INS claimed there were too few women to merit it.

In order to communicate with their attorneys, therefore, the women must rely primarily on telephone calls. However, all outgoing calls must be made collect. Attorneys cannot call into the facility even to convey a message to their client that they should call them.

The delegation was very concerned about one Chinese woman who was moved to San Francisco the day of its visit. Her attorney had not been informed of this transfer.

Not surprisingly, the women are very confused about the status of their cases. Advocates reported that at least one woman has indicated that she will give up and agree to deportation if she is not released by New Year's Day. Others indicated that they will endure detention until their claims are reconsidered under the new immigration law, which advocates have informed them might facilitate their release. Advocates stated that one woman was deported to China in October 1996. Although she had initially agreed to her deportation, she tried to reverse her decision after learning of passage of the new law. The INS refused her request and carried out her deportation.

Conclusions and Recommendations

- The prolonged detention of the Chinese women is arbitrary, cruel, and inhumane, and may very well be causing them serious psychological harm. It also violates international standards for the detention of asylum seekers.

- The Chinese women should be immediately released from detention pending the reconsideration of their asylum claims under the Immigration Act of 1996. They should not be held hostage to a legal system that inadequately addresses the basis of their asylum claims nor to concerns about the potential political costs of a further Chinese influx. The new law is clearly intended to facilitate the admission of individuals such as the Chinese women.

- At the very least, the INS should allow refugee organizations that are willing to care for the women to provide them with more suitable housing and the social services necessary to address their needs.

- The INS should discontinue its use of county prisons located in remote areas for the detention of asylum seekers. Ready access to attorneys must be a requirement for any contracted detention space.

- Under no circumstances should women asylum-seekers be penalized on the grounds that there are too few of them and deprived of services made available to male detainees. Education services that are provided to male detainees must be equally provided to the women. Transport to San Francisco for attorney consultations must also be equally available. Anything less constitutes an unacceptable form of discrimination.

- The transfer of detainees from facility to facility should be prevented, unless clearly required to facilitate access to a detainee by her attorney or family. Transfers should not be performed solely for the administrative convenience of the INS.

- The INS must retain ongoing authority over detention space. This includes developing detailed standards for detention that adequately address the special needs of asylum seekers. It also includes frequent and meaningful contact with detainees in its custody.

- The special needs of women asylum seekers must be fully addressed. This includes oversight and monitoring of facility staff to ensure that women are not exposed to any abuse or mistreatment. Only female guards should be assigned to supervise female detainees.

Addendum

Soon after the issuance of this report by the Women's Commission, President Bill Clinton ordered the INS to release the *Golden Venture* Chinese from detention. However, their ordeal is not over, as their claims to asylum still await adjudication. Moreover, the decision to release the *Golden Venture* Chinese was a political one, made in the context of tremendous media coverage and pressure from organizations such as the Women's Commission and concerned members of Congress, rather than a policy change.

Hundreds of women asylum seekers remain in detention, including, ironically, other Chinese who also left their home country to escape its coercive family planning program but who arrived in the United States on other vessels. The need for comprehensive reform of the U.S. detention system continues.

◆◆◆

CHAPTER ELEVEN

Women and the Military

In the United States most people grow up with pride in this country, its wealth, its power, and its superior position in the world. We learn the Pledge of Allegiance, a sense of patriotism, and that our way of life is worth fighting and perhaps dying for. Most families have at least one member who has served in the military. The United States is number one in the world in terms of military technology, military bases, training of foreign forces, and military aid to foreign countries (Sivard 1996). It also spends the most. The U.S. military budget exceeds the total military expenditure of the next twelve biggest spenders combined: Russia, China, France, Britain, Germany, Japan, South Korea, North Korea, Libya, Syria, Iraq, and Cuba (Sivard 1996). The largest proportion of our federal budget, $659 billion in 2000–2001 or 47 percent, supports current and past military operations, including the upkeep of over four hundred bases and installations at home and over two thousand of those abroad, the development and maintenance of weapons systems, pensions for retired military personnel, veterans benefits, and interest on the national debt attributable to military spending (War Resisters League 2000). Major companies with household names like Westinghouse, Boeing, and General Electric research and develop weapons systems and military aircraft. War movies are a film industry staple, portraying images of manly heroes. Many best-selling video games involve violent scenarios. G.I. Joe has a new female colleague, a helicopter pilot, dressed in a jumpsuit and helmet and armed with a 9mm Beretta. Even Barbie is in uniform.

The military shapes our notions of patriotism, heroism, honor, duty, and citizenship. President Clinton's avoidance of military service as a young man was heavily criticized by his detractors in both election campaigns, the suggestion being that this was unpatriotic and not fitting for a president of the United States, who is also the commander in chief of the armed forces. Politically, economically, and culturally, the military is a central U.S. institution.

The Need for Women in the Military

Although the vast majority of U.S. military personnel have always been male, the military has needed and continues to need women's support and participation in many capacities (D'Amico and Weinstein 1999; Enloe 1983; Isakson 1988; Weinstein and White 1997). It needs mothers to believe in the concept of patriotic duty and to encourage their sons, and more recently their daughters, to enlist or at least to support their desire to do so. It needs women nurses to heal the wounded and the traumatized. It needs wives and girlfriends back home, the prize waiting at the end of war or a period of duty overseas, who live with veterans' trauma or who mourn loved ones killed in action. During World War II, White, African American, and Latina women, symbolized by Rosie the Riveter, were needed for the war effort working in shipyards and munitions factories while men were drafted for active service overseas (Denman and Inniss 1999).

Currently the military needs women to work in electronics and many other industries producing weapons components, machine parts, tools, uniforms, household supplies, and foodstuffs for military contracts. It needs women working in nightclubs, bars, and massage parlors near foreign bases and ports providing R and R, rest and relaxation, for military personnel, or, as it is sometimes called, I and I, intoxication and intercourse (Enloe 1993a, 2000; Sturdevant and Stoltzfus 1992). And the military needs women on active duty, increasingly trained for combat as well as performing more traditional roles in administration, communications, intelligence, or medicine.

Having women in the military to the extent that they are today is a relatively new phenomenon. In 1972 women were only 1.2 percent of military personnel. The following year, after much debate, Congress ended the draft for men, though young men are still required to register for the draft when they turn eighteen. Many left the services as soon as they could, causing a manpower shortfall that has been made up by recruiting women, especially women of color. In 1997, 43 percent of the enlisted women in all services (Army, Navy, Marine Corps, and Air Force) were women of color (29 percent African American, 8 percent Latina, and 6 percent "other"); 20 percent of all women officers were women of color. The Air Force has the highest percentage of women (28 percent), although the Army, being more labor-intensive, has the greatest numbers. Among all officers in the armed services, 15 percent are women (U.S. Department of Defense 2000).

The Military as Employer

For many of these women, the military offers much better opportunities than the wider society: jobs with better pay, health care, pensions, and other benefits, as well as the chance for education, travel, and escape from crisis-torn inner cities in the United States. It enhances women's self-esteem and confers the status of first-class citizenship attributed to those who serve their country. Military recruiters emphasize security, professionalism, empowerment, adventure, patriotism, and pride. In noting the benefits of army life in the early 1950s, Jean Grossholtz (Reading 69) includes medical services, expanded opportunities, a ready-made community of women, and a sense of self-worth and accomplishment. Margarethe Cammermeyer served as a military nurse for twenty-six years, in the Army, the Army Reserves, and the National Guard; she was the highest-ranking officer to challenge military policy on homosexuality before being discharged in 1992 on the basis of sexual orientation. Her autobiography emphasizes the professionalism, structure, and discipline she experienced in military life and her keen sense of patriotism and duty (Cammermeyer 1994).

As we argued in Chapter 8, the U.S. labor market has changed markedly over the past three decades or so through automation and the movement of jobs overseas. In addition to a loss of jobs, there are few sources of funding for working-class women's (and men's) education. Government funding for education and many welfare programs was cut back during the 1980s and 90s, but despite the end of the cold war, enormous changes in the former Soviet Union, and cuts in U.S. bases and personnel, the U.S. military budget has been maintained at high levels. Women who enter the military are thus going where the money is. Their very presence, however, exposes serious dilemmas and contradictions for the institution, which we explore below. Another contradiction of this situation is the fact that massive government spending on the military diverts funds that could otherwise be invested in civilian job programs and inner-city communities.

Limitations to Women's Equal Participation in the Military

Support for women's equality within the military is based on a belief in women's right to equal access to education, jobs, promotion, and authority in all aspects of society, and to the benefits of first-class citizenship. Women's rights organizations, such as the National Organization for Women, have campaigned for women to have equal opportunity with men in the military, as have women military personnel, military women's organizations like the Minerva Center (Pasadena, Md.) and the Pallas Athena Network (New Market, Va.), and key members of Congress like former representative Pat Schroeder, who was on the Armed Services Committee for many years. After years of pressure, women who served in Vietnam were honored with a memorial in Washington, D.C. This advocacy and recognition, together with women's changing position in society, have also affected social attitudes. In the Persian Gulf War, for example, military women were featured in headline news stories around the country. Saying good-bye to their families as they prepared to go overseas, they were portrayed as professional soldiers as well as mothers.

Women's equal participation in the military is limited in several ways, however, these include limits on combat roles; a lack of access to some military academies; the effects of a general culture of racism, sexism and sexual harassment; and the ban on being openly lesbian.

Women in Combat Roles

Women served in the U.S. military during World War II, the Korean War, and the Vietnam War. They were generally designated as auxiliary, according to Katzenstein (1993), despite the fact that they performed a wider range of tasks than is usually recognized—as transport pilots (Cole 1992), mechanics, drivers, underground reconnaissance, nurses (Camp 1997), and administrators. The influx of women into the military since the mid-1970s and the question of whether to train women for combat have exposed a range of stereotypical attitudes toward women on the part of military commanders, Pentagon planners, and members of Congress, depending on the degree to which they believe that combat is male. From the late 1980s well into the 90s, countless news reports, magazine articles, editorials, and letters to the editor took up this issue.

War making is increasingly a high-tech, push-button affair, as exemplified in the bombing missions of the Gulf War, but old attitudes die hard. Combat roles are dangerous and demanding. Many argue that women are not physically strong enough, are too emotional, and lack discipline or stamina. They will be bad for men's morale, it is said, and will disrupt fighting units because men will be distracted if a woman buddy is hurt or captured. The country is not ready for women coming home in body bags.

Women in the military tend to have better performance records than men, according to Enloe (1993b). Military planners face a dilemma. They need women to make up the shortfall in personnel; at the same time they hold sexist or condescending notions about women. What counts as combat in modern warfare is not as simple as it might seem, however, and definitions of "the front" and "the rear" change with developments in military technology. Communications and supply, defined as noncombat areas where women work, are both likely targets of attack. Media attention on women's participation in the Persian Gulf War showed that many performed combat roles similar to those of men, and this led to changes in laws and regulations that had previously kept women out of combat assignments (Muir 1993; Peach 1997; Sadler 1997; Skaine 1998). In 1993 the rule barring women from dangerous jobs was changed, though some exceptions were preserved. Women can work on combat ships and jet planes but not in submarines or in direct offensive combat on the ground. Restricting women from combat roles has been a way of limiting their career advancement, as senior positions often require combat experience (Francke 1997; Stiehm 1989). By 1997 women filled only 815 of the 47,544 combat-related jobs that were opened to women in 1993 and 1994 (Study shows few women in combat jobs 1997).

Officer Training: Storming the Citadel

In 1975 Congress mandated that the three military academies were to admit women. Researching the experiences of the first women to enter the U.S. Military Academy at West Point, Yoder (1989) noted the severe pressure on these women to do well. They were a highly visible, very small minority, tokens in what had been constructed as an exclusively male institution. They faced tough physical tests designed for men; they were out of the loop in many informal settings and were routinely subjected to sexist notions and behavior by male cadets who did not accept them as peers (Campbell with D'Amico 1999). As a result, for the first four years at least, the dropout rate for women was significantly higher than it was for men, a fact that could be used by policy makers to justify exclusionary practices. Yoder concluded, however, that these women were not competing on equal terms with men, and she argued for changes in evaluation criteria and the overwhelmingly male culture of the academy, an increase in the number of women entering the academy, and greater commitment to women's full participation at an institutional level. More recently, women have entered other private military academies like the Citadel and the Virginia Military Institute with similarly mixed success. In January 1997, two of the first four women at the Citadel withdrew because of intolerable harassment (Applebome 1997). The other two became the first female cadets to graduate from the Citadel in 1999. Two women also completed their training at the VMI in the same year.

Sexism and Misogyny

Added to this chilly climate for women are overt sexual harassment and sexual abuse. An internal report from the Naval Academy, compiled by the Women Midshipmen Study Group and released in October 1990, noted that sexual harassment of female students was widespread. "The lack of acceptance [of female students] has created an environment in which steady low-level sexual harassment passes as normal operating procedure" (*Rocky Mountain News,* 1990, p. 35). Most victims do not complain, the report noted, for fear of reprisals. Even when women do report sexual harassment to superior officers, the majority of their complaints have been dismissed or ignored.

Melinda Smith-Wells notes her experience of sexual harassment in the Air Force (Reading 68), even though the Department of Defense has had a "specific policy prohibiting sexual harassment of military personnel for over fifteen years," summed up as "zero-tolerance" (Guenter-Schlesinger 1999, p. 195). A 1995 Department of Defense survey reported that 4 percent of all female soldiers said they had been the victim of a completed or attempted rape during their military service, and 61 percent said that they had been sexually harassed in the Army (High 1997). Ninety percent of women in a Veterans Administration study reported harassment, and a third said they had been raped by military personnel (*STAMP Newsletter* 1998/99). Paula Coughlin, a helicopter pilot, went public with her experiences of sexual as-

sault at the 1991 Tailhook naval aviators' convention at the Las Vegas Hilton, where women were subjected to sexual harassment, indecent assault, and indecent exposure. She testified that she endured relentless harassment from colleagues afterward and had since resigned her commission as a Navy lieutenant (Noble 1994). More than eighty other women also filed complaints, and a few also filed civil lawsuits.

After hearing testimony from servicewomen in 1992, a Senate Committee estimated that as many as 60,000 women had been sexually assaulted or raped while serving in the U.S. armed forces. Senator Dennis DeConcini commented, "American women serving in the Gulf were in greater danger of being sexually assaulted by our own troops than by the enemy" (Walker 1992, p. 6). In the fall of 1996 this issue surfaced publicly again, when women at the Aberdeen Proving Grounds Ordnance Center in Maryland complained of being sexually harassed and raped by drill sergeants during training. As part of its investigations into these allegations, the Army set up a toll-free hotline, which took four thousand calls in the first week relating to harassment at many military facilities (McKenna 1996/1997). *Time* magazine reporter Elizabeth Gleick (1996) described this issue as an abuse of power by superiors, threatening "to undermine the thing that many in the military hold sacred: the chain of command" (p. 28). Interviewed for the ABC weekly news program *20/20,* Alan Cranston, former U.S. senator from California, suggested three reasons for the intensity of sexual abuse in the military: men feeling threatened by women coworkers, the general "macho" military culture, and the fact that many military personnel have easy access to guns (Walters and Downs 1996). As the investigation spread, military commanders did their best to attribute any misconduct to "a few bad apples." Brigadier General Robert Courter, for example, commander of the 37th Training Wing at Lackland Air Force Base, was quoted as saying, "There are going to be incidents, but where we have those cases, we take action. . . . I feel certain the American people can be confident that their sons and daughters are going to be safe in the Air Force" (Military sex scandal 1996, p. A15). At the same time, many who oppose women's participation in the military have claimed that such incidents support their view that the military is, indeed, no place for women.

Racism

Although the armed services were officially integrated in 1948, decades before desegregation in the southern states, racism, like sexism, is still a common occurrence in the military between individuals and at an institutional level. The preponderance of women of color in the enlisted ranks of the military also demonstrates the institutionalized racism of the wider society. In 1994 a House Armed Services Committee investigation uncovered serious problems with institutionalized racism throughout the armed forces and warned about skinhead and other extremist activity on four military bases visited by investigators. In December 1995, for example, two African American civilians were random victims, shot and killed by three White servicemen, described in press reports as right-wing extremists, from the Army's 82nd Airborne Division at Fort Bragg, North Carolina (Citizen Soldier 1996). In December 1996, two African American airmen at Kelly Air Force Base (Texas) talked to the media about a racist incident in which they were taunted by men wearing pillowcases resembling Ku Klux Klan hoods and said that they were dissatisfied with the Air Force's response to their complaints (2 Black airmen 1996). Military statistics generally include Black women as part of the general category of "women in the military," whereas Black service personnel are assumed to be Black males. Official data do not take account of the intersectionality of race and gender. Hall (1999) notes that a 1994 U.S. House Armed Services Committee report found that service members of color perceived racial discrimination in opportunities for career-enhancing assignments or training. This information was not broken down by gender. Individuals experience racism and discrimination, but, given the lack of detailed information, it is impossible to track the extent of it at the institutional level.

Sexual Orientation

A final area of limitation for women—and men—in the military concerns sexual orientation. The Pentagon considers homosexuality incompatible with military service, and a series of regulations have precluded lesbians and gay men from serving openly, despite their continuing presence as officers and enlisted personnel (Scott and Stanley 1994; Webber 1993). In Reading 69 Jean Grossholtz notes the contradiction implicit in this policy: The military is based on male bonding, yet homosexuality is banned. Thousands of gay men and lesbians have been discharged over the years in what she refers to as "purges." Margarethe Cammermeyer (1994) notes that in June 1992 the General Accounting Office reported that fourteen hundred military personnel who had been trained for military service were discharged each year between 1980 and 1991, at an estimated cost of $494 million, not including the cost of investigations (p. 293). During his first presidential election campaign, Bill Clinton promised to lift the ban on gays in the military when he came into office in 1992. Concerted opposition from the Pentagon and many politicians made this impossible, however, and some argue that current policy, summed up as "Don't Ask, Don't Tell, Don't Pursue," is not much different than before. "Homosexual conduct," defined as homosexual activity, trying to marry someone of the same sex, or acknowledging one's homosexuality, is grounds for discharge. A number of lesbians and gay men have challenged this policy in court. Gay rights organizations, like the National Gay and Lesbian Task Force and Gay, Lesbian, and Bisexual Vets of America, continue to raise this issue as an example of lesbians' and gay men's second-class citizenship.

Reports of anti-gay harassment—including verbal abuse, beatings, death threats, and apparent killings—more than doubled in the late 1990s, increasing from 182 violations documented in 1997 to 400 in 1998 (Servicemembers Legal Defense Network 1999a). Military policy expressly forbids such harassment, but in April 1998, five years after the "Don't Ask, Don't Tell, Don't Pursue" policy was introduced, the Pentagon acknowledged that the service branches had not instructed commanders on how to investigate those who make anti-gay threats. The Department of Defense discharged 1,149 service members in 1998 for being lesbian, gay, or bisexual, compared with 997 in 1997. This was the largest number of gay discharges in more than a decade (Servicemembers Legal Defense Network 1999b). Women were 28 percent of those discharged, though they make up only 14 percent of active duty personnel.

In August 1999, the Department of Defense issued its updated policy on gays in the military requiring mandatory training on antiharassment guidelines for all troops, beginning in boot camp. In March 2000, Pentagon officials conceded that there is a "disturbing" level of gay harassment in the military (Richter 2000).

Military Wives

Military wives have been the subject of a number of studies in the past decade or so (D'Amico and Weinstein 1999; Enloe 1989, 2000; Weinstein and White 1997). The model military wife is a staunch supporter of her husband's career. She learns to manage the moves from base to base, the disruption of family life, and interruptions in her own work (and, increasingly, she may be in the military herself). Wives and children of military families also suffer abuse at the hands of servicemen husbands and fathers. Researchers attribute this to a combination of factors: the stress of military jobs, family responsibilities, relatively low pay, uncertainty about job security, training for combat, and relative powerlessness at work. Reports of spousal abuse of wives associated with the military rose from 18.6 per thousand in 1990 to 25.6 per thousand in 1996 (U.S. Department of Defense 1996). As is the case for the estimate of domestic violence in civilian families, this is inevitably a conservative estimate. Women abused by military personnel are often fearful of reporting incidents because of a combination of lack of confidentiality and privacy; limited victim services; lack of training and assistance on the part of military commanders; and disruption caused by moving from base to base.

According to official policy, violence against women and children is not to be condoned or tolerated. However, the message has not been clear and consistent throughout command leadership (Miles Foundation 1999). "The War at Home," which aired on *60 Minutes* in January 1999, helped to make this issue more public and to support victims of military violence. Survivors Take Action Against Abuse by Military Personnel (STAMP, Fairborne, Ohio) grew out of women's anger and frustration with the lack of accountability for sexual harassment and abuse of women in the armed forces by their colleagues and

superiors. The Miles Foundation (Waterbury, Conn.) has taken up the issue of violence within military families. Despite the existence of policies against sexual harassment, and an increase in sensitivity training for various military personnel, entrenched military culture blocks the implementation of such policies (Guenter-Schlesinger 1999).

The Impact of the U.S. Military on Women Overseas

The worldwide superiority of the United States — in political, economic, and military terms — is sustained by a wide network of U.S. bases, troops, ships, submarines, and aircraft in Europe, Asia, Latin America, the Caribbean, the Persian Gulf, and the Pacific. This U.S. presence relies on agreements with each particular government. In return the military may pay rent for the land it occupies. Some local people may be employed directly on the bases; many others work in nearby businesses patronized by U.S. military personnel. We consider four ways that U.S. military policies and bases abroad affect women: through militarized prostitution, through their responsibility for mixed-race children fathered by U.S. service personnel, through crimes of violence committed by U.S. troops, and through the harmful effects of atomic tests.

Militarized Prostitution

As a way of keeping up the morale of their troops, military commanders have long tolerated, and sometimes actively encouraged, women to live outside military camps to support and sexually service the men. With U.S. bases positioned strategically around the globe, especially since World War II, militarized prostitution has required explicit arrangements between the U.S. government and the governments of the Philippines, Japan (Okinawa), Thailand, and South Korea, for example, where many women work in bars and massage parlors, "entertaining" U.S. troops (Enloe 1990, 1993a; 2000; Sturdevant and Stoltzfus 1992). As a way of protecting the men's health, women who work in bars must have regular medical exams, on the assumption that they are the source of sexually transmitted diseases (Moon 1997).

If the bar women fail such tests, they are quarantined until they pass. They usually earn better money than they can make in other ways, though this may be harder as they grow older. By creating a class of women who are available for sexual servicing, the governments attempt to limit the sexual demands of U.S. military personnel to specific women and specific locations.

Despite the low opinion many local people have of bar women, their work is the linchpin of the subeconomy of the "G.I. towns" adjoining the bases, and many people, including store owners, salespeople, bar owners, restaurateurs, cooks, pimps, procurers, cab drivers, and security men, are in business as a result of their work. Some of the bar women are able to send money to their aging parents or younger siblings, an important part of being a good daughter, especially in countries with few social services or welfare supports. Occupational dangers for the women include psychological violence, rape, and beatings from some of their customers; health risks from contraceptive devices, especially IUDs; abortions; AIDS and other sexually transmitted diseases; drug use; and a general lack of respect associated with this stigmatized work. Despite the incursions of transnational corporations, there are few options for women's economic development in rural areas in South Korea and the Philippines, and there is a need for income-generating projects that pay decent wages. This is exactly the dilemma faced by the women of BUKLOD in the Philippines (Reading 70). Kathleen Barry (1995) argues that "military prostitution buys off women with higher wages than they can earn in the industrial wage labor sector" and is, in effect, "a dumping ground . . . between the patriarchal family structure and the industrializing labor force" (p. 163).

Mixed-Race Children Fathered by U.S. Troops

Many bar women and former bar women in Okinawa (Japan), South Korea, the Philippines, and Vietnam have Amerasian children, an often-neglected group. Some of these people, born during the Korean War or Vietnam War, are now in their forties and fifties; others are young children born to women recently involved with U.S. troops stationed in South Korea

or Okinawa. Most of them have been raised in poverty, further stigmatized by their mothers' occupation and their own mixed heritage. According to Okazawa-Rey (1997), many of the mothers of Amerasian children in South Korea had serious relationships with the children's fathers. Yu Bok Nim (1990), who founded a shelter, My Sister's Place, for Korean women involved with U.S. military men, notes that some three thousand marriages take place each year between Korean women and U.S. military personnel. Most of the men, however, simply leave. They may turn out to be already married in the United States—a fact they had not thought necessary to mention—or they just disappear. Many of the children of these unions have not had much schooling as a result of poverty and intimidation and harassment from their peers. In South Korea, Amerasians whose fathers are African American may gain some acceptance by doing well in stereotypically Black spheres like sports and music. Some of the girls become bar women like their mothers. A relatively small number of such children are adopted by U.S. families, but this is expensive and not possible for children whose births have not been registered.

Crimes of Violence against Women

The behavior of U.S. troops in other countries is governed by agreements between the U.S. government and the host government. Usually U.S. military personnel who commit crimes against civilians are dealt with, if at all, through military channels rather than the local courts. In many cases, U.S. troops are not held responsible for crimes they commit. Sometimes they are simply moved to another posting. This is a highly contentious issue, especially for those who do not support the U.S. military presence in their countries. In South Korea, for example, the National Campaign for Eradication of Crime by U.S. Troops in Korea was founded in 1993, growing out of a coalition of women, students, labor activists, religious people, and human rights activists that formed to protest the brutal murder of a young woman, Yoon Kum E, the previous year. The campaign collects information about crimes committed against Korean civilians by U.S. military personnel and cites a South Korean Assembly report that estimated 39,542 such crimes between 1967 and 1987, including murders, brutal rapes, and sexual abuse; incidents of arson, theft, smuggling, fraud, and traffic offenses; an out-flow of P.X. (on-base department store) merchan-dise; and a black market in U.S. goods (Ahn 1996). This situation is not known by many in the United States and is rarely publicized here. This customary silence, however, was broken in the fall of 1995 when a twelve-year-old Okinawan girl was abducted and raped by three U.S. military personnel. This incident is one of many; its brutality and the victim's age were important factors in generating renewed out-rage at the presence of U.S. bases by many Oki-nawans (Okazawa-Rey and Kirk 1996).

Atomic Testing

In the 1950s and early 1960s the United States mili-tary, as well as those of Britain and France, under-took a series of atomic tests in the Pacific that irradiated whole islands and contaminated soil and water for generations to come. The U.S. military con-ducted tests in Micronesia, which it administered as a United Nations Strategic Trust Territory, suppos-edly as a step toward the political independence of the islanders. Many Micronesian women have since given birth to children with severe illnesses or dis-abilities caused by radiation, including some "jelly-fish babies" without skeletons who live only a few hours (de Ishtar 1994; Dibblin 1989). Pacific Island women and men have contracted several kinds of cancer as a result of their exposure to high levels of radioactive fallout. Given the long-lasting effects of atomic material in the food chain and people's re-productive systems, these disabilities and illnesses are likely to last for many generations. Film footage of the U.S. tests, included in newsreels for U.S. au-diences, described the islanders as simple people, in-deed, as happy savages (O'Rourke 1985). In 1969, some years after the partial Test Ban Treaty (1963), which banned atomic tests in the atmosphere, the United States ended its trusteeship of Micronesia. Henry Kissinger, then secretary of state, was highly dismissive of the indigenous people in his comment "There's only 90,000 people out there, who gives a damn?" (Women Working for a Nuclear-Free and Independent Pacific 1987).

Many in Pacific Island nations see these atomic—and later nuclear—tests, which France continued until 1996, as imperialist and racist. Various activist organizations are campaigning for a nuclear-free and independent Pacific and see U.S. military bases in Hawaii and Guam, for example, and the activities of the U.S. Pacific fleet as a serious limitation on their sovereignty and self-determination (Trask 1999). Meanwhile, women take the lead in trying to keep their families and devastated communities together.

Women's Opposition to the Military

Early Peace Organizations in the United States

Activist organizations oppose the presence and im-pact of U.S. military bases in many countries, in-cluding those mentioned earlier. This opposition is sometimes based on nationalism, sometimes on ar-guments for greater self-determination, local control of land and resources, with more sustainable eco-nomic development. Women often play a key role in these organizations.

In the United States, too, although many women have supported and continue to support the military in various ways, there is a history of women's oppo-sition to militarism and war with roots in Quakerism and the nineteenth-century suffrage and temperance movements (Alonso 1993; Washburn 1993). Julia Ward Howe, for example, remembered as the author of the Civil War song "The Battle Hymn of the Re-public," was involved in the suffrage movement as a way of organizing women for peace. In 1873 she initiated Mothers' Day for Peace on June 2, a day to honor mothers, who, she felt, best understood the suffering caused by war. Women's peace festivals were organized in several U.S. cities, mainly in the Northeast and Midwest, with women speakers who opposed war and military training in schools. The Philadelphia Peace Society was still organizing in this way as late as 1909 (Alonso 1993). During the 1890s many women's organizations had peace com-mittees that were active in the years before U.S. en-try into World War I. In 1914 the Women's Peace Party was formed under the leadership of Carrie Chapman Catt and Jane Addams.

Despite difficulties of obtaining passports and wartime travel, over one thousand women from twelve countries, "cutting across national enmities," participated in a Congress of Women in the Hague,

Holland, in 1915, calling for an end to the war. The congress sent delegations to meet with heads of state in fourteen countries and influenced press and public opinion. A second congress at the end of the war proposed an ongoing international organization: the Women's International League for Peace and Freedom (WILPF), which is active in forty-two countries today and maintains international offices at the United Nations and in Geneva, Switzerland (Foster 1989). Among the participants at the second congress were Mary Church Terrell, a Black labor leader from the United States, and Jeanette Rankin, the first U.S. congresswoman and the only member of Congress to vote against U.S. involvement in both world wars. In the 1950s and again in the 1960s, more U.S. women than men opposed the Korean War and Vietnam War. Women Strike for Peace, founded in 1961 and still active through the 1980s, was initially concerned with the nuclear arms race, as well as the Vietnam War (Swerdlow 1993). These organizations attracted members who were overwhelmingly White and middle class, though many women of color have an antimilitarist perspective, as exemplified by Sonia Sanchez in Reading 73.

Feminist Antimilitarist Perspectives

Women's opposition to militarism draws on a range of theoretical perspectives, which we discuss briefly below. In any particular organization several of these perspectives may provide the basis for activism, but it is useful to look at them separately here to clarify different and sometimes contradictory positions.

Women's Peaceful Nature   Although some women — and men — believe that women are "naturally" more peaceful than men, there is no conclusive evidence for this. Differences in socialization, however, from infancy onward, lead to important differences in attitudes, behavior, and responsibilities in caring for others. In U.S. electoral politics since 1980, these differences have been described as creating a "gender gap," under which more women than men oppose high military budgets and environmental destruction and support socially useful government spending (Abzug 1984; Gallagher 1993). Many who oppose the military see the current division of labor in society between men's and women's roles as a fundamental aspect of military systems, whereby

men (and now a few women) "protect" women, children, and older people. They ask: Can we afford this dichotomy? Where does it lead? Those who support women's equal access to social institutions argue that everyone should have the opportunity to join the military and take on roles formerly reserved for men. Opponents argue that the abolition of war is dependent on changing this division of labor, with men taking on traditional women's roles and caring for infants and small children, the elderly, and the sick (Dinnerstein 1989).

Maternalism   Some women see their opposition to war mainly in terms of their responsibility to protect and nurture their children; they want to save the lives of both their own children and the children of "enemy" mothers. In the early 1980s, for example, when the U.S. and Soviet militaries were deploying more powerful nuclear weapons, Susan Lamb, who lived near USAF Greenham Common in England, a nuclear base, put it this way:

> I've got two young children, and I've taken responsibility for their passage into adulthood. Everyone tells me they are my responsibility. The government tells me this. It is my responsibility to create a world fit for them to grow up in. I can't say I'm responsible for my children not catching whooping cough and not responsible for doing anything about the threat of annihilation that hangs over them every minute of the day.
>
> *(Quoted in Cook and Kirk 1983, p. 27)*

Although this approach can sentimentalize motherhood, it is also powerful because mothers are behaving according to their roles and it is difficult for the state to suppress them. They expose contradictions: that the state, through militarism, does not let them get on with their job of mothering.

Diversion of Military Budgets to Socially Useful Programs   Another argument put forward by peace activists — women and men — concerns government spending. The Women's International League for Peace and Freedom (U.S. Section, Philadelphia) publishes a Women's Budget, which shows how a 50 percent reduction in military expenditures and redistribution of those funds could provide for social programs that benefit women and their families.

Human and Financial Costs of War

- Since 1900 there have been 250 wars and 109,746,000 war-related deaths, more than the combined populations of France, Belgium, Netherlands, and the four Scandinavian countries. In the 1980s, civilians constituted 74 percent of those killed.

- World military expenditure in 1995 amounted to $1.4 million per minute, despite a decline during the previous five years.

- Between 1990 and 1995, over three-fourths of arms sales by the United States to developing countries went to nations where citizens had no right to choose their own government.

- The cost of one Stealth bomber—$2.2 billion—could supply family planning services to 120 million women.

- The cost of a multiple launcher rocket system loaded with ballistic missiles (a long-range self-propelled artillery weapon widely used in the Gulf War), at $29 million, could supply one year's basic rural water and sanitation services for 2 million people in developing countries.

- In Cambodia, one of every 236 people is an amputee; there are as many land mines planted there as there are people (estimated 10 million mines and 9.9 million people).

Source: Sivard 1996.

Cuts in funding for nuclear weapons, chemical and biological weapons, and U.S. troops, ships, and aircraft carriers around the world, they argue, could fund job-training programs, public housing, education, urban development, environmental cleanup, and AIDS research, for example. They would enable cuts in Medicaid, food stamps, and child nutrition programs to be restored (see Reading 71).

Women's Action for New Directions (WAND, Arlington, Mass.) is organizing nationwide on the issue of the bloated military budget. When tax dollars are diverted from civilian programs like education and health care, where many women are employed, military spending is also at the expense of women's jobs (Anderson 1999). A 1991 research report, *Converting the American Economy* (Anderson, Bischak, and Oden 1991), showed the economic effects of cutting the military budget by $70 billion per year and transferring these funds into health care, Head Start, education, job training, mass transit, and the environment. This would have created 460,000 additional jobs for women. Anderson (1999) notes that "every $1 billion transferred from the Pentagon to these civilian expenditures generates a net gain of about 6,800 women's jobs" (p. 248).

The Military as a Sexist and Racist Institution
Opposition to the military also turns on the argument that, by its very nature, the military is profoundly antifeminist and racist and is fundamental to political systems that oppress women and peoples of color. Its ultimate effectiveness depends on people's ability to see reality in oppositional categories: us and them, friends and enemies, kill or be killed (Reardon 1985). To this end it is organized on rigidly hierarchical lines, demanding unquestioning obedience to superiors. Although the military uses women's labor in many ways, as mentioned earlier, it does so strictly on its own terms. The military environment also fosters violence against women. The higher incidence of domestic violence in military families than in nonmilitary families and crimes of violence against women committed near military bases in the United States and overseas are not coincidences but integral aspects of military life and training (Morris 1999). Moreover, though not publicly sanctioned, rape is a weapon of war (Peterson and Runyan 1993; Rayner 1997; Tétreault 1997), as mentioned in Chapter 6.

This opposition focuses not only on how the military operates but also on militarism as an underlying system and worldview based on the objectification of "others" as enemies, a culture that celebrates war and killing (Reardon 1985). The Women's Pentagon Action, for example, identified militarism as a cornerstone of the oppression of women and the destruction of the nonhuman world. Thousands of women surrounded the Pentagon in November 1980 and again in 1981. They protested massive military budgets; the fact that militaries cause more ecological destruction than any other institutions; the widespread, everyday culture of violence manifested in war toys, films, and video games; the connection between violence and sexuality in pornography, rape, battering, and incest; and the connections between militarism and racism. This was no routine demonstration but a highly creative action organized in four stages: mourning, rage, empowerment, and defiance, culminating in the arrest of many women who chose to blockade the doors of the Pentagon (King 1983). The Unity Statement of the Women's Pentagon Action is included as Reading 72.

At an Okinawan rally on violence and human rights violations against girls and women in September 1995, a women's declaration pointed to military training as a systematic process of dehumanization that turns "soldiers into war machines who inflict violence on the Okinawan community, only a chain-link fence away" (Okinawa Women Act against Military Violence 1996, p. 7). These activists see crucial connections between personal violence and international violence, both based on the objectification of others (see Reading 40, Chapter 6). Cynthia Enloe's (1990, 1993b) concept of a constructed militarized masculinity fits in here. Citing the sexual assault of women at the Tailhook meeting of Navy aviators in 1991, the general incidence of sexual assault on military women, men's resistance to women in combat, and fears about openly gay men and lesbians in the military, she argues that the U.S. military is based on very specific notions of "militarized masculinity" (Enloe 1993b). Thus, women in combat roles threaten the manliness of war and the very nature of militarism as male.

Women who oppose militarism have very different perspectives from those who enter the military. They may also have different class positions and more opportunities for education and work. Liberal feminists have criticized feminist peace activists for being classist and racist in their condemnation of the military as an employer when working women, especially women of color, have few employment options. The Unity Statement of the Women's Pentagon Action, for example, argues for equality between men and women but against participation in the military for either sex. Peace activists also argue that the military is no place for gay men and lesbians. Jean Grossholtz (Reading 69)

writes that, ironically, it was her involvement in the military, seeing casualties of the Korean War, that changed her views and led her to become a peace activist later in life. Barbara Omolade (1989) notes the contradictions of militarism for people of color in the United States, many of whom support the military because it provides economic opportunities that are lacking in civilian society. Military personnel of color fight for the United States, a country where they are oppressed. Since World War II, the people they have fought against and are trained to kill are other people of color in various parts of the world — Vietnam, Grenada, Libya, Panama, and Iraq — to take examples from the past several decades. Combatants of color are more likely to be killed than their White counterparts, as happened in Vietnam.

Redefining Adventure, Power, and Security

Antimilitarist activists have well-developed critiques of militarism as philosophy and institution. To rework the recruiters' slogan, they do not believe that joining the army is being all you can be. Yet military recruitment ads promise security, challenge, professionalism, empowerment, exhilaration, adventure, and pride for the individual who enlists. How can these concepts be redefined so that they are not limited to military activities? Feminist writings on power, empowerment, and security are relevant here (see, for example, Plant and Plant 1992; Reardon 1993, 1998; Shields 1994; Starhawk 1987).

Antimilitarists believe that a world that will sustain the lives of individuals, as well as communities and nations, must be built on the security of respect for differences of gender, race, and culture, not the creation of enemies; that the world's resources should be devoted to people's basic needs — housing, feeding, and schooling everyone; that gross inequalities between rich and poor countries and between rich and poor people within countries must be eradicated. Peace is not just an absence of war, and there can be no peace without justice. They believe in cultures that are generative rather than materialistic, where people recognize and appreciate that we are nurtured and sustained by the earth's wealth and that we need to live in sustainable ways. This view includes security for the individual — a major reason why women in the United States are currently drawn to enlist in the military — but this individual security also involves security at the meso and macro levels, for communities and nations (Boulding 1990; Reardon 1993). They think about the process of demilitarization—in economic, political, and practical terms and in terms of masculinity and the reconstruction of gender relations. They may work at practical projects that embody some small piece of this larger vision—teaching conflict resolution in schools; working as healers, on rape crisis lines, or in shelters for victims of domestic violence; establishing community gardens and alternative economic projects; or working with Amerasian children in South Korea or the Philippines. Women involved in antimilitarist work also imagine alternatives, exemplified in several of the writings we have included here. This redefinition of security is not an issue for women only, of course. Long-standing organizations like the War Resisters League and Jobs with Peace, and the conversion of military bases and technology, are also salient here. Much more needs to be done in this direction and against the conventional wisdom that the military is an inevitable fact of life as well as a major source of jobs in many states.

A crucial question for the future concerns security and safety for individuals, communities, and nations. Currently, notions of security usually rely on strength and force: building walls, gates, and fences; locking people up, keeping them in or out; carrying Mace, buying guns, and stockpiling weapons; and maintaining the military budget. These are all ways of separating people and maintaining hierarchies of haves and have-nots, people who are dominant and those who are inferior. It is leading to a world that is increasingly militarized, where people generally feel less, not more, secure.

◆◆◆
Questions for Reflection

As you read and discuss this chapter, think about these questions:

1. What purposes does the military serve in this society?

2. Who joins the military? Why?

3. Why has the issue of gays in the military surfaced as an issue of mainstream U.S. politics?

4. What makes you feel safe/unsafe at home? At school? In your community? On the streets? In communities you don't know? In cities or the countryside?

5. What can you do to improve your sense of safety/security in these different settings?

◆◆◆
Taking Action

1. Think about the ways you usually resolve conflicts or serious differences of opinion with your family, friends and peers, teachers, and employers. What are the dynamics involved in each case? Do you cave in without expressing your opinion? Do you insist that you are right? Does violence play a part in this process? If so, why?

2. List all the kinds of service you can imagine, as an alternative to military service, that would improve national security.

3. Analyze the representation of armed conflict and war in the news media or popular culture.

4. If you had $309 billion to spend (military expenditure for 2001), how would you spend it to achieve national security?

SIXTY-EIGHT

The Women in Blue

Melinda Smith-Wells

The advertising slogan says: "The United States Air Force, a great way of life!" Is it really? I beg to differ.

In order to fuel the war-fighting machine, and advance its economic and political goals, our government — the government I provide "muscle" for — embarked on a media campaign to attract young, adventurous dreamers like me. It has enticed and entrapped many.

"I promise to defend, honor and protect my country and fellow countrymen with my life, until the day that I die." In the early morning hours six years ago, in South Carolina, I swore to uphold and defend The Constitution of the United States against all enemies, foreign and domestic. In making this promise, I relinquished a substantial portion of my liberty to ensure that others would be able to have and enjoy their own. I did not foresee what the future had in store for me on that fateful morning that seems so long ago. Unaware of the consequences, I jumped in feet first, hoping to be successful and to achieve something great. Unfortunately, I seem to have landed in something bad.

Recruiting? I didn't need that; my father was "in." I thought I was doing the right thing at the time — securing my future and giving myself the opportunity to advance and excel in life. I wanted the finer things that life has to offer: education, training, travel, money: things that many only dream of. I must admit that I have received these things, more or less, but not the quality I was promised, and at a cost I didn't think would be so high.

I am a twenty-five-year-old woman of Portuguese–Puerto Rican ancestry, struggling to juggle my studies to attain a Bachelor of Arts Degree in Business Administration while serving as an active duty military member. Currently, I am a Maintenance Scheduler. I schedule maintenance for the various aircraft and support equipment in the Air Force inventory. During my six-year military career I have been stationed at three different Air Force bases in the U.S.: Homestead AFB, Florida; McCord AFB, Washington; and Beale AFB, California. I have had the opportunity to travel to South Korea and England on temporary duty.

The military has affected my personal life in two ways. First, I don't know my husband as well as I'd like to because I constantly go on temporary assignments to various locations. This can be very stressful on a relationship because it keeps us apart for six months at a time or longer. There are times when we need each other, but due to the circumstances we can't be together. We have been married for nearly four years, but have only spent 2.5 years together. Second, I don't have any "true" friends with whom to socialize. Once you get to the point where you consider someone a friend, either one of you may be moved to a different location. You have to get used to people leaving, and the transient nature of the "business."

The "trials and tribulations" of military life have definitely had an effect on me and many other women that I have worked with. Sexual harassment has been and always will be a sensitive issue in all organizations because of the narrow-minded, insecure individuals that exist in our world. In the military, sexual harassment — regardless of what the establishment says — is very much alive and well. In my experience, the military leadership tends to look the other way when it comes to this issue. I think they feel that "boys will be boys," and women should accept this because the military is a man's world.

Oh yes, when you see incidents like "Tailhook" or those involving the Army training instructors, those of you on the outside might say, "the military will get to the bottom of this and resolve these matters." Don't be naïve enough to think that happens. The military will resolve matters in the media but not in the various units around the military world. What the leadership does is to send out memorandums or have a 1–2 hour "crash training course" on sexual harassment as if this will eliminate the problem! Does that resolve the matter? What do you think? It's just another piece of training for people to brush aside.

If you should go so far as to file a sexual harassment complaint you may put your career in jeopardy. These matters are supposed to be confidential but they eventually get out. When they do, you walk around with a stigma attached to you. You become labeled a "bitch or whore" who wanted it to happen and couldn't handle it when it did. "You brought it upon yourself because you shouldn't walk around here looking and smelling nice." That's a great environment to live and work in, huh!

Although my overall experiences in the Air Force have been livable, I do not wish to endure them again for the simple fact that my military experience has not met my expectations. Budget cuts have had an intense impact on the quality of military life. Yes, the military offers educational benefits to its members if you can fit the classes into your hectic work schedule. Medical benefits have become nothing more than medical insurance, and the quality of care we receive is adequate at best. Then there are ongoing senseless changes, and the ongoing conversations and actions regarding sexual harassment.

Some of the "intangible benefits" of the military are achieving self-discipline and maturity. You must have both of these to keep from losing your composure, and maybe cursing someone out. It is very tough to do. Many military members judge your intelligence and ability by how many stripes you have on your sleeve instead of looking at you as an individual, and what you demonstrate through your work and conversation.

A disadvantage of the military is that military members are not compensated for the work we do.

Can you actually put a price on someone's life and liberty? No, you can't, but you can show them through the compensation they receive that they are a respected, valuable, and integral part of this nation. The military robs a person of their dignity and individuality. Your thoughts and actions are not your own. You have to focus on the mission and not on your own personal agenda. There are times when you are given an assignment and told how to do it, but the instructions you've been given are wrong. You can't deviate because the person who gave you the assignment has more stripes than you. The worst part is that when it comes out in the wash that the job was done wrong, who gets blamed—you. You are manipulated like a puppet on a string in a never-ending play.

I will not continue pursuing the military as a career after my enlistment ends, nor would I recommend it to other adventurous women because it's not what you are led to believe it is. I recommend that young women take the time to assess their lives and determine what they truly want for themselves and their future. There are other options out there, and you should weigh them all before you make a decision that can have a lasting effect on the rest of your life.

In the military there is a gap between perception and reality that can be compared to the myth of "The Great American Dream": something that never really existed, or not the reality of your own experience. If it sounds too good to be true, then it probably is.

The Search for Peace and Justice
Notes toward an Autobiography

Jean Grossholtz

I was standing in the sunlight on Pennsylvania Avenue watching the passing gays and lesbians, relishing the color, the noise, and the excitement. I saw them coming around the corner, men and women many in uniform carrying signs, "I'm gay and I served." I watched them as they passed, the pride in their faces, the confidence in their step. And suddenly there I was marching, tears streaming down my face, holding the hand of another woman beside me. Here I was, a 65-year-old dedicated peace activist, who had put my body on the line in such out of the way places as the Seneca Army Base, Greenham Common, and Diablo Canyon. I, who had courted federal prison and spent time in many jails for peace, was marching with the military for the rights of gays to serve in an institution I found distasteful in the extreme. But it was an institution in which I served for four years, nine months, and five days through the Korean War. It was an institution that had meant my personal survival, had honed my political passions to a fine level of anger, had given me a deep and everlasting commitment to end war.

Confused, conflicted, and still a strong lesbian political activist, I walked beside my newfound friend as we traded stories of the purges, the fears, the betrayals by our own and others as we had sought to survive in a hostile environment. I remembered sitting paralyzed in the mess hall while noncommissioned officers who outranked me discussed the dangers of getting too close to the "troops." I knew this was aimed at me. I had just returned from a weekend of love and lust with one of my "troops." It did not matter that I knew some of them were guilty of the same infractions. I was in danger and they were warning me.

It took some time to understand those warnings before I began to hear them. The Lieutenant who made fun of me for walking with my arm around my friend. "Childish," she called it, "high school," not the behavior of a grown woman and a noncommissioned officer. The Captain who mentioned a missing light bulb as a means of casually warning me there was to be a surprise bed check. There were many such warnings as we all did our best to be decent people in an atmosphere of constant betrayal. This way surely madness lies, this occupation of a totally alien space where what one was and wanted to be was denied and hidden and yet ever present.

So there I was marching in the Gay Pride March for a Simple Matter of Justice, reliving those old fears and betrayals, the times I denied, the times I turned my back as others felt the wrath of the Army's purging. This was an important moment. Did I really want to honor the right to serve in this institution? Was I marching for the right of women, of lesbians to join this killing machine?

I had grown up committed to the organization of the working class. I grew up believing in freedom and justice. I read about the strikes of the women textile workers in Lawrence in 1912, and shed real tears when I read of the awful things that happened to strikers. I read of the Pullman Company and their private police and the murdered men at Haymarket in Chicago in 1894. I read of the government's and businessmen's fears of anarchism and the scapegoating of two foreign-born working men, Sacco and Vanzetti. Account after account of those martyred for justice made me understand that capitalism grew in this country at great cost to ordinary people, to the workers whose labor made it all possible. And I dreamed of playing that role, of being the one burnt at the stake or beheaded. Overhearing my father talking with his friends, I learned of the Industrial Workers of the World and their dream of one big union for all the working class. I fell in love with the words of these men and women. Elizabeth Gurley Flynn and Joe Hill and Big Bill Haywood of the Industrial Workers of the World. Nicknamed the Wobblies by some Chinese workers unable to pronounce the "W," these organizers moved around the country lending their skills to local leadership, integrating grass roots groups, trying to build one big union. Throughout middle school and high school I chased after stories of these grand ideas of equality and justice.

I joined the Army, as did most of the women I met in the Women's Army Corps, to get out of what looked to me a dead end street. I was 17 years old and going nowhere, with nothing but drinking and living from one shit-level job to the next in my future. I had read enough war novels to know that the men in the Army were not all establishment puppets. I knew some of the people in the Army were the same people who walked the picket lines outside of factories. I did not make the connection between the Army, the state, and the destruction of the IWW. I only knew I had to get somewhere, go somewhere where I would be able to read, to think about these people and their ideas, to find people who used these words this way.

And I had another, deeper, darker secret for leaving my home town, I was a freak. I lusted after women. I did not like boys, could not relate to them except as friends, did not want to marry, or be what the women around me seemed to want. In the small town where I went to high school I was driven crazy by my inability to fit in, to even try, make an attempt. I did not know the words dyke, lesbian. I learned of homosexual and I heard people referring to sick people they called "queer" and I knew that was me. I had hopes and hints there were others like me. When I finally met one such, she was already going into the Army and she convinced me there would be others like us there.

But the driving force was economic. With a high school education all I could do was waitress, wash dishes, work in the laundry, stand all day on an assembly line. I had spent much of my life in small towns or on a farm; I was unused to being cooped up, unused to routine. I drifted from one job to another, failing as a waitress, having a brief happy fling for some months as a short order cook when the male cook got sick. Mostly it was jobs that were killing me, that I could not keep because my anger and despair led me to outraged rebellion. The middle-aged women who stood all day on an assembly line repeating the same movement endlessly hour after hour, having to ask permission to go to the toilet, tried to comfort me. They understood only that we had no choice, that the world offered only this to poor and uneducated people. When I raged they gave me cookies, when I spoke of strikes they laughed. My heart hurting, my body aching, my mind numbed, I would eventually explode at the foreman, the factory superintendent, the product we were making. And I would be fired and move to another factory to repeat the experience.

The Army saved me. Although it led me to some heavy drinking for a time, it also led me to reject that life full force and to see some hope in moving beyond this past to something new. For the first time we had medical care, good food, warm clothes. For many of us our first visit to the dentist. (I credit the Army for the fact that alone of all my siblings I still have real teeth at the age of 67.) I had the first medication for my chronic stomach ulcers that I never had a name for before. We laughed about our uniforms but it was for some of us the first time we were not in danger of being laughed at, criticized for what we wore and how we wore it. We had social services we never thought possible. The Army was the biggest welfare state in the world and it took great care of us. And in the end it gave me the GI Bill and a college education.

We complained and raged against the Army's peculiar ways of trying to break our spirit but all of us secretly gloried in our new wealth and were

shamed into lying about our pasts, making up stories that were nowhere near true. We would tell Dick and Jane stories of loving fathers who wore suits and carried briefcases, of mothers smiling and young-looking, of little white houses with shutters and pets. And when one of us would tell the truth of the shopworn mother, the abusive father, the rape by a brother, the fights over money, we would sit together in silence, loving one another and knowing we were all afraid to speak out as she had done, afraid to make ourselves so vulnerable.

I learned that I could be somebody. That I could do all the things they asked of me, that I could stand up against the harshest, most angry of my peers and survive. A lieutenant, angry at me and humiliated because I knew more than she did about what was happening in the world, set me impossible tasks over and over until I was made into a zombie by tiredness and lack of sleep. And I still led my platoon and won good soldier awards. I was a good teacher, a popular leader. I began to see there was a way to have integrity, to be able to live as I really was. Not at first, at first I lied, I passed myself off as what I was not, indeed never wanted to be. I tried on different faces of myself searching for the one that fit. The Army allowed me that space, that time. As long as I did my duty. And that proved easy.

I learned how to act in concert with others. I learned the discipline that group activity required. Much of what the Army thrived on struck me as dumb and not worth paying attention to. The Army demanded total unquestioned obedience. They called it discipline, and punished infractions with idiotic penalties. For example, once, for arguing with an officer, I was sent to remove all the coal from the coal bin, scrub the bin, and put all the coal back. I found this ridiculous. If I thought someone was wrong I needed to say so. Sometimes this worked in my favor and allowed me to blossom, at other times it caused me grief and I paid for my inattention to the Army's rules.

Over time I realized that people liked me, that I was smart, that the Army appreciated me despite all my rebellions. I was sent to Leadership School and the entire unit showed me they thought this was a fine idea, that I was worthy of respect as a leader.

I was sent to Leadership School in Carlisle Barracks, Pennsylvania. There I met some wonderful historians who told us stories of the battles and generals of the Civil War. I fell in love with the history and with the ease which these men told the stories of Grant and Meade and Robert E. Lee and cavalry charges across peach orchids. And then I saw the pictures, the dead strewn across the battlefields. And I remembered Walt Whitman who had become the poet of my liberation, of my becoming.

I learned to teach everything from map-reading to first aid to current events. I grew daily more confident, less confused. I met women who had been to college and we talked of many things. I learned to read the *New York Times,* not knowing then how much it was misshaping and confusing my principled politics of the working class. I was sent to a detachment working with an engineering battalion in the woods of Wisconsin and I became a newspaper editor. Me, the farm girl, editing an Army newspaper. I found myself at the heart of some of the more important activities of the camp.

I learned about war. War had been something I'd read about, something that people became heroes in. And a hero I wanted to be. I did not like the killing. Felt instinctively it was wrong and that nothing would justify it or ever make me take a weapon against another human being. I had grown up with brothers and fathers hunting, hunting for meat for our food. I could not stand the smell of them when they returned — the smell of fresh blood and dead animals. I did not eat the meat they brought so proudly. I did not look at the carcasses as they carved them up and canned the results. Still I wanted to be a hero. I did not altogether reject the idea of armies in battle, of enemies.

After I had been in the Army for a few months, the United States began what they called "a police action" against North Koreans. This reaction started with a movement by North Koreans across the border with South Korea. But 1950 was the height of the Cold War frenzy. Washington was in turmoil over who had "lost" China to the Communists. The inside view in Washington was that the border crossings and troop movements in the North were a precursor of a massive, Soviet-backed invasion. This never happened. Instead the Americans, failing to stop at just policing the border, invaded North Korea and headed for Manchuria. In response, the People's Republic of China entered the war and drove the Americans from the North in a massive and bloody retreat.

A small peacetime army was suddenly increased. Thousands of new recruits were brought in, trained, and sent to Korea. Many died within days of landing at Inch'on. One young man I met from Kansas had lied about his age, entered the Army at 17, was dead on his eighteenth birthday.

As the U.S. Generals pushed to the border, proclaiming victory, the terrible retreats, the terrible killing fields of the North came to haunt us. Pictures of young men, their feet wrapped in blankets, their eyes hollow with horror. "They brought their dead out," the generals crowed, as if that were a victory. I lay many nights in my cot listening to Taps and remembering the strong young men learning engineering skills in the woods of Wisconsin. I could no longer countenance war. I no longer wanted to be a hero. I wanted to stop war, this war, all wars.

I was transferred from Wisconsin to Fitzsimmons General Hospital in Denver and the wounded came flooding back. As editor of the hospital newspaper, my job was ostensibly to tout the patriotism of these young men. I had considerable freedom until I printed a story about the limited blood supply and then I was put under tighter rein.

As I haunted the wards talking with these men, I came to see what war was really about. I saw that the bravery I had identified with saving one's buddies was really the result of a foolish, meaningless slaughter. The broken bodies of the young men I met in those hospitals were the reverse image of the sweating healthy young men I had seen training in Wisconsin. I knew that I had to organize my life to destroy the idea that war and dying in war was glorious. This blatant disrespect for life was wrong.

The Army taught me that whatever else was true, war was never an answer to any political issue; that politicians and the Generals were not good judges of reality.

But the Army taught me also that I could not love my own kind. For many years I lived in fear and shame. Shame, because what I wanted was so far from what I was supposed to want. Shame, as I saw other WACs seeking private hideouts to live out their realities while maintaining a public posture rejecting that very reality. This option did not appeal to me, it demanded that I think of myself as less than what I was, what I wanted to be. Not being able to talk to each other honestly, not being able to be anything together, they turned to drink. I saw them drinking themselves into an oblivion where shame would be stilled and they could act on their feelings and for some brief moments forget the pain of their unacceptable existence. I could not do this. I felt confused, alienated from those who hated queers and those who would not admit to being queer except when drunk. I was unable to find a center for myself.

As confidence in my own abilities grew, confidence in who I was emerged and I came to understand that the Army's war on homosexuals was wrong, that there was nothing the matter with me that a little healthy acceptance wouldn't cure. I recognized an eerie similarity between the Army's relentless attack on homosexuality, the total rejection of love of your own sex, and the constant insistent bonding with your unit, your buddies. The Army runs on love for your buddies, the willingness to lay down your very life for the group.

The Army's internal war against homosexuality is a warning not to go too far, not to put your faith in individuals but in the unit. And the unit is the Army. Men must be willing to die for the Army, to see their manhood as coming out of the barrel of a gun and its use. It is our national idea of heroism. How many times have we seen U.S. Presidents (Ronald Reagan most especially) visiting caskets in an airplane hangar and declaring these were heroes. Sometimes men who only happened to be at the wrong end of the barracks when a "terrorist" ran his explosive-laden truck into the gate, or when an airplane crashed inadvertently. Heroes simply for being there. No one saw the heroism of the women left as single heads of family back home who still managed to raise their kids and keep them out of poverty in the face of terrible odds. If you put on a uniform you are a hero, you are somebody, you are your nation's finest. Even if you are treated like a pile of shit everywhere you go and are roughed up, discriminated against, called names, within the Army. Such a contradiction — love your buddy like your brother, do not love another man.

The Army's vicious, continuous, almost holy crusade against homosexuals, the periodic purges of the WAC detachments, and the continuous challenges to gay men were all means by which the Army kept its control. Gendered identities made men into soldiers willing to kill for their commanders, and women into either the girl back home or whores. There was no place for anyone who challenged these assumptions. A real man, a soldier, abjures homo-

sexuals even as he learns to put his hope, trust and daily livelihood in his buddies, his unit, his commander. Study what happens to men in battle. Read the war novels by men from every war. They are driven nearly crazy with fear and grief before they can turn to help one another, to express their love physically. How can this clearly "men loving men" organization keep its militaristic pose without undercutting the very thing it is built on?

The Army's relentless pursuit of homosexuals is one way a gendered power structure is kept in place. If women can be competent, active public agents, and men can access that part of themselves which shares the softer, life-enhancing qualities of womanness, what will happen to the killing force, to the automatic disciplined response to orders?

After I left the Army I watched the madness of the Korean War continue as the United States embarked upon a massive war economy, engaged in a worldwide contest with the "Evil Empire," the Soviet Union. I used the GI Bill to enter college and then went on to graduate school. I studied international relations and political economy. I became a specialist on Southeast Asian politics.

I came to know that the war machines were created not really to be used because that would be the end of the world, but to press the Soviets to spend their resources, to spend to bankruptcy. Meanwhile, American corporations feeding at the military trough developed technology to enter world markets at a great advantage, selling military equipment and technology developed at the taxpayers' expense. This military machine, now released by the fall of the Soviet Union, can be used to secure and guarantee the resources of a new global economic order. From Korea to Vietnam, Grenada, Afghanistan, and Kuwait, the American Army is used to keep imperialism solidly in place. Without the Soviet Army to oppose them, the U.S. military can freely intervene. The global success of the international capitalist economic system is ultimately guaranteed by that military force.

Years after I had left the Army, after I had earned a Ph.D. in Political Science, another American government entered into another war, reminiscent of the Korean War: Vietnam. An area of the world in struggle against colonial rule, a country also divided by international fiat into north and south. And again a U.S.-generated incident and a military response, and once again young men, barely out of basic training, sent to die and Generals chortling about how brave they were, how fine, counting up the numbers they killed as if at a football match.

And I now took to the streets and found myself many times on the opposite side of the Army. Standing holding hands with my colleagues staring into the faces of young men and women frightened by us and worried about their own self-esteem.

I began standing at the gates of Westover Air Base in Massachusetts with a remarkable woman named Frances Crowe. At first we were alone but in time others joined us. Other actions followed, lying in the streets to stop the buses taking the new draftees, blocking the doors of the New York Stock Exchange, surrounding the Pentagon, being dragged to police buses and jails. I learned remarkable strength as we faced our fears of what would happen, of how we would behave when threatened by the police. I sat through endless meetings processing and planning, and nights on church floors with hundreds of others, catching what little sleep we could before an action. I experienced wonderful togetherness in jail cells. And eventually there were the women's peace camps at Seneca and at Greenham Common. Public spaces where women met freely and as equals, seeking a new way of being, a new way of making decisions, a new way of resisting injustice. This it seemed to me was the real beginning of something new, something with hope for a different future.

I have seen women create community; create, without structured authority, large-scale actions and projects. These actions were not without problems and not, in the end, without being somewhat co-opted. But we did create and maintain organized effort, whether to bring attention to Cruise missiles stored at the Seneca Army Base or to keep constant attention on the delivery of Cruise missiles to Greenham. Communities formed, the discipline of consensus decision-making was accepted, and we learned to appreciate ourselves and each other as women. The Women's Peace Camps had their days of glory, of achievement, and to all who came there, something remains, the possibility, maybe only the hope, that another way of living, of making decisions, of sharing in a common life can happen. Those of us who experienced the camps changed our lives. We could hope for an alternative. Even if we had not found it altogether.

Later in New England I joined a wondrous group of women called the Women of Faith. We did monthly actions against the nuclear submarines and their D5 missiles being constructed at Electric Boat in Connecticut. We marched and demonstrated at each launching, sometimes getting arrested, sometimes simply doing guerrilla theater. But each month we did some action. Dancing at the gate one morning at 6:30, we shut down the missile business for 28 minutes and were inordinately proud of it. Another time we invaded their offices, several times we chained ourselves to gates or blockaded entrances.

We would think up our next action while we were waiting arraignment in the holding cell or sitting waiting as part of the support group in the courtroom. The night before the planned action we would meet to make signs, plan the press coverage, assign tasks. We would meet in a church or a private home near our action. For a couple of years we worked together without tension or friction, bringing new women into our group and learning how to talk to the media, handle the jail situation. What broke us up was some of the changes in the military situation and internal disruption caused by one new woman's inability to accept consensus. Until that time we had worked without a slip. Proving that it can be done.

I found some of the same camaraderie, the same sense of belonging to something bigger than one's self, the same willingness to accept others' decisions, as I found in the Army and this time aimed at peace, at justice, and at the creation of political community.

So why was I marching in a parade proclaiming the right of queers to serve in the military? What did I hope to accomplish by this? How did it fit with my peace activism?

I was marching along with hundreds of others to say "Yes, I was there. You can no longer deny my existence. Silencing me and all these others was useless because we know and you know what you are up to. Those of us in uniform are not just robots wound up and set out to kill and be killed at the bidding of the world economic order. We have lives that you do not approve of, we have thoughts and values that reject yours."

So I was marching for all of this, to challenge the Army's gendered system of power, to challenge its failure to honor the love of men and women for each other, to force them to change that reality. Because if they acknowledge the existence of queers in their ranks, in their leadership, and among those who make the decisions that vote them budgets, then they can no longer adhere to that male ideology of exclusion and machoism. Those qualities that have been assigned to women, the experiences and perceptions of women cannot so simply be dismissed. The Army as a male hierarchical institution is weakened.

And I was marching because I wanted to put the lie to all that we have been told was not possible, was dangerous. Contrary to what we are told, I have seen that this country can provide all the necessities of life, housing, food, clothing, health care, and education to hundreds of thousands of people in a very short time. An enormous army was assembled, housed, fed, and clothed in a very short time for the Korean War and again for the Vietnam War. Despite all we have heard of the dangers of the welfare programs and helping people out of trouble, the country did not go bankrupt, those people did not

become lazy or valueless. Providing young people with all the necessities of life and good health made them strong and efficient.

Contrary to the claim that we only act out of individual self-interest, I have seen men and women put the good of the community above their own individual wishes. I have seen that men and women can think collectively about how to live together and get a job done. And I have seen them do this despite, not because of, the barbarous discipline.

Equality and justice, my lifelong dreams, are not to be found in fighting, in militarism. Killing people does not bring peace. There are other ways to create common commitments, a willingness to put one's body on the line, the courage to take risks.

It is here we must start to remake the world.

S E V E N T Y

◆◆◆

What Are the Alternatives to a Military Base?

*Alma Bulawan and the Women of BUKLOD**

Presently, there are significant questions being raised about the continued existence of the U.S. bases here in our country. Many consultations are also being held in order to discuss these questions. At first glance, the primary problem and stumbling block would be the loss of work for the large numbers of Filipinos who work inside the base.

This issue is being seriously considered by the government and the large and strong sectors of the country. I wish to make known to everyone that there is one more sector that is in need of an alternative if the bases leave. This sector is the 9,000 women who work in the hospitality industry.[1] I am here therefore because I want to pass on to every-

one, and to you, the fact that there is a responsibility to make decisions about their serious needs. Please listen for a moment and consider what the women in this trade would like to have passed on.

Based on our questions and our knowledge as of now, one alternative to the U.S. bases is to make a free port at Olongapo City. We believe that this is not the answer to our situation and that, rather, the situation would become even worse. If many different ships came into port, there would simply be different kinds of customers—a situation that would induce many more women to work in the hospitality trade. This would add to the loss of suitable ways of caring for and control of foreigners who arrive.

One more alternative being considered is an industrial complex. This would mean that the women would work in factories. This is a possible answer to the situation if the regulations and conditions were just: for example, a proper salary, time away from the job for the different duties and responsibilities of women, benefits that respond to the situation of women, support for their needs in caring for their children and families, and the assurance that management would not make assessments according to

---

*This statement, based on discussions with women in Olongapo, was written by Alma Bulawan, a staff member at BUKLOD and formerly a waitress in a club, to present at a consultation on alternatives to U.S. bases in the Philippines.
[1]The figure of 9,000 used here refers to registered women in Olongapo. Estimates of the number of registered and unregistered women together are around 16,000.

high levels of education and experience. If this is not accomplished, nothing will change because the work in the factories will only lead to exasperation and frustration; and if the earnings are not sufficient, it is possible that the women will return to what they did before.

Our questioning indicated that if the government provided an alternative, a number of women would like to have some capital in order to start a small business. Perhaps this is one of several possible solutions to the problem and should be studied in detail. If so, there are additional considerations that need to be addressed: drawing from our limited experience, we know that many of the women who borrow even a small amount of capital are not able to repay it. There are at least three reasons for this: first, lack of business experience; second, lack of knowledge about the system of business dealings; and third, perhaps, a certain lack of responsibility. If there were capital available for business loans, proper training and experience would have to be provided as well. The training and experience should respond to the entirety of what is needed for the advancement of women. These are the following:

1. Consciousness raising so that the women may understand that it is not right to lose one's choice of livelihood and also feel

forced to barter this valuable resource (sexual labor) in order just to eat and stay alive.

2. Training about the rights and responsibilities of women.

3. Focus on an understanding of reproductive health and other health training.

4. The importance of nationalism and self-reliance.

5. Education and training in business: being careful, orderly, and clean; saving for the future; and recognizing the importance of work and one's fellow human beings.

Equally as important as education and experience is the methodology of implementation. The methodology must be suitable to the progress of the women's consciousness.

Finally, and perhaps of greatest importance, is the eradication of society's low regard for the women who have been forced to work in the hospitality trade. We must all endeavor to accept them without exception and without doubt as valuable members of the country of the Philippines.

When all this has been accomplished, we will be able to say that there are genuine alternatives for our women in Olongapo.

SEVENTY-ONE

Women's Budget

Women's International League for Peace and Freedom

The distribution of federal payments is heavily weighted toward military expenditures. Investments in programs that guarantee a social safety net for low income people, fund vital local services, and enrich the infrastructure of the country are seriously underfunded. In addition to the kinds of investments listed below, the government could enhance women's economic potential through policies such as full employment, a guaranteed adequate annual income, an increase in the minimum wage, universal access to health care, and the guarantee of child care for all who need it.

High levels of military spending are particularly damaging to women's economic prospects because women are severely under-represented in the military and in military contractor jobs, and because military spending creates fewer jobs than civilian spending. When the government spends money in the military sector, spending on consumer goods, state and local governments, schools, health care, and day care lose out, all sectors that have high concentrations of women. One billion transferred from military spending to civilian investment would create a net gain of 6,800 jobs, which means that a $350 billion transfer from military to civilian spending would create over 2 million jobs in five years.

Investments of $350 billion could be made in social investments over five years through military cuts. . . . Following are examples of investments that could be made:

Education   **$40 billion**
Increase funding for Head Start, Compensatory Education, Student Aid, enforcement of the Women's Educational Equity Act

Infrastructure   **$45 billion**
Increase spending for highways, bridges and airports, Mass Transit, Amtrak, Wastewater Collection and Treatment

Environment   **$20 billion**
Increase funding for Superfund cleanup, Municipal Solid Waste Program, Groundwater Protection, Forestry and Conservation, Renewable Energy and Energy Conservation

Housing   **$55 billion**
Increase investment in Public Housing and support services for the homeless

Income Support   **$60 billion**
Increase investment in Child Care, Aid to Families with Dependent Children (AFDC), Supplemental Security Income, Low-Income Energy Assistance, Unemployment Compensation

Health Care   **$50 billion**
Expand Medicaid, increase funding for Maternal and Child Health Block Grant, Community and Migrant Health Centers, the Family Planning Program, the Child Immunization Program, Office of Research on Women's Health

Nutrition   **$20 billion**
Expand the Women's, Infants' and Children's Program (WIC), the Older Americans Act Nutrition Programs, School Breakfast, Child Care, and Summer Food Programs, and Food Stamps

Employment & Training   **$25 billion**
Increase funding for the Economic Dislocation and Worker Act, Senior Community Services Employment Program, Occupational Safety and Health Administration (OSHA), the Wage and Hour Administration, and new initiatives to provide training targeted for low-income women

Special Women's Programs   **$15 billion**
Increase funding for Violence Against Women Act, Older Americans Act, Displaced Homemakers Self-sufficiency Act, transition programs and services for women entering the job market, the Women's Bureau

International Relations   **$20 billion**
Increase funding for U.S. development assistance for women, support goals of the Fourth World Conference on Women, pay debt to UN and increase contribution

Total Investments   **$350 billion**

Which Would You Choose?
The ballistic missile defense ("Star Wars") program ($91 billion) **OR** *Provide early education for 740,000 children under Head Start for 26 years?*

◆◆◆

Unity Statement

Women's Pentagon Action

We are gathering at the Pentagon on November 16 because we fear for our lives. We fear for the life of this planet, our Earth, and the life of the children who are our human future.

We are mostly women who come from the northeastern region of our United States. We are city women who know the wreckage and fear of city streets, we are country women who grieve the loss of the small farm and have lived on the poisoned earth. We are young and older, we are married, single, lesbian. We live in different kinds of households: In groups, families, alone, some are single parents.

We work at a variety of jobs. We are students, teachers, factory workers, office workers, lawyers, farmers, doctors, builders, waitresses, weavers, poets, engineers, homeworkers, electricians, artists, blacksmiths. We are all daughters and sisters.

We have come here to mourn and rage and defy the Pentagon because it is the workplace of the imperial power which threatens us all. Every day while we work, study, love, the colonels and generals who are planning our annihilation walk calmly in and out the doors of its five sides. They have accumulated over 30,000 nuclear bombs, at the rate of three to six bombs every day. They are determined to produce the billion-dollar MX missile. They are creating a technology called Stealth—the invisible, unperceivable arsenal. They have revised the cruel old killer, nerve gas. They have proclaimed Directive 59 which asks for "small nuclear wars, prolonged but limited." The Soviet Union works hard to keep up with the United States initiatives. We can destroy each other's cities, towns, schools and children many times over. The United States has sent "advisors," money and arms to El Salvador and Guatemala to enable those juntas to massacre their own people.

The very same men, the same legislative committees that offer trillions of dollars to the Pentagon have brutally cut day care, children's lunches, battered women's shelters. The same men have con-

cocted the Family Protection Act which will mandate the strictly patriarchal family and thrust federal authority into our home life. They are preventing the passage of ERA's simple statement and supporting the Human Life Amendment which will deprive all women of choice and many women of life itself.

We are in the hands of men whose power and wealth have separated them from the reality of daily life and from the imagination. We are right to be afraid.

At the same time our cities are in ruins, bankrupt; they suffer the devastation of war. Hospitals are closed, our schools deprived of books and teachers. Our Black and Latino youth are without decent work. They will be forced, drafted to become the cannon fodder for the very power that oppresses them. Whatever help the poor receive is cut or withdrawn to feed the Pentagon which needs about $500,000,000 a day for its murderous health. It extracted $157 billion dollars last year from our own tax money, $1,800 from a family of four.

With this wealth our scientists are corrupted; over 40% work in government and corporate laboratories that refine the methods for destroying or deforming life. The lands of the Native American people have been turned to radioactive rubble in order to enlarge the nuclear warehouse. The uranium of South Africa, necessary to the nuclear enterprise, enriches the white minority and encourages the vicious system of racist oppression and war.

The President has just decided to produce the neutron bomb, which kills people but leaves property (buildings like this one) intact. There is fear among the people, and that fear, created by the industrial militarists, is used as an excuse to accelerate the arms race. "We will protect you . . ." they say, but we have never been so endangered, so close to the end of human time.

We women are gathering because life on the precipice is intolerable. We want to know what anger in these men, what fear, which can only be satisfied by destruction, what coldness of heart and ambition drives their days. We want to know because we do

---

Statement from 1980.

not want that dominance which is exploitative and murderous in international relations, and so dangerous to women and children at home—we do not want that sickness transferred by the violent society through the fathers to the sons.

What is it that we women need for our ordinary lives, that we want for ourselves and also for our sisters in new nations and old colonies who suffer the white man's exploitation and too often the oppression of their own countrymen?

We want enough good food, decent housing, communities with clean air and water, good care for our children while we work. We want work that is useful to a sensible society. There is a modest technology to minimize drudgery and restore joy to labor. We are determined to use skills and knowledge from which we have been excluded—like plumbing or engineering or physics or composing. We intend to form women's groups or unions that will demand safe workplaces, free of sexual harassment, equal pay for work of comparable value. We respect the work women have done in caring for the young, their own and others, in maintaining a physical and spiritual shelter against the greedy and militaristic society. In our old age we expect our experience, our skills, to be honored and used.

We want health care which respects and understands our bodies. Physically challenged sisters must have access to gatherings, actions, happy events, work. For this, ramps must be added to stairs and we must become readers, signers, supporting arms. So close, so many, why have we allowed ourselves not to know them?

We want an education for children which tells the true story of our women's lives, which describes the earth as our home to be cherished, to be fed as well as harvested.

We want to be free from violence in our streets and in our houses. One in every three of us will be raped in her lifetime. The pervasive social power of the masculine ideal and the greed of the pornographer have come together to steal our freedom, so that whole neighborhoods and the life of the evening and night have been taken from us. For too many women the dark country road and the city alley have concealed the rapist. We want the night returned: the light of the moon, special in the cycle of our female lives, the stars and the gaiety of the city streets.

We want the right to have or not to have children—we do not want gangs of politicians and med-

ical men to say we must be sterilized for the country's good. We know that this technique is the racists' method for controlling populations. Nor do we want to be prevented from having an abortion when we need one. We think this freedom should be available to poor women as it always has been to the rich. We want to be free to love whomever we choose. We will live with women or with men or we will live alone. We will not allow the oppression of lesbians. One sex or one sexual preference must not dominate another.

We do not want to be drafted into the army. We do not want our young brothers drafted. We want *them* equal with us.

We want to see the pathology of racism ended in our time. It has been the imperial arrogance of white male power that has separated us from the suffering and wisdom of our sisters in Asia, Africa, South America and in our own country. Many North American women look down on the minority nearest them: the Black, the Hispanic, the Jew, the Native American, the Asian, the immigrant. Racism has offered them privilege and convenience; they often fail to see that they themselves have bent to the unnatural authority and violence of men in government, at work, at home. Privilege does not increase knowledge or spirit or understanding. There can be no peace while one race dominates another, one people, one nation, one sex despises another.

We must not forget the tens of thousands of American women who live much of their lives in cages, away from family, lovers, all the growing-up years of their children. Most of them were born at the intersection of oppressions: people of color, female, poor. Women on the outside have been taught to fear those sisters. We refuse that separation. We need each other's knowledge and anger in our common struggle against the builders of jails and bombs.

We want the uranium left in the earth and the earth given back to the people who tilled it. We want a system of energy which is renewable, which does not take resources out of the earth without returning them. We want those systems to belong to the people and their communities, not to the giant corporations which invariably turn knowledge into weaponry. We want the sham of Atoms for Peace ended, all nuclear plants decommissioned and the construction of new plants stopped. That is another war against the people and the child to be born in fifty years.

We want an end to the arms race. No more bombs. No more amazing inventions for death.

We understand all is connectedness. We know the life and work of animals and plants in seeding, reseeding and in fact simply inhabiting this planet. Their exploitation and the organized destruction of never to be seen again species threatens and sorrows us. The earth nourishes us as we with our bodies will eventually feed it. Through us, our mothers connected the human past to the human future.

With that sense, that ecological right, we oppose the financial connections between the Pentagon and the multinational corporations and banks that the Pentagon serves. Those connections are made of gold and oil. We are made of blood and bone, we are made of the sweet and finite resource, water. We will not allow these violent games to continue. If we are here in our stubborn thousands today, we will certainly return in the hundreds of thousands in the months and years to come.

We know there is a healthy, sensible, loving way to live and we intend to live that way in our neighborhoods and our farms in these United States, and among our sisters and brothers in all the countries of the world.

SEVENTY-THREE

◆◆◆

Reflection after the June 12th March for Disarmament

Sonia Sanchez

I have come to you tonite out of the depths
   of slavery
   from white hands peeling black skins over
   America;
I have come out to you from reconstruction eyes
   that closed on black humanity
   that reduced black hope to the dark
   huts of America;
I have come to you from the lynching years—
   the exploitation of blk/men and women by
   a country that allowed the swinging of
   strange fruits from southern trees;
I have come to you tonite thru the
   Delaney years, the Du Bois years, the
   B. T. Washington years, the Robeson
   years, the Garvey years, the
   Depression years, the you can't eat
   or sit or live just die here years,
   the Civil rights years, the black power
   years, the blk Nationalist years, the
   Affirmative Action years, the liberal
   years, the Neo-conservative years;

I have come to say that those years
   were not in vain—the ghosts of our
   ancestors searching this american dust for
rest were not in vain—black women
   walking their lives in clots were not
   in vain—the years walked
   sideways in a forsaken land were not
   in vain;
I have come to you tonite as an equal,
   as a comrade, as a Black woman
   walking down a corridor of tears,
   looking neither to the left or the right,
   pulling my history with bruised
   heels,
   beckoning to the illusion of America,
   daring you to look me in the eyes to
   see these faces—the exploitation of a
   people because of skin pigmentation;
I have come to you tonite because no people
   have been asked to be modern day people
   with the history of slavery, and still
   we walk—and still we talk—and
   still we plan—and still we hope and
   still we sing;
I have come to you tonite because there are
   inhumanitarians in the world. They are not
   new. They are old. They go back into history.
   They were called explorers, soldiers, mercenaries,
   imperialists, missionaries, adventurers—

but they looked at the world for what
it would give up to them and they violated
the land and the people, they looked
at the land and sectioned it up for
private ownership, they looked at the
people and decided how to manipulate
them thru fear and ignorance, they looked
at the gold and began to hoard and
worship it;
I have come to you because it is time
for us all to purge capitalism from
our dreams, to purge materialism
from our eyes, from the planet earth
to deliver the earth again into the hands
of the humanitarians;
I have come to you tonite not just for the
stoppage
of nuclear proliferation — nuclear
plants — nuclear bombs — nuclear
waste — but to stop the proliferation
of nuclear minds, of nuclear generals,
of nuclear presidents, of nuclear scientists,
who spread human
and nuclear waste over the world;
I come to you because the world needs to be
saved for the future generations who must
return the earth to peace — who will not
be startled by a man's/a woman's skin
color;

I come to you because the world needs sanity
now, needs men and women who will
not work to produce nuclear weapons,
who will give up their need for excess
wealth and learn how to share the
world's resources, who will never
again as scientists invent again just
for the sake of inventing;

I come to you because we need to turn our
eyes to the beauty of this planet, to the
bright green laughter of trees, to the beautiful
human animals waiting to smile their
unprostituted
smiles;
I have come to you to talk about our
inexperience
at living as human beings — thru death
marches and camps,
thru middle passages and slavery
and thundering countries raining hungry
faces;
I am here to move against
leaving our shadows implanted on the
earth while our bodies disintegrate in
nuclear lightning;
I am here because our scientists must
be stripped of their imperialist dreams;
I am here between the voices of our ancestors
and the noise of the planet,
between the surprise of death and life;
I am here because I shall not give the
earth up to non-dreamers and earth
molesters;
I am here to say to YOU:

My body is full of veins
like the bombs waiting to burst
with blood.
We must learn to suckle life not
bombs and rhetoric
rising up in redwhiteandblue patriotism;
I am here. And my breath/our breaths
must thunder across this land
arousing new breaths. New life.
New people, who will live in peace
and honor.

CHAPTER TWELVE

Women and the Environment

Place is a fundamental element in our lives whether we live in a spacious suburb, a vibrant — maybe overcrowded — downtown area, an old-established inner-city neighborhood, on a farm, a ranch, or a reservation (Anderson 1991; Barnhill 1999; Williams 1992). Places change over time so that a formerly Polish American or Italian American community may now be home to African Americans or Vietnamese immigrants; a poorer neighborhood may become gentrified as middle-class people move in and push up property values. Neighborhood facilities — churches, temples, synagogues, schools, stores, restaurants, parks, community centers — reflect the interests and concerns of people who live there. The quality of some local services and the physical space also reflect the standing of a particular community in the wider society. In general, middle-class and upper-middle-class communities have better school buildings, more sports facilities, more doctors' offices, and a wider range of stores than poorer neighborhoods. They are also farther from factories, oil refineries, sawmills, stockyards, railway terminals, highways, garbage dumps, and other sources of pollution, bad smells, and noise.

Many people contribute to safeguarding our physical environment. Federal legislation like the Clean Air Act and regulatory agencies like the Environmental Protection Agency limit toxic emissions from factories, homes, and cars. Cities or counties provide services like potable water, garbage disposal, street cleaning and repair, snow clearance, stop signs and traffic lights, town parks, and recreation centers. National environmental organizations have lobbied for the preservation of wilderness areas as national parks, for the protection of endangered species, and for stronger environmental regulation of industry. Community organizations clear trash from highways and vacant lots, or work in community gardens. Individuals mow lawns, trim trees, sweep the sidewalk, recycle reusable materials, compost organic matter, and buy "green," or environmentally safe, products like paper goods from recycled paper or biodegradable soaps and detergents. Important as they are, these efforts cannot keep up with the scale and pace of environmental degradation.

In the past thirty years or so, many people in the United States have become increasingly concerned with environmental issues. Hazardous industrial production processes have affected the health of workers and people who live near or downwind of industrial areas. Industrial pollutants, chemical pesticides and fertilizers, and wastes from nuclear power plants and uranium mines are seeping into the groundwater in many parts of the country as exemplified in feature films like *A Civil Action* and *Erin Brockovich*. Homes and schools have been built on land once used for toxic dumps. Deforestation, global warming, and the disappearance of hundreds of species are also hallmarks of vast environmental destruction worldwide. Given the enormous scale of the environmental crisis, however, the small steps mentioned earlier do not begin to touch the heart of the problem, though as we discuss later, there are many views as to what the heart of the problem is. United States environmental activists probably agree, however, that the greatest threat to environmental security worldwide comes from the waste-producing, industrialized, militarized economies of the North, especially North America, Europe, and Japan.

This chapter is concerned with environmental effects on women particularly and with women's activism around environmental issues. It assumes that there is an ethical dimension to living in any location: that we care for the environment for our own sake and for the sake of future generations. As the world has become more integrated, place is a more amorphous concept. Our home places are deeply affected by corporate and governmental decisions often made many miles away. As with other topics in this book, environmental issues are experienced at the micro and meso levels, but also have macro- and global-level dimensions, as made clear by the writers whose work we include here. The lenses of gender, race, class, and nation are also essential tools in this chapter.

In the United States the environmental crisis affects men as well as women, of course, but in terms of environmental health, women and children show the effects of toxic pollution earlier than men do, either because of low body weight or because women's bodies become what some have termed "unhealthy environments" for their babies (Nelson 1990). A significant number of babies without brains have been born to women on both sides of the Rio Grande, a river polluted by U.S.-controlled *maquiladora* industries on the Mexican side (Kamel and Hoffman 1999). (Working conditions in these *maquiladoras,* or subassembly plants, are described in more detail in Chapter 7.) Contact with pesticides has led to poor health for many women farmworkers in the United States and to chronic illnesses or severe disabilities for their children (Chavez 1993; Moses 1993). Several firms have tried to keep women of childbearing age out of the most noxious production processes — often the highest paid — or to insist that

they be sterilized, lest women sue them later for fetal damage (Chavkin 1984). Children's health in the United States is also compromised by environmental factors such as lead in paints and gasoline, air pollution, traffic hazards, and violence that often involves the use of handguns, with significant differences between those living in inner cities and those in suburban neighborhoods (Hamilton 1993; Phoenix 1993). The Akwesasne Mothers' Milk project in upstate New York, founded by Katsi Cook, is a Native American research project that was started in response to women's concern that their breastmilk might be toxic and that breast-feeding, supposedly the best way to nurture infants, could expose them to pollutants from birth (LaDuke 1999).

Many more women than men are involved in campaigning on behalf of environmental issues at a grassroots level. We do not see women as somehow closer to nature than men, as is sometimes argued, or as having an essentially nurturing, caring nature. Rather, we see women's environmental activism as an extension of their roles as daughters, wives, and mothers, caring for families and communities. Because of the gendered division of labor between home and work, women have a long-standing history of involvement in community organizing: campaigning against poor housing conditions, high rents, unsafe streets, lead in gasoline, toxic dumps, and so on. Ideally, taking care of children and other family members should be everyone's responsibility, as we argue in Chapter 5. We see organizing around environmental issues as part of this responsibility.

Theoretical and Activist Perspectives

Generally, theories grow out of and inform experience. Women who are concerned about environmental degradation draw on different theoretical and activist perspectives: deep ecology and bioregionalism, ecofeminism, and environmental justice. These are not unitary perspectives, though here we emphasize points of comparison between them rather than their internal variations.

Deep Ecology and Bioregionalism

Deep ecology is a term coined by Norwegian philosopher Arne Naess and taken up in the United States by Devall and Sessions (1985). It is premised on two fundamental principles: self-realization for every being and a "biocentric" equality among species. Many environmental activists in the United States who are drawn to deep ecology are critical of more mainstream environmental organizations like the Sierra Club, Natural Resources Defense Council, or the Environmental Defense Fund that focus on lobbying and legislation to improve air and water quality or to protect wilderness areas and endangered species. Although these efforts have contributed to growing public concern about environmental degradation, they are slow; they are cast in human-centered terms and invariably compromised by corporate interests. Earth First! is an activist network that exemplifies principles of deep ecology in practice. It has gained public recognition through direct action, particularly in opposition to the logging of old-growth forests in the Pacific Northwest and northern California (Davis 1991; List 1993).

At its worst, deep ecology is sometimes reduced to a rather simplistic view of the world in which nature is "good" and people are "bad." Deep ecologists argue for reducing human population, reducing human interference in the biosphere, and reducing human standards of living. As its name implies, Earth First! has been more interested in saving the earth than in safeguarding the human population. This has led to arguments that, for example, if AIDS didn't exist it would have had to be invented, or that starving people in Africa should be left to die so that the human population can be brought back into balance with the carrying capacity of the land (Thropy 1991). Deep ecologists value the preservation of nature in and of itself rather than for any benefit such preservation affords to humans. Nature is often seen in terms of romance: The virgin, feminized wilderness is vulnerable, innocent, and weak, and protecting "her" draws on old macho, militaristic iconography (King 1987). Wilderness is not thought of as the homeland of indigenous people but as a special place where people (at least athletic, nondisabled people, usually male) can get close to an "experience" of nature. Critics of U.S. deep ecology oppose its people vs. nature stance and argue that nature is not something far away, to be encountered on weekend hikes or occasional camping trips. Everyone is connected to nature in the most mundane but profound way: through the air we breathe,

the water we drink, and the food we eat, as embodied human beings in a continuum of life.

A significant development is the alliance between Earth First! and labor union members. In the 1980s and early 90s, people who tried to stop logging, for example, especially in old-growth forests of western states, often found themselves up against loggers who were dependent on timber companies for their livelihood. In urban areas, too, industrial jobs were often set against a cleaner environment. Corporations argued that they could not afford to clean up their operations or that cleaning up would be at the expense of jobs. This win-lose formulation, jobs vs. the environment, means that different groups will continue to fight among themselves. An alliance between environmentalists and labor organizers is essential. People need a livelihood as well as good environmental conditions, and the two are not mutually exclusive.

A biocentric view also prevails within the bioregional movement, which emphasizes decentralization, agricultural and economic self-sufficiency within bioregions, and a strongly developed attachment to place (Andruss, et al. 1990; Berg 1993; Sale 1985). Many ecofeminists and environmental justice activists are critical of this strand of *bioregionalism*. It does not analyze the structures of dominance among people in capitalist, patriarchal societies. It does not appear to be specifically committed to women's liberation or to opposing racism and has no principles for dealing with social and economic inequality within a bioregion. There is the assumption that decentralized, small-scale, regional structures and a shift from a human-centered to a biocentered perspective will solve all problems. Without an explicit social ethics this seems highly unlikely.

Ecofeminism

The term **ecofeminism** was first used by a group of French feminists who founded the Ecology-Feminism Center in 1974, and was based on their analysis of connections between masculinist social institutions and the destruction of the physical environment (d'Eaubonne 1994). A few years later, groundbreaking work in the United States by Susan Griffin (1978) and Carolyn Merchant (1980) put forward a central insight of ecofeminism, the connection between the domination of women and the domination of nature. These authors pointed to the ways in which Western thought and science from the time of Francis Bacon has seen nonhuman nature as wild and hostile, so much matter to be mastered and used:

> For you have to but follow and . . . hound nature in her wanderings, and you will be able when you like to lead and drive her afterward to the same place again. . . . Neither ought a man make scruple of entering and penetrating into these holes and corners, when the inquisition of truth is his whole object.
>
> *(Quoted in Merchant 1980, p. 168)*

In Western thought, nature is often feminized and sexualized through imagery such as "virgin forest," "the rape of the earth," and "penetrating" the wilderness. Vandana Shiva (1988) notes that in the Western model of development sources, living things that can reproduce life—whether forests, seeds, or women's bodies—are turned into resources to be objectified, controlled, and used. This makes them productive in economic terms. In this view, a forest that is not logged, a river that is not fished, or a hillside that is not mined, is unproductive (Waring 1988). A core point in ecofeminist analysis involves the concept of dualism, where various attributes are thought of in terms of oppositions: culture/nature; mind/body; male/female; civilized/primitive; sacred/profane; subject/object; self/other. Val Plumwood (1993) argues that these dualisms are mutually reinforcing and should be thought of as an interlocking set. In each pair, one side is valued over the other. Culture, mind, male, civilized, for example, are valued over nature, body, female, primitive, which are thought of as "other" and inferior. Plumwood argues that dualism is the logic of hierarchical systems of thought—colonialism, racism, sexism, or militarism, for example, which rely on the idea of otherness, enemies, and inferiority to justify superiority and domination. Ecofeminism links concerns with racism and economic exploitation to the domination of women and nature, as discussed by Starhawk (Reading 79) from the perspective of earth-centered spirituality.

Such a broad approach is open to many interpretations and ideas for activism. The first ecofeminist conference in the United States, titled "Women for Life on Earth," was held in Amherst, Massachusetts, as a response to the near-meltdown at the Three Mile Island nuclear power plant in 1980. One outcome of the conference was the Women's Pentagon Action, a major demonstration against militarism in the early 1980s, mentioned in Chapter 11 (also see King 1988). Currently, ecofeminism is explored and developed through newsletters and study groups, college courses, animal rights organizing, and long-term women's land projects. Some ecofeminist writers and researchers work with local activist groups or contribute to national and international debates. Significant examples include the National Women's Health Network's research and organizing around industrial and environmental health (Nelson 1990), critiques of reproductive technology and genetic engineering by the Feminist Network of Resistance to Reproductive and Genetic Engineering (Mies and Shiva 1993), and the Committee on Women, Population, and the Environment, which critiques simplistic overpopulation arguments that focus only on countries of the South rather than also addressing the overconsumption of the North (Hartmann 1995; Mello 1996; Silliman and King 1999). Women's Environment and Development Organization coordinated a major international conference in 1991 to work out a women's agenda to take to the U.N. Conference on the Environment and Development in Rio de Janeiro in June 1992. This group also was an active participant in the NGO Forum in China in 1995, as we noted in Chapter 7.

Charlene Spretnak (1990) embraces the eclectic nature of U.S. ecofeminism and notes its varied roots in feminist theory, feminist spirituality, and social ecology. This diversity in ecofeminist approaches raises the question of whether there is a sufficiently consistent, intellectually coherent ecofeminist perspective, and many academics claim that there is not. Some women of color argue that, as with U.S. feminism in general, ecofeminism emphasizes gender over race and class; other women of color argue that it focuses on abstract ideas about women and nature rather than on practical issues with a material base (Davis 1998; Smith 1997; Taylor 1997). Left-wing radicals, some environmentalists, and many academics reject ecofeminism as synonymous with goddess worship or on the grounds that it assumes women are essentially closer to nature than men. Joni Seager (1993), for example, develops a feminist understanding of environmental issues but does not use the term *ecofeminism* to describe her work. At present U.S. ecofeminism is very much the preserve of writers and scholars, albeit those who are often on the margins of the academy in part-time or temporary positions. Although this may lead to an activism of scholarship — by no means insignificant, as suggested earlier — it does not often connect directly with the reality of life for many women organizing around environmental issues (also see Epstein 1993; Kirk 1997; Sachs 1996). We argue that an ecological feminism can, and should, integrate gender, race, class, and nation in its analyses and that its powerful theoretical insights can, and should, translate into activism.

Environmental Justice

The people most affected by poor physical environments in the United States are women and children, particularly women and children of color. Many women of color and poor White women are active in hundreds of local organizations campaigning for healthy living and working conditions in working-class communities, communities of color, and on Native American land, which are all disproportionately affected by pollution from incinerators, toxic dumps, pesticides, and hazardous working conditions in industry and agriculture (Bullard 1990, 1993; Hofrichter 1993; Szasz 1994). Data show a strong correlation between the distribution of toxic wastes and race, which has been termed **environmental racism** (Lee 1987). The theory of environmental racism and the movement for **environmental justice** draw on concepts of civil rights, under which all citizens have a right to healthy living and working conditions. Organizationally, too, the environmental justice movement has roots in civil rights organizing, as well as in labor unions, Chicano land-grant movements, social justice organizations, and Native American rights organizations. Its tactics include demonstrations and rallies, public education, research and monitoring of toxic sites, preparing and presenting expert testimony to government agencies, reclaiming land through direct action, and maintaining and teaching traditional agricultural practices, crafts, and skills. Examples of local organizations include West Harlem Environmental Action (New York; see Miller 1993), the Center for Third World Organizing (Oakland, Calif.), and the Southwest Network for Environmental and Economic Justice (Albuquerque, N.M., and Austin, Tex.; see Kirk 1998).

Local organizations embrace different issues depending on their memberships and geographic locations. Some are primarily concerned to stop the location of toxic waste dumps or incinerators in their neighborhoods, an approach sometimes dubbed the Not-In-My-Back-Yard (NIMBY) syndrome. Most groups are quick to see that it is not enough to keep hazards out of their own neighborhoods if this means that dumps or incinerators will then be located in other poor communities. This has led to coordinated opposition on a local and regional level. Examples include Laotian-immigrant organizing against Chevron (Richmond, Calif.), the context for Bouapha Toommaly's work (Reading 75); Native Hawai'ian people's approach to sovereignty, tourism, and the environment (Mililani Trask, Reading 76); and Mexican American women's organizing in East Los Angeles (Mary Pardo, Reading 77).

Besides opposing hazardous conditions, the environmental justice movement also has a powerful reconstructive dimension involving sustainable projects that intertwine ecological, economic, and cultural survival. Examples include Tierra Wools (northern New Mexico), where a workers' cooperative produces high-quality, handwoven rugs and clothing and organically fed lamb from its sheep (Pulido 1993); the Native American White Earth Land Recovery Project in Minnesota, which produces wild rice, maple sugar, berries, and birch bark (LaDuke 1993, 1999); and many inner-city community gardening projects producing vegetables for local consumption (Bagby 1990; Hynes 1996; Warner 1987).

Although very few local environmental issues are exclusively the concern of women, women form the majority of local activists in opposing such hazards as toxic dumps. As noted, women have a history of community organizing. This activism may also be given special impetus if they have sick children or become ill themselves (see Reading 55, Chapter 9). Illnesses caused by toxics are sometimes difficult to diagnose and treat because they affect internal organs and the balance of body functioning, and symptoms can be mistaken for those of other conditions. Women have been persistent in raising questions and searching for plausible explanations for such illnesses, sometimes discovering that their communities have been built on contaminated land, as happened at Love Canal, New York, for example, or tracing probable sources of pollution affecting their neighborhoods (Gibbs 1995, 1998; Kaplan 1997). They have publicized their findings and taken on governmental agencies and corporations responsible for contamination. In so doing they are often ridiculed as "hysterical housewives" by officials and reporters and their research trivialized as emotional and unscholarly. By contrast, others — Nelson (1990), for example — honor this work as kitchen table science. In October 1991, women were 60 percent of the participants at the First National People of Color Environmental Leadership Summit in Washington, D.C. The conference adopted a statement called "Principles of Environmental Justice," included here (Reading 74). Many urban gardeners in northern cities are elderly African American women (e.g., Bagby 1990). In rural areas, women work on family subsistence garden plots, planting, harvesting, and processing fruits and vegetables for home use (Sachs 1996). Some know the woods or backcountry areas in great detail, as ethnobotanists, because they go there at different seasons to gather herbs for medicinal purposes. Among Mexican Americans, for example, *curanderas* — traditional healers — continue to work with herbal remedies and acquire their knowledge from older women relatives (Perrone, Stockel, and Krueger 1989).

In 1989 the Citizens' Clearinghouse for Hazardous Wastes organized a conference to address women's experiences as environmental activists (Zeff, Love, and Stults 1989). Excerpts from the conference report are included in Reading 78. When women become involved with environmental justice organizing, they become politicized (Gibbs 1995, 1998; Krauss 1993; Zeff, Love, and Stults 1989). They are suddenly caught up in meetings, maybe traveling to other towns and cities and staying away overnight. They spend much more time, and money, on the phone than before. They are quoted in the local papers or on the TV news. They often face new challenges, balancing family responsibilities, perhaps struggling with their husbands' misgivings about their involvement, or facing the tensions of being strong women in male-dominated communities. As mentioned in our discussion of antimilitarist activism in the previous chapter, motherhood also provides a powerful stimulus for environmental justice activism (Glazer and Glazer 1998), as exemplified in Reading 77 and Reading 78. Such women activists see their identity as women integrated with their racial and class identities, with race and/or class often more a place of empowerment for them than gender. While recognizing gender subordination, they are not interested in separating themselves from the men in their communities and frame their perspectives, as women, in class- and race-conscious ways.

Connectedness and Sustainability

Underlying and implicit in these various perspectives are ideas of connectedness, relationship, respect, and responsibility: among people, nonhuman species, and the natural world. The activists mentioned in this chapter all work from their sense of relationship and responsibility to maintain these connections or to remake them where they have been severed. Together such projects and movements draw on alternative visions and strategies for sustainable living, however small-scale and fragile they might be at present. At root this is about taking on the current economic system and the systems of power — personal and institutional — that sustain and benefit from it, working to transform relationships of exploitation and oppression.

The idea of sustainability is often invoked but means very different things to different people. For corporate economists, for example, it means sustained economic growth that will yield sustained profits; for ecologists it involves the maintenance of natural systems — wetlands, forests, wilderness, air and water quality; for environmentalists it means using only renewable resources and generating low or nonaccumulating levels of pollution (Pearce, Markandya, and Barbier 1990). Many concerned with environmental economics note the contradiction between the linear expansionism of current capitalist economies and long-term sustainability (Daly and Cobb 1989; Henderson 1991; O'Connor 1994). Maria Mies (1993) notes that for countries of the South to follow the development model of the industrial North there would need to be two more worlds: one for the necessary natural resources and the other for the waste. A more sustainable future for both North and South means rethinking current economic systems and priorities and emphasizing ecologically sound production to meet people's basic needs, as argued by H. Patricia Hynes (Reading 80). A sustainable future implies local control over transnational corporations, reduction of poor countries' foreign debt, and making money available for development that is ecologically sound, as we suggested in Chapter 7. At a local level in the United States it implies support for community gardens, farmers' markets, credit unions, and small-scale worker-owned businesses and markets, as we suggested in Chapter 8. It means valuing women's unpaid domestic and caring work, a key aspect of sustaining home and community life (Mellor 1992; Waring 1988). Mellor notes that this work is geared to biological time. Children need feeding when they are hungry; sick people need care regardless of what time of day it is; gardens need planting in the right season. She argues that, given a gendered division of labor, "women's responsibility for biological time means that men have been able to create a public world that largely ignores it," a world "no longer rooted in the physical reality of human existence" (pp. 258–59). A sustainable future must be based in biological time and will require emotional as well as physical and intellectual labor. Novels provide an effective way of showing the possibilities—positive and negative—of particular philosophies and societal arrangements, and they can help us to imagine different futures (e.g., Butler 1993; Piercy 1976; Starhawk 1993).

To create such a future will also mean changing current definitions of wealth that emphasize materialism and consumerism. A broader notion of wealth includes everything that has the potential to enrich a person and a community, such as health, physical energy and strength, safety and security, time, skills, talents, wisdom, creativity, love, community support, a connection to one's history and cultural heritage, and a sense of belonging. This is not a philosophy of denial or a romanticization of poverty, though it does involve a fundamental **paradigm shift,** or change of perspective, in a country—indeed, a world—so dominated by the allure of material wealth. Writers included in this chapter all implicitly or explicitly argue for a profound change in attitudes, in which human life and the life of the natural world are valued, cared for, and sustained. Reading 47 (Chapter 7) by Diverse Women for Diversity is also relevant here.

◆◆◆
Questions for Reflection

As you read and discuss this chapter, ask yourself these questions:

1. What does it mean to be part of an interconnected chain of life?

2. What are the main environmental issues in your area?

3. Is there a farmers' market in your area? Are there community gardens in your area?

4. Do you have access to a compost pile or worm box?

5. What are the main illnesses in your area? Are they linked to environmental causes?

6. Think about the practical projects mentioned in the readings for this chapter. What resources were used by the people involved? What worldviews are implicit in their actions?

7. What is your vision of a sustainable future?

◆◆◆
Taking Action

1. Find out about environmental organizations in your area. What are their goals and perspectives? What projects are they currently working on? How could you participate in or support their work?

2. Find out about the people who used to live where you live now. What happened to the Native American people who used to live on this land? Are there other groups who

used to live here? How did they support themselves? Why did they move? Where are they now? How are they living now?

3. How big is your ecological footprint? Work out how to make it smaller.

S E V E N T Y - F O U R

◆◆◆

Principles of Environmental Justice

The First National People of Color Environmental Leadership Summit

October 24–27, 1991
Washington, D.C.

Preamble

We, the people of color, gathered together at this multinational People of Color Environmental Leadership Summit, to begin to build a national and international movement of all peoples of color to fight the destruction and taking of our lands and communities, do hereby re-establish our spiritual interdependence to the sacredness of our Mother Earth; to respect and celebrate each of our cultures, languages and beliefs about the natural world and our roles in healing ourselves; to ensure environmental justice; to promote economic alternatives which would contribute to the development of environmentally safe livelihoods; and, to secure our political, economic and cultural liberation that has been denied for over 500 years of colonization and oppression, resulting in the poisoning of our communities and land and the genocide of our peoples, do affirm and adopt these Principles of Environmental Justice:

1. *Environmental justice* affirms the sacredness of Mother Earth, ecological unity and the interdependence of all species, and the right to be free from ecological destruction.

2. *Environmental justice* demands that public policy be based on mutual respect and justice for all peoples, free from any form of discrimination or bias.

3. *Environmental justice* mandates the right to ethical, balanced and responsible uses of land and renewable resources in the inter-est of a sustainable planet for humans and other living things.

4. *Environmental justice* calls for universal protection from nuclear testing, extraction, production and disposal of toxic/hazardous wastes and poisons and nuclear testing that threaten the fundamental right to clean air, land, water, and food.

5. *Environmental justice* affirms the fundamental right to political, economic, cultural and environmental self-determination of all peoples.

6. *Environmental justice* demands the cessation of the production of all toxins, hazardous wastes, and radioactive materials, and that all past and current producers be held strictly accountable to the people for detoxification and the containment at the point of production.

7. *Environmental justice* demands the right to participate as equal partners at every level of decision-making including needs assessment, planning, implementation, enforcement and evaluation.

8. *Environmental justice* affirms the right of all workers to a safe and healthy work environment, without being forced to choose between an unsafe livelihood and unemployment. It also affirms the right of those who work at home to be free from environmental hazards.

9. *Environmental justice* protects the right of victims of environmental injustice to receive full compensation and reparations for damages as well as quality health care.

10. *Environmental justice* considers governmental acts of environmental injustice a violation of international law, the Universal Declaration on Human Rights, and the United Nations Convention on Genocide.

11. *Environmental justice* must recognize a special legal and natural relationship of Native Peoples to the U.S. government through treaties, agreements, compacts, and covenants affirming sovereignty and self-determination.

12. *Environmental justice* affirms the need for urban and rural ecological policies to clean up and rebuild our cities and rural areas in balance with nature, honoring the cultural integrity of all our communities, and providing fair access for all to the full range of resources.

13. *Environmental justice* calls for the strict enforcement of principles of informed consent, and a halt to the testing of experimental reproductive and medical procedures and vaccinations on people of color.

14. *Environmental justice* opposes the destructive operations of multi-national corporations.

15. *Environmental justice* opposes military occupation, repression and exploitation of lands, peoples and cultures, and other life forms.

16. *Environmental justice* calls for the education of present and future generations which emphasizes social and environmental issues, based on our experience and an appreciation of our diverse cultural perspectives.

17. *Environmental justice* requires that we, as individuals, make personal and consumer choices to consume as little of Mother Earth's resources and to produce as little waste as possible; and make the conscious decision to challenge and reprioritize our lifestyles to ensure the health of the natural world for present and future generations.

Adopted, October 27, 1991
The First National People of Color
   Environmental Leadership Summit
Washington, D.C.

SEVENTY-FIVE

◆◆◆

Asians and Pacific Islanders in the Environment

Booapha Toommaly

My name is Bouapha Toommaly. I am from one of the Laotian tribal groups called Khmmu. We are considered the indigenous people of Laos. In fact, when we talk in the Khmmu language about Native Americans we call them the Khmmu of America.

We have had a hard time moving from the hills of Laos to Richmond. One day our folks were farmers and hunters — just like their ancestors — and the next day we were fighting a war for the United States, running into Thai refugee camps, and then taking a jet plane to the U.S.

As our people moved into many parts of the U.S. they heard through the grapevine about Richmond's weather. They heard about the jobs, and they moved because grandma and grandpa were already living here — the last reason is why my family moved from

San Francisco to the East Bay. It is important for us to be near our extended family because Laotians are used to living in small villages.

I thought that this situation was unique to my family. Then I learned that across many urban areas around the country, Southeast Asian refugees have settled in the poorest and most environmentally sick areas of their cities and they suffer alongside their African American and Latino neighbors. I don't think this stuff happened by chance.

We are overlooked because of our small numbers and because we don't speak English. Don't overlook us, we have lived off of the land for hundreds of years. We know some things about taking care of the land. To this day Laotian women still like to grow their own vegetables in their small yards and men in our community still go fishing in our toxic bay to put food on the table. Richmond should be clean enough so we can continue to think of the land and water as good things, not poisonous things.

I think we have a special role as indigenous people to teach people to respect the land, air, and water so that no matter where we live we can be healthy and happy.

SEVENTY-SIX

Native Hawaiian Historical and Cultural Perspectives on Environmental Justice

Mililani Trask

When you ask a Hawaiian who they are, their response is "Keiki hanau o ka aina, child that is borne up from the land." I am a Native Hawaiian attorney. I also have the great honor and distinction, and the great burden and responsibility, of being the first elected Kia'Aina of Ka Lahui Hawai'i, the sovereign nation of the Native Hawaiian people, which we created ourselves in 1987.

It's a great pleasure and honor for me to be here to address a group such as yourselves, such a momentous occasion, the first time that the people of color will gather to consider the impacts on our common land base.

I thought I would begin by giving a little bit of history about Hawaii Nei because many people are not aware of the crisis there and the status of the Native Hawaiian people. As we approach the United Nations' celebration of the discoverers, we are celebrating not only the arrival of Columbus but also of Cortez and Captain Cook. In Hawaii Nei we are celebrating 500 years of resilient resistance to the coming of the "discoverers."

In 1778 Captain James Cook sailed into the Hawaiian archipelago. He found there a thriving Native community of 800,000 Native people, living in balance on their lands, completely economically self-sufficient, feeding and clothing themselves off of the resources of their own land base. Within one generation, 770,000 of our people were dead—dead from what is called "mai haole, the sickness of the

white man," which Cook brought: venereal disease, flu, pox, the same tragic history that occurred on the American continent to Native American Indians and the Native people of Central and South America.

In 1893 the United States Marines dispatched a group of soldiers to the Island of Oahu for the purpose of overthrowing the lawful kingdom of Hawaii Nei. Prior to 1893, Hawaii was welcomed into the world family of nations and maintained over 20 international treaties, including treaties of friendship and peace with the United States. Despite those international laws, revolution was perpetrated against our government, and our lawful government overthrown. In two years we will mark the hundredth anniversary of when we had the right to be self-determining and self-governing.

In 1959, Hawaii was admitted into the Union of the United States of America. There were great debates that occurred in Washington, DC that focused on the fact that people were afraid to incorporate the Territory of Hawaii because it would become the first state in the union in which white people would be a minority of less than 25 percent. That was the reason for the concern when those debates were launched. In 1959, when Hawaii became a state, something happened that did not happen in any other state of the union. In all of the other states, when the U.S. admitted that state into the union, America set aside lands for the Native people of those states, as federal reserves. Today there is a policy that provides that Native Americans should be self-governing, should be allowed to maintain their nations, should be allowed to pass laws, environmental and otherwise, to protect their land base. That did not occur in the State of Hawaii. In the State

———————
*This paper was presented at the First National People of Color Environmental Leadership Summit, October 24–27, 1991, Washington, D.C.

of Hawaii in 1959, the federal government gave our lands to the state to be held in trust, and gave the Native Hawaiian people, of which there are 200,000, the status of perpetual wardship. We are not allowed to form governments if we are Native Hawaiian; we are not allowed to control our land base. To this day our lands are controlled by state agencies and utilized extensively by the American military complex as part of a plan designed by Hawaii's Senator Daniel Inouye.

In 1987 we decided to exercise our inherent rights to be self-governing. The Hawaii Visitors Bureau declared 1987 the Year of the Hawaiian for a great tourist and media campaign. We took a look at our statistics: 22,000 families on lists waiting for land entitlements since 1920; 30,000 families dead waiting for their Hawaiian homelands awards; 22,000 currently waiting. We thought to ourselves, how are *we* going to celebrate 1987? And we decided that the time had come to convene a constitutional convention to resurrect our nation and to exert our basic and inherent rights, much to the dismay and consternation of the state and the federal government, and certainly to the shock of Senator Inouye.

We have passed a constitution that recognizes the right and the responsibility of Native people to protect their land base and to ensure water quality, because Western laws have been unable to protect the environment. We decided to lift up and resurrect our nation in 1987, passing our constitution, and we are proceeding now to come out, to announce that we are alive and well, and to network with other people.

I have come to announce that a state of emergency exists with regards to the natural environment of the archipelagic lands and waters of Hawaii, and also a state of emergency exists with regards to the survival of the Native people who live there and throughout the Pacific basin. We have many environmental injustices and issues that need to be addressed; most of them have dire global consequences. The expansion of the United States military complex presents substantial threats to our environment.

Right now on the Island of Hawaii and on the Island of Kauai, Senator Inouye is pressing for what he calls the "space-porting initiative," which we all know to be Star Wars. It will distribute large amounts of toxic gases, it will scorch the earth beyond repair and, most importantly and offensive to us, the lands that have been chosen are lands set aside by the Congress in 1920 for the homesteading of Hawaiian

people. These are the lands that are pursued on the Island of Hawaii.

Our response to that is "kapu Ka'u." Ka'u is the district; kapu is the Hawaiian way for saying, "It is taboo." We cannot allow desecration of sacred lands, desecration of historic properties that are the cultural inheritance of our people to be converted for the military complex and for the designs of those who would further the interests of war against others. It is an inappropriate use of Native lands.

Other Threats

The United States Navy continues its relentless bombing of Kahoolawe Island. Not only have they denuded the upper one-third of that island, but as they have blasted away the lands, trees and shrubs, all that silt has come down to the channels between Kahoolawe and Maui Islands, the channels that are the spawning grounds of the whales that migrate every year to Hawaii Nei.

We now have information coming from Lualualie on the Island of Oahu that there is a very high incidence of leukemia and other cancers among the Hawaiian children who live there. We believe that this is due to electromagnetic contamination. In Lualualie the United States military is taking control of 2,000 acres of Hawaiian homelands, lands set aside by the Congress to homestead our people. These lands were taken over and converted for a nuclear and military storage facility. Ten years ago, in 1981, they issued a report saying that there's electromagnetic radiation there. After the report was issued all the military families were moved out of the base, but nobody told the Hawaiian community that lives in the surrounding area. We have taken it to the Western courts, we have been thrown out, because the court ruled that Native Hawaiians are wards of the state and the federal government. Therefore, Native Hawaiians are not allowed standing to sue in the federal courts to protect our trust land assets. We are the only class of Native Americans, and the only class of American citizens, that are not allowed access to the federal court system to seek redress of grievances relating to breach of trust.

Ka Lahui Hawai'i is pleased and proud to join all of the other Pacific Island nations in opposing the federal policy which is being perpetrated by Mr. Bush and Senator Inouye identifying the Pacific region as a national sacrifice area. What is a national sacrifice area? I did some legal research and I found out that national sacrifice areas usually occur on Indian reservations or in black communities. They are areas that the nation identifies primarily for the dumping of toxic wastes. As the Greens celebrate in Europe what they perceive to be an environmental victory in forcing America to remove its nuclear and military wastes from Europe, we in the Pacific region have been told that Johnston Island and other Pacific nations have been targeted for storage and dumping. We will not allow that and we will continue to speak out against it.

Tourist Evils

Tourism and its attendant evils continue to assault our island land base. Hundreds of thousands of tourists come to Hawaii every year. They are seeking a dream of paradise. They drink our water, they contaminate our environment. They are responsible for millions of tons of sewage every year, which is deposited into the Pacific Ocean. And, in addition, they are taking lands from our rural communities.

Tourism perpetuates certain Western concepts of exclusive rights to land. Tourists don't like to see other people on their beaches. Tourists don't like to allow Native people to go and fish in the traditional ways. And, because of toxification of the ocean due to release of sewage in Hawaii, there are many places where you can no longer find the reef fish. You cannot go there and take the opihi, the squid, or take the turtle, because they're gone now. So in the few remaining areas where there are fish, the state and federal governments have imposed public park restrictions to prevent Native people from going there to lay the net and take the fish. If the fish are taken out, what will the tourists see when they put on their snorkels? Native people are not allowed to fish so that tourists can view through their goggles what remains of the few species we have because their own tourist practices destroyed all the rest of the bounty of our fisheries.

Tourists need golf courses; golf courses need tons of pesticides, herbicides and millions of tons of water. Hawaii is an island ecology, we do not get fresh water from flowing streams. All the water that falls from the rain in Hawaii is percolated through the lava of the islands and comes to rest in a central basal lens underneath our island. As the rains percolate down they bring with them all the herbicides and pesticides that have been used for years by agribusiness: King Cane, Dole Pineapple, United States military. Already on the island of Oahu we have had to permanently close two of our drinking wells because of toxification. Nobody in the State of Hawaii or the Hawaii Visitors Bureau is going to tell you that at the present time there are 30 contaminants in the drinking water in the State of Hawaii.

The specter of geothermal development lays heavily upon our lands. For 25 years the United States and its allies have been developing geothermal energy in Hawaii. It is destroying the last Pacific tropical rain forest on the Island of Hawaii, Wao Kele o Puna Forest, sacred to the lands of Tutu Pele, our Grandmother Pele, who erupts and gives birth to the earth. This is her home, yet this is the place where they are developing geothermal. And as it proceeds, Native people are denied their basic right to worship there. We have taken this case to the United States Supreme Court. It was struck down along with the Native American freedom of religion cases because the court ruled that religious worship in America must be "site-specific." If you take the Akua, if you put God in the building, American courts will understand. But if you take God and say, "The earth is the Lord's and the fullness of it, the Black Hills of South Dakota, the lands and forests of Tutu Pele," American courts do not understand.

This past year we have had two geothermal explosions in the State of Hawaii. Despite the fact that we were in court to stop geothermal development while the Civil Defense removed 1,000 families and a state of emergency was declared, the governor and representatives of these developers issued press statements celebrating the explosion. They said it demonstrated that there was a great deal more energy they could harvest than initially anticipated. Their press releases ceased 48 hours after the explosion when it was reported that Hawaii had now recorded its first prenatal death as a result of geothermal toxicity. That case will proceed to court but I can tell you one thing: there is no jury award, no amount of Kala (the white man's dollar) that will compensate the family that lost that child. There's no dollar figure for that kind of loss.

International fishing practices, gill netting and drift netting, are genocide in the sea. As a result of these practices, the Native fisheries are diminished and depleted. In some areas our marine fisheries are depleted to the point that we can no longer harvest that resource.

What is the appropriate response to this environmental and human outrage? In Hawaii Nei we have undertaken to address these things through sovereignty and the basic exertion of the rights of Native people to govern and control their own land base. These are political issues, certainly. But they spring from a very ancient source, a source within our heart, a source that all Natives and people of color understand: our relationship in the global context. As Hawaiians say, "Keiki hanau o ka cuna, child that is borne up from the land," understanding that there is an innate connection to the earth as the Mother. We are called upon now as the guardians of our sacred lands to rise up in the defense of our Mother. You don't subdivide your Mother, you don't chop her body up, you don't drill, penetrate and pull out her lifeblood. You protect and nurture your Mother. And the Hawaiian value for that is aloha ai'na, love for the land, malama ai'na, care and nurturing for the land. It is reciprocal. It gives back to the Native people. Our people know that the Akua put us here on this earth to be guardians of these sacred lands. It is a God-given responsibility and trust that a sovereign nation must assume if it is to have any integrity. And so we in Ka Lahui have undertaken this struggle. Environmental racism is the enemy. The question is, What is our response? What really is environmental justice? I'll tell you one thing I learned in law school at Santa Clara. Do you know how they perceive and teach justice, the white schools of this country? A blind white woman with her eyes covered up by cloth, holding the scales of justice. And if you look at it, they're not balanced. The Native scale and the environmental scale are outweighed by other priorities.

Well, environmental justice is not a blindfolded white woman. When I saw the woman with the scales of justice in law school, I thought to myself, "You know, if you blindfold yourself the only thing you're going to do is walk into walls." You are not going to resolve anything. And that's where we are with Western law. I know that there are many attorneys here and others who are working on environmental cases. I support them. We have received a great deal of support from attorneys working in environmental law. But do not put your eggs in the basket of the blind white lady. We must try other approaches.

In closing, I would like to say in behalf of myself and the Hawaii delegation that we are very renewed in coming here, and that when we return to Hawaii in two or three days we will have good news to share with our people, that we have come ourselves these many thousands of miles, that we have looked in the faces of people of color, that we have seen there, in their hearts and in their eyes, a light shining, a light of commitment, a light that is filled with capacity and a light that is filled with love for the Mother Earth, a light that is the same that we have in our hearts.

I try to do one thing whenever I finish speaking. I try to leave the podium by telling people what the motto of Ka Lahui Hawaii is, the motto of our nation that we're forming now. I find it to be very applicable to the situations that we are in. We are facing a difficult struggle. Every bit of commitment and energy is needed to save our Mother Earth and to ensure the survival of our people and all of the species of the earth. It is a difficult row to hoe. There is going to be a great deal of strife and a great deal of pain. But we must proceed; we have no alternative. This is the same position that the native people of Hawaii Nei found themselves in 1987 when we committed to resurrecting our national government. And at the time that we passed that constitution we also adopted a motto. It is a motto that I think you might want to live by as we proceed in this environmental war that we are waging. That motto is: "A difficult birth does not make the baby any less beautiful."

◆◆◆

SEVENTY-SEVEN

Mexican American Women
Grassroots Community Activists
"Mothers of East Los Angeles"
Mary Pardo

The relatively few studies of Chicana political activism show a bias in the way political activism is conceptualized by social scientists, who often use a narrow definition confined to electoral politics. Most feminist research uses an expanded definition that moves across the boundaries between public, electoral politics and private, family politics; but feminist research generally focuses on women mobilized around gender-specific issues. For some feminists, adherence to "tradition" constitutes conservatism and submission to patriarchy. Both approaches exclude the contributions of working-class women, particularly those of Afro-American women and Latinas, thus failing to capture the full dynamic of social change.

The following case study of Mexican American women activists in "Mothers of East Los Angeles" (MELA) contributes another dimension to the conception of grassroots politics. It illustrates how these Mexican American women transform "traditional" networks and resources based on family and culture into political assets to defend the quality of urban life. Far from unique, these patterns of activism are repeated in Latin America and elsewhere. Here as in other times and places, the women's activism arises out of seemingly "traditional" roles, addresses wider social and political issues, and capitalizes on informal associations sanctioned by the community. Religion, commonly viewed as a conservative force, is intertwined with politics. Often, women speak of their communities and their activism as extensions of their family and household responsibility. The central role of women in grassroots struggles around quality of life, in the Third World and in the United States, challenges conventional assumptions about the powerlessness of women and static definitions of culture and tradition.

In general, the women in MELA are longtime residents of East Los Angeles; some are bilingual and

native born, others Mexican born and Spanish dominant. All the core activists are bilingual and have lived in the community over thirty years. All have been active in parish-sponsored groups and activities; some have had experience working in community-based groups arising from schools, neighborhood watch associations, and labor support groups. To gain an appreciation of the group and the core activists, I used ethnographic field methods. I interviewed six women, using a life history approach focused on their first community activities, current activism, household and family responsibilities, and perceptions of community issues. Also, from December 1987 through October 1989, I attended hearings on the two currently pending projects of contention—a proposed state prison and a toxic waste incinerator—and participated in community and organizational meetings and demonstrations. The following discussion briefly chronicles an intense and significant five-year segment of community history from which emerged MELA and the women's transformation of "traditional" resources and experiences into political assets for community mobilization.

The Community Context:
East Los Angeles Resisting Siege

Political science theory often guides the political strategies used by local government to select the sites for undesirable projects. In 1984, the state of California commissioned a public relations firm to assess the political difficulties facing the construction of energy-producing waste incinerators. The report provided a "personality profile" of those residents most likely to organize effective opposition to projects:

middle and upper socioeconomic strata possess better resources to effectuate their opposition. Middle and higher socioeconomic strata neighborhoods should not fall within the one-mile and five-mile radii of the proposed site. Conversely, older people, people with a high school education or less are least likely to oppose a facility.

The state accordingly placed the plant in Commerce, a predominantly Mexican American, low-income community. This pattern holds throughout the state and the country: three out of five Afro-Americans and Latinos live near toxic waste sites, and three of the five largest hazardous waste landfills are in communities with at least 80 percent minority populations.

Similarly, in March 1985, when the state sought a site for the first state prison in Los Angeles County, Governor Deukmejian resolved to place the 1,700-inmate institution in East Los Angeles, within a mile of the long-established Boyle Heights neighborhood and within two miles of thirty-four schools. Furthermore, violating convention, the state bid on the expensive parcel of industrially zoned land without compiling an environmental impact report or providing a public community hearing. According to James Vigil, Jr., a field representative for Assemblywoman Gloria Molina, shortly after the state announced the site selection, Molina's office began informing the community and gauging residents' sentiments about it through direct mailings and calls to leaders of organizations and business groups.

In spring 1986, after much pressure from the 56th assembly district office and the community, the Department of Corrections agreed to hold a public information meeting, which was attended by over 700 Boyle Heights residents. From this moment on, Vigil observed, "the tables turned, the community mobilized, and the residents began calling the political representatives and requesting their presence at hearings and meetings." By summer 1986, the community was well aware of the prison site proposal. Over two thousand people, carrying placards proclaiming "No Prison in ELA" marched from Resurrection Church in Boyle Heights to the 3rd Street bridge linking East Los Angeles with the rapidly expanding downtown Los Angeles. This march marked the beginning of one of the largest grassroots coalitions to emerge from the Latino community in the last decade.

Prominent among the coalition's groups is "Mothers of East Los Angeles," a loosely knit group of over 400 Mexican American women. MELA initially coalesced to oppose the state prison construction but has since organized opposition to several other projects detrimental to the quality of life in the central city. Its second large target is a toxic waste incinerator proposed for Vernon, a small city adjacent to East Los Angeles. This incinerator would worsen the already debilitating air quality of the entire county and set a precedent dangerous for other communities throughout California. When MELA took up the fight against the toxic waste incinerator, it became more than a single-issue group and began working with environmental groups around the state. As a result of the community struggle, AB58 (Roybal-Allard), which provides all Californians with the minimum protection of an environmental impact report before the construction of hazardous waste incinerators, was signed into law. But the law's effectiveness relies on a watchful community network. Since its emergence, "Mothers of East Los Angeles" has become centrally important to just such a network of grassroots activists including a select number of Catholic priests and two Mexican American political representatives. Furthermore, the group's very formation, and its continued spirit and activism, fly in the face of the conventional political science beliefs regarding political participation.

Predictions by the "experts" attribute the low formal political participation (i.e., voting) of Mexican American people in the U.S. to a set of cultural "retardants" including primary kinship systems, fatalism, religious traditionalism, traditional cultural values, and mother country attachment. The core activists in MELA may appear to fit this description, as well as the state-commissioned profile of residents least likely to oppose toxic waste incinerator projects. All the women live in a low-income community. Furthermore, they identify themselves as active and committed participants in the Catholic Church; they claim an ethnic identity—Mexican American; their ages range from forty to sixty; and they have attained at most high school educations. However, these women fail to conform to the predicted political apathy. Instead, they have transformed social identity—ethnic identity, class identity, and gender identity—into an impetus as well as a basis for activism. And, in transforming their existing social networks into grassroots political networks, they have also transformed themselves.

Transformation
as a Dominant Theme

From the life histories of the group's core activists and from my own field notes, I have selected excerpts that tell two representative stories. One is a narrative of the events that led to community mobilization in East Los Angeles. The other is a story of transformation, the process of creating new and better relationships that empower people to unite and achieve common goals.

First, women have transformed organizing experiences and social networks arising from gender-related responsibilities into political resources. When I asked the women about the first community, not necessarily "political," involvement they could recall, they discussed experiences that predated the formation of MELA. Juana Gutiérrez explained:

> Well, it didn't start with the prison, you know. It started when my kids went to school. I started by joining the Parents Club and we worked on different problems here in the area. Like the people who come to the parks to sell drugs to the kids. I got the neighbors to have meetings. I would go knock at the doors, house to house. And I told them that we should stick together with the Neighborhood Watch for the community and for the kids.

Erlinda Robles similarly recalled:

> I wanted my kids to go to Catholic school and from the time my oldest one went there, I was there every day. I used to take my two little ones with me and I helped one way or another. I used to question things they did. And the other mothers would just watch me. Later, they would ask me, "Why do you do that? They are going to take it out on your kids." I'd say, "They better not." And before you knew it, we had a big group of mothers that were very involved.

Part of a mother's "traditional" responsibility includes overseeing her child's progress in school, interacting with school staff, and supporting school activities. In these processes, women meet other mothers and begin developing a network of acquaintanceships and friendships based on mutual concern for the welfare of their children.

Although the women in MELA carried the greatest burden of participating in school activities, Erlinda Robles also spoke of strategies they used to draw men into the enterprise and into the networks:

> At the beginning, the priests used to say who the president of the mothers guild would be; they used to pick 'um. But, we wanted elections, so we got elections. Then we wanted the fathers to be involved, and the nuns suggested that a father should be president and a mother would be secretary or be involved there [at the school site].

Of course, this comment piqued my curiosity, so I asked how the mothers agreed on the nuns' suggestion. The answer was simple and instructive:

> At the time we thought it was a "natural" way to get the fathers involved because they weren't involved; it was just the mothers. Everybody [the women] agreed on them [the fathers] being president because they worked all day and they couldn't be involved in a lot of daily activities like food sales and whatever. During the week, a steering committee of mothers planned the group's activities. But now that I think about it, a woman could have done the job just as well!

So women got men into the group by giving them a position they could manage. The men may have held the title of "president," but they were not making day-to-day decisions about work, nor were they dictating the direction of the group. Erlinda Robles laughed as she recalled an occasion when the president insisted, against the wishes of the women, on scheduling a parents' group fundraiser—a breakfast—on Mother's Day. On that morning, only the president and his wife were present to prepare breakfast. This should alert researchers against measuring power and influence by looking solely at who holds titles.

Each of the cofounders had a history of working with groups arising out of the responsibilities usually assumed by "mothers"—the education of children and the safety of the surrounding community. From these groups, they gained valuable experiences and networks that facilitated the formation of "Mothers of East Los Angeles." Juana Gutiérrez explained how preexisting networks progressively expanded community support:

You know nobody knew about the plan to build a prison in this community until Assemblywoman Gloria Molina told me. Martha Molina called me and said, "You know what is happening in your area? The governor wants to put a prison in Boyle Heights!" So, I called a Neighborhood Watch meeting at my house and we got fifteen people together. Then, Father John started informing his people at the Church and that is when the group of two to three hundred started showing up for every march on the bridge.

MELA effectively linked up preexisting networks into a viable grassroots coalition.

Second, the process of activism also transformed previously "invisible" women, making them not only visible but the center of public attention. From a conventional perspective, political activism assumes a kind of gender neutrality. This means that anyone can participate, but men are the expected key actors. In accordance with this pattern, in winter 1986 an informal group of concerned businessmen in the community began lobbying and testifying against the prison at hearings in Sacramento. Working in conjunction with Assemblywoman Molina, they made many trips to Sacramento at their own expense. Residents who did not have the income to travel were unable to join them. Finally, Molina, commonly recognized as a forceful advocate for Latinas and the community, asked Frank Villalobos, an urban planner in the group, why there were no women coming up to speak in Sacramento against the prison. As he phrased it, "I was getting some heat from her because no women were going up there."

In response to this comment, Veronica Gutiérrez, a law student who lived in the community, agreed to accompany him on the next trip to Sacramento. He also mentioned the comment to Father John Moretta at Resurrection Catholic Parish. Meanwhile, representatives of the business sector of the community and of the 56th assembly district office were continuing to compile arguments and supportive data against the East Los Angeles prison site. Frank Villalobos stated one of the pressing problems:

We felt that the Senators whom we prepared all this for didn't even acknowledge that we existed. They kept calling it the "downtown" site, and they argued that there was no op-

position in the community. So, I told Father Moretta, what we have to do is demonstrate that there is a link (proximity) between the Boyle Heights community and the prison.

The next juncture illustrates how perceptions of gender-specific behavior set in motion a sequence of events that brought women into the political limelight. Father Moretta decided to ask all the women to meet after mass. He told them about the prison site and called for their support. When I asked him about his rationale for selecting the women, he replied:

I felt so strongly about the issue, and I knew in my heart what a terrible offense this was to the people. So, I was afraid that once we got into a demonstration situation we had to be very careful. I thought the women would be cooler and calmer than the men. The bottom line is that the men came anyway. The first times out the majority were women. Then they began to invite their husbands and their children, but originally it was just women.

Father Moretta also named the group. Quite moved by a film, *The Official Story,* about the courageous Argentine women who demonstrated for the return of their children who disappeared during a repressive right-wing military dictatorship, he transformed the name "Las Madres de la Plaza de Mayo" into "Mothers of East Los Angeles."

However, Aurora Castillo, one of the cofounders of the group, modified my emphasis on the predominance of women:

Of course the fathers work. We also have many, many grandmothers. And all this IS with the support of the fathers. They make the placards and the posters; they do the security and carry the signs; and they come to the marches when they can.

Although women played a key role in the mobilization, they emphasized the group's broad base of active supporters as well as the other organizations in the "Coalition Against the Prison." Their intent was to counter any notion that MELA was composed exclusively of women or mothers and to stress the "inclusiveness" of the group. All the women who assumed lead roles in the group had long histories of volunteer work in the Boyle Heights community;

but formation of the group brought them out of the "private" margins and into "public" light.

Third, the women in "Mothers of East L.A." have transformed the definition of "mother" to include militant political opposition to state-proposed projects they see as adverse to the quality of life in the community. Explaining how she discovered the issue, Aurora Castillo said,

> You know if one of your children's safety is jeopardized, the mother turns into a lioness. That's why Father John got the mothers. We have to have a well-organized, strong group of mothers to protect the community and oppose things that are detrimental to us. You know the governor is in the wrong and the mothers are in the right. After all, the mothers have to be right. Mothers are for the children's interest, not for self-interest; the governor is for his own political interest.

The women also have expanded the boundaries of "motherhood" to include social and political community activism and redefined the word to include women who are not biological "mothers." At one meeting a young Latina expressed her solidarity with the group and, almost apologetically, qualified herself as a "resident," not a "mother," of East Los Angeles. Erlinda Robles replied:

> When you are fighting for a better life for children and "doing" for them, isn't that what mothers do? So we're all mothers. You don't have to have children to be a "mother."

At critical points, grassroots community activism requires attending many meetings, phone calling, and door-to-door communications—all very labor-intensive work. In order to keep harmony in the "domestic" sphere, the core activists must creatively integrate family members into their community activities. I asked Erlinda Robles how her husband felt about her activism, and she replied quite openly:

> My husband doesn't like getting involved, but he takes me because he knows I like it. Sometimes we would have two or three meetings a week. And my husband would say, "Why are you doing so much? It is really getting out of hand." But he is very supportive. Once he gets there, he enjoys it and he starts in arguing

too! See, it's just that he is not used to it. He couldn't believe things happened the way that they do. He was in the Navy twenty years and they brainwashed him that none of the politicians could do wrong. So he has come a long way. Now he comes home and parks the car out front and asks me, "Well, where are we going tonight?"

When women explain their activism, they link family and community as one entity. Juana Gutiérrez, a woman with extensive experience working on community and neighborhood issues, stated:

> Yo como madre de familia, y como residente del Este de Los Angeles, seguiré luchando sin descanso por que se nos respete. Y yo lo hago con bastante cariño hacia mi comunidad. Digo "mi comunidad," porque me siento parte de ella, quiero a mi raza como parte de mi familia, y si Dios me permite seguiré luchando contra todos los gobernadores que quieran abusar de nosotros. (As a mother and a resident of East L.A., I shall continue fighting tirelessly, so we will be respected. And I will do this with much affection for my community. I say "my community" because I am part of it. I love my "raza" [race] as part of my family; and if God allows, I will keep on fighting against all the governors that want to take advantage of us.)

Like the other activists, she has expanded her responsibilities and legitimated militant opposition to abuse of the community by representatives of the state.

Working-class women activists seldom opt to separate themselves from men and their families. In this particular struggle for community quality of life, they are fighting for the family unit and thus are not competitive with men. Of course, this fact does not preclude different alignments in other contexts and situations.

Fourth, the story of MELA also shows the transformation of class and ethnic identity. Aurora Castillo told of an incident that illustrated her growing knowledge of the relationship of East Los Angeles to other communities and the basis necessary for coalition building:

> And do you know we have been approached by other groups? [She lowers her voice in em-

phasis.] You know that Pacific Palisades group asked for our backing. But what they did, they sent their powerful lobbyist that they pay thousands of dollars to get our support against the drilling in Pacific Palisades. So what we did was tell them to send their grassroots people, not their lobbyist. We're suspicious. We don't want to talk to a high-salaried lobbyist; we are humble people. We did our own lobbying. In one week we went to Sacramento twice.

The contrast between the often tedious and labor-intensive work of mobilizing people at the "grassroots" level and the paid work of a "high-salaried lobbyist" represents a point of pride and integrity, not a deficiency or a source of shame. If the two groups were to construct a coalition, they must communicate on equal terms.

The women of MELA combine a willingness to assert opposition with a critical assessment of their own weaknesses. At one community meeting, for example, representatives of several oil companies attempted to gain support for placement of an oil pipeline through the center of East Los Angeles. The exchange between the women in the audience and the oil representative was heated, as women alternated asking questions about the chosen route for the pipeline:

> "Is it going through Cielito Lindo [Reagan's ranch]?" The oil representative answered, "No." Another woman stood up and asked, "Why not place it along the coastline?" Without thinking of the implications, the representative responded, "Oh, no! If it burst, it would endanger the marine life." The woman retorted, "You value the marine life more than human beings?" His face reddened with anger and the hearing disintegrated into angry chanting.

The proposal was quickly defeated. But Aurora Castillo acknowledged that it was not solely their opposition that brought about the defeat:

> We won because the westside was opposed to it, so we united with them. You know there are a lot of attorneys who live there and they also questioned the representative. Believe me, no way is justice blind. . . . We just don't want all this garbage thrown at us because we are low-income and Mexican American. We are lucky

now that we have good representatives, which we didn't have before.

Throughout their life histories, the women refer to the disruptive effects of land use decisions made in the 1950s. As longtime residents, all but one share the experience of losing a home and relocating to make way for a freeway. Juana Gutiérrez refers to the community response at that time:

> Una de las cosas que me caen muy mal es la injusticia y en nuestra comunidad hemos visto mucho de eso. Sobre todo antes, porque creo que nuestra gente estaba mas dormida, nos atrevíamos menos. En los cincuentas hicieron los freeways y así, sin más, nos dieron la noticia de que nos teníamos que mudar. Y eso pasó dos veces. La gente se conformaba porque lo ordeno el gobierno. Recuerdo que yo me enojaba y quería que los demás me secundaran, pero nadie quería hacer nada. (One of the things that really upsets me is the injustice that we see so much in our community. Above everything else, I believe that our people were less aware; we were less challenging. In the 1950s—they made the freeways and just like that they gave us a notice that we had to move. That happened twice. The people accepted it because the government ordered it. I remember that I was angry and wanted the others to back me but nobody else wanted to do anything.)

The freeways that cut through communities and disrupted neighborhoods are now a concrete reminder of shared injustice, of the vulnerability of the community in the 1950s. The community's social and political history thus informs perceptions of its current predicament; however, today's activists emphasize not the powerlessness of the community but the change in status and progression toward political empowerment.

Fifth, the core activists typically tell stories illustrating personal change and a new sense of entitlement to speak for the community. They have transformed the unspoken sentiments of individuals into a collective community voice. Lucy Ramos related her initial apprehensions:

> I was afraid to get involved. I didn't know what was going to come out of this and I hesitated at first. Right after we started, Father

John came up to me and told me, "I want you to be a spokesperson." I said, "Oh no, I don't know what I am going to say." I was nervous. I am surprised I didn't have a nervous breakdown then. Every time we used to get in front of the TV cameras and even interviews like this, I used to sit there and I could feel myself shaking. But as time went on, I started getting used to it.

And this is what I have noticed with a lot of them. They were afraid to speak up and say anything. Now, with this prison issue, a lot of them have come out and come forward and given their opinions. Everybody used to be real "quietlike."

She also related a situation that brought all her fears to a climax, which she confronted and resolved as follows:

When I first started working with the coalition, Channel 13 called me up and said they wanted to interview me and I said OK. Then I started getting nervous. So I called Father John and told him, "You better get over here right away." He said, "Don't worry, don't worry, you can handle it by yourself." Then Channel 13 called me back and said they were going to interview another person, someone I had never heard of, and asked if it was OK if he came to my house. And I said OK again. Then I began thinking, what if this guy is for the prison? What am I going to do? And I was so nervous and I thought, I know what I am going to do!

Since the meeting was taking place in her home, she reasoned that she was entitled to order any troublemakers out of her domain:

If this man tells me anything, I am just going to chase him out of my house. That is what I am going to do! All these thoughts were going through my head. Then Channel 13 walk into my house followed by six men I had never met. And I thought, Oh, my God, what did I get myself into? I kept saying to myself, if they get smart with me I am throwing them ALL out.

At this point her tone expressed a sense of resolve. In fact, the situation turned out to be neither confrontational nor threatening, as the "other men" were also members of the coalition. This woman confronted an anxiety-laden situation by relying on her sense of control within her home and family—a quite "traditional" source of authority for women—and transforming that control into the courage to express a political position before a potential audience all over one of the largest metropolitan areas in the nation.

People living in Third World countries as well as in minority communities in the United States face an increasingly degraded environment. Recognizing the threat to the well-being of their families, residents have mobilized at the neighborhood level to fight for "quality of life" issues. The common notion that environmental well-being is of concern solely to white middle-class and upper-class residents ignores the specific way working-class neighborhoods suffer from the fallout of the city "growth machine" geared for profit.

In Los Angeles, the culmination of postwar urban renewal policies, the growing Pacific Rim trade surplus and investment, and low-wage international labor migration from Third World countries are creating potentially volatile conditions. Literally palatial financial buildings swallow up the space previously occupied by modest, low-cost housing. Increasing density and development not matched by investment in social programs, services, and infrastructure erode the quality of life, beginning in the core of the city. Latinos, the majority of whom live close to the center of the city, must confront the distilled social consequences of development focused solely on profit. The Mexican American community in East Los Angeles, much like other minority working-class communities, has been a repository for prisons instead of new schools, hazardous industries instead of safe work sites, and one of the largest concentrations of freeway interchanges in the country, which transports much wealth past the community. And the concerns of residents in East Los Angeles may provide lessons for other minority as well as middle-class communities. Increasing environmental pollution resulting from inadequate waste disposal plans and an out-of-control "need" for penal institutions to contain the casualties created by the growing bipolar distribution of wages may not be limited to the Southwest. These conditions set the stage for new conflicts and new opportunities, to transform old relationships into coalitions that can challenge state agendas and create new community visions.

Mexican American women living east of downtown Los Angeles exemplify the tendency of women to enter into environmental struggles in defense of their community. Women have a rich historical legacy of community activism, partly reconstructed over the last two decades in social histories of women who contested other "quality of life issues," from the price of bread to "Demon Rum" (often representing domestic violence).

But something new is also happening. The issues "traditionally" addressed by women—health, housing, sanitation, and the urban environment—have moved to center stage as capitalist urbanization progresses. Environmental issues now fuel the fires of many political campaigns and drive citizens beyond the rather restricted, perfunctory political act of voting. Instances of political mobilization at the grassroots level, where women often play a central role, allow us to "see" abstract concepts like participatory democracy and social change as dynamic processes.

The existence and activities of "Mothers of East Los Angeles" attest to the dynamic nature of participatory democracy, as well as to the dynamic nature of our gender, class, and ethnic identity. The story of MELA reveals, on the one hand, how individuals and groups can transform a seemingly "traditional" role

such as "mother." On the other hand, it illustrates how such a role may also be a social agent drawing members of the community into the "political" arena. Studying women's contributions as well as men's will shed greater light on the networks dynamic of grassroots movements.

The work "Mothers of East Los Angeles" do to mobilize the community demonstrates that people's political involvement cannot be predicted by their cultural characteristics. These women have defied stereotypes of apathy and used ethnic, gender, and class identity as an impetus, a strength, a vehicle for political activism. They have expanded their—and our—understanding of the complexities of a political system, and they have reaffirmed the possibility of "doing something."

They also generously share the lessons they have learned. One of the women in "Mothers of East Los Angeles" told me, as I hesitated to set up an interview with another woman I hadn't yet met in person,

> You know, nothing ventured nothing lost. You should have seen how timid we were the first time we went to a public hearing. Now, forget it, I walk right up and make myself heard and that's what you have to do.

SEVENTY-EIGHT

Empowering Ourselves
Women and Toxics Organizing
Robbin Lee Zeff, Marsha Love, and Karen Stults

Health Effects

The environmental justice movement would not exist today were we not concerned about the devastating health effects on our families from exposure to toxic wastes. We got involved because we want justice for ourselves and others who have already been harmed. We're concerned about protecting families against future harm from incinerators, leaking landfills and other sources of hazardous waste contamination. Involuntary exposure to toxic substances

is a form of persecution. We will no longer be victims to environmental persecution.

Since environmentally induced illness is such an overwhelming reality in all of our lives, we have devoted a large portion of this publication to the subject of health effects. . . . Three women who have faced the consequences of the environmental poisoning of their families and their communities tell their stories. Then we discuss the emotions we feel as we deal with illness and, finally, some obstacles and solutions for dealing with the health effects of toxic exposure.

Penny Newman

Penny Newman is a long-time veteran in the grassroots movement against toxics and a leader of Concerned Neighbors in Action of Riverside, California. Penny was one of the first to work with Lois Gibbs at Love Canal to discover that hazardous waste was in everyone's backyard. Penny is one of the key activists at the Stringfellow Acid Pits site in Riverside, California. She is now the western regional field organizer for CCHW [Citizens Clearinghouse for Hazardous Wastes].

"I Didn't Know the Danger."

We chose to move to our community because we thought it was the place to raise our kids. The small town atmosphere, the rural countryside, was the kind of place we wanted to be. I knew that when you go house hunting, you find out about the schools in the neighborhood. But I didn't know then that I had to ask whether the community had a toxic dump.

This community is near a Class 1 hazardous waste site. On the site there are volatile organics, TCE, DDT, the heavy metals. We have radiation. We have everything at Stringfellow. I didn't know it then.

When we moved there, I was three months pregnant. At 5½ months I miscarried. Eric was conceived just a few months after that. Eric was born 6 weeks premature. He had a lot of allergies from the very beginning and was always a fairly fragile child. It was routine not to sleep at night, because you lay there listening for his breathing. At any time you might have to rush him to the hospital for his injections.

"The Doctors Didn't Know What Was Wrong."

When Eric started school, instead of things getting better, like everybody told me he would, "he'd outgrow the asthma," he just got worse. We went through a year of really severe abdominal pains and the doctors just didn't know what was going on. Eric went through all kinds of tests. They finally said it was an epileptic stomach. It had to be a teacher who was putting pressure on Eric at school. That seemed really strange to me, because he had a very laid-back teacher.

One night he had to have emergency surgery. They thought it was appendicitis, but it wasn't. So they did exploratory surgery and took out Eric's gall bladder. They decided that's what it was. A six-year-old with a gall bladder problem! So unusual, they wrote articles in medical journals about him. On top of this, Eric was diagnosed as having a congenital defect which required being in braces. Eric also had no vision in one eye. They classified it as "lazy eye," but it wasn't quite that. So we went through a period of braces, glasses and an eye patch. He knocked out teeth, because he kept falling with his braces. He looked like a battered child. Every time we took him out, I'd have to say, "No, I really don't beat this kid." It was very embarrassing.

After the gall bladder surgery Eric seemed to do a little better. Every time the flu came around he wasn't drastically ill. Every time a cold came around he wouldn't be out of school for two weeks.

Shawn was always the healthy kid. I finally thought, "Aha, we've got one that is going to make it." Until he started school. The school is ¾ of a mile from the site. Shawn started with asthma, which he didn't have as a younger child. He seemed to develop it very quickly, as I did, because I had started working at the school. His skin would crack open and ooze. And he had ear infections, continuous ear infections.

"The Officials Didn't Tell Us."

In 1978, we had overflows from the site. They pumped 800,000 gallons of chemicals into the community. It flowed down the street and the flood canal, which goes directly behind the elementary school. It overflowed into the playground. The state officials didn't tell anyone they were doing this. They didn't want to panic the public.

The school district found out and decided they should do something. They didn't want to close the school, because they would lose state financing, based on the average daily attendance rates. So they set up an evacuation plan. They told the staff, "If you hear one bell, take the kids down to buses. If you hear two bells, it will be too late; the dam will be broken. Put the kids on the desks and hope for the best." The staff was instructed not to tell parents.

So we were sending our kids off to school every day, and the kids played in the puddles, as all kids do. They didn't know that they shouldn't be playing in that water; they thought it was rain water. We had foam in the community which they kept telling us was agricultural foam. The kids could actually make beards out of it. They put the foam on their faces.

"Doctors Ended Up Adding to the Problem."

After that, Shawn began having neurological symptoms—the blurred vision, the headaches. The headaches would get so bad he would just scream. It didn't do any good to put him in a dark room; it didn't do any good to give him aspirins. And then he'd start in with dizzy spells to the point of really being nauseous. And you'd actually have to hold on to him, so he could see he wasn't moving. He was in the 4th grade.

We went through two years of tests on him. It was probably the biggest nightmare I'd ever gone through. At that point I really began to hate doctors. They ended up adding to the problem rather than helping it, by telling a 4th grader that he had brain damage without giving him any explanation. By telling him later on that he was just doing it to get attention. They said this to a young man in his formative years.

Shawn graduated into junior high school, which is out of that immediate area. Things began to subside a bit. He was put on phenobarbital. And we never figured out if it was the medication or just removing him from the area. But he seemed to improve a little bit. However, he never, from that 4th grade period on, never did well in school again, as he used to. And Shawn had been recommended for the gifted program. He was extremely bright and very well coordinated. But he wasn't any more. Clearly there was a change. He noticed it more than I did. He became very conscious of it, to the point that he didn't want to participate in sports any more because he couldn't do things that he used to be able to do. He has also told me he simply can't concentrate.

"The State Says There Are No Significant Health Effects."

In the last year we've started having testing done, as part of our lawsuit. And despite what the state has said in their epidemiological studies—and our community has been studied like a zoo by the state—they kept saying there were no significant health effects. But we got ahold of an internal memo, where they outlined health effects that included an increase in cancer, urinary tract infections, respiratory problems, ear infections, heart problems. But they considered this "no significant health impact." A young man with terrific potential. That potential is reduced. They'll never be able to give that back to him.

I look back now and think: How stupid could I have been? But I just never made the connection. And it wasn't until we got a list of all the chemicals and their health effects that I started reading and thinking, "My God, that's Eric's problem, that's Shawn's problem."

"People Were Scared."

My kids are not the sickest kids in our community. They are considered pretty healthy kids. For a long time people didn't even want to discuss what was going on, because they were scared. Some suspected, mainly because of skin problems. You could see the rashes; you could see the sores. Sores that didn't respond to treatment. And so people would talk about that. The things they wouldn't talk about were the suicide tendencies of their kids, or the really emotional state that some of the people were in. They didn't talk about the reproductive problems they were having. And a lot of it was that they didn't associate those problems with those chemicals.

It's frightening to have a doctor go through this whole list of things that are wrong. And knowing that there are not any doctors around us who are even going to acknowledge that it's happening, much less provide treatment. That's a real problem. What do you do with people by telling them they have these problems and not being able to offer them any help?

Luella Kenny

Luella Kenny joined the grassroots movement for environmental justice in 1978 when her son Jon died from chemical exposure at Love Canal. Luella remains active as a member of CCHW's Board of Directors, the chairperson of the Love Canal Medical Trust Fund, and as a consultant to grassroots groups nationwide.

I was one of the original activists at Love Canal. And I'm ashamed to say that the only thing that got me involved was because my son died, because he was playing in his own backyard. Otherwise, I was just as complacent as the next person and didn't pay attention to what was going on.

Yet back in 1978 my 7-year-old son suddenly became ill. And I was too busy running back and forth from the hospital to pay attention. I knew that 1/10th of a mile from my house there was a lot of ruckus going on. People were protesting.

Both my husband and I are in the sciences. We went to the medical library and started reading. Jon had a kidney disease, known as nephrosis. We found out that this disease could be triggered if you're exposed to chemicals. I was told not to worry about it.

But 4 months later this little 7-year-old boy died. The members of the Love Canal Home Owners Association were interested because the death occurred in the immediate neighborhood. And New York State said that they were going to investigate Jon's death. Ironically, I worked for the New York State Dept. of Health for 29 years. I was very trusting. I thought this was what we should do. We should investigate it.

"The Commissioner of Health Didn't Look Me in the Eye."

It's not very easy for a mother to have to read her son's autopsy report and to try and deal with the officials. I thought it was important to know what had happened, so I sat down with the Commissioner of Health of New York State and tried to go over this autopsy report. Typical of most officials, his head down, not looking me straight in the eye, he had the nerve to tell me that little boys have the tendency to pick their nose and therefore they get bloody noses, not because they are exposed to chemicals. Nothing happens to little boys' kidneys because they are exposed to chemicals; it's because they play football and they fall down and rupture them.

Children have a gland called the thymus gland. It is what determines immune response. It usually disappears when children are 14 years old. The autopsy report indicated that Jon's thymus was already shrunk. In the medical journals, all of the animal studies showed that a shrunken thymus is an indicator of exposure to dioxin. That's what was in our backyard. Dioxin.

Who would have thought that my other son who was 10, was anorexic because of the appetite-suppressing chemicals at the creek? Who would have thought that the hundreds and hundreds of warts that were all over his body which we constantly had to have removed, who would have thought it was due to chemical exposures?

"Don't Be Intimidated by Doctors."

I had worked in the scientific field, and yet I was given stupid answers. I was considered an hysterical housewife. But the officials didn't address the issues any better when I tried to approach them without emotion. Because they are not ready to accept it.

I want to make one last point. Don't be intimidated by doctors. They are not gods. And don't take what they say. You have to go out and search for what you know is true. Don't let them focus only on cancer and miscarriages, which are the obvious things. David Axelrod, the Health Commissioner, told me, "Collect yourself, go back home, start your life again." It's impossible. This is 9 years later. I've started my life again, but certainly not in the direction he told me to.

Patty Frase

Born and raised in Jacksonville, Arkansas, Patty first became involved in the toxics issue when she lost her parents to toxics-related illnesses. Patty now lives in Benton, Arkansas, and directs the Environmental Congress of Arkansas, which works on a variety of issues such as hazardous waste incineration, deep well injection, and landfills.

"Don't Trust Government and Industry Research Studies."

When I hear these stories I get so angry. I want to go out and grab these doctors and throw them in the pit. I want to take them out there and let them drink our water.

We have "independent" studies we're supposed to rely on. The majority of those studies are funded by the chemical companies. So they're going to have a study that says, "It's o.k. Don't worry about what's in your landfill. There is nothing wrong with your landfill."

"CDC: Center for Diffusing Citizen Concern."

The government studies are also bogus. We just have to start out knowing that the Centers for Disease Control, the EPA, or any of these regulatory agencies are not telling the truth. When they come your way, tell them to go away. Tell them, "We don't need your studies." You don't need their studies, because then you are countering more than you were before they got there. Because now they are reinforcing that you're crazy. But you're not crazy; there is nothing wrong with you.

Some of the things that go on with the CDC and the EPA are so incredible that it's hard to believe that we're the ignorant ones. The CDC and the EPA came to town and said, "We're going to do you a favor. You've been asking for all this stuff, so we're going to test 10 people that have died in your community. We're going to do liver samples. We're going to do brain samples. We're going to do intestinal samples. We're going to do it all."

My Congressman's office calls me two weeks later and says, "Patty, I don't think you want that. You're the control group for Times Beach, Missouri." So I called the CDC and I asked them if this was true. And I called the press, like crazy. The next day the study was cancelled. Thank goodness. We were supposed to be the control group. We were. Our contamination level was just as high, if not higher, in some parts of our community, than Times Beach. They evacuated Times Beach at the 1 part per billion (ppb) level. Some of our homes have 2.8 ppb, 3.7 ppb, 4.6 ppb.

Don't let any of them tell you anything, because it's all b.s. The CDC was supposed to test for 10 chemicals. There were no established background levels for these chemicals, so they compared the levels of these chemicals with DDT, DDE, etc. So that they can show you that you're crazy.

The CDC got up at a press conference with an autopsy report, and they say 508 ppb 3,5 dichlorophenyl, 2,4,5,T. This is the autopsy of a little baby.

A baby that's never eaten anything. Been on canned formula. Canned formula. The CDC holds up the autopsy report and a can of moth balls and says, "These children are no more contaminated than if they ate these moth balls." They took the warning labels off the moth balls, and they held them up in front of us hysterical housewives to justify to us idiots that the children are no more contaminated than if they swallowed moth balls.

"They Don't Know How to Handle Us Hysterical Housewives."

They don't know how to handle us emotional people, which is wonderful. I thank God they don't, because otherwise we'd never win. I'm glad I'm hysterical. Now they're putting sociologists and psychologists in the field to come deal with us crazy people, us emotional people.

Health Effects: Obstacles and Solutions

Obstacles

Emotional Responses to Health Effects   Handling a serious illness in the family is difficult. Environmentally caused illnesses are all the more tragic and difficult for families because they are less understood, harder to treat, and caused by corporate carelessness. It is especially stressful for women since we are the primary caretakers of the ill family member. Whether we are dealing with illness or death, in ourselves or in others, we feel many emotions: denial, sadness, fear, and anger.

> **Denial:** You deny the death, hoping to cheer others up. You become a bit hard. You close off your feelings as you see someone dying.

> We are the strong ones. We have no one to break down with. We cannot show remorse, cry or be sad with our groups, whenever we feel like it. Most times, when it is time to cry, we are the ones helping others to express their grief, enabling the process, rather than participating in it for ourselves. As organizers we are involved in the recovery, the moving on.

Sadness: Yet it's hard to keep being pumped up. You're losing still another person in your support group. We have delivered eulogies to beloved community leaders and have felt the loss of the entire community and have expressed that with sadness.

Death of children at a site is the most devastating. We have children ourselves and when we counsel others on the loss of a child, we are reminded of our own child's vulnerability. We own the problem twice.

Fear: It's terrifying. You wonder who's next.

Anger: I really had to work off my anger. My daughter was contaminated and had symptoms and I was contaminated and exposed to the chemicals. "I'm going to get these people," I thought, "they just can't do this to me and get away with it." I wanted to get them back.

Solutions

It's o.k. to be emotional. Warm and caring people feel emotions. In our work, we are reclaiming the role of women as healers and nurturers. Acknowledge your emotions and let your sadness, anger, and fear lead you to ACTION.

Obstacles

Physicians' Lack of Knowledge on Illnesses Due to Toxic Exposure Your local family physician is not likely to know anything about toxic chemicals. Medical students receive only 4 hours of training on this subject in 4 years of medical school.

Solutions

It's our job to educate our doctors, so that they know what questions to ask us and how to treat our families when we become ill. Shortly after this conference CCHW began a newsletter called "Environmental Health Monthly" which is sent to doctors across the country to educate them about environmental health issues. Contact CCHW to get your local doctors on the mailing list.

Obstacles

Too Much Emphasis on Cancer Scientists and government agencies who study our communities have not validated all the types of health effects that may occur. In their view there's only a problem if a population shows up with cancers and reproductive problems. They are not so quick to acknowledge or accept, for example, neurological damage or immune system dysfunction.

Solutions

Be persistent. Don't give up. Trust your instincts. We are being forced to be living experiments of chemical exposure. If you believe there's a real problem which they're not acknowledging, don't accept what they tell you. Contact CCHW for advice about what to do.

Obstacles

Experts The environmental science field is not all that big. The same "experts" get called in to evaluate communities all over the country. Some of them do good work, but some of them do not. Many "experts" have bad reputations with environmental groups because they act more like "hired guns" than scientists and professionals.

Solutions

Let CCHW know of your experiences dealing with scientists and other experts. CCHW will keep a "Hit List" of names of people to avoid. If they are brought to your community, just say, "No thanks, we're not cooperating until this person is replaced." Try to check an expert's credentials and find out which other communities they have worked in. Call those communities to find out what kind of job they did. A national network of sympathetic doctors and industrial hygienists has also been created to help exposed workers and their families deal with work-related health problems. These professionals may be helpful to our local groups. Contact CCHW (now center for Health, Environment, and Justice) for more information.*

---

*P.O. Box 6806, Falls Church, VA 22040. (703) 237-2249

Obstacles	Solutions
Intimidation of Scientific Language Lots of scientific and medical terms are thrown at us by government agencies and scientists who study our communities. Learning the language they use and knowing how they operate can be confusing and difficult.	CCHW has a science department that can help you decipher technical reports and studies. There are books available for community groups that make science accessible to everyone. These books describe how epidemiological surveys are done and how to conduct your own health survey.

SEVENTY-NINE

◆◆◆

Power, Authority, and Mystery
Ecofeminism and Earth-Based Spirituality

Starhawk

Earth-based spirituality is rooted in three basic concepts that I call immanence, interconnection, and community. The first—immanence—names our primary understanding that the Earth is alive, part of a living cosmos. What that means is that spirit, sacred, Goddess, God—whatever you want to call it—is not found outside the world somewhere—it's in the world: it *is* the world, and it is us. Our goal is not to get off the wheel of birth nor to be saved from something. Our deepest experiences are experiences of connection with the Earth and with the world.

When you understand the universe as a living being, then the split between religion and science disappears because religion no longer becomes a set of dogmas and beliefs we have to accept even though they don't make any sense, and science is no longer restricted to a type of analysis that picks the world apart. Science becomes our way of looking more deeply into this living being that we're all in, understanding it more deeply and clearly. This itself has a poetic dimension. I want to explore what it means when we really accept that this Earth is alive and that we are part of her being. Right now we are at a point where that living being is nearly terminally diseased. We need to reverse that, to turn that around. We really need to find a way to reclaim our power so that we can reverse the destruction of the Earth.

When we understand that the Earth itself embodies spirit and that the cosmos is alive, then we also understand that everything is interconnected. Just as in our bodies: what happens to a finger affects what happens to a toe. The brain doesn't work without the heart. In the same way, what happens in South Africa affects us here: what we do to the Amazon rain forest affects the air that we breathe here. All these things are interconnected, and interconnection is the second principle of Earth-based spirituality.

Finally, when we understand these interconnections, we know that we are all part of a living community, the Earth. The kind of spirituality and the kind of politics we're called upon to practice are rooted in community. Again, the goal is not individual salvation or enlightenment, or even individual self-improvement, though these may be things and *are* things that happen along the way. The goal is the creation of a community that becomes a place in which we can be empowered and in which we can be connected to the Earth and take action together to heal the Earth.

Each of these principles—immanence, interconnection, and community—calls us to do something. That call, that challenge, is the difference between a spirituality that is practiced versus an intellectual philosophy. The idea that the Earth is alive is becoming an acceptable intellectual philosophy.

Scientists have conferences on the Gaia hypothesis without acknowledging that this is exactly what people in tribal cultures, what Witches, shamans, and psychics, have been saying for thousands of years. But there's a difference between accepting it as a scientific philosophy and really living it. Living with the knowledge that the cosmos is alive causes us to do something. It challenges us. Earth-based spirituality makes certain demands. That is, when we start to understand that the Earth is alive, she calls us to act to preserve her life. When we understand that everything is interconnected, we are called to a politics and a set of actions that come from compassion, from the ability to literally feel *with* all living beings on the Earth. That feeling is the ground upon which we can build community and come together and take action and find direction.

Earth-based spirituality calls us to live with integrity. Once we know that we're all part of this living body, this world becomes the terrain where we live out spiritual growth and development. It doesn't happen anywhere else, and the way we do it is by enacting what we believe, by taking responsibility for what we do.

These values are not limited to any particular tradition. They can be found in many, many different spiritual traditions and within many different political groups. For me, they come out of my tradition, which is the Pagan tradition, the Wiccan tradition, the old pre-Christian Goddess religion of Europe. We have a certain perspective that I believe can be valuable politically and that is, in some way, linked to what I see ecofeminism and the Green movement attempting. It's not that I think everyone has to be a Witch to be an ecofeminist, or that all Greens should be Witches—pluralism is vitally important in all our movements. It's that I do feel that Pagan values and perspectives can make important contributions to ecofeminist analysis and organizing.

A Pagan perspective might influence our approach to action. For example, I've participated in many political actions and organizations over the past 15 years. There have been times when it's been very exciting. In 1981, 1982, and 1983 the Livermore Action Group (LAG) was active in the [San Francisco] Bay Area. We were constantly blockading, demonstrating, risking arrest, and mobilizing large numbers of people.

What happened to LAG, though, is very interesting. At a certain point—in fact, after what was really our strongest, most solid and successful action in 1983—things began to fall apart. Organizing began to get harder and harder, and we were never able to organize a large, cohesive action again. At the same time this was happening to LAG—and we were having meeting after meeting, asking, "Where did we go wrong?"—the same thing was happening to the peace movement in general. Everybody was asking, "What's wrong? Why are we burning out?"

In 1981 and 1982 we were very much focused on the Cruise and Pershing missiles, which were going to be deployed in Europe. There was a strong sense that if we didn't prevent the deployment from happening, that would be it. Russia would go to launch on warning, which meant that computers with approximately a 6-minute margin for error would essentially be in charge of blowing the world up. It made people more than nervous: we were terrified. This was a great impetus for action. If ever there was a time to put your personal life aside, to put your body on the line, to get dragged away, to go to jail, this was it. So our organizing was apocalyptic. Every meal, we feared, was the Last Supper. Without realizing it, we were acting out a Christian myth, expecting the end of the world, the end of time.

Of course, what happened is that the missiles went in, in spite of all the times we went to jail. And that's the way that political organizing and action often work. You go out, twelve hundred people performing civil disobedience, holding solidarity for 2 weeks, but President Reagan doesn't wake up the next day and say, "Gee, all these people are in jail. They're so sincere. They must have a point." It doesn't work that way.

But then, five years later, after long negotiations, Reagan and Gorbachev decide to take those missiles out of Europe. That is a victory, a victory that is the fruit of the organizing that we did all those years. But this kind of victory is not one we're going to see immediately. This is where the Pagan perspective comes in.

What Witches and Pagans do is practice magic. I like the definition of magic that says, "Magic is the art of changing consciousness at will." I also think that's a very good definition of political change—changing consciousness on a mass scale in this country. And one of the things we learn when we practice magic is that the results don't necessarily happen immediately. They unfold over time, and they always unfold in surprising ways, which is why we talk about our spiritual tradition in terms of mystery rather than answers and dogma and certainty. We talk about what it is we don't know and can only wonder about and be amazed at.

There is a certain way that magic works: it is, in a sense, a technology. When we want to do something, to change consciousness, for example, we first need an image of the change we want to create. We need a vision.

The same is true for political work. If we want to change consciousness in this nation, we first need to have a vision in our minds of what we want to change it into. We need to have an image, and we need to create that image and make it strong. And we need to direct energy and, in some way, ground it in reality.

The vision we want to create must also reflect a different model of power, one rooted in our understanding of the Earth as alive. We live in a system where power is *power-over,* that is, domination and control; it is a system in which a person or group of people has the right to tell other people what to do, to make their decisions, to set standards they have to live up to. The system may be overtly coercive, like a prison, or it may be benign on the surface, but it is still a system of power. And we internalize the system of domination. It lives inside us, like an entity, as if we were possessed by it.

Ecofeminism challenges all relations of domination. Its goal is not just to change who wields power, but to transform the structure of power itself. When the spirit is immanent, when each of us is the Goddess, is God, we have an inalienable right to be here and to be alive. We have a value that can't be taken away from us, that doesn't have to be earned, that doesn't have to be acquired. That kind of value is central to the change we want to create. That's the spell we want to cast.

The way we can embody that vision, can create the living image of that value, is in the groups we form and the structures we create. In some ways, especially in the Bay Area, we often have done this well. That is why so many people found organizing around Livermore and Diablo empowering. The

Livermore Action Group and the Abalone Alliance (which organized the blockade at the Diablo nuclear power plant) were structured around small groups that worked by consensus. Now consensus can drive you out of your mind with frustration sometimes, but there is a very important principle in it. That is, everyone in the group has power, and everyone has equal power because everyone has value. That value is accepted, it's inherent, and it can't be taken away.

Along with the decision-making process goes a real care for the process that we use with each other. We listen to each other, we let each person have a say and hear each other and recognize that different people's opinions may be important, even if we disagree with them. Feminist process, as we call it, creates a strong sense of safety, and it changes people. I've known people in LAG who've said that their lives were profoundly changed by living for the first time in a society in which what they said was heard and considered important.

In a sense, that kind of decision making and organizing becomes a ritual. A ritual really is any kind of an intentional act we create that deepens our sense of value. The real heart of any ritual is telling our stories, that is, listening to each other and telling the sacred stories that we may have heard, that have been handed down and distilled from many people's experience, and telling the stories of our own experience.

Groups often seem to be most empowering when they are small. Only in a relatively small group can we really know each other as individuals. That's why LAG was organized in affinity groups, which are small, and why Witches are organized in covens, which traditionally have no more than thirteen members. When a group gets too large, people begin to become faceless. At the same time, small groups can also come together and form networks and coalitions and act together in larger ways. But the real base is always a small community of people who know and value each other personally.

We also need to have a sense of safety. A lot of people will say, "I feel unsafe in this group," meaning "I'm afraid someone's going to hurt my feelings." The truth is that someone will—someone always does—you can count on it. When we're honest, when we really interact with each other, there are always times when our needs or our style or our ways of communicating don't mesh. But when we each feel sure of our value to the group, conflict need not be devastating.

But real safety comes from something else. The groups we create and the ways we organize also have to be sustainable. If we weren't living in a state of denial all the time, the whole idea of sustainability would clearly be our first priority. How is it that we can live in a world where we use the Earth in ways that are destroying it and not worry? We all know we have to breathe; we all know we have to drink water; we all know we have to eat food; and, we all know it's got to come from somewhere. So why isn't the preservation of the environment our first priority? It makes such logical sense that it's irritating to have to say it.

In order to put the environment on the national agenda, we have to organize, but we also need to embody the principle of sustainability in our own groups. I think one of the flaws in our organizing, for example, in that period in the early 1980s, was exactly the apocalyptic sense coming out of that unconscious Christian myth that the end of time was near.

From a Pagan perspective, there is no end of time. Time is a cycle, and cycles come around and they go around and come back again. Our goal isn't to burn ourselves out as martyrs. Our model is the Earth, and the seed that is planted and springs up, grows, loses life, is planted and comes up again and again and again.

That, I think, is the kind of model we need for our politics. We need to see the process of changing our society as a lifetime challenge and commitment. Transforming consciousness so that we can preserve and sustain the Earth is a long-term project. We need the communities we create around that task to be sustainable. There are going to be times when we're active and it's exciting and we're obsessed by action, and there are going to be times when we pull back and nurture ourselves and heal and take care of ourselves. There are times when each of us gives a lot to a group, and times when each should get something back from the group, times when the giving and taking in a group balance out. Nobody should be stuck always having to be the leader, the organizer, or the one who pulls it all together. These tasks should rotate. And nobody should get stuck being

the nurturer, the one everyone complains to, the mediator, the one who smooths everything over.

It is true that sometimes doing political work involves making sacrifices, and it may involve suffering. It's also true that around the world, people are suffering tremendously right now because of the policies of this country, the historical decisions and choices this country has made. We have to oppose and change these policies, and to do that we have to be willing to take risks. But sometimes in the nonviolence movement there's a kind of idealization of suffering. And I don't think that serves us. It comes out of the fantasy that people will see us suffering for our cause, be impressed by our nobility and sincerity, and be attracted to join and suffer with us.

Gandhi was a great man, but his ideas don't always fit for a lot of us, particularly for women. Gandhi said we have to accept the suffering and take it in. Women have been doing that for thousands and thousands of years, and it hasn't stopped anything much — except a lot of women's lives. In some ways, it's also not ecological. Rather than absorb the violence, what we need to do is to find some way to stop it and then transform it, to take that energy and turn it into creative change. Not to take it on ourselves.

The actual unsung truth about a lot of organizing is that it feels really good, and that's why people do it, again and again and again. It feels good because when we're actually organizing and taking action to stop the destruction of the Earth, we're doing an act of healing and we are free. There are few times when we are free in this culture and this is one of them. We need to speak about the joy and wildness and sense of liberation that comes when we step beyond the bounds of the authorities to resist control and create change.

Finally, I think that the spell we need to cast, the model we need to create, has to be open to mystery, to the understanding that we don't know everything about what's going on and we don't know exactly what to do about it. The mystery can be expressed in many ways. For one person it might be expressed through ritual, through celebration, chanting, and meditation; in some groups it might be expressed through humor, through making fun of what everybody else is doing. In some groups it might be expressed both ways. We can't define how a group or individual is going to experience it, but we can attempt to structure things so that we don't have dog-mas and party lines, so we remain open to many possibilities of the sacred.

These are some ideas of how we build communities and what kinds of communities we might want to create. The other question is what we're going to organize these communities around. It's hard to get people together in a vacuum. One of the things that plagues our movements is that when we start looking at what's really going on with the Earth and the people on it, it's overwhelming. All the issues seem so important that it's very, very hard to know what to focus on, and we can easily get fragmented.

I had dinner recently with a man named Terry Gips who heads a group called the International Alliance for Sustainable Agriculture. He was telling me that he'd come to the conclusion that we have about 3 years to turn around the environmental destruction or it'll be too late. He had expressed this idea to his friends and reactions were so bad that he'd decided not to talk about it any more. People got very depressed. I could understand that because I'd gotten terribly depressed myself.

I said, "Well, I don't know if it's useful to think in those terms. When you said 'three years,' it didn't sound like enough time. It reminds me of that period in the early 1980s when we thought we had to get rid of those missiles now or never. At the same time, if you really believe that, what do we need to do? Do we need to smash capitalism in 3 years and totally transform society? I don't think we can do that."

He said, "No. Actually, there are some very concrete things to do in the next 3 to 5 years—however long we might have—that would reverse the destruction enough to give us time to make the deeper kinds of changes and transformations we need to make." He sat there talking, and I started thinking, and we came up with a campaign for turning the tide.

So this is what I think we should do, and, if I were setting an ecofeminist or a Green agenda, this is how I would organize it, the beginning of which I look at as a sort of magic circle.

Illustrated are the tree of life and the magic circle. The magic circle is a circle of the elements: air, fire, water, and earth. The tree has roots and a core, a center, a heart that's the same as the circle, and it has branches. If we think about it, all of these issues that we see as being so interconnected can fit into that magic circle.

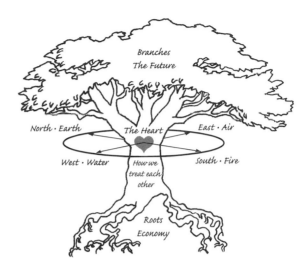

For example, let's talk about air. The ozone layer has holes in it and is rapidly being depleted. We should be organizing around this issue if we want our food crops and ocean plankton to survive, if we want to preserve the viability of the Earth. And such organizing has already had some success. Du Pont, which manufactures 25 percent of the world's chlorofluorocarbons, has voluntarily decided to phase out production. Several states, including Minnesota, are considering bills to ban these substances, and some fast-food franchises are phasing out packaging made from these substances. But even with these changes, the ozone will continue to diminish since chlorofluorocarbons remain in the Earth's atmosphere for up to 80 years. Yet these positive steps show us that public pressure can bring about important changes.

Another air issue is the destruction of tropical rain forests. If you wonder why I put that under air, it's because these forests are the lungs of the world. They are being cut down, and they are key to systems that regulate the Earth's weather patterns. There *should* be an international commission on the rain forest, and there should also be pressure on institutions like the World Bank and the International Monetary Fund to stop funding the destruction of rain forests. A lot of the destruction comes as rain forests are cut down so cattle can graze and our fast-food restaurants can turn out hamburgers. That's another thing we can organize around. A boycott of one fast-food chain, Burger King, convinced it to stop buying rain forest beef.

Now look at fire: we have nuclear issues. Nuclear power—what do we do with all that waste? Nuclear weapons, we should be working to ban them. Fire represents energy, and we need renewable sources of energy. We need our money put into those sources rather than into things that pollute and kill.

There are also important water issues. Acid rain is also killing trees and forests. Canada wanted some very simple things from us, like smoke scrubbers and curbs on acid rain, and then-President Reagan refused. We need to set standards and see that they're enforced. (Bush's new proposals sound good but actually lack strict standards.) We need to be talking about groundwater pollution. In Minnesota, "Land of a Thousand Lakes" as the license plate says, wells were tested and 39 percent were found to be contaminated; similar statistics exist for many areas. We also need to stop the pollution of the ocean, the oil drilling off the coasts, the depletion of fisheries, and the killing of whales.

Then, of course, there's the Earth. One of the things that would push us toward sustainable agriculture would be simply to stop subsidizing pesticides, which we do now in a lot of very subtle ways. For example, if a pesticide is banned, who is it that pays for storing and destroying it? It's us. It's our tax money, not the company that produces it. In California beekeepers lose thousands of dollars every year to pesticides. The government reimburses them, but the pesticide companies should be paying the price. It's estimated that there are four pesticide poisonings a minute, three-fourths of them in the Third World. We could make it uneconomical to poison the Earth and the human beings who grow and eat the food the Earth produces. We could make alliances with the United Farmworkers of America, who've been calling for a boycott of grapes and focusing attention on pesticide issues and labor practices.

We also need to preserve sacred lands such as Big Mountain and end the destruction of indigenous peoples and cultures. If the Earth is sacred to us, we must preserve the wilderness that's left because that's the place we go for renewal, where we can most strongly feel the immanence of the Goddess.

Also with Earth go feeding the hungry, sheltering the homeless. One of the advantages of seeing issues as integrated, rather than fragmented, is that it can help us avoid false dichotomies. For example, environmental issues *are* social justice issues, for it is the poor who are forced to work directly with un-

safe chemicals, in whose neighborhoods toxic waste incinerators are planned, who cannot afford to buy bottled water and organic vegetables or pay for medical care. Environmental issues are international issues, for we cannot simply export unsafe pesticides, toxic wastes, and destructive technologies without poisoning the whole living body of the Earth. And environmental issues are women's issues, for women sicken, starve, and die from toxics, droughts, and famines, their capacity to bear new life is threatened by pollution, and they bear the brunt of care for the sick and the dying, as well as for the next generation.

Environmental issues cannot be intelligently approached without the perspectives of women, the poor, and those who come from other parts of the globe, as well as those of all races and cultural backgrounds. To take only one example, we cannot responsibly approach questions of overpopulation without facing questions of women's power to make decisions about their own reproduction, to challenge traditional roles and restrictions.

If we approach any issue without taking into account the perspectives of all those it affects, we run the risk of accepting false solutions, for example, that famine or AIDS are acceptable answers to population problems. From a Pagan point of view, such "solutions" are entirely unethical because the ethics of integrity prevents us from accepting a solution for someone else that we are unwilling to accept for ourselves.

False solutions are also dangerous because they divert our attention from the real forces with which we must contend. Like an illusionist's tricks, they distract us from seeing what is really going on and from noticing what really works and what doesn't. What really works to stem population growth is not mass death—wars, famines, and epidemics have produced, at most, a ripple in the rising tide. What works is increasing the security of life for those who are already alive and, especially, increasing women's power and autonomy, women's control over our own bodies and access to work and economic compensation independent of our role in procreation. Feminists have been saying this for a long time, and environmentalists need to listen or their analysis will remain fragmented and shortsighted.

Unless we understand all the interconnections, we are vulnerable to manipulation. For example, we are often told that to end hunger we must sacrifice wilderness. But what will work to end hunger is not the further destruction of natural resources within the same system of greed and inequality that has engendered hunger. In their book, *World Hunger: Twelve Myths* (New York: Grove Press, 1986), Frances Moore Lappé and Joseph Collins make the point that people are hungry not because there isn't enough food in the world, but because they are poor. To end hunger we must restore control over land and economic resources to those who have been disenfranchised by the same forces that destroy, with equal lack of concern, the life of a child or a tree or an endangered species, in the name of profit.

And so we come to the roots of the tree—our economic base. Our economy reflects our system of values, in which profit replaces inherent value as the ultimate measure of all things. If we saw ourselves as interconnected parts of the living being that is the Earth, of equal existential value, we could no longer justify economic exploitation.

Our economy is one of waste. The biggest part of that waste is that it's an economy of war, which is inherently wasteful. We need to transform that into an economy that is truly productive and sustainable. To do that we need economic justice—economic democracy as well as political democracy.

Then we can support the branches of the tree, which reach out into the future, touching upon such issues as caring for our children, education, and the values that we teach people. Protecting the future also involves challenging potentially dangerous technologies like genetic engineering. It means basing our decisions, plans, and programs on our obligation to future generations.

In the heart of the tree, the center, is how we treat each other. To work on any of these issues, we must transform the power relationships and the hierarchies of value that keep us separate and unequal. We must challenge the relations of domination between men and women, between light people and dark people, between rich people and poor people; we must do away with all of those things that my friend Luisah Teish calls the "Ism brothers." Then we can really begin treating each other with that sense that each one of us has inherent value, that nobody's interests can be written off and forgotten.

These are the ways I see the issues as being interconnected. Ultimately, to work on any one of them, we need to work on all of them. To work on all of them, we can start at any place on that circle or part of the tree. What I would envision ecofeminist groups

saying is: "Let's do it. Let's turn the environmental destruction around. Let's have a movement we call Turning the Tide and commit ourselves to it. Not as a short-term thing that we're going to do for a year and then burn out, but as a way of transforming and changing our lives."

We can begin this long-term commitment by first getting together with people in a small way and forming our own action groups, our own circles for support, which can take on their own characters and their own personalities. Maybe you will form a circle where members take off their clothes and go to the beach and dance around and jump in the waves and energize yourselves that way. And then you'll all write letters to your congresspersons about the ozone condition. Maybe somebody else will form a circle in their church where members sit on chairs and meditate quietly and then go out to Nevada and get in the way of the nuclear testing. But whatever we do, our spirituality needs to be grounded in action.

Along with seeing issues as interconnected, we need to all be able to envision new kinds of organizing. We need to envision a movement where our first priority is to form community, small groups centered around both personal support and action, and to make that what people see as their ongoing, long-term commitment. We don't have to commit ourselves to some big, overall organization. We can commit ourselves to eight other people with whom we can say, "We can form a community to do political and spiritual work and find support over a long period of time." Then our communities can network and form organizations around issues and around tasks as needed, and can dissolve the larger organizations and networks when they're not needed.

I want to end with my vision of where this might all bring us. It's an optimistic one because, ultimately, I do believe that we can do it. We really can turn the tide—we can reverse the destruction of the Earth.

And so the time comes when all the people of the earth
　　can bring their gifts to the fire
　　and look into each other's faces
　　unafraid

Breathe deep
Feel the sacred well that is your own breath, and look
　　look at that circle
See us come from every direction
　　from the four quarters of the earth
See the lines that stretch to the horizon

the procession, the gifts borne
  see us feed the fire
Feel the earth's life renewed
And the circle is complete again
  and the medicine wheel is formed anew
  and the knowledge within each one of us
  made whole
Feel the great turning, feel the change
  the new life runs through your blood like fire
  and all of nature rises with it
  greening, burgeoning, bursting into flower
At that mighty rising
  do the vines rise up, do the grains rise up
  and the desert turns green
  the wasteland blooms like a garden
Hear the earth sing
  of her own loveliness
  her hillock lands, her valleys

  her furrows well-watered
  her untamed wild places
She arises in you
  as you in her
Your voice becomes her voice
Sing!
Your dance is her dance
  of the circling stars
  and the ever-renewing flame
As your labor has become her labor
Out of the bone, ash
Out of the ash, pain
Out of the pain, the swelling
Out of the swelling, the opening
Out of the opening, the labor
Out of the labor, the birth
Out of the birth, the turning wheel
  the turning tide

E I G H T Y

Consumption
North American Perspectives
H. Patricia Hynes

Sorting through a pile of books, pamphlets, and journal articles put aside for writing this piece on consumption, I came upon a report from a nongovernmental organization (NGO) promoting a simple, fairly low-cost solar cooker. The NGO, Solar Cookers International, recently undertook a pilot project with Somali women living in a refugee camp on Kenya's northeastern border with Somalia. A cadre of women was trained to teach some 2,000 other women in the camp how to use a solar cooker for cooking, baking, and boiling liquids.

When interviewed about the cookers' utility, refugee women described the hours they spent searching for sticks in the fragile desert environment (many left at 4 a.m. and returned at noon twice per week), the hazards of snakes and scorpions, the risk of being raped by bandits, and the need to trade food for fuel in the camp when fuel-gathering was inadequate. Solar cookers give them time, they said, for rest and for other tasks, including planting and nur-

turing trees in exchange for the cookers.[1] With the cookers, they are spared hours spent bending over open wood fires and inhaling wood smoke — the daily equivalent in some cases, of many packs of cigarettes and the proximate cause of acute respiratory infections (the "most pervasive cause of chronic illness in developing nations").[2] Fire hazards to children are eliminated. And the food, cooked slowly in its own juices, is moister and tastier than fire-cooked meals.

The connections between solar cookers and environmental health extend farther still. Two of the highest risk factors for mortality and loss of healthy life among people in developing countries are malnutrition and contaminated water supply with concomitant poor hygiene.[3] The cooker can pasteurize water and milk; it retains more nutrients in the cooking process and can be used to dry food for preserving. Moreover, the urban and rural poor — who pay upward of 20 percent of their disposal income

Figure 1. Share of Population, Hazardous Waste Production, and Natural Resource Consumption in the United States, Developing, and Developed Regions, 1990s

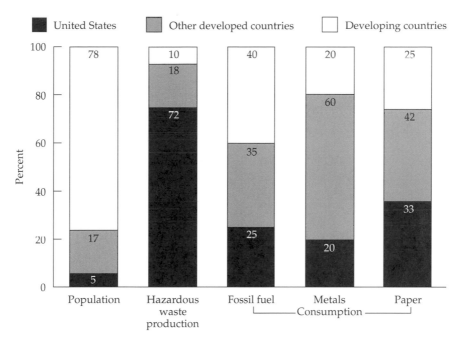

Source: Natural Resources Defense Council, in Lori S.Ashford, *New Perspectives on Population: Lessons from Cairo. Population Bulletin* (Washington, DC: Population Reference Bureau, Inc.), Volume 50, No. 1 (March 1995), 30.

for wood or charcoal—can buy fresh food in lieu of cooking fuel.[4]

Half of the world's people eat food cooked over wood and charcoal; more than three billion people depend on wood, biomass, and charcoal for the majority of their energy use.[5] Thus, the widespread dissemination of an easy-to-assemble and easy-to-use solar technology in sun-rich countries has enormous potential to save woodlands, to stem desertification and soil erosion, and to slow global climate change. (Who has more vested in saving local woodlands, pastures, and soil than the rural poor for whom these resources are the source of daily life?)

By chance, the solar cooker material lay near a pamphlet published by the Population Reference Bureau, Inc., which explicates the so-called population-environment nexus. A bar graph illustrates the consumption of primary materials (including fossil fuels, metal, and paper) and the production of haz-

ardous waste by aggregate populations in the United States, other developed countries, and developing countries [See Figure 1].

The accompanying analysis relies on the iconic population-consumption-technology formula, I = PAT, and a recent add-on variable called "carrying capacity": The impact of humans on the environment (I) is a function of their population size (P), their consumption of resources (A), the pollution impact of producing and consuming those resources (T), and the capacity of particular environments to support this human activity. The populous poor (such as the refugee women in northeastern Kenya), the author argues, have increased incentives to exploit marginal forest and soil resources because of poverty and lack of economic opportunity; thereby, they can and do cause acute environmental degradation. Although the very poor of the developing world consume and pollute little in comparison to

Figure 2. U.S. Household Ownership of Appliances, 1960–88

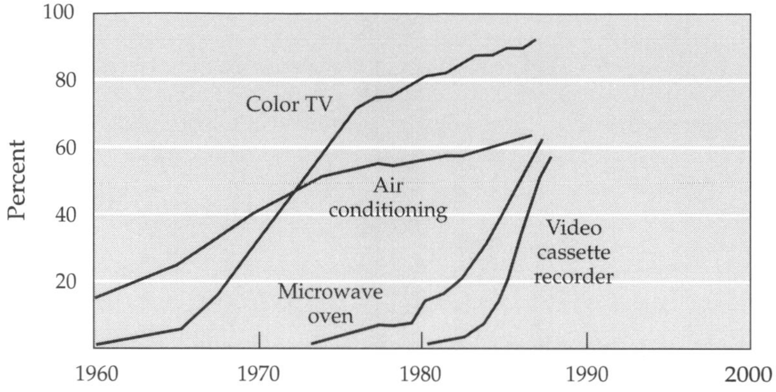

Source: Alan Durning. *How Much Is Enough?* (New York: W. W. Norton, 1992), 32.

the developed world (as Figure 1 amply illustrates), they often live in critical, degraded habitats with minimal capacity to support humans. Thus, every stick taken by a woman for cooking the next meal, the argument implies, contributes to lowered water tables, soil erosion, desertification, and landslides. Slowing population growth among the very poor is the imminent solution to saving critical habitats from the survival consumption of the poor.

In the chance juxtaposition of the Solar Cookers International report and the Population Reference Bureau pamphlet, I found the crux of my argument for this essay on consumption: The consumption of resources by individuals, by governments and ruling elites, by semi-autonomous and secretive institutions such as the military, and by macroeconomic systems is embedded within the matrix of political economy and cultural values. Yet consumption—like demographics-driven theories of "population"—has been reduced to a mere empirical, per capita phenomenon, as if it were detached from those structural and ideological forces that result in wealth-building for some and impoverishment and poor health for others. The huge discrepancy in natural resource use between the wealthiest and the poorest peoples of the world (and its compelling injustice) withers and dissipates when the very poor are accused of having incommensurate impact on their local ecosystems by their minimal efforts to survive. Thus, the issue of consumption needs no less debate than feminists have given to population-control ideology.

What, then, is the content of recent North American critiques of consumption and consumerism? What are their strengths and weaknesses? What core elements of a woman-centered analysis can we bring to them?

Within this decade, a handful of analyses and practice-based responses have emerged to characterize, critique, and provide alternatives to consumption patterns and consumerist ideology in industrialized countries. Among the chief prototypes are three approaches: the "demographics of consumption," movements to simplify life and make consumer choices that are less environmentally damaging, and the computation of the ecological footprint.

Demographics of Consumption

Asking the question "How much is enough?" Worldwatch Institute researcher Alan Durning has amassed quite a stunning picture of the explosion in the consumption of consumer goods and services in the United States and worldwide.[6] He traces the origins of "consumer society" in the United States to the 1920s, with the emergence of name brands, the entrée of packaged and processed foods, the rise of the car as the popular symbol of American upward mobility, and the birth of mass marketing through advertising. Consumerism was stymied by the Depression and World War II, but it picked up enormous momentum in the United States after the war and was rapidly disseminated worldwide, under the gospel of development and the democratization of consumerism, to gain markets for expanding U.S. industries. To cite a few supporting statistics on the radical change in post–World War II consumption: People in the United States own, on the average, "twice as many automobiles, drive two and a half times as far, use 21 times as much plastic, and cover 25 times as much distance by air as their parents did in 1950."[7]

Durning's data on the growth in household appliance ownership over time embody the triumph of the central message of mass marketing: Greater purchasing power and growing choice in the marketplace guarantee a better (and happier) life. Popular culture advertising underpins the macroeconomic maxim: An expanding economy—with rising per capita income and consumer spending—is a healthy economy.

Comparing global patterns of consumption leads Durning to a deeper inquiry into the qualitative differences in consumption among peoples in the world. He asks what kinds of resources people consume on a day-to-day basis and structures his answer around a comparison of consumption by diet, transport, and principal type of materials used. The result is three classes of consumption, the latter two being of much sounder environmental quality than the first, which has no sustainable characteristics.

The primary focus of this tripartite view of consumption in the world—emerging from Worldwatch Institute and a number of liberal environmental, economic, and alternative-lifestyle circles in the United States—is the plight of the consumer class in the United States. Economist Juliet Schor points out that people in the United States work more hours today in their jobs than they did two decades ago, even though we are twice as productive in goods and services as we were in 1948. Why, instead of working more and having less leisure, do we not work less and enjoy more leisure, she queries. Describing the pitfalls of consumerism and the manufacture of discontent that keep middle-class people locked into a work-and-spend cycle, she calls for overcoming consumerism, revaluing leisure, and rethinking the necessity of full-time jobs.[8]

Both Schor and Durning hinge a key part of their prescription—that people rethink and modify their consumerist work- and lifestyles—on the question of happiness. National polls conducted since the 1950s show no increase in the percentage of people who report being "very happy," despite the fact that people now purchase almost twice the number of consumer goods and services they did in the 1950s. Time spent enjoying two of the classic sources of happiness—social relations and leisure—has diminished as people work more to purchase more nondurable, packaged, rapidly obsolete, nonvital goods and services.

Durning advocates that the consumer class be wary of the estimated 3,000 advertising messages that bombard us per day cultivating consumer taste and needs, and that we climb a few rungs down the consumption ladder by choosing durable goods, public transportation, and low-energy devices. In other words, he points to the consumption patterns of the 3.3 billion "middle consumer class" people in Table 1 as more sound and sustainable for the environment.

Voluntary Simplicity Movement

Arising from these same cultural observations, the voluntary simplicity, or new frugality, movement offers a new road map for those of the consumer class who wish to live better with less. Begun in Seattle and strong in the Northwest, this movement was given a high profile by the best-selling book *Your*

Table 1. World Consumption Classes, 1992.

CATEGORY OF CONSUMPTION	CONSUMERS (1.1 BILLION)	MIDDLE (3.3 BILLION)	POOR (1.1 BILLION)
Diet	meat, packaged food, soft drinks	grain, clean water	insufficient grain, unsafe water
Transport	private cars	bicycles, buses	walking
Materials	throwaways	durables	local biomass

SOURCE: Durning, 27.

Money or Your Life, a pragmatic self-help approach to living securely on less money in order to spend one's time in more meaningful social, personal, spiritual, and environmentally sustaining ways.[9]

In this movement, people learn to assess their real financial needs (with generous distinctions made between "needs" and "wants"), how to budget and invest to achieve financial independence on a substantially reduced income, and how to calculate the impacts of their lifestyle on the environment through household audits of energy, products, and waste. More than 300,000 people have developed "new road maps" for their future lives, based on core values they have identified in the process of rethinking what ultimately matters to them. Most reduce their cost of living by 20 percent immediately and, eventually, by even more; many "retire" from careers and full-time jobs to pursue personal and social interests.

If It's Good for the Environment and Good for the Person, What's the Problem?

How can we fault the appeal to happiness and to core values that these critiques of the consumerist culture make? They result in people living "more softly" on the Earth. They reach deeper into a person's self than the green consumer movement, which redirects, but does not necessarily reduce or challenge, consumerism. How many green products are designed for durability and marketed as such? The majority of green product manufacturers employ mass marketing techniques, including the cultivation of "need," and use shallow appeals to feel-good environmentalism to sell their products. Green consumers get locked into seesaw debates over plastic versus paper, for example, never learning that the debate is a foil that deters deeper questions of product durability and necessity. At its best, says Durning, green consumerism outpaces legislation and uses market tactics to reform the market; at its worst, it is "a palliative for the conscience of the consumer class, allowing us to continue business as usual while feeling like we are doing our part."[10]

The primary shortcoming of the "consumer treadmill" critique is that it is socially and politically underdeveloped. Focusing on average per capita consumption, Durning and others make little dis-

tinction among the highly disparate economic classes of people within the United States. While our society as a whole is locked into meat, packaged food, soft drinks, and throwaways—with a McDonald's on every corner—the gap between the poorest fifth and richest fifth of the United States begs for an environmental policy that is based on "a hunger and thirst for justice" as well as national concern about global climate change and the decline of personal happiness. The prescriptions to live on less, to get out of the rat race and enjoy more leisure, to examine one's personal values and organize one's life by those values, may not necessarily result in a more equitable or humanistic society. Those who choose voluntary simplicity, durables, and bicycles may live happily and stress-free across town from the angry (or depressed) involuntary poor, with no more empathy, solidarity, or insight into undoing social injustice. (Alternatively, of course, by choosing to live on less, people may end up in less expensive mixed-income neighborhoods, join their neighborhood associations, and, in so doing, meet and collaborate with the involuntary poor on neighborhood betterment.)

The focus on the cultivation of need by mass marketing and the lack of personal fulfillment, when divorced from an inquiry into the patterns and structures that reward the well-off and punish the poor, creates islands of better-living and more personally satisfied people without necessarily generating a sense of a new social movement or new society. "Twelve-step" programs to break the consumer habit offer good techniques borrowed from self-fulfillment and self-control support-group settings, but they are no substitute for social responses to persistent poverty, to misogyny that sells women as sex to be consumed, to child labor and sweatshops, to the consumption engine of militarism and military spending that siphons the life force out of societies, and to all oppressions of "the other."

Social consciousness within the environmental movement on the other hand, speaks to people's civic and humanistic being, to their quest for a connectedness with others and the earth, to their desire to make the world more just and humane, as well as to the stressed, overworked, and seemingly optionless plight of individuals caught on the work-and-spend treadmill of late-20th-century industrial life. Taming consumption through a personal, spiritual quest is part of the answer, but not the whole one.

Table 2. The Ecological Footprint of the Average Canadian, in Hectares per Capita.

	ENERGY	BUILT ENVIRONMENT	AGRICULTURAL LAND	FOREST	**TOTAL**
Food	0.4		0.9		**1.3**
Housing	0.5	0.1		0.4	**1.0**
Transport	1.0	0.1			**1.1**
Consumer Goods	0.6		0.2	0.2	**1.0**
Resources in Services	0.4				**0.4**
TOTAL	**2.9**	**0.2**	**1.1**	**0.6**	**4.8**

SOURCE: Mathis Wackernagel, *How Big Is Our Ecological Footprint?* (Vancouver: University of British Columbia, 1993), 3.

The Ecological Footprint

The intriguing epithet "ecological footprint" is short-hand for an analysis that more successfully integrates the calculation of consumer impact on the earth with the responsibilities of government, the right of every human to a fair and healthful share of the Earth's resources, and a deep concern for not overloading or degrading global ecosystems.[11] Here, too, the focus is primarily the North American consumer lifestyle and an accounting of its impacts on the environment. However, the goal is to calculate the size of the Canadian and U.S. ecological footprint compared with that of others in lesser-industrialized and non-industrialized countries and to determine how the oversized North American footprint can be reduced through better regional planning, more ecologically conscious consumption, and the restructuring of industrial technology and economics.

This ecological accounting tool, as geographer Ben Wisner points out so well, inverts "carrying capacity" to ask: Given nearly six billion people in the world, how should we live so as to enable all to live within the limits of the biosphere?[12] The premise of the ecological footprint is that although half the world lives in cities (and by 2020 an estimated two-thirds of people will), we live in a biosphere much larger than the physical boundaries of our cities and towns when we buy goods that are grown or made from resources outside our municipality or region and when we dispose of our wastes in the global atmosphere and marine environments. The ecological footprint is calculated by translating key categories of human consumption — food, housing, transport, consumer goods and services — into

the amount of *productive land* needed to provide these goods and services and to assimilate their resultant waste.

Using assumptions about biomass substitutes for fossil fuels and so on, the authors of this method, Mathis Wackernagel and William Rees, calculate that the amount of land needed to support the average Canadian's present consumption, or ecological footprint, is 4.8 hectares.

In their calculations of ecologically productive land, Wackernagel and Rees estimate that an average of 1.6 hectares of land per capita is available worldwide for goods and services. In other words, the average Canadian uses three times as much of the earth's capacity as is available to every person; in other words, the average Canadian's ecological footprint is three times the size it ought to be, since everyone deserves a fair share of the global commons. Correspondingly, the average Indian ecological footprint is 0.4 hectare per person.

The average per capita consumption in Canada, as in every country, is a composite of the consumption of the rich, poor, and middle consumption classes. Thus, Figure 3 compares the ecological footprints of various Canadian households in order to show where the extremes of consumption lie and whose consumer lifestyle inordinately appropriates the carrying capacity of the Earth.

Three aspects of this analysis are particularly laudable. First, its starting point is the assumption that every human being has the same claim on nature's productivity and utility. Thus, it is inequitable and undesirable for North Americans to appropriate others' share of the global commons. Second, it promotes an urban and regional planning strategy

**Figure 3. Examples of Ecological Footprints of
Various Canadian Households, in Hectares per Capita**

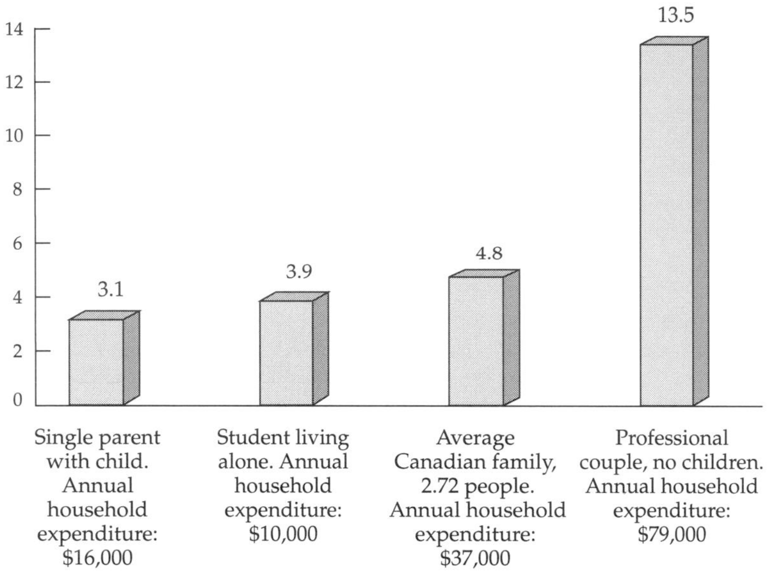

Source: Wackernagel, 3.

that would reduce North Americans' footprint on the global environment by reversing sprawl through integrating living, working, and shopping; promoting bike paths and public transportation; and favoring the local economy. Third, it calls for a massive reform of industrial society to free up the ecological space needed by the poor to raise their standard of living, while enabling the well-off to maintain their high material standards.[13] Wackernagel and Rees's recommendations for restructuring industrialism to achieve a smaller ecological footprint on the world include reforms that are simultaneously being advocated by radical environmental economists:

- Shift taxes from income to consumption and include the full costs of resources and pollution in consumer products through environmental taxes and fees. Including true environmental costs in the full cost of products will motivate industry to make cleaner products and consumers to buy them; it will favor reuse, repair, and reconditioning of products.

- Invest in research into energy- and material-efficient technologies to achieve the "four- to ten-fold reduction in material and energy intensity per unit of economic output" needed in industrial countries to reduce the ecological footprint to a sustainable size.

- Invest the anticipated economic gains from the enhanced efficiency in remediating and restoring critical ecosystems.[14]

Even with a more structural approach to macro-economic systems and the socially conscious goal of commonweal, certain footprints, in this analysis, remain invisible. Women have much less stake in the global economy than men—by virtue of having little political and economic power, as well as by holding different economic priorities, in many instances, from men. Thus, women have a smaller individual and structural footprint than men and male institutions. The economic and political institution of the military, for example ([which has an] extreme impacts on economies, cultures, and ecosystems), arises from patriarchal concepts of power and methods of conflict resolution.

What insights and efforts can a woman-centered analysis bring to the issue of consumption in order to further the goals of redistributing and humanizing our use of natural resources, consumer goods, and services, and of mitigating and reversing our pollution impacts on ecosystems?

Conclusion

The commentary of Somali women refugees, when interviewed about the benefits of the solar cooker, provides a robust framework for the elements of a woman-centered analysis of the consumption-environment nexus.

Why are more than a billion women and girls consigned to spending hours daily collecting wood and biomass and ingesting smoke when the dissemination of technologies such as more efficient cook stoves and solar cookers would ease their lives; save their health; and conserve woodlands, soil, water, and biomass in critical ecosystems? Authors Kammen and Dove have identified a bias in science against "research on mundane topics" in energy, agriculture, public health, and resource economics akin to the initial prejudice against the "mundane economics" of the Grameen Bank.[15] Their analysis of the fallacies that underlie the inattention to labor-, time-, health- and environment-saving technologies is consonant with feminist critiques of science culture and science values.[16] According to the canon of science, the premier scientific work is basic research, uncontaminated by the needs of real people and characterized by objective and detached thought. The potential of "breakthrough discoveries" charges the rarefied atmosphere of science research and relegates revisiting old, unsolved, human-centered problems to second-tier science. In this first-order science, abstract theory, mathematical modeling, speed, distance, and scale are privileged over social benefits, qualitative methods, and the local and small-scale applications of "mundane" science. In other words, what might be seen as the subjectivizing, sociologizing, and feminizing of science popularizes and banalizes it.

Why, when a woman leaves a refugee camp to collect fuel for the next meal, must she fear being raped by men in the desert? And why, when she returns without enough sticks or does not have enough food for her family, must she be forced to have sex with male camp guards for food and fuel? The links between rape, food, fuel, and poverty in the Somali refugee camp exemplify the interconnectedness of women's unequal status in society, their sexual exploitation by men, and gender differences in the consumption of goods and services.

Worldwide, in every society and in every economic class, women are less financially secure than men. Insecurity and the need for survival goods and services create dependency; dependency causes women to sell or trade sex for food. Men who buy sex—and also spend money on gambling, alcohol, cigarettes, pornography, and sports—are spending income, in many cases, that is needed by their families for food, health, education, and home improvements. Studies of household economics demonstrate that women and men spend their incomes differently: men spend more on "luxury" items, and women, earning on the average less than men, spend more on the household needs of their families.[17]

Additionally, health data give insight into gender differences in consumer spending. For example, alcohol use is the leading cause of male disability in developed regions and the fourth leading cause for men in developing regions, while for women in developed regions, it is the tenth leading cause of disability. Depression is the leading cause of disease burden for women in developing and developed countries; poor reproductive health and suicide are the other leading causes of poor health for women in developing countries.[18]

Social goodness and community health, as the "ecological footprint" analysis affirms, are requisites and indices of a sustainable community. In our effort to reduce overconsumption through distinguishing genuine needs and consumerist wants, we must confront the consumption of so-called goods and services that are based on the sexual exploitation of women and girls and are often a consequence of war and environmental degradation, such as prostitution, pornography, and mail-order brides. The impeccable logic of environmental justice—that poor communities of color have been systematically exploited by polluters and industry by reason of race, and suffer disproportionately from poor health—holds for women as well. Like racial justice, a sexual justice that seeks to eliminate the sexual exploitation of women is fundamental to environmental justice, to community health, and to social goodness.

Notes

1. *Delivering On a Promise,* annual report (Sacramento, CA: Solar Cookers International, 1995).

2. Daniel M. Kammen and Michael R. Dove, "The Virtues of Mundane Science," *Environment,* Vol. 39, No. 6 (July/August 1997), 12–13.

3. Christopher J. L. Murray and Alan Lopez, *The Global Burden of Disease: Summary* (Boston: Harvard School of Public Health, 1996), 28.

4. Kammen and Dove, "The Virtues of Mundane Science," op. cit., 12.

5. Ibid., 11.

6. Alan Durning, *How Much Is Enough?* (New York: W. W. Norton, 1992).

7. Ibid., 30.

8. Juliet Schor, *The Overworked American: The Unexpected Decline of Leisure* (New York: Basic Books, 1991).

9. Joe Dominguez and Vicki Robin, *Your Money or Your Life* (New York: Viking, 1992).

10. Durning, *How Much Is Enough?* op. cit., 125.

11. Mathis Wackernagel and William Rees, *Our Ecological Footprint: Reducing Human Impact on the Earth* (Gabriola Island, British Columbia, and Philadelphia: New Society Publishers, 1996).

12. Ben Wisner, "The Limitations of 'Carrying Capacity,'" *Political Environments* (Winter–Spring 1996), 1, 3–4.

13. Wackernagel and Rees, *Our Ecological Footprint,* op. cit., 144.

14. Ibid., 144–45.

15. Kammen and Dove, "The Virtues of Mundane Science," op. cit., 10–15, 38–41.

16. See Sue V. Rosser, *Female-Friendly Science* (New York: Teacher's College Press, 1990).

17. Sylvia Chant, *Gender, Urban Development and Housing* (New York: UNDP, 1996), 12–15.

18. Murray and Lopez, *The Global Burden of Disease,* op. cit., 21, 25–26.

◆◆◆

CHAPTER THIRTEEN

Creating Change:
Theory, Vision, and Action

In the last one hundred years, women in the United States have won the right to speak out on public issues, to vote, to own property in their own names, the right to divorce, and increased access to higher education and the professions. Developments in birth control have allowed women to have fewer babies, and family size is much smaller than it was in the early years of the twentieth century. Improved health care and better working conditions mean that women now live longer than ever before. Women's wage rates are inching closer to men's. Issues like domestic violence, rape, sexual harassment, and women's sexual freedom are public issues. As a group women in the United States are more independent—economically and socially—than ever before.

Although women have broken free from many earlier limitations, this book also shows how much still needs to be done. As we argue in previous chapters, many aspects of women's lives are subject to debate and controversy as **contested terrains.** These controversial issues include women's sexuality, reproductive freedom, the nature of marriage and family relationships, the right to livelihood independent of men, and the right to affordable health care. Gains have been made and also eroded, as conservative politicians aided by conservative religious leaders and media personalities attempt to turn the clock back. Suzanne Pharr notes the success of the religious Right in Reading 85 and argues for a revitalized progressive politics, not in the narrow party sense of Republican and Democrat, but in terms of broad-based coalitions and alliances.

Politics is about power: What is it? Who has it? How is it used? Who does it benefit and who is disadvantaged? It is easy to review the details of U.S. women's experiences of discrimination and to come away feeling angry, depressed, hopeless, and disempowered. The interlocking systems that keep women oppressed can seem monolithic and unchangeable. Major U.S. social movements of the past one hundred years—for the rights of working people; the civil rights of peoples of color; women's liberation; disability rights; gay, lesbian, bisexual, and transgender rights—have made gains and also seen those gains challenged and attacked.

In this final chapter we consider what is needed to tackle the problems for women that we have identified throughout the book. How can this be done in ways that address underlying causes as well as visible manifestations? More fundamentally, how can we—women and men—build relationships, systems of work, local communities, and a wider world based on sustainability and real security?

Each person needs to find meaning in his or her life. Knowing a lot of facts may be an effective way of doing well on tests and getting good grades, but this kind of knowledge does not necessarily provide meaning. Knowing what matters to you means that you can begin to take charge of your own life and begin to direct change. This process involves examining your own life, as suggested through the questions included in each chapter. Unless you examine your own life, you will be absent from your own system of knowledge.

The process of creating change requires a combination of theoretical insights and understandings, visions of alternatives, and action. This involves using your head, heart, and hands in ways that reinforce one another. The readings in this chapter include a blend of these three aspects.

Using the Head: Theories for Social Change

Throughout this book we have presented information, and analytical and theoretical writing, about women's lives as well as women's descriptions and analyses of their experiences. The issues, as we have presented them, are multilayered, especially when viewed in terms of the intersections of gender, race, class, and nation. As scholars and editors, we want readers to come away with a clear sense that women's lives are complex and are often affected by contradictory pressures and expectations. As we argued in Chapter 1, facts do not speak for themselves but through the framework in which they are placed. Key points that arise out of Chapters 1–12 provide examples of this. In very summary form they represent our understandings on which our ideas for change are based.

- Our personal identities — rooted in a complex mix of gender, race, class, nation, culture, and history — shape who we are, how we relate to others, and how we understand the world.

- We are embodied human beings. Through our bodies we sense and experience the world around us. Our bodies are also culturally constructed with reference to gender norms, ideal standards of beauty, and prevailing ideas about sexuality. Seemingly personal issues are also profoundly political.

- Through personal and family relationships we learn about ourselves and how to live with others. The larger social system affects personal relationships, as well as our situation and opportunities in this society. Women are not equally placed because of differences based on race, class, age, sexuality, disability, and nationality. Moreover, as a group, women are not equal to men in many aspects of life.

- Sexual violence and the fear of violence affect women's lives and can limit our confidence, our sense of possibility, and our actions.

- The global economy affects work opportunities worldwide.

- More women in the United States are working for wages than ever before. This brings opportunities and responsibilities, especially as most conditions of work are not geared to parenting. The polarization of the job market and greater restrictions on welfare payments to mothers who are not in paid work means that many women barely make a living.

- Women's health has improved overall, though there are differences linked to race and class. In general, the health system is not geared to research women's illnesses, to care for chronic illnesses that affect women more than men, or to use alternative therapies based on the concept of wellness.

- Many more women than ever before are incarcerated, especially poor women of color.

- More women are joining the military as a way to better their situation in life. Others oppose military values and argue for alternative ways of thinking about security.

- Women and children are particularly affected by environmental pollution. Many women are campaigning for clean air, water, and food and for healthy living and work environments.

As we pointed out in Chapter 1, doing something about an issue or a problem requires us to have a theory, an explanation, of what it is. The theory we create directly shapes what we think ought to be done about it. Thus *how* we theorize is a key first step in creating change. When people face difficult problems alone, they can draw only on their own insights. Although these are valuable, they are likely to be limited. In talking things over with others, we may discover that they are also facing a similar situation or have done so in the past, that their perspective sheds light on things we may have missed, or that they provide a whole different way to think about what we are dealing with. Similarly, if we only examine the specifics of an issue, examine each issue separately, or use a limited analytical framework, we will end up with limited understandings of women's lives. For a fuller picture we need to analyze issues individually and together, looking for commonalities, recognizing differences, and using frameworks that illuminate as many parts as possible.

This principle has guided our choices in making the selections for this book. Our theoretical ideas, which run through the previous chapters — sometimes explicit, sometimes implicit — are summarized here:

- A social-constructionist perspective allows us to see how social and political forces shape our lives and our sense of ourselves in ways we may not have been aware of. It encourages us to focus on the specificity of experience and also the diversity of experiences among people. It allows us to see that situations and structures are not fixed for all time but are changeable under the right circumstances.

- How an issue is defined and framed will affect how we think about the problem, where we look for probable causes, our ideas about what ought to be done about it, and who is likely to become involved.

- In analyzing social situations, it is necessary to look at them in terms of micro, meso, macro, and global levels and to understand how these levels affect one another. Strategies for change need to address all of these levels.

- There are many women's activist organizations and projects working on the issues discussed in this book.

- Efforts to create equal opportunities for women and equal access to current institu-

tions have made a difference for many women, but by themselves they cannot achieve a genuinely secure and sustainable world because these are not the goals of most institutions.

Theories for social change also involve ideas about how change happens. We see a key role for individuals, as change agents, working with others to envision alternatives and bring them into being through collective action.

Using the Heart: Visions for Social Change

Vision is the second necessary ingredient in creating social change — some idea of a different way of doing things, a different future for humankind, framed by explicit principles around which human relations ought to be organized. Otherwise, as the saying goes, "If you don't know where you're going, any road will get you there."

Visions are about values, drawing from inside ourselves everything we value and daring to think big. The many demands of our busy lives leave most people with little time or opportunity to envision alternatives. In school and college, for example, we are rarely asked to think seriously about our hopes and dreams for a more truly human world in which to live. Much of what we do is guided not by our own visions but in reaction to the expectations of others and outside pressures. Social issues, too, are framed in reactive and negative terms. People talk about "antiracism," for instance, not about what a truly multicultural society would be like.

Some people scorn this step as time-wasting and unrealistic. What matters, they say, is to come up with ideas that people feel comfortable with, that businesses will want to invest in, or that fit government programs and guidelines. Tackle something small and specific, something winnable. Don't waste time on grandiose ideas.

Because most of us are not encouraged to envision change, it may take a while to free ourselves from seemingly practical ideas. Our imaginations are often limited to what we know, and that makes it difficult to break out of our cramped daily routines and habits of thought. Envisioning something different also means putting on hold the voice inside your head that says: Are you *crazy*? This will never work! Who do you think you are? Where will you *ever* get the money? Better keep quiet on this one, people will think you're nuts. . . .

Go ahead. Envision the multicultural society, the women's health project, the community play/read/care program for elders and children, the Internet information business run by inner-city teenagers, the women's taxi service, the intimate relationship of your dreams, your blossoming sexuality. Envision it in as much detail as you can. Think it, see it, taste it, smell it, sing it, draw it, and write it down. Share it with others who you think will be sympathetic to it. This is where you're headed. Now all you need is to create the road. The projects we mention throughout this book, like this book itself, all started this way, as somebody's dream.

Using the Hands: Action for Social Change

The third essential ingredient for change is action. Through action, theories and visions are tested, sharpened, and refined to create even more useful theories and more creative visions. In Chapter 1 we referred to Rosenberg's (1988) distinction between *knowing* and *understanding*. Rosenberg further argues that understanding compels us to action, even though we may not initially want to change our habitual ways of thinking and being. When you understand something, you

> find that [your] world becomes a different world and that [you] must generate a new way to be in the new world. Since each person's way of being in the world is relatively fixed — and serves as protection against the anxieties of the unknown — integration is extremely hard. To give up a world in which one's life makes sense means undergoing great loss. Yet without the readiness to risk that loss we cannot hope to pursue understanding.
>
> *(p. 382)*

In previous chapters we mentioned various activist projects, which are all relevant to this discussion. In this chapter, readings by Suzanne Pharr (Reading 85), Cynthia Cohen (Reading 86), and Elizabeth Wilson-Compton (Reading 87) address spe-

cific projects. Here we suggest a range of avenues for trying to implement your visions. Some will be more appropriate than others, depending on your goals and theoretical perspectives. Some of the activities we list below may be impossible for students, who need to concentrate on getting degrees, to participate in. Progressive social change is a long-term project; there will be plenty to do after you graduate.

- Think of yourself as someone with something valuable to say, as someone who can take the initiative and start something you think is important. Think about what you want to do after college, how to live your values and ideals.

- Express your ideas: talk to others; write 'zines, poems, leaflets, speeches, letters to newspaper editors and politicians; put up flyers or posters; organize a film series; paint murals, dance, sing, or perform your ideas.

- Be a conscious shopper. Support fair-trade products; boycott products made in sweatshops, for example. Buy directly from farmers' markets or craft producers. Spend your money where it will support your values.

- Support women's organizations, environmental groups, antiracist organizations, or gay/lesbian/bisexual/transgender groups by letting them know you appreciate their work, letting others know these groups exist, attending events, donating money or something the group needs, volunteering your time, proposing ideas for projects, working as an intern for college credit.

- Work for institutional change. Within your family you may want to stop others from telling sexist or racist jokes, create greater understanding between family members, or develop more egalitarian relationships. At school you may want to set up study groups to work together, support teachers who help you, point out glaring gaps in the curriculum to teachers and administrators, challenge racism or sexual harassment.

- Participate in direct action politics. This includes interrupting, keeping silent, organizing groups of women to walk together at night, defending clinics where abortions are performed, participating in demonstrations and rallies, boycotts, picketing, rent strikes, tax resistance. Whatever the setting, take back the Nike slogan. Just Do It!

- Get involved in grassroots organizing. Join an existing group or consider starting your own. Meet with others and decide what you can do together to tackle some issue of shared concern. Look for allies, resources, funding. This kind of group may have various goals over time, depending on how long it holds together; it provides a place where people can speak out and express themselves, it creates services that people need, and it provides a base from which people can strategize about how to change things that affect them.

- Participate in coalition politics. Consider joining with other groups on an issue of shared concern so as to be more visible and effective. Coalitions are usually short-term efforts that mobilize the maximum number of people around a single issue or a few issues.

- Learn about local and national issues, and use your vote, even if you think there isn't much choice between candidates. The lesser of two evils is still the lesser of two evils. Let your representatives at city, state, and national level know your opinions. Urge them to use their offices to pass appropriate laws and regulations and to speak out in public situations and to the media. Help to elect progressive candidates. Support them if they get into office, and hold them accountable to their election promises.

- Learn more about international networks and organizations working on issues that concern you. Consider participating in international meetings and bringing the knowledge you gain there to your organizing work back home.

Taking action very often involves risk. A range of supports help us in taking risks: a sense of hope and conviction that women's lives can be improved, anger at current inequalities and injustices, reliable allies, well-thought-out strategies, knowing that others will step in to attend to responsibilities we may have to let go for a while — parents, partners, neighbors, friends, children, or total strangers who make a crucial contribution by freeing us so that we can take action.

Women and Politics

Politics involves the use of power. Sociologists and political scientists define **power** as the ability to influence others. This may be by persuasion, charisma, law, political activism, or coercion (Andersen 2000). As we argue throughout this book, individuals and groups have power based on a range of attributes (race, class, gender, age, education, etc.) that are valued in this society. In patriarchal cultures, for example, men use personal and institutional power to maintain dominance over women and children. This could be by active means or by passively accepting the status quo. Many people focus on the ways in which others exert power over us or on the fact that they have more power than we have. We generally pay less attention to the ways in which we have more power than others. This is true especially for members of oppressed groups, such as women and men of color in the United States, where some fundamental aspect of our existence, if not our identity, is predicated on being "the powerless" in many settings.

Power, then, is the ability to make things happen. Audre Lorde writes of women's personal power (Reading 27, Chapter 4), and several writers in this book refer to the importance of personal empowerment. People have power to make decisions that affect many others through institutions such as education, religion, corporations, the media, the law, the military, and all aspects of government. Sometimes this power can be exercised regardless of individual intent or knowledge of its existence (Baron 1970; Bulhan 1985). Power is expressed in the values and practices of institutions that compel people to think and behave in specific ways. For example, the heterosexist values embedded in our culture and its institutions define the family as a heterosexual couple, legally bound by marriage, and their children. The value and legitimacy attached to this institution is a powerful influence on everyone and is in itself a pressure to marry. Higher education operates out of values that are overwhelmingly Eurocentric, middle class, and masculinist. These values uphold particular ways of learning, certain kinds of discourse, and the use of a specific language. To succeed in college, a student must subscribe to these values, at least in a minimal way.

Power also operates at the community, macro, and global levels. Political scientists have focused on formal political organizations, especially the U.S. Congress, where there are relatively few women. As a result, past studies of women's political participation have seriously underestimated it. Feminist researchers have pointed out that women's political participation includes active membership in a wide range of local, state, and national organizations including women's clubs and labor unions, working in support of candidates for political office, organizing fund-raising events, circulating petitions, participating in letter-writing and call-in campaigns, as well as voting. Flammang (1997) notes that the "daily maintenance of the civil rights movement at the local level was in women's hands" and women were "the mainstay" of the National Welfare Rights Organization (p. 107). During the 1970s, community activism on the part of working-class White women and women of color "grew along with changes in the labor market, the unresponsiveness of local government, and the inadequacy of social services" (p. 108). This activism has continued in the 1980s and 90s, as described by Deanna Jang (Reading 36, Chapter 6), and Mary Pardo (Reading 77, Chapter 12) (also see West and Blumberg 1990; Naples 1997, 1998).

Identity Politics

A personal source of confidence and power is knowing who we are. As we discussed in Chapter 2, the development of identity is a crucial process, ongoing through life. Throughout this book many writers talk about identity and note significant changes in the way they think about themselves over time. Some mention the difficulties of coming to terms with who they are, the complexities of their contradictory positions, or breaking the silence surrounding taboo subjects, thoughts, and feelings. They also comment that coming to new understandings about themselves and being able to speak from a place of personal identity and self-knowledge is profoundly empowering.

Identity politics is a politics that puts identity at the center, based on, for example, age, race, ethnicity, or sexual orientation. It usually involves the assumption that this particular characteristic is the most important in the lives of group members and that the group is not differentiated according to other characteristics in any significant way. Identity politics is concerned with wider opportunities—maybe greater visibility and recognition in society, equality, justice, even liberation for ourselves and our group. Our authoritativeness comes from our experience of a shared identity, some common ground of experience that allows a group to say "we." This identity politics is the foundation for many student organizations, community groups, religious groups, national networks, and major social movements. Examples include women's groups or organizations run for and by students of color on campus, the Appalachian Women's Alliance (Christiansburg, Va.), Revolutionary Sisters of Color (Roxbury, Mass.), the Indigenous Women's Network (Lake Elmo, Minn.), and the many others mentioned in this book, as well as major social movements for labor rights or women's rights in the United States and many other countries (Basu 1995).

At the same time, identity politics has serious limitations, as mentioned by Suzanne Pharr in Reading 85. Groups tend to remain separate, focused on their own issues and concerns, often competing with each other for recognition and resources. The language of identity politics gives voice to people's discrimination and oppression. It does not encourage us to think about identity in a more complex way, as a mix of privilege and disadvantage. In Chapter 2 we introduced the idea that most people occupy multiple positions and that salient aspects of identity may vary significantly depending on the context. An African American graduate student who is about to receive her Ph.D., for example, may be highly respected by her teachers and peers, regardless of their race or hers. A White man walking past her in the street may insult and curse her because she is Black.

Understanding this notion of multiple positionality helps us to see how our personal and group identities are political and how the various identity groups fit together in the wider society. The specific context is crucial. In the public discourse about immigration, for example, there is a fear on the part of White people—usually hinted at rather than stated directly — of being overrun by Asians. When the context shifts to a discussion of peoples of color in the United States, however, Asians become the "model minority," the standard against which African Americans or Latinos are compared unfavorably. Understanding one's identity involves a recognition of the ways in which one is privileged as well as the ways in which one is disadvantaged, and the contradictions that this raises, as noted by Melanie Kaye/Kantrowitz in Reading 84. With this more nuanced perspective, one not only focuses on the circumstances and concerns of one's own group, but also can use the complexity of one's identity to make connections to other groups. Thus, a White, middle-class woman with a hearing disability can take all of these aspects of her identity and understand her social location in terms of privilege as well as disadvantage. This is important for building effective alliances with others, which we discuss in more detail later. Note how writers in this chapter draw on their identities — for example, as an African American woman, a lesbian, a Jewish American woman — as the starting point for their activist work.

Feminist Movements

At the beginning of the twentieth century, suffragists in the United States were nearing the end of a seventy-year-long campaign for women's right to vote, which was finally won in 1920. This campaign had its roots in the nineteenth-century movement for the abolition of slavery. Again in the 1960s, the struggle for racial equality was "midwife to a feminist movement" (Evans 1980, p. 24) as women in the civil rights movement began to look more closely at the ways they were oppressed as women. These two periods are sometimes referred to as the "first wave" and "second wave," respectively.

Feminist movements have centered on women's supposed shared identity as women. In emphasizing their oppression as women, White middle-class feminists of the 1960s and 70s generally glossed over inequalities based on race and class. This assumption of "sisterhood" ignored the experiences of women of color, working-class White women, and White women's racial privilege. Barbara Omolade's feminist activism grew out of her involvement in the civil rights movement in the mid-1960s when she was just out of college (Reading 81). Her mentor and role model was Ella Baker, a courageous and vibrant

African American leader, the executive secretary of the Southern Christian Leadership Conference. Omolade notes that Black nationalism provided a powerful liberatory vision for many young African American activists. Women worked hard alongside men, but became critical of and disillusioned with sexism in the civil rights movement and Black power organizations. In the 1970s and 80s, Omolade was involved in various campaigns, drawing on both the sisterhood of Black feminism and the militancy of nationalism. The greatest challenge for women's organizing has been building an inclusive movement. Barbara Macdonald criticized younger activists for excluding older women (Reading 82). The racism and classism of many White feminists, and the lack of attention to these key issues by established feminist organizations, have been widely criticized and are discussed by Gloria Yamato (Reading 83) and Melanie Kaye/Kantrowitz (Reading 84) (also see Moraga and Anzaldua 1981; Bunch and Myron 1974; Lorde 1984; Rich 1986c; Shah 1997; Smith 1983).

Despite these limitations, women's organizing since the 1960s has been a powerful force for change at micro, meso, and macro levels, and a transforming experience for those involved (Brenner 1996; Davis 1991; DuPlessis and Snitow 1998; Rosen 2000). Women identified sexism in every area of life, including their own personal relationships, traditional gender roles, language, children's play, and symbolic events like the Miss America pageant. They used their own life experience to theorize about patriarchal systems, and they envisioned women's liberation. Some challenged women's exclusion from well-paying jobs in blue-collar trades, higher education, the law, medicine, and the media, as well as seeking to increase pay and improve conditions for jobs based on women's traditional roles. Some organized alternative institutions for women like health centers, publishing projects, music events and recording companies, art, film, writing circles, poetry readings, dances, and women-owned land projects. Others campaigned to elect more women to political office at city, state, and federal levels, on the assumption that this would change law and policy to benefit women. Note that these different approaches were based on different theoretical positions, some women seeking equality with men within existing institutions, others wanting to change these structures to be more liberatory for women and men. Varying theoretical perspectives led to cleavages

Figure 13.1. Women's and Men's Representations in National Legislatures

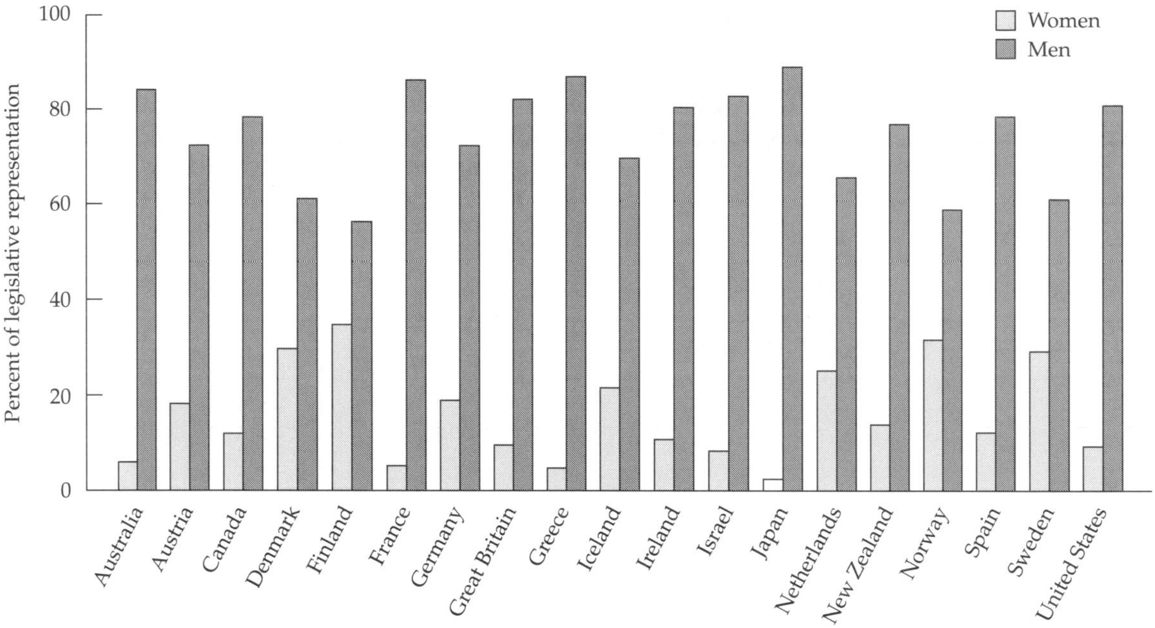

Source: Andersen, M. 2000. *Thinking about Women: Sociological Perspectives on Sex and Gender*, 5th ed. Allyn & Bacon. Data from R. Darcy, Susan Welch, and Janet Clark. 1994. *Women, Elections, and Representation.* Lincoln: University of Nebraska Press, p.78.

between groups, some bitter arguments about strategy and political direction, and a range of activist efforts. Activists moved from project to project as issues arose, as described by Omolade, who links her personal activist history with movement history. Feminist organizations—several of which are mentioned in this book—are one of the most fundamental developments in the United States in the past thirty years (Ferree and Martin 1995).

Women in Electoral Politics

A key strategy for many women has been to support women candidates for political office or to run for office themselves. This includes local offices like parent-teacher associations (PTAs), city council seats, statewide offices, and the U.S. Congress. In 1990 women were 5.6 percent of congressional representatives. According to Susan Carroll of the Center for American Women and Politics at Rutgers University (New Jersey), that put the United States

"about on a par with Iraq and Sri Lanka" (quoted in Davis 1991, p. 204). At that rate, it would be another fifty years before there was equality in state legislatures and at least another three hundred years before there were equal numbers of women and men in Congress. The proportion of women elected to political office has increased since then, though the United States has fewer women in office than many other countries (see Figures 13.1 and 13.2). In 1999 women held 65 (12.1 percent) of the 535 seats in the U.S. Congress: 9 percent of the 100 seats in the Senate and 56 (12.9 percent) of the 435 seats in the House of Representatives. Eighteen women in Congress were women of color. Of the 1,661 women state legislators nationwide, 15 percent were women of color (Center for American Women and Politics 1999). Andersen (2000) notes the impediments that limit women who want to run for political office: prejudice, socialization, and structural factors like lack of support from party leaders, lack of access to extensive political networks, and lack of money. At the

Figure 13.2. Women in the U.S. Congress

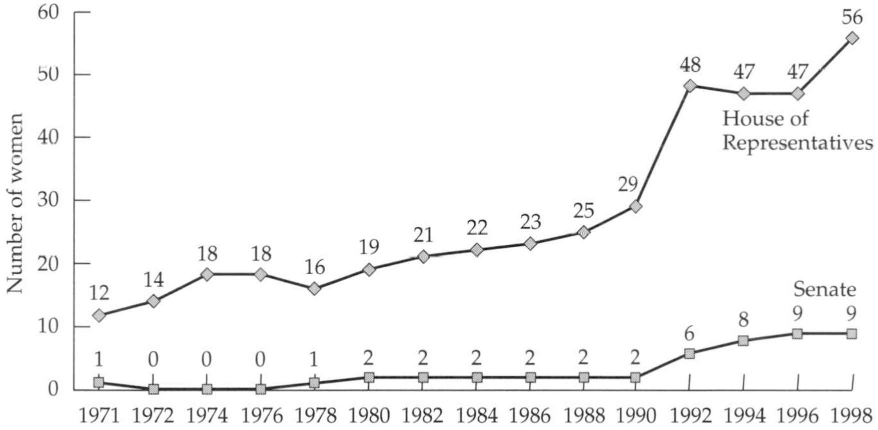

Source: Andersen, M. 2000. *Thinking about Women: Sociological Perspectives on Sex and Gender,* 5th ed. Allyn & Bacon. Data from Center for the American Woman and American Politics. 1995. *Fact Sheet on Women's Political Progress.* New Brunswick, NJ: Rutgers University; Center for the American Woman and American Politics. 1998. *Women's Electoral Success: A Familiar Formula.* New Brunswick, NJ: Rutgers University. Web site: www.rci.rutgers.edu/~cawp/98electpress.html.

same time, women seeking office and organizations like the Fund for a Feminist Majority and the National Women's Political Caucus are working to overcome these limitations (Burrell 1994; Woods 2000).

As elected officials and as voters, women are more likely than men to hold liberal views and to support the Democratic party. For example, more women than men support gun control, a national health-care system, social programs, tougher sentences for rapists and perpetrators of sexual assault and domestic violence, and workplace equality, as well as issues like women's right to abortion and gay/lesbian rights (Grunwald 1992). This **gender gap,** which continued to widen during the 1990s, can be significant in two ways: getting more liberal candidates—women and men—elected and giving greater focus to liberal issues once such candidates are in office (Abzug 1984; Gallagher 1993; Smeal 1984). Note that the gender gap is significant for White voters. The majority of African American and Latino voters hold liberal views, regardless of gender. The assumption of those who are working hard to elect more women is that policy will change when a crit-ical mass of women hold political office. In the mid-1990s there were more women in elected positions than ever before. A growing bipartisan Congressional Women's Caucus

served as a focus for some women's concerns on Capitol Hill. Janet Reno was appointed as the first woman U.S. attorney general in the nation's history, and Madeleine Albright the first woman secretary of state. More women also held high office at the state level, whether as governors, attorneys general, state treasurers, chief educational officers, and so on. Whether or not elected women can make a significant difference in political institutions and public policy that is overwhelmingly dominated by masculinist and corporate interests is a key question.

There are too few women in elected office at all levels, as well as in high appointed positions, to be able to evaluate their effectiveness, though there is some evidence that women can and do make a difference. Many are on committees concerned with health, education, and social services, and they bring their support for women and insights into women's experience to their work. Others are doubtless constrained by political considerations. Madeleine Albright, for example, has been very vocal about women's oppression in Afghanistan, but, following U.S. government policy, she has not pushed for an end to economic sanctions against Iraq—a step that would save the lives of many people, especially women and children. Nor has she intervened in any discernible way in incidents of U.S. military violence against women and children in East Asia, as discussed by Suzuyo Takazato (Reading 40, Chapter 6).

Overcoming Blocks to Effective Action

Political action does not always work; that is, a chosen course of action may not achieve our original goals. There are many possible reasons for this: inadequate theoretical understandings and analysis of the issues; choosing inappropriate or ineffective strategies; not following through on the course of action; not being able to get enough people involved for this particular strategy to be effective; wrong timing; the failure of the group to work together well enough; the failure of people whom you thought were allies to come through when needed; and so on. The other major reason, of course, is that the opposition—whether this is your sexist uncle, your boss, the university administration, the city school board, the opposing political party, or the U.S. Congress—was simply more powerful.

Feeling that an action has failed is disheartening and may lead people to give up, assuming that creating change is hopeless. But action *always* accomplishes something, and in this sense it always works. At the very least, activism that does not meet your goals teaches you something important. In hindsight, what may seem like mistakes are actually valuable ways to learn how to be more effective in the future. This is what we called "socially lived" theory in Chapter 1. Always evaluate what you did after some activity or event, personally and with the group. If it worked as you hoped, why did it work? What have you learned as a result? If it did not work, why? What will you do differently next time?

Personal blocks to activism may include practical factors like not having enough time or energy, or needing to focus on some other aspect of life. Emotional blocks include guilt—a paralyzing emotion that keeps us stuck—and cynicism—a frustrated idealism that has turned hopeless and bitter. Anger can be a very useful, high-octane fuel if you can channel it in a constructive direction. Overextending yourself is not a sign of your commitment to your ideals, and trying to do more than you can, under pressure, is one sure way to burn out quickly. Activism for progressive social change needs patience, humor, creativity, a wide range of skills and resources, an

ability to talk to other people, a willingness to listen and to change, a willingness to be reflective, refining your ideas, holding onto your visions.

In the 1980s and 90s right-wing organizations challenged feminist gains, especially on issues like abortion and gay/lesbian rights, as discussed by Suzanne Pharr (Reading 85). As values shift in the wider society, partly due to successful efforts of women, and men of color, there is a conflict between the pluralistic society that many want to see the United States become and the more authoritarian, monocultural society envisioned by right-wing organizations. Such organizations have often been visible and active following shifts toward greater equality: after the abolition of slavery, after the growth of labor unions in the 1930s, and after the gains of the Civil Rights Act of 1964 and feminist movements of the 1960s and 70s. This resurgence of organizing by conservatives currently manifests in campaigns against reproductive and sexual freedom, a drive for censorship of specific books and the arts in general, opposition to legal immigrants who are said to be taking American jobs, and support for reductions in welfare. Pharr argues for building strong alliances in order to be able to pursue a multi-issue agenda that could take up this range of issues and more. Our concern for security and sustainability at all levels requires large numbers of people working together.

Building Alliances for Social Change

Although one often hears of the failures, of times when alliances did not work, there have also been effective alliances across lines of difference. We emphasize the importance of such alliances for two reasons. First, the many inequalities among women, mentioned throughout this book, often separate us and make it very difficult to work together effectively. Those with power over us know this and often exploit differences to pit one group against another. Second, progressive social change is a slow process that needs sustained action over the long haul. Effective alliances, based on a deepening knowledge of others and learning whom to trust over time, are necessary for long-term efforts, in contrast to coalition work, where the important thing is to stand together around a single issue, regardless of other differences. Alliances across lines of difference are both a means and an end. Gandhi commented that there is no road to peace; peace *is* the road. Similarly, alliances across lines of difference provide both the process for moving toward, and some experience of, multicultural society. Melanie Kaye/Kantrowitz (Reading 84) and Gloria Yamato (Reading 83) offer insights for alliance building, especially across lines of race and class. Cynthia Cohen (Reading 86) and Elizabeth Wilson-Compton (Reading 87) describe projects that bring women together across significant differences.

Some Principles for Alliance Building

- Know who you are, what is important to you, what are your nonnegotiables. Know your strengths and what you bring to this shared venture.

- Decide whether you want to be allies with a particular person or group. What do they stand for? What are their values? What are they interested in doing in terms of creating social change? Are they open to the alliance? What is the purpose for coming together?

- Recognize, honor, and accept the ways you are different from others in the group. You may look different. You may have learned some very different messages from your own community.

- Check out the person or the group as the acquaintance grows. Are they who they say they are? Do they do what they say they believe in? Do you have reason to trust them to be there for you? Judge them by their track records and what actually happens, not by your fears, hopes, or expectations based on previous experiences.

- Commit yourself to communicate. Listen, talk, and listen more. Communication may be through conversations, reading, films, events and meetings, or learning about one another's communities. Work together on projects and support one another's projects. Go into one another's settings as participants, observers, guests. Get to know one another in different settings.

- Share the past. Talk about what has happened to you, what has been important, what you've hoped for. Talk about the ways you've changed. If I hear something negative about you, is it the "you" you are now?

- Wanting to understand, to hear more, to stay connected requires patience from the inside. It is not an abstract principle imposed from the outside. Allow one another room to explore ideas, make mistakes, be tentative. Hold judgment until you understand what's going on. Ask the other person to say more. Be committed to the process of communication rather than attached to a specific position.

- Honesty is the most important thing. Be authentic and ask for authenticity from others. If this is not possible, what is the alliance worth? Say honestly what you honestly need.

- Keep the process "clean." Call one another on bad things if they happen—preferably with grace, teasing maybe, firmly but gently, so that the other person does not lose face. Don't try to disentangle difficulties when it is impossible to do so meaningfully, but don't use externals (too late, too tired, too busy, too many other items on the agenda) to avoid it.

- Be open to being called on your own mistakes, admitting when you're wrong, even if it is embarrassing or makes you feel vulnerable. Tell the other person when his or her opinions and experiences give you new insights and help you to see things differently.

- Do some people in the group take up a lot of time talking about their own issues and concerns? Are they aware of it? What is the unspoken power dynamic among people? How does privilege based on gender, race, class, sexuality, disability, age, culture, or language play out in this relationship or alliance? Can you talk about it openly?

- What is the "culture" of your group or alliance? What kinds of meetings do you have? What is your decision-making style? If you eat together, what kind of food do you serve?

What kind of music do you listen to? Where do you meet? What do you do when you are together? Does everyone in the group feel comfortable with these cultural aspects?

- Work out the boundaries of your responsibilities to one another. What do you want to do for yourself? What do you need others to help with? When? How?

- Look for the common ground. What are the perspectives, experiences, and insights we share?

Impediments to Effective Alliances

Over and over again sincere and committed attempts at building alliances have been thwarted, despite the best of intentions. Several common impediments to creating effective alliances include the following beliefs and behaviors:

Internalized Oppression   This is a learned mindset of subservience and inferiority in oppressed peoples. It is the passive and active acceptance of labels, characteristics, prejudices, and perceptions promoted by the dominant society. Specific behaviors include self-hatred and dislike, disrespect for and hatred of others of the same group, isolation, and being satisfied, even grateful for being allowed to exist (Lipsky 1977; Pheterson 1990).

Internalized Domination   This is a mindset of entitlement and superiority among members of the dominant group, which includes the belief that inequalities are normal; thus those in the dominant group never realize that they are privileged. This belief is often accompanied by the contradictory feelings of self-righteousness and guilt. Behaviors such as always speaking first in group discussions, being unconscious of the large amount of physical and social space one takes up, and automatically assuming leadership roles are some manifestations of internalized domination (Pheterson 1990).

Operating from a Politics of Scarcity   This impediment results from a deeply held, sometimes unconscious, belief that there is not enough of anything — material things as well as nonmaterial things like power, positive regard, popularity, friendship,

time — and, more important, that however much there is, it will not be shared equally. In this view, inequality is simply a given that cannot be changed. It also justifies individualism and competition.

Subscribing to a Hierarchy of Oppression   This involves the placement of one oppressed group in relation to another so that one group's experiences of discrimination, prejudice, and disadvantage are deemed to be worse or better than another's. There is an assumption that these experiences can somehow be measured accurately and that a negative or positive value can be placed on certain kinds of experiences.

Not Knowing One Another's History   Ignorance about other persons' backgrounds often results in drawing incorrect conclusions about their experiences. This prevents us from recognizing the complexity of women's experiences and can hide the ways our experiences are both different and similar.

Creating a Secure and Sustainable World

Throughout the history of this country, countless numbers of women have worked on many fronts to improve women's lives. Some provide direct services, such as counseling, support groups, crisis lines, shelters, training schemes, and so forth. Others have become advocates and legislators to reform the existing social, political, and economic institutions so more women will have increased opportunities within these institutions. Still others have the goal of transforming those institutions and establishing values that are fundamentally different from those now in place. We call this third kind of effort at social change a transformational movement, in which one of the main goals is to change the core interpersonal, community, and societal values, not simply to alter or add to existing ones.

Providing services to women in need and reforming existing institutions to make them more responsive to those who are excluded are crucially important in the overall work of progressive social change and have made a difference to generations of women. The challenge for the future is to continue to expand this work. Given the many insecurities of life for women and for men, and the growing threat to the planet itself from increasing industrialization, militarization, and ecological devastation, what sense does it make for women to seek an equal piece of what Ynestra King (1993b, p. 76) has called this "rotten and carcinogenic" pie? In previous chapters we assume a fundamental interdependence between people as an absolute given. We see sustainability in terms of egalitarian relationships, redefined family values, supportive communities, livelihood, wellness, positive notions of security, ecological balance, and hope for the future.

This book is about U.S. women's lives and the kind of world we need to create for women's empowerment, development, and well-being. This world will be based on notions of security and sustainability, as we have suggested here. The project of human development—for both women and men—is one that has been in process for a very long time. Over time there have been important gains as well as serious setbacks. It is our challenge to take the next steps in this process. How can we settle for anything less?

◆◆◆
Questions for Reflection

As you read and discuss this chapter, think about these questions:

1. What are your assumptions about how people and societies change? What do you think needs changing, if anything?

2. Have you ever been involved in a social-action project or electoral politics? What was your experience like? If you have not, why not?

3. Have you ever tried to establish and maintain an ongoing relationship, friendship, or working partnership with someone from a background very different from your own? What happened? What did you learn from that experience? What would you do differently, if anything?

4. If you have had such a relationship, why did you become involved in the first place? Was that a good enough reason? Why or why not? If you never have, why not?

5. What do you know about the history of the various groups you are a member of? What do you know about groups that are not your own? How does knowing this history help, and how does not knowing it hinder you in making alliances across lines of difference?

6. What is your vision of a secure and sustainable personal relationship? Community? Society? World?

◆◆◆
Taking Action

1. List all the ways you are an activist. Review the suggestions for taking action at the end of each chapter. Commit yourself to continuing to involve yourself in issues that matter to you.

2. Think about how aspects of your identity can help you to make alliances with others. Support campus or community groups that are working together on an issue of shared concern.

3. Where do your elected officials (at the city, state, and national levels) stand on issues that matter to you? What is their voting record on these issues? Write to thank them for

supporting issues you care about (if they do), or urge them to change their positions. Present them with information from your course materials or other sources to make a strong case.

4. Many of the issues we have discussed have implications at the global level. What can you do that will have an impact at that level?

E I G H T Y - O N E

Ella's Daughters

Barbara Omolade

I worked with Ella Baker during the summer of 1964 at the Washington, D.C., office of the Mississippi Freedom Democratic Party (MFDP). She was already a legend in the Civil Rights Movement as the advisor to the radical and committed young activists in the organization she founded, the Student Nonviolent Coordinating Committee (SNCC).

Our Washington MFDP office staff included Ms. Baker, Walter Tillow, a white SNCC worker from New York, and myself, a recent college graduate who had been a part-time worker in the New York SNCC office. We were to gain support for seating the delegation from the MFDP instead of the regular Mississippi Democratic Party delegation at the National Democratic Party presidential convention in Atlantic City. We coordinated volunteers who lobbied Democrats on the Hill and raised funds to support MFDP activities.

Although a college graduate, I was so inept and anxious, most of my time was spent trying to deal with my newly discovered sexual freedom and autonomy—and marveling at Ms. Baker. She was everything I was not: self-assured and brilliant. Ms. Baker was able to easily communicate with and gain respect from "ordinary" people, young activists as well as powerful white men such as Attorney Joseph Rauh, a leading Democratic Party advisor. She immediately took command of every situation while I floundered and stumbled through the simplest chores.

In August, the bodies of three missing civil rights workers, Michael Schwerner, James Chaney, and Andy Goodman, were discovered. Andy had been my classmate at college and I had recruited him to participate in the Mississippi Freedom Summer Project. Because of his lynching and the gravity of

the efforts in Mississippi, that summer my identity as a woman became intertwined with becoming like Ms. Baker, an effective and respected organizer. Fighting injustice and oppression, making sacrifices for social causes became, for me, the indicators of true womanhood or manhood. However, as the Civil Rights Movement waned I became absorbed in personal journeys and travels, and then in marriage and motherhood.

However, my interest in Ms. Baker and my quest to emulate her was reawakened by my relationship to the women's movement. I was thrust into the heart of second wave feminism, not by choice or politics—I was a staunch nationalist at the time—but because I worked for white feminist organizations. In the mid-70s, I became the co-coordinator of Women's Survival Space, a 40-bed battered women's shelter located in Brooklyn, and then an administrator at the Women's Action Alliance, a national women's organization and resource center founded by Gloria Steinem and others.

The feminists around me constantly spoke about the roots of feminism being derived from books by Betty Friedan and Simone de Beauvoir, which raised women's consciousness and began a "second wave" of women's activism. Few acknowledged the contributions of white and Black women civil rights workers, or the critical role of the Civil Rights Movement, in general, to the material conditions which made the women's movement possible. The reality that much of Black and white feminist praxis and social theory came from the work and ideas of Ella Baker was ignored.

By the time Ella Baker founded SNCC, she had already been a full-time organizer for the NAACP in the Deep South from 1938 to 1946 and an executive secretary of the Southern Christian Leadership Conference. In 1943 she was named director of NAACP branches, in charge of establishing and maintaining the local chapters. At considerable risk to herself and her constituents, she traveled throughout the South enrolling southern Black people in the NAACP, an outlawed organization whose members were often harassed, tortured, killed, and run out of town. She helped community members identify local leaders and issues for struggle against segregation. This political work confronted the real possibility of torture and death because at the time the South was ruled by legalized apartheid. Not unlike police states and dictatorships worldwide, protesting Black southerners were "disappeared," their homes were bombed, or they were, at the very least, imprisoned. However, Ms. Baker was relentless and courageous in her determination to extend the mutual support and collectivity of Black communities to include active resistance to segregation.

In 1958, after living in New York for 12 years, Ms. Baker returned south at the age of 55 to become the executive secretary of the SCLC, founded by Martin Luther King, Jr. The conference was a network of Black ministers in southern cities who assumed local leadership of mass movements fighting segregation. One of Ms. Baker's assignments was to organize a meeting to mobilize the diverse and disparate groups of students who, during 1960, had "sat in" protesting segregated lunch counters and bus stations. Ms. Baker was outraged and walked out of a meeting where ministers mapped out plans to isolate students by region and pressure them to become part of an SCLC-dominated youth organization. Rejecting these high-handed pressure tactics, Ms. Baker held that "those who were under the heel were the ones to decide what action they were going to take to get from under their oppression." She encouraged the protesting students to establish their own organization, the Student Nonviolent Coordinating Committee (SNCC), and became its advisor, working part time for the Atlanta YWCA to support herself. She hired Jane Stembridge, a white student from Georgia, and Bob Moses, a Black high school teacher from New York, to become SNCC's first field secretaries.

SNCC became a racially mixed group of male and female field secretaries who from 1961 to 1966 organized voter registration and anti-segregation campaigns in Black communities throughout south-west Georgia, Alabama, and Mississippi. Its ambitious Mississippi Freedom Summer Project, organized with nominal support from the NAACP and SCLC, and in active partnership with CORE [Congress of Racial Equality], brought hundreds of northern students and volunteers into the state from 1963 to 1965 to organize Freedom Schools, medical and legal clinics, cultural programs and the MFDP.

Representing the fullest expression of Ella Baker's social praxis, SNCC and MFDP were more political collectives than organizations in the traditional sense. Ms. Baker's social theory and praxis is based upon face-to-face political work involving dialogue, where the organizer/initiator listens to the concerns of "local people," who articulate what they know, receive feedback about their ideas, and offer their own remedies, strategies, or solutions. From a series of dialogues held at people's homes or job sites, the organizer/initiator gathers together several people and calls a meeting—usually at a church. The meetings are usually accompanied by song and prayer, which continue earlier discussions, develop mutual courage, and enable members to resolve to execute an action to change some aspect of their political condition—a voting card, a traffic signal, a new policy. The activity must be decided upon by the consensus of those who will execute and be affected by the action.

The organizer is an "outsider" actively seeking anonymity and no personal rewards, while serving to facilitate the meetings and actions of local leaders and community members. The organizer without domestic or career ties is "called" to social action rather than employed by the civil rights organization.

Although many social theories and movements share Ms. Baker's approach to organizers and communities, hers is one of the few which emerged from an African American ethos of mutual aid and support. "Where we lived there was no sense of hierarchy, in terms of those who have, having the right to look down upon, or to evaluate as a lesser breed, those who didn't have" (Canterow, 60). An organizer's success depended upon "both your disposition and our capacity to sort of stimulate people—and how you carried yourself, in terms of not being above people" (Canterow, 71).

This ethos was expanded to include the collective power to challenge segregation and make social change in communities which were made up of "people from various and sundry other areas . . .

who had to learn each other . . . and begin to think in terms of a 'wider brotherhood'" (Canterow, 61). Class and gender, and even racial differences, were muted in this kind of organizing. White men and women SNCC workers became part of the community by rejecting their own racist backgrounds and communities in order to live and work among and *for* Black people.

Ms. Baker was not overtly ideological. She spouted no pre-packaged party line. She was not a Marxist, although she stood with the working class and the poor. She was not a professed nationalist, although she was deeply rooted in the African American ethos and community. Likewise, she was not a declared feminist but modeled for young Black and white women a powerful womanhood that was not tied to traditional domestic social roles. Ms. Baker was a "liberated" Black woman radical whose genius was her ability to develop democratic and activist political organizations and communities.

In giving students permission to organize on their own behalf and define their own role in the movement, Ella Baker transformed American politics. The organization she birthed, SNCC, took on a life of its own. Her philosophy affirming the right of Black poor people to organize gave rise to a political culture which is now commonplace. The idea of "grassroots" groups of ordinary people organizing to protest, petition, as well as develop their own agendas, was enlarged and expanded by Ella Baker to empower organizers to meet the needs of antisegregation struggles in the Deep South. She developed a network and apparatus among alienated and disparate community leaders during her NAACP organizing years. She connected activist ministers during her SCLC years, concretizing King's vision and enabling him to be a leader among other ministers in the movement. She produced young student leaders who became the movement's "shock troops." Unencumbered by family or jobs, they could go into southern towns and give local people inspiration and technical assistance.

Bringing white and Black college students into SNCC enabled Ella Baker to influence and train leaders who became part of national movements promoting changes in the academy, including the free-speech movement, and protesting the Vietnam War. The white men she mothered brought the New Left Movement into being. The white women she

mothered in the movement inspired others, creating second-wave feminism.

Many white students attribute their political evolution and enlightenment to SNCC, not realizing that SNCC was Baker's creation. Bob Moses, Jim Forman, Ruby Doris Smith Robinson, Dorie Ladner, and other admired SNCC members worked closely with Ms. Baker in *their* formative years.

Her Black daughters combined and took from feminism, nationalism and the New Left, adding their own unique notions, to birth womanism. During the late 1970s and 1980s, a network of Black feminists or womanists in central Brooklyn emerged to carry on the traditions of Ella Baker. These daughters developed organizations and campaigns in spite of sexism and antifeminist sentiments within Black nationalism and the Black community.

During the 1970s most politically active women in Black communities were connected in some way to the building of nationalist institutions and groups. At the heart of many of these efforts was the construction of more explicitly "African" cultural forms. Outwardly signaled by African names, attire, music, and religions, cultural nationalism rejected the "White World" and its values. Many women were attracted to the ideals of nationalism which affirmed their "womanhood" and beauty. However, male nationalists attempted to confine "womanhood" to mating and motherhood. In spite of the significance of Assata Shakur and Angela Davis, most women found themselves restricted by the rather narrow definitions of their role in nationalist organizations.

Many nationalists believed "the struggle" should restore the traditional gender roles destroyed by slavery, colonialism and racism: strong patriarchal warriors with supportive wives who mothered their children. Although some nationalist men believed women should be co-warriors in restoring the Black nation, ultimately their place would be caring for the home and family. Nationalist men sought to restrict women from leadership roles, though they continued to need Black women's labor, creativity, and resourcefulness.

Nationalist women often saw themselves as "warriors" in their own right. Among themselves, sisters balked at being mere supporters and complained of male chauvinism—while maintaining a united front with men against white racism. Many didn't realize that Black women in the past, especially radical organizers such as Ella Baker and revolutionary women around the world, were battling the same two colonialisms: patriarchy and white supremacy.

Although Ms. Baker and other SNCC leaders understood that the struggle was really about creating a more equitable and just society, its immediate goals and forms were straightforward. The issues were there in Black and white: politically powerless Black people fought against the white power structure for the franchise, access to opportunity, and for equal treatment before the law. Such a movement required unity and sacrifice among a critical mass of people to show collective resistance for even a brief and defined period of time—the time it took for a demonstration, protest, or campaign. In this sense, the combination of Ms. Baker's work empowering local people (using students as their legs and arms), NAACP legal strategies, and King's spiritual and inspiring leadership was successful: Blacks have gained the franchise, and access to public facilities. But the movement unearthed other issues: free speech, sexism, peace. African Americans were radically changed because as the high points of the southern movement were ebbing, new forms of nationalist politics were being formed.

Both Ms. Baker and Martin Luther King became overshadowed by Malcolm X's post–civil rights message, which offered an alternate paradigm to citizenship for Blacks. His message of Black self-determination, anti-colonialism, and transformed identification forced Blacks to look at what kind of society they were struggling to become citizens of.

Inspired by the possibilities of nationalism, two of Ella's sons: Kwame Toure (aka Stokeley Carmichael) and Jamil Abdullah Al-Amin (aka H. Rap Brown) abandoned her grassroots, passive resistance strategies for a more militant and ideologically confrontational politics in the Black Panther Party. The Panthers' nationalist positions and radical rhetoric demonstrated their break with the methods of the southern struggle, although they grew out of the party of the same name in Lowndes County, one of SNCC's Alabama projects. Ella's sons rebelled against her model, her philosophy, and her name. The nationalism of organizations and groups founded by nationalist men did not allow women like Ella Baker to participate in their leadership.

In spite of the domination of men, Black women remained active in Black nationalist organizations. Their sisterhood and connection to each other strengthened both their own commitment to all Black people and their definitions of nationalism. These organizations fought police brutality and racist schools while building alternative schools and cultural programs. They helped to foster "community" among those viewed as fragmented and brainwashed by white culture.

The East, founded in 1970 by Jitu Weusi, was the major nationalist institution in central Brooklyn. It began as an outgrowth of an alternative school for Black students expelled from a city high school after staging a tribute to Malcolm X; the protest had been viewed as anti-Semitic and militant by the school authorities. Uhuru Sasa, the East's Freedom School, soon drew hundreds of students supported by parents frustrated and angered at the racism in the public school system. It soon expanded into a cultural institution which included an annual street fair of Black merchants and craftsmen/women, musical concerts, and community forums.

"It is our belief that the most crucial work for this particular era of African existence is the building of Revolutionary Nationalist institutions. By 'institutions' we mean schools, political parties, cultural centers, military units, presses—all those programmatic structures that enable a people to see beyond survival; in short, the elemental ingredients of a viable nation" (*New Africa Education*). The East, at its height, was an internationally known model for this kind of vision.

Women such as Martha Bright, Abimbola, Atchuda Barkr, and Aminisha Weusi demonstrated that strong Black women continued to organize during the cultural nationalist era. Their hard work and strong women's circles enabled them to be effective in spite of male chauvinism. Ironically, most male leaders, needing skilled and loyal workers, expressed admiration and respect for "strong sisters." Some nationalists such as Kalamu ya Salaam and his wife Tayari attempted to address Black male chauvinism through a nonsexist practice involving study, seminars, and pamphlets. There were also some men in the East community who were struggling against their own sexism and its effect on the movement. In fact, during the late 1970s, Segun Shabaka encouraged me, a Black feminist and radical activist, by publishing my articles in the *Black News,* the East-sponsored journal he edited.

When I wrote those articles, I was a single mother of three children, working full time as an administrator at the Women's Action Alliance and part time as an adjunct in women's studies at a local college. As a result of my own search for an effective and hospitable political community, I threw myself into a flurry of activism. In addition to writing for *Black News,* I worked with white leftists, primarily in supporting normalized relationships between the United States and the People's Republic of China. I learned about Marxism and nationalist theory by attending meetings of many radical groups. In 1979, I was in a Black women's study group which included Susan McHenry, one of *Ms. Magazine*'s earliest Black woman editors, and Michele Wallace, when she first published *Black Macho and the Myth of the Superwoman.* I was also active in the Sisterhood of Black Single Mothers and the Women's Committee of the Black United Front. I demonstrated against and protested police brutality and South African apartheid. I spoke on feminism and activism to any group that asked me. I was trying very hard to be like Ms. Baker. Soon I kept meeting other activist Black women such as Daphne Busby, Safiya Bandele, Arlene Parker, Andree McLaughlin and others who could also claim to be Ella's daughters.

In 1972, Daphne Busby, a young single mother, founded the Sisterhood of Black Single Mothers, perhaps the first Black feminist grassroots group of the post–civil rights era not connected to any Black male organization. The Sisterhood always identified itself as a Black and female organization. By supporting Black single mothers and refusing to become embroiled in either feminist or nationalist ideological debates, the Sisterhood opened an entirely new arena for Black women's social activism. The Sisterhood was one of the first organizations to legitimate the connections between personal issues, such as sexuality and motherhood, and Black female consciousness.

Established to counteract the slandering of women who were regularly called "unwed mothers" of "broken homes" with "illegitimate" children, the Sisterhood defended and advocated for Black single mother families. Daphne Busby's pride in declaring herself the head of a "family that works" challenged critics to examine their own prejudices and sexist assumptions about Black single mothers.

The Sisterhood offered consciousness raising, social services, and social activities to diverse Black single mothers: professionals, welfare recipients, middle-age divorcees and teen mothers. As one of the first groups to work with these younger mothers and with Black single fathers, the organization pioneered in social policies and programs concerned with the Black family. While perfecting the white feminist movement's concern with connecting the personal to the political, which was merely a restating of Ella Baker's notion of dialogue, the Sisterhood deepened the Black community's traditions of self-help. Interestingly, the Sisterhood was able to simultaneously gain the respect of white feminists, Black nationalists, and Black single mothers, in part because of the timeless energy of Daphne Busby's outspoken and no-nonsense leadership, and in part for its tangible help for Black single mothers.

For nearly 20 years, the Sisterhood attracted scores of sisters like me who were searching for an authentic place to deal with our personal needs as mothers and women and who needed concrete help with our families. Safiya Bandele was one of the first women to answer Daphne Busby's call for interested Black single mothers to join her. Safiya worked steadfastly along with Daphne, and eventually became the Chair of the Sisterhood board.

By the mid 1970s, Safiya and I began to find ourselves at the same meetings of the Sisterhood, the Black United Front and other groups. She eventually became my closest *companera* because we both were searching for a sisterhood which had the feminism and supportiveness of the sisterhood of Black Single Mothers and the militancy and resistance politics of the Black United Front.

The Black United Front (BUF), founded in 1976 by Jitu Weusi and the Rev. Herbert Daughtry, was a multi-faceted political organization which mounted responses to police brutality and racial injustice, opposed apartheid, and supported radical international movements and human rights organizations.

The BUF women's committee was the largest and best fund raiser of the dozen committees of the organization. The committee was composed of women from the church, from the general membership of BUF, and activists like myself. Together we organized buses to demonstrate in Washington D.C., protesting attacks against affirmative action. We sponsored programs for the general membership and developed strategies for reforming the public schools.

While I worked in the women's committee, Safiya was an officer on BUF's executive board. In spite of the respect given the work of the women's committee and Safiya's executive position, women's leadership in the organization was resisted. Frustrated and restless because of our marginal roles in BUF, both of us also worked with Daphne at the sisterhood and for a myriad of other causes, conferences, and campaigns.

During this period, Safiya and I learned a great deal about the patterns of male chauvinism and the subordinate position of women within nationalist organizations. Across the country, challenges to Black male chauvinism were increasingly made by Black women whose expertise and experience had been downplayed by dominant males. By the end of the 1970s virtually every Black organization or initiative seemed to break down over the appropriate place of Black women in its leadership. Some organizations, such as the National Black Independent Political Party (NBIPP), tried to create a formal approach by requiring that Black women co-lead with Black men in each of its chapters.

Safiya and I continued to straddle both the Sisterhood and BUF, striving to do work which would give sisters an authentic political voice while defending Black people against injustice. We encouraged each other, but grew increasingly dissatisfied, observing and noting male chauvinism while continuing to lend our labor power to the work of their organizations.

In 1981, I called together five Black women activist friends, including of course, Safiya, to develop a Black female response to the missing and murdered children in Atlanta, whose mothers were being maliciously attacked as "unfit" in the media, yet whose murderers were not being actively sought.

Since white men were reportedly implicated in the ritual murders of the children, many Black groups began rallying support for community patrols and more effective police activity. Newspaper accounts, however, repeatedly stated that the murdered Black boys were hanging in the streets late at night unsupervised because they came from "broken homes" with "unfit mothers"—meaning from families headed by Black women.

Some mothers of the missing and murdered children called press conferences and rallies to respond to these negative attacks on their families.

Our group in Brooklyn wanted to demonstrate solidarity with the mothers of Atlanta's missing and murdered children. We gathered more Black women together and formed the Coalition of Concerned Black Women. We decided to have a Mother's Day march to highlight the plight of the children and their mothers. Over 300 people marched on Mother's Day, May 10, 1981, nearly two miles through Brooklyn in a demonstration supported by 54 organizations. It was one of the first political marches organized solely by Black women and featuring a significant number of Black women speakers on the program. Organized in 6 weeks, the march was a bold step in which Black women decided upon a goal to go forward and do something together and did it.

A year later, in 1982, I received a small grant from the Sisterhood to develop *The Rising Song,* a 13-week lecture series on Black women's history for the community. Held at the Restoration Corporation, a Brooklyn-based community development corporation, the lecture series attracted large audiences of community members. Week after week, noted Black women historians, activists, and poets provided information and vision about the historical accomplishments and achievements of Black women. The lecture series presented speakers such as Professor Myrna Bain speaking about the unremitting toil of African women's labor, the late Audre Lorde discussing sexuality, and poet Hattie Gossett showcasing Black women writers, singers, and "wild women."

While the lecture series occurred, protests were intensifying at nearby Medgar Evers College. Among faculty and student concerns were the competency of the college president and the lack of adequate support services and academic programs for the predominantly Black and female student body.

Medgar Evers College was founded in 1971 as a result of strong demands by the members of the Black community in Brooklyn that the City University of New York create "a new experimental and innovative institution which meets the needs of the community in which it is located and the needs of the City which it must serve." Once established, the college received little support and few resources from CUNY; its neglect and the lack of adequate leadership created a climate of discontent which erupted during the spring of 1982 into a four-month-long sit-in in the President's office, carried out by students and a few faculty members. The Student, Faculty, Community Coalition to save Medgar Evers College was founded to rid the college of its president and rebuild the college in the image of Medgar Evers, the man. The movement at MEC was eventually responsible for removing the President, for getting the Board to authorize new facilities and for establishing a woman's center. At the end of the four-month strike, a childcare center named in honor of Ella Baker and Charles Roman, a former professor at MEC, was started in the former President's quarters.

Embodying Ella's democratic notions of consensus, the sit-in's student, faculty, and community members argued, debated, and developed an agenda. The agenda presented the group's demands and set forth policies for governing the school. Because Black women students, faculty, staff, and community members performed support as well as leadership roles in all of its levels, the sit-in at MEC was perhaps the first political struggle in the post–civil rights era which connected an explicitly Black feminist praxis to a Black community struggle.

Unlike the students in the Civil Rights Movement, MEC students were workers and parents. The movement at MEC was sustained by women who were forced to strain the limits of their extended kin networks to get care for their children so they could be on the frontline. Some women brought their children with them, sleeping next to them on the floor and in chairs.

Four out of five officers of the Student government were women. The main security area in front of the President's office was staffed by a woman who at times literally put her body across the door. Women were prominent in maintaining a 24-hour watch down the halls and corridors from the office.

Inside another office, students ate together, slept together on the floor and shared resources and information. The domestic chores of cleaning, cooking, answering phones, which had been traditional roles for women in other political movements, were shared by all. Decisions were hammered out and executed democratically.

The militantly democratic nature of the protest, as well as its feminist and nationalist ideology, was ensured by the powerful experiences of its Black women faculty leaders: the student movement experience of Professor Andree McLaughlin, the political experience of Professor Zala Chandler, and the community and Black women's movement experience of Professor Safiya Bandele. Their role was matched by the dedication and power of women students such as Sharon Smith, Alice Turner and, Rhonda Vanzant. Students such as Trevor Belmosa,

Norman Coward, and Vincent Manuel demonstrated that Black men could work along with strong Black women. Not needing to dominate or cower, these men demonstrated the potency of a truly united effort among equals.

The Sisterhood, the Black United Front, Black Veterans for Social Justice, and other community organizations lent their support and expertise to the sit-in. I became a community representative to the Medgar Evers College Coalition which was created to support it. The MEC struggle brought many groups and individuals together in much the same way that the sit-ins and freedom rides had brought Black college students to SNCC decades before.

During the 1970s, the East and BUF were centers of male-dominated Black nationalist thought and practice. Black women were tentative in their search for an authentic place for their practice and ideas. After the struggle, Medgar Evers College became the center of explicit Black feminist concerns and womanist praxis.

A major issue of the sit-in at MEC had been the lack of support services, information, and scholarship which specifically addressed the needs of women students. Courageous women from the struggle demanded a women's center.

Directed by Safiya Bandele, the Center for Women's Development (CWD) opened its doors in April 1983. It has been one of the only women's centers in the country directed by a Black woman and established by Black women students. The center offers both individual and group counseling, especially for those who are depressed, battered and under stress. The CWD is also a referral service offering information about health, welfare, housing, and other support services. The CWD has sponsored and co-sponsored conferences, forums, and programs which reflect both the international and personal concerns of the student body. in 1985, the Center organized a delegation to attend the United Nations Decade for Women's Meeting in Kenya.

In 1985, Professor Andree McLaughlin, as coordinator of the Women's Studies, Research and Development, "piloted a Cross Cultural Black Women's Studies Curriculum" (Jackson, 2) which grew into a series of International Cross Cultural Black Women's Studies Summer Institutes. "Convening annually in different nations, the Institute is a world assembly of women activists, theorists, artists, writers, peasants, and workers who are concerned with learning about each other's realities to enable themselves to better control their destinies" (Jackson, 1).

Since its inception, the group has met in Zimbabwe, New Zealand, Berlin, and New York and discussed "Women and Communications," "Women and the Politics of Food," "Human Rights and Indigenous Peoples in the Information Age," and "Black People and the European Community." "This think tank for women and women's concerns has decided it is crucial to continue to address the legacies of colonialism and feudalism as well as the realities of patriarchy and imperialism which impact on their everyday existence in real ways . . ." (Jackson, 8–9). The Institutes, primarily led and developed by Andree McLaughlin, have created an international community of Black women which, like the anti-colonialist Pan African conferences at the beginning of the 20th century, will undoubtedly have a major impact in global politics in the future.

In addition to the exciting potential of this international work, by the end of the 1980s Black women in Brooklyn had institutionalized many womanist-inspired programs and institutions. In 1989, the Sisterhood founded Kianga House, a residential program for homeless teen mothers, one of the first places to institutionalize Black feminist approaches to this issue. Martha Bright, formerly of the East, joined with Esmeralda Simmons and others to develop parenting groups and legal services at the Medgar Evers College Center for Law and Social Justice. Alice Turner, the heroic student leader of the MEC struggle, after receiving her MSW degree, returned to run the Center for Women's Development counseling unit, developing and expanding its program.

In 1985, the CWD sponsored a Black Women's Conference with over 500 participants. The conference planning committee, composed of lesbians and heterosexual sisters, had hoped it would heal wounds among Black women, and create a common and on-going agenda. However, homophobic participants rejected lesbians who spoke openly about themselves and their issues. Although the conference failed to develop a true sisterhood, it encouraged CWD to do more intensive work on personal issues of sexuality and identity.

Gwen Braxton of the New York City Black Women's Health Project, a member of the conference planning committee, helped the CWD develop an agenda for its own members' health. The motto "if you are not working on yourself, you are not working" informed support groups and "internal work" among Center staff. The Center has implemented the self-help/support group/mutual-help model of the Black Women's Health Project, which emphasizes coming together to give and receive help, "not as expert, social worker, psychologist, organizer, physician, teacher, paid helper, and needy paying client helpee" (*NYC Black Women's Health Project*).

One of the women who helped the CWD institutionalize this approach is Arlene Parker, the first Black woman to receive a degree in Black women's studies from CUNY. Before working at the Center for Women's Development, Arlene worked at the Bedford Stuyvesant Restoration Community Development Corporation as Assistant to the President. Arlene brings a unique approach to her work by attending to the well-being of Black women. She affirms and connects women to each other by using the traditional approaches women have used to maintain kinship relationships: sending cards, phone calls, celebration of holidays, and birthdays. Arlene has fostered a sisterhood among the women at the Center for Women's Development.

The Center's special approach to Black women's self-help was consolidated in a series of workshops, "Healing Women Warriors," which grew out of an unpublished article I wrote with Andaye de la Cruz, a Latina activist and therapist. Both of us were recovering from our own "burnout" and overextension as activists, workers, and mothers. We looked around and saw that many of the women activists we worked with were themselves "sick" and overworked.

The "Healing Women Warriors" work enabled me to critically confront one of Ms. Baker's mottos: "She who believes in freedom cannot rest," a powerful yet dangerous message for overworked women activists. For more than a decade, I and other women were trying to work for the people and the sisters while we also worked for wages and raised families. Not only were we "burning out" and suffering from the same tragedies as other Black women—murder, rape, cancer, and depression—we were often neither effective, nor sisterly. Many of us realized that we could not remain wedded to a politics which tried to hold back the tide of diminishing political community, waning activism, and the avalanche of new and complicated social and personal issues, without strengthening and healing ourselves. Ella's daughters had to learn to rest and carve out time to recuperate. We also needed on-going support groups in order to be effective women and organizers.

Ms. Baker worked behind the scenes of major political organizations, doing the unrecognized toil of meetings and campaigns. Although she claimed not to want to "be in front," the tensions between the male authority in power and the authority she embodied were just below the surface of Ms. Baker's problems with SCLC and the NAACP. While Ella worked around gender issues in order to "contribute" to the Civil Rights Movement, today's Black women activists are compelled to focus on them—especially violence against women, women's development, homophobia, and challenges to male chauvinism.

Some of Ella's daughters have replicated her role as the "woman in front," the pioneer and initiator. The woman in front "puts her body into the movement." She, like Ella, is found working long hours, squeezing in family obligations and sacrificing personal pleasures. Policy, programs, and work evolves from and is most often initiated by her. Andree McLaughlin, founder and leader of the Cross Cultural Black Women's Institute, and Daphne Busby, founder and director of the Sisterhood of Black Single Mothers, are examples of the "woman in front" leadership model. In fact, because of the rise of such womanists in the Black community and in Black women's consciousness, more are daring to become "women in front."

Ella Baker's adherence to democratic collective work has inspired another womanist leadership model—the woman leader "in the circle." Groups of Black women work together on projects, campaigns, and programs and maintain friendships and personal relationships beyond their work. Safiya Bandele at the CWD has used this model in her work, empowering the women on staff to work on themselves as well as on the Center's tasks.

As Brooklyn's Black womanist community matures, it becomes clear that these two approaches— "woman in front" and "woman in the circle"—are not mutually exclusive. The "woman in front" leader often becomes "burned out," feels isolated, and truly needs to share her work and responsibilities with sisters in support groups and networks.

However, without the daring actions of these "women in front," women's circles can become overly concerned with raising the consciousness of their members. We, as Ella's daughters in central Brooklyn, have developed a praxis that uses and develops both kinds of Black women's leadership. Each woman in the group is encouraged to work on herself and her dreams, and somehow they all become part of the Center's mission and work.

Our Black womanist praxis is a process which utilizes the social distance between Black men and women to raise feminist consciousness. It enables women to see the social character of their personal and private oppression. It exposes male chauvinism and sexism as being detrimental to all Black life. It is a social movement concerned with the physical, emotional, political, and spiritual health of all members of the Black community. Our praxis attempts to bridge differences between lesbians and heterosexual women and tries to work and participate in an international sisterhood of Black women.

The Black Women's Health Project advocates resistance to all forms of oppression, and the complete elimination of oppression as essential to the Black Woman's struggle for and achievement of well-being. It considers violence a public health issue and seeks to eliminate the physical, institutional, psychological, and ideological violence perpetuated against Black women.

Furthermore, this social praxis is developing in the midst of a literary renaissance and an explosion of studies by and about Black women. More and more Black women who want to help their sisters and do something about the destitution and despair in the Black community are becoming leaders of unions and schools, owning their own businesses, and running for elected office.

There is also a transformation within the Christian Church because of the pro-woman praxis of Black women, laity and clergy. Not all Black women who sustain pro-active positions and commitments to social change consider themselves womanists. However, Black women activists and womanists alike rely on their personal relationship with God for guidance and determination. Like Ella Baker, they pray their feet be guided by God so their work will not be in vain. This faith informs and sustains their visions of social change.

Our praxis in the past has been to do anti-racist work with Black men, to do women's work with Black women within the Black community, and sometimes to do work on women's issues in coalition with white women and other women of color. The womanist praxis in Central Brooklyn has shown that when Black women develop their own power, consciousness, and skills, this resonates with Black people's overall survival, development, and peace. Andree McLaughlin challenges us to understand that our praxis must attempt to be nationalist, feminist, and socialist all at the same time, in opposition to the "multiple jeopardy which undermine the standard to all people's existence" (McLaughlin, 54).

Ella Baker believed, like many others, that a baton is passed from one generation to another to keep the struggle for social change alive. As the tireless "fundi" (a Swahili term for "the person in a community who passes on the crafts from one generation to another"), Ella Baker passed on her baton to me, a direct descendant of her praxis and her work. But I had to shape and redefine the baton to fit the requirements of my own time and needs. The power of her baton has grown to be shared with other women.

Our womanist praxis has been birthed, extended, and embraced by multiple circles of sisters, sometimes led by the "woman in front" and other times led by the "sister within the circle." While other children can afford the racial or gender privilege of ignoring or dropping the baton she offered them,

Black womanists can never forget that Ella Baker was our mother and that, as her daughters, we owe it to her to continue to struggle in her name.

References

Braxton, Gwen, *New York City Black Women's Health Project, Suggested 12 Step Program,* flyer.

Canterow, Ellen, with Susan Gushee O'Malley and Sharon Hartman Strom, "Moving the Mountain," *Women Working for Social Change,* Old Westbury, New York: Feminist Press, 1980: 52–93.

Jackson, Dr. Phyllis, *The International Cross Cultural Black Women Studies Seminar Institute Report (1987–1990).*

McLaughlin, Andree Nicola, "The International Nature of the Southern African Women's Struggle," *Network: A Pan African Women's Forum,* Harare, Zimbabwe, Vol. 1, No. 1, Winter, 1988: 49–56.

The Uhuru Sasa School Program, *Outline for New African Educational Institute,* Brooklyn, NY: Black Nation Education Series #7, 1971.

Ya Salaam, Kalamu, *Our Women Keep Our Skies From Falling,* New Orleans: Nkombo, 1980.

EIGHTY-TWO

An Open Letter to the Women's Movement (excerpt)

Barbara Macdonald

. . . The following are a few suggestions to all of us for working on our ageism:

- Don't expect that older women are there to serve you because you are younger—and *don't think the only alternative is for you to serve us.* . . .

- Don't believe you are complimenting an old woman by letting her know that you think she is "different from" (more fun, more gutsy, more interesting than) other older women. To accept the compliment, she has

to join in your rejection of old women.

- Don't point out to an old woman how strong she is, how she is more capable in certain situations than you are. Not only is this patronizing, but the implication is that you admire the way she does not show her age, and it follows that you do not admire the ways in which she does, or soon will, show her age.

- If an old woman talks about arthritis or cataracts, don't think old women are constantly complaining. We are just trying to get a word in edgewise while you talk and write about abortions, contraception, premenstrual syndromes, toxic shock, or turkey basters.

- Don't feel guilty. You will then avoid us because you are afraid we might become dependent and you know you can't meet our needs. Don't burden us with *your* idea of dependency and *your* idea of obligation.

- By the year 2000, approximately one out of every four adults will be over 50. The marketplace is ready now to present a new public image of the aging American, just as it developed an image of American youth and the "youth movement" at a time when a larger section of the population was young. Don't trust the glossy images that are about to bombard you in the media. In order to sell products to a burgeoning population of older women, they will tell you that we are all white, comfortably middle class, and able to "pass" if we just use enough creams and hair dyes. Old women are the single poorest

minority group in this country. Only ageism makes us feel a need to pass.

- Don't think that an old woman has always been old. She is in the process of discovering what 70, 80, and 90 mean. As more and more old women talk and write about the reality of this process, in a world that negates us, we will all discover how revolutionary that is.

- Don't assume that every old woman is not ageist. . . .

- If you have insights you can bring to bear from your racial background or ethnic culture—bring them. We need to pool all of our resources to deal with this issue. But don't talk about your grandmother as the bearer of your culture—don't objectify her. Don't make her a museum piece or a woman whose value is that she has sacrificed and continues to sacrifice on your behalf. Tell us who she is now, a woman in process. Better yet, encourage *her* to tell us.

EIGHTY-THREE

◆◆◆

Something about the Subject Makes It Hard to Name

Gloria Yamato

Racism—simple enough in structure, yet difficult to eliminate. Racism—pervasive in the U.S. culture to the point that it deeply affects all the local town folk and spills over, negatively influencing the fortunes of folk around the world. Racism is pervasive to the point that we take many of its manifestations for granted, believing "that's life." Many believe that racism can be dealt with effectively in one hellifying workshop, or one hour-long heated discussion. Many actually believe this monster, racism, that has had at least a few hundred years to take root, grow, invade our space and develop subtle variations . . . this mind-funk that distorts thought and action, can be merely wished away. I've run into folks who re-

ally think that we can beat this devil, kick this habit, be healed of this disease in a snap. In a sincere blink of a well-intentioned eye, presto—poof—racism disappears. "I've dealt with my racism . . . (envision a laying on of hands) . . . Hallelujah! Now I can go to the beach." Well, fine. Go to the beach. In fact, why don't we all go the beach and continue to work on the sucker over there? Cuz you can't even shave a little piece off this thing called racism in a day, or a weekend, or a workshop.

When I speak of *oppression*, I'm talking about the systematic, institutionalized mistreatment of one group of people by another for whatever reason. The oppressors are purported to have an innate ability to access economic resources, information, respect, etc., while the oppressed are believed to have a corresponding negative innate ability. The flip side of oppression is *internalized oppression.* Members of the target group are emotionally, physically, and spiritually battered to the point that they begin to actually believe that their oppression is deserved, is their lot in life, is natural and right, and that it doesn't even exist. The oppression begins to feel comfortable, familiar enough that when mean ol' Massa lay down de whip, we gots to pick up and whack ourselves and each other. Like a virus, it's hard to beat racism, because by the time you come up with a cure it's mutated to a "new cure-resistant" form. One shot just won't get it. Racism must be attacked from many angles.

The forms of racism that I pick up on these days are (1) aware/blatant racism, (2) aware/covert racism, (3) unaware/unintentional racism, and (4) unaware/self-righteous racism. I can't say that I prefer any one form of racism over the others, because they all look like an itch needing a scratch. I've heard it said (and understandably so) that the aware/blatant form of racism is preferable if one must suffer it. Outright racists will, without apology or confusion, tell us that because of our color we don't appeal to them. If we so choose, we can attempt to get the hell out of their way before we get the sweat knocked out of us. Growing up, aware/covert racism is what I heard many of my elders bemoaning "up north," after having escaped the overt racism "down south." Apartments were suddenly no longer vacant or rents were outrageously high, when black, brown, red, or yellow persons went to inquire about them. Job vacancies were suddenly filled, or we were fired for very vague reasons. It still happens, though the perpetrators really take care to cover their tracks these days. They don't want to get gummed to death or slobbered on by the toothless laws that supposedly protect us from such inequities.

Unaware/unintentional racism drives usually tranquil white liberals wild when they get called on it, and confirms the suspicions of many people of color who feel that white folks are just plain crazy. It has led white people to believe that it's just fine to ask if they can touch my hair (while reaching). They then exclaim over how soft it is, how it does not scratch their hand. It has led whites to assume that bending over backwards and speaking to me in high-pitched (terrified), condescending tones would

make up for all the racist wrongs that distort our lives. This type of racism has led whites right to my doorstep, talking 'bout, "We're sorry/we love you and want to make things right," which is fine, and further, "We're gonna give you the opportunity to fix it while we sleep. Just tell us what you need. 'Bye!!" — which *ain't* fine. With the best of intentions, the best of educations, and the greatest generosity of heart, whites, operating on the misinformation fed to them from day one, will behave in ways that are racist, will perpetuate racism by being "nice" the way we're taught to be nice. You can just "nice" somebody to death with naïveté and lack of awareness of privilege. Then there's guilt and the desire to end racism and how the two get all tangled up to the point that people, morbidly fascinated with their guilt, are immobilized. Rather than deal with ending racism, they sit and ponder their guilt and hope nobody notices how awful they are. Meanwhile, racism picks up momentum and keeps on keepin' on.

Now, the newest form of racism that I'm hip to is unaware/self-righteous racism. The "good white" racist attempts to shame Blacks into being blacker, scorns Japanese-Americans who don't speak Japanese, and knows more about the Chicano/a community than the folks who make up the community. They assign themselves as the "good whites," as opposed to the "bad whites," and are often so busy telling people of color what the issues in the Black, Asian, Indian, Latino/a communities should be that they don't have time to deal with their errant sisters and brothers in the white community. Which means that people of color are still left to deal with what the "good whites" don't want to . . . racism.

Internalized racism is what really gets in my way as a Black woman. It influences the way I see or don't see myself, limits what I expect of myself or others like me. It results in my acceptance of mistreatment, leads me to believe that being treated with less than absolute respect, at least this once, is to be expected because I am Black, because I am not white. "Because I am (*you fill in the color*)," you think, "life is going to be hard." The fact is life may be hard, but the color of your skin is not the cause of the hardship. The color of your skin may be used as an excuse to mistreat you, but there is no reason or logic involved in the mistreatment. If it seems that your color is the reason, if it seems that your ethnic heritage is the cause of the woe, it's because you've been deliberately beaten down by agents of a greedy system until you swallowed the garbage. That is the internalization of racism.

Racism is the systematic, institutionalized mistreatment of one group of people by another based on racial heritage. Like every other oppression, racism can be internalized. People of color come to believe misinformation about their particular ethnic group and thus believe that their mistreatment is justified. With that basic vocabulary, let's take a look at how the whole thing works together. Meet "the Ism Family," racism, classism, ageism, adultism, elitism, sexism, heterosexism, physicalism, etc. All these isms are systemic, that is, not only are these parasites feeding off our lives, they are also dependent on one another for foundation. Racism is supported and reinforced by classism, which is given a foothold and a boost by adultism, which also feeds sexism, which is validated by heterosexism, and so it goes on. You cannot have the "ism" functioning without first effectively installing its flip-side, the internalized version of the ism. Like twins, as one particular form of the ism grows in potency, there is a corresponding increasing in its internalized form within the population. Before oppression becomes a specific ism like racism, usually all hell breaks loose. War. People fight attempts to enslave them, or to subvert their will, or to take what they consider theirs, whether that is territory or dignity. It's true that the various elements of racism, while repugnant, would not be able to do very much damage, but for one generally overlooked key piece: power/privilege.

While in one sense we all have power, we have to look at the fact that, in our society, people are stratified into various classes and some of these classes have more privilege than others. The owning class has enough power and privilege to not have to give a good whinny what the rest of the folks have on their minds. The power and privilege of the owning class provide the ability to pay off enough of the working class and offer that paid-off group, the middle class, just enough privilege to make it agreeable to do various and sundry oppressive things to other working-class and outright disenfranchised folk, keeping the lid on explosive inequities, at least for a minute. If you're at the bottom of this heap, and you believe the line that says you're there because that's all you're worth, it is at least some small solace to believe that there are others more worthless than you, because of their gender, race, sexual preference . . . whatever. The specific form of power that runs the

show here is the power to intimidate. The power to take away the most lives the quickest, and back it up with legal and "divine" sanction, is the very bottom line. It makes the difference between who's holding the racism end of the stick and who's getting beat with it (or beating others as vulnerable as they are) on the internalized racism end of the stick. What I am saying is, while people of color are welcome to tear up their own neighborhoods and each other, everybody knows that you cannot do that to white folks without hell to pay. People of color can be prejudiced against one another and whites but do not have an ice-cube's chance in hell of passing laws that will get whites sent to relocation camps "for their own protection and the security of the nation." People who have not thought about or refuse to acknowledge this imbalance of power/privilege often want to talk about the racism of people of color. But then that is one of the ways racism is able to continue to function. You look for someone to blame and you blame the victim, who will nine times out of ten accept the blame out of habit.

So, what can we do? Acknowledge racism for a start, even though and especially when we've struggled to be kind and fair, or struggled to rise above it all. It is hard to acknowledge the fact that racism circumscribes and pervades our lives. Racism must be dealt with on two levels, personal and societal, emotional and institutional. It is possible—and most effective—to do both at the same time. We must reclaim whatever delight we have lost in our own ethnic heritage or heritages. This so-called melting pot has only succeeded in turning us into fast-food-gobbling "generics" (as in generic "white folks" who were once Irish, Polish, Russian, English, etc., and "black folks," who were once Ashanti, Bambara, Baule, Yoruba, etc.). Find or create safe places to actually *feel* what we've been forced to repress each time we were a victim of, witness to or perpetrator of racism, so that we do not continue, like puppets, to act out the past in the present and future. Challenge oppression. Take a stand against it. When you are aware of something oppressive going down, stop the show. At least call it. We become so numbed to racism that we don't even think twice about it, unless it is immediately life-threatening.

Whites who want to be allies to people of color: You can educate yourselves via research and observation rather than rigidly, arrogantly relying solely on interrogating people of color. Do not expect that people of color should teach you how to behave nonoppressively. Do not give into the pull to be lazy. Think, hard. Do not blame people of color for your frustration about racism, but do appreciate the fact that people of color will often help you get in touch with that frustration. Assume that your effort to be a good friend is appreciated, but don't expect or accept gratitude from people of color. Work on racism for your sake, not "their" sake. Assume that you are needed and capable of being a good ally. Know that you'll make mistakes and commit yourself to correcting them and continuing on as an ally, no matter what. Don't give up.

People of color, working through internalized racism: Remember always that you and others like you are completely worthy of respect, completely capable of achieving whatever you take a notion to do. Remember that the term "people of color" refers to a variety of ethnic and cultural backgrounds. These various groups have been oppressed in a variety of ways. Educate yourself about the ways different peoples have been oppressed and how they've resisted that oppression. Expect and insist that whites are capable of being good allies against racism. Don't give up. Resist the pull to give out the "people of color seal of approval" to aspiring white allies. A moment of appreciation is fine, but more than that tends to be less than helpful. Celebrate yourself. Celebrate yourself. Celebrate the inevitable end of racism.

EIGHTY-FOUR

◆◆◆

Jews, Class, Color, and the Cost of Whiteness

Melanie Kaye/Kantrowitz

asleep: dream. i walk down the street wearing shorts and a t-shirt and the new earrings my ex-lover just gave me for my birthday. i pass two young hip-looking women.

she's all japped out, *they say. about me. i cringe, self-conscious.*

then i look down at my shorts & t-shirt. i'm not even dressed up, except for the earrings. suddenly i understand that no matter what i wear i will be perceived as "all japped out."

When I wake I realize I've never heard the expression. But I know exactly what it means.

Awake: vision. I walk down 106th street, a big wide street, in the mostly Puerto Rican and Dominican neighborhood where I live, after 25 years away from New York. I spot a man I've seen before on Broadway, asking for money. He's out in the street, shaking his fist at cars, gesturing as if in a silent movie—he looks like he's shouting and no words come out, or at least I can't hear them. He moves in jerky, violent spurts so that when he veers toward the sidewalk, people scatter, afraid. I watch him for a bit, afraid he'll hurt himself, wondering if I should do something. I walk into the copy shop I sometimes use. Everyone's speaking Spanish. I don't, and so I ask, "Do you speak English?" Yes. I discuss the problem with the man behind the counter. We go out into the street and watch. We decide to phone 911, the emergency number.

First question they ask: *is he white black or hispanic?* Like the new baby question: *boy or girl?* Asian doesn't even exist.

White, I say, knowing it's only because he's white that I can phone cops on his behalf. If he were Black or Latino, I'd be afraid of how they'd treat him. I keep walking towards Broadway. So does the silently cursing man. He miraculously crosses Broadway to the traffic island without incident and plunks down on a park bench, one of two white men on the Upper West Side asking for money. I watch for a while. No police car arrives.

Awake: more vision. Last night on Broadway I saw the man who had asked me and Helena for money, and I ran across the street against the light and dangerously close to traffic to get away. He scares me. A couple of weeks ago we were walking home, we were almost on my block, 106th between

Amsterdam and Columbus, where no one ever asks for money because no one assumes anyone east of Amsterdam has any money. We told him, sorry, not today. I had just given money to two different people, and Helena had three dollars to her name.

By the time we reached the end of the block he'd circled back, stood in front of us, asking again. *You know, I don't want to rob or anything but I just might have to,* he says.

I'm not about to respond, but he keeps talking. *I don't want to be like this, asking for money on the street, but you know I need money, and I don't want to rob or anything.* . . . Finally Helena gives him a dollar.

It seems that he came back to us, rather than the dozen other people on the street, because he (a black man) assumes we have money (we're white) and will be afraid (we're women). The truth is, we are neither moneyed nor afraid, and we give (Helena) or not (me) for our own reasons. The truth also is, he's desperate and we're not.

The next night I'm walking home by myself, late, and there he is, practically in front of my building. He approaches, extends his hand. *I'm sorry about last night,* he says. We shake hands, smile. Then he says, *but I need some money again, could you give me some?*

Late and dark. I don't want to stand there going through my pockets and especially taking out my wallet. Most of all I'm disturbed that he knows me. I am afraid of him becoming mine: *my beggar.* I don't want to be responsible for him. I don't want him to expect anything from me. Half the movies I've ever seen rise up in me, and I know if this were a movie I'd run into him every day for a week and at the end of the week he'd stab me. Everyone watching would recognize the heavy symbolism.

I shove aside the racist movie images. I say, *I can't give you money today*—and now I am stuck with my lie. I could give something. But I want to keep moving, get home.

He demands, *I need money.*

I can't . . .

I need . . .

I can't . . .

I need . . .

until finally I say, *hey man, I dig it but do you hear me?*

He nods. We both know I'm lying, that I'm the one who gets to say yes or no. We say goodnight, smile.

Let me walk you around my neighborhood. On 106th street at Broadway, people of all colors and ages shopping, walking, sitting at street cafes, waiting for buses, heading for the subway, wheeling children in strollers. But notice the people, and there are many, stretched out asleep on the benches and even on the sidewalks—winter is harsh here and still they're in the street, sometimes without shoes—the people shaking cups, asking, *can you spare some change,* saying, *I'm very hungry, can you give me something, even a quarter.* They're almost all African American men, a few women, also African American. Look at the taxi drivers. Step into one of the hundreds of small shops, restaurants, groceries, stationery shops that line Broadway. I see owners and often their families, and hired clerks: Asian, Indian, Arab, Latino, Greek, Jewish, sometimes Caribbean Black. Rarely are they African American. Practically all of them speak English wrapped in the vowels and consonants of their mother tongue, which is not English; except their kids, teenagers who help out after school and Saturdays, as I used to help out in my parents' store, are fluently bilingual, perfect English, as well as rapid-fire Chinese, Korean, Spanish. . . . They will go to college, their kids will probably lose their language, their culture. This is the American dream.

South of 96th street the balance of color shifts from brown to white, Latino to yuppie. Gentrified, white graduates of elite colleges live in buildings with swimming pools and elaborate doormen, views of the George Washington bridge—men and women in their twenties whose parents, or trust funds, bought them apartments costing maybe a million dollars.

There are lots of old Jews, surviving still in their rent-controlled apartments that will probably turn co-op when they die. Lots of harried thirty-somethings and forty-something Jewish women and men, their Jewishness visible only to those familiar with the intricacies and codes of New York Jews. They had their kids late, they split economically between upper middle and middle, and politically between liberals and radicals. Some are insistent about sending their kids to public schools, and some have given up on the public schools, refusing, in their words, to sacrifice their kids to a principle. They are professionals who live on schedules so tight that any unforeseen disruption is a minor disaster. To cope with the stress of life by the clock, and because they were raised to, or have taught themselves to, expect some joy and fulfillment in life, they see therapists, acupuncturists, chiropractors, and belong to health clubs where they work out and stay in shape. On the Upper West Side (and all over New York City) class shows in well-developed calves and trim forms. Fat is sloppy. Fat is poor. I am sure that the average weight in my immediate neighborhood among the women is 15 pounds higher than 15 blocks south.

One more thing: in my immediate neighborhood, when you see women with children, they tend to be the same color, brown to black. A few blocks west or south, when I see a woman and child of the same color, I'm almost surprised; the norm is women of color caring for white children, what I've come to think of as the underbelly of feminism. Most of the women are immigrants. Some of the children are Jews.

Let me adjust the lens, for accuracy. Not all Jews are professionals (45% are working class or poor); not all African Americans are homeless or poor, generation after generation (though a full third live below the poverty line). Not all whites are yuppies, New York is not the nation, and the Upper West Side is not even all of New York.

For example, I recently visited Seattle; at the Asian community health clinic, the brochures come in ten different languages for clients from Hong Kong and the hills of Laos (imagine in the early part of this century, a "European" clinic had to serve Irish, Poles, Italians, Slavs, Greeks, Jews, and Swedes, from farms and *shtetlekh,* from Sicily, Dublin, Paris and Prague). In Seattle the homeless are white men, and anti-racist coalitions include Jews as a matter of course, because skinheads and other white supremacist groups mustering forces in Idaho target Jews and people of color. Or in New Mexico, where I used to live and where I still return as often as I can, the poor are Native American and after them, Chicano/a; Anglos buy up the beautiful old adobes; the issues are development and ecology, water table first and foremost. In Maine and Vermont, where I also have lived, and which share with New Mexico and Mississippi the honor of being the poorest states in the union, the poor are mostly white, nationally invisible because small-town and rural and the only news that counts happens in the big cities, where media thrive. For rural and small-town residents, the issues are not street violence; there are few streets and hardly anyone is anonymous, though women and children endure and resist violence in their homes. Rural issues are development and agriculture; the question is whether all food production will rest in the hands of a few multinational corporations.

But whatever is coming apart in the nation is doing so to some extent in New York first. When the public schools are essentially abandoned; when thousands upon thousands of people have no place to live, and everyone who does carries key rings heavy with metal, for the two to five locks required to simply get in one's apartment; when the threat of rape and other street violence against women controls our every decision about where to go, how long to stay, how much it will cost, and how much anxiety we can tolerate; when hate crimes of all kinds are on the rise, this is the future of our nation if something doesn't change. A recent survey found that even in rural areas, nearly half the people encounter on a daily basis people with no place to live. This is the human cost of our nation's priorities.

In the early and mid-eighties, I was working out some thoughts on racism and anti-Semitism, heavily influenced by these places I'd lived, and by my friends, many of whom were women of color, from both poor/working- and middle-class families, and white poor and working-class women. The way the debate was being framed as Black-Jewish or even Black-white obscured, I felt, the issue of class and the complexity of race. I wrote about the ways racism played out very differently against the various peoples of color—Chinese, Japanese, Arab, Native American. . . . I wrote about why I saw anti-Semitism as a form of racism, meaning racist ideology. This last seemed like a truism to me; the camps of Europe were revealed three months before I was born. And in New Mexico, Maine, Vermont, I was certainly an alien. And I said then, the difficulty some people have in grasping anti-Semitism as a serious concern and as a form of racism is that it hasn't kept Jews poor. (In fact, anti-Semitism often claims that all Jews are rich.) I also saw what was getting called Black-Jewish conflict as a mutual scapegoating—Jews were getting blamed for white racism and Blacks for christian anti-Semitism—as well as obscured class conflict.

But I have come to believe that this analysis needs to be pushed further. I am troubled, for example, by analogies between Asians and Jews, between Arabs and Jews, not because these analogies are not valid—with the difference that Asians almost always look Asian, while Jews and Arabs may often pass. What troubles me is this: while class and general principles of race-hate are illuminated by these analogies, something else gets obscured: the intransigence and virulence of oppression of African Americans . . . and something else.

The structure of apartheid is useful to contemplate here, not because things in the U.S. are so fixed and clear; they're not. But let me pursue the analogy. South Africa has not two racial categories, but three: white, black and colored. It's the particular buffer zone of colored that I want to examine. Colored are those who will never be white but at least aren't black. Colored are those who have more access to higher status and all that implies—better housing, jobs, education, health, leisure, safety, respect. I want to suggest that in many places in the U.S., Japanese, Korean, and some Chinese, Indians and Pakistanis, Arabs and lighter-skinned or wealthier Latinos get to be colored. Sometimes Caribbean Blacks, by virtue of their accent, their education, the strength of growing up as the majority, also get to be colored. And African Americans, I want to suggest, are not the only "blacks," though they are the most visible. Many Latinos are black—dark in color—and also those most Indian of Chicanos, tracked in the lowest social and economic status. Immigrants from Southeast Asia hold some of the hardest, worst-paying jobs in the nation. And in the Southwest and sometimes Northwest, where there are few African Americans, native Americans are kept the lowest of the low, and every cruel stereotype of inferiority shows up in local racist culture.

As I've said, these categories are not totally fixed. There is a certain permeability that characterizes the class-race system in the U.S., a certain amount of passing—literally, for those with skin light enough, who shed their accents, language, culture; and approximately, for those who, laboring under the heavy burden of racism, through luck and extraordinary heroism and sometimes through hardness against their own people, still squeak through. Clarence Thomas rises up from poverty to hobnob with the white male club called the Senate precisely by abandoning his people's concerns.

The point of this white/colored/black classification is not to violate the hope of solidarity among people of color by dividing them, but to recognize divisions that exist and must be named in order to bridge them. The Iraqi-Black conflicts in Detroit; Korean-Black in Flatbush and L.A.; Cuban-Black in Miami. Conflicts which a generation ago often were Jewish-Black because they are in part the inevitable result of who owns what in whose community, and who is poor, and who is accessible.

You could say, as my sister did when I was sharing these thoughts with her, aren't you talking about class? Yes and no. I'm talking about *caste as access to class,* as representing the probability either of moving up or standing still. And in the years of Reagan and Bush, standing still means things get worse.

Let me meander for a moment in the swamp of class. Top down, billionaires, millionaires: control and power; wealth so beyond the needs of one person, one family, it staggers the mind; here we find unlimited access to health care, comfort, resources; mostly WASP. 70% of Congress comes from this class. While most white people aren't in it, most people in it are white, some Jews.

Middle class includes low-level managers, social workers, small shopkeepers, and teachers—K-12, secondary school, junior college, university—as well as business people, doctors, lawyers, and other professionals with incomes of $200,000 a year and more ($200,000, the dividing line under Reagan/Bush, between the rich getting richer and everyone else getting poorer). When a class category includes both those piling up assets and those applying for food stamps, we should recognize an obsolete term and come up with something else. Here is where we find over half the Jews in the U.S., spread throughout the category, and a fair number of people of color, mostly represented at the lower end of the class.

Working class is also problematic as an economic category. The nonunionized women in the chicken factories, Black in the South, white in Maine; Asians and Latinas in the endlessly transforming, infinitely stable New York City sweatshops once worked by Italian and Jewish women: these are working-class, and, as we see, part of the problem with the category is gender. Working class also includes the racially diverse members of the UAW, the men whose sons used to be guaranteed the best paid laboring jobs in the U.S.—but today Michigan, heart of the auto industry, endures 35% unemployment. Working class excludes the endemic poor, the poor without a prayer of breaking out of it, not those who perform backbreaking work of past generations of immigrants but those who can find no work at all, or can only find work that pays so badly that, for example, women with children can't afford to give up welfare to earn money that will all get swallowed by child-care costs. They are African American, Latino, Native American, Asian. As for the rural white poor, because there are no jobs, their children leave for the cities, become essentially immigrants, and in the cities their white skin serves them in finding work — but, like other immigrants, they lose their culture. Working class spans well-paid unionized fields, many of which are now threatened because of automation, and because successful unionization has challenged owners' greed and sent manufacturing jobs abroad to pay workers less and maximize profits. Whole industries abandon communities of workers who have served them for generations; even keypunch work which requires English is shipped to Ireland (lest we miss the dominance of class/poverty as theme, and mistake it entirely for race/color), because Irish women are so poor as to demand so little. The two fields of labor still growing in the U.S., the hardest to organize and the worst paid, are office work and the service industry, including maids and restaurant workers.

Who does this office and service work? Women. People of color, especially immigrants, a replenishing, flexible pool of cheap labor, thankful to work hideously long hours for little money, because it is more than they had, and because they came here, often, not for their own betterment but for their children's. And so they groom their kids to escape the parents' lives, to assimilate, much as I, raised passionately pro-union, was groomed to escape the working class, and even the lower-middle-class shopkeeping existence at which my parents had succeeded.

It is precisely this access to better-paid working-class jobs or lower-middle-class small business opportunities, along with access to education for the next generation, that characterizes the experience of "colored" in the U.S. It is precisely this lack of better working-class jobs and small business opportunities along with systematic disadvantaging and exclusion by the educational system, that characterizes the experience of "blacks" in the U.S. Sherry Gorelick's *City College and the Jewish Poor* describes how City College was created as a path to upward mobility to distract the radical Jewish poor from the revolutionary class struggle predicted by Marx; the path of higher education was taken by thousands and thousands of poor and working-class Jews. But college was free for us, and there was room, if not at the top, then certainly in the middle. Where are the free colleges now? Private colleges cost more than $20,000 a year. And where is room in the middle, when even the middle is suffering?

This shared economic disaster could and should unite most people across lines of color. But the illusory protection of "whiteness" offers a partial escape route toward which anyone who can scrambles. This desire to identify with whiteness, as well as bigotry and fear, blocks solidarity.

In this white-colored-black scheme, where are the Jews?

Of the groups I've named as targeted by a general hate I'll call race-hate, Jews are the closest to white. Many would say we are white, and indeed a common-sense visual response suggests that many of us are.

But listen to the prophet James Baldwin: "No one was white before he/she came to America," Baldwin wrote in the mid-eighties.* "It took generations, and a vast amount of coercion, before this became a white country. . . ."

> It is probable that it is the Jewish community — or more accurately, perhaps, its remnants — that in America has paid the highest and most extraordinary price for becoming white. For the Jews came here from countries where they were not white, and they came here in part because they were not white; and incontestably — in the eyes of the Black American (and not only in those eyes) American Jews have opted to become white. . . .

Now, the point is not for us, Jews, to escape the category "white," to evade confronting our own racism, nor is it to insert ourselves artificially into a category of oppression, as sometimes happens in our movements where oppression in some puny paradoxical way confers privilege. It is to recognize a continuum where we are the closest of the coloreds to white, or the closest of the whites to colored.

---

*James Baldwin, "On Being 'White' and Other Lies," *Essence* (April, 1984).

This is hardest to see in New York City, where Jews can hardly be called a minority. If there is the diaspora and Eretz Yisroel, I have come to think of New York as a third category, somewhere between the two. "I'm in exile from Brooklyn," I used to joke, but it's no joke. Jews in New York City, except for select neighborhoods, experience the luxury of normality. To assume christianity in New York is to be hopelessly provincial. In New York one finds Jewish culture on a broad spectrum: orthodox, secular, lesbian and gay, Sephardic, Yiddishist, feminist. . . . The paradoxical result is a majority of Jews who operate without consciousness of their Jewishness. It's not an issue. Anti-Semitism is occasional, focused, and historical, and in recent years, for New Yorkers, has been associated mostly with African Americans. Quite the opposite from what's going on in the farm belt, the Northwest, and the South, where alliances between Jews and people of color are obvious to everyone.

Yet I'm suggesting that progressive Jews recognize our position in between colored and white, a source of tension but also of possibility. I can envision a powerful coalition between Jewish and Asian women, against the JAP stereotype. I can also envision a nightmare coalition between Jewish and Asian men against affirmative action. The challenge is to build progressive coalitions not only among the coloreds but between the coloreds and the blacks, and between these and the economically struggling whites—and then to expand still further. The issue of hate crimes, for example, can unite Jews with people of color, and with lesbians and gays; and we should insist on the legal—and moral—classification of violence against women as a hate crime. That will be a powerful coalition indeed.

What I want to focus on is this: in James Baldwin's phrase, "the extraordinary price of becoming white."

Many of us chose, or had chosen for us, a white path. A path of assimilation, of passing, often accompanied by extreme cultural loss. How many of us speak or read Yiddish or Ladino or Judeo-Arabic? What do we know of our own histories, our literature, our music, our cultural diversity, our rich traditions? What do we know beyond or besides the now-usual sources of American Jewish identity, which are, in a nutshell, religion, Israel, and the Holocaust. Nothing wrong with these sources—but as the sum total of Jewish identity, this is limited.

Where does this restricted focus leave secularists or confirmed diasporists? What happens when we disagree, as we do, about solutions to the Israeli-Palestinian conflict? How does this restricted focus help us create and strengthen an authentic Jewish American identity? How does it enable us to see the Holocaust in a context of Jewish history, the tragedy of which was not only the destruction of millions of lives—as though that were not tragedy enough—but also the destruction of a rich and varied culture.

It's called assimilation. We, like others who pass or partly pass, can choose where to direct our allegiance: upward and whitening, restricting our Jewishness to that which assimilation increasingly demands, *a Jew at home, a "man" in the streets,** white people who go to Jewish church, i.e., synagogue; or we can deepen both our identity and our affiliation, with the other "others," the outsiders: the coloreds and the blacks.

Think about shedding whiteness. I don't mean to pretend that Jews who are white endure the same visual vulnerability as people of color; though we should recognize that many Jews, especially outside the U.S., simply *are* people of color, that the definition of Jews as automatically "European" is incorrect. In addition, many Sephardi and also many Ashkenazi Jews are sufficiently dark to be readily perceived, at least in the South and in the heartland, as people of color. Think also about the Hasids; think about wearing a Jewish star, or other item that identifies you as a Jew; think about never taking it off. Think about driving through Mississippi.

So: is fighting anti-Semitism a diversion from fighting racism? Do we think we can fight anti-Semitism without fighting racism? Do we think Jews can be safe within a white supremacist society?

I do not. I believe, along with a great many other Jews, that a color/class barrier means injustice, and our culture teaches us to pursue justice. I also believe that a color/class barrier threatens Jews, in two ways:

1. Because race hate will never exclude us. As long as the world is divided into us and them, minorities are vulnerable. Fascism is on the rise. In our century, can we be naive about the danger?

2. Because the particular nature of anti-Semitism, which defines Jews as money, as powermongers—

---

*The phrase was used to characterize the "modern" Jew of the European Enlightenment.

especially marks us as scapegoats for the abuses of capitalism, and we are living through a time of rampant abuse.

It's also a hard time to be talking about the abuses of capitalism, when it seems that so many people living under communism have rejected it, or tried to. Even allowing for lies and misperceptions, the American left is going through something as massively disruptive to our way of describing and envisioning the world as were the fifties' exposés of Stalinism on one hand, and persecutions by McCarthy on the other. I know that some of us who came to adulthood calling Lyndon Baines Johnson a fascist have a perspective problem, one which Reagan and Bush have helped us address. But we have not yet dealt, even theoretically, with the re-emergence in Europe and the former Soviet Union of toxic nationalism, nor with the dazzling speed with which internationalization of capital is matched by internationalization of labor: "guest workers" in Germany, Kuwait, Saudi Arabia; "illegals" in the U.S. What do national boundaries or national identity mean at [the 20th] century's end?

Jews with any sense of history are scanning the airwaves for disaster. What I think we must keep poised in response to our knowledge that communism as practiced has failed; *so has capitalism.* We cannot accept what we have as tolerable. It's not okay that, in the richest country in the world, millions are without health care. It's not okay that one out of five children grows up in poverty, or that the figure for Black children is one out of two.

The rich get richer. And who does the dominant culture blame? Jews; Asians, especially Japanese; Arabs; foreigners; let's face it, "the colored" get blamed for various contributions to economic disaster; for controlling the economy, or making money on the backs of the poor; for raising the price of oil; for stealing or eliminating jobs (by importing goods or exporting production); for taking the jobs. African Americans, Latinos, Native Americans, "the blacks," get blamed for urban violence and chaos, for drugs, for the skyrocketing costs and failures of social programs. That is, coloreds get blamed for capitalism's crimes; blacks for capitalism's fallout. Do I need to point out who escapes all blame?

When we are scapegoated we are most conscious of how we feel humiliated, alienated, and endangered. But the other function of scapegoating is at least as pernicious. Scapegoating protects the source of the problem we are being scapegoated for, the vi-

cious system of profit and exploitation, of plenty and scarcity existing side by side.

And let me address briefly, because it is the glaring omission so far, the pain and difficulty many of us have experienced from hearing about or facing anti-Semitism from African Americans. How are we supposed to be allies? people ask, not unreasonably.

But I want us to understand a few things. First, just as a racist remark by Jackie Mason does not reveal the inherent racism of all Jews, let us not assume that an anti-Semitic remark by Leonard Jeffries, or by ten Leonard Jeffries, reveals the heart of the African American community. We need to recognize the destructive role played by the media in fanning the flames of the "Black-Jewish Conflict." Cornel West, bell hooks, Richard Green, Barbara Christian, Henry Louis Gates, Marian Wright Edelman, Nell Painter, Albert Raby. . . . Why are these names not as well known outside the African American community as the names of Louis Farrakhan or Leonard Jeffries? Are they, in their diversity and dynamism, less representative of the African American community?

Second, no more than racism in the Jewish community should surprise us, should we be surprised by anti-Semitism in the christian and Muslim communities, which includes African Americans. Nor should we be surprised by racism among people of color against each other. We all learn the same lies about one another. Part of our work is untangling these lies.

I want to make one last point about Jews and class, and this is about privilege and power. Hatred, chauvinism, oppression always function to keep people from their power, to mute their strength. Because they're laboring under heavier odds. Because they're taught to feel bad about themselves.

Anti-Semitism has a peculiar edge because the myth is that we're too powerful, too rich, and much too pushy. I began with my dream, where displaying a simple gift of earrings, walking down the street daring to feel okay, means: *she's all jupped out.* Any particle of this that we absorb makes us afraid of our strength, loath to use our power, embarrassed by the relative economic and social success of Jews as a people, afraid it will be used against us (and it will).

Jewish progressives often buy into this scheme of contempt for "most Jews," assumed to be uniformly well off, or they experience a nostalgic longing for the time when Jews were authentically the right class, that is, poor and working-class.

I think we need to look critically at this attitude. First, because it erases working-class Jews and poor Jews. Second, because it writes off the political energy and concerns that exist sometimes apart from class, the ripe possibilities for coalition of feminist Jews, of lesbian and gay Jews, of Jewish educators and cultural workers, of Jewish seniors, and on and on, not to mention Jews who see anti-Semitism for what it is, a form of race hate which must be fought along with other forms of race hate, and those who are simply hungry for economic and social justice. Who do not wish to spend our lives deciding whether or not to give quarters or dollars to other human beings who need more than we can possibly give; who do not wish to abandon the cities with their fabulous human variety because of the stresses of economic inequality, alienation, and violence; who still believe a better way is possible.

Third, because this attitude of contempt for Jews who are not poor, which is, after all, a form of internalized anti-Semitism, ignores the fact that education, choice, comfort are all valuable. One cannot walk the streets of any of our cities, see people living in cardboard boxes or wrapped in torn blankets, and not appreciate the material basis for human ex-

istence. The problem is not relative Jewish success. The problem is a severe class system that distributes success so unequally.

Used well, education, choice, even comfort, can strengthen people, individually and collectively. As for money—let me say the dirty word—nothing gets done without it. The question is, what do we do with our education, our choice, privilege, skills, experience, passion for justice: our power. Don't racism and anti-Semitism make you sick? Doesn't hatred scare you? Don't you feel at least a little desperate about the way things are going unless something intervenes?

I think Jews need to gather our power, make it visible, and use it right. I'm sick of the more conservative wing of the Jewish community speaking for all of us. Everyone knows that Jews are all over progressive movements, what I've come to think of as the political diaspora. Maybe our task is to ingather the Jews, just a little, into a new civil and human rights coalition, in which we are present and visible as Jews. It means being proud of our collective strength, confident that we can use it right. Someone will always call us pushy. Isn't it time to really push?

E I G H T Y - F I V E

Multi-Issue Politics

Suzanne Pharr

At the National Gay and Lesbian Task Force's Creating Change Conference, I was asked to give a luncheon speech to the participants of the People of Color Institute and the Diversity Institute. Right off, I told them that I thought I was an odd choice for these groups because I don't really believe in either diversity or identity politics as they are currently practiced. Fortunately, people respectfully stayed to hear me explain myself.

First, diversity politics, as popularly practiced, seems to focus on the necessity for having everyone (across gender, race, class, age, religion, physical ability, etc.) present and treated well in any given setting or organization. An assumption is that everyone is

oppressed, and all oppressions are equal. Since the publication of the report, "Workforce 2000," that predicted the U.S. workforce would be made up of 80% women and people of color by 2000, a veritable growth industry of "diversity consultants" has arisen to teach corporations how to "manage" diversity. With integration and productivity as goals, they focus on the issues of sensitivity and inclusion—a human relations approach—with acceptance and comfort as high priorities. Popular images of diversity politics present people holding hands around America, singing "We Are the World."

I have a lot of appreciation for the part of diversity work that concentrates on making sure everyone is included because the history of oppression is one of excluding, of silencing, of rendering people invisible. However, for me, our diversity work fails if it does not deal with the power dynamics of difference and go straight to the heart of shifting the balance of power among individuals and within institutions. A danger of diversity politics is becoming a tool of oppression by creating the illusion of participation when in fact there is no shared power. Having a presence within an organization or institution means very little if one does not have the power of decision-making, an adequate share of the resources, and participation in the development of the workplan or agenda. We as oppressed people must demand much more than acceptance. Tolerance, sympathy and understanding are not enough, though they soften the impact of oppression by making people feel better in the face of it. Our job is not just to soften blows but to make change, fundamental and far-reaching.

Identity politics, on the other hand, rather than trying to include everyone, brings together people who share a single common identity such as sexual orientation, gender, or race. Generally, it focuses on the elimination of a single oppression, the one that is based on the common identity, i.e., homophobia/heterosexism, sexism, racism. However, this can be a limited, hierarchical approach, reducing people of multiple identities to a single identity. Which identity should a lesbian of color choose as a priority—gender, race, or sexual orientation? And does choosing one necessitate leaving the other two at home? What do we say to bisexual or biracial people? Choose, damnit, choose??? Our multiple identities allow us to develop a politic that is broad in scope because it is grounded in a wide range of experiences.

There are positive aspects of organizing along identity lines: clarity of single focus in tactics and strategies, self-examination and education apart from the dominant culture, development of solidarity and group bonding, etc. Creating organizations based on identity allows us to have visibility and collective power, to advance concerns that otherwise would never be recognized because of our marginalization within the dominant society.

However, identity politics often suffers from failing to acknowledge that the same multiplicity of oppressions, a similar imbalance of power, exists within identity groups as within the larger society. People who group together on the basis of their sexual orientation still find within their groups sexism and racism that have to be dealt with—or if gathering on the basis of race, there is still sexism and homophobia to be confronted. Whole, not partial, people come to identity groups, carrying several identities. Some of the major barriers of our liberation movements to being able to mount a unified or cohesive strategy, I believe, come from our refusal to work directly on the oppressions—the fundamental issues of power—within our own groups. A successful liberation movement cannot be built on the effort to liberate only a few and only a piece of who we are.

Diversity and identity politics are responses to oppression. In confronting oppressions, we must remember that they are more than people just not being nice to one another: they are systemic, based in institutions and in general society, where one group of people is allowed to exert power and control over members of another group, denying them fundamental rights. Also, we must remember that oppressions are interconnected, operating in similar ways, and that many people experience more than one oppression.

I believe that all oppressions in this country turn on an economic wheel; they all, in the long run, serve to consolidate and keep wealth in the hands of the few, with the many fighting over crumbs. Oppressions are built in particular on the dynamic intersection of race and class. Without work against economic injustice, against the excesses of capitalism, there can be no deep and lasting work on oppression. Why? Because it is always in the best interest of the dominators, the greedy, to maintain and expand oppression—the feeding of economic and social injustice.

Unless we understand the interconnections of oppressions and the economic exploitation of oppressed groups, we have little hope of succeeding in a liberation movement. The religious Right has been successful in driving wedges between oppressed groups because there is little common understanding of the linkages of oppressions. Progressives, including lesbians and gay men, have contributed to these divisions because generally we have dealt with only single pieces of the fabric of injustice. We stand ready to be divided. If, for example, an organization has worked only on sexual identity issues and has not worked internally on issues of race and gender, then it is ripe for being divided on those issues.

The Right has had extraordinary success in using homosexuality as a wedge issue, dividing people on the issues clustered around the Right's two central organizing points: traditional family values and economics. An example is their success in using homosexuality as a way to organize people to oppose multicultural curricula, which particularly affects people of color and women; while acting to "save the family from homosexuals," women and people of color find themselves working against their own inclusion. If women's groups, people of color and lesbian and gay groups worked on gender, race and sexual identity issues internally, then perhaps we would recognize the need for a coalition and a common agenda for multicultural education.

An even more striking example is how the Right, in its "No Special Rights" campaign, successfully plays upon the social and economic fears of people, using homosexuality as the wedge issue, and as the *coup de grace,* pits the lesbian and gay community against the African-American community. Ingeniously, they blend race, class, gender and sexual identity issues into one campaign whose success has profound implications for the destruction of democracy.

In summary, the goal of the "No Special Rights" campaign is to change the way this nation thinks about civil rights so that the groundwork is laid for the gradual elimination of civil rights. This is not an easy idea to present to the general public in a straightforward manner. Therefore, the religious Right has chosen homosexuality and homophobia to open the door to thinking that is influenced by racial hatred and its correlatives, gender and class prejudice.

Depending upon the persuasion of racism, sexism and homophobia, the religious Right seeks these basic twisted and distorted changes in our thinking about civil rights:

1. **They suggest that** civil rights do not already exist in our Constitution and Bill of Rights; they are a special category for "minorities" such as people of color and women. The religious Right refers to these people as having "minority status," a term they have invented to keep us focused on the word **minority.** Most people think of minorities as people of color. Recently in Oregon, signs appeared that read, "End Minority Status." They did not specify gay and lesbian: the message was

about **minorities** and what that so-called "status" brings them.

2. **Then they say that** basic civil rights are themselves "Special Rights" that can be given or taken away by the majority who has ordinary rights, not "special rights."

3. **They argue that** "Special Rights" should be given to people based on deserving behavior and hardship conditions (especially economic) that require special treatment. In their words, people who "qualify" for "minority status."

4. **Then they introduce the popular belief that** "Special Rights" given to people of color and women and people with disabilities have resulted in the loss of jobs for deserving, "qualified" people through affirmative action and quotas. This introduces the notion that rights for some has an economic cost for others; therefore the enhancement of civil rights for everyone is not a good thing.

5. **They argue that** lesbians and gay men have no hardship conditions that would require extending "Special Rights" to them. Further, homosexuals **disqualify** themselves from basic civil rights because, by the nature of who they are, they exhibit bad behavior. They do not, according to the Right's formula, "qualify" for "minority status."

6. **Then there is the pernicious connection:** There are other people who already have "Special Rights" who exhibit bad behavior and prove themselves undeserving as they use and deal drugs and commit crimes of violence and welfare fraud. The popular perception is that these are minorities. However, the Right also extends its description of the undeserving to those who bear children outside of two-parent married families, women who choose abortion, and even those who receive public assistance.

7. **And finally, their logical and dangerous conclusion:** Because giving "Special Rights" to undeserving groups is destroying our families, communities and jobs for good people, who deserves and does not deserve to be granted "Special Rights" should be put to the popular vote and good, ordinary citizens allowed to decide who gets them and who gets to keep them.

Clearly, the religious Right understands the interconnection among oppressions and in this campaign plays directly to that interweaving of racism, sexism, classism and homophobia that is virtually impossible to tease apart. To see this campaign as single issue, i.e., simply about lesbians and gay men, is to ensure defeat of our efforts in opposing it. It has to be responded to as the multi-issue campaign that it is. If the "No Special Rights" campaign is successful, everyone stands to lose.

The question, as ever, is what to do? I do not believe that either a diversity or identity politics approach will work unless they are changed to incorporate a multi-issue analysis and strategy that combine the politics of inclusion with shared power. But, you say, it will spread us too thin if we try to work on everyone's issue, and ours will fall by the wayside. In our external work (doing women's anti-violence work, working against police brutality in people-of-color communities, seeking government funding for AIDS research, etc.), we do not have to work on "everybody's issue" but how can we do true social change work unless we look at all within our constituency who are affected by our particular issue? People who are infected with the HIV virus are of every race, class, age, gender, geographic location, yet when research and services are sought, it is women, people of color, poor people, etc., who are usually overlooked. Yet today, the AIDS virus rages on because those in power think that the people who contract it are dispensable. Are we to be like those currently in power? To understand why police brutality is so much more extreme in people-of-color communities, we have to understand why, even within that community, it is so much greater against poor people of color, prostituted women and gay men and lesbians of color. To leave any group out leaves a hole for everyone's freedoms and rights to fall through. It becomes an issue of "acceptable" and "unacceptable" people, deserving and undeserving of rights.

Identity politics offers a strong, vital place for bonding, for developing political analysis, for understanding our relationship to a world that says on the one hand that we are no more than our identity, and on the other, that there is no real oppression based on the identity of race or gender or sexual identity. Our challenge is to learn how to use the experiences of our many identities to forge an inclusive social change politic. The question that faces us is how to do multi-issue coalition building from

an identity base. The hope for a multi-racial, multi-issue movement rests in large part on the answer to this question.

Our linkages can create a movement, and our divisions can destroy us.

Internally, if our organizations are not committed to the inclusion and shared power of all those who share our issue, how can we with any integrity demand inclusion and shared power in society at large? If women, lesbians and gay men are treated as people undeserving of equality within civil rights organizations, how can those organizations demand equality? If women of color and poor women are marginalized in women's rights organizations, how can those organizations argue that women as a class should be moved into full participation in the mainstream? If lesbian and gay organizations are not anti-racist and feminist in all their practices, what hope is there for the elimination of homophobia and heterosexism in a racist, sexist society?

When we grasp the value and interconnectedness of our liberation issues, then we will at last be able to make true coalition and begin building a common agenda that eliminates oppression and brings forth a vision of diversity that shares power and resources. In particular, I think there is great hope for this work among lesbians and gay men. First, we must reconceptualize who we are and see ourselves not as the wedge, not as the divisive, diversionary issue of the religious Right—but as the bridge that links the issues and people together. If we indeed represent everyone—cutting across all sectors of society, race, gender, age, ability, geographic location, religion—and if we develop a liberation politic that is transformational, that is, that eliminates the power and dominance of one group over another within our own organizations—we as old and young, people of color and white, rich and poor, rural and urban lesbians and gay men can provide the forum for bringing people and groups together to form a progressive, multi-issue, truly diverse liberation movement. Our success will be decided by the depth of our work on race, class and gender issues.

Instead of the flashpoint for division, we can be the flashpoint for developing common ground, a common agenda, a common humanity. We can be at the heart of hope for creating true inclusive, participatory democracy in this country.

EIGHTY-SIX

Common Threads
Life Stories and the Arts in Educating for Social Change
Cynthia Cohen

Introduction

The Oral History Center for Education and Action, (OHC), a community organization currently located at the Center for Innovation in Urban Education at Northeastern University in Boston, uses oral history methods and the arts for the purpose of strengthening communities. Our work is informed by a strong multi-cultural and anti-racist perspective; it is designed to facilitate the kinds of understanding needed to build alliances across differences.

The OHC's model is based on the idea that everyone has an important story to tell. It emphasizes an attentive quality of listening that can be transformative for both the listener and the teller. It also integrates the arts, in ways that nourish people's imagination, validate diverse cultures, and reach large audiences. The model evolved out of two projects I coordinated under the auspices of The Cambridge Arts Council, in 1980 through 1982: The Cambridge Women's Oral History Project (CWOHP) and the Cambridge Women's Quilt Project (CWQP). This article describes those two projects, as well as others the OHC sponsored during the years when I was its director, from 1982 through 1990.

The Cambridge Women's Oral History Project

In the CWOHP, high school students collected stories from their own and others' cultural communities. We chose the theme "transitions in women's lives" because the young women themselves were undergoing many transitions, and also because it could embrace the experience of women from all groups in the city, including recent immigrants. The young women conducted interviews (mostly in English, but also in Haitian Creole, Portuguese and Spanish), indexed tapes, and created a visual exhibit incorporating photographic portraits, excerpts of oral narrative, and brief biographies. Working with the staff of the project, they created a slide-tape show "Let Life Be Yours: Voices of Cambridge Working Women," which focuses on the theme of work in women's lives. "Let Life Be Yours" asks a question: How have women's cultural and economic backgrounds affected their ability to make choices in their lives? Answers can be found in the women's stories.

> Antonia Cruz, a recent immigrant from Puerto Rico: "My father wanted to take me out of school, because it was too expensive, he said. They were poor, they took me out of school in the fifth grade."

> Addie Eskin, a Jewish woman born near Boston: "'What do you mean you have to go to high school, what do you have to go to high school for?' she said. 'Your father is very sick, what do you think, you're gonna go to school and hold your hand out?' And I said, 'Auntie, if I have to wear this middy blouse for the next four years, I'm going to graduate from high school.'"

> Henrietta Jackson, a black woman born in Cambridge: "One of the newspapers called Cambridge High and Latin School, and asked the office practice teacher if she had any good student who might want a few hours every day after school in the newspaper office. I was considered one of the fastest typists and I went with two other girls. I was rejected immediately. And she called them and she was practically told they weren't quite ready for a black person. She said that it will be a long time before there won't be this kind of unfair treatment of a person whose only fault is that she happens to have a black face."

> Catherine Zirpolo, an Italian woman born in Boston: "1914. I was fortunate, I didn't have to

go to work . . . being an only child. . . . When I became of age to go to high school, I wasn't a bit interested in high school. I wanted to be an actress even then. . . ."

When the older women who participated in the Cambridge Women's Oral History Project told stories about the obstacles they faced, they revealed inspiring spiritual strength. The project's political message (i.e., opposing oppression based on race, class and gender) is all the more powerful because their language is personal and accessible, devoid of rhetoric. In evaluation interviews at the end of the project, the young women involved reported that their participation in the project had changed their ideas about older people, about the study of history, and about working with women:

> Books are dull, but this way I get enjoyment out of history. . . . Winona and I have had really different lives. She's black and I'm white; I have more opportunities with education, work, and money. She's religious. There's a strength about her, so it's nice to talk to her. She's the kind of inspiring person that makes us want to go out and read and read good books and take it in. She makes you see how somebody can be at peace with things. Part of this is kind of making up for what I couldn't find from my own grandmother.

> The people changed my opinions a lot. . . . Older people are pretty active in the community; they have a lot to say, most of them. They are just older, not feeble or anything. I used to see them like stereotypes, as people who sat back and watched the world go by. But they have a big part while it goes by. I never realized that. I got a lot out of seeing women work together. It gives you a sense of self-respect, a sense that I'm a valuable person. You see women working together and taking each other seriously and you know it's there and you know it should be there all the time.

Since its completion in 1984, "Let Life Be Yours" has been translated into Portuguese, Haitian Creole and Spanish. It has been used as the basis for community education programs on women's history, multicultural issues, older people's lives, and oral history methods.

The Cambridge Women's Quilt Project

The Oral History Center's second major project involved sixty women and girls, ranging in age from eight to eighty, working in collaboration with two fabric artists to create images from their lives in fabric. The project was designed as a study of the historical, social and cultural factors that influenced changes in women's lives. Also we intended to reflect on quilt-making: its function in women's lives, and its relationship to oral tradition. Through the project, we were able to enact the very subjects we were studying. For instance, many women and girls found that their participation in the project was itself producing changes in their lives. As has been a part of the American quilting bee tradition historically, participants in the project shared medical and political information, reflected together on their relationships with boys and men, and gained perspective on the decisions they were facing. They felt themselves becoming part of a community.

The fabric artists supported each woman to create her own image of a story from her own life. One was about braiding a daughter's hair and another about a great-grandmother quilting. Others were about lighting Sabbath candles, dressing up to go to church, riding a donkey in Haiti, making wine in Italy, the dream of walking freely outside at night, hitchhiking throughout Europe and Africa, making life rafts during World War II, giving birth at home, reading alone in one's bedroom, reading to a group of neighborhood children, a childhood picking cotton in the South and a childhood dream of becoming a ballerina.

Our respect for each woman's expression was put to the test when one woman depicted in her quilt patch a child, pants rolled down, being spanked by his parent. When asked to document something important for history, this participant had chosen to represent "a time when parents cared enough about their children to set limits, to punish them when necessary." Other participants were upset by the expression of what they took to be violent: not only the spanking itself, but the humiliation of the child, with his bare bottom exposed. Through discussion, compromise was reached: the patch remained, but restitched with rolled-up pants.

In other ways too, the project created a congruence between the content and methods of our inquiry. For instance, women and girls depicted women weaving rugs, making lace and quilting, and here we were, making a quilt. Several patches honored women as bearers of traditional food ways: a Jamaican aunt carrying fruits home from market on her head, a Mennonite grandmother baking a cherry pie, and an Irish Nana heating tea. As we shared traditional foods and recipes at our potlucks, we were enacting as well as documenting this dimension of women's experience.

A total of 52 fabric images were sewn into two vibrant quilts. Some of the participants tape recorded interviews about the meaning of each patch; these oral narratives were edited into a catalog. Finally, a group of younger women worked with singer/songwriter Betsy Rose to compose a ballad, sung to a traditional Portuguese melody, based on the stories of the quilt patches. The ballad became the audio background for a slide-tape on the making of the quilts.

Informal conversations as well as the more formal sharing of stories in interviews were understood to be an important aspect of the projects. As one participant said,

> People who came were very shy and really, you couldn't see a visible importance about their lives. But once the little quilt square opened it was like they came alive. Everybody was so enthusiastic and one story led to another. . . . Maybe the most important thing about the quilt project was that the women who did it enjoyed each other and talked to each other. . . . There was no performance, and no being performed. Everybody is on stage. Everybody's the song. Everybody's the story teller.

Since their completion in 1982, the quilts have been exhibited in the neighborhoods of the city, at local festivals, and in libraries, stores, churches, schools and cultural and social service organizations. They have traveled to several other New England cities, and as far away as the International Women's Forum in Nairobi, Kenya, and to meetings of the Belize Rural Women's Association in Central America. In one of our most engaging exhibits, viewers of the quilts at the Boston Children's Museum could use nearby computer terminals to call up edited versions of the interview narratives according to a number of different categories.

Common Threads

As we watched women and girls from different ethnic communities interacting as they sewed the quilts, it became clear that fabric arts were familiar media in which many women felt comfortable expressing themselves. In fact, many of the participants in the quilt project were steeped in the skills and customs of rich fabric traditions such as Portuguese lacemaking, Haitian embroidery, African-American appliqué quilting, as well as knitting, crocheting and sewing. Activities using fabric gave women and girls the chance to feel a sense of accomplishment for their skills (generally unacknowledged, even within their own communities), and to learn about one another's lives and cultures.

We used these insights to design Common Threads, an exhibit and series of events which highlighted the stories and work of ten traditional and contemporary fabric artists, each from a different local ethnic community. The exhibit, displayed at a branch of the local library and in the high school, consisted of samples of fabric art such as lace, embroidery, batik, appliqué and crochet, along with the life stories of the women who created the pieces. At several events, members of English-as-a-Second-Language classes and others in the community were invited to bring their own fabric work and other crafts, and to share stories about their lives and their work.

Following the exhibit, the OHC collaborated with several local organizations to sponsor a visit to Cambridge of two Chilean *arpilleristas,* women who use small burlap tapestries to depict the harsh realities of daily life under the dictatorship of Augusto Pinochet. One of the *arpilleristas,* for instance, used a series of her tapestries to document her ten-year search for her son, detained by the military police shortly after Pinochet came to power. Many of the community women who participated in Common Threads and the Cambridge Women's Quilt Project attended a workshop with the *arpilleristas,* making an immediate connection through their common interest in storytelling through fabric. The following year, the OHC built on this awareness by sponsoring our own Stories-in-Fabric workshop, and the resulting tapestries were taken to the International Women's Forum in Nairobi, Kenya.

Because the Common Threads exhibit was temporary, we created a slide-tape show, which explores the social, political, economic and artistic meanings of fabric art in the lives of women. The slide show has been used in educational programs with groups of older people, fabric artists and students of women's history.

Lifelines

In addition to conducting women's oral history projects in community settings, the OHC also collaborated with teachers to adapt its model to a classroom context. Lifelines was a curriculum development project, designed to support fifth through eighth grade and bilingual teachers to incorporate oral history into on-going Social Studies and Language Arts curricula. Two teachers, for example, worked with students on labor history projects. In one case, students created a visual exhibit combining excerpts of interviews with parents and older workers with statistical analyses of the shifting economic base of the city. In the other classroom, students interviewed six women who worked in Cambridge factories during the 1930s and 1940s, and produced an illustrated timeline, visual exhibit, and slide-tape show about the changing patterns of women's work in the Depression, World War II, and the post-war eras. Three Lifelines classes explored topics in family and ethnic studies.

The arts were especially important in a Lifelines project in a Haitian bilingual class. The project was designed specifically to enhance self-esteem. The Haitian students were at the bottom of the social hierarchy at their school. They were teased about their language, their body odor, the possibility of being carriers of AIDS. These assaults on their integrity were sustained while they were struggling to learn a new language, to adjust to separation from members of their families, and often while they were recovering from the political violence and the extreme poverty that had led their families to leave the island whose landscape and culture they still cherished.

Students who had been in the U.S. for just two or three years interviewed Haitian adults who worked in careers of interest to the children. As they began to hear the stories of the adults of their own community validated and celebrated in their classroom, there began an outpouring of expression from them: stories and especially pictures of their lives in Haiti and their bewildering encounters with an American city. With help from a student intern from Harvard, the students created a slide-tape show, "We Are Proud of Who We Are," in which they narrated the stories told them by adults. They also worked with a storyteller to prepare performances of their own narratives. The children's stories and artwork, exhibited in the school corridors, provided contexts for relationship-building between the teachers and administrators in the school's monolingual program and the Haitian children. In subsequent years, students created notecards embellished with their drawings of images from their lives, and sold the cards to raise funds for an eye clinic in Haiti. The entire school participated in that effort, and later a group traveled to Haiti to visit a sister school. Through this project, the students began to realize the possibilities inherent in their own expression, and to understand that they were not only documentors, but makers, of history.

A Passion for Life: Stories and Folk Arts of Palestinian Women

During the same years we were working in collaboration with the Cambridge Public School on Lifelines, one of the women drawn to our Stories-in-Fabric series became involved in the OHC. Her name was Feryal Abbasi Ghnaim, and she worked as a traditional Palestinian embroiderer. Her interests and skills helped define our next major oral history project, A Passion for Life: Stories and Folk Arts of Palestinian and Jewish Women. The project was designed to explore whether stories and folk arts could be used to facilitate communication not just across differences, but across the chasm created by long-standing political conflict and violence.

The project's final exhibition displayed the stories of eight Jewish and Palestinian women, along with objects of folk expression, such as baskets, embroidered dresses, family photographs and cooking utensils. Eighteen public events preceded and accompanied the exhibition; these ranged from sessions of sharing recipes, songs, dance and visual arts, to a theoretical discussion on the role of folk arts in communities in crisis and a workshop on challenging stereotypes of Arab and Jewish people. The members of the project's Directions Committee, which consisted of both Jewish and Palestinian women and others, wrote at the time that we were looking for modes of expression which would invite people in conflict to reach beneath their defenses and their fears, so they could come to recognize each other's humanity:

> In spite of our many differences, we believe there is wisdom in the perspectives of women, who are striving day to day, sometimes under harsh oppression, to create their lives and to recreate culture and community for their children. There is value in the stories of these regular common people who do the mundane but richly detailed work of sowing seeds and harvesting fruits, preparing foods and cleaning homes, fixing remedies and stitching cloth, selling goods and listening to the stories people share when they come together to celebrate, to grieve and to pass on traditions.

> The stories and works of art in our exhibition include descriptions of the tragedy of the Palestinian Diaspora and the oppression of Palestinian people under Israeli occupation. They speak to the terrible persecution which Jewish people have endured throughout history, most horrifyingly manifested in Europe during World War II.

> We bring these stories together in one exhibition not to suggest any simple parallels, but to create a vision broad enough to embrace them all. As we listen to stories from both Jewish and Palestinian women, we share feelings of sadness and anger, sometimes outrage. We believe that nothing excuses acts of inhumanity. Has the world not seen enough of families divided, homes and communities destroyed? Have there not been enough precious heirlooms confiscated, people imprisoned, children murdered? How can this fragile fabric of our lives, which we and our mothers and our grandmothers have stitched so carefully — note by note, spoonful by spoonful, caress by caress, story by story — be so brutally torn to shreds?

> We engage with this work out of a deep love for our own traditions and an appreciation for the richness of the others'.

> We recognize the deep-seated fears of both Palestinian and Jewish people. We are working towards a world in which we all are safe to preserve and develop our cultures. We are inspired by the passion for life which permeates these women's stories and their art: the impulse to create beauty, to nourish children, to take risks, to resist oppression, to celebrate community; and the determination to survive, both physically and spiritually, against forces of brutality and destruction.

> Take inspiration from these stories to reach out to each other with openness and respect. Let them motivate you to take a stand for justice and to work for peace.

A Passion for Life proved to be more difficult than we ever could have imagined at the outset. Sometimes it seemed to be little more than a snarl of ethical dilemmas, demanding relationships and intense emotions. At times, both Feryal and I, the project's co-directors, felt pressured by members of our families and communities to withdraw from the project. Key people from both communities chose not to participate, and in a couple of cases, backed out at the last minute. In retrospect, it seems like a miracle that we ever managed to bring the eight women's stories under one roof, even for just a couple of months.

Among the many conflicts we needed to resolve in the course of the project, the most contentious were misunderstandings about language, and our lack of awareness of the meanings and resonances of specific words for members of each other's communities. For many Palestinians, for instance, the word "peace," unless immediately followed by the word "justice," had come to signify a criticism of Palestinian resistance to the Israeli occupation. It was a kind of a code, understood by many Jewish people, who had themselves come to perceive the word "justice" as pro-Palestinian. The word "1948" also resonated very differently for members of each community. For Palestinians, 1948 is the year of the *nakba,* or disaster. It is the year of the dispersion, when many Palestinians were dispossessed of their land, the year when the fabric of their lives was permanently rent. Nineteen-forty-eight is the year of the massacre of the citizens of Deir Yessin, a Palestinian village plundered by members of two Jewish right-wing terrorist organizations. Thousands of Palestinians fled from their homes in fear of a repetition of Deir Yessin. For most Jewish people, on the other hand, 1948 marks the creation of the state of Israel, a time of rejoicing in the fulfillment of a dream of a homeland — a symbol that evokes images of security, justice, democracy, and the possibility of a post-holocaust renewal. It isn't just that one group views the history as victors and the other as a people defeated, but that each places the events of the year within a different frame of historical reference.

The most problematic and emotionally charged meanings were encoded in the phrase "the Holocaust." The emotional resonances which surround the memory of the holocaust, the politically motivated abuses of holocaust imagery by both sides, and the disparate meanings which are attached to the word may be among the central barriers to Palestinian-Jewish reconciliation. While most Palestinians and Jews understand each others' readings of the words "peace" and "justice," often they are unaware of the different resonances of references to the holocaust. For most Jews of Eastern European background, the holocaust is a sacred memory. Less than [sixty] years ago, a third of the Jewish people were killed, and this fact still defines communal reality.

What happened in Europe — the systematic obliteration of thousands of communities; the destruction of Yiddishkeit as a living culture; the challenge to Jewish understanding of God, and justice and faith; the magnitude of the suffering and the devastation underscoring the meaning of being homeless in the world — all of this is the context in which contemporary Jews of European heritage came to define their individual and collective identity.

From a Palestinian perspective, "the holocaust" is what they have repeatedly heard as an excuse for the inexcusable brutality and injustice to which they have been subjected. European and American guilt about it was a major factor in turning world opinion to support the Zionist claim to Israel. Palestinian people feel that they are being made to suffer for Europe's crimes, and that somehow the significance of their own suffering diminishes when it is compared to the holocaust. A Palestinian friend once said to me: "Don't put me beside a holocaust survivor; I feel like nothing. How can my suffering compare?"

While Jewish people feel a need to honor the memory of the holocaust by retelling the story and by bearing witness to the tragedy, many Palestinian people are weary of hearing the story. "Why do they have to tell us this story?" asked Feryal. "We are the ones who are suffering now." The documentaries and fictional renditions of the holocaust story on TV often culminate with hopeful references to the new state of Israel, accompanied by images which either demonize Arabs or render their true experience invisible. These are especially painful because of the media's relative silence about Palestinian history and culture, its muteness about Palestinian suffering and legitimate needs for security.

Throughout A Passion for Life, in spite of these misunderstandings of words, there were moments when Palestinian and Jewish people began to understand each other's point of view, to feel each other's suffering, to recognize themselves in each other's aspirations. This happened through hearing each other's stories, and seeing and appreciating each other's artistic work. After hearing the stories of Palestinian women who had become friends, one Jewish woman acknowledged for instance that she had never realized that Jewish people in Israel were living in the actual dwellings which had once belonged to Palestinian families. One Palestinian woman said that although she had known about the holocaust before, she had never truly felt the enormity of it. After seeing Feryal describe the symbols in her embroidery, an older Jewish man, a committed supporter of Israel, commented that he had never realized that Palestinian women were telling stories in their embroidery.

Often, A Passion for Life seemed like an enormous landscape, clouded by terror and confusion. It often seemed that what we were attempting was actually impossible. But, all along, there were moments when the terrain would shift, creating new contours of possibility. These openings, made possible by our caring for each other and by the power of stories and the arts, enlarged our imagination and deepened our yearning for reconciliation. These were the moments that sustained us in our work. Once after a particularly difficult phase of the project, Feryal and I spoke together at a gathering of people from both communities. She showed her beautiful tapestry of a Palestinian woman holding aloft a dove. In its beak is an envelope carrying this message:

Women of the world: Women love peace to raise their children in, so why don't you make peace your number one goal? I as a Palestinian know intimately that there are two kinds of peace. (1) Peace that is built on the bodies of those brutalized and murdered to silence their calls for their just rights; (2) peace which comes from understanding a people's suffering, sitting down with them to genuinely solve and resolve their problems, so that justice and equality can be the code of the land, not death and suffering.

Why don't we, women, raise our voices high and strong in the service of true peace to preserve our children, our future as human beings? I ask you to support my call for true peace for my people. We are not subhumans. We are people with history and civilization. We are mothers and fathers and children. We have had enough killing and Diaspora. I smuggled my dreams in my hidden wishes and crossed the ocean in hope for peace; for my Palestinian sisters who lost their children in wars and who have been widowed at an early age. I ask you for true peace for my people.

I followed Feryal by reading an excerpt from the extraordinary autobiography of Heda Margolius Kovaly, in which she recounts the events of her life in Prague from 1941 through 1968:

Three forces carved the landscape of my life. Two of them crushed half the world. The third

was very small and weak, and, actually, invisible. It was a shy little bird hidden in my rib cage an inch or two above my stomach. Sometimes in the most unexpected moments the bird would wake up, lift its head, and flutter its wings in rapture. Then I too would lift my head because, for that short moment, I would know for certain that love and hope are infinitely more powerful than hate and fury, and that, somewhere beyond the line of my horizon there was life indestructible, always triumphant.

The first force was Adolf Hitler; the second was Iosif Stalin. They made my life a microcosm in which the history of a small country in the heart of Europe was condensed. The little bird, the third force, kept me alive to tell the story.

When I finished reading Kovaly's words, Feryal leaned over and pointed to the dove in her tapestry. "You see," she whispered, "it's the same bird."

The Oral History Center for Community Education and Action is located at the Center for Innovation in Urban Education, 403 Richards Hall, Northeastern University, Boston, MA 02115. Oral history resources mentioned in this article can be ordered from the OHC by mail or by phone: 617-373-4814, or fax: 617-373-8482. Requests can also be directed to the author, c/o the Department of Education, University of New Hampshire, Durham, NH 03824.

EIGHTY-SEVEN

The Anti-Violence Coalition of Kentucky
An Experience in Alliance-Building
Elizabeth Wilson-Compton

Bowling Green, Kentucky 1996

Western Kentucky University's campus spreads itself out along a steep hill and reminds the onlooker that they are in Kentucky. Pine trees sporadically show themselves among the majestic oaks and maples, and thick, rich bluegrass covers the lawns. Once a Normal School for teachers, Western is now a state university that actively recruits people of diverse backgrounds to fill its faculty positions as well as seeking diversity among its student body. WKU has a Women's Studies Department, an African American Studies Department, and an International Studies Department, complete with a progressive recruitment of foreign students. I have been at Western since the summer of 1994 and, until I attended a conference in Washington, D.C. in spring 1996 on "Building Alliances and Coalitions," I believed it to be a great place for my children to grow up. Now, I realize that it is a great place to begin changing before my children grow up.

I ended up receiving the skills to change my part of the world in a very unexpected way. While between classes reading the postings on a bulletin board, I saw a letter about the Women as Leaders Conference, an enrichment seminar sponsored by the Washington Center in Washington, D.C. The idea of a "girls only" vacation in D.C., highlighted by academic work, appealed to me. So I applied and was accepted into the program. A scholarship covered most of my expenses, freeing up my finances to explore the sights of the city.

The sights I ended up being most enthralled with, however, were free. I spent a great deal of time standing, walking, or just sitting and watching people of the Capitol. Suddenly, political awareness was not something I studied in a "Controversial Issues" class, and the concerns of African Americans, Native Americans, gay and lesbian people, people with disabilities, and Asian Americans were not just words on a page, they were an integral part of policy and life. I visited the buildings where the American Indian Movement had holed up in protest of continual broken promises from our government. I walked on the grass where civil rights marches took place and, more recently, where a mass wedding of gays and lesbians was held. I could almost feel the heat from the bras that burnt in protest of our paternalistic government when I stood on the steps of the Supreme Court building.

Still, even more inspiring were the people of D.C. The women I met really cared about equality, some of them had dedicated their entire lives to it. Blacks and whites walked down Pennsylvania Avenue and laughed together. Men and women in the traditional dress of their native countries or tribes walked, unnoticed, among the crowds. I was deeply affected by the contrast between this city and mine, and it moved something in me that had been stirring for a long time.

I lay in my hotel room that night and thought about what I had seen. I acknowledged that, had I not gone out of my way to take classes that forced me to look at other people's perspectives — American Institutions and Minorities, Psychology, Honors, and Sociology classes — I might not have noticed

these differences so clearly. However, I felt dumbfounded about how to bring this knowledge home in a real way. Simply retelling my experience would be no more effective than having my friends and family read a book. I wanted them to *feel* the experience of seeing life, all aspects of it, through someone else's eyes.

At the conference I learned about tools to catalyze change and the yearning within me to give this empowerment, especially to other women, became overwhelming. The following is an excerpt from my journal:

> The women here are all strong. At home I felt special because I was strong. That my upbringing or something in my mother caused me to be different. But I am not different. I have just been given the opportunity to see things through a wider lens. I didn't come to school to get my MRS and I have closed myself off to the women who have, but if I can show them what I see, lend them the experiences that bring about insight, maybe we can all be strong — Together.

I began to develop a strategy. I would form a coalition of people and organizations to put on a Clothesline Display Project. We would call it the Anti-Violence Coalition of Kentucky. The Clothesline Display Project, a visual display of T-shirts created by victims of violence, their friends, or family members, had been successfully initiated in over 250 cities since its inception in the early eighties. Like the founders, I wanted to bring attention to the problem of violence and the ability of women to survive; but I also had other dreams for this project: Strength, solidarity, and insight.

Back home, I sat in the lobby of the Plaza Hotel, less than two weeks after my return from D.C., waiting for Marlice Pillow, the director of our local spouse abuse shelter. Marlice was a very classy lady who exuded strength and tenacity, and who had led many alliances and mentored many people throughout her life. We went to a seat in the dining room and I told her about my past (I had been in an abusive marriage that robbed me of my childhood as well as my high school education) and about the Clothesline Project itself.

"I see this as a chance to draw women into this project who have not been involved with much before. For them to experience the empowerment of helping others and to work with different people on an important issue. I may be being idealistic, but I think this could be the start of bringing about a change in some of the women who only come to school to get married. Women with enormous potential who cannot see beyond today, or their boyfriend, or whatever keeps them from being like those women I met in D.C.," I said enthusiastically.

Marlice smiled and said many encouraging things. That lunch, alongside the image of the sixteen women in my small group in Washington, gave me the strength that I was too excited to realize I would need over the next few months.

After meeting with Marlice and the director of the Rape Crisis Center, Phyllis Millstaugh, I began calling organizations and people that I believed would be interested in the project. My first letdown occurred within the first week when I called the Pregnancy Help Center. In organizing my list of contacts I had included Black, white, pro-life, pro-choice, Republican, Democrat, straight, gay, conservative, liberal, and neutral organizations. I expected some to refuse, as the national Clothesline Display Project included "women assaulted because of their sexual orientation," but I was still hurt by the director's response.

"I'm sorry, Miss, what was it? Wilson?" he asked.

"Wilson-Compton," I replied, knowing full well that even my hyphenation was an offense to many conservatives.

"Yes, well. I really don't think we would be interested. It sounds like your agenda is a little too feminist/political for us."

"My mother is a pastor and I have worked with affiliates of yours. Do you know Dena in Somerset?" I queried, feeling insulted, but trying to draw on my personal past to engage him in dialogue.

I tried to draw him into the conversation and he thawed a little. "Yes, I know Dena well," he said with some warmth, but went on to say, "Listen, why don't you drop off the information and we'll call you if we're interested." Of course, he wasn't interested, nor were any of the other thirty Christian organizations I called.

I refused to let it get me down. I went out to the abuse center and talked with Marlice for about an hour and toured the facilities, fascinated and distracted. Later, I put the picture of my small group in the front of my day-runner and started calling prospective board members and sponsors again. The Plaza Hotel was our first corporate sponsor, then Women's Studies, and the list grew. Eventually we raised over $1000 in cash and over $500 in supplies.

I sat at my computer working one morning when the phone rang. It was Larry Calliout, head of the Christian Fellowship of Faculty/Staff (CFFS) of WKU. CFFS is a very visible group on campus that takes out a full-page ad twice a year, announcing its membership roster. Larry told me that CFFS wanted to throw their hat into the ring as board members AND sponsors! I discussed my problems in getting a response from the Christian community with Larry at length and he encouraged me to keep trying. He and I talked two or three more times over the course of the next few months and he sent representatives to several board meetings.

Another phone call brought the news that Marlice had died from a long-term illness. Though our friendship had been very brief, this discovery cut me to the quick. Marlice's treatment of me had been nothing short of inspiring and her contribution to the coalition had been profound. I let myself cry openly for a long time, concentrating on the enormity of this loss to our community. She had served as the first female police officer, a faculty member at Western, and in various other positions before coming to the spouse abuse shelter. Her wide influence was attested to by the diverse crowd at her funeral, and we decided to dedicate the Bowling Green Clothesline Display Project to her. She had left us with a hard, but worthy, act to follow.

As the coalition gathered steam we were a diverse group partly due to Marlice's influence. Our board included an openly gay man, a lesbian, a Native American Christian, an atheist, a male social worker (sporting an earring), several women (including a police officer, myself (sporting an eye-ring), several older members, one who was 19, and working closely with us was Take Back the Night, a predominantly black group on our campus. Volunteers came from all walks of life and all segments of the college and community. We had counselors from a Christian firm, from the Rape Crisis and Spouse Abuse Centers, and from the Campus Counseling Service. We set up booths at the Kentucky Victims Advocate Conference, the International Festival, and the National Coming Out Day celebration on campus.

At those sessions, women, and more than a dozen men, who created shirts talked with us and touched us with stories too horrible to repeat, but too profound to forget. One incident I remember vividly was that of an eighteen-year-old gay man who had been raped by another man. Words failed me as he told his story. All I could do was hold him. Another story came from my relatives in northeastern Kentucky. My cousin had found a ten-year-old girl raped and sodomized. Many mothers stopped by our pre-display booths and talked to us. A local eight-year-old girl had been recently kidnapped from her yard. People were frightened for their children. Women from the Spouse Abuse Center created shirts in their therapy sessions. One was on a white, one-piece infant outfit and read "No, no, please don't hurt me." This shirt had a powerful impact on the crowds at our displays—one downtown and one on campus. Young white couples picked up brochures on how to talk to their kids about abuse and about a local drop-in daycare center. Children wore bear stickers that said "Stop Child Abuse." Black women stopped and took brochures; Asian women used an interpreter to talk with me briefly. Women from all walks of life and all backgrounds shared stories and concerns, and made T-shirts for themselves or someone they knew.

I made a shirt too. My shirt had a weeping willow drawn on it and said "My Family Tree Is a Weeping Willow: Grandpa raped his daughters and beat daddy. Daddy raped my sister and beat us all. Brother raped me and my sister." At the bottom I wrote a promise to my children that the cycle stops with me. Another promise I make to them every day is that I will show them the world through the widest possible lens. I don't mind being the only white family in the Martin Luther King Jr. Day march. I don't mind having my house broken into and my life threatened because gay men and lesbians are welcome in my home. I don't mind being out of place or feeling different. *That is the essence of building alliances, that is the essence of change. And only when we are willing to leave the security of the known and venture into the "other" do we stretch and grow and learn.* And somewhere along the road we look back and realize that the greatest thing we have learned is that we can work together and that each of us has a unique and valuable contribution to give.

At the end of the conference in Washington, our group performed a skit where a wire hanger was shaped into a woman's figure and each member of our group brought up a personal item (glasses, keys, scarf, . . .) and attached it to the woman as I read the following. This "model woman" is who we must all aspire to be, as the alliance begins inside of us.

Mysterious Woman

Numerous, seemingly unrelated parts go into her
*   construction.*
A bit of wit from her mother.
A bit of self-esteem from her teacher.
Humility, through failures she dares not forget.
Bigotries she hopes to erase.
Sunsets which bring her a glimpse of serenity.
Wars, which force upon her rage.
Injustices which bring her unrest.
Internal conflicts whose resolutions change her
*   very appearance,*
and somewhere—before the final artwork is
*   unveiled—*
A sense that all that is wrong,
all that is painful,
all that causes others to cry out in desperation
*   or hunger,*
fear or loneliness,
ALL THAT IS . . .
Can be irrevocably altered . . .
by her.

She is the homeless mother.
She is the woman in Africa whose genitals were
*   mutilated during childhood.*
She is the woman who kicked at the bricks of the
*   Berlin wall.*
She is the self-conscious fourth grader.
She is the political prisoner.
She is the girl from the suburbs.
She is a hundred shades of brown.
She is the hope.
She is the salvation.
She is the leader.
The woman—she, my friend, is YOU.

Since October, when the Clothesline Display Project was packed into boxes (until next year), I have become more active in the newly re-formed Lesbian/Bisexual/Straight/Gay Alliance, where I am putting what I have learned to work for that organization. "What I learned" encompasses both my acquired knowledge from the Washington Center's Women As Leaders Seminar and the more subtle things I learned from my experiences with the Anti-Violence Coalition. The suggestions that follow are a synthesis of the two.

Learn about People Who Are Different from You You cannot work with people from different backgrounds if you have no knowledge of those backgrounds. A few books or a couple of multiculturalism classes will give you a great start. You will probably find that some cultures or issues interest you more than others; that is fine. Understand that any culture or issue you understand well will give you the tools to communicate with members of that group or persons interested in that issue MUCH better than if you are simply tolerant. A good example is the issue of Christianity here in Bowling Green. Though I am now an atheist, I grew up in a Christian home and attended Bible School for two years. There have been numerous occasions where displaying my knowledge of the Bible, my understanding of modern theology, or my simply mentioning that I went to Bible School has opened communications with colleagues. I was not "selling out" or advocating their position, I was simply showing them that I understood their point of view. This is a powerful tool, to be sure.

Ask Questions If you don't understand someone's argument, whether they are siding with you or not, ask them open-ended questions in a neutral manner. An example would be "Really, Nancy? That's an interesting way of looking at the euthanasia issue. What makes you see it as a breach of the doctor's contract?" "Can you elaborate?" is another great opener. If you are hostile — in tone or body language — then the person will respond defensively. Defensiveness is the quickest way to end all communication.

Stay on Task If you are working on school reform, abortion issues have no place in your meeting. Do not bring side issues up, and quickly change the subject when they are brought up. This can be difficult, but I have found it helpful to say things like, "we're getting a little off track here," or "that brings up a number of issues, maybe after the meeting you could discuss it, but for right now, we need to vote on. . . ." I often make a joke after tense moments like these, sometimes making a joke of the intervention itself. "Okayyyyy kids. If talking about abortion will solve our staffing problem, I'm all for it, but other-wise — help, help, help!!" Having served as VP of Protocol for LBSGA, the primary job of which was to keep things on-task, I recognize that *this can be the single hardest problem in alliances.*

Be Organized, but Flexible Never come to a meeting without an agenda. If you have an issue to contend with, make up several suggestions beforehand (calling members for suggestions is very helpful and builds one-on-one communication) and introduce them, asking for feedback/further suggestions. I strongly recommend not making any major decisions without doing this, though. You want as many people in on the decision making as possible. *If people do not feel like their opinion is valued (this means being flexible and listening intently to their comments), they will not continue in alliance with you.*

Look for Strengths in Odd Places We tend to count on the most outspoken people the most, but I have found that people who are not a part of the main group represented (usually Anglo-Saxon, abled, heterosexual, men from the middle class) are far less outspoken. While this trend is changing in some areas (e.g., women represent much of the anti-violence work I do), it is holding fast in most. I try very concertedly to draw out people who are quiet and I intentionally assign them duties. I have met with great success on this front. A case that comes to mind is a shy young man I am working with in LBSGA. Aside from his shyness, his inexperience and tendency to act or speak in socially inappropriate ways cause him to be overlooked for leadership/responsibility roles. After some discussion with him, he confessed that he would like to do more for the group (his shyness faded within a year of becoming a member, but the other problems persisted). Two weeks ago we voted him in as my assistant and I assigned him as stage manager for an upcoming benefit concert. The belief I have shown in him has not been unwarranted, as he has attended the meetings faithfully and gotten his tasks done more quickly and accurately than some veteran members. *Some of the best alliances come from having confidence in people's abilities regardless of how they may appear.*

Glossary

This glossary contains many of the key concepts found in this book. The first time the concept is used in the text it is shown in **bold.** Refer to the definitions here to refresh your memory when you come across the terms again later.

able-bodyism — Attitudes, actions, and institutional practices that subordinate people with disabilities.

adultism — Attitudes, actions, and institutional practices that subordinate young people on the basis of their age.

ageism — Attitudes, actions, and institutional practices that subordinate elderly persons on the basis of their age.

alliance — Working with others, as a result of a deepening understanding of one another's lives and experiences.

analytical framework — A perspective that allows one to analyze the causes and implications of a particular issue, rather than simply describing it.

anti-Semitism — Attitudes, actions, and institutional practices that subordinate Jewish people (the term *Semite* is used also to refer to some Arabs).

biological determinism — A general theory holding that a group's biological or genetic makeup shapes its social, political, and economic destiny. This view is used to justify women's subordination, or the subordination of peoples of color on the argument that they are biologically or genetically different from, and usually inferior to, men or White people.

capitalism — An economic system in which most of the **capital** — property, raw materials, and the means of production (including people's labor) —

and goods produced are owned or controlled by individuals or groups — capitalists. The goal of all production is to maximize profit making.

classism — Attitudes, actions, and institutional practices that subordinate working-class and poor people on the basis of their economic condition.

coalition — Usually a short-term alliance of organizations in which the strategy is to stand together to achieve a specific goal or set of goals around a particular issue, regardless of other differences among the organizations.

commodification — The process of turning people and intangible things into things, or commodities, for sale; an example is the commodification of women's bodies through advertising and media representations.

comparable worth — A method of evaluating jobs that are traditionally defined as men's work or women's work — in terms of the knowledge and skills required for a particular job; the mental demands or decision making involved; the accountability or degree of supervision involved; and working conditions, such as how physically safe the job is — so as to eliminate inequities in pay based on gender.

conscientization — A methodology for understanding reality, or gaining a "critical consciousness," through group dialogue, critical analysis and examination of people's experiences and conditions that face them, which leads to action to transform that reality (Freire 1989).

contested terrain — An area of debate or controversy, in which several individuals or groups attempt to impose their own views or meanings on a situation.

criminalization—The process of turning people's circumstances or behaviors into a crime, such as the criminalization of mothers with HIV/AIDS or homeless people.

cultural relativism—The view that all "authentic" experience is equally valid and cannot be challenged by others. For example, White-supremacist views of Ku Klux Klan members are seen to be equally as valid as those held by antiracist activists. There are no external standards or principles by which to judge people's attitudes and behaviors.

culture—The values, symbols, means of expression, language, and interests of a group of people. The **dominant culture** includes the values, symbols, means of expression, language, and interests of people in power in this society.

discrimination—Differential treatment against less powerful groups (such as women, the elderly, or people of color) by those in positions of dominance.

ecofeminism—A philosophy that links the domination of women with the domination of nature.

environmental racism—The strong correlation between the distribution of toxic wastes and race; the movement for **environmental justice** draws on concepts of civil rights, whereby all citizens have a right to healthy living and working conditions.

essentialism—The view that people have some inherent essence, or characteristics and qualities, that define them. Some people argue, for example, that women are essentially more caring and nurturing than men.

eugenics—The White-supremacist belief that the human race can be "improved" through selective breeding.

feminization of poverty—Women and children constitute the vast majority of poor people in the United States and throughout the world, a result of structural inequalities and discriminatory policies that do not address this issue.

fertility rate—The number of children born to women between fifteen and fifty-four, considered by official census reports to be the child-bearing years.

first-wave feminism—Organizations and projects undertaken by suffragists and women's rights advocates from the 1840s until 1920 when women in the United States won the vote. See **liberal feminism.**

gender bending—Adopting clothing, body language, or behavior that challenges and undermines conventional gender norms and expectations.

gender gap—A significant difference between the political attitudes and voting patterns of women and men.

gendered division of labor—A division of duties between men and women under which women have the main responsibility for home and nurturing and men are mainly active in the public sphere. Also referred to as **gender roles.**

gender socialization—The process of learning the attitudes and behaviors that are considered culturally appropriate for boys or girls.

glass ceiling—An unseen barrier to women's promotion to senior positions in the workplace. Women can see the senior positions in their company or field, but few women reach them because of negative attitudes toward senior women and low perceptions of their abilities and training.

global level of analysis—A term used to describe the connections among people and among issues as viewed from a worldwide perspective.

heterosexism—Attitudes, actions, and institutional practices that subordinate people on the basis of their gay, lesbian, bisexual, or transgender orientation.

ideology—Ideas, attitudes, and values that represent the interests of a group of people. The dominant ideology comprises the ideas, attitudes, and values that represent the interests of the dominant group(s). Thus, for example, the ideological role of the idealized nuclear family is to devalue other family forms.

internalized oppression—Attitudes and behavior of some oppressed people that reflect the negative, harmful, stereotypical beliefs of the dominant group directed at oppressed people. The behaviors include holding negative beliefs about people in their own group. An example of internalized sexism is the view of some women that they and other women are inferior to men, which causes them to adopt oppressive attitudes and behaviors toward women.

intersectionality — An integrative perspective that emphasizes the intersection of several attributes, for example, gender, race, class, and nation.

liberal feminism — A philosophy that sees the oppression of women as a denial of equal rights, representation, and access to opportunities.

libertarianism — The belief in unrestricted liberty.

macro level of analysis — A term used to describe the relationships among issues, individuals, and groups as viewed from a national perspective.

marginality — The situation in which a person has a deep connection to more than one culture, community, or social group but is not completely able to identify with or be accepted by that group as an insider. For example, bisexual, mixed-race/mixed-culture, and immigrant peoples often find themselves caught between two or more social worlds.

marginalization — Attitudes and behaviors that relegate certain people to the social, political, and economic margins of society by branding them and their interests as inferior, unimportant, or both.

matrix of oppression and resistance — The interconnections among various forms of oppression based on gender, race, class, nation, and so on. These social attributes can be sources of disadvantage as well as privilege. Even negative ascriptions may be the source of people's resistance based on shared identity.

medicalization — The process of turning life processes, like childbirth or menopause, into medical issues, where the dominant model is based on sickness. Thus, menopause becomes an illness to be treated by medical professionals with formal educational qualifications and accreditation. By the same token, experienced midwives are considered unqualified because they lack these credentials.

meso level of analysis — A term used to describe the relationships among issues, individuals, and groups as viewed from a community, or local, perspective.

micro level of analysis — A term used to describe the connections among people and issues as seen from a personal or individual perspective.

militarism — A system and worldview based on the objectification of "others" as enemies, a culture that celebrates war and killing. This worldview operates through specific military institutions and actions.

militarized masculinity — A masculinity constructed to support militarism, with an emphasis on heroism, physical strength, lack of emotion, and appearance of invulnerability (Enloe 1990, 1993a).

misogyny — Woman-hating attitudes and behavior.

neocolonialism — Continuing economic inequalities between rich and poor countries that originated in colonial relationships.

objectification — Attitudes and behaviors by which people are treated as if they were "things." One example is the objectification of women through advertising images.

objectivity — A form of understanding in which knowledge and meaning are believed to come from outside oneself and are presumably not affected by personal opinion or bias.

offshore production — Factory work or office work performed outside the United States — for example, in Mexico, the Philippines, or Indonesia — that is done for U.S.-based companies.

oppression — Prejudice and discrimination directed toward whole socially recognized groups of people and promoted by the ideologies and practices of all social institutions. The critical elements differentiating oppression from simple prejudice and discrimination are that it is a group phenomenon and that institutional power and authority are used to support prejudices and enforce discriminatory behaviors in systematic ways. Everyone is socialized to participate in oppressive practices, either as direct and indirect perpetrators or passive beneficiaries, or — as with some oppressed peoples — by directing discriminatory behaviors at members of one's own group.

paradigm shift — A complete change in theoretical perspective.

patriarchy — A family, social group, or society in which men hold power and are dominant figures. Patriarchal power in the United States plays out in the family, the economy, the media, religion, law, and electoral politics.

peer marriage — An intentionally egalitarian marriage with an emphasis on partnership, cooperation, and shared roles that are not highly differentiated along gender lines.

postmodern feminism — A type of feminism that repudiates the broad-brush "universal" theorizing of liberalism, radical feminism, or socialism, and emphasizes the particularity of women's experiences in specific cultural and historical contexts.

poverty level — An income level for individuals and families that officially defines poverty.

power — The ability to influence others, whether through persuasion, charisma, law, political activism, or coercion. Power operates informally and through formal institutions and at all levels (micro, meso, macro, global).

power elite — A relatively small group — not always easily identifiable — of key politicians, senior corporate executives, the very rich, and opinion makers such as key media figures who influence political and economic decisions in the country. Although this group shifts over time, and according to the issue, it is relatively closed.

praxis — Reflection and action upon the world in order to transform it; a key part of socially lived theorizing.

prejudice — A closed-minded prejudging of a person or group as negative or inferior, even without personal knowledge of that person or group, and often contrary to reason or facts; unreasonable, unfair, and hostile attitudes toward people.

privilege — Benefits and power from institutional inequalities. Individuals and groups may be privileged without realizing, recognizing, or even wanting it.

public vs. private dichotomy — The view that distinguishes between the private and personal (dating, marriage, sexual habits, who does the housework, relationships between parents and children) and the public (religion, law, business). Although these two spheres affect each other, according to this view they are governed by different rules, attitudes, and behavior.

racism — Racial prejudice and discrimination that are supported by institutional power and authority. In the United States, racism is based on the ideology of White (European) supremacy and is used to the advantage of White people and the disadvantage of peoples of color.

radical feminism — A philosophy that sees the oppression of women in terms of patriarchy, a system of male authority, especially manifested in sexuality, personal relationships, and the family.

reproduction of labor — Women's unpaid domestic work in producing, nurturing, and socializing the next generation of workers and citizens; caring for adult members by providing meals and clean clothes, as well as rest, relaxation, love, and sexual intimacy, so that they are ready to face another working day.

second shift — Responsibilities for household chores and child care after having already done a full day's work outside the home, mostly done by women.

second-wave feminism — Feminist projects and organizations from the late 1960s to the mid-1980s that campaigned for women's equality in all spheres of life and, in some cases, that argued for a complete transformation of patriarchal structures. See **liberal feminism, radical feminism, socialist feminism.**

sexism — Attitudes, actions, and institutional practices that subordinate women because of their gender.

situated knowledge — Knowledge and ways of knowing that are specific to a particular historical and cultural context.

S/M or **sado-masochism** — A sexual encounter or relationship in which one partner plays a dominant role and the other a subordinate role. In sado-masochistic sexual relationships, this inequality is presumed to be consensual.

social constructionism — The view that concepts that appear to be immutable and often solely biological, such as gender, race, and sexual orientation, are defined by human beings operating out of particular cultural contexts and ideologies. The definitions are systematically transmitted, and appropriate attitudes and behaviors are learned through childhood socialization and life experience. In this view, for example, heterosexuality is something learned — socially constructed — not innate.

social control — Attitudes, behaviors, and mechanisms that keep people in their place. Overt social controls include laws, fines, imprisonment, and violence. Subtle ones include ostracism and withdrawal of status and affection.

social institutions — Institutions such as the family, education, the media, organized religion, law, and government.

socialist feminism — A view that sees the oppression of women in terms of their subordinate position in a system defined as both patriarchal and capitalist.

social location—The social features of one's identity incorporating individual, community, societal, and global factors such as gender, class, ability, sexual orientation, age, and so on.

speciesism—Attitudes, actions, and institutional practices that subordinate nonhuman species; usually used in discussions of environmental and ecological issues.

standpoint theory—The view that different social and historical situations give rise to very different experiences and theories about those experiences. See **situated knowledge.**

state—Governmental institutions, authority, and control. This includes the machinery of electoral politics, lawmaking, government agencies that execute law and policy, law enforcement agencies, the prison system, and the military.

subjectivity—A form of understanding in which knowledge and meaning come from oneself and one's own experiences.

sustainability—The ability of an ecologically sound economy to sustain itself by using renewable resources and generating low or nonaccumulating levels of pollution. A more sustainable future means rethinking and radically changing current production processes, as well as the materialism and consumerism that support excessive production.

theory—An explanation of how things are and why they are the way they are; a theory is based on a set of assumptions, has a perspective, and serves a purpose.

third-wave feminism—Feminist perspectives adopted in the 1990s often by younger women, with an emphasis on personal voice and multiple identities, ambiguity, and contradictions.

References

Abbey, S., and A. O'Reilly, eds. 1998. *Redefining motherhood: Changing identities and patterns.* Toronto: Second Story Press.

Abramovitz, M. 1996. *Regulating the lives of women.* Rev. ed. Boston: South End Press.

Abramovitz, M., and F. Newton. 1996. *Challenging AFDC Myths with the Facts.* Available from the Bertha Capen Reynolds Society, Columbus Circle Station, P.O. Box 20563, New York, NY 10023.

Abzug, B. 1984. *Gender gap: Bella Abzug's guide to political power for American women.* Boston: Houghton Mifflin.

Adler, F. 1975. *Sisters in crime: The rise of the new female criminal.* New York: McGraw-Hill.

Agarwal, B. 1992. The gender and environment debate: Lessons from India. *Feminist Review* 18(1): 119–57.

Ahn, I. S. 1996. Great army, great father. In *Great army, great father,* edited by T. H. Yu. Seoul, South Korea: Korean Church Women United.

Aisha. 1991. Changing my perception. *Aché: A Journal for Lesbians of African Descent* 3(3): 28–29.

Alcoff, L. 1988. Cultural feminism versus post-structuralism: The identity crisis in feminist theory. *Signs* 13(3): 405–36.

Alexander, J., and C. T. Mohanty, eds. 1997. *Feminist genealogies, colonial legacies, democratic futures.* New York: Routledge.

Allen, P. G. 1986. *The sacred hoop: Recovering the feminine in American Indian traditions.* Boston: Beacon Press.

Allison, D. 1992. *Bastard out of Carolina.* New York: Dutton.

Alonso, H. H. 1993. *Peace as a women's issue: A history of the U.S. movement for world peace and women's rights.* Syracuse, N.Y.: Syracuse University Press.

American Association of Retired Persons. N.d. *America's changing work force: Statistics in brief.* Washington, D.C.: American Association of Retired Persons.

American Civil Liberties Union. 1999. In stunning civil rights victory, VT court directs state to give same-sex couple marriage benefits. *ACLU News* [online], 20 December. Accessed 21 December 1999. http://www.aclu.org/news/december99.html

American Correctional Association. 1990. *The female offender: What does the future hold?* Washington, D.C.: St. Mary's Press.

American Federation of State, County, and Municipal Employees. 1988. *Stopping sexual harassment: An AFSCME guide.* Washington, D.C.: American Federation of State, County, and Municipal Employees.

American Friends Service Committee. 1989. *AFSC perspectives on the employer sanctions provisions of the Immigration Reform and Control Act of 1986.* Philadelphia: American Friends Service Committee.

American Heritage Dictionary. 1993. 3d ed. Boston: Houghton Mifflin.

American Society of Plastic Surgeons. *National clearinghouse of plastic surgery statistics, 1998.* Accessed 6 January 2000. http://www.plasticsurgery.org/mediactr/98avgsurgfees.htm

Amnesty International USA. 1999. *"Not part of my sentence": Violations of human rights of women in custody.* New York: Amnesty International USA.

Amott, T. 1993. *Caught in the crisis: Women and the U.S. economy today.* New York: Monthly Review Press.

Amott, T., and J. Matthaei. 1996. *Race, gender, and work: A multicultural economic history of women in the United States.* Rev. ed. Boston: South End Press.

Andersen, M. 2000. Women, power and politics. Pp. 290–322 in *Thinking about women: Sociological perspectives on sex and gender,* 5th ed. Boston: Allyn and Bacon.

Anderson, L., ed. 1991. *Sisters of the earth: Women's prose and poetry about nature.* New York: Vintage Books.

Anderson, M. 1999. A well-kept secret: How military spending costs women's jobs. Pp. 247–52 in *Gender camouflage,* edited by F. D'Amico and L. Weinstein. New York: New York University Press.

Anderson, M., G. Bischak, and M. Oden. 1991. *Converting the American economy.* East Lansing, Mich.: Employment Research Associates.

Anderson, M. L., and P. H. Collins, eds. 1995. *Race, class, and gender: An anthology.* 2d ed. Belmont, Calif.: Wadsworth.

Anderson, S., J. Cavanagh, and D. Ranney. 1999. NAFTA: Trinational fiasco. Pp. 104–7 in *The maquiladora reader: Cross-border organizing since NAFTA,* edited by R. Kamel and A. Hoffman. Philadelphia: American Friends Service Committee.

Andre, J. 1988. Stereotypes: Conceptual and normative considerations. In *Racism and sexism: An integrated study,* edited by P. S. Rothenberg. New York: St. Martin's Press.

Andruss, V., C. Plant, J. Plant, and S. Mills. 1990. *Home!: A bioregional reader.* Philadelphia: New Society.

Anglin, M., and Y. Hser. 1987. Addicted women and crime. *Criminology* 25: 359–94.

Angwin, J. 1996. Pounding on the glass ceiling. *San Francisco Chronicle,* 24 November, p. C3.

Anzaldua, G. 1987. *Borderlands la frontera: The new mestiza.* San Francisco: Spinsters/Aunt Lute.

Applebome, P. 1997. Citadel's president insists coeducation will succeed. *New York Times,* 14 January, p. A1.

Arcana, J. 1994. Abortion is a motherhood issue. Pp. 159–63 in *Mother journeys: Feminists write about mothering,* edited by M. Reddy, M. Roth, and A. Sheldon. Minneapolis: Spinsters Ink.

Archibold, R. C. 1999. "A chill at Stuyvesant High: Prudence, or paranoia, after sexual abuse by teacher?" *New York Times,* 21 September, p. B1.

Arditti, R., R. D. Klein, and S. Minden, eds. 1984. *Test-tube women: What future for motherhood?* Boston: Pandora Press.

Associated Press. 1999. Most leaving welfare remain poor. *San Francisco Chronicle,* 12 May, p. A6.

Atkins, D., ed. 1998. *Looking queer: Body image and identity in lesbian, bisexual, gay, and transgender communities.* New York: Haworth Press.

Ayres, B. D., Jr. 1994. U.S. crackdown at border stems illegal crossings. *New York Times,* 6 October, pp. A1, A14.

Baca Zinn, M. 1989. Family, race, and poverty in the eighties. *Signs* 14: 856–74.

Bagby, R. 1990. Daughter of growing things. Pp. 231–48 in *Reweaving the world: The emergence of ecofeminism,* edited by I. Diamond and G. Orenstein. San Francisco: Sierra Club.

Baker, B. 1993. The women's convergence for national health care. *The Network News,* July/August, 1, 3.

Baptists in Texas reject a call for wives to "submit" to husbands. 1999. *New York Times,* 10 November, p. A21.

Barnett, R., and C. Rivers. 1996. *She works, he works: How two-income families are happier, healthier, and better-off.* New York: HarperSanFrancsico.

Barnhill, D. L., ed. 1999. *At home on the earth: Becoming native to our place.* Berkeley: University of California Press.

Baron, H. M. 1970. The web of urban racism. In *Institutional racism in America,* edited by L. L. Knowles and K. Prewitt. Englewood Cliffs, N.J.: Prentice Hall.

Barry, K. 1995. *The prostitution of sexuality: The global exploitation of women.* New York: New York University Press.

Bart, P., and P. O'Brien. 1993. *Stopping rape: Successful survival strategies.* New York: Teachers College Press.

Bartlett, J. 1994. *Will you be a mother? Women who choose to say no.* London: Virago.

Bass, E., and L. Davis. 1988. *The Courage to Heal.* New York: Harper & Row.

Basu, A. 1995. *The challenge of local feminisms.* Boulder, Colo.: Westview Press.

Beasley, M., and D. Thomas. 1994. Violence as a human rights issue. Pp. 323–46 in *The public nature of private violence: The discovery of domestic abuse,* edited by M. A. Fineman and R. Mykitiuk. New York: Routledge.

Benard, C., and E. Schlaffer. 1997. "The man in the street": Why he harasses. Pp. 395–98 in *Feminist frontiers IV,* edited by L. Richardson, V. Taylor, and N. Whittier. New York: McGraw-Hill.

Benjamin, M., and A. Freedman. 1989. *Bridging the global gap: A handbook to linking citizens of the first and third worlds.* Cabin John, Md.: Seven Locks Press.

Bennett, K. 1992. Feminist bisexuality: A both/and option for an either/or world. Pp. 205–31 in *Closer to home: Bisexuality and feminism,* edited by E. R. Weise. Seattle, Wash.: Seal Press.

Benston, M. 1969. The political economy of women's liberation. *Monthly Review* 21(4): 13–27.

Berg, P. 1993. Growing a life-place politics. In *Radical environmentalism: Philosophy and tactics,* edited by J. List. Belmont, Calif.: Wadsworth.

Bergen, R. K. 1996. *Wife rape: Understanding the response of survivors and service providers.* Thousand Oaks, Calif.: Sage.

———. 1999. *Marital rape.* Department of Justice Online Resources. http://www.vaw.umn.edu/vawmet/mrape.htm

Bergmann, B. R. 1986. *The economic emergence of women.* New York: Basic Books.

Bernstein, R., and S. C. Silberman, eds. 1996. *Generation Q.* Los Angeles: Alyson.

Bhattacharjee, A. 1997. A slippery path: Organizing resistance to violence against women. Pp. 29–45 in *Dragon ladies: Asian American feminists breathe fire,* edited by S. Shah. Boston: South End Press.

Bin Wahad, D. 1996. Speaking truth to power: Political prisoners in the United States. In *Criminal injustice: Confronting the prison crisis,* edited by E. Rosenblatt. Boston: South End Press.

Bird, C. 1995. *Lives of ours: Secrets of salty old women.* New York: Houghton Mifflin.

Bird, C., and S. W. Briller. 1969. *Born female: The high cost of keeping women down.* New York: Pocket Books.

Black Women's Health Project. 1995. *Reproductive health and African American women. Issue brief.* Washington, D.C.: Black Women's Health Project.

Blakely, M. K. 1994. *American mom: Motherhood, politics, and humble pie.* Chapel Hill, N.C.: Algonquin Books.

Blau, J. 1999. *Illusions of prosperity: America's working families in an age of economic insecurity.* New York: Oxford University Press.

Blauner, R. 1972. *Racial oppression in America.* New York: Harper & Row.

Blee, K. M. 1998. Radicalism. Pp. 500–501 in *The reader's companion to U.S. women's history,* edited by W. Mankiller, G. Mink, M. Navarro, B. Smith, and G. Steinem. Boston: Houghton Mifflin.

Bleier, R. 1984. *Science and gender: A critique of biology and its theories on women.* New York: Pergamon Press.

Bloom, B., M. Chesney-Lind, and B. Owen. 1994. *Women in California prisons: Hidden victims of the war on drugs.* San Francisco: Center on Juvenile and Criminal Justice.

Bloom, C., A. Gitter, S. Gutwill, L. Kogel, and L. Zaphiropoulos. 1994. *Eating problems: A feminist psychoanalytic treatment model.* New York: Basic Books.

Boesing, M. 1994. Statement to the Court. Pp. 189–91 in *Mother journeys: Feminists write about mothering,* edited by M. Reddy, M. Roth, and A. Sheldon. Minneapolis: Spinsters Ink.

Boggs, G. L. 1994. Fifty years on the left. *The Witness,* May, 8–12.

Bohmer, C., and A. Parrot. 1993. *Sexual assault on campus: The problem and the solution.* New York: Lexington Books/Macmillan.

Booth, W. 1997. Ex–Black Panther freed. *Washington Post,* 11 June, p. A1.

Bordo, S. 1993. *Unbearable weight: Feminism, Western culture, and the body.* Berkeley: University of California Press.

Borkovitz, D. K. 1995. Same-sex battering and the backlash. *NCADV Voice,* Summer, 4.

Bornstein, K. 1995. *Gender outlaw: On men, women, and the rest of us.* New York: Vintage/Random House.

———. 1998. *My gender workbook: How to become a real man, a real woman, the real you, or something else entirely.* New York: Routledge.

Boston Women's Health Book Collective. 1992. *The new our bodies, ourselves.* New York: Simon & Schuster.

———. 1994. *The new ourselves growing older.* New York: Simon & Schuster.

———. 1998. *Our bodies, ourselves for the new century: A book by and for women.* New York: Simon & Schuster.

Boswell, J. 1994. *Same-sex unions in premodern Europe.* New York: Villard Books.

Boumil, M., and J. Friedman. 1996. *Deadbeat dads: A national child support scandal.* Westport, Conn.: Praeger.

Boulding, E. 1990. *Building a civic culture: Education for an interdependent world.* Syracuse, N.Y.: Syracuse University Press.

Bourbeau, H. 1998. U.S. companies under fire for using Chinese sweatshops. *Financial Times,* 19 March, p. 8.

Bowlby, J. 1963. *Child care and the growth of love.* Baltimore: Penguin Books.

Braidotti, R., E. Charkiewicz, S. Häusler, and S. Wieringa. 1994. *Women, the environment and sustainable development: Towards a theoretical synthesis.* London: Zed Books.

Brant, B., ed. 1988. *A gathering of spirits: A collection by North American Indian women.* Ithaca, N.Y.: Firebrand.

Brennan, S., J. Winklepleck, and G. MacNee. 1994. *The resourceful woman.* Detroit: Visible Ink.

Brenner, J. 1996. The best of times, the worst of times: Feminism in the United States. Pp. 17–72 in *Mapping the women's movement,* edited by M. Threlfall. London: Verso Books.

Bright, S. 1994. *Herotica 3.* New York: Plume.

Brown, B. R. D. 1996. White North American political prisoners. In *Criminal injustice: Confronting the prison crisis,* edited by E. Rosenblatt. Boston: South End Press.

Browne, J. 1996. The labor of doing time. In *Criminal injustice: Confronting the prison crisis,* edited by E. Rosenblatt. Boston: South End Press.

Brownmiller, S. 1975. *Against our will: Men, women, and rape.* New York: Simon & Schuster.

Brumberg, J. J. 1997. *The body project: An intimate history of American girls.* New York: Random House.

Buchwald, E., P. Fletcher, and M. Roth, eds. 1993. *Transforming a rape culture.* Minneapolis: Milkweed.

Bulhan, H. A. 1985. *Frantz Fanon and the psychology of oppression.* New York: Plenum Books.

Bullard, R. D. 1990. *Dumping in Dixie: Race, class, and environmental quality.* Boulder, Colo.: Westview Press.

———, ed. 1993. *Confronting environmental racism: Voices from the grassroots.* Boston: South End Press.

Bullough, V. L., and B. Bullough. 1993. *Cross dressing, sex, and gender.* Philadelphia: University of Pennsylvania Press.

Bunch, C. 1986. *Passionate politics: Essays 1968–1986.* New York: St. Martin's Press.

Bunch, C., and R. Carillo. 1991. *Gender violence: A human rights and development issue.* New Brunswick, N.J.: Center for Women's Global Leadership, Rutgers University.

Bunch, C., and N. Myron, eds. 1974. *Class and feminism: A collection of essays from the Furies.* Baltimore: Diana Press.

Bunch, C., and N. Reilly. 1994. *Demanding accountability: The global campaign and Vienna Tribunal for women's human rights.* New Jersey: Center for Women's Global Leadership, Rutgers University; New York: UNIFEM.

Bureau of Justice Statistics. 1991. *Special report: Women in prison in 1986.* Washington, D.C.: U.S. Department of Justice.

———. 1992. *Women in jail in 1989.* Washington, D.C.: U.S. Department of Justice.

———. 1994a. *Special report: Women in prison in 1991.* Washington, D.C.: U.S. Department of Justice.

———. 1994b. *National crime victimization survey, violence against women.* Washington, D.C.: U.S. Department of Justice.

———. 1995. Violence against women: Estimates from the redesigned survey. Washington, D.C.: U.S. Department of Justice.

———. 1998. *Criminal victimization 1997: Changes 1996–97 with trends 1993–97.* Washington, D.C.: U.S. Department of Justice.

———. 1999a, December. *Special report: Women offenders.* Washington, D.C.: U.S. Department of Justice.

———. 1999b, August. *Bulletin: Prisoners in 1998.* Washington, D.C.: U.S. Department of Justice.

———. 1999c. *Rates of HIV infection and AIDS-related deaths drop among the nation's prisoners.* Washington, D.C.: Bureau of Justice Statistics.

Bureau of Labor Statistics. 1998. *Employment and earnings.* Washington, D.C.: Bureau of Labor Statistics.

Burke, P. 1996. *Gender shock: Exploding the myths of male and female.* New York: Anchor Books.

Burrell, B. 1994. *A woman's place is in the House: Campaigning for Congress in the feminist era.* Ann Arbor: University of Michigan Press.

Burton, N. 1998. Resistance to prevention: Reconsidering feminist antiviolence rhetoric. Pp. 182–200 in *Violence against women: Philosophical perspectives,* edited by S. French, W. Teays, and L. Purdy. Ithaca, N.Y.: Cornell University Press.

Bury, J., V. Morrison, and S. McLauchlan, eds. 1992. *Working with women with AIDS.* New York: Routledge.

Bush-Baksette, S. R. 1999. The 'war on drugs' a war against women? In *Harsh punishment: International experiences of women's imprisonment,* edited by S. Cook and S. Davies. Boston: Northeastern University Press.

Butler, J. 1990. *Gender trouble: Feminism and the subversion of identity.* New York: Routledge, Chapman, & Hall.

Butler, O. 1993. *The parable of the sower.* New York: Warner Books.

Calvo, J. 1996. Health care access for immigrant women. Pp. 161–81 in *Man-made medicine: Women's health, public policy, and reform,* edited by K. L. Moss. Durham, N.C.: Duke University Press.

Cammermeyer, M. 1994. *Serving in silence.* New York: Viking.

Camp, L. T. 1997. *Lingering fever: A World War II nurse's memoir.* Jefferson, N.C.: McFarland and Co.

Campbell, D., with F. D'Amico. 1999. Lessons on gender integration from the military academies. Pp. 67–79 in *Gender camouflage: Women and the U.S. military,* edited by F. D'Amico and L. Weinstein. New York: New York University Press.

Campbell, J. 1999, October. *Health insurance coverage 1998.* Washington, D.C.: U.S. Department of Commerce, Economics and Statistics Administration.

Candib, L. 1995. *Medicine and the family: A feminist perspective.* New York: Basic Books.

Caplan, P., ed. 1987. *The cultural construction of sexuality.* London: Tavistock Publications.

Caputi, J., and D. E. H. Russell. 1990. "Femicide": Speaking the unspeakable. *Ms.,* September/October, 34–37.

Carlen, P. 1989. Feminist jurisprudence, or women-wise penology. *Probation Journal* 36(3): 110–14.

Cavin, S. 1985. *Lesbian origins.* San Francisco: Ism Press.

Center for American Women and Politics. 1999. *Fact sheet: Women in the U.S. Congress 1999.* New Brunswick, N.J.: Center for American Women and Politics, Rutgers University.

Center for Reproductive Law and Policy. N.d. *The facts about contraceptive coverage in private and government insurance.* New York: Center for Reproductive Law and Policy.

Centers for Disease Control and Prevention. 1996. *Sexually transmitted disease surveillance.* Atlanta: U.S. Department of Health and Human Services.

———. 1999. *HIV/AIDS surveillance report* 11(1). Rockville, Md.: Centers for Disease Control and Prevention.

Chalker, R. 1995. Sexual pleasure unscripted. *Ms.,* November/December, 49–52.

Chambers, V. 1995. Betrayal feminism. In *Listen up: Voices from the next feminist generation,* edited by B. Findlen. Seattle, Wash.: Seal Press.

Chapkis, W. 1986. *Beauty secrets: Women and the politics of appearance.* Boston: South End Press.

Chavez, C. 1993. Farm workers at risk. Pp. 163–170 in *Toxic struggles: The theory and practice of environmental justice,* edited by R. Hofrichter. Philadelphia and Gabriola Island, B.C.: New Society Publishers.

Chavkin, W. 1984. *Double exposure: Women's health hazards on the job and at home.* New York: Monthly Review Press.

Chernin, K. 1985. *The hungry self.* New York: Times Books.

Chesler, P. 1972. *Women and madness.* New York: Avon.

Chesney-Lind, M. 1986. Women and crime: A review of the literature on the female offender. *Signs: Journal of Women in Culture and Society* 12(1): 78–96.

———. 1987. Female offenders: Paternalism reexamined. In *Women, the courts and equality,* edited by L. Crites and W. Hepperle. Newbury Park, Calif.: Sage.

———. 1995. Rethinking women's imprisonment: A critical examination of trends in female incarceration. In *Women, Crime, and Criminal Justice,* edited by B. R. Price and N. Sokoloff. New York: McGraw-Hill.

———. 1997. The female offender: Girls, women and crime. Thousand Oaks, Calif.: Sage.

———. 2000, February. From bad to worse. Review of *Hard punishment: International experiences of women's imprisonment. Women's Review of Books* 17(5): 7.

Chesney-Lind, M., and R. G. Shelden. 1992. *Girls, delinquency and juvenile justice.* Pacific Grove, Calif.: Brooks/Cole.

Chodorow, N. 1978. *Reproduction and mothering: Psychoanalysis and the sociology of gender.* Berkeley: University of California Press.

Chrichton, S. 1993. Sexual correctness: Has it gone too far? *Newsweek,* 25 October, 55.

Churchill, W. 1992. Introduction: The Third World at home. In *Cages of steel: The politics of imprisonment in the United States,* edited by W. Churchill and J. J. Vander Wall. Washington, D.C.: Maisonnueve Press.

Citizen Soldier. 1996. *Newsletter.* New York: Citizen Soldier.

Clinton, H. R. 1996. *It takes a village and other lessons children teach us.* New York: Simon & Schuster.

Cobble, D. S., ed. 1993. *Women and unions: Forging a partnership.* Ithaca, N.Y.: ILR Press.

Cole, J. H. 1992. *Women pilots of World War II.* Salt Lake City: University of Utah Press.

Collins, P. H. 1990. *Black feminist thought: Knowledge, consciousness, and the politics of empowerment.* Boston: Unwin Hyman.

Comité Fronterizo de Obreras-American Friends Service Committee. 1999. *Six years of NAFTA: A view from inside the maquiladoras.* Philadelphia: AFSC.

Commonwealth Fund. 1997. *The Commonwealth Fund Survey of the health of adolescent girls: Highlights and methodology.* New York: The Commonwealth Fund.

Connell, R. W. 1990. The state, gender, and sexual politics: Theory and appraisal. *Theory and Society* 19(4): 507–44.

Cook, A., and G. Kirk. 1983. *Greenham women everywhere: Dreams, ideas, and actions from the women's peace movement.* Boston: South End Press.

Coontz, S. 1992. *The way we never were: American families and the nostalgia trap.* New York: Basic Books.

———. 1997. *The way we really are: Coming to terms with America's changing families.* New York: Basic Books.

Cooper, E. 1992. When being ill is illegal: Women and the criminalization of HIV. *Health/PAC Bulletin,* Winter, 10–14.

Cooper, M. 1997. When push comes to shove: Who is welfare reform really helping? *The Nation,* 2 June, 11–15.

Corea, G. 1985. *The mother machine: Reproductive technologies from artificial insemination to artificial wombs.* New York: Harper & Row.

———. 1987. *Man-made women: How reproductive technologies affect women.* Bloomington: Indiana University Press.

Cox, T. 1999. *Hot sex: How to do it.* New York: Bantam Books.

Crenshaw, K. 1993. The marginalization of sexual violence against Black women. Speech to the National Coalition Against Sexual Assault, 1993 Conference, Chicago. http://www.ncasa.org/marginalization.html

Dalla Costa, M., and S. James. 1972. *The power of women and the subversion of the community.* Bristol, England: Falling Wall Press.

Daly, F. 1994. Perspectives of Native American women on race and gender. In *Challenging racism: Alternatives to genetic explanations,* edited by E. Tobach and B. Risoff. New York: The Feminist Press.

Daly, H. E., and J. B. Cobb Jr. 1989. *For the common good: Redirecting the economy toward community, the environment, and a sustainable future.* Boston: Beacon Press.

Daly, K. 1994. *Gender, crime, and punishment.* New Haven, Conn.: Yale University Press.

Daly, M. 1976. *Gyn/ecology: The metaethics of radical feminism.* Boston: Beacon Press.

D'Amico, F., and L. Weinstein, eds. 1999. *Gender camouflage: Women and the U.S. military.* New York: New York University Press.

Danaher, K. N.d. *Seven arguments for reforming the world economy.* http://www.globalexchange.org/economy/econ101/sevenArguments.html

Dankelman, I., and J. Davidson. 1988. *Women and the environment in the Third World.* London: Earthscan.

Dargan, C. A. 1995. *Statistical record of health and medicine.* Detroit: Gale Research.

Davis, A. Y. 1983a. Racism, birth control, and reproductive rights. In *Women, race, and class.* New York: Vintage Books.

———. 1983b. *Women, race, and class.* New York: Vintage Books.

———. 1997. A plenary address. Paper presented at conference, Frontline Feminisms: Women, War, and Resistance, 16 January, at University of California, Riverside.

Davis, F. 1991. *Moving the mountain: The women's movement in America since 1960.* New York: Simon & Schuster.

Davis, J., ed. 1991. *The Earth First! reader: Ten years of radical environmentalism.* Salt Lake City: Peregrine Smith Books.

Davis, M. 1998. Philosophy meets practice: A critique of ecofeminism through the voices of three Chicana activists. Pp. 201–31 in *Chicano culture, ecology, politics: Subversive kin,* edited by D. G. Peña. Tucson: University of Arizona Press.

d'Eaubonne, F. 1994. The time for ecofeminism. In *Ecology,* edited by C. Merchant. Atlantic Highlands, N.J.: Humanities Press.

de Beauvoir, S. 1973. *The second sex.* New York: Vintage Books.

Deen, T. 1998. Globalisation devastates women, say unions. *InterPress Service,* 4 March.

de Ishtar, Z. 1994. *Daughters of the Pacific.* Melbourne: Spinifex Press.

D'Emilio, J. 1984. Capitalism and gay identity. Pp. 100–13 in *Powers of desire: The politics of sexuality,* edited by A. Snitow et al. New York: Monthly Review Press.

D'Emilio, J., and E. Freedman. 1997. *Intimate matters: A history of sexuality in America.* 2d ed. Chicago: University of Chicago Press.

Denman, J. E., and L. B. Inniss. 1999. No war without women: Defense industries. Pp. 187–99 in *Gender camouflage: Women and the U.S. military,* edited by F. D'Amico and L. Weinstein. New York: New York University Press.

De Oliveira, O., T. De Barbieri, I. Arriagada, M. Valenzuela, C. Serrano, and G. Emeagwali. 1991. *Alternatives: The food, energy, and debt crises in relation to women.* Bangalore, India: DAWN.

DePalma, A. 1996. Why that Asian TV has a "Made in Mexico" label. *New York Times,* 23 May, p. D1.

Devall, B., and G. Sessions. 1985. *Deep ecology: Living as if nature mattered.* Salt Lake City: Smith Books.

Diamond, I., and G. F. Orenstein, eds. 1990. *Reweaving the world: The emergence of ecofeminism.* San Francisco: Sierra Club Books.

Diamond, S. 1995. *Roads to dominion: Right-wing movements and political power in the United States.* New York: Guilford Press.

Dibblin, J. 1989. *The day of two suns: U.S. nuclear testing and the Pacific Islands.* New York: New Amsterdam Books.

Dickersin, K., and L. Schnaper. 1996. Reinventing medical research. Pp. 57–76 in *Man-made medicine: Women's health, public policy, and reform,* edited by K. L. Moss. Durham, N.C.: Duke University Press.

Dinnerstein, D. 1976. *Sexual arrangements and the human malaise.* New York: Harper & Row.

———. 1989. Surviving on earth: Meaning of feminism. In *Healing the wounds,* edited by J. Plant. Philadelphia: New Society Publishers.

Disability Statistics Center. 1999. *How many Americans have a disability?* [online]. Accessed 1 August 2000. http://www.dsc.ucsf.edu/

Dittrich, L. 1997. Sociocultural factors that influence body image satisfaction in women. Doctoral dissertation, California Institute of Integral Studies, *Dissertation Abstracts International.*

DNA testing: A new military invasion. 1996. *Citizen Soldier.* Available from Citizen Soldier, 175 Fifth Ave., #2135, New York, NY 10010.

Donchin, A., and L. M. Purdy. 1999. *Embodying bioethics: Recent feminist advances.* Lanham, Md.: Rowman and Littlefield.

Doress, P. B., and D. L. Siegal. 1987. *Ourselves, growing older: Women aging with knowledge and power.* New York: Simon & Schuster.

Doyal, L. 1995. *What makes women sick: Gender and the political economy of health.* New Brunswick, N.J.: Rutgers University Press.

Drill, E., H. McDonald, and R. Odes. 1999. *Deal with it! A whole new approach to your body, brain and life as a gurl.* New York: Pocket Books.

Duberman M. B., M. Vicinus, and G. Chauncey Jr. 1989. *Hidden from history: Reclaiming the gay and lesbian past.* New York: New American Library.

Duff, K. 1993. *The alchemy of illness.* New York: Pantheon.

Duggan, L., and N. Hunter. 1995. *Sex wars: Sexual dissent and political culture.* New York: Routledge.

Dujon, D., and A. Withorn, eds. 1996. *For crying out loud: Women's poverty in the United States.* Boston: South End Press.

Dula, A. 1994. The life and death of Miss Mildred: An elderly Black woman. *Clinics in Geriatric Medicine* 10(3): 419–30.

———. 1996. An African American perspective on reproductive freedoms. Panel on Reproduction, Race, and Class at the Third World Congress of Bioethics, Feminist Approaches to Bioethics, November, San Francisco.

DuPlessis, R. B., and A. Snitow, eds. 1998. *The Feminist Memoir Project: Voices from women's liberation.* New York: Three Rivers Press.

Duran, J. 1998. *Philosophies of science/feminist theories.* Boulder, Colo.: Westview Press.

Dworkin, A. 1987. *Intercourse.* New York: Free Press.

Dziemianowicz, J. 1992. How we make the stars so beautiful. *McCall's,* July, 105.

Echols, A. 1989. *Daring to be bad: Radical feminism in America 1967–1975.* Minneapolis: University of Minnesota Press.

Edison, L. T., and D. Notkin. 1994. *Women en large: Images of fat nudes.* San Francisco: Books in Focus.

Efon, S. 1997. Tsunami of eating disorders sweeps across Asia, *San Francisco Examiner,* 19 October, p. A27.

Ehrenreich, B., and D. English. 1973. *Witches, midwives, and nurses: A history of women healers.* Old Westbury, N.Y.: Feminist Press.

———. 1978. *For her own good: 150 years of the experts' advice to women.* Garden City, N.Y.: Anchor/Doubleday.

Ehrenreich, B., E. Hess, and G. Jacobs. 1986. *Remaking love: The feminization of sex.* New York: Anchor/Doubleday.

Eisenstein, Z. R. 1979. *Capitalism, patriarchy, and the case for socialist feminism.* New York: Monthly Review Press.

———. 1988. *The female body and the law.* Berkeley: University of California Press.

———. 1998. Socialist feminism. Pp. 218–19 in *The reader's companion to U.S. women's history,* edited by W. Mankiller, G. Mink, M. Navarro, B. Smith, and G. Steinem. Boston: Houghton Mifflin.

Ekins, R. 1997. *Male femaling: A grounded theory approach to cross-dressing and sex-changing.* New York: Routledge.

Elliott, L. 1999. Britain ends Third World debt. *The Guardian,* 18 December, p. 1.

Eng, D. and A. Y. Hom, eds. 1998. *Q & A: Queer in Asian America.* Philadelphia: Temple University.

Enloe, C. 1983. *Does khaki become you? The militarization of women's lives.* Boston: South End Press.

———. 1988. *Does khaki become you? The militarization of women's lives.* London and Winchester, Mass.: Pandora Press.

———. 1990. *Bananas, beaches and bases: Making feminist sense of international politics.* Berkeley: University of California Press.

———. 1993a. *The morning after: Sexual politics at the end of the cold war.* Berkeley: University of California Press.

———. 1993b. The right to fight: A feminist Catch-22. *Ms.,* July/August, 84–87.

———. 2000. *Maneuvers: The international politics of militarizing women's lives.* Berkeley: University of California Press.

Ensler, E. 1998. *The vagina monologues.* New York: Villard/Random House.

Epstein, B. 1993. Ecofeminism and grassroots environmentalism in the United States. Pp. 144–52 in *Toxic struggles: The theory and practice of environmental justice,* edited by R. Hofrichter. Philadelphia and Gabriola Island, B.C.: New Society Publishers.

Erdman, C. 1995. *Nothing to lose: A guide to sane living in a larger body.* San Francisco: HarperSan Francisco.

Erez, E. 1992. Dangerous men, evil women: Gender and parole decision making. *Justice Quarterly* 9(1): 105–27.

Eridani. 1992. Is sexual orientation a secondary sex characteristic? In *Closer to home: Bisexuality and feminism,* edited by E. R. Weise. Seattle, Wash.: Seal Press.

Evans, S. 1980. *Personal politics.* New York: Vintage Books.

Facts on the global sweatshop. 1997. *Rethinking Schools: An Urban Education Journal* 11(4): 16.

Faderman, L. 1981. *Surpassing the love of men: Romantic friendship and love between women from the Renaissance to the present.* New York: William Morrow.

Fallon, P., ed. 1994. *Consuming passions: Feminist perspectives on eating disorders.* New York: Guilford.

Faludi, S. 1991. *Backlash: The undeclared war against women.* New York: Crown.

Family Violence Prevention Fund. 1995. International peace begins at home. Pp. 2–3 in *News from the homefront.* San Francisco: FVPF.

———. 1998. *Domestic violence is a serious, widespread social problem in America: The facts.* Available from the Family Violence Prevention Fund, 383 Rhode Island Ave., San Francisco, CA 94103.

Fanon, F. 1967. *Black skin, white masks.* New York: Grove Press.

———. 1968. *The wretched of the earth.* New York: Grove Press.

Farnsworth, M., and R. Teske Jr. 1995. Gender differences in felony court processing: Three hypotheses of disparity. *Women and Criminal Justice* 6(2): 23–44.

Fausto-Sterling, A. 1993. The five sexes: Why male and female are not enough. *The Sciences,* March/April, 20–24.

Federal Bureau of Investigation. 1992. *Uniform crime reports 1991.* Washington, D.C.: U.S. Department of Justice.

———. 1997. *Crime in the United States 1996*. Washington, D.C.: FBI, U.S. Department of Justice.

Federation of Feminist Health Centers. 1995. *A new view of a woman's body*. 2d ed. Los Angeles: Feminist Health Press.

Feinberg, L. 1993. *Stone butch blues*. Ithaca, N.Y.: Firebrand Books.

———. 1996. *Transgender warriors: Making history from Joan of Arc to RuPaul*. Boston: Beacon Press.

———. 1998. *Trans liberation: Beyond pink or blue*. Boston: Beacon Press.

Ferguson, A. 1989. *Blood at the root: Motherhood, sexuality, and male dominance*. London: Pandora.

Ferguson, M., and J. Wicke, eds. 1992. *Feminism and postmodernism*. Durham, N.C.: Duke University Press.

Ferree, M. M., and P. Y. Martin. 1995. *Feminist organizations: Harvest of the new women's movement*. Philadelphia: Temple University Press.

Ferreyra, S., and K. Hughes. 1991. *Table manners: A guide to the pelvic examination for disabled women and health care providers*. San Francisco: Sex Education for Disabled People and Planned Parenthood Alameda.

Ferriss, S., and R. Sandoval. 1997. *The fight in the fields: Cesar Chavez and the Farmworkers movement*. New York: Harcourt Brace.

Fiduccia, B. W., and M. Saxton. 1997. Disability feminism: A manifesto. *New Mobility: Disability Culture and Lifestyle* 8(49): 60–61.

Findlen, B., ed. 1995. *Listen up: Voices from the next feminist generation*. Seattle, Wash.: Seal Press.

Fineman, M. A., and R. Mykitiuk, eds. 1994. *The public nature of private violence: The discovery of domestic abuse*. New York: Routledge.

Finger, A. 1990. *Past due: A story of disability, pregnancy, and birth*. Seattle, Wash.: Seal Press.

Firestone, S. 1970. *The dialectics of sex: The case for feminist revolution*. New York: Morrow.

Flammang, J. A. 1997. *Women's political voice: how women are transforming the practice and study of politics*. Philadelphia: Temple University Press.

Foley, L., and C. Rasche. 1979. The effect of race on sentence, actual time served and final disposition of female offenders. In *Theory and research in criminal justice*, edited by J. Conley. Cincinnati: Anderson.

Forrest, M. Silk. 1992. Groups: Powerful medicine for our deepest wounds. In *The Healing Woman: The Monthly Newsletter for Women Survivors of Childhood Sexual Abuse*, July, 1, 10–11.

Foster, C. 1989. *Women for all seasons: The story of W.I.L.P.F.* Athens, Ga.: University of Georgia Press.

Fox-Genovese, E. 1994. Beyond individualism: The new Puritanism, feminism, and women. *Salmagundi* 101(2): 79–95.

Francis, D. 1999. Rich man's plan seen as stingy. *Christian Science Monitor*, 24 June, p. 6.

Francke, L. B. 1997. *The gender wars in the military*. New York: Simon & Schuster.

Frankenberg, R. 1993. *White women, race matters: The social construction of whiteness*. Minneapolis: University of Minnesota Press.

Franklin, D., and J. Sweeney. 1988. Women and corporate power. Pp. 48–65 in *Women, power and policy: Toward the year 2000*, 2d ed., edited by E. Boneparth and E. Stoper. New York: Pergamon Press.

Fraser, L. 1997. *Losing it: America's obsession with weight and the industry that feeds it*. New York: Dutton.

Freedberg, L. 1996. 1,000 more agents will be sent to the border. *San Francisco Chronicle*, 9 February, p. A3.

Free trade vs. fair trade. N.d. Available from Global Exchange, 2017 Mission St., Rm. 303, San Francisco, CA 94110.

Freire, P. 1989. *Pedagogy of the oppressed*. New York: Continuum.

Freudenheim, E. 1995. *Healthspeak: A complete dictionary of America's healthcare system*. New York: Facts on File.

Friedan, B. 1963. *The feminine mystique*. New York: W. W. Norton.

Frye, M. 1983. Oppression. Pp. 1–16 in *The politics of reality: Essays in feminist theory*. Freedom, Calif.: The Crossing Press.

———. 1992. *Willful virgin: Essays in feminism 1976–1992*. Freedom, Calif.: The Crossing Press.

Fuchs, L. 1990. The reaction of Black Americans to immigration. In *Immigration reconsidered*, edited by V. Yans-McLaughlin. New York: Oxford University Press.

Fuentes, A., and B. Ehrenreich. 1983. *Women in the global factory*. Boston: South End Press.

Fund for a Feminist Majority. 1997. *Right-wing investment funds scare corporations away from RU 486 and contraceptive research*. http://www.feminist.org/rrights/rwfact1.html

Fuss, D., ed. 1991. *Inside out: Lesbian theories, gay theories*. New York: Routledge.

Gaines, P. 1994. *Laughing in the dark: From colored girl to woman of color — a journey from prison to power.* New York: Anchor Books.

Gallagher, N. W. 1993. The gender gap in popular attitudes toward the use of force. Pp. 23–37 in *Women and the use of military force,* edited by R. Howes and M. Stevenson. Boulder, Colo.: Lynne Rienner Publishers.

Garber, M. 1992. *Vested interests: Cross-dressing and cultural anxiety.* New York: HarperPerennial.

Gardner, M. 1999. The family-leave law, and beyond. *Christian Science Monitor,* 4 August, p. 17.

Garner, D. M. 1997. The 1997 body image survey results. *Psychology Today,* January/February, 31–44, 75–84.

George, S. 1988. Getting your own back: Solving the Third World debt crisis. *New Statesman & Society,* 15 July, 20.

Gibbs, L. 1995. *Dying from dioxin: A citizens' guide to reclaiming our health and rebuilding democracy.* Boston: South End Press.

———. 1998. *Love canal: The story continues.* Gabriola Is. BC, New Society Publishers.

Gilfus, M. 1992. From victims to survivors: Women's routes of entry and immersion into street crime. *Women and Criminal Justice* 4(1): 62–89.

Gill, C. 1996. Cultivating common ground: Women with disabilities. Pp. 183–93 in *Man-made medicine: Women's health, public policy, and reform,* edited by K. L. Moss. Durham, N.C.: Duke University Press.

Giordano, P., S. Kerbel, and S. Dudley. 1981. The economics of female criminality. In *Women and crime in America,* edited by L. Bowker. New York: Macmillan.

Glazer, P. M., and M. P. Glazer. 1998. *The environmental crusaders: Confronting disaster and mobilizing community.* University Park: Pennsylvania State University Press.

Gleick, E. 1996. Scandal in the military. *Time,* 25 November, 28–31.

Glover, P. 1997. Ithaca HOURS makes social change pay: "Print money locally and make revolution globally." *Resist* 6(4): 3.

Gluck, S. 1976. *From parlor to prison: Five American suffragists talk about their lives.* New York: Vintage Books.

Gold, J., and S. Villari, eds. 2000. *Just sex: Students rewrite the rules on sex, violence, activism, and equality.* Lanham, Md.: Rowman and Littlefield.

Goldberg, G. S., and S. Collins. 1999. *Washington's new poor law: Welfare "reform" and the roads not taken, 1935–1998.* New York: Apex Press.

Goodman, E. 1996. Predators and jailbait. *San Francisco Chronicle,* 21 February, p. A17.

———. 1999. Working moms do no harm. *San Francisco Chronicle,* 4 March, p. A23.

Gordon, L. 1988. *Heroes of their own lives: The politics and history of family violence, Boston 1880–1960.* New York: Viking.

———. 1997. Killing in self-defense. *The Nation,* 24 March, 25–28.

Gould, J. 1997. *Juggling: A memoir of work, family, and feminism.* New York: The Feminist Press.

Grahn, J. 1984. *Another mother tongue: Gay words, gay worlds.* Boston: Beacon Press.

Gray, C. 1999. *Corporate cash: Few nations can top it.* Eugene, Oreg.: Author.

Gray, J. 1992. *Men are from Mars, women are from Venus: A practical guide for improving communication and getting what you want in your relationships.* New York: HarperCollins.

Greenfeld, L. A., et al. 1998, March. *Bureau of Justice Statistics factbook: Violence by intimates.* Washington, D.C.: Bureau of Justice.

Greenhouse, L. 1999. High court limits who is protected by disability law. *New York Times,* 23 June, p. A1.

Greenhouse, S. 1997. Nike shoe plant in Vietnam is called unsafe for workers. *New York Times,* 8 November, p. A1.

Greider, W. 1997. *One world ready or not: The manic logic of global capitalism.* New York: Simon & Schuster.

Griffin, S. 1971. Rape: The all-American crime. *Ramparts* 10(3): 26–35.

———. 1978. *Woman and nature: The roaring inside her.* San Francisco: Harper Colophon.

———. 1986. *Rape: The politics of consciousness.* 3d ed. San Francisco: Harper & Row.

Grossholtz, J. 1983. Battered women's shelters and the political economy of sexual violence. Pp. 59–69 in *Families, politics, and public policy: A feminist dialogue on women and the state,* edited by I. Diamond. New York: Longman.

Grossman, R. 1998a. Can corporations be accountable? (Part 1). *Rachel's Environment and Health Weekly,* 30 July, 1–2.

———. 1998b. Can corporations be accountable? (Part 2). *Rachel's Environment and Health Weekly,* 6 August, 1–2.

Grunwald, L. 1992. If women ran America. *Life Magazine,* June, 37–46.

Guenter-Schlesinger, S. 1999. Persistence of sexual harassment: The impact of military culture on policy implementation. Pp. 195–212 in *Beyond zero tolerance,* edited by M. Katzenstein and J. Reppy.

Haiken, E. 1997. *Venus envy: A history of cosmetic surgery.* Baltimore: Johns Hopkins University Press.

Hall, G. M. 1999. Intersectionality: A necessary consideration for women of color in the military? Pp. 143–61 in *Beyond zero tolerance,* edited by M. Katzenstein and J. Reppy.

Hamer, D., and B. Budge. 1994. *The good, the bad and the gorgeous: Popular culture's romance with lesbianism.* London: Pandora.

Hamilton, C. 1993. Coping with industrial exploitation. In *Confronting environmental racism: Voices from the grassroots,* edited by R. Bullard. Boston: South End Press.

Hammonds, E. 1995. Missing persons: African American women, AIDS, and the history of disease. Pp. 443–49 in *Words of fire: An anthology of African-American feminist thought,* edited by B. Guy-Sheftall. New York: New Press.

Harman, B. 1996. Happy ending. Pp. 286–90 in *"Women in the trees": U.S. women's short stories about battering and resistance, 1839–1994,* edited by S. Koppelman. Boston: Beacon Press.

Harne, L., and E. Miller, eds. 1996. *All the rage: Reasserting radical lesbian feminism.* New York: Teachers College Press.

Hartmann, B. 1995. Dangerous intersections. *Political Environments,* no. 2 (summer): 1–7. Publication of the Committee on Women, Population and the Environment, Hampshire College, Amherst, Mass.

Hartmann, H. 1981. The unhappy marriage of Marxism and feminism: Towards a more progressive union. In *Women and revolution: A discussion of the unhappy marriage of Marxism and feminism,* edited by L. Sargent. Boston: South End Press.

Hartsock, N. 1983. *Money, sex, and power: Toward a feminist historical materialism.* New York: Longman.

Harvey, E. 1999. Short-term and long-term effects of early parental employment on children of the National Longitudinal Survey of Youth. *Developmental Psychology* 35(2): 445–459.

Havemann, J. 1999. Former welfare recipients got more jobs in past 3 years. *San Francisco Chronicle,* 27 May, p. A3.

Hayden, D. 1981. *The grand domestic revolution: A history of feminist designs for American homes, neighborhoods, and cities.* Cambridge, Mass.: MIT Press.

Healey, S. 1997. Confronting ageism: A MUST for mental health. Pp. 368–76 in *In our own words: Readings on the psychology of women and gender,* edited by M. Crawford and R. Unger. New York: McGraw-Hill.

Heise, L. 1989. Crimes of gender. *World Watch,* March/April, 12–21.

Heise, L., J. Pitanguy, and A. Germain. 1994. *Violence against women: The hidden health burden.* World Bank Discussion Papers #255. Washington, D.C.: The World Bank.

Henderson, H. 1991. *Paradigms in progress: Life beyond economics.* Indianapolis: Knowledge Systems.

Hennessy, R., and C. Ingraham, eds. 1997. *Materialist feminism: A reader in class, difference, and women's lives.* New York: Routledge.

Herman, J. 1981. *Father-daughter incest.* Cambridge, Mass.: Harvard University Press.

———. 1992. *Trauma and recovery.* New York: Basic Books.

Hesse-Biber, S. J. 1991. Women, weight, and eating disorders: A socio-cultural analysis. *Women's Studies International Forum* 14(3): 173–91.

———. 1996. *Am I thin enough yet?* New York: Oxford University Press.

Hetherington, M., and G. Clingempeel. 1992. *Coping with marital transitions: A family systems perspective.* Chicago: Chicago University Press for the Society for Research in Child Development.

Heywood, L. 1998. *Bodymakers: A cultural anatomy of women's body building.* New Brunswick, N.J.: Rutgers University Press.

Heywood, L., and J. Drake. 1997. *Third wave agenda: Being feminist, doing feminism.* Minneapolis: University of Minnesota Press.

Hicks, G. 1994. *The comfort women.* New York: W. W. Norton.

High, G. 1997. Combating sexual harassment. *Soldiers* 52(2): 4–5.

Hill, J. 1993. Outrageous acts. Unpublished class assignment, Antioch College.

Hinchman, H. 1997. *A trail through leaves: The journal as a path to place.* New York: W. W. Norton.

History Project. 1998. *Improper Bostonians: Lesbian and gay history from the Puritans to Playland.* Boston: Beacon Press.

Hite, S. 1994. *Women as revolutionary agents of change: The Hite Report and beyond.* Madison: University of Wisconsin Press.

——. 1995. *Hite Report on the family: Growing patriarchy.* New York: Grove Press.

Hochman, A. 1994. *Everyday acts and small subversions: Women reinventing family, community, and home.* Portland, Oreg.: Eighth Mountain Press.

Hochschild, A. R. 1989. *The second shift: Working parents and the revolution at home.* New York: Viking.

——. 1997. *The time bind: When work becomes home and home becomes work.* New York: Henry Holt.

Hofrichter, R., ed. 1993. *Toxic struggles: The theory and practice of environmental justice.* Philadelphia and Gabriola Island, B.C.: New Society Publishers.

Holmes, S. A. 1995a. Ousters of undocumented immigrants set a record. *San Francisco Chronicle,* 28 December, p. A13.

——. 1995b. The strange politics of immigration. *New York Times,* 31 December, p. E3.

hooks, b. 1984a. *Feminist theory: From margin to center.* Boston: South End Press.

——. 1984b. Feminist movement to end violence. Pp. 117–31 in *Feminist theory: From margin to center,* edited by b. hooks. Boston: South End Press.

——. 1993. *Sisters of the yam: Black women and self recovery.* Boston: South End Press.

——. 1994. Seduced by violence no more. Pp. 109–13 in *Outlaw culture: Resisting representations,* edited by b. hooks. New York: Routledge.

Hubbard, R. 1989. Science, facts, and feminism. In *Feminism and science,* edited by N. Tuana. Bloomington: Indiana University Press.

——. 1990. *The politics of women's biology.* New Brunswick, N.J.: Rutgers University Press.

Human Rights Campaign. 1999. *State of the workplace report.* Washington, D.C.: HRC.

Human Rights Watch. 1999a. *World report 1999. United States: Human rights developments.* New York: Author.

——. 1999b. No guarantees: Sex discrimination in Mexico's maquiladora sector. Pp. 31–35 in *The maquiladora reader: Cross-border organizing since NAFTA,* edited by R. Kamel and A. Hoffman. Philadelphia: American Friends Service Committee.

Humm, A., ed. 1992. *Feminisms: A reader.* New York: Harvester Wheatsheaf.

Hurtado, A. 1996. *The color of privilege: Three blasphemies on race and feminism.* Ann Arbor: The University of Michigan Press.

Hutchins, L., and L. Kaahumanu. 1991. *Bi any other name: Bisexual people speak out.* Boston: Alyson.

Hynes, P. 1996. *A patch of Eden.* White River Junction, Vt.: Chelsea Green.

Inciardi, J., D. Lockwood, and A. Pottieger. 1993. *Women and crack cocaine.* New York: Macmillan.

In Phoenix chain gangs for women. 1996. *New York Times,* 28 August, p. C1.

Institute for Women's Policy Research. 1998. *Social Security reform and women: A factsheet.* Washington, D.C.: IWPR.

Ireland, M. S. 1993. *Reconceiving women: Separating motherhood from female identity.* New York: Guilford Press.

Isakson, E., ed. 1988. *Women and the military system.* New York: St. Martin's Press.

Jaggar, A. M. 1983. *Feminist politics and human nature.* Totowa, N.J.: Rowman & Allanheld.

——, ed. 1994. *Living with contradictions: Controversies in feminist social ethics.* Boulder, Colo.: Westview Press.

Jetter, A., A. Orelck, and D. Taylor, eds. 1997. *The politics of motherhood: Activist voices from left to right.* Hanover, N.H.: University Press of New England.

Johnson, A. G. 1997. *The gender knot: Unraveling our patriarchal legacy.* Philadelphia: Temple University Press.

Jones, A. 1980. *Women who kill.* New York: Holt, Rinehart, and Winston.

——. 1994a. Is this power feminism? Living with guns, playing with fire. *Ms.,* June/July, 36–44.

——. 1994b. *Next time, she'll be dead: Battering and how to stop it.* Boston: Beacon Press.

Jones, J. 1985. *Labor of love, labor of sorrow: Black women, work, and the family, from slavery to present.* New York: Vintage Books.

Kadi, J. 1996. *Thinking class: Sketches from a cultural worker.* Boston: South End Press.

Kamel, R. 1990. *The global factory: Analysis and action for a new economic era.* Philadelphia: American Friends Service Committee.

Kamel, R., and A. Hoffman, eds. 1999. *The maquiladora reader: Cross-border organizing since NAFTA.* Philadelphia: American Friends Service Committee.

Kaplan, T. 1997. *Crazy for democracy: Women in grassroots movements.* New York: Routledge.

Katz, J. N. 1995. *The invention of heterosexuality.* New York: Plume.

Katzenstein, M. F. 1993. The right to fight. *Women's Review of Books* 11(2): 30–31.

Katz-Rothman, B. 1986. *Tentative pregnancy: Prenatal diagnosis and the future of motherhood.* New York: Viking.

Katzenstein, M. F., and J. Reppy, eds. 1999. *Beyond zero tolerance: Discrimination in military culture.* Lanham, Md.: Rowman and Littlefield.

Kaye/Kantrowitz, M., and I. Klepfisz, eds. 1989. *The Tribe of Dina: A Jewish women's anthology.* Boston: Beacon Press.

Kerr, J., ed. 1993. *Ours by right: Women's rights as human rights.* London: Zed Books.

Kessler-Harris, A. 1990. *A woman's wage: Historical meanings and social consequences.* Lexington: University Press of Kentucky.

Kich, G. K. 1992. The developmental process of asserting a biracial, bicultural identity. Pp. 304–17 in *Racially mixed people in America,* edited by M. P. Root. Newbury Park, Calif.: Sage.

Kilbourne, J. 1994. Still killing us softly: Advertising and the obsession with thinness. Pp. 395–418 in *Feminist perspectives on eating disorders,* edited by P. Fallon, M. K. Katzman, and S. C. Wooley. New York: Guilford Press.

———. 1999. *Deadly persuasion: Why women and girls must fight the addictive power of advertising.* New York: Free Press.

Kim, E., L. V. Villanueva, and Asian Women United of California. 1989. *Making waves.* Boston: Beacon Press.

———. 1997. *Making more waves: New writing by Asian American women.* Boston: Beacon Press.

Kimmel, M. S., and T. Mosmiller, eds. 1992. *Against the tide: Pro-feminist men in the United States, 1776–1990.* Boston: Beacon Press.

King, Y. 1983. All is connectedness: Notes from the Women's Pentagon Action, USA. In *Keeping the peace,* edited by L. Jones. London: The Women's Press.

———. 1987. Letter to the editor. *The Nation,* 12 December, 702, 730–31.

———. 1988. Ecological feminism, *Z Magazine,* July/August, 124–27.

———. 1991. Reflection on the other body: Difference, disability and identity politics. Unpublished paper.

———. 1993a. The other body. *Ms.,* March/April, 72–75.

———. 1993b. Feminism and ecology. Pp. 76–84 in *Toxic struggles: The theory and practice of environmental justice,* edited by R. Hofrichter. Philadelphia and Gabriola Island, B.C.: New Society Publishers.

———. 1998. Ecofeminism. P. 207 in *The reader's companion to U.S. women's history,* edited by W. Mankiller, G. Mink, M. Navarro, B. Smith, and G. Steinem. Boston: Houghton Mifflin.

Kingston, M. H., 1976. *The woman warrior: Memoirs of a girlhood among ghosts.* New York: Knopf.

Kirk, G. 1997. Ecofeminism and environmental justice: Bridges across gender, race, and class. *Frontiers: A Journal of Women's Studies* 18(2): 2–20.

———. 1998. Ecofeminism and Chicano environmental struggles: Bridges across gender and race. Pp. 177–200 in *Chicano culture, ecology, politics: Subversive kin,* edited by D. G. Peña. Tucson: University of Arizona Press.

Klein, R., and L. J. Dumble. 1994. Disempowering midlife women: The science and politics of hormone replacement therapy (HRT). *Women's Studies International Forum* 17(4): 327–43.

Klepfisz, I. 1990. *Dreams of an insomniac: Jewish feminist essays, speeches and diatribes.* Portland: Eighth Mountain Press.

Koedt, A., E. Levine, and A. Rapone, eds. 1973. *Radical feminism.* New York: Quadrangle Books.

Kohl, H. 1992. *From archetype to zeitgeist: Powerful ideas for powerful thinking.* Boston: Little Brown.

Kohn, S. 1999, June. *The NGLTF domestic partnership organizing manual.* Washington, D.C.: National Gay and Lesbian Task Force.

Komesaroff, P., P. Rothfield, and J. Daly, eds. 1997. *Reinterpreting menopause: Cultural and philosophical issues.* New York: Routledge.

Koppelman, S., ed. 1996. *"Women in the trees:" U.S. women's short stories about battering and resistance, 1839–1994.* Boston: Beacon Press.

Koss, M. P. 1988. Hidden rape: Sexual aggression and victimization in a national sample of students in higher education. Pp. 3–25 in *Rape and sexual assault,* edited by A. W. Burgess. New York: Garland.

Koss, M. P., E. T. Dinero, and C. A. Seibel. 1988. Stranger and acquaintance rape: Are there differences in the victim's experience? *Psychology of Women Quarterly* 12: 1–24.

Koss, M. P., L. Goodman, A. Browne, L. Fitzgerald, G. P. Keita, and N. F. Russo. 1994. *No safe haven:*

Male violence against women at home, at work, and in the community. Washington, D.C.: American Psychological Association.

Krauss, C. 1993. Blue-collar women and toxic-waste protests: The process of politicization. Pp. 107–17 in *Toxic struggles: The theory and practice of environmental justice,* edited by R. Hofrichter. Philadelphia and Gabriola Island, B.C.: New Society Publishers.

Krieger, L. 1998. RU-486 abortion pill is still not widely available in the U.S. *San Francisco Examiner,* 27 January, p. A1.

Krieger, N., and E. Fee. 1996. Man-made medicine and women's health: The biopolitics of sex/gender and race/ethnicity. Pp. 15–35 in *Man-made medicine: Women's health, public policy, and reform,* edited by K. L. Moss. Durham, N.C.: Duke University Press.

Krieger, N., and S. Sidney. 1996. Racial discrimination and blood pressure: The CARDIA study of young Black and White adults. *American Journal of Public Health* 86(10): 1370–78.

Kruttschnitt, C. 1980–81. Social status and sentences of female offenders. *Law and Society Review* 15(2): 247–65.

Kurz, D. 1995. *For richer, for poorer: Mothers confront divorce.* New York: Routledge.

LaDuke, W. 1993. A society based on conquest cannot be sustained: Native peoples and the environmental crisis. In *Toxic struggles: The theory and practice of environmental justice,* edited by R. Hofrichter. Philadelphia and Gabriola Island, B.C.: New Society Publishers.

———. 1999. *All our relations: Native struggles for land and life.* Cambridge, Mass.: South End Press.

LaFramboise, T., J. S. Berman, and B. Sohi. 1994. American Indian Women. In *Women of color: Integrating ethnic and gender identities in psychotherapy,* edited by L. Comas-Díaz and B. Greene. New York: Guilford Press.

Lahey, K. 1985. Until women themselves have told all they have to tell. *Osgoode Hall Law Journal* 23(3): 519–41.

Lakoff, R. T., and R. L. Scherr. 1984. *Face value.* Boston: Routledge & Kegan Paul.

Lancaster, R. N., and M. di Leonardo, eds. 1997. *The gender/sexuality reader: Culture, history, political economy.* New York: Routledge.

Larkin., J., and K. Popaleni. 1997. Heterosexual courtship violence and sexual harassment: The private and public control of young women. Pp.

313–26 in *In our own words: Readings on the psychology of women and gender,* edited by M. Crawford and R. Unger. New York: McGraw-Hill.

Lasch, C. 1977. *Haven in a heartless world: The family besieged.* New York: Basic Books.

LaVigne, P. 1989. "Take a little off the sides": Baby boomers boost plastic surgery biz. *Utne Reader,* September/October, 12.

Lawe, C., and B. Lawe. 1980. The balancing act: Coping strategies for emerging family lifestyles. In *Dual career couples,* edited by F. Pepitone-Rickwell. Beverly Hills, Calif.: Sage.

Lazarre, J. 1976. *The mother knot.* New York: McGraw-Hill.

Lee, C. 1987. *Toxic wastes and race in the United States.* New York: New York Commission for Racial Justice United Church of Christ.

Lehrman, K. 1993. Off course. *Mother Jones,* September/October, 45–55.

Leidholdt, D., and J. Raymond. 1990. *The sexual liberals and the attack on feminism.* New York: Pergamon.

Leonard, A., ed. 1989. *SEEDS: Supporting women's work in the Third World.* New York: The Feminist Press.

Lichtenstein, A. C., and M. A. Kroll. 1996. The fortress economy: The economic role of the U.S. prison system. In *Criminal injustice: Confronting the prison crisis,* edited by E. Rosenblatt. Boston: South End Press.

Lieberman, T. 1997. Social Security: The campaign to take the system private. *The Nation,* 27 January, 11–16, 18.

Light, J. 1996. Rape on the border. *The Progressive,* September, 24.

———. 1999, October. Prison industrial complex. *Corporate Watch.* San Francisco: Transnational Resource and Action Center.

Lips, H. 1991. *Women, men, and power.* Mountain View, Calif.: Mayfield.

Lipsky, S. 1977. Internalized oppression. *Black Reemergence,* Winter, 5–10.

List, P. C., ed. 1993. *Radical environmentalism: Philosophy and tactics.* Belmont, Calif.: Wadsworth.

Lobel, K., ed. 1984. *Naming the violence: Speaking out about lesbian battering.* Seattle, Wash.: Seal Press.

Lorber, J. 1994. *Paradoxes of gender.* New Haven, Conn.: Yale University Press.

Lord, S. A. 1993. *Social welfare and the feminization of poverty.* New York: Garland.

Lorde, A. 1984. *Sister outsider.* Freedom, Calif.: The Crossing Press.

Los Angeles Times. 1999. 38% of ex-welfare recipients jobless. 15 January, p. A21.

Lowy, J. 1999. Gay adoption backlash growing. *San Francisco Examiner.* 7 March, p. A-20.

Lublin, N. 1998. *Pandora's box: Feminism confronts reproductive technology.* Lanham, Md.: Rowman and Littlefield.

Luebke, B. F., and M. E. Reilly. 1995. *Women's studies graduates: The first generation.* New York: Teachers College Press.

Luker, K. 1996. *Dubious conceptions: The politics of teenage pregnancy.* Cambridge, Mass.: Harvard University Press.

Lunneborg, P. 1992. *Abortion: A positive decision.* New York: Begin and Garvey.

Lusane, C. 1991. *Pipe dream blues: Racism and the war on drugs.* Boston: South End Press.

MacKinnon, C. 1987. *Feminism unmodified: Discourse on life and law.* Cambridge, Mass.: Harvard University Press.

———. 1991. From practice to theory, or what is a white woman anyway? *Yale Journal of Law and Feminism* 4(13–22): 1281–1328.

———. 1993. Turning rape into pornography: Postmodern genocide. *Ms.,* June/July, 24–30.

———. 1998. Rape, genocide, and women's human rights. Pp. 43–54 in *Violence against women: Philosophical perspectives,* edited by S. French, W. Teays, and L. Purdy. Ithaca, N.Y.: Cornell University Press.

Maher, F. A., and M. K. T. Tetreault. 1994. *The feminist classroom.* New York: Basic Books.

Mahoney, M. 1994. Victimization or oppression? Women's lives, violence, and agency. Pp. 59–92 in *The public nature of private violence: The discovery of domestic abuse,* edited by M. A. Fineman and R. Mykitiuk. New York: Routledge.

Mainardi, P. 1992. The politics of housework. *Ms.,* May/June, 40–41.

Mainstream. 1997. 15(2): 14–16.

Mairs, N. 1990. Carnal acts. In *Carnal acts: Essays.* Boston: Beacon Press.

Majaj, L. S. 1994. Boundaries: Arab/American. Pp. 65–86 in *Food for our grandmothers: Writings by Arab-American and Arab-Canadian feminists,* edited by J. Kadi. Boston: South End Press.

Mann, C. R. 1995. Women of color and the criminal justice system. In *The criminal justice system and women,* edited by B. R. Price and N. J. Sokoloff. New York: McGraw-Hill.

Martin, G. 1986. *Socialist feminism: The first decade.* Seattle, Wash.: Freedom Socialist.

Martin, J. A., B. L. Smith, T. J. Mathews, and S. J. Ventura. 1999. Births and deaths: Preliminary data for 1998. *National Vital Statistics Reports,* vol. 47, no. 25. Hyattsville, Md.: National Center for Health Statistics.

Martinez, E. 1998. *De colores means all of us: Latina views for a multi-colored century.* Boston: South End Press.

Martinez, L. A. 1996. Women of color and reproductive health. In *Dangerous intersections: feminist perspectives on population, immigration, and the environment,* edited by T. Reisz and A. Smith. Amherst, Mass.: Committee on Women, Population, and the Environment, Hampshire College.

Mason, M. 1998. *USA: Supreme Court strengthens sexual harassment law,* 30 June. http://www.igc.org/igc/wn/hl9806304896/hl1.html

Mauer, M., and T. Huling. 1995. *Young Black Americans and the criminal justice system five years later.* Washington, D.C.: The Sentencing Project.

McCarthy, C., and W. Crichlow, eds. 1993. *Race, identity, and representation in education.* New York: Routledge.

McGinn, M. 1995. How GATT puts hard-won victories at risk. *Ms.,* March/April, 15.

McIntosh, P. 1988. *White privilege and male privilege: A personal account of coming to see correspondences through work in women's studies.* Wellesley, Mass.: Center for Research on Women, Wellesley College.

McKenna, T. 1996/1997. Military culture breeds misogyny. *Women Against Military Madness,* December/January, 1.

Mello, F. V. 1996. Population and international security in the new world order. *Political Environments,* no. 3 (winter/spring): 25–26. Publication of the Committee on Women, Population and the Environment, Hampshire College, Amherst, Mass.

Mellor, M. 1992. *Breaking the boundaries: Towards a feminist green socialism.* London: Virago Press.

Members of the AIDS Counseling and Education Program of the Bedford Hills Correctional Facility. 1998. *Breaking the walls of silence: AIDS and women in a New York State maximum security prison.* Woodstock, N.Y.: Overlook Press.

Merchant, C. 1980. *The death of nature: Ecology and the scientific revolution.* San Francisco: Harper & Row.

Messerschmidt, J. W. 1986. *Capitalism, patriarchy, and crime: Toward a socialist feminist criminology.* Totowa, N.J.: Rowman & Littlefield.

Mies, M. 1986. *Patriarchy and accumulation on a world scale: Women in the international division of labor.* London: Zed Books.

———. 1993. The need for a new vision: The subsistence perspective. In *Ecofeminism,* edited by M. Mies and V. Shiva. London: Zed Books.

Mies, M., and V. Shiva, eds. 1993. *Ecofeminism.* London: Zed Books.

Miles Foundation. 1999. E-mail communication from Christine Hansen, Miles Foundation, to Gwyn Kirk, 11 October 1999.

Military sex scandal extends to Air Force base. 1996. *San Francisco Chronicle,* 15 November, p. A15.

Milkman, R., ed. 1985. *Women, work, and protest: A century of U.S. women's labor history.* London: Routledge & Kegan Paul.

Miller, V. D. 1993. *Building on our past, planning our future: Communities of color and the quest for environmental justice.* Pp. 128–135 in *Toxic Struggles: The theory and practice of environmental justice,* edited by Richard Hofrichter, Philadelphia and Gabriola Is., B.C.: New Society Publishers.

Mills, J. 1986. *The underground empire: Where crime and governments embrace.* New York: Doubleday.

Mintz, S., and S. Kellogg. 1988. *Domestic revolutions: A social history of American family life.* New York: Free Press.

Mitchell, J. 1971. *Woman's estate.* New York: Pantheon.

———. 1990. Women: The longest revolution. In *Women, class, and the feminist imagination,* edited by K. V. Hansen and I. J. Philipson. Philadelphia: Temple University Press.

Mohanty, C., A. Russo, and L. Torres, eds. 1991. *Third World women and the politics of feminism.* Bloomington: Indiana University Press.

Moon, K. 1997. *Sex between allies: Military prostitution in U.S.-Korea relations.* New York: Columbia University Press.

Moraga, C., and G. Anzaldua, eds. 1983. *This bridge called my back: Writings by radical women of color.* New York: Kitchen Table: Women of Color Press.

Morgan, R. 1996. Dispatch from Beijing. *Ms.,* January/February, 12–15.

Morell, C. M. 1994. *Unwomanly conduct: The challenge of intentional childlessness.* New York: Routledge.

Morris, M. 1999. In war and peace: Incidence and implications of rape by military personnel. Pp. 163–94 in *Beyond zero tolerance: Discrimination in military culture,* edited by M. F. Katzen-

stein and J. Reppy. Lanham, Md.: Rowman and Littlefield.

Morrison, A., R. White, E. Van Velsor, and the Center for Creative Leadership. 1992. *Breaking the glass ceiling: Can women reach the top of America's largest corporations?* Reading, Mass.: Addison-Wesley.

Morrison, T., ed. 1992. *Race-ing, justice, en-gendering power: Essays on Anita Hill, Clarence Thomas, and the construction of reality.* New York: Pantheon.

Morrow, D. 1999a. Maker of Norplant reaches settlement in suit over effects. *New York Times,* 27 August, p. A1.

———. 1999b. A moveable epidemic: Makers of AIDS drugs struggle to keep up with the market. *New York Times,* 9 September, p. C1.

Moses, M. 1993. Farmworkers and pesticides. Pp. 161–78 in *Confronting environmental racism: Voices from the grassroots,* edited by R. Bullard. Boston: South End Press.

Movement for a New Society. 1983. *Off their backs . . . and on our own two feet.* Philadelphia: New Society Publishers.

Mudrick, N. R. 1988. Disabled women and the public policies of income support. In *Women with disabilities: Essays in psychology, culture, and politics,* edited by M. Fine and A. Asch. Philadelphia: Temple University Press.

Muir, K. 1993. *Arms and the woman.* London: Hodder and Stoughton.

Mullings, L. 1997. *On our own: Race, class, and gender in the lives of African American women.* New York: Routledge.

Musil, C. M., ed. 1992. *The courage to question: Women's studies and student learning.* Washington, D.C.: Association of American Colleges.

Myers, A., J. Taub, J. F. Morris, and E. D. Rothblun. 1998. Beauty mandates and the appearance obsession: Are lesbians any better off? Pp. 17–25 in *Looking queer: Body image and identity in lesbian, bisexual, gay, and transgender communities,* edited by D. Atkins. New York: Haworth Press.

Nadelson, C. C., and T. Nadelson. 1980. Dual-career marriages: Benefits and costs. In *Dual career couples,* edited by F. Pepitone-Rickwell. Beverly Hills, Calif.: Sage.

Nader, R. 1993. *The case against free trade.* San Francisco: Earth Island Press.

Naffine, N. 1987. *Female crime: The construction of women in criminology.* Boston: Allen & Unwin.

Naidus, B. 1993. *One size does not fit all.* Littleton, Colo.: Aigis Publications.

Naples, N., ed. 1997. *Community activism and feminist politics: Organizing across race, class, and gender.* New York: Routledge.

———. 1998. *Grassroots warriors: Activist mothering, community work, and the war on poverty.* New York: Routledge.

National Cancer Institute. 1996. *SEER monograph: Racial/ethnic patterns of cancer in the United States, 1988–1992.* Washington, D.C.: National Cancer Institute.

National Center for Health Statistics. 1996a. *Health United States, 1995.* Hyattsville, Md.: Public Health Service.

———. 1996b. *Monthly vital statistics report on final mortality, 1994.* Hyattsville, Md.: National Center for Health Statistics.

———. 1999a. *Final data for 1997,* vol. 47, no. 19, p. 108. Hyattsville, Md.: National Center for Health Statistics.

———. 1999b. *Infant mortality statistics from the 1997 period linked birth/infant death data set,* vol. 47, no. 23, p. 24. Hyattsville, Md.: National Center for Health Statistics.

National Clearinghouse on Marital and Date Rape. 1998. http://members.aol.com/ncmdr/index.html

National Institute of Justice and Centers for Disease Control and Prevention. 1998. *Prevalence, incidence, and consequences of violence against women: Findings from the National Violence Against Women Survey.* Washington, D.C.: National Institute of Justice and Centers for Disease Control and Prevention.

National Victim Center. 1992. *Rape in America. A report to the nation.* Arlington, Va.: Author.

National Women's Studies Association. 1994. *NWSA directory of women's studies programs, women's centers, and women's research centers.* College Park, Md.: National Women's Studies Association.

Navarro, M. 1996. Lesbian loses court appeal for custody of daughter. *New York Times,* 31 August, p. A7.

Navarro, V. 1993. *Dangerous to your health: Capitalism in health care.* New York: Monthly Review Press.

Nechas, E., and D. Foley. 1994. *Unequal treatment: What you don't know about how women are mistreated by the medical community.* Philadelphia: Temple University Press.

Nelson, L. 1990. The place of women in polluted places. In *Reweaving the world: The emergence of ecofeminism,* edited by I. Diamond and G. Orenstein. San Francisco: Sierra Club Books.

Nestle, J., ed. 1992. *The persistent desire: A femme-butch reader.* Los Angeles: Alyson.

Neuborne, E. 1994. Cashing in on fear: The NRA targets women. *Ms.,* June/July, pp. 45–50.

Newman, L. 1991. *SomeBody to love: A guide to loving the body you have.* Chicago: Third Side Press.

News Services, 1998. Pope warns against dangers of capitalism. *St. Louis Dispatch,* 26 January, p. A1.

NiCarthy, G. 1986. *Getting free: You can end abuse and take back your life.* Seattle, Wash.: Seal Press.

———. 1987. *The ones who got away: Women who left abusive partners.* Seattle, Wash.: Seal Press.

Nicholson, L., ed. 1990. *Feminism/postmodernism.* New York: Routledge.

Nike: Just don't *do it.* 1997. Special report available from Global Exchange, 2017 Mission St., Rm. 303, San Francisco, CA 94110.

Noble, K. 1994. Woman tells of retaliation for complaint on Tailhook. *New York Times,* 5 October, p. A10.

Norsigian, J. 1996. The women's health movement in the United States. Pp. 79–97 in *Man-made medicine: Women's health, public policy, and reform,* edited by K. L. Moss. Durham, N.C.: Duke University Press.

Norwood, R. 1986. *Women who love too much.* New York: Pocket Books.

NOW Legal Defense and Education Fund. 1999. *Violence against women legislative advocacy packet.* http://www.nowldef.org/html/policy/violence.htm

O'Connor, M., ed. 1994. *Is capitalism sustainable? Political economy and the politics of ecology.* New York: Guilford Press.

O'Connor, P. 1992. *Friendships between women: A critical review.* New York: Guilford Press.

Odubekun, L. 1992. A structural approach to differential gender sentencing. *Criminal Justice Abstracts* 24(2): 343–60.

Ogur, B. 1996. Smothering in stereotypes: HIV-positive women. In *Talking gender: Public images, personal journeys, and political critiques,* edited by N. Hewitt, J. O'Barr, and N. Rosebaugh. Chapel Hill: University of North Carolina Press.

Okazawa-Rey, M. 1994. Racial identity development of mixed race persons: An overview. In *Diversity and human service education,* edited by J. Silver-Jones, S. Kerstein, and D. Osher. Council of Standards in Human Service Education Monograph Series, No. 4.

———. 1997. Amerasians in GI town: The legacy of U.S. militarism in South Korea. *Asian Journal of Women's Studies* 3: 1.

Okazawa-Rey, M., and G. Kirk. 1996. Military security: Confronting the oxymoron. *CrossRoads* 60: 4–7.

Okin, S. M. 1989. *Justice, gender, and the family.* New York: Basic Books.

Okinawa Women Act Against Military Violence. 1996. *An appeal for the recognition of women's human rights.* Naha, Okinawa: Author.

Okinawa women's America peace caravan. 1996. Unpublished program. February 3–17. Naha City, Okinawa: Okinawa Women Act Against Military Violence.

Oliker, S. J. 1989. *Best friends and marriage: Exchange among women.* Berkeley: University of California Press.

O'Melveny, M. 1996. Lexington Prison High Security Unit: U. S. political prison. In *Criminal injustice: Confronting the prison crisis,* edited by E. Rosenblatt. Boston: South End Press.

Omolade, B. 1986. *It's a family affair: The real lives of Black single mothers.* New York: Kitchen Table: Women of Color Press.

———. 1989. We speak for the planet. In *Rocking the ship of state: Toward a feminist peace politics,* edited by A. Harris and Y. King. Boulder, Colo.: Westview Press.

Ong, P., E. Bonacich, and L. Cheng. 1994. *The new Asian immigration in Los Angeles and global restructuring.* Philadelphia: Temple University Press.

O'Reilly, B. 1991. Cooling down the world debt bomb. *Fortune,* 20 May, 123.

O'Rourke, D. 1985. *Half life: A parable for the nuclear age.* Video.

O'Shea, K. 1998. *Women and the death penalty in the United States, 1900–1998.* Westport, Conn.: Praeger.

O'Toole, L., and J. Schiffman. 1997. *Gender violence: Interdisciplinary perspectives.* New York: New York University Press.

Owen, B., and B. Bloom. 1995. Profiling women prisoners. *The Prison Journal* 75(2): 165–85.

Oxfam International. 1998. *Making debt relief work: A test of political will.* http://www.oxfamamerica.org/advocacy/Test_of_Political_Will.htm

Paglia, C. 1990. *Sexual personae: Art and decadence from Nefertiti to Emily Dickinson.* New Haven, Conn.: Yale University Press.

———. 1992. *Sex, art, and American culture.* New York: Vintage Books.

———. 1994. *Vamps and tramps.* New York: Vintage Books.

Paley, G. 1998. The illegal days. Pp. 13–20 in *Just as I thought.* New York: Farrar, Straus, Giroux.

Parenti, C. 1999, September. The prison industrial complex: Crisis and control. *Corporate Watch.* San Francisco: Transnational Resource and Action Center.

Patai, D. 1998. *Heterophobia: Sexual harassment and the future of feminism.* Lanham, Md.: Rowman and Littlefield.

Pateman, C. 1988. *The sexual contract.* Stanford, Calif.: Stanford University Press.

Peach, L. J. 1997. Behind the front lines: Feminist battles over combat. Pp. 99–135 in *Wives and warriors: Women and the military in the United States and Canada,* edited by L. Weinstein and C. White. Westport, Conn.: Bergin & Garvey.

Pearce, D., A. Markandya, and E. B. Barbier. 1990. *Blueprint for a Green economy.* London: Earthscan.

Perrone, B., H. H. Stockel, and V. Krueger. 1989. *Medicine women, curanderas, and women doctors.* Norman: University of Oklahoma Press.

Petchesky, R. 1990. *Abortion and woman's choice: The state, sexuality, and reproductive freedom.* Rev. ed. Boston: Northeastern University Press.

———. 1997. Fetal images: The power of visual culture in the politics of reproduction. Pp. 134–50 in *The gender/sexuality reader,* edited by R. Lancaster and M. di Leonardo. New York: Routledge.

Peters, J. 1997. *When mothers work: Loving our children without sacrificing ourselves.* Reading, Mass.: Addison-Wesley.

Petersen, B. 1991. *Dancing with Daddy: A childhood lost and a life regained.* New York: Bantam Books.

Peterson, R. R. 1996. Re-evaluation of the economic consequences of divorce. *American Sociological Review* 61(3): 528–53.

Peterson, V. S., and A. S. Runyan. 1993. *Global gender issues.* Boulder, Colo.: Westview Press.

Pharr, S. 1988. *Homophobia: A weapon of sexism.* Inverness, Calif.: Chardon Press.

Pheterson, G. 1990. Alliances between women: Overcoming internalized oppression and internalized domination. In *Bridges of power,* edited by L. Albrecht and R. M. Brewer. Philadelphia and Gabriola Island, B.C.: New Society Publishers.

Phoenix, J. 1993. Getting the lead out of the community. In *Confronting environmental racism,* edited by R. D. Bullard. Boston: South End Press.

Piercy, M. 1976. *Woman on the edge of time.* New York: Fawcett Crest.

Pitter, L., and A. Stilmayer. 1993. Will the world remember? Can the women forget? *Ms.,* March/April, 19–22.

Plant, C., and J. Plant, eds. 1992. *Putting power in its place: Create community control!* Philadelphia and Gabriola Island, B.C.: New Society Publishers.

Plumwood, V. 1993. *Feminism and the mastery of nature.* New York: Routledge.

Pollack, J. 1994. The increasing incarceration rate of women offenders: Equality or justice? Paper presented at Prisons 2000 Conference, Leicester, England.

Pollitt, K. 1994. Subject to debate. *The Nation,* 11 July, 45.

Pratt, M. B. 1995. *S/he.* Ithaca, N.Y.: Firebrand Books.

Press, E. 1997. Breaking the sweats. *The Nation,* 28 April, 5–6.

Prison Activist Resource Center. 1997. *Women in prison.* Fact sheet prepared by Prison Activist Resource Center, Berkeley, Calif.

Pulido, L. 1993. Sustainable development at Ganados del Valle. In *Confronting environmental racism: Voices from the grassroots,* edited by R. Bullard. Boston: South End Press.

Quindlen, A. 1994. Feminism continues to grow and reach and affect us all. *Chicago Tribune,* 21 January, sec. 1, p. 21.

Rafter, N. 1990. *Partial justice: Women, prisons and social control.* New Brunswick, N.J.: Transaction.

Rape Abuse Incest National Network. 1999. RAIN-News. http://www.rainn.org/news/stat.html

Raphael, J., and R. Tolman. 1997. *Trapped in poverty, trapped by abuse: New evidence documenting the relationship between domestic violence and welfare.* Project for Research on Welfare, Work, and Domestic Violence. A collaboration between Taylor Institute and University of Michigan Development Center on Poverty, Risk, and Mental Health.

Rasmussen, V. 1998. Rethinking the corporation. *Food and Water Journal,* Fall, 17–21.

Raymond, J. G. 1986. *A passion for friends: Toward a philosophy of female affection.* Boston: Beacon Press.

———. 1994. *The transsexual empire: The making of the she-male.* 2d ed. New York: Teachers College Press.

Rayner, R. 1997. Women in the warrior culture. *New York Times Magazine,* 22 June, 24–29, 40, 49, 53, 55–56.

Reagon, B. J. 1987. *Ode to the international debt.* Boston: Songtalk.

Reardon, B. A. 1985. *Sexism and the war system.* New York: Teachers College Press.

———. 1993. *Women and peace: Feminist visions of global security.* Albany, N.Y.: SUNY Press.

———. 1998. Gender and global security: A feminist challenge to the United Nations and peace research. *Journal of International Co-operation Studies* 6(1): 29–56.

Redwood, R. 1996. The glass ceiling. *Motion Magazine.* http://www.inmotionmagazine.com/glass.html

Renzetti, C. M. 1992. *Violent betrayal: Partner abuse in lesbian relationships.* Newbury Park, Calif.: Sage.

Reti, I., ed. 1992. *Childless by choice: A feminist anthology.* Santa Cruz, Calif.: Her Books.

Reynolds, M. 1992. *Erotica: Women's writing from Sappho to Margaret Atwood.* New York: Fawcett Columbine.

Rich, A. 1976. *Of woman born: Motherhood as experience and institution.* New York: W. W. Norton.

———. 1986a. Compulsory heterosexuality and lesbian existence. In *Blood, bread, and poetry.* New York: W. W. Norton.

———. 1986b. *Of woman born: Motherhood as experience and institution.* 10th anniversary ed. New York: W. W. Norton.

———. 1986c. Notes towards a politics of location. Pp. 210–31 in *Blood, bread, and poetry.* New York: W. W. Norton.

Richie, B. 1996. *Compelled to crime: The gender entrapment of battered Black women.* New York: Routledge.

Richter, P. 2000. Armed forces find "disturbing" level of gay harassment. *Los Angeles Times,* 25 March, p. A1.

Rierden, A. 1997. *The Farm: Inside a women's prison.* Amherst: University of Massachusetts Press.

Riley, D. 1988. *Am I that name? Feminism and the category of "women" in history.* Minneapolis: University of Minnesota Press.

Risman, B. J. 1998. *Gender vertigo: American families in transition.* New Haven, Conn.: Yale University Press.

Roberts, D. 1997. *Killing the Black body: Race, reproduction, and the meaning of liberty.* New York: Pantheon.

Roberts, M. M., and T. Mizuta, eds. 1993. *The reformers: Socialist feminism.* London: Routledge/Thoemmes Press.

Roediger, D. R. 1991. *The wages of whiteness: Race and the making of the American working class.* New York: Verso.

Roiphe, K. 1993. *The morning after: Sex, fear, and feminism.* Boston: Little Brown.

Root, M. P. P., ed. 1996. *The multiracial experience: Racial borders as the new frontier.* Thousand Oaks, Calif.: Sage.

Rosen, R. 2000. *The world split open: How the modern women's movement changed America.* New York: Viking.

Rosenberg, A. 1988. The crisis in knowing and understanding the Holocaust. In *Echoes from the Holocaust: Philosophical reflections on a dark time,* edited by A. Rosenberg and G. E. Meyers. Philadelphia: Temple University Press.

Rosenblatt, E., ed. 1996. *Criminal injustice: Confronting the prison crisis.* Boston: South End Press.

Ross, A., ed. 1997. *No sweat: Fashion, free trade, and the rights of garment workers.* New York: Verso.

Ross, L. 1993. Major concerns of imprisoned American Indian and White mothers. In *Gender: Multicultural perspectives,* edited by J. Gonzalez-Calvo. Dubuque, Iowa: Kendall Hunt.

Rubin, G. 1984. Thinking sex: Notes for a radical theory of the politics of sexuality. Pp. 267–319 in *Pleasure and danger: Exploring female sexuality,* edited by C. S. Vance. Boston: Routledge and Kegan Paul.

Ruddick, S. 1989. *Maternal thinking: Toward a politics of peace.* Boston: Beacon Press.

Russell, B. 1935. *In praise of idleness and other essays.* New York: W. W. Norton.

Russell, D. 1995. *Women, madness, and medicine.* Cambridge, England: Polity Press.

Russell, D. E. H. 1975. *The politics of rape: The victim's perspective.* New York: Stein and Day.

———. 1986. *The secret trauma: Incest in the lives of girls and women.* New York: Basic Books.

———. 1990. *Rape in marriage.* Rev. ed. Bloomington: Indiana University Press.

Russo, N. F., and M. A. Jansen. 1988. Women, work, and disability: Opportunities and challenges. In *Women with disabilities: Essays in psychology, culture, and politics,* edited by M. Fine and A. Asch. Philadelphia: Temple University Press.

Sachs, C. 1996. *Gendered fields: Rural women, agriculture, and environment.* Boulder, Colo.: Westview Press.

Sadler, G. C. 1997. Women in combat: The U.S. military and the impact of the Persian Gulf War. Pp. 79–97 in *Wives and warriors,* edited by L. Weinstein and C. White.

Safe, J. 1996. *Beyond motherhood: Choosing a life without children.* New York: Pocket Books.

Sajor, I. L., ed. 1998. *Common grounds: Violence against women in war and armed conflict situations.* Quezon City, Philippines: Asian Center for Women's Human Rights.

Sale, K. 1985. *Dwellers in the land, the bioregional vision.* San Francisco: Sierra Club Books.

Sanday, P. 1990. *Fraternity gang rape: Sex, brotherhood, and privilege on campus.* New York: New York University Press.

Sanders, B., and M. Kaptur. 1997. Just do it, Nike. *The Nation,* 8 December, 6.

Saporito, B. 1998. Can Nike get unstuck? *Time,* 30 March, 47–53.

Schulman, K. A., J. Berlin, W. Harless, J. Kerner, S. Sistrunk, B. Gersh, R. Dubé, C. Talghani, J. Burke, S. Williams, J. Eisenberg, and J. Escarce. 1999. The effects of race and sex on physicians' recommendations for cardiac catheterization. *New England Journal of Medicine* 340(8): 618–26.

Schwartz, P. 1994. *Love between equals: How peer marriage really works.* New York: Free Press.

Scott, W. J., and S. C. Stanley. 1994. *Gays and lesbians in the military: Issues, concerns, and contrasts.* Hawthorne, N.Y.: Aldine de Gruyter.

Seager, J. 1993. *Earth follies: Coming to feminist terms with the global environmental crisis.* New York: Routledge.

Sedgwick, E. K. 1990. *Epistemology of the closet.* Berkeley: University of California Press.

Segal, L. 1994. *Straight sex: Rethinking the politics of pleasure.* Berkeley: University of California Press.

Segell, M. 1996. The second coming of the Alpha male: A prescription for righteous masculinity at the millennium. *Esquire,* October, 74–82.

Segrest, M. 1994. *Memoir of a race traitor.* Boston: South End Press.

Seidman, S. 1992. *Embattled eros: Sexual politics and ethics in contemporary America.* New York: Routledge.

Seigel, L. 1997. The pregnancy police fight the war on drugs. Pp. 249–59 in *Crack in America: Demon drugs and social justice,* edited by C. Reinarman and H. G. Levine. Berkeley: University of California Press.

Sen, G., and C. Grown. 1987. *Development, crises, and alternative visions: Third World women's perspectives.* New York: Monthly Review Press.

Sengupta, S. 1999. Squeezed by debt and time, mothers ship babies to China. *New York Times,* 14 September, p. A1.

Serna, I. 1992. *Locked down: A woman's life in prison.* Norwich, Vt.: New Victoria Publishers.

Servicemembers Legal Defense Network. 1999a. *Conduct unbecoming. Fifth annual report on "Don't ask, don't tell, don't pursue."* http://www.sldn. org/scripts/sldn.ixe?page=pr_03_15_99

———. 1999b. Pentagon fires record number of gays. http://www.sldn.org/scripts/sldn.ixe? page=pr_01_22_99

Shah, S., ed. 1997. *Dragon ladies: Asian feminists breathe fire.* Boston: South End Press.

Sharf, J. 1997. Guess again: Sweatshop violations continue. *Jews for economic and racial justice,* Bulletin 33. Available from JREC, 64 Fulton St., #605, New York, NY 10038.

Sherrill, R. 1997. A year in corporate crime. *The Nation,* 7 April, 11–20.

Shields, K. 1994. *In the tiger's mouth: An empowerment guide for action.* Gabriola Island, B.C.: New Society Publishers.

Shiva, V. 1988. *Staying alive: Women, ecology and development.* London: Zed Books.

Showalter, E. 1987. *The female malady: Women, madness, and English culture, 1830–1980.* London: Virago.

Shugar, D. R. 1995. *Sep-a-ra-tism and women's community.* Lincoln: University of Nebraska Press.

Sidel, R. 1996. *Keeping women and children last: America's war on the poor.* New York: Penguin Books.

Siegal, N. 1995. Girl trouble. *San Francisco Bay Guardian,* 29 November, pp. 16–18.

———. 1998. Women in prison. *Ms.,* September/ October, 64–73.

Silliman, J., and Y. King, eds. 1999. *Dangerous intersections: Feminist perspectives on population, environment, and development.* Cambridge, Mass.: South End Press.

Simon, R. 1975. *Women and crime.* Lexington, Mass.: Lexington Books.

Singh, G. K., and S. M. Yu. 1995. Infant mortality in the United States: Trends, differentials, and projections, 1950 through 2010. *American Journal of Public Health* 85(7): 957–64.

Sivard, R. L. 1995. *Women . . . a world survey.* 2d ed. Washington, D.C.: World Priorities.

———. 1996. *World military and social expenditures 1996.* 16th ed. Washington, D.C.: World Priorities.

Skaine, R. 1998. *Women at war: Gender issues of Americans in combat.* Jefferson, N.C.: McFarland and Co.

Skolnick, A. 1991. *Embattled paradise: The American family in an age of uncertainty.* New York: Basic Books.

Smart, C. 1989. *Feminism and the power of law.* London: Routledge & Kegan Paul.

———. 1995. *Law, crime, and sexuality: Essays in feminism.* London: Sage.

Smeal, E. 1984. *Why and how women will elect the next president.* New York: Harper & Row.

Smelser, N. 1994. *Sociology.* Cambridge, Mass.: Blackwell.

Smith, A. 1997. Ecofeminism through an anti-colonial framework. Pp. 21–37 in *Ecofeminism: Women, culture, nature,* edited by K. Warren. Bloomington: Indiana University Press.

Smith, B. 1998. *The truth that never hurts: Writings on race, gender, freedom.* New Brunswick, N.J.: Rutgers University Press.

Smith, B., ed. 1983. *Home girls: A Black feminist anthology.* New York: Kitchen Table: Women of Color Press.

Smith, M. 1997. When violence strikes home. *The Nation,* 30 June, 23–24.

Snitow, A., C. Stansell, and S. Thompson, eds. 1983. *Powers of desire: The politics of sexuality.* New York: Monthly Review Press.

Spelman, E. V. 1988. *Inessential woman: Problems of exclusion in feminist thought.* Boston: Beacon Press.

Spretnak, C. 1990. Ecofeminism: Our roots and flowering. In *Reweaving the world: The emergence of ecofeminism,* edited by I. Diamond & G. Orenstein. San Francisco: Sierra Club Books.

Stacey, J. 1993. Untangling feminist theory. Pp. 49–73 in *Thinking feminist: Key concepts in women's studies,* edited by D. Richardson and V. Robinson. New York: Guilford Press.

———. 1996. *In the name of the family: Rethinking values in the postmodern age.* Boston: Beacon Press.

———. 1999. The family values fable. Pp. 487–90 in *American families: A multicultural reader,* edited by S. Coontz with M. Parson and G. Raley. New York: Routledge.

Stanworth, M., ed. 1987. *Reproductive technologies.* Cambridge, England: Cambridge University Press.

Starhawk. 1987. *Truth or dare: Encounters with power, authority, and mystery.* San Francisco: Harper & Row.

———. 1993. *The fifth sacred thing.* New York: Bantam Books.

State of the Workplace Report. 1999. Washington, D.C.: Human Rights Campaign.

Steedman, C. 1986. *Landscape for a good woman: A story of two lives.* New Brunswick, N.J.: Rutgers University Press.

Stefan, S. 1994. The protection racket: Rape trauma syndrome, psychiatric labeling, and law. In *Northwestern Law Review,* 88(4): 1271–1345.

Stein, A. 1997. Sisters and queers: The decentering of lesbian feminism. Pp. 378–91 in *The gender sexuality reader,* edited by R. Lancaster and M. di Leonardo. New York: Routledge.

Stein, D., ed. 1991. *From inside: An anthology of writing by incarcerated women.* Minneapolis: Honor Press.

Steinberg, J. 1989. At debt's door. *Ms.,* November, 78.

Steinem, G. 1983. *Outrageous acts and everyday rebellions.* New York: Holt, Rinehart, & Winston.

Stewart, A., A. Copeland, N. L. Chester, J. Malley, N. Barenbaum. 1997. *Separating together: How divorce transforms families.* New York: Guilford Press.

Stewart, I. 1997. Vietnam's fed-up workers striking for rights. *San Francisco Chronicle,* 23 June, p. A10.

Stiehm, J. H. 1989. *Arms and the enlisted woman.* Philadelphia: Temple University Press.

———, ed. 1996. *It's our military too! Women and the U.S. military.* Philadelphia: Temple University Press.

Stocker, M., ed. 1991. *Cancer as a women's issue: Scratching the surface.* Chicago: Third Side Press.

———. 1993. *Confronting cancer, constructing change: New perspectives on women and cancer.* Chicago: Third Side Press.

Stoller, E. P., and R. C. Gibson, eds. 1994. *Worlds of difference: Inequality in the aging experience.* Thousand Oaks, Calif.: Pine Forge.

Stonequist, E. V. 1961. *The marginal man: A study in personality and cultural conflict.* New York: Scribner & Sons.

Storr, M., ed. 1999. *Bisexuality: A critical reader.* New York: Routledge.

St. Paige, E. 1999. *Zaftig: The case for curves.* Seattle, Wash.: Darling and Co.

Study shows few women in combat jobs. *San Francisco Chronicle,* 21 October 1997, p. A6.

Sturdevant, S., and B. Stoltzfus. 1992. *Let the good times roll: Prostitution and the U.S. military in Asia.* New York: New Press.

Survivors take action against abuse by military personnel. 1999. *Newsletter 1998/99.* Fairborn, Ohio: Author.

Sward, S. 1997. S.F. police panel puts off FBI proposal. Feds want to team up to fight terrorism. *San Francisco Chronicle,* 16 January, p. A18.

Swerdlow, A. 1993. *Women strike for peace: Traditional motherhood and radical politics in the 1960s.* Chicago: University of Chicago Press.

Szasz, A. 1994. *Ecopopulism, toxic waste and the movement for environmental justice.* Minneapolis: University of Minnesota Press.

Takaki, R. 1987. *Strangers from a different shore: Perspectives on race and ethnicity in America.* New York: Oxford University Press.

Tan, A. 1989. *The Joy Luck Club.* New York: G. P. Putnam's Sons.

Tan, C. I. 1997. Building shelter: Asian women and domestic violence. Pp. 108–17 in *Dragon ladies: Asian American feminists breathe fire,* edited by S. Shah. Boston: South End Press.

Tannen, D. 1990. *You just don't understand: Men and women in conversation.* New York: Morrow.

Taueber, C. 1991. *Statistical handbook on women in America.* Phoenix: Oryx Press.

Tax, M. 1993. Five women who won't be silenced. *The Nation,* 10 May, 624–27.

Taylor, D. E. 1997. Women of color, environmental justice, and ecofeminism. Pp. 38–81 in *Ecofeminism: Women, culture, nature,* edited by K. Warren. Bloomington: Indiana University Press.

Tenenbeing, S. 1998. Power, beauty, and dykes. Pp. 155–60 in *Looking queer,* edited by D. Atkins. Binghampton, N.Y.: Harrington Park Press.

Tétreault, M. A. 1997. Accountability or justice? Rape as a war crime. Pp. 427–39 in *Feminist frontiers IV,* edited by L. Richardson, V. Taylor, and N. Whittier. New York: McGraw-Hill.

This Bud's for you. No, not you, her. 1991. *Business Week,* 4 November, 86.

Thompson, B. W. 1994. *A hunger so wide and so deep.* Minneapolis: University of Minnesota Press.

Thorne, B. 1997. *Gender play: Girls and boys in school.* New Brunswick, N.J.: Rutgers University Press.

Thornhill, R., and C. T. Palmer. 2000. *A natural history of rape: Biological bases of sexual coercion.* Cambridge: MIT Press.

Thropy, M. A. 1991. Overpopulation and industrialism. In *Earth First! reader,* edited by J. Davis. Salt Lake City: Peregrine Smith Books.

Tong, R. 1989. *Feminist thought: A comprehensive introduction.* Boulder, Colo.: Westview Press.

Tooher, N. L. 1999. For Mexican women, sexism is a daily battle. Pp. 38–40 in *The maquiladora reader: Cross-border organizing since NAFTA,* edited by R. Kamel and A. Hoffman. Philadelphia: American Friends Service Committee.

Torre, A. de la. 1993. Key issues in Latina health: Voicing Latina concerns in the health financing debate. In *Chicana critical issues,* edited by N. Alarcon, R. Castro, E. Perez, B. Pesquera, A. S. Riddell, and P. Zavella. Berkeley, Calif.: Third Woman Press.

Townsend, R., and A. Perkins. 1992. *Bitter fruit: Women's experiences of unplanned pregnancy, abortion, and adoption.* Alameda, Calif.: Hunter House.

Trask, H.-K. 1999. *From a native daughter: Colonialism and sovereignty in Hawai'i.* Rev. ed. Honolulu: University of Hawaii.

Trujillo, C., ed. 1991. *Chicana lesbians: The girls our mothers warned us about.* Berkeley, Calif.: Third Women Press.

———. 1998. *Living Chicana theory.* Berkeley, Calif.: Third Women Press.

Tuana, N., ed. 1989. *Feminism and science.* Bloomington: Indiana University Press.

Tucker, C. 1996. Women's practical vote for Clinton. *Chicago Tribune,* 9 November, p. 3.

Turk, A. T. 1995. Transformation versus revolutionism and reformism: Policy implications of conflict theory. In *Crime and public policy: Putting theory to work,* edited by H. Barlow. Boulder, Colo.: Westview Press.

2 black airmen allege racial discrimination. 1996. *San Francisco Chronicle,* 4 December, p. A9.

Tyagi, S. 1996. Writing in search of a home: Geography, culture, and language in the creation of racial identity. In *Names we call home,* edited by B. Thompson and S. Tyagi. New York: Routledge.

Umansky, L. 1996. *Motherhood reconceived: Feminism and the legacies of the sixties.* New York: New York University Press.

Unnecessary cesarean sections: Halting a national epidemic. 1992. *The Network News,* November/December, 7.

U.S. Bureau of the Census. 1996. *Statistical abstract of the United States: 1996.* 116th ed. Washington, D.C.: U.S. Bureau of the Census.

———. 1998. *Vital statistics of the United States.* Washington, D.C.: U.S. Bureau of the Census.

———. 1999a. *Health insurance coverage 1998.* Washington, D.C.: U.S. Bureau of the Census.

———. 1999b. *Current population reports. Series P-60.* Washington, D.C.: U.S. Bureau of the Census.

U.S. Department of Defense. 1992. *Department of Defense worldwide list of military installations (major, minor, and support).* Washington, D.C.: U.S. Department of Defense.

———. 1996. *FY 1990–96 spouse and child maltreatment.* Washington, D.C.: U.S. Department of Defense.

———. 2000. *Women in the military.* Washington, D.C.: U.S. Department of Defense.

U.S. Department of Health and Human Services. 1996. *Health, United States 1995. Chartbook: Women's health.* Washington, D.C.: U.S. Department of Health and Human Services.

U.S. Department of Justice. 1997. Violence-related injuries treated in hospital emergency departments. Michael R. Rand. Washington, D.C.: Bureau of Justice Statistics

———. 1998. *Criminal victimization 1997: Changes 1996–97 with trends 1993–97.* Washington, D.C.: U.S. Department of Justice.

———. 2000. Extent, Nature, and Consequences of Intimate Partner Violence: Findings from the National Violence against Women Survey. Washington, D.C.: U.S. Department of Justice.

U.S. Department of Labor. 1993. *Facts on working women* (No. 93-2). Washington, D.C.: U.S. Department of Labor.

U.S. Department of Labor, Bureau of Labor Statistics. 1999. *Employment and earnings.* Washington, D.C.: U.S. Department of Labor.

U.S. Department of Labor, Women's Bureau. 1996. *Facts on working women. Domestic violence: A workplace issue.* Washington, D.C.: U.S. Department of Labor.

———. 1997. *First national working women's summit, June 5, 1997, Washington, D.C.* http://www.dol.gov/dol/wb/welcome.htm

———. 1999. *Facts on working women.* Washington, D.C.: U.S. Department of Labor.

U.S. Immigration and Naturalization Service. 1996. *Immigration to the United States in fiscal year 1995.* Washington, D.C.: U.S. Immigration and Naturalization Service.

Usdansky, M. L. 1996. Single motherhood: Stereotypes vs. statistics. *New York Times,* 11 February, p. E4.

Ussher, J. 1991. *Women's madness.* Hemel Hempstead, England: Harvester Wheatsheaf.

Vance, C., ed. 1984. *Pleasure and danger: Exploring female sexuality.* Boston: Routledge and Kegan Paul.

Van Every, J. 1995. *Heterosexual women changing the family: Refusing to be a "wife"!* Bristol, Pa.: Taylor and Francis.

Ventura, S. J., J. A. Martin, S. C. Curtin, and T. J. Mathews. 1999. Births: Final data for 1997. *National Vital Statistics Reports,* vol. 47, no. 18. Hyattsville, Md.: National Center for Health Statistics.

Ventura, S. J., W. D. Mosher, S. C. Curtin, J. C. Abma, and S. Henshaw. 2000. Highlights of trends in pregnancies and pregnancy rates by outcome: Estimates for the United States, 1976–96. *National Vital Statistics Reports,* vol. 47, no. 29. Hyattsville, Md.: National Center for Health Statistics.

Wade-Gayles, G. 1993. *Pushed back to strength: A Black woman's journey home.* Boston: Beacon Press.

Waldman, A. 1997. Labor's new face: Women renegotiate their role. *The Nation,* 22 September, 11–15.

Walker, J. 1996. The prison industrial complex. *RESIST Newsletter* 5(9): 4–6.

Walker, L. 1979. *The battered woman.* New York: Harper & Row.

———. 1984. *The battered woman syndrome.* New York: Springer.

Walker, M. 1992. Sex attacks "rife" on U.S. servicewomen. *London Guardian,* 2 July, p. 6.

Walker, R. 1995. *To be real: Telling the truth and changing the face of feminism.* New York: Anchor/Doubleday.

Walters, B., and H. Downs. 1996. *20/20,* November 15. New York: American Broadcasting Company.

Waring, M. 1988. *If women counted: A new feminist economics.* New York: Harper & Row.

Warner, S. B. 1987. *To dwell is to garden: A history of Boston's community gardens.* Boston: Northeastern University Press.

War Registers League. 2000. *Where your income tax money really goes.* War Registers League, 339 Lafayette St., New York, NY 10012.

War Resisters League. 2001. *Where your income tax money really goes: The United States federal budget for fiscal year 1998.* New York: War Resisters League.

Washburn, P. 1993. Women and the peace movement. Pp. 135–48 in *Women and the use of military force,* edited by R. Howes and M. Stevenson. Boulder, Colo.: Lynne Rienner Publishers.

Wasserman, C. 1992. FMS: The backlash against survivors. *Sojourner: The Women's Forum,* November, 18–20.

Watterson, K. 1996. *Women in prison.* Rev. ed. Boston: Northeastern University Press.

Webber, W. S. 1993. *Lesbians in the military speak out.* Northboro, Mass.: Madwoman Press.

Weedon, C. 1987. *Feminist practice and poststructuralist theory.* New York: Blackwell.

Weinstein, L., and C. White, eds. 1997. *Wives and warriors: Women and the military in the United States and Canada.* Westport, Conn.: Greenwood Press.

Weise, E. R., ed. 1992. *Closer to home: Bisexuality and feminism.* Seattle, Wash.: Seal Press.

Wendell, S. 1992. Toward a feminist theory of disability. Pp. 63–81 in *Feminist perspectives in medical ethics,* edited by H. B. Holmes and L. M. Purdy. Bloomington: Indiana University Press.

West, G., and R. L. Blumberg, eds. 1990. *Women and social protest.* New York: Oxford University Press.

White, E. C. 1985. *Chain, chain, change: For Black women dealing with physical and emotional abuse.* Seattle, Wash.: Seal Press.

———, ed. 1990. *The Black women's health book: Speaking for ourselves.* Seattle, Wash.: Seal Press.

White, L. 1988. *The obsidian mirror: An adult healing from incest.* Seattle, Wash.: Seal Press.

Wider Opportunities for Women. 1989. *Women, work, and childcare.* Washington, D.C.: Wider Opportunities for Women.

Wilchins, R. A. 1997. *Read my lips: Sexual subversion and the end of gender.* Ithaca, N.Y.: Firebrand.

Williams, L., ed. 1997. *Gender equity and the World Bank group: A post-Beijing assessment.* Washington, D.C.: Women's Eyes on the World Bank-U.S.

Williams, T. T. 1992. *Refuge: An unnatural history of family and place.* New York: Vintage.

Wilson, M. 1993. *Crossing the boundary: Black women survive incest.* Seattle, Wash.: Seal Press.

Will the new corporations rule the new world order? 1992. *World Citizen News,* March, 9.

Wingspan Domestic Violence Project. 1998. *Abuse and violence in same-gender relationships: A resource for lesbian, gay, bi, and transgendered communities.* Tucson, Ariz.: Wingspan Domestic Violence Project.

Withorn, A. 1999. Temp work: "A devil's bargain" for women. *Sojourner: The Women's Forum,* October, 9.

Wittig, M. 1992. *The straight mind and other essays.* Boston: Beacon Press.

Wolf, N. 1991. *The beauty myth.* New York: Doubleday.

———. 1993. *Fire with fire: The new female power and how it will change the 21st century.* New York: Random House.

Women harassed at Naval Academy. 1990. *Rocky Mountain News,* 10 October, p. 35.

Women of Color Resource Center. 1996, December. Solicitation letter to donors. Berkeley, Calif.: Women of Color Resource Center.

Women's Environment and Development Organization (WEDO). 1998. *Mapping progress: Assessing implementation of the Beijing Platform.* New York: WEDO.

Women Working for a Nuclear Free and Independent Pacific, ed. 1987. *Pacific women speak.* Oxford, England: Green Line.

Wong, L. 1995. U.N. women's conference platform for action. *Sojourner,* October, 7.

Wood, S. 1997. Blood, sweat, and shears. *Corporate Watch Features,* 22 September. San Francisco: Corporate Watch.

Woods, H. 2000. *Stepping up to power: The political journey of American women.* Boulder, Colo.: Westview Press.

Working Group on the WTO. 1999. *A citizens' guide to the World Trade Organization.* New York: Apex Press.

World March of Women in the Year 2000. www. ffq.qc.ca/marche2000/

Yans-McLaughlin, V., ed. 1990. *Immigration reconsidered.* New York: Oxford University Press.

Yen, M. 1989. Refusal to jail immigrant who killed wife stirs outrage. *Washington Post,* 10 April, p. A3.

Yoder, J. 1989. Women at West Point: Lessons for token women in male-dominated occupations. In *Women: A feminist perspective,* edited by J. Freeman. Mountain View, Calif.: Mayfield.

Young, I. 1980. Socialist feminism and the limits of dual systems theory. *Socialist Review,* 10(2–3): 174.

Young, M. E., M. A. Nosek, C. A. Howland, G. Chanpong, and D. H. Rintala. 1997. Prevalence of abuse of women with physical disabilities. *Archives of Physical Medicine and Rehabilitation* 78: S34–S38.

Young, W. A. 1997. Women and immigration. Unpublished manuscript produced for Women's Commission for Refugee Women and Children, Washington, D.C.

Yu, B. N. 1990. Voices of hope and anger: Women speak out for sovereignty and self-determination. *Listen ReaLoud: News of Women's Liberation Worldwide* 10(1–2): 20. Philadelphia: Nationwide Women's Program, American Friends Service Committee.

Zambrano, M. Z. 1985. *Mejor sola que mal accompanda: For the Latina in an abusive relationship.* Seattle, Wash.: Seal Press.

Zaretsky, E. 1976. *Capitalism, the family, and personal life.* New York: Harper & Row.

Zavella, P. 1987. *Women's work and Chicano families: Cannery workers of the Santa Clara Valley.* Ithaca, N.Y.: Cornell University.

Zeff, R., M. Love, and K. Stults, eds. 1989. *Empowering ourselves: Women and toxics organizing.* Falls Church, Va.: Citizens Clearinghouse for Hazardous Wastes.

Zepernick, M. 1998a. The sovereign people are stirring. *The Cape Cod Times,* 27 November, p. A15.

———. 1998b. A lesson in democracy. *The Cape Cod Times,* 11 December, p. A15.

Zinn, H. 1995. *People's history of the United States: 1492–present.* Rev. and updated ed. New York: HarperPerennial.

Zita, J., ed. 1997. Special issue: Third wave feminisms. *Hypatia: A Journal of Feminist Philosophy,* vol. 12, no. 3 (summer).

Credits

RANDY ALBELDA and CHRIS TILLY, "It's Not Just Welfare: Policies As If Families Really Mattered" from *Glass Ceilings and Bottomless Pits*. Boston: South End Press, 1997, pp. 147–164. Used by permission.

DOROTHY ALLISON, "A Question of Class" from *Sisters, Sexperts, Queers* by Arlene Stein. Copyright © 1993 by Arlene Stein. Used by permission of Dutton Signet, a division of Penguin Putnam, Inc.

TERESA AMOTT and JULIE MATTHAEI, "The Transformation of Women's Wage Work" from *Race, Gender, and Work: A Multi-Cultural Economic History of Women in the United States*. Revised Edition. Boston: South End Press, 1996, pp. 317–354. Used by permission.

MARGARET ANDERSEN, tables on pp. 540, 541 from *Thinking About Women: Sociological Perspectives on Sex and Gender,* Fifth Edition. Copyright © 2000 by Allyn & Bacon. Reprinted by permission.

RITA ARDITTI with Tatiana Schreiber, "Breast Cancer: The Environmental Connection — a 1998 Update." Article reprinted with permission from the *Resist Newsletter,* May/June, 1992, published by Resist, Inc., 259 Elm St., Somerville, MA 02144. Resist has been funding social change since 1967. Copyright © 1998 Rita Arditti and Tatiana Schreiber.

SILVIA BARALDINI, MARILYN BUCK, SUSAN ROSENBERG, and LAURA WHITEHORN, "Women's Control Unit: Marianna, FL." Used with permission of Prison News Service.

GRACE CAROLINE BRIDGES, "Lisa's Ritual, Age 10" from *Resourceful Woman,* edited by Shawn Brennan, Julie Winklepleck, and G. MacNee. Copyright © 1994 Visible Ink Press. All rights reserved. Reprinted by permission of The Gale Group.

ALMA BULAWAN and THE WOMEN OF BUKLOD, "What Are the Alternatives to a Military Base?" from *Let the Good Times Roll: Prostitution and the U.S. Military in Asia* by Saundra Pollock Sturdevant and Brenda Stoltzfus, published by The New Press. Copyright © 1992 The New Press. Reprinted by permission.

CHARLOTTE BUNCH, "Not by Degrees: Feminist Theory and Education" from *Passionate Politics* by Charlotte Bunch. Copyright © 1987 by Charlotte Bunch. Reprinted by permission of St. Martin's Press, LLC.

ANDREA R. CANAAN, "Girlfriends" from *Making Face, Making Soul/Haciendo Caras: Creative and Critical Perspectives by Feminists of Color.* Copyright © 1990 by Gloria Anzaldúa. Reprinted with permission from Aunt Lute Books (415) 826-1300.

CARIBBEAN ASSOCIATION FOR FEMINIST RESEARCH AND ACTION, "The Debt Crisis: Who Really Owes Whom?" from *CAFRA News,* March–May 1990. Used with permission of CAFRA.

the feminine power of birth. She is the editor of *Minnesota Parent,* a regional journal devoted to the voices of mothers, fathers, and children. Jeannine lives and writes in Center City, Minnesota, with her husband, John, and their three small children.

H. PATRICIA HYNES, "Consumption: North American Perspectives" from *Dangerous Intersections: Feminist Perspectives on Population, Environment, and Development,* edited by Ynestra King and Jael Silliman. Boston: South End Press, 1999, pp. 189–201. Used by permission.

DEANNA L. JANG, "Asian Immigrant Women Fight Domestic Violence" from *CrossRoads,* March 1994. Reprinted by permission of the publisher.

ALLAN G. JOHNSON, "Patriarchy, the System: An It, Not a He, a Them, or an Us" from *The Gender Knot: Unraveling Our Patriarchal Legacy.* Copyright © 1997 by Allan G. Johnson. Reprinted by permission of Temple University Press. All rights reserved.

ERIKA JONES, "Toward a More Perfect Union" from *Sojourner: The Women's Forum,* October 1999, vol. 25, no. 2. Copyright © 1999 by Sojourner Feminist Institute. Reprinted by permission.

JOANNA KADI, "Moving from Cultural Appropriation toward Ethical Cultural Connections" from *Thinking Class: Sketches from a Cultural Worker.* Boston: South End Press, 1996, pp. 115–127. Used by permission.

MELANIE KAYE/KANTROWITZ, "Jews, Class, Color, and the Cost of Whiteness" from *The Issue Is Power: Essays on Women, Jews, Violence and Resistance.* Copyright © 1992 by Melanie Kaye/Kantrowitz. Reprinted with permission from Aunt Lute Books (415) 826-1300.

SURINA A. KHAN, "The All-American Queer Pakistani Girl." Used with permission of the author. She is an Associate Analyst at Political Research Associates, a think tank and research center that monitors authoritarian, anti-democratic movements. She has contributed to the *Boston Phoenix, Sojourner,* the *Washington Blade, Gay Community News,* and the *Harvard Gay and Lesbian Review,* among other publications.

MICHAEL S. KIMMEL, "Clarence, William, Iron Mike, Tailhook, Senator Packwood, Spur Posse, Magic . . . and Us," from *Transforming a Rape Culture* (1993), edited by Emilie Buchwald, Pamela R. Fletcher, and Martha Roth, pp. 120–138. Minneapolis: Milkweed Editions. Copyright © 1993, 2000 by Michael S. Kimmel. Used by permission of the author.

NANCY KURSHAN, "Behind the Walls: The History and Current Reality of Women's Imprisonment." Reprinted by permission of Nancy Kurshan. She has been a political activist for the past 30 years. Through her activities in the political movements of the 1960s she developed an understanding of the racist nature of the prison system, as well as the important role prisons play in the containment of social change. Ms. Kurshan is a founding member of the Committee to End the Marion Lockdown (CEML), which has been organizing to abolish control unit prisons since 1985. You can contact her at CEML, P.O. Box 57812, Chicago, IL 60657.

JUDITH LORBER, "The Social Construction of Gender" from *The Paradoxes of Gender* (1994). New Haven: Yale University Press. Used by permission of Yale University Press.

AUDRE LORDE, "Uses of the Erotic: The Erotic as Power" reprinted from *Sister Outsider: Essays and Speeches* by Audre Lorde. Freedom, CA: The Crossing Press. Copyright © 1984 Audre Lorde. Used with permission of the publisher.

MIRIAM CHING LOUIE and NGUYEN LOUIE, "The Conversation Begins" from *Conversation Begins: Mothers and Daughters Talk about Living Feminism* by Christina Baker-Kline and Christina Looper Baker. Copyright © 1996 by Christina Looper Baker and Christina Baker-Kline. Used by permission of Bantam Books, a division of Random House.

BARBARA MACDONALD, "Do You Remember Me?" and an excerpt from "An Open Letter to the Women's Movement" in *Look Me in the Eye* by Barbara Macdonald with Cynthia Rich. San Francisco: Spinsters Ink, 1983. Available from Spinsters Ink, 32 East First Street, #330, Duluth, MN 55802. Reprinted by permission.

HAKI R. MADHUBUTI, "On Becoming Anti-Rapist" from *Claiming Earth: Race, Rage, Rape, Redemption: Blacks Seeding a Culture of Enlightened Empowerment.* Copyright © 1994 by Haki R. Madhubuti. Reprinted by permission of Third World Press, Inc. Chicago, Illinois.

JULIANNE MALVEAUX, "Work, Worth, and Popular Culture" from King Features Syndicate, April 24, 1997. Reprinted with special permission of King Features Syndicate.

ELIZABETH MARTINEZ, "A Word about the Great Terminology Question" from *De Colores Means All of Us: Latina Views for a Multi-Colored Century.* Boston: South End Press, 1998, pp. 1–3. Used by permission.

GWENDOLYN MINK, "Feminists, Welfare Reform, and Welfare Justice" from *Social Justice,* vol. 25, no. 1 (1998). Reprinted by permission from *Social Justice.*

CHANDRA TALPADE MOHANTY, "Defining Genealogies: Feminist Reflections on Being South Asian in North America" from *Our Feet Walk the Sky: Women of South Asian Diaspora.* Copyright © 1990 by Women of South Asian Descent Collective. Reprinted with permission from Aunt Lute Books (415) 826-1300.

TONI MORRISON, "The Coming of Maureen Peal" from *The Bluest Eye* by Toni Morrison. Copyright © 1970 by Henry Holt & Co. Reprinted by permission of International Creative Management, Inc.

LEITH MULLINGS, "Households Headed by Women: The Politics of Race, Class, and Gender" from *On Our Own Terms: Race, Class, and Gender in the Lives of African American Women.* Copyright © 1997 by Leith Mullings. Reproduced by permission of the author and Taylor & Francis, Inc./Routledge, Inc., http://www.routledge-ny.com.

EILEEN NECHAS and DENISE FOLEY, "Fallen Women: Alcoholics and Drug Abusers." Reprinted with permission of Simon & Schuster from *Unequal Treatment: What You Don't Know About How Women Are Mistreated by the Medical Community* by Eileen Nechas and Denise Foley. Copyright © 1994 by Eileen Nechas and Denise Foley.

SIA NOWROJEE and JAEL SILLIMAN, "Asian Women's Health: Organizing a Movement" from *Dragon Ladies: Asian American Feminists Breathe Fire,* edited by Sonia Shah. Boston: South End Press, 1997, pp. 73–89. Used by permission.

BARBARA OMOLADE, "Ella's Daughters" from *The Rising Song of African American Women.* Copyright © 1994 by Routledge. Reprinted by permission of the author.

LISA ORLANDO, "Loving Whom We Choose" from *Bi Any Other Name: Bisexual People Speak Out,* Loraine Hutchins and Lani Ka'ahumanu, eds. Reprinted by permission.

MARY PARDO, "Mexican American Women Grassroots Community Activists: Mothers of East Los Angeles." Originally published as "Mexican American Women Grassroots Community Activists: 'Mothers of East Los Angeles'" by Mary Pardo in *Frontiers: A Journal of Women's Studies,* vol. xi, no. 1, 1990. Copyright © 1990 Frontiers Editorial Collective.

SUZANNE PHARR, "Multi-Issue Politics" from *Transformation,* January/February 1994, the quarterly newsletter of the Women's Project, 2224 Main St., Little Rock, AR 72206. Used with permission of the publisher.

MINNIE BRUCE PRATT, "Who Am I If I'm Not My Father's Daughter" from "Identity: Skin Blood Heart" in *Rebellion* by Minnie Bruce Pratt. Firebrand Books, Ithaca, NY. Copyright © 1991 by Minnie Bruce Pratt. Used by permission of the publisher.

DOROTHY E. ROBERTS, "Punishing Drug Addicts Who Have Babies: Women of Color, Equality, and the Right of Privacy" from *Harvard Law Review,* May 1991, #1419. Used with the permission of the publisher and the author.

KALIMA ROSE, "Taking on the Global Economy," from *CrossRoads,* March 1996. Copyright © 1996 CrossRoads. Reprinted by permission.

SONIA SANCHEZ, "Reflection after the June 12th March for Disarmament." This poem has been reprinted from *Peace and Freedom,* Sept./Oct. 1985, the magazine of the Women's International League for Peace and Freedom (WILPF).

SASKIA SASSEN, "Immigrants in a Global Economy" from *CrossRoads,* November 1993. Copyright © 1993 CrossRoads. Reprinted by permission of the publisher.

MARSHA SAXTON, "Reproductive Rights: A Disability Rights Issue" from *Sojourner,* July 1995. Used with permission of the author.

RACHEL ABER SCHLESINGER, "Personal Reflections on Being a Grandmother: L'Chol Dor Va Dor" from *Celebrating the Lives of Jewish Women: Patterns in a Feminist Sampler,* by Rachel Josefowitz Siegel and Ellen Cole. New York, NY: Haworth Press, Inc. Used by permission of Haworth Press, Inc.

LESLIE MARMON SILKO, "The Border Patrol State." Reprinted with the permission of Simon & Schuster from *Yellow Woman and a Beauty of Spirit: Essays on Native American Life Today* by Leslie Marmon Silko. Copyright © 1996 by Leslie Marmon Silko. Originally appeared in *The Nation.*